LEO BAECK INSTITUTE

YEAR BOOK

1992

After the liberation
Jewish service in Berlin, 1945

LEO BAECK INSTITUTE

YEAR BOOK XXXVII

1992

SECKER & WARBURG · LONDON
PUBLISHED FOR THE INSTITUTE
LONDON · JERUSALEM · NEW YORK

FOUNDER EDITOR: ROBERT WELTSCH (1956–1978)
EDITOR: ARNOLD PAUCKER (1970–1992)

Editorial office: Leo Baeck Institute
4 Devonshire Street, London W1N 2BH

THE LEO BAECK INSTITUTE

was founded in 1955 for the study of the history and culture of German-speaking Central European Jewry

The Institute is named in honour of the man who was the last representative figure of German Jewry in Germany during the Nazi period

LEO BAECK INSTITUTE

JERUSALEM: 33 Bustanai Street
LONDON: 4 Devonshire Street, W1
NEW YORK: 129 East 73rd Street

© Leo Baeck Institute 1992
Published by Martin Secker & Warburg Limited
Michelin House, 81 Fulham Road, London SW3 6RB
ISBN 0 436 25551 0
Photoset by Wilmaset Limited, Birkenhead, Wirral
Printed in Great Britain by Richard Clay (The Chaucer Press), Limited,
Bungay, Suffolk

Contents

Preface and Introduction by Arnold Paucker IX

I. JEWISH CULTURE AND RELIGION

DAVID SORKIN: Jews, the Enlightenment and Religious Toleration –
Some Reflections 3
FALK WIESEMANN: Jewish Burials in Germany – Between Tradition, the
Enlightenment and the Authorities 17
ISMAR SCHORSCH: History as Consolation 33
RACHEL HEUBERGER: Orthodoxy versus Reform: The Case of Rabbi
Nehemiah Anton Nobel of Frankfurt a. Main 45

II. EMANCIPATION RE-ASSESSED

ARNO HERZIG: The Process of Emancipation from the Congress of Vienna
to the Revolution of 1848/1849 61
MICHAEL GRAETZ: From Corporate Community to Ethnic-Religious
Minority, 1750–1830 71
WERNER E. MOSSE: Integration and Identity in Imperial Germany:
Towards a Typology 83
WOLFGANG BENZ: The Legend of German-Jewish Symbiosis 95
HERBERT A. STRAUSS: Emancipation History – Limits of Revisionism in
the Post-Holocaust Period – Comments on the Papers of Arno Herzig,
Michael Graetz, Werner E. Mosse and Wolfgang Benz 103

III. JEWISH IDENTITY AND ANTISEMITISM

ROBERT S. WISTRICH: Socialism and Judeophobia – Antisemitism in
Europe before 1914 111
JEHUDA REINHARZ: Jewish Nationalism and Jewish Identity in Central
Europe 147
JOHN M. EFRON: The "Kaftanjude" and the "Kaffeehausjude": Two
Models of Jewish Insanity – A Discussion of Causes and Cures among
German-Jewish Psychiatrists 169
STEVEN E. ASCHHEIM: Nietzsche and the Nietzschean Moment in Jewish
Life (1890–1939) 189
ERIK LINDNER: Houston Stewart Chamberlain: The Abwehrverein and
the "Praeceptor Germaniae", 1914–1918 213
JACOB TOURY: Jewish Aspects as Contributing Factors to the Genesis of
the Reichsbanner Schwarz-Rot-Gold 237

IV. HISTORY THROUGH THE BOOK

WOLF KAISER: The Zionist Project in the Palestine Travel Writings of German-speaking Jews 261

FRANK EYCK: A Diarist in fin-de-siècle Berlin and her Family: Helene, Joseph and Erich Eyck 287

MICHAEL BRENNER: East and West in Orthodox German-Jewish Novels (1912–1934) 309

V. WAR AND RESISTANCE

AVRAHAM SELIGMANN: An Illegal Way of Life in Nazi Germany .. 327

ALBERT H. FRIEDLANDER: A Muted Protest in War-time Berlin – Writing on the Legal Position of German Jewry throughout the Centuries: Leo Baeck – Leopold Lucas – Hilde Ottenheimer 363

HORST R. SASSIN: Liberals of Jewish Background in the Anti-Nazi Resistance 381

SIMONE ERPEL: Struggle and Survival – Jewish Women in the Anti-Fascist Resistance in Germany 397

JOHN P. FOX: German and Austrian Jews in Britain's Armed Forces and British and German Citizenship Policies 1939–1945 415

GUY STERN: In the Service of American Intelligence – German-Jewish Exiles in the War against Hitler 461

VI. ATTITUDES TO PREJUDICE

BRUCE F. PAULEY: The United States and the Jewish Question in Austria 481

HELMUT ESCHWEGE: The Churches and the Jews in the German Democratic Republic 497

VII. REFUGEES AND THE FILM INDUSTRY

KEVIN GOUGH-YATES: Jews and Exiles in British Cinema 517

VIII. BIBLIOGRAPHY 543

IX. LIST OF CONTRIBUTORS 655

X. INDEX 661

Illustrations

Religious service .. .. Frontispiece

After the liberation .. .. between pp. XVIII–XIX

Cemeteries .. .. between pp. 20–21

Nehemiah Anton Nobel .. .. .. opp. p. 52

Eyck family; Erich Eyck .. .. .. between pp. 292–293

Leo Baeck, Leopold Lucas .. .. opp. p. 372

Liberal resistance .. .. between pp. 388–389

Women in the resistance .. .. .. between pp. 404–405

Memorial tablet .. .. opp. p. 500

Emigrés in the cinema .. .. .. between pp. 532–533

Preface/Introduction

BY ARNOLD PAUCKER

German Jews were always amongst those who professed themselves the willing servants of the *Aufklärung*. Were they not right in doing so? Was not their entry into the modern world inextricably linked with it? Yet David Sorkin who opens this Year Book paints a picture of an Enlightenment relationship fraught with ambiguities. Full acceptance of the Jew was conditional on regeneration; there were Jewish reservations and, moreover, mutual toleration remained an ideal never fully attained. As Falk Wiesemann shows, even the Jewish way of death was an aspect of Judaism which gave offence to the enlightened mind. Hasty interment and traditional Jewish styles of burial with their perceived lack of decorum jarred on the nerves of those who wished to remove Jewish "imperfections". Compliance with Gentile burial norms became yet another yardstick of assimilation.

Ismar Schorsch offers a further contribution to Zunz scholarship in his analysis of Zunz's *Memorbuch*, enhancing Jewish "collective memory". Zunz's advocacy of a marriage of continuity with modernity was also a Jewish answer to Enlightenment demands for a Jewish willingness to embrace a "superior" world. If Judaism was to live, a "balance between piety and progress" was clearly indicated – but how far was adaptation to be carried? The Jewish Reform movement believed in a large measure of integration and religious compromise which was bound to provoke a backlash of traditionalism. Rachel Heuberger deals with the clash between Orthodoxy and Reform as exemplified by Nehemiah Nobel, whose re-assertion of the traditional way of Jewish life was consonant with moderation – and also with German patriotism. How to come to terms with modernity, yet retain a Jewish identity and preserve a living Judaism, is a constant theme reverberating through the first section of this Year Book.

The 'Acculturation and Identity' of the German Jew was the topic of a panel of the September 1990 meeting of the German historians in Bochum, the papers of which are printed here. The topics of the first two Year Book sections thus overlap, but the conference papers continue the theme up until the destruction of Jewish existence in Germany. Apart from the perennial strife over the term "symbiosis", the session was marked by the usual clash of opinion as to whether "integration" or "co-existence" or – after all – "symbiosis" was ever feasible or no more than wishful thinking on the part of the Jewish minority. Basically either optimistic or pessimistic, both Jewish and German participants were divided in their outlook. Arno Herzig speaks of over-compensation in the process of acculturation and dwells in particular on the role of the Jew as an anti-symbol in

periods of economic upheaval. The enemies of the Enlightenment and of Liberal
solutions arose again and again, and yet the Jews did not lack allies. Michael
Graetz outlines the destruction of Jewish autonomy for which there was no place
in modern society. From a closed, corporate community, in a development
spearheaded by a rising Jewish middle class, German Jewry became a religious
minority; to belong to it an act of individual will. His stress on ethnicity is
consonant with a National Jewish approach. Werner Mosse dwells on the
successful entry of certain Jewish groups into modern German society and hits
out against Gershom Scholem's simplistic negation of its ever having been
achieved. His examples of Jewish elites, which integrated whilst preserving a
Jewish identity, he believes of validity for other Jewish groups. A degree of
acceptance without "assimilationism" was a distinct possibility. The Scholem
thesis is defended by a German scholar, himself dismayed by the Jewish
catastrophe in Germany; Wolfgang Benz sees no reciprocity, no partner, no
acceptance and almost total rejection and exclusion. The elimination of German
Jewry by the Nazis is for him the supreme proof of the fallacy of Jewish
emancipation, with the general German population willingly accepting "legal"
measures to that end. Herbert Strauss, neatly summing up the session, seems to
warn of exclusive rival interpretations of the conflicting evidence in the history of
the Jews in Germany from the Enlightenment to the Nazi revocation of their
emancipation. There are inherent pitfalls in the post-Holocaust re-evaluation of
the rich and varied German-Jewish past.

Although much of the next substantial section of this Year Book could also be
summarised under the heading 'The Jewish Question in Imperial and Weimar
Germany', most of the six authors concerned, in keeping with the broadening
scope of this annual, transcend these boundaries. Robert Wistrich's discussion of
anti-Jewish trends in the labour movement reminds one of Nathan Birnbaum's
prophetic words about centuries of latent antisemitism in Socialist societies of the
future.[1] His gloomy prognosis was borne out in a far briefer span. The debate on
the degree of "Socialist antisemitism" continues,[2] and Wistrich, who has given
the topic a European dimension, traces the cross-fertilisation in European labour
movements' Judeophobia. As far as Germany is concerned, there was a definite
diminution of Socialist antisemitism in the late nineteenth century, with parallels
in tsarist Russia. The SPD would seem to have given up their opportunist
flirtation with antisemitic ideas. The Jew as the villain of the piece did not

---

[1]"Und wenn schon nach langen und heftigen Kämpfen die neue Gesellschaftsordnung . . . alle
Widerstände besiegt haben wird, dann werden noch immer Jahrhunderte lang manche Wellen der
alten Welt in die neue hinübergleiten. Eine solche Welle wird der Judenhass sein, diese jedenfalls
secundäre Geschichtsursache kräftigster Wirkung." 'Die Jüdische Moderne'. Vortrag gehalten im
Akademischen Vereine "Kadimah" in Wien von Matthias Ascher [Nathan Birnbaum], Leipzig
1896.
[2]For a further contribution to the debate see now also the conference volume of a Steinheim Institute
and London Leo Baeck Institute seminar, Mülheim, December 1990: Ludger Heid and Arnold
Paucker (eds.), *Juden und deutsche Arbeiterbewegung bis 1933. Soziale Utopien und religiös-kulturelle
Traditionen*, Tübingen 1992 (Schriftenreihe wissenschaftlicher Abhandlungen des Leo Baeck
Instituts 49).

convince the German proletariat and there were enough Socialist leaders who realised that antisemitism posed a real danger to the labour movement. This ran concurrently with Jewish intellectuals joining the Socialist movement in great numbers – Arnold Zweig's moving words about their pact with the German working class spring to mind.[3] One can add that in the last years of Weimar, when the Liberal centre had collapsed, large sections of the bourgeois Jewish community could turn only to the Socialist working class. Yet the lack of immunity to xenophobia and racism found amongst Socialist leaders and Socialist-led in over a century of European Socialism remains a chilling thought.

Jehuda Reinharz, who sketches the development of Jewish Nationalism in Central Europe, links the early Zionist movement to the rising militancy in defence of Jewish positions; gradually Jewish consciousness became no less strong within the much derided "assimilationist" majority. Both sides are seen as engaged in a rivalry for supremacy as defenders of Jewish rights, which ushered in half a century of Jewish activism – and one notes that the life styles of German-Jewish functionaries in both groups were very similar. The ethnic element, of much importance in Austria and Bohemia, was totally absent in Germany. Reinharz in his comparative treatment of Zionism in three lands stresses the psychological function of German Zionism and the sharpening clash of Jewish ideologies.

German-Jewish psychiatrists is John Efron's theme; those whose practices and cures were a Jewish retort to a kind of pathological isolation of the Jews as having their own strictly defined mental illnesses. Zionist and "assimilationist" practitioners differed sharply in their assessment of who was a psychologically healthy Jew, with one group castigating the Western degenerate, a nervous victim of "assimilationist" mimicry and identity crisis; the other the *Ostjuden* suffering from the monstrosities of a bastard language (Yiddish) or diagnosing Zionists as victims of dangerous and debilitating fallacies – and *vice versa* . . . Here politics bedevilled scientific approaches – as with other ethnic groups even today – and the subject needs and receives a commendable degree of irony.

Jewish champions of Nietzschean thought and Jews as purveyors and critics of Nietzsche's philosophy are analysed in Steven Aschheim's contribution. While Jewish attitudes are often ambiguous, Nietzsche as the non-Jewish opponent of racism and antisemitism who extolled himself and Heine as Germany's foremost artists of the German language also commended himself to an otherwise Enlightenment-tied German Jewry. It is no wonder that the *Centralverein* made lavish use of Nietzsche's writings in its defence activities. We see the manifold adaptation and appropriation of Nietzscheanism by the "official" Jewish community and his positive reception by a respectable Jewish middle class (which differed from that of their German "Klassengenossen"). Aschheim shows how Nietzsche became the intellectual diet of a second Zionist generation, even

---

[3]". . . jenes Bündnisses, das wir jüdischen Intellektuellen mit den Arbeiterparteien geschlossen hatten. Wir gaben ihnen die geistige Führung, die selbst zu erwerben der Machtstaat sie hinderte, sie verbürgten uns die Sicherheit unseres Lebens und die Grundlagen unserer Arbeit als Juden. Es war ein anständiger ungeschriebener Vertrag . . ." Arnold Zweig, *Bilanz der deutschen Judenheit 1933. Ein Versuch*, Amsterdam 1934, pp. 281–282.

influencing the Marxist *Hashomer Hazair*, and finally how under the Nazis, with their take-over of the philosopher, a new Jewish Nietzsche-strategy was required.

That a British turncoat should become the bane of patriotic German Jewry in the First World War is yet another ironic twist in its history. Erik Lindner's painstaking examination of how the *Abwehrverein* took on Houston Stewart Chamberlain provides an entire catalogue of the contortions of defence. The "Evangelist of Race"[4] was clever enough to attack the German Jews indirectly by "internationalising" the Jew, since at the time, after all, they were serving their country – something he grudgingly acknowledged. Chamberlain may have been an astute tactician, but it is saddening that some of the best minds available had to waste their time in refuting his pseudo-scientific twaddle. The persistence of this stuff in the Europe of 1992 is depressing.

An admirable example of what careful archival research can achieve is presented by Jacob Toury's reconstruction of the Jewish role in the formation of early Republican defence organisations in certain regions and the eventual creation of the *Reichsbanner Schwarz-Rot-Gold*. It has, in fact, remained largely unknown that in Bremen, Hamburg and other areas the Jewish factor was quite formidable. Although essential for Jewish security, co-operation with the emerging *Reichsbanner* on the *Reich* level was, however, haphazard. Jewry was only gradually groping towards Republican consciousness. There was *Reichsbanner* mistrust of the Jewish community and there were Jewish misgivings about anti-Jewish prejudices in the *Reichsbanner* rank and file. A true and intensive collaboration was only achieved at a late hour during the final crisis of the ill-fated Weimar Republic.

The section that follows illustrates how travel accounts, memoirs and fiction can reflect the mentality and conflicting aims of German-speaking Jews. Wolf Kaiser in his survey of Jewish visitors to Palestine from Germany, Austria and Bohemia shows us not only a country of pioneers, seen through the eyes of the non-resident, but reveals much of the psyche of the "Jewish tourist" (those with National Jewish leanings idealise the sons of toil at the expense of the spineless Diaspora Jew etc., etc.). The Arab-Jewish confrontation is, of course, commented on by many of the writers, but whether itinerant Zionist stalwarts, travelling "assimilationists" or devout pilgrims, they reveal only a glimmering awareness of the coming explosion of nationalisms and wars which would face the State of Israel. Frank Eyck's memoirs of his family exemplify German-Jewish interaction or co-existence. (Here we have an outlook similar to that in Werner Mosse's exposition of forms of Jewish integration in Germany.) The author complements the family diaries with a short biography of his father, Erich Eyck, a noted Weimar Liberal who, as a refugee in England, became the author of a classic history of the destroyed Weimar Republic. Michael Brenner recaptures Orthodox Jewish life in Germany in his analysis of Orthodox German-Jewish fiction. This rather didactic genre is, as he himself points out, only of limited

---

[4]Geoffrey G. Field, *Evangelist of Race. The Germanic Vision of Houston Stewart Chamberlain*, New York 1981, remains the standard work on the racist "philosopher".

literary value; these writers cannot compete with a German-Jewish Fontane such as Georg Hermann. Designed for readers in religious Jewish homes, these novels deserve resurrection as they tell us much about growing Jewish alienation and how Orthodox writers attempted to cope with the deteriorating situation of German Jewry.

With the second of the two most substantial sections of this Year Book we return once again to the fate of German Jewry under the onslaught of Nazism, but with special emphasis on the war years. Six authors deal with the responses of those who were trapped when the frontiers of *Grossdeutschland* were finally closed, and those fortunate enough to have escaped to freedom in time – beyond the European continent – and who had reached the shores of the two Western democracies.

Avraham Seligmann concerns himself with the Jews who went underground in Germany to avoid deportation. There are various ways of defining resistance. It can be restricted to active anti-Fascism, but this narrowest of definitions certainly will not do in the case of German Jewry. Evasion of deportation, the refusal to comply with the orders of an almighty totalitarian dictatorship, is an act of defiance which deserves to be classified as resistance in the broadest sense of the term. Seligmann, in a dispassionate study, analyses the motivation and the lot of up to 15,000 German Jews who opted for the illegal way of life and of whom close to 4,000 survived in hiding. Even if the figures are to be treated with some caution they are quite remarkable when confronted with the usual picture of a legality-bound and passive German Jewry. It is also a tribute to the many brave Germans who were willing to risk their lives for Jews on the run and who followed not the dictates of the State but those of conscience.

German resistance to Nazi rule spanned the whole range from the ultra-Conservative reactionary Right to revolutionary Socialists and Communists. Jewish co-operation and involvement with the resistance – where it took place – quite logically extended to all these groups, reflecting the outlook of a community which, even under relentless pressure, had retained the divergent political orientations which had been formed in the German Empire and the Weimar Republic. This is well brought out in the essays of Albert Friedlander, Horst Sassin and Simone Erpel.

The more "conservative" Jewish representatives of the *Reichsvertretung/Reichsvereinigung* had, apart from their natural "Liberal" links, contacts with the emerging Conservative resistance. Unfortunately, we have been able to learn too little about these relations. Leo Baeck said towards the end of his life that there was at least a possibility of his writing about them,[5] but he never did so and the knowledge which has come down to us is scanty and unsatisfactory. As influential Conservative resistance groups are on record as having expressed quite forcefully that they had no intention of according full restoration of civil

[5]Hans Reichmann, 'Aufzeichnung über eine Unterredung', in *Worte des Gedenkens für Leo Baeck*. Im Auftrag des Council of Jews from Germany – London. Herausgegeben von Eva G. Reichmann, Heidelberg 1959, p. 238; *idem*, 'Excerpts from Leo Baeck's Writings. Foreword: The Fate of a Manuscript', in *LBI Year Book III* (1958), p. 361.

rights to the Jews after the overthrow of Hitler,[6] the problematic character of this Jewish/Conservative co-operation must surely be self-evident. We can only assume that the "Conservatives" who put their trust in Leo Baeck were marked by a more "philosemitic" stance. In view of what we know today it is more than curious, it is incongruous, that it was Baeck's draft of an appeal or manifesto directed to the German people and to be issued on the day of the "liberation" which was apparently chosen in a kind of "conservative" essay competition.[7] And it was at the behest of the Conservative resistance that Baeck had undertaken to write a history of the Jewish "Rechtsstellung" for the benefit of the "freed" German population, the textual examination of which is here undertaken by Albert Friedlander. It was surely "Recht" and "Entrechtung"; the question of their "Rechtsstellung" with which the Jewish outcasts were concerned. The voluminous work is the historical documentation of another act of defiance, as Friedlander demonstrates, of a spiritual resistance to Nazism which does great honour to Leo Baeck and his collaborators, Leopold Lucas and Hilde Otten-heimer.

Horst Sassin criticises the comparative neglect of the part played by Jews in the Liberal resistance; an imbalance in resistance historiography which he seeks to redress. That here, too, the Jewish share was considerable is now beyond doubt – the author's definition of who is "Jewish" is generous and elastic, but there is surely no need to quibble on this point. There are some disconcerting "conservative" echoes in the programme of the main Liberal group under discussion here; with an advocacy of a very gradual restoration of Jewish rights in a reborn German democracy, a tactical manoeuvre which could only have been based on a negative assessment of their German compatriots as standing in need of much re-education. Jewish participation in Liberal resistance activities does of course accord with a general Jewish commitment to Liberalism which, however, did not always display a convincing militancy.

Where Jewish youth sought the path of active anti-Fascist resistance in Germany they almost invariably aligned themselves with the illegal movements of the Left, and particularly the Communists. The evidence for this is incontrovertible; they regarded the Communists as the most determined and skilled opponents of Nazism. Simone Erpel in her contribution concerns herself with the resistance of Jewish women in general and then presents four studies of Jewish women in the Communist resistance. One need not be a feminist to agree with her claim that an assessment of the special position of Jewish women resistance fighters is long overdue. It could be said that women – who are so much more adaptable and qualified for undercover work – enjoyed, at best, a tenuous equality with men in the resistance movements in Europe.[8] As Erpel stresses, with increasing persecution Jewish motivation also became stronger for

---

[6]There is conclusive and reliable documentary evidence for these attitudes. Christof Dipper's excellent essay, 'Der deutsche Widerstand und die Juden', in the special issue, *Juden in Deutschland zwischen Assimilation und Verfolgung*, of *Geschichte und Gesellschaft* (edited by Reinhard Rürup), IX, No. 3 (1983), pp. 349–380, may serve as an example for a host of recent literature on this sore topic.

[7]H. Reichmann, 'Aufzeichnung', *loc. cit.*, p. 238; *idem*, 'Fate of a Manuscript', *loc. cit.*, pp. 361–362.

[8]Italian women, who fought heroically alongside the men in the North Italian partisan brigades, found themselves quickly relegated to the kitchen after the liberation.

these women, despite their main loyalty to the outlawed German labour movement. This is again a common feature in accounts of the resistance and one cannot help but wonder about the heart-searchings among Jewish activists during the lull in anti-Fascist activity in the Communist sector of the resistance from the period of the Hitler-Stalin pact to the invasion of the Soviet Union. These are questions which must be asked, but it does not diminish our respect for these courageous young Jewish women who fought and died in the struggle against the Nazi regime.

As Guy Stern observes at the beginning of his essay, a history of the Jews fighting in the war against Nazi Germany is yet to be written. In such a work many chapters would have to be devoted to the part played by the Jews from Germany who joined the Allied Armies.[9] The contributions to this volume by John Fox and Stern should be viewed as two further studies towards such a comprehensive work. Both authors could easily have opted for statistical methods, a mere enumeration of the groups which volunteered and the units in which they served; a reiteration of numbers and individual feats. They have chosen rather to concentrate on more specialised topics. John Fox is mainly concerned with official British attitudes to the thousands of German- and Austrian-Jewish "aliens" who had flocked to fight in the British Forces. They were, at times, only hesitantly accepted and British officialdom was apparently much occupied, throughout the war, with avoiding a state of affairs in which the United Kingdom would find itself lumbered with all these foreigners once hostilities had ended. Much of it makes unpleasant reading and it is only fair to say that this bureaucratic wrangle had a happy ending. The "alien" Jewish ex-servicemen were naturalised after the war and successfully integrated into English life. The United States, a country of immigration, with set laws and rights for newcomers, was without this particular problem. Guy Stern has taken as his subject the role of German Jews in American Intelligence, where they rendered valuable services. It should be noted here that former members of German-Jewish youth movements were a marked presence in both the United States Units of the Office of Strategic Services and the British Special Services; many fought behind the lines; a number were captured and executed.

The penultimate section of this Year Book is on the persistence and revival of prejudice. Bruce Pauley deals with American reactions to Austrian antisemitism, composed as it is of particularly nasty ingredients, and Helmut Eschwege concerns himself with the reaction of the Churches to the now defunct German Democratic Republic's singular "Judenpolitik". Although the first essay covers a century of Austrian politics – and four different forms of state – while the second deals only with a more evanescent state creation, the topics can be seen in juxtaposition and also as different aspects of a "Bewältigung der Vergangenheit", which in both areas is far from complete. Perturbation and disgust has

---

[9]The pioneer study for the United Kingdom remains, of course, Norman Bentwich, *I Understand the Risks. The Story of the Refugees from Nazi Oppression who fought in the British Forces in the World War*, London 1950.

always been voiced in the United States about the manifestations of Austrian antisemitism, though the chorus of complaints was, admittedly, largely orchestrated by a vocal Jewish lobby. Recent Austrian history and current opinion polls are not reassuring. In Germany, the Lutheran Church, especially, carries a heavy responsibility for the past. Therefore the Churches of the East must be commended for their response, over the last two decades, to the GDR's denial of the very uniqueness of the persecution of the Jews by German Fascism and of the European Holocaust – accompanied as it was by its very own brand of intemperate anti-Zionism. While the drawing of analogies between Nazi and Communist rule in Eastern Germany is a dangerous pastime, which can only result in the whitewashing of the infinitely more evil Nazi regime, the products of educational neglect and indoctrination in the former GDR are now with us in the form of outbreaks of frightening xenophobia.

Some ten years ago in Year Book XXVII Hans Feld surveyed the part played by the Jews in the German film industry, a nascent industry in which the outsider had a marked impact. There is a continuity in this volume when Kevin Gough-Yates analyses the role played by the exiles from Nazi Europe in British cinema – among them were many refugee directors and actors from Weimar Germany. The author also fills a real gap, as this was one of the subjects not covered in the history of the German-speaking refugees and immigrants who chose Great Britain, which was published last year by the London Leo Baeck Institute.[10]

This Preface/Introduction has, of necessity, a very personal note as this is the last volume of the Year Book I shall edit. I have been connected with the Year Book of the Leo Baeck Institute since 1959 when I was first appointed Director of the London LBI. As an associate of Robert Weltsch I assisted in the editing of ten early volumes, becoming the Year Book's *de facto* editor in 1970. Having been responsible for a total of 23 volumes would seem to indicate that a change of editorship and in some ways also of direction is now called for, even if I were a somewhat younger man; however I am almost 72 and a firm believer in change and rejuvenation.

   The fact that this is a sort of valedictory volume must also go some way to account for its size.[11] While I apologise for this to the reader, I should perhaps explain that many of my personal friends and colleagues, who have been involved in German-Jewish studies over a long period and have helped to shape this publication, wished to contribute to my last volume. The question of reserving some of their studies for another volume could not of course be entertained, in fact I am deeply grateful for their commitment. That the Year

[10]Werner E. Mosse (co-ordinating ed.), Julius Carlebach, Gerhard Hirschfeld, Aubrey Newman, Arnold Paucker, Peter Pulzer (eds.), *Second Chance. Two Centuries of German-speaking Jews in the United Kingdom*, Tübingen 1991 (Schriftenreihe wissenschaftlicher Abhandlungen des Leo Baeck Instituts 48).
[11]I must here also acknowledge the generosity of friends who have contributed to the costs of this Year Book.

Book has achieved the scholarly eminence it enjoys is surely due to a small group of some one hundred scholars in England, Germany, Israel and the United States, who are strongly represented in this and the two preceding volumes. As retiring editor I must acknowledge this here.

The Year Book will remain firmly anchored in London. The Leo Baeck Institute has appointed Professor John Grenville, Chairman of the Department of History of Birmingham University as the next Editor. His Associate Editor will be Professor Julius Carlebach, at present Rector of the *Hochschule für Jüdische Studien* in Heidelberg. Both are members of the Executive of the London Leo Baeck Institute. That the Institute has been so fortunate as to enlist the services of two such distinguished scholars is immensely gratifying. The Year Book could hardly be transferred into safer hands and it is with a great deal of satisfaction that I introduce them here.

Completing such a long "tour of duty" gives one, I feel, a right to take stock. Certainly, as the official organ of the Leo Baeck Institute the Year Book fulfils its main purpose as the forum of German-Jewish historiography, as we always like to describe it. Yet it is surely inevitable that some personal element enters editorial policy, that it was also formed by the experiences of the particular group I myself come from. What we have tried to achieve in the Year Book between 1970 and, say, 1990 can of course only be touched on briefly here. And even though I am constrained to restrict myself to certain aspects in this summary,[12] a repetition of some of the points of view stressed in more recent Year Book prefaces is unavoidable.

The Year Book was founded 37 years ago by Robert Weltsch, who first of all succeeded in mobilising the surviving émigré scholars as an indispensable reservoir of authors. (We usually refer to them as the "founding fathers".) Certainly their own testimonies had to be recorded before it was too late. The early Year Books were welded together by Weltsch in his essay-introductions in which he distilled the experiences of his generation. Many historians have rightly called them small historiographical masterpieces.[13]

The "founding fathers" set the tone of the early Year Books. They firmly believed – having, rightly, a high opinion of their own worth – that the history of their community could only be written by those who, rooted in the past, had

---

[12]The following remarks are largely based on two papers as yet unpublished: (1) Arnold Paucker, 'Die deutsch-jüdische Geschichte im Jahrbuch des Leo Baeck Instituts', delivered at a conference of the Leo Baeck Institute and the Max-Planck-Institut für Geschichte, Schloss Ringberg/Tegernsee, on *Deutsch-jüdische Geschichte. Zur Entwicklung der historischen Forschung und Darstellung seit 1945. Ergebnisse, Kritik, Aufgaben*, 25th–28th November 1987; (2) *idem*, 'History in Exile. Writing the Story of German Jewry', delivered at a symposium on *German-speaking Exiles in Great Britain*, Aberdeen 24th–26th September 1990 (publication forthcoming). I have also drawn on the excellent analysis of Christhard Hoffmann, 'Deutsch-jüdische Geschichtswissenschaft in der Emigration. Das Leo-Baeck-Institut', in Herbert A. Strauss, Klaus Fischer, Christhard Hoffmann, Alfons Söllner (eds.), *Die Emigration der Wissenschaften nach 1933. Disziplingeschichtliche Studien*, München – London – New York – Paris 1991, pp. 257–279. Hoffmann deals with the evolution of the Year Book in pp. 267–273.

[13]See, for instance, my obituaries of Robert Weltsch in *AJR Information*, London, February 1983, and *The Wiener Library Bulletin*, Special issue, 1983, pp. 51–53.

themselves been part of German-Jewish "co-existence". As an absolute maxim, of course, such an approach does not hold. If the presence of participant-observers is an *a priori* condition for reliable historiography then who could write Greek or Roman history today? On the other hand, the first generation not only gave an impetus to German-Jewish history, they stimulated further research and added, as living primary sources in themselves, much flavour and spice to what might well have become an arid raked-over subject, and provided inside knowledge of events which would otherwise have vanished into oblivion.

However, long before 1970 we had realised that if we were to continue the Year Book, amongst whose authors professional historians were in a minority, it had to be transformed; and it had to be brought in tune with modern methods of research. Naturally, change was bound to come with the years, but we also embarked on it as a deliberate policy. Professionalisation went together with generational change, and the composition of the body of the authors altered at first gradually and then markedly. Soon the Year Book was no longer the preserve of former German Jews, or only of Jews for that matter. There is no need to work out percentages here. Charts and tables have been compiled by others. Suffice it to say that while a second German-Jewish generation, already largely educated outside Germany, and their descendants, have retained a certain prominence – something the subject of our annual made inevitable and which remains important – the Year Book is written today by Gentiles and Jews, by Germans and Jews, by secular and Orthodox Jews, by Catholics, Quakers and Methodists. As the voice of the recognised academic discipline of German-Jewish studies, as a scholarly, historical publication, it has won general acclaim. However modest we may wish to be, we are surely entitled to state that the transformation has been successfully accomplished.

It is a very noticeable feature of the second phase in the history of the Year Book that we have increasingly transcended any narrow definition of "Jewishness" in the choice of topics. I venture here on controversial ground; I know that it is difficult to achieve complete agreement as to how to define a Jew for the purpose of historical research. Again the "older generation" tended to restrict its attention to those who, however nominally, continued to adhere to or practise the Jewish faith. That was a time-honoured attitude, but it is surely now outdated. For instance, the *Centralverein* in Weimar Germany countered antisemitic accusations of "Jewish Bolshevism" – such as the entire leadership of the Bavarian Soviet Republic having consisted of Jews – with the argument that these men had long ago left the faith of their fathers; patriotic German Jews as the leaders of the *Centralverein* were, they felt that they had to refute such insinuations as groundless – and declared that there was not a single Jew amongst the revolutionaries of Munich![14] Of course such clumsy apologetics led them nowhere. It is simply a truism that, when tracing the communal history of German Jewry, treating the development of Jewish thought or the inner-Jewish controversies – to give only a

[14]For defence argumentation re Jews and Bolshevism see the various editions of *Anti-Anti. Tatsachen zur Judenfrage* published by the *Centralverein* in Berlin until the *Machtübernahme*.

After the liberation
Procession of the Berlin Jewish community

After the liberation
Two Jewish boys at the first Jewish service in Berlin

After the liberation

The first performance of Lessing's 'Nathan der Weise' in Berlin
Paul Wegener as Nathan and Eduard von Winterstein as Klosterbruder

After the liberation – in Italy
Above: Jewish soldiers with German prisoners
Below: Soldiers of the Jewish Brigade with Italian children

few examples – the concerns should be solely limited to those within the fold. If you wish to analyse the "Jewish Question" in Germany, the relations and tensions between Jews and Gentiles, or to understand the cultural impact of the Jews on Germany (and how can you leave out the converts here?), persecution and resistance, continuing adherence to the Jewish religion or even affirmation of a Jewish people or nationhood cannot be the yardstick. Most historians have long since accepted that for the scholarly investigation of the history of the Jews in Germany all those were to be included who were descended from the Jewish group, who had been seen by the outside world as Jews, and who had suffered the Jewish fate. No justice can be done to German-Jewish history in all its variety by any other method. Any contention that in this we are tainted by racial concepts must be rejected. Broadly guided by this approach I have published an essay on the "Jewish Christians" of the *Paulus-Bund*[15] and once allotted almost a quarter of a Year Book to the Nazi persecution of converts and those of partly Jewish descent.[16]

One amongst those subjects to which the Year Book has always given particular attention is that of the political orientation and voting patterns of German (and Austrian) Jews. There is now a general consensus that the political allegiances of a largely middle-class Jewish community were not in keeping with its more conservative life style and class interests, but that it was relentlessly driven to the Left by an antisemitic German Right. Eva Reichmann's dictum on this Jewish class anomaly – the result of an emancipation incompletely carried out – has retained its validity.[17] The steady move from the National Liberals after 1878 to *Fortschritt/Freisinn* and, after 1918, the DDP; up until the mass migration of Liberal Jews to the Social Democrats after the disintegration of the Liberal centre in 1932 has been studied by the Leo Baeck Institute and in its Year Book again and again; from Jacob Toury's magisterial work[18] to Barbara Suchy's[19] and George Mosse's[20] essays, which delve into the problematic affinities of German Jewry to Liberalism, and Peter Pulzer's balanced and differentiated study[21] – surely the last word on this subject. The thesis of the Jewish group as a

[15]Werner Cohn, 'Bearers of a Common Fate? The "Non-Aryan" Christian "Fate-Comrades" of the Paulus-Bund, 1933–1939', in *LBI Year Book XXXIII* (1988), pp. 327–366.

[16]Ursula Büttner, 'The Persecution of Christian-Jewish Families in the Third Reich'; and Jeremy Noakes, 'The Development of Nazi Policy towards the German-Jewish "Mischlinge" 1933–1945', in *LBI Year Book XXXIV* (1989), pp. 267–354.

[17]Eva, G. Reichmann, *Die Flucht in den Hass. Die Ursachen der deutschen Judenkatastrophe*, Frankfurt a. Main [1956], p. 172; original English edn.: *Hostages of Civilisation. The Social Sources of National Socialist Anti-Semitism*, London 1950, pp. 144–145.

[18]Jacob Toury, *Die politischen Orientierungen der Juden in Deutschland. Von Jena bis Weimar*, Tübingen 1966 (Schriftenreihe wissenschaftlicher Abhandlungen des Leo Baeck Instituts 15).

[19]Barbara Suchy, 'The Verein zur Abwehr des Antisemitismus (I). From its Beginnings to the First World War', in *LBI Year Book XXVIII* (1983), pp. 205–239; *idem*, 'The Verein zur Abwehr des Antisemitismus (II). From the First World War to its Dissolution in 1933', in *LBI Year Book XXX* (1985), pp. 67–103.

[20]George L. Mosse, 'German Jews and Liberalism in Retrospect. Introduction to Year Book XXXII', in *LBI Year Book XXXII* (1987), pp. XIII–XXV.

[21]Ernest Hamburger and Peter Pulzer, 'Jews as Voters in the Weimar Republic', in *LBI Year Book XXX* (1985), pp. 3–66.

progressive factor in German society has been substantiated. There was some Jewish withdrawal from Liberalism after the Nazi seizure of power, but it was a passing phenomenon. The largely Liberal/Left-Liberal/Social Democratic leanings of the German Jews are, moreover, reflected in their political behaviour in the countries of their emigration; the former German Jews and their descendants are a moderate, tolerant, humanistic factor, particularly in Israel. It is also interesting to see that the authors of the Year Book, Jews and Gentiles alike, reflect in their political outlook almost that of the German-Jewish community before the catastrophe. This is not accidental; one could almost say that to some extent here the object of research exerts an influence on the researcher. There are, of course, individual motives and impulses which lead a scholar in the direction of certain specific studies.

It was always stressed that when the Leo Baeck Institute was founded ten years after the war, the various contending German-Jewish groups which had emerged unscathed had agreed to bury the hatchet. Today this statement needs qualification. Initially there was indeed harmony, but we began also to see a renewed growing apart which certainly had its effect on the Year Book. The three main groups of former German Jews have made their lives under very different conditions – in America, Israel and England – and undoubtedly their specific contributions to German-Jewish historiography have, to some extent, been shaped and moulded by this. There is a stimulating diversity of approach – there are those who lean more to a Judeo-centric view, seeing the histories of the Jews in different countries primarily as one, a history of the Jewish Diaspora; and those who would place modern German-Jewish history more firmly within the German dimension. This diversity has at times resulted in a tension at once inspiring and fruitful. I would contend that the Jewish group in the United Kingdom is less subject to outside pressure; and in this respect things are somewhat different in both Israel and the United States. I would further put forward the idea that the social climate in Britain, with its greater inclination to intellectual tolerance, is perhaps more conducive to an objective and detached view of the past; moreover, the second German-Jewish generation here, strongly rooted, seems to have imbibed the pragmatic approach. So much for assimilatory processes. I feel that London has been a good choice, slightly more of a "neutral" ground for the location of the Year Book. The diversity of the three Institutes deserves to be stressed, and brings great benefits to our work, though it should not be exaggerated.

Neither should one over- or underestimate the differences in the approach to German-Jewish history between Jews and Gentiles, or German and Jews. Undoubtedly one can discern in some contributions, for instance on the problems of emancipation, a more "Jewish" and a more "German" point of view. Yet to allocate to Jewish authors more of the "inner-Jewish" history and more of an "externalised" history to non-Jewish scholars is not warranted. Judging by the experience of the Year Book, it would be injudicious to earmark the essence of Judaism as mainly a Jewish preserve. Any such facile divisions are unjustified and were at no time entertained. The Year Book has also shown that genuine intuition and insight into the inner development of German Jewry can come from the most unexpected quarters.

Two German-Jewish movements which figure strongly in the Year Book are the *Zionistische Vereinigung für Deutschland* and the *Centralverein deutscher Staatsbürger jüdischen Glaubens*; with a certain preponderance of studies by National Jewish historians over those who would qualify as latter-day protagonists of the Jewish Defence. This impinges on the central German-Jewish clash of ideologies which runs like a marker-thread through all the Year Books. Although Zionism has its place only in the last third of Modern German-Jewish History and Zionists were an unrepresentative minority in German Jewry before 1933, one must, of course, measure Zionism by its eventual significance in the history of the Jewish people. Moreover, many of our post-war historians originally came from the Zionist German-Jewish youth movements,[22] which affected their outlook and formed their future lives. However, one should stress the remarkable even-handedness of many "Zionist" historians. Their approaches are not necessarily guided by an automatic castigation of the failure of "assimilationism", with the return to Israel as the only salvation. There are those who point to an unhealthy *völkisch* romantic influence on segments of German Zionism; and others who have investigated its humanist component and the advocacy of Arab-Jewish understanding. There is much critical evaluation of Zionist policies in Wilhelminian and Weimar Germany; and no unanimity in the assessment of the *Centralverein*. Some of the most positive evaluations of the Jewish Defence can be found in the contributions of Israeli historians. C.V. historiography was actually initiated in London in the early 1960s. By 1984, in a not completely exhaustive bibliography, we were able to list some 70 studies exclusively or largely dedicated to the *Centralverein*;[23] only part of them published in the Year Book – today we are close to 200. The *Centralverein* has advanced from being the slighted "assimilationist" stepchild of Jewish historiography, via rehabilitation and praise for militant Jewish self-defence, to being in the centre of a renewal of the classic controversies.[24] In earlier years taboos and restraints imposed by some of the still formidable antagonists from both sides of the Jewish fence posed some hindrance; but this

---

[22]I have mentioned above that a certain personal element was bound to colour editorial policy. The many essays on the Jewish youth movements, Zionist or non-Zionist, are such a case in point. I would single out here the important two-part studies of Jehuda Reinharz, 'Hashomer Hazair in Germany . . .', I and II, in *LBI Year Books XXXI/XXXII* (1986/1987); and Chaim Schatzker, 'The Jewish Youth Movement in Germany in the Holocaust Period . . .', I and II, in *LBI Year Books XXXII/XXXIII* (1987/1988).

[23]Arnold Paucker, 'Die Abwehr des Antisemitismus in den Jahren 1893–1933', in Herbert A. Strauss and Norbert Kampe (eds.), *Antisemitismus. Von der Judenfeindschaft zum Holocaust*, Bonn 1984, and several later editions (Schriftenreihe der Bundeszentrale für politische Bildung 213), pp. 143–171, bibliography pp. 164–171. See also *idem*, 'The Jewish Defense against Antisemitism in Germany, 1893–1933', in Jehuda Reinharz (ed.), *Living with Antisemitism. Modern Jewish Responses*, Hanover, N.H. – London 1987 (The Tauber Institute for the Study of European Jewry Series 6), pp. 104–132.

[24]'Two Debates', 'The German-Jewish Centralverein in Historical Perspective' and 'The German Zionists and the Centralverein', Preamble by A[rnold] P[aucker] and Papers by Chaim Schatzker, Abraham Margaliot, Evyatar Friesel, Jehuda Reinharz and Marjorie Lamberti, in *LBI Year Book XXXIII* (1988), pp. 95–128.

has long since been overcome. There remains only the necessity to stress the sharp topicality of these studies. In the Jewish world a majority in the West has opted for integration into pluralist societies, defending its position with methods not unlike those of the *Centralverein*; while millions have chosen the Jewish State. The subject is by no means exhausted.

The greatest change the Year Book has seen in its second phase is the much larger measure of space now given to the period 1933 to 1945. To some extent this was unavoidable; there has been in the last fifteen years a marked shift to Holocaust studies, almost a realignment of research interests, which any editor was bound to take into account. However, the change was also another act of deliberate policy on our part. When the Leo Baeck Institute was formed, the initial programme for the study of Modern German Jewry did not really go much beyond 1933. True, the "catastrophe" does figure – almost marginally it would seem – in the guidelines formulated in 1956 by Siegfried Moses, the Institute's President,[25] but it was tacitly understood (this on good authority) that the Institute should above all concentrate on the 150 years before the Nazi seizure of power; the ostensible reason being that there were already several other Jewish institutes which concerned themselves with persecution and the Holocaust – an argument which always seemed rather lame. When material on the period of the Third *Reich* did figure in our research programme, a voluntary restriction was more or less implied, and it was the constructive features of Jewish reaction to the Nazi measures, the so-called *Aufbau im Untergang*, which were emphasised – with scant attention to post-1933 Jewish policies and behavioural patterns. To this the Institute and its Year Book adhered for a considerable period.

I have argued in these pages and elsewhere[26] that here we made a great mistake – and that those accounts we have do not tell the whole story. It is more than mere surmise to believe that there were psychological stumbling blocks and one must appreciate that some fears may have had their justifications. In a dangerous time, the relations between the "unfree" Jewish representatives and the underlings and henchmen of the Nazi potentates were clouded and complex and lend themselves to misinterpretation and misrepresentation. Quislings and collaborators were few, most of those involved – exposed as they were – had acted honourably, despite considerable pressure, and had nothing to hide. But anxiety and timidity resulted in an abdication which was to leave the field wide open to ill-equipped and biased "historians"; to agitators and to third-rate dramatists with a political axe to grind. All this has led to much distortion of the historical position of the Jewish community, to charges of collaboration and much else besides, only too easily absorbed by a gullible public. This is something which had to be redressed by a new generation of professional historians working on the source material which is now becoming increasingly available.

[25]Siegfried Moses, 'Leo Baeck Institute of Jews from Germany', in *LBI Year Book I* (1956), pp. XI–XVIII, esp. pp. XV–XVI. See also *idem*, 'The First Ten Years of the Leo Baeck Institute', in *LBI Year Book X* (1966), pp. IX–XV.

[26]See my remarks in the more recent Year Book introductions and *Jüdischer Widerstand . . .* , *Jewish Resistance . . .* (note 34 below).

Yet the onus should have been on us to provide, at a much earlier date, a critical assessment of all aspects of a German Jewry subjected to a merciless dictatorship. For it is all too easy to compile an anthology made up of the reprehensible utterances of self-elected war veterans and of National German Jews or of the ingratiating approaches to *Edelnazis* from some Zionist quarters. There are some over-emphatic pronouncements from Leo Baeck or a few Orthodox rabbis issued in the first phase of Nazi power, on Jewish loyalties to the state, declaring that patriotic Jews had nothing in common with godless Communists (who were already at that time, together with so many other enemies of the regime, being tortured in prisons and Nazi concentration camps). It speaks for the moral stature of Leo Baeck that he later regretted these statements.[27] Granted all this, it remains nevertheless true that virtually all "official" utterances by representatives of German Jewry under a totalitarian regime which controlled all expressions of public opinion must be taken with a grain of salt. Sources and documentation are all very well, but the scholar must know how to interpret them, how to read between the lines. It is a vexed question for the researcher that very little can be taken at face value.[28] Drawing valid conclusions from comic sounding "laments" such as that the Jews were mortified by their exclusion from the festival of national resurrection; and taking this as proof that they were only too willing to jump on the bandwagon of the National Revolution are rather far off the mark. Although there were certainly some misguided Jewish minority groups, any such assumptions go counter to the traditions of German-Jewish history, a history which had not begun yesterday. While some disenchantment with Liberalism has been recorded, there is no indication that Germany's Jews had abandoned their faith in liberal moderation and democratic Socialism. There was a large Jewish sector which had been active in the German labour movement and there were Jewish youth movements of a pronounced Leftist orientation, many of which had also fervently embraced another kind of Nationalism. Undoubtedly, unfortunately, illusions that National Socialism might after all prove a passing phase[29] were rife within the Jewish leadership (as also amongst Jews in general) and their misreadings of the situation were nurtured by their equally deluded "philosemitic" contacts who remained within the German bureaucracy.

[27]Information obtained from Hans Reichmann and Robert Weltsch in the early 1960s. One of their conversations with Leo Baeck is mentioned above. There could be no more reliable witnesses.
[28]All surviving editors of Jewish papers published under the Nazi regime have corroborated this. See now also Arno Herzberg, 'The Jewish Press under the Nazi Regime. Its Mission, Suppression and Defiance. A Memoir', in *LBI Year Book XXXVI* (1991), pp. 367–388.
[29]C. C. Aronsfeld is probably right in correcting the apocryphal notion that Leo Baeck said as early as 1933 that the "thousand-year-long history of the German Jews has come to an end", *Die Zeit*, 8th November 1991, p. 67; *Tribüne*, vol. 30, No. 120 (1991), pp. 216–221. I am informed by Professor E. G. Lowenthal, Berlin, that the only similar statement on record was one made by Baeck as late as 1948, in a Frankfurt press conference when he said that the "einzigartige Geschichte der Juden in Deutschland, die Männer des Geistes hervorgebracht habe, wie kaum anderswo, sei zu Ende, zu Ende etwa wie die Geschichte der Juden in Spanien und Portugal in den Jahren 1492 und 1497". 'Dr. Baeck vor der Frankfurter Presse', *Jüdisches Gemeindeblatt*, vol. 3, No. 17 (22nd October 1948), p. 8. Yet to present a misguided Jewish optimism and to substantiate these general Jewish attitudes by quoting statements from the controlled and censored Jewish press, as Aronsfeld does, will be objected to by most historians.

These observations are meant only as an intimation of the complexities which face the investigator of Jewish life in Nazi Germany. In this Year Book and in other publications[30] the Institute has tried in recent years to mend previous neglect by careful analysis and to put the record straight. These are mere beginnings. The definitive history of the German Jews under the Nazi regime remains to be written. It is yet another task to be undertaken in order to counter that historical revisionism which has of late warped contemporary historiography, an ill-intentioned revisionism which we ignore at our peril.

It has been noted more than once that, particularly in the last ten years or so, German-Jewish history has been presented in the Year Book with a strong dash of anti-Fascism. That this is so surely needs no apology. The term is here used advisedly, though perhaps with some circumspection; as any historian of the period is aware of its early party-political origins and its subsequent post-war devaluation and debasement. However, many, the generation which saw the Popular Fronts, the International Brigades[31] and the war against Nazi Germany, did see themselves as anti-Fascist, in a broader sense which transcended narrow party confines or partisan politics. And, as Jewish anti-Fascists, they had come to realise that they had to combat all manifestations of Fascism or racism, whether openly antisemitic or not; that solidarity with all threatened minorities and with all victims of Fascist oppression and racial intolerance was also vital to Jewish interests. Very little is learned from history, but if we have not learned this, then we as Jews have learned nothing at all. Similar conclusions, it could be said, had already been arrived at in the last years of the Weimar Republic – certainly in a more rudimentary and hesitant form – by younger middle-class functionaries of the so often unjustly maligned *Centralverein*.[32] They were born of bitter experience and must also shape our understanding of the Jewish past.

Jewish resistance in Nazi Germany and the service of former German Jews in the armies of the anti-Fascist alliance in the Second World War are again subjects which mark the second phase of the Year Book as distinct from the first. A theme such as the illegal anti-Nazi activities of some young Jewish groups did not feature in the earlier volumes and in fact I found myself facing some opposition

---

[30]Arnold Paucker with Sylvia Gilchrist and Barbara Suchy (eds.), *Die Juden im Nationalsozialistischen Deutschland/The Jews in Nazi Germany 1933–1945*, Tübingen 1986 (Schriftenreihe wissenschaftlicher Abhandlungen des Leo Baeck Instituts 45).

[31]While the Jewish volunteers for the International Brigades came largely from the Left of the political spectrum – with a preponderance of Communists – there was widespread support for the cause of the Spanish Republic in the world Jewish community, amid growing realisation that the fight against Hitler and against Franco was one. (Cf. Arno Lustiger, 'German and Austrian Jews in the International Brigade', in *LBI Year Book XXXV* [1990], pp. 297–320; *idem, Schalom Libertad! Juden im spanischen Bürgerkrieg*, Frankfurt a. Main 1989.) The only sizeable Jewish communities who would not/could not indulge in such "official" backing were, of course, those of Germany and Italy (Portugal and, for different reasons, South Africa also qualify).

[32]Arnold Paucker, *Der jüdische Abwehrkampf gegen Antisemitismus und Nationalsozialismus in den letzten Jahren der Weimarer Republik*, Hamburg 1968, 2nd edn. 1969 (Hamburger Beiträge zur Zeitgeschichte IV); *idem*, 'Jewish Defence against Nazism in the Weimar Republic', in *The Wiener Library Bulletin*, vol. XXVI, Nos. 1/2, new series, Nos. 26/27, pp. 21–31, esp. p. 28.

when, in 1970, Jewish resistance historiography was introduced as a topic in the Year Book.[33] This "resistance" against "resistance" has been evaluated elsewhere.[34] It, too, is linked with the definition of what is "Jewishness", since many active Jewish anti-Fascists could be termed peripheral Jews who saw their work in the anti-Nazi underground as part of the struggle of the German working class. In this respect the "older" generation of more "conservative" historians was overruled. Resistance history has now become, in its turn, part of the Year Book volumes. Of course, Jews fought Nazism in many ways. And here I must declare a personal interest. To those of us who volunteered *en masse* for the Allied Armies after 1939 and 1941 this is important. Thus we have emphasised the part played by German Jews world-wide in the military defeat of Nazi Germany.[35] Yet there is more here than the bare facts. What motivated so many German-Jewish refugees or exiles to volunteer varied. They fought in their own defence, to avenge what they had suffered, as anti-Fascists and – who would deny it – in Palestine also to create the kernel of a future Jewish army, but there were those who still had an affection for what had once been a better Germany, despite having been cast out, and they felt that they were fighting to rid that country of a monstrous tyranny. Who would dispute this? Objectively seen, Germans who fought in Hitler's armies betrayed their country; the German resistance were true patriots. Those German Jews who had not entirely shaken off old loyalties could surely make a similar claim.

The end of Jewish history in Germany is seen in the popular imagination almost entirely in terms of deportation and mass murder. Yet the German Jews were not only unresisting victims. Tens of thousands also fought back wherever and however they could; in the German underground, as partisans in occupied Europe and in the massed armies of the Western Allies.[36]

In this brief rounding-up I have had to be selective and it is natural that I have chosen to discuss subjects which during my editorship were of particular interest to me. I would add that we have attempted to break out of an inherited Prussian parochialism, that we have gradually introduced comparative studies of min-

---

[33]Helmut Eschwege, 'Resistance of German Jews against the Nazi Regime', in *LBI Year Book XV* (1970), pp. 143–180.

[34]Arnold Paucker, *Jüdischer Widerstand in Deutschland. Tatsachen und Problematik*, Berlin 1989 (Beiträge zum Widerstand 1933–1945 37), pp. 4–5 and *passim*; expanded English version *Jewish Resistance in Germany. The Facts and the Problems*, Berlin 1991 (Publications in English of the Gedenkstätte Deutscher Widerstand), pp. 4–5 and *passim*. See also *idem*, 'Self-Defence against Fascism in a Middle-Class Community: The Jews in Weimar Germany and Beyond', in Francis R. Nicosia and Lawrence Stokes (eds.), *Germans against Nazism. Nonconformity, Opposition and Resistance in the Third Reich. Essays in Honour of Peter Hoffmann*, New York–Oxford 1990, pp. 59–79, esp. p. 71.

[35]For those who fell while serving in the British Forces, see Henry Morris, *We will remember them. A Record of the Jews Who Died in the Armed Forced of the Crown 1939–1945*, ed. by Gerald Smith, London 1989, which lists all the German and Austrian volunteers who died in the war against Nazi Germany. Unfortunately some of the names in the special sections for enemy aliens and Palestinian Jews are misspelt or garbled.

[36]It is probable that up to 8,000 former German Jews were in the British and American Forces poised for D-Day; and there were many thousands of German Jews with the Fifth and Eighth Armies in Italy, including the Jewish Brigade.

orities and comparative studies of different Jewish communities and emigration history; that we have aimed at a greater integration of German-Jewish historiography into general historiography. This seems to be a pointer to the future. On the other hand I am fully aware of our shortcomings. What we broadly define as the inner-Jewish history of German Jewry needs far more elaboration. But this is also a question of the material available – an editor depends on studies of good quality – and in some areas they have not always been forthcoming. I have also refrained from outlining the general task of German-Jewish historiography as exemplified in the Year Book. The reader is not only referred to the sources quoted,[37] but to the far-reaching historical surveys of Reinhard Rürup[38] and Michael Meyer[39] which introduced Year Books XXXV and XXXVI.

Those who founded the Leo Baeck Institute and its Year Book not only wanted to write the history of their destroyed community but were most anxious to preserve and to transmit what they called the "values" of German Jewry to their offspring and to coming generations. I for one – and I am not alone in this – have never accepted such a programmatic postulate. While one can sympathise with this wish, it is ideology and not historiography. Though myself a secular Jew, I am convinced that there are such specific German-Jewish values, not only in the religious sense – where they are obvious – but that there is something of a humanistic, liberal, tolerant essence, often intangible, hard to define. If, as a result of our historical research, such values are in some way handed on and bear fruit in Jewish life, well and good, only as a "mission", such a task it cannot constitute part of the editorial programme of the publication of a historical research institute.

As to the transformation of this Year Book into the recognised platform for German-Jewish studies; it has become a publication in which all trends of historical thinking are represented, all controversies are articulated, in which there is no tutelage or censorship. Today it largely serves, as Ismar Schorsch put it so succinctly in 1980 in his introduction to Year Book XXV, "as the international forum in which young American, Israeli, German and English academics, whose own historical experience lies this side of 1933, exhibit and test the products of their craft".[40] To this, twelve years later, I can have nothing to add.

In 1991 the Leo Baeck Institute lost three men who were very close to us.

[37]See note 12.
[38]Reinhard Rürup, 'An Appraisal of German-Jewish Historiography. Introduction to Year Book XXXV', in *LBI Year Book XXXV* (1990), pp. XV–XXIV.
[39]Michael A. Meyer, 'Jews as Jews versus Jews as Germans. Two Historical Perspectives. Introduction to Year Book XXXVI', in *LBI Year Book XXXVI* (1991), pp. XV–XXII.
[40]Ismar Schorsch, 'The Leo Baeck Institute: Continuity amid Desolation: Introduction to Year Book XXV', in *LBI Year Book XXV* (1980), pp. IX–XII, quotation, p. IX.

Erwin Rosenthal, the orientalist and Judaist, died on 5th June 1991 in Cambridge, in his 87th year. He belonged to our founder generation and was a much-loved member of the London Board of the LBI. Born in Heilbronn, he studied at Heidelberg, Munich and Berlin. His first publication was a work on the fourteenth-century Tunisian historian Ibn Khaldun, which appeared in 1932. Deprived of an academic career by the Nazis, he came to England in 1933, teaching first at University College London, eventually becoming Reader in Oriental Studies at Cambridge University and Fellow of Pembroke College. He had numerous scholarly publications to his credit, but what he himself regarded as his single most important contribution was *Averroes' Commentary on Plato's Republic* (1952). For the Leo Baeck Institute, in 1963, he opened Year Book VIII with a masterly essay on Ismar Elbogen. A wise and kindly counsellor to the Editor, he will be remembered with great affection.

Curt Wormann, the Germanist and pre-eminent librarian, died on 2nd July 1991, in Jerusalem, in his 92nd year. He, too, belonged to the founders of our Institute and was a member of the Jerusalem Board of the LBI from the beginning. It was Wormann who built up the modern library system in Israel and he became Director of the Jewish National and University Library, Jerusalem. He was also the founder and Director of the Graduate Library School, Jerusalem. He wrote many works on library science, general literature and adult education. In 1970 he contributed an incisive study on the cultural situation of the German Jews in Israel to our Year Book.

Gerson D. Cohen, the eminent Judaist, died on 16th August 1991 in New York at the age of 67. He was a Fellow of the New York LBI and a member of its Board. For thirteen years he was Chancellor of the Jewish Theological Seminary of America and Professor of Jewish History there and at Columbia University. Under his direction, the Seminary established its Institute for the Study of European Jewry. He was a prolific writer, the most recent of his works being *Studies in the Variety of Rabbinic Cultures*. He was a valued adviser to our New York Institute; and in 1970 he wrote a stimulating and profound Introduction to our Year Book: 'German Jewry as Mirror of Modernity'.

As retiring Editor my first thanks must be to those who year by year put this annual together. Sylvia Gilchrist, who joined us in 1978, has been Assistant Editor for over ten years. Her skill and dedication have been invaluable. It is her meticulous care which has smoothed the entire process of the production of the Year Book. The Bibliography is noted as an especial feature of our publication. It was initiated by Ilse Wolff in 1956. The fascination of bibliography attracts its devotees who can become almost obsessive in its pursuit, as was Bertha Cohn who worked for us until 1979. We were fortunate in Irmgard Foerg's enthusiasm and expertise for the task she undertook from then until 1990. It is now carried out by Barbara Suchy who is herself a historian of German Jewry. Continuity is provided by Annette Pringle who has been responsible, over many years, for the English-language material. Janet Langmaid, our excellent indexer has now also completed the manuscript of the General Index Volume for Year Books XXI to XXXV. Dora Segall, Editorial Assistant to Robert Weltsch in the first ten years; and Ilse Shindel, who retired as Editorial Secretary in 1974, have both continued to assist us in many ways. The late Lux Furtmüller was our brilliant translator for many years, a task now taken on adroitly by Louise Willmot. Emma Morgan has been a much valued Editorial Assistant for the last three years. Pauline Paucker was pressed into service as English lector by Robert Weltsch in 1959 and continued unremittingly – and for the Institute she has done so much more besides.

I would like to thank here our publishers Secker & Warburg/Heinemann who have produced for us twenty-one volumes with care and understanding; and in particular Dan Franklin and Mary Gibson who were responsible for the publication in the most recent years. We are very appreciative of Richard Clay, our printers, and Wilmaset, the photosetters, for their patient co-operation. The London Institute and the editorial office of the Year Book have been housed for 33 years in the same building as the Wiener Library; and to the latter the Editor would like to express his gratitude; without its resources and the unstinting help of its staff, the editing work would have been beset by the greatest difficulties.

The Editor owes a particular debt to his friends and colleagues on the London Executive of the LBI, Esra Bennathan, Julius Carlebach, Hans Feld, John Grenville, Werner E. Mosse, Peter Pulzer and David Sorkin for their constant support. But I must single out Werner Mosse, our Chairman of almost fifteen years, for his energetic backing, and our treasurer Hans Feld who has helped us to weather many a financial storm. In New York, Max Gruenewald, who resigned as International President of the LBI in 1991, under whose presidency the Institute enjoyed a most successful phase, and Fred Grubel, its Director until 1991 and now the Institute's Vice President, have used their wide contacts in the United States to great advantage for the Year Book; a path now continued by its new Director, Robert Jacobs. Michael Meyer and Ismar Schorsch, one now International President of the Institute and the other President of the New York LBI, both leading Judaists, have lent their intellectual authority and advice. In Jerusalem, five successive Directors, from the wise and level-headed Shalom Adler-Rudel, and Jochanan Ginat, to Joseph Walk, Daniel Brecher and now Shlomo Mayer, have also aided us in many ways.

A great many individuals, who cannot all be named here, have assisted the Year Book and the Editor; the following have given exceptional help in the past few years: Werner T. Angress, Berlin; Avraham Barkai, Israel; Werner Becker, Bonn; Ingrid Belke, Marbach; Guiseppe Bevilacqua, Florence; Peter Brod, Prague; Ursula Büttner, Hamburg; David Cesarani, London; Susie Cohen, Jerusalem; Avi Dinshaw, Channel Islands; Helga Eberhard, Hamburg; Ze'ev

Estreicher, Tel-Aviv; Albert H. Friedlander, London; Evyatar Friesel, Jerusalem; Kate Gardiner, London; Robert Gavron, London; Nachum Tim Gidal, Jerusalem; Günter Ginzel, Cologne; Gisela Greive, Cologne; Ludger Heid, Duisburg; Gerhard Hentrich, Berlin; Gerhard Hirschfeld, Stuttgart; Christhard Hoffmann, Berlin; Stefi Jersch-Wenzel, Berlin; Werner Jochmann, Hamburg; James Joll, London; Marion A. Kaplan, New York; Ian Kershaw, Sheffield; Konrad Kwiet, Sydney; Ernest K. Litthauer, Birmingham; Cécile Lowenthal-Hensel, Berlin; Ernst G. Lowenthal, Berlin; Arno Lustiger, Frankfurt a. Main; C. T. Marx, London; Yogi Mayer, London; Gerhard Moest, Leipzig; George L. Mosse, Madison, Wisconsin; Francis R. Nicosia, Colchester, Vermont; Liliana Picciotto Fargion, Milan; Jehuda Reinharz, Waltham, Mass.; Monika Richarz, Cologne; Michael A. Riff, New York; Werner Rosenstock, London; Tom Rosenthal, London; Reinhard Rürup, Berlin; Ernst Schulin, Freiburg; Joshua A. Sherman, New York; Hermann Simon, Berlin; Albert Sternfeld, Vienna; Herbert A. Strauss, New York; Bernhard Suchy, Düsseldorf; Jacob Toury, Israel; Rudolf Vierhaus, Göttingen; Hans Walz, Hanover; Tony Wells, London; Christa Wichmann, London; P. B. Wiener, Birmingham; Alexandra Wiessler, London; Robert Wistrich, London/Jerusalem and Moshe Zimmermann, Jerusalem.

Finally, I owe a tremendous debt to the generation which moulded German-Jewish studies in our century and was closely associated with the work of the Leo Baeck Institute. And in these last sentences I must pay my own personal tribute to three people who had a formative influence on me: Salomon A. Birnbaum, the Yiddishist and Hebrew paleographer who first aroused my love for Jewish learning; Robert Weltsch, the writer and editor, who taught me my craft; and Eva G. Reichmann, the sociologist and historian, who inspired my research.

It is in their spirit that I have striven to edit the Year Book of the Leo Baeck Institute.

London in the Summer of 1992 *Arnold Paucker*

Jewish Culture and Religion

Jews, the Enlightenment and Religious Toleration – Some Reflections

BY DAVID SORKIN

When pronounced in German, "*Juden und Aufklärung*" has a special resonance. It was the German-speaking Jews of Central Europe who transformed the Enlightenment into a cult central to their self-definition. Only they had a "patron saint" such as Moses Mendelssohn who equally personified the "Jews" and the "*Aufklärung*" and whose friendship with Lessing supplied an ideal relationship between Christians and Jews; only they created a significant Jewish version of the *Aufklärung* in the eighteenth century, the *Haskalah*.[1] They alone enshrined the *Aufklärung* as representing a new era in their history. Elsewhere in Europe it was different. In England the Jews understood the resettlement of the seventeenth century to have incorporated them into the Whig tradition, the unfolding of English liberties since 1688.[2] In France the Jews identified with the Revolution of 1789 that had granted them citizenship, and the Napoleonic Sanhedrin that had wedded them to the state. In these historic nations the symbols of Jewish self-representation were primarily political, even if the causes of resettlement and the criteria for integration patently were not. In the politically belated German nation, in contrast, culture could be the foundation for citizenship and politics. It could serve as compensation for an incomplete emancipation, consolation for an imperfect social integration, or a secure anchorage when the social and political waters turned rough.

That German Jews relentlessly celebrated the cult of "*Juden und Aufklärung*" goes without saying. A few examples of the historic ritual will suffice. The centenary of Mendelssohn's birth in 1829 was commemorated with sermons, articles and books. The preacher and scholar, Leopold Zunz, typically asserted

---

This article is dedicated to Arnold Paucker, who, as editor of the Year Book, has done so much to encourage young scholars.

[1]For the phrase "patron saint" see Alexander Altmann, 'Moses Mendelssohn as the Archetypal German Jew', in Jehuda Reinharz and Walter Schatzberg (eds.), *The Jewish Response to German Culture. From the Enlightenment to the Second World War*, Hanover–London 1985, p. 18.

[2]I am indebted to Dr. David Cesarani of the Wiener Library, London, for allowing me to read his unpublished paper, 'Dual Heritage or Duel of Heritages? Englishness and Jewishness in the Heritage Industry'.

of Mendelssohn that: "As a man and a writer, he was at once teacher and model."[3]

In 1838 the lawyer, political activist and future Vice-President of the Frankfurt Assembly, Gabriel Riesser, appealing to his fellow "Israelites" for contributions to a Lessing memorial, identified Lessing with "education of mankind, love of mankind, Enlightenment, freedom of conscience", and the "struggle against intolerance, religious animosity, intellectual oppression". He then asked.

> "Whose heart beats louder over the thoughts of freedom, toleration, love of mankind, the struggle against religious animosity and moral constraint than that of the German Jew, when he is able to comprehend his position and vocation?"

But of course Lessing's relationship with the Jews was more intimate still. The cause of the Jews inspired Lessing's muse in *Nathan der Weise*:

> "Since Judaism had suffered longest and hardest from oppression, hatred and persecution, Lessing's muse chose it for the cornerstone of the poetic temple of reconciliation and love of mankind."

And, of course, his friendship with Mendelssohn was a model of moral relations:

> "Where are we to find a purer and more sublime model than in Lessing's and Mendelssohn's friendship?"[4]

Such views were not limited to liberals or Reform Jews. Orthodox Jews also belonged to the subculture, participating fully in the cult by elevating the triad of Lessing, Schiller and Kant. Samson Raphael Hirsch, the patriarch of Frankfurt Neo-Orthodoxy, in 1859 claimed Schiller for Judaism.

> "Are these not Jewish thoughts and perceptions with which he has penetrated the heart of the German people and for which the entire German people rises to offer Schiller its heartfelt jubilation?"[5]

In 1905 a lesser Orthodox leader, Raphael Breuer, reiterated this view:

> "At the moment Israel has more in common with Schiller's genius than those for whom he wrote."[6]

The 1929 bicentenary of Mendelssohn's and Lessing's birth provided another opportunity, with representatives of all the competing viewpoints weighing in: Reform, Orthodox, Zionist and Right-wing veterans. It comes as no surprise that the first play the ostracised Jewish artists who comprised the *Jüdischer Kulturbund* performed on 1st October 1933 was Lessing's *Nathan der Weise*. It is also not

---

[3]Leopold Zunz, *Rede gehalten bei der Feier von Moses Mendelssohns hundertjährigen Geburtstage*, Berlin 1829.

[4]Gabriel Riesser, *Einige Worte über Lessings Denkmal; an die Israeliten Deutschlands gerichtet*, Frankfurt a. Main 1838.

[5]Samson Raphael Hirsch, 'Worte gesprochen bei der Schillerfeier, 1859', in *idem, Gesammelte Schriften*, 6 vols., Frankfurt a. Main 1912, vol. VI, p. 311.

[6]*Der Israelit*, 46 (1905), p. 736; quoted in Mordechai Breuer, 'Das Bild der Aufklärung bei der deutsch-jüdischen Orthodoxie', in *Wolfenbütteler Studien zur Aufklärung*, 14 (1990), pp. 131–142.

surprising that in the 1930s younger intellectuals, such as Hannah Arendt, began to question the cult of *"Juden und Aufklärung"*.[7]

Such celebration belonged, of course, to the reception of *"Juden und Aufklärung"*: it was an essential part of German Jewry's self-understanding, its subculture. Yet reception-history and history are not identical. The cult long obscured the historical reality of the *Aufklärung* by making its relationship to the Jews a norm. The same holds for the Jews' relationship to the *Aufklärung*. The *Haskalah* has been subsumed to the issues of emancipation and assimilation rather than being studied in its own terms. I would like to examine both sides of that relationship before proceeding to one of the less-known points at which the two met. My purpose is to highlight the ambiguities which beset this historical turning point.

I

Let us look first at the *Aufklärung*'s relationship to the Jews. Historians have revised the subculture's view of that relationship by putting the politics back in. They have taught us, in the first place, that the role the *Aufklärung* played in altering the Jews' situation was more modest than the subculture would have allowed. A few dates will be helpful. The *Aufklärung* in Germany can be dated to the closing decades of the seventeenth century. Christian Thomasius's major works began to appear in the 1690s; the first of Christian Wolff's series of treatises (*Vernünftige Gedanken*) was published in 1719; the "moral weeklies" appeared in force in the 1720s; the University of Halle was founded in 1694, Göttingen in 1736; the Berlin Academy in 1700, the Bavarian Academy in 1759. Yet the Jews were allowed to resettle in Berlin in 1671, Anhalt-Dessau in 1672, Kurhessen in 1653. Not the *Aufklärung*, but a combination of absolutist ambition and mercantilist policy brought significant numbers of Jews back into the German territories. This return constituted a virtual resettlement. Jewish residence since the Middle Ages had survived plague, persecution and expulsion in only a few areas, most notably in the West (centred around Frankfurt a. Main) and the South East. The rest of the German territories had largely been emptied of Jews.

> "By 1570 the Jews had been cleared from every major German secular territory except Hesse, and from every Imperial Free City of any importance except Frankfurt."[8]

Resettlement took place during and after the Thirty Years' War as sovereigns came to regard the Jews as a source of revenue, an aid in restoring economic activity and a means to circumvent the Estates. This was an example of mercantilist practice forging ahead of mercantilist theory and law. A striking example is Brandenburg. The Peace of Westphalia had established the toleration

---

[7]Elizabeth Petuchowski. 'Zur Lessing-Rezeption in der deutsch-jüdischen Presse. Lessings 200. Geburtstag (22. Januar 1929)', in *Lessing Yearbook*, 14 (1982), pp. 43–59; Hannah Arendt-Stern, 'Aufklärung und Judenfrage', in *Zeitschrift für die Geschichte der Juden in Deutschland*, 4 (1932), pp. 65–77.

[8]Jonathan Israel, *European Jewry in the Age of Mercantilism, 1550–1750*, Oxford 1985, p. 23.

of private worship for the three recognised religions – Lutherans, Calvinists and Catholics, but not for dissenters. In 1662 Friedrich Wilhelm promulgated an edict declaring a "Christian toleration and moderation . . . so that the truth can be sought, and found, in peace"; in 1664 he extended *tolerantia Ecclesiastica* to Protestant sects; and in 1671 defied the Estates by declaring "that the Jews and their commerce seem not detrimental to us and the country but rather beneficial" and admitted fifty Jewish families recently expelled from Vienna.[9] Such practice of *raison d'état*, of politics independent from religion, was not legally codified until the Wöllner decrees of 1788. It also went beyond mercantilist theory: in Germany and England at the time its major theorists argued that the Jews were a liability, and not an asset.[10]

The result of such a policy was that from 1648 to the end of the *ancien régime* the Court Jew became a common figure. By serving a prince or other sovereign, he was often able to establish new Jewish settlements (Berlin, Dessau) or to renew old ones (Dresden, Leipzig, Kassel, Brunswick, Halle). This resettlement represented a distinct historical stage in the development of toleration towards Jews. This was toleration the ruler granted by will. This toleration did not imply rights, such as personal freedom of religion. It also did not entail uniform rights of worship: the Peace of Westphalia had distinguished between at least three forms (public worship, private worship, domestic devotion). Such toleration, in other words, was part of a corporate society in which the ruler granted privileges to groups or individuals on the basis of political and economic expediency.[11]

That expediency prevailed in the admission of Jews is self-evident in the distinctions made between rich and poor. Rulers who granted admission to wealthy Jews often exempted them from Jewish law courts by placing them under personal jurisdiction. The *Schutzjuden* were allowed to have families and the retainers they required for their households and businesses. The sorts of privileges granted to them evolved in the course of the eighteenth century: from the original *Schutzbrief* giving the individual personal, untransferable privileges; to a *Generalpatent* that applied to a widow and children; to a *Generalprivileg* which gave the same rights as Christian merchants (Prussia, 1761); to a *Naturalisationspatent* granting citizenship without the right of political participation; to full *Staatsbürgerliche Rechte* (in Prussia in the 1790s).[12] The few who enjoyed such benefits – *Hoffaktoren*, merchants – constituted a new mercantile elite. Yet they also suffered from numerous disabilities, which taxed their purses, but, even worse, their pride.

---

[9]Quoted in Gerhard Besier, 'Toleranz', in *Geschichtliche Grundbegriffe. Historisches Lexicon zur politisch-sozialen Sprache in Deutschland*, vol. VI, Stuttgart 1990, pp. 496–497.

[10]Shmuel Ettinger, 'The Beginnings of the Change in the Attitude of European Society Towards the Jews', in *Scripta Hierosolymitana*, 7 (1961), pp. 211–212. Ettinger's examples are William Petty in England and Johann Joachim Becher in Germany.

[11]Walter Grossmann, 'Religious Toleration in Germany, 1684–1750', in *Studies on Voltaire and the Eighteenth Century*, 201 (1982), pp. 115–141; Hermann Conrad, 'Religionsbann, Toleranz und Parität am Ende des alten Reiches', in Heinrich Lutz (ed.), *Zur Geschichte der Toleranz und Religionsfreiheit*, Darmstadt 1977, pp. 164–171.

[12]Heinrich Schnee, *Die Hoffinanz und der moderne Staat. Geschichte und System der Hoffaktoren an deutschen Fürstenhöfen im Zeitalter des Absolutismus*, 6 vols., 1953–1967, vol. 3, pp. 214–215.

Those who suffered most from such disabilities were, of course, the poor. It has been estimated that in 1750 there were 60,000–70,000 Jews in the areas that were to constitute Imperial Germany. Some 50–60% lived below the level of the guild masters and well over half lived a marginal existence of petty trade, begging and thievery. Mercantilist policy and *raison d'état* dictated that these *Betteljuden* and *Trödeljuden* be excluded or, as in the case of Prussia in 1750, expelled. Gaining the right of residence was often unachievable, unless one was in the employ of the mercantile elite. And even those who found domicile in a village or rural hamlet often struggled to eke out a living because of occupational restrictions and other disabilities, the most humiliating being the *Leibzoll*, a transit tax otherwise applicable only to cattle.[13]

If *raison d'état* and mercantilism brought the Jews back to the Germanies and determined their legal status, then what effect did the *Aufklärung* have? At what point did it impinge on the Jews? One early form was intervention by the state in communal autonomy. This belonged to the states' general effort to reduce corporate institutions in the name of administrative centralisation and fiscal independence. Jewish communal autonomy was an easy target. In some cases the original settlement privileges limited legal jurisdiction, powers of taxation and the right to admit additional Jews (e.g. Berlin). In other cases the lack of historic privileges and dependence on the ruler made the Jewish community especially vulnerable. Such encroachment, which increasingly integrated the Jews into the mechanisms of the all-pervasive bureaucratic state, can also be seen as an outgrowth of *Aufklärung* political ideals. An unmediated relationship between state and subject was one goal of natural rights theory, since it was a prerequisite for the realisation of individual rights. Yet such administrative integration remained compatible with the *Polizeistaat* that also discriminated against the Jews. Here is an example of *Aufklärung* in the service of absolutism.[14] Such administrative integration was necessary, but not sufficient to bring about the next stage in toleration – emancipation. This required a different image of the Jews as well as a major reorganisation of state and society (e.g. Baden, 1809; Prussia, 1812).

The *Aufklärung* provided this image by creating a discourse of universal humanity. But historians have taught us – we now come to the second point about the *Aufklärung* – that in this regard the *Aufklärer* were ambivalent, indeed fundamentally so. The idea of universal humanity presumed a universal morality. Virtue was to take the place of belief as the criterion of admission. The *Aufklärer* envisioned a society of virtuous men rather than a society of believers, though they might be that as well. The problem was that throughout Europe the enlighteners had grave doubts about the Jews' actual or even potential *Tugend*. They were torn by conflicting images of the Jews. Eighteenth-century (though

---

[13]Much work needs to be done on the Jewish poor in the eighteenth century. See Rudolf Glanz, *Geschichte des niederen jüdischen Volkes in Deutschland*, New York 1968; Azriel Shohat, *Im Hilufei Tekufot*, Jerusalem 1960. and see now Steven M. Lowenstein, 'Two Silent Minorities. Orthodox Jews and Poor Jews in Berlin, 1770–1823', in *LBI Year Book XXXVI* (1991), pp. 3–26.

[14]Selma Stern, *Der preussische Staat und die Juden*, 8 vols., Tübingen 1962–1975 (Schriftenreihe wissenschaftlicher Abhandlungen des Leo Baeck Instituts 7, 8, 24 and 32).

not earlier) proponents of economic utility had joined Protestant philosemites enamoured of the Bible in propagating a favourable image. But opponents of established religion used the Jews as a stick to beat the Church: from the English deists onwards the immorality of the Old Testament and, by extension, of contemporary Jews, was used to excoriate Christianity. As a result, the *Aufklärung* transmuted the inherited Christian notion of the Jews' theological inferiority into a secular notion of moral inferiority. This was evident in France, where Montesquieu's positive image based on *raison d'état* clashed sharply with that of Diderot, D'Holbach and Voltaire, who saw the Jews as personifications of clericalism, superstition and, especially in the case of Voltaire, irremediable corruption.[15]

This issue of morality was at the heart of the German *Aufklärung's* attitude to the Jews. Around mid-century the elements began to appear that made possible an argument for toleration, and eventually emancipation. Cameralists recognised the Jews' economic utility. Writers such as Christian Gellert and Lessing devised the figure of the "edler Jude" who established the claim, at least in theory, to Jewish virtue. In addition, these writers and others began to promote the environmentalist argument that the Jews' faults – so obvious among the poor – were the result of discrimination and disabilities rather than of national character or religion. These arguments had crystallised and were widely circulated by the 1770s.[16] Yet the fundamental ambivalence remained. To take one example, Christian Gellert's 1746 novel, *Leben der Schwedischen Gräfin*, featured a Russian Jew who proved:

> "that there are pure hearts even among that people which seems least likely to have them"

and in addition to that:

> "Perhaps many of these people would have better hearts if, with our contempt and cunning violence, we did not make them abject and deceitful in their transactions; and did not through our ideas often force them to hate our religion."

Yet in a letter Gellert could write of an old Jew he had just seen:

> "an old worthy Jew, if such exists".

Gellert's "edler Jude" was a literary construct.[17]

The consequence of this ambivalence is that toleration and emancipation were made contingent upon regeneration. This comes to the fore in Christian Wilhelm Dohm's *Über die bürgerliche Verbesserung der Juden* (1781). Dohm vigorously

[15]Ettinger, 'The Beginnings of the Change', *loc. cit.*; Paul H. Meyer, 'The Attitude of the Enlightenment Towards the Jews', in *Studies on Voltaire and the Eighteenth Century*, 26 (1963); Arthur Hertzberg, *The French Enlightenment and the Jews*, New York 1970.

[16]Jacob Toury, 'Die Behandlung jüdischer Problematik in der Tagesliteratur der Aufklärung (bis 1783)', in *Jahrbuch des Instituts für deutsche Geschichte*, 5, Tel-Aviv 1976, pp. 13–47.

[17]Jürgen Stenzel, 'Idealisierung und Vorurteil. Zur Figur des "edlen Juden" in der deutschen Literatur des 18. Jahrhunderts', in Stéphane Mosès and Albrecht Schöne (eds.), *Juden in der deutschen Literatur*, Frankfurt a. Main 1986, pp. 114–126.

propounded the environmental argument. "The Jew is more man than Jew."[18] The Jews were debased as a result of disabilities and restrictions; once these were removed they would improve. "Bürgerliche Verbesserung" thus meant regeneration as well as an improvement of civil status.

From Dohm onwards emancipation came to be conceived as a contract in which rights were predicated upon a regeneration encompassing education, occupations and religion. Dohm had the political sagacity to see that rights had to come first: only the ennobling conditions of freedom could transform the oppressed. Others did not share this view. Most *Aufklärer* thought emancipation should be a step-by-step exchange. Nor did the states follow Dohm. Jewish emancipation became an incremental process of regeneration under state tutelage. The Jews' regeneration was consequently a public issue. It was debated in the first half of the nineteenth century in respect to emancipation, in the last third of the century and during the Weimar Republic in terms of the "*Judenfrage*". In other words, it bedevilled Germans and German-Jews from the *Aufklärung* until the bitter end. And its companion piece was, of course, the German-Jewish cult of the *Aufklärung*: the more virulent the debate, the more energetic the celebration of the cult.

One historian has argued in the case of France that the Enlightenment's presumption to reshape the Jews was the source of modern antisemitism.[19] This claim is exaggerated. But I think we should not shrink from acknowledging the *Aufklärung*'s ambivalence and its consequences. The *Aufklärer* had the courage to see the Jews as men. They lacked the conviction unconditionally to treat them as such.

II

So much for the *Aufklärung*. What about "*Juden*"? Here I would like to focus on the Jewish version of the *Aufklärung*, the *Haskalah*. The *Haskalah* is generally dated from the 1770s. It is associated with such figures as Moses Mendelssohn, Naphtali Herz Wessely and David Friedländer. Its best known literary creations were the Hebrew journal *Hame'asef*, Wessely's educational manifesto *Words of Peace and Truth* (*Divrei Shalom ve-Emet*) and Mendelssohn's German translation of the Bible (printed in Hebrew script) with a Hebrew commentary known as the *Biur*; its best known institution was the Berlin *Freischule* (1778). Most historians regard it as an effort "to return the Jews to the world of reality" – a campaign of reform in imitation of the *Aufklärung* designed to gain emancipation.[20] This view makes the *Haskalah* primarily a response to external developments. Yet the concern with emancipation came only in the 1770s and 1780s. The *Haskalah*

[18]Christian Wilhelm Dohm, *Über die bürgerliche Verbesserung der Juden*, 2 vols., Berlin–Stettin 1781–1783, vol. I, p. 28. For Dohm see Robert Liberles, 'Dohm's Treatise on the Jews. A Defence of the Enlightenment', in *LBI Year Book XXXIII* (1988), pp. 29–42.

[19]Hertzberg, *The French Enlightenment and the Jews, op. cit.*

[20]Isaac Barzilay, 'The Ideology of the Berlin Haskalah', in *Proceedings of the American Academy of Jewish Research*, 25 (1956), p. 1.

began instead as an indigenous effort to renew Judaism; contact with the *Aufklärung* helped give it shape; only later did it become an effort to reform the Jews.

Historians have a tendency to treat the Judaism of early modern Europe as timeless, or "traditional". This was not so. It was a particular interpretation of the tradition – let us call it baroque Judaism – and like any other, had its strengths and weaknesses. Its strength was its single-minded concentration on the study of Talmud and law, which it often supported with mystical i.e., kabbalistic ideas. Its weaknesses were the method of Talmud study – a casuistry often at odds with literal meaning – its neglect of Hebrew, the Bible and the Jewish philosophical tradition and its cultural insularity manifest in a disdain of foreign languages and science.

The *Haskalah* was not an attack on tradition, but instead an attempt to revise baroque Judaism. It emerged from a number of sources. There was a line of pedagogical critics from the late sixteenth century deeply dissatisfied with the curriculum of the schools, and especially the predominance of casuistry in the study of Talmud. Complementing these critics were admirers of the Sephardic Jewish schools, which systematically taught the Bible and the Hebrew language, preferred the literal to the casuistic study of Talmud, and included vernacular languages, science and mathematics. In the first half of the eighteenth century, works of various sorts appeared that contributed to a different vision of Judaism: Hebrew dictionaries and grammars; popular manuals of science in Hebrew; exegetical works that argued the indispensability of science and mathematics for a correct understanding of Bible and Talmud; study aids for medieval Jewish philosophy. In 1742 Maimonides's *Guide for the Perplexed*, one of the central texts of medieval Jewish philosophy, was republished for the first time in almost two centuries.[21]

One work at mid-century perhaps gives a sense of what the *Haskalah* represented and how contact with the *Aufklärung* influenced it. In 1755 Moses Mendelssohn issued a few numbers of a Hebrew journal, the *Preacher of Morals (Kohelet Musar)*. Modelled on the "moralische Wochenschriften", it presented a fresh reading of biblical, rabbinic and medieval philosophical texts, which were explicated with the categories of Christian Wolff's philosophy. The articles embraced the *Aufklärung*'s ideal of the "virtuous" man who was committed to religious-metaphysical truth and the fulfilment of ethical obligations. Mendelssohn also made a plea for Hebrew, showing it to be equal to other languages by

---

[21]I have discussed these at length in, 'From Context to Comparison. The German Haskalah and Reform Catholicism', in *Tel-Aviver Jahrbuch für deutsche Geschichte*, XX (1991), pp. 23–58. For early *maskilic* figures see Steven and Henry Schwarzschild, 'Two Lives in the Jewish Frühaufklärung. Raphael Levi Hannover and Moses Abraham Wolff', in *LBI Year Book XXIX* (1984), pp. 229–276. For the influence of the Sephardim see Ismar Schorsch, 'The Myth of Sephardic Supremacy', in *LBI Year Book XXXIV* (1989), pp. 47–53. For Hebrew publishing see Menahem Schmelzer, 'Hebrew Printing and Publishing in Germany, 1650–1750. On Jewish Book Culture and the Emergence of Modern Jewry', in *LBI Year Book XXXIII* (1988), pp. 369–383.

translating some contemporary English verse (Edward Young's *Night Thoughts*).[22]

The *Haskalah*'s alternative to baroque Judaism was, then, a reasonable understanding of Judaism consisting of the study of Hebrew language, grammar and the Bible; a literal construction of the Talmud; a revival of medieval philosophy and philosophical exegesis; and an end to cultural insularity through the study of languages, science and mathematics. The Enlightenment also had its place, primarily in the form of science and Wolffian philosophy. The *Haskalah* was a new means of expounding Judaism that was entirely within the boundaries of authority and piety. As an effort at intellectual renewal it had much in common with the Protestant *theologische Aufklärung* or Reform Catholicism, both of which aspired to replace scholasticism with a reasonable reading of their respective religion that utilised the new science (Newton) and philosophy (Wolff).

The 1770s and 1780s brought a major change by inextricably binding the *Haskalah* to emancipation. The public discussion culminating in Dohm's tract, as well as Joseph II's *Toleranzpatent*, politicised the *Haskalah*. The educational issues it addressed to renew Judaism were now enlisted to reform the Jews. Some things escaped this politicisation, at least to start with. The Berlin *Freischule*, founded in 1778, taught the children of the poor in the spirit of the *Haskalah*, offering Jewish subjects (Bible, Hebrew, Talmud), but also secular ones such as languages and arithmetic. Mendelssohn's Bible translation and commentary epitomised the *Haskalah*'s ideal of a reasonable Judaism, making the Bible accessible by linking the best of contemporary knowledge (aesthetics and Bible study, science and philosophy) with the best of the rationalist tradition of Judaism (medieval philosophy, philosophical exegesis and grammar). Wesseley's *Words of Peace and Truth* (1782) caught the full force of controversy. Joseph II's *Toleranzpatent* legislated compulsory education for Jewish children including secular subjects. Wessely tried to support Joseph II by showing that such a reform did not threaten Judaism but promised to enhance it: he thought that if such changes were introduced in the spirit of *Haskalah* they could both renew Judaism and transform the Jews. Wessely's pamphlet drew criticism from influential rabbis. In subsequent years these same rabbis criticised Mendelssohn's *Biur* (one claimed the difficult German made Hebrew "a maidservant to German") as well as the *Freischule*, whose press (*Die orientalische Buchdruckerei*) was placed under a ban.

If the 1770s and 1780s bound the *Haskalah* to emancipation, the 1790s bound it to assimilation. Lax or lapsed observance among the wealthy; including apostasy and intermarriage among the young; and calls by some radical thinkers (e.g. Lazarus Ben-David, Saul Ascher) for an abrogation of the law because it was an insurmountable obstacle to emancipation – all these now became identified with the *Haskalah*. These were, however, a disfiguration. The *Haskalah* was not alone in suffering such a fate. Reform Catholicism and the *theologische Aufklärung* were also politicised during the *Spätaufklärung*, becoming associated

[22]Meir Gilon, *Kohelet Musar le-Mendelssohn al Reka Tekufato*, Jerusalem 1979.

with ideas and policies that were hardly in keeping with their origins. The
Haskalah was an indigenous effort at religious renewal that was influenced by the
Aufklärung and diverted by emancipation.[23]

III

One little known point at which *Aufklärung* and *Haskalah* met was the attitude of
the established religions to toleration. The nineteenth century shrouded this
issue in myth. *Kulturprotestantismus* assigned Catholics an eternal monopoly on
intolerance. Catholics accused Protestants of religious indifference. German
Jews asserted that Judaism had always been tolerant. The facts show otherwise.
In the sixteenth and seventeenth centuries the idea of toleration had been the
preserve of heterodox sects, humanists, irenicists, proponents of *raison d'état* or
early enlighteners.[24] In eighteenth-century Germany all three religions had to
learn toleration. This was neither simple nor painless. Justifying toleration
required major theological adjustments, whether in the interpretation of central
beliefs (e.g. revelation) or in the understanding of Church or synagogue as an
institution. Protestant *theologische Aufklärer*, Reform Catholics and Jewish *maskilim* all made these alterations by reconciling the language of natural right and
reason with belief.

In general, secular practice preceded religious theory. In the Protestant case,
as we have seen, some princes extended toleration in the latter half of the
seventeenth century. This was in advance of the provisions of the Peace of
Westphalia and made civic toleration and the privilege of private worship moot
points.[25] When Protestant theologians debated the issue in the eighteenth
century they were concerned with dogmatic toleration and full civic equality
linked to the right of public worship. The debate turned on the understanding of
revelation. One can see this in the case of a prominent opponent of toleration,
Johann Melchior Goeze, the Hamburg pastor made infamous by his polemics,
especially with Lessing. He construed the Lutheran concept of revelation as an
exclusive claim to the entire life of the believer. Since this understanding
established an absolute truth in which belief was paramount, dogma dictating
ethics, it was inherently intolerant. Goeze accepted, for example, that members
of other faiths might be sincere and moral, yet true Lutheran belief in Christ was
the only guarantee.

> "Only those who are righteous in Christ Jesus have a sincere heart in its authentic and full
> sense."

---

[23]Sorkin, 'From Context to Comparison', *loc. cit.* For the *Maskilim* and the Talmud see Moshe Pelli,
'The Attitude of the First Maskilim in Germany towards the Talmud', in *LBI Year Book XXVII*
(1982), pp. 243–260. For a moderate *Maskil* see Nehama Rezler-Bersohn, 'Isaac Satanow. An
Epitome of an Era', in *LBI Year Book XXV* (1980), pp. 81–99.

[24]Henry Kamen, *The Rise of Toleration*, London 1967.

[25]Grossmann, 'Religious Toleration in Germany', *loc. cit.*; Conrad, 'Religionsbann, Toleranz und
Parität', *loc. cit.*; Ernst Wolff, 'Toleranz nach evangelischer Verständnis', in Lutz (ed.), *Zur
Geschichte der Toleranz und Religionsfreiheit, op. cit.*, pp. 135–154.

Goeze agreed that the State must grant freedom of conscience and civil toleration. He also urged brotherly love between members of different confessions. Yet he rejected the right of public worship to Calvinists in Hamburg, opposing the construction of a church.[26]

Among those who made the theological argument for toleration was Johann Lorenz von Mosheim, church historian and Professor of Theology at Tübingen. Mosheim was a proponent of the "collegialist" theory of church law which made the Enlightenment's regard for individual freedom and autonomous reason integral to Christianity and the Church. Using ideas of natural law and contract theory he argued that the Church was a free society of equal members. It was distinguished from other societies merely by its divine purposes.

> "A sacred society is distinguished from others not by its character and disposition but only by its object."[27]

Yet he understood this to have been the work of Jesus and the Apostles. Freedom of conscience and toleration were the "clearest and most distinct injunctions of Christ and the Apostles".[28] Mosheim's interpretation of scripture and his view of the Church turned the claim of revelation into a demand for toleration. At the same time, it also legitimised reforms within the Church. Although Protestants continued the debate till the end of the century, such views were well-formulated by mid-century, and were to reverberate among Catholics and Jews.

Catholic theory also followed Catholic practice, though a generation or more after the Protestants. The debate became serious in the 1780s with Joseph II's *Toleranzpatent* and such incidents as the *Kölner Toleranzstreit* (1787–1789).[29] There were two major theoretical obstacles to Catholic toleration. The first was the status of the believer: were non-Catholics wilful disbelievers who deserved punishment (i.e. formal heretics) or were they inculpable since they acted from "invincible ignorance" (i.e. material heretics)? The second was the status of the Church: was it the "sole church of salvation" or was salvation to be had elsewhere?

Most Reform Catholic theologians addressed the status of the believer. They used natural rights theory to advocate civil toleration by arguing that freedom of conscience and individual rights were not to be violated since they were quintessentially Christian. Bishop Herberstein of Laibach argued in a pastoral letter of 1782, for example, that "since each individual has the inherent right to adhere to that religious group which, after conscientious examination, appears to him to be the true one",[30] God alone had the right to examine the individual's conscience. The state should tolerate all who were obedient and productive.

---

[26]Harald Schultze, 'Toleranz und Orthodoxie. Johann Melchior Goeze in seiner Auseinandersetzung mit der Theologie der Aufklärung', in *Neue Zeitschrift für systematische Theologie*, 3–4 (1961–1962), pp. 197–219.

[27]*Allgemeines Kirchenrecht der Protestanten*, Helmstädt 1760, p. 478.

[28]*Ibid.*, p. 261.

[29]Ernst Heinen, 'Der Kölner Toleranzstreit, 1787–1789', in *Jahrbuch des kölnischen Geschichtsvereins*, 44 (1973), pp. 67–86.

[30]Bishop Herberstein, *Hirtenbrief an die Geistlichkeit und an das Volk der laybachischen Diöces von dem Bischofe zu Laybach* [no place] 1782, p. 57.

Such an argument from natural right was perfectly compatible with the religious one that distinguished the heresy from the heretic. The heretic deserved love in imitation of God's love for his creatures. As the neo-Jansenist Marc Wittola put it: "Tolerance is . . . the lowest form of love." Moreover: "only he who gladly tolerates all men, including false religious relations, is a good Catholic".[31] Yet love of the heretic did not imply acceptance of the heresy. The heresy was to be corrected and indeed "love, meekness and virtue", following the example of Jesus, were the most effective means.[32] All compulsion was to be avoided, but conversion was still to be sought.

Another argument for civil toleration was made by Catholic professors of canon law who used "collegialist theory". Franz Xavier Gmeiner, Professor of Canon Law at Graz, asserted the harmony of natural law and revelation.

> "The laws of natural right are immutable and incapable of change; indeed, they are so holy that revelation not only cannot abolish them, but in fact must confirm them."[33]

The Church must, therefore, be based on natural law by being constituted as a free society of men. Yet Gmeiner used collegial theory to justify compulsion within the Church, rather than to abolish it. Revelation transformed this free society, giving it powers over its members, e.g. the ban, as well as justifying hierarchy, which is essential to its preservation. Yet this did not preclude toleration. Natural law informs the State, which the Church supports in promoting security and felicity (*Glückseligkeit*). Toleration is in the gift of the sovereign and should be granted so long as it is not injurious to society. In addition, it would be a violation of natural right were religious differences to impinge on civil status.[34]

Only a handful of extreme rationalists within Reform Catholicism grappled with the more formidable obstacle of the status of the Church or dogmatic toleration. Some argued that the Church must renounce its claim to infallibility, acknowledge that it was a human institution, grant doctrinal freedom to its adherents and tolerate those outside it.[35] Others suggested that the Church relinquish its claim to a monopoly on salvation and cease trying to convert non-believers.[36] Such radical views made little headway. The main line of Reform Catholic thinking was to justify civil toleration by altering the believer's status.

The *Haskalah* addressed toleration tangentially; emancipation made it an issue. Toleration in Judaism turned on the concept of the "sons of Noah" (Genesis II:16). Those who observed six prohibitions (idolatry, blasphemy, murder, adultery, theft, eating the flesh of a living animal) as well as having a

[31]Marc Anton Wittola, *Schreiben eines österreichischen Pfarrers über die Toleranz nach den Grundsätzen der katholischen Kirche*, Vienna 1782, pp. 5–6.

[32]Herberstein, *Hirtenbrief, op. cit.*, p. 62.

[33]Franz Xavier Gmeiner, *Kirchenrecht*, 2nd edn., Graz 1790, p. 10.

[34]*Ibid.*, pp. 165, 235–236.

[35]Felix Anton Blau, *Kritische Geschichte der kirchlichen Unfehlbarkeit*, Frankfurt a. Main 1791.

[36]For the case of Eulogius Schneider see Wilhelm Forster, 'Die kirchliche Aufklärung bei den Benediktinern der Abtei Banz im Spiegel ihrer von 1772–1798 herausgegebenen Zeitschriften', in *Studien und Mitteilungen zur Geschichte des Benediktiner-Ordens und seiner Zweige*, vol. 64 (1952), pp. 176–177.

legal system to enforce them, qualified as "sons of Noah" and were to be tolerated in this world and granted a place in the world to come. Muslims had long been considered sons of Noah. For much of the Middle Ages Christians were not. They were thought to be idolaters because of the doctrine of the Trinity.[37]

In the mid-eighteenth century Rabbi Jacob Emden of Altona argued against this view. He asserted that Judaism and Christianity were fundamentally similar religions of revelation and that Christianity and Islam were God's chosen instruments to eradicate idolatry and disseminate belief. Christians thus qualified as sons of Noah. Although his view was innovative, his argument rested exclusively on internal categories.[38]

The emancipation debate politicised these ideas. The doubts of the *Aufklärer* about the Jews extended to Judaism: was Judaism a tolerant religion? If not, could Jews be emancipated? The first *Maskil* to use natural law was Naphtali Herz Wessely. Wessely's educational concerns brought him to a new understanding of the Noahide laws. He identified them with the secular knowledge he wanted Jews to acquire (the "teaching of man" or "human law"). Such knowledge was universally accessible to reason and the basis of society and moral order. All who possessed it were sons of Noah and deserving of toleration.[39]

Moses Mendelssohn took Wessely's argument a step further. On the basis of natural law he argued for a strict separation of Church and State. Using collegial theory he envisaged Judaism as a free society of equal members exercising solely the power of admonition and persuasion. Yet Mendelssohn went further still: he posited that Judaism made no claim to "an exclusive revelation of eternal truths that are indispensable to salvation".[40] He designated Judaism a "divine legislation" (and not a "revealed religion") whose truths were constantly represented to its adherents through their observance of the commandments. Such a Judaism was tolerant and compatible with a multi-religious society.

In his famous *Letter Concerning Toleration* John Locke had called "mutual toleration" the "Characteristical Mark of the True Church".[41] That was, however, a "mutual toleration" largely among Protestants. He excluded atheists because there could be no morality without God, Catholics because of their seditious loyalty to Rome. The toleration advocated by influential members of the three faiths in Germany was similarly imperfect. All denied atheists toleration. In addition, Reform Catholics and Protestant *theologische Aufklärer* shared the ambivalence of their secular counterparts when it came to the Jews. Reform Catholics relegated Jews to a separate category of "gratuitous toleration" (*tolerantia gratiosa*), which the sovereign granted at will and could revoke.

---

[37]Jacob Katz, *Exclusiveness and Tolerance. Jewish Gentile Relations in Medieval and Modern Times*, New York 1969; David Novak, *The Image of the Non-Jew in Judaism*, Toronto 1983.

[38]Blu Greenberg, 'Rabbi Jacob Emden. The Views of an Enlightened Traditionalist on Christianity', in *Judaism*, 27, No. 3 (1978), pp. 351–363.

[39]Naphtali Herz Wessely, 'Divrei Shalom ve-Emet', in *Mikhtavim Shonim*, Vienna 1827.

[40]*Moses Mendelssohn's Gesammelte Schriften, Jubiläumsausgabe*, ed. by Fritz Bamberger *et al.*, 19 vols., Stuttgart 1971ff., vol. VIII, pp. 159–164.

[41]John Locke, *A Letter Concerning Toleration*, 2nd edn., London 1689.

Theological *Aufklärer* made toleration conditional on regeneration. Yet to stress such imperfections is to miss the point. The true significance of these arguments was their ability to embrace toleration without relativising faith. Members of all religions who opposed toleration feared that it entailed indifference, scepticism or the relativising of belief and revelation. Mosheim, Gmeiner and Mendelssohn showed that this was not the case. By reconciling faith and natural law they were able to speak a language of toleration common to believing Protestants, Catholics and Jews.

CONCLUSION

I have concentrated on the ambiguities of "*Juden und Aufklärung*". The *Aufklärer* advocated emancipation of the Jews, yet made it conditional. The *Haskalah* began as an effort at religious renewal, yet emancipation diverted it into social reform. The established religions advocated toleration without relativising faith, yet it was imperfect. These ambiguities are worth bearing in mind. Through its cult the German-Jewish subculture attempted to idealise "*Juden und Aufklärung*". The events of the twentieth century have threatened to vilify it. "*Juden und Aufklärung*" did mark a turning point in the relationship between Jews and European society, but like all historical events of importance, it cannot be painted in terms of either black or white. History requires a palette of many colours and tones.[42]

---

[42]An abbreviated German version of this essay was given at the Ludwig-Maximilians-Universität, München, on the 15th July 1991, at the invitation of the C.H. Beck Verlag and the University.

Jewish Burials in Germany – Between Tradition, the Enlightenment and the Authorities

BY FALK WIESEMANN

Because of the rapid physical deterioration of the gravestones, current research into Jewish cemeteries in Germany has concentrated on photographing what still exists and recording the inscriptions and iconographic elements. Understanding what has been recorded, however, requires a lot more than simply taking photographs. Jewish cemetery design and burial practice changed considerably in the course of the nineteenth century and, to explain these changes, we need to investigate the ideas and forces which lay behind them. Fortunately, the historical sources on such matters are extensive. There are, for example, literary sources, newspapers and journals and there are also a great many archival records. Yet most of this material has never been systematically analysed by historians. Thus, the present paper sets out to introduce some of the more significant changes in Jewish attitudes and practice with respect to death, mourning and burial. And it analyses these changes in the light of parallel developments in the attitudes and behaviour in the non-Jewish environment.[*]

In the eighteenth century, the social and cultural lives of Jews and Christians remained almost entirely independent of each other. As the classical descriptions of Jewish life written during the period reveal, the two groups mourned for and buried their dead in a different manner and completely separately from one another.[1] Christian communities, however, often deliberately impeded Jewish

---

[*]Author and Editor would like to thank Dr. Mark Roseman, Birmingham, for his translation of this essay from the original German.

[1]Johann Jakob Schudt, *Jüdische Merckwürdigkeiten* . . . Frankfurt a. Main–Leipzig 1715; Paul Christian Kirchner, *Jüdisches Ceremoniel, oder Beschreibung dererjenigen Gebräuche, welche die Juden so wol in und ausser dem Tempel . . . in acht zu nehmen pflegen* . . . Nuremberg 1726 (reprinted Hildesheim 1974); Johann Christoph Georg Bodenschatz, *Kirchliche Verfassung der heutigen Juden sonderlich derer in Deutschland*, 4 parts, Erlangen 1748 and Coburg 1749; idem, *Aufrichtig teutsch redender Hebräer, welcher gründlich zeiget den Ursprung und die Schicksale des jüdischen Volcks, wie auch deroselben Kirchenwesen*, 4 parts, Frankfurt a. Main and Leipzig 1756; for the early nineteenth century see Joseph von Obernberg and Majer Bretzfeld, *Der Kultus der Juden*, Munich 1813, pp. 193–208; P. J. Schneider, 'Medizinisch polizeiliche Würdigung einiger Religionsgebräuche und Sitten des israelitischen Volkes, rücksichtlich ihres Einflusses auf den Gesundheitszustand derselben', in *Zeitschrift für die Staatsarzneikunde*, 5 (1825), pp. 213–301. See also Max Simonsohn, 'Trauervorschriften und Trauerbräuche', in Friedrich Thieberger (ed.), *Jüdisches Fest – Jüdischer Brauch*, Berlin 1936 (reprinted Königstein/Ts. 1979), pp. 434–446; Hermann Pollack, *Jewish Folkways in Germanic Lands (1648–1806). Studies in Aspects of Daily Life*, Cambridge, Mass.–London 1971 (pp. 40–49: 'Death and Burial'); Eva Groiss-Lau, 'Tod–Begräbnis–Trauer. Gesetze und Gebräuche bei jüdischen Beerdigungen', in *Jüdische Landgemeinden in Franken. Beiträge zu Kultur und Geschichte einer Minderheit*, Bayreuth 1987, pp. 93–98.

religious practices; many parishes were barred to Jewish funeral processions, thus forcing the Jews to find alternative routes to bring their dead to the burial ground. This happened in Floß, in the Upper Palatinate, where until the nineteenth century an administratively separate Jewish ghetto existed at the edge of the town. The cemetery lay on the other side of Floß, but, denied access through the town, the Jews were forced to lay a new stone path across marshy fields to carry their dead to the ground.[2] Sections of this path were still visible until building work destroyed them a few years ago.

After the expulsions from the towns in the late Middle Ages, the vast majority of Jews lived on the land and most lived in the small states of Southern and South-Western Germany. It was there that large, so-called group cemeteries (*Verbandsfriedhöfe*) were established, serving several communities at once. "Jews' Hill" near Kleinbardorf in Lower Franconia, for example, provided a burial ground for the dead of, in all, 20 congregations. For some of those communities, the journey to the cemetery could take as much as seven and a half hours.[3]

Until the eighteenth century the Jews were able to bury their dead according to religious law (*Halakha*) and custom (*Minhag*) with little interference from the state authorities. The local rulers restricted themselves essentially to raising revenue. There were land taxes and rents from the cemeteries, levies on funeral processions and a payment to be made for every death reported.

Around 1750, however, non-Jews, and Jews who had been influenced by the Enlightenment, began to question the Jewish way of death and to seek to change it. Among the enlightened circles of the day the belief had taken hold that many people were being buried alive.[4] The then increasingly popular "Gothick" novels were full of stories of individuals apparently dead but in reality still alive. Enlightenment spokesmen therefore warned against burying the dead too rapidly. Instead, the interval between death (or apparent death) and burial should be extended as long as possible in order to rule out any possibility of error.

The new attitudes towards death and dying which emerged during the Enlightenment were the result of deep-seated changes in consciousness during this period. When it came to explaining natural phenomena, modern thinkers were no longer prepared to accept the binding validity of religion, tradition and inherited wisdom. Instead, they turned towards the methods and findings of the natural sciences. As far as death was concerned, for instance, there were extensive discussions about what were the most reliable and precise ways of establishing that an individual had indeed died. True, there were limits to what the scientific method could achieve. It is clear from the discussions that it proved impossible to find exact signs of death; the decomposition of the corpse seemed to be the only sure indicator. Yet this uncertainty about the exact moment of death was, for enlightened thinkers, all the more reason for taking the decision as to whether an individual had died out of the hands of lay people and transferring

[2] Peter Kraus, 'Der Judenberg in Floß', in *Oberpfälzer Heimat (Weiden)*, 19 (1975), pp. 63–75.
[3] List, 5th August 1864, Staatsarchiv Würzburg, Regierungsabgabe 7084.
[4] Christoph Wilhelm Hufeland, *Der Scheintod oder Sammlung der wichtigsten Thatsachen und Bemerkungen darüber in alphabetischer Ordnung (1808)*, ed. and introduced by Gerhard Köpf, Bern–Frankfurt a. Main–New York 1986.

responsibility to the "health police", the physicians. The family, the Christian priest or the Jewish burial society *Chevra Kaddisha* could no longer be entrusted with the task. Gradually, under the influence of the Enlightenment, new regulations appeared on how deaths were to be ascertained and certified and on the proper interval between death and burial. As a result the doctors gained ever more power. It was in keeping with this general trend that in 1798 the Prussian King, Friedrich Wilhelm III, issued a terse and forthright edict concerning Jewish burial practice which stated that the question whether someone was dead or not was a matter not for religion but for science.[5]

In 1772, the Duke of Mecklenburg-Schwerin issued what were the first set of German regulations about Jewish burials to be influenced by the new anxieties about being buried alive. These regulations required Jews to allow at least three days to elapse between death and burial.[6] They thus stood in flat contradiction to the Jewish practice of burying the dead as soon as possible.

The *Halakhah* defines the dead as "impure". Those who come into contact with the dead or remain with them under the same roof become ritually impure themselves. The members of the *Chevra Kaddisha* perform the last services to the dead, i.e. washing the body, cutting hair and nails and reciting the accompanying prayers. This can take place in the house of the deceased or in a room in the synagogue. Usually, however, it takes place in the *Beth Tahara* ("cleansing house") within the burial ground.

In a few cemeteries, some rural, some urban, the old *Beth Tahara* can still be found. However, many were destroyed in the Nazi period or even torn down in the post-war era. Where measures have been taken to preserve or renovate Jewish cemeteries, it has often been with no knowledge of the buildings' ritual functions. As a result many culturally and historically significant elements have been removed.

One *Beth Tahara* which still bears clearly the marks of its former function can be found in the great cemetery of Walsdorf, which served the community of Bamberg and its environs. The half-timbered building was built in 1742. To the right of the entrance hall are two rooms, one for the *Chevra* and one for the bereaved. To the left at the rear of the house is a room with a brick well-head and a fireplace for boiling water. The front room contains a plinth on which rests the thick, slightly inclined stone table for washing the dead. Three engraved plaques, two in Hebrew and one in Yiddish, record the charitable donations made to the *Beth Tahara*.

Sources from the turn of the eighteenth/nineteenth centuries tell us that the dead were brought to the cemetery within 4–6 hours of dying. People who died in the evening were buried the following morning. Where a death took place early on Friday, every effort would be made to carry out the burial on the same day before the beginning of the Sabbath. Then, as now, no burials were carried out

---

[5]Reskript, 15th January 1798, Bayerisches Hauptstaatsarchiv München, MInn 65777; see also Staatsarchiv Nürnberg, Regierung Mittelfranken, Abgabe 1932, Tit. Judensachen 37 I.
[6]Siegfried Silberstein, 'Mendelssohn und Mecklenburg', in *Zeitschrift für die Geschichte der Juden in Deutschland*, 1 (1929), pp. 233–244, 275–290, here p. 233.

on the Sabbath itself or the first days of the festivals, and so far as possible burials were also avoided on the second and intermediate days of the festivals as well. The legend grew amongst Christians – who had very little real knowledge of Jewish practices – that the dying were "helped" to die before the beginning of the Sabbath. One can still sometimes hear this myth being advanced as a serious proposition.[7]

The practice of early burial derived partly from the laws of ritual cleanliness, partly from certain other considerations which will not be examined here, but also from the belief that the soul of the deceased is fully released from the body only once the grave is covered with earth. A far more practical reason for early burials is that the seven-day period of strict mourning begins on the day of burial. The next of kin must spend this period in the house of the deceased with fasting and prayers. Only after the seven days may they return to earning a living.

It was in Mecklenburg-Schwerin that the conflict over early burials first emerged, and with it a fundamental problem of Jewish emancipation. Could the Jews satisfy the demands of an enlightened society and the drive for uniformity of a modern state administration without giving up their culturally distinct lifestyle with its own traditions and religious laws? In the case of Schwerin, the traditionally inclined Jewish population did not want to abide by the new regulations. The Jews turned in their distress to the renowned Rabbi Jacob Emden of Altona. He, in turn, confirmed the correctness of their position.[8] At the same time the Schwerin congregation also asked Moses Mendelssohn for his opinion, not because they had any sympathy for his enlightened views, but because they hoped that he might make a favourable impression on the Duke. Mendelssohn wrote that:

> "In my opinion, following this ducal decree will not involve the breach of any religious laws . . . According to the unanimous views of the best medical opinion there is no fully reliable sign of death . . . Should the Duke insist on full compliance with the regulation, you can do no better than to follow the example of our forefathers and build a vault within the burial ground. There the departed can be cleaned according to the custom, then watched over for three days and only then laid to rest."[9]

Mendelssohn concluded by saying:

---

[7] In 1929, Julius Streicher's *Der Stürmer* informed its readers about the "Jewish custom of 'finishing off' moribund Jews before 'Schabbes' so that the day itself is not desecrated by their death": 'Der Blutmord von Manau', in *Der Stürmer*, No. 13 (March 1929). Evidently this was an old antisemitic stereotype, which can be found as early as 1700 in Eisenmenger's *Entdecktes Judentum*. Leopold Zunz, *Die synagogale Poesie des Mittelalters, Teil 2: Die Ritus des synagogalen Gottesdienstes*, Berlin 1859 (reprinted Hildesheim 1967), p. 178, cites an author from 1783 as saying that "the Jews commissioned a man, whom they called the Angel of Death, to strangle the deceased before burial".

[8] Silberstein, *loc. cit.*, *passim*; see also Meyer Kayserling, *Moses Mendelssohn. Sein Leben und Wirken*, Leipzig 1862 (reprinted Hildesheim 1972), pp. 276–280 ('Die Begräbnisfrage'); Ludwig Geiger, 'Mitteilungen aus der Geschichte der Juden Berlins, 4. Aktenstücke über die frühe Beerdigung der Todten', in *Zeitschrift für die Geschichte der Juden in Deutschland*, 3 (1889), pp. 211–223; Kurt Wilhelm, 'Die Frage der frühen Beerdigung der Juden in Braunschweig', in *Zeitschrift für die Geschichte der Juden in Deutschland*, 4 (1932), pp. 204–207.

[9] Silberstein, *loc. cit.*, pp. 280–282; see also Alexander Altmann, *Moses Mendelssohn. A Biographical Study*, Alabama 1973, pp. 288–294.

Marcus Herz

über

die frühe Beerdigung

der Juden.

An die Herausgeber des hebräischen Sammlers.

Zweyte verbesserte und vermehrte Auflage.

Berlin, 1788.
Bey Christian Friedrich Voß und Sohn.

Title page of 'Über die frühe Beerdigung der Juden' by Marcus Herz
The engraving by Wilhelm Chodwiecki (1765–1805)
shows a visitor to the grave of Moses Mendelssohn in Berlin

Above: Eighteenth-century Beth Tahara
at the cemetery at Walsdorf near Bamberg

Below: Cleansing table in the seventeenth-century Beth Tahara
at the cemetery near Kleinbardorf, Lower Franconia

Above: Urns at the Jewish cemetery in Würzburg

Below: The separate area in the Jewish cemetery
in Nuremberg assigned to those who had been cremated

Above: Old country cemetery in Burgkunstadt
with eighteenth-century gravestones

Below: Modern town cemetery in Amberg, Oberpfalz

"I know that you will not do what I suggest; the force of habit is strong. After reading my proposals you may even see me as a heretic."

Mendelssohn's response, however, did have some effect in that the regulations were amended. They now ceased to refer to a three-day period and instead laid down that "from now on none of your deceased shall be buried until they have been inspected by a recognised physician and their death certified by him".[10] That was, however, by no means the end of the debate about early burial. On the contrary, the issue now began to excite attention on a broader front. The participants were primarily doctors, priests and civil servants who often interspersed their deliberations with asides aimed at the "Jews' stiff-necked adherence to their practices and malpractices".[11]

Within the Jewish community, too, deep rifts were opened up by the burial question. Marcus Herz, a close associate of Mendelssohn, emerged as the leading spokesman of the Enlightenment party. In 1787 Herz published a well-respected pamphlet that went into a second edition within a year of publication. In it, the writer promised to bring a "rational case" to bear against "prejudice and custom", though he himself was unable to refrain from invoking the contemporary Gothick spectre of being buried alive:

"My brothers, you simply can never have imagined the true horror of what it must be like for someone to awake in the grave! . . . Follow me into that musty grave, which only yesterday received its incumbent, not dead but slumbering. Only now he rouses from his slumber, his energies revive, his heart regains its beat, his face its colour and his soul returns to consciousness. The first thought which rises from the darkness is heartfelt gratitude to the gracious Creator who has called him back to the joys of life. Now a thousand ecstatic thoughts criss-cross his mind: of good deeds in the future to render him worthy of such divine grace; of the happiness of his spouse who had almost died of grief at her loss; the leaping for joy of his children who had so nearly been orphaned . . .
Now his recovery has progressed still further. He opens his eyes; around him everything is dark and desolate . . . He groans, cries, pleads with all the powers that he has struggled so hard to regain: to no avail, he languishes unheard. He touches his bed and grasps, not the soft down of a bedspread, but instead a clod of damp, wormy earth."[12]

Jewish traditionalists, on the other hand, were united in their opposition to the new ideas and addressed their own texts to the public.[13] "The new writers",

[10]Silberstein, *loc. cit.*, pp. 238–239.

[11]Report of the Landgericht Würzburg, 27th February 1809, Staatsarchiv Würzburg, Regierungsabgabe 7088.

[12]Marcus Herz, *Über die frühe Beerdigung der Juden. An die Herausgeber des hebräischen Sammlers*, 2nd edn., Berlin 1788, pp. 30–32 (1st edn., Berlin 1787); see also Ludwig Geiger, 'Markus Herz über die frühe Beerdigung der Juden', in *Zeitschrift für die Geschichte der Juden in Deutschland*, 4 (1890), pp. 55–57 (see also *ibid.*, p. 315); Joel Loewe, *Schreiben an die würdigen Mitglieder sämmtlicher löblichen und wohlthätigen Chebroth Gemilus Chasadim. (Mit hebr. Buchstaben gedruckt)*, Berlin 1794; Lazarus Adler, 'Übereinstimmung der Staatsgesetze mit den Vorschriften der jüdischen Religion in Ansehung der Beerdigung der Todten', in *Die Synagoge*, 2 (1839), pp. 338–352.

[13]M. J. Marx, *Über die Beerdigung der Todten*, Hannover 1788; Salomon Seligmann Pappenheim, *An die Barmherzigen zu En-dor oder über die zu früh scheinende Beerdigung der Juden*, Breslau 1794; *idem, Die Nothwendigkeit der frühen Beerdigung*, Breslau 1797; *idem, Deduction seiner Apologie für eine frühe Beerdigung der Juden*, Breslau 1798 (unfortunately, Pappenheim's works were unobtainable); 'Widerlegung der von Dr. E. Altschuhl zu Prag aus dem Talmud geschöpften vermeintlichen Gründe für den Scheintod. Von einem unbefangen Prüfenden', in *Der Treue Zions-Wächter*, 2 (1846), pp. 238–239, 334–336.

wrote the executive of the Jewish community in Strelitz to the government, "venture to undermine old customs and want to destroy the Jewish law; who knows what will follow. Perhaps they, like the French Revolutionaries, are out to bury the Jewish religion."[14]

The conservative burial societies clung grimly to established practice and would not countenance any changes. Growing minorities within the communities, however, formed separate burial societies, which agreed not to bury their dead before three days had passed and to abandon certain other elements of the traditional ritual. The first society of this kind, founded in Breslau, had to seek police protection in order to carry out a new style burial against the bitter resistance of the old *Chevra Kaddisha*. Breslau even saw the creation of a third burial society which wanted to abide by the old ritual but to abandon the practice of early burial.[15]

In Germany, as the modern constitutional and legal state replaced older state forms, the official administrations developed the idea of linking Jewish emancipation to "improving" and "refining" the behaviour of the Jew. The Jew should receive the rights of the citizen – but only if he modified the way he earned his living, improved his standard of education and changed his religious practices and customs. The emergence of such official aspirations to control and alter behaviour can be illustrated by contrasting a decree from Ansbach in 1793 with one passed by the ruler of Aschaffenburg on 17th February 1809. The Ansbach decree laid down that "in view of the strong sense of tradition which is well known to characterise the Jewish race and in view of the burdensome . . . difficulties associated with keeping the corpses for longer periods . . . the Jews' request to be freed from the police-law [against early burial] will for the time being be granted".[16] The Aschaffenburg regulation, on the other hand, betrays the new spirit of the controlling state:

> "The decree issued on 9th February 1784, proceeding from those principles of religious freedom and tolerance which are due to the Jews, sought to ensure that no-one of that persuasion should, through misapplication of their religious laws, be buried too early or alive. It therefore ruled that irrespective of age or sex no Jew should be buried witout a death certificate being issued by the district, town or parish doctor . . .
> The good intentions and tolerant spirit from which this law proceeded, its recognition that there must always be exceptions to the law where other lives are in danger, would incline one to expect gratitude and prompt obedience from those to whom it applied. Instead, objections were thrown up based on distortions of Mosaic and Talmudic law which even the more understanding Jews condemned. The regulations were not kept, or were followed in so arbitrary and devious a manner that their intention was completely undermined.
> For many years, the authorities were lenient in their enforcement of these regulations. They hoped that the passing of time and quiet consideration would persuade the Jews to change their attitude and show more consideration for the lives of their fellow religionists. After several years, however, it became clear that the Jews were blind to their best interests, clung to

[14]Silberstein, *loc. cit.*, pp. 239–240.

[15]Max Freudenthal, 'Die ersten Emancipationsbestrebungen der Juden in Breslau', in *Monatsschrift für Geschichte und Wissenschaft des Judentums*, 37 (1893), pp. 565–579.

[16]Preußische Regierung Ansbach, 12th December 1793, Staatsarchiv Nürnberg, Ansbachische Oberamtsakten 3612.

their false ideas and resisted the guiding hand of the authorities which sought to lead them in a direction which Jews in other states have long since taken."[17]

By 1820 or thereabouts all the German states had issued burial regulations allowing burial only after two or three days had elapsed (24 hours in exceptional cases) and requiring certification from an officially accredited doctor. The Jewish communities attempted to fight the prohibition on early burial with petitions and rabbinical opinions, but to no avail. Cases where the authorities learned that the laws had not been followed, were vigorously pursued.[18] The Jews tried in a variety of different ways to circumvent the impact of the regulations; for instance through giving false information about the causes and time of death. In addition, on the land at least, the obligatory official inspection of the body was often not carried out because there were too few doctors.[19] Often it was difficult to get to the official doctors and sometimes they could be prevailed upon to furnish death certificates to order – naturally in return for a higher than usual fee:

"Some doctors and surgeons make a good living from this important decree [decree of 10th October 1809]. For inspecting the body, they receive a generous fee from the Jews who will pay anything to be allowed to continue to indulge their absurd prejudices. Some issue certificates without even having seen the body."[20]

An officially accredited physician reported from Baden on the basis of personal experience:

". . . no sooner has the patient died than the Israelites race to get the corpse out of bed, put on the burial clothing, close the eyes and mouth and place the body on the floor. Then they besiege the physician from all sides to obtain permission to carry out a speedy burial. To that end they always put back the time of death and employ any conceivable trick to have the burial carried out 6 – 8 – 12, at most 24 hours after death has taken place."[21]

In every parish, priests were obliged to maintain a separate register of deaths for Jews (in Bavaria this applied between 1813 and 1875) and using this register it is possible to observe the gradual imposition of the state regulations. Here, the Jewish register from Segnitz in Lower Franconia has been taken as an example.[22] From the register we can see that initially the burials took place on the day of death or at the latest the following day:

"Year of Our Lord 1814. Ballin, small trader here, died early on 20th October, between 7 and 8 o'clock, from an ailment of the lungs. With permission of the doctor he was buried on this same day – age 35 years.
Year of Our Lord 1825. Hirsch Lazarus Grünewald, Master Butcher, died here from old age

---

[17]Staatsarchiv Würzburg, Regierungsabgabe 7087.
[18]See the numerous reports to the district authorities from the first part of the nineteenth century; Staatsarchiv Würzburg, Regierungsabgabe 7088 and 7089; Staatsarchiv Nürnberg, Regierung Mittelfranken, Abgabe 1932, Tit. Judensachen 37 I/II.
[19]See the files on 'Leichenbeschau, Leichenhäuser, Verfahren bei Unglücksfällen und Scheintodten' 1769–1883, Bayerisches Hauptstaatsarchiv München, MInn 65776–65782.
[20]Report of the Patrimonialgericht Pfaffendorf, 29th November 1809, Staatsarchiv Würzburg, Regierungsabgabe 7088.
[21]Schneider, *loc. cit.*, p. 289.
[22]Pfarrarchiv Segnitz, Unterfranken.

and lung disease on the evening of 5th April, 5 o'clock, at the age of 74 and was buried on the 6th with permission from the doctor.

1840. Bernhard Ballin, third child of the first marriage of Ballin, Master Butcher, died on the morning of the 26th February 10 o'clock from an inflammation of the bowel aged 2 months and 3 days. Without the knowledge or consent of the parish he was buried on 27th, upon which judicial proceedings were instituted. Doctors Weinrich and Roth."

After a tightening up of the regulations at the end of the 1830s a waiting time of two days between death and burial became the norm. Early burial became restricted to cases where there was a danger of the spread of infectious diseases. An entry from 1868 contains a comparatively late reference to an early burial which was carried out because of the approaching festival of Passover:

"1860. Friederike Moßbacher, sixth child of the first marriage of the wine merchant Elias Mosbacher residing here, died here on the evening of 30th October at 5.30 from scarlet fever with cerebral pains and paralysis of the limbs at the age of 3 years, 7 months and 16 days. With medical permission burial took place at 1 p.m. on 1st November at Rödelsee. The doctor was Dr. Merk in Marktbreit.

1868. Hayum Stern, businessman and landowner residing here, married, died in the night of 11th April after 11 o'clock from tubercular disease of the lungs. Because of the approaching festivals and the fact that the corpse was beginning to rot, the district physician gave approval for burial to take place at Rödelsee on the 12th of the month at 3 o'clock. Physicians were Dr. Mayer in Marktbreit and district physician Dr. Henke in Kitzingen."[23]

The rural Jews had a particularly strong sense of established tradition and could not be persuaded by warnings or appeals to reason to abandon the practice of early burial.[24] As a result, the threat and application of heavy punishment was used. In cases where it could be proven that the law had been broken deliberately, those involved had to pay the extraordinarily high fine of 100 Talers. Even these heavy personal fines, however, had little impact on the behaviour of the Jewish community as a whole and, moreover, were often difficult to extract. The authorities in Bavaria, therefore, began to make the respective Jewish congregations collectively responsible. Thus, just as in the pre-emancipation period, the Jews were, in effect, treated as if they were still under exceptional law.

The executives of the congregations and the rabbis were used by the state as a means of enforcing the law. The authorities' aim was not just to prevent early burial but also to regulate and control the whole burial procedure, to unify the practice and regulations in the various different Jewish cemeteries and to bring them into line with those of their non-Jewish counterparts. The synagogue

---

[23]In Bavaria a ministerial decree from 20th November 1885 laid down that Jewish burials could take place less than 24 hours after death only in those cases where applying the official waiting time of 48 or 72 hours would have led the burial to coincide with the Sabbath or a major festival; Isidor Silbernagel, *Verfassung und Verwaltung sämtlicher Religionsgenossenschaften in Bayern*, 4th edn., Regensburg 1900, p. 444. When a festival was imminent, the burial ceremonies were often shortened considerably, as for example in Schwabach because of the approaching *Rosh Chodesh Nissan*, *Der Israelit*, 1889, p. 617.

[24]'Eine Mahnung an die israel. Gemeinden, wo noch nach altem Mißbrauch eine zu frühe Beerdigung stattfindet', in *Allgemeine Zeitung des Judenthums*, 1846, p. 143.

executives were now made responsible for ensuring proper decorum was maintained and for reporting to the authorities.[25]

When a burial was about to take place, the chairman was obliged to make known in writing to the congregation the precise time and composition of the funeral procession, the names of the pallbearers and of the other participants. This imposed order was often alien to the communities, a fact which emerges clearly from the following public announcement made during morning prayers at the Synagogue of Untermerzbach in Lower Franconia:

> "Unfortunately we have once again been witness to that indecorous behaviour that used to characterise our funerals. Several individuals from one house, wearing only dirty suits and caps, suddenly appeared to walk a few steps with the coffin, just so that they could exercise the *mitzvah haleveiath hameth* [duty of accompanying the dead]. Indeed, the misconduct, as it may fairly be called, went so far that most of the members of the funeral procession had already left before the coffin had been placed down.
> We earnestly request the members of this Israelite community, if God forbid there should be another death, please to accompany the dead in well-ordered pairs, in decent suits with a proper hat. We also urge the women not to group together in a huddle or to follow the coffin in a disorderly group. Instead, we expect that the women will – as they generally have done until now – maintain proper decorum, dress in decent clothes and follow the procession in ordered pairs.
> Those who fail to keep to these rules are in serious breach of the laws of this land and will be reported to the Royal State Court at Ebern."[26]

The burial societies which had once been the most important organisations in maintaining the separate religious-cultural practices of the Jews, and had symbolised their separate corporate status, now found their rights and freedom severely circumscribed. It was the rabbis who now led and controlled the burial services. Deaths had to be reported immediately to them or to cantors acting as their representatives. The societies were allowed to continue to exist and to participate, but they now had to follow the instructions of the rabbi.[27]

The synagogues were obliged to keep a register of all burials in duplicate. The cemeteries had to be surrounded by a wall with a fence or hedge around it and kept locked. The gravestones had to be numbered in sequence. Children had to

---

[25]Rules to ensure discipline and decorum in funeral processions were also included in the cemetery regulations drawn up by the Jewish congregations, initially in big city communities such as Vienna and Berlin; see 'Religiöse Gebräuche bei Leichenbestattungen', in *Israelitische Annalen*, 1 (1839), pp. 307–308; 'Neue Beerdigungs-Anordnung in der Israelitischen Gemeinde zu Berlin', in *Sulamith*, vol. VII, No. 11, pp. 337–344.

[26]Bekanntmachungen, 27th January and 26th February 1841, Staatsarchiv Würzburg, Landratsamt Ebern 4022; see also the complaint of the city magistrate of Fürth, 28th September 1823: ". . . Jewish funerals are enacted in most unseemly fashion. A swarm of Jews surrounds the coffin and pall bearers, and the coffin is then carried off in indecent haste and with no decorum. You would think that the carcass of an animal was being taken away, rather than a human being to whom, as surely all civilised races would acknowledge, respect is due even after death," Staatsarchiv Nürnberg, Regierung Mittelfranken, Abgabe 1932, Tit. Judensachen 37 I; see also the complaint of a Jewish observer in Bavaria: "In most of our congregations funeral processions take place with no sort of discipline. In the country, they're often more like a pantomime", in *Allgemeine Zeitung des Judenthums*, 1852, p. 501.

[27]'Leichenbegräbniß-Ordnung für die israelitischen Kultusgemeinden in dem Regierungsbezirke Unterfranken und Aschaffenburg', 22nd June 1839, in *Intelligenzblatt von Unterfranken und Aschaffenburg*, 1839, pp. 487–490.

be buried separately from adults "as is the usual practice amongst Christians".[28] This last practice was in many areas no imposition, since the Jews themselves had often buried children separately, as well as maintaining separate burial areas for the *Kohanim*, the descendants of the priests, and for women who died in childbirth.

A complaint from the Christian population in 1864 led the Bavarian regional administration for Lower Franconia to undertake an extensive investigation into Jewish funeral processions. According to the complaints "fumes" and "fluid" had been seen emanating from one of the coffins. Hostile civil servants wanted to restrict the Jews' right to transport their coffins so that in the summer they would be able to transport them only at night. As a result of the investigations, it emerged that the Jews used home-made wooden coffins. These were covered with a black cloth and carried to the cemetery on a bier or, for longer distances, on a simple wooden handcart. The state authorities, acting from the premise that the "Jews should bury their dead in the same way as the Christians",[29] ordered that the dead could be carried only in firmly closed coffins, sealed with pitch, in closed wagons. This order met with considerable resistance from the poor rural Jews, partly because of the cost, but also because it eroded yet another element of the Jews' separate burial practice.[30]

As a result of legal emancipation, the Jews became more geographically mobile and the regional distribution of their cemeteries therefore changed. True, even after migration to the cities, nearby rural cemeteries continued to be used for a while. But increasingly the Jews began to buy up plots within the town borders. In the country, too, individual communities withdrew from the existing group cemetery arrangements and created their own – something which in the past lack of resources or official resistance had prevented. Particularly in Bavaria, where restrictive official policy hindered the Jews' social and regional mobility for longer than in other areas, a large number of small rural cemeteries emerged. Built in the expectation of communal growth, many of these cemeteries contain only a few dozen gravestones because of the subsequent dramatic drain of members away from the rural communities.

In the towns, the Jews were predominantly liberal in their religious orientation and abandoned many old-established religious practices.[31] Alongside the liberals emerged a minority of so-called Neo-Orthodox who, while regarding many customs as no longer in keeping with the times, were all the more

---

[28]Regierungsentschließung für den Untermainkreis, 8th March 1842, Staatsarchiv Würzburg, Landratsamt Ebern 4029.

[29]Report of the Patrimonialgericht Pfaffendorf, 10th October 1809, Staatsarchiv Würzburg, Regierungsabgabe 7088.

[30]Staatsarchiv Würzburg, Regierungsabgabe 7084.

[31]See also the discussion of the Reform rabbis about the removal of mourning customs: Abraham Kohn, 'Über die jüdischen Trauergebräuche', in *Wissenschaftliche Zeitschrift für jüdische Theologie*, 3 (1837), pp. 214–235; see also the positions of Joseph Aub, Leopold Stein, Bernhard Wechsler and Abraham Geiger, *ibid.*, 4 (1839), pp. 39–60, 352–354; *Protokolle und Aktenstücke der zweiten Rabbiner-Versammlung abgehalten zu Frankfurt am Main, vom 15ten bis zum 28ten Juli 1845*, Frankfurt a. Main 1845, pp. 270–273; *Protokolle der dritten Versammlung deutscher Rabbiner, abgehalten zu Breslau, vom 13. bis 24. Juli 1846*, Breslau 1847, pp. 279–290 and 305.

committed to defending *halakhic* law against the encroachments of the liberals. The most bitter conflicts took place over the synagogue services, questions of circumcision, ritual purity and the dietary laws and also over all matters connected with burial and mourning.

The first morgues had been built at the behest of enlightened state leaderships at the end of the eighteenth century.[32] For the Jews, as we have seen, Mendelssohn recommended that suitable buildings be found temporarily to house the bodies. Marcus Herz believed that in most cases the *Beth Tahara* would be the most suitable building in which to house the morgue:

> "What prevents us from waiting four hours after the last signs of life have gone, taking the body to the cleansing house, leaving it for a few days watched over either by someone paid for the task or by a voluntary society, and only then, when death is certain, carrying out the burial?"[33]

In recognition of the problems this would raise for existing practice, Herz suggested that:

> "The burial ceremonies can take place only after the end of the period of waiting at the real burial. However, mourning at home should start on the day the body is taken out of the house . . . A large number of rules to cover problem cases will have to be developed and agreed by wise rabbis and experienced doctors. If only our brethren were men enough to break free from an unworthy tradition against which all humanity is up in arms!"

Because the Jews clung so long to the tradition of early burial and also because they did not want to use the general, largely Christian morgues, the rabbis instructed their congregations to build their own morgues.[34]

Here is an imaginative description of an ideal morgue in the countryside. It was conceived by a Jewish school teacher – with literary as well as Reform ambitions – in Middle Franconia:

> "The new building . . . was well designed for its purpose. One attractive room, its walls adorned with the paintings of famous Israelites, serves the mourners. Here, the prayers for the dead are read, while next door the burial society's committee meetings take place to make the necessary planning and decisions. Then there is a small library of improving works and next to it a small registry. From here two glass doors lead into another room, in the middle of which is the covered bier on which the deceased is laid. The room corresponds exactly to the design recommended by modern medical opinion, a design which should avert the danger of being buried alive. Four wires hang down from the warden's room above and are fastened to the hands and feet of the deceased. The tiniest movement sets off the alarm in the room upstairs and thus alerts the warden."[35]

[32]Hans-Kurt Boehlke, 'Über das Aufkommen der Leichenhäuser', in *Wie die Alten den Tod gebildet. Wandlungen der Sepulkralkultur 1750–1850*, Mainz 1979, pp. 135–146.

[33]Herz, *Über die frühe Beerdigung, op. cit.*, pp. 52–60. Cf. the proposal of Joseph Friedländer that mourning should commence when the body was placed in the coffin and not wait for the burial, in *Sulamith*, vol. 8, No. 4 (1842), pp. 259–260. Incidentally, on the direction of the Berlin rabbinate both Herz and Mendelssohn were, against their prior instructions, buried within 24 hours of death! Silberstein, *loc. cit.*, p. 238.

[34]*Allgemeine Zeitung des Judenthums*, 1848, pp. 195–197 (Jastrow); P. L. Hurwitz, 'Über Scheintod und Leichenhäuser. Nach Ansichten des alten Judenthums. Eine Aufforderung an sämmtliche jüdischen Gemeinden, und besonders an die Berliner', *ibid.*, 1837, pp. 227 and 238–239; David Einhorn, 'Über die Notwendigkeit der Einrichtung von Leichenhäusern', in *Sinai* (Baltimore), 1862, pp. 213–214 and 243.

[35]Simon Krämer, 'Frankenheim', in *idem, Jüdische Erzählungen*, Nürnberg 1851, pp. 106–107.

In the second half of the nineteenth century, the *Beth Tahara* was generally designed to conform to current medical and scientific opinion[36] and was thus able to serve as a morgue as well.[37] Nevertheless, liberal and Orthodox Jewry continued to argue about the most appropriate manner in which to design and appoint the buildings.[38]

During the nineteenth century, responsibility for cemeteries passed into the hands of the municipalities and this was bound to generate conflict between the burial traditions of the Christian majority and those of the Jewish minority. Whereas it is common in Christian cemeteries for burial plots to be rededicated after the passing of some decades, or for plots no longer in use to be given over to some other purpose, Jewish graves are supposed to remain intact forever. Reburial of someone's buried remains is permissible only in exceptional circumstances. Yet town councils and administrations – influenced no doubt by the fact that Christian society was becoming increasingly deconfessionalised – felt able to make plans and decisions that simply ignored the Jews' special burial practices.[39] Indeed, they demanded of Jewish communities that they share common cemeteries with their Christian neighbours. For most Jews, this represented a major attack on their religion. Had not, they asked, Abraham their forefather bought his own burial plot in which to lay his wife Sarah to rest? Since then every Jewish community had regarded it as one of its primary duties to establish its own burial plot and to ensure that its dead found their "eternal rest". Even the committed Reformer Ludwig Philippson wanted to ensure that Jewish burial plots were kept strictly separate:

> "In their churchyards and graves, the Christian churches naturally display the crosses and crucifixes which are the symbols of Christianity. These symbols express the special features of the Christian creed and thus those features of Christianity to which Judaism is most resolutely opposed. As long as Christianity upholds these different beliefs – and to remain Christianity it must do so – they will represent an unbridgeable divide between Christianity and Judaism. Thus, for the sake of the feelings and beliefs of the dead but also of the survivors, no Jewish grave can be placed in a churchyard or next to graves which carry these symbols . . . They [the different beliefs and symbols] manifest a division between Judaism and Christianity which reaches from the cradle to the grave, though they should never prevent the two sides from living alongside each other with common duties and rights, and with love and respect."[40]

Jewish sections within municipal cemeteries were established for the first time in the 1870s. Düsseldorf, Alzey, Gießen and Schweinfurt were the pioneers, though in each case the sections were established only after the Orthodox had managed to make important modifications. By threatening to leave the congregations,

---

[36]See Max Pettenkofer, 'Über die Wahl der Begräbnisplätze', in *Zeitschrift für Biologie*, 1 (1865), pp. 45–68.

[37]Cf. 'Synagogen und jüdische Begräbnisplätze, bearb. von Baurath E. Oppler, ergänzt von Architekt A. Haupt', in *Deutsches Bauhandbuch*, vol. II, Berlin 1884, pp. 270–285, here p. 285.

[38]'Das Harmonium in einer jüdischen Leichenhalle und dessen Mitwirkung bei Beerdigungen', in *Der Israelit*, 1905, pp. 1219–1221 and 1227–1229.

[39]Conflicts on this issue appeared first in France and England; see *Israelitische Annalen*, 3 (1841), pp. 214–215, 220–222 and 318; Abraham Gilam, 'The Burial Grounds Controversy between Anglo-Jewry and the Victorian Board of Health 1850', in *Jewish Social Studies*, 45 (1983), pp. 147–156.

[40]Ludwig Philippson, 'Die Begräbnißplatzfrage', in *Allgemeine Zeitung des Judenthums*, 1867, pp. 509–511, 529–531 and 549–552, here p. 529.

they were able to insist on complete physical separation and separate entrances for the Jewish sections.[41]

Another issue which generated a conflict between modern and traditional Jews in the second half of the nineteenth century was that of cremation, which was then becoming increasingly popular among non-Jews. There was a bitter debate over whether cremation was acceptable under Jewish law and whether the ashes could be buried in Jewish cemeteries.[42] Here too, Ludwig Philippson could be found with the "conservatives", arguing that cremation was completely unacceptable to Jewish law. Another rabbi went so far as to argue that "our dead should turn to ash not in a Siemens furnace but in mother earth, surrounded by flowers and greenery and good natural carbon".[43] Even Reform rabbis doubted whether cremation would ever become popular among Jews. Writing in opposition to the views of Ludwig Philippson, Rabbi Szántó of Hungary, for example, could not hide a certain resignation:

> "There was no Jewish law of burial. All Jewish practices in this area are simply *Minhag*, i.e. in plain language following the old rut, but, as is well known, nothing can be allowed to come before *Minhag*, not the *Halakhah*, not even the holy Torah itself."[44]

The very different pace at which different groups within the Jewish community became assimilated was manifest in the way different Jewish communities responded to the cremation issue. In the generally liberally orientated urban communities, the rabbis tended to tolerate cremation and allow the ashes to be buried. The fact that the burials were normally in a separate section of the cemetery, with no Hebrew inscription on the stones, showed, however, that the dead were regarded as having distanced themselves from Jewish tradition. Cremations in fact remained the exception and in 1890 there were only 153 cremations in the whole of Germany (by 1918 the figure had risen to 466). This compared with 3,236 Protestant cremations (13,824 in 1918) though only 299 (891 in 1918) for a Catholic population which was many times larger than the Jews.[45]

In 1906, an Orthodox rabbi in Würzburg, Nathan Bamberger, refused to

[41]'Die Friedhofs-Frage in der israel. Gemeinde Düsseldorf', in *Der Israelit*, 1876, pp. 138–141; 'Die Friedhofs-Angelegenheit', *ibid.*, 1876, pp. 1005–1007; 'Die Friedhofsfrage in Düsseldorf', *ibid.*, 1877, pp. 441–443; H. Sänger, 'Zur Friedhof-Frage', *ibid.*, 1877, p. 1083; see also 'Die Friedhofsangelegenheit in Brüssel', *ibid.*, 1878, pp. 856–858.

[42]See above all the controversy between Rabbis Kohn und Wiener in the *Jüdisches Literaturblatt* (Magdeburg), 1886–1888 on the issue of 'Erd- und Feuerbestattung nach Bibel und Talmud', and the positions of Simon Scherbel, Moritz Krakauer, Moritz Steckelmacher, Wolff (Aurich) and Goldschmitt (Birkenfeld), *ibid.*; see also Daniel Fink, 'Das Verbrennen der Leiche vom Standpunkte des Judenthums gewürdigt', in *Der Israelit*, 1900, pp. 855–856, 879–880, 959–960, 991–992 and 1097–1098; Isak Unna, *Die Leichenverbrennung vom Standpunkt des Judenthums. Ein Vortrag. Nebst einem Anhang: Kritik des Wiener'schen Gutachtens über die Feuerbestattung*, Frankfurt a. Main 1903.

[43]K. Kohler, 'Trauerbräuche und ihre Bedeutung. Eine kulturgeschichtliche Studie', in *Neuzeit* (Wien), 1876, p. 403.

[44]Simon Szántó, 'Die Frage der Leichenverbrennung', in *Neuzeit*, 1874, pp. 119–121, 127–129 and 144–145; Hirsch B. Fassel, *ibid.*, 1874, p. 145.

[45]'Betriebsergebnisse der deutschen Krematorien im Jahre 1908', in *Zeitschrift für Demographie und Statistik der Juden*, 5 (1909), p. 48; 'Die Betriebsergebnisse der deutschen Krematorien im Jahre 1918', in *Die Flamme*, 1919, pp. 19–20.

agree to the burial of an urn, whereupon he was overruled by the synagogue executive by ten votes to three. With the signatures of 248 members of the community, Bamberger turned to the authorities for aid, but the synagogue executive stuck to its opinion "that the laws of the state and not the beliefs of a rabbi determine whether someone can be considered to have left the Jewish religion. An Israelite cemetery does not cease to be an Israelite cemetery just because someone's ashes have been buried there." The authorities were of the view that the dispute should be settled without the intervention of the state. In the end, the matter took two and a half years to be resolved, at which point an agreement was reached that a special building should be established in the cemetery where, without the usual ceremonial and with no rabbi present, the ashes of cremated Jews would be placed.[46] In the more traditional rural communities within his area of jurisdiction, Rabbi Bamberger faced no such problems. The statutes of the cemetery in Geroda, which were approved by Bamberger, included the clause that "urns containing ashes from cremations will not be allowed into the cemetery", and a postscript laid down that "in the case of bodies which are to be cremated, neither the community nor the *Chevra* may offer assistance; the cleansing and washing must not be carried out".[47]

As a result of the process of assimilation, the cemeteries threatened to lose their specifically Jewish character. From the first half of the nineteenth century onwards, German inscriptions appear alongside Hebrew ones on the grave-stones. Indeed, the gradual increase of German-language inscriptions and the eventual almost complete disappearance of Hebrew from Jewish gravestones serves as a gauge of the degree to which the Jews were being absorbed into the wider culture or, alternatively, were holding on to their traditions. In Breslau in 1830, a dispute arose when the old *Chevra Kaddisha* refused to allow German inscriptions. Eventually, the King decreed that the name of the deceased could appear in German and Hebrew, but there should be no dates according to the Christian calendar.[48] In the Cologne cemetery, situated in what is now the suburb of Deutz, we find from around 1880 onwards gravestones bearing lines from Goethe. On the other hand, in Burgpreppach in Lower Franconia, one of the centres of rural Orthodoxy, we find nothing but Hebrew inscriptions right up to the demise of the congregation in 1942.

Another development was the emergence of costly monuments bearing witness even in death to differences in wealth and social prestige within the community. There was also a new habit of planting flowers on the graves. Just like their Christian counterparts, Jewish gravestones were increasingly likely to be decorated with neo-classical ornamentation and designs.

In the twentieth century, the long-established criticism from traditionalists of the effects of assimilation in the cemeteries was taken up by the *Kulturzionisten*.[49]

[46]Staatsarchiv Würzburg, Regierungsabgabe 7110.

[47]Statutes, 6th and 16th November 1910, Staatsarchiv Würzburg, Landratsamt Brückenau 260.

[48]Freudenthal, *loc. cit.*, p. 576.

[49]Rahel Wischnitzer-Bernstein, 'Alte Friedhofskunst', in *Der Jude*, 2 (1917/1918), pp. 682–691; Erich Toeplitz, 'Jüdische Friedhofskunst', *ibid.*, 5 (1920/1921), pp. 493–499. There was also revived interest in the burial grounds of Eastern Jews; see Arthur Levy, 'Jüdische Grabmalkunst in Osteuropa', in *Jeschurun*, 10 (1923), pp. 317–348 and 389–416.

The Zionists demanded that the authentic, autonomous elements of Jewish culture be revived as a conscious expression of Jewish identity:

> "The old Jewish cemetery presents a pleasing picture and one which nature renders steadily more beautiful, that is if it is not prevented from so doing by some over-zealous gardener. The modern Jewish cemetery, on the other hand, resembles nothing so much as a confused crate of bricks. The garish colours of the flowers and wreaths jar against the landscape . . . The old cemeteries preferred simplicity. The proportions of the gravestones remained modest even when no jealous authority was keeping accounts. The materials used were modest too, even though many could have afforded far better stones than these. What could not be attained in life, namely, equality, could at least be realised after death in the 'house of eternity'. This rule of equality was broken only in the case of the resting place of the rabbis. How characteristically Jewish that special homage in death should be paid to those who devoted their lives to study!"[50]

At the beginning of the period under review, the Jews found themselves confronted by demands for religious change, demands which had their roots in the ideas of the Enlightenment and often drew on scientific arguments for support. The conservative Jewish congregations vigorously opposed these demands. Gradually, however, the influence of Jewish Reformers in conjunction with pressure from state authorities forced the Jewish communities to abandon a large part of their distinctive religious and cultural life. The state pressure was, unlike that of earlier periods, no longer motivated by religious sentiment. Yet the massive use of antisemitic stereotypes continued to be a characteristic feature of the state's behaviour towards the Jewish minority. The official programme of "educating" the Jews to become modern citizens was aimed at the disciplining and homogenisation of society. Alongside these pressures, the demographic transitions of the nineteenth century – in particular urbanisation – also helped to change Jewish mentality and behaviour. Without denying the existence of Neo-Orthodoxy in the towns or the pockets of traditional piety to be found in rural areas, it is fair to say that, by the end of the period, religious liberalism and cultural assimilation were the dominant characteristics of a German Jewry which believed itself to be in the vanguard of modernity, progress and Enlightenment.

---

[50]Erich Toeplitz, 'Jüdische Friedhöfe einst und jetzt', in *Jeschurun*, 9 (1922), pp. 229–235; see also Karl Schwarz, 'Moderne jüdische Grabmalskunst', in *Allgemeine Zeitung des Judent[h]ums*, 1913, pp. 547–549; Magnus Weinberg, 'Synagoge und Friedhof der Gemeinde Sulzbürg', in *Bayerische Israelitische Gemeindezeitung*, 1928, pp. 86–88.

History as Consolation

BY ISMAR SCHORSCH

Hermann Cohen once remarked to Franz Rosenzweig that Leopold Zunz "could have been a great historian, but actually was only an antiquarian".[1] Not so. A tad of truth should never be taken for the whole. For all his attention to facts, Zunz was not a pedant. A pedant would never have chosen for his motto an affirmation as ringingly pro-active as "echte Wissenschaft ist thaterzeugend – genuine scholarship creates deeds".[2] Zunz left Judaism transformed. His work repositioned a faith awash in *midrashic* thinking on the firm foundation of historical knowledge. He softened the resistance to Reform, forged alternate bonds of loyalty, and compelled respect for a long-disdained religion. In an era dominated by the institution of the synagogue, Zunz excavated the rich deposits of its literary creativity (both prose and poetry) and then portrayed it as the bearer of national consciousness. Crafted over the course of a lifetime of self-denial, his majestic and intricate history of the synagogue endowed emancipated Judaism with the certitude of unbroken continuity, a new centre of religious gravity, and a revitalised sense of self.[3]

Whereas pedants are unerringly deaf to the human need for relevance, Zunz's work pulsated with relevance. In a climate of critical scholarship, meaning simply welled up from fresh springs. Even Zunz was not averse to reaching beyond the facts and on one occasion ingeniously turned chronological sequence

---

[1]Hermann Cohen, *Jüdische Schriften*, 3 vols., Berlin 1924, vol. I, p. 332. Recently, Professor Michael Stanislawski laid to rest the well-known version of a visit by Judah Leib Gordon to the aged Zunz that was fabricated to deliver the same charge (*For Whom Do I Toil?*, New York–Oxford 1988, pp. 123–124).

[2]Solomon Schechter, 'Leopold Zunz', in *idem*, *Studies in Judaism*, 3 vols., Philadelphia 1945, vol. III, p. 117.

[3]In addition to the essay by Schechter and the early biography by Shaul Pinchas Rabinowitz, *R. Yomtov Lipman Zunz. His Life, Times and Books* (in Hebrew), Warsaw 1897, one may now consult the accumulating recent scholarship on Zunz: *Leopold Zunz. Jude – Deutscher – Europäer. Ein jüdisches Gelehrtenschicksal des 19. Jahrhunderts in Briefen an Freunde*. Herausgegeben und eingeleitet von Nahum N. Glatzer, Tübingen 1964 (Schriftenreihe wissenschaftlicher Abhandlungen des Leo Baeck Instituts 11), pp. 3–72; Michael A. Meyer, *The Origins of the Modern Jew*, Detroit 1967, pp. 144–182; Ismar Schorsch, 'From Wolfenbüttel to Wissenschaft – The Divergent Paths of Isaak Markus Jost and Leopold Zunz', in *LBI Year Book XXII* (1977), pp. 109–128; *idem*, 'The Emergence of Historical Consciousness in Modern Judaism', in *LBI Year Book XXVIII* (1983), pp. 413–437; *idem*, 'Breakthrough into the Past: The Verein für Cultur und Wissenschaft der Juden', in *LBI Year Book XXXIII* (1988), pp. 3–28; *idem*, 'Emancipation and the Crisis of Religious Authority – The Emergence of the Modern Rabbinate', in *Revolution and Evolution. 1848 in German-Jewish History*, edited by Werner E. Mosse, Arnold Paucker, Reinhard Rürup, Tübingen 1981 (Schriftenreihe wissenschaftlicher Abhandlungen des Leo Baeck Instituts 39), pp. 239–242.

into theological solace. The unparalleled tragedy of the Spanish expulsion, for example, prompted him to allude to the presence of divine concern.

> "The day of departure on which the temporary delay [of three months] for Spanish Jewry ended, 2nd August 1492, was the fast day of *Tisha B'Av*, long stamped as a day of calamity. But with the very next day consolation arrived, though inaudible to those suffering: on 3rd August, Columbus set sail to discover a new world and a new freedom."[4]

The focus of this essay is one of Zunz's last publications, an unheralded instance of his abiding exertion to nourish Jewish collective memory. In 1872, as his powers began to ebb, he produced a second enlarged edition of a small book of eighty pages, now called *Die Monatstage des Kalenderjahres* (The Days of the Month of the Calendar Year). The unwieldy title was surely a euphemism in place of the blunter title, *Sterbetage* (Days of Death), of the incomplete first edition, which had failed to defer to middle-class sensibilities, though the subtitle *Ein Andenken an Hingeschiedene* (A Remembrance of Those Departed) in both served to convey a sense of the contents.[5] Arranged by the days of the secular year beginning with 1st January, the volume records the *Yahrzeit* of nearly eight hundred Jews and non-Jews, including twenty-two women, as well as the dates of some seventy medieval persecutions of Jews. In most cases, the name is accompanied by a pithy, often piquant, description of what made the person memorable. A synopsis of Jewish history, this highly personal assemblage of facts in the service of faith is a window on its author through which no one as yet has been curious enough to cast a glance.

The genesis of this project takes us back to a decade of intense scholarly and public activity, the 1840s, when Zunz stood at the height of his powers. Prussia was politically astir again, with its Jews on edge over impending legislation that threatened to curb their rights and reverse the movement towards full equality. As director of the teachers' seminary of the Jewish community in Berlin, Zunz occupied an important public post, enhanced it by his scholarly reputation, and imbued it with the fullness of his being. He never let up on his basic research (publishing *Zur Geschichte und Literatur* in 1845 and completing the editing of Krochmal's *Moreh Nevukhei ha-Zeman* in 1846) even as he taught, administered, counselled the government, and wrote a medley of vigorous popular essays on Judaism. In a letter from the summer of 1843, he sketched for Krochmal's impatient son-in-law a rare and vivid self-portrait.

> "Absorbed by my writing, holding an official post, and set upon by the events and battles of the day, I sometimes envy the lot of those tranquil souls who live in modest retirement with the good fortune to be forgotten by the world, free of trouble and without knowledge of the pain all over."[6]

---

[4]Leopold Zunz, *Zur Geschichte und Literatur*, Berlin 1845, p. 526; cf. Yitzhak Baer, *A History of the Jews in Christian Spain*, 2 vols., Philadelphia 1961, vol. II, pp. 439, 512.
[5]Leopold Zunz, *Sterbetage*, Berlin 1864; *idem*, *Die Monatstage des Kalenderjahres*, Berlin 1872.
[6]Ismar Schorsch, 'The Production of a Classic: Zunz as Krochmal's Editor', in *LBI Year Book XXXI* (1986), p. 299.

In short, the record of that decade not only offers the most trenchant refutation of
Cohen's characterisation, but also forms the context of Zunz's memorial
calendar.

The intensity of Zunz's engagement bursts forth with unique clarity from his
essays, which tackle artfully contemporary issues from the perspective of Jewish
history. So, for example, on the occasion of the coronation of Frederick William
IV in October 1840, Zunz delivered, in the main synagogue, an earnest plea for
religious renewal and self-respect without any trace of grovelling patriotism.

> "There is so much yet to do for the awakening of our religious souls, for the honour of Israel,
> for the salvation of our children. Do not wait till the divine spark in them [your children] has
> died out and they turn coldly away from you and your faith, till they trample on God's
> covenant and seal a covenant with the world, because they are consumed by the thirst for your
> vanities, a thirst which nothing can slake, neither gold nor title . . . If we are ashamed of our
> faith, if we betray it for base profit, then we are duplicitous with both God and fatherland. We
> will have sunk to the level of barbarians who trade a treasure for a toy."[7]

One month later Zunz opened the new seminary with an invocation of the
spiritual alliance between school, synagogue and seminary as curators of Jewish
consciousness. Again he rose to speak for the supreme value of Jewish continuity.

> "That we are a single Israelite totality, wish to be and must be, that every one of us should
> grow up and mature in this sentiment – for that purpose you need, as the bearer of this
> knowledge, spiritual institutions to preserve the holy fire, a fire that can bring individual coals
> to burn collectively even as it melts down the metallic hardness of many a heart. Hospitals
> alone contribute nothing towards that end."[8]

Nowhere did Zunz enunciate his conservative value system more forcefully
than in an 1844 defence of circumcision, the nineteenth-century version of our
current "who is a Jew" question. Political pressure and personal distaste
combined to induce a growing number of assimilating Jews to reject the rite for
their sons. Asked by Baron Amschel Mayer Rothschild of Frankfurt to address
the problem publicly, Zunz did much more: he spoke of his conception of
Judaism.

> "Nearly all of our ceremonial laws are in their form and in the living ideas which accompany
> them the product of history. The great foundation of this historical edifice that binds us to the
> Bible is called Talmud. But we teach our children that the Talmud is not sacred, is not a law
> book, is not folk literature, is not an instrument of education . . ."[9]

His integrated view of Judaism sought to preserve the historical structure while
doing justice to the welter of new historical information. It also explains why
Zunz still allotted nearly one third of the seminary curriculum to the study of
Talmud. The canopy of Oral Law wedded development to continuity.[10]

Yet Zunz would definitely not have countenanced setting "the goddess of
history . . . over the God of Abraham".[11] He repudiated the facile historicising of

---

[7]Leopold Zunz, *Gesammelte Schriften*, 3 vols., Berlin 1875–1876, vol. II, pp. 119, 124.
[8]*Ibid.*, p. 127.
[9]*Ibid.*, p. 198. On the genesis of Zunz's essay, see The Jewish National and University Library
Archives, Jerusalem, 4°792/F2, p. 35.
[10]Schorsch, 'From Wolfenbüttel to Wissenschaft', *loc. cit.*, p. 122, note 55.
[11]Zunz, *Gesammelte Schriften, op. cit.*, vol. II, pp. 199–200.

radical Reformers that led to trashing much of Judaism by emptying it of all religious specificity.

> "Since circumcision is a sign of the unity and eternity of Israel, a visible act of conferring and bequeathing God's law – its omission would be decisive for the next generation: a son left uncircumcised on principle will hardly stay loyal to Judaism on principle. An abrogation of both the Talmud and the Messiah [as was the case with the Frankfurt Reform Association], that is with a surrender of both past and present, severs Judaism squarely in the middle. Suicide is no reform."[12]

For Zunz the entire class of ceremonial law was an expression of historical loyalty. "Not a single law", he declared in the truculent spirit of Mendelssohn, "was to be sacrificed for equality".[13]

In still another popular essay from that period, Zunz blamed his fellow historians for the indifference towards Jewish history of most literate Jews. Bereft of empathy and integrity, all too many of them cast Jewish history entirely in terms of degeneration. Their works bristled with contempt for their subject, disregarded or distorted the facts, and traduced the major players. As gate-keepers to the past, such historians wholly lacked the tools, knowledge and disposition to unlock the grandeur of the Jewish saga.

> "If the ties of language, history and religion, the idea and its national forms, are thus constantly sundered, don't be amazed if our fashionable Jews quickly sell or put away their Hebrew books and care not a whit about the heroes of our history . . . It is far better to praise Israel's ancient history two or three times than to defame it once . . . Wherever art goes under, the artists have preceded it."[14]

Similarly, then, the compilation of *Yahrzeit* dates was a product of that selfsame decade in which Zunz often addressed an audience far larger than that of his scholarly peers. In 1847 he published a first instalment of his *Sterbetage* that went as far as 29th March.[15] A second instalment appeared a year or two later, but only in New York, reaching to the end of June.[16] Finally, and surprisingly, the first slender book edition of 1864, which reprinted the first two instalments, extended the days of death only down to 30th September. Not till 1872 did Zunz seem to have actually completed the project by providing at least one *Yahrzeit* for nearly every single day of the year. In fact, by then, the number of *Yahrzeit*s per day had also increased substantially. Zunz, thus, clearly persisted with this unusual project for a quarter of a century as his larger research agenda yielded the biographical and chronological data of Jewish history.

The originality of the work lies in the effort to turn the Gregorian calendar into an instrument of Jewish consciousness. Brilliantly, Zunz made of the traditional *Yahrzeit* a portal into the unfolding world of Jewish history. His memorial calendar of the ordinary year offered a poignant synopsis of the last two millennia of the Jewish experience. And it was no accident that the first instalment was

---

[12]*Ibid.*, p. 199.
[13]*Ibid.*, p. 203.
[14]*Ibid.*, pp. 186, 190.
[15]*Idem*, 'Sterbetage', in Isidor Busch (ed.), *Kalender und Jahrbuch für Israeliten auf das Schaltjahr (1848) 5608*, 6 (1847–1848), pp. 87–94.
[16]Listed by M[oritz] S[teinschneider], *Die Schriften des Dr. L. Zunz*, Berlin 1857, p. 15.

published in an annual pocket-size calendar and year book for Jews that contained a melange of religious and practical information, of short stories and light history.

The subject of death was very much on Zunz's mind in the 1840s. In 1845 he had published an absorbing essay of one hundred and fifty pages, unequalled to this day, on the manner in which Jews historically sought to preserve the memory of the dead.* Structured thematically and developmentally, 'Das Gedächtniss der Gerechten' (The Remembrance of the Righteous), assembled a staggering amount of information on a vital range of topics, from honorifics used in conjunction with the dead, to the fate of the dead, to the question of whether Judaism admits of a life-after-death to righteous non-Jews, with Zunz concluding that most authorities do, to the evolution of tombstones, to the importance of their inscriptions for reconstructing family history. Amid a plethora of primary sources, philology became the key to unravelling the history of Jewish practice and theology in regard to the dead.[17]

Zunz himself had been orphaned at an early age. His father and first teacher died in 1802, when Zunz was but eight, and a year later, when he was shipped off to the archaic *yeshivah* of Wolfenbüttel, he saw his mother, who was to die in 1809, for the last time.[18] So one senses, beneath the hard surface of Zunz's compressed style, a scintilla of personal anguish when he came to write of what he most lacked as a child.

> "Parents occupy first place among the living as among as the dead. The lofty position assigned to parents by the Law in the very middle of the Ten Commandments, was later emphatically preserved . . . This religious dogma created in Israel a family life worthy of envy by the Caucasian race, which contributed so vitally to Jewish survival."[19]

I would like to imagine that Zunz's scholarly interest in the unexplored area of commemorating the dead had its deepest roots in his own deprived childhood.

But there is nothing funereal about this majestic survey. Its brisk pace vibrates with a mix of empathy, reverence and anti-Christian animus, while its ultimate intent is decidedly practical – to prompt Jewish communal leaders to set about preserving the tombstones that have survived the ravages of Christian plunder and Jewish indifference.

> "Above all, Jewish communities themselves must invest greater care in the preservation of their monuments, an obligation they owe both to the dead and the living. Towards that end, the official registering of all tombstones along with a copy of their inscriptions would be a great initial act of both religious and scholarly piety."[20]

This pioneering and exhaustive piece of scholarship most likely triggered the idea of a memorial calendar. Zunz stressed the age-old duty in Judaism to

---

* See also the preceding essay by Falk Wiesemann, 'Jewish Burials in Germany. Between Tradition, the Enlightenment and the Authorities', in this volume of the Year Book – (Ed.).

[17] Zunz, *Zur Geschichte, op. cit.*, pp. 304–458.

[18] Markus Brann, 'Mittheilungen aus dem Briefwechsel zwischen Zunz und Kaufmann', in *Jahrbuch für jüdische Geschichte und Literatur*, 5 (1902), p. 190; David Kaufmann, *Gesammelte Schriften*, 3 vols., Frankfurt a. Main 1908–1915, vol. I, p. 334.

[19] Zunz, *Zur Geschichte, op. cit.*, p. 319.

[20] *Ibid.*, p. 404.

venerate the names of the departed, with children often named after their parents.

> "In this manner, names were passed down as objects of veneration. In the Middle Ages, the names of relatives, of famous teachers and benefactors, of persons who had served their community well were formally blessed at public services. One would give charity in their behalf, offer prayers for their salvation, and record their names in the 'memorial book'."[21]

The specific reference to *Memorbücher* suggests that Zunz's memorial calendar may well have been intended as a modern, secular version of this well-known medieval Ashkenazic genre.

Liturgically inspired in the post-Crusade period and consisting of three distinct sections, the *Memorbuch* lay on the reader's *almemor* table in the middle of the synagogue (hence the name) for frequent public use. It contained the special prayers to be recited after reading the Torah, an ever-growing necrology of local and national leaders individually described, and a martyrology that preserved the names of places and people struck down by persecution. After the pogroms of the Black Death, the *Memorbuch* became a staple of German-Jewish liturgy, a tool for socialising the young to the uncertainty of Jewish life and for enriching the content of collective memory.[22] Remarkably, the contents of Zunz's final memorial calendar correspond throughout to the necrology and martyrology of the *Memorbuch*.

Not so his first edition, which failed to record dates of persecutions or acts of martyrdom. What expanded the conception of the popular format was Zunz's monumental work on the liturgical poetry of the medieval synagogue. In 1855 he had published his elegant survey of the corpus known to him, with countless examples in translation. Unexpectedly, *Die synagogale Poesie des Mittelalters*, after a short introduction on the Psalms, starts off with a detour, a searing chronicle of Jewish suffering, whose memorable opening lines betoken its angry, elegaic mood.

> "If there is a ladder of suffering, then Israel has reached the top. If the span of pain and the patience with which it is borne ennoble, then Jews surely are a match for the nobility of any land. If a literature with but a few classic tragedies be deemed rich, what are we to make of a fifteen-hundred-year tragedy recorded in prose and poetry by the heroic victims themselves?"[23]

Yet the reason for the detour is basic: the poetry of the synagogue mirrors the precariousness of reality. The poet often gave voice to the anguish and resentment of the oppressed. Political context alone, Zunz argued, explains the strange commingling of the purest religious sentiments with the most shuddering imprecations for revenge.[24]

In due time, then, Zunz's avocation, his memorial calendar, took on the character of a true *Memorbuch*, with a martyrology as well as a necrology. Of the seventy odd persecutions entered, many were simply transferred from the

---

[21] *Ibid.*, pp. 318–319.
[22] Magnus Weinberg, 'Untersuchungen über das Wesen des Memorbuches', in *Jahrbuch der jüdisch-literarischen Gesellschaft*, 16 (1924), pp. 253–320.
[23] Leopold Zunz, *Die synagogale Poesie des Mittelalters*, Berlin 1855, p. 9.
[24] *Ibid.*, p. 58.

chapter compiled for *Die synagogale Poesie*. For example, Zunz had recorded therein that "in the year 1481, in Seville, Jews were slaughtered four times, namely on 10th January, 26th March, 21st April and 4th November".[25] In the later memorial calendar, each onslaught is listed separately under its appropriate day of the year, with the last accompanied by a typical specimen of Zunz's stinging sarcasm. "On 4th November 1481, in Seville, God was entertained with an *auto-da-fé*."[26]

Indeed, the memorial calendar depicted the reign of terror for Jews as extending well beyond the middle of the sixteenth century, at which point *Die synagogale Poesie* had stopped, by taking special note of the *autos-da-fé* of the seventeenth century. Witness the following two entries:

> "On 5th May 1624, the priests of Coimbra [Portugal] burned Dr. Antonio Homem along with three baskets of books, because he admitted to being a Jew.
> On 10th May 1682, Abraham Lopez Pereira and Isaac de Fonseca were burned in Lisbon. This form of sacrifice, as is well known, did not fall into disuse until after the period of Bayle, Voltaire and Frederick the Great."[27]

The contempt for Christianity is barely disguised. More important, the addition of the martyrological mode accorded with the traditional and still prevailing view of Jewish survival: a dialectic of suffering and learning, of torment and Torah.

The necrology, of course, addressed the spiritual side of the ledger. At the outset Zunz cautioned not to impute too much significance to the individual names salvaged from the wreckage of the Jewish past. Each fragment enlarged our picture of the whole, and the Jewish experience comprised a valuable part of the total human odyssey. The brief introduction, which went unchanged from 1847 to 1872, intoned his reverential and polemical design.

> "Since the muse of Jewish history seldom favours her devotees with the age of her heroes, how thankful must we be when the day of death is noted. Thus let us not press too hard as to why one person is considered and another more important overlooked. For where many are wronged and much goes unheard and some still lie buried waiting for a quickening love, there we should not seek to censure or judge, but rather to preserve the memory of those who, if not singlehandedly surely as partners, laboured mightily for a common idea. Accordingly, the following pages of remembrance are given over to all those who do not choose to ignore the spokesmen of the spirit if they be Jews or individuals who admired or defended things Jewish."[28]

Nevertheless, the final mosaic bristles with subjectivity. The names chosen and the comments added offer a luminous view of Zunz's own value system. To begin with, his unique erudition is graced by an encompassing spirit of humanity. More than five per cent of the names entered belong to non-Jews, who, often at great risk, had dared to study Judaism fairly, to defend it publicly, or to advance the cause of political emancipation. Thus Zunz paid tribute to his own teacher of Bible at the University of Berlin, Wilhelm de Wette, "in whose

[25] *Ibid.*, p. 51.
[26] *Idem, Die Monatstage, op. cit.*, p. 60.
[27] *Ibid.*, pp. 25, 27.
[28] *Ibid.*, 'Vorwort'.

works an undogmatic critical spirit fought against mindless fundamentalism",[29] and to the scientist Alexander von Humboldt who "bore the most famous name of our day and [who] regarded the Jews as his equal. His word, as his life, were a death knell to the exclusivism of the clerics and to the arrogance of an impoverished nobility."[30] Some like Columbus were listed because, as we saw, they benefited Jews indirectly,[31] and a few like Benjamin Franklin, simply because Zunz admired them: "For him it was enough to be a good man. By means of magnetism, he attracted both flashes of lightning and human hearts."[32] Even Luther's death was noted, though without comment, probably in gratitude for his early defence of Jews.[33]

The magnanimity of Zunz's spirit extended even to those who had chosen to abandon Judaism. A number he knew personally. His own view seemed to accord with that of Lazarus Bendavid, the free-thinker who had directed the Jewish Free School of Berlin for twenty years without pay and whom he quoted approvingly. "They [i.e. the converts to Christianity] are splinters, that must be painfully extracted from a clumsy giant. The giant thereby will only get stronger."[34] More concretely, the attrition hurt, but was not life-threatening. On occasion, Judaism's loss became mankind's gain, and Zunz fearlessly honoured their memory. Besides passing references to Spinoza, Heine, Josef von Sonnenfels (the Councillor to Joseph II), and the medieval historian Philipp Jaffé, Zunz singled out his lifelong friend Eduard Gans, "who converted to Christianity in Paris on 12th December 1825, but whose finest period of development fell between 1818 and 1823 (i.e. the period of the *Verein für Cultur und Wissenschaft der Juden*), a period entirely passed over by Heinrich Laube in his biography".[35] The pathos of the past was intensified by the continued injustice of the present. The creation of a single German *Reich* in 1870 had failed to diminish the ubiquitous hostility towards Jews, as Zunz wittily remarked while commenting on the converted writer Ludwig Börne: "On this day [13th February 1837] L. Börne died in Paris. In 1821 he had written *Der ewige Jude* [a hard-hitting defence of the Jews], and if he were still alive in 1871, he could have written it once again."[36]

But in the final analysis, it is the Jewish cameos of Zunz's gallery that are most captivating. The study of Jewish history had begun to reshape the contours of collective memory. Zunz's empathy heralded the known and enfranchised the forgotten. Though his necrology bore a distinct German complexion, it also revealed a bias for Italian Jews and a steady interest in Jews around the world from Kovno (Abraham Mapu) to New Orleans (Gerson Adersbach).[37] In consequence, the gallery unveiled the bracing diversity of Jewish expression –

[29] *Ibid.*, p. 34.
[30] *Ibid.*, p. 26.
[31] *Ibid.*, p. 28.
[32] *Ibid.*, p. 20.
[33] *Ibid.*, p. 9; see also *idem, Die synagogale Poesie, op. cit.*, p. 55.
[34] *Idem, Die Monatstage, op. cit.*, p. 15.
[35] *Ibid.*, p. 26.
[36] *Ibid.*, p. 8.
[37] *Ibid.*, pp. 48, 52.

political leaders and religious teachers, *halakhists* and *aggadists*, Karaites and Kabbalists, poets and philosophers, scientists and historians, preachers and printers, commentators and grammarians, and, remarkably, the names of over twenty women like Judith Montefiore, "the wife of Moses and the author of a diary of her trip to Palestine".[38] Throughout, Zunz is at pains to note what survives unpublished of their literary legacy: our knowledge remains so fragmentary.

As curator of this exhibit, Zunz achieves an admirable balance between piety and progress. He recalls the memory of rabbinists and Reformers graciously by focusing on the positive. This is not a forum for settling scores. What does offend him deeply, though, is trifling with Judaism. "Already in the year 1813 Abraham Muhr [a prominent Prussian Jewish attorney who died in 1847] had admonished that in matters of religion we ought not to tear down old pillars to replace them with the trivia of modernity."[39] Yet Zunz was no less exercised by the wilful ignorance of coercive fundamentalists. "On the same day of the month [7th September 1848], while in Germany, three parliaments proclaimed freedom of conscience, the respected preacher and author Abraham Cohn of Lemberg was poisoned by his pious enemies."[40] The passion lies in the juxtaposition.

The encomium Zunz penned for Naphtali Herz Wessely, the finest Hebraic writer of Mendelssohn's circle, allowed a glimpse of his own quest for equilibrium. "A man aglow for beauty and human welfare, who dared to include his love for Israel. He taught his generation that Orthodoxy need not consist of decay and ignorance, nor of hatred and intolerance for other religions."[41] Zunz drove home the same point in what he chose to stress in the life of Marcus Herz, the physician who fell under the spell of Immanuel Kant. "Herz had on more than one occasion reprimanded the exclusivists, who condemn or ridicule all knowledge outside their own. He regarded freedom of thought, that is the articulation of what is thought, as a key factor imbuing whole nations with a measure of good taste."[42] Indeed, the affinity Zunz evinces for such catalytic figures as Rashi, Jacob ben Meir Tam, Abraham Ibn Ezra, David Gans, Efraim Lentschutz, Yomtov Lipman Heller, Nachman Krochmal, Isaac Benjacob, Salomon Steinheim and Shlomo Yehudah Rapoport is rooted in the conviction that insularity can only serve to warp a wholesome faith.

By the same token, Zunz displayed a firm reserve towards *Kabbalah*, enunciated with amusing subtlety. On occasion, facts are marshalled to deflate a myth, as in the case of Isaac Luria, who died in Safed on 15th July 1572. "The Kabbalists of the seventeenth century elevated him to a hero and wonder worker, in much the same manner as the authors of the *Zohar* had once done with Simeon ben Yohai. Yet his contemporaries, including R. Joseph Caro, had no inkling of such glory."[43] And where the facts were still unknown to Zunz, juxtaposition

---

[38] *Ibid.*, p. 53.
[39] *Ibid.*, p. 33.
[40] *Ibid.*, p. 50.
[41] *Ibid.*, p. 14.
[42] *Ibid.*, p. 4.
[43] *Ibid.*, p. 40.

could serve the same purpose. "10th September 1676 is the day of death of the alleged Messiah Sabbatai Zvi, who left behind no other trace of his activity than the sarcastic and polemical tracts called forth by his following. Jewish literature does owe an eternal debt of gratitude to Edward Pococke [Professor of Arabic and Hebrew at Oxford as well as biblical scholar], who died the same day [1691] in Oxford."[44] Finally, Zunz saw fit to praise Jacob Emden, who merited an ambivalent entry, for undermining the traditional view which attributed the *Zohar* to R. Simeon ben Yohai. "To this powerful zealot [Emden] goes the honour of being the first to dethrone the mighty *Zohar*, which he did in the same year that Mendelssohn's *Phädon* appeared [1767]."[45]

In contrast, Zunz betrayed no estrangement from the Hebrew language. It had been his first writing medium back in the *yeshivah* of Wolfenbüttel. Samuel Meyer Ehrenberg, "his unforgettable teacher and mentor", loved the language deeply, and his own mastery of all its literary and linguistic strata was unrivalled.[46] In consonance with that background, Zunz wrote of the decline of Hebrew at the turn of the eighteenth century with felt emotion. Witness how he chose to etch for us the memory of Isaac Euchel, who had died in Berlin on 14th June 1804: "The biographer of Mendelssohn, the editor of [a new edition of] Maimonides's *Moreh Nevukhim*, and a co-founder of the epoch-making Hebrew periodical *The Collector* [Hame'asef] in April 1783. In the summer of 1800 he lamented already the growing neglect among Jewish youth of the study of Hebrew."[47]

More poignant still is the immediacy of the recollection of Aaron Wolfssohn, who had died on 23rd March 1835 in Fürth at the age of 79.

> "One of those men who in the last decades of the previous century worked for enlightenment through translations and Hebrew journals. At the end of 1797, *Hame'asef* had only 120 subscribers and closed down. Indeed, at the time Wolfssohn said: 'It would truly be sad if we should find our hopes dashed and if among all the Jewish inhabitants in Germany there would not be 200 people who would be prepared to offer up two taler annually.' Nevertheless, *Hame'asef*, after it had served its time, did close down and thus provided yet another example that individuals are only the servants of Providence but never Providence itself."[48]

The tone of resignation is nuanced by nostalgia. Zunz was clearly distressed by the erosion of Hebrew as a living language. In retrospect, his selfless decision to edit Krochmal's Hebraic torso should also be regarded as a valiant effort to sustain and enrich the ancient tongue.

It is hoped that this scrutiny of the memorial calendar has mounted a case for celebrating Zunz as one of the great servants of Providence. As Degas taught us, beauty is often viewed best obliquely. From the perspective of his occasional essays, Zunz emerges as anything but a mindless and indifferent pedant. Although he graciously crowned Rapoport as "the founder of the critical phase of

[44]*Ibid.*, p. 50.

[45]*Ibid.*, pp. 20–21.

[46]Isaak M. Jost, 'Vor einem halben Jahrhundert', in *Sippurim*, III, ed. by Wolf Pascheles, Prague 1854, pp. 150–152; Leopold Zunz, *Samuel Meyer Ehrenberg*, Braunschweig 1854, p. 43.

[47]*Idem, Die Monatstage, op. cit.*, p. 33.

[48]*Ibid.*, pp. 13–14.

Jewish scholarship",[49] no one did more than Zunz himself in rethinking Judaism historically. By the time he finished, historical consciousness was well on the way to replacing revelation as the ground of Jewish existence. His memorial calendar sought to pour that new wine into old bottles – the institutions of the *Yahrzeit* and the *Memorbuch* – for large scale consumption.[50] Paradoxically, despite the change in *mentalité*, Zunz perpetuated the traditional bipolar vision of the Jewish past as consisting solely of victims and scholars.

[49]*Ibid.*, p. 57.

[50]Shaul Pinchas Rabinowitz, in his generally sympathetic biography of Zunz, roundly criticised him for omitting the Hebrew date of each *Yahrzeit*. To Rabinowitz, one of the great transmitters of German-Jewish *Wissenschaft* to the Jews of Eastern Europe, the use of the Hebrew calendar was a matter of national pride and religious integrity. While Rabinowitz deemed the rise of a sense of history as a vital step towards national revival, he abhorred the readiness to assimilate, as exemplified in the choice of calendars (Rabinowitz, *op. cit.*, pp. 327–328).

Orthodoxy versus Reform
The Case of Rabbi Nehemiah Anton Nobel
of Frankfurt a. Main

BY RACHEL HEUBERGER

In the nineteenth century the decisive controversies between Jewish Orthodoxy and the Reform movement took place in Germany.[1] A Jewish Reform movement came into existence, that intended first of all to reform the traditional liturgy, but then soon aimed to adapt Judaism to the surrounding society, which was determined by Christianity. Central commandments of rabbinical Judaism were abolished and new beliefs formulated.[2] For the adherents of the Reform movement integration into German society went hand in hand with an increasing loss of Jewish knowledge, Jewish tradition and Jewish values.

By the sixties and seventies it was Orthodoxy that had to fight for survival.[3] But in the meantime Orthodoxy itself had undergone essential changes. Samson Raphael Hirsch had developed a specific ideology of education (*Bildungsideologie*), since then famous under the slogan "*Torah im Derech Erez*", which would enable the Orthodox Jews to integrate into the German bourgeois society while at the same time continuing to keep their strict adherence to Jewish law (*Halakhah*).[4]

By the end of the nineteenth century the different religious movements were established within the Jewish community. While Reform was recognised as one of the trends in Judaism, Orthodoxy had reasserted itself. After the passing of the law of 1876 (*Austrittsgesetz*), which granted members of the independent congre-

---

[1]This article is based on a study of Nobel as part of a dissertation in the History Department of the Hebrew University in Jerusalem. My thanks are due to my supervisors Professors George L. Mosse and Moshe Zimmermann who encouraged me to undertake this study and to Dr. Monika Richarz for her comments.

[2]The most comprehensive recent work on the Jewish Reform movement is Michael A. Meyer, *Response to Modernity. A History of the Reform Movement in Judaism*, New York–Oxford 1988. And see now also *idem*, 'Recent Historiography on the Jewish Religion', in *LBI Year Book XXXV* (1990), pp. 3–16. Basic research on the German rabbinate in the period dealt with in this article is found in Alexander Altmann, 'The German Rabbi: 1910–1939', and Alfred Jospe, 'A Profession in Transition. The German Rabbinate 1910–1939', both in *LBI Year Book XIX* (1974), pp. 31–59.

[3]Meyer, *Response to Modernity, op. cit.*, p. 183.

[4]Mordechai Breuer, *Jüdische Orthodoxie im Deutschen Reich 1871–1918. Die Sozialgeschichte einer religiösen Minderheit*, Frankfurt a. Main 1986, Veröffentlichung des Leo Baeck Instituts, pp. 27–34, argues for the concept of "Neo-Orthodoxy" in light of the innovations in modern German-Jewish Orthodoxy. For a critical review of this concept see Julius Carlebach, 'The Foundations of German-Jewish Orthodoxy. An Interpretation', in *LBI Year Book XXXIII* (1988), pp. 88–91.

gations freedom from payment of community taxes, Orthodoxy established its own separate communities or was strengthened within the community (*Einheits-gemeinde*) where it came to some kind of arrangement with Reform.[5]

The number of Orthodox Jews continued to decrease steadily. Whereas until 1848 the majority of the German Jews had been traditional, at the end of the First World War the Orthodox Jews numbered only between 10–20%.[6] This shrinkage did not alter German-Jewish Orthodoxy's view of itself as representing German Jewry as a whole. However, they did fear for their continuing ability to meet the needs of Orthodox Jews in the predominantly liberal *Einheitsgemeinden*.

Orthodoxy continued to see itself as the only legitimate form of Judaism. It was from this platform that they waged their fight against the changes intended by Reform. This meant that the Orthodox rabbis in the so-called *Einheitsgemein-den* – which included both Orthodox and Reform within their framework – were facing new challenges every day in their relationship to the Reform movement. On the one hand they had to keep up the Orthodox claim of being the sole representative of Judaism; on the other they not only had to tolerate their liberal colleagues and community members, but also to co-operate with them in various community matters.

In this essay the Orthodox rabbi Nehemiah Anton Nobel and his role in the community in Frankfurt a. Main will serve as a model to illustrate how these contrasting requirements were realised within their social context. Nobel was one of the most prominent representatives of German-Jewish Orthodoxy. Even one of his pronounced adversaries characterised him as "one of the outstanding personalities of contemporary German Jewry".[7] In 1921 he was the first Orthodox rabbi to be elected as President of the *Allgemeiner Deutscher Rabbinerver-band*.[8] He had been its executive director already since 1919. Nobel embodies the dilemma of the Orthodox within the community facing Reform.[9] Besides demonstrating his attitude towards Reform in Frankfurt a. Main, the second largest Jewish community in Germany, his position serves simultaneously as an example of the Orthodox camp and as a light upon the way the Orthodox led their fight against Reform.

[5]Robert Liberles, *Religious Conflict in Social Context. The Resurgence of Orthodox Judaism in Frankfurt am Main 1838–1877*, Westport, Conn. 1985.

[6]Monika Richarz (ed.), *Jüdisches Leben in Deutschland*, vol. II: *Selbstzeugnisse zur Sozialgeschichte im Kaiserreich*, Stuttgart 1979, Veröffentlichung des Leo Baeck Instituts, p. 48; Breuer, *op. cit.*, p. 6.

[7]He was characterised that way by his opponent Jakob Rosenheim, founder of *Agudath Israel* and leading figure in the *Israelitische Religionsgesellschaft*, the Frankfurt *Austrittsgemeinde*, in Jakob Rosenheim, *Ohalei Jakob. Ausgewählte Aufsätze und Ansprachen*, vol. II, Frankfurt a. Main 1930, p. 478.

[8]*Jüdische Presse*, 52, No. 23 (1921), p. 171.

[9]The Orthodox within the community were called *Gemeindeorthodoxie* or "conservative" (*Konservative*), whereas those organised in secessionist congregations (*Austrittsgemeinden*) were called "Orthodox". The term "Orthodox" itself was frowned upon by Nobel and his predecessor Marcus Horovitz as well as by members of the *Austrittsgemeinden*. See Nobel, *Die Richtlinien. Predigt gehalten in der Gemeindesynagoge am Börneplatz*, Frankfurt a. Main 1912, p. 10; Joseph Wohlgemuth, 'Etwas über die Termini "Orthodoxes und gesetzestreues Judentum" ', in *Festschrift zum 70. Geburtstage D. Hoffmanns*, Berlin 1914, pp. 435–453. Nobel advocated the term "*gesetzestreu*". The different terminology grew out of Jewish communal politics, not out of matters of religion. Therefore the term "Orthodox" is used in this article for those organised within as well as outside of the community.

Nehemiah Anton Nobel was born on 8th November 1871 in Nagy-Atad, a small place in Hungary.[10] He grew up in Halberstadt, one of the oldest and most important Jewish communities in Germany. After matriculation in 1892 he went to Berlin to study philosophy and literature at the university. At the same time he studied at the Orthodox *Rabbiner-Seminar* of Esriel Hildesheimer, who considered him his model pupil and occasionally entrusted him with giving the Talmud lessons.[11] After his ordination in 1895, he did his one year's military service before being appointed rabbi of the Orthodox private *Hevrat Talmud Torah* congregation in Cologne. In 1897 he received his doctorate at the university of Bonn for a thesis on Schopenhauer and his theory of beauty.[12] The next year he married Julie Weil from Viersen, and their only child, Ruth, was born in 1905.[13]

In August 1900 he became rabbi of the Orthodox secessionist congregation *Adass Isroel* in Königsberg in Prussia. After a few months he resigned in order to study in Marburg under Hermann Cohen. A long-lasting and close friendship developed in these years between the two very different personalities, Cohen, the representative of Neo-Kantian thought and liberal in religious terms and Nobel, the Orthodox rabbi. Both shared philosophical idealism and Nobel always expressed his admiration for his teacher. Long before Cohen's great work, *Die Religion der Vernunft*, was posthumously published, Nobel had already pointed out the importance of Cohen's views on Judaism and rationalism.[14] Inspired by Cohen, Nobel was perhaps "the only true philosopher amongst German-Jewish Orthodoxy".[15]

Nevertheless at the same time he had always stressed the differences in their views and had rejected Cohen's position "beyond positive Judaism, beyond the belief of revelation". "We believe that Judaism could never have become a universal religion", he wrote, "had it confined itself to a system of abstract thought. The prophets do not teach pure abstract ethicism. They are not opposing the observance of law, but its mechanical observance, the miserable belief, which has always been the catechism of sanctimoniousness (*Werkheiligkeit*) and which holds that man can have religion without morality. The prophets abound in national tendencies, they are possessed of that healthy nationalism which, as Cohen himself remarks, is compatible with world citizenship."[16] With

---

[10]These details are taken from of his doctoral thesis. Information about the date and place of his birth vary in the different biographical essays and obituaries.

[11]Jeschajahu Wolfsberg, *The Rabbi Nechemja Zwi Nobel* (in Hebrew), Jerusalem 1943, p. 10. He was told this by Nobel's widow.

[12]N. A. Nobel, *Schopenhauers Theorie des Schönen in ihren Beziehungen zu Kants Kritik der ästhetischen Urteilskraft*, diss., Köln 1897.

[13]Eugen E. Mayer, 'Nehemiah Anton Nobel', in *Guardians of our Heritage (1724–1953)*, New York 1958, pp. 566–567, gives a short genealogical survey on Nobel's family. Nobel's wife Julie died in 1938 in Haifa.

[14]Hermann Cohen, *Die Religion der Vernunft aus den Quellen des Judentums*, Leipzig 1919. This work was published posthumously. Nobel's appraisal of Cohen appeared in an editorial, 'Hermann Cohen zu seinem 60. Geburtstag', *Jüdische Presse*, 33, No. 27 (1902), pp. 255–256.

[15]Alexander Altmann, 'Theology in Twentieth-Century German Jewry', in *LBI Year Book I* (1956), p. 211.

[16]*Jüdische Presse*, 33, No. 27 (1902), p. 233. If not otherwise stated, the translations are mine. This one is taken from the essay by Mayer, 'Nobel', *loc. cit.*, p. 568.

these words Nobel unequivocally positioned himself with Orthodox Judaism in its historically transmitted form. At the same time he hinted at the basis of his Zionism as an open-minded self-understanding of the Jewish people, that was based on the nationalism of the prophets.

Nobel always admired Cohen for his personal engagement in defending the rights of the Jews and his battle against anti-Jewish prejudices, particularly those generating from the Bible exegesis of Christian theologians. In that manner Cohen had brought back to Judaism "quite a few Jewish students who had cast an eye at the baptismal font" and had contributed to the strength of Judaism.[17] When Cohen died in 1918 Nobel was designated to compose the inscription on his tombstone.[18]

In 1902 Nobel was appointed as rabbi at the *Adass Jeschurun* in Leipzig, a secessionist congregation that had been established the year before. Five years later he became communal rabbi in Hamburg. After the death of the Orthodox Frankfurt rabbi Marcus Horovitz in March 1910, Nobel was appointed as his successor in the *Börneplatzsynagoge*. Here he held his inaugural sermon on 30th September 1910 and served as rabbi until his early death on 24th January 1922.[19]

During the early years of the First World War, Nobel expressed in emphatic sermons his enthusiasm for the German war effort and prayed for the victory of the German armies.[20] Although he was a Zionist, he fully identified with German war aims and was not among those few who had a critical attitude towards the war.[21]

In his sermons he spoke about the "holy soil of the German fatherland" and declared war to be a "pious and solemn undertaking".[22] Nobel raised the concrete political confrontation of war to the metaphysical level of good and bad and put religion in the service of German Nationalism. In these sermons Nobel, like Cohen, turned the State into the bearer of ethical ideas, so that the State itself became an ethical value.

---

[17]Nobel, *Jüdische Presse*, 33, No. 27 (1902), p. 255.

[18]The inscription read: "Platons strahlende Welt und Kants erdunkelnde Tiefen / Strahlten Dir, Großer, in Eins. Musisch erklangen sie Dir. / An der prophetischen Glut entbrannte die lodernde Fackel. / Sterbliches bargen wir hier. Lodere heller, o Glut!" Mayer, 'Nobel', *loc. cit.*, p. 568, translated it the following way: "Platon's radiant world and Kant's profoundness and darkness Fused together in you, Muses intoning the tune. Ardour of prophets did kindle the glow of the torch and its blazes. Buried are mortal remains, Glow ever brighter, oh torch!"

[19]Nobel's literary bequest in the Archives of the Jewish National and University Library, Jerusalem (JNUL), MS Varia 299, consists of a collection of manuscripts. One contains his inauguration address in Frankfurt. *Der Israelit*, 8, No. 40 (1910), p. 9, stressed the fact that Nobel acknowledged the genius of Samson Raphael Hirsch in his address. For the exact date of his death, see Stadtarchiv Frankfurt a. Main, Magistratsakten, S 408.

[20]*Gebetordnung für Feldgottesdienste*, ed. by N. A. Nobel, Frankfurt a. Main 1914; N. A. Nobel, *Kriegspredigten, gehalten in der Gemeindesynagoge am Börneplatz. 1. Vor der Vereidigung. 2. Wo finde ich Dich*, Frankfurt a. Main 1914, 2. Folge, *Der Tag des Kampfes*, Frankfurt a. Main 1915.

[21]Neither Mayer, 'Nobel', *loc. cit.*, nor Ernst Simon, 'N. A. Nobel als Prediger (1961)', in *idem, Brücken. Gesammelte Aufsätze*, Heidelberg 1965, pp. 375–380, mentioned these war sermons in their detailed biographical essays on Nobel, while his biographer Jeschayahu Wolfsberg found only excuses for them.

[22]Nobel, *Kriegspredigten, op. cit., Vor der Vereidigung*, pp. 5–8.

When Cohen provoked a vehement controversy in the Jewish press with the publication of his essay 'Deutschtum und Judentum' in 1916, Nobel took his stand on the side of Cohen. In this essay Cohen expressed his view that there existed a profound affinity, "an inner coherence", between Germanism and Judaism, which were congenial states of mind.[23] When the Orthodox and Zionist Gustav Witkowsky wrote a harsh review criticising Cohen in the *Jüdische Presse*, Nobel reacted with personal polemical attacks against Witkowsky.[24] He rebuked Witkowsky's critique without refuting it, and misread the rejection of Cohen's ideas as a personal attack on Cohen.[25]

Nobel defended Cohen's view, that the ethos of the German state was in harmony with that of prophetic Judaism, because he too felt the "deep correlations and associations" that Cohen had expressed. Nobel's sermons during the First World War show that he had not only been caught up in the general mood of German war ecstasy, but believed that German Nationalism and Jewish religiousness mutually enhanced each other. Nobel had no moral doubts about the "German mission", the duty of Germany to stand up as the keeper of European civilisation and to impart its own ethical values to other nations.[26]

After the war Nobel founded a circle of young Jewish intellectuals, among them Erich Fromm, Siegfried Kracauer, Leo Löwenthal, Franz Rosenzweig, Ernst Simon, Nahum N. Glatzer and others. Together they launched a Jewish renaissance whose impact rejudaicised broad circles outside Orthodoxy.[27] During his years of activity in Frankfurt, Nobel was highly respected and became famous, far beyond his own congregation, as a preacher surrounded by "the secret of a mythical mystery".[28] At the same time Nobel was generally recognised as a talmudic authority. He embodied the "Raw in the old sense", who knew the *Halakhah* better than most Orthodox Jewish scholars in Germany.[29] In Frankfurt he carried out two important *halakhic* decisions, the institution of an *Eruv* and the imposition of women's suffrage in the *Israelitische Gemeinde*.[30]

Nobel was one of the few Orthodox rabbis in Germany professing adherence to

---

[23]Alfred Jospe, *loc cit.*, p. 57, puts forward that the German rabbis did not adhere to their "proclaimed political neutrality", but supported German Nationalism.

[24]Gustav Witkowsky, *Jüdische Presse*, 46, Nos. 39/40 (1915), p. 454.

[25]Nobel, *Christliche Welt*, 30, No. 3 (1916), p. 53.

[26]Egmont Zechlin, *Die deutsche Politik und die Juden im Ersten Weltkrieg*, Göttingen 1969, pp. 87ff.

[27]Leo Löwenthal, *Mitmachen wollte ich nie. Ein autobiographisches Gespräch mit Helmut Dubiel*, Frankfurt a. Main 1980, pp. 18–20.

[28]Caesar Seligmann, *Erinnerungen*, ed. by Erwin Seligmann, Frankfurt a. Main 1975, p. 150.

[29]Shlomo Dow (Fritz) Gotein, in *Nachrufe auf Rabbiner N. A. Nobel*, Hrsg. vom Vorstand der Israelitischen Gemeinde Frankfurt a. M., Frankfurt a. Main 1923, p. 40.

[30]The issue of *Eruw* and women's suffrage are specified elsewhere and cannot be dealt with here. See Nehemiah Anton Nobel, *Porat Josef. Quuntres odot tiqun eruvin bevranqfurt a'n moin* (in Hebrew), Frankfurt a. Main 1914. Briefly mentioned in Peter Freimark, 'Eruw/"Judentore". Zur Geschichte einer rituellen Institution im Hamburger Raum (und anderswo)', in Peter Freimark, Ina Lorenz and Günter Marwedel (eds.), *Judentore, Kuggel, Steuerkonten. Untersuchungen zur Geschichte der deutschen Juden, vornehmlich im Hamburger Raum*, Hamburg 1983, esp. pp. 10–16 and 52–53. Women's suffrage in Marion A. Kaplan, *The Jewish Feminist Movement in Germany. The Campaigns of the Jüdischer Frauenbund, 1904–1938*, Westport, Conn. – London 1979, pp. 147–168.

Zionism. Already as a young rabbi in Cologne he had joined the Zionist Movement. At the 4th conference of the *Zionistische Vereinigung für Deutschland* (ZVfD), which took place in Cologne on 19th and 20th March 1899, he was elected to the board of the ZVfD.[31] Like Herzl, whom he adored, he was a representative of political Zionism. "Zionism represents for me essentially political and economical thinking. Towards its realisation the religiously different-minded can work together more easily than within the *Allgemeiner Deutscher Rabbinerverband*, where religious questions must necessarily be dealt with."[32] With these words he defined his position within Zionism and at the same time tried to convince his fellow rabbis to change their negative attitude towards Zionism. On the grounds of adhering to political Zionism, he backed Herzl at the VIth Zionist Congress in Basel in August 1903 in the well-known controversy about the Uganda-plan. Functioning as the Vice-Chairman of the *Misrachi* he declared his confidence in Herzl and the Action-Committee in the name of his party.[33]

Nobel played a decisive role in establishing the *Misrachi* in 1904 and functioned as the Vice-President of the Preßburg Congress in August 1904.[34] He was elected by the *Misrachi* Congress as President of the newly founded West European Central Committee of the *Misrachi*, located in Frankfurt a. Main.[35]

One year later he left the Zionist organisation and refrained from supporting the Zionist case in public.[36] After the First World War he once again advocated Zionism publicly and participated as a delegate of *Misrachi* in the XIIth Zionist Congress, that took place in Karlsbad in August 1921. As President of the *Allgemeiner Deutscher Rabbinerverband*, a position he held from 1921, he succeeded in passing a pro-Zionist resolution that spoke about Palestine as the future new homeland for great parts of the Jewish people.[37]

Nobel believed that Jewish history could not be assessed on religious values alone, but that it was also the expression of national development. At the same time he was deeply rooted in German culture and was known as an expert on Goethe, with whom he felt close bonds. He was well aware of these two divergent

---

[31] *Der Durchbruch des politischen Zionismus in Köln. 1890–1900. Eine Dokumentation. Briefe, Protokolle, Flugblätter, Reden*, ed. and rev. by Henriette Hanna Bodenheimer, Köln 1978, p. 273.

[32] Nobel to Jeremias in a letter, Central Zionist Archives (CZA), K 11/58.

[33] *Stenographisches Protokoll der Verhandlungen des VI. Zionistenkongresses in Basel, 23.–28.8.1903*, Wien 1903, p. 98.

[34] *Frankfurter Israelitisches Familienblatt*, 2, No. 33 (1904), p. 2.

[35] *Ibid.*, Beilage zu No. 34.

[36] JNUL, MS Varia 299, contains the draft of Nobel's letter to the board of the *Israelitische Gemeinde* Frankfurt a. Main of the year 1910, in which he claims that he left the Zionist movement 4½ years ago, because of his religious persuasion. In all biographical essays and personal memoirs, however, he is described as being a Zionist throughout all this time. Therefore it seems that he left the Zionist movement, knowing that his professional prospects would otherwise be hampered by anti-Zionist attitudes of the community boards. In a letter to David Wolffsohn he explained his being turned down as rabbi in Cologne and accepted in Leipzig by his Zionist position, CZA W 55/II. Wolfsberg, *Der Rabbiner Nobel, op. cit.*, p. 24 comes to the same conclusion. Kurt Wilhelm, 'Der Zionistische Rabbiner', in *In Zwei Welten, Siegfried Moses zum 75. Geburtstag*, ed. by Hans Tramer, Tel-Aviv 1962, p. 61, is wrong in claiming that "a conservative rabbi in Germany did not have to face any serious difficulties because of his Zionist ideology."

[37] *Jüdische Presse*, 52, No. 21 (1921), p. 21.

convictions and stated: "I am rooted in the sphere of national Jewish thought. It is not a conviction that I have absorbed: it is my very life. But, on the other hand, I cannot conceive of this life without Goethe, the poet of the Germans. There works in me this synthetic force, which binds together and unites both nationalisms. I realize that each one in itself is strong enough to be allied with the other."[38]

As a rabbi, Nobel always stood up for Orthodox Judaism, basing his struggle against Reform on specific issues. At the same time he was tolerant and showed understanding towards those who had different religious and political views. He did not allow differences in principle to be transferred to the personal realm. Still a young rabbi at the very beginning of his career, he demonstrated his own understanding of the rabbinate by giving his view of the office in the following words:

> "I hold that a rabbi can fulfil his task successfully only if he stands above all parties within and outside his community. He himself must have a firm and unflinching standpoint on all religious issues of his time. For myself, this standpoint is that offered by Judaism in its historical tradition. This alone seems to me to guarantee development and sound progress. But I consider it my duty to examine every religious trend within Judaism, to meet it with objective arguments only, and to treat the representatives of contrary persuasion with that kind of respect owed to ardent opponents, as well as to lay greater stress in my public activities on that which different trends have in common than on that which separates them . . . This is my ideal of a rabbi; to strive for it is my life's task."[39]

The paradox underlying his words, the notion of a rabbi's neutrality on the one hand and his identification as Orthodox on the basis of historically transmitted Judaism on the other, marks the two poles that would have a decisive effect on Nobel's activities as a rabbi. It is characteristic of Nobel to formulate his "confessed higher estimation of Orthodox Judaism" (bekenntnismäßige Höherbewertung des konservativen Judentums) in a highly discreet manner, so as to respect others and nevertheless maintain his own position.[40]

He consequently endorsed the existence of the community as *Einheitsgemeinde*, and believed this to be the only adequate form of organisation for the Jewish

---

[38]Nobel in a letter to Max Warburg, dated 10th April 1921, quoted in English from Mayer, 'Nobel', *loc. cit.*, p. 570.

[39]Nobel's application on 30th April 1897, to the Board of the *Synagogengemeinde Köln*; in his manuscripts.

[40]Nobel's application was published in the *Festschrift*, with which his friends and disciples honoured him on his 50th birthday, *Gabe Herrn Rabbiner Dr. Nobel zum 50. Geburtstag dargebracht von . . .* (the names of 13 contributors follow), Frankfurt a. Main 1921. When the contributors put their names below the application, Franz Rosenzweig had to alter the dedication after protests by Martin Buber. Originally Rosenzweig wanted them all to sign with the following dedication: "With these words, written 25 years ago, you have expressed the views of all of us on the essence and task of the rabbi's profession." After Buber's protest, Rosenzweig realised that "taken seriously, not only Buber, but three quarters of those, who signed, myself included, could not have endorsed this formulation, because Nobel's words expressed a confessed higher estimation of Orthodox Judaism, even if it was formulated very tolerantly, typically Nobel (*eben so Nobelsch*) . . ." Rosenzweig composed the following, impersonal dedication that was signed by all, including Buber: "This view of the honour and burden (*Würde und Bürde*) of the rabbinical profession you have written down 25 years ago." Franz Rosenzweig in a letter to Rudolf Hallo, December 1922, in Franz Rosenzweig, *Briefe*, unter Mitwirkung von Ernst Simon. Ausgew. und hrsg. von Edith Rosenzweig, Berlin 1935, p. 460.

entity, because he was convinced of the principle of unity of Judaism. "Listen my Israel, there is a unity of Judaism. That unity is guaranteed by the eternity of the Torah. It is guaranteed to us by the common history, which we have experienced."[41]

He rejected any kind of separatism on the basis of communal politics or religion and advocated co-operation with Reform. Nevertheless he always defended vigorously the interests of Orthodox Judaism. "Tolerance towards a view of Judaism that does not in our opinion correspond to historically transmitted Judaism would stop being a virtue if it turned into intolerance against ourselves."[42] He was not discouraged, although he knew that there were some, like the members of the *Israelitische Religionsgesellschaft* in Frankfurt, who interpreted this position as weakness. "Tolerance is a weakness, when it grows out of anxious wavering. Tolerance is a strength, when it is based in a firmly grounded and deeply rooted persuasion."[43]

Yet he felt obliged to oppose Reform when the controversy focused on objective matters. He advocated "recognising the biblical-talmudical religious law as binding for the life of the individual and the community".[44] The *Halakhah* played a central role in his creed as the virtual basis on which historical Judaism came into existence. Therefore, he advocated

> "the holy persuasion that beside belief there must stand the law, its accomplishment, its realisation, the knowledge of it, its deepening and its stimulation. Therefore, whoever attacks the existence of the law, attacks the existence of Judaism itself. And he walks, willingly or not, in the footsteps of Paul."[45]

Again and again in his sermons and publications he declared himself for the Jewish law. "Studying the law, studying the great art, to gain through this law a consistent approach to life . . ." this had been most important for him since the beginning of his work in Cologne.[46] Maintaining Orthodoxy in its strictest sense was the basis of his struggle against Reform, a fight he had started for the first time when he was still a young rabbi in Königsberg in order to pick it up later in Frankfurt a. Main with great determination.

He attacked the Reform Movement for the first time in his inaugural sermon to the *Adass Jisroel* in Königsberg, stating it as his aim to fight against the Reformers. Simultaneously he declared R. Meir Loeb ben Jechiel Michael, called Malbim, a talmudist, radical and uncompromising adversary of any Reform tendencies, to be his ideal. He denounced the *Me'asfim*, the representatives of the nascent Jewish Enlightenment, and accused them of "lack of religious depth and national seriousness (*Ernst*)". The changes of Reform seemed to him to be only an imitation of a non-Jewish or even un-Jewish cult which distorted

---

[41]N. A. Nobel, *Fünf Reden, gehalten am Versöhnungstage und am Schlußfeste des Jahres 5673 (1912)*, Frankfurt a. Main 1912, p. 28.
[42]*Jüdische Presse*, 33, No. 27 (1902), pp. 255–256.
[43]Nobel, *Fünf Reden, op. cit.*, p. 35.
[44]'Deutschtum und Judentum', in *Christliche Welt*, 30, No. 3 (1916), p. 53.
[45]Nobel, *Die Richtlinien, op. cit.*, p. 10.
[46]Nobel, *Fünf Reden, op. cit.*, p. 9.

Nehemiah Anton Nobel
(1871–1922)

Judaism and stripped it of all its precious possessions.[47] The harsh way in which his judgement was formulated may be rooted in the fact that Nobel was still a young rabbi speaking to a separatist community. However, his principal attitude towards Reform did not change in later years, as one sees in his sermon 'The Guidelines', delivered on 9th November 1912.

These 'Guidelines', which Nobel condemned in his sermon of the same name, had been unanimously approved by the liberal rabbinate and were presented as 'Guidelines towards a Programme for Liberal Judaism' to the members of the *Vereinigung der liberalen Rabbiner Deutschlands* at their convention in October 1912 in Poznań. Having been drafted mainly by the liberal rabbi Caesar Seligmann, Nobel's colleague in the community of Frankfurt, the 'Guidelines' were to demonstrate the dogmas of liberal Judaism and serve as a kind of "liberal Schulchan Aruch". Divided into 13 major paragraphs, this programme differentiated between the eternal truth and ethic values of Judaism on the one hand, and the ritual commandments as historical means on the other, by which Judaism has been transmitted throughout the centuries. The 'Guidelines' negated the obligatory character of the Jewish law as well as its divine origin.[48]

The harsh reaction of the Orthodox rabbis came immediately. Both unions of Orthodox rabbis – the *Vereinigung der traditionell-gesetzestreuen Rabbiner Deutschlands*, which had been established in 1897 by Esriel Hildesheimer, and the *Verband der orthodoxen Rabbiner Deutschlands*, which was formed on the basis of the issue of secession (*Austritt*) – published declarations which condemned the 'Guidelines', but differed in formulation. The Orthodox rabbis pointed to the gap that had been created ultimately between Orthodox and liberal Judaism by laying down the 'Guidelines' and announced that future measures would have to be taken towards liberal rabbinates. They threatened that *halakhic* decisions of rabbis, who declared themselves acting on the basis of the 'Guidelines' would lose their validity, and this would, as in the case of divorce, have grave effects on future community life.

The *Verband der orthodoxen Rabbiner Deutschlands* stressed that "the Guidelines reveal the essence of Reform (*Neologie*) to be a total break from the principles of Judaism, as the Orthodox camp had long ago realised" and repeated that there existed no "religious unity of Judaism".[49] The *Vereinigung der traditionell-gesetzes-treuen Rabbiner Deutschlands* laid emphasis on the problems that would occur in future in the joint work of the *Einheitsgemeinde*. Especially religious education given by the liberal rabbis and based on the 'Guidelines' would constitute "a danger for Jewish youth".[50]

Although he was a member of the *Vereinigung der traditionell-gesetzestreuen Rabbiner Deutschlands*, Nobel did not sign this statement, which was signed by

---

[47] *Ibid.*, pp. 21–22.
[48] *Liberales Judentum*, hrsg. von Caesar Seligmann, 4, No. 9 (1912), p. 210ff. See also Seligmann, *Erinnerungen, op. cit.*, p. 146ff. and especially the introduction by Michael A. Meyer, pp. 17ff. Also Meyer, *Response to Modernity, op. cit.*, pp. 210–212.
[49] *Jüdische Presse*, 43, No. 48 (1912), p. 454.
[50] *Ibid.*, No. 47, p. 455.

111 of his colleagues.[51] The undifferentiated and severe rejection may have prevented him from doing so. He was also not prepared to support the actions threatening the liberal rabbis and renouncing all future co-operation. But he fully approved the content of the 'Guidelines' rejection, as his own sermon on the 'Guidelines' shows. However, he had differentiated between the personal intentions of the rabbis who composed the 'Guidelines' and their meaning.

> "First of all let us appreciate in justice and honesty, that the motivations of the authors of the Guidelines have been pure and fine ones. These men are labouring under the mistaken notion that they can rally around the ruins of that proud and imposing edifice, which for thousands of years resisted storms, round that vast crowd, that much too vast crowd, of which they consisted, drifting apart. To present Judaism to them as something definitive, to prevent them and their children from taking the last fatal step, is the outspoken and unspoken intention of the Guidelines."[52]

"Thanking" the authors for their intentions, Nobel nevertheless condemned the content of the 'Guidelines' as being un-Jewish. To Nobel, the 'Guidelines' represented only an imitation of the Protestant faith. By denying Shabbat, the revelation and the law (*Gesetzlichkeit*), which were the pillars of Judaism, they undermined the foundation of Judaism. Keeping Jewish law was the precondition of Judaism. Any attack on its lawfulness endangered the vital nerve of Judaism and served to disparage it.

In his sermon Nobel accused the authors of the 'Guidelines' of trying to characterise historical Judaism as being solely a religion of laws. They had tried to draw a sharp line between *Halakhah* and the ethical values expressed by the prophets. Thereby they had misunderstood the ethical values, which were inherent in the laws. They degraded Judaism and negated its "dignity as a universal religion". They played right into the hands of those for whom the "suppression and degradation of the law was nothing else than the glorification of Paul and his teachings".[53] Thus the authors of the 'Guidelines' contributed involuntarily to the continuation of traditional Christian misinterpretation and disdain for the Jewish faith and even reinforced it.

Nobel, on the contrary, argued that the prophets had not raised their voice against the law, but rather against the "degeneration of and alienation from the law". He concluded, that the division between *Halakhah* and prophecy was drawn artificially. Basing himself upon the Sages, he protested against partitioning the Jewish faith into different sections that were then shown to be contrary to one another.[54]

> "For me, there is no division between 'rigid' *Halakhah* and 'flowing' prophetism, between the sobriety of the law and the intoxication of poesy. The law too proves its strength to us only

---

[51]*Ibid.*, No. 52, p. 495, specifies this number. Altmann in 'The German Rabbi', *loc. cit.*, p. 37, states 136 signatures of members of both Orthodox rabbinical unions.

[52]Nobel, *Richtlinien*, *op. cit.*, p. 3.

[53]*Ibid.*, p. 11.

[54]*Ibid.*, p. 11, quoted from the Sages the verse: "Malachi is no one else than Esra" and wrote: "As if they [the Sages] had anticipated, that science of our days would try to declare Esra, the representative of pure lawfulness (*Gesetzlichkeit*) to be the opponent of the prophets."

when it accompanies our lives with rhythmical harmony just as poetry can proceed proudly and safely only through the coherence of its inner laws."[55]

These words reflect his synthetic comprehension of Judaism underlying his conviction of the inner coherence of Judaism. Nobel was not at all "conservative more out of an enthusiastic love for his people and their tradition of a thousand years, than out of dogmatic conviction", as Caesar Seligmann has characterised him.[56] On the contrary, in his sermon against the 'Guidelines' Nobel expressed again his inner conviction of the sacrosanct primacy of Jewish law and the necessity for absolute conformity to it (*Gesetzestreue*).[57] Simultaneously he pointed out the dangers that the 'Guidelines' did pose to the unity of Judaism, especially by changing the marriage laws.

The religious controversy between Orthodoxy and Reform continued in the sphere of communal politics. After the sharp protests of both Orthodox unions against the 'Guidelines', the boards of the Jewish communities of Berlin and Frankfurt, the two greatest in Germany, expressed in public their position in this matter on 1st December 1912. They resolutely protested against the future sanctions that the Orthodox rabbis had threatened and declared them to be presumptuous as well as being an interference in community affairs. "We regard with disapproval and regret a certain group of rabbis claiming the right to declare invalid or dangerous the religious decisions taken, functions exercised or religious education offered by rabbis whom the Jewish communities have duly elected."[58]

Thus Orthodoxy and the community boards entered into a controversy concerned with rabbinical competence. Other Jewish communities, including Cologne, Munich, and later to some extent Königsberg, joined Berlin and Frankfurt, supporting their statement. Both Orthodox unions of rabbis countered with new protests, maintaining again that the duty of the rabbis is "to guard the unimpaired preservation of the Torah, to point to every announcement, that endangers its survival and to warn the public". The rabbis for their part now accused the boards of communities of having interfered with their statement of 1st December 1912 on the competence of rabbis and of having infringed their authority. Against this they entered a "protest with all decisiveness".[59]

The statement of the board of the *Israelitische Gemeinde* in Frankfurt continued to provoke vehement and long-lasting protests from Orthodox community members. At the beginning of 1914 the board had to revoke its earlier statement and to reaffirm the competence of the Orthodox community rabbi. After long

[55]Nobel, *Fünf Reden, op. cit.*, p. 12.

[56]Seligmann, *Erinnerungen, op. cit.*, p. 150.

[57]This conformity to law formed the basis of his friendship with the Orthodox rabbi of Marburg, Dr. Leo Munk. When Munk died, Nobel called him in his funeral oration "the closest ally of my religious persuasion". In *Dr. Leo Munk. Ein Gedenkbuch. Lebensgang, Trauerreden, Nekrologe*. In Druck geg. durch Jakob Rothschild, Marburg 1918, p. 15.

[58]*Jüdische Presse*, 43, No. 49 (1912), p. 465. It may be assumed that Nobel's sermon on 9th November 1912, and fear of his influence had urged the board of the Frankfurt community to protest in public.

[59]*Jüdische Presse*, 43, No. 50 (1912), p. 477.

deliberations, the representatives of the Frankfurt community determined that "with its statement of 1st December 1912 the board had had no intention of giving its opinion on the 'Guidelines' and according to its understanding has not done so. With its decision the board had intended to assure the peaceful development of the Frankfurt community (*Einheitsgemeinde*) and had not wanted to forbid the Orthodox rabbis the right to criticise the 'Guidelines'. On the contrary, the board recognises that from the point of view of Orthodox rabbis it is their duty to criticise this trend." However, the concessions the community board had to grant went even further. The board gave assurance that "liberal rabbis have not dealt any differently with matters concerning marriage law and religious education as a result of the 'Guidelines', nor will they change their handling of these matters in the future".[60]

Thus within the Frankfurt Jewish community the Orthodox under Rabbi Nobel were victorious. They had succeeded in preventing the Reform movement from carrying out substantial changes now and in the future. The religious *status quo* of the *Einheitsgemeinde* was preserved. It had been established after long and bitter fights in 1878 with the assumption of office of Marcus Horovitz in the *Börneplatzsynagoge*.[61] The community as a framework within which both religious trends could coexist, could continue to function only if none of the trends – neither Orthodox nor Reform – was allowed to enlarge its existing privileges. Otherwise the shaky balance between Orthodoxy and Reform – observed carefully from outside by the *Austrittsgemeinde* – would have been destroyed. Had the 'Guidelines' been realised in daily community life, not only would the *Austrittsgemeinde* feel confirmed in its allegations that Orthodoxy within the community supported transgressions of Judaism carried out by Reform, but the institutionalisation of changes advocated by Reform through the 'Guidelines' would also have created a deep rupture within the community in the long run. This had been prevented by the moderate, but firm, position of Nobel. Nobel's reputation rose, and his position was strengthened at the outcome of this conflict.

The controversy about implementing the 'Guidelines' was the last time Reform tried to undertake changes within existing community norms. New issues became important within the community, such as the phenomenon of Zionism and rising antisemitism.[62] The few years left to the community, until it was dissolved ultimately by the Nazis in April 1939, were years of fruitful co-operation between Orthodox and liberals in the community. They worked together on the community board and in other institutions, and brought about a rich and pluralistic community life.[63]

Nobel had had his part in strengthening the basis of the Frankfurt *Einheitsge-meinde*. It was the unity of the Jewish entity, *Klal Israel*, that he was concerned with in the first place. He possessed, as Leo Baeck stressed in his obituary, "the

---

[60]*Ibid.*, 45, No. 1 (1914), p. 5.
[61]Paul Arnsberg, *Die Geschichte der Frankfurter Juden seit der Französischen Revolution*, Darmstadt 1983, vol. I, pp. 844–859.
[62]Meyer, *Response to Modernity*, *op. cit.*, p. 212.
[63]Rachel Heuberger and Helga Krohn, *Hinaus aus dem Ghetto . . . Juden in Frankfurt am Main 1800–1950*, Frankfurt a. Main 1988, pp. 145–168.

strong and lively feeling for Jewish community wholeness (*Gesamtheit*)".[64] His belief, that there existed a Jewish entity and a Jewish solidarity resulting from it, was fundamental. The feeling of obligation to *Klal Israel* always made him tolerant towards representatives of the Reform movement and made him a strict adversary of separatist community politics. "Both trends have enough in common, so that the consciousness of belonging together and forming one entity can develop its social, political and religious creative strength. The majority of the German Jews take the Solomonic view that the maternal love of conviction proves itself in its love to the whole."[65]

Yet Nobel had already recognised the paralysis and degeneration that had started in Orthodox Judaism as a result of Orthodox Jewish integration into German bourgeois society. The reality of Orthodox Jews who adapted more and more to their non-Jewish surroundings stood in contradiction to an extremely idealised image of a lively Eastern European Jewry.[66] Nobel wanted to revive Orthodox Judaism and to start its process of restoration. Judaism should not only be a ritual, but become for all Jews, the Orthodox included, their aim in life (*Lebensinhalt*). Thus he became a critic of Orthodoxy from within, pursuing the same goal, the renaissance of Orthodox Judaism.

Historically transmitted Judaism that had created the Jewish entity, the *Klal Israel*, was founded on the *Halakhah*. Nobel was therefore convinced that Judaism could only be revived if the *Halakhah* would once again become the guideline for the individual's acting within his entity. The answers to present-day problems of the Jews could only come from the *Halakhah*. *Halakhah*, in turn, could only then keep its position as the sole, valid law if it stood the test in modern reality. Nobel did not doubt that *Halakhah* could do so, if only the rabbis would utilise it.

In his sermon 'The Sabbath' Nobel dealt at length with the role of *Halakhah*. "It is true that the rabbis have encircled and fenced in the law of the Sabbath. But are there only rigid trellis fences? There exist also living fences which play a part in the life of the noble flora entrusted to their protection . . ."[67] Jewish law was, in Nobel's view, not rigid and fixed. It meant for him a framework, in which the Jew could unfold himself freely. He saw his task and duty as continuing to carry out the Jewish religious law according to the traditional commentaries. He attached the greatest importance to showing the inner substance of the law and its creative power.*

[64]Leo Baeck, in *Nachrufe, op. cit.*, p. 31.
[65]*Christliche Welt*, 30, No. 3 (1916), p. 53. In these words Nobel characterised the controversies between Orthodoxy and Reform in his reply to the Protestant theologian Michael Rade.
[66]Eugen Mayer, 'Räumet, räumt, macht Bahn!' in *Gabe, op. cit.*, p. 85, has sarcastically described the changes for the worse of assimilated Orthodoxy. "How do the righteous of our time appear? In the morning they put their religion with their prayer-thongs in their tefillin cases and go about their daily work as if nothing has happened. *Minhag* supersedes the Law, ignorance becomes the norm, religion becomes a sport."
[67]'Der Sabbat', in *Soziale Ethik im Judentum*, hrsg. vom Verband der Deutschen Juden, Frankfurt a. Main 1913, pp. 111–119.
* The reader is also directed to Nobel's critique of Nietzsche, as described by Steven E. Aschheim in his essay, 'Nietzsche and the Nietzschean Moment in Jewish Life (1890–1939)', in the current volume of the Year Book, pp. 199–200 – (Ed.).

Keeping the *Halakhah* was, therefore, to Nobel a pre-condition absolutely necessary for the revival of Judaism. His uncompromising fight against Reform was based on this belief. At the same time this was the foundation of his Zionism. Only in *Eretz Israel* could the Jews create their own political and economic framework in which a Jewish community could be formed that lived according to *halakhic* laws. The Zionist ideology of the *Misrachi* was used by Nobel in order to bring the Jews back to the Torah. Only in *Eretz Israel* could the Torah develop without any restrictions. Only there could the Torah's claim to totality in all spheres of private as well as public life be fully realised.

Nobel, therefore, demanded the restitution of Jewish law within the Zionist programme and believed this to be an important contribution to Jewish cultural politics. He especially urged the use of Jewish labour legislation and property laws as the legal basis for Jewish colonisation in *Eretz Israel*, as was done by the *Misrachi* in the religious Kibbutz movement.

"Religious renaissance must be the ultimate aim of the new achievement. It is not through narrow-mindedness and intolerance that we shall instill the spirit into *Eretz Israel* . . . Genuine exponents of the religious ideal are not so fearful as to be intolerant. Religion only flourishes on fertile soil. Orthodoxy itself is in need of resurrection. The holy land will produce a noble maternal instinct and bring about a new rebirth . . ."[68] To Nobel Israel meant the centre of the Jewish religion that would revive Orthodox Judaism. His Zionism, as well as his fight against Reform, served to prevent Judaism from losing its national character in the religious sense and becoming just a religious denomination.

---

[68]Nobel in a letter to Max Warburg, dated 10th April 1921, in Mayer, *loc. cit.*, pp. 170–171.

Emancipation Re-assessed

The Process of Emancipation from the Congress of Vienna to the Revolution of 1848/1849

BY ARNO HERZIG

The period under investigation here, from 1815 to 1848,* is marked by serious contradictions. After the promising movement towards acculturation and emancipation in the Age of Enlightenment and the Napoleonic era, came 1815 followed by years of disruption, which seemed to make further advance in this direction virtually impossible during the subsequent decades. Attempts to prevent any further integration were not the sole prerogative of the state and most of its officials; within society itself, overt resistance to emancipation was articulated in pamphlets, plays and newspaper articles as well as being manifested in numerous acts of protest during this apparent *Biedermeier* epoch. Nevertheless, the decisive step towards legally regulated emancipation was taken in the short revolutionary period from 1848–1850. How were these contradictions resolved, or did they actually remain despite the legal settlement?

At the end of the Napoleonic era, German Jewry faced one of its gravest crises. At least in part, this crisis was the result of economic factors. Developments during the eighteenth century had led to the growth of important social distinctions within the Jewish communities. Alongside the tiny group of court factors, agents and moneylenders (who remained vital for the development of banking in Germany in the first half of the nineteenth century), the majority of German Jews – apart from a small well-to-do middle class – remained on the edge of poverty. Constantly threatened with the loss of safe-conduct, they always faced the prospect of falling through the social safety-net. Even when the Jewish communities took some form of responsibility for the wandering Jewish beggars, their mode of existence was very far from desirable. Interestingly, however, even the criminal members of this group – the Jewish robber gangs – remained loyal to Jewry.

It is not possible to provide exact figures for the relative size of the individual social groups during the eighteenth century and the Napoleonic period. Nevertheless, it can be assumed that more than half of German Jews lived in constant danger of falling to the level of beggars, even though the poor were at first largely maintained by the communities and were not driven from community to community. Trade and moneylending, the most important and basic livelihoods, were constantly threatened by the crises of the *ancien régime* and

---

*Although the following essay by Michael Graetz begins with the eighteenth century, we print the papers here in the sequence they were given at the panel of the September 1990 Bochum meeting of German historians. See pp. IX and 103 – (Ed.).

particularly by war. The modest prosperity of a Jewish trader or moneylender could be transformed into extreme poverty almost overnight, if their customers suddenly became unable to pay. In addition, and particularly in Prussia, taxes had been increasing inexorably since the Seven Years' War.[1]

However, in the nineteenth century the new capitalist economic system also provided opportunities for Jews to make use of their accumulated experience as businessmen and moneylenders. Knowledge acquired over the centuries, frequently in the most difficult circumstances, could now be put to good use. Moreover, it proved possible to ignore all the advice about re-education which had been recommended to the Jews from Dohm on by officials and the proponents of the Enlightenment. Such thinkers, who included the Jewish rationalists with the exception of Mendelssohn, had argued that Jews should become farmers and artisans. Yet it was now apparent that these professions had themselves been thrown into crisis by the new economic order. On the other hand, these developments gave sustenance to the specious argument that the Jews preferred to live at the expense of others rather than work themselves. Even the intellectual representatives of Jewry had so internalised this falsehood that they actively advocated re-training through the *Vereine* and other institutions, and made enormous efforts to explain away every failure.[2] Most Jews stubbornly refused to change their profession and insisted on making use of the new opportunities in their traditional spheres. Many of them had some success. In the nineteenth century, many formerly impoverished Jewish dealers managed to achieve the respected position of businessman.[3] However, this was a process which was completed over several generations, Jacob Toury has convincingly calculated that even at the end of this period, in 1848, up to 50% of the Jews in Germany were still living a marginal – not bourgeoisified – social existence. This was particularly true of those Jews who lived in the countryside. Nevertheless, he also argues that between 15% and 30% of the Jewish minority in Prussia and Bavaria can be reckoned to belong to the upper and middle bourgeoisie and, correspondingly, between 25% and 40% to the petty bourgeoisie.[4]

Apart from the economic crisis, which showed some signs of moderating, German Jewry was also burdened by an identity crisis during this period. Admittedly, most Jews had probably not been affected by criticism of the beliefs of traditional German Jewry; in general this had been confined to the intellectual sphere and the thinking of the Jewish rationalists. However, a new situation had

[1]Joseph Isaak, *Unmaßgebliche Gedanken über Betteljuden und ihre bessere und zweckmäßigere Versorgung*, Nürnberg 1791; Hermann Arnold, 'Bemerkungen über die soziale Grundschicht des deutschen Judentums im 18. und frühen 19. Jahrhundert', in *Wort und Wirklichkeit. Festschrift E.L. Rapp zum 70. Geburtstag*, Meisenheim 1976, pp. 132–152.

[2]Arno Herzig, 'Das Assimilationsproblem aus jüdischer Sicht (1780–1880)', in Hans Otto Horch and Horst Denkler (eds.), *Conditio Judaica. Judentum, Antisemitismus und deutschsprachige Literatur vom 18. Jahrhundert bis zum Ersten Weltkrieg*, Pt. 1, Tübingen 1988, pp. 10–28.

[3]*Jüdische Minderheit und Industrialisierung. Demographie, Berufe und Einkommen der Juden in Westdeutschland 1850–1914*, Avraham Barkai unter Mitarbeit von Schoschanna Barkai-Lasker, Tübingen 1988 (Schriftenreihe wissenschaftlicher Abhandlungen des Leo Baeck Instituts 46), pp. 32ff.

[4]Jacob Toury, *Soziale und politische Geschichte der Juden in Deutschland 1847–1871*, Düsseldorf 1977, pp. 100ff.; Friedrich Battenberg, *Das europäische Zeitalter der Juden*, vol. II, Darmstadt 1990, pp. 110ff.

undoubtedly been created by the disappearance of the old *Landjudenschaften* and their institutions. A first wave of urbanisation, which began in the Napoleonic era and could not be checked even after 1815 despite the measures of the state authorities, made traditional Jewish life impossible. The outlines of a new Jewish consciousness, as proposed by the representatives of Reform Jewry, were not taken up by most communities, particularly in the countryside; the conception of a "New Orthodoxy" did not occur until the 1870s. Instances of serious conflict between Reformers and traditionalists in the communities remained rare. Yet even those Jews who were committed to traditional and Orthodox Jewry saw their entire way of life unsettled.[5] In the public emancipation debate of the *Vormärz*, traditional Orthodoxy – and thus the majority of German Jews – played little part. Not until 1848 was this group too affected by the "inner Jewish turning point" (Toury). Despite their traditional ties they were no longer committed to a closed cultural system, but instead took an increasing part in the general cultural life of the towns and even the countryside. The Jewish spokesmen in the emancipation debate, men such as Philippson and Riesser, were close to Reform Jewry and numbered the liberal communities among their supporters. Despite the setbacks after 1815, they had not abandoned the hope that the process of emancipation would be sustained. In the tradition of the Berlin *Verein für Cultur und Wissenschaft der Juden (Culturverein)* they attempted to bring the traditional heritage of Jewry into European culture. The purported backwardness of Jewish culture led them to a degree of over-compensation in the process of acculturation. Success in their eyes was measured by the acceptance of Jewish citizens by society in general: it was documented in the acceptance of Jewish members by *Vereine*, other associations and municipal governments. (The *Allgemeine Zeitung des Judenthums* is full of such reports.) Despite many setbacks and apparently against all the odds, this persistence would finally lead to the Jews regaining the equality they had obtained in the Napoleonic era.

At the Congress of Vienna, the Hanseatic cities had forced through an amendment to Article 16 of the Confederation constitution to the effect that the Jews should continue to hold the civil rights granted *by* rather than *in* the various states. This change, for example, allowed the city-state of Lübeck to expel the Jews who had settled there during the Napoleonic era, as in the Middle Ages.[6] Meanwhile, Prussia neglected to extend the 1812 Edict of Emancipation, introduced as part of the process of "defensive modernisation", uniformly through all parts of the monarchy. The government restored over twenty old *Judenordnungen*, some of which dated from the Middle Ages but which had been in force in the various parts of the kingdom before and even during the Napoleonic period. As far as the treatment of the Jews was concerned, Prussia was prepared

[5]Heinz Moshe Graupe, *Die Entstehung des modernen Judentums. Geistesgeschichte der deutschen Juden 1650–1942*, 2nd rev. edn., Hamburg 1977, pp. 128ff.; Mordechai Breuer, *Jüdische Orthodoxie im Deutschen Reich 1871–1918. Sozialgeschichte einer religiösen Minderheit*, Frankfurt a. Main 1986, Veröffentlichung des Leo Baeck Instituts, pp. 15ff; Michael A. Meyer, *Response to Modernity. A History of the Reform Movement in Judaism*, New York–Oxford 1988, pp. 100f.
[6]Rainer Erb and Werner Bergmann, *Die Nachtseite der Judenemanzipation. Der Widerstand gegen die Integration der Juden in Deutschland 1780–1860*, Berlin 1989, pp. 97ff.

to depart from all the rules of *raison d'état* aiming at the creation of a unified Prussian state.[7] Where Napoleonic laws remained in force, as in the Rhineland and to an extent in Westphalia, recourse was had until 1847 to the exceptional regulations of the "*Schändliches Dekret*" (infamous decree) or special laws were created, as in the four Westphalian *Kreise* of Warburg, Höxter, Büren and Paderborn.[8] In 1815 Hardenberg had still been attempting to win the support of the Hanseatic cities for the Prussian solution in the form of the Edict of 1812. However, his first abandonment of efforts at reform came in the sphere of Jewish emancipation. The policy of reform was advocated by a small elite only. Particularly as regards the emancipation of the Jews, this elite was opposed by a broad phalanx of different social groups, ranging from the nobility through the craftsman-based petty bourgeoisie to the peasantry. Ultimately the reformers did not dare continue the policy of emancipation against this broad coalition. Ideologically the opposition was held together by the "Germanomania" which had emerged in the struggle against Napoleon and wanted to eliminate the Jews from the "German national body".

Apart from Prussia, the other states did not feel compelled to retract their efforts to emancipate the Jews, since no great progress had been made even during the Napoleonic era. Best situated were the Jews in Baden (1.7% of the population), where the Constitutional Edicts of 1808 and 1809 had declared them to be *erbfrei* state citizens but without automatically granting them the right of local citizenship (*Ortsbürgerrecht*). Even the reforming *Landtage* of the 1830s had failed to bring about any improvement here. In fact, they had tended to worsen the situation since now the status of *Schutzbürger* was held only by Jews in the municipalities. In Bavaria (roughly 1.4% of the population) the Registration Law of 1813 had virtually re-introduced the status of the old *Judengeleit*. In other states, such as Hesse, the principle of linking emancipation and education was followed and the right of state citizenship and in many cases also of local citizenship was granted only to "well-to-do and productive Jews".[9]

It is not immediately apparent why, in their development towards becoming modern economic states, most German states chose to place restrictions on their economically active Jewish minorities and thereby, as in Prussia, incurred significant administrative expense. The reason for it lay partly, perhaps, in the role which the Jews played as an anti-symbol for broad sectors of the population during this turbulent period of economic and social upheaval. For most social groups, the Jewish minority was perceived as symbolically embodying the dark

[7]Ludwig von Rönne and Heinrich Simon, *Die früheren und gegenwärtigen Verhältnisse der Juden in den sämmtlichen Landestheilen des Preußischen Staates*, Breslau 1843, p. XI.

[8]Arno Herzig, *Judentum und Emanzipation in Westfalen*, Münster/W. 1973, pp. 37ff.; Rainer Erb, '"Jüdische Güterschlächterei" im Vormärz. Vom Nutzen des Stereotyps für wirtschaftliche Machtstrukturen dargestellt an einem westfälischen Gesetz von 1836', in *International Review of Social History*, 30 (1985), pp. 312–341.

[9]Toury, *op. cit.*, pp. 277ff.; Reinhard Rürup, 'Die Emanzipation der Juden in Baden', in *idem*, *Emanzipation und Antisemitismus. Studien zur "Judenfrage" der bürgerlichen Gesellschaft*, Göttingen 1975, pp. 37ff.; Manfred Treml, 'Von der "Judenmission" zur "Bürgerlichen Verbesserung". Zur Vorgeschichte und Frühphase der Judenemanzipation in Bayern', in *idem et al.* (eds.), *Geschichte und Kultur der Juden in Bayern. Aufsätze*, München 1988, pp. 247ff.

side of the new system and its apparently insuperable difficulties. Most governments were careful to take account of these simplistic attempts at explanation. They did not dare to continue promoting equal rights and integration, particularly since the majority of parliamentary committees – where these existed – opposed it. As the example of the cabinet order of 1836 for the East Westphalian *Kreise* reveals, Prussia was even prepared to take the tactical step of rescinding the status the Jews had already achieved. A contributory factor was that reformist concepts were seen to have failed and it was hoped to eliminate unrest in the population by introducing anti-Jewish measures. In this particular case – the *Ausnahmegesetz* for East Westphalia – it was also significant that it was the nobility who gained from this special law; they were being thwarted by competition from Jewish buyers at the public auctions of bankrupt farms. This was the weakest point of "defensive modernisation". Nor was there any "offensive modernisation" as at the time of the French Revolution, to grant the Jews immediate rights of state citizenship. In *Vormärz* Germany, using the ideology of the "Christian state", an attempt was made to evade the demand for the integration of the Jewish minority. According to this ideology, all European states were based on the principle of Christianity and no non-Christian should or could hold any vital position in them. The Prussian King Friedrich Wilhelm IV even wanted to deprive the Jews of the rights as state citizens that they had thus far been granted and to remove them from the *Staatsverband* as an independent corporation. In this attempt he failed in the general Prussian *Landtag* of 1847; this, despite its reservations about the Jews, regarded a segmented society within the state as inconsistent with modern development.[10] Numerous Prussian politicians, even Wilhelm von Humboldt, regarded baptism as a suitable means to a desired end. This would have eliminated any Jewish identity, though it was calculated that it would still take generations until "typically Jewish" characteristics were finally overcome. In fact it was an illusion to believe that baptism and special laws could provide a solution.

Governments did not bear the prime responsibility for putting the brakes on development towards a bourgeois society in which the Jews would have an equal place. The chief role was taken by those groups which had been privileged by the old economic system, were opposed to any reorganisation, and were, therefore, happy to portray the Jews as the beneficiaries or initiators of the new system.[11] Inaccurate images of the Jews as the enemy were offered as superficial explanations for modern developments, thereby rendering unnecessary any rational justification for preventive strategies. In this process, religious motives were frequently advanced in order to cover economic ones. The aggression of craftsmen's and merchants' guilds against Jewish pursuit of "free trade", which had its roots in the Middle Ages, largely determined the protests of the Restoration period and the *Vormärz*. These have been further clarified for us by

---

[10]Annegret H. Brammer, *Judenpolitik und Judengesetzgebung in Preußen 1812 bis 1847. Mit einem Ausblick auf das Gleichberechtigungsgesetz des Norddeutschen Bundes von 1869*, Berlin 1987, pp. 251ff.

[11]Barbara Vogel, *Allgemeine Gewerbefreiheit. Die Reformpolitik des preußischen Staatskanzlers Hardenberg (1810–1820)*, Göttingen 1983, pp. 227ff.

the results of intensive regional research.[12] A pamphlet of the "Good and Righteous" makes it clear that the riots of 1819, which began in Würzburg and lasted there until well into the 1820s, were directed against the Jews for rejecting the "time- and tradition-honoured Franconian laws" by setting up "public shops". The groups responsible, consisting of shopkeepers and probably craftsmen, were fully prepared to act in the most brutal manner. They made themselves spokesmen for all the "Good and Righteous" and felt "strong enough to resist anyone" and "to cleanse ourselves of the Jewish vermin . . . with fire, dagger and sword". The pamphlet ended with an appeal to the "protector and maker of justice" and for his "blessing over us and over our dear Frankish land".[13] Pamphlets of this kind were greeted with the "greatest acclaim" in the coffee houses; these, like the *Alsterpavillon* in Hamburg, were the starting-points for pogroms in both 1819 and 1830. However, small business- and craftsmen, who with the peasants were the main perpetrators of almost every anti-Jewish measure between 1815 and 1848, were a relatively small group. It was therefore important for them to involve the "mob" in the protest actions, a process which had the additional benefit of allowing the blame to be shifted in the aftermath. Where the lower orders did become involved, as in Hamburg, they tended to pursue their own objectives which were not related to the aims of the shopkeepers and craftsmen.[14]

Anti-Jewish motives can be detected only rarely in the protests of the lower strata between 1815 and 1848. As far as we know, they emerge only in the Luddite-style attacks in Prague in 1844 and during the start of the March 1848 revolution in the Vienna suburbs. In these cases, the trouble was caused mainly by down-graded craftsmen who were trying to arrest their own social decline by fomenting machine-wrecking in Jewish factories.[15] For their part, the shopkeepers and craftsmen who became involved in anti-Jewish actions were aiming to weld together a broader front. If their efforts to draw together apparently large crowds to support the protests did not produce success, the attempt was made to push religious motives to the fore in order to disguise economic ones. When the Minden shopkeepers called for pogroms against the Jews in 1844, they argued that the "ruin of the Jews" was justified because they were "betrayers of our Saviour" as well as "bloodsuckers of Christians".[16]

For small shopkeepers' guilds and the craftsman class, the aim was to defend their privileges according to the old concepts of a "fair livelihood". On the other

---

[12]Rainer Wirtz, *"Widersetzlichkeiten, Excesse, Crawalle, Tumulte und Skandale"*. *Soziale Bewegung und gewalthafter sozialer Protest in Baden 1815–1848*, Frankfurt a. Main 1981, pp. 60ff.; Moshe Zimmermann, 'Antijüdischer Sozialprotest? Proteste von Unter- und Mittelschichten 1819–1835', in Arno Herzig, Dieter Langewiesche and Arnold Sywottek (eds.), *Arbeiter in Hamburg. Unterschichten, Arbeiter und Arbeiterbewegung seit dem ausgehenden 18. Jahrhundert*, Hamburg 1983, pp. 89ff.

[13]Erb and Bergmann, *op. cit.*, pp. 225ff. Quotations also taken from here.

[14]*Ibid.*, p. 226; Zimmermann, *loc. cit.*, p. 91; Helmut Berding, *Moderner Antisemitismus in Deutschland*, Frankfurt a. Main 1988, pp. 66f.

[15]Arno Herzig, 'Die Reaktion der Unterschichten auf den technologischen Wandel der Proto- und Frühindustrialisierungsphase in Deutschland', in *Archiv für Sozialgeschichte*, 28 (1988), pp. 1–26, esp. pp. 12f.

[16]Herzig, *Judentum und Emanzipation in Westfalen*, *op. cit.*, p. 86.

hand, a fear for their bare existence often seems to have been the decisive factor behind the anti-Jewish actions of agricultural workers, particularly the lower levels. Anti-Jewish protests by the latter first began during the agrarian reform, when none but Jewish moneylenders, in many cases, were available to meet the high payments required. At this time the protagonists resorted to the punitive actions of social protest, stealing promissory notes and destroying furniture and feather beds in Jewish homes on the grounds that these were the fruits of unjustly acquired wealth. In Catholic areas these actions tended to be legitimised by reference to the blood libel and ritual murder accusations of the Middle Ages. From many personal accounts, it is clear that this argument also had an influence in Protestant regions.[17] Thus petty bourgeois and agricultural labourers resorted to public protest actions in an attempt to save their existence or their livelihood and to punish those who were held to blame: the Jews. On the other hand, during the same period the nobility, the upper-middle class and the intellectuals employed more skilful tactics to prevent the integration of the Jews into society. The Jewish salons of the later Age of Enlightenment, in which barriers of rank, sex and religion appeared to have been removed, were opposed by the Christian-German *Tisch-Gesellschaft*; this re-established sex and religion as criteria for acceptance or rejection "according to the *reformständische* concept of the state" (Frühwald). The Jews were to be excluded culturally. Many an aristocratic romantic writer, such as Arnim and Eichendorff, created negative Jewish figures in their work, thereby avenging themselves for their own or their fathers' inability to maintain themselves economically after speculating with their lands and property. As well as the "Jewish tea-tables with their playbills and aesthetic drivel", Brentano derided "humanity and enlightenment" in general.[18] In a play by Voss (1804), the figure of *Nathan der Weise* was "downgraded to the level of an old, grimy and piffling little (*kleinkariert*) shopkeeper" (Bayerdörfer); linguistically Nathan was made to speak a *Juden-deutsch* pedantically enriched with Hebraisms, for which Voss also provided the glossary. A well-chosen contrast to the conduct of the father is provided by the studious standard German of Recha, which is also made the subject of caricature only partly because of the contrast with the father's *Judendeutsch*.[19] Here, as in Sessa's play *Unser Verkehr*, which was banned by Hardenberg, all Jewish efforts at acculturation were cynically dismissed as farcical. In the view of these authors and the public which applauded them, such efforts were intended only to disguise Jewish avarice, lust for power and acquisitiveness.[20]

---

[17]Arno Herzig, *Unterschichtenprotest in Deutschland 1790–1870*, Göttingen 1988, pp. 58ff.; Stefan Rohrbacher, 'Die "Hep-Hep-Krawalle" und der "Ritualmord" des Jahres 1819 zu Dormagen', in Rainer Erb and Michael Schmidt (eds.), *Antisemitismus und jüdische Geschichte. Studien zu Ehren von Herbert A. Strauss*, Berlin 1987, pp. 135–148; Max Lazarus, *Erinnerungen*, Dortmund 1967, pp. 31f.

[18]Wolfgang Frühwald, 'Antijudaismus in der Zeit der deutschen Romantik', in Horch and Denkler (eds.), *Conditio Judaica, op. cit.*, Pt. 2, 1989, pp. 72–91, esp. p. 87.

[19]Hans-Peter Bayerdörfer, ' "Harlekinade in jüdischen Kleidern"? – Der szenische Status der Judenrollen zu Beginn des 19. Jahrhunderts', *ibid.*, pp. 92–117, esp. p. 104.

[20]Horst Denkler, ' "Lauter Juden". Zum Rollenspektrum der Juden-Figuren im populären Bühnen-drama der Metternichschen Restaurationsperiode (1815–1848)', in Horch and *idem* (eds.), *op. cit.*, Pt. 1, pp. 149–163.

In the famous letter to her brother Ludwig Robert (24th August 1819), Rahel Varnhagen blamed the cultural exclusion of Arnim, Brentano and the play *Unser Verkehr* for the antisemitic outburst of that year. However, she also related it to the "Germanomania" of Professors Rühs and Fries and the new piety of Romanticism.[21] It must remain an open question how far there were direct links between them. Nevertheless, intellectuals and poets contributed significantly to a hostility towards Jews and helped to increase the obstacles facing them.

What moved the intellectual pamphleteers to their orgies of hostility? Why did the turn to "Germanomania" and the "Christian state" occur, putting an end to all the positive approaches of the Enlightenment? As we have seen, the economic and mental difficulties brought by the new order of society and the economy were projected onto the Jews as an anti-symbol. Paradoxically, however, Jewry was also regarded as a "state within the state" which endangered the emerging bourgeois state. Even in 1793, in his defence of the French Revolution, Fichte had linked the threatened bourgeois state with the idea of the powerful and hostile Jewish state, which was constantly at war with every other and pressed "dreadfully hard on the citizens".[22] The idea was connected with the myth of the "typical Jewish nature", acquisitive and avaricious; even bourgeois democrats such as Marx saw these characteristics as the embodiment of Jewry. Strategies of physical destruction, though only as metaphor, had already been demanded by Fichte. Beyond the Age of Emancipation, many Germans felt that the most convincing embodiments of Jewishness were provided by figures such as Veitel Itzig or Schmulchen Schievelbeiner.

Despite these prejudices, during the 1840s the belief was gaining ground that in a bourgeois society there should be no second-class citizens, particularly when the citizens concerned were active and economically innovative. The conviction first took root at local level, where Jewish citizens took an active part in economic, social and parliamentary life. Petitions and applications to parliamentary bodies and the votes within them are witness to the trend. The breakthrough occurred in the Rhenish *Landtag* of 1843, when 58 delegates supported the emancipation of the Jews (with 5 votes against). Thereafter, town councillors, magistrates and citizens of various towns such as Königsberg, Bielefeld, Paderborn and Hamm/Westphalia also voted in favour of equal rights for the Jews. Everywhere the petitioners pointed to the principle of equality which – according to the argument in the Düsseldorf *Landtag* – had been in force in the Rhineland for 40 years, since the promulgation of the *Code Napoléon*. To counter supporters of the theory of the Christian state, supporters of emancipation argued that the theory was an idea of "modern philosophy" which contradicted the Christian principle of the equality of all men. Against the Germanomanes, reference was made to the sacrifices made for Germany by Jews during the Napoleonic Wars. And when antisemites talked of the profits made by Jewish speculators in the new economic system, the supporters of emancipation pointed

---

[21]Rahel Varnhagen, *Briefwechsel*, vol. IV, München 1979, p. 504.
[22]Erb and Bergmann, *op. cit.*, pp. 174ff.

to the large number of poor Jews and, especially, those who had lost their possessions through lending money.[23]

Despite a flood of anti-Jewish pamphlets after the resolution of the Rhenish *Landtag*, increasing numbers of citizens came to accept the principle that equal rights must also apply to Jews. When their enemies repeatedly pointed to the "national unreliability" of the Jews, their supporters countered by indicating the achievements of Jewish politicians in Holland, France and England and of Jewish representatives in many Prussian municipal parliaments. In the last analysis, behind the demand for equality and justice for the Jews in Germany, which led after 1848 to (admittedly not full) equal rights for the Jews in most German states, was the view that the modern bourgeois state required the equality of all its citizens.[24]

Notwithstanding with the victory of the liberal approach, the old reservations and prejudices remained even in 1848/1849. In fact they were actually on the increase during this period, giving rise to numerous pogroms in both town and countryside. Jewish citizens tended to play down the significance of these incidents and to dismiss them as "sacrifices" which had to be made in return for freedoms newly obtained.[25] But after 1848/1849 still it was the attitudes revealed by the pogroms which remained the determining factor of subsequent history, rather than the liberal position which ultimately led to the elimination of all legal restraints in the German states in 1870/1871. The liberal position was always under threat in Germany. Anti-Jewish resentments could always be revived. The element of danger which had been revealed so clearly in the years from 1815 to 1848 remained only just below the surface even in liberal phases of German history.

[23]Herzig, *Judentum und Emanzipation in Westfalen*, *op. cit.*, pp. 101ff.; Frühwald, *loc. cit.*, p. 7.

[24]Reinhard Rürup, 'European Revolutions and Emancipation', in *Revolution and Evolution. 1848 in German-Jewish History*, edited by Werner E. Mosse, Arnold Paucker and Reinhard Rürup, Tübingen 1981 (Schriftenreihe wissenschaftlicher Abhandlungen des Leo Baeck Instituts 39), pp. 1–53, esp. pp. 45ff.

[25]Erb and Bergmann, *op. cit.*, pp. 251ff.; Toury, *op. cit.*, pp. 288ff.

From Corporate Community to Ethnic-Religious Minority, 1750–1830

BY MICHAEL GRAETZ

I. THE DECLINE OF THE CORPORATE COMMUNITY

In 1812 King Friedrich Wilhelm III of Prussia granted an Edict of Emancipation[1] to the Jews. Under Paragraph 30 it laid down that: "In no case may rabbis and Jewish Elders arrogate to themselves either a jurisdiction or a tutelary institution and direction." The clause meant the abolition of a central agency of Jewish autonomy. It was thus a heavy, though not a fatal, blow to the community.

The emancipation of the Jews in the German states was not a single event, but a struggle which involved setbacks as well as advances. Government policy in most parts of Germany was marked by contradictions, with the result that civil emancipation was achieved over decades. Only a year before the outbreak of the 1848 Revolution, Friedrich Wilhelm IV submitted to the Prussian *Landtag* a draft law which was intended to reinforce the corporate character of the Jewish community and its patronage by the State.

The Bavarian Edict of 1813, designed to improve the civil status of the Jews in the course of an overall policy of reform, was accompanied by the *Matrikelgesetz* (registration law). This restricted freedom of movement and obliged the Jewish *Vorsteher* to enforce strict supervision of their co-religionists. In particular, itinerant Jewish traders without a registration number were to be prevented from gaining a foothold in the community. It was the duty of the *Vorsteher* to inform against these Jews and ensure their removal. Such regulations make it clear that the opening of the ghetto gates did not mean that the State was abandoning the concept of "collective liability" of the Jews.

Just as civil equality did not become a reality overnight, so the corporate character of the Jewish community did not disappear immediately. Instead, the decline of the old community order should be seen as a lengthy process which began in the first half of the eighteenth century and accelerated after 1750. Only then does it become possible to speak of a destruction of Jewish autonomy.

What were the reasons for this development? Absolutism, whether enlightened or not,[2] was certainly one of them. Though with varying degrees of determination, absolutist rulers sought to extend the central power of the State

---

[1] Ismar Freund, *Die Emanzipation der Juden in Preußen*, Berlin 1912, I, pp. 208–226, II, pp. 455–459.
[2] Rudolf Vierhaus, *Deutschland im Zeitalter des Absolutismus*, Göttingen 1978, pp. 116–150.

and to restructure the German territorial states by suppressing the estates and all particularist forces. This powerful centralising drive on the part of absolutist rulers also led to an increasing interference in the internal affairs of the Jewish community.[3] Ever stricter control was exerted over its members, the selection of *Vorsteher* and rabbis was closely supervised and there was particularly tight control over revenues from taxation and expenditure for education and poor relief. The bookkeeping of the community administration had to be done in German to make it easier for the officials of the absolutist state to keep control.

When the Great Elector, Friedrich Wilhelm, enabled the renewal of Jewish settlement in Brandenburg-Prussia in 1671, he ordered no restrictions on community autonomy. His successors, by contrast, pursued a systematic policy of tutelage and the restriction of self-administration. To that end they appointed agencies within the central machinery of state. Thus Friedrich Wilhelm I created the *Judenkommissariat*, and under Friedrich II the *Generaldirektorium der Kriegs- und Domänenkammer* was entrusted with the task of supervision.[4] The *Judenreglement* (Jewish regulations) of 1750 laid down that the *Vorsteher* of the community had to deliver an exact monthly statement of accounts to the *Generaldirektorium*, covering every change of *Zivilstand* among the members of the community.

These regulations provide clear evidence of the policies of the absolutist rulers, which accelerated the decline of the Jewish corporate body. Paragraph 31 restricted rabbinical jurisdiction to the specifically religious sphere, to disputes affecting Jewish ceremonies, marriages, wills etc. Civil and economic actions, on the other hand, could not be judged by the rabbi and his assessors.[5] The curtailment of the rights of the autonomous Jewish court, which had been demanded repeatedly before 1750, was thus enforced by the State. One of the main elements of Jewish autonomy, the Jewish court was the symbol of a long-lost political sovereignty and had remained inviolate over centuries during the Middle Ages. It was gravely weakened by the *Judenreglement* and was to disappear in a matter of decades.

In the same Paragraph 31, Friedrich II stipulated: "We further desire that all the *Schutzjuden* living in Berlin and our other cities should join with the whole Jewish community in religious matters, by subjecting themselves to the Elders and the rabbi in religious and church matters." At first sight this wording appears to offer respectful support for self-administration and its will to survive. But let there be no mistake; the absolutist rulers – and not only in Prussia – chose to retain the corporative structure for the time being simply because it seemed the instrument best suited to helping them collect the many taxes which were imposed on the Jews. At the same time, however, the noose was being tightened over the leadership of the community so that it eventually lost almost all its freedom of choice.

---

[3]Jacob Katz, *Out of the Ghetto. The Social Background of Jewish Emancipation, 1770–1870*, New York 1978, pp. 31–33.
[4]Selma Stern, *Der preußische Staat und die Juden*, 8 vols., Tübingen 1962–1975 (Schriftenreihe wissenschaftlicher Abhandlungen des Leo Baeck Instituts 7, 8, 24 and 32), I/1, pp. 21–30, III/1, pp. 255–269.
[5]Freund, *op. cit.*, II, pp. 52–54.

It would be a mistake to attribute sole blame for the destruction of the time-honoured autonomy of the Jewish community to the policies of the absolutist governments and their officials, many of whom were committed to the principles of the Enlightenment and to concepts of the State based on natural law. The forces of destruction also grew from within, from Jewish society itself. The relatively rapid changes in community life caused by absolutism would have been inconceivable without the active participation of a comparatively narrow element in Jewish life – a new and rising elite. Nor was its willingness to participate solely the result of external pressure.

Businessmen, bankers, court agents – in short, the first representatives of a Jewish property-owning middle class – took a leading role here. These men had integrated successfully into the state-directed mercantilist proto-industrial system: their successors, provided they had retained their wealth into the nineteenth century, then joined forces with the new industrial entrepreneurs. Alongside them there appeared the first representatives of an educated Jewish bourgeoisie which, with the exception of men such as Mendelssohn and Friedländer, was not part of the economic elite in terms of its occupation and income. These were mostly self-educated men since, except for the study of medicine, the universities were still closed to them. Some worked as private tutors; others were employed in the growing network of Jewish schools which were dedicated to the ideas of the Enlightenment; still others were active, after the beginning of the nineteenth century, in Reform synagogues and communities.[6]

In the period of interest here, the rising Jewish educated middle class (*Bildungsbürgertum*) – in contrast to its Christian counterpart – had no civil servants in the state administration and no lecturers at the universities. These careers were still closed to them. There were also very few Jews in the liberal professions. In 1798 there was not a single Jewish lawyer in Berlin. (Only in the 1820s did this profession, now regarded as thoroughly middle-class, begin to open itself to Jews: in 1824 in Frankfurt a. Main, in 1834 in Bavaria.[7]) By contrast, there were then eleven Jewish doctors in Berlin, as Jews had been able to study medicine at German universities since the first half of the eighteenth century (59 Jews had qualified as doctors in Halle in the years between 1724 and 1800!).

Doctors, whose numbers increased steadily, comprised an influential element in the educated Jewish middle class. They took a leading part in ensuring the penetration of the Enlightenment and its change in values and norms into the community. Doctors were among the first in the process of acculturation: they wrote and spoke the German language and even adapted their appearance by shaving and wearing swords and wigs.

One such doctor was Marcus Herz, an adherent of Mendelssohn and an

---

[6]Monika Richarz, *Der Eintritt der Juden in die akademischen Berufe. Jüdische Studenten und Akademiker in Deutschland 1678-1848*, Tübingen 1974 (Schriftenreihe wissenschaftlicher Abhandlungen des Leo Baeck Instituts 28), pp. 13–82.

[7]Jacob Toury, *Der Eintritt der Juden ins deutsche Bürgertum. Eine Dokumentation*, Tel-Aviv 1972, pp. 273–289; Richarz, *op. cit.*, pp. 47–54, 172–178.

enthusiastic Kantian who had qualified in Halle. Herz made his salon in Berlin into a centre of education and scholarship, giving talks to Jews and non-Jews on philosophy and the natural sciences. He also expressed his views in a dispute within the Jewish community, between the conservative majority and the spokesmen of the Enlightenment over the early burial of the dead.* It was the custom to bury the dead on the day of their death, though the practice was not based on the Talmud and was increasingly questioned by the rationalists on scientific and medical grounds. Mendelssohn had already stated his own opposition to early burial in 1772 in a response to the community in Mecklen-burg-Schwerin.[8] Overall the issue was not significant. Nevertheless, it helped to draw up the lists within Jewish society, in which modernists and conservatives were beginning to clash with increasing severity. In the process, moreover, they frequently sought assistance from outside, from government and its officials.

There was a much more important problem around which the forces within the Jewish community tested their strength in the eighteenth century. This was the issue of rabbinical jurisdiction and the use of the ban (*Cherem*). As a penal sanction within the community, it provided a certain substitute for absent police power, being designed to secure collective interests but also for use against individuals if necessary.

To the absolutist regime this use of the ban was a thorn in the flesh. It therefore endeavoured to eliminate it, or at least to limit its application within the framework of a policy of rationalisation in justice and administration. Strong support for this policy was obtained from within the Jewish community itself, from the rising middle class.

Complaints were made by members of the middle class concerning the incompetence of the rabbis and abuses of judicial functions. Time and time again, requests for liberation from rabbinical jurisdiction played into the hands of absolutist rulers by making it easier for them to interfere in the internal affairs of the corporate community and encouraging the abolition of certain functions.[9] The autonomy of the court was clearly threatened when community members took disputes about ceremonial and ritual matters, as well as quarrels over money and trade, before the regular courts. They thereby helped to undermine what remained of the old rabbinical authority.

The decline of the Jewish corporation and the rise of the Jewish middle class were, therefore, closely linked. In addition, it was those who were best situated, the "privileged" and "naturalised" Jews, who did their utmost to free themselves from their community obligations – from its jurisdiction, from collective obligations in taxation and so forth. These were men like Itzig, Veitel Ephraim, Gumpertz, Friedländer, Riess and Bendix. By income, property and profession, these men were regarded by the government as standing high in the Jewish social

*For Jewish burial practices see the essay by Falk Wiesemann, 'Jewish Burials in Germany. Between Tradition, the Enlightenment and the Authorities', in the preceding section of the current Year Book – (Ed.).

[8]Marcus Herz, *Über die frühe Beerdigung der Juden. An die Herausgeber des hebräischen Sammlers*, Berlin 1787; Alexander Altmann, *Moses Mendelssohn. A Biographical Study*, Alabama 1973, pp. 288–289.

[9]Stern, *op. cit.*, II/1, pp. 30–33, II/2, p. 274, III/1, pp. 255–268.

hierarchy, because they were expected to be of most use to the State. When the banker Daniel Itzig (1723–1799) obtained his *Naturalisationspatent* in 1792, he acquired not only the right of citizenship in the city of Berlin, but also exemption from rabbinical jurisdiction for himself and his family.[10]

Within the rising Jewish middle class there was a transformation of lifestyle – in clothing, customs, language and social gathering – which imitated that of the parallel class in Christian society. This class, and particularly its businessmen, bankers and the *Hofjuden*, thus contributed to the disintegration of the corporate community.

At first it was Sephardic, and later Ashkenazic, Jews who inclined to this middle-class transformation. Rabbis and preachers from the conservative majority responded with bitter criticism. They warned against the practice "of dressing in the style of Christian citizens, against the shaving of the beard and the easy-going mixing in *Vereine*, in coffee-houses and in salons with card- and dice-games, against visits to the opera and theatre". Fears were expressed that this form of acculturation would very soon lead to a turning away from Jewish law, from the daily obligation to prayer, from the observance of rest on the Sabbath and of fast days (for example, the day of mourning for the destruction of the Second Temple).[11]

The change in external behaviour was a source of constant conflict. As well as taking place within the wider framework of the community between traditional-ists and innovators, this conflict also began to be felt within the family circle. For the first time, the documents record a generational conflict, with fathers and sons quarrelling over opposing values and norms. The echo of their confrontation can be heard in the literature of the age, in the satires[12] of Aaron Wolfsohn Halle (1754–1835) and Isaac Euchel (1756–1804), both of whom were pupils of Mendelssohn.

In the dramas *Leichtsinn und Frömmelei* (1796) and *Reb Chenech – ein Familienge-mälde* (1797), they portray, with comedy but also realism, the clash of fathers with the changing lifestyles of their children. Change was replacing continuity; a break was taking place in the area which for centuries had been the stormproof centre of Jewish society.

Wills dating from this period also testify to the conflict between the generations. In their last wills, some fathers made the adherence of the children to the law and tradition of Israel into a condition of their share in the inheritance. This decision was made, for example, by Isaac Jacob Gans, the grandfather of Eduard Gans in Celle, and by Mayer Amschel Rothschild with his five sons in Frankfurt.

The theory which encouraged the forces of destruction within the traditional community was conceived by the supporters of the Enlightenment, the *Maskilim*, the first representatives of an educated Jewish middle class. In the eighteenth century it was largely self-educated men who brought the zeal and perceptive-

[10]Toury, *op. cit.*, pp. 65–68; Haim Hillel Ben-Sasson (ed.), *Geschichte des jüdischen Volkes*, Munich 1980, III, pp. 35–39.

[11]Katz, *op. cit.*, pp. 145–146.

[12]Israel Zinberg, *A History of Jewish Literature*, 8 vols., New York 1976, VIII, pp. 140–150.

ness of the talmudic school to bear as they advanced into the new territory of a previously taboo secular culture. In particular, they began to study philosophy and other areas of enlightened-humanist teaching.

No less a figure than Moses Mendelssohn (1729–1786) pleaded for the removal of the rabbinical ban (*Cherem*) and thereby endorsed one of the demands of the absolutist regime. In *Jerusalem – oder über religiöse Macht und Judentum* (1783) he argued: "The right to ban or censure, which the state may allow itself from time to time, diametrically opposes the spirit of religion." His argument was based on Locke's view that Church and State should be separate; there should be tolerance for religious convictions and conduct on the grounds that these were matters for the individual, which should not be subjected to external compulsion.

The Rationalists were also sharply critical of the tradition-bound Jewish education system. This they condemned as one-sided and backward because it concentrated exclusively on the Talmud to the exclusion of other knowledge. Here too the source of their inspiration lay outside the community tradition. They looked to men such as Basedow and Pestalozzi, who called for consideration of the nature of the child and his capacity to absorb information, which varied according to age and development.

Plans for a radical reform of Jewish methods of education were published in 1782 by Naphtali Herz Wessely (1725–1805), a friend and colleague of Mendelssohn. These were a direct response to the *Toleranzpatent* of Joseph II in which he called for Jewish children to be given secular education.[13]

To the Orthodox majority, all these schemes appeared to be an attempt to overturn a system of values which had been sanctified by the tradition of centuries. The desire to put liberal humanist education, if not actually above talmudic religious education, then at least on a par with it, was regarded by the rabbis and the conservative majority as an attack by "heretics" on the vital nerve of the Jewish community. It was scarcely surprising that they contemplated the use of the ban to defeat these "heretics", just as the rabbinical court of the Amsterdam Jewish community had excommunicated Baruch Spinoza some hundred years before as punishment for his views on Jewry and Jewish autonomy. But historical conditions had changed. Governments frequently prevented the imposition of the ban (in Hamburg, Raphael Cohen, and in Frankfurt, Rabbi Horovitz). In general, the emergence of an internal Jewish opposition was part of a comprehensive restructuring process of state and society in the German-speaking lands. Unlike Spinoza and those who shared his views, therefore, the rising middle class could no longer be completely isolated and driven out of Jewish society.

II. BETWEEN TWO SOCIETIES – THE EMERGENCE OF NEW JEWISH SOCIAL FORMS

There was one further aspect to the outcome of the conflict. The Jewish middle class in this period (1750–1830) did not exert a purely negative effect as the

[13]Katz, *op. cit.*, pp. 66–68; Naphtali Herz Wessely, *Divrei Shalom veEmet* (in Hebrew), 1782.

catalyst of destruction in the old society. It also made constructive contributions and acted as a positive force in creating cells of renewal – societies or *Vereine* – on the periphery of the old Jewish community. These societies had very varied objectives. Some were established as reading and discussion groups, while others existed to promote welfare and education, to prepare poor Jewish children for farming and trades, to promote science and culture, to reform religous ritual, or even simply to enable Jews to mix sociably.

The initiative should come as no surprise. In this period, the non-Jewish middle class had come to regard the *Verein* as the ideal form of organisation to reflect its ideals and interests. The older order of society, based on estates and corporations, was dissolving under the pressure of central state power. At such a time, the *Verein* gave members of a rising social group the opportunity to create a community of like-minded individuals and to strive for a Utopian model of society.[14]

There is no doubt that the rising Jewish middle class was strongly influenced by the parallel Christian group in society. The origins of the innovation, nevertheless, must be sought within Jewish society itself. From the Middle Ages until the eighteenth century, the Jews lived in their community as a self-contained and cohesive society. Even where there were no ghetto walls, the norms and laws of rabbinical Jewry surrounded every sphere of life both inside and outside the synagogues and Talmud schools. No group or individual could for long escape the power of the community leadership, which was sanctioned by the ruler – king, prince or bishop.

The circle which had enclosed the corporate community over centuries was now broken by the rising middle class. Its members formed groups on the periphery of the community, establishing a new type of sociability which, though generally opposed to the old leadership elites and to normative Jewry, must still be regarded as Jewish according to sociological and ethnic criteria.

Such new social forms developed from the situation of conflict in which the Jewish bourgeois class found itself. The rising Jewish elite moved in the area of tension between two societies: an old, traditional Jewish society from which they had not completely broken free, and a modernising Christian society which placed serious obstacles in the way of social advance. The conflict between the Jewish and Christian middle classes was perceptible to Jews as soon as they became candidates for membership of groups such as reading societies, free-masons' lodges and *Burschenschaften*.

After the Wars of Liberation and the Congress of Vienna (1815), the activity of the *Burschenschaften* intensified among students in university towns such as Bonn, Göttingen, Giessen, Jena, Heidelberg and Berlin. As the number of Jewish students increased after 1812, they were confronted with the problem of membership of these societies, which dominated the student scene. Young Jews, mostly from middle-class families, were soon convinced that even at the

---

[14]Thomas Nipperdey, *Deutsche Geschichte 1800–1866*, Munich 1983, pp. 180–182; Hans-Ulrich Wehler, *Deutsche Gesellschaftsgeschichte*, I (*1700–1815*), Munich 1987, pp. 317–328.

universities their Christian counterparts were pursuing strongly discriminatory policies.

From 1816 the *Burschenschaften* at the universities of Giessen, Erlangen, Jena and Heidelberg adopted the "*Judenparagraphen*", which ran as follows: "As the *Burschenschaft* is a society of German young men, only young men whose mother tongue is German can be members. Jews are excluded as enemies of our folk character."[15] The other *Burschenschaften* soon followed this lead in the aftermath of the Wartburg meeting of 1818. The draft constitution of the Berlin *Burschenschaft* stated: "Foreigners as well as Jews can be accepted after it is explained to them that the whole life of the *Burschenschaft* of this place is a Christian-German one and a declaration is made by them that they are drawn to this aspiration and wish to collaborate in it enthusiastically." In other words, Jewish students were to abandon completely their Jewish identity.

It is significant that the freemasons refused to accept Jews. Such actions were wholly contradictory to the ideas of brotherhood and world citizenship, the Enlightenment and humanism to which they purported to be committed, and flew in the face of their claim that differences of class and ethnic and religious origin were irrelevant.[16] In Berlin, three Grand Lodges opposed the admission of Jews: *Die Grosse Landesloge, Die Grosse National-Mutterloge, Die Königliche York Loge.* Nor was the situation any better in Frankfurt a. Main and other places where Jews requested admission to lodges. Consequently, representatives of the propertied and educated middle class began to found Jewish lodges such as *Die Loge zur aufgehenden Morgenröthe* (1807) and *Zum Frankfurter Adler* (1832) in Frankfurt a. Main.[17]

Ludwig Börne clearly expressed the feeling of frustration and dissonance aroused by this conflict:[18]

> "You gentlemen of the Frankfurt Scholars Society, answer me: Why can no Jewish scholar become a member of this society?
>
> You gentlemen of the Frankfurt Museum for Art and Science, answer me: Why do you admit no Jewish friend of art and science, no Jewish scholar or artist?
>
> You gentlemen of the Frankfurt reading societies, answer me: why may no Jew sit among you and read the *Allgemeiner Anzeiger*?
>
> . . . You men of the Frankfurt *Casino*, I do not ask you why you do not tolerate Jews among you, for you are tradesmen."[19]

Why was this rejection by the middle-class *Vereine* of the German cultural sphere so particularly wounding? Quite simply, because, well into the nineteenth century, these societies had been the preferred frame of reference for all shades of the ascendant Jewish bourgeoisie. In no other country, perhaps, did the latter identify so strongly with the model of bourgeois society and with those of its segments which took as their basis its catalogue of virtues and its lifestyle.[20] The

---

[15]Richarz, *op. cit.*, p. 154; Oskar Fritz Scheuer, *Burschenschaft und Judenfrage. Der Rassenantisemitismus in der deutschen Studentenschaft*, Berlin 1927, p. 12; *Verfassung der Erlanger Teutonia*, 1817.

[16]Wehler, *op. cit.*, p. 323.

[17]Jacob Katz, *Jews and Freemasons in Europe, 1723–1939*, Cambridge, Mass. 1970, pp. 54–94.

[18]Ludwig Börne, *Sämtliche Schriften*, II, Düsseldorf 1964.

[19]*Idem, Der ewige Jude*, 1821.

[20]Jürgen Kocka, *Bürger und Bürgerlichkeit im 19. Jahrhundert*, Göttingen 1987, pp. 28, 44–49.

Jewish middle class felt a high degree of identification with the parallel group in the majority community, with which it shared much common ground. Members of the Jewish and Christian middle class were in constant contact in their professional lives, as businessmen, bankers, doctors, academics and students (this, indeed, was a sign of the "opening" of modern society). In these circumstances, exclusion from non-Jewish *Vereine* caused a deep personal injury. If the resulting feelings of frustration were to be overcome, an answer had to be found. The step was thus taken to found parallel Jewish *Vereine*.

The first to be mentioned is the *Gesellschaft der Freunde*, founded in Berlin in 1792 by a group of young Jews including Joseph Mendelssohn (1770–1848, the eldest son of Moses Mendelssohn), Isaac Euchel and Aaron Wolfssohn, editors of the first Hebrew journal *Hame'asef*, and other businessmen and intellectuals. They cited the desire to combat "the abuse of too early burial" as the main reason for their initiative. This indicates the internal conflict within the Jewish community, based on antagonism between the conservative majority and a minority which was committed to the ideas of the Enlightenment and hoped to introduce more "reason and aesthetic sense and less irrational custom and superstition" into Jewish religious life. Joseph Mendelssohn concluded his speech to the inaugural meeting with the hope "that no-one who has at heart the true improvement of our nation, which depends solely on its greater enlightenment, will refuse to enter this society".[21]

But there is clear evidence that external conflict, with the Christian middle class, was also an important motive for the founders of the society. Thus the chronicle of the society reported on the pleasure members gained from:[22]

> ". . . spending the time in part on friendly discussion, in part on the reading of interesting new writings. But it must also have been a source of attraction that Jews, who were not granted entry to any Christian resource and were unable to feel at ease even at public places of entertainment where they were treated with rejection, suddenly found a social circle where they could forget the cares of life, where mutual goodwill and friendliness ruled without discrimination between persons."

The *Gesellschaft der Freunde* had 127 members in its first year and 382 in 1830, in a Berlin community which had increased from 3,400 in 1790 to about 5,500 in 1830.[23]

A glance at the membership list reveals that many belonged to the propertied and educated middle class of Jewish society. The situation was similar in the *Vereine* established elsewhere. According to their statutes and stated objectives, these hoped to fulfil a number of specific roles within the Jewish population, such as the reform of education and religion and the promotion of scholarship and knowledge among the Jews. Nevertheless, their overall emphasis was on those concepts and views which were common to the Jewish and Christian middle class. Thus, they stressed education, individual achievement through work and personal initiative, order and morality coupled with reason and directed towards

---

[21]Ludwig Lesser, *Chronik der Gesellschaft der Freunde*, Berlin 1842, pp. 8–29.
[22]*Ibid.*, pp. 29, 53.
[23]Herbert Seeliger, 'Origin and Growth of the Berlin Community', in *LBI Year Book III* (1958), pp. 159–168.

a rational-universal vision in contrast to the particularist outlook of a society based on estates and corporations.

In the discourse of the Jewish middle class, the stress was placed on concepts such as the brotherhood and unity of the human race and the elimination of ethnic-religious conflicts. Jewish art and literature were also committed to this purpose. The painter Moritz Oppenheim (1799–1882), famous for his portrayals of the family life of the Jewish middle class, articulated this striving for harmony in a painting dedicated to Mendelssohn and his salon. This shows Lessing and other Christian representatives of the Enlightenment together with the Jew Mendelssohn. It seems as though Oppenheim was trying to say: "Lo and behold, a new era has dawned with the emergence of citizens who meet in social concourse unconstrained by consideration of ethnic-religious affiliations." In fact, the painting was a contribution to the myth of symbiosis.

This symbiosis was presented as a real goal by various members of the Jewish middle class: by the founders of a *Reformtempel* (in Berlin, Hamburg and Breslau); by members of a society for the creation of a "free school"; and by others who wanted to promote crafts, knowledge or scientific study among the Jews. For some the vision of the future was a symbiosis in the light of religion – a coming together of all monotheists. For others it was the prospect of a brotherhood of Jews and non-Jews in knowledge. One of the founders of the *Verein für Cultur und Wissenschaft der Juden* in Berlin in 1819 gave his own version of the goal:[24]

> "The Jews must again prove themselves vigorous collaborators in the common work of humanity, they must raise themselves and their principle to the level of science, for this is the level of European life. At this level the relationship of foreignness, in which Jews and Jewry previously stood to the outside world, must disappear."

Clearly, as a vision of the future, it was not lacking in Utopian excess.

CLOSING REMARKS

In the period under investigation, both Christian and Jewish parts of society were undergoing decorporatisation and restructuring, and beginning to open up. In the area of tension which was produced, new Jewish social forms were created. With a genuine emancipatory élan, a close network of associations, institutions and centres of cultural activity took shape. These formed a secularised sphere of life alongside the old, tradition-bound structures of the Jewish community. The intensity of the emancipatory zeal can be seen in the simple fact that, between 1800 and 1849, no fewer than 39 *Vereine* to promote crafts among the Jews were founded; literally hundreds of Jews joined societies with a wide range of different aims.[25]

[24]Immanuel Wolf (Wohlwill), 'Über den Begriff einer Wissenschaft des Judenthums', in *Zeitschrift für die Wissenschaft des Judenthums* (1822), p. 24.
[25]David Sorkin, *The Transformation of German Jewry 1780–1840*, Oxford–New York 1987, pp. 107–123, 208–209.

This development was frequently accompanied by serious conflicts between the conservative Jewish leadership elite and the advocates of a secularised Jewry. The new Jewish sociability mirrored developments in the non-Jewish community and was part of bourgeois society and its continued extension.[26] Common interests between the two groups were unmistakable and can be recognised as a phenomenon of the bourgeoisie and its way of life. Nevertheless, the Jewish middle class did not completely lose its identity. Though it was no longer embedded in a corporate community, in its conduct and mentality the Jewish middle class continued to reflect its affiliation to an ethnic-religious minority, within a majority society which was increasingly developing according to the criteria of the modern nation state.

In conclusion, the following elements of this affiliation should be emphasised:
1. Even outside the ghettos or the special Jewish streets, there was a distinct tendency for Jews to live together in certain quarters and streets within the towns, to intermarry and to establish specifically Jewish groups (though these did not always have cultural-religious objectives).

Furthermore, there was a desire to give a Jewish complexion to the ideas and concepts deriving from a fundamentally bourgeois view of the world. This was done by linking them with symbols, words and terms from the Jewish tradition (with the monotheism of Israel, with its messianic faith, with the ethics of the prophets etc.). In speaking of *Wissenschaft*, people would add *Wissenschaft des Judentums* (the science of Judaism) as though *Wissenschaft* could actually be defined according to ethnic-religious affiliation. Thus it is possible to speak of a discourse among the rising Jewish bourgeoisie.
2. The Jewish bourgeoisie suffered discrimination at the hands of the majority society. This discrimination, emanating not only from the anonymous state power but also from the Christian social group with which it identified and felt linked, produced a "*Judenschmerz*" of frustration. Nevertheless, it did not lead to any fundamental reorientation; the German bourgeoisie and its culture continued to be the point of reference, and the Jewish bourgeoisie continued to adhere to its position between the societies.

It was the first group to break out of the closed circle of the corporate community, though maintaining an extremely complex and weakened link with that community. As a result, the community could still exert an influence on elements of the Jewish minority. The bourgeoisie became a positive force, originally in matters of culture and through the establishment of *Vereine*, and later, in the course of the nineteenth century, in the political life of the Jews.
3. The decline of the corporate Jewish community has frequently been described with nostalgia. With much the same anxiety and regret, it should be noted, de Tocqueville regarded the disappearance of the structures and lifestyles of the *ancien régime* in France. He believed that an irreparable breach in society had been created by the almost total eradication of the groups (province, city, guild) which had once stood between domestic and political society, and in which all had been obliged to participate. Yet thinkers such as Durkheim, Tönnies and

[26]Nipperdey, *op. cit.*, pp. 174–205.

Simmel[27] have shown that new forms of group formation can be perceived in the social web of the bourgeoisie and that these have a vitalising effect.

Jewish society too was revitalised after the decline of the corporate community. In this process a new group – the bourgeoisie – played a decisive part. The contribution of the Jewish middle class lay partly in its creation of its own forms of sociability. In addition, there emerged a new self-awareness which was clearly different from that of normative Jewry but not identical with that of the non-Jewish *Bürgertum*. This self-awareness demanded a certain level of erudition and consciousness. Its advantage was that it enabled Jews to remain Jews in an opening society. However, it could no longer be maintained by sanctions, either from within or without.

The choice of whether or not to be a Jew would in future rest on a personal decision, a daily "plebiscite". The individual, not the collective alone, was asked to use his reason, his emotions, his catalogue of virtues – in short, to act in a thoroughly bourgeois manner – in order to reach a decision: "I wish – or do not wish – to share the living conditions of an ethnic-religious minority."

---

[27]Emil Durkheim, *Moral und Gesellschaft*, Frankfurt a. Main 1984, p. 268.

Integration and Identity in Imperial Germany: Towards a Typology

BY WERNER E. MOSSE

The Empire, for the Jews of Germany, was the post-emancipatory age. The attainment of formal legal equality with the rest of the population (1869–1871) opened the way – in theory – for their complete integration into German society. Under the constitution, they enjoyed full civic rights and equality before the law. Remaining discrimination was extra-legal. A majority of Jews was by this time completely accultured and they were, as a group, "*verbürgerlicht*". Whilst preserving a distinctive Jewish identity and self-awareness they had yet in many respects become assimilated to the Gentile middle and upper-middle classes.

Among German Jews – a number of intellectuals apart – it was the mainly commercial *haute bourgeoisie* and their offspring who enjoyed the greatest opportunities for successful integration. Wealth and position in the commercial world, on occasion generous patronage and large scale philanthropy, partially compensated in the eyes of at least part of Gentile society for the ineradicable stigma of "Jewishness". A generation of "heirs" and "heiresses" born with silver spoons in their mouths, possessed, among Jews, the widest choices of occupation, life styles, leisure pursuits and last, but not least, marriage strategies. How far, against the background of these opportunities, was the *haute bourgeoisie* able to achieve a successful integration into Imperial German society? To what extent did it attain smooth and stable professional and social relations with its Gentile counter-part? How far and in what form did its members, at the same time, retain their Jewish identity?

I. INTRODUCTION

It is of course a well-established fact that, collectively and individually, Jewish integration in the German body politic as in post-emancipatory society remained patchy and incomplete. Political integration was impeded by many forms of extra-legal discrimination; social integration by the pervasive and ever-present ground-swell of antisemitism. Only in two spheres, the economic and, to a great extent, the cultural was a high degree of integration a practical possibility.

About the actual degree of integration achieved in these conditions there has been a good deal of sweeping, ill-conceived generalisation in (scientifically misapplied) terms of an alleged "symbiosis", whether "failed" or otherwise. Sweeping statements by Gershom Scholem and his disciples have become for many the conventional wisdom.[1] They have been accompanied by blanket assertions about an alleged dissociation from Jewish concerns, propensity for mixed marriages and conversion of members, more particularly, of the "assimilationist" *haute bourgeoisie.*

The time has come, at long last to look at the evidence. If one considers the records left by some members of the *haute bourgeoisie* of Imperial Germany about themselves and their families, it is immediately apparent that there existed, in a situation of some social and psychological fluidity, various forms of partial integration combined with distinctive perceptions of identity. All generalisation is unwarranted. What the evidence does suggest instead is the existence of some typical forms of integration and corresponding self-identification determined by a variety of factors in both the Gentile environment and in the Jewish sphere. Occupation plays a major part, as do geography, personality and an element of chance. With time, it would be possible to elaborate a fairly sophisticated and differentiated pattern of "integration" and "identities", with any given family or individual approximating more or less closely to one or other of these types. What follows is a first attempt to identify through the experience of a number of individuals or families, some of the basic forms of integration and identity. The families selected, partly on account of the available information, are the Wallich, Salomonsohn, Tietz, Hirsch (Halberstadt) and lastly, as an individual Paul Singer, joint leader of the Social Democratic Party.[2]

II. THE WALLICHS

Hermann Wallich (1833–1928) was co-founder in 1870 of the *Deutsche Bank* and until his retirement in 1893 one of its leading directors. Offspring of an observant Jewish family in Bonn – though with a "liberally-inclined" Jewish mother from Alsace – he had from an early age lost much of his Jewish identification. After years overseas in the service of a Paris bank, Wallich moved to Berlin in 1870. Five years later, he married Anna Jacoby from a wealthy "assimilated" family. Her musical talents created for the somewhat lonely bachelor isolated in uncongenial Berlin – she was twenty years his junior – a congenial social circle. "Dank dem musikalischen Talent meiner Frau" (his memoirs record[3]), "sie sang vorzüglich, sammelte sich ein kleiner, aber netter Kreis um uns, und unser sogenanntes 'Kränzchen', wie andere unserer Gesellschaftsabende, wurde mit

[1]For a classic statement see Gershom Scholem, 'On the Social Psychology of the Jews in Germany. 1900–1933', in *Jews and Germans from 1860 to 1933. The Problematic Symbiosis*, ed. by David Bronsen, Heidelberg 1979, pp. 14ff.

[2]Three of these families have been dealt with individually in great detail in earlier essays: see Werner E. Mosse, 'Problems and Limits of Assimilation. Hermann and Paul Wallich 1833–1938', in *LBI Year Book XXXIII* (1988), pp. 43–66; *idem*, 'Terms of Successful Integration. The Tietz Family 1858–1923', in *LBI Year Book XXXIV* (1989), pp. 131–161; and *idem*, 'Integration through Apartheid. The Hirschs of Halberstadt 1780–1930', in *LBI Year Book XXXV* (1990), pp. 133–150.

[3]Hermann Wallich, *Aus meinem Leben* [in] *Zwei Generationen im deutschen Bankwesen 1833–1914*, Schriftenreihe des Instituts für bankhistorische Forschung e. V., Band 2, Frankfurt a. Main 1978.

Vorliebe besucht".[4] Later, with an established position in commercial Berlin and a substantial inheritance from his wealthy father-in-law, Wallich had social relations mainly with his colleagues and some business friends, whether Jewish or Gentile.

In Berlin, Wallich was confronted for the first time with the problem of his identity (overseas he had met little antisemitism) during the Stoecker agitation of the late seventies and eighties. His first reaction was to emigrate, a plan he abandoned at the instance of his wife. In return he stipulated that, should children be born to them – the marriage had been childless for five years – these should be baptised and brought up as evangelical Christians. In 1882 the son Paul was accordingly baptised (together with his slightly older sister). In his memoirs, written for his children, Wallich seeks to explain (and to justify) the step:

> "Ich war zu der Erkenntnis gekommen, dass das Judentum sich überlebt, dass die Sucht nach materiellen Gütern längst die religiösen Ideen untergraben, dass es demnach töricht wäre, Märtyrer einer Sache zu sein, für die man nicht mehr das volle Gefühl hatte."[5]

> "Wenn ich auch persönlich aus Achtung vor dem Andenken meiner Vorfahren an einen Glaubenswechsel nicht denken konnte, so hatte ich doch kein Recht, Kinder ohne Glauben in die Welt zu setzen."[6]

His object in having his children brought up as Christians was, he claims, at the same time religious and civic:

> "Nicht äusserer Vorteil hat mich zu diesem Schritt geleitet, sondern der Gedanke, meinen Kindern eine wirkliche Religion zu geben, sie von einer Ausnahmestellung zu befreien und sie aufgehen zu lassen in der Allgemeinheit des Landes, in dem sie geboren waren."[7]

> "Und wird hoffentlich der Erfolg zeigen, dass wir das Richtige getroffen haben."[8]

Paul Wallich, Hermann's son, began his university studies in 1901. "Als ich nach Freiburg kam", he writes in his memoirs (dating from 1916), "war ich Antisemit, mehr als ich es je wieder gewesen".[9] The antisemitism is, of course, understood in a social context, a compulsive desire to avoid all relations with Jews and a corresponding craving for aristocratic or, at least "Aryan" contacts. The desperate quest for non-Jewish society is described in compelling detail. It was crowned with indifferent success: "Dass ich das Schwergewicht meines Verkehrs in eine rein arische Richtung zu legen suchte", Wallich sums up with some exaggeration, "hat mir den ganzen Freiburger Aufenthalt verdorben. Ich habe dadurch eben gar keinen Verkehr gehabt."[10]

During his military service, Wallich strained every nerve to become an officer of the reserve. His overall objective, at this time was to raise his own social status and that of his family:

---

[4]*Ibid.*, p. 130.
[5]*Ibid.*, p. 133.
[6]*Ibid.*
[7]*Ibid.*, p. 134.
[8]*Ibid.*, p. 132.
[9]Paul Wallich, *Lehr- und Wanderjahre eines Bankiers* [in] *Zwei Generationen, op. cit.*, p. 161.
[10]*Ibid.*, p. 162.

"Mein ausgesprochenes Weltanschauungsideal war damals die Hebung des sozialen Standards der Familie . . . Dazu gab es nur drei Wege, die möglichst alle drei hätten beschritten werden müssen . . . der Eintritt in ein Korps, der Reserveoffizier und die Gattin von 'Familie'."[11]

Not without irony, Wallich describes the modest successes of his endeavours to attain his objectives, more particularly his comic and increasingly desperate quest for a wife "of family". Only one of his aims was eventually achieved – and brought him little pleasure: election (not without difficulty) into the officers' mess of a distinctly inferior regiment. Before long he in fact resigned his commission. His wife, though a blond "Aryan" was hardly "of family", being the educated daughter of an instructor at a military school. The marriage despite a distinct difference in the spouses' social status turned out to be a happy one.

A spell as a volunteer in a Hamburg commerical firm (in which he was accepted reluctantly thanks to Hermann Wallich's friendly relations with its head) saw further pathetic efforts to gain admission into "good society". Graphically, and in his later ironic style, Wallich describes his varied experiences. These in fact finally laid "den Grundstein für eine allmähliche Ernüchterung".[12] Wallich came to realise the futility of his snobbish endeavours and to accept his natural position as a well-to-do banker of Jewish extraction, a bibliophile and amateur poet with an ethnically mixed circle of acquaintances. He finally appears to have found a measure of not unacceptable integration "between the two races".

Paul's son Henry C. Wallich would one day write about the "assimilationist" endeavours of his father and grandfather:

"Das jüdische Thema und das verzweifelte Streben nach Assimilierung klingt in den Memoiren von Vater und Sohn immer wieder durch. Des Vaters frühe Absicht, sich taufen zu lassen, scheitert an der Frömmigkeit seiner jüdischen Verwandten. Spätere Schritte unterbleiben, obgleich er seine Kinder taufen lässt. . . In Pauls Memoiren ist vieles nur unter dem Aspekt des Assimilierungsstrebens zu verstehen. Die Reserveoffizierskarriere, Wahl seiner Studienkollegen und schliesslich seiner Frau stehen unter diesem Zeichen . . . Mit der Zeit ging der jugendliche Snobismus . . . über in eine seriösere Haltung . . ."[13]

The "assimilationist" model is thus characterised by imperfect social integration combined with a weak sense of identity. Ethnically Jewish informal networks could not be shaken off overnight. Entry into "good" Gentile society remained unattainable. Even though "Jewishness" was rejected, it remained an inescapable present in the presence of a "crypto-Jewish" environment and of increasingly racialist antisemitism in society at large.

III. THE SALOMONSOHNS

Adolf Salomonsohn (1835–1919) born in Inowraclav (Poznań), descendant of a rabbinical family, was appointed *Syndikus* (chief legal adviser) in 1863 of the *Direction der Disconto-Gesellschaft*. From 1869 until his retirement in 1888 he was a

---

[11]*Ibid.*, pp. 167f.
[12]*Ibid.*, p. 219.
[13]Henry C. Wallich, in *Zwei Generationen, op. cit.*, p. 13.

Teilhaber (partner) and one of the bank's leading members. Like his wife, Sara Rinkel, he came from a modest, observant background in a small provincial town. Following a rapid social rise in Berlin, the Salomonsohns' circle consisted largely of Gentile colleagues:

> "Mit Hecker, Russell und dem im Jahre 1877 hinzugetretenen Sozius Alfred Lent und ihren Frauen [their son Georg would later recall] haben unsere Eltern die Bande innigster und treuester Freundschaft verbunden. Uns Kindern, die wir in diesem Kreise aufgewachsen sind . . . war die sich aus dieser Gemeinschaft ergebende Geistesverwandtschaft der durch das Institut verbundenen Familien das selbstverständliche Rückgrat der eigenen Entwicklung."[14]

Another and somewhat surprising friend of Adolf Salomonsohn was Emil Kirdorf, the forceful Managing Director of the *Gelsenkirchener Bergwerks AG* (GBAG). Theirs was a friendship "die auf besonders starker Gesinnungsgleichheit beruhte".[15]

> "Vater gehörte dem Aufsichtsrat der GBAG seit deren Gründung an und fühlte sich zu Emil Kirdorf hingezogen, sobald dieser auf dem Plan erschien. Beiden Männern war furchtlose Unerschrockenheit eigen, die vor keinem Götzen halt machte, und so fanden sich beide in der Ueberzeugung, dass Wilhelm II Deutschland zugrunde richten werde. Beide Männer waren überzeugte Monarchisten und warmherzige Patrioten."[16]

> "Wir Jüngeren haben, wenn wir mit Vater und Kirdorf im offenen Lokal zu Tisch sassen, uns beim Anhören der von beiden mit Vehemenz geäusserten Majestätsbeleidigungen oft ängstlich umgesehen ob auch kein Unberufener in Hörweite sässe."[17]

For Sara Salomonsohn, her husband's growing position involved great representative obligations of which she acquitted herself with distinction.

> "Was war es nun was ihr, die aus kleinen Verhältnissen kam, ermöglicht hat, sofort ihren Platz auszufüllen, als wäre sie für ihn geboren, und grade und aufrecht . . . auf diesem Platz zu stehen, auch als in den kommenden Dezennien die Wogen des Antisemitismus hochschlugen . . . ? Freiheitsdrang zur Wahrheit bildete den Grundzug ihres Wesens und liess sie untrüglich auch in schwierigen Lagen den richtigen Weg gehen."[18]

The young woman developed into "eine Aristokratin an Lebensführung, die jeden, der in ihren Kreis trat, in ihren Bann schlug".[19]

In social relations, necessitating on occasion contacts with antisemites, not only did the Salomonsohns never attempt to conceal their Jewishness but sometimes would even draw attention to it. Adolf Salomonsohn's attitude to Judaism is characterised as "sehr einfach und klar". He would tell his son:

> "Das Judentum hat der Welt bereits den Monotheismus gegeben, und es wird die Welt auch die Toleranz lehren. Die sich daraus für jeden kultivierten Juden ergebende Belastung seines Lebens ist eine gute Schule für das Vorwärtskommen."[20]

---

[14]Georg Solmssen, *Gedenkblatt für Adolf und Sara Salomonsohn zum 19. Mai 1931*, Berlin 1931. See also Werner E. Mosse, *The German-Jewish Economic Elite 1820–1935. A Socio-Cultural Profile*, Oxford 1989, pp. 6ff.
[15]Solmssen, *Gedenkblatt, op. cit.*, p. 12.
[16]*Ibid.*, p. 13.
[17]*Ibid.*
[18]*Ibid.*, pp. 24f.
[19]*Ibid.*, p. 24.
[20]*Ibid.*, pp. 20f.

There was thus, writes the son "für Kindheit und Jugend den Kindern der Gedanke eines Glaubenswechsels völlig ausgeschlossen". "Trotz dieses Festhaltens an dem Ueberkommenen waren beide Eltern nichts weniger als orthodox und besonders hellhörig und hellsichtig für alle Fehler der Juden."[21]

When, however, Georg, after an extensive encounter with social antisemitism in the USA, explained to his father that he wished to be baptised and to change his name to Solmssen, Adolf Salomonsohn raised no objection:

"... er habe gegen ein völliges Untergehen im Deutschtum, dass sich auch äusserlich dokumentiere, nichts einzuwenden, vorausgesetzt, dass es nicht aus Feigheit geschähe. Der Sohn erwiderte, dass er dafür sorgen werde, dass dieser Verdacht nie entstehen könne."[22]

He did this by publishing a technical study, the fruit of his American researches, under his original name. Arthur Salomonsohn, Adolf's nephew, who took his place in the bank after his retirement remained a Jew. Georg Solmssen who, in turn replaced him, remained a prominent member of the German banking community until the advent of National Socialism.

Adolf Salomonsohn is an example of what might be termed successful occupational or professional integration on an ideological base of Liberal Conservatism with, possibly, some capitalist overtones. The harmonious blend of professional and personal relations is significant. The Salomonsohns' self-understanding appears to have combined unproblematically German and Jewish elements – if perhaps in unequal proportions. Thanks to this, they were able to stand up successfully to antisemitic influences to which Hermann Wallich succumbed. The strong integrative forces were shared professional interests and a community of *Weltanschauung*.

IV. THE TIETZ FAMILY

Oscar Tietz (1858–1923) came from a humble observant family – his father was a carter – in Birnbaum (Poznań). He was destined to become the owner of what would become the most important department-store chain in Imperial Germany. Holding strong democratic views, "ganz dem Fortschritt zugetan auf allen Gebieten ... aus eigener Neigung stand er zwischen den Ideologien des Liberalismus und der Sozialdemokratie",[23] he could be described as a convinced "Left-wing Liberal". His son Georg (1889–1953) describes entertainingly his self-assured (not to say "cheeky") and usually successful dealings with various representatives of Imperial authority. After moving to Berlin (from Munich) in 1900 he became within three years the owner of three flourishing stores. In 1903 he was elected chairman of the newly formed *Verband deutscher Waren- und Kaufhäuser*. He was to occupy that position for the next twenty years. As a leading member of the commercial community, he played a prominent role in its professional activities.

---

[21] *Ibid.*
[22] *Ibid.*, p. 21.
[23] *Hermann Tietz, Geschichte einer Familie und ihrer Warenhäuser*, berichtet von Georg Tietz, Stuttgart 1965, Veröffentlichung des Leo Baeck Instituts, p. 48.

"Durch seinen Vorsitz im Warenhausverband war er unter anderem stellvertretender Vorsitzender der Berufsgenossenschaft (staatliche Zwangsunfallversicherung der Angestelltenschaft), sachverständiges Mitglied des Reichsversicherungsamtes ... Mitglied der Reichsbankenkommission und Ältester der Kaufmannschaft. Ausserdem war er Repräsentant der Berliner Jüdischen Gemeinde ... und vieler anderer ähnlicher Institutionen."[24]

Oscar Tietz, like his son Georg, took an active part in the affairs of the Jewish community:

"'Als Grossvater Jacob die Augen schloss', berichtet Georg Tietz, 'liess er sich von seinen Kindern versprechen, dass sie Glauben und Gesetze der Väter hielten'. Dem Wunsch seines Vaters folgend ist Oskar Tietz stets ein treuer Jude geblieben. Wie er die Feier des Freitagabend zu schätzen weiss, so hat er die Feiertage geheiligt und stets an ihnen alle seine Kaufhäuser geschlossen."[25]

Oscar Tietz became a leading figure of Liberal Judaism:

"Mit aller Kraft setzte er sich für seine Glaubensgenossen ein. Als Repräsentant der Berliner Jüdischen Gemeinde hat er jahrelang die Verwaltung des grössten jüdischen Gemeinwesens in Deutschland aufs stärkste beeinflusst. Nicht nach aussen aber nach innen ist er der Führer der jüdisch-liberalen Bewegung in Deutschland. Er betont neben dem Judentum stets sein Deutschtum, was ihm 'heftige Kämpfe sowohl mit den Zionisten wie mit den Konservativen eintrug'."[26]

Georg also reports:

"Am ersten Sonnabend nach meinem erreichten dreizehnten Lebensjahr wurde ich in der Synagoge Lützowstrasse, deren Kultus weder orthodox-konservativ, aber auch keineswegs reformiert war, in den Kreis der Erwachsenen unserer Glaubensgemeinschaft in den althergebrachten Formen aufgenommen."[27]

The Russian pogroms of 1905 led Georg Tietz to reflect on the problem of his identity and the relation between the Jewish and German components:

"Ich begriff schon damals, dass ich in religiös-ethischem Sinne Jude bin ... dass ich in politischer und kultureller Beziehung aber Deutscher war, wobei es kein protestantisches, katholisches oder jüdisches Deutschtum geben konnte. Mit anderen Worten, man habe dem Kaiser zu geben, was des Kaisers ist, und Gott, was Gottes ist. So meinte ich es wenigstens damals und betete, niemals vor die Frage, ob ich Deutscher oder Jude sein wolle, gestellt zu werden."[28]

During the war, in curious circumstances in Constantinople, Georg Tietz's visit to the synagogue would pay unexpected dividends.[29]

Overall, the Tietz family (including its senior member Hermann Tietz, of whom nothing is said here) presents a picture of successful integration based on a synthesis of Jewish and "German" elements. It could be described as an instance of "Left-Liberal" integration, characteristic also of some other families. Its success rested on a number of factors:

---

[24]*Ibid.*, pp. 93f.
[25]Kurt Zielenziger, *Juden in der deutschen Wirtschaft*, Berlin 1930, p. 216.
[26]*Ibid.*
[27]Tietz, *op. cit.*, p. 64.
[28]*Ibid.*, p. 67.
[29]*Ibid.*, pp. 178ff.; see also Mosse, 'Terms of Successful Integration', *loc. cit.*, pp. 155f.

i. great commercial success, considerable wealth and resulting influence and esteem not only in business, but also in official cricles.
ii. marked self-assurance based on success, independence and personality, manifested in dealings with the authorities at times bordering on "chuzpah".
iii. conscious renunciation of all social ambition[30] or of attempts to play a part on the public stage beyond the defence of professional interests. Only during the war did Oscar Tietz, in relation to economic matters, and Georg, as a convinced pacifist, step outside these limits.[31]
iv. close social – or socio-political – relations with Left-Liberal and Social-Democratic *Gesinnungsgenossen* (journalists, publicists, politicians, industrialists) irrespective of religion or race.
v. a harmonious and supportive extended family, also in commercial and financial matters.
vi. steadfast involvement in the affairs of the Jewish community.

V. THE HIRSCHS OF HALBERSTADT

Linked in double marriage with the Orthodox rabbinical family of Auerbach, the metal traders and manufacturers Hirsch in Halberstadt (later also Eberswalde and Berlin) led a social and religious life largely insulated from their Gentile surroundings. Successive members lived in Halberstadt as leaders of the Jewish community, devoted to the daily fulfilment of their religious obligations. They became leaders of Neo-Orthodoxy. By marriage, they became related to the Hildesheimer family.

At the same time, the Hirschs prospered in their commercial activities both as traders and manufacturers. They gained important positions in professional organisations and in the international metal trade. One member of the family became the only non-British founding member of the London Metal Exchange. *Aron Hirsch & Son* enjoyed the esteem of the international metal-trading community.

The key-figure and for many years patriarch of the family, Benjamin Hirsch (1840–1911) and his wife Julie (Julchen), née Auerbach, watched zealously over the observance of Jewish ritual and tradition. Clerical staff (though not those engaged in manufacture) were drawn almost exclusively from Orthodox Jewish families. For several generations, marriages between relatives (cousins, and even uncles and nieces) were common, as were those with members of a small number of already related families. Where none of these was possible, it was the dowries which played the decisive role.

A characteristic incident illustrates Benjamin's attitude. A rare exception to the prevailing practice of the firm was the admission as a trainee metal trader of

---

[30]For the social ambitions of Oscar's wife, Betty, kept in check with difficulty by her husband and son, see Tietz, *op. cit.*, pp. 49ff.
[31]For details of the Tietzes' involvement in the peace movement towards the end of the war and of the overlapping groups frequenting their salon at the time, see *ibid.*, pp. 183f.

Ludwig Vogelstein, son of a leading Reform rabbi in Stettin. During seven years in Halberstadt, Vogelstein won golden opinions from members of the family alike as a person and a man of affairs. He became in fact Benjamin's right-hand man. When, in due course, he applied for a partnership, he enjoyed the support of several members of the family. Benjamin Hirsch interposed his veto:

"Vogelstein ist kein Hirsch. Er wird von mir, wie er und Ihr wisst, in Tüchtigkeit und als Mensch geschätzt. Aber eben 'kein Hirsch' und seit unberufen 1837, der Gründung durch meinen Grossvater und Vater waren nur Hirsche Inhaber. – Aber dann ist L.V. schliesslich der Sohn des Reformrabbiners Heinemann Vogelstein in Stettin, des Haupt-Kämpfers für die Reform der Orthodoxie. Nein und abermals nein! Mit ihm würde die Reform der alten Tradition von AH&S in vielem beginnen. Wo würde sie 'Gott soll hüten' enden?!"[32]

Denied a partnership, Ludwig Vogelstein emigrated to the USA, where he became a leading industrialist. He was elected Chairman of the Union of American Hebrew Congregations, the highest lay position in the American Reform movement.[33] At the same time, he remained a good friend and close business associate of the Hirsch family and its enterprises.

The Hirschs thus developed a form of integration and identity within a largely self-enclosed environment. Though the manufacturing branch of the family gradually abandoned the tenets and practices of Benjamin and Julchen, their older sons remained observant to the end. The house in Halberstadt, on the eve of the Great Depression, had to be moved to Berlin and merge with another firm.

VI. PAUL SINGER

Paul Singer (1844–1911), a prosperous industrialist had, in 1869, become co-founder in Berlin of a firm producing ladies' overcoats. During the seventies, he had joined the *Sozialdemokratische Partei Deutschlands* (SPD). In 1884 he was elected to the *Reichstag* and three years later gave up his commercial activities. Two years later, he was expelled from Berlin, but returned in 1890. From 1890 until his death in 1911 he filled the office of joint chairman of the SPD.

"Singer war der populärste sozialistische Führer Berlins. Er verstand sich mit den Berliner Arbeitern ausgezeichnet. Er war ein echter Repräsentant der Hauptstadt, deren Bewohner in der Theorie radikal, zuweilen hyperradikal waren und in der Praxis viel common sense zeigten . . . Die Mischung von theoretischem Radikalismus und nüchtern-praktischem Sinn bestimmte Singers Wirken."[34]

Whilst other prominent Social Democrats registered themselves as Dissidents, Paul Singer (like Eduard Bernstein) chose to remain a member of the Jewish community. Clearly it must have been a deliberate choice. At the same time, Singer kept in the background when Jewish issues were discussed in public. At

[32]Siegmund Hirsch, *Die Kupferhirschs in Halberstadt 1780–1830.* Typewritten revised ms., dating, probably, from 1962, p. 83; see also Mosse, 'Integration through Apartheid', *loc. cit.*, p. 134.
[33]Communication from Professor Michael A. Meyer, Cincinnati.
[34]Ernest Hamburger, *Juden im öffentlichen Leben Deutschlands. Regierungsmitglieder, Beamte und Parlamentarier in der monarchischen Zeit, 1848–1914*, Tübingen 1968 (Schriftenreihe wissenschaftlicher Abhandlungen des Leo Baeck Instituts 19), p. 421.

the International Socialist Congress in 1891, he tried to prevent the inclusion of an item on antisemitism on the agenda. In 1884, however, on his election to the *Reichstag* over an antisemite opponent, he expressed his satisfaction that at the height of the antisemitic campaign Berlin workers had ostentatiously rejected it.

There is, unfortunately, no evidence to show what problems, if any, were presented by the combination of Singer's full Socialist integration and his residual Jewishness. There is no doubt about his popularity with the Berlin working class, his wholehearted acceptance by his SPD comrades and his total devotion to the Party. There is at the same time no evidence that his deliberately maintained membership of the Jewish community ever created problems. It is reported that when Singer's coffin left one of the Berlin stations, whilst vast crowds of Berlin workers were gathered outside, representatives of the SPD on one platform, those of the Jewish community on another, bade him their last farewell.[35]

VII. CONCLUSION

Several typical forms of Jewish integration (or attempted integration) in Imperial Germany with distinctive senses of identity can thus be picked out. Although the examples presented here are deliberately chosen from the ranks of the *haute bourgeoisie* – the most conspicuous and best documented Jewish group and the subject of Scholem's generalisations – the evidence would seem to suggest the validity – to a greater or lesser extent – of the typology for broader middle-class groups. Certainly many Jewish "upper-class" families approximated in conduct and attitudes to one or other of the models outlined. Their relatively high degree of successful integration was, of course, favoured by economic success with its concomitant wealth, status and self-assurance and, above all, relative independence. The basis of integration could be commercial and professional achievement, capitalist solidarity, shared ideology, common cultural pursuits, personal sympathies and shared aversions.

Different variants of more or less successful integration (how, in any case, does one measure the degree of success?) undoubtedly existed in Imperial Germany. The hypothesis may even be ventured that these embraced the bulk of the Jewish *haute bourgeoisie*. Moreover, on the basis of at least partial integration, identity problems, even in the face of widespread antisemitism, would lose a great deal of their sharpness. It was often possible to associate with the like-minded and the unprejudiced.

To talk of a "failed symbiosis" – whatever that woolly concept may mean – appears (on the evidence) unwarranted. So does all "portmanteau" generalisation. The relative frequency of mixed marriages (and, for that matter, conversions) suggests otherwise. There was a highly successful integration in commercial affairs, documented by the conspicuous part played by Jews and those of Jewish origin in professional associations. And outside the mainstream,

[35]Communication from Professor Laurenz Demps, Berlin.

there were the forms of integration and identity represented respectively by Benjamin Hirsch and Paul Singer. The great majority were, in the end, content to define themselves as "German citizens of the Jewish faith". Whilst this, of course, only partly reflected realities, it was an approximation which, so long as Germany remained a *Rechtsstaat*, could form the basis for an incomplete but none the less real integration into surrounding society* and for a German-Jewish sense of identity.

* See also the essay of Frank Eyck, 'A Diarist in fin-de-siècle Berlin and her Family. Helene, Joseph and Erich Eyck', in this volume of the Year Book, pp. 287–307 – (Ed.).

The Legend of German-Jewish Symbiosis

BY WOLFGANG BENZ

The emancipation of the Jews by the principles of the French Revolution was linked with the expectation that it would be accompanied by assimilation. Count Clermont-Tonnerre's plea that: "One must refuse the Jews everything as a nation and grant them everything as individuals",[1] also became the watchword of emancipation in Germany. By means of cultural assimilation it was – in large part – realised. Educated Jews in Germany were known as "Germans by Goethe's grace", and there was much truth in the term. Yet the dictum also revealed that Jews were not wanted everywhere; in spheres like the military, the universities and the student corporations, not even baptism could guarantee equal rights to those of Jewish origin. Nevertheless, the fact of cultural assimilation has encouraged the fallacy that there was a German-Jewish symbiosis. Retrospectively, the significance of this supposed symbiosis has been almost transfigured.

Undoubtedly, as Hannah Arendt reported, German-speaking Jewry was a "unique phenomenon, even in the area of the normal history of Jewish assimilation". At least as regards the educated bourgeois class, the rapprochement in the previous century had progressed much further than was the case with comparable historical parallels, such as Hellenist Alexandria in ancient times or Spain under the Moors. But was the cultural and intellectual assimilation of the German-speaking Jews, as Gershom Scholem claimed, no more than "a one-sided declaration of love"?[2]

Though baptism – and thus the abandonment of the Jewish identity – was the precondition for social recognition, the gates to major careers generally remained closed. In Wilhelminian society it was still very rare to find Jewish staff officers, university professors, genuinely senior civil servants and chairmen of *Vereine*. When the *Stiftungsuniversität* of Frankfurt was founded with Jewish money, one of its aims was, therefore, to facilitate the appointment of Jews to professorships. In these circumstances, doubts about the perfection of emancipation are surely justified.

Following Max Weber, Hannah Arendt defined the existence of the Jews in Europe as that of a pariah people; this was most clearly understood by those "on whom the ambiguous freedom of emancipation and the even more ambiguous equality of assimilation was tried out". In the lands of emancipation most Jews had either to yield to the temptation of this foolish mimicry or to pursue a *parvenu*

[1] Robert Badinter, *Libres et égaux . . . l'émancipation des Juifs 1789–1791*, Paris 1989.
[2] Gershom Scholem, 'Jews and Germans', in *Commentary*, 42 (November 1966), pp. 31–38.

career. The worst fate, admittedly, befell those who sought a third way, which involved "taking the glad tidings of emancipation seriously, as had never been meant, and deciding, as Jews, to be men. This 'misunderstanding' began that splendid process in which Jews, to whom political freedom and direct *Volksnähe* were denied, liberated themselves as people, as individuals, in passionate opposition to their Jewish and non-Jewish environment and achieved *Volksnähe* in the imaginative power of head and heart, so to say on their own initiative."[3]

This formulation, made public for the first time in Spring 1944, contains the radical counterposition to the assumption of a German-Jewish symbiosis.

The most serious argument against the theory of the "German-Jewish symbiosis", which is said to have existed until Hitler's rise to power in 1933, is provided by antisemitism. Here I am not referring to the rowdy mob antisemitism of the *völkisch* groups and the National Socialists, but to bourgeois antisemitism. Motivated by religious, social and economic factors, bourgeois antisemitism began with the discussion of the "Jewish Question" and ended by looking on in silence when the "solution" was found under the National Socialist regime. It spread alongside the flourishing of Jewish freedom in Germany at the end of the nineteenth and beginning of the twentieth centuries. As a response to such antisemitism, the *Verein zur Abwehr des Antisemitismus* was founded shortly before the turn of the century. This organisation, which supported Democratic and Liberal goals and was not dominated by Jews, was of steadily diminishing significance. Nevertheless, its very existence can be taken as an argument against German-Jewish symbiosis. At the beginning of 1933 there were still some 20,000 subscribers to its newspaper (the *Abwehrblätter*); at its general assembly in Dresden in 1932 it was argued that in Germany more people than ever were seeking the solution to social problems in radical antisemitism.[4]

Despite the claims of hostile propaganda, the Jews in Germany were not a homogeneous group politically, sociologically or even in religious matters. Nevertheless, setting aside the various religious groupings within Jewry and the distance which all German Jews maintained from the immigrating *Ostjuden*, two major tendencies can be detected. The dominant trend was represented by the *Centralverein deutscher Staatsbürger jüdischen Glaubens*; the other by the Zionists. While the Jews organised in the *Centralverein* espoused national and cultural aspirations identical to those of the non-Jewish German middle class, the Zionists propagated the counter-programme to assimilation, the consciousness of a specifically Jewish cultural tradition.

Despite all the conflicts aired in the newspapers of the two tendencies, the Zionist *Jüdische Rundschau* and the *C.V.-Zeitung*, the gap between them was not unbridgeable; at least until 1933 it was limited to theoretical position-taking. Thomas Mann, who shared the scepticism of the assimilated Jews towards the attempts at Jewish settlement in Palestine, could still argue in 1931:

[3]Hannah Arendt, 'Die verborgene Tradition', in *idem, Sechs Essays*, Heidelberg 1948, pp. 82–83; see also Hannah Arendt, *The Jew as Pariah. Jewish Identity and Politics in the Modern Age*, ed. by Ron H. Feldman, New York 1978.
[4]Barbara Suchy, 'The Verein zur Abwehr des Antisemitismus (II). From the First World War to its Dissolution in 1933', in *LBI Year Book XXX* (1985), p. 99.

"It would be a misunderstanding to believe that Zionism demands a mass return of the Jewish people to its traditional homelands. Such a demand would be foolish, since the great majority of Jews is much too firmly rooted in western civilisation and in the culture of its various native lands for it to be able to separate from them and settle once again into the land of its forefathers."[5]

Two years later, in 1933, the Zionist programme became more attractive to some German Jews, but by no means the majority. Most Jewish citizens of Germany yielded to no-one in their loyalty to the Fatherland. They rested their hopes in the legality of the Hitler regime and its perceived symbol, President Hindenburg, and in the constitution, three articles of which appeared to guarantee the equality of all Germans, access for all citizens to public offices, and freedom of faith and conscience. But the process of dissimilation had begun with Hitler's Chancellorship at the latest; the dream of German-Jewish symbiosis was over. This change first began in the universities. Here Jewish professors, under pressure from *völkisch* and Nazi students with support from German Nationalist notables in the faculties, had been forced from their posts. Two examples here are Theodor Lessing (Hannover 1926) and Emil Julius Gumbel (Heidelberg 1932).

Symbiosis is a term which derives from the natural sciences. It describes the process by which different life forms live together, mutually complementary and providing necessary functions in reciprocal exchange. There are two indicators that such a symbiosis did not exist in the German-Jewish relationship. First, reciprocity through equality was not present; a section of the Jewish community was always forced to remain in the ghetto despite the process of assimilation. This remained true in the religious and spiritual sphere even though the German *Kaiser* had paid a visit to a synagogue and assured the *Centralverein der deutschen Staatsbürger jüdischen Glaubens* of his goodwill. And in social affairs it was true even for baptised Jews (from whom this official separation from Jewry was demanded as a precondition of social advance). Secondly, it remained the case that though non-Jewish Germans mixed with Jews on business and official matters, these relations rarely extended to the private sphere. When they did, it was the exception rather than the rule.

Full participation in social life had not been granted to the Jews as the fruit of assimilation. Consequently, they searched for a substitute. Consolation was found in an extensive and intensive family life, which was a source of strength, helping members to withstand the disappointments and humiliations of daily existence. Solace was also found in cultural traditions, in increased sensitivity to nature, in music and spirituality, and the awareness that the true home of the Jews was exile.[6] Some also sought comfort in patriotism: no-one should be allowed to accuse the Jews of not trying to be the best Germans, the most patriotic, the most loyal to the *Kaiser*. Many recognised with horror only in the

---

[5]'Eine lebende menschliche Wirklichkeit', radio talk 1931, quoted in Thomas Mann, *An die gesittete Welt. Politische Schriften und Reden im Exil*, Frankfurt a. Main 1986, p. 850.
[6]See also Friedrich Georg Friedmann, ' "Deutsch-jüdische Symbiose: Fiktion oder Wirklichkeit?" Gedanken zu einem komplexen Verhältnis in der Nachfolge Franz Rosenzweigs', in *Frankfurter Allgemeine Zeitung*, 20th March 1989.

ghettos and extermination camps of the East that their First World War decorations were not worth the metal they were made of. Once their wearers had believed that such medals would win them social recognition; much later, they had hoped that this proof of their patriotism might at least save their lives.

Looking back, a resident of Jerusalem recalls that as a youth, he and two other Jewish *Gymnasium* pupils had frequently dared to venture into their class only in the company of the teacher. This was in Munich at the beginning of the 1920s. And Perez Harburger's memoirs contain further evidence of the condition of the Jews in Germany: "We were 'German citizens of the Jewish faith', in which the 'German' was writ large and the 'Jewish' small. We made do with formal equality, which was usually purchased with assimilation: Just don't attract attention! Just don't emphasise the Jewish side!"[7]

In the memoirs and reflections of non-Jewish Germans dealing with the persecution and extermination of the Jews, there are many references to Jewish schoolfriends, neighbours, colleagues etc. Very rarely, however, is there evidence that deep contacts were sought with them outside school, the office, or the business environment. Yet if the Jews had been completely emancipated in Germany, such relations would have been the norm. Jews and non-Jews listened to Wagner and Beethoven together in the concert halls and opera houses, they visited the same theatres, they revered the same artists, but afterwards they went their separate ways home and locked their doors. The mention of private contacts with Jews is generally something of a demonstration or an alibi, but is always something out of the ordinary – and that is the vital criterion.

On the other hand, when Jewish contemporary witnesses look back they often emphasise the close cultural and intellectual links between the groups. They cite as evidence the names of great German-Jewish writers such as Zweig, Werfel, Kafka and Wassermann. Yet their arguments also show that the idea of German-Jewish symbiosis was a dream to them, whose collapse at the end of the Weimar Republic filled them with a pain which still lingers even today. That is especially true of those who were committed to Jewish traditions whilst being genuinely receptive to German culture.[8]

The relations between Jewish and non-Jewish Germans in the social sphere (not intellectually and culturally) was akin to that between patricians and plebeians. With emancipation, Jews were granted the *ius commercii* but not the *ius connubii* – understood in the broadest sense of social equality, and mindful of the existence of many "*Mischehen*" between Jews and non-Jews. Despite external appearances of equality, the Jews – at least the Jewish middle class – did not belong to the social network of German society. Bourgeois Jews regarded themselves as German *Gymnasiasten* and German students, they might even be recognised as *primus omnium* in school, yet socially they never quite belonged. Once their studies were completed, they discovered that although they might be respected colleagues in lawyers' chambers during the day, they would not be

---

[7]Perez Harburger, 'Meine Eltern waren nicht nur gute Deutsche, sondern auch gute Münchner', in *Jugendbilder (Geschichtswettbewerb der Stadt München)*, Gauting 1988, pp. 61–67.
[8]Conversation with Norbert Wollheim, April 1989, New York.

accepted as friends in drawing-rooms in the evening. The Jewish middle class continued to yearn for acceptance into society of the kind achieved by the Rathenau family, which stood for the Jewish patriciate. Its hopes were almost always in vain.[9]

The First World War had crystallised these hopes. According to an appeal of 1st August 1914, the German Jews were ready to devote their efforts to the Fatherland "beyond the limits of duty". A hundred thousand Jewish soldiers went to war, not simply to prove their patriotism; "I went into the field as a German to protect my troubled Fatherland. But also as a Jew, to gain full equality for my co-religionists", records the will of a Jewish lieutenant.[10] The Jewish total of 100,000 men was high in proportion to the Jewish share of the population (around 550,000), as was also the total of 12,000 deaths. But the sacrifice was in vain. So too was the tireless propaganda of the Jewish veterans' association, the *Reichsbund jüdischer Frontsoldaten*, which sought recognition for Jewish patriotism throughout the Weimar Republic.

This hope of recognition for Jewish achievements, and particularly the high level of cultural and intellectual assimilation, prevented many German Jews from recognising in time that the Nazis intended to make them outlaws and even to bring about their physical destruction. The period between the First World War and the end of the Weimar Republic brought the German Jews the high point of their cultural assimilation, but also the beginnings of social dissimilation. Antisemitic propaganda looked for scapegoats for the humiliating consequences of the war; the impoverished, *déclassé* petty bourgeois, full of fear of the future and damaged national pride, blamed "the Jews" as the cause of Germany's ills. Doubts about the national reliability of the Jews and accusations of dual loyalty ("first a Jew, then a German") revealed a desire to treat them as outcasts. It reached its first climax in the boycott of April 1933, accompanied by the insinuation that "the Jews" had declared war on the German people in Spring 1933.

As a gesture of threat and notification of intent, the boycott was followed some days later by the *Gesetz zur Wiederherstellung des Berufsbeamtentums* (Law for the Restoration of the Professional Civil Service). Germany was set on the road which would lead in five stages to the destruction not only of the achievements of the Enlightenment and emancipation, but of the physical existence of two thirds of European Jewry.[11] It is important to remember the interaction of propaganda with legislative and administrative measures in this process. Though the Germans appeared to respond with distaste to the brutal stage-management of the boycott in 1933 or the pogrom of 1938, they proved willing to accept measures which bore the stamp of formal legality, such as the Nuremberg Laws of 1935, even when these served only to implement racial antisemitism in its grossest form. The steps towards discrimination and the outlawing of the Jews

---

[9]Interview with Fred Grubel, April 1989, New York.

[10]Quoted in Heinrich Walle, 'Deutsche jüdische Soldaten 1914–1945', in Militärgeschichtliches Forschungsamt (ed.), *Deutsche Jüdische Soldaten 1914–1945*, Herford–Bonn 1983, p. 14.

[11]See Alex Bein, *Die Judenfrage. Biographie eines Weltproblems*, vol. I, Stuttgart 1980, pp. 303–304.

were taken with a speed which is also evidence against the existence of a German-Jewish symbiosis.

The first stage involved defamation and measures to lower the social standing of German Jews. Between the beginning of 1933 and Autumn 1935, Jews were expelled from public positions: doctors, lawyers, civil servants, army officers and college teachers were deprived of their influence by means of legal measures and with the assistance of the *Arierparagraphen*.

The second stage was reached in September 1935 with formal deprivation of rights and racial segregation through the Nuremberg Laws. Jews were now officially and legally second-class citizens of the state with limited rights (as decreed by the *Reichsbürgergesetz*); according to the regulations of the *Gesetz zum Schutze des deutschen Blutes und der deutschen Ehre* (Law for the Protection of German Blood and German Honour) they were an inferior race, forbidden to marry or have sexual relations with "citizens of German or related blood". This was not only the definitive rejection of the *ius conubii* in the narrow meaning of the term, but also served to degrade and criminalise Jews by means of the new criminal offence of *Rassenschande* (racial defilement). The *Reichsbürgergesetz*, with its clearly formulated and limited content, was expanded by 13 decrees until Autumn 1944 and by countless further implementation orders. It served to take away from the Jews first their rights as state citizens, then their human rights, then their human dignity and, finally, their lives.

From the end of 1938, the third stage involved destroying the economic existence of the Jews. It was achieved through the "Aryanisation" of businesses, the imposition of taxes on Jews escaping from Germany, the billion Mark contribution after the November Pogrom, the plundering of the remaining economic possessions of the Jews, and the exploitation of the labour force.

After the outbreak of war the fourth stage of isolation and expulsion began. During it the Jews lost their homes, were placed on starvation rations and subjected to vicious harassment of every kind. Measures designed to humiliate and outlaw them, worked out in the offices of the bureaucracy and then put into practice, included bans on keeping domestic pets, on sitting on park benches, and on using public transport.

The final stage, the physical destruction of the Jews, was achieved by the compulsory wearing of the Star of David from September 1941, the deportations which were already under way, and by genocide in the execution pits and extermination camps of Eastern Europe.

After the defeat of the Nazi regime, the initial reaction to events was one of silence and horror. It was followed by various responses to the catastrophe, sometimes existing side-by-side and sometimes consecutive. After Auschwitz – and even because of it – unconscious guilt and distress combined to produce a new antisemitism. This was articulated in many ways, in anti-Zionism and criticism of Israel as well as through more traditional forms.[12] However, there

[12]See Werner Bergmann and Rainer Erb (eds.), *Antisemitismus in der politischen Kultur nach 1945*, Opladen 1990; Herbert A. Strauss, Werner Bergmann, Christhard Hoffmann (eds.), *Der Antisemitismus der Gegenwart*, Frankfurt a. Main–New York 1990.

was a step forward in that antisemitic prejudices could no longer be played on in public on German soil.

A diametric reaction against disguised hostility to Jews is unconsidered philosemitism, the exponents of which frequently lack any knowledge either of Jewish culture and identity or of the historical facts. But both these responses, the antisemitic and the philosemitic, are limited to a minority. The majority of Germans were first overcome by the emotional horror of events at the end of the 1970s, as a consequence of the television series *Holocaust*. Even though the effect was short-lived, there is no reason for arrogance – from historians, for example – about the use of non-academic methods in the attempt to enlighten and explain. Whatever its faults, the *Holocaust* series made more people think about what had happened than ever before.

The most recent reaction, created from a combination of underlying philosemitism and regret over the loss of cultural substance caused by Nazi racial policy, has been a revival of the legend of German-Jewish symbiosis. Possibly this also occurred as an unconscious rejection of mass emotions, since the invocation of symbiosis is naturally a matter for the intellectuals.

The legend of an intimate co-existence of "Germans" and "Jews" to the benefit of both – for that is what symbiosis means – is false. For one thing, it is held to refer to the conditions of prominent assimilated Jews, to men such as Samuel Fischer and Walther Rathenau, Albert Einstein and Bruno Walter. Yet these are men whose Jewishness can be defined only by the fact that, despite their assimilation, they remained targets for antisemitic abuse. Retrospectively, they are now being reclaimed for German culture, as Jews, in order to support the theory of symbiosis. On the other hand, it never occurs to anyone to use Jewish cattle-dealers and stockbrokers to make the point instead.

In fact, the theory was based on Jews no longer behaving in a Jewish way. For that reason, baptism was demanded as an avowal of German culture and patriotism, and non-Jews regarded prominent Jews as Germans only on a provisional basis. As soon as people thought they could detect "Jewish characteristics", then the response – according to the level of education – was to say "Aha!" or even "*Saujud*".

Furthermore, the co-existence of Jewish and non-Jewish Germans which was called symbiosis – and which was generally tolerable for the minority – functioned only when conditions were good. Long before Hitler came to power the Jews had adequate reason to fear physical and psychological violence, although it was not an everyday event before 1933.[13] Thereafter, however, they quickly found it impossible to rely on even a minimum of solidarity and decency or even the barest sense of justice; these should surely have been available as a matter of course in the social life of a cultured nation, particularly given the high degree of assimilation of the German Jews. It took less than two years – from the Jewish boycott of 1st April 1933 to the Nuremberg Laws of September 1935 – to destroy the foundations of co-existence. This in itself is a strong argument

---

[13]Numerous examples in Werner Jochmann, *Gesellschaftskrise und Judenfeindschaft in Deutschland 1870–1945*, Hamburg 1988, esp. pp. 99ff.

against any assumption of a symbiosis. Though many German Jews could not fully comprehend the destruction of their social existence and tolerated the loss of their livelihood, the increasing discrimination and deprivation of rights; though they found it almost impossible to believe that even their lives were under threat – these facts cannot be used to support the legend of symbiosis.

Many Jews feel a particular aversion to the term symbiosis because of the link with the natural sciences and the potential association with parasitism. In fact, parasitism is quite different from symbiosis. But even if the analogy stands, would the Jews have been the parasites and the non-Jews – simply by right of numbers – the generous host? If we examine the "Aryanisation" of Jewish wealth, the accompanying circumstances as well as the financial value, it is easy to come to the opposite conclusion to the one so tirelessly propagated by Goebbels.

It remains to ask who the advocates of the legend of German-Jewish symbiosis are, and why Jews should be concerned with it. Is it an attempt, based on ignorance and good will, to repair something which never existed and which, if it had existed, could never be repaired in any case? Or is it an attempt to simplify history, arising from lack of knowledge? Such an attempt would be disastrous, particularly in its tendency to limit the origins of the catastrophe to the actions of a small minority of powerful criminals. Another effect would be to exclude from consideration the great majority of Germany's half a million Jews, by reclaiming for German culture only those Jews who took a prominent role in art, science and intellectual life (though not, it should be noted, the great businessmen and bankers).

The names cited in such arguments are always Nobel Prize winners like Albert Einstein, Lise Meitner and Fritz Haber, writers such as Lion Feuchtwanger and Kurt Tucholsky, publishers like Schocken and Ullstein, philosophers such as Martin Buber and Hannah Arendt, actors such as Fritz Kortner and Therese Giese, musicians and painters such as Otto Klemperer, Leo Blech, Max Liebermann and Max Oppenheimer. One consequence is already emerging. The mourning for Germany's cultural losses amounts to virtual self-pity, and sometimes takes on the nature of a reproach directed towards those German Jews who managed to escape, on the grounds that they were removing themselves from German culture.

In the logic of this reproach there lies another: that, by their actions, the émigrés actually did harm to German culture. In the last analysis, this kind of stress on the legend of German-Jewish symbiosis can even give rise to new accusations against the émigrés and the murder victims. Then, indeed, the circle of misconception would once again be complete.

Emancipation History – Limits of Revisionism in the Post-Holocaust Period

Comments on the Papers of Arno Herzig, Michael Graetz, Werner E. Mosse and Wolfgang Benz

BY HERBERT A. STRAUSS

For reasons worth pondering, German Jewry's post-mortem standing in the estimate of scholars and within the wider community has reached levels it did not enjoy consistently during its lifetime. There is growing recognition that the process of culture change which began in the eighteenth century, most visibly in the German states, was just that, a multiform social process, not subject to individual decision. Jewry has become part of the modern world, however one wishes to define Jewish "modernity".* As the late (and much mourned) Gershom Cohen and others formulated it, German Jewry has emerged in its post-modern image as the "mirror of modernity".[1]

Some of the consequences of this understanding have appeared in post-1945 German-Jewish historiography. As Reinhard Rürup has pointed out,[2] what the Leo Baeck Institute began in 1956 has become a major international enterprise beyond the wildest dreams of the founders. The last decade or two have witnessed expanded and intensified work in the USA, Israel, Great Britain, and by no means last or least, the German Federal Republic. It has allowed new generations to enter the field, and new perspectives to be gained, *Erkenntnisziele*

Scholars and scholarship on German Jewry owe immense gratitude to Arnold Paucker, whose tenure as editor of the Year Book of the Leo Baeck Institute ends with this issue. He has made the difficult succession he stepped into a brilliant success, as the Year Book continued to be kept open for the major innovations in our discipline. That the Year Book has stayed in the forefront of international research under his editorship, during a period of major expansion and intensification, has laid the foundation for continued excellence. I shall be among the many who will miss his broad grasp of the field, his integrity, and his warm humanity.

*The papers to which the following comments refer were presented at the 38th *Versammlung Deutscher Historiker* in Bochum on 27th September 1990. The panel (Section 6 of nineteenth- and twentieth-century history) was sponsored by the *Verband zur Erforschung der Geschichte der deutschen Juden* under the title: 'Akkulturation und Identität: Deutsche Juden im Spannungsfeld der Modernisierungen'. The author is grateful to the President of this *Verband*, Professor Alfred Haverkamp, Trier, for assistance and advice in the organisation of the panel at the *Historiker-Versammlung*.

[1]Gershom Cohen, 'German Jewry as Mirror of Modernity', Introduction to *LBI Year Book XX* (1975), pp. IX–XXXI.
[2]Reinhard Rürup, 'An Appraisal of German-Jewish Historiography', Introduction to *LBI Year Book XXXV* (1990), pp. XV–XXIV.

have diversified, the archival and source bases have been broadened, research and writing have focused on new topics. One of the more significant results of this generational change is a thorough professionalisation. The conceptual framework of German-Jewish history has been searched for its intellectual, political, or social context, e.g. terms like emancipation, assimilation,[3] normalis-ation, Nationalism, German-Jewish symbiosis, in fact the implications of Jewish existence in the German context, between Eastern European and, say, American culture. German-Jewish history, by becoming the prototype of Jewish modernity – for better and for worse, of course – has been de-ideologised and de-mythologised. As the dust has settled, individuals have become "social types", their behaviour has begun to be understood as beyond praise or blame and political invective; their choices limited by the cultural range of their periods and life situations.

Specifically, German-Jewish historiography has been approached with the intellectual tools of a vastly expanding, even amorphous discipline – history – and thus has fulfilled the methodological postulates of *Wissenschaft des Judentums* for broad conceptual inclusiveness. *Geisteswissenschaftlich* preferences have been complemented and in significant areas by-passed by social science concepts and methods, and not only in the related field of research on antisemitism.

The four short papers to be commented upon reflect this intellectual situation. They were of course subject to the limitation of space and time, and their authors wisely did not attempt to impart basic information or construct coherent narratives. This was to be expected, given the enormous expansion of the field. The contributions were to reflect on research frontiers. Arno Herzig chose the German background of emancipation in the *Vormärz* period; Michael Graetz dwelled on the internal development of Jewish communal organisation in the eighteenth and early nineteenth centuries; Werner Mosse interpreted the role of German Jews in Prussian "high society" during the *fin de siècle*; Wolfgang Benz, finally, concentrated on German-Jewish relations as a problem in cross-cultural "symbiosis". Thus, what united the presentations was the topic of Jewish modernisation as conceptualised in the value-free terms "acculturation" (the fusion of cultural traits in situations of cultural encounters) and "identity" (the auto-stereotype in which the continuities and discontinuities of behaviour and attitudes are fixed), in this case especially in a culture or cultures deriving moral values from fixed identities or prescribed significant behaviour .

The following comments will concentrate on concepts and methods, and their relevance for the present state of German-Jewish history.

Arno Herzig uses social history methods to examine the key factors in the slow advance of emancipation legislation after 1815. His literary design – after so much resistance how is it that emancipation succeeded within two years after 1848? – points to the use he has made of recent and current research[4] on the

[3]Cf. David Sorkin, 'Emancipation and Assimilation. Two Concepts and their Application to German-Jewish History', in *LBI Year Book XXXV* (1990), pp. 17–33.
[4]Rainer Erb and Werner Bergmann, *Die Nachtseiten der Judenemanzipation. Der Widerstand gegen die Integration der Juden in Deutschland 1780–1860*, Berlin 1989.

Nachtseiten (the dark undersides) of emancipation. Concentrating on the social composition of the opposition, he brings his considerable experience with topic and period to bear on a sombre picture of classes made insecure by the transition from agrarian, semi-feudal, or guild-controlled systems to the free market. "Governments did not bear the prime responsibility for putting the brakes on development towards a bourgeois society in which Jews would have an equal place, but . . . groups [once] privileged . . . [now] opposed to any reorganisation and [typecasting] Jews as beneficiaries or initiators of the new system." His reading of the (admittedly hard to interpret) sources suggests to him that resistance was centralised in the old (petty trading) bourgeoisie and the guild-controlled artisans, whom he also sees at work behind the violent protests (riots) of the period, from the "hep hep" disturbances starting in Würzburg in 1819 to the widespread unrest of 1848 directed against government, land-owning nobles and, precisely, Jews as symbols of the new system imposed from above in South-West Germany and elsewhere. In including references to the analysis of violent protest movements, Herzig represents an effective and innovative trend in German social history (to which he has made previous important contributions).[5]

Thus, his study becomes a thesis paper, postulating a constant trend: "The liberal position was always under threat in Germany. Anti-Jewish resentments could always be revived. The element of danger . . . remained only just below the surface even in liberal phases of German history." Herzig extends the German *Sonderweg* into the *Vormärz*. As applied to the politics of emancipation in the *Bundesstaaten*, however, it offers several difficulties. Social history as applied here amounts to a rationalist fallacy, if the negative image is derived from the interest calculations of opponents alone: the period saw riots based on religious traditions (accusations of ritual murder); Protestant pastors and synods passed resolutions opposing emancipation, etc. Stereotype precedes the selective perception of a "counter-symbol". The identification of the opposition with pre-modern strata bars the insight into the division beginning between Liberals and Democrats (populists) and the social conditions of newly disadvantaged groups below and to the Left of the bourgeoisie. Social analysis should be applied to bureaucrats as well, precisely because their social and economic interests (foreign and finance ministries) and their support for government-sponsored *laissez faire* (economics ministries) had made them influential actors in the cumbersome search for consensus. Even Friedrich Wilhelm IV of Prussia was unable to stop modernising legislation if it helped Prussia's power, army, or economy.

A shift to day from night aspects of emancipation controversies within the state systems and a return to clear periodisation for structural changes would correct some of the imbalances in the important insights this paper offers. The

---

[5]For the first comprehensive analysis of anti-Jewish riots 1815–1849 see Stefan Rohrbacher, *Antijüdische Ausschreitungen in Deutschland in der Zeit der Restauration, Vormärz und Revolution (1815–1848/49)*, phil. diss., Technische Universität Berlin, 1990 (being prepared for publication), bibl. pp. 349–366.

solution to the author's rhetorical query might lie in extending focus and social-political analysis to these "day" aspects as well.

Michael Graetz's discussion of the transformation of Jewish communal structures adds some significant touches to a well-researched story. Like Selma Stern-Taeubler, he conceives the break-up of traditional autonomy in the context of absolutist power politics and economic statism. Because states needed Jews to provide funds for central authorities, they extended increasing control over their source, the community, just as they fought bitter battles with the estates of their as yet motley territories to secure military and fiscal ascendancy. Jewish businessmen and financial agents are seen as the driving forces of communal self-destruction which, quite correctly, is linked with the politics of rationality in dispensing justice and administration. It may be too modish to call the very thin layer of businessmen, physicians, petty traders and petty craftsmen, that early, a *Besitzbürgertum*, just as the term *Bildungsbürgertum* is several rungs too high for the minuscule and diverse secular intelligentsia (almost invisible outside Berlin and probably a few other settlements). Like Stern-Taeubler, Graetz sees the core of organisational transformation in the loss of the court monopoly of the rabbis or communal functionaries. As social component (*Trägerschicht*) for this transition period (up to 1830) Graetz correctly identifies a rising Jewish middle class, however defined, and contrasts their self-image with the actuality of in-group behaviour as expressed in informal associations (*Vereine*). The conclusion is that German-Jewish emancipation created an ethnic type of religious minority (the term subculture might have been more suggestive and operational compared to the more questionable, primarily political, term "minority"). The "Eigenständigkeit" (particularism) of the Jewish *embourgeoisement* is properly alluded to even if the dimensions (religious, settlement pattern, sociability, sense of universal rejection – "*Judenschmerz*") appear too narrow for subculture analysis. (Were not Jews "bourgeois" before *Bürgertum*?)

This, of course, puts forward the revisionist view, well represented in what one may call the "Jerusalem school" whose tendency to see national trends in every period Graetz avoids by using the term "ethnic", as in American research. The paper does not fully avoid moral censure and nostalgic projections inconsistent with the social history approach. It personalises where process and structure explain reality better. It should also be remembered that to focus on rabbinical jurisdiction as a symbol of cultural break-up is much too narrow: rabbis never had jurisdiction in criminal cases, criticisms of rabbinical objectivity were frequent before new classes demanded that procedure and decision-processes be less subjective. Government interferences in communal organisation – including those requested by the Orthodox – were legion, etc. The newly emancipated as well as the locally elected Jewish representatives in the numerous *Gemeinden* had long tried to replace rabbinical leadership and jurisdiction for their own benefit and interest, not those of government tax collectors. Here, in the social analysis of Jewish structures, the choice of topic has limited the range. I would question whether by 1830 German political thought or behaviour formed society "according to the criteria of the modern nation state": that the new *Vereine* had not been modelled after the considerable intermediate associational structure characteristic of pre-emancipation congregations from Poznań to Cologne, and that the political and social environment in which Jews moved at the time was as globally hostile as generalised by the author in his closing remarks. Given the incomplete state of research for the period, the author's understanding of continued Jewish ethnicity needs to be related a.o. to the expanding Jewish role in local politics, increasing administrative links between Jews and bureaucracies on nearly all levels, including compulsory military service (1845). Jewish *Honoratioren* (among them Rubo, Zunz and Muhr for Berlin, Akiba Eger for Poznań, etc.), advised on the preparation of the law of 1847, and instead of dissolving Jewish communal structures this law, however deficient in many aspects, created a firm communal structure, based on compulsory membership, for Jewish life in Prussia.

The last two papers finally reviewed here, centre around a similar historic problem, but approach it with dissimilar methods and assumptions. Mosse lives up to the challenge of the original panel, to relate identity to integration as the main issue in German-Jewish modernisation. Selecting the family as the basic unit of analysis – in adaptation of Namierite prosopographic techniques – Mosse constructs thumb-nail sketches of some of the most successful clans among this small and *nouveau arrivé* top group among (mostly Berlin or North-German) Jews. They are judiciously selected to cover the range of "social types" (Simmel/Troeltsch) with respect to maintenance of Jewish communality, ritual, associational ties, endogamy, or sociability, and their integration is pronounced a success within the range of attitude clusters (also over generations) representing the different types constructed.

One may question whether making a lot of money also makes a man a representative archetype of the group he comes from. German Jewry, recent research has increasingly stressed, was made up of diverse population groups, who found themselves at a great variety of points on the acculturation continuum that must be used to operationalise "integration". Two of Mosse's typical families originate from Poznań; one from one of the numerous pockets and regions of solid (and stolid) German-Jewish Orthodoxy. Silesian and Poznań Jewries provided much of the dynamics of Berlin or Breslau Jewries, followed by Eastern European immigrants embarking subsequently on acculturation processes. The break-up of rural Jewry does not necessarily imply cultural urbanisation, i.e. loss of orthoprax orientation or communal loyalty – a common error of ecologists. Thus, forms and types of modernisation (acculturation, Jewish roles in culture, business, or politics) would offer more representative avenues to the variety of cultural situations in question. German Jewry has been too frequently reconstructed from sources centring on a few and select cosmopolitan groups (because they were there . . . ?) whose local settlement roots usually did not reach beyond one or two generations. At present, emphasis lies on local and group studies along carefully constructed methodological lines, linked with increasing clarification of the conceptual foundations and working hypotheses.

But does Mosse answer the provocatively argued restatement of Scholem's life-long and ever-renewed attack on the viability of Diaspora Jewish dialogue with their Christian (-German) environment proffered in Wolfgang Benz's passionate *plaidoyer*? It is somewhat ironic that the thesis of the illusionary symbiosis between Germans and Jews during emancipation is revived by Benz as a critique of post-war German attitudes towards the Holocaust, Nazism, Israel and Jews in general. Its roots, of course, were in the revolution of Jewish politics brought about by pre-1914 Zionism and the controversial and intensely passionate function it served in the (very Germanic-authoritarian) storm and stress between the generations in the Scholem family. Scholem's re-interpretation of Jewish history (recently under attack)[6] and his *sh'liluth hagolah* form the political background, a form of a Jewish national counter-myth, in Frantz Fanon's verbiage, against the myth of the euphoric harmony of Berlin Jewish life as Scholem knew it. Scholem's one attempt (the only one known to this writer) to present the observation in more than autobiographical form[7] falls short of the quantitative precision needed for demographically based observations, but is a far cry from the stereotyped use made of his charmingly provocative forays in cultural journalism. He knew full well the differentiation and complexity of German acceptance of Jews. It has long been an empirically established commonplace that minorities do not seamlessly fuse with majorities once and for all – and in all situations of mutuality and encounter. Identity as an empirical concept is as much in need of deconstruction as is the myth that the infinite numbers and kinds of social roles assumed by both sides in infinitely varied situations can be generalised in one-dimensional concepts. Symbiosis, biological handbooks tell us, covers a great variety of animal and plant behaviour, from mutual exploitation to life-giving co-operation.[8] The empirical weight of one hundred and fifty years of emancipation history – and the post-Holocaust ubiquity of modernisation – require demythologisation to give full rein to this "mirror of modernity" in the self-understanding of the present.

[6]David Myers, 'The Scholem-Kurzweil Debate and Jewish Historiography', in *Modern Judaism*, October 1966, pp. 261–286.
[7]Gershom Scholem, 'Zur Sozialpsychologie der Juden in Deutschland 1900–1930', in Rudolf von Thadden (ed.), *Die Krise des Liberalismus zwischen den Weltkriegen*, Göttingen 1978, pp. 250–277.
[8]That symbiosis was an acceptable term to Zionist functionaries to describe the entire range of Jewish activities in German society (not only culture, as suggested by the title) was established in 1956 by Siegfried Moses, then Comptroller of the State of Israel, who became President of the Leo Baeck Institute on the death of Leo Baeck. Cf. *LBI Year Book I* (1956), p. XV. All agreed that it had its problems, but none questioned its existence. When Scholem used it, it denoted a broad range of biological behaviour; cf. the popular dtv, *Atlas zur Biologie*, München 1987, pp. 254–257.

Jewish Identity and Antisemitism

Socialism and Judeophobia – Antisemitism in Europe before 1914

BY ROBERT S. WISTRICH

The relationship between Socialism and antisemitism is a rather obscure chapter in European history which only began to attract the attention of historians in the aftermath of the Second World War. Perhaps the first systematic attempt by a historian to investigate the attitudes of Social Democracy in Central Europe to the phenomenon of antisemitism was made by Paul Massing in his book, *Rehearsal for Destruction*. Massing, himself an exiled (non-Jewish) Social Democrat forced to flee from Nazi Germany, came to the conclusion that:

> "the socialists never wavered in their stand against all attempts to deprive Jews of their civil rights. They treated with contempt the antisemitic agitators and the groups behind them. They never gave in to the temptation – considerable at times – to gain followers by making concessions to anti-Jewish prejudice."[1]

Massing's thesis, based exclusively on the analysis of positions adopted by the German labour movement before 1914, argued that the Social Democrats were the most consistent champions of equal rights for the Jewish minority in Imperial Germany and that they became immunised during this period against antisemitic tendencies. Indeed, Massing claimed that not only did the German Social Democrats consistently battle against antisemitism, they were also the first theoreticians to provide a coherent sociological analysis of the phenomenon. He pointed out that they correctly perceived the special attraction of antisemitism for the decaying *Mittelstand*, for the small peasantry, a section of the Junker aristocracy and the semi-proletarianised intelligentsia.

The antisemitism of these social groups, adversely affected by industrialisation and modernisation, was, according to the German Socialists, the product of their mistaken view of the role played by Jews in the capitalist economy. Once these declining social strata came to grasp the real nature of their misery and to realise that the allegedly exploitative role of the Jews was a temporary, historically-conditioned phenomenon, they would gravitate towards Social Democracy. The "Jewish Question", according to this view (pioneered by Friedrich Engels and August Bebel), was an incidental by-product of the class struggle in modern bourgeois society. It would be resolved by the victory of

I would like to acknowledge here the dedicated and highly professional editorial work, over many years, of Arnold Paucker and to thank him for his help as Editor with my own contributions to the Year Book.

[1] Paul W. Massing, *Rehearsal for Destruction. A Study of Political Antisemitism in Imperial Germany*, New York 1949, p. 151.

Socialism which was opposed in both theory and practice to all forms of antisemitism. Massing's account of the position adopted by the German Social Democrats was in broad terms accepted by many later historians – Marxist and non-Marxist alike. Indeed, modern Communist historiography has invariably stretched this line of argument to claim that Socialism, in general, is by its very nature immune to antisemitism.[2]

The Communist position, echoed on this point by Trotskyist and New Left historiography in the West, defines antisemitism in purely instrumental class terms as:

> "one of the most brutal weapons, which the exploiting classes utilise to stabilise and extend their position of power (*Machtposition*)".[3]

Since capitalism and its exploiting classes are held to be responsible for the existence of a "Jewish Question" and for aggravating antisemitism, it is a self-evident truth for many Marxists that Socialism – as part of the solution to the problem – must be *a priori* immune to anti-Jewish prejudice.[4] We find another influential variation on the Marxist position in Jean-Paul Sartre's sweeping assertion that there are "hardly any anti-Semites among the workers", because "the workman sees society as the product of real forces acting in accordance with rigorous laws".[5] Sartre's assumption, like that of many more orthodox Marxists, is that the socio-economic conditions of the working class and the way its individual members supposedly view the world (i.e. through the prism of historical materialism) preclude the proletariat from adopting antisemitic attitudes. Independent sociological investigations such as the study by James Robb of the British working class in East London have, in fact, long ago shown this thesis to be empirically false.[6] Yet many sociologists have found it difficult to abandon.

More surprising, perhaps, is the readiness of some Liberal historians to credit the idea of an inborn immunity of the labour movement to antisemitism. A typical variant of this argument is presented by Peter Pulzer, who suggests that because Social Democracy has been concerned traditionally with universal emancipation, with spreading education, combating poverty, tyranny and evil, it is inevitably opposed to the antisemitic creed which "set forth the primacy of the national and the integral over the universal".[7] In more recent years, this assumption that Socialism with its universalist, emancipatory ideals is somehow irreconcilable with an antisemitic "world-view" has been clearly disproved by developments in contemporary history.

Already, the anti-Jewish motifs in the "anti-cosmopolitan" campaigns that occurred in the Socialist countries, e.g. the Soviet Union (1948–1953) and

---

[2]E.g. Walter Mohrmann, *Antisemitismusideologie und Geschichte im Kaiserreich und in der Weimarer Republik*, Berlin (East) 1972.

[3]*Ibid.*, p. 11; see also I. Rennap, *Anti-Semitism and the Jewish Question*, London 1942.

[4]Abram Leon, *The Jewish Question. A Marxist Interpretation*, New York 1970, pp. 257ff.

[5]Jean-Paul Sartre, *Anti-Semite and Jew*, New York 1973, pp. 35–36.

[6]James Robb, *Working-Class Anti-Semite. A Psychological Study in a London Borough*, London 1954.

[7]Peter G. J. Pulzer, *The Rise of Political Anti-Semitism in Germany & Austria*, 2nd revised edn., London 1988, p. 252.

Eastern Europe, began to shake the confidence of more independent-minded Liberal and Marxist scholars. The so-called "anti-Zionist" crusades directed against Jews in post-Stalinist Russia, in Communist Poland (1967–1968, 1970, and again as recently as 1981), in Czechoslovakia (1968–1970) and the militant antisemitic type of anti-Israelism still manifested by sections of the Western old and new Left, have further called into question many long-held assumptions about the relation of Socialism to antisemitism. This and other factors have led even some modern German historians on the Left of the political spectrum to reassess, a little more critically, the record of the Social Democrats on the "Jewish Question". Reinhard Rürup acknowledges, for example, that the pre-1914 Socialists seriously underestimated the strength and staying-power of antisemitism and that a negative image of Jews was quite widespread among the working classes of Central Europe. Official Party opposition to political antisemitism, he admits, was not necessarily incompatible with anti-Jewish resentment and prejudices among many rank-and-file Socialists, though he tends to play down the significance of the latter phenomenon.[8]

Another study of German Social Democracy, written from a Socialist viewpoint, has shown that while the party-political press and most of its major leaders did indeed fight against antisemitism before 1914, their struggle was not carried over successfully into the cultural sphere. In popular working-class literature, in caricatures, *feuilletons*, anecdotes, verses, short stories and serial novels, traditional antisemitic stereotypes continued to flourish unchecked. Though derivative in other respects, this study breaks new ground in showing that the Social Democratic subculture in Imperial Germany, its vocabulary, images and associations remained as tainted with familiar anti-Jewish values and modes of thought as the dominant bourgeois German culture.[9] The glaring gap between the political and cultural work of the Social Democrats meant, therefore, that conventional prejudices against Jews remained largely unaffected by the official opposition of the leadership to antisemitism in the German labour movement. Nevertheless, while more differentiated than Massing's original thesis, both Leuschen-Seppel and Rürup basically repeat the standard contention that Social Democracy as an emancipatory movement was uncompromisingly opposed to political antisemitism.

A diametrically contrary theory was propounded over thirty years ago by the Israeli scholar Edmund Silberner who wrote that modern Socialism in general is characterised by a "long-standing antisemitic tradition", so much so that "Socialist antisemitism" can be classified as a specific brand of modern antisemitism.[10] Silberner's pioneering study, the first major interpretation that discussed the antisemitic tradition in modern Socialism as a whole, drew on a

[8]Reinhard Rürup, 'Sozialismus und Antisemitismus in Deutschland vor 1914', in Walter Grab (ed.), *Juden und Jüdische Aspekte in der Deutschen Arbeiterbewegung 1848–1918*, Tel-Aviv 1976, pp. 203–227.
[9]Rosemarie Leuschen-Seppel, *Sozialdemokratie und Antisemitismus im Kaiserreich*, Bonn 1978, pp. 231–279.
[10]Edmund Silberner, 'The Anti-Semitic Tradition in Modern Socialism', Inaugural Lecture, Hebrew University, 4th January 1953; *idem*, *Ha-Sotsialism ha-maravi ve-shelelat ha-yehudim*, Jerusalem 1955. More recently Silberner reiterated his earlier thesis in *Kommunisten zur Judenfrage*, Opladen 1983, adding some new material on Polish and German Communism.

broad range of sources in various European languages and did not confine itself solely to the German case. Silberner claimed that there was a consistent anti-Jewish mode of thought which was characteristic of European Socialist ideologues and political leaders. He regarded the youthful essay of Karl Marx, *Zur Judenfrage*, written in 1844, as "the source" of this basic endemic antisemitism. Silberner's work was attacked, even by those who relied on his documentation, for quoting selectively and out of context; it was pointed out by critics that Marx's position had to be analysed in the framework of his overall thought at the time and that his articles of 1844 had little actual effect on the further development of German or Russian Social Democracy. Similarly, it was argued that anti-Jewish remarks made by other Socialist politicians, ideologues or writers did not necessarily constitute a structural phenomenon called "Socialist antisemitism" which could be differentiated from bourgeois antisemitism.

Silberner's simple definition of antisemitism as a "hostile" or "unfriendly" attitude to Jews was regarded, with some justification, as too sweeping and methodologically inadequate. According to such a definition (or lack of definition) it was suggested that only very small, marginal groups in European society could be considered as non-antisemitic. In so far as Silberner's critics did acknowledge a partial validity to his thesis they have generally confined it to the early (pre-Marxist) Socialist movement, in contrast to the class-conscious organised labour movement that developed in advanced capitalist countries. The sweeping identification of Jews with capitalism by early Socialists was characterised as part of the birth-pains of the labour movement which in its mature phase could and did dispense with "primitive" antisemitic stereotypes. We intend to show later with examples from France, Germany, Russia, Britain and Austria-Hungary that the evidence does not warrant this apologetic interpretation.

An extension of Silberner's thesis first appeared in 1968 with George Lichtheim's seminal article on 'Socialism and the Jews', which analysed the anti-Jewish current in the European labour movement before 1914 as being:

> "rooted in a complex of attitudes going back to the French Revolution and its impact upon traditional society".[11]

Lichtheim, while drawing extensively on Silberner's source material shifted the focus of his attention to

> "the complex process whereby European socialism in general, and French socialism in particular, *shed* its anti-Semitic aspects".[12]

He considered the intertwining of the anti-capitalist and the anti-Jewish theme in nineteenth-century Socialist literature to be a consequence of the French Revolution, which had simultaneously unshackled the Jews and the market economy. Antipathy to Jewish emancipation and bourgeois liberalism was not, therefore, accidental among the early Socialists (e.g. the Fourierists) who advocated a return to communitarian values and were hostile to the economic

[11]George Lichtheim, 'Socialism and the Jews', in *Dissent* (July–August 1968), p. 314.
[12]*Ibid.*

individualism of modern capitalist society, exemplified for them by Jewish high finance (*la haute banque*). Because he focused on French rather than German Socialists, Lichtheim's analysis tended to reinforce Silberner's thesis, although on a philosophical rather than historical level. At the same time it also appealed to some Marxist critics by arguing that:

> "anti-Semitism could and did become an element of the *primitive* system of ideas in which the anti-capitalist reaction of the 1830s and 1840s at first presented itself".[13]

Lichtheim followed Silberner in characterising the French Socialists, Alphonse Toussenel (1803–1885), Pierre Leroux (1797–1871), Pierre Joseph Proudhon (1809–1865) and Auguste Blanqui as "antisemites" who saw in the Jews the incarnation of the spirit of Mammon, the inventors of the banking system and the representatives of a new industrial feudalism. However, he also pointed to the streak of primitive barbarism, the hostility to "civility" and urban civilisation which, in his view, linked the Russian revolutionary anarchist Bakunin with Proudhon and lay behind the visceral antisemitism of both men. Lichtheim did not deny that Socialist Judeophobia in France continued to be a factor throughout the nineteenth century, but suggested that the Marxist "internationalist" wing of the labour movement gradually prevailed over the tradition of purely "French" antisemitic Socialism, whether Fourierist, Blanquist or Proudhonist.

During the Dreyfus Affair (1894–1906) the national "Socialist" antisemitism of the French Left was allegedly vanquished by a republican, universalist non-antisemitic Socialism represented by Jean Jaurès. One problem with this thesis is that the anti-Dreyfusard, antisemitic type of national "Socialism" did not disappear in France in the twentieth century and was indeed to enjoy a kind of belated revival under the Vichy regime (1940–1944). Moreover, the anarcho-syndicalists, beginning with Georges Sorel at the turn of the twentieth century, continued to employ the standard vocabulary of antisemitism and this provided one of the primary roots for their *rapprochement* on the eve of the 1914 war with the integral Nationalists of *Action Française*. The extreme Left and the Nationalist Right found common ground in France after the Dreyfus Affair in their hatred of Jewish finance, Jewish intellectualism, Liberal-Republican democracy and bourgeois parliamentarianism. The Proudhonist tradition of national Socialism was revived in France by both Left and Right, as demonstrated by Zeev Sternhell, providing one of the major ideological roots of modern fascism during *La Belle Epoque*.[14] Earlier research by the American historian George L. Mosse, since then more extensively confirmed by Sternhell, has shown, moreover, that the French Right did penetrate the working classes with national "Socialist", xenophobic and racist-antisemitic ideas before 1914.[15] This has still further

---

[13]*Ibid.*, p. 319.

[14]Zeev Sternhell, *La Droite Révolutionnaire 1885–1914. Les Origines Françaises du Fascisme*, Paris 1978, pp. 177–214; see also *idem, Ni Droite ni Gauche. L'idéologie fasciste en France*, Paris 1983.

[15]George L. Mosse, 'The French Right and the Working Classes. Les Jaunes', in *Journal of Contemporary History*, vol. VII, Nos. 3–4 (July–October 1972); Sternhell, *La Droite Révolutionnaire, op. cit.*, pp. 245–316.

undermined the simplistic notion that the industrial proletariat is necessarily immune to what Marxists usually classify as "reactionary bourgeois ideologies" like antisemitism.

Empirical historical research focused on France has tended, therefore, to indicate that some of the principal themes of twentieth-century antisemitism derived from a cross-fertilisation of concepts between Left and Right and that they resulted from the fusion of Socialist, Nationalist and Conservative ideology which eventually constituted a major component in inter-war fascism. A more far-reaching, if dubious variation on this theme, *L'idéologie française* (Paris 1981) by Bernard-Henri Lévy, argues indeed that just as Germany was originally the fatherland of Marxism, so France was and remains the classic land of fascism and "national" Socialism. The tradition of Socialist antisemitism can be looked at and analysed from this viewpoint as a component part of the dominant "French ideology", centred on the formula "France for the French" invented by such *fin-de-siècle* Nationalist thinkers as Edouard Drumont and Maurice Barrès. Antisemitism is then perceived as the most effective integrationist ideology to have transcended the Left-Right schism in French society.

Current historiography dealing more narrowly with Marx and his writing on the "Jewish Question", long ago challenged the conventional wisdom that Marxism as an internationalist ideology is impervious to antisemitism. The Franco-Jewish philosopher, Robert Misrahi, in his *Marx et la question juive* (Paris 1972) showed, for example, that structural antisemitism was indeed rooted in the mode of thought of the young Marx. But he argued that this was an archaic pattern of prejudice, a victory of passion over reason, a manifestation of opportunism and subjective choice rather than a sociological or political necessity for the labour movement. Others suggested that in the case of Marx and many of his Jewish disciples in the Socialist movement, anti-Jewish stereotypes had been internalised through the impact of the Christian cultural and Nationalist context in which they operated.[16]

More unequivocal is the verdict of those historians who, on the basis of their correspondence and journalistic articles, charge both Marx and Engels with antisemitic and racist tendencies.[17] They stress the extent to which Marx's antisemitism was in the past played down and even ignored: "in some popular socialist accounts of Marx's career published in the West and intended for radical and socialist consumption".[18]

In the 1970s, a painstakingly researched study by Julius Carlebach carefully re-examined the claim that Marx is the *fons et origo* of Socialist antisemitism as well as the subsequent polemical literature on the subject. Carlebach pointed out that the young Marx was indeed aggressively hostile to Jews and Judaism, but argued that once his conception of historical materialism had matured, his attitude became more balanced. In Marx's final period, Jews "ceased to be of

[16]Cf. Robert S. Wistrich, *Revolutionary Jews from Marx to Trotsky*, London 1976.
[17]W. H. Chaloner and W. O. Henderson, 'Marx/Engels and Racism', in *Encounter*, vol. XLV, No. 1 (July 1975), pp. 18–23.
[18]*Ibid.*, p. 22.

interest or consequence" to the author of *Das Kapital*.[19] Carlebach accepted that the second half of the young Marx's essay "must be regarded as an antisemitic document", one which gave an aura of social and philosophical respectability to ancient popular stereotypes. But Carlebach's book did not really tackle the crucial question as to how far and in what ways Marx's opinions on the Jews influenced the European labour movement.

This is indeed the principal theme of my study, which not only traces Marx's ideological influence, but demonstrates the multiple causes of antisemitism in the labour movement; these include retarded economic development in Central and Eastern Europe, the Christian cultural inheritance, the fragility of political Liberalism outside Western Europe, the intensity of national conflicts and the quality of leadership and class consciousness within the proletariat itself.[20] Without taking this multiplicity of factors into account within the broad context of late nineteenth- and early twentieth-century European society, culture and politics, one cannot hope to disentangle the complex relationship between Socialism and antisemitism from the coils of ideological partisanship and *a priori* dogma.

Having already looked at the historiography, I propose to begin this pan-European survey with an analysis of the period between 1830 and 1880, before the emergence of fully-fledged labour movements in the industrialising nations of the Continent. These were crucial, formative years, not only in the development of different schools of European Socialism, but also in the crystallisation of anti-Jewish stereotypes (some inherited from the Middle Ages and others of more recent origin) among radical ideologues of the Left.[21]

Before the 1880s the existing labour movements in Europe had not yet evolved into distinctive mass parties of industrial workers with a fully developed class-consciousness, an independent subculture or a virtually autonomous political ideology. Marxism had not yet been endorsed as the dominant ideology of any single European labour movement, though by 1880 it was beginning to consolidate its grip in Germany, partly as a result of Bismarck's anti-Socialist law which had outlawed the Social Democrats. Similarly, this was a period in which antisemitism itself had not yet matured in the form of organised political parties, though the late 1870s saw the embryonic beginnings of a mass movement in Germany, from whence it spread rapidly to Austria, Hungary and France.

For our purposes, the significant fact about the literary, ideological "anti-semitism" of the pre-1880 period (the term "antisemitism" was itself only invented by the German journalist, Wilhelm Marr, in 1879) was the extent of its debt to an earlier radical critique of Judaism pioneered in France and Germany during the 1840s. It was precisely this earlier period that had seen the emergence

[19]Julius Carlebach, *Karl Marx and the Radical Critique of Judaism*, London 1978, p. 357.
[20]Robert S. Wistrich, *Socialism and the Jews. The Dilemmas of Assimilation in Germany and Austria-Hungary*, London 1982.
[21]See *idem*, 'Radical Antisemitism in France and Germany', in *Israel and the Nations. Essays presented in Honor of Shmuel Ettinger* (in Hebrew), Jerusalem 1987, pp. 157–184, which discusses the years between 1840 and the mid-1870s.

of the concept of the "Jewish Question" and an extensive debate on emancipation, centred mainly in Germany.[22] It was in Young Hegelian circles, i.e. that section of the nascent radical German intelligentsia which stood outside established institutions in the Prusso-Christian state, that one can first observe in Germany the transition from a traditional anti-Judaism (rooted in Christian theological teaching) to a secular, "scientific" form of Jew-hatred.[23]

Modern racial antisemitism in Germany, like Marxism itself, grew out of this secular anti-Judaism expressed in the writings of such radicals as Bruno Bauer, Ludwig Feuerbach, Friedrich Daumer, Friedrich Wilhelm Ghillany, Richard Wagner and Wilhelm Marr. The Young Hegelians themselves built on the post-Christian (and anti-Christian) tradition of eighteenth-century French Enlightenment *philosophes* such as Voltaire and d'Holbach whose rationalist attack on the Old Testament held Jewry and Judaism responsible for the "barbarism", fanaticism and intolerant obscurantism which the Catholic Church had inflicted on the world.[24]

From Voltaire and the Baron d'Holbach through to Bruno Bauer and Karl Marx, Judaism was attacked as the root of Christianity and as a symbol of human self-alienation. The early French and German radicals bequeathed to the European labour movement not only their rationalist anti-clericalism, but a "scientific" negation of Judaism as a fossilised religion, tradition and way of life, as well as a hostile view of Jewry as an anti-social element. The leader of the Left Hegelians, Bruno Bauer, in his *Die Judenfrage* (1843) depicted Jews as an ahistorical people whose stubborn particularism conflicted with the law of progess. The Jewish "essence" was presented as unchanging, separatist, bound to an illusory Mosaic law which excluded Jews from participating in the real life of nations and made it impossible for the Christian state to grant them emancipation.[25]

Twenty years later, Bruno Bauer was to emerge as one of the founders of the new antisemitism in Germany, arguing that Jews were racially incompatible with the German *Volk*.[26] Bauer, as in 1843, continued to emphasise the unchanging character of the Jewish Law and the isolationism of the Jewish people; only now these characteristics were attributed to blood and race-factors which could not be eliminated by conversion to Christianity or total assimilation. Karl Marx's polemic against Bauer in 1844 significantly did not take issue with the anti-Jewish elements in his ex-mentor's writings. Indeed Marx emphasised that Bauer's critique of the Jewish religion, of "the religious opposition between Judaism and Christianity" and of the Christian State had been carried out "with

[22]Jacob Toury, 'The Jewish Question – A Semantic Approach', in *LBI Year Book XI* (1966), pp. 85–106.

[23]Shmuel Ettinger, 'Biqoret hadat ha-yehudit shel ha-Hegelianim ha-Tsairim', in *Ha-antishemiut ba-et ha-hadesha*, Tel-Aviv 1978; see also Wistrich, 'Radical Antisemitism in France and Germany', *loc. cit.*, pp. 157ff.

[24]Arthur Hertzberg, *The French Enlightenment and the Jews*, New York 1968.

[25]Zvi Rosen, 'The Anti-Jewish Opinions of Bruno Bauer (1838–1843)' (in Hebrew), in *Zion*, XXXIII (1968), pp. 59–76.

[26]Bruno Bauer, *Das Judentum in der Fremde*, Berlin 1863.

dash, clarity, wit and profundity, in a style which is as precise as it is pithy and vigorous".[27]

Where then did the founder of "scientific Socialism" (mature Marxism is generally dated from 1845/1846, a year or so after this essay, but Marx, it should be noted, never repudiated the writings of his youth) differ from the "antisemitic" Bauer? Here is Marx himself:

> "Let us consider the real Jews, not the *sabbath Jew*, whom Bauer considers, but the *everyday Jew*. Let us not seek the secret of the Jew in his religion, but let us seek the secret of his religion in the real Jew. What is the profane basis of Judaism? *Practical* need, *self-interest*. What is the worldly cult of the Jew? *Huckstering*. What is his worldly god? *Money*. Very well: then in emancipating itself from *huckstering* and *money*, and thus from real and practical Judaism, our age would emancipate itself.
> An organization of society which would abolish the preconditions and thus the very possibility of huckstering, would make the Jews impossible . . . In the final analysis, the *emancipation* of the Jews is the emancipation of mankind from *Judaism*."[28]

In these and other passages, Marx goes beyond Bruno Bauer and makes it clear that there will be no place for the Jew or Judaism in a truly liberated, human society (i.e. under conditions of Socialism). The Jew through whom "money has become a world power", who has "judaised" bourgeois society and "the practical spirit of the Christian nations", is for Marx the embodiment of egoism, commercialism and the capitalist spirit:

> "The god of the Jews has been secularized and has become the god of this world. The bill of exchange is the real god of the Jew."[29]

Marx's "solution" for the "Jewish Question" was indeed accepted in theory by the Marxist-orientated labour movement especially in Germany and Austria-Hungary – the assumption being that the overthrow of capitalism would remove "the *empirical* essence of Judaism – huckstering and its conditions". A Socialist society based on human needs would abolish the sway of material self-interest and the alienation of man from man. It would, therefore, make impossible the "Jew" understood as a symbol of capitalism. "The *social* emancipation of the Jew is the *emancipation of society from Judaism*."[30]

Undoubtedly, Socialists with antisemitic inclinations could and did interpret this identifying of Judaism with the practice of buying and selling in an anti-Jewish way. Such Socialists were, of course, impervious to the fact that Marx's concept of the capitalist Jew applied, if at all, at best to a minority of Jews in Western Europe (Germany, France, England, Holland etc.) and not at all to the majority of world Jewry who lived in the small towns or urban ghettos of tsarist Russia and Poland. Furthermore, it must be remembered that the 1844 essay (admired by Engels) was accompanied later by many highly uncomplimentary anti-Jewish remarks which appear in the Marx-Engels correspondence. (The first editors of this correspondence, the German Socialist leaders, August Bebel

[27]Karl Marx, 'On Bruno Bauer's *The Jewish Question*', in *Karl Marx. Early Writings*, transl. and ed. by T. B. Bottomore, New York 1964, pp. 1–40.
[28]*Ibid.*
[29]*Ibid.*
[30]*Ibid.*

and Eduard Bernstein, carefully excised these remarks from their edition – a fact which may attest to their own embarrassment at this aspect of the early Marxist legacy.) In many cases, Marx would add to the proper name of a Jew such expressions as "der Jud", or "der verfluchte Jude" while both he and Engels referred to their Socialist rival Ferdinard Lassalle (himself a self-hating Jew) as "Baron Itzig", "Jüdel Braun" or "Ephraim Gescheit" – all derogatory, anti-semitic epithets widely used in Germany at that time. Moses Hess, an associate of Marx, Engels and Lassalle in the German Socialist movement, observed in his Zionist classic, *Rome and Jerusalem*, of his own party comrades

> "that in every personal controversy they make use of this [antisemitic] 'hep' weapon, which in Germany seldom fails to have its effect".[31]

It was not only in private letters to Engels that Marx engaged in antisemitic outbursts. He savagely attacked Jewish financiers – Königswarter, Raphael, Stern, Rothschild, Mendelssohn, Bleichröder, Fould and many others – for co-operating in raising loans for the Russian government to finance the Crimean War.

> "Thus we find every tyrant backed by a Jew, as is every Pope by a Jesuit. In truth, the cravings of oppressors would be hopeless, and the practicability of war out of the question, if there were not an army of Jesuits to smother thought and a handful of Jews to ransack pockets."

Marx went on to lash out at the "loan-mongering Jews" of Amsterdam:

> "many of whom are engaged in this gambling and jobbing of securities . . . Here and there and everywhere that a little capital courts investment, there is ever one of these little Jews ready to make a little suggestion or place a little bit of a loan."

Marx concluded his article by recalling:

> "The fact that 1855 years ago Christ drove the Jewish money-changers out of the temple, and that the money-changers of our age enlisted on the side of tyranny happen again chiefly to be Jews, is perhaps no more than a historical coincidence. The loan-mongering Jews of Europe do only on a larger and more obnoxious scale what many others do on one smaller and less significant. But it is only because the Jews are so strong that it is timely and expedient to expose and stigmatise their organisation."[32]

There is a bitter irony in the fact that Marx, who so clearly detested his own race, should himself have been attacked as a Jew and the political movement he led stigmatised as a "Jewish conspiracy" by Socialist and anarchist rivals such as the Frenchman Proudhon, the Russian Bakunin and the German Eugen Dühring. Proudhon's celebrated quarrel with Marx was one factor which led the most influential thinker in the early French labour movement to observe in December 1847:

> "Jews – Write an article against this race which poisons everything, by meddling everywhere without ever joining itself to another people – Demand their expulsion from France, with the

---

[31]Moses Hess, 'Sechster Brief', in *idem, Rom und Jerusalem, die letzte Nationalitätsfrage*, Leipzig 1862, p. 47.

[32]The article, which originally appeared in the *New York Tribune*, 4th January 1856, was reprinted in Karl Marx, *The Eastern Question*, 1897, new edn. 1969, pp. 600–606. It is quoted in Chaloner and Henderson, *loc. cit.*

exception of individuals married to Frenchwomen – Abolish the synagogues; don't admit them to any kind of unemployment; pursue finally the abolition of this cult.

It is not for nothing that the Christians call them deicides. The Jew is the enemy of the human race. One must send this race back to Asia or exterminate it.

H. Heine, A. Weil, and others are nothing but secret spies; Rothschild, Crémieux, Marx, Fould – malignant beings, bilious, envious, acrid, etc., etc., who hate us. By fire or fusion, or by expulsion, the Jew must disappear . . .".[33]

These savage remarks were for private consumption only, though in published work, Proudhon showed that his hatred for Marx did not prevent him from sharing the latter's views on the "parasitic" role of the Jews and expressing this antipathy in brutal racist language.

"The Jew is by temperament an anti-producer, neither a farmer, nor an industrialist, nor even a true merchant. He is an intermediary, always fraudulent and parasitic, who operates in trade as in philosophy, by means of falsification, counterfeiting and horse-trading. He knows but the rise and fall of prices, the risks of transportation, the incertitudes of crops, the hazards of demand and supply. His policy in economics has always been entirely negative, entirely usurious. It is the evil principle, Satan, Ahriman incarnated in the race of Shem, which has already been twice exterminated by the Greeks and by the Romans, the first time at Tyre, the second time at Carthage."[34]

Bakunin and his followers, along with the Proudhonists, represented the chief opponents of Marx in the period of the First International (1864–1871), and were no less racist and antisemitic. The founder of Russian anarchism described the Jews as

"an exploiting sect, a bloodsucking people, a unique devouring parasite, tightly and intimately organised . . . cutting across all the differences in political opinion".[35]

In a passage dating from the end of 1871, Bakunin even asserted that Marx and the Rothschilds were linked by secret sympathies – the classic "Jewish conspiracy" thesis which was so effectively used by National Socialist propaganda during the twentieth century. Here is Bakunin's version:

"This may seem strange. What can there be in common between communism and high finance? The communism of Marx wants a mighty centralisation by the State, and where this exists there must nowadays inevitably be a Central State bank, and where such a bank exists, the parasitical Jewish nation, which speculates on the labour of the people, will always find a means to sustain itself."[36]

Bakunin's antisemitism was in fact shared by a section of the Russian revolutionary populists who later defended the pogroms of 1881 in Russia as a rising of the masses against the "Jewish Tsar", the nobility and the Jewish "exploiters". Typical of their prejudices was the reaction of the Ukrainian revolutionary, Yantsin, who wrote an angry letter in 1876 to the exiled Russian populist leaders Lavrov, Smirnov and their circle in London protesting against

[33]*Notebooks of P. J. Proudhon*, Paris 1960–1961, vol. II, pp. 337–338.

[34]Pierre Joseph Proudhon, *Césarisme et Christianisme*, Paris 1883. This was first published eighteen years after Proudhon's death and is quoted in Lichtheim, *loc. cit.*, p. 322.

[35]A. Lehning, A. J. C. Rüter and P. Scheibert (eds.), *Bakunin-Archiv*, Leiden 1963, vol. I, Part 2, pp. 124–126.

[36]'Rapports personnels avec Marx', in Bakunin, *Oeuvres*, vol. III, pp. 298–299. Quoted in Lichtheim, *loc. cit.*, p. 338.

the efforts of Aron Liberman[n], the first Hebrew Socialist, to integrate the struggle of the Jewish masses with the Russian revolutionary movement. Rejecting the idea of class divisions among the Russian Jews, the Ukrainian Socialist claimed that:

> "the weight of their [the Jews'] exploitation is great and their harmfulness unlimited . . . If we find it possible to preach revolution, and only revolution against the nobles, how can we defend the Jews? . . . We cannot have any faith in the laughable Yiddish International nor in the sympathies of the Yids for the Revolution."[37]

Another leading Ukrainian Socialist, Serge Podolinsky, declared in June 1876 that "in my view Yidophobia is as indispensable for every Russian socialist as is hatred of the bourgeoisie".[38] Podolinsky explicitly denied:

> "even the possibility of the existence in Russia (not only in the Ukraine) of socialist *Zhidy* [derogative term meaning "Yid"] being completely sincere in their behaviour as a socialist should be".[39]

The antisemitic prejudices of the Russian and Ukrainian Social Revolutionaries of this generation, active in the 1870s and early 1880s, were themselves shared by many Jews who had rebelled against their traditional Jewish heritage, were alienated from the Jewish collectivity and had adopted Russian culture. Vladimir Iokhelson, a friend of Aron Liberman and one of these Socialist Jews, explained their complete indifference to all things Jewish and their willingness to refer to Jews as kikes (*zhidy*) as a result of:

> "our estrangement from the culture of the Russian Jews and . . . our negative assessment of their religious and bourgeois leaders. Regarding the Jewish lower classes we thought that the liberation of the whole of Russia would bring along the liberation of all nations living there . . . One has to admit that Russian literature has instilled in us a view that Jewry was not a nation but a parasite class."[40]

The efforts of these Jewish radicals in the 1870s to "go to the people", to the Russian *moujiks* (peasants) in an attempt to identify themselves socially with the peasantry, failed miserably. They did not succeed in overcoming peasant hostility or the radical antisemitism prevalent in the Populist movement and as a result some, like Aron Liberman, acquired a renewed interest in the liberation of the Jewish people. The pogroms of 1881 and the indifferent, or even supportive, attitude of the Russian revolutionaries towards them shocked the Jewish radicals. On 30th August 1881 the executive committee of the revolutionary terrorist organisation of *Narodnaya Volya* (The People's Will) issued a proclamation to the Ukrainian people which vindicated the pogroms in Bakuninist style as a popular, anti-capitalist movement.

> "The damned police beat you, the landowners devour you, the kikes, the dirty Judases, rob you. People in the Ukraine suffer most of all from the kikes. Who has seized the land, the woodlands, the taverns? The kikes. Whom does the peasant beg with tears in his eyes to let him near his own land? The kikes. Wherever you look, whatever you touch, everywhere the

[37]Quoted in Jonathan Frankel, *Prophecy and Politics. Socialism, Nationalism, and the Russian Jews, 1862–1917*, Cambridge 1981, p. 34.
[38]*Ibid.*, p. 567.
[39]Boris Sapir, 'Jewish Socialists around *Vpered*', in *International Review of Social History* (1965), p. 369.
[40]*Ibid.*, p. 383.

kikes. The kike curses the peasant, cheats him, drinks his blood. The kike makes life unbearable."[41]

This antisemitic attitude of the populist revolutionaries prompted Paul Axelrod, a leading Socialist Jew and one of the founders of the first Russian Social Democratic organisation (Liberation of Labour) and later the Menshevik wing of the labour movement, to write a pamphlet describing the disillusion of young Jewish radicals. Axelrod admitted that the greatest disappointment of all for the Jewish student youth came:

"when they realized that the socialist-minded Russian students sympathized with the crusade against the Jewish masses and, worse yet, exhibited their antisemitic feelings toward their Jewish fellow-revolutionaries".[42]

The pogroms made a sizeable part of the Jewish Socialist intelligentsia in Russia feel that they had made a mistake in forsaking the Jewish masses in the name of cosmopolitanism. For the first time they understood that the majority of Russian society, including the radical elements,

"considered all Jews – a pious Jewish worker, a petit bourgeois, a moneylender, an assimilated lawyer, a socialist prepared for prison or deportation – as kikes, harmful to Russia, whom Russia should get rid of by any and all means".

Nor was there any basis for believing in the indigenous labouring masses for:

"they lacked not only cosmopolitan feelings and ideas, but were wanting even in the idea of class solidarity among the poorer classes of Russia's nationalities".[43]

Clearly then, in Russia, as in Western and Central Europe, Socialism in this period before the rise of an organised, class-conscious Social Democratic labour movement was easily reconcilable with antisemitic stereotypes and encouraged a negative view of the Jews as a parasitic element in the agrarian economy. The Russian Socialist-Revolutionary and Yiddishist, Chaim Zhitlovsky, recalled in his memoirs that his first encounter with Socialist ideas in Russia forced him to conclude that Jews were, in the main, "parasites"; that as merchants, store-keepers, bankers, manufacturers, landowners, they were "exploiters, living . . . on the body of the labouring people, sucking their lifeblood, and condemning them to eternal poverty and enslavement". Zhitlovsky did not actually say that the new Socialist ideology promoted antisemitism, "but if I would then have asked 'Are you for us or against us', the answer definitely could not have been 'for you'". Zhitlovsky makes it clear that: "Socialism was a stream of ideas containing elements inimical to Jewish existence in the Diaspora" and that "between my Judeophilia and this socialism which regarded the whole Jewish people as a multitude of parasites yawned a chasm which I had to vault".[44]

Zhitlovsky's embrace of a Socialism which had a pronounced Russian

---

[41]Quoted in Lucy S. Dawidowicz, *The Golden Tradition. Jewish Life and Thought in Eastern Europe*, London 1967, p. 406.
[42]*Ibid.*, p. 410.
[43]*Ibid.*, p. 410.
[44]*Ibid.*, p. 415.

populist, agrarian-Socialist character, made him reject with contempt all "philosemitism" as "justifying Jewish merchantry".

> "Wherever I turned my eyes to ordinary, day-to-day Jewish life, I saw only one thing, that which the antisemites were agitating about: the injurious effect of Jewish merchantry on Russian peasantry. No matter how I felt, from a socialist point of view, I had to pass a death sentence not only on individual Jews but on the entire *Jewish* existence of individual Jews."[45]

However, by 1884, like many of his generation in Russia, the young Zhitlovsky had come to the conclusion that assimilation was bankrupt and for the rest of his active life sought to find ways to reconcile his Socialist ideas with Jewish Nationalism and the problems of Jewish life. On the other hand, by the late 1880s the growing influence of Marxism and Western-style "Social Democracy" in the Russian labour movement, along with the emergence of an industrial proletariat, encouraged Jews to join the revolutionary ranks in greater numbers. This, in turn, contributed to a diminution of the earlier antisemitic tendencies – a trend similar to that in the German labour movement.

The German workers' movement in its early phase, that is to say in the 1860s and 1870s, had undoubtedly made tactical concessions to prevailing antisemitic sentiments in German society, especially those unleashed in the wake of the post-1870 speculative boom (*Gründerjahre*). This was especially true of the *Allgemeiner Deutscher Arbeiter-Verein* (ADAV) founded by Ferdinand Lassalle in 1863, the year before his death. At this time the workers' movement was primarily a movement of artisans – not until the 1880s and 1890s did the industrial proletariat take over as the dominant social force in the ranks of the Social Democratic Party and the trade unions. Among German artisans, who feared proletarianisation and social decline, the tendency to equate Jews with modern capitalism had long been evident. In the 1860s there were antisemitic overtones evident from time to time in the German Socialist press, which blamed Jewish usurers for the plight of the artisans. But the main focus of antisemitic agitation in the ADAV was directed against the Jewish intelligentsia, the so-called "Press Jews". This built on a tradition first created by Lassalle himself who had sometimes used antisemitic arguments in his polemics against the Liberal-bourgeois press.[46]

Lassalle's successor as head of the ADAV, Johann Baptist von Schweitzer, also used antisemitic jargon in his attacks on Jewish capitalists like Leopold Sonnemann who were sympathetic to the workers and sought to develop a social-liberal programme. On the other hand, the fact that Lassalle himself (like Marx) was a Jew also tended to inhibit antisemitic tactics and propaganda to the extent that it showed that not all Jews sided with the bourgeoisie and that some of them had indeed embraced the cause of the German working class, providing it with outstanding leaders and men of science. However, there were relatively few Jews in the ADAV after 1870 as opposed to the *Sozialdemokratische Arbeiterpartei* (SDAP), the "Marxist" wing of the German labour movement, possibly a reflection of the antisemitic tendencies in the Lassallean organisation. The

[45]*Ibid.*, p. 418.
[46]Wistrich, *Revolutionary Jews, op. cit.*, chap. 2.

conflict between the two Socialist organisations encouraged the ADAV to use anti-Jewish rhetoric as a weapon against the rival SDAP which was depicted as a "party of intellectuals" and as agents of the bourgeoisie. The editor of the *Neuer Social-Demokrat* (the main press organ of the ADAV), Wilhelm Hasselmann, was particularly aggressive in his attacks on the "Press Jews" as the greatest danger to the workers' movement. This anti-intellectual type of antisemitism was also shared by the leading neo-Lassallean agitator, Tölcke, and the new President of the movement, Hasenclever, who in 1872 wrote in the *Neuer Social-Demokrat*:

> ". . . only in Lassalle's organisation, only in the *Allgemeiner Deutscher Arbeiter-Verein* can workers find the fulfilment of their aspirations, where all other organisations, spawned by the overheated imagination of arrogant Jew-boys and other mischief-makers, are falling apart . . ."[47]

Tölcke denounced efforts to unite the two workers' parties as inspired by "boundless, typically Jewish arrogance" and accused "Jewish speculators" of being behind the rival SDAP labour movement. The origins of Jewish members of the Marxist SDAP like Eduard Bernstein were stigmatised ("that honest-to-God little Jew") and the organ of the SDAP, *Volksstaat*, was dismissed as a "Jewish rag".[48] Agitators of the ADAV in the Berlin area did not hesitate to exploit the primitive antisemitic prejudices nourished by the post-1871 speculative boom and stock-market crash. Some, like the joiner Carl Finn, eventually joined the antisemitic Berlin movement of the 1880s. As members of the ADAV, Finn and other agitators characterised their Socialist opponents as *Mühlendammer* (after the Berlin district of *Mühlendamm* where Jewish retail shops and second-hand clothes dealers were concentrated) – claiming they behaved with all the "pushiness", deceit and low cunning of Jewish traders. Wilhelm Hasselmann went furthest in the demagogic use of antisemitism, distinguishing between Judaism as a "religious sect" and Jewry as a tribe of "worldly jobbers". Hasselmann claimed that:

> "we shall never object to the paring of the flesh in the Judaic rite of circumcision, while strenuously opposing the Jewish habit of the paring of ducats".[49]

In election speeches Hasselmann encouraged farmers to believe that "the Jew" was responsible for their economic plight and in his journalistic articles he tried to prove with quotations from Marx, Lassalle and Heine (all radical Jews)

> "that the Jews are the embodiment of egoism and that for centuries past they have been burrowing, haggling and deceiving".

Hence it was necessary not only to exterminate the (Jewish) "press bandits", but to "lead the Jews altogether, with a few exceptions, not through, but into, the Red Sea". Hasselmann's macabre solution was as brutally racist as anything in Proudhon or Bakunin.

---

[47] *Neuer Social-Demokrat*, 18th September 1872; on Wilhelm Hasenclever see Shlomo Na'aman, 'Social Democracy on the Ambiguous Ground between Antipathy and Antisemitism – The Example of Wilhelm Hasenclever', in *LBI Year Book XXXVI* (1991), pp. 229–240.

[48] *Neuer Social-Demokrat*, 22nd January 1873.

[49] Quoted in Arno Herzig, 'The Role of Antisemitism in the Early Years of the German Workers' Movement', in *LBI Year Book XXVI* (1981), p. 253.

"Egoism must be exterminated, and for those who will not renounce it, death by drowning would only mean liberation from the bondage of devilish egoism."[50]

Although bitterly anti-Marxist (he denounced the "Marxist" SDAP as controlled by "Jewish wire-pullers") he nonetheless invoked Karl Marx's 1844 essay on the Jews to support his theses. Indeed, he was the first German Socialist to reprint the essay, claiming that Marx, and with him,

"all other clear-headed Socialists look upon the Jewish tribe as the nucleus of bourgeois society [*Bourgeoisgesellschaft*] and as the enemy of the workers' causes, bound to perish when the hour has come for the emancipation of the proletariat".[51]

Hasselmann clearly used Marx's 'On the Jewish Question' for antisemitic purposes but went beyond the radical critique of Judaism (fashioned by the Young Hegelians in the 1840s) and the concept of Jewish social parasitism developed by Marx. In an article entitled *Der Jüdische Stamm* published on 6th November 1872, Hasselmann abandoned any pretence at a Socialist analysis of class society and denounced the "naked selfishness" of the Jews as a "congenital defect of that tribe" which had "a pernicious effect on all nations and all states". "The Jewish Tribe", Hasselmann concluded, "is exploitation of the workers personified" – it is *the* enemy of the proletariat. This racial type of antisemitism with its naturalistic imagery of the Jews as an alien *Volkskörper* corroding the national organism was exactly parallel to and in effect preceded that which developed in Germany after 1880 in the writings of Wilhelm Marr, Otto Glagau and Eugen Dühring. All of them were radical writers and journalists with a quasi-Socialist background. In the climate of social aggression engendered by the stock-market crash and the assault on Manchester Liberalism in the 1870s, this type of antisemitism (distinctly "Leftist" in flavour) flourished. Otto Glagau, the pamphleteer whose best-selling book on the stock-exchange "swindlers" had been published in 1876, had, like Hasselmann, identified the social with the "Jewish" question, *homo capitalisticus* with the iniquities of Jewish merchants and bankers. He consciously appealed to the embittered artisans and small business-men who had been badly hit by the crash, offering them a scapegoat – the "Semites" – who allegedly aimed at imposing their tribal racial domination over German Christians through the banks, the stock-exchange, the liberal parties and the State. The message of Wilhelm Marr was similarly tinged with the democratic radicalism and the anarchism of the 1840s when he had been a utopian Communist. His hatred of Jews, like that of his contemporaries who had come from the Left of the political spectrum, owed nothing to Christian theology. Marr, a veteran revolutionary of 1848, explicitly rejected the notion of "religious hatred", just as did Socialist antisemites of the Hasselmann/Dühring variety. He was violently anti-clerical, as bitterly anti-Catholic as he was anti-Jewish – convinced like Voltaire, Feuerbach, Bruno Bauer, Daumer and other radical Hegelians of the 1840s, that Judeo-Christian monotheism was "a malady of human consciousness", the root of all tyranny and evil. Like Dühring (and the French Socialist disciples of the virulent anti-clerical atheist, Auguste Blanqui),

[50]*Neuer Social-Demokrat*, 3rd November 1872; Herzig, *loc. cit.*, p. 252.
[51]*Neuer Social-Demokrat*, 20th September 1872, 8th November 1872.

Wilhelm Marr saw the struggle against Semitism as a racial struggle against Judaism and Christianity, which had to be superimposed on the class-struggle over which it took precedence.[52]

Dühring, the academic Socialist who exercised a great influence on the German labour movement in the mid-1870s (significant enough to oblige Engels to devote an entire book to demolishing his theories), took Marr's antisemitism even further in a racial-biological direction. By 1881 he was calling for a Jewish return to the ghetto and a war of liberation of the modern "Aryan" peoples against the Judeo-Christian "yoke" of the Old and New Testaments. Christianity (for Dühring as for Marr) was part of the problem rather than the solution. It was a product of the "Asiatic" legacy of Semitism to the West which had to be stripped off, if the Germanic peoples were ever to emancipate themselves. Both Dühring and Marr insisted, like all the Socialist antisemites, that the Jews were not merely a religious group but a tribal-racial community (*Stamm*) whose characteristics were incompatible with the German people – a view already put forward in the early 1860s by Bruno Bauer.

It is not surprising that this racial "anti-Christian" type of antisemitism (building on older culturally determined Christian stereotypes) caused considerable confusion in the early German workers' movement, as it did in France and Belgium, where it found expression in the writings of the prominent Belgian Socialist, Edmond Picard. It was put forward by radicals, who certainly shared the intense anti-liberalism of the workers' movement, but sought to solve the "social question" entirely through the elimination of the Jews. During the 1860s and 1870s there was, therefore, a certain overlap between the Socialist and the antisemitic critique of liberal capitalist culture and this continued as long as the German labour movement was still internally divided and influenced by a demagogic neo-Lassalleanism and petty-bourgeois anarchist trends.

Such ideological confusion allowed radical antisemitism to masquerade as an acceptable form of "Socialism" in the eyes of some members of the labour movement. Nevertheless, the efforts of Hasselmann, Dühring and others did not succeed in persuading the rank and file that Jewish capital was the prime enemy of the German working class. The "Jew" as anti-symbol ultimately proved insufficient as a rallying-point for the frustrations and animosities of the German proletariat. By 1880 both Hasselmann and Dühring had left the labour movement which began to firmly oppose the efforts of the Protestant court preacher Adolf Stoecker to win over workers to his antisemitic Christian-Social Party in Berlin.[53]

It should be pointed out, however, that Dühring's influence over the German Social Democrats, which had reached its peak between 1874 and 1877, declined for reasons largely unconnected with his antisemitism. Neither Eduard Bernstein nor August Bebel, who had been among his early disciples, dealt with or opposed his antisemitic remarks (directed *inter alia* against Marx and Lassalle)

[52] For a discussion of the concept of anti-Christian antisemitism, see Uriel Tal, *Christians and Jews in Germany. Religion, Politics and Ideology in the Second Reich, 1870–1914*, Cornell 1974.

[53] Robert S. Wistrich, 'German Social Democracy and the Berlin Movement', in *Internationale Wissenschaftliche Korrespondenz* (December 1976), pp. 323–333.

nor did the Jews in the Party – nearly all of them highly reticent about their origins. Only Engels mentioned the problem of antisemitism in passing in his *Anti-Dühring* (1878) describing Dühring's hatred of the Jews as "if not specially Prussian, at any rate specifically East Elbian", characteristic of the Junkers (landed gentry) and hence as a Conservative weapon against the working class.

The change in attitude of Engels (whose correspondence with Marx shows to what extent he had previously shared the latter's anti-Jewish prejudices) appears to have had a political motivation, one which largely explains the official opposition of the German Social Democrats after 1880 to antisemitism. It was clearly a reaction to the anti-Socialist laws of 1878 and to the efforts of Bismarck's spiritual *gendarme* in Berlin, the court preacher Adolf Stoecker, to win the workers over to "Governmental Socialism" and to foment a deliberate campaign to channel their frustrations against the Jews. It was the danger of the Stoecker agitation to their own survival as an independent labour movement, rather than sympathy for the Jews (whose identification with liberal capitalism still made them appear in Socialist eyes as linked with the class enemy), which ensured the opposition of the workers' leaders to the Protestant court preacher and his antisemitic crusade. Hence in the 1880s the battle against political antisemitism became part of the Socialist struggle against the Conservative ruling classes in Germany (a similar development was to occur in tsarist Russia) who were perceived as using anti-Jewish agitation to divide and persecute the workers. This struggle to prevent their own supporters from falling for the clerical antisemitic slogans of the Conservatives did not perhaps fundamentally alter the existing negative stereotypes of German Jewry – perceived as a section of the exploiting bourgeois class, largely opposed to Socialism – nor did it eliminate altogether the antisemitic vocabulary of the pre-1880 period. But it did largely hold in check open expressions of political hostility to the Jews in the German labour movement.

It was in France, the cradle of European Socialism, that Left-wing antisemitism had its oldest tradition, one which survived both the belated impact of Marxism on the workers' movement and the Dreyfus Affair. It appeared already in the writings of the Fourierists and Proudhonists and cannot be reduced simply to the personal eccentricities of Charles Fourier or Pierre Joseph Proudhon. The Socialists of the 1830s and 1840s reacted to what they regarded as the consequences of the emancipation of the Jews, which had occurred forty years earlier as part of the thrust of the victorious French bourgeoisie towards establishing a modern economy, based on free trade, social mobility and economic individualism. Fourier regarded this emancipation of the Jews as among the most "shocking actions" of the great French Revolution –

> "doubly impolitic in that it opens the door to parasites and unproductive people, all of whom are devoted to trade and not to agriculture. An enlightened policy would have excluded these people as a social contagion."[54]

[54]Quoted in Edmund Silberner, 'Charles Fourier on the Jewish Question', in *Jewish Social Studies*, vol. VIII, No. 4 (October 1946), pp. 245–266.

Fourier's abuse of Jews as "parasites", "merchants" and "usurers" – as a race which "had achieved nothing in art and science" and "are distinguished only by a record of crime and brutality" was echoed by his followers and intensified by the rivalry between his school and the rival Saint-Simonian movement in France. The "philosemitism" and sympathy with Jewish Messianism of the Saint-Simonians was well-known, as was their affirmation of the Industrial Revolution.[55] The Fourierists, on the other hand, were violently hostile to the progress of commercial-industrial civilisation, to the banking and capitalist system, denouncing Jewish financiers with the same fervour that the Saint-Simonians had extolled their civilising mission. Fourier's disciple, Alphonse Toussenel, sharply expressed this populist hatred of capitalism in his *Les Juifs, Rois de l'Époque* – which was the Bible of French antisemitism until the appearance of Edouard Drumont's even more scurrilous *La France Juive* forty years later – a best-selling work in which he was consciously influenced by his Socialist predecessor. From the outset, Toussenel (like Marx who had published his 'On the Jewish Question' in Paris a year earlier) defined

> "by the despised name of Jew every dealer in money, every unproductive parasite living off the work of someone else. Jew, usurer, money-dealer – all are synonymous to me."[56]

For Toussenel, as for the Christian Socialist, Pierre Leroux, the "Jewish spirit" was identical with capitalism and money-worship. As Leroux put it in 1846, "*l'esprit juif*" was a synonym for "the mentality of gain, of profit, of exploitation, the mentality of banking".[57] This updating of the medieval Christian image of the Jew as moneylender to fit the new social realities of early industrial capitalism in France (which developed under the auspices of the "Bourgeois Monarchy" of Louis Philippe between 1830 and 1848) was especially popular in Socialist circles. However, in Toussenel's lexicon, the term "Jew" was stretched to cover every capitalist, irrespective of nationality or religious denomination and was used especially as a weapon against the French Jews and the *bourgeoisie protestante* (the Protestant bourgeois oligarchy), who together with the Rothschilds and their associates, then dominated French banking and government. In addition to denouncing Jewish-Protestant influence, Toussenel's antisemitic vocabulary had an Anglophobic edge – a theme echoed by Proudhon in 1847 who wrote in his diary: "the hatred of the Jew, as that of the English, must be an article of our political faith".[58]

Victorian England, it must be remembered, was regarded by French Socialists with particular venom. It was not just the hereditary enemy (this element of Nationalist rhetoric continued throughout the century, though after 1870 it tended to be partly displaced by Germanophobia), but the cradle of the Industrial Revolution and commercial imperialism, responsible for the "per-

---

[55] J. L. Talmon, *Political Messianism. The Romantic Phase*, 1961, pp. 77ff.
[56] Alphonse Toussenel, *Les Juifs, Rois de l'Époque. Histoire de la Féodalité financière*, Paris 1845, 1847.
[57] Pierre Leroux, 'Les juifs, rois de l'époque', in *Revue Sociale* (January 1846). Quoted in Victor M. Glasberg, 'Intent and Consequences. The "Jewish Question" in the French Socialist Movement of the Late Nineteenth Century', in *Jewish Social Studies*, vol. XXVI, No. 1 (January 1974), pp. 61–71.
[58] *Notebooks of P. J. Proudhon*, *op. cit.*, vol. II, pp. 337–338.

nicious" doctrines of classical economics, unrestrained liberal individualism and
Malthusianism. For some French Leftists, children of a Catholic agrarian
culture and at the same time powerfully influenced by the revolutionary
Nationalism of 1789 which Protestant Britain had sought to frustrate, hatred of
the Bible-fearing, rapacious English (the "nation of shopkeepers" in Napoleon's
famous phrase) went hand in hand with Judeophobia. Toussenel, like the
integral Nationalists of *Action Française* at the beginning of the twentieth century,
saw the root of the modern exploitative ethic in the Judaic teaching absorbed by
the Protestant nations, beginning with Great Britain and followed by the
Americans, Dutch and Swiss.

> ". . . Who says Jew also means Protestant, and it is inevitable that the Englishman, the
> Dutchman and the Genevan who learn to read the will of God in the same book as the Jew [the
> Bible], profess the same contempt as the Jew for the laws of equity and the rights of the
> workers."

Unlike the Englishman, "the Jew" represented, however, an internal enemy who
had successfully seized control of France and inaugurated the reign of a new
industrial feudalism:

> "The French people, supposedly emancipated by the revolution of '89 from the yoke of the
> feudal nobility, has only changed masters."

By obtaining a monopoly control over the banks and railways, the cosmopolitan
Jewish financiers like Rothschild, Fould, Péreire etc. had become "the kings of
the epoch". Under their sway

> ". . . Europe is entailed to the domination of Israel. This universal domination, of which so
> many conquerors have dreamed, the Jews have in their hands."[59]

Toussenel's antisemitic Socialist vocabulary, his image of the Jews as "a nation
within the French nation", as a conquering cosmopolitan tribe and a deicidal
race especially hostile to Catholicism, exercised a great influence on the founder
and high-priest of late-nineteenth-century antisemitism, Edouard Drumont,
who admitted:

> "my sole ambition after long literary labour would be that my book might take its place beside
> his in the libraries of those who would understand the causes which have brought ruin and
> shame to our country".[60]

Toussenel, it might be argued, was an antisemite who happened also to be a
Socialist, were it not for the consistency with which his arguments and
vocabulary were repeated by other French Socialists throughout the nineteenth
century. We have already cited Proudhon, who noted in the summer of 1847
under the heading 'Work to be done' that, with regard to the Jews, "what the
people of the middle ages hated by instinct, I hate upon reflection, and
irrevocably". The only solution Proudhon could see was, as he put it, to
accomplish the wish of Voltaire – "I hate this nation . . . it must be sent back to

[59]Toussenel, *op. cit.*; Lichtheim, *loc. cit.*, p. 320.
[60]Edouard Drumont, *La France Juive*, Paris 1886.

Jerusalem".[61] As in the case of Fourier, this antisemitically motivated "Zionism" was little more than a rhetorical gesture.

It is, however, curious that although an atheist anti-clerical, Proudhon felt obliged to blame the Jews for not following Jesus and at the same time denied the Jewish ancestry of the founder of Christianity. Proudhon also insisted on the "Aryan" origins of monotheism – one of several indications that already in the 1860s the myth of "Aryan" superiority to the "Semites" had begun to infiltrate French Socialist circles. It was, however, the followers of the revolutionary insurrectionist and militant atheist, Louis Auguste Blanqui, who first systematically developed this racial type of antisemitism in the French labour movement – thereby popularising the doctrines which had originally been invented in France in the 1850s by the Comte de Gobineau and Ernest Renan.

Blanqui himself was originally a "Socialist" antisemite in the eighteenth-century rationalist tradition of Voltaire and Baron d'Holbach. His primary target was the Catholic Church and he regarded Christianity as the most ferocious of the "terrible monotheistic sects" whose function was to reduce the people to a mass of docile beasts in the hands of clerics, capitalists and aristocrats. The watchword of Blanqui and his Socialist followers, *Ni Dieu, Ni Maître*, expressed the central role of the war against all religion and authority in their ideology – especially the destruction of Judeo-Christian monotheism. At the same time, Blanqui and his chief lieutenant Gustave Tridon, who wrote *Du Molochisme juif* in 1868 (it was first published only in 1884), soaked up the new racialism, expressing the hatred of "Semitism", which became fashionable at the end of the Second Empire. Tridon presented the Semites as the "evil genius of the world" who worshipped a perverse, sadistic God, practised cannibalism, ritual murder and human sacrifice. Jewish Moloch-worship with its alleged blood-lusts (this myth had been developed in the 1840s by the Young Hegelians in Germany like Daumer, Ghillany, Bruno Bauer and even Moses Hess) was, according to the Blanquists, the root of Christian sacrifice, which in turn was related to the lust for profit of modern capitalism. Tridon, like Blanqui and Proudhon, regarded the Jews as a nation of rapacious "swindlers" and "Shylocks" and the origins of exploitation in the contemporary era as going back to the Bible and the covenant by which Israel had been given universal domination over the nations. The Jews were the archetype of "Semitism" (the "shadow in the picture of civilisation") – whom the Liberal French scholar Ernest Renan had already "proved" to be inferior to the Aryans in culture and creativity. It was, therefore, the task of revolutionary Socialists "to fight the Semitic spirit and ideas" in the name of the "Indo-Aryan race".[62]

The racist antisemitism of the Blanquists was also much appreciated by Edouard Drumont who had recognised, among the French Socialists, some of his most important precursors. "Of all the revolutionaries", he wrote in *La Fin d'un Monde* (1899), "only the Blanquists have had the courage to refer to the Aryan race and to proclaim that race's superiority." It was no accident that during the Dreyfus Affair, the Nationalist wing of the Blanquist party adopted an extreme

[61]*Notebooks of P. J. Proudhon, op. cit.*, vol. II, p. 150.
[62]Gustave Tridon, *Du Molochisme juif*, Paris 1884, p. 5.

anti-Dreyfusard and antisemitic position, branding French Jews as "Prussians from within", agents of the enemy across the Rhine and of an international capitalist conspiracy against the working class.

In France there was no immediate turning-point in Socialist attitudes to the "Jewish Question" after 1880, similar to that which pertained in Germany or tsarist Russia. The continuity in Left-wing antisemitism was maintained and not challenged until the Dreyfus Affair suddenly demonstrated that Jew-hatred could become a powerful political weapon of the French Right, the Church and the Army in its struggle against the Republic, and was, therefore, ultimately dangerous to the working class. In the 1880s and 1890s, however, Socialist antisemitism actually became more respectable than previously in France – partly as a result of the crash of the Catholic bank *Union Générale* in 1882 (widely attributed to the machinations of the Rothschilds) and a series of financial scandals culminating in the Panama Affair of 1893 in which a number of German-Jewish financiers were involved. Even the mainstream Socialist theoretical journal, *Revue Socialiste* edited by Benoît Malon, adopted an antisemitic line in the 1880s (Malon had been influenced by Proudhon and Bakunin in his earlier years) – publishing, for example, a series of articles entitled 'Aryens et Sémites' from 1887–1889. Their author, an ex-Communard and Blanquist, Albert Regnard, claimed that capitalism was mainly a "Jewish creation" whereas Socialism "is a Franco-German creation, i.e. Aryan in the fullest sense of the term".[63]

Regnard, drawing heavily on the ideas of Gobineau, Renan and others, sought to prove "Aryan" (which included Graeco-Roman, Indian, Persian cultures etc.) superiority over the nomadic, sterile, materialistic "Semitic" race. Though scarcely different from the racist antisemitic stereotypes in *La France Juive*, Regnard's "scholarly and superb study", which breathed the spirit of genuine "Aryanism", was welcomed by Malon, who also took the trouble to introduce his friend Drumont to Parisian working-men. Moreover, Malon threw open the columns of *Revue Socialiste* to Auguste Chirac, a Socialist antisemite who sought to adapt Toussenel's lexicon to the conditions of the Third Republic. Chirac's attacks on the *féodalité financière* used the same sweeping definition of *la juiverie* (Jewry in a pejorative collective sense) which claimed to embrace capitalists of all denominations – Jewish, Protestant, even Catholic. However, it was apparent to all that Chirac's "Kings of the Republic" were primarily Jewish international financiers engaged in shady deals that were ruining France as well as in secret conspiracies to undermine the tsarist and other European states.[64]

The rise of the chauvinist wave of revanchism associated with General Boulanger in 1886 favoured a coalition of Conservative, Catholic, Nationalist and Socialist elements, leading for the first time in France to the use of antisemitism as an electoral political weapon. It was on the back of this Boulangist hysteria that demagogic politicians and journalists like Edouard

---

[63]See Edmund Silberner, 'French Socialism and the Jewish Question 1865–1914', in *Historia Judaica*, XVI (April 1954), pp. 6–7.
[64]Auguste Chirac, *Les Rois de la République*, Paris 1888.

Drumont, Maurice Barrès, Henri Rochefort and the Marquis de Morès developed a national-Socialist ideology in which antisemitism was a central element. They blamed *la haute banque juive* (the Rothschilds above all) for working-class misery and argued that the expropriation of Jewish fortunes would be a revolutionary act of liberation. In his *Le Testament d'un antisémite* (1890), Drumont even predicted that the day would come when "a man of the people", "a Socialist leader" independent of the "synagogue" would take up his campaign and rally the *déclassés* – the oppressed, the disinherited and uprooted of all classes – around his national-social-antisemitic banner. The Boulangist deputy, Maurice Barrès adopted a similar line in the 1890s, as did other French antisemitic leaders like the Marquis de Morès and Jules Guérin who embellished their populist demagogy with "Socialist" rhetoric designed to attract the workers. It was Guérin, for example, who coined the phrase: "Plus on est loin des juifs, plus on est près du peuple" and defined antisemitism as "a precise and formal claim of national labour against Jewish speculation". The antisemitic "Socialists" of this type, like the Socialist antisemites who preceded them, regarded the "Jew" as the embodiment of capital and as the enemy of the worker. During the Dreyfus Affair, however, they went even further and attacked the official Socialists as mercenaries of Rothschild and the "Jewish system", for supporting the Republic dominated as it was by Jews, Protestants, freemasons, liberal cosmopolitans and the yoke of finance capital which had reduced the French workers to "slaves of the Jew".

The struggle against the rehabilitation of Captain Dreyfus became, for the antisemitic section of the French Left, part of their general struggle against the organised "Jewish syndicate" which they believed was out to ruin France for its own profit. Even the official Marxist Left led by Jules Guesde and the mainstream pro-republican Socialists who followed Jaurès, believed for a time that the agitation on behalf of Dreyfus's release was nothing but an attempt by the Jewish financial bourgeoisie to regain its hegemonic position. It was only Emile Zola's forceful intervention on behalf of Dreyfus and against the military clique that first split this consensus of the parliamentary Socialist group. The "moderates" argued that Dreyfus's cause was unpopular and that intervention on his behalf was electorally imprudent; Jaurès, Guesde and Vaillant (leader of the Blanquist-Marxist wing) were converted to a more positive view, but the manifesto they composed on 19th January 1898 still claimed that "the Jewish capitalists, after all the scandals which have discredited them, needed to rehabilitate themselves" and "to wash out the stains of Israel".

The French Socialists like their German, Austrian and Polish comrades, when accused of being lukewarm or indifferent to the danger of antisemitism, invariably still replied that the antisemites were "incipient Socialists". Even the cry of "Death to the Jews", which was sweeping France in early 1898, was initially shrugged off as a prelude to proletarian revolution. The Dreyfus case did, however, lead some French Socialists and anarchists to reject antisemitic chauvinism and to use the Affair as a means to rally the workers against their traditional enemies, the Army and the Church. Not a few, who had flirted with an antisemitically-tinged Socialism before 1900, changed their spots once they understood that it was a powerful weapon in the hands of the counter-revolutionary Right.

Although the Marxist *Parti Ouvrier Français* declared its neutrality in the Affair, the more liberal wing of French Socialism led by Jaurès came to see in antisemitism a political danger to the labour movement no less serious than militarism, clericalism and extreme nationalist hysteria. The emergence of a "Dreyfusard" Socialism ready to defend the Republic did not, however, eliminate Left-wing antisemitic stereotypes in France – especially among the syndicalist intellectuals like Georges Sorel, Edouard Berth and Robert Louzon. They greeted the victory of the Dreyfusard forces as a triumph for "the Jewish party" over its Catholic rivals. Some syndicalists like Emile Janvion and Emile Pataud even claimed that the Jews, through their alleged control of high finance and freemasonry, had infiltrated and neutralised the labour movement. Together they sponsored a mass meeting in Paris in April 1911 which was advertised as "a great anti-Jewish and anti-Masonic demonstration".[65]

The antisemitic syndicalists who claimed that Socialist internationalism only benefited the "kikes" at the expense of honest French workers, clearly had some popular support. Their campaign against capitalism, philosemitism, Jewish immigrant workers and also the "Dreyfusard" Socialists led by Jaurès, was enthusiastically welcomed by the Nationalist Right. The most important of the syndicalist intellectuals in France, Georges Sorel, who had once been a Dreyfusard, went in a similarly antisemitic direction, once he turned his back on bourgeois democracy and rejected Jaurès's moderate, parliamentary Socialism. Sorel's concern for the national tradition, his obsession with myth, his hatred of liberalism and compromise – above all, his irrationalism – influenced his turn to antisemitism. Between 1908 and 1914 he was one of the driving forces of the *Cercle Proudhon* which attacked democracy as a "Jewish" invention that had substituted "the laws of gold for the laws of blood"; like the integral Nationalists and monarchists of *Action Française*, the Socialist Sorel blamed Jews for the decomposition of traditional European culture, for the nefarious impact of liberalism, capitalism and rationalism. A specifically Socialist variant of antisemitism continued to exist, therefore, both within the French labour movement and on its intellectual fringes, before 1914. The evidence suggests, however, that the crisis provoked by the Dreyfus Affair weakened its grip, at least among those in the labour movement who came to see in antisemitism a direct menace to republican democracy.

The tenacity of Socialist antisemitism in nineteenth- and early twentieth-century Europe is even more strikingly illustrated by its survival in England, the mother of parliaments and liberal democracy, which in 1900 was described by Theodor Herzl as "the one spot left throughout the whole world in which God's ancient people are not detested and despised". Although Great Britain appeared to many Jews as an island of tolerance and sanity compared to the rampant antisemitism

---

[65]Edmund Silberner, 'Anti-Jewish Trends in French-Revolutionary Syndicalism', in *Jewish Social Studies*, vol. XV, Nos. 3–4 (1953).

that had spread across the European continent, it was by no means free of the anti-Jewish virus and British Socialists played a not insignificant part in fuelling it. The marked increase in alien Jews, mainly from Russia and Poland, who fled persecution in Eastern Europe and arrived in England in the 1880s and 1890s increasingly provoked fears of the indigenous proletariat for their jobs. This was especially true in the East End of London where most new immigrants were concentrated and the problem of social pauperism was already acute. It was not too difficult for political agitators to fan the irrational hatreds and prejudices of the slum-dwellers against "destitute aliens" (read Russian Jews); claiming that they were driving British workmen out of the labour market, lowering the moral tone of their neighbourhoods, reducing wages and encouraging nihilist violence, etc.[66]

Radical and trade-union leaders, no less than Conservatives and imperialists, saw the vote-catching potential of anti-alienism and calls for the restriction of foreign immigration. Virtually all the big British unions, from the dockers to the miners, engineers, carpenters, shoemakers and tailors favoured restriction of immigration. Trade-union leader John Hodge, presiding over a session of the twenty-fifth Trades Union Congress (TUC) at Glasgow (September 1892), condemned the "enormous immigration of destitute aliens" who "take work at any price", so that "the tailoring and kindred trades have been practically ruined". The TUC passed, not for the last time, a resolution calling for government legislation to stop the entry of pauper aliens. The fact that immigrants' trades were mostly sweated trades, that the Yiddish-speaking Jews kept to themselves and that they were more socially mobile than working-class Gentiles, added to tension in a period of economic stress and unemployment. The Socialist Beatrice Webb, who observed the Jews of Whitechapel in the late 1880s, even claimed that they were altogether indifferent to class solidarity and professional ethics, that they had no desire for trade-union organisation and undercut the wages of their fellow-workers. They were solely concerned with preserving themselves and their families, motivated by the love of profit and unmoved by sentiment or moral considerations. The Jewish immigrant, according to Beatrice Webb, "seems to justify by his existence those strange assumptions which figure in the political economy of Ricardo – an always enlightened selfishness, seeking employment or profit with an absolute mobility of body and mind . . ."[67]

Alien Jews were constantly being accused, by representatives of such British trades as the tailors and the bakers and confectioners, of malpractice, of monopolising local trade, of depressing business and by other trade-union leaders of blacklegging (strike-breaking). In 1894 and 1895 the TUC repeated its resolutions against the admission of "pauper aliens". In the East End, anti-alienist sentiment was spreading in spite of genuine public distaste (expressed in Parliament and the press) for Russian-style pogroms or for the antisemitism in France at the time of the Dreyfus Affair. Most of the British working-class reaction was probably more xenophobic than antisemitic, an outgrowth of

[66]William J. Fishman, *East End Jewish Radicals 1875–1914*, London 1975, chap. 3: 'Briton and Alien'.
[67]*Ibid.*, p. 82.

economic conflict and traditional native insularity; antisemitism as an ideology was indeed officially condemned by many in the British Socialist movement as being in conflict with their civic norms of tolerance and internationalist ideals of brotherhood. Nevertheless, there was an indigenous English radical tradition hostile to Jews which had manifested itself in the writings of William Cobbett and in some of the Chartist propaganda in the first half of the nineteenth century; there was also a growing economic antisemitism in Socialist circles directed at the rich Jews of Hampstead, Bayswater and the West End, and those prominent in international finance.[68]

This Socialist ideological antisemitism exploded during the Boer War (1899–1902), the most controversial conflict in British imperial history, with the radical anti-war movement exploiting the Jewish origins of prominent financiers in South Africa to influence public opinion and discredit the Conservative government. "Jewish finance" came to symbolise in the eyes of the Left everything shady and disreputable about the South African war; Jewish entrepreneurs like Barney Barnato, the Hamburg-born Alfred Beit, Lionel Phillips, the Albu brothers, and others with banking and business connections who had become millionaires through the discovery of diamonds and then of gold, symbolised a *nouveau riche* class of cosmopolitan financiers who were blamed for the imperialist machinations that had drawn Britain into the South African war. By seizing on a monolithic "Jewish" factor (even though many of the "Jewish" magnates had only marginal ties with Judaism, were frequently in conflict with each other and pursued individual or class rather than specifically Jewish communal interests), a section of the Left evidently hoped by these means to discredit British imperialism itself. The chief organ of the Marxist Social Democratic Federation (SDF), *Justice*, edited by Henry Hyndman, led this virulent campaign against the "capitalist Jew", whom he saw as the soul of a sinister "Gold international", destined to be locked in mortal conflict with the Socialist "Red international". Hyndman and his followers had repeatedly identified Judaism with the corrupt domination of money during the 1880s and openly sympathised with the Leftist antisemitic campaign that developed in France during the Panama Scandal. In 1893 Hyndman even described Jewish newspaper magnates in Britain as "poisoners of the wells of public information" and protested that "capitalist Jews of the baser sort are already influential in both our political parties".[69]

It was however the nexus between international Jewry and late-nineteenth-century British imperialism, especially in Egypt and South Africa, which mainly preoccupied him and other radicals. In a virulently hostile essay entitled 'Imperialist Judaism in South Africa', he charged that Beit, Barnato and their fellow-Jews were planning "an Anglo-Hebraic Empire stretching from Egypt to Cape Colony and from Beira to Sierra Leone".[70] Hyndman, Harry Quelch and other Left-wing radicals blamed the outbreak of the South African war on the

---

[68]John A. Garrard, *The English and Immigration. A Comparative Study of the Jewish Influx (1880–1910)*, London 1971.
[69]*Justice*, 21st January 1893.
[70]*Justice*, 25th April 1896.

"Jew-jingo" gang and the "Jew press", which had allegedly brainwashed the British public into supporting "piratical imperialism in the Transvaal and elsewhere". The Jewish financiers personified in Socialist eyes "that gold international which today dominates the Government and jingo press of all countries". *Justice* consistently referred to the South African war as the "Jew war in the Transvaal" engineered by a "Jew clique" around Joseph Chamberlain and Arthur Balfour, a war in which it was "us common Englishmen [who] shall have to pay . . . in blood".[71]

The blatant Judeophobia of Hyndman and his colleagues aroused some criticism in the columns of *Justice*, especially among Jewish members of the SDF. In a letter to the editor on 21st October 1899 Rothstein wrote:

> ". . . in Hyndman and in you [Harry Quelch] the Socialist movement of this country has two leaders ready – in theory, at least – to go hand in hand with Lueger [leader of the Austrian antisemites], Stoecker, Drumont and others . . . [*Justice* is] preaching from its pulpit rank anti-Semitism. Is it not a strange and sad spectacle? . . . Referring recently to the part which you imagine Jew-capitalism had been playing all along in the Transvaal business, you express yourselves to the effect that you would not be surprised if an anti-Semitic movement were to arise in this country, as it did on the Continent. Nor should I, I may tell you candidly, were I sure of the wide influence of *Justice*; that very sentence is enough to have an anti-Semitic effect on the mind . . ."

Rothstein went on to ask how Jewish Socialists could combat Zionism in the face of such Left-wing antisemitism. How they could expect that Jew-hatred would disappear in a Socialist society, given the hostile line that *Justice* had taken on "the subject of Jew-capitalism"? Other critics also objected to the race prejudice that Hyndman and his followers had "imbibed with their mother's milk" and to their "unsocialist attack on Jews" and by 1900 the overtly antisemitic campaign in *Justice* was moderated. One factor in this was the realisation that such rhetoric damaged Socialist prospects of organising the largely Jewish proletariat in such areas of London's East End as Tower Hamlets. At heart, however, Hyndman, Quelch and their colleagues continued to believe in the "Jewish conspiracy", in a secret cabal that dominated the press and the stock exchanges of the world and was responsible for the imperialist plot to seize the gold-rich Boer lands in the Transvaal in order to enrich World Jewry.

The less ideologically-orientated *Reynolds News*, which saw itself as the guardian of the British working class, was no less hostile to the Jews, whether rich capitalists or poor foreign immigrants. It focused its attacks on the financiers, mostly "of German Jewish origins", on the danger to British labour from impoverished Jewish aliens and on the racial solidarity of the Jews:

> "who, by refusing to intermarry with the people among whom they dwell, and by their ever growing control of the money markets and Press of all civilized states, may probably establish . . . a dominancy which will keep the entire world in subjection".[72]

The Jews were presented as a strange Asian people, as only nominally English, or as a "secret order established in the heart of every nation" in which each branch supported the other internationally – the classic argument of continental

[71] *Justice*, 7th October 1899.
[72] *Reynolds News*, 12th November 1899.

antisemitism. These outpourings of the popular press were echoed even by such sophisticated radicals as John Hobson who, in 1900, published his influential *The War in South Africa, its Causes and Effects* and by the most prominent Labour leaders, Keir Hardie and John Burns. They all shared the view, expressed by Hardie that:

> "modern imperialism is really run by half a dozen financial houses, many of them Jewish, to whom politics is a counter in the game of buying and selling securities".[73]

Indeed the anti-war movement in Britain as a whole was easily sucked into the conspiratorial view that the British government was itself in the hands of Jewish capitalists and "foreign financiers". Inevitably, the campaign soon escalated into the antisemitic terminology which characterised all Jews as "bloodsuckers" and corrupt vampires preying on innocent victims. John Burns, the Labour MP for Battersea, considered an outstanding leader of the Socialist movement in Britain, fully subscribed to the mythic view of a Jewish conspiracy. In a speech in the House of Commons on 6th February 1900 he declared:

> "Wherever we go in this matter we find the same thing. Wherever we examine, there is the financial Jew, operating, directing, inspiring the agonies that have led to this war. They were supreme at the South African Committee in 1897. I thought I had landed myself in a synagogue when I went to hear the trial of the Johannesburg prisoners before the Chief Justice . . . The trail of the financial serpent is over this war from beginning to end."[74]

Burns's public rhetoric against the war at times resembled the antisemitic "Socialism" rampant in France during the 1890s and his diaries reveal that he regarded all Jews, rich and poor, capitalist and proletarian, native and alien, with a similar hatred and contempt. The allegations of a "Jewish plot" spread by Burns and to be found in the pamphlet literature put out by the anti-war leagues were also accepted by the trade-union elite. In September 1900, the TUC passed a resolution condemning the war as designed "to secure the gold fields of South Africa for cosmopolitan Jews most of whom had no patriotism and no country".[75]

However, the British working class as a whole either supported the South African war or was indifferent to the issue, so that no systematic Jew-baiting on continental lines ultimately developed in Great Britain, though "anti-alien" agitation continued to be a central public issue. Even the crusading zeal of John Hobson, who relentlessly attacked "Jew power" in South Africa and denounced the manipulation of British foreign policy by a secret "racial confederacy", failed to mobilise public opinion. Ironically, the image of a sinister Jewish elite seeking world domination was much more successful on the Continent where it became linked with the Anglophobia that swept France and Germany in 1900 in the wake of the Boer War. Thus the alleged "robbery committed by international Jewry" was invariably linked by continental antisemites (especially on the Right) with British imperialist piracy against the plucky Boers fighting for self-determination.

[73] *Labour Leader*, 24th February 1900.
[74] Quoted in Claire Hirshfield, 'The British Left and the "Jewish Conspiracy". A Case Study of Modern Antisemitism', in *Jewish Social Studies*, vol. XLIII, No. 2 (Spring 1981), p. 105.
[75] *Ibid.*, pp. 106–107.

In Germany and Russia, as we have argued, such antisemitic conspiracy theories which became the staple diet of the Radical Right, were much less common in the labour movement after the early 1880s. With a few exceptions, the German Social Democrats, who were going from strength to strength in electoral terms, resisted antisemitism as the "Socialism of fools" in the classic phrase of their leader, August Bebel. There were isolated attacks on Jews, mainly by Right-wing Socialists like Wolfgang Heine (who resented the influence in the German Party of Russian- and Polish-born revolutionaries such as Rosa Luxemburg) or Richard Calwer who wrote in 1894:

> "For every good Jewish writer there will be found at least half a dozen who are altogether worthless, but who possess an extraordinary power of self-assertion and an inexhaustible flow of words, but no real understanding of Socialism."[76]

But such barbs were much milder than the virulent hatred of Jewish Socialist intellectuals expressed twenty years earlier by German Left-wingers like Dühring and Hasselmann. More typical was the Socialist ambiguity towards Jews that derived from the long-standing anti-liberalism in the Party and expressed itself in a bizarre campaign against philosemitism in the 1890s. The leading exponent of this line of thought was Franz Mehring, a highly regarded journalist and historian on the Left wing of the *Sozialdemokratische Partei Deutschlands* (SPD), whose views on the "Jewish Question" were strongly influenced by Karl Marx. Mehring denounced liberal philosemitism as a defence of capitalist privileges, as a hypocritical whitewash of rich Jews, while partly justifying German antisemitism in the 1890s as a movement of the downtrodden, exploited peasantry and lower middle class.

> "In considering the brutalities which antisemitism with words rather than deeds commits against Jews, one should not overlook the brutalities which philosemitism with deeds rather than words, is committing against everyone, be he Jew or Turk, Christian or pagan, who opposes capitalism."[77]

Mehring believed that the defence of capitalist Jews was a much greater crime or danger to the labour movement than antisemitism, which he saw as a primitive form of anti-capitalism and he re-interpreted Marx's attack on "Judaism" in this spirit.[78] Mehring's hostility to *Geldjuden* and the anti-Jewish stereotypes he derived from Marx were prevalent and widely shared in the German labour movement, even by Social-Democratic leaders like August Bebel who strongly opposed political antisemitism. In his speech to the SPD Party Congress in 1893 Bebel, quoting Fourier and Marx, even linked the Jewish preference for commerce to acquired racial characteristics. It was in his view "indisputable that the spirit of commerce – as Fourier calls it . . . is developed to a high degree in the Semitic race". Bebel argued that "our whole society is based

[76]Richard Calwer, *Das Kommunistische Manifest und die heutige Sozialdemokratie*, Braunschweig 1894, p. 41.
[77]See Robert S. Wistrich, 'Anti-Capitalism or Antisemitism? The Case of Franz Mehring', in *LBI Year Book XXII* (1977), pp. 35–54.
[78]*Idem*, 'Karl Marx, German Socialists and the Jewish Question, 1880–1914', in *Soviet Jewish Affairs*, vol. III, No. 1 (1973), pp. 92–97.

on haggling and money-making and therefore a Judaised society (*verjudete Gesellschaft*)", but that the "peculiar essence of the Jews" would disappear with the abolition of bourgeois society.[79]

In contrast to Marx and Mehring, Bebel, however, emphasised that the Jews were an oppressed race and that the social role of Judaism was a result of Christian persecution and medieval legislation. Together with other leading German Marxist theoreticians like Engels and Kautsky, his negative stereotype of the social role of some Jews was balanced by recognition that there was a growing Jewish proletariat and labour movement in Eastern Europe.[80] Bebel held the view, first articulated by Friedrich Engels, that antisemitism was the product of backward semi-feudal societies and declining social classes threatened by capitalism with which the German labour movement should have nothing to do. Moreover, the Gentile leaders of the Social Democratic Party in Germany were conscious of the debt they owed, not only to Marx and Lassalle as founders of the European labour movement, but also to the many other Jewish intellectuals who had joined their ranks. Recognition that "the Jews have become an eminently revolutionary factor", as Karl Kautsky put it, counteracted the Socialist dislike and even contempt for Judaism itself as a "reactionary factor", a clerical, obscurantist relic of the Middle Ages. German Socialists looked forward to the disappearance of corporate traditional Judaism as an obstacle to human progress. But increasingly they welcomed the participation of Jews as individuals in the revolutionary movement in Germany and throughout Europe as a whole.

A similar attitude of hostility to Jewish religion and tradition combined with appreciation of the role of assimilated Jewish revolutionaries developed in the Russian Marxist parties after the 1890s, strongly influenced as they were by the example of the German Social Democratic Party. The impact of German Marxist theory and the growth of an industrial proletariat in tsarist Russia, together with the barbarous use of pogromist antisemitism as a counter-revolutionary weapon by the autocratic Russian government, obliged the Russian Social Democrats to instigate a campaign against the deeply-rooted Judeophobia of the peasant masses. The revolutionary movement in Russia, swelled by the presence of many Jews driven into its arms by persecution and oppression, increasingly emerged as a defender of Jewish civil rights, though it did not always succeed in preventing Russian and Ukrainian workers from participating in pogroms, as for example in 1905.

However, the different factions in Russian Social Democracy (Bolshevik, Menshevik etc.), while opposed to antisemitism, fought equally hard against Zionism and the national "separatism" of the *Bund*, the leading Jewish Social Democratic organisation in tsarist Russia and Poland. Basing themselves in part on the orthodox Marxist theories of Karl Kautsky, Russian Social Democrats,

---

[79] *Ibid.*, p. 95.
[80] See Nathan Weinstock, *Le Pain de Misère. Histoire du Mouvement ouvrier juif en Europe*, 2 vols., Paris 1984, for a recent historical synthesis describing this phenomenon.

whether Bolshevik or Menshevik, denied that Jews (in Russia or elsewhere) constituted a nation, but classified them instead as a "caste" which continued to exist as a collectivity only because of the artificial segregation of the Pale of Settlement and the reactionary policies of the tsarist government. This was the position of Lenin, Trotsky, Stalin, Martov and other Russian Marxist leaders – all of whom opposed antisemitism as an extreme form of political reaction and as an attempt to divert the natural hatred of workers and peasants from their exploiters towards the Jewish minority. But they also rejected equally strongly the slogan of national culture or cultural-national autonomy for the five million Russian Jews in the Tsar's Empire. In their struggle with the Jewish labour movement, the Russian Marxists denounced the advocacy by the *Bund* of federalism, non-territorial cultural autonomy and its claims to be "the sole representative of the Jewish proletariat" as bourgeois nationalism.[81] Plekhanov, the founder of Russian Marxism, was especially contemptuous of the Jewish Socialist *Bund* and his opinions were antisemitically tinged. According to Lenin's notes:

> "He declared straight out that this is not a Social Democratic organization, but simply an organization of exploitation – to exploit the Russians. He felt that our goal is to kick the Bund out of the Party, that the Jews are all chauvinists and nationalists, that a Russian [*ruskaia*] party must be Russian and not 'give itself into captivity to the tribe of Gad', etc. . . ."[82]

Lenin's polemics against the *Bund* were also extremely harsh and as part of this ruthless ideological struggle, he declared in 1903 that "the idea of a separate Jewish people is politically reactionary and scientifically untenable". Indeed, in Lenin's view the notion of a specifically Jewish culture was inherently bourgeois: "Jewish national culture is the slogan of the rabbis and the bourgeoisie, the slogan of our enemies." At the same time, however, Lenin identified himself with the progressive elements in Jewish culture as manifested in the Western world and with the contributions of Jewish revolutionaries to the Social Democratic movement. This was a significant difference between his position and that of Stalin, whose *Marxism and the National Question* (1913) also dealt extensively with the *Bund* and the "Jewish Question". Stalin saw only the negative sides of Jewish culture and stressed the desire of the *Bund* to isolate itself from everything non-Jewish as a nationalist betrayal of Marxism. The defence of Yiddish, Jewish hospitals, schools and traditional holidays was branded as separatist and isolationist. The Jews could not, in any case, legitimately claim national rights since they were in Stalin's opinion, a nebulous, amorphous entity, lacking all the attributes of nationality – e.g. common language, territory, economic life and community of culture.

Stalin's position was within the tradition of doctrinal Marxist orthodoxy but tinged, even before 1914, with a Russian nationalism that was hyper-centralist and potentially intolerant of minorities. Referring back to his Bolshevik

---

[81]John Mill, *Pionirn un Boyer*, 2 vols., New York 1946–1949; see also Henry J. Tobias, *The Jewish Bund in Russia from its Origins to 1905*, Stanford 1972; Nora Levin, *Jewish Socialist Movements 1871–1917*, London 1978, pp. 109–112, on the attitude of the Socialist International to the *Bund* before 1914.
[82]Quoted in Frankel, *op. cit.*, p. 229.

comrades in Baku during the 1907 London Congress of the Russian Democratic Party, Stalin was unfavourably struck by the high percentage of Jews in the rival Menshevik faction. He felt compelled to record that

> ". . . one of the Bolsheviks . . . jestingly remarked that the Mensheviks were a Jewish faction while the Bolsheviks were *truly Russian* [my emphasis] and hence it would not be amiss for us Bolsheviks to instigate a pogrom in the party".[83]

The "jest" was perhaps a significant pointer to latent anti-Jewish feeling within a section of Russian Social Democracy and to the pathological antisemitism of Stalin which exploded at the end of his life.

The Austrian Social Democrats, who like the Russian party operated in a multi-national environment with a substantial Jewish population (1.2 million excluding Hungary), were no less opposed to Jewish national autonomy, even though they had accepted it for other smaller peoples in the Habsburg Monarchy. Their chief theoretician, Otto Bauer (himself a Jew but estranged from Judaism and Jewish culture) argued that "the Jewish workers should not demand national autonomy", because the Jews were a nation without a future, whose assimilation was historically inevitable. Even if one assumes that Otto Bauer was devoid of antisemitic prejudice, it is remarkable that he denied to Jews what the Austro-Marxists accepted as valid for Germans, Poles, Czechs, South Slavs etc. in Austria-Hungary – i.e. the right to develop their language, national individuality, independent schools and culture, etc.[84]

Bauer's terminology derived from Marx, assuming that Judaism and Christianity were only superstructures on a capitalist, economic basis and that the Jews were a "non-historical nation". Like other Austrian Democrats and their Polish allies in Galicia, Otto Bauer's disqualification of East European Jewry as a national entity with a future, had a self-evident political purpose – to weaken Jewish Nationalism while strengthening the assimilation of *Ostjuden* to the common class-struggle. He felt that the Jewish masses (especially in Galicia) were backward, under the sway of clerical obscurantism and a petrified tradition which represented the antithesis of a Marxist approach to the "Jewish Question". But his attitude was also partly the consequence of a self-hatred displayed by many assimilated Jewish leaders of the Austrian Social Democratic Party, which was founded and guided for nearly thirty years (1889–1918) by a converted Jew, Victor Adler, who in his youth had been a Pan-German Nationalist.[85]

What is especially significant is that the Socialist antisemitism which developed in Austria during these years was more deep-rooted and persistent than elsewhere in Europe (except France), yet distinct from both its racist and clerical rivals as manifested in the antisemitic mass movements led by Georg von

---

[83]J.V. Stalin, 'Londonskii Syezd Rossiskoi Sotzial-Demokraticheskoi Rabochei Partii', in *Sochineniya*, vol. II (*1907–1913*), Moscow 1949, pp. 50–51.

[84]Wistrich, *Socialism and the Jews, op. cit.*, pp. 335–343.

[85]*Idem, Revolutionary Jews, op. cit.*, chap. 5; *idem, Socialism and the Jews, op. cit.*, pp. 240ff.

Schoenerer and Karl Lueger between 1880 and 1914.[86] Antisemitism had first infiltrated the Austrian labour movement in the period of "anarchist" confusion during the early 1880s – precisely because the antisemitic movement was more "oppositional", more "democratic" and radical in Austria than in Germany. In 1884 Karl Kautsky wrote to Engels from Vienna:

> ". . . it has been proved that a part of the anarchist leaders are in the pay of the antisemites. The latter are becoming significant in Austria; thanks to anarchist muddleheadedness the workers fall to them and we have trouble in keeping our own people from fraternising with the antisemites."[87]

The petit-bourgeois, artisan background of the Austrian working class and the influence of German Nationalism on some of its leaders like Victor Adler, Engelbert Pernerstorfer and Heinrich Braun ensured that an antisemitic undercurrent would remain strong in the labour movement even after the collapse of the anarchist trends and even though it was never part of the official Marxist ideology. The strength of clerical and Nationalist antisemitism as mass movements in Austria – especially the electoral successes of the Christian Socialist Party led by Karl Lueger – drove the Socialists further on the defensive. Though they rejected an exclusive struggle against "Jewish" capitalism, the Socialists shared the unrelenting hostility of the antisemitic parties to Austro-Liberalism and its philosemitism. Liberalism (with its strongly Jewish colouring in Austria) was regarded by the Socialists as the hereditary enemy of the labour movement and the so-called *Judenpresse*, which included such influential Liberal newspapers as the *Neue Freie Presse*, was often viewed as far more dangerous than the antisemitic press. Moreover, the leaders of the Social Democrats realised that, given the electoral popularity of antisemitism in Austria, there was nothing to be gained politically by defending Jews. On the contrary, such a defence would play into the hands of the antisemites who, in any case, had branded Austrian Social Democracy as a "Jewish protective guard" because of its high percentage of Jewish-born leaders.

Thus in Austria the Socialists took an opportunist position, not infrequently exploiting antisemitism in their attacks on Liberalism and even branding their Christian-Socialist rivals as "agents of Jewish capital".[88] Efforts at Jewish self-defence were stigmatised as an attempt to justify the financial power of the Rothschilds, the Jewish capitalists and the Liberal press. The "struggle against antisemitism" was branded as an egoistic mask for preserving Jewish-Liberal privileges, while Socialists defended the antisemitic movement in Austria as a "persecuted" party of the masses. Jewish Nationalism was frequently ridiculed by the Socialists (especially those of Jewish origin) as a clerical, reactionary return to the ghetto.

[86]On the Lueger movement, see the major work by John Boyer, *Political Radicalism in Late Imperial Vienna. Origins of the Christian Social Movement 1848–1897*, Chicago–London 1981; Robert S. Wistrich, *The Jews of Vienna in the Age of Franz Joseph*, Oxford–New York 1989.
[87]Karl Kautsky to Friedrich Engels, 23rd June 1884, in Benedikt Kautsky (ed.), *Friedrich Engels' Briefwechsel mit Karl Kautsky*, Wien 1955, p. 125.
[88]Robert S. Wistrich, 'Socialism and Antisemitism in Austria before 1914', in *Jewish Social Studies*, vol. XXXVII, Nos. 3–4 (Summer-Fall 1975), pp. 323–333.

At the 1897 Austrian Social Democratic Party Congress there were even protests that too many bourgeois Jews were entering the workers' movement. Victor Adler himself preferred to put up "Christian" candidates in the elections and, if possible, to restrict the number of Jewish intellectuals – a policy of *numerus clausus* that remained informal and failed to prevent the Party from being dominated largely by Jews. Nevertheless, the Jewish leaders of the Austrian Social Democrats went to great lengths to dissociate themselves from capitalist Jewry and even to justify antisemitism. Typical of this stance was the attitude of Friedrich Austerlitz, editor of the central Party newspaper, *Arbeiterzeitung*, who wrote that before Lueger came to power in Vienna in 1897 there had been "a conspiracy in favour of the Jews". Nothing, according to Austerlitz, "so promoted Viennese antisemitism as the fact that for a long time the Viennese press has been controlled by the Jews".[89] The Polish Socialists, like their colleagues in Vienna, even justified the antisemitic pogroms in Galicia during the summer of 1898 as an understandable reaction of oppressed Polish peasants against Jewish middlemen and usurers.[90] The leader of the Russian *Poale Zion*, Ber Borochov, who lived for several years in Vienna at the beginning of the twentieth century, summed up accurately enough the attitude of the pan-Austrian Social Democratic Party to the "Jewish Question":

> ". . . their own newspapers never deem it necessary to oppose antisemitism unequivocally. Its manifestations in everyday life, in the press and in the trade unions, are tolerated by the Social Democrats. They generally tend either to dismiss the Jewish Question and to pass it over in silence, or to ridicule it with antisemitic jokes."[91]

The Austrian Social Democrats, like their colleagues in the labour movements of Germany, Russia, Poland, France, Belgium and Great Britain, denied, of course, that they were antisemitic or that they "tolerated" anti-Jewish utterances. They did, however, generally admit, as Otto Bauer put it in 1910, that "Marx's essay on the Jewish Question already differentiated us sharply from Liberal philosemitism" and they often asserted (especially in countries like Germany, Austria, Poland and Russia where Jews were prominent in leadership positions) that Social Democracy was not "a Jewish protective guard". Officially, the Socialist position remained one of neutrality – neither for nor against the Jews. As the Second Congress of the Socialist International held in Brussels (1891) put it, both anti- and philosemitic outbursts (!) were to be condemned "as one of the means by which the capitalist class and reactionary governments seek to divert the Socialist movement and divide the workers". In reality, of course, the Socialist International was being evasive, for it had been asked (by the American Jewish delegate, Abraham Cahan) to condemn unequivocally open antisemitic persecution in Russia. Instead, under the influence of French and Belgian Socialists (supported by two leaders of Jewish origin, Victor Adler and

---

[89]*Ibid.*, p. 330.

[90]Robert S. Wistrich, 'Austrian Social Democracy and the Problem of Galician Jewry 1890–1914', in *LBI Year Book XXVI* (1981), pp. 107–109.

[91]Ber Borochov, *Ketavim* (in Hebrew), Tel-Aviv 1955–1966, vol. III, p. 121. On Borochov see *Class Struggle and the Jewish Nation. Selected Essays in Marxist Zionism*, edited with an Introduction by Mitchell Cohen, New Brunswick–London 1984.

Paul Singer, a prominent SPD deputy) it had also equally condemned "philose-mitism", as if Jews organised pogroms against Gentiles or Jewish bankers had interests and privileges different from Christian bankers![92]

The equivocacy of the Socialist International reflected, as we have shown, a much deeper ambiguity and tradition of hostility, indifference and contempt for Jews apparent in the Socialist movements of almost all European countries, including even liberal Great Britain. Socialists throughout Europe were reluc-tant to distinguish between anti-capitalism and antisemitism and frequently lent their support to a Leftist variety of Judeophobia which equated capitalist and "Jew". Many European Socialists believed, moreover, that in the last analysis, antisemitism served to advance the cause of Socialism, just as the *narodniki* in Russia had welcomed the pogroms as the prelude to social revolution. At times, the German Social Democrats, too, as we have seen, flirted with the proposition that antisemitism was ultimately beneficial to the Socialist cause, precisely because it was accelerating the disintegration of bourgeois society. As the veteran Social Democratic leader, Wilhelm Liebknecht, put it in 1893: "Yes, the antisemites plough and sow, and we Social Democrats will reap. Their successes are therefore not at all unwelcome to us."[93] This opportunist stance was also common in France and Austria-Hungary and indicated the reluctance of many Socialists to risk openly combating the antisemitic wave at its height.

The Austrian Social Democrats signally failed in their endeavours to channel the discontent of the petty bourgeois masses in a Socialist direction, by indulging in their own anti-capitalist variant of popular antisemitism. Like many other Socialists in *fin-de-siècle* Europe, far from immunising the workers against Judeophobic prejudices, the Austrian Social Democrats unwittingly reinforced their potency, even when claiming to be fighting against antisemitism.[94] As we have seen, even the German Social Democrats, who persistently defended Jewish equality whenever it was threatened by German antisemites, were not immune to this tendency.[95] Moreover, they consistently underestimated antisemitism, assuming that it was doomed to disappear along with the declining *Mittelstand*. All over Europe this distinct Socialist tradition of Judeophobia, would, with varying degrees of intensity and success, continue to identify Jews with the hated capitalist system, at least until the First World War.

---

[92]James Joll, *The Second International*, London 1955, p. 68.
[93]Wistrich, *Socialism and the Jews, op. cit.*, p. 115.
[94]*Idem*, 'Social Democracy, the Jews, and Antisemitism in *Fin-de-Siècle* Vienna', in Jehuda Reinharz (ed.), *Living with Antisemitism. Modern Jewish Responses*, Hanover–London 1987, pp. 193–209.
[95]Questions of Judeophobia and antisemitism were dealt with at a recent symposium, 'Soziale Utopien und religiös-kulturelle Traditionen. Juden und deutsche Arbeiterbewegung bis 1933', sponsored by the Steinheim-Institut, Duisburg and the London Leo Baeck Institute, which took place in Mülheim in December 1990. The papers have been published in Ludger Heid and Arnold Paucker (eds.), *Juden und deutsche Arbeiterbewegung bis 1933. Soziale Utopien und religiös-kulturelle Traditionen*, Tübingen 1992 (Schriftenreihe wissenschaftlicher Abhandlungen des Leo Baeck Instituts 49).

Jewish Nationalism and Jewish Identity in Central Europe

BY JEHUDA REINHARZ

Jewish liberals, who dominated most of the Western and Central European communities, were faced with a dilemma in the last part of the nineteenth century. They had to come to terms with the discrepancy between the promise of full social and political emancipation on the one hand and the reality of being a group that was at best tolerated, at worst discriminated against and oppressed, on the other.* Thus, in managing their communities they needed to do more than rely solely on religious toleration to solve the Jewish problem. They developed programmes and organisations that promoted the cultural, social and economic amelioration of the Jews' situation, while urging their co-religionists to prove their right to emancipation by reforming voluntarily.[1]

The outcome of this process was another paradox. Despite all obstacles, emancipation was accompanied by a remarkably successful acculturation, economic advance and – to an extent – social assimilation of the Jews. But this very success became the grounds for new, increasingly virulent forms of antisemitism. By the late nineteenth century even conversion could not make the Jews acceptable to their enemies in Europe, for the new antisemitism erected the insuperable barrier of racism.

Until Zionism emerged as a potent force, Jewish liberals adjusted to this anomaly in practice, while evading it intellectually. Excluded from the various clubs, fraternities and orders in the lands of their residence, Jews formed societies that were purportedly "non-sectarian", but in actuality exclusively Jewish bodies. The local Jewish community, which nominally organised for purely cultural functions, actually formed a considerable variety of mutual welfare services. While claiming to engage in general philanthropy, quite a few organisations within the Jewish community performed purely ethnic functions. Under the impact of Zionism, leaders of these organisations were from time to time forced to acknowledge their Jewishness. Almost invariably, they did so only

This essay is dedicated to my dear friend and esteemed colleague, Dr. Arnold Paucker. I am personally indebted for both his pathbreaking studies and insightful comments on my own work. The entire field of German-Jewish history is forever in his debt.

*This essay was enriched by suggestions made by Benjamin Ben-Baruch. I am especially grateful to him for some references in the fields of sociology and psychology – J.R.

[1]See Jehuda Reinharz, *Fatherland or Promised Land? The Dilemma of the German Jew, 1893–1914*, Ann Arbor 1975, chaps. 1 and 2.

under duress; with time, however, they moved closer to an open declaration of ethnic identity while continuing to deny the existence of a national element.

The ideological challenge of Zionism was less clear and immediate for traditionalists than for the modernist liberal establishment. The ideas that the new radical Zionists themselves considered most revolutionary – that antisemitism was a permanent, structural feature of life in the Diaspora, and only the restoration of the Jews to national autonomy in their own land could eradicate it – sounded to traditionalists like echoes of the ancient Jewish mythos of Exile and Redemption. What made them wary was the intrusion of secularists – even by way of partial rapprochement with tradition – into an area held especially sacred: Jewish settlement in the Holy Land. Some of those long associated with support of the *Yishuv*, both through the *halukka* and the other Orthodox organisations, fell away from the new movement because of the active involvement of unbelievers and transgressors. Others, who continued in the new framework, had to keep close watch against the threat of importing infidelity into Zion, the sanctuary of religious commitment.

For the reform-minded Western philanthropists who concerned themselves with the *Yishuv* and the Jewish refugee question, ideological Zionism was immediately perceived as an acute problem. The main issues of the debate in the Jewish community after the pogroms were practical, to be sure, rather than ideological: they were centred primarily on the relative advantages and drawbacks of supporting the immigration of Jewish refugees to Palestine or to the Americas. The "practical" arguments in favour of Palestine (for example, that Jewish loyalty to tradition would be better preserved in the Holy Land than in America) obviously rested on deeper assumptions (that emancipation in the Exile threatened the survival of Judaism through assimilation), widely held among the traditionalists in opposition to the ruling consensus among Western Jewish philanthropists. But since the only programme of action that these assumptions entailed among traditionalists was a defensive retreat to self-seclusion, together with reliance on the divinely-appointed messianic redemption, this presented no real challenge to modernism. But ideologically explicit secular Zionism, in spite of its own modernism, was seen as a direct attack on the established programme of integration into the nation-state, which renounced Jewish nationality and retained only the (rather loose) tie of religion. This gave the debate over practical issues a sharper polemical edge when conducted between Zionists and the establishment modernists.

But practical considerations quickly forced the secular Zionists to moderate their position, at least with regard to the programme of immediately relevant action. The Romanian pro-Palestine movement found within a few years that the obligations it incurred to support settlers were far beyond its means. Only the intervention of Baron Edmund de Rothschild saved the settlements that Romanians had begun to build in the valley east of Safed and the upland plain south of Haifa. Relieved of this responsibility, the Romanian organisation lapsed into virtual dissolution. When the 1884 Kattowitz conference created a new, international centre for the *Hovevei-Zion*, the Romanian movement was incapable of participating. The prime movers in that conference were the Russian *Hovevei-*

Zion.[2] Their main concern was to build a more effective organisation for carrying out the responsibilities they had assumed: to support those remaining new settlements in Palestine which Rothschild had not, at that time, undertaken to maintain. They, too, were fully aware of their dependence on support from Western Jews. This led their chosen leader, Leon Pinsker, to suppress the ideological contentions of his earlier position, stated in the brochure *Autoemanzipation*, and set forth a programme confined to practical, humanitarian aid for resettlement in Palestine, on lines calculated to propitiate the leaders of emancipated Western Jewish communities.

But while their working programme was adapted to non-Zionist specifications, the Russian *Hovevei-Zion*, and the *Maskilim* and intellectuals associated with their movement, carried on a lively ideological debate in the Hebrew and Russian press. Divisions within the movement were sharply defined and developed in more complex articulation. The practical work in Palestine sufficed to keep the organisation alive, in spite of the handicaps under which it laboured in the Diaspora and in Palestine. But the compromises it was compelled to accept were a source of constant frustration to those young *Maskilim* and radical intellectuals who shared in a cultural revival inspired by the mythos of auto-emancipation.

Eastern Europe was the cradle of Zionism, but from its earliest days the movement developed significant relations with Jewish communities in the West. Oppressive conditions in its original Russian base hampered the movement in its work and compelled Zionism to seek support in countries of greater freedom. The waves of emigration from Russia, Romania and Austria-Hungary included a scattering of Zionist adherents who went to cities like Berlin, Paris, London, Zürich and New York, building Zionist cells wherever they settled. Often it was the Eastern Europeans who had moved westwards – men like Leo Motzkin, Shmarya Levin and Chaim Weizmann – who became the leaders of Zionist societies in the West.[3]

At the same time, Western Zionism always had in its ranks – and often as its local leaders – native-born or fully integrated Western Jews. Such recruits shared, broadly speaking, their Eastern comrades' assumptions about the general nature of the "Jewish problem", but came to Jewish Nationalism by a different route: from a background of experience which they shared with some of their Western non-Zionist contemporaries.

One source of Western sympathy for Zionism was the tradition of supporting the *Yishuv*, the Jewish community in the Holy Land. Philanthropists who carried on that tradition in the nineteenth century did so in a new, modernising spirit. Their benefactions were not simply acts of pious charity, but also an extension overseas of the programme of enlightenment and socio-economic "amelioration" that they pursued on behalf of fellow Jews at home, in the campaign for civic emancipation. The traditionalist community in Palestine, however, showed a

---

[2]Israel Klausner, *Behitorer am. Hatnuah lezion be-Russyah* (in Hebrew), Jerusalem 1962.
[3]See Jehuda Reinharz, *Chaim Weizmann, the Making of a Zionist Leader*, New York 1985, pp. 65–91.

stiff resistance to modernisation, particularly in its opposition to secular studies, the mainstay of the Westerners' programme.

The Zionists were no less committed than the philanthropists to projects of secular education, vocational retraining and agricultural settlement. Co-operation with them was, therefore, an attractive option for Westerners – but only if the Zionists would play down their dangerous nationalist intentions. When they did so (under the pressure of Ottoman restrictions), co-operation with Western non-Zionists was indeed achieved. Meanwhile, there were from the beginning Western Jews who found Zionism itself ideologically acceptable. These men joined and frequently became leaders of early Zionist movements in such countries as Germany, the United Kingdom and the United States.

One factor that predisposed such Western Jews to become Zionists was the tendency towards a more militant, self-assertive style in the defence of Jewish rights and interests. Early protagonists of enlightenment and civic emancipation had usually accepted that Jews must earn their equal rights by reforming traditional ways, economic and social as well as religious. This attitude led many – notably in America – to eschew separatist political activity, such as that clearly implicit in Zionism. But by the time Zionism itself arose, a different, activist attitude was held by an entire generation of self-assured Jewish liberals. They considered civic equality to be an absolute right that must not be made conditional or withheld until Jews fulfilled demands for "amelioration". Moreover, it became clear by the 1870s that not only legal discrimination but social prejudice against Jews, culminating in the rise of political antisemitism, required militant Jewish action, and therefore organisation for self-defence.

The *Alliance Israélite Universelle*, formed in France in 1860 as an international Jewish body, and the *Centralverein deutscher Staatsbürger jüdischen Glaubens* (C.V.), organised in Germany in 1893 to combat antisemitism, were founded by leaders of this activist inclination. Their avowed commitment to emancipation according to the principles of the French Revolution was, of course, in direct conflict with the Zionist slogan of auto-emancipation; their anti-Zionist militancy was often due to the implicit challenge to their own leadership in the activist, militant and political defence of Jewish interests. These conflicts frequently took the form of differences over tactics; what the non-Zionist leadership shared with the Zionists was a fundamental strategy of activism rather than passive, inner-directed accommodation in seeking to define the Jewish position in a Gentile world.

Theodor Herzl, the founder of the World Zionist Organisation, belonged to a generation of young Jews in German lands whose sensitivity to the insults of antisemitism was strongly implanted in their student years. The 1880s saw some German and Austrian political parties rise to heights of menacing strength. Even if the antisemites' electoral strength receded in Germany during the 1890s, students at the universities continued to be harassed and humiliated by antisemitic fraternities. In consequence of the rejection they encountered, Jews organised their own student societies; some were professedly non-sectarian, though overwhelmingly Jewish in composition; others were proudly, if not defiantly, committed to positive programmes of Jewish self-assertion. The wounded pride, which that generation held in common was expressed in the *Centralverein*'s militant defence of Jewish rights, and by men like Max Boden-heimer, Franz Oppenheimer and Herzl in Zionism.

With the rise of Herzl, Zionism could no longer be viewed as an essentially Eastern European movement with marginal Western supporters and sympath-isers. To be sure, even before Herzl, Western sympathisers had played a vital role in the proto-Zionist movement, the *Hibbat Zion*. The Parisian Baron Edmund de Rothschild had taken over the financial sponsorship of nearly all its Palestinian settlements, and *Hibbat Zion* had set up headquarters in Paris in an attempt to overcome handicaps imposed by the Russian government. But in convening the Zionist Congress in 1897, Herzl projected the movement boldly and effectively into the domain of international affairs – not as a pragmatic solution to the local problems of certain oppressed Jewish communities in Eastern Europe, but as the claim of Jews throughout their dispersion to be liberated as "a nation, one nation". In this bold manoeuvre he was able to revive the original impulse of auto-emancipation among the Zionists in the East and – by a positive expression of Jewish pride – to attract a following among men like himself in the West. He put Zionism forward once again as an ideological challenge to all Jews and as a solution for a problem that affected them all alike.

For Westerners, however, this meant identifying with an ideology and a prescription for action that found its clearest application in the situation of Eastern European Jews. Herzl did not shy away from this conclusion, arguing that the crisis clearly approaching Russian and Romanian Jews was eventually bound to befall Jews everywhere. Other Zionist leaders (like Max Bodenheimer of Cologne) might agree in principle that the basic Jewish situation was most clearly exemplified in Eastern Europe, but would regard the case of Germany as a fortunate exception; the plea of exceptionalism was one that Western Jews in many nations, and Western Zionist leaders among them, made with respect to their home countries.[4] But in their understanding of the position of Jews generally, as a single people, such Zionists recognised the Eastern European situation, and the diagnosis and prescription appropriate to it, as the paradigma-tic case.

One further element which made Zionism attractive to some Western Jews was the growing disquiet over the effects of the rationalist universalism of Jewish religious Reform and of secularist liberalism. Young Jews brought up in such a milieu too frequently dismayed their parents by abandoning tribal loyalties; alternatively, the young themselves found their parents' secularism or reformed religion to be distasteful expressions of a bourgeois lifestyle. Either situation could lead to a heightened appreciation of the solid ethnic roots believed to characterise the Eastern European community. Zionism, as an expression of this quality, drew some German Jews of Orthodox religious background in the early years. Later, especially after closer contacts with Eastern Europe during the First World War, an *avant-garde*-ist group of young Zionists in Berlin, Prague and

---

[4]See Max Bodenheimer, *Wohin mit den russischen Juden? Syrien ein Zufluchtsort der russischen Juden*, Cologne 1891.

other centres of modernist culture came to lead the German Zionist movement. As in other Western Jewish communities, Zionism was taken up, like the vogue for neo-*hasidism* inspired by Martin Buber and others, as part of a broader rebellion of the young against the older establishment.

It was during the First World War that Western Jews – particularly German Jews – met their Eastern European brethren – often for the first time – and established the kind of ties that would endure afterwards. German Zionists considered the East European Jews to be "better Jews" than they, in closer touch with their tradition and culture. Those of the older generation recognised the differences between German Jews and their East European brethren, but did not draw any implications from this for their own lives. The younger generation, however, looked to the *Ostjuden* as Jews worthy of emulation. This was largely a romantic idealisation, however, since very few German Jews had actually come into close contact with the *Ostjuden* prior to the First World War. Many young Zionists assumed that the assimilated West European Jew had personality flaws which accounted for the moral and national decline of Western Jewry. Identification with the *Ostjuden* was one vehicle for checking this decline. Idealisation of the *Ostjuden* and their East European culture became the answer to the young Zionists' basic and deep personal needs.

One may state that the First World War constitutes a turning point in the attitude of German Zionists towards the *Ostjuden*. They were henceforth viewed not merely as objects of philanthropy, but as valuable political and ideological partners in the cause of Zionism and as active participants in alleviating their own miserable condition. Moreover, many German Zionists perceived in the *Ostjuden* a needed source for their own Jewish strength and vitality. An increasing number of German Zionists sought out the East European Jews who lived in their own midst.[5]

It has often been pointed out that German Zionism was a post-assimilation phenomenon; that it was shaped and defined by people who were expected to advocate assimilation in its various manifestations with universalistic and liberal rhetoric, but instead adopted a nationalist/particularistic ideology out of step with the views of the majority. Indeed, German Zionism was an anomaly – its ideology largely transplanted from the East – at a time when the acculturation of German Jewry was proceeding apace amid a favourable political and cultural climate. It is, therefore, not surprising that German Zionists did, in fact, resemble their liberal cohort along the entire spectrum of social indicators. It was largely in the realm of ideology that the German Zionists tried to define for themselves a separate and distinctive role that would distance them from the majority of German Jews.

Zionism in Germany emerged as both an ideology and a social movement. As an ideology, Zionism had as its chief proponents those who seemed to be "class defectors". As a social movement, it sponsored organisational activities that

[5]See Jehuda Reinharz, 'East European Jews in the Weltanschauung of German Zionists, 1882–1914', in *Studies in Contemporary Jewry*, I (1984), pp. 55–95.

seemed geared primarily towards consciousness-raising rather than to any practical fulfilment of its programme. Practical work was, for the most part, limited to fund-raising and propaganda. Zionism in Germany was not primarily a response by the majority of German Jewry to the consequences of their own social position. Rather, it was largely an effort by an organised minority to educate German Jewry towards a national Jewish self-definition.

The similarity of socio-economic background, occupations and lifestyles among the leaderships of the *Zionistische Vereinigung für Deutschland* (ZVfD) and the major liberal German organisation, the C.V., has been noted before.[6] The two organisations were ideological competitors with diametrically opposed conceptions of the needs and interests of German Jewry. Yet, when we examine what compelled some German Jews to join one organisation and some the other, we find that social and class factors cannot provide sufficient explanation. German Zionists saw Germany as their homeland and very few of them emigrated to Palestine, or even had the intention to, until events after 1933 forced the issue.

Psychological factors may be pertinent here. German Zionists themselves stressed the psychological function of Zionism, arguing as a major theme in their writings that Zionism offered a cure for an unhealthy personality.* Richard Lichtheim, Max Bodenheimer, Kurt Blumenfeld, Siegfried Kanowitz, Adolf Friedemann and many others recalled the psychological changes taking place during their "conversion" to Zionism.[7] Martin Buber, at an address to the XIIth Zionist Congress in Karlsbad, spoke in similar terms, though couched within a larger theoretical framework.[8]

All these individuals were exposed in their young adulthood to the Zionist analysis of the causes and consequences of the social position of the Jews. They accepted this analysis because it seemed to define objectively their own social position. It gave them an insight into their own situation and the forces shaping the objective conditions of their lives, an insight that constituted for many of them a sense of rebirth. Abraham Maslow has described this process as a "peak experience" – the revelation that comes when one suddenly sees the connections among the various causes and consequences under study and is able to make

---

[6]See Jehuda Reinharz, 'Consensus and Conflict between Zionists and Liberals in Germany before World War I', in Michael A. Fishbane and Paul R. Flohr (eds.), *Texts and Responses. Studies presented to Nahum N. Glatzer on the Occasion of his Seventieth Birthday by his Students*, Leiden 1975, pp. 226–238.
*See the following essay by John M. Efron, 'The "Kaftanjude" and the "Kaffeehausjude". Two Models of Jewish Insanity. A Discussion of Causes and Cures among German-Jewish Psychiatrists', in this volume of the Year Book – (Ed.).
[7]See Richard Lichtheim, *Rückkehr. Lebenserinnerungen* 1970, Veröffentlichung des Leo Baeck Instituts, pp. 65–66, 68; Max Bodenheimer, *Prelude to Israel. The Memoirs of M.I. Bodenheimer*, New York 1963, pp. 60–61; Kurt Blumenfeld, *Erlebte Judenfrage. Ein Vierteljahrhundert Deutscher Zionismus*, Stuttgart 1962, Veröffentlichung des Leo Baeck Instituts, p. 39; Siegfried Kanowitz, 'Vom post-assimilatori-schen Zionismus zur post-Zionistische Assimilation', in *Rückblick und Besinnung, Aufsätze Gesammelt aus Anlaß des 50. Jahrestages der Gründung der Verbindung Jüdischer Studenten "Maccabaea"*, Tel-Aviv 1954, pp. 22, 92; Adolf Friedemann, 'Was will der Zionismus?', in *Jüdische Rundschau*, VIII (1903).
[8]Martin Buber, *Israel and the World*, New York 1963, pp. 217–219.

sense of the whole, to integrate the various parts into a *Verstehen*.[9] According to Maslow, when one has had a cognitive peak experience, one integrates the new understanding with one's concept of self. This process leads to a commitment to this creative endeavour as a vocation, or what the existentialists call *engagement*.[10] For the Zionists, a new Jewish consciousness emerged that could not be reconciled with the prevailing assimilationist ideology of German Jewry.

The accepted ideology among German Jewry – as expressed by the *Central-verein* – was accommodation and integration which equated civil emancipation and acceptance into the German *Volk*. It postulated the continuous development of political Liberalism within Germany and strove for the complete acculturation of German Jews into German culture and society. At some point, however, some middle-class assimilated or assimilating German Jews perceived this basic assumption to be false. Not their identity, but their social position had to be re-assessed. What, then, was the meaning of this new self-definition?

The threshold of a new social consciousness was crossed when the first generation of German Zionists claimed that whereas Jews could never become fully integrated into the German nation, they had the right to preserve their own ethnic identity while remaining loyal Germans.[11] In so doing, the Zionists rejected the postulate of the continuous development of German liberalism – the desirability of complete acculturation. This was the meaning of the "Jewish Question" for the Zionists and the essence of the debate between them and the liberals. This is why so much of the debate centred on the definition and redefinition of the terms of *Deutschtum* and *Judentum*, a theoretical debate that was even more salient in their writings than themes like the problem of identity, the meaning of "personality disorder", or the act of conversion to Zionism.[12]

The C.V. was both a defence organisation (*Abwehrverein*) and a proponent of a specific ideology (*Gesinnungsverein*). These dual functions were intimately related in the organisation's basic platform, which consistently stated that antisemitism could be defeated by those who professed utter loyalty to *deutsche Gesinnung*. Despite consistency on this point, the *Centralverein*'s ideological position was in a continual process of modification in response to the external and internal events between 1893 and 1938. The First World War, the Balfour Declaration, the influx of *Ostjuden* into Germany, and the demands of the younger C.V. generation during the late 1920s were, among other factors, instrumental in these changes. An analysis of the C.V.'s attitude towards *Deutschtum* and *Judentum* before the First World War is, therefore, crucial to a proper understanding of the evolution of its ideology up to 1938.

[9]Abraham Maslow, *The Farther Reaches of Human Nature*, New York 1971; *idem*, *Toward a Psychology of Being*, 2nd edn., New York 1968. Maslow was also influenced by Buber. I would like to thank Benjamin Ben-Baruch for drawing my attention to Maslow's work. Parts of my analysis here derive from our previous collaboration.

[10]Maslow, *Toward a Psychology of Being*, *op. cit.*, p. 110.

[11]Jehuda Reinharz, 'Three Generations of German Zionism', in *The Jerusalem Quarterly*, No. 9 (Fall 1978), p. 97.

[12]See Jehuda Reinharz, 'Deutschtum and Judentum in the Ideology of the Centralverein deutscher Staatsbürger jüdischen Glaubens, 1893–1914', in *Jewish Social Studies*, vol. XXXVI, No. 1 (January 1974), pp. 19–39.

In its early years the C.V. emphatically declared that it was solely a defence organisation which aimed to protect the honour of the German Jews in the face of antisemitic insults. This statement plainly contradicts the first paragraph of the C.V. statutes which demanded "German-mindedness" from its members. This demand meant that membership in the C.V. was conditional on loyalty to *Deutschtum* above all other loyalties, including loyalty to *Judentum*, and this was the overriding position of the C.V. before the First World War. Despite its stress on patriotism and love of everything German, the C.V. did not neglect to define its stand towards *Judentum*. A major task of the C.V. before the First World War was, therefore, to make both *Judentum* and *Deutschtum* components of the *Weltanschauung* of the German Jew.

Before the founding of the C.V. in 1893, there had been many attempts to define the place of the Jew within the German state. These definitions, philosophical, historial and polemical, were painstakingly constructed to prove the same thesis – that the Jews were solely a religious body, analogous to the Catholics and Protestants, completely integrated within the state. This definition is the essence of the liberal ideology of integration and accommodation, developed and refined from the eighteenth century on. Foremost among the men who shaped this ideology were Gabriel Riesser, Moritz Lazarus, Hermann Cohen and Eugen Fuchs. Riesser, Lazarus and Cohen were influential in formulating the theoretical ideology of the general German-Jewish community while Fuchs, the acknowledged ideologue of the C.V., related their theories to the specific needs of the organisation.[13] The names of these four exponents of the synthesis of *Deutschtum* and *Judentum* appear continuously in the C.V. publications, especially in *Im deutschen Reich* and *C.V.-Zeitung*. The philosophy of the C.V. was derived wholly from these four men.

Zionism offered the psychological liberation that comes from self-affirmation; Zionists identified themselves in terms of their relations among Jews, not in terms of their place in German society. Their self-affirmation frequently led them to re-evaluate their relationship to other Jews and hence to redefine their status and role within the Jewish community. For the first generation of German Zionists self-affirmation meant reaffirming their bonds to the Jewish community. But for the second and third generations who frequently romanticised the *Ostjuden*, it often meant re-learning Jewish culture and Jewish values.

Thus far we have looked at the psychological factors that may account for the emergence of the Zionist idea in Germany. We ought to look at the emergence of the Zionist organisation in order to understand how it differed from the liberal organisations. Especially pertinent are the Jewish youth movements and other early Zionist social structures that formed an important component of the ZVfD

---

[13]See e.g. Gabriel Riesser, 'Besorgnisse und Hoffnungen für die künftige Stellung der Juden in Preussen', in *Gesammelte Schriften*, edited by M[eyer] Isler, vol. III, Frankfurt a. Main 1867, pp. 417ff.; Moritz Lazarus, 'Was Heisst National?', in *Treu und Frei. Gesammelte Reden und Vorträge über Juden und Judentum*, Leipzig 1887, pp. 115–155; Hermann Cohen, 'Deutschtum und Judentum', in Bruno Strauss (ed.), *Jüdische Schriften*, vol. II, Berlin 1924, pp. 302–318; Eugen Fuchs, *Um Deutschtum und Judentum, Gessammelte Reden und Aufsätze*, edited by Leo Hirschfeld, Frankfurt a. Main 1919.

and/or merged into the federated structure of the umbrella organisation, for these groups were the locus for the articulation of ideology and the mediation of the psychological factors.

As is well known, fraternities were a common form of student organisation in Germany during the 1890s.[14] Jewish students, like others of their class, joined fraternities in large numbers. Many of these young Jews, if not all, came from assimilated backgrounds and wished to participate in the various forms of German culture as fully as possible. However, as the decade wore on, increasing antisemitism in these fraternities made it difficult – psychologically, if not always legally – for Jews to join or remain in them. Their response was to form separate fraternities that emulated the forms and structures of their German counterparts. Ostensibly these new fraternities were open to Jews and Gentiles, but in practice they became exclusively Jewish.

This process led to dissonance. On the one hand these young Jews maintained the attitudes and values of assimilationism and liberalism into which they had already been acculturated. On the other hand, they were acting in a parochial manner within the context of a closed Jewish fraternity.

Jews resolved this dissonance in two ways. Some maintained that there was no dissonance at all, that the apparent incongruity was merely a manifestation of their need to organise to combat antisemitism and thus fight for German liberalism. The struggle against antisemitism was seen as necessitating (a) self-improvement and further acculturation, in order to demonstrate worthiness to join German fraternities, and (b) direct attacks on the common antisemitic attitude. Thus the existence of parochial fraternities was rationalised as a necessary temporary phenomenon on the road to full integration. This approach was the most common resolution of the dissonance and was typical of the large liberal majority and of the C.V.

The second way of resolving the dissonance was by rejecting notions of acculturation or assimilation. Those Jews who could not or would not avoid recognising the incongruence in their own lives asserted that exclusively Jewish fraternities were no mere temporary stop-gap, but actually preferable as instruments for fostering Jewish pride and unity. This new attitude towards Jewish national pride re-established congruence between actions and attitudes. Eventually members of this group developed a more coherent Zionist ideology and organised Zionist groups that were the precursors of the ZVfD or joined it after its establishment. It is not coincidental that many of these groups included Russian-born men and women who had been influenced by the *Hovevei-Zion*.

Significantly, a parallel process was evident within the liberal-assimilationist student groups. They slowly drifted towards a more fully developed new formulation of a German-Jewish ideology that stressed the need for Jewish defence, focusing on which Jewish interests should be defended, and how, in concert with German political Liberalism. The organisational activities of these

---

[14]For a general background on Jewish youth during the Second *Reich* see Chaim Schatzker, *Jüdische Jugend im zweiten Kaiserreich. Sozialisations- und Erziehungsprozess der jüdischen Jugend in Deutschland, 1870–1917*, Frankfurt a. Main 1988.

groups expanded. They used the press vigorously to attack antisemitism as being in conflict with German law and with Liberal principles, and they cultivated German culture within the Jewish community.

Similar developments took place in other Jewish youth movements. Like the fraternity students of the 1890s, Jewish youth in the first and second decades of the twentieth century established associations based on the German *Wandervogel* and other German youth movements from which they were excluded.[15] Once again there was incongruence between the assimilationist attitude and the parochial action. But, particularly after the First World War, this dissonance was more frequently resolved by a change of attitude, by an embracing of Zionism, than through avoidance or rationalisation.[16]

Given their background and experience in the last third of the nineteenth century, it is not at all surprising that assimilated German Jews should at first try to avoid the contradictions between reality and liberal ideology. It must also be kept in mind that until well into the 1920s the liberal ideology had attractive features. It promised continued upward mobility and full acceptance into German society. It postulated greater economic and even political – not to speak of cultural – opportunities for Jews. Zionism, on the other hand, appeared as a negative phenomenon, criticising and deprecating their very existence as Jews in the Diaspora.

The more permanent the contradictions became in the social structure, however, the more difficult it became to avoid the dissonance. Nevertheless, until the First World War the general pattern was to avoid facing the contradiction; few German Jews rejected the liberal ideology outright. But from about 1912 on, and particularly during the crises of liberalism and the increase of *völkisch* antisemitism of the Weimar era, the contradiction became more salient. This, and other developments outside Germany proper, propelled increasing numbers of German Jews to turn to Zionism.

This conflict between liberal assimilationism and Zionism in Germany, hardly touched the social, cultural, political or economic life of German Jewry. Zionism in Germany was an ideology only and its attraction for German Jews was not in practical or concrete deeds. Nevertheless the ZVfD did have a set of concrete goals: to provide organisational resources for the World Zionist Organisation, to provide support for the Palestinian labour movement, to raise funds for a variety of Zionist enterprises,[17] and to help Eastern European Jews emigrate to Palestine as well as to aid them in Germany. This last goal also had, of course, ideological implications, in the sense that the first generation of

---

[15]See Chaim Schatzker 'The Term "A-Semitism" in the German Youth Movement', in *Mehkarim be-Toldot Am Israel ve-Eretz Israel* (in Hebrew), ed. by B. Oded *et al.*, vol. III, Haifa; Walter Z. Laqueur, 'The German Youth Movement and the Jewish Question', in *LBI Year Book IX* (1961); and Chanoch Rinott, 'Major Trends in the Jewish Youth Movements in Germany', in *LBI Year Book XIX* (1974).

[16]Schatzker, 'The Term "A-Semitism" ', *loc. cit.*

[17]The Zionists even took some part in community elections – either directly or indirectly. See Shmuel Maayan, *Ha-behirot be-kehilat Berlin, 1901–1920* (in Hebrew), Givat Havivah 1977; see also Michael Brenner, 'The Jüdische Volkspartei. National-Jewish Communal Politics during the Weimar Republic', in *LBI Year Book XXXV* (1990), pp. 219–243.

German Zionists appear to have regarded the situation of Russian and Romanian Jews as the genuine Jewish Problem, and their own German situation as exceptional. In any case, none of these activities necessitated Zionist involvement in communal or national politics, or called for more concrete personal involvement in Palestine along the lines of the Posen Resolution of 1912.

In order to achieve its major ideological and other goals, the ZVfD had to combat the liberals and raise the consciousness of German Jews. The very divergence of the Zionist view from that of the liberal majority worked to its advantage here, giving it in essence, the same thing – high and constant visibility within the community. Other strategies included, primarily, the use of propaganda, among small groups and local chapters, at public lectures and in printed materials. The major resources in this campaign were individuals who could make the Zionist idea plausible to German Jews. These men and women, either paid staff or volunteers, devoted a great deal of their time to their task. Almost without exception, they were German-born, post-assimilation Zionists whose common background, language, manner and style made it possible for them to find resonance among the highly acculturated German liberal middle class.

Owing to the clear direction of ideology in German Zionism, there was a remarkable streamlining in the goals of the ZVfD, enabling it to mobilise effectively resources within its structure and activities. German Jews were attracted to Zionism as an idea that made sense psychologically and socially. In sum, the early structure of the ZVfD emerged from a confluence of social, historical and psychological forces that shaped its Zionism in ideological rather than practical terms until the Nazis came to power in 1933.

The interaction between Zionist and Jewish Nationalists on the one hand and members of the Austrian, and particularly the Viennese, liberal community on the other, took quite a different form than in Germany.[18] Here they clashed not only in their respective definitions of Jewishness but also on how to implement their definitions and the decisions they entailed in public life. The battle between them was over two issues: the general political posture of the Jews *vis à vis* the Gentile community[19] and political dominance in the *Israelitische Kultusgemeinde* itself.[20] In both cases the battle forced both sides – but particularly the liberal-

---

[18]For an overview, as reflected in the newspapers, see Jacob Toury, *Die jüdische Presse im Österreichischen Kaiserreich. Ein Beitrag zur Problematik der Akkulturation 1802–1918*, Tübingen 1983 (Schriftenreihe wissenschaftlicher Abhandlungen des Leo Baeck Instituts 41); see also Albert Fuchs, *Geistige Strömungen in Österreich, 1867–1918*, Vienna 1978; Abraham Palmon, 'Ha-kehilah ha-yehudit be-Vina ve-ha-rapublikah ha-ostrit ha-rishonah (1918–1938)', in *Historyah Yehudit*, vol. I, No. 1 (Spring 1986), pp. 9–32; Robert S. Wistrich, *The Jews of Vienna in the Age of Franz Joseph*, Oxford 1989, pp. 421–493. For a comparative, general assessment, see Julius Bab and Willi Handl, *Wien und Berlin. Vergleichendes zur Kulturgeschichte der beiden Hauptstädte Mitteleuropas*, Berlin 1918.

[19]See 'Eine Judenkurie in Österreich', in *Die Welt*, No. 49 (8th December 1905), pp. 1–2; 'Jüdische Autonomie und Jüdische Wählerkurien', in *Die Welt*, No. 3 (19th January 1906), p. 16; see also 'Eine Wiener Massenversammlung für die nationale Autonomie der Juden', in *Die Welt*, No. 50 (15th December 1905), pp. 7–8.

[20]See e.g. 'Die Zionisten und die Wahlen in der Wiener Cultusgemeinde', in *Die Welt*, No. 47 (23rd November 1900), pp. 1–3.

assimilationist camp – to rethink their definitions of Jewishness and Austrian patriotism.[21]

In the multinational Austro-Hungarian empire, the ethnic aspect of the Jewish situation was enhanced by the additional factor of an ethnically divided electorate. The curial system permitted a number of Jewish representatives to be chosen even under the conditions of a highly restricted, as well as easily manipulated, franchise.[22]

The Liberal Jewish deputies who were the spokesmen for the established community leadership, however, adopted a singular policy. Whereas all other deputies grouped themselves according to ethnic interests and openly defended these interests in parliament, the Jews understood their role to be the submergence of their ethnic identity. They felt that they had to deny the existence of a Jewish people in order to achieve a neutral identification with the Austrian state, but the irony was that there was no "Austrian" national entity with which to identify.[23] The "Dual Monarchy" was based on an arrangement through which the Germans, dominant over the empire generally, also recognised Magyar dominance in Hungary and the dominance of Conservative Polish aristocrats in Galicia.[24] Thus Jews demonstrated that they were Austrian primarily by identifying with the German Liberals, but if they were elected in Galicia they also joined the "club", or bloc, of Polish deputies,[25] while in Hungary German-speaking Jewish notables stood politically with the dominant Magyars. Moreover, despite the guise of "Austrian" neutrality, the Jewish deputies also defended specifically Jewish interests.[26]

Jewish Liberals held that Jews were simply a religious group, indistinguishable in all other respects from their fellow countrymen; at the same time, they engaged in patently ethnic practices.[27] They conducted distinctly Jewish activities in the field of communal social welfare, both local and international, and even undertook political action, both domestic and international, in defence of Jewish interests.[28] When Jewish Nationalists sought to widen these functions by democratising the structure of the Jewish community, they found it already constituted on a fairly wide ethnic base. Consequently, "Nationalism", the issue on which the Jewish Nationalists differed radically from the Jewish establish-

[21]See the interesting article by Hugo Bergmann, 'Der Weg ins Freie', in *Ost und West*, 8/9 (August/September 1908), pp. 492–496. This is a review of the play by Arthur Schnitzler dealing with the theme of Austrian Jewish assimilation.

[22]The following discussion relies on the work of Marsha L. Rozenblit, *The Jews of Vienna 1867–1914. Assimilation and Identity*, Albany 1983, and the manuscript by Ben Halpern and Jehuda Reinharz, 'The Emergence of the Jewish State, 1880–1948'. See also, William A. Jencks, *The Austrian Electoral Reform of 1907*, New York 1974.

[23]See Peter G. J. Pulzer, 'The Austrian Liberals and the Jewish Question, 1867–1914', in *Journal of Central European Affairs*, XXIII (1963), pp. 131–142.

[24]On the nationality conflict see C. A. Macartney, *The Habsburg Empire 1790–1918*, New York 1969.

[25]See the detailed discussion in Nathan M. Gelber, *Toldot ha-tnuah ha-zionit be-Galizia* (in Hebrew), 2 vols., Jerusalem 1958ff.

[26]See Anna Drabek, Wolfgang Häusler, Kurt Schubert *et al.*, *Das Österreichische Judentum, Voraussetzungen und Geschichte*, Vienna–Munich 1974, pp. 103–140.

[27]See Steven Beller, *Vienna and the Jews, 1867–1938. A Cultural History*, Cambridge 1989.

[28]See Walter B. Simon, 'The Jewish Vote in Austria', in *LBI Year Book XVI* (1971), pp. 97–121.

ment, expressed itself not only in their theory, but also in the practice of Jewish social policy.

Rather than viewing the activities of Jewish organisations as humanitarian, as did their co-religionists, Jewish Nationalists interpreted them from an openly ethnic perspective and radicalised and politicised the whole range of already existing functions that had developed as a result of the anomalous Jewish situation.[29] They promoted, of course, an emigration that was to produce an autonomous, concentrated settlement in a Jewish homeland. But they paid just as much attention to local and welfare activities that were to play a role in developing the principle of auto-emancipation. The aim of cultural reform should no longer be to introduce European culture into the Jewish ghetto in whatever language was convenient. Rather, the national language – Hebrew or, alternatively, Yiddish – should be cultivated as the instrument of distinct cultural individuality. The aim of vocational reform should no longer be to remove complaints against Jewish usury and make Jews acceptable in Gentile society. Instead, vocational retraining, producers', consumers' and credit co-operatives and political and trade union struggles were proposed to fight for the rights and protect the interests of oppressed Jewish workers. The social integration sought, contended the Jewish Nationalists, should be one that solidified and activated an inner Jewish, autonomous consensus, not one that established Jews as a fully absorbed part of Gentile society. And, finally, Jewish political activity should serve openly Jewish ends, whether directed towards the international problem of Jewish migration or the local problems inherent in domestic politics. These were views to which the Zionists were most clearly and comprehensively committed.[30]

In the Austrian, as well as the German context there was, of course, an inherent irony in Jewish liberals feeling compelled by the pressure of public opinion to conduct their affairs on the basis of ethnic policy.[31] But the Zionists had a similar ideological problem. The distinctive feature of Austrian Zionism was not "auto-emancipation" – a slogan that other factions in the Jewish community had also adopted. Rather, Zionism's distinctive trait was its doctrine that the road to emancipation necessitated an exodus from Diaspora countries to Zion. If adhered to, such a doctrine would obviously preclude the Zionists' concern with the domestic policies of the countries they planned to leave. But Zionism was no more doctrinaire than any other ideological movement. The fact that the Basle Programme had to contend with already existing cultural, ethnic,

---

[29]See Kurt Stillschweig, 'Nationalism and Autonomy among Eastern European Jewry', in *Historia Judaica*, 6 (1944), pp. 27–68.

[30]See the lively description of some of these debates in Anschel Reis, *Bisearot hatkufah* (in Hebrew), Tel-Aviv 1982, pp. 37–43. See also Shabtai Unger, 'Poalei Zion ba-Kesarut ha-ostrit, 1904–1914', unpubl. Ph.D. thesis, Tel-Aviv 1985, esp. chap. 2, pp. 175–235.

[31]See Werner J. Cahnman, 'Adolf Fischhof als Verfechter der Nationalität und seine Auswirkung auf das jüdisch-politische Denken in Österreich', in *Studia Judaica Austriaca*, Band 1, *Das Judentum im Revolutionsjahr 1848*, Vienna 1974, pp. 78–91; see also Harriet Pass Freidenreich, *Jewish Politics in Vienna, 1918–1938*, Bloomington 1991.

Socialist and other forms of Jewish Nationalism – in Austria-Hungary and elsewhere – precluded its rigid application.

Theodor Herzl understood this from the outset and, in order to retain the support of Zionists in various national and ethnic contexts, he maintained a flexible attitude towards them, while ignoring their differences as best he could. The result was that a variety of Jewish Nationalists – themselves not always agreeing on strategy and aims – continued to oppose the Jewish *Reichsrat* deputies who conducted a pro-German rather than ethnic Jewish policy. Jewish Nationalists were also critical of the Jewish establishment which controlled institutions by means of a restricted community franchise and they sharply opposed official anti-Jewish discrimination.[32] Similarly, they did not hesitate to attack Polish and German antisemitic politicians and Social Democratic leaders who ignored the existence of a Jewish proletariat while equivocating on the issue of antisemitism.

Socialist and labour Zionist groupings appeared in Russia and Austria during the turbulent years that bridged the nineteenth and twentieth centuries. At the VIIth Zionist Congress, in 1905, they were no longer represented merely by individual delegates, but appeared as organised factions in the World Zionist Organisation.

Jewish labour parties arose out of the same anomalous situation that produced Zionism itself, as well as all other modern Jewish ideologies. Because Jews were both a dissident religion and an oppressed group, the liberal leaders of Western Jewries found they could not rely solely on civic emancipation and religious toleration to solve the Jewish problem. They had to develop programmes of cultural, social and economic amelioration. The late nineteenth-century Leftist ideologues, who were primarily concerned with social and economic issues, similarly found that they could not deal with the problems of Eastern and East-Central European Jewries without confronting the issues of emancipation and antisemitism. Because Liberals and Leftists focused on different aspects of the same anomalous general-Jewish situation, and developed in different regions at different periods, they formed their views in response to characteristically different Gentile counterparts or adversaries.

The debate between Zionists and the liberal leaders of Western Jewry was over what Zionists called "assimilationism". It centred on the assumption of the Western liberals that, once emancipated, Jews should not differ from their fellow-countrymen in anything other than their "religion" and that, too, was to be redefined in the narrowly ecclesiastical sense of Western churches and reshaped in the style of the locally dominant Christian denomination.

In practice, the non-Zionist West did not, or could not, fully abide by the logic

---

[32]On antisemitism in Austria see Peter G. J. Pulzer, *The Rise of Political Anti-Semitism in Germany and Austria*, 2nd revised edn., Cambridge, Mass. 1988; see also Carl E. Schorske, 'Politics in a New Key. An Austrian Triptych', in *Journal of Modern History*, 39 (1967), pp. 343–386. For a more recent, comprehensive discussion of the subject see, Leopold Spira, *Feindbild "Jud". 100 Jahre politischer Antisemitismus in Österreich*, Vienna–Munich 1981; Robert S. Wistrich, 'Social Democracy, the Jews and Antisemitism in Fin-de-Siècle Vienna', in Jehuda Reinharz (ed.), *Living With Antisemitism. Modern Jewish Responses*, Hanover, N.H. – London 1987, pp. 193–209.

of this assumption. Emancipation was followed by remarkably successful acculturation, economic advance and – to an extent – social assimilation of the Jews. But this very success became the grounds for the recurrent rise of new, increasingly virulent forms of Jew-hatred. As noted earlier, until the emergence of Zionism, Jewish modernists adjusted to the anomaly in practice, while evading it intellectually, within a general ideology of liberalism. Excluded from Masonic orders, student *Burschenschaften* or *Korps*, Jews formed their own parallel societies; but, in theory, they conducted these as "non-sectarian" bodies. The local Jewish community, nominally organised purely for functions of worship and ceremony, actually performed a considerable variety of intra-communal welfare services. Special agencies, like the *Alliance Israélite Universelle*, were active on an international scale, conducting a range of cultural, economic and political projects no less comprehensive than those later envisaged by the Zionists; but they presented these activities in the guise of "philanthropic" assistance to one's "co-religionists". Under the publicly acceptable titles of general philanthropy and of a special responsibility for the need of one's own church, these quite evidently ethnic functions veiled their national character.

Western Jewish philanthropy extended to the Jewish community in Palestine made possible Zionist co-operation with non-Zionists and, at the same time, gave cause for disputes over strategic and tactical theories. The roots of difference were ideological, but co-operation in practice became possible when underlying ideological issues were covered over by reciprocal, or one-sided, concessions.

Leftist Zionism arose in a confrontation with Socialist or Social-Revolutionary Jewish ideologies, primarily in the Russian and Austro-Hungarian empires. It had to contend with a Jewish opposition, usually dominant among the local Left-orientated elements, that did not propose to reshape the Jewish community as a Western-style religion purged of ethnic attributes, but rather regarded Jewishness, whether religious or ethnic, as an historical irrelevancy and a present-day encumbrance. That Jews were at once a religiously and ethnically defined community, a group classified by faith and nationality, was not a matter of debate in Eastern and East-Central Europe. The question was how this undisputed fact was to be dealt with in practice. Given the curial system and a divided electorate, this was a particularly difficult problem in the Austro-Hungarian context.

The Liberal Jewish deputies, spokesmen for the established community leadership, adopted a singular policy. In a parliament where all other deputies grouped themselves according to ethnic interests and openly defended them, Jews alone took the mandate of their Jewish electors as instructions to submerge their ethnic identity. They were like the editor of the *Neue Freie Presse*, about whom Herzl ironically remarked that he belonged to a species the Zionist leader had never seen before: "he is an Austrian".[33] They needed a neutral identification with the state in order to deny the existence of a Jewish people.

[33]See Wistrich, *The Jews of Vienna*, *op. cit.*, p. 449.

The situation in the Czech lands was at least as complicated as in Austria. Here the main forces vying for hegemony within the Jewish communities were German Liberalism, the Czech Jewish movement and Zionism.[34] Since the focus of this paper is on German-speaking lands it will concentrate on Bohemia, or more specifically on Prague, the centre of the Zionism-Liberalism struggle.[35]

Although the beginning of the Jewish National movement in Prague can be traced to the founding of the "Maccabaea" in 1893,[36] Zionist activities were initiated in a sustained fashion only after the Ist Zionist Congress, probably stimulated by Theodor Herzl's call in the pages of *Die Welt*.[37] The Zionist movement offered to both German- and Czech-speaking Jews the solution of a credible middle road in the nationalist controversy. Its intent was not only to renounce both German and Czech "chauvinism", but also to affirm a positive, Jewish national identity. This was the public stance of the first overtly Zionist organisation in Bohemia, the *Jüdischer Volksverein "Zion"*. Simultaneously, Czech-speaking university students founded the bi-lingual *Bar Kochba, Verein Jüdischer Hochschüler in Prag*. They were the first to challenge the assimilationists in the Czech-Jewish National Union.[38]

Assimilationists feared the inroads Zionism was making in their own territory,[39] for the Zionists' insistence on self-defence and the maintenance of Jewish honour struck a responsive chord, especially among provincial Czech Jewry. Students, whether originally Czech- or German-speaking, discovered in Jewish Nationalism both a social alternative to a hostile environment and an honest response to the culture they did not accept. For the Jewish students of *Bar Kochba*, Zionism was a personal, spiritual revelation, a reclaiming of Judaism as a living culture. They drew their main inspiration from Ahad Ha'Am through the

[34]See Karl Fischl, 'Die Juden in Böhmen', *Die Welt*, No. 10 (9th March 1900), pp. 2–3; Felix Weltsch, 'The Rise and Fall of the Jewish-German Symbiosis. The Case of Franz Kafka, in *LBI Year Book I* (1956), pp. 255–276; Ruth Kestenberg-Gladstein, 'The Jews between Czechs and Germans in the Historic Lands, 1848–1918', in *The Jews of Czechoslovakia. Historical Studies and Surveys*, vol. I, Philadelphia–New York 1968, pp. 21–71; See also Wilma A. Iggers, 'The Flexible National Identities of Bohemian Jewry', in *East Central Europe*, vol. VII, No. 1 (1980), pp. 38–48.

[35]The discussion in this section has benefited from the unpublished dissertation of Michael A. Riff, *The Assimilation of the Jews of Bohemia and the Rise of Political Antisemitism*, University of London 1974 and the book of Hillel J. Kieval, *The Making of Czech Jewry. National Conflict and Jewish Society in Bohemia, 1870–1918*, New York 1988.

[36]See the following studies in Hebrew: Ruth Kestenberg-Gladstein, 'Athalot Bar Kochba', in *Prag Vi-Yerushalayim*, ed. by Felix Weltsch, Jerusalem 1954, pp. 86–110; Nathan M. Gelber, 'Kavim le-kadmut toldoteha shel ha-zionut be-Bohemia-u-Moravia', *ibid.*, pp. 36–51; see also Chaim Yahil, *Dvarim al Hazionut ha-Czechoslowakit*, Jerusalem 1967.

[37][T. Herzl], 'Die Jagd in Boehmen', *Die Welt*, No. 23 (5th November 1987), pp. 1–2; see also Stuart A. Borman, *The Prague Student Zionist Movement, 1896–1914*, unpubl. Ph.D thesis, University of Chicago 1972.

[38]The diaries of Hugo Bergman are indispensable for an understanding of the history of Zionism in Bohemia. See Schmuel Hugo Bergman, *Tagebücher und Briefe, Band I, 1901–1948*, Königstein/Ts 1985. Veröffentlichung des Leo Baeck Instituts, esp. pp. 3–100 for this discussion.

[39]Concerning the level of assimilation see Michael A. Riff, 'Assimilation and Conversion in Bohemia. Secession from the Jewish Community in Prague 1868–1917', in *LBI Year Book XXVI* (1981), pp. 73–88.

mediation of Nathan Birnbaum, Martin Buber[40] and others. At the same time they acknowledged that they were, if not a by-product of the nationality controversy in the Czech lands, then certainly inspired by the great nationalist leaders of the time, particularly Thomas Masaryk.

The emergence of Jewish Nationalism in Prague threatened the equilibrium of organised Jewish life. Prague Zionism was interpreted by many to be a defection from the ranks of German-speaking Jewry, an internal weakening of the German cultural edifice. In fact, all the German institutions of the city – not only those identified with the Jewish community – reacted to the activities of the Prague Zionists with immediate disapproval.[41]

The Prague Zionists, through their organ, *Selbstwehr*, claimed that assimilation was a lie that had to be challenged by the newly aroused Jewish national consciousness. They pointed out that modernising and emancipatory pressures had twisted the natural inclinations of the Jews of Bohemia, and German cultural values had been foisted on them without regard for their genuine well-being. Moreover, all avenues of acculturation – be they Czech or German – served merely as arrangements of convenience.[42] When the Austrian *Reichsrat* elections of 1907 resulted in the election of four Jewish deputies, *Selbstwehr* seemed to view events as a possible model for Czech Jewry. Like their Austrian counterparts, Czech Zionists also believed that Zionism had a mission to perform in Europe as well as in Palestine.[43]

But by 1910 Bohemian Jewish culture, which had been largely a German-Jewish alliance, had turned in the direction of a Czech-Jewish orientation, that became increasingly alienated from Austrian German Liberalism and self-consciously bilingual.[44] Whether Czech or Zionist in political orientation, the culture of Bohemian Jewry after the turn of the century, could only be expressed in national terms. Even those institutions that had earlier identified Liberal politics and liberal German culture with a general cosmopolitanism, now demonstrated a German national stance. These strong national tendencies resulted in an undercurrent of hostility and intense competition.[45] Despite the vitality and longevity of the German-Jewish cultural pattern, Czech-speaking

[40]See e.g. Hans Kohn, 'Rückblick auf eine gemeinsame Jugend', in *Robert Weltsch zum 70. Geburtstag von seinen Freunden*, ed. by Hans Tramer and Kurt Loewenstein, Tel-Aviv 1961, p. 115; Hugo Bergmann, 'Die nationale Bedeutung Achad Haams', in *Der Jude* (1916–1917), pp. 358–361; Jehuda Reinharz, 'Ahad Ha'Am, Martin Buber, and German Zionism', in *At the Crossroads. Essays on Ahad Ha'Am*, ed. by Jacques Kornberg, Albany 1983, pp. 142–155.

[41]Kieval, *The Making of Czech Jewry, op. cit.*, pp. 154–163; See also Hans Tramer, 'Prague – City of Three Peoples', in *LBI Year Book IX* (1964), pp. 305–306.

[42]*Selbstwehr*, No. 21 (27th May 1910), pp. 1–2. On *Selbstwehr*, and its aims and contributors, see *Das jüdische Prag. Eine Sammelschrift*, Mit Texten von Max Brod, Martin Buber *et al.*, Kronberg/Ts. 1978; Hartmut Binder, 'Franz Kafka and the Weekly Paper "Sebstwehr"', in *LBI Year Book XII* (1967), pp. 135–148.

[43]See Robert S. Wistrich, 'Austrian Social Democracy and the Problem of Galician Jewry 1890–1914', in *LBI Year Book XXVI* (1981), pp. 89–124.

[44]See 'Das Ende des deutschen Liberalismus', *Selbstwehr*, No. 9 (4th March 1910).

[45]See Michael A. Riff, 'Czech Antisemitism and the Jewish Response Before 1914', in *Wiener Library Bulletin*, vol. XXIX, Nos. 39/40 (1976), pp. 8–20.

Jews challenged both the political assumptions and cultural strategies of the larger community.[46]

In this situation Zionism emerged as a serious cultural option for large segments of the educated and professional class. It offered instead, as we have noted, the chance to affirm a positive, Jewish identity – hence its conscious rejection of liberal prescriptions for Jewish emancipation.[47]

To the eye of a Zionist, as to many other modernist critics, the traditional Jewish community, in spite of its "tribal" cohesion and unparalleled religious solidarity through centuries, seemed to lack a firm social consensus which could serve as a basis for dealing with critical modern problems. The traditional firmness and unity of the Jews, according to such critics, depended on the ghetto or other forms of medieval isolation from the Gentile world. The values and institutions upon which it was based – the uniformity of religious practice, the loose but comprehensive, worldwide communal organisation, the universal intensive education in the Jewish tradition – seemed suitable only for adjustment to the problems of ghetto life. Once the ghetto was broken open, Jewish solidarity based on these foundations could no longer be sustained. Accordingly, the nineteenth-century Jews emerging from the "ghetto" were considered by modernist critics of all kinds as a disorganised throng of individualists, unable to subordinate their egoistic motives to the common interest – however the latter might be defined.

The advocates of general enlightenment and civic emancipation of the Jews as the solution of the modern Jewish problem felt that a consensus must be created among Jews such as would unite them with Gentile fellow citizens in a common body politic. Apart from whatever common Jewish religious values remained after Judaism, developed by Reform and Orthodox sects, other values and institutions specific to the Jews and common to all Jews should be replaced by new values and institutional bonds specific to the secular state in which each group of Jews lived and common to all its citizens. Jewish languages and folk customs should give way to the national languages and customs of modern Europe. The independent discipline of the Jewish community should be abandoned as far as necessary for its proper subordination to the state.

Zionists, on the other hand, demanded a new basis of social consensus such as could unite nineteenth-century Jews with each other throughout the world in the face of the modern Jewish situation. That consensus, they held, could no longer be religious alone but must be national: for it had to unite not only diverse religious groupings within Judaism, but also believing and unbelieving Jews; and, in addition, it had to organise the Jews not for the pious, passive acceptance of oppression but for the rebellious, active struggle for liberation. The Hebrew

[46]See e.g. Max Brod, *Im Kampf um das Judentum*, Vienna–Berlin 1920; Eva Bock, 'The German-Jewish Writers of Prague – Interpreters of Czech Literature', in *LBI Year Book XXIII* (1978), pp. 239–246; Gary B. Cohen, 'Jews in German Liberal Politics: Prague, 1880–1914', in *Jewish History*, vol. I, No. 1 (Spring 1986), pp. 55–74; see also Kieval, *The Making of Czech Jewry*, *op. cit.*, p. 123.

[47]*Ibid.*, p. 201. See for the later period: Antony Polonsky and Michael Riff, 'Poles, Czechoslovaks and the "Jewish Question", 1914–1921. A Comparative Study', in Volker R. Berghahn and Martin Kitchen (eds.), *Germany in the Age of Total War*, London 1980, pp. 63–101.

(or Yiddish) language was promoted as the cultural medium and the Zionist organisation was created as the prototype of the general Jewish representative agency that should embody that aim.

But political organisations expressing the same principle of collective auto-emancipation were created by other Jewish nationalist and autonomist movements, distinctly antagonistic to the Zionists. Some decried as escapist or defeatist the Zionist proposal to solve the Jewish problem by removing Jews from their homes to a land of their own. They proposed instead a form of collective emancipation of the Jewish people, or of Jewish culture, in their existing habitations through establishing their rights as a recognised minority. Such views were promoted, for example, by the *Sejmist* party or by the general Jewish workers' union, the *Bund*, in Eastern Europe. Others, agreeing with the Zionists that concentration of the Jews in a territory of their own was essential for solving the Jewish problem, tried to find a country other than Palestine, and, to their mind, more suitable, in which they hoped to resettle them. The international Jewish Territorialist Organisation (ITO) was founded by Israel Zangwill in 1905 to pursue this aim after he and his followers left the World Zionist Organisation because it rejected the so-called "Uganda" offer.

CONCLUSION

When we attempt to compare the ideology and practice of the Zionist movements in Germany, Austria and Bohemia, the differences are immediately apparent, reflecting the cultural and political frameworks within which they each developed and clearly mirroring the constraints and opportunities these systems afforded. Zionism in Germany, unlike its counterparts, was a movement for which questions of *Gegenwartsarbeit* – the battle against antisemitism and involvement in the details of local and national politics – were of secondary importance.[48] German Zionism was Palestino-centric from its inception. Thus, the battle for hegemony between Zionists and liberals in Germany was fought in the realm of ideology; it was fought for the souls of German Jewry, or at most for its funds, but not for its votes. In the Austro-Hungarian Empire, however, the same battle was fought in the arena of politics both in the *Gemeinde* and on the national scene. Ironically here, where Theodor Herzl resided, his call for the *Eroberung der Gemeinden*, meant only as a consciousness-raising device, was implemented literally. In Bohemia, even more than in Austria-Hungary, Jewish Nationalism owed its very popularity to the national conflict itself. In both regions, however, the conflicting demands of the various national movements, compounded by a growing intolerance towards Jews, were factors in producing the Jewish response of self-affirmation.

In all three cases the Zionist movement served to clarify the position of Jews who had to a smaller or larger degree been previously outside the traditional

---

[48]See Jehuda Reinharz, 'The Zionist Reponse to Antisemitism in Germany', in *LBI Year Book XXX* (1985), pp. 105–140.

Jewish community. At issue was the role of the Jews *vis à vis* their social environment. At the same time Zionism engaged in an effort to transform both the content and thrust of Jewish culture itself. In all three political entities Zionism represented a deliberate turning away from the liberal German culture of the Jewish community. Zionists criticised their liberal opponents for adopting a national culture that was not theirs. They made a deliberate effort to halt the course of Jewish history in Western and Central Europe since the Enlightenment. They rejected the synthesis of *Deutschtum* and *Judentum* as artificial and harmful. They insisted that full equality meant the right to develop their own natural culture. They all looked to the *Ostjuden* for their own cultural renaissance.

The period prior to the First World War witnessed the Zionists' most intensive struggle with their respective liberal communities. In the aftermath of the war's upheaval, they were finally able to implement a number of their pre-war ideological and political goals.

In sum, it can be stated that the Zionists had to contend not only with the opponents who still maintained that civic enfranchisement of the Jews as individuals would solve the Jewish problem, and with traditionalists who were suspicious of all attempts to solve it, but also with opposing organisations inspired by the same underlying principle, if not the same formulated aims, as themselves. On the other hand, the institutions created by Zionism enjoyed the co-operation of many non-Zionists. Their specific aims and functions were so defined that many who shared only the Jewish heritage and not the Zionist idea could ally themselves or even accept membership in them. This was particularly important for those organisations – the central institutions from the point of view of any nationalist movement – which claimed to act in a representative capacity for the whole Jewish people. Two such organisations, created after the First World War, the Jewish Agency for Palestine and the *Vaad Leumi*, formed in Palestine under the British Mandate, were available as foundations, when the time came to build the governmental institutions of Israel.

The "Kaftanjude" and the "Kaffeehausjude":
Two Models of Jewish Insanity
A Discussion of Causes and Cures among
German-Jewish Psychiatrists

BY JOHN M. EFRON

From the beginning of modern medicine and physical anthropology (both initially related disciplines) in the eighteenth century, German practitioners regarded the Jews as physically different from non-Jews.[1] Although they classified Jews as part of the "White" race, comparative anatomists and physical anthropologists such as Göttingen's Johann Friedrich Blumenbach (1752–1840) and Berlin's Karl Asmund Rudolphi (1771–1832), stressed the uniqueness of both the physical appearance and the pathology of Jews, especially noting their easy identifiability, irrespective of geographic locale.[2]

While the works of such men were not explicitly antisemitic, they formed the basis of a tradition in the German biological sciences that persisted into the twentieth century – the separate anthropo-medical classification of Jews on the basis of perceived racial differences.[3]

It is no accident that from at least the late eighteenth century, German medicine and anthropology tended to isolate Jews and refer to them as a separate group. Jews were scientifically classified in a way that served to mirror their social isolation. This, I argue, reflected the Jews' social position of existing both inside and outside German society. By this is meant that by the time of the founding of the *Kaiserreich*, nearly one hundred years after Moses Mendelssohn

---

[1] This article is based on a part of my doctoral dissertation, *Defining the Jewish Race. The Self-Perceptions and Responses of Jewish Scientists to Scientific Racism in Europe, 1882–1933*, Columbia University 1991. I owe a significant debt of gratitude to my dissertation supervisor Professor Yosef Hayim Yerushalmi, as well as Professors Nancy Stepan, Sander L. Gilman, and Michael A. Meyer, all of whom provided me with important critical comments on this paper. The preparation of this article was made possible by a grant from the Memorial Foundation for Jewish Culture.

[2] For their evaluations of Jews see Johann Friedrich Blumenbach, *On the Natural Varieties of Mankind*, New York 1969, p. 234; and D. Karl Asmund Rudolphi, *Beyträge zur Anthropologie und allgemeinen Naturgeschichte*, Berlin 1812, p. 153. On the general history of racial thinking during the Enlightenment see George L. Mosse, *Toward the Final Solution: A History of European Racism*, Madison, Wisconsin 1985; and Léon Poliakov, *The Aryan Myth. A History of Racist and Nationalist Ideas in Europe*, New York 1974.

[3] By the late nineteenth century, these views were, of course, easily adopted by antisemitic scientists, who not only stressed Jewish difference, but Jewish racial incompatibility with Germans.

had attempted to reconcile traditional Judaism with *Deutschtum*, thereby establishing a model for future Jewish integration into the modern state, German Jews of the late nineteenth century were still largely a group apart. Social integration had remained incomplete and culturally too, while it cannot be denied that German Jews enthusiastically partook of German culture, recent research has begun to show that German Jews creatively developed a unique Jewish subculture designed to co-exist with and complement German culture.[4]

The medical profession at the *fin-de-siècle* responded to these developments by expressing its concerns with the paradoxes of Jewish life in Germany – professional integration and social isolation; high visibility and numerical marginality; physical and linguistic indistinctiveness and ethnic independence – by reflecting the Germans' own concerns about the anomolous position of the Jews. In sum, it was the elements of these paradoxes that combined to form the "Jewish Question". German medicine and anthropology lent its prestige, and more importantly its authority to the debate, attempting to provide scientific evidence to determine whether biological or indeed racial peculiarities were the cause that gave rise to the *Judenfrage*.

According to mainstream medicine at this time, the nature of illnesses suffered by Jews was generally thought to be unique to them, and racial factors were largely held to be the etiological origin of these maladies.[5] It was believed that Jews were especially prone to diabetes, known in German as the *Judenkrankheit*, respiratory ailments, haemorrhoids, cancer (but neither penile nor uterine due to circumcision), conjunctivitis trachoma and colour-blindness.[6]

By the turn of the twentieth century, the pathological isolation of the Jew was expanded to include his mental state as well. In one branch of medicine, psychiatry, there was widespread belief that Jews displayed a higher incidence of insanity than non-Jews. By insanity, we mean here a group of disparate psychopathologies that were regarded in the late nineteenth century as indicators of mental illness. These ranged from clinically diagnosable schizophrenia, to the more subjective and commonly referred to *fin-de-siècle* condition of neurasthenia.

Two of the most influential psychiatrists of the nineteenth century, Emil Kraepelin (1856–1926), and Richard von Krafft-Ebing (1840–1902) expressed mainstream psychiatry's evaluation of the Jews. In his *Psychiatrie. Ein Lehrbuch*, which was first published in 1883 and went through nine editions by 1927, Kraepelin noted that it was really impossible to tell which of the various influences; race, life-long habits, climate, diet, or general health conditions were

[4]On the development of this Jewish subculture see Shulamit Volkov, 'Jüdische Assimilation und jüdische Eigenart im deutschen Kaiserreich. Ein Versuch', *Geschichte und Gesellschaft*, 9 (1983), pp. 331–348; and *idem*, 'The Dynamics of Dissimilation: *Ostjuden* and German Jews', in Jehuda Reinharz and Walter Schatzberg (eds.), *The Jewish Response to German Culture. From the Enlightenment to the Second World War*, Hanover, N.H.–London 1985, pp. 195–211; and David Sorkin, *The Transformation of German Jewry, 1780–1840*, New York 1987.
[5]Georg Buschan, 'Einfluß der Rasse auf die Form und Häufigkeit pathologischer Veränderungen', *Globus*, 67 (1895), pp. 21–24, 43–47, 60–63, 76–80.
[6]For the fullest discussion of the racial pathology of the Jews see Maurice Fishberg, *The Jews. A Study of Race and Environment*, New York 1911, pp. 270–355.

responsible for mental illness. But with the Jews, Kraepelin was sure that race did play an etiological factor in their insanity, He observed:

"... that the peculiarity of a people can play a role [in causing insanity] is proven by the case of the Jews who can be compared to the surrounding population without making great [statistical] errors. The comparison shows that at least in Germany, and likewise in England, the Jews are inclined to mental and nervous disease in considerably higher numbers than the Teutons. Certainly alcoholic forms of insanity are rare amongst them; on the other hand we see such extraordinary disturbances caused by hereditary degeneration."[7]

Krafft-Ebing was inclined to see the higher frequency of mental illness among Jews as a consequence of their religious fervour, which in turn encouraged deviant sexual practices such as consanguineous marriage:

"Very often excessive religious inclination is itself a symptom of an originally abnormal character or actual disease, and, not infrequently, concealed under a veil of religious enthusiasm there is abnormally intensified sensuality and sexual excitement that lead to sexual errors that are of etiologic significance."[8]

German psychiatry's marginalisation of the Jew, its burdening him with a unique psychopathology, completed the attempt of the medical profession in general to represent Jews as a biologically peripheral group. Whether portrayed as physically different (and this could even mean beautiful, especially when speaking of Sephardic women) or psychologically distinct from Germans, whose supposedly contemplative "nature" was more apt to result in chronic melancholia as opposed to the hot-blooded Semitic Jew who suffered more frequently from various manias, German medicine, with its authority and prestige sought to return Jews to a theoretical ghetto.

Challenged by the claims of mainstream medicine, Jewish psychiatrists began a European-wide debate on the mental illness of the Jews, producing a considerable corpus of literature on the subject. In this essay I will specifically examine the image of the Jew as presented by Jewish psychiatrists, and trace the dynamics of their response to mainstream psychiatry's marginalisation of the Jew.

A study of the Jew in what we may call "Jewish psychiatric literature" reveals the adoption of clear ideological trends by the psychiatrists. Jewish practitioners tended to delineate between Eastern European and Western European Jews, creating distinctions between what they believed were the different psychopathologies of the two groups. However, over time, a paradigm shift took place in this construct. There was a change in the representations as to which Jew, the German or the Polish, best represented a model of Jewish insanity. The original image of the mentally sound Jew, the *Westjude*, which dominated the discourse

---

[7]Emil Kraepelin, *Psychiatrie. Ein Lehrbuch*, I, Leipzig 1903, p. 106. For a fuller explanation of Kraepelin's degeneration theory see his, 'Zur Entartungsfrage', *Zentralblatt für Nervenheilkunde und Psychiatrie*, 31 (October 1908), pp. 745–749.

[8]Richard von Krafft-Ebing, *Text-Book of Insanity*, transl. by Charles Gilbert Chaddock, Philadelphia 1904, p. 143. In keeping with the ambivalent attitude of the German medical profession to Jews, Krafft-Ebing, despite his above-quoted views, could treat individual Jews rather differently. In 1897, he, together with Hermann Nothnagel, head of the Division of Internal Medicine at the University of Vienna, proposed Sigmund Freud for the position of *Ausserordentlicher Professor*. Individual Jews were always more acceptable than Jews *en masse*.

throughout the nineteenth century, gave way by the *fin de siècle* to one which identified the *Ostjude* as typifying the psychologically healthy Jew. This shift was fully crystallised with the advent of "Nationalist psychiatry", that is, psychiatry written from the Zionist perspective. The assimilated German Jew was portrayed by Zionist physicians as mentally unfit, a creature psychologically tormented by a crisis of identity, while the East European Jew, secure in his cultural identity, was held up as the representative of sound Jewish mental health.

Unlike their more famous Jewish contemporaries such as Sigmund Freud, Max Eitingon, or Karl Abraham, the doctors whose work is to be examined here focused their research specifically on the mental illnesses of the Jews. Almost all were clinical psychiatrists practising between 1900 and 1939 at famous clinics such as the *Burghölzli* in Zürich, large city institutions such as the *Irrenanstalt zu Frankfurt am Main*, or at private Jewish mental hospitals in Eastern Europe. Their written findings, therefore, were based on close observation of Jewish patients in a hospital setting. This, plus the fact that Jewish psychiatrists sometimes undertook large scale studies, allowed them to claim the objective-scientific high-ground – a feature many of them felt was absent in the work of non-Jewish psychiatrists. Most of the psychiatrists also had a broader impact on Jewish life, in that many published popular versions of their scientific papers in mass-circulation Jewish newspapers, periodicals and even literary magazines. The issue of mental illness among Jews had become, by the end of the First World War, a common topic in Jewish communal life in both Eastern and Western Europe.

Two primary factors motivated the work of these men. First, Gentile psychiatrists' limited clinical experience with Jewish patients and Jewish life in general, led Jewish psychiatrists to challenge what they perceived at the time, as the lack of objectivity in the work of their non-Jewish colleagues. For the Jewish psychiatrists to be studied here, Jews were the major focus of their work, and not an interesting but quite insignificant theme, as they were in the writings of men such as Emil Kraepelin, Richard von Krafft-Ebing and Eugen Bleuler. For unlike much of the anthropological literature on Jews, which was often guided by hostile non-Jews, the psychiatric literature on Jews was mainly produced by Jewish psychiatrists who came to dominate the discourse, define its terms and set its boundaries. Second, many of the Jewish psychiatrists were in complete accord with the findings of non-Jewish doctors, accepting the claims about the higher Jewish incidence of and pre-disposition towards nearly all forms of mental illness. What prompted them to carry on their work was not so much inspired by differences concerning etiology, but, rather, the cure of Jewish insanity. It is in this far more important way that they differed. They rejected the Kraepelian paradigm of hereditary degeneration, opting for one that held out the hope of psychological redemption and rehabilitation.

In the course of their work, Jewish psychiatrists tested hypotheses, challenged commonly-held assumptions and, far from achieving the desired objectivity, were highly polemical. Their personal politics, their geographic location, and the patients they saw came to determine the focus of their works, the questions they asked and the solutions they offered. A partial list of the questions which formed the core of their enterprise reads as follows: are Jews more frequently predisposed to mental illness than non-Jews? If so, which illnesses and why? Was there a specific *Psychosis Judaica*? Was the predominance of a particular illness due to heredity or environment? If it was environment, what was it about Jewish life that promoted insanity? On the other hand, if Jews were immune to certain diseases or mental disorders, was this caused by something peculiar to the "race" or, rather, the conditions under which they lived? Could it perhaps be due to the observance of endogamous marriage resulting in the development of an immunity? Or was the converse true? Was the sex life of European Jewry detrimental to its physical and mental well-being? Was there any significant psychological difference between East and West European Jewry? Above all, as men dedicated to healing, all the psychiatrists were occupied with the most important question; was there a cure? It is the aim of this essay to show how Jewish psychiatrists dealt with these themes.

The image that Jewish doctors had of the mental health of Jews and one that was to last until the beginning of the present century was largely established during the *Haskalah*, the Jewish Enlightenment, in Germany during the last third of the eighteenth century. In 1777, a Jewish doctor from Metz, Elkan Isaac Wolf, discussed the mental state of the Jews in his important treatise, *Von den Krankheiten der Juden*.[9]

Wolf identified the two major causes of disease among Jews as poverty and the Jewish mode of prayer. The first, of course, led to malnutrition, the inability to dress correctly so as to protect oneself from the elements, and the evil results of living in overcrowded houses.[10] But, according to Wolf, the Jews not only lived in a state of physical despair; they were mentally ill as well. Wolf's book thus becomes one of the first modern medical texts by either a Jewish or a Gentile physician to charge the Jew with mental illness. It was a combination of the exigencies of daily life, and the traditional Jewish way of worship, that Wolf concluded was the cause of Jewish neuroses:

> "It is also not difficult to grasp why most of my brothers are thin, living skeletons and from where their tawny colour and the extraordinary sensitivity of their nervous system derives. The incessant, corrosive grief caused by constant reflection on daily living expenses, the agonising apparition of decreased vitality in the future, the loss of riches through withering capital and illegal exchange . . . is immensely disadvantageous for the nerves. It is also little wonder, therefore, that among us we observe so much hypochondria, which little by little degenerates into irritability and melancholia. From thence there develops the constant disturbance of their mental powers, so that one observes in Jews a constant *Delirio* with all kinds of changes in appearance and conduct.
> This sensitivity of the nerves is caused by our mode of prayer . . ."[11]

---

[9] On Wolf and his place within seventeenth- and eighteenth-century Jewish medical literature see M. Dienemann, 'Hygiene der Juden im 17. und 18. Jahrhundert', in *Die Hygiene der Juden. Im Anschluss an die Internationale Hygiene-Ausstellung Dresden 1911*, ed. by Max Grunwald, Dresden 1911, pp. 265–267.

[10] Elkan Isaac Wolf, *Von den Krankheiten der Juden, seinen Brüdern in Deutschland gewidmet*, Mannheim 1777, pp. 11–12.

[11] *Ibid.*, pp. 12–13.

What we read in the work of Wolf, a *maskilic* physician, is that it is the traditionally observant Jew, the unenlightened or Eastern Jew, the one whose life revolves around the synagogue and the eking out of a miserly existence, who is in desperate need of rehabilitation so as to prevent his physical and mental deterioration.

In a different context, Wolf's views were echoed in 1790 by the Königsberg physician Moishe Marcuse. His *Seyfer Refues*, is regarded as the first scientific medical text in the Yiddish language, and was thus directed at a Polish-Jewish readership.[12] Like Wolf's work, Marcuse's was also largely an uncompromising critique of traditional Jewish life. He focused especially on the practice of popular medicine and folk cures as not only bad in and of themselves, but more generally representative of the backwardness of the culture in general.

The diagnoses of Wolf and Marcuse, which called for a cure entailing a programme of *Selbstbildung*, and auto-emancipation, would appear with different emphases in the works of acculturated and assimilated Jewish psychiatrists into the twentieth century.

Heirs to that stream in *Haskalah* ideology which encouraged the abandonment of traditional ritual, regarding it as harmful, the earliest modern Jewish psychiatrists such as Moritz Benedikt (1835–1920) and Hermann Oppenheim (1858–1918), perpetuated and elaborated upon the Wolfian stereotype of mentally ill Jews. While Wolf and other *Maskilim*, such as Marcuse, targeted all traditional Jews as ill in some way or another, requiring the curative effects of secularisation, Benedikt and Oppenheim, who practised in Vienna and Berlin respectively, cities where the bulk of Jews had already abandoned ritual, specifically targeted the East European Jew. To them, the *Ostjude* was the modern incarnation of what German Jews had been before modernisation, the bearers of ill health.

In 1900, Benedikt, a Viennese neurologist, challenged an English psychiatrist Cecil Beadles, who claimed that the Jews were racially predisposed to mental illness.[13] Benedikt's rebuttal to Beadles, a description of the "mental and nervous qualities" of the Jews, contrasted starkly with Beadles's highly jaundiced judgement of their immorality.[14]

Benedikt argued for the Jews' intellectual and moral maturity. Indeed, it was the very possession of original "Jewish" character traits that prepared them to become the bearers of Mosaic teaching and act as the spiritual forebears of Christianity:

[12]Moishe Marcuse, *Seyfer Refues* (in Yiddish), Poritsk 1790, n.p. It is significant that, unlike Wolf, Marcuse elected to write in a Jewish language. This was to be a defining feature of East European Jewish Reformist movements into the twentieth century, and typical of the difference between the East European and the German *Haskalah*. Marcuse noted that just as Maimonides had written medical texts in Arabic, so too would he write in the vernacular Yiddish, so that the Jewish public could benefit from his advice (p. 6).

[13]Cecil Beadles, 'The Insane Jew', *The Journal of Mental Science*, XLVI, 195 (1900), pp. 731–737.

[14]Moritz Benedikt, 'The Insane Jew. An Open Letter to Dr. C. F. Beadles', *The Journal of Mental Science*, XLVII, 198 (1901), pp.503–509.

"No nation in ancient times was so fit to receive abstract ideas on Cosmogeny and the fundamental questions of metaphysics as the Jewish people were, fifteen centuries before Christ. Moses must have recognised this quality in his followers, for he made the bold experiment of imparting to them knowledge of the highest importance from Hamitic and Semitic philosophers . . . The second psychical quality which was necessary in order that a people might bear this burden was, that high ethical predisposition to sacrifice their political, social, and economic interest to profound ideas and convictions."[15]

This affirmation of the high moral standard of the Jewish people notwithstanding, Benedikt drew the line at extending those qualities to contemporary East European Jews. Like Elkan Isaac Wolf before him (and many other Jewish physicians), Benedikt blamed the victim as it were, charging that a lapsed ethical standard was to blame for the psychopathologies of Eastern Jews. He was convinced that the unique sociology of Jewish family life, especially in the East, contributed to the high incidence of mental disorders among the Jews. This came about as a result of the lack of access Jews had to the outside world. Essentially cut off, Jews turned inward, developing a family life that "often resulted in excessive sexual intercourse, *inter matrimonium*".[16]

It is true that a number of non-Jewish psychiatrists had also charged the Jews with this. However, their descriptions of Jews were static, undifferentiating and all-encompassing, including both Western and Eastern Jews. But Benedikt, as a Jew, practising in Vienna, was more selective. To him it was Orthodox Jewry, and in the Vienna of 1900 that primarily meant that it was the sexual life of Eastern European Jews which was called into question:

> "The females chiefly suffered by these excesses, and even at the present day, among Orthodox Jews, every female is condemned from maturity till the menopause to an uninterrupted series of pregnancies, parturitions, and lactations. No wonder, then, that *hysteria gravis* is so frequent among Jewish women . . ."[17]

While the Eastern European Jew remained for Benedikt a character whose way of life and language promoted insanity, his prognosis was a hopeful one. He was convinced that although "the inherent qualities of the Jews have persisted for many centuries . . . they are endowed with a great aptitude for variation, both mentally and physically".[18] All that was required to stimulate the metamorphosis from traditional, afflicted Jew, to modern, healthy one, was a change of milieu. A modern education and the adoption of the ideas and sentiments of this new environment would ensure that the latent mental qualities of the Jews (the necessary prerequisites for the receipt of Mosaic law to begin with) would again surface.

Benedikt's studies of Orthodox Jews forced him to re-evaluate the accepted

---

[15]*Ibid.*, pp. 505–506.

[16]*Ibid.*, p. 506.

[17]*Ibid.*, p. 506. It is pertinent to point out that one element that "Jewish psychiatry" shared with that of mainstream medicine in general is its gender bias. Men were rarely diagnosed as suffering from hysteria, and women, especially among the Jews, were primary objects of psychiatric research. Having said this, in the antisemitic discourse common to much late *fin-de-siècle* medicine, the Jews were often regarded as an effeminate race and therefore Jewish males were often diagnosed as suffering from the same ailments as Christian women.

[18]*Ibid.*, p. 507.

causes of degenerative neuroses and general paralysis – alcoholism and syphilis. While Jews suffered from the entire gamut of neuropathological disorders there was a marked absence of either drunkenness or venereal disease. "From these facts", wrote Benedikt, "I am convinced *a priori*, that the modern etiological theory is erroneous." Since Jewish insanity was, for him, Eastern European Jewish insanity, Benedikt concluded that the two major causes of general paralysis among Jews were persecution and ill-treatment.[19] These two historical conditions were a feature of contemporary Russian-Jewish, not German-Jewish life. It is clear from this that Benedikt dismissed any theory of hereditary insanity based on race. It was the Eastern European environment, both Jewish and Gentile, and nothing about the physical or psychological constitution of the Jews themselves that fostered mental illness.

At the end of the First World War, Benedikt contributed an article to the German literary monthly *Nord und Süd* in which he continued to pursue the theme of Eastern European Jewish mental illness.[20] After a study of an epidemic of paralysis among Jewish tailors in London's East End that occurred in 1901, Benedikt went on to discuss the etiology of Jewish insanity in more general terms. For him, the mental illness of Eastern European Jews was caused by their specific mode of Diaspora existence, and the way they adapted to it. Specifically, he referred to Jewish alienation from artistic and agricultural pursuits.

But, according to Benedikt, what was especially responsible for the increase of insanity among these Russian Jews was the persistence of traditional Jewish education. "From childhood years on, especially in religious circles, the dialectics of the Talmud are forced on capable and incapable brains, whereby paralysis is actually bred."[21] Here again it is the Eastern European Jew who, for Benedikt, is the victim of mental illness. These psychopathologies were not only a direct result of external pressures (pogroms) but also internal obscurantism. Benedikt's assessment bears a striking similarity to Wolf's diagnosis of 140 years earlier, when the latter attributed the mental illness of the Jews to their "mode of prayer".

To appreciate fully that for Benedikt, the "*geisteskranker Jude*" was the *Ostjude*, it is important to be aware of the context in which his discussion took place. His discussion was not only a piece on the paralysis epidemic in London of 1901, but also a polemic aimed directly at the most important Zionist psychiatrist, Dr. Rafael Becker (whose contributions will be discussed below) and a fierce denunciation of *Ostjudentum* in general. Benedikt was responding to the fact that, by 1918, Zionist psychiatrists had made significant contributions to diagnosing both Western and Eastern European Jewish psychopathologies. In doing so, the Zionists set the terms of the debate over Jewish insanity, and most importantly, prescibed cures in keeping with the nationalist *Zeitgeist*. It must be noted at this point that in the intellectual world of early German Zionism, the movement for

---

[19]*Ibid.*, p. 509.
[20]Moritz Benedikt, 'Der geisteskranke Jude', *Nord und Süd. Eine deutsche Monatsschrift*, CLXVII, 43 (1918), pp. 266–267.
[21]Benedikt, 'Der geisteskranke Jude', *loc. cit.*, p. 269.

the repatriation of the Jews to Palestine was meant as a solution to the plight of Eastern European Jewry only, and it was never intended that the mass of German Jews should depart Europe for ever.[22] Benedikt's denunciation of Becker concerned the latter's point that it was German Jewry that stood to gain the most from the Zionist enterprise. Although he was no Zionist, Benedikt implicitly adopted the standard German-Jewish line on Zionism; that if it was to be for any one group, then it was to be for the Jews of Eastern Europe.

While Becker identified Western European Jewishness as the etiology of Jewish insanity, for Benedikt, Eastern European Jewishness was in itself a pathological condition. It was the cause of both physical and mental degeneration:

> "Dr. Becker . . . expects a racial-hygiene improvement through Zionism. [Zionism] is a bold posture, contributing much, and in place of the generally scatterbrained ideas [of *Ostjudentum*] generates a healthy concept of discipline. [But] his goal of a national rebirth strikes great difficulty. This rebirth is chiefly an *ostjüdisch* question. And there stands in the way, above all, the Yiddish language. It has stirred up much disaster . . . In Italy, France, and the Anglo-Saxon world, just as in the Germanic and Scandinavian, and also in a part of the Slavic world, the Jews have adapted culturally, nationally, and politically, as well as amalgamated with the population. Rude bodily forms, especially posture, etc., disappear mostly in the next generation. [But] the Eastern European Jewish emigration to England and the United States sees the monstrous language hang on. These countries, with their tolerance, have gone so far, that this so-called language has even been conferred with official status . . . One wants a perfect national language, and one has come into being . . . and as far as can be evaluated . . . [the newly developed Hebrew] is in as good shape as modern Greek."[23]

Thus, for Benedikt, a Hungarian Jew, Eastern European Jewishness in general, and the Yiddish language in particular, was both a sign of and contributor to the mental illness of the Jews. It was an impediment to the healthy integration of Jews such as had taken place in Central and Southern Europe.[24] In the end, Benedikt held that not only did language cause insanity, but so too did politics. For him, Zionism, despite his gratuitous claim that it was a "bold posture", was itself a sign of psychopathology. As a political idea it was a dangerous fantasy, symptomatic of a disturbed mind. Tersely, he wrote: "But also the madness must disappear from the surface – so that in Palestine a kind of national state can be created."[25] For Benedikt, Zionism only appeared palatable when compared to all other aspects of Eastern European Jewish culture.

The Jewish psychiatrists of the older generation never reconciled themselves to Eastern European Jewry, retaining an antipathy towards that group which resonated in their professional and personal lives. Unlike the younger generation of psychiatrists and other intellectuals in Germany who came of age between 1900 and 1918, they did not participate in the cult of the Eastern European Jew. Rather, they steadfastly clung to the belief that it was Western European Jewry,

---

[22]Stephen M. Poppel, *Zionism in Germany, 1897–1933. The Shaping of Jewish Identity*, Philadelphia 1977.

[23]Benedikt, 'Der geisteskranke Jude', *loc. cit.*, pp. 269–270.

[24]Not only was it a barrier to integration, but, as Sander Gilman has pointed out, Yiddish, because of its similarity to German, was regarded as a threat by German-speaking Jewry, long sensitive to accusations of linguistic corruption. See Sander L. Gilman, *Jewish Self-Hatred. Anti-Semitism and the Hidden Language of the Jews*, Baltimore–London 1986.

[25]Benedikt, 'Der geisteskranke Jude', *loc. cit.*, p. 270.

with its secularism, its *Kultur*, its *Deutschtum*, that was the ideal symbol of modern Jewry, an ideal to which all Jews should aspire.[26] They identified the integrated and educated Western European Jews as being mentally healthy, while Eastern European Jewry, stuck in a quagmire of poverty and religious obscurantism, was afflicted with all forms of psychoses and neuroses.

In 1908, the celebrated Berlin neurologist Hermann Oppenheim published an important article in the prestigious *Journal für Psychologie und Neurologie* entitled, 'On the Psychopathology and Nosology of the Russian-Jewish Population', in which he noted that "approximately three quarters of all Russian-Jewish patients are neuropaths and hypochondriacs".[27] According to Oppenheim, the high frequency of mental illness among Russian Jews was directly attributable to their environment. He listed four principal causes: the pogroms; the mental and physical strain of every-day life; the poor hygienic conditions which resulted from poverty, narrow apartments and being herded in together (*Zusammenpferchung*); and the Eastern European Jewish obsession with study (even after a full days's work) in enclosed, unventilated rooms.[28]

All these features of Jewish life in Russia were obviously rectifiable, in theory. However, under existing conditions in the East, the possibility of reform was very unlikely, and Jews continued to leave, seeking better conditions in the West. In attempting to account for the inordinately large numbers of Eastern European Jews in Western Europe specifically seeking medical care, Oppenheim painted a picture that fitted into his world view of the superiority of German science, and life in general, especially as it applied to Jews:

> "A further factor is the world-wide renown of our German spas, Austrian baths and mineral springs, and Tyrolean mountain health-resorts – the way to all of them leads through Berlin. When one further considers that Russia does not possess many such spas and that staying in [those that do exist] is off limits to Jews, then the rush of Russian Jews to our surgeries is fully explained."[29]

In short, pre-First World War Russia was, for Oppenheim, a bad place for Jews to be. It offered them nothing but misery and torment, and was the cause of myriad mental disorders. All of this stood in marked contrast to the conditions that prevailed in the German-speaking lands, where reason, science, advanced medicine, a high living standard and tolerance towards Jews were the hallmarks

[26]On the cult of the Eastern European Jew see Steven E. Aschheim, *Brothers and Strangers. The East European Jew in German and German-Jewish Consciousness, 1800–1923*, Madison 1982, esp., pp. 185–214.
[27]The charge of hypochondria is one that does not occur with much frequency in the works of the younger generation of Jewish psychiatrists. By describing it as a specific malady of Eastern European Jewry, Oppenheim belongs within that earlier trend of Jewish medicine which identified the traditionally Orthodox Jew as the psycho-pathological personality. Indeed, in 1777, Wolf identified hypochondria, stomach disorders and haemorrhoids as the three most common ailments of adult Jews. Wolf, *Krankheiten*, *op. cit.*, p. 84.
[28]Hermann Oppenheim, 'Zur Psychopathologie und Nosologie der russisch-jüdischen Bevölkerung', *Journal für Psychologie und Neurologie*, 13 (1908), pp. 2–3.
[29]*Ibid.*, p. 3.

of a more civilised society, one where Jews had been allowed to integrate themselves, and had, as a consequence, become paragons of mental health.[30]

In comparing his Russian-Jewish patients with those from Germany and other countries, Oppenheim concluded that they were in possession of certain traits and characteristics that would be of special interest to the psychologist and psychopathologist. The primary one that Oppenheim diagnosed was nosophobia, a morbid fear of disease. "The nosophobia", he wrote, "is either the illness itself, or only an appendage to the real suffering, covers it, and overlays it, and thus becomes the main source of the complaint . . . The patient suffers much less from his illness, than from his reflections upon it, and sometimes these reflections are his only suffering."[31]

Oppenheim also identified distrust and suspiciousness as specifically Eastern European Jewish psychological traits. Refusing to believe the word of just one physician, Eastern European Jews consulted as many specialists as possible, in what Oppenheim referred to as a *"furor consultativus"*. The progress of this was only impeded by the fact that the Jew generally ran out of money.[32]

The etiology of the distrust itself lay with the low level of occupational structure of Russian Jews, most of whom were engaged in jobs which encouraged the deployment of cunning and deception. "It is no wonder that this gradually passed into the flesh and blood and became a fundamental characteristic."[33] Thus, Oppenheim's diagnoses of Eastern European Jewry's mental health problems were based on both the cultural and class distance he observed and indeed felt. For Oppenheim, the enormous, hypochondriacal Russian-Jewish proletariat stood in marked contrast to the mentally fit, solidly bourgeois community of German Jewry.

By the turn of the century, however, younger, dissenting voices among Jewish psychiatrists were beginning to be heard, and with them, the paradigm shift identified above began to gain momentum. In 1902, a Jewish physician in Vienna, named Martin Engländer, delivered a public lecture at the Zionist fraternal lodge, *Zion*. His address was published as a book, entitled *The Conspicuously Frequent Appearances of Illnesses of the Jewish Race*.[34]

As a Zionist, Engländer drew a distinction between Eastern European and Western European Jews that was very different from the one drawn by Benedikt and Oppenheim. Despite what he perceived to be the physical inferiority of Eastern European Jews, brought on by their socio-economic conditions, their material poverty only deprived them of their physical, not their mental well-

---

[30]Despite his faith in German civilisation Oppenheim himself was the victim of that country's institutional antisemitism. He had earned an international reputation based among other things on his widely translated *Lehrbuch der Nervenkrankheiten für Aerzte und Studierende* (1894), which became a standard textbook for neurologists throughout the world for decades. Despite a unanimous recommendation by the medical faculty of the University of Berlin that he be appointed to the Chair of Neurology, he was turned down by the Prussian government unless he accepted baptism. This he steadfastly refused to do. See *Jüdisches Lexikon*, vol. IV, Berlin 1930, cols. 583–584.

[31]Oppenheim, *loc. cit.*, p. 3.

[32]*Ibid.*, p. 4.

[33]*Ibid.*, p. 5.

[34]Martin Engländer, *Die auffallend häufigen Krankheitserscheinungen der jüdischen Rasse*, Vienna 1902.

being.[35] Conversely, the relative economic prosperity of Western European Jews had serious repercussions for the psychological state of this more assimilated group:

> "Finally, I would like to mention that the degenerative process of the central nervous system – the main topic in the discussion about the condition of the Jews in the West – is also a consequence of over-striving and over-fatigue (*Überanstrengung und Übermüdung*) of the brain. [This occurs] in the form of nervous disorders and mental disturbances, and is to be found considerably more frequently among Jews than among the non-Jewish population."[36]

Thus, by the turn of the twentieth century, Zionist psychiatrists succeeded in creating a new model of Jewish insanity. The *maskilic* image of the unhealthy *yeshivah* student, first elaborated in the eighteenth century, had now been replaced with that of the assimilated Western Jew. It was this individual whom the younger generation of Jewish psychiatrists held to be the archetypal representative of the neurasthenic, hysterical type.

In concurrence with two of the most influential psychiatrists of the nineteenth century, Emil Kraepelin and Richard von Krafft-Ebing, Engländer confirmed that Western European Jews found themselves at a serious level of degeneration. But in contrast to the more organic view of Jewish mental illness as expressed by the two Germans, Engländer found the cause to be strictly environmental. The impetus for this manifest behaviour of mental decline was release from the ghetto. It was at this point that the Jews were cast onto the great battlefield of international competition and found themselves in the front line of battle. As Engländer observed; "This struggle, haste and drive, the hunt for happiness cannot but have left its trace on the nerves of the people."[37]

But this competition which Engländer so horrifyingly described was an open one. Why then was Western European Jewry more severely affected than other Europeans? The answer lay squarely in Jewish history. While the recent struggle in the bourgeois marketplace was a new experience for Christians, it was, for Jews, but a mere continuation of their ancient struggle for existence. This latter struggle, shared by all Jews throughout their history, only came to have profound psychological consequences for Jews in the West. For when the time came for them to pursue their *embourgeoisement*, a necessary corollary of emancipation, they were an exhausted, spent people:

> "The struggle for a cozy existence is a struggle against the brain. The Jewish brain, however, has already fought a difficult fight for centuries. Until emancipation it was just a naked struggle for the necessities of existence.
> The multifarious convulsions which the Jews have endured in their two-thousand-year Diaspora and life of suffering, cannot but have caused a reaction on their central nervous system. By whatever measure, the brain of the Jews was already, prior to their entrance into the above-described competitive struggle, less resistant, more vulnerable than the brain of non-Jews . . ."[38]

---

[35]Engländer identified some of the more prevalent diseases among "ghetto Jews" such as: weak bone, muscular, and respiratory development; tuberculosis, trachoma and myopia. Engländer, *op. cit.*, pp. 11–12.

[36]*Ibid.*, pp. 12–13.

[37]*Ibid.*, p. 16.

[38]*Ibid.*, p. 17.

His critique of Jewish life in the West constituted an attack on the Jewish preference for big-city life, their participation in intellectual or business professions, their lack of physical exercise, their extreme susceptibility and emotion at the slightest instance, their timidity and helplessness. These were all taken as factors contributing to Jewish degeneration.[39] In a pointed criticism of Central European Jewish life, Engländer implored German Jews "not to be so unreasonable as to drag [your] children around to coffee-houses and restaurants. The young need to sit inside less and move around and play more in the open."[40]

In the nineteenth century the term "degenerate" was used to describe groups as varied as criminals, prostitutes, *avant-garde* artists and foreign races. Perhaps, above all, the term degenerate was applied in popular and medical usage to describe the sexual deviant. Gentile psychiatrists who often questioned Jewish sexual practices such as intra-marriage, maintained that the etiology of Jewish insanity lay in their degenerate sexual practices. In particular, the Jews were charged with inbreeding. Endogamous marriage among a relatively small population over thousands of years had led to insane offspring and was the reason why so many more Jews than non-Jews were mentally ill. According to the sexologist Richard von Krafft-Ebing:

> "This is a phenomenon [inbreeding] similar to that observed in certain highly aristocratic and wealthy families, whose members, whether from motives of honor or money, constantly intermarry, and thus have many insane relatives."[41]

Similarly, Emil Kraepelin declared that Jews suffered from an extraordinarily high incidence of mental illness, brought on by hereditary degeneration, most likely caused by the Jewish preference for consanguineous marriage.[42] There is a syllogism in operation in much of this type of work: the insane are degenerates; the Jews are insane; therefore the Jews are degenerate.

Jewish psychiatrists such as Martin Engländer, Max Sichel, and Leo Sofer, all firmly rejected the inbreeding theory. Engländer stated that Jews had, for centuries, been aware that inbreeding led to generations of neuropathically burdened individuals and, as such, Mosaic law had forbidden it. "Is then", he asked, "the Jewish race of today one large family which sprang from the loins of Abraham and the womb of Sarah and can only continue to multiply from within itself?" Relying on the authority of historians and natural scientists who argued that the Jews had mixed with other nations, Engländer denied the existence of a Jewish race and by extension, the possibility that mental illness among the Jews was based on racial factors. Rather than inbreeding, it was business and the conditions of life that were responsible for the neuroses of the Jews.[43]

Max Sichel, who was an assistant psychiatrist at the Frankfurt a. Main City

[39]On the theory of degeneration as it permeated the discourse of science, art and politics in the nineteenth century, see the collection of essays edited by J. Edward Chamberlain and Sander L. Gilman, *Degeneration. The Dark Side of Progress.* New York 1985.

[40]Engländer, *op. cit.*, p. 29.

[41]Quoted in Sander L. Gilman, *Difference and Pathology. Stereotypes of Sexuality, Race, and Madness,* Ithaca–London 1985, p. 155.

[42]Emil Kraepelin, *Psychiatrie. Ein Lehrbuch, op. cit.,* I, p. 106.

[43]Engländer, *op. cit.*, pp. 24–25.

Mental Asylum, stated that the purported connection between consanguineous marriage and insanity was not borne out by his clinical observations. "Of the 128 cases we observed, only two had parents who were blood relatives. Inbreeding as an etiological factor among our ill plays no demonstrable role and so it must be due to other important factors . . ."[44] Thus, even while accepting that there was a considerable number of Jewish patients in his asylum, Sichel flatly rejected any theory that assigned the cause of their presence there to sexual promiscuity.

Other Jewish physicians went further than Sichel in claiming that there was no link between Jewish insanity and consanguineous marriage. Leo Sofer, a Viennese Jewish physician, boldly claimed that endogamous marriage bore a prophylactic property in combatting physical and psychological disease. Among those diseases which many European and American doctors thought Jews were immune to, were tuberculosis, pleurisy, typhus and malaria. Sofer approvingly quoted a Dr. Reibmayer who wrote of the Jews, "[t]hey can give up all their customs; as long as they do not give up in-breeding they will not lose their biostatical advantage".[45]

The major "biological advantage" that Jews were perceived to hold over non-Jews was sobriety. Alcoholism, a central theme in nineteenth-century psychiatry, was unanimously referred to by all psychiatrists as the one mental disorder that Jews did not suffer from. Again, however, the views of Jewish and Gentile psychiatrists differed with regards to prognosis. In the far more static conceptions of the Jew held by the non-Jewish doctors, there is no indication in the literature that Jews would ever become intemperate. Often spoken of as having a racial immunity to drink, Jews, it was believed, were free of all alcohol related neuro-psychoses including epilepsy. For non-Jewish psychiatrists, the Jewish condition was cause for wonderment, even envy, while for Jews it was both a source of great pride and concern.

This anxiety of the Jewish psychiatrists was prompted by their belief in the power of the environment to effect change. In an important study on the connection between alcohol use and criminality among Jews undertaken in 1907, Hugo Hoppe sent out a warning signal to his fellow Jews that things were changing. He maintained that increased criminality among Jews occurred as a result of their "assimilation to the drinking habits [of non-Jews]". Maintaining that the temperance of the Jews through many generations was the result of original religious proscriptions, Hoppe held that the innate aversion to alcohol had finally acquired the form of an inherited characteristic. But this acquired racial property was not indelible, and that just as the custom of abstention had developed, so too could that of alcoholism:

> "Their [the Jews'] ancient temperance, their immunity to alcoholism, is, unquestionably, in a
> slow process of decline. If no inner movement to counter it ensues and the general movement

---

[44]Max Sichel, 'Über die Geistesstörungen bei den Juden', *Neurologisches Centralblatt*, 27 (1908), p. 360.
[45]Leo Sofer, 'Zur Biologie und Pathologie der jüdischen Rasse', *Zeitschrift für Demographie und Statistik der Juden*, II, 6 (1906), p. 89.

against alcohol cannot stop it, the time will soon appear when the Jews will be alcoholics like their neighbours and within one generation will not differ from them."[46]

Hoppe thus becomes part of an early chorus of Jewish physicians with Zionist sympathies to point out boldly that not all the after-effects of emancipation and subsequent assimilation were to the Jews' benefit. Irreplaceable social mores and biological benefits were being lost in the wake of Jewish integration into the majority culture. Jewish psychiatrists, who were largely convinced that Jews were highly susceptible to mental illness, were especially concerned that Jews would now acquire the few psychopathological disorders to which they had hitherto been immune.

The phenomenon of Jewish insanity was particularly perplexing for European psychiatry at the turn of the century, because while the high incidence of it was rarely in question, Jews did not suffer to any significant extent from two of the most commonly held causes of mental illness – alcoholism (as discussed above) and syphilis.

Significantly, the issue of assimilation once again becomes a compelling theme in the literature on syphilis among the Jews. Although the data were numerically insignificant, the evidence pointed to a higher incidence of the disease among Western European Jews as opposed to those in Eastern Europe. All Jewish psychiatrists identified the cause of this as being environmental. Especially for the Zionist physicians, it was the very conditions of ghetto life in the East, such as strict adherence to ancient customs, habits and regulations that held luetic infection at bay. By way of contrast, one psychiatrist declared, "thanks to his assimilation, his social position, his profession, and his prosperity, the emancipated Western European Jew [suffers] from a more frequent occurrence of [syphilitic] progressive paralysis".[47]

As Max Sichel argued in an article that appeared in the journal of the famous homosexual-rights leader and Berlin Jewish physician, Magnus Hirschfeld, the cause of the low incidence of syphilis among Eastern European Jews was the resistance they had built up as a result of living for centuries in a state of moral and ethical purity. By contrast, he argued, the Jew of Western Europe, by his very entry into the big city lost a good deal of his Jewishness, his religiosity, and thereby, had forfeited the surest protection against that which can only come from wild and indiscriminate sexual intercourse – syphilis. Sichel also pointed to the early marriage of Eastern European Jews as a custom of a biologically prophylactic nature, and a contributing factor to the infrequency of syphilis among these people.[48]

The paradigm shift identified above, was, by the end of the First World War coming into sharper focus. No longer is it the Eastern European Jew who is the psycho- and socio-pathic model, but, rather, it is now the deracinated, culturally bankrupt Western European Jew. According to Zionist doctors, while emanci-

[46]Hugo Hoppe, 'Die Kriminalität der Juden und der Alkohol', *Zeitschrift für Demographie und Statistik der Juden*, III, 4 (1907), p. 56.
[47]Jizchok Taitz, *Psychosen und Neurosen bei Juden. Inaugural-Dissertation*, Basel 1937, p. 28.
[48]Max Sichel, 'Paralyse der Juden in sexuologischer Beleuchtung', *Zeitschrift für Sexualwissenschaft*, VI, 3 (1919), pp. 98–104.

pation, greater acculturation, prosperity and *embourgeoisement* ensured that the physical condition of *Westjudentum* would be superior to that of *Ostjudentum*, their new life-styles, the speed and way with which they integrated themselves into non-Jewish society made them victims to myriad psychotic and neurotic disorders. By contrast, Jewish psychiatrists saw Eastern European Jews as physically unhealthy, victims of diseases brought on by poverty such as rickets or tuberculosis, but, because of their spiritual and cultural completeness, they were mentally sound in a way that Western European Jews, suffering above all from an identity crisis, were not.

This view was most fully elaborated by Rafael Becker (b. 1891) unquestionably the most prolific and influential of the Zionist psychiatrists. With this Russian Jew from Saratow, who took his medical degree at the University of Zürich in 1917, the paradigm shift referred to above can be said to have been completed.

From the appearance of his first work on Jewish mental illness in 1918, to his final publications in the 1930s, he was the most widely quoted, oft referred to, and indeed controversial of all the Jewish psychiatrists examined here. Aside from his high standing within the profession, what may account for his widespread contemporary recognition is that he published extensively in three languages, German, Yiddish and Polish, and held various hospital appointments in both Switzerland and finally in Poland, where he perished some time during the Holocaust.

Following the completion of his medical studies, Becker took up an appointment as assistant to Eugen Bleuler at the *Burghölzli* clinic in Zürich, where Freudian psychoanalysis was being applied for the first time in a psychiatric hospital setting.[49] Becker's first research assignment was a comparative study of "Jewish and non-Jewish patients to determine whether the work done by earlier investigators could be validated with the psychoanalytic approach".[50] Becker presented the findings of his research to a Zürich academic Zionist fraternity called *Hechawer*, on 4th March 1918.[51]

His speech began dramatically. "All of humanity has become nervous", he declared. Not only did the war have terrible consequences for the nerves of people, but, indeed, "the war itself was a product of the pathological spirit of man". It was in the context of this proposition that Becker sought to elucidate specifically the problem of the psycho-pathology of the Jews. While much work on this had already been done, Becker lamented that the results bore very little "goodwill". Typical of this genre was the view that mental illness had recently increased among the Jews and that many proclaimed them to be a "perishing and degenerate race". It was exactly this view that Becker's study intended to test.[52]

---

[49]See Gilman, *Difference and Pathology, op. cit.*, p. 159; and Manfred Bleuler, 'Geschichte des Burghölzlis und der psychiatrischen Universitätsklinik', in *Zürcher Spitalgeschichte*, 2, Zürich 1951, p. 396.
[50]Gilman, *Self-Hatred, op. cit.*, pp. 294–295.
[51]Published as *Die jüdische Nervosität. Ihre Art, Entstehung und Bekämpfung*, Zürich 1918.
[52]*Ibid.*, p. 3.

"Was there a specific Jewish mental illness or in medical terms, a *Psychosis Judaica*"? he asked rhetorically. "There is no specific Jewish nervous disorder, just as there are no specific Jewish anthropological characteristics, the [supposed] existence of which are used to prove the inferiority of the Jewish race." But Becker was forced to concede that on the basis of all modern research, Jews did indeed suffer from a higher frequency of mental illness than non-Jews. Not only was the incidence of insanity among Jews higher than among Gentiles, but it was also on the increase. The following figures were for Prussia and Bavaria but could be duplicated all over Europe:

TABLE

| | Mentally ill per 100,000[53] | | |
	Protestants	Catholics	Jews
1871	236	234	423
1895	291	250	498

Becker concurred that syphilis and alcoholism, as had long been thought, did not afflict Jews with great frequency. But they were, he lamented, on the rise in Western Europe, where the crashing of the ghetto walls had led to the adoption of Christian morals, the subsequent increase in syphilis, paralysis and feeble-mindedness, as well as a predilection for "Christian champagne".[54] In sum, the insanity of German Jewry was a direct result of its assimilation.

In contrast to this, the ghetto, and the inbreeding that took place there for centuries, leading to the racial purity that the Eastern Jews currently enjoyed, was "the best security for the great psychical and physical productiveness of a people".[55] Central to the mental well-being of the Eastern Jews was the retention of religious faith.

It is no wonder that Becker glorified medieval Jewish life, seeing its social and religious organisation as the fountain-head of Jewish vitality and the source of Jewish perseverance. The Jewish Middle Ages were not a *Leidensepoche*, but, rather, a time characterised by Jewish spiritual integrity and, therefore, psychological contentment and well-being. To Becker, it was the contemporary period that witnessed the most Jewish suffering. According to him, the modern Western European Jew had abandoned his faith in his drive to assimilate. In this respect, Becker parted company with Freud, arguing instead for the psychological efficacy of religious observance.[56] Rather than regard religion as the

[53]*Ibid.*, p. 9.
[54]*Ibid.*, p. 10.
[55]*Ibid.*, pp. 14–15.
[56]Freud expressed his belief in the relationship between individual obsessions and organised religious practice when he wrote, "In view of these resemblances and analogies one might venture to regard the obsessional neurosis as a pathological counterpart to the formation of a religion, to describe this neurosis as a private religious system, and religion as a universal obsessional neurosis." See his 'Obsessive Acts and Religious Practices' (1907), in Sigmund Freud, *Collected Papers*, II, ed. by Ernest Jones, New York 1961, pp. 25–35. See also Freud's fuller exposition on religion in *The Future of an Illusion*, transl. and ed. by James Strachey, New York 1961.

collective analogue of individual neurosis, Becker held that it was profound piety
and devotion to ceremony that had historically provided Jews with psychological
stability and insuperability:

> "Yes, Ladies and Gentlemen, in these modern times, Jews live in much greater torment than
> their forefathers in the Middle Ages, and even the earlier times of persecutions, tortures, and
> *Autos-da-fe*. At that time, the Jew went to his death without angst and fear, with firm faith in
> his religion . . . with proud readiness, with the *Shema Israel* on his lips.[57]
> However, the earlier Jews were much more fortunate than we are now. They had the firm
> belief that God punished them for their sins and dispersed them to all the corners of the world,
> but that the time would come, that with their Messiah, the Jews would again be fortunate and
> returned to their ancient homeland. This belief we do not have now."[58]

While Becker extolled the faith of his ancestors, he did not remain at the
simplistic level of lamenting a bygone age of Jewish piety and observance, seeing
that alone as the only salvation for this exiled, suffering people. Nor did he
advocate that a theocratic state be established for the Jews. For Becker, the
Western Jews' loss of religious faith was symptomatic of their loss of faith in
general; a loss characterised in the first instance by those who did not believe in
the Zionist dream, and in the second place, by those who no longer believed in
the Jews themselves:

> "And if some of us believe that our national rebirth, through our firm, great will can come
> about, and that we can be freed from *Galut*-life and lead a new, normal, national life, then
> indeed another, and unfortunately a larger part of us, has lost its belief in this."[59]

Thus, it is the anti-Zionist, irrespective of his political or cultural persuasions
that Becker identifies as the mentally ill Jew. For the path of assimilation had led
many German Jews down the road of self-hatred:

> "The Jew, whether he is a conscious assimilationist or even a Nationalist Jew who sees how
> badly his national rebirth is going, begins to believe what the antisemites say: that his God is a
> wicked God, that his morals are base morals, that his entire race is not of high quality and is of
> no value. In a word the Jew begins to feel himself inferior."[60]

Becker thus analysed the social and psychological constitution of the Jews
(primarily anti-Zionists) within the dissenting paradigm of neurosis developed
by the one-time disciple of Freud, Alfred Adler (1870–1937). Becker had read
Adler's *Über den nervösen Charakter* (1912), and applied its principle of "Every
neurosis can be understood as an attempt to free oneself from a feeling of
inferiority in order to gain a feeling of superiority",[61] as characteristic of the
Jewish mental condition. The Jews who refuse to pursue the Zionist path to
national rebirth are weak-willed, and further, they refuse to do so because they
are suffering from a raging inferiority complex. And this syndrome is in turn

[57]Becker, *op. cit.*, pp. 16–17. Due to Becker's influence, the issue of religion and psychiatry became a
celebrated theme in some of the Jewish periodicals after the First World War. For example, see
Felix Resek, 'Die jüdische Nervosität', *Der Israelit*, 27 (1918), p. 2; and Hermann Seckbach, 'Die
Nervenkranke', *Der Israelit*, 1 (1919), pp. 2–3.

[58]Becker, *op. cit.*, pp. 16–17.

[59]*Ibid.*, p. 17.

[60]*Ibid.*

[61]Franz G. Alexander and Sheldon T. Selesnick, *The History of Psychiatry. An Evaluation of Psychiatric
Thought and Practice from Prehistoric Times to the Present*, New York 1966, p. 232.

exacerbated, in part, because they have come to accept as fact, the hostile discourse of their enemies.[62]

The hopelessness of Jewish life in the Diaspora demanded the "most radical therapy" – a Jewish national homeland in Palestine. It could not be any other way. For, as Becker assessed, the assimilationist Jew was still classified as a Jew by Gentiles, and the Nationalist Jew was unable to garner any respect from his fellow Jews. Battered from without and within, the Jew was a helpless victim of his European environment.

Since the primary victims of these myriad mental disorders were the assimilated, indistinguishable, Western European Jews, then Zionism, the solution, was for Becker, unlike for Benedikt, a Western European Jewish problem. The creation of a Jewish homeland in Palestine would cure the deracinated *Westjude* of his inferiority complex, the source of his insanity.

With the conclusion of his clinical research at *Burghölzli*, Becker took up a number of other hospital appointments in Switzerland and then sometime between 1920 and 1925, left Central Europe for Poland, where he became director of the Jewish mental asylum *Zofyowke* in Otwosk, near Warsaw.

In Poland, working with a Jewish population of an entirely different character from that which he had treated in Switzerland, Becker was driven to ask new questions and challenge some of his older theories. He now confronted a traditional Jewish community, confident and proud of its heritage, speaking a Jewish language, Yiddish, possessed of a vibrant Jewish culture, and largely observant. His paradigm of the "Jewish Complex", that feeling of Jewish inferiority that he used to explain the cause of insanity among Western European Jews, simply did not fit here.

To be sure, Becker was able to point to certain similarities between the clinical pictures of Eastern and Western European Jews. The infrequency of epilepsy, syphilis, and alcohol-related psychoses was also in evidence in Poland, but because of the tenacity of tradition, it seemed unlikely that a change, as was slowly occurring in the West, would take place here. But important differences did exist. In the West, Jews suffered more from schizophrenia, manic-depressive insanity, progressive paralysis, senile dementia and mental deficiency than non-Jews.[63] Cocaine and morphine addiction, on the rise in the West, was seldom found among Polish Jews.[64]

However, in Poland, only two psychoses marked off the Jewish population from both the non-Jewish, and the Western European Jewish communities. The frequent incidence of schizophrenia and manic-depression, the former affecting 60% of all Jewish patients, and the latter being twice as frequent among Jews as among Poles, convinced him that a psychogenetic explanation for these diseases,

---

[62]See Gilman, *Self-Hatred, op. cit.*, for a discussion of the appropriation of antisemitic discourse by Jews.

[63]Rafael Becker, 'Ein Beitrag zur Frage der Verbreitung der Geisteskrankheiten bei den Juden in Polen', in *OSE-Rundschau. Zeitschrift der Gesellschaft für Gesundheitsschutz der Juden*, 1 (January 1930), pp. 2–4.

[64]Rafael Becker, 'Die Geisteserkrankungen bei den Juden in Polen', *Allgemeine Zeitschrift für Psychiatrie*, 96 (1932), p. 50.

which he previously explained in the West by recourse to the inferiority complex, was inadequate in this environment. Instead, Becker became convinced of the organic foundation of the illnesses. He was not yet prepared to say that race played a factor in the spread of these illnesses among Polish Jews, but he was stymied as to their etiology, and called for more detailed research, insisting on the need for genealogical, occupational, economic and sociological studies.[65]

Even though Becker's large scale studies of institutionalised Jewish mental patients enabled him to speak of the nosology of mental disorders among Polish Jews, he was unable to fit them into any etiological paradigm (other than adverse living conditions) that would explain the widespread existence of schizophrenia and manic-depression among them. As a consequence of this, when in Eastern Europe he also proposed a eugenic solution to the problem, calling for the implementation of a programme of negative eugenics, or the need for Jewish society to self-regulate unhealthy marriages among the mentally and physically ill, or between cousins.[66] Encouraged by the success of such eugenics laws in the United States, England, Germany and Czechoslovakia, Becker advocated a large scale propaganda campaign among the Jewish masses.

In summing up, we have highlighted four important themes that require reiteration. First, it has been shown that the early twentieth century witnessed a shift in the way Jewish psychiatrists observed the mentally ill among the Jewish people. The *Haskalah*-inspired model of secular (German) Jewish sanity versus Orthodox (Eastern European) Jewish insanity was replaced with its mirror image. Second, the debate among Jewish psychiatrists, irrespective of which side they held, contained an important element of unity that helped mark it off from mainstream psychiatry. Unlike the latter, which mainly saw Jewish mental illness as a function of racial factors, Jewish psychiatrists were firmly rooted in an Enlightenment tradition that identified the environment as capable of determining psychological characteristics and behaviour.

Third, this examination is instructive in a broad sense in that it shows clearly the interaction of politics with science. We have seen how the politics of the psychiatrists, assimilationism versus Zionism, and *Deutschtum* versus *Ostjudentum*, determined their medical diagnoses and prescriptions for cure.

Finally, through this study of how Jewish psychiatrists constructed an image of the Jewish "Other", an important theme in modern Jewish history, namely the encounter of the Western European and Eastern European Jew in the early part of the twentieth century, is broadened. With recourse to medical texts, we have seen that the traditional image of the German Jew, holding his Russian-Polish co-religionist in contempt, was not a one-way street. Within the circumscribed, yet important field of psychiatry, the "*Kaftanjude*" was more than a match for the "*Kaffeehausjude*".

---

[65]*Ibid.*, p. 54.

[66]Rafael Becker, 'Di nerven-krankheytn un der kampf kegn zey', *Folksgezunt*, 1 (1924) [in Yiddish], pp. 13–16; and 'Die Bedeutung der Rassenhygiene für die jüdische Familie', *Jüdische Familien-Forschung*, IV, 1 (1928), pp. 2–6. In the latter article, Becker accepted those categories of "inferior individuals", who should be prevented from propagating, from the German sexologist Hermann Rohleder. They were: the mentally inferior, the physically inferior and the socially inferior.

Nietzsche and the Nietzschean Moment in Jewish Life (1890–1939)

BY STEVEN E. ASCHHEIM

Friedrich Nietzsche's impact upon twentieth-century sensibilities has been quite extraordinary. His influence has been insistently international,[1] lightly traversing geographical and cultural boundaries.[2] In protean manner, his mediated legacy has permeated manifold – and often openly contradictory – areas of political and cultural life. This was certainly true for Germany where the philosopher's informing presence was most dense, sustained and, indeed, fateful. Nietzschean impulses penetrated, and were remoulded to fit, a remarkably broad range of *avant-garde*, religious, Socialist, Nationalist and *völkisch*, anarchist, radical Right and National Socialist, feminist, expressionist and Youth Movement currents.[3]

Given the pervasive nature of this influence, and the fact that – however one chose to interpret it – the Jewish dimension occupied a prominent place within Nietzsche's corpus, it was bound to intersect densely with Jewish concerns. The

I should like to dedicate this essay to Dr. Arnold Paucker. Under his exemplary stewardship the scholarly and editorial standards of the Year Book have been of the highest order.

[1]Recognition of this began early. See, for instance, Guy De Pourtales, *Nietzsche en Italie*, Grasset 1929; Geneviève Bianquis, *Nietzsche en France*, Paris 1929. More recent studies of his impact upon national cultures include Gonzalo Sobejano, *Nietzsche en Espana*, Madrid 1967; Patrick Bridgwater, *Nietzsche in Anglosaxony. A Study of Nietzsche's Impact on English and American Literature*, Leicester 1972; David S. Thatcher, *Nietzsche in England 1890–1914. The Growth of a Reputation*, Toronto 1970; Bernice Glatzer Rosenthal (ed.), *Nietzsche in Russia*, Princeton 1986.

[2]Nietzsche's impact throughout the Habsburg Empire is clearly evident in the volume edited by Laszlo Peter and Robert B. Pynsent, *Intellectuals and the Future in the Hapsburg Monarchy 1890–1914*, London 1988. This influence was not limited to "Western" spheres. In Japan, beginning as early as the 1890s, Nietzsche functioned as a "modernising" force, the most influential articulator of an individualism foreign to traditional Japanese culture. See Hans Joachim Becker, *Die frühe Nietzsche-Rezeption in Japan (1893–1903). Ein Beitrag zur Individualismusproblematik im Modernisierungsprozess*, Wiesbaden 1983. His shaping presence is felt to this day. Nietzsche is probably the most inspirational figure in currently fashionable post-structuralist, deconstructionist and post-modernist trends. On some of these connections see David B. Allison (ed.), *The New Nietzsche. Contemporary Styles of Interpretation*, Cambridge, Mass. 1985; and Clayton Koelb (ed.), *Nietzsche as Postmodernist. Essays Pro and Contra*, Albany 1990.

[3]We cannot here enter into a detailed discussion of the peculiar qualities of the Nietzschean *oeuvre* that made it so attractive and congenial to these manifold appropriations. I have attempted a synoptic analysis of this influence, from its beginnings through the present, in *Nietzsche in Germany, 1890–1990*, Berkeley–Los Angeles 1992.

task of this paper will be to chart the complex roles that Nietzsche and Nietzschean impulses played in Jewish representations within the German *Kulturbereich* (and, to some extent, in Eastern Europe).[4] We shall not be able to deal here with the modes in which Nietzscheanism was harnessed by antisemites to become an integral part of their lethal arsenal. This negative history we must leave for a later time. But the fact that opposed interests – in this instance, Jewish as well as antisemitic – could simultaneously harness divergently conceived notions of Nietzscheanism for their own purposes, will not come as a surprise to anyone familiar with the vagaries of Nietzsche reception. Ironies of this kind constitute the rule rather than the exception. For a crucial characteristic of the determinedly experimental and anti-systemic Nietzsche corpus was its congeniality to multiple, indeed opposed, interpretations.

Some form of casuistry was, of course, endemic to the way in which these – and all – interested appropriations of Nietzsche operated. Nietzsche, clearly, was not identical with any appropriations made in his name. As a rule his sprawling, aphoristic and apparently self-contradictory *oeuvre* offered hints, gleanings and references that were able to lend such manifold annexations at least a semblance of plausibility. But all those who appealed to his authority (and not just Jews and Zionists) were obliged to explain (or explain away) how Nietzsche, despite obvious contradictions or even hostility, was in effect compatible with one's favoured position, perhaps even its most enthusiastic representative. Placing Nietzsche within any "framework" entailed a filtering system in which desired elements were highlighted and embarrassing ones deleted or played down. Inevitably, the "real" or "deep" (German, Christian, Jewish, Socialist) Nietzsche had to be located and distinguished from the merely apparent one. Nietzsche was constantly decoded and recoded; "correct" readings made to yield the desired underlying and "authentic" meanings and messages.

We will focus here on the Nietzschean impulse within explicitly acknowledged and defined Jewish frames and on organised streams of community life. Individual Jews will similarly be considered only insofar as their encounter with Nietzsche was informed by explicitly Jewish concerns. After all, the role of "unaffiliated" Jews in the general interpretation, transmission and political transmutations of Nietzsche and Nietzscheanism has been (and continues to be) very substantial. The long list ranges from (and is nowhere nearly exhausted by) the early enthusiasm of Siegfried Lipiner[5] and the pioneering popularising expositions of Georg Brandes,[6] the aristocratic *Lebensphilosophie* of Georg

---

[4]In this paper we shall be concerned, in the main, with those individuals and groups who, in more or less critical ways, championed either Nietzsche or (their understanding of) his views. It goes without saying that many others rejected this legacy and actively opposed it.

[5]See Siegfried Lipiner, *Der entfesselte Prometheus*, Leipzig 1876; and *idem, Buch der Freude*, Leipzig 1876. Nietzsche, incidentally, also expressed his admiration for Lipiner. See William J. McGrath, *Dionysian Art and Populist Politics in Austria*, New York–London 1974, especially pp. 1, 64, 70.

[6]See his famous 'Aristokratischer Radikalismus. Eine Abhandlung über Friedrich Nietzsche', *Deutsche Rundschau*, 63, No. 7 (April 1890), pp. 52–89. See, too, his 'Friedrich Nietzsche', in *idem, Menschen und Werke. Essays*, Frankfurt a. Main 1893, pp. 137–225. The same essay also appeared in *Deutsche Persönlichkeiten*, Munich 1902.

Simmel,[7] the poetry and criticism of Stefan George disciples like Karl Wolfskehl[8] and Friedrich Gundolf,[9] the messianic Socialism of Ernst Bloch,[10] the anti-centralist anarchism of Gustav Landauer[11] and the sophisticated, wary post-Marxist ruminations of the Frankfurt School (Adorno, Horkheimer, Marcuse etc.),[12] to the contemporary deconstructionist impulses of Jacques Derrida.[13] But this catalogue, impressive as it may be, possesses no intrinsic Jewish significance. All these endeavours were made in the name of general, not Jewish, culture. Neither the conscious intentions nor the results of the encounter could, in any meaningful way, be described as "Jewish".

To be sure, not all Nietzscheans perceived it this way. From the 1890s on, pro-Nietzsche antisemites argued that the philosopher's deepest essence was in reality Germanic and that this spiritual fact had been systematically hidden from public consciousness by Jews who had monopolised his mediation and who had distorted him into a nihilist and internationalist, consonant with their own rootless and destructive interests.[14] Not only rabid antisemites propounded this line. As late as April 1933, none other than that complex but always passionate Nietzschean, Thomas Mann, could confide to his diary:

> "But for all that, might not something deeply significant and revolutionary be taking place in Germany? . . . It is no calamity after all that Alfred Kerr's brazen and poisonous Jewish-style imitation of Nietzsche is now suppressed, or that the domination of the legal system by Jews

[7]Simmel's enthusiasm began early. See his 'Friedrich Nietzsche. Eine moralphilosophische Silhouette', *Zeitschrift für Philosophie und philosophische Kritik*, No. 2 (1896), pp. 202–215; and 'Der Nietzsche-Kultus', *Deutsche Literaturzeitung*, No. 42 (23rd October 1897), pp. 1645–1651. He considered his later book on Nietzsche to be his most important work. See his *Schopenhauer und Nietzsche. Ein Vortragszyklus*, Leipzig 1907.On Nietzsche's determinative influence see Klaus Lichtblau, 'Das "Pathos der Distanz". Präliminarien zur Nietzsche-Rezeption bei Georg Simmel', in Heinz-Jürgen Dahme and Otthein Rammstedt (eds.), *Georg Simmel und die Moderne*, Frankfurt a. Main 1984, pp. 231–281. Of course, strictly speaking Simmel was not a Jew, neither in terms of religion nor self-definition. His Jewish father converted to Catholicism and his mother came from a Jewish family that baptised her as a Lutheran. Simmel himself was baptised and married a non-Jewish wife. But, despite all this, the perception that Simmel was Jewish persisted throughout his life (and after). See Peter Gay, 'Encounter with Modernism', in his *Freud, Jews and Other Germans. Masters and Victims in Modernist Culture*, New York 1978, especially p. 98.

[8]See Wolfskehl's poem 'Zarathustra', *Blätter für die Kunst* (May 1901), p. 7 and his comments in 'Die Blätter für die Kunst und die Neue Literatur', *Jahrbuch für die geistige Bewegung*, 1 (1910), p. 1.

[9]See Friedrich Gundolf, *Dichter und Helden*, Heidelberg 1921; and *Caesar im neunzehnten Jahrhundert*, Berlin 1926.

[10]The most graphic and accessible examples of Bloch's Communist annexation of Nietzsche are now available in the English translation of his *Erbschaft dieser Zeit*, by Neville and Stephen Plaice under the title, *Heritage of Our Times*, Berkeley–Los Angles 1990. See especially, but not exclusively, pp. 299–331.

[11]The peculiar Nietzschean influence upon, and transmutation by, Gustav Landauer is well analysed in Eugene Lunn, *Prophet of Community. The Romantic Socialism of Gustav Landauer*, Berkeley 1973.

[12]For an illuminating analysis of the general relationship see Reinhart Maurer, 'Nietzsche und die Kritische Theorie', *Nietzsche Studien*, 10/11 (1981–1982).

[13]See his *Spurs/Nietzsche's Styles*, translated by Barbara Harlow, Chicago–London 1979; and 'Otobiographies. The Teaching of Nietzsche and the Politics of the Proper Name', in *The Ear of the Other. Otobiography Transference Translation*, edited by Christie V. McDonald, translated by Peggy Kamuf and Avital Ronell, New York 1985.

[14]For an Austrian example see 'Friedrich Nietzsche und die Modernen', *Deutsche Zeitung*, Morgen Ausgabe, No. 10294 (28th August 1900). See too Lenore Ripke-Kühn, 'Nietzsche der ewige Deutsche', *Deutschlands Erneuerung*, 6 (1919), pp. 420, 424.

has been ended. Secret, disquieting, persistent musings. Come what may, much will remain that in a higher sense, is repellent, base, and unGerman. But I am beginning to suspect that in spite of everything this process is one of those things that have two sides to them . . ."[15]

With the advent of Nazism, and the elevation of Nietzsche to State prophet, Jewish commentators also began to argue for the existence of a special (though, of course, differently evaluated) Jewish-Nietzsche relationship. They too now approvingly emphasised the ethnic background of those Jews who had first "discovered" the philosopher and courageously sought, quite against the prevalent grain, to diffuse his controversial ideas.[16]

But, of course, the claim of a peculiarly "Jewish" affinity to Nietzsche does not stand up to scrutiny.[17] This is not merely because the most historically influential Nietzscheans and Nietzsche interpreters have been non-Jews (Ernst Bertram, Stefan George, Ludwig Klages, Karl Jaspers, Carl Gustav Jung, Martin Heidegger spring immediately to mind). More pertinent here is the fact that while many of Nietzsche's ardent admirers were, indeed, such "unaffiliated" Jews, so too were his most vociferous critics. It was, after all, Max Nordau who, in his pre-Zionist phase, penned perhaps the most authoritative dismissal of Nietzsche as a prime symptom of *fin-de-siècle* "degeneration".[18] This was as true in the realm of politics as it was for *Kulturkritik*. Liberal and Socialist Jews – writing, of course, not as Jews but as representatives of general political positions – were amongst Nietzsche's most severe critics.[19] We should not forget, moreover, that it was Georg Lukács who literally helped to outlaw Nietzsche and who lastingly defined the vehement Marxist orthodoxy on the philosopher.[20]

There certainly was more "Jewish" criticism of Nietzsche than there was of the other great cultural icons before whom acculturated German Jewry stood in awe – Humboldt, Lessing, Goethe, Schiller, Kant and so on. This should come as no

[15]See the entry of 10th April 1933 in Thomas Mann, *Diaries 1918–1939*, transl. by Richard and Clara Winston, London 1984, p. 150.

[16]See, for instance, Leo Hirsch on Lipiner, '"Beinahe Echt?". Nietzsche und der jüdische Prometheus', *C.V.-Zeitung*, XIV, No. 25 (20th June 1935).

[17]Jacob Golomb has recently argued that precisely their marginality predisposed Jewish individuals (more than any others) to adopt a peculiarly passionate interest in, and sensitivity to Nietzsche (whose corpus was especially conducive to their post-traditional and assimilatory needs). There are cases where Nietzsche indeed fulfilled these functions. But within a wider context the claim of Jewish exceptionality does not hold up. Individual Jews were not exceptions but rather reflections of a remarkable, general interest in the philosopher that encompassed a variety of social, religious and ideological currents. Nietzsche enthusiasm – as well as Nietzsche rejection – was a generalised not an ethnic phenomenon. See Jacob Golomb, 'Nietzsche and the Marginal Jews', in *Jerusalem Studies in Jewish Thought*, 4 (1985), pp. 97–143 (in Hebrew).

[18]Max Nordau, *Degeneration*, New York 1968, especially Book III, Chapter V. The work appeared first in 1892 and was widely translated.

[19]For a liberal critique of Nietzsche's "aristocratic reaction to democracy" see Ludwig Bamberger's 'Unsere Neuesten', *Die Nation*, No. 43 (July 1892), pp. 640–643. For an early Socialist (if at times somewhat ambivalent) rejection see Kurt Eisner's aptly named *Psychopathia Spiritualis. Friedrich Nietzsche und die Apostel der Zukunft*, Leipzig 1892.

[20]For his classical exposition – based on writings from the thirties and forties and completed in 1952 – see *The Destruction of Reason*, transl. by Peter Palmer, Atlantic Highlands, N.J. 1981. The orthodoxy in Soviet Russia remained intact to the end. See Bernice Glatzer Rosenthal, 'Current Soviet Thought on Nietzsche', in Sigrid Bauschinger, Susan L. Cocalis and Sara Lennox (eds.), *Nietzsche heute. Die Rezeption seines Werkes nach 1968*, Bern–Stuttgart 1988.

surprise. For these philosophers had provided Jews with a continuing emancipatory creed, a tolerant, humanist and Enlightenment model of German culture.[21] In a certain sense, it is true, Nietzsche's resistance to Nationalist chauvinism, his emphasis on criticism and individualism, genuine *Kultur* and inner *Bildung* perpetuated this line of thinking.[22] At the same time, however, his "immoralism" and *Lebensphilosophie* irrationalism, his radically anti-Enlightenment, anti-Liberal, anti-humanist strictures were regarded by many as the gravest threat to that tradition.[23] If, as George Mosse has argued, cultural humanism was inseparable from the mental make-up of the German-Jewish intelligentsia, then Nietzsche's place in such a constellation was necessarily far more tentative and ambiguous than that of other classic thinkers.

But we must turn now to the organised German-Jewish community. The differentiated but, by and large, mainly positive response of even its most conservative and official organs from the 1890s on reflected, at least to some extent, the complex centrality of the Jews and Judaism within Nietzsche's work itself. Whether or not one regards these views as a unified and coherent element of Nietzsche's larger outlook or as disparate, changing and self-contradictory,[24] is not relevant here. In assessing the Jewish reception of Nietzsche's ideas one must pay attention to their varied uses and selective annexations rather than the "truth" value or the "validity" or "invalidity" of such appropriations and interpretations. Clearly, from the Jewish point of view, there was much in this *ouevre* that both required confrontation and could be usefully and interestedly mined.

From early on, Jewish analysts were aware that (like much of the rest of his thinking) Nietzsche's reflections on Jews and Judaism were stated in rather radical terms covering both negative and positive extremes. On the one hand he endowed the Jews with a world-historical stain. *On the Genealogy of Morals*, held the "priestly people" responsible for nothing less than beginning "*the slave revolt in morality*: that revolt which has a history of two thousand years behind it and which we no longer see because it – has been victorious".[25] The history of Israel,

[21] On this whole question see George L. Mosse, *German Jews Beyond Judaism*, Bloomington 1985.

[22] This was the line taken by Nahum Goldmann. The successors of Kant, Wolff and Leibniz, he wrote, were Goethe, Fichte, Hegel, Schopenhauer, Nietzsche and Meinecke. What these artists and creators had in common was their cultural universality. They were not national thinkers but men concerned with world history and world philosophy, representatives of an ongoing tradition based not on a narrow provincialism but a broad supranationalism. See Nahum Goldmann, *Der Jude im deutschen Kulturkreise. Ein Beitrag zum Wesen des Nationalismus*, Leipzig 1930, p. 48. On this tendency see Sidney M. Bolkosky, *The Distorted Image. German Jewish Perceptions of Germans and Germany, 1918–1935*, New York 1975, especially p. 93.

[23] On the complexities of Nietzsche's relation to the classical tradition of *Bildung* see Chapter 8 of W. H. Bruford, *The German Tradition of Self-Cultivation. "Bildung" from Humboldt to Thomas Mann*, Cambridge 1975.

[24] This is not the place to examine the role of Nietzsche's views on the Jews and Judaism in relation to his whole philosophy. For three recent attempts to do this see Arnold M. Eisen, 'Nietzsche and the Jews Reconsidered', *Jewish Social Studies*, XLVIII, No. 1 (Winter 1986); Willard Mittelman, 'Nietzsche's Attitude toward the Jews', *Journal of the History of Ideas*, XLIX, No. 2 (April–June 1988); Jacob Golomb, 'Nietzsche's Judaism of Power', *Revue des études juives*, CXLVII (July–December 1988).

[25] First Essay, Section 7 of *On the Genealogy of Morals*, transl. by Walter Kaufmann and R. J. Hollingdale (together with *Ecce Homo*, transl. by Walter Kaufmann), New York 1969, pp. 33–34.

as depicted in *The Antichrist* consisted of the *ressentiment* denaturing of natural values. The Jews, with their desire to survive at any price, were "the *most catastrophic* people of world history". They radically falsified

> "all nature, all naturalness, all reality, of the whole inner world as well as the outer . . . out of themselves they created a counter-concept to *natural* conditions: they turned religion, cult, morality, history, psychology, one after the other, into an *incurable contradiction to their natural values* . . . by their aftereffect they have made mankind so thoroughly false that even today the Christian can feel anti-Jewish without realizing that he himself is *the ultimate Jewish consequence*".[26]

These were the gravest of all possible charges and became an important ingredient in the formation of a murderous modern anti-Christian antisemitism. Careful readers will note that Nietzsche referred in the main to the priestly period: "Originally, especially at the time of kings", he wrote, "Israel stood in the right, that is, the natural relationship to all things."[27] Interested appropriators, of course, seldom bothered with such qualifications, a tendency made all the easier by the extremity of Nietzsche's rhetoric. Much of that rhetoric was couched in terms of an ongoing discourse concerning the dangers of "Judaisation".[28] In some of his moods, Nietzsche regarded Christianity as merely an expression of this process. "Everything", he wrote, "is visibly becoming Judaized, Christianized, mobized (what do the words matter!)."[29]

> "This Jesus of Nazareth . . . was he not this seduction in its most uncanny and irresistible form, a seduction and bypath to precisely those Jewish values and ideals? Did Israel not attain the ultimate goal of its sublime vengefulness precisely through the bypath of this 'Redeemer', this ostensible opponent and disintegrator of Israel? What is certain, at least, is that *sub hoc signo*, Israel, with its vengefulness and revaluation of all values, has hitherto triumphed again and again over all other ideals, over all *nobler* ideals."[30]

These convictions notwithstanding, Jewish readers also found in Nietzsche perhaps the most pronounced non-Jewish opponent of the racist and antisemitic "swindle", and the most outspoken admirer of the energy, intellect and capacities of the European Jews of his time.[31] And in typically self-subverting fashion, Nietzsche ironically inverted the logic of Judaisation discourse to which he himself had fatefully contributed. No other German thinker could conceivably have penned the following reflections (the kind that gave even the most

---

[26] *The Antichrist* (24) in *The Portable Nietzsche*, edited and translated by Walter Kaufmann, New York 1968, pp. 592–593. The italics are Nietzsche's.

[27] *The Antichrist*, op. cit. (25), p. 594. Sections 25 and 26 elaborate on this distinction.

[28] On the history of "Judaisation" and its modes see my ' "The Jew Within". The Myth of "Judaization" in Germany', in Jehuda Reinharz and Walter Schatzberg (eds.), *The Jewish Response to German Culture. From the Enlightenment to the Second World War*, Hanover–London 1985.

[29] *On the Genealogy of Morals*, op. cit., p. 36.

[30] *Ibid.*, p. 35. "In Christianity", Nietzsche wrote in *The Antichrist*, "all of Judaism, a several-century-old Jewish preparatory training and technique of the most serious kind, attains its ultimate mastery as the art of lying in a holy manner. The Christian, this *ultima ratio* of the lie, is the Jew once more – even three times more." *Op. cit.*, p. 620.

[31] Nietzsche's pro-Jewish – and very often, related anti-German remarks – are legion. For a convenient summary of these more positive views see Walter Kaufmann, *Nietzsche. Philosopher, Psychologist, Antichrist*, Fourth Edition, Princeton 1974, especially Chapter 10. In this respect, however, Kaufmann's work, first published in 1950, presents a rather sterilised, even apologetic, portrait of the philosopher's views.

casuistically adroit Nietzschean antisemites great difficulty[32] and which prompted many others simply to disavow him[33]):

> "Whoever reads me in Germany today has first *de-Germanized* himself thoroughly, as I have done: my formula is known, 'to be a good German means to de-Germanize oneself'; or he is – no small distinction among Germans – of Jewish descent. Jews among Germans are always the higher race – more refined, spiritual, kind. – *L'adorable* Heine, they always say in Paris."[34]

Which other major German thinker had expressed such favourable views on the Bible, and in explicit contrast to the New Testament?

> "The *Old* Testament – that is something else again: all honour to the Old Testament! I find in its great human beings, a heroic landscape, and something of the very rarest quality in the world, the incomparable naiveté of the *strong heart*; what is more, I find a people. In the New one, on the other hand, I find nothing but petty sectarianism, mere rococo of the soul, mere involutions, nooks, queer things . . ."[35]

Interested (and opposed parties) invoked these extreme – negative and positive – positions and selectively harnessed them to their own causes.[36] They also had to negotiate and suitably interpret ambiguous passages like the one in *Morgenröte* (Book III, 502), with its curious mix of anti- and philosemitic elements, its simultaneously prophetic, affirmative and ominous tone:

> "Among the spectacles to which the coming century invites us is the decision as to the destiny of the Jews of Europe. That their die is cast, that they have crossed their Rubicon, is now palpably obvious: all that is left is for them either to become the masters of Europe or to lose Europe. They themselves know that a conquest of Europe, or any kind of act of violence, on their part is not to be thought of: but they also know that at some future time Europe may fall into their hands like a ripe fruit if only they would just extend them. To bring that about they need, in the meantime, to distinguish themselves in every domain of European distinction and

---

[32]Perhaps the most notorious Nietzschean Nazi, Alfred Bäumler, rationalised Nietzsche's anti-antisemitic comments thus: "Anyone familiar with the philosopher knew how opposed to the Jews he really was. His philosemitic comments were really designed as an attention-gaining device – playing the Jews against the Germans was part of his strategy to get the Germans to listen to him!" See his, *Nietzsche der Philosoph und Politiker*, Leipzig 1931, p. 157.

[33]Precisely because of Nietzsche's philosemitic views and his anti-German remarks many antisemites were not persuaded to attempt such casuistry and remained determinedly anti-Nietzschean. On this see Chapters 4, 5 and 8 of Aschheim, *Germany and the Nietzsche Legacy, op. cit.*

[34]These words were intended to be included in 'Why I Write such Good Books', 2, *Ecce Homo*, note 1, of Walter Kaufmann's translation and commentary (together with *On the Genealogy of Morals*), New York 1969, p. 262. It was discarded but their spirit is nevertheless contained in innumerable, other published passages. Indeed, to the outrage of many, Nietzsche mockingly employed his admiration for Heine to subvert favourite antisemitic themes even further, rendering only "impure" – Jewish and Polish – Germans as the ultimate masters of the German language! "The highest concept of the lyrical poet", he wrote, "*Heinrich Heine* gave to me. I seek in vain all the realms of thousands of years for an equally sweet and passionate music. He possessed that divine malice without which I cannot imagine perfection. I estimate the value of human beings, of races, according to the necessity by which they cannot conceive the god apart from the satyr./And how he handles his German! One day it will be said that Heine and I have been by far the foremost artists of the German language – at an incalculable distance from everything mere Germans have done with it." See *Ecce Homo*, 'Why I Am So Clever', 4, p. 245.

[35]*On the Genealogy of Morals, op. cit.*, Third Essay, Section 23, p. 144.

[36]Thus in its publications *Centralverein* spokesmen quoted liberally from Nietzsche in order to demonstrate that the Old Testament was generally considered by great non-Jews to be the foundation of Western culture and values. See Fritz Goldschmidt, 'Deutschtum und Judentum zu den Grundlagen unseres Seins', *C.V.-Zeitung*, XII (8th June 1933).

to stand everywhere in the first rank until they have reached the point at which they themselves determine what is distinguishing . . . Then, when the Jews can exhibit as their work such jewels and golden vessels as the European nations of a briefer and less profound experience could not and cannot produce, when Israel will have transformed its eternal vengeance into an eternal blessing for Europe: then there will again arrive that seventh day on which the ancient Jewish God may *rejoice* in himself, his creation and his chosen people – and let us all, all of us, rejoice with him!"[37]

Discussions and appropriations of Nietzsche within the German-Jewish community began to appear parallel to his general popularisation from 1890 onwards. Clearly, they were not intended to be uninterested expositions but, rather, interwoven with Jewish purposes and interests. There was, of course, an awareness of the disturbing elements but, by and large, the celebratory, apologetic and defensive uses of Nietzsche were most emphasised. It was quickly recognised that no other contemporary European (let alone German) thinker of similar stature had been more complimentary to the Jews and more scathing of its enemies. This predisposed the overwhelmingly liberal middle-class Jewish community to look more favourably upon Nietzsche than did other sectors of the "established" German bourgeoisie. For, at least prior to the First World War, Nietzsche was championed by decidedly "unrespectable", dissident and radical groups. "Establishment" classes, for the most part regarded him as an insane and dangerous subversive. Within the Jewish community there were, of course, also outright opponents of Nietzsche and his appropriation was seldom totally uncritical. Nevertheless, more than elsewhere within "respectable" middle-class groupings there was reason for a more positive reception.

Beginning as early as 1892, the spokesman for liberal German Jewry, the *Allgemeine Zeitung des Judentums*, carried a number of admiring and balanced (if in certain places mildly critical) expositions, celebrating Nietzsche, his praise for Jewry and hopes for a Jewish renaissance.[38] Similar positive, if differentiated, assessments appeared throughout the community in better-known,[39] as well as comparatively obscure sources,[40] and in more scholarly works.[41]

Much of this went beyond mere exposition. Nietzsche was often employed as an authoritative crutch in continuous polemics and defence activities against

---

[37]For the whole of this remarkable, multi-levelled document see 205, 'Of the people of Israel', *Daybreak. Thoughts On The Prejudices of Morality*, transl. by R. J. Hollingdale, Cambridge 1982, pp. 124–125.

[38]See, for instance, Leo Berg, 'Friedrich Nietzsche über das Judenthum', *Allgemeine Zeitung des Judentums*, LVI (1892), pp. 282–284; Maximilian Stein, 'Friedrich Nietzsche und das Judenthum', *Allgemeine Zeitung das Judentums*, LXIV (1900), pp. 451–453.

[39]Thus Auguste Steinberg, 'Nietzsche und das Judentum', *Ost und West*, 3, No. 8 (1903), pp. 547–556. This highly respectful piece was, however, written from a viewpoint sympathetic to Zionism and takes Nietzsche to task for envisaging Jewish renaissance in terms of its absorption into Europe and not taking into account the re-awakening of a modern Jewish national self-consciousness.

[40]See the anonymous 'Nietzsche und das Judenthum', *Dr. Adolf Brüll's Populär-Wissenschaftliche Monatsblätter*, 21, No. 3 (1st March 1901), pp. 49–52. The incorrect spelling remained throughout. This article stressed that while Nietzsche viewed Jews from without – he had no contact with the intimate details of Jewish life – he was nevertheless the "great ethnological analyst of the Jewish problem", (p. 52).

[41]See the long section on Nietzsche in the work by Albert Lewkowitz, a teacher at the Jewish theological seminary in Breslau, in his *Religiöse Denker der Gegenwart. Vom Wandel der modernen Lebensanschauung*, Berlin 1923.

antisemitism (where, often, he himself was portrayed as its victim).[42] It was not just Nietzsche's scathing dismissals of antisemites and racists, but also some of his central concepts that proved useful in the battle. Thus, in the 1930s, Jewish exiles from National Socialism diagnosed antisemitism as essentially a phenomenon of *ressentiment* (when first propounding the concept Nietzsche, of course, had designated the Jews as the *ressentiment* people *par excellence*!). Antisemitism, they argued, was perhaps the most quintessential of all forms of *ressentiment*. In his quirky 1939 polemic *Friedrich Nietzsche and the Jews*, the exiled jurist Richard Maximilian Cahen insisted that Nietzsche understood the antisemitism of his time as nothing but the most recent "revolt of the slaves", the work of small, spiteful, deracinated people linked to no class or *Volk*.[43]

For Jews who remained within the Third *Reich* such analyses were, of course, out of the question. In a regime which had made Nietzsche into an official State prophet, entirely new forms of apologetics and accommodations were required. The "Jewish" role in the anti-positivist and anti-materialist revolt and in the discovery of Nietzsche was now highlighted and made into a virtue, a mode of inverting older antisemitic accusations: "Today one must hammer into the brain", wrote one Jewish commentator in 1934, "that it was Jews who, almost alone, took a stand for Nietzsche and against trite materialism: Georg Brandes in the North, Henri Bergson in the West, Berdyczewski in the East". It was a total – but prevalent – misconception to believe that "at the beginning of the century there were only *Kommerzienräte* and 'historical' materialists amongst our parents. The opposite is the case."[44]

These were not the only general functions Nietzsche fulfilled in Jewish life. As elsewhere in German political and cultural discourse, the Nietzschean idiom, its slogans and catchwords, soon took on a familiar life of its own and was applied to a variety of Jewish situations. They helped, for instance, as tools in the formulation of a newly conceptualised sense of Jewish solidarity and identity. Thus the popular German-Jewish magazine *Ost und West* – a journal devoted to mediating the largely pre-emancipated Jewish world of Eastern Europe to an acculturated German-Jewish audience and engaged in somehow overcoming the

[42]See, for instance, the anonymous 'Nietzsche, ein Opfer des Antisemitismus', *Mitteilungen des Vereins zur Abwehr des Antisemitismus*, No. 15 (1901) and in the same journal, anonymous, 'Nietzsche und der Antisemitismus', No. 14 (1904). For the later period, 'Nietzsche und der Antisemitismus', *Allgemeine Zeitung des Judentums*, LXXXII (1918), pp. 89–90; 'Friedrich Nietzsche als Wegbereiter völkischer und judenfeindlicher Strömungen?', *Bayerische Israelitische Gemeindezeitung*, VII, No. 1 (1st January 1931), pp. 1–2; K. W. Goldschmidt, 'Nietzsches Stellung zum Judentum', *Berliner Gemeindeblatt* (February 1931). Such activities were not confined to Jews. See the publication by the *Deutsche Demokratische Partei*, *Wider den Nationalsozialismus*, Berlin 1932, in particular August Weber, 'Die Nationalsozialisten sind auf dem Wege des politischen Mordes vorangegangen!', pp. 51–52. See P. B. Wiener, 'Die Parteien der Mitte', in *Entscheidungsjahr 1932. Zur Judenfrage in der Endphase der Weimarer Republik*. Ein Sammelband herausgegeben von Werner E. Mosse unter Mitwirkung von Arnold Paucker, Tübingen 1966 (Schriftenreihe wissenschaftlicher Abhandlungen des Leo Baeck Instituts 13), p. 297.

[43]This work, written under the pseudonym of Lonsbach, has recently been republished. See Richard Maximilian Lonsbach, *Friedrich Nietzsche und die Juden*, ed. by Heinz Robert Schlette, Bonn 1983, pp. 52–53. See too Theodor Lessing, *Deutschland und seine Juden*, Prague 1933.

[44]Leo Hirsch, 'Friedrich Nietzsche und der jüdische Geist', *Der Morgen*, 10 (1934), p. 187.

historic distance between them[45] – without even mentioning Nietzsche's name, portrayed the mutually antithetical yet complementary qualities of Eastern and Western Jewry in categories derived directly from *The Birth of Tragedy*. Eastern Jews had fundamentally "Dionysian" properties while Western Jews were characterised by their opposite "Apollonian" nature. Their mutually fruitful meeting and the ensuing synthesis of emotion and order would bring about the same kind of Jewish renaissance which Nietzsche had envisaged for Germany.[46] The overall conversion of Nietzschean slogans into conventional folk-wisdom also had its consolatory Jewish uses. In coming to terms with the Jewish situation under Nazism and in the attempt to provide a modicum of hope and meaning to the prevalent suffering, German-Jewish leaders repeatedly turned to the famous aphorism: "whatever does not destroy me makes me stronger".[47]

Precisely because the Nietzschean idiom was rapidly integrated into everyday usage, part of the world of accessible cultural associations, it was as easily employed to undermine as to bolster Jewish solidarity. Thus in his 1910 "assimilationist" tract, Friedrich Blach transmuted Jewish assimilation into a life-affirming Nietzschean act. Forcefully advocating collective Jewish self-immolation he wrote: "Well then, so be it, free and joyful suicide. For I no longer want to be the self that I was born. 'Die at the right time: thus spake Zarathustra.' We have endured too long."[48] Richard Maximilian Cahen (Lonsbach) also advocated a form of radical assimilation on Nietzschean grounds[49] and in terms of what he described as the point of Nietzsche's great cultural-biological politics: the creation of a regenerated European *Herrenrasse*, a New Man and breed, formed not on the basis of antisemitism but rather through race mixture of its best elements.[50] During the thirties there were also other rather exotic attempts to invoke Nietzscheanism as definitive of a non-Nazi, but nevertheless racist, vision that would include the Jews in the *Herrenrasse* of a

---

[45]On the general history and dynamics of this question see my *Brothers and Strangers. The East European Jew in German and German-Jewish Consciousness, 1800–1923*, Madison 1982.

[46]Fabius Schach, 'Ost und West', *Ost und West*, III, No. 8 (1903), p. 548. (The article appears on pp. 547–555.) Schach did not use the terms Apollonian and Dionysian, but a quick glance at only part of the passage demonstrates its clear relationship.

[47]See Fritz Goldschmidt, 'Mehr Selbstvertrauen', *C.V.-Zeitung*, XII (28th September 1933), 'Rosch Haschana 5696', *C.V.-Zeitung*, XIV (26th September 1935); Rabbi Ernst Jacob, 'Freiheit durch Bindung. Pessachbetrachtung', *C.V.-Zeitung*, XIII (29th March 1934). Quoted in Jacob Boas, 'Countering Nazi Defamation – German Jews and the Jewish Tradition, 1933–1938', in *LBI Year Book XXXIV* (1989), p. 219.

[48]Friedrich Blach, *Die Juden in Deutschland*, Berlin 1911, p. 42.

[49]As always textual gleanings could be found. Nietzsche wrote in his 'European man and the abolition of nations', that "the entire problem of the *Jews* exists only within national states . . . As soon as it is no longer a question of the conserving of nations but of the production of the strongest possible European mixed race, the Jew will be just as usable and desirable as an ingredient of it as any other national residue." The passage is worth reading *in toto*, however, for it manages both to state that "perhaps the youthful stock-exchange Jew is the most repulsive invention of the entire human race" and (again inverting the thrust of the Judaisation thesis) that while "Christianity has done everything to orientalize the occident, Judaism has always played an essential part in occidentalizing it again". See Book 8, 475, 'A Glance at the State', *Human, All Too Human. A Book for Free Spirits*, transl. by R. J. Hollingdale, Cambridge 1986, pp. 174–175.

[50]Lonsbach, *Friedrich Nietzsche und die Juden, op. cit.* See the chapter 'Synthese'.

regenerated martial Europe, intent on fighting off its non-European coloured enemies.[51]

But these were all, more or less, incidental uses. There were far more direct and substantive confrontations and appropriations. It is an interesting measure of the popularity of Nietzsche-like slogans that a leading liberal rabbi – Caesar Seligmann – coined the much-quoted phrase: "the will to Judaism".[52] Seligmann presents an interesting example of the multi-layered response Nietzsche induced within circles of liberal Judaism. On the surface this was a meeting of total opposites. Seligmann typified the liberal *Bildung* tradition of mainstream German Jewry. There was nothing less Nietzschean than his emphasis on the quiet, settled, industrious and patriotic life. Yet, as a liberal rabbi, Seligmann felt it imperative to be open to the currents of modern thought and the confrontation with Nietzsche, Seligmann had no doubt, was a central and vital part of this enterprise. He praised Nietzsche as an embodiment of modernity, a non-dogmatic seeker of truth with no final or closed system, a latterday prophet who, try as one may, would not be silenced or made to die.[53] Although he was quite aware of the more dubious dimensions of Nietzsche's version of Jewish history, he was more impressed by the fact that, as he put it, not even the most chauvinist Jew had endowed Jews and Judaism with greater significance than Nietzsche.[54]

For Seligmann the encounter itself was of significance, a sign of Jewish cultural openness. Ultimately, however, his *Bildung* liberalism entailed a rejection of the Nietzschean message. The problem, he wrote, was not the prophetic idea of morality, as Nietzsche believed, but rather its lack of fulfilment. For Judaism, unlike Nietzsche, it was not man but the *Unmensch* that had to be overcome.[55]

The prominent Orthodox personality Rabbi Nehemiah Anton Nobel, in the last analysis, also rejected Nietzschean illiberalism. Nietzschean immoralism and contempt for the weak was unacceptable. "There is", wrote Nobel, "only one morality and it is democratic, cultivates no disproportionate cult of genius, advocates no romantic, mystic love of the distant but says, 'Love thy neighbour as thyself'."[56] For all that, Nobel – also very much concerned with the open encounter with modernity – went considerably further than Seligmann and in 1898, in tandem with some Protestant exegetic formulations of the same

---

[51]See the (rather Spenglerian) reflections of Alfred Rosenthal, *Nietzsches "Europäisches Rasse-Problem". ("Der Kampf um die Erdherrschaft")*, Leiden 1935.
[52]On the phrase and Seligmann himself see George L. Mosse, 'The Secularization of Jewish Theology', in *Masses and Man. Nationalist and Fascist Perceptions of Reality*, New York 1980, pp. 257–259; and *idem*, *German Jews Beyond Judaism*, op. cit., pp. 74–75.
[53]See Caesar Seligmann, 'Nietzsche und das Judentum', in *idem*, *Judentum und moderne Weltanschauung*. *Fünf Vorträge*, Frankfurt a. Main 1905, especially pp. 76–79.
[54]*Ibid.*, especially pp. 69–70. Seligmann especially emphasised Nietzsche's love for the Hebrew Bible and his preference for it over the New Testament.
[55]*Ibid.*, pp. 86–89.
[56]See Nehemiah Anton Nobel, 'Friedrich Nietzsche's Stellung zum Judenthum', *Die Jüdische Presse*, 31, Nos. 36, 37, 39 (7th, 14th, 28th September 1900), pp. 373f., 389f., 413f. For the quote see p. 414. This was originally given as a lecture in Winter 1898 to the Cologne "Verein für jüdische Geschichte und Literatur".

period,[57] expounded perhaps the first version of a continuing German-Jewish temptation to (at least partially) Nietzscheanise Judaism (and, at times, Judaise Nietzsche). For Nobel, the prevalent fashion – simply favourably chronicling what Nietzsche had said about the Jews and antisemitism – did not penetrate to the core. Far more essential was the comparative inner relationship between the structures of Judaism and Nietzsche's thought.[58] Like Nietzsche, Nobel proclaimed, Judaism had always stressed the volitional, the element of will. Indeed, it was precisely this voluntary ingredient that had provided Judaism with its glory.* Moreover, the Nietzschean call for *Übermenschen*, the notion of the development of humanity in terms of ever-higher goals, was the basis of the Jewish messianic faith. Here Nietzsche and the prophets were one.

As against the pessimistic Schopenhauerian worldview, Judaism had always been characterised by a kind of affirmative Nietzschean *Lebensphilosophie*:

> "Insofar as Jewish morality holds world-flight and renunciation to be immoral, it creates very immanent, very earthly moral values. The commandments of Judaism relate to life itself in all its details. It elevates the most common matters in the sphere of religion: it ennobles work and rest, food and drink. Every Jew who consciously fulfils one of the so-called ceremonial laws, thereby enacts the transvaluation of values of which Nietzsche spoke . . ."[59]

These kinds of pontifical statements were not universally popular. It was one thing for Jews to study and confront Nietzsche, an indignant critic of these tendencies complained, and quite another, for rabbis – of all people – to transform Nietzsche into a Jewish prophet. The hysterical rabbinical attempt to "turn the German philosopher into a Hebrew" was nothing short of laughable, yet another misguided instance of Jewish "modernism".[60]

Criticised or not, this casuistic Nietzscheanisation of Judaism was (and continues to be[61]) a temptation. Writing in 1925, in a liberal journal associated with the *Centralverein*, Isaac Heinemann, for example, presented the Nietzschean model of *übermenschtum* – ideal individuals able to reach heights far beyond the grasp of the great masses – as normative to Judaism and, in different ways, central to the systems of Philo, Jehuda Halevi and Maimonides. While maintaining Judaism's *übermenschlich* dimension Heinemann, however, sought to temper it with a more human, less elitist face. There was no pure analogy,

---

[57]On this whole episode see Aschheim, 'After the Death of God. Varieties of Nietzschean Religion', *Nietzsche-Studien*, 17 (1988); and Chapter 7 of *idem, Germany and the Nietzsche Legacy, op. cit.*

[58]Nobel, *loc. cit.*, p. 374.

*On Nobel see also the essay by Rachel Heuberger, 'Orthodoxy versus Reform: The Case of Rabbi Nehemiah Anton Nobel of Frankfurt a. Main', in the first section of this Year Book – (Ed.).

[59]Nobel, *loc. cit.*, pp. 413–414.

[60]David Neumark, 'Die jüdische Moderne', *Allgemeine Zeitung des Judentums*, LXIV, No. 45 (9th November 1900), p. 536.

[61]In present-day Israel this idiosyncratic equation of Nietzsche as ultimate Judaic prophet persists – in the most unlikely incarnation. Rebbe Arye Weissfisch, a pious *hared* from the highly Orthodox Mea Shearim quarter in Jerusalem, has made his life into an obsessive mission to spread the word. In this version, Nietzsche stands as a reinforcement of Jewish piety, revealing to Jews the inner meaning and significance of their own faith. Here Nietzsche is the philosopher who rejected only "the God of Christianity" while in Judaism and Jews he perceived the "striving for morality, for the sanctity of man". For one of the few accessible English language descriptions of Weissfisch's involvement with Nietzsche, see Abraham Rabinovich, 'Gathering of Foes', *The Jerusalem Post* (26th April 1986).

Heinemann insisted, for Judaism softened and redirected the *übermenschlich* mission. It encouraged bonds between the leaders and the masses, it linked the higher individuals with the people. Great knowledge, far from increasing distance, automatically entailed greater responsibility. Heinemann's resultant Jewish *Übermensch* was thus the synthesis of the Greek notion of the higher man with Jewish conceptions of responsibility and solidarity.[62]

This was a critical application of Nietzschean categories to Judaism. Others were far less measured. In 1932, perhaps reflecting the more general tenor of the times, Heinrich Berl proclaimed Nietzsche to be nothing less than the "prophet of the Jewish spirit" ("Der Prophet des jüdischen Geistes"). Here was a relationship that had to be understood in terms of congeniality rather than consanguinity. Judaism and Nietzsche coincided in their psychology and ethics and shared the same paradigmatic mentality.[63] Nietzsche, he argued in a moment of eccentricity rare even amongst Nietzscheans, preferred "musical, Dionysian" Judaism to what he regarded as "plastic, Apollonian" Greece.[64]

For Berl there were crucial Jewish-Nietzschean parallelisms. Jewish ethics was a *Gattungsethik* (species ethic) based upon an essentially Nietzschean *Gattungsethik:* "the pathos of distance". Judaism, moreover, was a morality which – in its single-minded devotion to Jahwe – stood beyond good and evil. Nietzsche, Berl proclaimed, erred in his depiction of Jewish slave morality: throughout their history Jews had possessed primal Nietzschean characteristics! What Nietzsche had overlooked was that the slaves' will to domination was more powerful than the masters' because the latter already possessed external power while the slaves remained hungry for it![65]

Given both their religious and establishmentarian provenance these hermeneutic appropriations may well have been surprising, but they were, nevertheless, all variations on a conserving theme, identifying parallels and integrating – if sometimes also making distinctions between – Judaism and the Nietzschean thematic. They were all the products of circles concerned with the perpetuation, in some way or another, of normative Judaism.

But this was not the most typical function of Nietzscheanism. Nietzscheans were, in general, dissidents and idiosyncrats, concerned above all with upsetting conventional patterns of thought and action. This was as true for the Jewish world as it was elsewhere. The philosopher's impact was most intensely felt within non-conformist, and innovative elements of the community. It was amongst such groups that Nietzsche became a radicalising, dynamic presence, a galvanising element in the post-traditional quest for regenerative Jewish forms and post-liberal modes of identity.

It is hardly surprising that in the life and thought of Franz Rosenzweig (1886–1929), the most innovative German-Jewish theologian of the twentieth century, Nietzsche – the man and his mode of thinking (if not always the content of his

---

[62]See Isaac Heinemann, 'Der Begriff des Übermenschen in der modernen Religionsphilosophie', *Der Morgen*, I (1925).
[63]Heinrich Berl, 'Nietzsche und das Judentum', *Menorah* (1932), p. 68.
[64]*Ibid.*, especially pp. 59–60, 67–68.
[65]*Ibid.*, pp. 60–61, 67.

philosophising[66]) – stood as a shining beacon. For Rosenzweig's was a theology of radical renewal, a body of thought – typical of so many pathbreakers brushed by the Nietzschean grain – characterised by its questioning breakdown of accepted categories. As Gershom Scholem described it in 1930 there was an "obvious impossibility of recognizing the realms of orthodoxy or liberalism in Rosenzweig's world".[67] Rosenzweig described his work as "quite fantastic, entirely unpublishable, equally scandalous to 'Christians, Jews and heathens' ".[68]

Nietzsche was centrally present in Rosenzweig's rejection of Hegelian idealism and abstract academic scholarship, his discovery of a "living" Judaism, his epistemological emphasis on "becoming" and insistence upon a personal philosophy (in which man had to be the starting point of thought).[69] In 1918 he wrote of Hegel: "It's a pity about him! Only Nietzsche (and Kant) pass muster!"[70]

Rosenzweig called for a type of theologian-philosopher always impelled to translate "theological problems into human terms" and to bring "human problems into the pale of theology".[71] Nietzsche the heretic was precisely the embodiment of such a vision. As Rosenzweig put it, in his 1921 *magnum opus, The Star of Redemption*, Nietzsche

> "was one man who knew his own life and his own soul like a poet, and obeyed their voice like a holy man, and who was for all that a philosopher. What he philosophized has by now become almost a matter of indifference. Dionysiac and Superman, Blond Beast and Eternal Return – where are they now? But none of those who now feel the urge to philosophize can any longer by-pass the man himself, who transformed himself in the transformation of his mental images, whose soul feared no height, who clambered after Mind, that daredevil climber, up to the steep pinnacle of madness, where there was no more Onward. The fearsome and challenging image of the unconditional vassalage of soul to mind could henceforth not be eradicated . . . For the philosopher, philosophy was the cool height to which he had escaped from the mists of the plain. For Nietzsche this dichotomy between height and plain did not exist in his own self: he was of a piece, soul and mind a unity, man and thinker a unity to the last."[72]

If Rosenzweig's work was a conscious part of the German-Jewish impulse to renewal, it remained a densely personal endeavour, connected only in tenuous

---

[66]Robert A. Cohen has recently sought – rather unpersuasively in my view – to minimise Nietzsche's influence on Rosenzweig. See his 'Rosenzweig vs. Nietzsche', *Nietzsche-Studien*, 19 (1990), pp. 346–366. The fact that like other – particularly religious – appropriations, Rosenzweig's usage of Nietzsche was always partial, interested and often critical does not necessarily lessen the influence. On the contrary, what is of interest here is the remarkable ability of Nietzsche to influence modes of thought and action far removed from his own.

[67]Gershom Scholem, 'On the 1930 Edition of Rosenzweig's Star of Redemption', in *The Messianic Idea in Judaism*, New York 1972, p. 320. See too his comments on its profoundly revolutionary nature and impact.

[68]Letter of 27th August 1918 to Gertrud Oppenheim, quoted in Nahum N. Glatzer (ed.), *Franz Rosenzweig. His Life and Thought*, New York 1976, p. 81.

[69]See Glatzer's 'Foreword' to *The Star of Redemption*, transl. by William W. Hallo, Boston 1971; and the 'Introduction' to his *Franz Rosenzweig, op. cit.*

[70]August 27th 1918 letter to Gertrud Oppenheim in Glatzer (ed.), *Franz Rosenzweig, op. cit.*, p. 81.

[71]For an instructive analysis of Rosenzweig's conception of the relation between philosophy and theology see Paul Mendes-Flohr, 'Franz Rosenzweig's Concept of Philosophical Faith', in *LBI Year Book XXXIV* (1989). For the above quote see p. 368.

[72]*The Star of Redemption, op. cit.*, p. 9.

ways to any larger social and political movement. For the Nietzschean impulse within a larger, organised movement we must turn to Zionism.

Classical Zionism, conceived orginally as a secular and modernising movement, possessed a clear consciousness of the crisis of Jewish tradition and its supporting institutions. Nietzsche was enlisted by many as an authority for articulating the movement's ruptured – though complex – relationship with the past, a force in its drive to "normalisation" and its activist ideal of the self-creating new Hebrew Man. Unlike the circles mentioned above, Zionist circles were not particularly interested in harmonising Judaism with Nietzscheanism. It was not Nietzsche's writings on Judaism and the Jews that inspired them. What moved them was, rather, Nietzsche's radical anti-traditionalism, his overall rebellious, transvaluative attitudes which they could bring to bear on their own Jewish experience. At the same time, it is important to recognise that there were always inbuilt tensions within Zionism – pressures to Jewish continuity as against the imperative to rebel[73] – which tended either to mute this Nietzschean impulse or to deflect it into more conserving directions.

In the early (pre-1918) years it was the radical Nietzschean note that functioned as a pervasive, if at times purposely vague, means for the expression of activist and redemptive Zionist hopes. In 1902, for instance, the future first President of the State of Israel, Chaim Weizmann, wrote from Switzerland to his then sweetheart Vera Khatzman, "Vera, my joy, I am sending you Nietzsche: learn to read and understand him. This is the best and finest thing I can send you."[74] Weizmann never spelled out the reasons for his admiration yet it was, perhaps, implicit in an earlier comment he had made: "The French", he exclaimed, "are incapable of understanding Nietzsche. They are too superficial for a revaluation of all values."[75] Presumably the Jews – impelled by Zionism and operating within its framework – were not.[76]

Within the specifically German *Kulturbereich* the Zionist attraction to

[73]For a superb analysis of this tension see Gershom Scholem, 'Zionism – Dialectic of Continuity and Rebellion', in Ehud Ben Ezer (ed.), with a Foreword by Robert Alter, *Unease in Zion*, Jerusalem 1974.

[74]Letter of 3rd August 1902 (No. 266), in Leonard Stein (ed.), in collaboration with Gedalia Yogev, *The Letters and Papers of Chaim Weizmann*, vol. I (Summer 1885–29th October 1902), London 1968, pp. 340–341.

[75]Letter to Vera Khatzman of 14th(?) March 1901 (No. 63), *ibid.*, pp. 94–96. The quote appears on p. 95. "When you can read German", Weizmann promised Vera in a letter of 28th July 1902 (No. 257), p. 326, "I'll get a *wonderful* edition of Nietzsche's 'Zarathustra' for you, but a really wonderful one. So go on, my sweet, and we shall read it regularly and without fail." For all that, it should be clear that this was the younger Weizmann. In later years Weizmann hardly mentioned Nietzsche.

[76]The transvaluative task, admittedly, was vast and could only be gradual. For, as Weizmann wrote in his Nietzsche-influenced diagnosis of the Jewish problem of his day, "the stench of decay hits one at every step. And years will pass, and many will still fall victims to these terrible conditions, before creative, constructive work starts. Are we going to see all that? No, I doubt it. Our fate, the fate of a people who live in a time of transition, is to be given activities of a purely negative character. To understand and ponder over old Jewish values, to understand them only to discard them perhaps, and to reappraise them at a later stage – my God, this is agonising labour, agonising work, and we, the feeble and the weak, have to bear it on our shoulders." Instructively, this passage did not mention Nietzsche but the next paragraph (perhaps unconsciously) immediately passes on to the subject of the philosopher – and his misuse by Socialists! See *ibid*, Letter No. 85 to Vera Khatzman, 8th June 1901, pp. 122–123.

Nietzsche was very much a generational affair.[77] The first Zionist generation, far from being a part of the widespread, Nietzsche-influenced revolt against liberal rationalism and positivism, in many ways embodied its values. The official journal of the Zionist Movement, *Die Welt*, remained unmoved by the Nietzsche cult at the turn of the century.[78] It was, after all, Theodor Herzl's close friend and the most famous Zionist of his time, Max Nordau, who in his *Degeneration*, as we have seen, had penned perhaps the most unbridled attack on Nietzsche (and what he considered to be the other related "irrationalisms" of the *fin de siècle*.) Herzl himself paid hardly any attention to Nietzsche, referring to him only once – as a "madman".[79]

A "radicalised" second German Zionist generation challenged the Zionism of its fathers, defining it not as a philanthropic and diplomatic matter but primarily as the imperative for personal metamorphosis and cultural rejuvenation. Jewish renaissance was increasingly transposed from the external and political to the cultural and existential plane, conceived as a question of personal identity and realisation. It was in this context that the Nietzschean moment entered German Zionism. The intellectual leadership of this generation no longer took the rationalist Enlightenment tradition for granted. The wider anti-bourgeois, neo-romantic mood of the day, with its emphasis on activist self-creation and the creative role of myth, admirably fitted the needs of a Zionism whose emphasis had shifted from formal institutions and political diplomacy to questions of collective regeneration and personal authenticity.[80]

Nietzschean themes and imagery and the rhetoric of "transvaluation" formed part of the staple intellectual diet of this generation.[81] On one level, Nietzsche acted as a kind of model of rebellious authenticity for what constituted the new secular kind of Jew, a radicalising force against fossilised tradition and religious ceremonial. Robert Weltsch cited the prevalent paradoxical contention of the time that Nietzsche (and Hölderlin) would create stronger Jews than "a forced return to a ritual in which we do not believe".[82] In 1922 Hans Kohn – then still a

---

[77]See Gert Mattenklott, 'Nietzscheanismus und Judentum', in *Archiv Bibliographia Judaica, Frankfurt a. Main, Jahrbuch I (1985). Probleme deutsch-jüdische Identität*, ed. by Norbert Altenhofer and Renate Heuer, Bad Soden/Ts. 1986, p. 57.

[78]The only relevant article to appear was the rather diluted, non-committal piece by Ernst Müller, 'Gedanken über Nietzsche und sein Verhältnis zu den Juden', *Die Welt*, No. 40 (5th October 1900).

[79]The context and commonality should also, however, be noted. In a conversation with Leo Franckel, Herzl explained that he was "against the democracies": "'So you are a disciple of Nietzsche', he [Franckel] said. I: 'Not at all. Nietzsche is a madman. But one can only govern aristocratically.'" See Raphael Patai (ed.), *The Complete Diaries of Theodor Herzl*, transl. by Harry Zohn, 5 vols., London 1960, vol. I, p. 191.

[80]For a summary of these trends see Aschheim, *Brothers and Strangers, op. cit.*, Chapters 4 and 5.

[81]See for example the collection by German and Czech Zionists, *Vom Judentum. Ein Sammelbuch*, Leipzig 1913, especially the contributions by Moses Calvary and Moritz Goldstein. Even where Nietzsche was criticised – or, indeed, not even specifically mentioned – the categories were his and the influence palpable.

[82]Cited in George L. Mosse, 'The influence of the Volkish Idea on German Jewry', in *idem, Germans and Jews. The Right, the Left and the Search for a "Third Force" in Pre-Nazi Germany*. London 1971, p. 96.

Zionist – portrayed Nietzsche as the father of a new kind of humanising , de-institutionalised form of Nationalism, one that was "becoming a question of personal ethics, personal shaping of life":

> "Everywhere people feel the desperation of a time without faith or myth, the fatigue of termination, but people are trying to get away from these things. A new song of life affirmation and powerful courage is to begin. Nietzsche, the unique genius, as lonesome as a gigantic figure, who overshadows the decline of an era of faith, is the father of this desperate temerity, this endless hope for a new heaven."[83]

Some of this Nietzschean dynamism went beyond rhetoric into Zionist *praxis*. The radical Zionist youth movement *Hashomer Hazair*, founded in Vienna in 1916, clearly incorporated the Nietzschean thematic into the *mélange* of its other influences – Gustav Wyneken, Freud, Gustav Landauer, Hans Blüher and so on. It actively aimed at creating a sexually and spiritually liberated, anti-bourgeois youth culture based upon voluntary and elitist communal forms, rejecting all "mechanical" relationships and party organisation.[84] Transplanted into newly-developing Palestine this radical Central European youth culture ethos soon achieved notoriety. The *Hashomer Hazair* commune, "*Bitania*", constantly clashed with party functionaries who sought to co-opt them into prevailing political structures. They loudly proclaimed their independence from all imposed ideology and organisation. Their outspoken insistence upon establishing "agitated" (*T'sisa*) and dynamic, rather than settled and ordered, modes of communal life as the basis for their central goal of perpetual self-creation, their strident cries for erotic and intellectual freedom were part and parcel of the Nietzschean cloth they had packed into the cultural baggage they had brought from Vienna.[85]

Even within a less harsh environment it would have been difficult to maintain such a self-sustaining sectarian Nietzschean dynamic outside of a mediating ideological framework. It is hardly surprising that around 1926–1927 the group adopted a revolutionary Marxist ideology, replete with doctrines of historical materialism and class warfare. Yet their origins left a permanent imprint: the earlier insistence upon voluntarism and individual freedom remained strong.

All the above-mentioned circles were in one way or another affected by the most important intellectual influence on the generation of young Jews, Martin Buber (1878–1965). It was through him, above all, that Nietzsche was assimilated into German Zionism. His particular mediation illustrates well both the

---

[83]Hans Kohn, 'Nationalism', in *The Jew. Essays from Martin Buber's Journal 'Der Jude', 1916–1928*, edited and introduced by Arthur A. Cohen and transl. by Joachim Neugroschel, Alabama 1980, p. 28. The essay appeared originally in *Der Jude*, VI (1921–1922), pp. 674–686.

[84]For a useful overview see Jehuda Reinharz, 'Hashomer Hazair in Germany (I), 1928–1933', in *LBI Year Book XXXI* (1986), especially pp. 173–174.

[85]On the history and documentation of these developments and polemics see Muki Tzur (ed.), *K'hilateinu* (in Hebrew), Jerusalem 1988. For the most characteristic expression of this tendency see the article by the remarkable spiritual leader of the group Meir Ya'ari, 'M'toch Hatsisa', *ibid.*, pp. 266–269. I thank Rina Peled and David Biale for drawing my attention to this reference.

possibilities and the limits which Nietzscheanism presented for the incorporation into organised and religio-national frameworks.

This is not the place to record Buber's passionate, complicated changing relationship to Nietzsche over the years nor the profound and differentiated impact Nietzsche had on the style, substance and course of his work.[86] The young Buber found Nietzsche intoxicatingly threatening,[87] but his public pronouncements were adulatory and fully supportive of the Nietzschean notion of dynamic self-creation and a suitably adapted *Lebensphilosophie*. Nietzsche, wrote Buber in his 1900 eulogy, belonged to those thinkers who were the "apostles of life" and whose greatness was as indefinable as life itself. He was a visionary who could intuit future human forms in ways that went beyond everyday language and longings. He was the prophet of immanence and creative renewal – "out of dead cultures he gathered elements of new formations into light". He "erected before our eyes the statue of the heroic man who creates himself and goes beyond himself . . . Against the God of Genesis he brought a great adversary: the God of becoming, in whose development we may share."[88]

It was precisely these vitalist and liberational values which informed Buber's influential *fin-de-siècle* vision of a Zionist Jewish renaissance, of a revivified nation composed of free and creative individuals. This renaissance was envisaged in Nietzschean terms not as a going backward but as a form of creative – individual and collective – rebirth, "the way out of medieval asceticism to a warm, flowing, life-feeling, out of the coercion of narrow-minded communities to freedom of the personality. The secret of the new, the rich sense of the discoverer, the free life of risks and the overflowing creative impulse (*Schaffenslust*) dominate this time." The Jewish renaissance of 1900 was not a return to old traditions and practices but, Buber wrote in strikingly Nietzschean language, one conceived and led by people "possessed by a sense of the future (*das Kommende*)".[89]

In Buber's early Zionist vision, the historical precondition for Jewish rebirth entailed overcoming the "life-denying", disempowering abnormalities of *Galut* (Exile) and the distortions of the "unfree spirituality" of the ghetto. The sources

---

[86] For a superb extended analysis of this question as well as an examination of the overall shift in Buber's thinking see Paul Mendes-Flohr, *From Mysticism to Dialogue. Martin Buber's Transformation of German Social Thought*, Detroit 1989.

[87] When he was seventeen, Buber later recalled, *Zarathustra* "took possession" of him "not in the manner of a gift but in the manner of an invasion which deprived me of my freedom, and it was a long time until I could liberate myself from it". See his 'Autobiographical Fragments', in Paul Arthur Schilpp and Maurice Friedman (eds.), *The Philosophy of Martin Buber*, La Salle, Illinois 1967, p. 12. In a very early unpublished piece, *Zarathustra*, both the admirable potency and fear of Nietzsche's work was evident. "Whoever could not work through Nietzsche", he wrote, "had better lay him aside." What was ultimately admirable about Nietzsche was his scepticism towards all systems – a mark of respect was therefore defection (*Abfall*) from him. His later works were certainly dominated by critical comments. For all that Nietzsche's influence was always there – if only in terms of some of the mature Buber's *Fragestellung*.

[88] Martin Buber, 'Ein Wort über Nietzsche und die Lebenswerte', *Die Kunst im Leben* (December 1900), p. 13.

[89] Martin Buber, 'Jüdische Renaissance (1900)', in *idem, Die Jüdische Bewegung. Gesammelte Aufsätze und Ansprachen 1900–1914*, Berlin 1920, pp. 10–11.

for this recovery were contained in the still healthy materials and *Ur*-powers of the Jewish *Volk* itself. Buber's use of Nietzsche, like other Nationalist appropriations, had somehow to reconcile the emphasis on "overcoming", on activist transvaluation, with the belief in the eternal, organic properties of the nation. Buber effected the compromise between Jewish tradition and Nietzschean creativity by arguing that only a dynamic movement such as Zionism would be able to tap and liberate the unbroken, but historically repressed, "life-feeling of the Jews".[90] Such an expansive "life-feeling", the necessary antidote to "pure intellectuality" (*reine Geistigkeit*), was in urgent need of recovery. Exile – consisting of external dependence and internal legal coercion – had dislocated this vitality "from its natural expression, the free creation in reality and art . . ."

Zionism, in this early Buberian rendering, was, then, akin to an act of Nietzschean renaturalisation, an aesthetic, vitalist vision in which Jews would once again be able to lead freely creative, joyful and healthy lives.[91] Even Buber's conception of the creative life itself was provided with a kind of nationalised Nietzschean character reminiscent of *The Birth of Tragedy* (for obvious reasons, the work most extensively used for all *völkisch* appropriations of Nietzsche). "The redemptive affirmation of an antagonism", he wrote, "is the essence of all creation". And the two basic forces that made up the creative life were "rootedness" and "die gebundene Tragik".[92]

Buber's youthful Zionism of renaturalisation never stressed the martial, warlike aspects of Nietzsche, nor, unlike the nascent German radical Nationalist versions, did it elevate one national group over another in terms of its will to power. Buber's version demonstrated that Nietzschean vitalism could be pressed equally into humanist as well as anti-humanist service. At the same time, the *Lebensphilosophie* component of Buber's Zionism was increasingly muted, indeed, deflected by his ever-more dominant *Erlebnismystik*. More and more the activist impulse was tamed by the Buberian emphasis on sanctity, deradicalised by a mystic interpretation of Nietzsche's "*Einheitslehre*".[93] Buber went on to construct a mysticism centred upon heightened inner experience. This, of course, was one reason for his attraction to – and sustained mythologisation of – *Hasidism*, which seemed to provide a living model of community of such experience. On the surface, at least, this seemed quite removed from Buber's earlier, far more vitalistic and radical use of Nietzsche.

This, however, did not exhaust the uses of such vitalism within the sphere of German Zionism. Different times generated new versions. A species of Nietzschean *Lebensphilosophie* was, for instance, at the heart of the writings of the controversial German-Jewish philosopher Theodor Lessing (1872–1933), during

---

[90] *Ibid.*, p. 13.
[91] *Ibid.*, pp. 14ff.
[92] '*Die Schaffenden, das Volk und die Bewegung* (1902)', *ibid.*, especially pp. 71ff.
[93] This mystic turn and appropriation of Nietzsche is illuminatingly analysed in Mendes-Flohr, *op. cit.*, Chapter 3, 'Buber's *Erlebnis*-Mysticism'.

the late 1920s and early 1930s. Lessing's theories were written under the shadow of Nazism (of which he was an early victim) and as a kind of last-ditch attempt to provide a Jewish answer. He had already written a number of general works on Nietzsche[94] as well as general philosophical-cultural critiques very much in the Nietzschean mode.[95] He now applied many of these Nietzschean themes in his analyses of, and solutions to, the contemporary Jewish condition. Lessing's diagnosis of Jewish self-hate – insights largely derived from his own share in that affliction – as well as his prescribed Zionist cure, flowed from a kind of *völkisch-*Nietzschean creed. Jewish self-hatred was a product of exile, of an "unnatural", over-intellectual life, alienated from nature and the earth. In this unnatural situation – and in response to their hostile environment – the Jews turned their own over-spiritualised characteristics against themselves. The result was a pathological psychology.

Lessing envisaged the transformation from this pathological state to one of healthy self-acceptance in explicitly Nietzschean terms, invoking the philosopher's injunction: "Become what you are."[96] Obviously, for Lessing, as with so many Nietzscheans, becoming what one was was far removed from conventional bourgeois Jewish self-acceptance. It meant rather a kind of Nietzschean process of re-naturalisation, the assertion of a Jewish "*Machtwille*" and a virile, even instinctual, activism. The old *Galut* Jew had to be metamorphosised into the new Zionist Man, forged in the spirit of the "Old Testament pagan *Naturmythos*".[97]

Of course, Lessing's late Nietzschean remedies were not animated by joy but desperation. For an indication of the really liberational Nietzsche within Zionism one must turn to the East European Hebrew intelligentsia, for it is there that he had the most sustained and radical impact. "No European thinker", the Israeli critic Menachem Brinker has recently pointed out, "had the same profound influence upon Hebrew literature during this period".[98] The reasons for this should be immediately apparent. German (and Western European) Zionism was essentially a "post-assimilationist" phenomenon, a project of "return" to forgotten Jewish materials.[99] In pre-emancipation Eastern Europe it

[94]See Theodor Lessing, *Schopenhauer – Wagner – Nietzsche. Einführung in Moderne Philosophie*, München 1906; *idem, Nietzsche*, Berlin 1925.

[95]*Idem, Geschichte als Sinngebung des Sinnlosen. Oder die Geburt der Geschichte aus dem Mythos*, Leipzig 1927, 4th edn.

[96]See *idem, Der jüdische Selbsthass*, Berlin 1930.

[97]See Lessing's 'Jüdisches Schicksal', *Der Jude*, 9 (1928). The quote appears on p. 17. The reference to "*Machtwille*" appears in Lessing's *Deutschland und seine Juden, op. cit.*, p. 14. See too Golomb, 'Nietzsche and the Marginal Jews', *loc. cit.*, pp. 125–126.

[98]See Menachem Brinker, 'Nietzsche's Impact on Hebrew Writers of the Russian Empire', in Bernice Glatzer-Rosenthal (ed.), *Nietzsche and Russia*, Princeton (forthcoming) 1992. I am indebted to Professor Brinker for providing me with a copy of this paper from which I freely draw for the following section.

[99]See, in this respect, Jehuda Reinharz, *Fatherland or Promised Land. The Dilemma of the German Jew, 1893–1914*, Ann Arbor 1975; Stephen M. Poppel, *Zionism in Germany 1897–1933. The Shaping of a Jewish Identity*, Philadelphia 1977.

functioned as a major secularising force, a modernising mode of escape from the constrictions of a continuing – though not untroubled – traditional Jewish life.[100] Whereas Buber addressed a post-assimilationist audience for whom the break with the past could be taken for granted, the Hebrew Nietzsche was designed for a public that had not severed the cord. In the East European context Nietzsche's hammer was employed to facilitate the break from the traditions and institutions of normative Judaism, to bring about liberation from what were regarded as repressive rabbinic-legal and communal restraints. This anti-traditional Nietzsche – although criticised by many – made immediate sense in Eastern Europe precisely because its public was still being actively shaped by that tradition.[101]

Nietzsche's visibility was, of course, enhanced by a historical coincidence: the "Europeanisation" of these East European Jewish intellectuals coincided with the period when Nietzsche was most in vogue. Nietzscheanism – in both its critical and affirmative guises – was thus easily channelled into, and plausibly able to articulate, some of the major thematics of the Zionist national revolt.

While the Nietzsche influence in Eastern Europe was pervasive,[102] we must limit ourselves to the most famous and vocal Hebrew Nietzschean – perhaps the most acute and controversial critic in all of modern Hebrew letters – Micha Josef Berdichevsky (1865–1921; pseudonym bin Gorion).[103] The explicitly Nietzschean title of his collection of essays written between 1890 and 1896 – *A Transformation of Values (Shinui Arachim)* – proclaimed his agenda.[104] Berdichevsky enunciated nothing less than a Nietzschean critique of Jewish ethics, a

---

[100]On Zionism generally – and some of the differences between the Eastern and Western modes – see the 'Introduction' by Arthur Hertzberg to *idem* (ed.), *The Zionist Idea*, New York 1975; and Walter Laqueur, *A History of Zionism*, London 1972.

[101]Some German Zionists were aware of the differences in situation and warned against a similar radicalism in their own deracinated context. See Gerhard Holdheim and Walter Preuss, *Die theoretischen Grundlagen des Zionismus*, Berlin 1919.

[102]This is not the place to trace the influence in detail. See Brinker, *loc. cit.*, for a list of relevant Hebrew luminaries such as Shaul Tschernikovsky, David Frischman and Hillel Zeitlin. As usual the use was selective. Perhaps the most interesting and sophisticated – as well as critical – of these was Y. H. Brenner who was acutely sensitive to the Nietzschean themes of perspectivism and the fictionality of interpretations.

[103]Needless to say, Berdichevsky's brand of Nietzscheanism aroused opposition amongst other Zionist and Hebrew writers. This is not the place to elaborate. The significant point here is that in attempting to refute him, many critics themselves incorporated a variety of Nietzschean assumptions, themes and categories into their own counter-arguments and systems – yet another sign of Nietzsche's importance. This was certainly true for Berdichevsky's most prominent and prestigious critic, Achad Ha'am (Asher Ginzburg). As Leon Simon remarks in his 'Introductory Note' to Achad Ha'am's essay 'Judaism and Nietzsche' (1898): In the course of the essay Achad Ha'am "adumbrated a sort of Jewish version of Nietzscheanism, with the substitution of morality for power as the ideal of the superman, and with the further postulate of the 'super-nation'.", in L. Simon (ed.), *Achad Ha-am: Essays. Letters. Memoirs*, Oxford 1946, pp. 76ff. See too the essay in the same volume, 'The Supremacy of Reason'. For 'The Transvaluation of Values' (1898) see L. Simon (ed.), *Selected Essays of Achad Ha-'Am*, New York 1970.

[104]These are not, alas, available in English. See *Shinui Arachim* in Berdichevsky's *Collected Essays* (in Hebrew), Tel-Aviv 1960.

Lebensphilosophie applied to the whole of the Jewish experience.[105] In its radical dismissal of both the Diaspora and the normative tradition with its anti-individualist constraints,[106] the early Berdichevsky posited a Zionist transvaluation of Jewish values based upon the perceived need for – and intrinsic value of – Jewish empowerment.

In Berdichevsky's view the Jewish religious and ideological establishment had rendered a pathetic powerlessness as a moral virtue. Lacking national power and the capacity to affect history the Jews were simply "below good and evil". Only their re-establishment into a national entity based upon power and responsibility would render them again capable of doing good and committing evil.[107] Nietzscheanism was perhaps the most radical means by which this stream of Zionism could enunciate its drive towards empowerment and "normalisation".

Nietzschean intellectual "irrationalism" and *Lebensphilosophie* centrally informed Berdichevsky's radical rereading of the Jewish past, its enslavement to history and the perpetual privileging of the "book" over the "sword".

> "There is a time for men and nations who live by the sword, by their power and their strong arm, by vital boldness. This time is the hour of intensity, of life in its essential meaning. But the book is no more than the shade of life, life in its senescence. The blade is not something abstracted and standing apart from life; it is the materialisation and substantial likeness. Not so the book."[108]

Berdichevsky was important to the shift in (mainly Zionist) historiography that placed renewed "monumental" emphasis on Jewish power and sovereignty as against the virtues of its vaunted spirituality and political passivity. The priestly-rabbinic stranglehold on Jewish life, he wrote, had emasculated the vitality of the people by repressing its original vital natural religion – the "anti-natural" Torah of Moses was a later imposition – and transforming it into an abstract, spiritualised doctrine. The prophets had also contributed to this process: their substitution of ethics for life had so weakened the national fibre that exile inevitably followed. David Biale has described this as a kind of Nietzschean "counter-history",[109] one that sought those vital elements and traditions which had been repressed in the distortive construction of a mono-lithic, anti-pluralist "historic Judaism". Berdichevsky believed that within the

---

[105]Bin Gorion was reasonably well known in Germany where he spent some time. Many of his works were translated into German. It is not surprising that it was, above all, Buber's journal that mediated him to a German-Jewish audience. See for instance Baruch Krupnick, 'Micha Josef Berdyczewski. Seine Wahrheiten und Dichtung', *Der Jude*, 3 (1918–1919) and Markus Ehrenpreis, 'Gespräche mit Berdyczewski', *Der Jude*, 6 (1921–1922).

[106]"In every other people, nationality is the single storehouse in which are preserved human individualities, and where the individual sees his achievements secured and his gains safeguarded. Among us, the individual finds in his Jewish nationality a power hostile to what is in his heart. Every one of us feels this opposition the moment he begins to improve himself and seek for culture . . ." See 'The Question of Culture' (1900–1903) reprinted in Hertzberg, *The Zionist Idea, op. cit.*, pp. 297–299. The quote appears on p. 298.

[107]Menachem Brinker develops this point extremely well. See his paper, *loc. cit.*, also for relevant sources.

[108]'In Two Directions' (1900–1903), reprinted in Hertzberg, *The Zionist Idea, op. cit.*, pp. 295–297. The quote appears on p. 295.

[109]David Biale, *Gershom Scholem. Kabbalah and Counter-History*, Cambridge 1979, pp. 37–43. Much of the present analysis is drawn from Biale.

rich reservoir of the Jewish tradition itself the materials for a vitalist recovery could be found, especially in those pre-Mosaic traditions of the sword and its orgiastic identifications with nature. Basing himself upon the Nietzschean insistence on destruction as precondition for creation, he maintained: "in order to build a temple, it is necessary first to destroy a temple".[110]

Yet, it is important to note, even for the most enthusiastic Jewish Nationalist Nietzscheans internal tensions were always present. Some kind of compromise or domestication or taming always seemed to be necessary. There were inbuilt limits, inevitable ironies, surrounding the Nietzschean revolt against Jewish normative tradition and the drive towards naturalisation and empowerment. Despite Berdichevsky's deep longings for such "normalisation", for overcoming the unnatural distortions of ghetto and exilic life, he embodied an ongoing and quite unresolved internal Zionist tension between normalcy and moral uniqueness, the traditional past and the open future. "When we defeat the past", he wrote, "it is we ourselves who are defeated. But if the past conquers, it is we, and our sons and the sons of our sons, who are conquered . . . Elixir and poison in one and the same substance. Who shall show us the way? Who shall clear us a path?"[111]

Ultimately Berdichevsky accepted what his critics had argued – that after the modern Jewish nation had been created and sovereignty restored it would, indeed, be governed by the same moral spirit he had so castigated.[112] The later Berdichevsky turned to forgotten aspects of the Jewish tradition, including of course *Hasidism*, and other neglected legends, sayings and folklore.[113] These too may have been elements of his vaunted "counter-history", avenues to the lost alternatives of the Jewish past. Nevertheless, Berdichevsky increasingly regarded himself as an historian, a chronicler rather than conscious mythologiser (and destroyer) of the Jewish past, and in later collections of his work often deleted his references to Nietzsche.[114]

In 1934 a German-Jewish commentator could write of both Berdichevsky's and Buber's turn to legends and *Volksmärchen* that this was not a conservative turning away from Nietzsche but a logical continuation of the interest in him. It was the point "where the extremes touch and the *Übermensch* is transformed into the *Volksgeist*. (The way from the Baalschem to Nietzsche and from Nietzsche to the Baalschem is possible, only that of the *Kommerzienrat* and the party functionary to the Baalschem or to Nietzsche cannot lead there.)"[115] Moreover, the commentator insisted, there were clear commonalities: "With Nietzsche and

---

[110]Quoted *ibid.*, p. 40.

[111]'The Question of Our Past' (1900–1903) in Hertzberg, *The Zionist Idea, op. cit.*, pp. 299–301. The quote appears on p. 301.

[112]This has been perceptively pointed out by Menachem Brinker, *loc. cit.*, p. 23. Nevertheless, Berdichevsky insisted that the precondition for sanctity, for being a holy people, entailed a normal national livelihood and framework. See his 'On Sanctity' (1900) in Hertzberg, *The Zionist Idea, op. cit.*, pp. 301–302.

[113]Contemporaries and later generations were unanimous in their praise of this remarkable undertaking. His volume *Die Sagen der Juden*, published in 1913 and 1919, has appeared in English under the title *Mimekor Israel*, Bloomington 1976.

[114]See Biale, *Kabbalah and Counter-History, op. cit.*, p. 43 and note 23, p. 235.

[115]Leo Hirsch, 'Friedrich Nietzsche und der jüdische Geist', *Der Morgen*, 10 (1934), p. 189.

Hasidism bin Gorion shared passion with passion, life-affirmation . . . and the mistrust against all words, slogans and programmes."[116] In fusing Nietzsche and *Hasidism* the plastic possibilities of even the most casuistic Jewish Nietzscheanism were stretched to their outmost limits.

"Nietzscheanism" as such did not conquer Jewish or Zionist life. There never was a "pure" Nietzscheanism, a set ideology backed by a central organisation with clear and independent guidelines. Indeed, only through its mediations did and could it become an effective cultural and political force. This was not a weakness. Its penetrative strength lay precisely in the fact that it was an elastic, infiltrative sensibility capable of being grafted on to numerous institutions, ideologies and systems. It was thus that, in manifold ways and different guises, Nietzschean impulses permeated various aspects of the Jewish and Zionist world, performing a number of important, even contrary, functions. Nietzscheanism acted variously as an apologetic and legitimising agent, as an inspirational solvent, catalyst and gadfly, challenging (and sometimes transforming) established modes of identity and self-understanding and questioning conventional postures and categories – while at the same time being recreated and "domesticated" by them. The historically mediated renderings of Nietzsche's messages, the rich symbolic meanings and expressivist uses of his transmuted legacy – while always controversial and far from being universally accepted – provided him with a complex and intriguing role in the twentieth-century representation of Jewish interests and the reshaping of its consciousness.

[116]*Ibid.*

Houston Stewart Chamberlain: The Abwehrverein and the "Praeceptor Germaniae", 1914–1918

BY ERIK LINDNER

"I know nothing whatsoever about history – I never could remember a number or a name. I am even more ignorant than Jean Jacques Rousseau; I have always used a kind of dream image, into which, as need arose, I temporarily incorporated events here and there."

Houston Stewart Chamberlain to Cosima Wagner, 18th February 1896.[1]

I. INTRODUCTION

Towards the end of the nineteenth century, the spread of antisemitism in Wilhelminian Germany resulted in the creation of a Jewish movement of self-defence. In 1890, some years before the *Centralverein deutscher Staatsbürger jüdischen Glaubens* had been established, the *Verein zur Abwehr des Antisemitismus* was formed, supported by middle-class Liberal Jews and Christians who sought to oppose the anti-Jewish movement by elucidation and explanation. This body, known as the *Abwehrverein* and characterised by Ismar Schorsch as "help from outside"[2] because of its Christian membership, lasted over forty years before its self-abrogation in 1933. The organisation published the *Mitteilungen aus dem Verein zur Abwehr des Antisemitismus* (hereafter *Mitteilungen*), which appeared every two weeks, having a circulation of about 10,000, and was distributed to members for a modest subscription. Barbara Suchy has written the history of the *Abwehrverein*, evaluating its notable contribution in forty years of struggle against antisemitism.[3]

The continuing aim was to counter antisemitic agitation with clear information and, basically, to combat false notions and faulty teaching. Contributors to the *Mitteilungen* realised from the beginning that anti-Jewish stereotypes were mainly spread by unthinking stories, slanders and rumours. Here, together with

[1]Paul Pretzsch (ed.), *Cosima Wagner and Houston Stewart Chamberlain im Briefwechsel 1898–1908*, Leipzig 1934, p. 444.
[2]Ismar Schorsch, 'Help from Outside, Verein zur Abwehr des Antisemitismus, 1891–1914', in *idem*, *Jewish Reactions to German Antisemitism, 1870–1914*, New York–London 1972, pp. 79–101.
[3]Barbara Suchy, 'The Verein zur Abwehr des Antisemitismus (I). From its Beginnings to the First World War', in *LBI Year Book XXVIII* (1983), pp. 205–239; *idem*, 'The Verein zur Abwehr des Antisemitismus (II). From the First World War to its Dissolution', in *LBI Year Book XXX* (1985), pp. 67–103. See also Arnold Paucker, *Der jüdische Abwehrkampf gegen Antisemitismus und Nationalsozialismus in den letzten Jahren der Weimarer Republik*, 2nd edn. Hamburg 1969, pp. 35–36 and *passim*.

lectures by prominent members or election speeches, scholarly essays could be effective. Whilst many historical authors have often cited and indeed commended the *Mitteilungen*, a detailed analysis of the *Abwehrverein*'s programme and method of counter-attack has so far been lacking. This essay will deal with the *Mitteilungen aus dem Verein zur Abwehr des Antisemitismus* during the First World War,[4] a period chosen because then, among such changes as the fall of the German *Reich* and the rise of revolution, antisemitism itself underwent modification. Analysis of the journal clearly shows how the *Abwehrverein* functioned in its fight against widely effective antisemitic propaganda amidst the pressures of war-time patriotism.

At that time, Houston Stewart Chamberlain was the most famous and colourful representative of the *völkisch* antisemitic movement: he and his publications formed the chief opponent and target of the *Mitteilungen* during the war years. The subject has been treated chronologically, so facilitating analysis of the *Mitteilungen*'s strategy and style in dealing with the issue. What follows should be regarded as a thematic addition to Geoffrey Field's seminal study of Chamberlain as the "Evangelist of Race".[5]

Chamberlain, from an early date the leading representative of the *völkische Weltanschauung*, was an Englishman born in Portsmouth. After publishing some pseudo-scientific essays and books about *völkisch* thinking, characterised by racialism and a mystical Christian religiosity, he achieved a considerable degree of success in Germany: his work on "cultural antisemitism", *Die Grundlagen des 19. Jahrhunderts*, first published in 1899, had reached twelve printings by 1914.[6] Like Guido von List, he was among those who developed the "Aryan myth" which presented the Teutonic Germans as the only real originators of culture worldwide. In his view, they were in fact the creators of modern European civilisation.[7]

From 1870 onward, Chamberlain lived in Germany, the country of his choice, continuing as an active writer almost up to his death in 1927 during the Weimar Republic. After the outbreak of the First World War, the race-theoretical writings of this "hero of *völkisch* publication"[8] visibly shifted to war politics. In the superficial calm (created by the military censorship) of the warring *Reich*, he produced a flood of *Kriegsaufsätze* displaying his apparently cosmopolitan and objective view of the basic elements of the struggle: the German character, German might, the German-British antithesis, German love of peace, the importance of the German language worldwide, the question of war guilt and

---

[4]This essay is based on the author's thesis, University of Münster, 1989. This version rendered into English by Janet Langmaid, Petra Lindner and Lillian Heifetz.

[5]Geoffrey G. Field, *Evangelist of Race. The Germanic Vision of Houston Stewart Chamberlain*, New York 1981.

[6]Hermann Greive, *Geschichte des modernen Antisemitismus in Deutschland*, Darmstadt 1983, pp. 78, 80.

[7]Jost Hermand, *Der alte Traum vom neuen Reich. Völkische Utopien und Nationalsozialismus*, Frankfurt a. Main 1988, pp. 73–75, 228; Geoffrey G. Field, 'Antisemitism and Weltpolitik', in *LBI Year Book XVIII* (1973), pp. 65–91, here p. 72; Houston Stewart Chamberlain, *Grundlagen des neunzehnten Jahrhunderts*, München 1899, part II, see here chap. 9 A, 'Die Germanen als Schöpfer einer neuen Kultur', particularly pp. 700, 725–726.

[8]*Mitteilungen aus dem Verein zur Abwehr des Antisemitismus* (hereafter *Mitteilungen*), 17th November 1915.

"German Peace".[9] While supporting the German position as a true patriot, Chamberlain catered for the general interest in cultural military topics during the first year of the war.[10] His writing had to be passed by the censors, who sometimes changed his texts.[11] Geoffrey Field regards Chamberlain's war essays as "the fullest expression he ever gave of his political philosophy".[12] They accordingly provide an extremely significant source for the historian.

II. THE FIGHT AGAINST THE RACIST

Chamberlain, the Social Darwinist *par excellence*[13] who succeeded in introducing a mystical triumphalist concept of racism, appeared to the *Abwehrverein* as the chief *völkisch* opponent. Extensive analyses of the *Kriegsaufsätze* and earlier publications are to be found in the *Mitteilungen*, more sparsely in the first months of the war, but from the beginning of 1915 in almost every issue. They are typified by harsh epithets and violent verbal attacks on their adversary. The *Mitteilungen*'s arguments were based on the many clearly antisemitic stereotypes occurring in the essays, which the contributors perceived as assaults upon the *Burgfrieden* existing in the *Reich*. For example, when Chamberlain referred to British groups of power and influence, he directed his polemics at "the Jewish-dominated press"; branding alleged "Jewish internationalism" as a conspiracy was a subtle allusion to the Jews in Germany. The *Mitteilungen* onslaught was not confined simply to the war-political writings of this *Deutschtümelnder* (German jingoist), but also vented itself on his chimerical racist publications such as *Arische Weltanschauung*. Since the arena of debate extended beyond the pages of the *Mitteilungen*, other voices of the German press could be brought into play and papers like the *Vossische Zeitung* or the *Zentrumspartei*'s *Kölnische Volkszeitung* were quoted to disprove and discredit him.

During the First World War, 1915 saw the height of confrontation with Chamberlain in a number of wide-ranging articles. In the issue of 27th January 1915, the *Mitteilungen* declared that this German-lover, one of the "loudest *deutsch-völkisch* standard-bearers", the born-and-bred Briton who had arrogated to himself the role of judge as a "super-German and as *praeceptor Germaniae*", the proliferator of antisemitism, had earned an anthology of his effronteries. In the *Kölnische Volkszeitung* of 21st January 1915, Professor Messer of Giessen commented on Chamberlain's hostile statements concerning the *Reichstag* and the parliamentary system embodied in it; these had included the pointed remark that parliaments were unnecessary because: "Silence is strength. . . Idle chatter

---

[9]Houston Stewart Chamberlain, *Kriegsaufsätze*, München 1915; *idem*, *Neue Kriegsaufsätze*, München 1915.

[10]*Mitteilungen*, 7th April 1915. The first edition of the *Kriegsaufsätze* numbered 75,000 copies.

[11]Chamberlain, *Neue Kriegsaufsätze*, *op. cit.*, see Chamberlain's introduction and conclusion in which he blames the censors for the awkward transitions between chapters.

[12]See Field, *Evangelist*, *op. cit.*, p. 368.

[13]Patrick von zur Mühlen, *Rassenideologien. Geschichte und Hintergründe*, Berlin–Bonn-Bad Godesberg 1977, pp. 122, 239.

enfeebles to the point of idiocy."[14] Messer, as reported by the *Mitteilungen*, made a satirical reference: "Perhaps Herr Chamberlain might apply his words to his own person and draw a practical conclusion." The *Mitteilungen* agreed: "We can only subscribe to this advice." Citing the widely-read *Kölnische Volkszeitung* provided an illustration of the many strata of opposition to Chamberlain and carried the discussion and clarification further. An important point was the avoidance of quotation from any Jewish newspaper or from publications of such Jewish defence associations as the *Centralverein*; the aim was to agitate on behalf of German Jewry without referring to "Jewish" press sources.

Apart from Chamberlain's attacks on parliamentarianism, the *Mitteilungen* exposed his more complex arguments in the field of racial theory, even those published before the war, dubbing him the "Oberkonfusionarius der Rassen-theoretiker".[15] To counter his vigorous and (as evidenced by the circulation figures) highly effective style, its readers were offered contrasting and clarifying views on racist theories by well-known scholars. For example, the issue of 5th May 1915 carried a discussion of Friedrich Hertz's *Rasse und Kultur*, which challenged Chamberlain and other racialists. The article quoted the final chapter of the second revised edition, entitled 'Rassenglaube und Persönlich-keit',[16] in which Hertz, while summarising other authors who condemned racist theories out of hand, declared: "An individual's vehement manifestation of belief in racism not infrequently shows a certain intellectual and moral inferiority."[17]

Since Hertz had made a profound study of the *Grundlagen des 19. Jahrhunderts*, the *Mitteilungen* could use his statements to counter Chamberlain's polemics against "Semites" and their "race-specific" character traits. The *völkisch* Chamberlain had developed a theory that the Jews were a mixture of various races: therefore, he decided by a wild leap of generalisation, if a person is inconsistent in character, this is due to racial mixing or, to use his own word, "bastardisation".[18] Hertz answered with a rhetorical question: in view of the contradictions which abounded on every one of his pages, to what extent was Chamberlain himself a mixture? To round off this criticism, the *Mitteilungen* also called in aid Professor Hugo Münsterberg, who described racism as a "poor

[14]See Field, 'Antisemitism and Weltpolitik', *loc. cit.*, p. 68. Chamberlain became hostile to the *Reichstag* and parliamentarianism when he joined the Wagner-*Kreis* in Bayreuth.

[15]*Mitteilungen*, 15th December 1915.

[16]Mühlen, *Rassenideologien, op. cit.*, p. 298, characterised Hertz as the "classic" critic of racialism in German-speaking countries. In the second edition of *Moderne Rassentheorien*, published as *Rasse und Kultur* in 1915, the Social Democrat Hertz compiled a list of the racialists' inconsistencies, to show the incredible and vacuous character of racial theory.

[17]*Mitteilungen*, 5th May 1915, quoted from Hertz, *Rasse und Kultur*. On Hertz see Field, *Evangelist, op. cit.*, p. 228, note 10. Hertz's views were widely discussed in the Jewish defence press: at the beginning of the century he had already confronted racists such as Chamberlain and had unmasked their subjective and irrational arguments in *Sozialistische Monatshefte*, 1902.

[18]Chamberlain, *Die Grundlagen, op. cit.*, part I, pp. 372, 377–388. Jews were said to comprise 5% Semites, 50% Hittites, 10% Amorites and 35% undefined forms, conformably with their character mix: 5% Volition, 50% Averageness, 10% Decency.

substitute for a *Weltanschauung*, the end result of an anti-philosophical era".[19] Readers were also invited to obtain the revised second edition of Hertz's book on racialism, which was praised for its brilliant presentation of different opinions from philosophers and contemporary writers, including Richard Dehmel, one of whose plays included characters debating *Rasse und Kultur*.[20] The *Mitteilungen* discussion of racism was reasoned, illuminating and literary, a kind of enlightenment which was especially interesting since it was independent of topical events in the war and was written in an academic and informative style.

On 30th June 1915, reviews of *Rasse und Kultur* appeared in the *Mitteilungen*. Contrary to the usual anonymity, the writers were identified by name or initials: *Geheimrat* Eduard König of Bonn recommended Hertz's work for its wealth of sound material, leading to the conclusion that the capacity for culture in no way depended on a person's race: many peoples had contributed to the development of civilisation, not merely Chamberlain's glorified Indo-Germanic-Aryan race. König noted that antisemites like Theodor Fritsch had exploited passages about the angry and vengeful Yahwe for their own purposes: Fritsch, head of the *Reichshammerbund* and editor of the *Handbuch zur Judenfrage*, always announced new books on evolutionary theory under the heading "Mein Beweismateriel gegen Jahwe". König regarded the partly undifferentiated perspective of Hertz's chapters on Judaism as weaponry for *völkisch* opposition to Jewry.

The next reviewer, identified only as "Dr. I. St.", made a sweeping assault on Chamberlain and Count Gobineau, the father of racialist philosophy in France, stressing approvingly that Hertz had found the cradle of racism in Gobineau's works and had sketched his influence on Richard Wagner and Chamberlain. Gobineau had founded the modern Aryan cult: Chamberlain, on the other hand, had had the audacity to class the English as "of particularly pure Germanic type". The reviewer blamed not only the racists' homelands, but also Germany: while a Frenchman and a Briton championed the racialist belief, most of its supporters were German. Dr. I. St. praised the book's methodical and extremely strict examination of Chamberlain's theories as well as Hertz's evidence of many misrepresentations and false quotations. Similar proof of such errors had often appeared in the *Mitteilungen*, where the "addlepated" Chamberlain and "his repeated examples of abysmal ignorance and shallow thinking" had been exposed time and again.[21] With its scholarly appeal, Hertz's work, Dr. I. St. thought, was a fitting instrument to break down racialist writings like those of

---

[19]*Mitteilungen*, 5th May 1915. Münsterberg, born in Danzig, taught philosophy at Harvard University from 1892 onward. Even before his death in 1916, he supported an understanding between Germany and the USA.

[20]See Richard Dehmel, 'Kultur und Rasse', in *Gesammelte Werke, Bd. 8. Betrachtungen über Gott, Kunst & die Welt*, Berlin 1909, pp 162–192, here p. 164. In a philosophical discussion with a Jewish painter, a German poet finally declares that he no longer believes in "the dogma of race". In general, Dehmel here expresses the modern humanist belief in progress. He rejected the term "race" as a culture determinant because it was impossible to explain the existence of talent by "this hypersimple sign of superficial differentiation".

[21]*Mitteilungen*, 30th June 1915.

"this mystical muddler".[22] As in 1905, when the first edition of *Rasse und Kultur* had appeared, Chamberlain failed to respond.

Two months later, another area of his basic ideas was targeted: his view that in the current war between Britain and Germany, the Germans were fighting for Christianity. *Mitteilungen* writers emphasised that while Chamberlain was now "wildly waving the banner of Christendom", he had earlier particularly attacked "Judaised Christianity": a psychological riddle no less puzzling than his protean temperament. As evidence of these inconsistencies, the *Mitteilungen* simply quoted Chamberlain's expositions of racial and anti-Christian arguments, chiefly from *Arische Weltanschauung*, published in 1905, in which he had expressed a positive admiration for the religious teaching of the ancient Indian philosophers and poets, while depicting Christianity and its allies with extreme hostility. In Europe, he had written, foolish superstition had spread, coupled with a bloated and pervasive priestly dominion, and this was increasing even more markedly than a century ago:

> "Whoever reflects that the true old Aryans – happy creatures! – had no church nor a priestly hierarchy . . . will think that the kingdom of God is vanishing further and further away."[23]

(Among the Jews of biblical times there were also prophets who tried to abolish organised religion.) The *Mitteilungen* stressed the contrast between Chamberlain's dislike for the Jewish origins of Christianity and his enthusiasm for the completely "Yahwe-free Indian teaching". The relevant passage read:

> "In all the history of Indo-Germanic spirituality, only the ancient Indian thought and poetry are free from any connection with the Semitic mind and therefore pure, candid, real, unique."[24]

Arische Weltanschauung included a racial discourse concerning Europe, which the *Mitteilungen* specially wished to draw to readers' attention. Within contemporary Europe, Chamberlain had "discovered" strange and nameless elements, similar to "ourselves" and, therefore, all the more dangerous because their souls were "specifically other". He constructed an evolutionary theory, in which he spoke of the true European, the Indo-Germanic, who in his passage westward and southward became hemmed in by foreign, ethnically extremely mixed elements of inferior mind who, "favoured by physical and in particular sexual strength coupled with relatively limited intelligence", multiplied in great

---

[22]Chamberlain's style was highly eclectic and pseudo-scholarly; Field, 'Antisemitism and Weltpolitik', *loc. cit.*, p. 71. He regarded history as a "poem imitating truth"; *ibid.*, p. 69. "His thought revealed a process of intellectual plundering, the scores of authorities he cited were ransacked merely to substantiate his own prior convictions." This is not too harsh a judgement, considering the assessment by Chamberlain's disciple Hermann Keyserling (*Reise durch die Zeit*, Vaduz 1948, p. 134): "Indeed throughout his life Chamberlain seldom had ideas of his own. But in the morning when he climbed his library ladder and leafed through his books, some quotations 'flashed' on him, of which he later made much use. Beyond the quotations used in his writings, Chamberlain had, with a few exceptions, read little of their authors and very rarely so in his later life. In this sense he was the most 'immoral' reader and quoter that I have ever known."

[23]Houston Stewart Chamberlain, *Arische Weltanschauung*, München 1905, here quoted from *Mitteilungen*, 11th August 1915.

[24]*Mitteilungen*, 11th August 1915.

numbers and so infiltrated the "Germanic stock". Moreover, according to the eugenic researches of Felix von Luschan, there developed "a demonstrable reduction of the cranial capacity and brain size, and consequently the ability to become civilised – in short the stultification of entire peoples", caused by mixing with markedly Mongolian elements.[25] The conclusion drawn by Chamberlain in *Arische Weltanschauung* was no less spectacular: "Ignatius Loyola, the Basque, child and type of these innate enemies of our civilisation is a thousand times more dangerous for our culture than the Jew."[26]

The *Mitteilungen* commented: "So the founder of the Jesuits is now the chief enemy; another typical contribution to this will-o'-the-wisp mind's sudden passionate love for Christianity." With this last thrust against St. Ignatius, Chamberlain seemed to have abandoned any possible credibility: his opponents felt that his stunning agility in changing from one enemy image to another – from Judaised Christendom to degenerate primeval Europeans who diminished Indo-Aryan capacity for culture – disqualified his war-time publications from being taken seriously. His judgement of Germany, the *Entente* powers and the character of the war was that of an eccentric racist and Germanophile. His arguments, such as those on European races and Ignatius Loyola, took on an air of fantasising which, divorced from reality, can only be called incomprehensible if not pathological.

The *Kriegsaufsatz* 'England', completed in Bayreuth on 9th October 1914, provoked the *Mitteilungen*'s special attention.[27] Chamberlain characterised Britain as the home of "mammonism" produced by "racial mixing". He concluded his attack on British materialism by referring to the "devilish maxims of English policies": war, commerce and piracy had for centuries of unbroken tradition been used, not to further a moral idea, but solely for gain.[28] A general decline in good behaviour, also manifested as materialism, was also blamed on racial mixing.[29] Although many war-time German writers had denied that the English were still Germanic, Chamberlain thought that some of them might be purer examples of the race than could be found in Germany.

Mitteilungen writers criticised Chamberlain's asseveration that many British Jews behaved like rabid British Nationalists and were indignant at his favourable (in Germanic terms) picture of the enemy Britain while he criticised the

---

[25]*Ibid.*

[26]*Ibid.* It is noteworthy in the quotation of this racial-biological chapter by Chamberlain that St. Ignatius is said to be "a thousand times more dangerous for our culture than the Jew". The first edition of *Arische Weltanschauung* appeared in 1905 as part of the series *Die Kultur* (Bard, Marquardt & Co., Berlin), edited by Cornelius Gurlitt; this contains (p. 32) a passage on Ignatius Loyola corresponding with the 1915 quotation in the *Mitteilungen*. In the seventh edition (München 1934) a significant difference appears on p. 40: the Basque Ignatius is "as dangerous as the Jew". The author is not aware whether this case of distorting a text during the Third *Reich* is unique or whether there was a politically motivated system of revising the work of highly-esteemed Nationalist and antisemitic authors. This particular modification is significant and shows the need for continuing scholarly analysis of first and subsequent editions of a publication.

[27]'Englisch-Jüdisch', in *Mitteilungen*, 11th August 1915.

[28]Chamberlain, 'England', in *Kriegsaufsätze, op. cit.*, p. 57.

[29]*Ibid.*, p. 55.

patriotism of British Jews. Contrastingly, Chamberlain approved the attitude of German Jews during the war:

"No-one should raise the question of Jewish influence, which is great indeed in the current British government; in Germany there are ten times as many Jews and where are they now? As though washed away by this immense upheaval, they are no longer to be found as 'Jews' because they are doing their duty as Germans in the face of the enemy or on the home front; while the British Jews, who are really and truly brothers and cousins of the German Jews, frantically join in everything shameful there, quickly change their German names for English ones. And in the press, which they almost entirely own, they put themselves at the head of the campaign of defamation."[30]

The *Mitteilungen* had no doubt that, with a patriotic attitude corresponding to that of the German Jews, British, French and Italian Jews would fight for their native countries, not for a phantom "Jewish world empire" as portrayed by the "low, backbiting press".[31] Chamberlain was credited with his words of praise for German Jewry, as coming from a declared Germanophile and antisemite: "We can at least take to heart this candid admission of such an 'authority' as Chamberlain: German Jews are doing their duty as Germans in the face of the enemy or on the home front."

The use of Chamberlain as a key witness in favour of German Jewry is noteworthy; singular, too, that the *Mitteilungen* should quote him during the war. In general, the *Kriegsaufsätze* contained a great many antisemitic phrases and slanders, mainly, it is true, directed against Jews in the Allied forces, but at a deeper level also incriminating German Jews. Here again we see the subtlety as well as the danger of a man like Chamberlain.

III. THE VÖLKISCH BRITON AND THE ALLIED POWERS

In the *Mitteilungen* of 11th August 1915, Chamberlain the racial theorist was once more the subject of discussion; by declaring in an essay entitled 'Zuversicht' that an "army of Antichrists" was on the march against Germany, he put the European conflict into the heroic light of a religious war. In the *Mitteilungen*'s view, "Antichrists" was a code word to refer to the march of "Juden und Judengenossen", a style of propaganda which exactly agreed with Chamberlain's usual practice. In order to show how grotesque such statements were, the paper undertook an analysis of opinion in enemy countries. By assessing press reports, the *Mitteilungen* found that in Britain and France the highest clerical dignitaries joined in the campaign against Germany and the "German mind". Religious thought in France was harnessed to chauvinism, according to Dr. Brief, a contributor to the foremost German Catholic paper, the *Kölnische Volkszeitung*. Churches in Paris were hotbeds of jingoistic propaganda and the Belgian army and the "Belgian race" in general were everlastingly extolled. In France, the Gallic mind – "the spirit of arrogance, of catchphrases, of self-intoxication by

---

[30]*Ibid.*, p. 46.
[31]*Mitteilungen*, 11th August 1915.

resounding words instead of sober patient work" – had gained the upper hand.[32] This article was quoted, in the words of the *Mitteilungen*, to illustrate "the Catholic clergy's fanatical hatred of the Germans". If Dr. Brief's patriotic, vigorous tone and the relevant passages in the *Mitteilungen* are compared with Chamberlain's parallel statement about "the Frenchman" in his war essay 'Grundstimmungen in England und Frankreich',[33] the substance is found to be similar:

> "His mind moves within narrow insurmountable confines, yet with dexterity; his language – very limited in comparison with German – exactly fulfils his needs. He handles it skilfully."

It is understandable that writers in the *Mitteilungen* tried, as patriots, to combat the jingoism of other nations. Yet it is disquieting to note that they held similarly chauvinist opinions and used parallel terms to depict the "abominable" arrogance of the French enemy, for here the *Mitteilungen* seems to join forces with Chamberlain, the German by choice. If in fact France had long been using the Joan of Arc cult as spiritual pro-French propaganda, this could hardly have gone unremarked for many years,[34] as the article of 11th August 1915, 'Die christlichen Kirchen und der Krieg', alleged. Though the statement was open to criticism, the *Mitteilungen* would have done well to scrutinise its own style: however, it must be realised that in war-time supposedly humanist ideals transcended verbal barriers.

The *Mitteilungen* discovered other articles dealing with "spiritual barbarity" in the French Catholic Church,[35] and a further batch on the broad alliance of British atheists and Christians against Germany.[36] One of these sources contained the following statement by the secretary of the largest British missionary association: "The German Empire started the march to destruction with Nietzsche as a prophet and Bernhardi as an evangelist."[37] Similarly, the secretary of the British Evangelical Alliance Committee declared that the war was a struggle between Christ and the Devil, and that Christ had given his sword into British hands. The war was not only being fought to overcome rapacious militarism and its methods, which were contrary to Christianity and the New Testament, but also to bring about "the overthrow of a false and anti-Christian philosophy by Nietzsche, Treitschke and other German minds"; it might be called a war between Christ and Nietzsche. In these two sources, the *Mitteilungen* saw the embodiment of an outbreak of hatred from Britain's "godliest of the godly"; the Christian front in France and Britain was moblising an army against the German *Reich*. Turning the topic against Chamberlain, the writers asked how

[32]*Ibid.*, quoting Dr. Brief in the *Kölnische Volkszeitung*.

[33]Chamberlain, *Neue Kriegsaufsätze, op. cit.*, pp. 7–29, especially p. 14. The date of this introduction is given as 21st December 1914.

[34]*Mitteilungen*, 11th August 1915.

[35]*Ibid.*, quoting an article by Dr. Julius Bachem from *Der Tag*.

[36]*Ibid.*, quoting the *Kreuzzeitung* and *Reichsbote*.

[37]General Friedrich Bernhardi, member of the *Alldeutscher Verband* (ADV), author of *Deutschland und der nächste Krieg* (1912), in which he maintained the actual biological necessity of war for the existence of races and peoples. In the years immediately before the First World War, such racial-ideological ideas were not peculiar to Germany: they also existed in e.g. France. See Mühlen, *Rassenideologien, op. cit.*, pp. 191f.

he had set in motion the idea of Antichrists inspiring a conspiracy of nations against Germany. The closing sentence might have annoyed Chamberlain: faithless to his native country, this spiritually rootless writer evoked "Homeric laughter" in Britain as the sole answer to his assertions.

In the issue of 17th November 1915 the *Mitteilungen* noted that during the pre-war period the "dragon's seed of nationalism" had run like wildfire through every nation, to the delight of warmongering journalists. It concluded that the war – so far as it was one of peoples – had been systematically prepared and brought about by "press agitation about nationalism stirred up to boiling point". What was significant in this respect was that in the second year of war the *völkisch* papers and Chamberlain felt free to conjure up the notion of Jewish influences in the international press. The *Mitteilungen* cited the first group by reference to the picture given by the functional journal *Deutschvölkische Blätter*, which reminded readers that in 1912 the *Tägliche Rundschau* had demanded that every inflammatory anti-German article should show a photograph of its author so that it should become readily apparent that it was not the British or French but "Jewish scene-setters . . . who sought to maintain enmity between peoples".[38]

In contrast, in the *Kriegsaufsatz*, 'Grundstimmungen in England und Frankreich', Chamberlain had asserted that all the editorial staff of *The Times*, the *Daily Mail* and *Le Matin* belonged to the same nation as Ernst Lissauer, the Jewish writer of the 'Hymn of Hate' (*Hassgesang gegen England*), Germany's most patriotic war-time poem. Moreover, he declared, probably 90 per cent of Paris journalists came from Poland or Frankfurt.[39] The *Mitteilungen* undertook research into these allegations; although at the time concrete information about *The Times* or the *Daily Mail* was apparently unavailable, an article on the foreign press was announced. In view of the grave accusations made by the slippery Chamberlain, the *Mitteilungen* had far-sightedly collected data on the journalistic background of foreign papers in order to delve more deeply into supposed Jewish influence. The outline of the international press, which as published dealt mainly with the supply of items by the news agencies, was a well chosen subject. According to the *Mitteilungen*, in Britain it was Reuters, in France the *Agence Havas* and in Italy the *Agenzia Stefani* which had most influence on the news. Reuters had indeed been founded by a German Jew but the family connection had long ceased, and it was now a limited company: any Jewish influence there might once have been no longer came into question. In war-time, too, the agencies could only provide news already passed by the censor, so that they were no more than mouthpieces for officially sanctioned information.

Nevertheless, the *Mitteilungen* had to gain time to be able to look more closely into the details of Chamberlain's recriminations against the "Judaised British war press", and accordingly promised its readers an article dealing specifically

---

[38]'Die Presse und der Krieg', in *Mitteilungen*, 17th November 1915, quoting *Deutschvölkische Blätter*.
[39]Chamberlain, *Neue Kriegsaufsätze, op. cit.*, here 'Grundstimmungen . . .' (Bayreuth, 21st December 1914), pp. 2–29, especially pp. 8f.: "Treitschke remarks that German good nature scarcely knows hate. The author of the *Hassgesang gegen England* fights like a good German, but he stems from a people that – in contrast to the Germans – has always fostered hatred as its main characteristic, and the whole editorial staff of *The Times*, the *Daily Mail* and *Le Matin* comes from the same people . . ."; see Field, *Evangelist, op. cit.*, pp. 379–380.

with *The Times* and Chamberlain. In its last issue of 1915 there appeared a detailed explanation of the character of *The Times* and its ownership. After referring to Graham, *The Times*'s correspondent in St. Petersburg, as "an out-and-out antisemite", the *Mitteilungen* declared that it had no proof of Jewish dominance in the editorial staff, so that Chamberlain's statement was not confirmed by more precise information. Moreover, the British paper *Labour Leader*, as quoted by the Social-Democratic *Vorwärts*, had published a list of all *The Times*'s stockholders, amongst whom were some with German names.[40] Since these were all Conservatives and aristocrats, it was highly improbable that there could be a dominant Jewish element in its editorship. The article ended with the telling charge that "Chamberlain and his imitators" were suffering from overheated imaginations about Jewish influence.

The *Mitteilungen*, it must be realised, despite all its research into the facts and all its quotations, could not actually disprove Chamberlain's allegations. The latter had indeed suggested in the *Tägliche Rundschau* – under the title 'Des Weltkriegs letzte Phase' – that the real instigators of British propaganda were journalists from Frankfurt and Cologne, who manipulated the British militarist capitalist party. Although the *Mitteilungen* had at the end of 1915 again pointed out the complete falsity of such statements, in the absence of evidence to the contrary it had to rest its case on probability. The debate clearly illustrates the awkwardness of the writers' task. To obtain information during the war about the religious affiliations of journalists working for enemy papers must have been an extraordinarily complicated and risky undertaking; this is an obvious example of the difficulty and limited effect of an argument based on research in comparison with the ease of printing conformist propaganda.

IV. CHAMBERLAIN AND THE VÖLKISCH MOVEMENT

To discredit Chamberlain, perhaps the most influential antisemitic journalist in Germany, one major strategy was to belittle him for his "European" roots. In its issue of 25th August 1915, the *Mitteilungen* followed that line in criticising certain publications under the title 'Ist das Burgfrieden?'. Theodor Fritsch and Chamberlain[41] had denied parliamentarianism any right to exist, Fritsch in his journal *Der Hammer, Blätter für deutschen Sinn*, Chamberlain with the essay 'Deutschland als führender Weltstaat'.[42] Although these had been published

[40]*Mitteilungen*, 29th December 1915: ". . . Baroness Elisa von Rotberg, Rheinweiler (Baden), Baroness Katherina Hall von Arnim (Karlsruhe) and Agnes A. von Maltzahn (Demmin). This information appeared so incredible that for a long time we hesitated to transmit it. We assumed that the leading German Conservative papers – the *Kreuzzeitung* and *Reichsbote* – would be in a position to deny the report, having members of these aristocratic families among their readership. Although *Vorwärts* published this interesting information from the *Labour Leader* many weeks ago, so that the Conservative German press has had time enough to issue a denial, no such correction has as yet appeared. So 'Jewish influence' on *The Times* exists only in the rabid fantasy of Chamberlain and his imitators."

[41]See above; quotation from the *Kölnische Volkszeitung*, 21st January 1915 ("Silence is strength . . .").

[42]Chamberlain, *Kriegsaufsätze, op. cit.* (Bayreuth, 8th September 1914), pp. 36–43.

some months earlier, the *Mitteilungen* only now printed an article in refutation. In January 1915, Messer's article alone had been quoted, yet before the *völkisch* essays were available in book form, they had already appeared in the press.[43] In the intervening ten months the *Mitteilungen* had actively fought against the anti-parliamentarian "pamphleteer", describing him as "completely rootless nationally, with no sense of responsibility, and a phrasemonger untroubled by moral scruples", who unequivocally slandered the *Reichstag* before the whole world. Chamberlain had had the impudence to assert that "in the unbearably trivial guise of the *Reichstag*" the strength of German nationhood parodied itself:

> "In truth, all the nations on earth are glutted with parliaments, satiated with this sacrosanct universal suffrage. Silence is strength . . . Idle chatter enfeebles to the point of idiocy: this will be the latter end of our contemporary parliaments."[44]

Chamberlain considered the *Reichstag* to be an un-German legacy of the French Revolution, and debate itself as foreign to "the German substance". The British Parliament, on the other hand, displayed some of the living "great traditions of the true old Teutonism", so that it "perhaps retained more than the mere pretence of a dignity lacking in the German *Reichstag*".

In sum, Chamberlain's theories were chaotic and inconsistent. Nor was it tactful to single out the British Parliament for its "old Teutonic traditions" in contrast to the *Reichstag*. The *Mitteilungen* assessed these chapters as a blunder by an unworldly fanatic, somewhat crankish and stubborn. Similarly, Theodor Fritsch was judged as "inspired by fanatical hatred for our parliaments".[45]

As an effective agitator, Chamberlain apparently attempted to collect moralistic tools for defence of the *Kaiserreich* on every level. The *Mitteilungen* of 25th August 1915 responded to the attacks on "international high finance", developed by Chamberlain and other *völkisch* antisemites whenever the war guilt question became "too boring". This topic was expounded by the economist Werner Sombart (whose *Händler und Helden* appeared in the seventh month of the war),[46] as well as Chamberlain who, said the *Mitteilungen*, exploited public interest in war books to address a wide audience. In the *Tägliche Rundschau* of 9th June 1915, he declared emotionally:

> "Germany's enemy is not this people or that, but a combination of *jobbers* utterly deficient in soul, heart or honour who have resolved to enslave the whole human race under Mammon . . . In contrast to this *devil's brood*, Germany stands forth as God's champion: *Siegfried against the Serpent, Saint George the dragon-slayer*."

In similar vein, a writer in *Der Hammer* of 1st July 1915 described high finance:

[43]The introduction to Chamberlain's *Kriegsaufsätze* contains important facts as to the character and publication of these essays. He writes that the texts of the *Gesammelte Aufsätze* (apart from the essay 'Deutschland') had already appeared during September/October 1914 in *Internationale Monatsschrift*, *Volkserzieher*, *Deutsche Tageszeitung*, *Tägliche Rundschau*: papers which may be regarded as an epitome of the *völkisch* and major Conservative press. The introduction is dated 28th October 1914.

[44]Chamberlain, *Kriegsaufsätze, op. cit.*, 'Deutschland als führender Weltstaat', p. 38, quoted verbatim in *Mitteilungen*, 25th August 1915.

[45]*Mitteilungen*, 25th August 1915.

[46]Werner Sombart, *Händler und Helden. Patriotische Besinnungen*, München–Leipzig 1915. Re the date of publication see introduction to the first edition.

"It has gained incredible power in the civilised states and now seeks to reach its goal with iron ruthlessness. Led by a foreign or alienated national spirit [*Volksgeist*], it does not ask what will benefit any one people, but how it can increase its own power."[47]

The *Mitteilungen* had good reason to answer such anti-materialism and its vituperation against "international powers alien to the national spirit". Since "Jewish Mammonism", "banking systems" and "stock exchange finance" had in the past been lumped together, attacks by *völkisch* journalists on the *Entente* and its alleged links with "international capital" eventually turned into an anti-Jewish campaign.[48] Couching their accusations in international terms, they succeeded in "internationalising" the Jews, so that the latter appeared separated from the people of the *Reich*. Indeed, many prominent Jewish families, such as the Rothschilds or the Ricardos, had historically presented cosmopolitan aspects, a fact exploited by *völkisch* propagandists to brand Jews as representatives of "impenetrable high finance", "utterly deficient in soul, heart and honour": in this way the image of the Jew became that of an enemy to civilisation. The *Mitteilungen* was quite right to display sensitivity to this particular argument from *völkisch* Germans and its reaction is significant as to both documentation and comment.

On 20th October 1915, the *Mitteilungen* added another dimension to the repeated cycle of recognition, comment and refutation of Chamberlain's words. An *Alldeutscher Verband* paper had reacted belligerently on learning that the inscription 'Dem deutschen Volke' was to appear in Roman lettering on the façade of the *Reichstag*. A storm of indignation broke out from the Right wing, who regarded the matter as one of *völkisch* dignity in time of war – "always the victor on the battlefield, always the loser when it came to *völkisch* sense of honour". The Right-wing groups felt it scandalous to use Roman letters, the script of Germany's enemies: Gothic *Fraktur* lettering alone could appear on the façade of the *Reichstag*. Apparently an official denial was issued, since the *Mitteilungen* informed its readers that the whole affair had originated in a canard. Nevertheless, an extraordinary discussion about the "enemy alphabet" and "German script" had begun.

The topic had been discussed by Ferdinand Avenarius in his *Kunstwart*, and the *Mitteilungen* quoted him, even though in the "Kunstwart Debate" of 1912 he had accused the *Abwehrverein* of stimulating antisemitism.[49] Avenarius had applied the lines laid down by some *alldeutsch*, *völkisch* papers to consign all the users of Roman letters to the national pillory. Lettering in *Antiqua* (the Italianate script used in Germany during and after the Renaissance) was to be found in ancient German cathedrals and had been used by Dürer, the brothers Grimm, Goedeke in his *Deutsche Literaturgeschichte* and Hermann Paul's *Germanische Philologie*: even the "prophet of Teutonism" Chamberlain and Richard Wagner

---

[47] *Mitteilungen*, 25th August 1915.

[48] See Field, *Evangelist*, *op. cit.*, p. 378: certain catch-phrases were readily accepted by the German public as having antisemitic associations. Chamberlain used this indirect anti-Jewish agitation because of the censorship.

[49] Barbara Suchy, 'The Verein zur Abwehr des Antisemitismus: (II)', *loc. cit.*, p. 222. The antisemite and publisher of the *Semi-Kürschner* and the *Semi-Gotha*, Philipp Stauff, also wrote for the *Kunstwart*. These "reference works" named scholars and aristocrats who were Jewish or of Jewish descent.

had used this script. Such findings, Avenarius declared, meant that anyone conscious of race and tradition must damn three-quarters of his whole library. In his guise as a "national" writer, Avenarius was even more disturbed by the use of Gothic print in the headings of the anti-German enemy press in Britain and France: the *Daily Mail, The Times*, the *Standard*, the *Daily Telegraph, Le Matin, Le Temps* and others. In short, the call for banishment of "Roman script" on patriotic grounds was "monstrous rubbish". The *Mitteilungen* enjoyed this neat *reductio ad absurdum*, agreeing with Avenarius that to bicker about the use of Roman script as a component of "Germandom" was ridiculous.*

The *Mitteilungen* slyly pointed out that Graf Reventlow's latest book had been printed in Roman script and even the "super-German" Chamberlain had published all his books, apart from the Wagner biography, in the same print. It ironically referred to an "offence against the German spirit" for such *völkisch* authors to publish in "our enemies' lettering". To round off its report, the *Mitteilungen* carried an item from the Agrarian paper *Zeitfragen* attacking Chamberlain for his "Fremdtümelei (alien jingoism)". The *völkisch* writer Karl Engelhard declared that Chamberlain's 1912 work on Goethe jarred on him with its Roman print and numerous foreign words. Anyone lacking education would scarcely be able to read the book without a dictionary of loan-words, nor would it be easy even for an educated person. The *Mitteilungen* was content to savour Engelhard's praise of two books about Goethe by the Jew Eduard Engel, which had appeared in "German" print. What was more, Engelhard had said, Engel had gone further with his doughty fight for a language free from foreign borrowings. As the *Mitteilungen* commented: "It could not have been easy for Engelhard, the famous literary pioneer of the *völkische Weltanschauung* to bestow such high praise on the work of a Jew, Eduard Engel, all the more because it was at the expense of Houston Stewart Chamberlain, the protagonist of Aryan glory."[50]

Besides these critical voices, the *Mitteilungen* noted others favourable towards Chamberlain. On 22nd September 1915, it cited one of his defenders, Johannes John of Flensburg, who had published a reply in the *völkisch* paper *Bühne und Welt* to an article on the *Kriegsaufsätze* in the *Kunstwart*, calling Chamberlain antisemitic. John had said that, far from being an antisemite, Chamberlain was an admirer of "the advantages of the Jewish race". He should not be judged antisemitic simply because he described the various races of Jews and Germans and the "inorganic", hampering effect of Judaism in "our culture", nor for his educational writings on the mixing of races. In contrast, Hermann Ahlwardt was a man whose life-work was completely dependent on his opinion of the Jews, so that he became a total antisemite. Chamberlain did not fit this image, since he was superior to it. In answer, the *Mitteilungen* replied that John had evidently not

---

* For the discussion of "Antiqua" versus "Fraktur" and confused Nazi notions on their use see Justin Howes and Pauline Paucker, 'German Jews in the Graphic Arts', in *LBI Year Book XXXIV* (1989), pp. 461–462 – (Ed.).

[50] *Mitteilungen*, 20th October 1915. The literary historian Eduard Engel (1851–1938) published his biography of Goethe in 1910.

read Chamberlain's books attentively; moreover, his arguments were based on Fritsch's *Antisemiten-Katechismus* and, therefore, untrustworthy.[51]

In an article entitled 'Moderne Bilderstürmer', the *Mitteilungen* criticised an ignorant claim of some *völkisch* writers.[52] Chamberlain and other German jingoists had demanded that German instead of English should be the global language: German schools should reduce the teaching of foreign languages, particularly English, since the English-speaking culture was of little value. In its reply to this piece of chauvinism, the *Mitteilungen* took a studiedly neutral position, its authors stressing the importance of the English language and illustrating their argument by quotations from, for example, Hugo von Hofmannsthal, the educationalist Adolf Matthias and the *Vossische Zeitung*. The statements cited showed that the arrogance expressed in a linguistic concentration on German would be foolish, as it could only be harmful. In the knowledge of other nations' culture and language were to be found, according to the *Mitteilungen*, the basis of commerce, advantages in establishing colonies and associated possibilities for improving the general welfare. This counter to the demands of Chamberlain and the *Alldeutsche* also shows that, even in a Liberal group like the *Abwehrverein*, there was no lack of "colonial" ways of thought.

V. CHAMBERLAIN'S POPULAR APPEAL

Chamberlain was by no means a lone agitator, no outsider haranguing the populace. For twenty years, he had been writing as a *völkisch* advocate, so that his opinions paralleled those of large groups and their publications, as well as political parties. Over and above that, he had gained fame at the highest level in Germany. However much he was portrayed by the *Mitteilungen* and by many of its readers as a crank and slanderer, he achieved considerable prestige. At the end of 1915, the *Kaiser* presented him with the Iron Cross "am weissen Band". This award evoked much press comment, from which the *Mitteilungen* drew some interesting views and information. The *Alldeutsche Blätter* noted: "This is . . . the first time that an author active in the field of Germanic thought has been graciously honoured by Kaiser Wilhelm II."[53] In the *Mitteilungen's* view, the decoration was of far-ranging significance: not so much the fact of the award but the "symbolic consequences for a particular political direction". At the most recent general meeting of the *Abwehrverein*, a famous journalist had demonstrated, by quoting published material, "that people in authoritative positions during the war were of the opinion that a man so honoured could not be publicly criticised and that nothing could be written against him".[54]

---

[51]See Theodor Fritsch, *Handbuch zur Judenfrage. Die wichtigsten Tatsachen zur Beurteilung des jüdischen Volkes*, 31st completely revised edn., Leipzig 1932. This was a sequel to the so-called *Antisemiten-Katechismus*.

[52]*Mitteilungen*, 7th April 1915.

[53]*Mitteilungen*, 1st December 1915.

[54]*Ibid*. It is not clear whether the allusion is to the censorship by the War Press Office (*Kriegspresseamt*) or possibly to the military leadership of the *Reich*.

This statement evidently struck the *Abwehrverein*. In his pamphlet *Politische Ideale* Chamberlain had described the *Reichstag* as a "talking-shop" and the parliament as a "selection of small-minded and empty-talking men", and this led the *Mitteilungen* to enquire whether the *Reichstag* was no longer allowed to confront this "artist of abuse". Moreover, Chamberlain had also denigrated German scholars,[55] a fact which similarly called for an answer. Should they be left defenceless and at the mercy of such low abuse? The *Mitteilungen* had to recognise with alarm that Chamberlain's fanatical admirers had triumphed, since by his *Kriegsaufsätze* he had become perhaps the most popular writer in Germany. The essays were extensively advertised throughout the country and eventually an edition for the trenches came on the market, discounted at just 13 *Pfennige* per copy if purchased in quantities of a thousand.[56] The antisemite Alfred Roth[57] rejoiced at the increasing effect of Chamberlain's *Weltanschauung*. Writing in the *Deutschvölkische Blätter* he proclaimed:

> "Whoever has observed, as I have, the profound effects that Chamberlain's essays have had on the battlefields and in the trenches among thousands of our soldiers may, in view of this development, be of good cheer."[58]

The *völkisch Deutschnationaler Handlungsgehilfenverband*, as the largest union of white-collar employees, had deliberately striven for this result by distributing Chamberlain's essay 'Zuversicht' in the trenches.[59]

Nationalistic emotion was to be found outside the rhetoric of the *völkisch* movement, as shown by the *Mitteilungen*'s declaration that the great majority of the German *Volk* refused to be taught about the real spirit of German-ness by a man "who juggles with his self-chosen Germanity just as he does with his words". In the foreword to the translation of the *Kriegsaufsätze*, Chamberlain asserted his pride in his purely English descent, the love of his British motherland and his

---

[55]Chamberlain, *Politische Ideale*, München 1915, quoted in the *Mitteilungen*, 1st December 1915: professors were "arrogant narrow-minded *Kathederpfaffen*", their findings were "an empiric swamp", their thoughts a "bugbear made of theories" and their community "a clique alienated from nature, comprising men who, under the honorary title of scholars, have enjoyed a completely unjustified reputation".

[56]Chamberlain, *Kriegsaufsätze*, *op. cit.*, publisher's note. The back cover displays an advertisement by the publishers, F. Bruckmann of Munich, offering a "Trenches Edition" of the essays 'England' and 'Deutschland', included in the *Kriegsaufsätze*, at the price of 20 *Pfennige*: "a welcome gift for our fighting men in the field". *Neue Kriegsaufsätze*, *op. cit.*, carried a parallel advertisement. The standard price of the pamphlets was 1 *Reichsmark* while the "Trenches Edition" cost 20 *Pfennige* per copy; 15 *Pfennige* each for 500 and only 13 *Pfennige* each for 1,000 copies. The price of 13 *Pfennige* per copy if bought in quantities of 100, as mentioned by the *Mitteilungen*, cannot be verified from the advertisements.

[57]On Alfred Roth, see Uwe Lohalm, *Völkischer Radikalismus. Die Geschichte des Deutschvölkischen Schutz- und Trutz-Bundes 1919–1923*. Hamburg 1970, p. 56. From 1900, Roth served in the *Deutschnationaler Handlungsgehilfenverband* (DHV): he became a lieutenant and was wounded in 1914. After 1912 his main interest was in the *Reichshammerbund*. In 1914 he joined its leadership and worked closely with Theodor Fritsch. Roth was the author (under the pseudonym Otto Arnim) of the antisemitic *Die Juden im Heere. Eine statistische Untersuchung nach amtlichen Quellen*, München 1919.

[58]*Mitteilungen*, 1st December 1915; see also Field, *Evangelist*, *op. cit.*, p. 390.

[59]*Mitteilungen*, 3rd November 1915. The paper complained about the antisemitic agitation which, despite the censorship, was reaching the trenches. The DHV prided itself on distributing the war essay as a broadsheet.

warm feelings towards France, where he had gone to school. The *Mitteilungen* answered that this "international trouble-maker and blusterer" would not be missed by Germany if he settled in his country of birth or country of education. "Let him delight these two countries with his confused racialism, seeing that they were indeed the true birthplaces of such racial pastimes."[60] Such sarcasm towards a bestselling author, whose *Kriegsaufsätze* ran into 300,000 copies and, the *Abwehrverein* estimated, had reached three million readers, has an air of hopelessness.[61] The allegation that a good majority of the German people was rejecting Chamberlain and his publications remains questionable, since the award by the *Kaiser* of the Iron Cross had raised his prestige even higher.

The consequent polarisation of the fronts is characteristic of the ensuing conflict between the *Mitteilungen* and Chamberlain, its dearest enemy; it is not recorded whether he made any reply to the paper. At the end of 1915, the process of refutation appears somewhat mechanical: *Mitteilungen* authors had discovered the following remarks in the *Neue Kriegsaufsätze*: "Within the present German *Reich* . . . Germans and Slavs had mixed to produce a wonderfully talented and active stock", an admission in blatant contrast to the views of the *Alldeutscher Verband* and Chamberlain's political allies. In consequence, the *Mitteilungen* branded further racial statements of the "Oberkonfusionarius der Rassentheoretiker" as a dubious collection of contradictions:[62] anyone who pronounced King David an Aryan and Ignatius Loyola a Jew could only be a fantasist. Yet the paper had to conclude resignedly: "Not only do the foolish masses listen trustingly to such a scholar-charlatan, but likewise no small part of our so-called 'educated people'."[63]

VI. THE MITTEILUNGEN AND CHAMBERLAIN DURING THE LAST PHASE OF THE WAR

The attacks against Chamberlain and his books, carried on intensively up to the end of 1915, continued thereafter only cursorily until the fall of the *Reich*. For one thing, the author was no longer publishing so many or such controversial war essays as in the first phase of the war. For another, the *Mitteilungen* had shifted its main interest to German political groupings, concentrating on the *Alldeutscher Verband*, internal political relationships (on which the ADV had considerable influence) and on the increased antisemitism. Accordingly Chamberlain was

---

[60]*Mitteilungen*, 1st December 1915.

[61]*Ibid.*

[62]Chamberlain became more and more confused. On the one hand, he referred, in the *Neue Kriegsaufsätze*, to Fichte's recognition that the French, Spaniards and Italians were of Germanic origin: on the other hand, in the *Grundlagen des 19. Jahrhunderts*, he spoke of Celtic and Slavonic Germanics. He also differentiated between the physiognomy of Northern Europeans and others born and nurtured in Germany. Earlier he had philosophised about the "incestuous crime" which led to racial chaos and bastardisation (*Grundlagen, op. cit.*, part I, pp. 372–375, 531), whereas he now said that the "mixed tribes" showed wonderful qualities.

[63]*Mitteilungen*, 15th December 1915: see also Field, 'Antisemitism and Weltpolitik', *loc. cit.*, pp. 82–83, concerning Chamberlain's popularity and esteem among writers, professors and students.

seldom thought to be worth a whole article, but still offered many targets for polemical reaction or refutation.

The *Mitteilungen* often seized on howlers made by the "Chamberlain cult". The *Politisch Anthropologische Monatsschrift* referred to Chamberlain (who had called the world-wide use of German a "necessity") as "Leibniz raised to a higher power", while the *Bühne und Welt* praised him as the spiritual heir of Shakespeare.[64] With quiet satisfaction, *Mitteilungen* journalists noted that "the fluent Phraseus [phrasemonger]" did not meet with unqualified enthusiasm from the *völkisch* camp. His homilies addressed to Germans about their essence were unfavourably received in the April edition of *Bühne und Welt*, which had apparently discovered that Chamberlain's character was more British than German. His claim and that of his disciples to be spiritual heirs to the writers of the Wars of Liberation (1813–1815), was flatly rejected by the *Mitteilungen*: while Goethe had always striven towards the highest level, for purity, wisdom, generosity and love, Chamberlain's works were nothing more than amateurish egoistic theories.[65]

It was a long time before Chamberlain managed to obtain German nationality and immediately after naturalisation he joined the *Alldeutscher Verband*.[66] To emphasise the ambiguous morals of the *deutschvölkisch* group, the *Mitteilungen* reported that in Britain Chamberlain was branded as a traitor to his own country. His entire life-style was that of a renegade, though his admirers applauded and glorified it as *völkisch* heroism. Naturalised Americans of German-Jewish origin, however, if they were in any way anti-German were vilified by these same people. And, the *Mitteilungen* charged, Chamberlain's behaviour was, nationally speaking, "self-castration".[67]

In order to discredit Chamberlain further, the *Mitteilungen* continually pointed out his erroneous quotations and falsifications and in August 1918 "Dr. I. St." undertook a sweeping argumentation, starting from an open letter by Chamberlain in the radical paper *Deutschlands Erneuerung* which dealt with the Romanian-Jewish question. This was in fact a slightly abridged version of an article first published in 1901, when Chamberlain had been accused of including a quotation from Goethe, falsified to appear anti-emancipatory and anti-Jewish.[68] The "open letter", commenting on the present-day "Jewish Question" on the occasion of German-Romanian peace negotiations in Bucharest, repeated this fabrication. "Dr. I. St." was biting: "Such a method is not German: these are the practices of Lord Northcliffe. We will not have the British Chamberlain ruining, desecrating

[64] *Mitteilungen*, 14th June 1916, quoting the May issue of *Bühne und Welt*.

[65] *Mitteilungen*, 14th June 1916. However, it should be realised that earlier Ernst Moritz Arndt and Johann Gottlieb Fichte were regarded as important poets of the Wars of Liberation. Their ideals differed from those of Goethe, but from the *völkisch* point of view they were noteworthy. The *Mitteilungen* was in error in referring to Goethe in this context.

[66] *Mitteilungen*, 23rd August 1916. On 3rd May 1916, it had already spoken of the "thoroughbred European", born in England and educated in France, who had paid the needful stamp duty on his naturalisation papers. This item was connected with the hint to *völkisch* circles who did not criticise Chamberlain's conversion of nationality, but rather fêted him as an ideal German.

[67] *Mitteilungen*, 13th June 1917, quotation from the edition of 3rd October 1917.

[68] *Mitteilungen*, 7th August 1918. In the weekly *Deutsche Heimat*, an allegedly verbatim quotation from Goethe's *Dichtung und Wahrheit* had been exposed as a falsification by Chamberlain.

or falsifying our Goethe in this way." The anonymous author considered that this method of misquotation was quite usual with Chamberlain,[69] but the problem was the authority which his publications had gained, especially the *Grundlagen des 19. Jahrhunderts*, from which German antisemites could draw turns of phrase and arguments. Goethe should not be exploited in favour of antisemitism. "Dr. I. St." affirmed Chamberlain's incapacity for scholarly research: his faulty education led to errors and ultimately to systematic falsification.[70]

The same subject had been dealt with in the previous year in reference to Chamberlain's work on Goethe, published in 1912, in which, after describing the Talmud, the Bible and rabbinical writings, he finally asserted that Jews were in no way prevented by their religion from lying to or stealing from those of other faiths. Chamberlain tried to support this proposition by quotation from Goethe. The *Mitteilungen* of 13th June 1917 had already emphasised that he had copied these vilifications of the Talmud from the antisemitic lampoonists Eisenmenger, Rohling, Wahrmund, Deckert and Fritsch. Detailed counter-analysis by Rabbi Dr. Horovitz of Frankfurt appeared in the *Mitteilungen* of September 1917, where the quotations were unmasked as falsifications:[71] Chamberlain had created a work on Goethe which disqualified itself through his arrogance and impudence. He had tried to exploit the poet as an antisemite by misinterpreting a dramatic passage, so turning the enlightened character of the play into antisemitism.[72]

Chamberlain, now settled in Bavaria, did not desist from the belligerence with which he had long attacked the Liberal press. While in the summer of 1916 the *Mitteilungen* could quote his abuse of "the jackals of the press in Berlin and Frankfurt",[73] in September 1918 it could provide details of a lawsuit springing from a defamatory attack on the *Frankfurter Zeitung* in the *Deutsche Zeitung* of 9th

---

[69]*Mitteilungen*, 7th August 1918. In *Rasse und Kultur*, Friedrich Hertz had referred to various falsifications by Chamberlain. Dr. I. St. adduced Hertz's page numbers to enable readers to confirm his argument. Lord Northcliffe was the proprietor of *The Times*, which was seen as one of the papers most hostile to Germany during the war.

[70]*Mitteilungen*, 7th August 1918. Dr. I. St. offered two examples. Chamberlain had wrongly cited the Alexandrian philosopher Philo: "Only the Israelites are human beings in the true sense of the word." From this developed the antisemitic stereotype of the Jew who despises people of other religions as non-human. Furthermore, a similarly misused quotation – shown to be Chamberlain's own – was earlier mentioned by him as "according to Stoecker".

[71]*Mitteilungen*, 19th September 1917, article signed by Dr. Horovitz. Readers could check his refutations, since the page numbers of Chamberlain's book on Goethe were given. Chamberlain had referred to Goethe's satirical drama *Das Jahrmarktsfest zu Plundersweilern*, which contained a dialogue between Haman and Ahasverus about usury and Christian as against Jewish character traits. Omission of part of the quotation had changed the meaning. Dr. Horovitz also considered the explanation of the Talmud and rabbinical writing as misinterpreted to conform to the theory of "criminal" ethics towards other religions.

[72]See pamphlet issued by the *Abwehrverein* (*Schwurzeugen des Antisemitismus?*, Berlin 1928), a collection of essays by Professor August Ziegler from the *Abwehrblätter* (the later name of the *Mitteilungen*), 1928. Here Luther, Goethe, Herder, Fichte, Mommsen and Bismarck were critically analysed and their adaptation to antisemitism was considered to be untenable. On Goethe in particular, see *ibid.*, pp. 16–19.

[73]*Mitteilungen*, 23rd August 1916. On the conflict between the paper and Chamberlain, which aroused great interest, see Field, *Evangelist, op. cit.*, pp. 392–394.

November 1917; Chamberlain had declared that this influential paper was in
enemy hands and that even Bismarck had recognised that Britain made use of it
against German interests.[74] The *Frankfurter Zeitung* reacted by bringing a suit for
defamation, which was rejected by a lower court (*Schöffengericht*) but proceeded to
the *Landgericht*. The defendant Chamberlain did not attend the hearings, which
opened on 9th August 1918, but was represented by two known Right-wing
lawyers, Heinrich Claß (head of the *Alldeutscher Verband*) and Alfred Jacobsen.
The court declared Chamberlain, now a sick man aged 63, guilty of defamation
under Section 186 of the *Reich*'s penal code, but merely imposed a fine on him.[75]
In the judgement, the accusation that the paper was "in enemy hands" was
deemed untenable. The *Mitteilungen* felt that this abuse was tantamount to a
charge of high treason against the *Frankfurter Zeitung* and also that the paper's
alleged common interest with high finance was not established. Nevertheless, the
court accepted that Chamberlain's statements were no more than an expression
of political opinion, whereas the *Mitteilungen* regarded it as the sharpest attack in
war-time on a German paper. His British origins were taken in mitigation and
the judges were unwilling to pass a prison sentence on a first offender who was
also "a prominent writer".[76]

The ensuing comment in the *Mitteilungen* had a double aim: on the one hand it
depicted the credibility of the *Frankfurter Zeitung*, which was proud to receive the
approbation of the *Reich*'s political leaders,[77] while on the other hand it was
stressed that no other German political writer (apart from the gutter press) had
abused his opponents so sordidly. Claß had claimed that his client, in the words
of the *Mitteilungen*, the "Pope of *völkisch* journalism", was not obliged to quote
exactly, but might do so from memory. The *Mitteilungen* considered the
defendant's behaviour disgraceful in the extreme and criticised his lenient
judges. In the same article, it described as "threatening" the total of his war-time
publications, which by the summer of 1918 had reached 800,000 copies: he had

---

[74] *Mitteilungen*, 5th September 1918. Chamberlain's article in the *Deutsche Zeitung*, November 1917,
was entitled 'Die deutsche Vaterlandspartei'. The source was a short essay by August Eigenbrodt,
'*Berliner Tageblatt* und *Frankfurter Zeitung* in ihrem Verhalten zu den nationalen Fragen 1887–1914'.
The *Mitteilungen* criticised the censorship for its inaction against Eigenbrodt's inflammatory
writing. One of Chamberlain's invectives against the *Frankfurter Zeitung* ran: "Everything that is
German is attacked and combatted by this paper and, if possible, destroyed."

[75] *Mitteilungen*, 5th September 1918. The prosecutors were the trustees and editors of the *Frankfurter
Zeitung*. According to Claß, his client had never read this paper; he had merely heard about it from
reliable friends. Chamberlain had to pay 1,500 *Mark* and legal expenses. In addition, he was
obliged to publish the judgement in twenty-one of the most important German newspapers of all
political colours. See also Field, *Evangelist, op. cit.*, pp. 392–394.

[76] *Mitteilungen*, 5th September 1918. The Court used the expression, "He was despised by his
adversaries and honoured in the same degree by his admirers."

[77] *Ibid*. The *Reich* leadership used the *Frankfurter Zeitung* political reports for 15 years, because in this
respect it was the most reliable source. Its reports on Russia were also highly regarded during the
war. Even the *alldeutsch* reporter for the *Kreuzzeitung*, Professor Otto Hoetzsch, considered the paper
as the best source for Moscow information. The *Mitteilungen* referred to the *Kreuzzeitung*, No. 358
(1918).

clearly appealed precisely to the "mood of the time".[78] The *Mitteilungen* and its writers felt that Chamberlain and his *Kriegsaufsätze* had caused incalculable damage to Germany in foreign countries.

Despite the paper shortage marking the last stage of the First World War, the *Mitteilungen* wrote a four-and-a-half page article on Chamberlain and his trial. The final passage disclosed the justification for the length of this report: the *Frankfurter Zeitung* and the *Berliner Tageblatt* as targets for *völkisch* attacks were mere "covering addresses"; the sights were really set on the declared enemy, "Pan-Judaism". Contrastingly, the *Mitteilungen* tried with all its might to reveal the connection between the outrageous and legally proven criminal contentions made by Houston Stewart Chamberlain with the no less dangerous thrust of the *alldeutsch* movement against Jews and Liberalism. The ADV honoured Chamberlain after his conviction as a stalwart of their cause and accordingly at the autumn conference of 1918 in Hanover "German thanks for Chamberlain" were called for and money was collected for his campaigns and for his publisher's legal expenses.[79]

VII. CONCLUSION

Houston Stewart Chamberlain was an active and successful writer in the Wilhelminian *Reich*. His ambivalent qualities were clearly evidenced by such books as the *Grundlagen des 19. Jahrhunderts* and the *Arische Weltanschauung*, as well as by those on Wagner and Goethe. Racial theories and Aryan mystic fanaticism bound up with a Germanic cult concealed a hidden time-bomb. Chamberlain's ideas, together with other theories on the nature of Jewish, Aryan and other "races", provoked and required discussion. The *Mitteilungen* had to continue the method of "scholarly discourse" during the war, reviewing or quoting scholars such as Friedrich Hertz and Hugo Münsterberg when they replied to material on Chamberlain. Precisely because the internal *Burgfrieden* had proved illusory soon after the first euphoria of August 1914, Jewish defence had to concentrate and continue its endeavours even though the *Abwehrverein* had declared at the outbreak of war that it proposed to halt its work for the duration. For various reasons, refutation of Chamberlain was seen as an absolute necessity. On the one hand, it was not possible to dismiss him as a lunatic because his writings had achieved such high circulation and helped to spread forms of "race-specific" theories. Moreover, in 1912, in his antisemitic *Wenn ich der Kaiser wär'*, the *alldeutsch* leader Heinrich Claß had appealed to Chamberlain and Gobineau as

---

[78]On Chamberlain's importance in the period of German *Weltpolitik*, see Field, 'Antisemitism and Weltpolitik', *loc. cit.*, p. 70.

[79]*Mitteilungen*, 2nd October 1918. In Hanover, the campaign was supported by the slogan: ". . . a thousand-*Mark* note for every war profiteer!". The *Mitteilungen*'s cynical comment was: "So the *völkisch* war profiteers in heavy industry certainly did the decent thing!"

authorities on racial-biological theory.[80] In addition, Chamberlain had a considerable reputation as a personality in public life – as Cosima Wagner's son-in-law and a man on conversational terms with the *Kaiser*, even if only rarely.[81] That alone meant that the *Mitteilungen* saw a pressing need to deal comprehensively with Chamberlain's ideological character and influence, since he was extremely prominent both as a *völkisch* writer and as a "cultural antisemite" during the last phase of the *Kaiserreich*.

After August 1914 this "Herold des Ariertums", in the words of Poliakov, made a new name for himself amidst the flood of war publications as the champion of the German cause. Chamberlain primarily gave his opinions as a German patriot who could also appreciate Jewish activities for *Kaiser* and *Reich*. However, in the second place, he imported many antisemitic stereotypes into his essays, with their "trenchant, dogmatic style" (Field), hidden behind his anti-British or anti-French chauvinism. His portrayal of "Jewish Internationalism", the power of the allegedly Jewish-dominated "agitation" press in foreign countries, meant that the *Abwehrverein* could not avoid opposing him during the war, notwithstanding the *Burgfrieden*. One problem for the *Mitteilungen* was to separate his pro-German sentiments from his antisemitism. Naturally, the *Mitteilungen* recognised love of Germany as a valid war-time tool in the fight against enemy nations, as can be seen from many patriotically slanted phrases in the journal.

A reading of the *Kriegsaufsätze* shows that the *Mitteilungen* analysed only the passages which in some way attacked Jews, the internal political situation in Germany or the Church. However chauvinist, Chamberlain's emphatic statements about Britain, "perfidious Albion",[82] were ignored, possibly through lack of space (a standard issue consisted of 4–8 pages). It is, however, conceivable that such slanders against the Allied Powers, even if uttered by Chamberlain, were

[80]It is important to note that Chamberlain as a thorough-going disciple of Darwin refused to rely on Gobineau. On Chamberlain's ideology, see Mühlen, *Rassenideologien*, *op. cit.*, p. 95; see also Field, 'Antisemitism and Weltpolitik, *loc. cit.*, p. 76; Daniel Frymann, *Das Kaiserbuch. Patriotische Wahrheiten und Notwendigkeiten* (the final title), Leipzig [7]1925, p. 32; Iring Fetscher, 'Die Entstehung des politischen Antisemitismus in Deutschland', in Hermann Huss and Andreas Schröder (eds.), *Antisemitismus. Zur Pathologie der bürgerlichen Gesellschaft*, Frankfurt a. Main 1966, pp. 9–33, here p. 27. Fetscher added that Claß had called Chamberlain and Gobineau as "key witnesses" to the racial biological *Weltanschauung*, and to the negative materialistic influence of the Jews: thus the Germans were infected by the Jews and had lost their instincts. These explanations showed terminological affinities with the *Grundlagen*, *op. cit.*, part I, pp. 372–373, where Chamberlain reported the awakening of instinct in the Jewish race after their country had been destroyed and their continuance endangered. He and Gobineau had given a theoretical basis to the racial myth, but Claß formulated detailed political programmes, designed to discriminate against the Jews in law, i.e. force them back to pre-emancipated status. Twenty-one years after the publication of Claß's *Wenn ich der Kaiser wär'* the National Socialists transformed the main components of his anti-Jewish programme into reality.

[81]The relationship between the *Kaiser* and Chamberlain after 1901 has been described by Lamar Cecil, 'Wilhelm II. und die Juden', in *Juden im Wilhelminischen Deutschland 1890–1914*. Ein Sammelband herausgegeben von Werner E. Mosse unter Mitwirkung von Arnold Paucker, Tübingen 1976 (Schriftenreihe wissenschaftlicher Abhandlungen des Leo Baeck Instituts 33), pp. 313–347, here pp. 330–332.

[82]See Chamberlain, *Neue Kriegsaufsätze*, *op. cit.*, pp. 21ff.: the Englishman's political thinking was in general "nearly as primitive as that of a Congolese negro".

regarded as legitimate and above criticism in time of war. Although the *Mitteilungen* attacked the experienced writer, the man on whom the *Kaiser* had pinned the Iron Cross, it was solely as an antisemite and not as a German patriot. In this respect, Chamberlain had secured his position, for example by opening the pamphlet *Deutschlands Kriegsziel* (1916) with a quotation from Hindenburg: "Let us hope that the war will last until all things have yielded to our will."[83]

Apart from these complications, it came as some relief for the *Mitteilungen* that Chamberlain and his *völkisch confrères* had polemicised harshly against the *Reichstag*, certain scholars and the Church, so that his image could be unfavourably presented not merely as an antisemite, but as a parliament-hater, an opponent of learning, an enemy of the Church. The *Abwehrverein*, on the other hand, acquired the patina of a defender of such institutions. Chamberlain's "internationalism" also benefited the *Mitteilungen*: as a self-professed "Germanic Englishman", was he really ordained to judge the German essence and predominance in the world – or was he suspect? In Britain he was regarded as an out-and-out apostate whose choice of Germany as his home was heatedly denounced.[84] *Völkisch* agitators in the *Reich* violently attacked "renegade" German-Jewish Americans who took the part of their new country against Germany, yet Chamberlain, culpable in the highest degree on the same charge, was hailed by his allies as a genius.

Two major aspects of its system of argument characterised the *Mitteilungen*. The bourgeois-Liberal stance of the *Abwehrverein* obviously precluded any approach to Zionism; the *Mitteilungen* avoided quotation from the Zionist press (except during the outburst of jingoism at the outbreak of war) and refrained from expressing approval of the movement. Similarly, it never referred to the *Centralverein*'s, *Im deutschen Reich* (and later to the *C.V.-Zeitung*). Clearly the paper shunned published support from the chief association of German Jewry, not wishing to offer a "Jewish profile" as a target to the opposition. In 1981 Geoffrey Field noted that in the division of labour between the *Centralverein* and the *Abwehrverein*, the latter concentrated on reproducing non-Jewish criticisms of Chamberlain.[85] The *Mitteilungen* could use many critiques and editorials from other papers to uncover Chamberlain's frequent inconsistencies and sought to diminish his reputation in this way. However, the large circulation of the *Kriegsaufsätze* in comparison to that of the *Mitteilungen* and similar publications must not be forgotten. Whereas Chamberlain's war-time writings were eventually sent to troops in the trenches as charitable gifts, the *Mitteilungen* had about 10,000 subscribers, so that in this scholarly, intellectual and polemic discussion

---

[83]Houston Stewart Chamberlain, *Deutschlands Kriegsziel*, Oldenburg i. Gr. 1916.
[84]Field, *Evangelist, op. cit.*, p. 366. In 1915 *The Times* described Germany as that "unhappy country" which harboured the renegade.
[85]Field, *Evangelist, op. cit.*, p. 246, note 59, on the struggle against the *Grundlagen des 19. Jahrhunderts*. See also Paucker, *Der jüdische Abwehrkampf. op. cit.*, pp. 35–36.

its influence was very limited.[86] A further point to be noted is the possible interdependence of defence activities and antisemitism: debates in defence journals drew attention to the question and concern was aroused not for the Jews but for their opponents. The antisemitic *Reichstagsabgeordneter* Hans Leuß had already mentioned this effect as early as 1894.[87] Defence activities in themselves increased publicity for the conflict, and this too might have unfavourable consequences.

Even at the end of the war, Chamberlain enjoyed great popularity and journalistic influence. The *Abwehrverein* extended its activities by founding more local groups. According to a report by the political department of the Leipzig police authority, it wished "simply to carry out opposition to antisemitism" which would seem unavoidably to entail "a very considerable effect on politics".[88] Defence activity during the First World War chiefly focused on the *Alldeutscher Verband* and other *völkisch* mass organisations, which were not lacking in followers, finance, agitators, supporters in the army and government, or the targets set by radical antisemitism. It was this rising tide of anti-Jewish campaigning on which the *Abwehrverein* planned to concentrate. The image of Houston Stewart Chamberlain, as reflected in the *Mitteilungen*, was that of the most prominent and the most fiercely attacked individual during the war years. But he ignored these assaults, shifting to prophecy as early as 1916: "The chief war aim will be attained so soon as Germany's distress shall have created a splendid man, intrepid and unshakeable, with the heart of a lion."[89]

[86]As to the possibility of influencing racial theories by writings in print, see Mühlen, *Rassenideologien, op. cit.* pp. 251, 262. He acknowledges that these publications never really succeeded; there was little political effect from such works and arguments. Rather, the racists protected themselves by libelling their opponents, saying that their books exuded a spirit of "Jewish destructiveness" or "inferiority". Chamberlain never reacted to the *Mitteilungen*: had he done so, it would have printed his response, just as it published the attacks and calumnies by other *völkisch* authors in 1916.

[87]On the essay in Maximilian Harden's *Die Zukunft*, see Arnold Paucker, 'Zur Problematik einer jüdischen Abwehrstrategie in der deutschen Gesellschaft', in *Juden im Wilhelminischen Deutschland, op. cit.*, pp. 479–548, here pp. 541–542.

[88]*Mitteilungen*, 12th June 1918. See Staatsarchiv Leipzig, Polizeipräsidium Leipzig, PP-V Nr. 3470, Verein zur Abwehr des Antisemitismus.

[89]Chamberlain, *Kriegsziel, op. cit.*, p. 16.

Jewish Aspects as Contributing Factors to the Genesis of the Reichsbanner Schwarz-Rot-Gold

BY JACOB TOURY

I

Karl Rohe's carefully researched study *Das Reichsbanner Schwarz-Rot-Gold*,[1] still unequalled in its field,[2] devotes some attention to the pre-history of this central Republican defence movement. Rohe describes a relatively large number of early local Republican defence groups, which sprang up more or less spontaneously in several particular trouble-spots, such as the Hanseatic cities of Hamburg and Bremen; Munich, Nuremberg and Würzburg; the Prussian province of Saxony, and to an extent also Greater Berlin.[3] However, Rohe's work is very little concerned with the Jewish issue, which has been made the main part of this paper.

Nevertheless, Rohe's book does provide a certain amount of information on early Jewish defence groups which may serve as a starting point for further research. For Hamburg in 1922, immediately after the murder of Rathenau, Rohe mentions among several Republican groups, such as a Social Democratic *Vereinigung Republik*; a "Republican Circle" consisting of members of the *Deutsche Demokratische Partei* (DDP) and also a *"Bund jüdischer Frontsoldaten* (not to be confused with the *Reichsbund jüdischer Frontsoldaten*)".[4] Similarly in Kassel, he names "a special section within the *Bund jüdischer Frontsoldaten* which was concerned mainly with defence against antisemitic attacks" and existed along-side the workers' defence associations.

A detailed study by Ulrich Dunker of the *Reichsbund jüdischer Frontsoldaten* (R.j.F.), which has been completed since Rohe's book was published, makes no mention of a Hamburg section of the R.j.F., although it does describe "Defence

---

This English version of a lecture, originally intended for a German audience, has been enlarged and brought up to date for this volume by kind invitation of the editor, Dr. Arnold Paucker. Thus it seems only fitting to thank him herewith for this and for all his dedicated editorial skill, to which the Year Book and its contributors owe so much during a period of more than two decades.

[1]Karl Rohe, *Das Reichsbanner Schwarz-Rot-Gold. Ein Beitrag zur Geschichte und Struktur der politischen Kampfverbände in der Weimarer Republik*. Beiträge zur Geschichte des Parlamentarismus, 34, Düsseldorf 1966.
[2]The compilation by Helga Gotschlich, *Zwischen Kampf und Kapitulation. Zur Geschichte des Reichsbanners Schwarz-Rot-Gold*, (East) Berlin 1987, can hardly be regarded as a serious contribution to the theme.
[3]Rohe, *Das Reichsbanner, op. cit.*, pp. 29–43.
[4]*Ibid.*, p. 30. Rohe's parenthesis.

Groups" (*Abwehrgruppen*) within the R.j.F. branches of Berlin, Breslau, Königsberg, Munich and Kassel, as well as rather nebulous supra-regional umbrella
organisation for these defence groups, the "AW".[5] However, Dunker's statements ought to be amended as his perusal of the archival sources concerning the
"AW" was not at all exhaustive. Attentive reading of the relevant file[6] leads to
the conclusion that the Jewish defence organisations existing in many places
from autumn 1923 to spring 1924 comprised not only ex-soldiers of the R.j.F.,
but also members of Jewish students' organisations and even schoolboys
affiliated with the youth-movement *Kameraden*.[7] The second amendment to be
made bears upon the mention of Kassel as a centre of organised Jewish self-
defence. It seems that this was occasioned by a police report from Kassel. This
report dealt with an informer who had penetrated a meeting of the R.j.F. in
Cologne, at which the establishment of an operation for gathering anti-
antisemitic information had been proposed. However, the information received
had not been acted on by the Cologne police, allegedly because of the influence of
a prominent Jew, *Regierungsrat* Bier, who had been nominated as Vice-Chairman
of the R.j.F.[8]

Another fact to be amended is the extent and the size of the "AW" on the eve of
1924. One instance ought to suffice: the "Landesverband" Silesia of the R.j.F.
reported more than 800 "AW" members in about ten local chapters with at least
three more in the planning stage.[9] Perhaps the most illuminating figures came
from Görlitz, whose R.j.F. branch numbered 23 members, while the local "AW"
was reported to have exactly double this figure (46)!

If one asks what these particulars have to do with the founding of the
Reichsbanner Schwarz-Rot-Gold, it should be pointed out that the "AW" seems to
have terminated its activities[10] on 1st April 1924, i.e. barely a month after the
founders' meeting of the *Reichsbanner* in Magdeburg (22nd–24th February 1924)
and exactly two days after the publication of its first manifesto in the *Vorwärts* and
most other Republican papers. And if this seems a mere coincidence, there
remains the question of Hamburg's *Bund jüdischer Frontsoldaten*, mentioned by
Rohe as a precursor of the *Reichsbanner*, as well as new archival evidence on a
Verein jüdischer Frontsoldaten in Bremen[11] – not mentioned either by Rohe or by
Dunker – both of these Jewish groups were closely connected with the first
appearance of the *Reichsbanner* in the Hanseatic towns.

[5]Ulrich Dunker, *Der Reichsbund jüdischer Frontsoldaten 1919–1938. Geschichte eines jüdischen Abwehrvereins*,
   Düsseldorf 1977, pp. 54f., 58, 257ff.
[6]Geheimes Staatsarchiv (Geh. St. A.: previously Deutsches Zentralarchiv [DZA]), Merseburg, Rep.
   77, Tit. 4043, new No. 402.
[7]The first mention of the *Kameraden* for defence work in Kolberg (autumn 1920); *Jüdische Volkszeitung*,
   Breslau, Nr. 7 (1921), p. 3. Also personal recollection of the present author, borne out by *ibid.*, p. 21a,
   being a letter by the (Orthodox) *Vereinigung jüdischer Akademiker*, Berlin, to the heads of the AW,
   signifying a certain readiness to recommend its members joining AW-units.
[8]*Ibid.*, pp. 27–31. Bier did not accept the nomination and the whole "information" seems to have been
   blown up out of all proportion, except for the report on anti-antisemitic activities of the R.j.F. in
   Cologne.
[9]*Ibid.*, p. 9.
[10]*Ibid.*, p. 36.
[11]Cf. below, notes 14–23.

II

It seems probable that the previously mentioned authors were somewhat confused by the different names given to the Hamburg organisation and to others such as the one in Bremen, although these local groups had existed from an early stage and their nuclei reach back to 1919. In fact their use of different names is easily explained. The first local association, founded in Berlin, had called itself the *Vaterländischer Bund jüdischer Frontsoldaten*; however, it quickly dropped the patriotic epithet *vaterländisch*, which was increasingly being misused by the extreme Right. When the various local groups of the R.j.F. came together (from 1919/1920 onwards), many local branches retained their original names.[12] One of these was the Hamburg *Vaterländischer Bund jüdischer Frontsoldaten*, which was founded soon after the Berlin association and was certainly in existence in November 1919. Another was the Bremen *Verein jüdischer Frontsoldaten*, the origins of which can also be traced back to the prevailing local conditions of 1919.

At this point, some attention must be devoted to the way in which big organisations developed from local initiatives and out of local problems. The *Reichsbanner* itself had a whole series of local and regional forerunners. Certainly it did not emerge, fully organised and with its headquarters in Magdeburg, on the sudden order of one of the Party leaders or even from Otto Hörsing's private initiative. This argument, often heard, was rightly dismissed as a "myth" by Rohe, and the *Arbeiternotwehr* of Magdeburg[13] certainly existed as early as April 1923.

Thus, it should come as no surprise that the Jews of Bremen followed their own specific route to the R.j.F. and the *Reichsbanner Schwarz-Rot-Gold*. As in other towns, Bremen's Jews participated in the city-wide residents' and citizens' defence associations. However, in the large area of the city-state with a relatively low population density and a very small Jewish proportion of the population (not exceeding 0.4–0.5%), Jewish involvement carried little weight in citizens' defence organisations, which by themselves had only limited success. In Bremen, the solution adopted was to keep control over endangered living-quarters, harbour installations or warehouses by establishing a professional guard.

One of its patrons, and possibly also one of the initiators of the whole guard service (later: *Wach- und Schließgesellschaft*)[14] in 1919, was Julius Bamberger, the owner of a large department store and second Chairman of the *Centralverein deutscher Staatsbürger jüdischen Glaubens* (C.V.). The surviving documents do not reveal exactly when, with Bamberger's encouragement, the Jewish war veterans

[12]See Dunker, *Der Reichsbund, op. cit.*, p. 32; *ibid.*, Dokument I, pp. 186ff., appeal of January 1919, from Berlin (signed: *Vaterländischer Bund* etc.), p. 188. For Hamburg see Ina Lorenz, *Die Juden in Hamburg zur Zeit der Weimarer Republik. Eine Dokumentation*, Hamburg 1987, vol. I, foreword, p. CXXXI: "The *Vaterländischer Bund jüdischer Frontsoldaten* as Hamburg local branch of the R.j.F. . . ."; also vol. II, documents, pp. 1137–1165.

[13]'Erinnerungen' by Werner Bruschke, in IfGA (Institut für die Geschichte der Arbeiterbewegung), Berlin (Ost), EA 1319/1 pp. 97f. IfGA contains the archives of the former *Sozialistische Einheitspartei Deutschlands*.

[14]Staatsarchiv (StA) Bremen, 4, 65 contains a special volume of documents on the private guards and their subscribers.

of Bremen founded their own local organisation. However, several reports from the police intelligence service in spring 1923 refer to an active *Verein jüdischer Frontsoldaten* under the chairmanship of Rudolf Apt, also active in the C.V., and Julius Bamberger.

One remarkable feature of the local association in Bremen was the decision of Apt – with Bamberger as spokesman – to give confidential information to the police intelligence service on 28th April 1923. Police officers were told that "in order to protect themselves against alarming incidents" of an antisemitic nature in Bremen, the Jews had "banded together and created an association of Jewish veterans which would protect their meetings. They also intended to set up boxing lessons so that personal attacks could be repelled on the spot."[15]

At the time of this conversation, police intelligence had already received a report about a big C.V. meeting of some 1,000 people on 14th April, which had been actively and effectively protected.[16] This had so impressed the observing officers that they had given detailed descriptions of the controls at the entrance and the way invitations were exchanged for numbered seat tickets after the invited guests had been identified. The police stressed that invitations had even been sent to "*völkisch* representatives" and to about ten members of the *Deutschnationale Volkspartei* (DNVP). These ticket-holders were directed to "seats along the main aisle of the hall", under the eyes of a "bodyguard" of forty to fifty people. The report pointedly noted that the members of this *Stoßtrupp* looked as though they belonged to the Communist Party, and possibly to the *Seemannsbund* and the "Syndicalists". As evidence, the officers argued that their leader had greatly resembled a notorious Communist "master butcher".[17]

Clearly, Julius Bamberger and Rudolf Apt were not betraying any secrets when, fourteen days after the meeting, they reported to the police that a squad had been established under the aegis of the *Verein der Frontsoldaten* to protect the hall. They omitted only to explain that it was quite impossible to collect sufficient well-trained young Jews in the whole of Schleswig-Holstein including the Hanseatic cities. The R.j.F. was certainly no mass movement and, in any case, the observing police officers were not wholly incorrect in claiming that a goodly proportion of the "Schutzgarde" at the Bremen C.V. meeting were non-Jews. But they were unlikely to have been "Communists" and "Syndicalists", despite the fact that at the beginning of 1924 the police managed to seize, on the premises of a Communist district leader, notepaper bearing the heading "Bezirksverband der jüdischen Jugendvereine Nordwestdeutschlands, Sitz Bremen"; in the police view, this was "particularly significant regarding the repeated information" that the Jews were making use of "Left Radical circles to combat the antisemitic movement".[18] Such facts serve only to confirm the experience of Hamburg and

---

[15]StA Bremen, 4,65/1125, Bl. 3V–5 R (Polizeidirektion-Nachrichtenstelle), typewritten record: "Dem Herrn Pol. Präs. vorzulegen". The term "Verein" seems to correspond to the official name.

[16]*Ibid.*, Bl. 17ff. The document seems to have been written down only after the conversation of 28th April and been dealt with late (last copy 3rd May, on Bl. 24R).

[17]Quoted from *ibid.*, Bl. 17V.

[18]StA Bremen, 4,65/1125, Bl. 35.

Berlin, and probably many other places, that the police itself was composed of "Leftists" and "Rightists" in unequal parts. As far as the innuendo of Jewish Left-wing Radicalism is concerned, we know that Bamberger, like many other Jews, belonged to the *Verein Republik* which had been active in the city of Bremen since 1922, and had given particular encouragement to its youth group, named *Reichsadler*.[19] *Die Freie Hanse*, the newspaper of the *Verein Republik*, initiated the union of the Bremen group with the *Deutscher Republikanischer Reichsbund*, which had existed in rudimentary form since 1921 and had more Democrats than Social Democrats in senior positions. Subsequently, the members of this organisation described it as a civil organisation for people who were not, or were no longer, applicable for *Reichsbanner* membership.[20] But in the eyes of Rightist policemen, all adherents of such alignments were "Reds".

The aforementioned *Saalschutz-* and *Ordner*-formations (protection squads) naturally also worked for the Social Democrats and other organisations of the Left. These groups, along with the *Reichsadler* youth group, joined the *Reichsbanner* in 1924.[21] Since no membership lists have survived, it is impossible to know how many Jewish activists in Bremen were among them and made their way to the *Reichsbanner* in this way. Anyway, from the conditions prevailing in Bremen, we can be certain that the city's Jewish organisations believed they had found a legal way to protect their activities and the safety of their members. In any case, it was this ratiocination that led them to the *Reichsbanner*. Thus it may be stated that the Bremen branches of the R.j.F. and C.V. contributed to the consolidation of the *Reichsbanner* in the city. Not surprisingly, therefore, the Rightist press claimed that the owners of two Bremen department stores had provided fairly large gratuities and running expenses for the recruitment of *Reichsbanner* members.[22]

Further evidence of the unique spirit of the Bremen *Reichsbanner* was provided when attempts were made to revive a *Reichsbanner* group in the city after the war (December 1953). But squabbles about its necessity and about the political views of its rather Leftist initiators led to the abandonment of the project.[23] Of course, it is an open question whether inferences about the Weimar period are permissible after such a lapse of time.

---

[19]This Republican youth-organisation also aroused the interest of the *Reichskommissar für die öffentliche Ordnung*. Cf. Lageberichte R. Ko. Inn, No. 103 (16th April 1924), Anlage No. 9. One example in PA Bonn R 98280. The Bremen antisemites then circulated defamatory leaflets about Bamberger. StA Bremen, 4, 65/1125 and 4, 65/1026, B1, 137, 137a (November 1924) *et al.*

[20]The *Deutscher Republikanischer Reichsbund* was by no means purely Socialist, but it was still on the "Left", and that was enough for many. On the Bremen groups see Herbert Schwarzwälder, *Geschichte der Freien Hansestadt Bremen*, III, Hamburg 1983, p. 202. Also StA Bremen, 4, 65/1012, 1013. Further material in Forschungsstelle für die Geschichte des Nationalsozialismus in Hamburg, Ordner 411, with special thanks to Dr. Ursula Büttner for her friendly advice.

[21]StA Bremen, 4, 5/165, 1027. During the transition period it called itself *Republikanischer Selbstschutz* or *Selbstwehr* (RSW).

[22]*Hamburger Echo*, 15th November 1924, 'Tagesberichte'. One of the owners of the department stores might have been Julius Bamberger himself.

[23]StA Bremen, V 2, Nr. 1432.

III

A unique way to the *Reichsbanner*, perhaps even more spectacular than that of Bremen, appears to have been found by Hamburg Jewish circles. The special relations existing between Hamburg Jews and the forerunners of the *Reichsbanner* undoubtedly played a part in this development. Ina Lorenz has given cautious but relevant testimony regarding the issue of the legality of this development, though she was apparently unable to provide proof of the actual events. She writes that the official Jewish organs refused "any form of active self-defence for the community (*Gemeinde*)". Lorenz was not able to establish from the sources "whether a minority of the Jewish leadership elite . . . seriously pursued the idea". However, she quotes the Chairman of the *Vaterländischer Bund jüdischer Frontsoldaten*, Dr. Siegfried Urias, who in 1929 described his organisation as a "powerful, active *Abwehrgruppe*" after it had been in existence for ten years. Urias will receive ample mention again later on. But even from certain "indirect references", Ina Lorenz was able to conclude that there were Jewish "links with the *Reichsbanner*", which itself included "not a few Jews". She also stated that in 1932 "the community organs" tentatively welcomed the individual entry of Jewish youths into the "Iron Front".[24]

However, direct archival evidence has now been found to show that members of the *Vaterländischer Bund jüdischer Frontsoldaten* were among the founding members of the Hamburg *Reichsbanner*, and possibly even belonged as a group to its initial core. In any case, as in Bremen, they had been involved with the forerunners of the *Reichsbanner* in one form or another.[25] The Hamburg *Reichsbanner* emerged from a number of *Kameradschaften*, which had in part existed since 1921 or 1922. Their core had been formed initially by pro-Republican police officers, who had pressed for the cleansing of reactionary forces from the Hamburg police; such as the "black" paramilitary units set up by Lettow-Vorbeck at the beginning of 1919, which had aided and abetted the unrest and looting of 25th–26th June of that year.[26] The formation of the Republican *Kameradschaften* appears to have been accelerated by the Kapp Putsch in March 1920. Additional impetus came later from the Republican members of the Inhabitants' Defence Associations (*Einwohnerwehren*) who responded to the dissolution of their associations on 3rd November 1921 by establishing the *Vereinigung Republik* (analogous to the *Verein Republik* in Bremen) and organising it according to the districts of the city. Its members, belonging mostly to the *Mehrheits*-SPD turned out for "military sports exercises and joint police patrols" –

[24]Lorenz, *Die Juden, op. cit.*, pp. CL–CLIII. The proposal for collective entry came from the Zionist side (Dr. Ernst Kalmus) – pp. CLIIIf.

[25]I am grateful for these references to the helpfulness and expertise of Mr. Jürgen Sielemann, my adviser at the Staatsarchiv (StA) Hamburg, who devoted much time and trouble to my quest and enabled me to trace the widely scattered and hidden material.

[26]On the Hamburg police see Wolfgang Schult, 'Geschichte der Hamburger Polizei', MS (1964) in St A Hamburg; Lothar Danner, *Ordnungspolizei Hamburg – Betrachtungen zu ihrer Geschichte*, Hamburg 1958. Detailed report on the unrest; *Mitteilungen aus dem Verein zur Abwehr des Antisemitismus*, 24th July 1919, pp. 116–117, also published in Lorenz, *op. cit.*, vol. II, pp. 1010ff., note 7.

the word "joint" expressing close co-operation with the Hamburg police force.[27] The fact that Hamburg's Jews took a rather active part in the now disbanded Inhabitants' Defence Associations, was demonstrated as early as Christmas 1919, when they volunteered to take over all guard duties, whilst their Christian colleagues celebrated the festive season.[28]

Moreover, in Hamburg as in Bremen, there existed a private guard association named *Heimschutz Groß-Hamburg*.[29] Although no specifically Jewish element has so far come to light in the latter company, it may be stated that the precursors of the *Reichsbanner* in the two Hanseatic cities of Bremen and Hamburg seem to have developed along more or less parallel lines.

In fact, the participation of Hamburg Jews is rather striking, although only provable at the moment of final union of the *Kameradschaften* and *Vereinigungen* early in 1924. As elsewhere in Germany, this development was prepared in periods of feverish political eruptions, such as the Kapp Putsch, the murder of Erzberger or Rathenau. It consolidated during the year 1923 and led to the establishment of the *Reichsbanner Schwarz-Rot-Gold*, in Hamburg as in Magdeburg, at the end of February 1924. The leading role of Hamburg was briefly referred to in the new organ of the movement, *Das Reichsbanner*.[30]

Two of the Hamburg *Kameradschaften*, No. 7 and No. 8, had either a partially or an unequivocally Jewish character. Since the *Kameradschaft jüdischer Frontsoldaten* (probably No. 7) was celebrating its flag dedication ceremony on 23rd November 1924, it seems likely that it had been in existence from the beginning of the *Reichsbanner* or even before; indeed, it was probably the section set up by the *Vaterländischer Bund jüdischer Frontsoldaten* to protect its meetings from 1923 or perhaps even earlier. Evidence to support this belief is provided by the fact that the speaker at the flag ceremony[31] was none other than the central figure of the R.j.F. in Hamburg and its first Chairman, the severely disabled war veteran Dr. Siegfried Urias. The leader of this Jewish *Kameradschaft* and its local administrator was Ludwig Rothstein, and the invitations to the ceremony bore his signature and address. Though the existence of a purely Jewish section within a general defence association is surprising, there had been at least one precedent for a separate Jewish defence section in Hamburg, dating back to 1916/1918. When during the First World War, youth companies were called into being for

---

[27]Danner, *Ordnungspolizei Hamburg, op. cit.*, p. 48. On co-operation with the police see p. 82. Danner emphasises (p. 205) the influence of these developments in Hamburg on the "decision . . . to found the *Reichsbanner*", which is not mentioned in any other source.

[28]*Im deutschen Reich*, 1920, p. 40.

[29]Ursula Büttner, *Politische Gerechtigkeit und sozialer Geist. Hamburg zur Zeit der Weimarer Republik*, Hamburg 1985, p. 104, note 124.

[30]*Das Reichsbanner*, I, No. 8 (1st September 1924), p. 9: "In Hamburg trat das RB schon bei der *Gründung der Groß*organisation auf den Plan . . ." (italics are mine). No other mention of Hamburg's role has come to light.

[31]StA Hamburg, CL VII, Lit. Q d, Nr. 533/fasc. I. This contains only a letter of invitation to the flag ceremony "An einen hohen Senat", the positive answer of the senate, and two printed complimentary tickets with a heading identical to the letterhead: "RB SRG. Kameradschaft jüd. Frontsoldaten, Hamburg". The number 7 became customary for this group at a later date – possibly after the *Kameradschaft* had ceased to present itself as a purely Jewish group, the C.V. having voiced strong opposition when the Jewish affiliation of the group became public knowledge. See *C.V.-Dienst* IV, No. 1/2 (15th January 1927), p. 12.

pre-military training, the Hamburg Zionist sport association *Bar Kochba* had set up the "Ninth Youth Company". In 1917 this unit was deployed to put out a moorland fire and was publicly praised by the deputy general commanding. Even so, the C.V. newspaper had protested against such "separatism",[32] and later on, at the end of 1926, when the *Völkischer Beobachter* got wind of what was called by the Nazis a "Judenschutz" section in the *Reichsbanner*, the C.V. appears to have exerted pressure on the R.j.F. to end such objectionable public displays. At the beginning of 1927 the C.V. announced that the "only separate section existing in the German *Reich*" would "no longer appear *outwardly* as a Jewish group". It was explained that "Jewish *Reichsbanner* members" had simply made themselves available "from personal interest as *individuals* to protect meeting places".[33] For the C.V., the theory that the Jews were not a minority group was thus saved. Nevertheless, the "individuals" of the renamed *Kameradschaft* No. 7 continued to make enthusiastic collections among the Jews of Hamburg in order to secure the financing of their further activities.[34]

As we have seen, since the founding of the Hamburg branch of the *Reichsbanner* a democratic *Kameradschaft*, bearing the number "8", had also been in evidence. Though it did not appear as a Jewish group, it had in all probability a large proportion of Jewish members. At any rate, the group was led by a certain Philipp Auerbach, a young man from a respected Jewish family in the city. The flag dedication of the *Kameradschaft* did not take place until a year after that of the *Frontsoldaten*, and it seems certain that this group No. 8 was formed after No. 7.[35] It is likely that *Kameradschaft* No. 8 was also largely financed by Jewish donations and that – similar to the Bremen forerunners of the *Reichsbanner* associated with Apt and Bamberger and their weekly paper *Die Freie Hanse* – it had no affiliation with the Social Democratic Party. Certainly, the situation in Hamburg, as in Bremen, bears out the statement that the Jewish link with the *Reichsbanner* ought not in itself be regarded as a Jewish commitment to Social Democracy.

IV

This was also borne out by the state of affairs in other German regions, and especially in the South. The trauma of the revolutionary period between November 1918 and April 1919 in Bavaria, and mainly in its capital of Munich, not only resembled conditions in the Hanseatic cities, but was even more exacerbated. With malicious over-simplification, the Bavarian government chose to answer Jewish protests against repeated verbal and physical attacks from various Right-wing antisemitic groups by reminding the protesters "that . . . Jews stand at the summit of the Left-Radical movement".[36] Moreover, the

---

[32]*Hamburger Jüdische Nachrichten*, No. 4 (1921), pp. 34–35; *Im deutschen Reich*, 1917, p. 420.

[33]*C.V.-Dienst*, IV, No. 1/2 (15th January 1927). Some emphases in original, some by present author.

[34]Lorenz, *Die Juden, op. cit.*, appeal for the year 1928, pp. 1024–1025.

[35]StA Hamburg, CL VII, Lit. Q d, Nr. 533, fasc. 4; also Staatliche Pressestelle I-IV, Nr. 4392, Bd. I.

[36]*Ministerpräsident* Held on 31st July 1924, according to 'Auszug Ministerrat', Bayerisches Hauptstaatsarchiv (Bay. HStA) München, MA 10016 Bl. 134.

government itself averred "that in certain Jewish figures one sees the exponents of that which is particularly odious in business and political life".[37] Thus, if Jewish self-defence and co-operation with Republican forces were needed anywhere, it was surely in Bavaria.

And in fact the Jews of Bavaria faced a similar situation to that which had led their co-religionists in Hamburg and Bremen to commit themselves to the *Reichsbanner*, and they responded to it in a similar manner. In cities such as Munich, Nuremberg and Würzburg, and even in smaller Bavarian towns, they were highly active. Although some Jews appear to have supported Kurt Eisner and the *Räteregierung* in 1918/1919, there is also evidence of a strange Jewish participation in the rather reactionary *Einwohnerwehren*, and even in some *Freikorps* groups.[38] Needless to say, the Jews received no thanks for it, nor for their activities in the Upper Silesian *Selbstschutz*, i.a. as members of the Bavarian corps *Oberland*. Anyhow, the *Freikorps* and the *Selbstschutz* organisations everywhere remained hotbeds of the most virulent antisemitism.

Eventually, the local branch of the *Reichsbund jüdischer Frontsoldaten* in Munich was faced with the need to establish a defence section, specifically to protect Jewish institutions and the meetings of Jewish organisations. According to police undercover reports from November 1922, the R.j.F. was able to mobilise up to 150 men for this purpose in the Isarmetropole.[39] In Munich, there is very little evidence of the sympathy of the R.j.F. for Left-Republican groups which we noted in the Hanseatic cities. Where such sympathy existed at all, it was limited to a few individuals who worked outside the Jewish community and whose activities are, therefore, difficult to document.

That is also true of certain Jewish veterans of the *Mehrheits*-SPD who, after May 1919, were brave enough to resist the "white terror" of the Nationalist groups and the government in the city and the state. One of the few was Carl Landauer, whose account of the period was not written until after the Second World War. Landauer had worked for the Social Democratic *Münchener Post* since 1920. He was one of the creators of the Party's first Munich squads set up to protect meetings and later of their "security section", whose news and information services he organised and whose financing he undertook himself, advised by the lawyer Max Hirschberg and his partner Philipp Löwenfeld.[40]

After the murder of Rathenau, when Landauer – aware of the growing danger of a Right-wing *coup d'état* – was frantically looking for more money to arm and activate his security sections, it may have been Löwenfeld who, to that end, established first contacts with the office of the Munich C.V. (Wilhelm Levinger).

[37]Bay. HStA München, MA 100403, 18th August 1921, in reply to the protest of a Jewish delegation under the leadership of Dr. Elias Straus regarding antisemitic outrages in Memmingen.
[38]Jewish activities in April 1919 in Munich's Marienplatz and the main station, which was stormed i.a. by Jewish members of the Würzburg *Freikorps*, documented from archival sources by Dunker, *Der Reichsbund jüdischer Frontsoldaten, op. cit.*, p. 252, note 8.
[39]Bay. HStA München, M.Inn. 73685, Police Report of 14th November 1922.
[40]The text and quotations here are taken from the autobiographical contribution of Carl Landauer, 'Erinnerungen an die Münchener Sozialdemokratie', in Hans Lamm (ed.), *Von Juden in München*, Munich 1958, pp. 311–317. Landauer worked until 1926 for the *Münchener Post*, latterly as editor. He then went to Berlin.

In any case, Landauer succeeded in reaching Paul Nathan and Ludwig Holländer, the later syndic of the Berlin C.V. As the result of a "loose agreement" between them, a source of money for the Munich SPD-squad was opened up, although it did not flow as freely as Landauer had hoped. By chance the link became known to the Munich police – and was at once passed on to antisemitic groups. The co-operation between "Jewish capitalists and Social Democratic bigwigs" provided effective propaganda material for the Right, and also made it easier for von Kahr's government to disarm the Munich "security sections" at a time when the danger of a Putsch by Bavarian Right-wing extremists was at its height (end of September 1923).[41]

In Munich, therefore, instead of the normal tendency of the R.j.F. to co-operate with forces defending the Republic, it was the local C.V. which emerged for the first time as supporter of a Republican defence organisation. However, this occurrence was not repeated and was carried out in secret and with insufficient resources, which in any case came from Berlin rather than from Munich itself. There were two reasons for this restraint. Firstly, the great majority of C.V. members and leaders were at least critical of Social Democracy – if not wholly opposed to it – for social, organisational and ideological reasons, which do not need to be investigated here.[42] Secondly, and more specifically, it was a principle of the C.V. that financial assistance could be made to general organisations only "on condition" that the money be used for actual defence against antisemitism. Until the principle itself was abandoned (rather late!), this condition was relaxed only reluctantly and in specific individual cases.[43]

In addition to the above, one further specific fact with regard to the Jewish organisations of Munich and Bavaria ought to be mentioned: the C.V. branch in the city – from its Chairman Ludwig Wassermann and subsequent *Syndikus* Werner Cahnmann[44] down to the middle- and lower-middle-class members – was inclined to see its political salvation in the *Bayerische Volkspartei*. Moreover, until 1924 Jewish public opinion was strongly pushed in that direction by the most widely read Jewish newspaper of Bavaria, Rabbi Seligmann Meyer's

[41] *Ibid.* For a brief summary see also Donald L. Niewyk, *Socialist, Anti-Semite and Jew. German Social Democracy Confronts the Problem of Anti-Semitism, 1918–1933*, Baton Rouge 1971, pp. 58–59.

[42] On the historical pros and cons in the relationship of Jews and Socialism see Jacob Toury, 'Die Dynamik der Beziehungen zwischen Juden und Arbeiterbewegung im Deutschland des 19. Jahrhunderts', in *Jahrbuch des Instituts für deutsche Geschichte*, Beiheft 2, Tel-Aviv 1977, pp. 47–62.

[43] Quoted from the unjustly neglected memoir of Dr. Julie Meyers, former secretary of the Nuremberg C.V. and the *Verband Bayerischer Israelitischer Gemeinden*. She belonged to the SDP and had close links with the *Reichsbanner*. After emigrating she worked in New York at the New School of Social Research. Her mimeographed manuscript is entitled, 'Jewish Anti-Defamation Work in Pre-Hitler Germany', published by the Jewish Labor Committee, New York, undated [1943]. Quoted here from pp. 23, 24.

[44] On Wassermann see Landauer, 'Erinnerungen', *loc. cit.*, p. 317. Cahnmann has left some personal records. His autobiographical note is held in the Leo Baeck Institute, London, but is not universally accessible. I am grateful to the director, Dr. Arnold Paucker, for granting my request to examine it.

Laubhütte[45] (Regensburg). On the other hand, in Nuremberg, and particularly in Würzburg and the surrounding area, Jewish relations with the Left-wing defence sections seem to have been more friendly than in Munich, where they were concentrated mainly in the small circle round Carl Landauer, even after the *Reichsbanner* had emerged as the official new Republican organisation in 1924.

In Nuremberg, Julie Meyers provided some liaison between Jewish organisations and the *Reichsbanner*, ostensibly not without success. For already on 31st July 1924, *Ministerpräsident* Held referred in the Bavarian *Ministerrat* (item No. 4 of the agenda):

> ". . . to the increasing appearance of the *Bund Schwarz-Rot-Gold*, which in Nuremberg already has over 3,000 members and is particularly supported by the Jews. The movement must be accorded close attention . . ."[46]

Significantly, the *Ministerpräsident* made no comment about Julius Streicher's poisonous Jew-baiting in Nuremberg and the Franconian hinterland. Apart from the memoirs of Julie Meyers, Jewish sources provide no information from the early period of the *Reichsbanner* which would support the conclusion that there was generous support for it in most of Bavaria, perhaps with the exception of certain small places (see below) and of Nuremberg, thanks to its Democratic mayor Dr. Luppe, who himself was an active supporter of the *Reichsbanner* and might have been supported by Jews. Thus, it stands to reason that until about 1929, the "main donations came from *individual* Jews . . . very often in *small* towns, where the Jews were the *only* ones to contribute to the local organisation of the *Reichsbanner*".[47]

The truth was that the authorities, particularly the police intelligence services, concentrated on gathering information about Jewish and Socialist activities, as though these were the only potential disturbers of the peace.

V

For example, the activity of the National Socialist propagandist Miss Ellend(t) in the Würzburg area was not the subject of official interest in 1923 and 1924. It is known to us only as the result of Jewish complaints about antisemitic outrages at Jewish meetings.[48] However, these reports also make it clear that some opposition was forming in the villages and was seeking to break up Nazi meetings. The documents record that this happened when Ellendt appeared in

---

[45]Rabbi Dr. S. Meyer, in his *Deutsch-Israelitische Zeitung* and supplement *Die Laubhütte* (on its foundation, and occasionally later, this was the main title of the paper), advocated loyal Jewish support for the *Bayerische Volkspartei*. He attempted to persuade the party leadership to combat all antisemitic incidents among its membership (1919–1924). Meyer died in 1925.

[46]See Julie Meyers, 'Jewish Anti-Defamation Work', *loc. cit.*, and Bay. HStA München, MA 100421, 'Ministerrats-Auszug' of 31st July (year not given but probably 1924 as other extracts bear this date). Further political miscalculations by Dr. Heinrich Held enabled Adolf Hitler to return to the political stage that same year.

[47]As note 43. Emphasis by present author. On Dr. Luppe see text below and note 55.

[48]Bay. HStA München, M.Inn. 73725, unpaginated collection in rough chronological order. Here, extract from *Fränkische Tagespost*, 29th January 1925.

Gerolzhofen in April 1923, though the official report notes only that a subsequent Jewish "information meeting" passed off without disturbance.[49] The identity of the disruptors of the first meeting, and the protectors of the second, was not revealed.

A unique witness to these issues is provided by Meyers for the years of the second Nazi organisational breakthrough from 1925 on. She mentions a place identifying it only as "J", which she describes as a "stronghold of antisemitic activities". This was probably a small Franconian town in Streicher's sphere of influence. There "Jewish businessmen, who were not at all rich, provided uniforms for the local branch of the *Reichsbanner* and looked after the unemployed". Before the founding of the *Reichsbanner* the Jews had "not dared to venture onto the streets after nightfall, or to go to an ale-house etc.", but now the situation was changed as a result of the co-operation of Jews and workers. However, this could not be discussed freely, for "when brought out into the open, [it] disgraced the organisations concerned . . ."[50]

When co-operating more or less openly, organisations such as the *Reichsbanner*, the C.V. and R.j.F. (and possibly the Zionists – see below) provided rich material for anti-Republican and antisemitic propagandists. Moreover, in Bavaria (and later elsewhere) the government insisted on treating the *Reichsbanner* as a "political" organisation[51] and subjecting it to close observation, as if it were a mere Social Democratic Party association. Consequently, the police did not hesitate to vent its suspicion that these signs of resistance in Gerolzhofen, and later in "J", were inspired from either Nuremberg or Würzburg Left-wing and Jewish circles.

In Würzburg a local branch of the *Republikanische Beschwerdestelle e.V.*, Berlin, had been established to keep watch over the constitutional conduct of civil servants and government offices. Its submissions and questions made life so uncomfortable for the organs of government that in Württemberg, for example, its complaints were not answered at all, on instructions from above.[52] Particular suspicion was aroused by the Berlin branch[53] and by the Würzburg Secretary Alfred Semank. In addition to all his constitutional interpellations, Semank was also Chairman of the Würzburg district of the *Reichsbanner* and Party Secretary of the DDP. "Semank also worked in co-operation with organisations such as the SPD, Republican youth associations . . . *Republikanischer Reichsbund, Reichsbund jüdischer Frontsoldaten*". As far as the Munich government was concerned, these

---

[49]Bay. HStA München, M.Inn. 73725. Report by Bezirks-Amt Gerolzhofen to Regierungs-Präsident, Würzburg, 5th January 1924.

[50]The whole description of "J" in Julie Meyers, 'Jewish Anti-Defamation Work', *loc. cit.*, pp. 24–25.

[51]On the basis of paragraphs 36 and 37 of the *Wehrgesetz*, as explained by the *Reichskommissar* for the Maintenance of Public Order, according to decision 196.7.24 of 5th August 1924. On the same day the *Deutscher Republikanischer Reichsbund* was also so classified. Dates given in Staatsarchiv (StA) München, Pol. Dir. 6899, Bl.2, V&R.

[52]An entire file on its *Beschwerdestelle* (complaints office), Deutsches Zentralarchiv (now Bundesarchiv Abt.) (ZA) Potsdam, RMdI (15.01)/25668/13. On the Würzburg branch see text and note 56 below.

[53]Developed in 1923 from a youth group called *Republikanischer Jugendbund Schwarz-Rot-Gold* and headed by Alfred Falk, called Cohn by the Nazis. He had to flee Germany early in 1933. ZA (BA Abt.) Potsdam, as in note 52, and *ibid.*, file no. 13193, fols. 218, 253.

activities were tantamount to hostility to the state.[54] Out of a similar bias, the above mentioned Nuremberg Mayor Luppe was also faced with great difficulties,[55] and like most of the politicians to the Left of the *Zentrumspartei* and the BVP, he was virtually accused of being a Communist. A similar mentality had already been demonstrated in the police reports of the North German city of Bremen. What makes Würzburg interesting, however, is the fact that it was the only place in Bavaria where there was a personal union between leadership of the *Reichsbanner* and membership of the R.j.F. In Würzburg there occurred another incident which has not been documented anywhere else in Germany. According to a police informer's report, at a joint meeting of the Würzburg Jewish community's board and the C.V. on 20th November 1930, the decision was taken to found a purely Jewish self-defence section, because the *Reichsbanner* and SPD could "not offer" adequate protection. Only one participant, a member of the *Reichsbanner*, opposed the decision, but was unable to prevent it from being implemented. On that same evening, ten men registered for the section,[56] although nothing more has transpired on its activities.

In all, these observations lead to the conclusion that co-operation between the *Reichsbanner* and R.j.F. and/or C.V. was much more the exception than the rule. In this sense, Julie Meyers's memoir sums it up by stating that open co-operation between the two sides was apt to heap "disgrace" on both sides.[57] Furthermore, while the leaders of the Jewish organisations were unable to restrain their overemphasis on patriotic loyalty which had been instilled into them, the members of the *Reichsbanner* found it extremely difficult to curb their long-standing anti-Jewish prejudices.

VI

The Federal Chairman of the *Reichsbanner*, *Regierungspräsident* Otto Hörsing in Magdeburg, was a man completely without personal prejudice who had proved his immunity to antisemitism on more than one occasion. Therefore, it appears to have been more than mere lip-service, when the founding-manifesto of the *Reichsbanner*[58] castigated those "cantankerous demagogues, who . . . hide their

---

[54]Bay. HStA München, M.Inn. 73725, 'Lagebericht', undated [1925], unpaginated. The bias of the quotation against all these organisations is almost lost in the translation.

[55]StA München, Pol. Dir. 6899. Extract from 'Lagebericht' Nr. 820/II of 5th February 1925, Bl. 3: "It is a considerable loss for the *Reichsbanner* that Mayor Dr. Luppe wishes to withdraw from any public activity for the *Reichsbanner* till further notice." The cause was certainly that – like leading Republicans (Scheidemann, Walter Loeb etc.) – he was embroiled in a trumped-up perjury trial. A libel suit that had been forced upon the first *Präsident* of the Republic, Friedrich Ebert, had heralded the struggle against Social Democracy at the judicial level and belongs to the pre-history of the *Reichsbanner*. A central, if not very successful, part of the defensive work of the *Reichsbanner* was a series of trials involving Otto Hörsing (re: Oskar Hamburger and esp. the Haas-Helling affair), Geheimes Staatsarchiv (Geh.StA) Dahlem, Rep. 84a, 11764; Historische Kommission, (HiKo) Berlin, Nl, Hörsing, maps 19, 21.

[56]Bay. HStA München, M. Inn. 73725, Pol. Dir. Würzburg, 28th November 1930.

[57]Julie Meyers, 'Jewish Anti-Defamation Work', *loc. cit.*, pp. 23ff.

[58]*Vorwärts*, 30th March 1924; *Das Reichsbanner*, No. 1 (15th April 1924).

own guilt and their clandestine designs behind disgraceful Jew-baiting". The declaration expressly mentioned the Jewish comrades among the fallen and wounded of the First World War, concluding that "this stupid antisemitism . . . is ridiculous and . . . constitutes a danger for German internal and external policy". Some of these blunt expressions may well have come out of Hörsing's arsenal, for he never minced his words. Moreover, he chose as one of his confidantes the Jewish merchant Paul Crohn from Magdeburg[59] and had him appointed Federal Treasurer of the organisation.

However, there is no evidence that a Jewish treasurer had the ability to mobilise more Jewish money than a non-Jewish one. There even seems to have been very little material help from another of Hörsing's intimates in Magdeburg, namely Felix Heimann, the Jewish lawyer and secretary of the C.V. In the province of Saxony, Heimann was appointed to the *Bundesleitung* (federal leadership) of the *Reichsbanner* without actually being a member of the association – a fact which was quickly picked up and publicised by a Bavarian news-gathering intelligence unit of the German army.[60] From 1926 Heimann, who was extremely well-informed and active in Jewish affairs, edited a *Jüdisches Wochenblatt* which was openly sympathetic to the *Reichsbanner*,[61] but could do no more for it.

Paul Crohn was less involved in Jewish life than Heimann, but more committed to the *Reichsbanner*. He typified what has already been stated on the links between the *Reichsbanner* and Jewish organisations, especially in cities with a relatively large Jewish population (around 3,000 Jews lived in Magdeburg in 1925): everywhere *Reichsbanner* offices received a great deal of printed material about Jewish defence, but little in the way of hard cash.

Specifically in Berlin – Germany's biggest Jewish community – there seems to have been no link at all between Jewish organisations and the forerunners of the *Reichsbanner*. For their part, those Jews who were active in the early Republican associations did not tend to join purely Jewish organisations. As an example of this tendency one may adduce the Democratic youth associations of Berlin. In 1921/1922 they had united in the *Reichsorganisation der deutsch-demokratischen Jugend*, working hard to include all the forces from the *Windthorst-Bund* to the *Mehrheits-SPD* youth. Especially after the murder of Rathenau, the organisation was prepared to give full support to the government and even to Chancellor Wirth personally.[62] From our point of view, the significant fact is that these forces, paving the way for the non-partisan *Reichsbanner*, did not appear from the records

---

[59]On him see Rohe, *Das Reichsbanner*, *op. cit.*, *passim*, index.

[60]StA München, as note 51, Bl.5, V&R, under the handwritten heading: 'Von der Reichswehr zusammengestellt'.

[61]Full title: *Jüdisches Wochenblatt für Magdeburg und Umgebung*. The paper is rare today. In Nl Hörsing (HiKo Berlin), Mappe 22 is deposited the edition of 12th August 1927 with Heimann's eulogy of Hörsing on his retirement as *Oberpräsident* of the province of Saxony.

[62]Bundesarchiv (BA) Koblenz, R 43 I/2661, for example Bl. 18 V&R. It should be pointed out that Wirth, and the Christian unions, actually had much sympathy for the *Reichsbanner* and occasionally took part in *Reichsbanner* gatherings. The opposition in the *Zentrumspartei* was concentrated initially round Wilhelm Marx during his Chancellorship. Two subsequent centres of opposition appear to have emerged in the Upper Silesian Centre Party (*Kreuzschar*) and in Württemberg.

to include any Jews in significant positions. Moreover, Jewish sources took no notice of them whatsoever.

In short, in Berlin the picture is that of a complete dichotomy. On the one hand, Jewish organisations made preparations to defend themselves on their own initiative;[63] and on the other, Jewish Social Democrats took a very active part in the work which led to the founding of the *Reichsbanner*. Erich Kuttner is an excellent example of a Jewish Social Democrat who had been involved in organising war-veterans from an early stage (1916),[64] but belonged to the second rank of the party rather than to its leadership.[65] Kuttner, who since 1924 also worked on the *Reichsbanner* newspaper, was not a member of its governing board but only of the *Reichsausschuß*; this rather unwieldy and inert body contained – alongside two members from the *Zentrumspartei* – several other Jewish members, particularly the Democrats Ludwig Haas and Theodor Wolff, Georg Bernhard and Dr. K. Simon.[66] The Berliners among them were not prominent in either the R.j.F. or the C.V.

From Berlin, we know of only two examples where leading members of Jewish organisations also played parts in the *Reichsbanner* and the SPD. One, Art[h]ur Schweriner, seems originally to have been close to the DDP[67] and appeared as an active representative of the central Berlin apparatus of the C.V. in various provinces, especially during elections.[68] For a number of years he was a speaker at *Reichsbanner* meetings. Within the C.V., Schweriner advocated a switch to "educational work for an *effect on the masses*",[69] using the blunt propaganda techniques of the extreme Right – jokes, cartoons, satire – in order to "raise the alarm" among the population. *Alarm* was the name he later gave to the satirical

---

[63]See Dunker, *Der Reichsbund jüdischer Frontsoldaten, op. cit.*, for the period 1919–1923, also the description in Hebrew by Jacob Toury, 'Self-Improvement and Self-Defence', in *Yalqut Moreshet*, 42 (1986).

[64]Rohe, *Das Reichsbanner, op. cit.*, p. 126, mentions the first initiative of the war veterans Friedrich Stampfer, Erich Kuttner *et al.*, who in autumn 1916 recognised the "need for organisation" of the returning soldiers. In 1919 Kuttner was a company commander in the *Regiment "Reichstag"*, afterwards editor of the party press, member of the Prussian *Landtag* etc. Yet he was never in the first rank of the party. See also note 65 below.

[65]On Kuttner see Bart de Cort, *'Was ich will, soll Tat werden' – Erich Kuttner 1887–1942. Ein Leben für Freiheit und Recht*. Hrsg. vom Bezirksamt Tempelhof, Berlin 1990.

[66]Membership list of the governing board (*Bundesvorstand*), mostly Magdeburg men, on first page of *Das Reichsbanner*, 15th April 1924. Names of the members of the *Reichsausschuß* were published in subsequent issues of the paper.

[67]For details see Arnold Paucker, *Der jüdische Abwehrkampf gegen Antisemitismus und Nationalsozialismus in den letzten Jahren der Weimarer Republik*, Hamburg 1968, pp. 120–121, 160–161; and on Art[h]ur Schweriner see now, *idem* 'Self-Defence Against Fascism in a Middle-Class Community: The Jews in Weimar Germany and Beyond', in *Germans against Nazism. Non-conformity, Opposition and Resistance in the Third Reich. Essays in Honour of Peter Hoffmann*, ed. by Francis R. Nicosia and Lawrence Stokes, Oxford 1990, pp. 59–60, 72; see also Niewyk, *Socialist, op. cit.*, pp. 140–150, and the sources in note 68 below.

[68]Thus in the election in Upper Silesia (autumn 1924) he worked i.a. with Ernst Behrendt-Beuthen, active in the local *Reichsbanner*-leadership, also a committee member of the C.V. and secretary of the union of white-collar workers. The local youth group of the *Kameraden* seems also to have been roped in for electioneering purposes. *C.V.-Zeitung* (1924), pp. 588–589.

[69]*C.V.-Zeitung*, Nr. 3 (1924), leading article, signed Artur Schweriner. Emphasis by present author.

paper[70] published and edited by him from 1929, which was close to the SPD but also accepted funds indirectly from the C.V. Though Niewyk maintains that Schweriner gave up his offices in the C.V., this is not confirmed by the reports of the *C.V.-Zeitung* or by other sources.[71] On the other hand, the C.V. failed to provide unequivocal support for Schweriner's move to the Left; even in May 1931, a young Social Democrat was forced to give an apologetic answer in the *C.V.-Zeitung* to the question whether a Social Democrat could or should be a member of the C.V.[72] The group round Schweriner in the C.V. was apparently neither numerous nor influential.

As regards the Berlin *Reichsbund jüdischer Frontsoldaten*, it is clear that this branch behaved with considerably more caution than those in Bremen, Hamburg, Würzburg (and possibly other areas for which details are lacking, such as Cologne and smaller towns). This can be explained by the desire of the Berlin governing board to maintain strict adherence to its own guidelines for the activity of the organisation, whose last paragraph reads as follows (§3):[73]

> "On questions of internal Jewish policy, of internal *German* policy, of religion, the *Frontsoldaten-bund* adopts no position, it therefore also *rejects any activity* in the above-named directions."

So far as can be judged, the Berlin leaders of the R.j.F. had no links with the forerunners of the *Reichsbanner* nor with the *Reichsbanner* formations themselves. Any practical measures of self-defence that they took were adopted purely on their own initiative and with the more or less active involvement of other Jewish associations.[74] Thus, it seems quite obvious that a Communist agent, probably from Munich, fell victim to over-eagerness when in his report for the year 1925 he stressed the collective affiliation of the whole R.j.F. with the *Reichsbanner*: "den . . . korporativen Übertritt des Bundes 'Jüdischer Frontsoldaten' mit 48,000 Mitgliedern".[75] Also later, despite the few exceptions mentioned above, the Berlin board of the R.j.F. remained aloof.

The Zionists also attempted to go it alone in resisting the threat of pogroms, although they were possibly the first major Jewish organisation trying to do so.[76] It appears that Alfred Klee was given the "defence portfolio" not only in the

[70]The first issue of *Alarm* (now very difficult to trace) of 1st November 1929 can be found in Hauptstaatsarchiv (HStA) Düsseldorf, Reg. Aachen/23763.

[71]In 1932 the *C.V.-Zeitung* calls him the "deputy legal adviser" and even "*Landesverband* legal adviser" (Leipzig), so that Niewyk's remark that he had left active Jewish work in favour of the *Reichsbanner* appears incorrect.

[72]Heinz Cohn, in *C.V.-Zeitung*, 29th January 1931.

[73]ZA Potsdam, 75 Ge 1/601, Bl. 2 (from the former *Gesamtarchiv der deutschen Juden*). Emphasis by present author.

[74]Apart from the "AB" mentioned above, this refers particularly to the defence measures in November 1923 and the attempts of 1927 to create an all-Jewish defensive organisation "JAD". See Dunker, *Der Reichsbund jüdischer Frontsoldaten, op. cit.*, *passim*, esp. pp. 63–64.

[75]IfGA II 1131, Bl. 2–12: "Von Gröhl auf seiner Schreibmaschine geschrieben (1. Februar 1924)". Spelling mistakes being disregarded by the present author, except for the membership of 48,000, which should probably read: 18,000.

[76]See the unsigned report of March 1920 in Central Zionist Archives (CZA) Jerusalem, NL Klee, A-142/87/40. Dunker also believes that this report from the days of the Kapp Putsch was written by Klee himself. Two years later Klee travelled to Beuthen during the excesses there in autumn 1923. Source for the last point: Toury, 'Self-Improvement', *loc. cit.*

Berlin association but in the entire *Zionistische Vereinigung für Deutschland* (ZVfD). In fact, Klee was another of those few Berlin Jewish leaders who later moved towards the SPD and the *Reichsbanner*. He was previously known for his orientation to the Right of Centre, but since the days of the Kapp Putsch and the threat of pogroms, in his anxiety over the safety of the Jews he had undergone a significant change of attitude. During the pogrom-scare in the days of Kapp, he had used his relations with Fritz Rathenau in the Ministry of the Interior in order to establish contact with Berlin police headquarters. On the other hand, he did not neglect to make use of his personal acquaintance with the Left-wing Socialist Oscar Cohn in order to keep himself informed about the situation in the country. Eventually the acute danger of pogroms receded as the Kapp Putsch collapsed. As a result, the tentative attempts of 1920 by an all-Jewish committee to construct a joint defence organisation also came to an end.[77] But it is significant that Klee remained convinced by his impressions gained during the Putsch that "the workers, where they could, opposed all such [anti-Jewish] endeavours". He therefore strengthened his links with Social Democracy and also began to appear as a lawyer for Left-wing defendants. The most notorious case involved a certain Georg Sklarz who, alongside his other businesses,[78] had organised guard services to protect against plundering in Berlin since the end of 1919. During the Spartacist disturbances Sklarz helped to feed and pay the *Republikanisches Regiment Reichstag* and also provided important assistance to the *Mehrheits*-SPD. He was also a personal friend of Philipp Scheidemann.[79]

During the Sklarz trial, the defence lawyer, Dr. Klee, was actually arrested for three days (16th-19th August 1924) for refusing to reveal the whereabouts of the accused. This traumatic experience of the manipulation of the judicial system by the Nationalists ended any remaining sympathy Klee might have felt for the Right-wing parties.[80] Later, when trials of Jews who had emigrated from the East began to increase, these were exploited for propaganda against the *Reichsbanner* – a fact which must have greatly distressed Klee and other members of the Republican organisation, who were abused as "Barmatrepublikaner" and followers of the "Sklarekbanner".[81]

Klee's transition to the SPD and the *Reichsbanner* was made easier because the first public appearance of the new Republican defence organisation coincided with a change in the policy of the ZVfD. Under the influence of Kurt Blumenfeld, this organisation had begun to assert an unequivocally Palestine-centred policy and was tending to abandon domestic tasks, including defence

[77]NL Klee, as in previous note, p. 4.
[78]Trude Maurer, *Ostjuden in Deutschland 1918–1933*, Hamburg 1986, p. 141, though the description is based upon extracts from antisemitic sources. Therefore see also the following note.
[79]To verify the account the *Schwäbische Tagwacht* of 28th January 1920, edited by the young Kurt Schumacher, was used and Maurer's arguments softened.
[80]For the whole affair, trial and arrest, CZA, A–142/24/15–20. The comments in the text are based on a report in the *Jüdisches Echo*, XI (1924), pp. 235–236, which may be quoted here because of its condemning that ". . . major attack on the position of the defender" with its rather striking argument: "We have not heard, for example, that the defenders of the 'wanted man' Lieutenant Erhardt have been taken into detention as accessories." In a later number of the *Echo* it was reported that incapacitation proceedings were under way against the arresting *Landgerichtsrat*.
[81]*Völkischer Beobachter*, 27th/28th September 1925; 20th/21st December 1931.

against antisemitic attacks. But active defence was a central concern of Klee and the *Jüdische Volkspartei* he had founded. Thus, the hope for understanding from the Left strengthened him in his "affiliation to Social Democracy" and his "active work with the *Reichsbanner*".[82]

Moreover, Klee's son-in-law was Hans Goslar,[83] a *Regierungsrat* and later *Ministerialrat* in the Prussian government, who was also a *Reichsbanner* activist. Of course, Klee (who was about 50 years old) and his intellectual son-in-law did not march with the crowds or do field exercises. Yet Klee's legal knowledge, and his work as *Syndikus* of the *Schutzverband deutscher Schriftsteller*,[84] may have been almost as important to the *Reichsbanner* and its writers (many of whom were Jewish[85]) as the central position of Hans Goslar in the Prussian Ministry of State.

VII

From the outset, the problem of the relationship of Jews and the *Reichsbanner* was characterised by a certain contradiction. On both the intellectual and the financial level, Jews took a not insignificant place among the contributors to the organisation; their presence in the ranks, however, despite exceptions such as the Hamburg *Kameradschaften* Nos. 7 and 8, was often missing.

The writings of Jewish intellectuals in the periodicals and pamphlets of the *Reichsbanner* were of only marginal interest to the enemies of the Jews. Thus, it was not widely known that one of the youngest activists of the Berlin C.V., Alfred Hirschberg, had written an anonymous pamphlet for the *Reichsbanner*, entitled *The True Face of National Socialism*, which went through two editions, or even more.[86]

In stressing Jewish literary activity for the *Reichsbanner*, and especially Jewish contributions to the funds of its defence sections,[87] it is important not to fall prey to an inverted form of the mania for exaggeration which characterised the

---

[82]Testimony of Georg Kareski at his trial in Jerusalem, Central Archives for the History of the Jewish People (CAHJP), J-m, p. 82/24 b, Bl.l. Later Klee seems to have considered seeking an SPD-candidature for the Prussian *Landtag*. See Ernest Hamburger and Peter Pulzer, 'Jews as Voters in the Weimar Republic', in *LBI Year Book XXX* (1985), p. 64.

[83]On Goslar see Trude Maurer, 'Auch ein Weg als Deutscher und Jude – Hans Goslar', in Julius H. Schoeps (ed.), *Juden als Träger bürgerlicher Kultur in Deutschland*, Stuttgart–Bonn 1989, pp. 193–239.

[84]Polit. Archiv AA Bonn, Rep. Presse-Abtlg. P 20, vol. 1, L1418/378225, 378448.

[85]Of Jewish workers for the newsapers and other publications of the *Reichsbanner*, only those names encountered during the preparation of this article are listed herewith: Arthur Silbergleit, Theodor Wolff, Samuel Bergner, Hans Goslar, Artur Schweriner, Otto Landsberg, Friedrich Stampfer, Erich Kuttner, Ludwig Wronkow, Erich Kaiser. The last two names have been added through the good offices of Mrs. Christa Wichmann, Chief Librarian of the Wiener Library, London, to whom I am grateful for her patient assistance.

[86]See note 87, and Niewyk, *Socialist, op. cit.*, pp. 129–130, 191, who speaks of one or two leaflets by Hirschberg in 1929. However, I was able to locate only the second edition of the anonymous piece (Magdeburg 1928). Perhaps a third edition appeared in 1929?

[87]On the latter theme Hirschberg, in the 'Notizen über die C.V.-Arbeit', an unpubl. ms. in Leo Baeck Institute, London, gives a German translation of Julie Meyers's already quoted observations on the local contributions, and adds: "To me it seems impossible to give even a rough figure." (But millions it surely was not! J.T.)

propaganda of the Radical Right in its efforts to demonise the "black-red-mustard Jew-protectors". This caption appeared in a Munich Nazi newspaper[88] shortly after the Bavarian Held government had permitted the Nazis to resume political activity. The article under the insulting headline contains the argument – so often repeated in Bavaria and other German states – that the *Reichsbanner* was simply a "Social Democratic Party organisation to protect the big capital of the exploiters – in short, the Jews . . ."[89] Perhaps this explains the necessity, even today – of listing the Jewish contributors' names in the "national" press during the years of Weimar and to examine the weight of their contribution wherever possible.

As has briefly been mentioned, the owners of two Bremen department stores were among the first to be named as donors to the local *Reichsbanner*. To this category of "department store owners", a Communist list later added "Jewish owners of big gents' and ladies' outfitters" of Stettin, whose names, however, were withheld.[90] The only name published in this connection was that of "department store owner Tietz", and since there were several people of this name in that line of business,[91] the detail was uninformative.

More specific were rumours from Hamburg, according to which the Warburgs, and even Carl J. Melchior, had been generous contributors. However, the only written evidence links the *Bankhaus Warburg* with another Jewish financier, the founder and first President of the Thuringia State Bank, Walter Loeb, who had assisted the *Reichsbanner* with donations "until recently"; before being forced to resign in September 1924 by the Right-wing-sponsored government of Thuringia. The latter (Communist) source[92] even names a figure for the Warburg donation – 100,000 RM; Loeb's share was not mentioned because it probably was very much less than this round sum. Yet even before these names were mentioned the source listed the *Reichsbund jüdischer Frontsoldaten* as one of the "main supporters" of the movement to "combat Communism and antisemitism", though without naming the amount of money it was supposed to have contributed; appearing in fifth place on the list, the R.j.F. was the very first Jewish organisation to be mentioned. Inevitably, the impression was created that the R.j.F. was making large donations to *Reichsbanner* funds.[92] In the early days this may indeed have been the case in Bremen and/or Hamburg as a response to local developments; elsewhere, particularly in Berlin and smaller towns, moderate sums may have been paid from time to time in return for the

[88]*Der Nationalsozialist*, Nr. 3 (29th November 1924). Press-cutting in StA München, Pol. Dir. 6889, Bl.34.

[89]*Der Nationalsozialist*, Nr. 3, as in note 88.

[90]First source: outlines for indoctrination of the *Roter Frontkämpferbund* in StA München, Pol.Dir. 6889, Bl. 6–29.

[91]BA Koblenz, R 134/36, Bl.42, paras. 3, 4.

[92]Quoted in: StA München, Pol.Dir. 6889, Bl. 6–29. Also oral information kindly added by Dr. Ursula Büttner of the *Forschungsstelle für die Geschichte des Nationalsozialismus in Hamburg*. However, Dr. Büttner also mentioned that Fritz Warburg and Carl Melchior "gave money to the Right too". See also below in text and note 102.

[93]This Communist "information" precedes the rumours on a collective entry of the R.j.F. into the *Reichsbanner*. See above note 75.

despatch of *Reichsbanner* units to protect meetings.[94] However, the generalisations of both Right- and Left-wing sources can only be regarded as attempts at deliberate political manipulation.

In fact, a *Reichswehr* intelligence agency in Bavaria manipulated the above report on the R.j.F. too obviously: on 10th April 1925, it mentioned in a short summary on the *Reichsbanner* (point 3):

> "Sources of money *for the most part Jewish*. Significant participation by *C.V. deutscher Staatsb. jüd. Gl.*"[95]

As this piece of disinformation demonstrates beyond any doubt, many of the other claims were inaccurate too. Moreover, until 1928, the C.V.-clause dealing with grants by that association ensured, as mentioned above, that every donation had to be used directly to combat antisemitism. Only in 1929, when the C.V. established a special office to direct the fight against National Socialism – the *Büro Wilhelmstraße* – was it able to operate with more freedom.[96]

As the *Reichsbanner* Chairman, Otto Hörsing, "openly admitted", this did not prevent him and his local commanders from applying for aid to "financially powerful circles, 'including Jews and Jewish organisations' ".[97] And indeed, regional and local committees occasionally directed their requests for assistance "to the industrialists and businessmen" of their areas; these were then not infrequently publicised by newspapers of the extreme Right and Left in order to disparage the *Reichsbanner* by citing the names of Jewish addressees.[98] Karl Rohe is therefore correct to stress the fact that in the case of "collections and contributions . . . by pro-Republican circles in the wholesale trade and among merchants . . . it was quite often a question of Jewish donors, who were sometimes linked in business to the *Reichsbanner* as suppliers". But he dismisses the widespread rumours about donations by "big-money earners of the inflation", such as "Michel (meaning Jakob Michael), Parvus-Helphand, the Barmats, and the Sklarek firm" as "not verifiable in individual cases", confining them to the sphere of "hostile" claims.[99] Certainly such rumours were spread with ill intent – for which we may cite the maliciously formulated claim of *Die Zeit* that *Ostjuden* were a main source of contributions to the *Reichsbanner*.[100] Yet

[94]Rohe, *Das Reichsbanner*, *op. cit.*, p. 76, note 4: "Frequently the *Reichsbanner* requested a small financial *quid pro quo* when tasks of hall protection were requested."

[95]StA München, Pol.Dir. 6889, Bl. 5, extract from a report dated 10th April 1925, handwritten title: 'Von der Reichswehr zusammengestellt'. Abbreviation as in original. Emphasis by present author.

[96]See Paucker, *Der jüdische Abwehrkampf*, *op. cit.*, pp. 110–129. In his book Paucker deals in detail with the co-operation between the *Reichsbanner* and the C.V. in the last years of the Weimar Republic.

[97]Rohe, *Das Reichsbanner*, *op. cit.*, p. 76, note 6 quoting (*Illustrierte*) *RB-Zeitung*, 1st November 1924.

[98]For instance: circular of *Gauvorstand* Groß Berlin–Brandenburg, quoted in the "outlines" contained in StA München, Pol.Dir. 6889, Bl. 6–29; petition from Mönchen-Gladbach was cited in *Völkischer Beobachter*, 5th December 1930; ditto from Kaiserslautern, *Völkischer Beobachter*, 31st July 1929. See also form-letter of Hörsing himself "An Fa. . . ." (request for funds for an officers' training school): DZA Potsdam, RMdI (15.01)/25668–10, Bl. 175 seq. (February 1929).

[99]Rohe, *Das Reichsbanner*, *op. cit.*, p. 76, note 3 with sources.

[100]Quoted from *Vorwärts*, 3rd January 1925, in Niewyk, *Socialist*, *op. cit.*, p. 67, note 5. *Die Zeit* was then close to the *Deutsche Volkspartei* of Stresemann (DVP) but quickly moved further to the Right.

there may have been some factual substance behind some of the rumours.[101] Thus there was even a grain of truth in the cynical and malicious remarks of the commentator in *Das Landvolk* when he surveyed the position of Jewish donations in 1931:

> "The frightened Jews, the men of finance, are paying large sums, and – however grotesque it sounds – to the most diverse parties . . . The monies are certainly a form of insurance to cover every eventuality."[102]

These words probably depict the disposition of large parts of German Jewry in the last phase of the Weimar Republic much more accurately than in the formative years of the *Reichsbanner*.[103] Before things came to such a pass, the *Reichsbanner* had been given some five years to consolidate itself and to prove its value as a stabilising influence in the struggle against Right-wing extremism and antisemitism. From the viewpoint of the Jewish situation in Germany during these years, it may be worthwhile to examine various aspects of the work of the *Reichsbanner* more closely, and to devote particular attention to the problems which eventually doomed it to failure.[104]

---

[101]For instance: on 30th September 1930 *Der Tag* described the *Deutscher Automobil Club*, set up by the *Reichsbanner*, as a Left-wing paramilitary "transport organisation" dependent "on Mosse's grace". This was an exaggeration, but justified to the extent that it could withstand a possible *Preßprozess*.

[102]*Das Landvolk*, Nr. 33 (9th February 1931), examined in DZA Potsdam, RMdI 25965, Bl. 199. And see above note 92, for the comment by Dr. Büttner.

[103]See Jacob Toury, 'Gab es ein Krisenbewußtsein unter den Juden während der "Guten Jahre" der Weimarer Republik 1924–1929?' in *Tel Aviver Jahrbuch für deutsche Geschichte*, XVII (1988), pp. 145–168.

[104]For a shorter German version of my essay see Jacob Toury, 'Die Judenfrage in der Entstehungsphase des Reichsbanners Schwarz-Rot-Gold', in Ludger Heid and Arnold Paucker (eds.), *Juden und deutsche Arbeiterbewegung bis 1933. Soziale Utopien und religiös-kulturelle Traditionen*, Tübingen 1992 (Schriftenreihe wissenschaftlicher Abhandlungen des Leo Baeck Instituts 49).

History through the Book

The Zionist Project in the Palestine Travel Writings of German-speaking Jews

BY WOLF KAISER

"For 40 years, since Ludwig August Frankl's journey to Jerusalem, no book in German that describes journeys to the Promised Land has been published from the Jewish point of view."[1] This statement is put forward by Willy Bambus in the preface of his travel book about his journey to Palestine in 1895.

Thirty years later the publisher Felix Weltsch noted: "The public's demand for Palestine reports seems to be satisfied."[2]

Indeed, a lot of German-Jewish travel books had been written during these decades and in spite of Weltsch's statement – also to be found in a description of a journey, of course – many others were to follow during the thirties.

Altogether 38 descriptions of visits in or journeys through Palestine by Jewish authors writing in German were published as books or booklets by various publishers in the forty years before the Second World War. Furthermore, a lot of articles were published in journals and newspapers. They, however, are not considered here. The fact that an average of almost one book a year written from a Jewish point of view was presented to the public, mainly to a specifically Jewish public, shows a very lively interest in this subject. In reality the publications are, of course, not so evenly distributed over this period. In 1925/1926 for example, following the first successes of Zionist settlement, six books were published, whereas there was only one during the years of crisis at the end of the twenties. This distribution is not accidental, because the interest of the Jewish visitors to the Holy Land is mainly directed towards the Zionist project, whatever the difference in their views might be. Their books are part of a controversial and vivid discussion within German-speaking Jewry about *Eretz Israel* and Zionism. Contrary to other contributors to this discussion the travellers refer to their personal experiences in the country and integrate their opinions, feelings and concepts into their descriptions and reports.

There are various factors that greatly shape the writers' perception of Palestine and its inhabitants. The selection of what is seen and the emotional attitude towards it are determined by their deep-rooted religious and political orientation, and they are also influenced by present experiences both at home and during the visits to Palestine. Therefore, these books have to be seen against a

---

[1] Willy Bambus, *Palästina. Land und Leute. Reiseschilderungen*, Berlin 1898, p. 5. Bambus was a merchant and editor of journals, who as a member of the *Hibbat Zion* movement ardently promoted Jewish settlements in Palestine.

[2] Felix Weltsch, *Land der Gegensätze. Eindrücke einer Palästinareise*, Prague 1929, p. 3.

double background: the social and cultural situation of German-speaking Jewry in its numerous factions and the state of Palestine's Jewish population, especially of the Zionist project, as well.

It is not surprising that Palestine is described in most of the books from the Zionist point of view, but there are also several authors with an Orthodox religious outlook and others whose patterns of interpretation and judgements are determined by their German patriotic opinions. The Jewish-Orthodox travel books in some respects follow the patterns of Christian reports on pilgrimage. Interest in Jewish monuments predominates, but there are also descriptions of the institutions and facilities of the Orthodox Jews in the "Old *Yishuv*", a term which distinguishes the community of the native Palestinian Jews and of the Orthodox Jews who had immigrated for religious reasons, from the "New *Yishuv*" of the Jewish settlers. The Orthodox travellers see the Jewishness of the "Old *Yishuv*" as the real representatives of Jewry in Palestine.

The Zionist view is focused on the "New *Yishuv*" and in particular on the agrarian settlements of the Jews. According to certain patterns of interpretation and argumentation the texts can be related to different factions in Zionism. But one thesis can be found in the books of *Allgemeine Zionisten* and Revisionists, of religious Zionists and followers of *Arbeiterzionismus*: the assumption that the very nature of the land and the people of Israel makes them depend on each other for their prosperity and the expectation that they would "redeem" each other. Signs of such a redemption heighten the travellers' enthusiasm – an enthusiasm they also try to convey to the reader.

The authors belonging to the *Centralverein deutscher Staatsbürger jüdischen Glaubens* (C.V.), did not share this enthusiasm. On the contrary, their reports from the twenties aim at creating or maintaining the reader's emotional detachment from the Zionist project. Their view is focused on the economic, cultural and political conflicts in Palestine. In their opinion these conflicts could only be resolved by giving up all political aims when supporting Jewish settlement in Palestine. They were afraid that the status of the German Jews as members of the German nation could be endangered if they supported colonisation in *Eretz Israel* which the public generally identified with Jewish-national aspirations. The views of this Jewish faction changed, after the German Jews had lost their rights as German citizens during the Nazi period anyway: the *Yishuv* was now considered as a potential centre of Jewish life even by officials of the C.V.[3] Thus their position comes to resemble the Zionist point of view, that Palestine is central for Jewish history, as well as being the centre of the Jewish people's present and future. As a result of the development in Germany in the thirties there was almost no criticism of Zionism any longer within German Jewry, the majority of which had been non- or even anti-Zionist until the end of the twenties. It was not the attractiveness of the Zionist construction of *Eretz Israel*, so enthusiastically described by the Zionist travel books which caused the change in the German Jews' attitude, but the experience of the antisemitic threat. This aspect, however, plays almost no part in the travel books – in contrast to programmatic texts of

[3]Cf. Werner Cahnmann, *Unruhe in Palästina. Reisebericht und Folgerungen aus dem Jahr 1936*, n.p. or d. [Berlin 1936], p. 9.

Zionism and also to Zionist novels – although the legitimation of the Zionist project, in the context of the inner-Jewish debate and directed to a wider public, is one of their most important demands. Rarely is it mentioned that Palestine could provide refuge from persecution. The authors of the travel books never use this argument which, as is well known, has been of considerable importance in the development of Political Zionism and constitutes the core of Zionist argumentation after the Holocaust, in the context of the Arab-Jewish conflict. The reason is that, according to Zionist ideas, immigration into Palestine was an *Aliyah*, an ascent of the Jews to a higher, national form which should be based on conviction, not on compulsion, whatever the circumstances in the countries of birth were. Thus the Zionists who immigrated after 1933 did not see themselves as refugees, but as pioneers of the future; in accordance with this view Palestine never appears as an asylum in the travel books, but as a country which demands sacrifices and also allows self-realisation.

From this viewpoint the authors also describe the life of the Jewish immigrants from Germany and discuss their specific problems and ways of behaviour. Those German Jews, who had decided to immigrate only under the pressure of the Nazi regime and who usually brought with them neither a sufficient knowledge of Hebrew, nor the agricultural or mechanical training needed in Palestine, became a central issue in German-language travel books, whereas in the years before they had only been mentioned sporadically, mainly because of their low numbers. Alfred Wiener states that in 1924/1925 they formed just 1.3 per cent of all Jewish immigrants.[4]

The authors do not assume, however, that all Jews from Germany should or could immigrate to Palestine. The capacity of the country to absorb people was discussed basically in terms of the British mandatory policy, not in terms of saving the German Jews, in spite of the fact that many of their readers were interested in Palestine mainly because of their own personal distress. The writers' main theme is – partly by presenting positive examples – which prerequisites are thought necessary for the potential immigrant to have, in order to integrate successfully into Palestine. Even in a book which already promises asylum in its title, *Palestine. The Permitted Country*, the author Grete Fischer describes the new immigrants from Germany somewhat reprovingly in the following way:

> "Most of them only think of themselves. And only a few have come to realise, how their present and future lives are connected with the security of the new fatherland which they are allowed to enter."[5]

The dominant aspect in the Zionist texts is still the possible contribution to the construction of Jewish Palestine, and not asylum from antisemitic persecution which was Herzl's starting point when he wrote the programme for Political Zionism. Two main factors were seen as a precondition for taking part in the construction of Palestine: on the one hand a shift, particularly from the over-abundant supply of members of the academic profession, to farming or craft

[4]Alfred Wiener, *Kritische Reise durch Palästina*, Berlin 1927 (Jüdische Siedlung und Wirtschaft, I), p. 45.
[5]Joseph Amiel [i.e. Grete Fischer], *Palästina, das erlaubte Land*, Paris 1934, p. 11.

work, and on the other hand the necessity also for a new attitude to physical labour, a change, in fact, in the immigrants' mental and physical habits in accordance with the Zionist image of man.*

Neue Menschen auf alter Erde (new men on ancient soil), that is what the Viennese feuilletonist Felix Salten, Theodor Herzl's friend and his successor at the *Neue Freie Presse*, called his description of a journey to Palestine in 1924.[6] This title is programmatic. His expectation was that the Jews should undergo a radical renewal in Palestine and at the same time preserve tradition.

In his travel book Salten again and again refers to the biblical tradition. His concept is based on a philosophy of history according to which Jewish history can be understood as alternating expulsion from and homecoming to Palestine and Zionist immigration as a contemporary parallel to the homecoming of the people of Israel under the leadership of Moses. He begins the account of his journey with the way through the Sinai and depicts how that great trek through the desert becomes a present-day experience to him. He prudently leaves the reader in the dark about the means of conveyance he used. He certainly did not cross the desert on horseback or on a camel, but took the train from El Kantara to Lydda. For Salten at least as important as the visualisation of Jewish history is the assurance that labour on the "ancient soil" produces "new men", that it will heal "the wounds which have been inflicted a thousandfold upon the Jewish soul and the Jewish mind".[7]

He is not the only one who hopes for a healing renewal of Jewry in Palestine. And this expectation shapes perception as well as the form of that which is perceived in Salten's and in other travel books. When looking at the Jews in Palestine the travellers search for the embodiment of an ideal preconceived before their journeys begin. Against this ideal they evaluate the reality with which they are confronted, or, *vice versa*, they project their ideal values onto the people in Palestine. Thus their descriptions not only teach us something about Palestinian Jews, but at the same time about the ideals of German Jews of differing ideological affiliations, in particular about their ideas regarding the desired changes in life styles and of the qualities thought to be characteristic of Jews.

The origin of the values which are put forward by Jewish travel writers is by no means exclusively Jewish. For some Zionist authors the ideals of the *Jugendbewegung* are very important. To give an example, the *Bericht von der ersten Palästinawanderfahrt* (report of the first walking tour in Palestine), in a passage about a gymnastic display, emphasises "the enjoyment of physical strength and agility"[8]

---

*A comprehensive study on this subject will be published under the title *Palästina – Erez Israel. Deutschsprachige Reisebeschreibungen jüdischer Autoren von der Jahrhundertwende bis zum Zweiten Weltkrieg*, Hildesheim (Schriftenreihe wissenschaftlicher Abhandlungen des Salomon Ludwig Steinheim-Instituts für deutsch-jüdische Geschichte, vol. II).

[6] Felix Salten, *Neue Menschen auf alter Erde. Eine Palästinafahrt*, Berlin–Wien–Leipzig 1909; new edition by Alex Carmel, Königstein/Ts. 1986.

[7] Salten, *op. cit.*, p. 54.

[8] *Bericht der ersten Palästinawanderfahrt zur Orientierung für die nächsten Fahrten*. Mit einem Geleitwort von Dr. Theodor Zlocisti. Herausgegeben vom Comité für Palästinawanderfahrten jüdischer Turner und Studenten, Berlin 1913, p. 7.

as the decisive element which – apart from their Jewish national conviction – unites the participants.

The glorification of physical health and strength is related to the traditional ideal of making the Jews "productive". The demand to assimilate the Jews to the physically labouring sector of the population is already to be found at the end of eighteenth century. At that time David Friedländer prophesied – and he did not intend this statement to be in any way satirical – that an integration into society would make the Jews "more stupid and stronger"[9] and thus suited to military service.

In a description of a journey to Palestine in 1914 one finds a full confirmation of this view. Moses Calvary, a pedagogue, writes:

> "The colonies will easily take care of curing our urban intellectualism. I will never forget the simple and natural pride of a boy from Petach-Tikvah – once a promising student of a *Yeshivah* – who together with some friends at the beginning of the World War immediately decided to volunteer for the Turkish Army and who, noticing my somewhat surprised glance, remarked in almost injured tone, 'I hope you don't think me to be too cowardly to do this!'"[10]

From the Age of Enlightenment and increasingly so since the second half of the nineteenth century, theoretical reflections were complemented by practical endeavours to make the Jews "productive", especially by means of their "return to the soil". These efforts were not very successful in Germany,[11] but in *Eretz Israel* this dream seemed to come true. However, only the Zionists demanded in a programmatic manner that the Jews should become "productive". The Orthodox authors who travelled through Palestine before the First World War, indeed express the hope that Palestine could nourish hundreds of thousands of Jewish farmers[12] and they praise the craft training for young Jews in Jerusalem,[13] but they do not question in any way the contemplative existence of Jews who dedicate their lives to religion. The Zionist authors, however, condemn the *halukka* on which these pious Jews depended, and demand their integration into the developing economic life of the New *Yishuv*.

The urge to work productively, devotion to the soil, and tenacious efforts to construct *Eretz Israel* were considered the main virtues which, in addition to the "love of the Palestinian fatherland", an unbroken self-esteem and the courage to defend oneself, were attributed to, or expected from, the modern Palestinian Jews by Zionist authors. These ideals resulted on the one hand from the Jews' dissatisfaction with their situation in Europe, their being forced by circumstance to conform and to confine themselves to intellectual work. On the other hand, the

---

[9]David Friedländer, *Akten-Stücke die Reform der Jüdischen Kolonien in den Preußischen Staaten betreffend*, Berlin 1793, p. 5, quoted from Wanda Kampmann, *Juden und Deutsche. Die Geschichte der Juden in Deutschland vom Mittelalter bis zum Beginn des Ersten Weltkrieges*, Frankfurt a. Main 1979, p. 114.

[10]Moses Calvary, *Durch Palästina*, Berlin 1920 (Jüdische Jugendbücher, No. 5) (Schriften des Ausschusses für jüdische Kulturarbeit), p. 123.

[11]Cf. the thorough study by Tamar Bermann, *Produktivierungsmythen und Antisemitismus. Eine soziologische Studie*. Wien 1973.

[12]Cf. Wilhelm Reich, *"Misrachah". Nach Osten. Eine jüdische Gesellschaftsreise nach Palästina. Reisebericht*, Frankfurt a. Main 1905, pp. 17f.

[13]Cf. Wilhelm Alexander, *Die Gesellschaftsreise nach Palästina im Jahre 5670–1910*, Sátoraljaujhely 1910, p. 106.

ideals were shaped by the values developing in the New *Yishuv* and propagated by Zionism. The Zionist travellers wanted to find the incorporation of these values among the rural population.

Before the First World War, the existence of the Jewish peasant in Palestine is wished for rather than thought to be a reality. "Peasants with calloused hands and frank faces",[14] admired by an Orthodox traveller in Petach-Tikvah at the beginning of our century are rarely to be found in travel books before the war. The travellers of the 1920s and 1930s, however, find their ideals embodied among the *Chaluzim* working as farmers in the kibbutzim. The answer to the question why people in the countryside are presented as ideals, often to the point of glorification, can be found in the functions Zionist concepts attribute to rural colonisation. Firstly, Zionist authors presume – as already stated in a travel book dating from before the First World War – "that the core of Jewish colonisation in Palestine has to be a Jewish peasantry".[15] Later, when the striving for hegemony in Palestine reaches a climax, the meaning of this phrase is expressed more clearly. In the thirties, Hugo Herrmann, a Zionist journalist and propagandist of the *Keren Hayesod*, repeatedly emphasises that the peasant is always "the master of the land"[16] and that a swift development of Jewish cities and city districts alone cannot turn Palestine into a Jewish country, if the village remains Arab. Then, too, Zionist travel descriptions voice the opinion that – sociologically speaking – the Jewish people are incomplete and therefore sick. The cure is seen in the creation of a class of labouring peasants.[17] The third and dominant motive for glorifying country life is the idea that by "returning to the soil" the Palestinian Jews would become "new men".

This idea of a "new man" is important for the overall development of a Zionist view of man in two ways: it serves as a goal to be reached and at the same time has an apologetic function.[18] It counters widespread antisemitic prejudice, and repudiates the charge that the Jews are rootless and live as parasites at the expense of the non-Jewish population. Faced with Jewish pioneers who drained swamps and cultivated the ground, even antisemitic Nazis could no longer speak of sponging and rootlessness.[19] But this rebuttal of the antisemites has a problematic drawback. Even though the ideal of a "new man" refutes the validity of antisemitic stereotypes and its underlying racism by pointing out that the Jews in Palestine are different, such an argumentation fails to expose the irrational character of antisemitism, often a projection of its proponents, and looks for the cause of the prejudice in the Jews themselves. Thus prejudices against European Jews are implicitly or even explicitly confirmed, because the hope that the Jews in Palestine will undergo a change presupposes a decidedly negative opinion of

---

[14]Reich, *op. cit.*, p. 19.

[15]Cf. Jacobus Henricus Kann, *Erez Israel. Das jüdische Land. Reiseerinnerungen*, Köln–Leipzig 1909, p. 123.

[16]Hugo Herrmann, *Palästina heute. Licht und Schatten*, Tel-Aviv 1935, p. 227.

[17]Cf. e.g. Salten, *op. cit.*, pp. 90f.

[18]Felix Pinner had already pointed to this in his book, *Das neue Palästina. Volkswirtschaftliche Studien*, Berlin 1926, pp. 31f.

[19]Cf. LIM [i.e. Leopold Itz Edler von Mildenstein], 'Ein Nazi fährt nach Palästina', in *Der Angriff*, Nos. 226 to No. 237 (26th September to 9th October 1934), particularly No. 234 (5th October).

the Jewish way of life and mentality in Europe. Nahum Goldmann, visiting Palestine shortly before the First World War, describes his thoughts and feelings before his arrival in the following way:

> "What will it be like there? Anxiously you ask yourself this, for you sense how much depends on the answer: a complete ideal, a whole life of hope and belief! Every time you encounter another product of our inner strife and our lack of dignity in the *Galut*, you console yourself again and again: there it is different. The hope that in Palestine the Jew lives a completely different life is perhaps the most powerful force that still strengthens us and enables us to work in the *Galut*."[20]

These sentences are not only a typical example of contemporary criticism of the *Galut*. At the same time they denominate the important functions which the stylisation of Palestinian Jews as "new men" have in Zionist travel books. The authors outline a counter image to the situation of Jews in Europe which they perceive as undignified, and at the same time give verve and persistence to the Zionist commitment.

The devaluation of Jewish life in Europe, of course, ran into stiff opposition from those who saw themselves as Jewish Germans. Only some of the anti-Zionist authors, however, went so far in their reactions as to question in principle the participation of young German Jews in pioneer work. These writers warn the sons and daughters of the bourgeoisie of their social decline if they pursue their goal of leading a life on the land in Palestine. Furthermore, they maintain that emigrating to Palestine and settling there means "giving up all the achievements which Jews have obtained in a long and painful struggle since their emancipation in Germany",[21] namely participation in European culture.

Zionist texts differ quite markedly, when it comes to the importance which culture is to have in the pioneers' lives. This is related to the very different qualities the authors attribute to the wished-for Jewish peasant in Palestine. Two main versions of the ideal are to be found: on the one hand the "simple, unlearned, but muscular peasant, full of the joy of living",[22] on the other hand a "new type of peasant",[23] who, in spite of all the work in the fields, does not neglect his intellectual interests. The former image is close to the prevalent picture of a peasant in Germany, mentally dull but close to the soil, tranquil and therefore happy.

This praise of the physical strength and closeness to the soil of Jewish peasants, together with a harsh criticism of the excessive intellectualism of the Jews in the *Galut* or in general of the Jews in the city, is to be found in travel books of the twenties and thirties, particularly in those whose authors are decidedly bourgeois and must be included in the Right wing of Zionism.[24] The Zionist Labour movement, however, wanted an educated Jewish peasant who was

---

[20]Na[c]hum Goldmann, *Erez-Israel. Reisebriefe aus Palästina*. Frankfurt a. Main 1914, p. 3; new edition Darmstadt 1982 (Judaica, vol. 4).

[21]Bruno Weil and (Staatsrat a.D.) Hermann Cohn(-Dessau), *Palästina. Reiseberichte*, Berlin 1927, p. 18.

[22]Goldmann, *op. cit.*, p. 62.

[23]Pinner, *op. cit.*, p. 50.

[24]Cf. e.g. Otto Abeles, *Besuch in Erez Israel*, Wien 1926, pp. 25, 55, 93; Oskar Neumann, *Fahrt nach Osten. Impressionen einer Erez-Israel-Fahrt*, Mukačevo 1933, pp. 193f.

pictured as an enthusiastic farmer, pursuing social, political and cultural interests as well. The ideal was, in general, the kibbutznik, working tirelessly and at the same time actively involved in his community.

This type of peasant was also envisaged by most of the Liberal middle-class authors of travel books, particularly in the twenties, although for them, too, the prime task of the Jewish settler was to strike deep roots. They did not think that these goals were easily compatible, as the pronouncements of Felix Pinner, a financial journalist, show. He demands that education in the rural settlements should aim at "making children into something which parents coming from other professions have not yet completely succeeded in becoming: *one hundred per cent real peasants*, who have no other wish and no other aim (consciously or subconsciously), but to remain settled fast on the soil conquered by their fathers".[25] Therefore, he deems it questionable, if the generation of pioneers that partly descends from the intelligentsia and had to "force themselves into the narrowness of peasant life" does the right thing "in giving their children, the second generation, an *intellectual training* which could one day make it difficult for them to remain in that narrow life". Pinner himself questions this argument, however, by making the following reflection:

> "Perhaps we Europeans are caught up in prejudice in believing that a deeply rooted peasantry is not possible without a certain narrowness. Perhaps a *new type of peasant* will develop in Palestine; one of a different nature, who by sheer willpower can compensate for what he lacks in attachment to the soil and in heavy dull instinct."

With determination the philosopher Felix Weltsch, a member of the Prague Circle, argues in favour of an educated Jewish peasant. He states categorically:

> "Personally I judge the Jews' change of profession into agriculture or other occupations demanding physical labour to be fortunate only if their intellectual horizon remains intact, if the people concerned remain open and interested in all intellectual events in the world, if they continue to play a lively role in science and arts, in short that they do not grow dull and stupid. I only want a Jewish peasant who does not become a yokel (*einen jüdischen Bauern, der nicht verbauert*)."[26]

The pioneers in the collective agrarian settlements were not only admired by travellers who hoped that taking root would redeem the Jews from all their real or alleged suffering and weaknesses. Their community, based as it was on solidarity and a radical egalitarian way of life, was also extolled by Socialists as an attempt to put the Socialist ideal into practice. When Arthur Holitscher, in his time the most renowned of all the travel writers whose texts are discussed here, journeyed through Palestine in 1921, for him the young *Chaluzim* are a "hope of mankind", although he vehemently opposes Zionism as a nationalist ideology. As in revolutionary Russia, about which he reported shortly before, he is enthusiastic about the willingness to make sacrifices which he finds among the "small flock"[27] of determined revolutionaries who dedicate their lives to the "service of mankind"[28] in order to create a human community free from

[25]This and the following quotations Pinner, *op. cit.*, p. 50.
[26]Weltsch, *op. cit.*, p. 60.
[27]Arthur Holitscher, *Reise durch das jüdische Palästina*, Berlin 1922, p. 126.
[28]Arthur Holitscher, *Mein Leben in dieser Zeit. Der "Lebensgeschichte eines Rebellen" zweiter Band (1907–1925)*, Potsdam 1928, p. 192.

exploitation and oppression. He is interested in their attempt to create Socialist ways of living and working together, and starting from the *kvutzot*, to develop a Socialist perspective for the future of all of society.

He expects most from the *Gedud Haavodah* whose most eminent minds really ascribed to it an important function for all of society. But it soon proved to be an illusion that the *kvutzot* were germ cells of a Socialist society. A few years later, during his second visit for the opening of the Hebrew University, Holitscher was already doubtful whether his hopes would come true, because the predominantly middle-class Fourth *Aliyah* had already shifted the interplay of forces.[29] Later, at the beginning of the thirties he pronounced the Zionist project "a drain on Jewish strength, activity and confidence in the future",[30] because its fate would be tied up with the doomed capitalist economic system.

The development in Palestine, however, also irritated those who set their hopes not on the creation of a Socialist way of life, but above all on the return to the land, although their disillusionment did not – as in Holitscher's case – result in a radical withdrawal from the Zionist project.

Since the beginning of the thirties, confidence that the Jews immigrating into Palestine would be moulded into "new men" was called into question by an important change in the country: the rapid urbanisation and the growth of the petty bourgeoisie. Under the pressure of organised antisemitism, middle-class Jews, too, emigrated to Palestine in great numbers. Many of them, especially the intellectuals and members of academic professions, had to change their jobs, though most of them remained in the cities or at best established themselves in so-called middle-class settlements. This development was not only advanced by non-Zionists in order to counter the idealised image of the Jewish immigrant, attached to the soil and finally doing productive work, it was also discussed by authors who were Zionists. Concerned about the discrepancy between Zionist ideology and Palestinian reality, the journalist Alfred Kupferberg asks how the enormous expansion of Tel-Aviv fits into the ideas of the Zionist readers who expect Palestine to be the "solution of the Jewish Question".

> "They know – what matters is the creation of a 'healthy society'. They are aware that a 'healthy society' in the first and perhaps also in the last place means that the largest possible number of Jews must take root in the *agricultural* settlements of Palestine . . . Certainly, cities are necessary in the context of such a complete economy . . . But: does that mean that this Tel-Aviv must exist, this 'hydrocephalus' which grows from month to month in frightening dimensions?"[31]

Kupferberg does not answer the question of the relationship between rural colonisation and city agglomeration. He quietly switches the problem to questions of economic stability and the "Jewish-cultural"[32] meaning of Tel-Aviv.

---

[29]Arthur Holitscher, *Das unruhige Asien. Reise durch Indien – China – Japan*, Berlin 1926, about Palestine pp. 36–76.

[30]Arthur Holitscher, 'Die Juden in der heutigen Zeit', in Heinrich Mann, Arthur Holitscher, Lion Feuchtwanger *et al.*, *Gegen die Phrase vom jüdischen Schädling*, Prague 1933, p. 316; the volume is an extract from *"Der Jud ist schuld . . . ?"*, Prague 1932.

[31]Alfred Kupferberg, *Deutsche Juden im jüdischen Land, Palästina-Bericht eines jüdischen Journalisten*, Hamburg 1934, p. 45.

[32]*Ibid.*, p. 46.

Non-Zionist authors did not fail to point to the contradiction between Zionist theory and practice in Palestine. In 1936, Werner Cahnmann, a former official of the C.V., but not at all hostile to Jewish colonisation in Palestine, pointed out that among the immigrants during those years were many who must be called human flotsam and jetsam and stated:

> "Theoretically, the countryside and within the rural settlements the *kvutzot* movement has primacy, but in real numbers the city population predominates, and there an ideologically completely unformed, culturally undeveloped and morally uninhibited element by far outweighs the former sound strata of pioneers."[33]

If Cahnmann, later a distinguished sociologist in the USA, grasped an essential trend, he called into question what also impressed many non-Zionist travellers most when they visited the country. They, too, saw the qualities and patterns of behaviour they regarded as particularly precious mainly among the Jews living and working in the countryside, though also among the workers in the city, whereas they were critical not only of the Jews of the old *Yishuv* but also of the urban middle class.

A mid-position was held by the settlers of the "old colonies" which had been developed with Baron Rothschild's aid and were supported by the Palestine Jewish Colonisation Association (PICA). The inhabitants of these *Moshavot* were private farmers, often owners of plantations, who employed hired labourers. Judgements about them are very different according to the respective political positions of the travellers.

In general they are not dealt with in terms of the antagonism, focused upon in Europe, between capital and labour. Looking critically at the settlers of the first generation, who had meanwhile become wealthy and employed Jewish and Arab workers in their *Pardessim*, the authors did not emphasise the conflicts resulting from this working relationship, but tended to stress cultural, ideological and political characteristics, which distinguished the colonists of the PICA-settlements from the Zionist community-settlements. This approach can be understood from the history of the Jewish immigration and colonisation. Since the immigrants of the Second *Aliyah*, who saw themselves as Socialists, had established themselves as the politically and ideologically strongest force, the settlers of the pre-Zionist colonies were deprecated as still mentally rooted in the ghetto and as narrow-minded philistines. Only the small group of the *Biluim*, which because of its co-operative ideas could be called a precursor of the Second *Aliyah*, was exempt from this judgement.[34]

Criticism of the planter-colonies and enthusiasm for the kibbutzim is closely connected with the aim of "becoming productive". Disparagement of the pre-Zionist planter-colonies of Judea prevails primarily where the yardstick is the aforementioned ideal of the Jewish peasant attached to the soil, or, more commonly, the ideal of the new Jewish man. The colonists are criticised because they did not "redeem the soil" with their own hands, but employed Arab workers.[35]

[33]Cahnmann, *op. cit.*, p. 2.
[34]Cf. Goldmann, *op. cit.*, pp. 21–23.
[35]Cf. e.g. Neumann, *op. cit.*, p. 81.

For most of the anti-Zionist authors economic prosperity is the sole criterion. Here, the PICA-colonies that had economically consolidated during the twenties did very well.[36] To his regret Alfred Wiener, the syndic of the C.V., had to concede, however, that these settlements also were influenced by the National-Jewish concept.[37] Such a rapprochement with Zionist ideas was detected very early by Zionist authors who welcomed it, of course. Even before the First World War the leading German Zionist Adolf Friedemann refers to this,[38] and in the twenties Felix Pinner confirms that the Nationalist spirit gained strength in the Rothschild settlements.[39]

Nevertheless, the contrast between the "old" and the new colonies was always present during the period studied here. The main source of the persistent conflict was the use of Arab workers in the settlements based on private property. The employment of Arab workers was regarded as a problem of all Jewish workers, even if they had already settled in a kibbutz; a problem not only because of the Nationalist demand to employ Jewish labourers exclusively, but also because the kibbutzniks were confronted with this practice, when they worked outside the kibbutz as hired hands in order to increase the income of the kibbutz. Economically the new immigrants could only survive by hiring themselves out, until the *Keren Kayemeth le' Israel* (Jewish National Fund) assigned land to them, and the young *kibbutzim* were dependent on their members' labour outside the kibbutz because the subsidies from the *Keren Hayesod* did not meet their chronic deficit. Under these circumstances hired labour proved to be a precondition for the kind of autonomous, self-determined (*selbstbestimmt*), productive agrarian work the Zionist-Socialist pioneers strove for. The employment of Jewish workers in the colonies, therefore, was a prerequisite for "making the Jews productive" and thus for the creation of "new men" as defined by the Zionist ideology.

When Jewish workers struggling for their living, demanded employment in the plantation-colonies, the fight did not only arouse social conflict, it also had an ideological and political dimension. It is not accidental that a military term was used: "kibbush haavodah", conquest of labour. But first the social motives dominated. The "conquest of labour" started with the Second *Aliyah*, when Jews from the tsarist Empire came to Palestine without means and without support from any organisation, and were thus dependent on paid employment. During the twenties the difficulties arising from the economic situation and the social motives of the Jewish workers are still emphasised in the travel books of Socialist and Left-Zionist provenance, when the "kibbush haavodah" is discussed. Arthur Holitscher writes in 1922:

> "The colonists from Rishon do not employ Jewish workers – but those nomad Bedouins and Fellaheen from the other end of their colony. They are cheap, undemanding, satisfied with

[36]Cf. Weil and Cohn, *op. cit.*, p. 23; Wiener, *op. cit.*, p. 38.
[37]Cf. Wiener, *op. cit.*, p. 115.
[38]Adolf Friedemann, *Reisebilder aus Palästina. Mit Nachbildungen von Originalradierungen und Handzeichnungen von Hermann Struck*, Berlin 1904, p. 89.
[39]Cf. Pinner, *op. cit.*, p. 50.

minimal wages. But hundreds of young Jewish workers, for lack of work, roam hungrily
through the streets of nearby Jaffa, Tel-Aviv. They cannot compete with the Arab labourers,
their organisations demand higher standard wages, they will never settle for the low standard
of living of the Arabs. Therefore the Jewish colonist refuses the Jewish worker."[40]

The conflicts between Arab and Jewish workers and between the latter and
Jewish employers became worse at times of economic crisis and increased
immigration, with the ensuing periods of unemployment. But just at such times
it was very often not the social aspects of these struggles which were emphasised,
but the national ones. In a travel book of 1934 the immigration of German Jews is
discussed as follows: "They strengthen the Jewish minority, Jewish capital and
. . . the conquest of labour."[41] Here the original problem is reversed. The point is
no longer to fight for the poor immigrants' opportunity to find work: on the
contrary, the increase in immigration is seen as the prerequisite for the
opportunity to get on with the replacement of Arab workers. This shows that the
national aim of the "conquest of labour" dominates the social aim.

This kind of argumentation is not confined to the thirties. Already before the
First World War, when Arab labour in Jewish colonies first became a problem
for the travellers, the national motive is turned against Jewish owners of
plantations; obviously certain Zionist authors are only interested in the
"conquest of labour" from national aspects. Thus Nahum Goldmann does not
ask whether Jewish workers are jobless because of the employment of Arabs in
Jewish colonies; he is full of understanding for the economic motives of the
colonists, but he sharply criticises their "indifference to the question of Jewish
labour", which gives evidence "of a low level of national feeling", and blames the
colonists of Rishon-le-Zion for not showing "concern for national interests, or
endeavouring to help fulfil urgent national tasks".[42] From this point of view
"conquest of labour" has the task of serving the national concord and the
dynamic of the expansion of the *Yishuv*.

In the travel accounts we find many references to conflicts which resulted from
the "conquest of labour". There is mention that Jewish workers, unable to
compete with the Arabs on the purely economic level, because the Arabs
generally ran an agrarian subsistence farming production in their own villages,[43]
used non-economic means to extort employment. As well as appeals to the
nationalism of the colonists, they carried out strikes, blockades and boycotts and
even used physical force against Jews who co-operated with Arabs,[44] and against
Arab competitors. Therefore "conquest of labour" contributed a great deal to
straining the Jewish-Arab relationship.

However, in the Zionist texts written after the First World War, almost all of
which mention the "conquest of labour", consequences for Arab-Jewish relations
are played down or completely ignored. Hugo Herrmann even maintains in 1925
that carrying through the principle of Jewish labour helped to improve relations:

[40]Holitscher, *Reise, op. cit.*, p. 75.
[41]Amiel, *op. cit.*, p. 68.
[42]Goldmann, *op. cit.*, p. 17.
[43]Cf. Herrmann, *Palästina heute, op. cit.*, p. 215.
[44]Cf. Erich Gottgetreu, *Das Land der Söhne. Palästina nahe gerückt*, Wien 1934, p. 92.

"When the first Jewish *kvutzot* said: Away with Arab labour – the experts shook their heads with foreboding: that means declaring war on the Arabs, it means driving them to open hostility. But look! The Jewish worker who himself cultivated his field and the Arabian Fellah who did the same close by understood each other much better than the nabobs and the coolies of Petach-Tikvah, Rehobot, or Rishon. They understand each other, they learn from one another – not just the Arab from the Jew, but also the Jew from the Arab – they help each other out."[45]

The author thinks to disprove the objection that the "conquest of labour" aggravates the Jewish-Arab opposition by arguing that the Jews performing physical labour would diminish their differences with the Arab working population so far that good neighbourliness and co-operation would become possible. "Becoming productive" would thus lead to a dismantling of class-opposition and to an understanding between Jews and Arabs.

This argument is paradoxical, because Herrmann put his trust in a class solidarity the preconditions for which are thought to be achieved in partly violent struggles between Jewish and Arab workers.

Arthur Holitscher had already questioned this kind of argumentation three years earlier by pointing out that in his opinion the subjective preconditions for an arrangement did not exist. He considered solidarity of the Arab Fellaheen and workers with Jewish workers on the basis of a common experience of physical labour to be unlikely.

"The humble Arab, so I was often told, persecutes the Jewish worker, whom he sees working, with less hatred than the Jewish townsman whose work he cannot comprehend, and the colonist, for whom he carries out harsh and badly paid drudgery. I cannot believe in such an evaluation (any more than I believe at all in a primary and primitive hatred of the Arabs for the Jews). The friendly glance at the working stranger and closeness on the basis of common work presupposes a much higher moral plane than the Arab has attained today."[46]

On the contrary, the Fellaheen would quickly lose the "respect he still feels for the foreign master race (*Herrenrasse*)",[47] if he sees the *Chaluz* reducing his economic condition to a level (*Anspruchslosigkeit*) similar to his own.

Here we see a remarkable reversal of positions. The radical Socialist Holitscher is convinced that a visible class difference between the immigrant Europeans and the Arabian peasants is necessary for the protection of the Jews. In fact, he does not understand the conflicts between Jews and Arabs as racially based, as could be inferred from his use of the term "Herrenrasse" – he is, on the contrary, convinced that the European imperialist powers have brought hatred into the Arabian population[48] – but in his opinion it is the differences in intellectual and moral development which are decisive, not the social ones.

Hugo Herrmann, in contrast, the follower of Jewish Nationalism, believes that national differences could be overcome by getting rid of class-conflict and he postulates, "let us be confident that two working peoples, both loving their country, will hold out their hands to each other".[49]

[45] Hugo Herrmann, *Eine werdende Welt. Reiseeindrücke aus Palästina*, Prague 1925, p. 39.
[46] Holitscher, *Reise, op. cit.*, p.82.
[47] *Ibid.*
[48] *Ibid.*, pp. 83f.
[49] Herrmann, *Eine werdende Welt, op. cit.*, p. 42.

Herrmann bases his optimism on the argument that only the urban upper class was interested in political struggle, whereas the rural population did not know much about it. Until the end of the twenties Arab-Palestinian politics were indeed almost exclusively run by the ruling clans in the cities. Therefore Herrmann's judgement is understandable as far as his first book about Palestine (published in 1925) is concerned. But he repeated the quoted passages in his book *Palästina wie es wirklich ist*, which is based on the previous one, but was published after the violent riots of 1929, in which Arab peasants played an important role. In the later text he only added a paragraph emphasising that the riots made it more difficult and time-consuming to settle the "neighbour-question", but at the same time made a much wider circle of people aware of the necessity for settling that question.[50] Herrmann stuck to the hope that there would be understanding between the labouring classes of both people, because it was pivotal to his political concept. This hope must not fail if an expansion of Zionist settlement (for which Herrmann as one of the most important propagandists of the *Keren Hayesod* was very active), and an Arab-Jewish arrangement were to be compatible. He advocated such an arrangement because of his basically humanistic attitude, and also because of the international support needed for the Zionist project. This was a precondition for any expectation that the ideal of Jewish pioneers "becoming productive" and forming their "attachment to the soil" could be realised without use of force.

"Conquest of labour" appeared as a national aspiration of first priority because of its centrality to the Zionist concept. It is, therefore, not surprising that Zionists tried to illegitimise objections to this policy as expressing partiality. Settlers of the "old colonies", who warned that the "kibbush haavodah" would aggravate Jewish-Arab differences, were accused of covering up their interest in cheap Arab labour by making such objections. Herrmann writes about them in 1933:

> "There are also some who pretend to have political motives, i.e. the fear that the exclusion of Arab labour would lead to a boycott by the Arab majority against the Jewish minority; but I think this political argument is a later self-justification if not just a pretext."[51]

This assessment might be right. But it does not change the fact that many planters, because of their economic interests, tended towards a policy of agreement with the Arab population, whereas the slogan "100 per cent Jewish labour", proclaimed by the workers' organisations, resulted in a bitter fight by workers, who generally saw themselves as Socialists, against their Arab class-comrades. The password "conquest of labour" was rejected only on the extreme Left, principally by the Communists, and with reservations by *Hashomer Hazair*, which refused to take sides against the struggle of the permanently employed Arab workers and therefore opposed the slogan "100 per cent Jewish labour", but

---

[50]Cf. Hugo Herrmann, *Palästina wie es wirklich ist*, 2nd revised edn., Wien–Leipzig 1933, pp. 74f. (first publ. 1933).
[51]*Ibid.*, pp. 212f.

participated in the "conquest of labour", as far as seasonal labour or new jobs were concerned.[52]

The playing down by certain Zionist authors of the conflicts resulting from the "conquest of labour", was categorically questioned by non-Zionists. Alfred Wiener in his book, *Kritische Reise durch Palästina* warned of the "important political dimension" of pushing through the principle of Jewish labour without any compromise.

> "The Arab workers are driven out, sometimes violently. At the very least, this does not establish friendship. And in this radical way of thinking, moreover, the seed of strong chauvinist exaggeration is hidden, the fruits of which will not be at all welcome."[53]

In the thirties, Werner Cahnmann, after criticising attempts to boycott all products of Palestinian Arabs, makes the statement that it was illogical to ask for a hundred per cent Jewish labour on the one hand, and on the other hand to point out at the same time that the standard of living of the Arab population had been raised by Jewish immigration. Cahnmann does not deny that Arabs who found work in Jewish colonies and could take advantage of the generally higher wage level were better off economically than before Jewish immigration. But he asks the reader to consider that this "had been an unintentional, keenly fought side-effect of Jewish immigration". One should not expect Arabs to feel grateful when their employment had been for purely economic reasons and had been accompanied by violent agitation against it from Jews.[54]

The settlements of the pioneers opened up a second field of conflict at least as explosive as that resulting from the "conquest of labour", mainly because it could not be done without the acquisition of land. There had, however, been Jewish land purchases even before the commencement of the Zionist settlement policy; their acquisitions covered a far greater extent than the purchases of the *Keren Kayemeth*, whose share of the whole area of Jewish agrarian settlements was still less than 20 per cent in 1930.[55] But with regard to the Arab-Jewish relationship the acquisition of land by Zionist funds was of special importance, because of the Zionist principle that the soil should be cultivated by Jews themselves without the employment of Arab hands.

From the beginning, the travellers to Palestine were interested in the growth of the real estate in Jewish hands, and some of them deal intensively with the questions related to this. Until the eve of the First World War, however, whenever Jews' purchases of land in Palestine are discussed, nobody asks about the consequences for the Arab peasants, but they concentrate instead on the future attitude of the Ottoman State towards Jewish ownership. Neither the Orthodox authors, who trust in the security which Ottoman rule provided for

---

[52]Cf. Eleasar Prai, *Was geht in Palästina vor? Eine marksistische [sic] Analyse der letzten Ereignisse*. Tel-Aviv n.d. [1936], pp. 44f.

[53]Wiener, *op. cit.*, p. 61.

[54]Cahnmann, *op. cit.*, p. 12.

[55]Cf. the precise numerical data in Alfred Bonne, *Palästina. Land und Wirtschaft*, Leipzig 1932, pp. 132, 134f.

religious minorities,[56] nor the Zionist travellers anticipate major conflict between Jews and Arabs in Palestine. The land is not only described as being sparsely populated, but even as almost devoid of people. Here one should take into account that in most areas the land purchases were not yet made on a large scale and social consequences were usually at that time still slight. Purchase of ground was not even connected with the settlement of Jews in every case. Rothschild's extensive estates at Tiberias and in the Hauran "had to be let to Arabs because of the lack of Jewish peasants",[57] as one traveller is sorry to state. Even at places where Jewish colonists settled, the consequences remained limited, because for the most part Arab workers were employed.

The situation changed with the beginning of the Zionist colonisation in 1907 which was decided on within the concept of "synthetic Zionism", i.e. political as well as practical Zionism. In order to provide a material basis for the future home of the Jewish people, the Zionist organisation made an effort to buy land which in the desired areas was mostly the property of big Arab landowners. Zionist funds propagated the "redemption of the soil", and this choice of words is taken over in the Zionist travel books. It is based on a biblical legal term, but here it means more than merely a legal or economic process.[58] Because of the connotations of the word "redemption", the purchase of land and the tilling of the soil gain a virtually metaphysical dimension. It can be assumed that this elevated terminology did not make it any easier to deal with the economic, social and political consequences of buying and cultivating the land.

In the travel books "redemption of the soil" on the one hand means freeing the ground from stones, watering it and draining swamps so that the soil can be used for relatively intensive agriculture, i.e. the soil is redeemed from the state of wilderness, of being a desert or a swamp. On the other hand "redemption" also implies the liberation of the soil from the Arabs who used to own and cultivate it. It is instructive to see which of the two aspects is emphasised. Here are two examples: a text published in 1920, which refers to a journey made immediately before the First World War, reports about a visit to Merhavia.

> "The ground is almost virgin territory, and on a lentil field of scarcely two acres forty male and female Jewish workers are toiling barefoot in the heat of the end of April clearing the rampant weeds. *Geulath haaretz*: the redemption of the soil! In a strange way the Arab village which existed here before, serves the future of the new colony; the vacated village seems to be just a heap of rubble, but it only needs to be taken off with a spade and carried to the fields to have a beneficial effect: this is because it contains the most valuable ingredients the soil needs: the dung of centuries."[59]

[56]Cf. Reich, *op. cit.*, pp. IV and 37; Alexander, *op. cit.*, p. 90; Josef Grünbaum, *Das Land, das jedem heilig ist. Miscellen aus einer palästinensischen Reisegesellschaft*, Budapest 1912, p. 75.

[57]Kann, *op. cit.*, p. 117.

[58]Max Dienemann in his article under the heading of 'Erlösung' in *Jüdisches Lexikon*, ed. by Georg Herlitz and Bruno Kirschner, Berlin 1927–1930, vol. II, pp. 473–477, quotations p. 473, has explained that "in the Bible redemption means the material, juridical recovering e.g. of real estate"; "today" (1928) the word is used "in the same sense for recovering the land of *Eretz Israel*". Already in 1904 a society with the name of "Geula" (redemption) was founded in Warsaw, which managed the purchase of ground in Palestine (cf. *Encyclopedia of Zionism and Israel*, New York 1971, vol. I, p. 435).

[59]Calvary, *op. cit.*, p. 39.

The ousting of Arab tenants is already mentioned here indirectly and the process of erasing their traces is also described, but the displacement is not considered, nor is it seen in connection with the term of "redemption".

This is dealt with differently in the travel book by Oskar Neumann, a leading Zionist of Slovakia. In his text written at the beginning of the thirties there is a chapter entitled 'In the Centre of the Redemption of the Soil'.[60] But it was not Emek Yezreel or another place of Jewish settlement which was regarded as the "centre of the redemption of the soil", but the offices of the *Keren Kayemeth le'Israel* (KKL), which organised the purchases of land. The acquired land is called "this soil redeemed by the *Keren Kayemeth le'Israel*".[61] This implies that the term "redemption" is seen here as connected in the first place with the purchase of land and not with its cultivation. The main aspect of "redemption" is the Nationalist one: the transfer of land into Jewish hands. The author discusses the principles of its purchase of land by writing that the KKL had the task:

> "to redeem as much land as possible in *Eretz Israel*, to transfer it to the Jewish people as their inalienable property and to keep it forever. This land may never be sold again or disposed of in any other way. It is national property which can be handed over as hereditary tenure or leasehold to every Jew who is ready to till this soil with his own hands and to redeem it."[62]

The purchase of land, as the author points out, is meant to form the basis for occupational retraining and social relocation and for making the Jewish youth "productive". The remarks quoted reveal the consequences the rules of the KKL have for the Arab population: because the land purchased by the KKL must not be sold, it is removed from the market and thus inaccessible to Arab customers. Only Jews are allowed to be tenants, and they have to cultivate the land themselves. Thus Arab tenants cannot have free disposal of this land, nor can Arab hired labourers use it to earn their living .

The question therefore arose, of whether Palestine still had sufficient land for agricultural use by both groups of the population, the Jews and the Arabs. This question was of immediate political and practical importance because, with the acknowledgement of the Churchill White Paper in 1922, the Zionist Organisation had agreed to prove in each case that Jewish immigration did not exceed the economic capacity of the country to absorb new arrivals and that extension of colonisation was possible without any harm as far as the rights of the native population were concerned. Partly because of statements made on behalf of the British government, e.g. in Sir John Hope Simpson's report, Zionist authors felt challenged to comment on the question of how many people Palestine could provide space for. The authors argue differently in detail, but all, not just extreme Nationalists, include Transjordan in their considerations. In so doing the authors, however, generally do not claim sovereignty for this region.

Only the journalist Wolfgang von Weisl, who belonged to the Right wing of Zionism the followers of which – in contrast to the other Zionist parties – as early as the twenties propagated not only a national home, but a Jewish state as the

[60]Neumann, *op. cit.*, p. 164.
[61]*Ibid.*, p. 165.
[62]*Ibid.*, pp. 164f.

objective of Zionism, puts the purchase of land directly into a political perspective. When he discusses the consequences of the Fourth *Aliyah*, he finds a condensed formula for the meaning which the ownership of land had for those Zionists who aimed at establishing a Jewish national state.

> "Parallel to the increased tempo of immigration there began intensified land purchase in Palestine, whose political importance is evident: without land there is no state, without agriculture no people."[63]

As the purchase of land is thus regarded as an essential element of *Staatszionismus*, its possible political dimension comes to the surface. Thereby a different light is shed on the ban on resale of land and on the duty to work it oneself. Seen from this perspective the statutes of the KKL – as a present critic of Zionism formulates – "seem to be an instrument used to transform land from being the basis for *agricultural* production into *national* territory".[64] Thus the Zionists' purchase of land does not only endanger the individual existence of the tenants concerned, but also threatens the Arabs' collective political existence in Palestine, so long striven for by the Arab national movement. It was therefore seen as a threat, although the purchase of land was not yet very extensive and the number of tenants who had to leave the ground made up only a small percentage of the total number of Fellaheen. Those Zionist authors who rejected Revisionism and fixed their hopes on some kind of agreement with the Arab population, either did not see or ignored the political implications of land purchase. Alfred Wiener, an opponent of Zionism, however, clearly formulates this problem:

> "The Jewish policy moves in the direction – and has no other choice – of reaching the *majority in the country* . . . of buying as much land as possible and populating it . . . The assumption that the Arabs would let themselves be bought out of their homeland bit by bit, crushed without batting an eyelid, is built on shaky foundations."[65]

The warning, already expressed in 1927, apparently fell on stony ground. At least as far as travel books are concerned, Zionist authors continue to limit their thoughts to the individual social or economic consequences that the purchase of land and the Jewish settlement may have for the Arab. They do not mention the political dimension of the problem. In justification they point to the fact that tenants were assigned land in other parts of the country, and that they received compensation, which was meant to facilitate transition from agricultural work to labour in urban areas.[66]

Signs of the process of dislocation, which led to the proletarianisation of tenants, were not easy to detect, mainly because only a small number of people was directly involved. Unlike today, visitors could rarely see abandoned Arab houses, because they were frequently demolished when Jewish settlements were established on the sites of Arab villages, as described in Calvary's book of 1920. Therefore, we should not consider it as blindness or as a sign of deliberately

---

[63]Wolfgang von Weisl, *Der Kampf um das Heilige Land. Palästina von heute.* Berlin 1925, p. 129.
[64]Dan Diner, *"Keine Zukunft auf den Gräbern der Palästinenser".* Eine historisch-politische Bilanz der Palästinafrage, Hamburg 1982, p. 83.
[65]Wiener, *op. cit.,* p. 80.
[66]Cf. Herrmann, *Eine werdende Welt, op. cit.,* p. 56; Herrmann, *Palästina wie es wirklich ist, op. cit.,* p. 223.

ignoring reality when, for example, Felix Salten, describing the farm of Migdal in 1925, does not give any hint of former Arab inhabitants,[67] although we can read in Nahum Goldmann's travel book, written eleven years before, that the owners still had a lot of difficulties with the Arabs who "formerly lived on this land and do not want to leave".[68]

Whereas many authors play down the consequences when they refer to the ousting of Arab tenants, justification is usually not considered necessary when the Bedouins are concerned. In almost none of the texts is the introduction of the rules of private property into a society governed by different rules considered to be a problem. It seemed to be self-evident that the Bedouins' right to pasture their cattle must end with the transition of the soil into Jewish hands. The ousted Bedouins were seen as aggressors, as "bands of robbers",[69] against whom Jewish colonists had to defend themselves by force of arms, when they drove their cattle to the land the Jews had purchased by a legal treaty.

The question whether there were Bedouin rights which had to be respected became important at the beginning of the thirties, when *Chaluzim* settled in the Wadi Chavarit near Chedera, which Bedouins claimed as pasture land. As can clearly be seen in a travel book of this time it was difficult for the European visitor to pay the least attention to the Bedouins' existence. On the one hand the author describes the tents and flocks belonging to Bedouins and does not conceal that the Wadi "has always been the undisputed domain of pasturing Bedouins".[70] On the other hand he maintains in the same context:

> "The Wadi is large, spacious, stretching a vast distance, undulating and empty! There is space for twenty settlements, for two thousand farmers, for fields, gardens, houses and stables, for sorrows and happiness – and empty!"[71]

When he considers the resistance of the Bedouins, however, the author laconically states that the living space of cattle-breeding nomads everywhere in the world is becoming more narrow and that this "primitive form of economy . . . has to make room for more economical and modern forms everywhere".[72]

In view of the national antagonism and the tension which could be felt especially during the twenties and the thirties, the question arose, how the problem of the Jewish-Arab relationship could be solved. The authors do not usually develop a coherent concept, but present observations, patterns of explication and prognoses which obviously imply a certain understanding of the problem. They see the tension as a symptom of a developmental problem, which was a result of the transformation from a still feudally structured society into a modern society. This transformation, initiated or expedited by the Jewish immigrants, is said to have run into opposition from conservative circles interested in the conservation

[67]Cf. Salten, *op. cit.*, p. 240.
[68]Goldmann, *op. cit.*, p. 70.
[69]Calvary, *op. cit.*, p. 45.
[70]Herrmann, *Palästina wie es wirklich ist, op. cit.*, p. 154.
[71]*Ibid.*, p. 156.
[72]*Ibid.*, p. 233.

of the established social conditions. To the same degree that this resistance could be overcome, would the tension between Jews and Arabs be diminished.

Blaming the Effendis, the big Arab landowners, is usually the core of this reasoning. Already in Arthur Holitscher's book, published in 1922, Effendis (next to the imperialist powers) are held responsible for the riots in the preceding years. The author maintains that the Effendis were disappointed because the Jews brought less money into the country than expected and that, therefore, the big landowners were not able to get rid of their debts quickly by selling their land for high prices. In addition the Effendis were said to be dissatisfied because the wages for farm labourers had gone up, since they could now work for the Jews, too:

> "Since the new Jews have come into this country the Fellah is no longer quite such an apathetic half-human creature."[73]

Holitscher denies the legitimacy of the Effendis' opposition by pointing to their exploitative practices. But he is also aware of the fact that by this statement the most decisive question is still not answered. "Whether the Arabs' 'national liberation movement' is in response to a real inner need of the Arab people or whether it has to be regarded as mere invention by the Effendis who want to hinder the Jews' immigration from selfish motives?"[74] Holitscher poses the question, but leaves it unanswered.

In later texts by other authors the thesis that "the Effendis who were concerned about their ground rent"[75] were the puppet-masters of riots and anti-Jewish actions can be found in various forms. The Arab peasants on the contrary – this is stated again and again – would profit from the Jewish settlements and agriculture, but, against their own interests let, themselves be incited by nationalist propaganda.

This pattern of explanation proved to be convincing enough, thanks to the fact that members of the class of big landowners actually were in leading positions in the Palestinian National movement. Hugo Herrmann, propagandist of the *Keren Hayesod*, accused this group "of pretending to be intransigent Nationalists", whilst at the same time "they plunder Jewish immigrants and Jewish organisations shamelessly".[76] After the Zionists' purchases of land, the reason for the Effendis' anti-Zionist involvement is no longer seen to be their disappointment over the Jews not spending as much money as they were expected to do. Herrmann maintains, in fact, that Effendis agitated amongst the Fellaheen against immigration, because they thought it would speed up the infiltration of European ideas and endanger the feudal system. He assumes that the Arab upper classes were not only disturbed because of raised wage standards, but also because of the whole social and cultural development which would shatter their own traditional social positions.

---

[73]Holitscher, *Reise, op. cit.*, p. 82; cf. also p. 35.
[74]*Ibid.*, p. 83.
[75]Eugen Hoeflich [M.j. ben gawriël], *Die Pforte des Ostens. Das arabisch-jüdische Palästina vom panasiatischen Standpunkt aus*, Berlin–Wien 1923, p. 56; cf. also Gottgetreu, *op. cit.*, pp. 55f.
[76]Herrmann, *Palästina heute, op. cit.*, p. 217.

Within this process of modernisation endangering "the Palestinian feudal system", he attributes to the Jewish settlers the function of serving as a model for the Fellaheen. In this context, too, as we see here, the independent labour of Jews in primary production is considered to be very important. It appears to contribute to progress in Arab society and thus to promote peace in the country.

The socio-psychological supposition of Herrmann's argument, that the "spirit of freedom and autonomy which inspired the settlers"[77] would be very attractive to the Fellaheen, was by no means shared by all travellers. In contrast to this optimistic view we find the assumption that the Fellaheen would feel the cultural divide between them and the *Chaluzim* as a threat. According to this view the settlement of Jews as peasants, which confronted the Arab peasants directly with a completely alien culture, had the opposite effect and heightened the tension between the two national groups. This assessment was shared by non-Zionist and by Revisionist authors, but they come to different conclusions.

Alfred Wiener contrasts the "typical" Fellah with the "typical" *Chaluz* as representatives of their people and remarks that they live in completely different worlds. He points especially to the differences in ways of production, in social conditions and intellectual attitudes. With these differences in mind, one must "prepare the ground skilfully and systematically in the long term",[78] even just to open a way to an approach. Wiener believes that it was particularly necessary "to withdraw the Revisionist-chauvinistic element from the political attitude of the *Chaluz* or at least of the rising generation and to make them somewhat more Palestinian, more Arab". This would be "an almost insoluble task", but there was no acceptable alternative.

The vast majority of the *Chaluzim* were not followers of Revisionism, of course, but they played an important role in the calculations of Revisionist politicians and ideologists. The Revisionist position among German-speaking travellers to Palestine is represented by the Viennese physician and journalist Wolfgang von Weisl, who later became a member of the radically Nationalist faction of the Jewish National Council in Palestine. His book is based on the aim of the establishment and development of a position of which ought to guarantee the realisation of maximum demands. Opinions like Weisl's were rejected by the majority of the Zionist authors. But an alternative plan for overcoming Jewish-Arab discord, which would mean more than manifesting readiness to find an arrangement, can hardly be found in their travel books.

This is not true in the case of the Viennese writer Eugen Hoeflich, who called himself Moshe Ya-akov Ben-gavriêl from the early twenties. Ben-gavriêl, an adherent to *Hapoel Hazair* and an admirer of Martin Buber, has worked out an elaborate radical counter-plan to the Revisionist concept in his books and articles about Palestine. It is worthwhile to enter into the particulars of Weisl's and Ben-gavriêl's books, not only because, even in the first years after the Balfour Declaration, they mark the extreme poles of the Zionist discourse, but also

---

[77]Hugo Herrmann, *Die Araberfrage Palästinas*, ed. by the J[üdisch-] A[kademische] Verb[indung] "Barissia", Prague 1932 (Schriften zur Diskussion des Zionismus, No. 6), p. 28.
[78]This and the following quotations from Alfred Wiener, 'Juden und Araber in Palästina. Zur Erkenntnis der jüngsten Vorgänge', in *Der Morgen*, V (1929), p. 503.

because they exemplify how the authors' political opinions shape their perceptions and their descriptions of the situation and the processes in Palestine.

In his often-quoted *The Struggle for the Holy Land. Palestine today*, Weisl maintains that the Arab resistance against the Jewish immigration was "absolutely necessary" (*naturnotwendig*).[79] In being confronted with the European culture of the Jewish immigrants and their superior work practices the Arabs faced a dilemma; they had either to give up their old culture in order to be able to compete with the Jews or stick to their traditional way of life and methods of production and leave the hegemony in Palestine to the Jews. As they would lose in either case they had to offer resistance. Therefore, every attempt at compromise would be hopeless and the Jews had no other choice but to gain their ends by political and military means.

In Weisl's opinion the Jews could only hold their ground in Palestine with British support, because after the disbanding of the Jewish Legion the Jews did not have any instruments of military power of their own left. He maintains that there could have been a possibility for agreement, if the Jewish Legion had not been demobilised and if the Jewish immigration had been enforced, for then the Jews would have been taken seriously in negotiations by their Arab counterparts. In his opinion the end of any such negotiations had to be the establishment of a Jewish state – an aim that was definitely out of question for the Arabs in the twenties. Therefore, one can hardly believe that his pleading for an Arab-Jewish agreement was intended seriously. Weisl clearly reveals how he thinks this goal will be realised when he discusses the possibility of building up a new Jewish army. By this means, in the long run, the Zionists could overcome their dependence on Britain and push through their interests on their own authority.[80]

How Weisl's idea influences the description of his impressions of Palestine may be seen by his depiction of the walk to the Wailing Wall, an obligatory chapter in all books about Palestine, even the Christian ones. Weisl reports that near the Wailing Wall which he visited at the Ninth of Av, he had boxed the ears of some Arab boys, because they had disturbed those praying by deliberately making a noise. When he did this a Jew stopped him and warned him, "we have no right to pray here . . ." Weisl comments:

> "'We have no rights here . . .' Maybe it is as well that Jews are reminded of this sentence before they start reading the laments of the Prophet Jeremiah. For living in the Jerusalem of today, the Jew feels free and proud. And the complaints about the 'city which lies deserted' lose relevance in the new Jerusalem, where new houses are being built in every quarter. Thus, from the historical point of view it is probably quite good to be reminded of the fact that all these new achievements are only on the surface: that hatred and contempt and injustice still exist from Jeremiah's time on until today – in the heart of Jerusalem. Otherwise the laments of Jeremiah would be found – obsolete."[81]

The changes in the situation of the Palestinian Jews, which Weisl makes obvious by pointing to new housing estates in Jerusalem, at first seem to be superficial and unimportant. Furthermore they seem to encourage self-decep-

---

[79]Weisl, *op. cit.*, p. 136.
[80]*Ibid.*, pp. 262–264.
[81]*Ibid.*, p. 191.

tion. But Weisl closes the chapter describing the marching up of the "young Jerusalem":

> "Wearing Russian blouses or the open shirts of the German *Blau-Weiss*, alone or in groups, many of them with their girlfriends – *Chaluzim* at the Wall of the Temple . . . Towards midnight I went home together with an American rabbi and some of his friends. There were still new crowds moving towards the Wall – endlessly. Thousands and thousands of people . . .
> Behind us a group of young workers' brigadists suddenly appeared, returning from the Wailing Wall. Four abreast, in military order, they moved with echoing songs through the sleeping streets of Jerusalem.
> My companions stood still shaking their heads, looking after the young people. 'They are singing – on the Ninth of Av they are singing! Dreadful!'"[82]

Weisl's sympathies are obviously not directed towards the religious people, to whom traditions are more important than the new Nationalist movement, but towards the young Zionists drawn up in military order. The passage about the Wailing Wall not only illustrates the inferior position of the Jews in Jerusalem, but also the changes in terms of power, and it depicts at the same time the demands central to Weisl's political concept for Palestine: Jewish mass immigration and the fight for respect and rights by the establishment of military power. The "legionary Zionism" as supported by Weisl was sharply opposed by Ben-gavriêl. He postulates:

> "The organic solution of the Arab question is the touchstone of the practical possibilities of Zionism and its moral motivations. This solution is vital for Zionism, which is meant to be more than merely the programme of some colonising association."[83]

In Ben-gavriêl's opinion an "organic solution" did not just demand the renunciation of any violent attempt to enforce Zionist interests. He thought that the re-orientalisation of the Jews was necessary to reach the goal which to him was the deeper sense of Zionism, "a brotherly alliance of Arab and Jewish communities in a free Arab-Jewish Palestine".

He sees signs of such a re-orientalisation when he is observing Jewish youth in Palestine. "These young people are bound up in nature and because of this withdrawn from cultural over-refinement, more dependent on themselves . . . than young people in Europe."[84] His descriptions of the young Jews are meant to witness their adjustment to the Orient.

> "I have seen Jewish boys, almost children, riding on galloping horses. I have seen them shooting, bringing in the harvest, suntanned, the Keffije wound around their heads, hardly to be distinguished from the Arab, singing Hebrew reaping songs . . ."[85]

In another passage he describes wedding-celebrations of Jews from the Yemen and of *hasidim* from Poland.[86] He believes that he can discern similarities between the Yemenite and the *hasidic* dances and songs and from this concludes that the Yemenite music has an old-Jewish origin and that *hasidic* music has an Oriental

---

[82]*Ibid.*, p. 195.
[83]Hoeflich, *Die Pforte des Ostens, op. cit.*, p. 70.
[84]Eugen Hoeflich, *Der Weg in das Land. Palästinensische Aufzeichnungen*, Wien 1918, p. 23.
[85]*Ibid.*, p. 24.
[86]Cf. *Ibid.*, p. 69–77.

origin. This line of argument is supposed to prove his central allegation that the Jews are an Oriental people. Though exile has stigmatised the Jews who live in Europe, it could not destroy their very nature, the characteristics and abilities running in their blood. He therefore calls them "half-Orientals" and his judgements do not allow any doubt about his wish that they should become complete Orientals again, get rid of the internalised restraints they were burdened with in Europe, and be integrated into the great community of the Oriental people. The Jews should prove themselves friends of the Arabs in a common fight against the European influence over the Orient,[87] they should thus gain their confidence and together with them form a new society without establishing a state.[88]

Other authors, also advocating an agreement between the two peoples, do not go as far as demanding that the Jews free themselves from European customs and values, but they, too, emphasise that Jews and Arabs are kin. In addition they refer to the ethos of the Bible, in particular to the ethos of the Decalogue and the Prophets, to prove the possibility of and demand the readiness for an agreement.[89]

Most of the Zionist authors confine themselves to expressing general approval of the readiness for an arrangement with the Arabs, but do not come to a far-reaching conclusion in respect of policy in Palestine. Propositions and ideas mostly aim at improving relations in every-day life, whereas the political dimension is missing. Frequently these suggestions are not postulated directly, but the authors, by using the narrative possibilities of a travel description, report examples of open-mindedness and good neighbourliness: medical aid for Arab villagers, invitations to feasts, lending out of seeds and agricultural machines to Arab farmers and so on.[90] Thus, by referring to their own concrete experiences, the authors try to suggest their optimistic expectation as to a possible agreement.

Every-day experiences also serve to demonstrate the Arab neighbours' readiness for friendly contacts with the Jews, when the Arabs are not incited and do not appear in fanatical masses.[91] Such positive examples can be taken as a call for good neighbourliness, but they also give the impression of being representative of the existing situation, as if the relations between the different groups of the population were developing in such a way that – as was occasionally remarked[92] – only the stubbornness of the politicians hindered a definitive peaceful solution of the Arab question in Palestine.

Even in generalisations about the state of Arab-Jewish relations, references to every-day life often supersede the political dimension of the conflict between the two populations. Grete Fischer writes in 1934:

> "Relations between the two Semitic peoples are indeed not very close. But they are neighbours: sometimes for the better, sometimes for the worse. They inveigh against each

[87]Cf. *Ibid.*, p. 27.
[88]Cf. Hoeflich, *Die Pforte des Ostens, op. cit.*, p. 35.
[89]Cf. Salten, *op. cit.*, pp. 65–67, 148, 155; Abeles, *op. cit.*, p. 74.
[90]Cf. Gottgetreu, *op. cit.*, pp. 74, 77f.; Abeles, *op. cit.*, p. 57; Herrmann, *Palästina heute, op. cit.*, pp. 85–91.
[91]Cf. Kupferberg, *op. cit.*, pp. 132f.
[92]Cf. Herrmann, *Eine werdende Welt, op. cit.*, p. 47.

other, cut one another out of competition if possible, separate their occupations and businesses. But Arabs travel by Jewish buses and Jews by Arab vehicles, they buy at the same market places. What they like best, however, is to disregard each other."[93]

These comments aimed at making it appear likely that the conflict would gradually become less harsh, can also be read "against the grain": then the tendency for mutual isolation of Arab and Jewish Palestine becomes prominent, making it more and more unlikely that the Arab-Jewish antagonism could be overcome by co-operation, an aim which can be considered the core of Ben-gavriêl's rationale.

At that time a solution to the conflict, even on the political level, could only be achieved (if at all) at the cost of giving up the fight for hegemony in Palestine. But even those Zionist authors who supported an open-minded and friendly attitude towards the Arab population were obviously not ready to do this – with the exception of Ben-gavriêl. When contentious political issues are mentioned at all, the authors reject any making of concessions to Arab demands and keep to the ideas which were advocated by the majority of the Zionists. They argue against the formation of a parliamentary representation, in which the Arab side would, of course, have the majority, and advocate an economic separation of Arabs and Jews.

It is not surprising, therefore, that the ideas of the *Brith Shalom* were rejected, not only by authors who regarded the Arabs as enemies, but also by those who supported an accommodation.[94] For the *Brith Shalom* in its endeavour to reach a Jewish-Arab agreement, opposed the striving for a Jewish majority and supported the economic integration of the Arab and the Jewish Palestine with the aim of forming a bi-national society.

Such ideas, however, were accepted by some non-Zionist authors, although not by all of them.[95] Alfred Wiener clearly shows his sympathy for the group around Arthur Ruppin, Hugo Bergmann and others, although he is sceptical about the chances for *Brith Shalom*'s efforts, because he believes that Zionism could not renounce the Balfour Declaration, continued Jewish immigration and the purchase of land without itself giving up. Nevertheless he asked the Zionists to support the Arabs' plans for self-administration in Palestine and by doing so to stick to democratic convictions, even if they were afraid of the inevitable Arab majority in a parliamentary assembly.[96]

In 1936 Werner Cahnmann still maintained that Jewish-Arab co-operation in the field of economy was necessary,[97] and he supported suggestions for "common Jewish-Arab autonomy in Palestine within the context of a pro-British Arab

---

[93]Amiel, *op. cit.*, p. 70.
[94]Leopold Goldschmied, *Palästina. Ein Tagebuch*, Prague 1933, p. 39; Kupferberg, *op. cit.*, p. 154.
[95]Selig Schachnowitz, editor of the leading journal of the *Agudas Jisroel*, in a very polemic way criticises the followers of the *Brith Shalom* because of the way they try to reach an Arab-Jewish arrangement and rates their suggestions as unrealistic. His theme, however, is not the struggle for a Jewish majority and an autonomous Palestine, but the experience of the pogrom-like riots of 1929, particularly the destruction of the Orthodox community of Hebron. Cf. Selig Schachnowitz, *Zwischen Ruinen und Aufbau in Erez-Israel. Eindrücke von einer Erez-Israel-Reise mit der Palästina-Centrale der Agudas-Jisroel*, ed. by the Palästina-Centrale der Agudas-Jisroel, Frankfurt a. Main 1932, p. 61.
[96]Cf. Wiener, 'Juden und Araber', *loc. cit.*, pp. 498–501, 508.
[97]Cahnmann, *op. cit.*, p. 12.

federation".[98] Though for the present – in view of the riots in Palestine and the unyielding attitude on the part of the Arabs – he believed it to be the task of the Palestinian Jews to strengthen their positions of defence,[99] he asked them, nevertheless, even while the fighting was going on, to think about compromises which could lead to permanent peace.

[98]*Ibid.*, p. 19.
[99]*Ibid.*, p. 18.

A Diarist in fin-de-siècle Berlin and her Family Helene, Joseph and Erich Eyck

BY FRANK EYCK

In November 1938 my father Erich Eyck, the historian, and my mother received their belongings from Germany, which they had left slightly more than a year previously. The property in question had been released after payment of the *Reichsfluchtsteuer* (the so-called capital flight tax), but still showed the labels of the earlier – as it turned out temporary – confiscation by the authorities. The furniture and household goods were a great help to Hedwig Eyck in the guest-house she took over in the London suburb of Hampstead to provide the livelihood for her family, and the books invaluable to Erich Eyck in the historical writing that was to win him international renown.[1] The papers that arrived in London included a number of family letters and two notebooks containing the journal Erich Eyck's mother kept in Berlin in the two decades before her death in 1898.[2] The journal gives a vivid picture of the life of an educated German-Jewish middle-class family in the German capital and throws light on the early development of Erich Eyck.[3]

Helene Veitel was born in Halle in May 1857, the daughter of the businessman (*Kaufmann*) Adolph Veitel and his wife Theresa née Gottschalk.[4] Early in 1877 Helene – who by this time resided in Leipzig with her family – married Joseph Eyck,[5] who for many years was a broker at the grain exchange in Berlin. Joseph

This article is dedicated to Dr. Arnold Paucker, a long-time friend, in gratitude for his outstanding contribution to the development of the study of German-Jewish history.

[1] See *inter alia* William H. Maehl, 'Erich Eyck', in S. William Halperin (ed.), *Essays on Eminent Europeans. Some 20th Century Historians*, Chicago 1961, pp. 227–253; Klaus Hildebrand, 'Erich Eyck', in Hans-Ulrich Wehler (ed.), *Deutsche Historiker*, vol. II, Göttingen 1971, pp. 98–119.

[2] The papers of Erich Eyck, including his mother's journal, are in my sole ownership. I deposited copies of most of the papers in the *Bundesarchiv* in Koblenz. There is continuing interest in the life and work of Erich Eyck, and I have dealt with a number of enquiries over the years, making material available whenever possible. Unfortunately, a doctoral dissertation at a German university failed to materialise, after I had spent considerable time on arranging for the student to do the research.

[3] I gratefully acknowledge here the financial contribution to the expenses for the work on the journal given to me through a research grant from the University of Calgary, using funds provided by the Social Sciences and Humanities Research Council of Canada. My thanks also go to my sisters, Mrs. Irene Reuter and Mrs. Eleanor Alexander, as well as my cousins Dr. F. Gunther Eyck, Mrs. Marianne Scheck and Mr. Gerhard Rosenberg for information on the history of our family supplied by them.

[4] Most of the details concerning the birth and descent etc. of Joseph and Helene Eyck are taken from the information kindly supplied by *Standesamt Charlottenburg von Berlin*.

[5] The date emerges from Adolph Veitel's letter from Leipzig of 3rd January 1877 about the reading of the banns.

had been born at Freystadt (Kreis Rosenberg), West Prussia in November 1846 and was thus about ten years older than his wife. Helene was well-educated and her first entries in the journal were made in 1876, while she was reading Goethe's *Wahlverwandtschaften*. Goethe provided a strong link to German culture for educated German Jews. Her second son Erich (born in December 1878) – like at least some of his siblings – was certainly strongly influenced by Goethe, whose works he knew thoroughly and whom he honoured deeply.

The journal was kept as a record of the development of the children, for later consultation by them and their parents.[6] It describes in detail the story of a growing family, the development of the children, the attitude to Judaism and relations with the Christian outside world. The first post-matrimonial entry in the journal is dated 4th June 1881, by which time three children had been born; Hans, the oldest, in 1877, with Erich the following year and Erna in 1881. Hans was to be a successful patent lawyer in Magdeburg and Erna to marry a relative from her mother's side, Fedor, a capable architect, whose surname had been adapted from Veitel to Feit. There were three more children. Trude (born in 1883) married Arthur Nussbaum, the distinguished jurist; Ernst, born in 1886, who went into business; and Lilli, born in 1893, who became a language teacher and married the physician Hermann Pineas. There are many references in the journal to infectious diseases,[7] which, given the state of medical knowledge at the time, could easily be fatal. Remarkably all six children survived to adulthood, but the youngest two died of tuberculosis, Ernst at about forty and Lilli at thirty-three.

With a cook and a maid, and often a *Fräulein* for the children, the household thus eventually grew to eleven, the supervision of which constituted a major task for Helene.[8] One sometimes wonders whether the pressure "to live according to one's estate"[9] was not a burden. Certainly for the husband and father, Joseph, the struggle to keep up middle-class standards and to secure the means of providing a cultured home for the family involved frequent worry. This is reflected both in the journal and in the letters Helene wrote to her husband from that part of the prolonged family summer holidays during which he had to work in Berlin. Husband and wife face these problems together, in a spirit of partnership. Obviously Helene is well-informed about their situation. Even so, as early as 1884 there are references to monetary worries,[10] and in 1891 to their not very secure financial circumstances.[11] However, even that year Joseph and

---

[6]Journal, 4th June 1881.
[7]They were tonsilitis, pneumonia, whooping-cough, measles and diphtheria (which was treated with serum).
[8]Journal, 7th October 1895.
[9]"Man mußte standesgemäß leben." This characterisation of the financial pressures on higher officialdom in the period by Ernst Heilborn, *Zwischen zwei Revolutionen*, vol. II, Berlin 1929, pp. 214f., is quoted in John C. G. Röhl, *Kaiser, Hof und Staat. Wilhelm II. und die deutsche Politik*, Munich 1987, p. 153.
[10]Journal, 2nd June 1884.
[11]Journal, 1st January 1891.

Helene had their holidays in Switzerland, one of two major trips they undertook without their children;[12] the other spent in Scandinavia in 1895.[13] In 1896 there appears to be another serious monetary crisis for the family, which leads to the abandonment of all plans to go away for the usual summer holidays.[14] The following year Joseph's appointment as manager of the Berlin brewery firm *Krugbier-Gesellschaft* brought some hope. Helene's father anticipated a splendid future for the firm, and hoped to support the enterprise by concluding agreements with breweries and beer distributors in Leipzig, presumably also in the interest of his son-in-law.[15] Helene was more sceptical, believing that for several reasons (which she did not state) the success of the company was not assured. Also the previous years, when Joseph had been a broker at the grain exchange, had not gone too well,[16] so that there was a great deal to be made up. Helene fully recognised the effort involved for the head of the family in earning all the money for the daily bread of his loved ones and for the provision of their educational needs, such as musical instruction. Joseph found the new job physically very exhausting.[17] Interestingly enough, Helene considered the post to be a particular burden because she regarded her husband at the age of 51 as a man of advanced years (*im vorgerückten Lebensalter*). In response to the difficulty of making ends meet, Helene repeatedly suggested making economies, though she did not indicate where the cuts should be made. In any case, in many ways the family lived in quite a simple style. For the children a buttered roll and sugar on an ordinary week-day were something quite special.[18] While she felt that it would not do the children any harm if their standard of living were somewhat reduced, she regretted her and her husband's nervousness due to their financial worries. The punishments the children received – corporal ones only as a last resort after due warning – would otherwise sometimes have been milder.

For many years the growing family lived in the increasingly cramped quarters in Oranienburger Straße 59, in central Berlin (in what was to form part of the Eastern sector of the city after 1945). This was a few houses away from the liberal synagogue at Oranienburger Straße 30, which had been completed in 1866. Originally designed by the famous architect Eduard Knoblauch, the synagogue had oriental features to distinguish it from churches. At the same time the architecture demonstrated its character as a public building as it was set facing the street, whereas at one time the Jews had to hide away their places of

---

[12]Journal, 18th and 22nd July 1891.
[13]Journal, 26th August 1895.
[14]Journal, 17th July 1896.
[15]Adolph Veitel to Joseph Eyck, 21st September 1897.
[16]Possibly this may have had something to do with the severe decline in grain prices. See J. H. Clapham, *The Economic Development of Germany and France 1815 to 1914*, Cambridge 1961, pp. 211ff.; Erich Eyck, *Das persönliche Regiment Wilhelms II. Politische Geschichte des Deutschen Kaiserreiches von 1890 bis 1914*, Erlenbach–Zürich 1948, esp. pp. 68 and 77.
[17]Journal, 26th November 1897.
[18]Journal, 6th September 1883 and 20th October 1884.

worship.[19] Incidentally the synagogue could accommodate a congregation of three thousand, about twice the capacity of the *Kaiser-Wilhelm-Gedächtniskirche*.[20]

In spite of all obstacles, however, in 1893 the family moved to a "better" district in the West of the city, in the proximity of the *Tiergarten*. At first they lived in Klopstockstraße and in 1897 went to live in the then rather quiet Augsburgerstraße (roughly parallel to the Tauentzienstraße on its southern side).

In her efforts to bring up her children, Helene does not spare herself. Any idea of thinking in modern feminist terms of "self-realisation" is alien to her. She has a task – both joyful and worrisome[21] – to which she has been called; to work together with her husband for the good of their family. The supervision of the upbringing of their children is primarily left to her, but here, too, she is assisted by her husband, whose authority constitutes a power of last resort with the children. Her reward is the love and affection her family have for her and any success that her pedagogy may yield with her children over the long term. She is open to new methods and in October 1882 arranges for the children to be taught by a *Kindergarten* teacher employing the Fröbel method[22] focusing on the natural and spontaneous development of the child, which turns out very well.[23] She watches the development of her children with great care and quite realistically, trying to develop positive features and correcting so far as possible negative ones, such as laziness or a quick temper. Her aim is that both the boys and the girls should one day be able to stand on their own feet as decent people. She is not over ambitious for them in intellectual or professional respects, but she wants them to realise their potential, for their own satisfaction. She attaches great importance to getting on with other people and is pleased if any of them are well liked. Helene is particularly happy at any feeling of sympathy or care for others that her children show. She emphasises the need for good manners, including at table, partly for reasons of hygiene, as well as of proper posture because of the health aspect.[24]

In many respects, the home Joseph and Helene Eyck provided for their children would have found many parallels in Christian families of the period in Germany, both Protestant and Catholic. Was there anything characteristically Jewish about the way they lived together? How did they react to the Christian society around them? How much contact did they have with it?

Joseph (to a greater extent than Helene) had received a Jewish upbringing, from parents who continued practising their religion.[25] Kreis Rosenberg, in which Joseph's birthplace Freystadt was situated, had belonged to the Duchy of Prussia ("East Prussia") which the Electors of Brandenburg inherited from their

[19]*Wegweiser durch das jüdische Berlin. Geschichte und Gegenwart*, Berlin 1987, pp. 108ff. I owe the gift of this book to the *Informationszentrum Berlin* on the occasion of an invitation by my native city for its 750th anniversary in 1987.
[20]*Ibid.*, p. 92.
[21]Journal, 10th June 1891.
[22]Journal, 9th October 1882.
[23]Journal, 25th April 1883.
[24]Journal, 31st December 1888, 2nd January 1891 and 17th July 1896.
[25]Apparently Jakob Eyck, Joseph's father, commissioned a Torah which was destroyed in the November 1938 "*Kristallnacht*".

Hohenzollern relatives in 1619.[26] The district was only later allocated to West Prussia, as part of an administrative re-arrangement following the annexation of that territory from Poland.[27] Freystadt itself was a small township with a population of upwards of two thousand inhabitants, with a cattle market and a grain trade. There was a Protestant church and a synagogue.[28] In a Jewish congregation which was not too large for all the families to know each other, religious observance must have played a vital role. It was not easy to miss out on it, as in the comparative anonymity of a large city. Also generally in the Eastern territories – like West Prussia, Silesia and Poznań – strong bonds within the Jewish community must have been required as bulwarks against the more numerous ethnic Germans and Poles in the region.[29] As in other parts of the Prussian territory conquered earlier by the Teutonic Knights, the landed nobility played a considerable part. The local *Reichstag* constituency, Marien-werder-Rosenberg, was represented by Protestant Conservative land-owners and former *Landräte*, usually from the nobility, from the establishment of the North German Confederation up to the end of the monarchy, except for one break. From 1890 to 1898 the riding was held by a Roman Catholic physician in the Polish interest.[30] The Neudeck estate, which was to become well-known as the home of Joseph Eyck's near-contemporary President Hindenburg was only five kilometres away from Freystadt.[31] When Joseph grew up in Freystadt, Field Marshal Hindenburg's grandparents still owned Neudeck.[32]

For Joseph the departure from a comparatively rural area was fraught with consequences. The transfer to the city from the countryside or a small township (corresponding to an East European *shtetl*) often brought in its train the abandonment of the keeping of religious customs, such as the dietary laws and the maintenance of the Sabbath.[33] All too easily, the greater assimilation to German culture the westward move appeared to bring within reach could lead to a loosening of the ties to the faith, at any rate to its rites. In Berlin, from the time he became more independent from his parents, Joseph moved away from strict

[26]Early in the Nazi period, the presence of the Eyck family on "German" territory was traced back to 1685.

[27]Paul von Hindenburg, *Aus meinem Leben*, Leipzig 1929, p. 4. The preface to this later edition is dated September 1919.

[28]These details are taken from E. Uetrecht (ed.), *Meyers Orts- und Verkehrs-Lexikon des Deutschen Reichs*, vol. I, Leipzig 1912, p. 512. The population of Freystadt is given as 2,607.

[29]The Polish presence did not necessarily impinge strongly on Freystadt itself.

[30]Max Schwarz, *MdR. Biographisches Handbuch der Reichstage*, Hannover 1965, p. 146, and detailed biographies of members.

[31]*Meyers Orts- und Verkehrs-Lexikon des Deutschen Reichs*, vol. II, Leipzig 1913, p. 260.

[32]Some time after the end of the First World War, the estate passed out of the possession of the Hindenburg family. But in 1927, as a present for his eightieth birthday, the *Feldmarschall* and *Reichspräsident* received the gift of the former family home purchased with money provided mainly by German industry. Erich Eyck, *Geschichte der Weimarer Republik*, vol. II, Erlenbach–Zürich 1956, pp. 333–334, which also describes the motives of the leader of the East Prussian agrarian lobby, von Oldenburg-Januschau, in initiating the gift, as well as some dubious tax aspects of the transaction on President Hindenburg's part. For the connection of the Hindenburg family with Neudeck see also von Hindenburg, *op. cit.*, pp. 4–5.

[33]See Monica Richarz (Hrsg.), *Jüdisches Leben in Deutschland. Selbstzeugnisse zur Sozialgeschichte im Kaiserreich*, Stuttgart 1979. Veröffentlichung des Leo Baeck Instituts, esp. pp. 48f.

religious observance. Sabbath observance in the household of Joseph and Helene was not very strict, but Friday was kept as a kind of half-holiday.[34] Also the children certainly said their prayers regularly.[35] Helene records in May 1898 that Lilli, the youngest, had got into the habit – instead of saying prayers – of reciting a poem out of a picture book. Helene felt that the poem thus received a proper consecration.[36] That biblical knowledge is imparted to the children is apparent from a remark of the oldest daughter about her youngest brother. When Ernst (aged four) leaned over the side of his bed and bragged about his good behaviour, the nine-year-old Erna commented: "He behaves like a Pharisee, he leans out of the window and proclaims his good deeds!"[37] Dietary laws are not kept strictly; there are several references to ham being eaten.[38] However, ritually cooked fish is served on Fridays[39] and there is some aversion to non-kosher food.[40] The children receive their presents on *Weihnachtsabend*.[41] In 1882 Helene suggests having the two elder boys instructed in Hebrew, partly to please Joseph's parents, but the husband would not agree, and thus the project was not pursued for the time being.[42] However, this must have been made up later on, for both had their barmitzvah when it was due. Helene thought of Hans's barmitzvah with great joy, "for it was, whatever one may otherwise think about the religious aspect of the celebration, a real family festival".[43] In Erich's case, about a year later, Helene uses the German term *Einsegnung* rather than barmitzvah when recording the event in the journal. The family character of the religious custom is once more stressed, but additionally hope is expressed "that an admonition and a recollection of this day will always recall him [Erich] to his duty, more than the threat of punishment".[44] When Joseph's father Jakob died in Berlin in 1895, Erich apparently said Kaddish for the required period.[45]

It is clear from all this that the ethic of Judaism – which has much in common with other religions – was imbibed, indeed that it was taken for granted. Joseph and Helene shared Jewish moral values, thanks to their upbringing, even if they had abandoned much of the ritual, as the great majority did when they moved away from the countryside and settled in large cities, such as Berlin.[46] They were convinced that they could pass on this moral heritage without exposing their children to the degree of religious observance to which Joseph, at any rate, had been accustomed at home. But to what extent could this particular moral

[34] Journal, 2nd January 1891.
[35] There are references to this in the journal of 21st February 1884, 2nd January 1891 and 16th May 1898.
[36] Journal, 16th May 1898.
[37] Journal, 2nd January 1891.
[38] For instance in Helene's letter to Joseph of 9th August 1878 from Arnstadt.
[39] Journal, 2nd January 1891.
[40] There is a reference to the purchase of kosher sausages: "I do not like to eat the others any more". Helene to Joseph from Arnstadt, 20th July 1878.
[41] Journal, 2nd January 1891.
[42] Journal, 9th October 1882.
[43] Journal, 17th January 1891.
[44] Journal, 4th January 1892.
[45] Recollection of a reminiscence of Erich Eyck.
[46] Richarz (Hrsg.), . . . *im Kaiserreich, op. cit.*, p. 48.

Joseph and Helene Eyck with five of their children, Berlin c. 1888
From left to right: Hans, Erich, Trude, Ernst and Erna

Erich Eyck as a young man

heritage be maintained beyond the generation which had still practised the Judaism on which it was based? To what degree was there any prospect that the ethical code could continue beyond the next generation, in which the children had still been able to witness the example of parents who had been observant, at least during their youth? In what measure was the move away from ritual connected with assimilation and acculturation? Was there a problem of reconciling an adherence to German culture with continuing to follow the faith of one's ancestors?

Legally, there was no requirement relating to the possession of German citizenship which depended on belonging to any particular faith or which affected the exercise of an individual's worship. A German could be Jew, of any particular complexion, from the Orthodox to the most liberal. A Jew also had the right to leave the congregation and to declare himself a dissident, or to convert to a Christian denomination. It did not occur to Helene and Joseph Eyck or to their children to take any of these steps away from Judaism. They all remained and married within the faith. Ties within the extended family, which included "in-laws" were very close, as is shown, for instance, by the fact that three marriages took place between the Eycks and the Veitels.[47]

Was there some kind of a subtle pressure in the German environment to weaken the ties to Judaism? German Nationalism saw religious division as a nuisance from the point of view of national unity, but in this respect Protestants actually often regarded Roman Catholicism as much more of a real threat than Judaism. While it is true that, at any rate during certain periods, German Roman Catholics found themselves branded as enemies of the *Reich* and as *prima facie* disloyal, owing to their greater numbers they were better able to deal with the emotional shocks they suffered than the Jewish minority.

Jewish families formed friendships mainly within their faith, as the journal, which goes up to 1898, and the surviving letters confirm. Among families mentioned are the Calés, including the later poet Walter Calé, then a boy.[48] Emma Weiß – the mother of Bernhard Weiß, the later Deputy Police Commissioner for Berlin in the Weimar period – was particularly dear to Helene, who was deeply shaken by her early death.[49] Erich Eyck was later on very close terms with Bernhard Weiß[50] both in Berlin and, after their emigration, in London. Dr.

---

[47]Besides the two mentioned in the text, there was a marriage between James Eyck and Anna Veitel in 1880, which broke up around 1902 (Erich Eyck papers).

[48]In a letter from Helene to Joseph from Friedrichroda of 4th August 1890. Helene described Martin Calé, Walter's father, a *Kaufmann*, as an educated, fine man. See also 'Walter Calé', in Theodor Lessing, *Der jüdische Selbsthaß. Mit einem Essay von Boris Groys*. Munich 1984, pp. 152–166. This citation does not necessarily imply that the present writer agrees with Lessing's categorisation of a brilliant young poet, who took his life in Berlin in 1904, in his twenty-third year.

[49]Journal, 28th March 1892.

[50]For Bernhard Weiß see Werner Röder and Herbert A. Strauss (eds.), *Biographisches Handbuch der deutschsprachigen Emigration nach 1933/International Biographical Dictionary of Central European Emigrés 1933–1945*, 3 vols., München–New York–London–Paris 1980–1983, vol. I, p. 809; 'Bernhard Weiss remembered. Courageous Prussian Jew', in *AJR Information*, November 1981; Dietz Bering, 'Isidor – Geschichte einer Hetzjagd. Bernhard Weiß, einem preußischen Juden zum Gedächtnis', in *Die Zeit*, 14th August 1981; and *idem*, *Der Name als Stigma. Antisemitismus im deutschen Alltag 1812–1933*, Stuttgart 1988, *passim*.

Peltesohn was the physician Helene and Joseph consulted for themselves and their sons and daughters. Presumably the domestic staff, including the *Fräulein*, were usually Christian. Thus, during the first years of their life, the children were comparatively sheltered from the problems of contact with the Christian majority and those posed by antisemitism. But all this changed once they began their school education, by which time Helene was certainly very conscious of current anti-Judaism in word and deed. Like all her generation, she was deeply shocked by the antisemitic outbreaks in Russia following the killing of Tsar Alexander II by a bomb set off by terrorists. She was obviously worried, too, by the antisemitic propaganda conducted by the court preacher Adolf Stoecker in Germany itself, to which she referred in a letter to her husband in July 1881, while on holiday:

> "Altogether the newspaper can make one ill and nervous. [There is] nothing in it but incitement against the Jews, infernal machines, and bloodshed. How badly that fits in with our lovely stay [here], how little one understands the hatred of human beings, you will know best."

She added that she would not worry about any newspaper any more once her husband had joined her.[51]

Helene thus had antisemitism partly in mind when she wrote about her children in September 1883, before the eldest entered school:

> "If only one could for rather a long time preserve for them untroubled their childlike nature and their genuine cheerful spirit; if only their contact with their fellow students would not break this bloom and the hazy veil of poetry, which is only found in the soul of a child, and drive them all too soon from this children's paradise, in which they live so innocently without concern for the future and view each day as a new miracle and as a new playground."[52]

The two elder boys had been told that, when the time came, they would be going to the *Friedrichsgymnasium*, one of the leading schools in Berlin providing a classical education:

> "What a role the school, which they do not know, already plays with them and with what pride they say 'our school, the *Friedrichsgymnasium*'; may they find joy and happiness at school, in learning, in all that is great and beautiful, and may they be spared a hatred and ill-will which easily affects them as Jews; and may we as parents be allowed to surround them with love, care and every good until they make their own way in the world, so that in their mind's eye they may see their parental home for a hundred years as a radiant and peaceful place and that they may carry within them the good seed and bring it once more to good fruition."[53]

Helene felt that childhood was too short and that school, with the considerable demands it made on children, encroached too early and too much on it. She, therefore, decided to delay as long as possible the school entry of the girls, believing that starting half a year later would not matter much to them.[54] When the fifth child, Ernst, reached school age, she was, in any case, not looking forward to being without him for much of the day, as she loved his company. But

---

[51]Helene to Joseph from Friedrichroda, 29th July 1881.
[52]Journal, 6th September 1883.
[53]*Ibid*.
[54]Journal, 26th January 1886.

when the matter had to be settled in the spring of 1892, there was an even weightier reason for hesitation:

"... probably he [Ernst] will be going from Easter onwards to school [apparently to the *Friedrichsgymnasium*], to which I am reluctant to send him as at the present an indescribable antisemitism prevails there from which the boys of the middle forms, to which Erich belongs, suffer very much; for not only do the fellow-students show an incredible impudence, but the *Untertertia* form master is so inconsiderate as to punish a boy who had used the word 'Goy' to defend himself more severely than the Christian students who had uttered the most incredible insults; on the contrary he more or less expressed the opinion that the Jewish students could actually thank God 'that they had been admitted at all as Germans and Prussians through the emancipation!' Thus spoken in the year of grace 1892, *fin de siècle*!

If such sentiments were not promoted [artificially] from above, they could not exist. Of course, at a time when the Emperor himself condescends to give speeches such as the one at the end of February to the *Landtag* of the Mark [Brandenburg], we can look forward to the strangest and most dangerous developments! The disturbances in the streets have passed without special mishaps, but there, too, one tries to drag in antisemitism, although the masses attacked the stores to be plundered without making any distinction between different religions."[55]

At the banquet of the Brandenburg provincial assembly on 24th February 1892, the Emperor had complained about those who consistently criticised the measures of the government. He asked whether it would not be better if these discontented grumblers shook the German dust from their feet. He invoked God and expressed his "unshakeable conviction that our old ally of Roßbach and Dennewitz [Prussian victories respectively over the Austrians in 1757 and the French in 1813] would not forsake him. He [God] had taken infinite trouble with our old Mark and with our dynasty." Wilhelm added that he would lead his Brandenburgers towards glorious days.[56]

Among those who shared Helene's concern with the Emperor's speech was the famous diarist, the Baroness Spitzemberg, wife of the Württemberg minister in Berlin. She was an intimate member of the Bismarck circle and an admirer – though not an uncritical one – of the founder of the *Reich*. She recorded in her diary on 28th February: "We are all very dismayed and distressed at the Emperor's recent speech in the provincial *Landtag*, which is the worst that he has made in this respect up to date and which really makes one fear megalomania [in him]."[57]

There cannot be any doubt that the antisemitism he experienced at school left scars on Erich. That his experience was not unusual is clear from a statement by Walther Rathenau, the later Foreign Minister, which derives additional weight from the fact that he belonged to a successful, well-connected family: "In the youth of every German Jew there is a painful moment which he remembers all his life: when he becomes fully conscious for the first time that he has entered the world as a second-class citizen and that no ability and no merit can free him from this situation."[58] However, in spite of the incidents mentioned, Erich held the

[55] Journal, 6th March 1892.
[56] A.O. Klaußmann (ed.), *Kaiserreden. Reden und Erlasse, Briefe und Telegramme Kaiser Wilhelms des Zweiten. Ein Charakterbild des Deutschen Kaisers*, Leipzig 1902, pp. 400–402.
[57] Rudolf Vierhaus (ed.), *Das Tagebuch der Baronin Spitzemberg. Aufzeichnungen aus der Hofgesellschaft des Hohenzollernreiches*, Göttingen 1960, p. 297.
[58] Walther Rathenau, 'Staat und Judentum. Eine Polemik', in *idem*, *Gesammelte Schriften*, vol. I, Berlin 1918, p. 189. Quoted in Richarz (Hrsg.), ... *im Kaiserreich*, *op. cit.*, p. 38.

Friedrichsgymnasium as such in great esteem and appreciated the encouragement he received from some of his teachers, particularly in the senior classes. In spite of all the turmoil in the early part of 1892, Erich, in fact, did better in April than his mother and father expected. He was promoted to the next class with a good ranking. So far as the objectivity of the school report was concerned, Helene regarded criticisms of Erich made in it (such as bad posture) as justified. She knew – as did the teachers at school and as Erich later freely admitted – that he was at times simply lazy. However, things began to change in 1894, when he – against expectation – passed his *Einjähriges*, the promotion to *Obersekunda* which carried with it a reduction of the period of compulsory military service to one year. Helene recorded with delight that the school principal, Professor Vogt, had spoken favourably of Erich and had called him "a very gifted boy", who during his last two years at school was certain to acquire the serious attitude to study which he might be lacking at present.[59]

By 1896, the parents already benefit from the moral support they receive from their eldest child. Hans, now nineteen years old, is praised by his mother for his sterling character, "treu wie Gold". She adds:

> "He feels and thinks with us. He surrounds us with the most tender love and very much senses the worries which burden us, particularly his father, at the present time."[60]

The mother is now convinced that Hans will, in due course, make good in his chosen profession. Erich, too, was beginning to make his way. For many years the parents showed grave doubts about the staying power and diligence of the two elder boys. Towards the end of his *Gymnasium* schooling Erich was beginning to show his great intellectual gifts and knowledge:

> "Erich has read much, very much and good [things], and his historical and literary knowledge is very significant, and his wish would be to study these subjects, but as a Jew and as the son of parents who are not rich he is prevented from doing so and has to follow the well-trodden path of the legal profession."[61]

Naturally Erich could have followed his own inclination and studied history, instead of the law, but at that time a university career was liable to progress very slowly, if at all. There were comparatively few paid professorial posts in a subject like history. While waiting for one of these to come up, there was usually a prolonged period of service in the unsalaried position of *Privatdozent*. The possession of private financial means was, therefore, almost a necessity for the academic aspirant. For example, Arthur Nussbaum, the future husband of Trude Eyck,[62] was thus enabled to risk the long wait required before receiving a salaried position. In Nussbaum's case this was liable to be even longer as he was a Jew. During the Empire the promotion of Jews to "full" professor (*Ordinarius*)

---

[59]Journal, 8th January 1895.

[60]Journal, 29th December 1896.

[61]*Ibid.*

[62]Nussbaum met his future wife through the lawyer Curt Rosenberg, who attended an economics seminar at the University of Berlin with Erich Eyck. Rosenberg introduced Eyck to Nussbaum. See Curt Rosenberg, 'Jugenderinnerungen', in Richarz (Hrsg.) . . . *im Kaiserreich, op. cit.*, pp. 303–304. Rosenberg married Else Stein, Helene Eyck's niece. His piece contains many interesting insights into the German-Jewish relationship.

was a rarity. Berlin University appointed Nussbaum *Dozent* in 1914, titular professor in 1918 and *außerordentlicher Professor* in 1921. He was dismissed in 1933, and from 1934 to 1950 was Research Professor of Public Law at Columbia University, New York. Nussbaum acquired an international reputation as a scholar whose work ranged widely over many aspects of the law. He died in New York in 1964.[63]

The journal does not chronicle daily events and is not primarily concerned with politics, except where – as we have seen – general events impact on the family. The reference to Emperor Wilhelm II in 1892 is negative. Joseph and Helene appear to have tended to Left-Liberalism in the sense of the *Deutsche Fortschrittspartei*. The early death of Friedrich III in 1888 after a reign of only ninety-nine days was perceived as a severe blow. Friederich's proclamation '*An Mein Volk*', with its liberal constitutional message, was treasured and apparently had a place of honour in the home. Helene was certainly devoid of any strong German nationalist feelings. A few weeks after the publication of the treaty with Great Britain which ceded Heligoland to Germany, Helene expressed her regret not to have visited the island while an English governor and English coastguards carried on their activities there: "Who knows whether it will later still have its charm, when the 'German representative' has hoisted his flag." She added that she found the newspaper press altogether quite abominable, that it abounded in accidents and crimes.[64]

Looking back on the journal and the surviving letters, it is often difficult to distinguish Jewish and German elements, as they were so closely interwoven. The family life that emerges from these records is impressive in the combination of both, intimately bound up with German culture without any surrender of the spiritual Jewish heritage. Family life was intimate. The sense of justice and duty, combined with the importance of caring for others and of mutual respect, was emphasised.

Helene made the last entry in her journal on 4th September 1898. She was full of joy over the development of her youngest child, Lilli, who was by now five years old. She felt that she was experiencing a second youth with her.[65] Helene was deeply thankful for her daughter's affection, which she warmly reciprocated, and for her intelligence and quick-wittedness. Incidentally, although he was fifteen years older, the relationship between Erich and his younger sister Lilli was particularly close. After many years of worry about her second son, Helene now had the highest terms of praise:

> "Erich has become good and capable, his character is industrious and frugal, and if he continues to utilise his fine gifts so felicitously, something will become of him (according to his father)."

His health had benefited from his stay in Freiburg, where he was studying law, and his independence had done him good.[66]

[63]Röder and Strauss (eds.), *op. cit.*, vol. II, p. 689; *New York Times* obituary, 22nd November 1964.
[64]Helene to Joseph Eyck from Friedrichroda, 9th August 1890.
[65]Journal, 16th May 1898.
[66]*Ibid.*

Helene died on 26th December 1898 at the age of 41. It was Hans, the eldest, by that time a student, who helped the desolate father by reporting the death to the authorities at the *Standesamt*. Husband and children were shattered. Helene may have had a premonition that she would pass from this earth before her time. In September 1883 she confessed her fears for the future of her children in the journal. She hoped to be able to complete the education of the children at the side of her husband,

> "but if things were ordered differently . . . would I know anybody to whom I would want to entrust my place, of whom I would believe that he [sic] could continue in my sense the work that has been started? I believe not, for – though there may be many women who would be better at educating, would they bring along the mother's heart, the acquaintance with the potential, characteristics, faults, which rest in *our* children? No and a thousand times no."[67]

When Helene died, a void was left for husband and children. Naturally the younger children were affected with particular severity, possibly Trude most as an adolescent of fifteen years of age. All the children held the memory of their mother very dear.

Joseph did not remarry and was eventually looked after by a housekeeper. For a time he was Berlin representative of a number of business firms with head offices elsewhere.[68] He was apparently a director of the *Viktoria Mühle*, a highly reputed feed-and-seed business corporation. Although Joseph never did brilliantly in business, unlike his brother-in-law Ludwig Stein,[69] who took over the delicatessen firm of Rollenhagen, he does seem to have commanded a great deal of respect among his peers. However, Joseph was elected president of the Greater Berlin branch of the *Hansabund für Gewerbe, Handel und Industrie*.[70] The preponderantly Liberal *Hansabund* was founded in 1909 as a counterweight to agrarian – and particularly large land-owning – interests represented mainly by the Conservatives. In the 1912 *Reichstag* election, the organisation, up to a point, scored considerable successes against these groups. The association, which was dominated by an oligarchy of banking, wholesale and industrial circles, had close links with Liberals of both the Right (*Nationalliberale Partei*) and Left (*Freisinn*). The policy of the *Hansabund* was largely determined by the National Liberal *Reichstag* deputy Jakob Riesser, who was president of the central association of German bankers. Riesser, by religion a Protestant, belonged to a prominent, originally Jewish family closely connected with the emancipation movement in 1848.[71] Berlin, where the *Hansabund* was founded, remained its focal point. Joseph Eyck was elected chairman of the Berlin branch, which honoured him at

---

[67]Journal, 6th September 1883.
[68]Adolf Veitel to Joseph Eyck, 22nd April 1902.
[69]The husband of Helene's younger sister Louise ("Lieschen").
[70]On the association, see Siegfried Mielke, *Der Hansabund für Gewerbe, Handel und Industrie 1909–1914*, Göttingen 1976.
[71]In the constitutional debate in the Frankfurt Parliament during August 1848, Gabriel Riesser cited the discrimination he had himself suffered, in his speech supporting the removal of legal disabilities for Jews. See Frank Eyck, *The Frankfurt Parliament 1848–49*, London 1968, pp. 242–243.

a celebration for his seventieth birthday in November 1916, at which Riesser spoke.[72]

The most useful source on the last decade of Joseph Eyck's life proved to be the husband of his youngest child, Lilli. Hermann Pineas[73] was born in Düsseldorf in 1892 and served as a medical officer in the German army during the First World War. He was at first stationed on the Eastern front, but spent some time back in Germany as he was ordered by the army authorities to take his final medical examinations there. During his stay in Berlin, for his studies, he got to know Lilli Eyck, whom he married in July 1918. Dr. Leo Baeck, who had taught Pineas about Judaism while he was a schoolboy in Düsseldorf, officiated at the wedding, which took place in Joseph Eyck's apartment at Passauer Straße 26 in the Charlottenburg district in the old West of Berlin. Erich Eyck was among those who held the *Huppah* at the wedding. Leo Baeck, who stayed on for the wedding meal after the ceremony, had, incidentally, arranged for the bride to be given some religious instruction before the wedding, as he had found she had some deficiencies in this respect. Pineas himself was a practising Jew. Joseph Eyck was a member of the *Jüdische Gemeinde zu Berlin*, belonging to the synagogue in the Oranienburger Straße. However, at that time he did not fast or attend synagogue on the High Holy Days. He gave his admission tickets for the synagogue service to Dr. Pineas, who attended with his wife. There were no longer any special arrangements for the Sabbath in the home of Joseph Eyck, who had a Christian housekeeper, Fräulein Fischer.

The Eycks showed a strong family spirit and Pineas expressed special gratitude to his wife's older sister Erna and to her husband Fedor Feit for arranging his transport to Berlin from the military hospital in Weimar, where he was treated after being severely wounded on the Western Front in mid-October 1918. The Feits were also most generous and helpful to other members of the family. It is interesting to note that Helene Eyck spotted some of these features in Erna quite early, when her daughter was only nine:

---

[72]Cutting from unidentified monthly journal of November/December 1916 in Erich Eyck papers, which also contain material on the arrangement for the celebration. I had the pleasure of meeting the former executive director of the *Hansabund* in the decade up to 1933, Professor Hans Reif (by then a *Freie Demokratische Partei* deputy in the *Bundestag*), in 1954. Reif still remembered Joseph Eyck from his work with the *Hansabund*.

[73]By chance I stumbled on the piece by Hermann Pineas in the section 'Überleben in Deutschland 1941–1945', in Monika Richarz (Hrsg.), *Jüdisches Leben in Deutschland. Selbstzeugnisse zur Sozialgeschichte 1918–1945*, Stuttgart 1982. Veröffentlichung des Leo Baeck Instituts, pp. 429–442, while working in the *Staatsbibliothek* in Munich in 1986. I remembered that he had been married to Lilli Eyck, who died in the second half of the twenties. Fortunately Dr. Fred Grubel of the Leo Baeck Institute, New York, was able to confirm that Dr. Pineas was still alive and I was able to have three days of discussion with him. Dr. Pineas died in 1988. I also want to thank Dr. Michael Riff, formerly of the Leo Baeck Institute, for allowing me to consult him while I was in New York. I thank the Department of History and the Faculty of Social Sciences of the University of Calgary, as well as the Calgary Institute for the Humanities, for financial aid and encouragement. Dr. Gordon Hamilton gave me much useful advice while we were both fellows of the Institute during the academic year 1985–1986.

"Erna . . . shows extraordinary goodness to her fellow-creatures, especially towards subordin-
ates and gives away everything without a moment's consideration, in order to give joy to
somebody."[74]

In general Helene Eyck was quite shrewd in her positive observations on her
children, loving but not uncritical. Negative comments mainly applied to phases
of gradual development.

During the early days of their marriage, Hermann and Lilli Pineas regularly
dined with Joseph Eyck, as Hermann's earnings as a physician were meagre at
the beginning of his professional career. Lilli taught commercial French at the
Privathandelsschule in the Wittenbergplatz, the square in which they also had their
apartment. By this time Joseph Eyck had retired from the Berlin grain exchange,
but he still acted as a referee in disputes there. This activity, like that in the
Hansabund, reflects recognition from the non-Jewish community in Berlin.
Incidentally Joseph returned to his West Prussian birthplace in July 1920, when
he voted in the plebiscite on the future of the territory, presumably lending his
support for its continuance with Germany and rejecting its transfer to the re-
established Poland. As a result of the overwhelming majority for Germany in the
plebiscites in the region, the *status quo* was maintained in the areas in question.

Joseph died of old age in Berlin in his apartment in Passauer Straße on 17th
November 1925, honoured as a patriarch by his children and grandchildren. By
the time of his death his children were well established, among them Erich Eyck,
with whom the remainder of the article is concerned.

Although Eyck would have preferred to have read history as his main subject,
he settled down well to his law studies at Freiburg, before he returned to Berlin to
complete his degree there. But he kept up his broad interests. Even from his early
twenties onwards, he was able to combine in a remarkable way a whole variety of
interests, particularly in the law, politics and writing. Following the Left-Liberal
bent of his parental home, he became associated with one of the parties
connected with it, the *Deutsche Volkspartei*,[75] which had its adherents mainly in
Southern Germany, and one of whose leaders was Leopold Sonnemann, the
owner of the influential *Frankfurter Zeitung*. Eyck made his debut as an author
around June 1899, when he was only twenty years old, with a pamphlet on
unemployment and unemployment insurance published under the auspices of
the *Deutsche Volkspartei*.[76] It is thus not surprising that he chose as the subject of
his doctoral dissertation at the University of Berlin, which he did in history
rather than law, a topic connected with the origins of the German workers'
movement. He examined the history of the *Vereinstag Deutscher Arbeitervereine*
formed in 1863 to provide an alternative to Ferdinand Lassalle's programme. A
leading sponsor of this movement was Leopold Sonnemann, who strongly
opposed the class struggle concepts of Lassalle on the one hand, and Marx and
Engels on the other. Sonnemann believed that the problems of society could only
be solved by co-operation between the bourgeoisie and the workers. He

[74]Journal, 2nd January 1891.
[75]This party was quite distinct from that founded by Stresemann at the end of 1918.
[76]Erich Eyck, *Die Arbeitslosigkeit und die Grundfragen der Arbeitslosen-Versicherung*, Frankfurt a. Main
1899.

emphasised the importance of self-help and of individual responsibility. However, the new movement was short-lived, as it was taken over in 1868 by supporters of the class struggle, who in due course proceeded to form the Social Democratic Party.[77] In the foreword to his dissertation, Eyck thanked Sonnemann, whose attention he had already attracted earlier through his treatise on unemployment,[78] for suggesting the topic and for providing him with material. Apparently Sonnemann was very pleased with Eyck's work, as he became a kind of patron of his,[79] received him when he came to Berlin and later – when Eyck visited Britain – agreed to publish his reports in the *Frankfurter Zeitung* whenever possible. In 1904 Eyck received his doctorate *cum laude*.[80] He had four distinguished examiners, the philosopher and pedagogue Friedrich Paulsen, the economists Gustav Schmoller and Adolf Wagner, and the historian Hans Delbrück. He regarded Delbrück as a model because of the independence and candour he displayed.[81]

While continuing to be an avid reader of historical literature, which proved a boon when he turned to writing his major books, he concentrated on his career as a lawyer, which was, after all, to provide his livelihood. The obstacles to a Jew succeeding in the legal profession were comparatively few. The career had been tried by other Jews, who could be consulted by new entrants and who could employ them in their partnerships.

There may well be another major reason for the attraction the legal profession had for Jews. This has something to do with the emphasis on the law in the Torah. Jews had an advantage in imbibing some training in legal concepts through their biblical study. However, there are clearly many other avenues to law and justice.

Once the decision for a career in law had been taken, Eyck concentrated on making it a success. He discharged the obligatory period of court service as a *Referendar* in Luckenwalde, just south of Berlin, which he enjoyed, after which he was promoted to *Assessor*. In 1906 he established himself as a lawyer in Berlin, at first taking a job with a partnership of lawyers who were also Jews. In 1910 he set up in practice on his own. This was soon after his marriage to Hedwig Kosterlitz in May 1910. The introduction came through two sisters, Trude Goldschmidt and Agnes Riegner[82] (nées Arnheim), both married to lawyers, so that the law proved useful in more ways than one. Hedwig Kosterlitz had been born in Pless,

[77]While recognising many of the merits of the Social Democrats during the Empire, Eyck criticised their dogmatic bias and class isolation. See Erich Eyck, *Die Sozialdemokratie*, Berlin 1912, which came out under the imprint of the book-publishing firm of the journal *Die Hilfe*.
[78]See the letter from the *Frankfurter Societäts-Druckerei* to Eyck of 7th October 1898 (Erich Eyck papers).
[79]See Eyck's letter to Carlheinz Gräter of 6th January 1962 (Erich Eyck papers). Eyck received a personal copy of Heinrich Simon, *Leopold Sonnemann. Seine Jugendgeschichte bis zur Entstehung der "Frankfurter Zeitung". Zum 29. Oktober 1931* (privately printed at the *Frankfurter Societäts-Druckerei*).
[80]The title of the dissertation was: *Der Vereinstag deutscher Arbeitervereine 1863–1868. Ein Beitrag zur Entstehungsgeschichte der deutschen Arbeiterbewegung*, Berlin 1904. The dissertation was published in 1904 by Georg Reimer in Berlin under the same title.
[81]Erich Eyck to the Dean of the Faculty of Philosophy, *Freie Universität* of Berlin, 3rd April 1964.
[82]The son of Heinrich and Agnes Riegner, Dr. Gerhard Riegner, served as General Secretary of the World Jewish Congress.

Upper Silesia in 1888, but had as a small girl moved to Berlin, where her father set up a demolition firm. Adolf Kosterlitz, a practising Jew, was initially not entirely happy with the religious background of his son-in-law,[83] but time was a great healer and Hedwig's family was won over by the happiness of the young couple. Hedwig proved a wonderful helper to her husband through the ups and downs of life and supported fully all his professional activities, culminating in his historical scholarship.

Eyck took great care over his legal work and served his clients with intelligence, knowledge and integrity. He became a member of a circle of like-minded colleagues, mainly Jewish, among them Rudolf Isay (who converted to Protestantism and married a Catholic),[84] Heinrich Riegner (Agnes Riegner's husband), Richard Calé (a brother of the poet Walter Calé), Heinrich Veit Simon (a member of one of the leading families of the Jewish congregation)[85] in Berlin and later Max Maier,[86] who practised in Frankfurt.

Thanks to great determination, seemingly boundless energy and generally robust health, Eyck was able to combine his legal work with a host of other activities, mainly to do with writing and politics. As a lawyer he gained considerable experience in the interpretation of documents and the weighing of evidence, as well as in their evaluation through his written briefs (*Schriftsätze*) and court pleadings. He was admitted to the bar of the *Kammergericht*, the supreme court of Prussia, in Berlin, and eventually was also appointed public notary.

In time, Eyck became an accomplished writer and speaker. He immersed himself in the contemporary political scene, adhering to a Left-Liberal stance. He took advantage of the wonderful opportunities Wilhelminian Berlin offered to a young man eager to find things out for himself. He often watched debates in both the *Reichstag* and the Prussian *Landtag* and, thanks to his knowledge of *Debattenschrift*, was able to practise alertness by taking the proceedings down in shorthand. Of the speakers, he was drawn particularly to Theodor Barth, one of the Left-Liberal leaders, who edited the weekly journal *Die Nation*, to which Joseph Eyck had been a loyal subscriber for many years, and which Erich had begun to read avidly even during his schooldays at the *Gymnasium*. He himself contributed to the journal from 1902 onwards.[87] As a university student, Erich Eyck consulted Barth on an economics paper he was attempting. He was at once impressed by Barth's friendliness and by the absence of any air of superiority towards much younger people. Eyck was privileged to be entertained by Barth in

---

[83]I owe this information to the late Dr. Erika Suchan, a close friend of the family, who was told by Hedwig Eyck. Apparently, at the bridegroom's wish, there was only a registry ceremony.

[84]See Rudolf Isay, *Aus meinem Leben*, Weinheim/Bergstr. 1960.

[85]For Veit Simon see Ernst G. Lowenthal, *Juden in Preussen. Biographisches Verzeichnis. Ein repräsentativer Querschnitt*. Herausgegeben vom Bildarchiv Preußischer Kulturbesitz, Berlin 1981, p. 232. See also *Hermann Veit Simon. Geboren am 8. Mai 1856, gestorben am 16. Juli 1914. Zum Gedächtnis*, privately printed, Berlin 1915.

[86]See Max Hermann Maier, *In uns verwoben, tief und wunderbar. Erinnerungen an Deutschland*, Frankfurt a. Main 1972; idem, *Ein Frankfurter Anwalt wird Kaffeepflanzer im Urwald Brasiliens. Bericht eines Emigranten 1938–1975*, Frankfurt a. Main 1975; Matilde Maier, *Alle Gärten meines Lebens*, Frankfurt a. Main 1978.

[87]I am greatly indebted to Dr. Helmut Goetz for the bibliography of Erich Eyck's works compiled by him. The list totals about 280 items.

a small circle at his Tiergarten residence in Berlin. To the end of his life he regarded him as one of the two great masters of politics at whose feet he had sat, the other one being Friedrich Naumann.[88] He met Barth frequently at various political functions and for many years this parliamentarian with his free trade views, his opposition to all forms of state tyranny and his support for an opening to the Social Democrats best represented his views. While Eyck fully recognised the outstanding parliamentary expertise and strength of conviction of Eugen Richter, leader of the *Deutsche Fortschrittspartei* and then of the *Deutsche Freisinnige Partei*[89] into which it merged, he disapproved of a certain rigidity in both his ideas and in his tactics. Above all Eyck was critical of Richter's conduct in 1893, when he insisted on expulsion from the parliamentary group of those *Reichstag* deputies who had broken ranks by voting in favour of Chancellor Caprivi's army bill. This split the Left-Liberals, because the expelled deputies formed their own party, the *Freisinnige Vereinigung*, which Barth also joined, although he had voted against the bill. All this was past history when Eyck began to take an active part in political life at the turn of the century, but undoubtedly it influenced his attitude. He was opposed to any further splintering of Liberal forces and attributed the decline of the Left-Liberals mainly to their divisions.[90] In restrospect, from a historian's perspective, he also questioned the wisdom of Liberal opposition to the government after Caprivi had taken over from Bismarck. At any rate, when he began his political work, it was for the *Freisinnige Vereinigung* of Theodor Barth,[91] rather than for the *Deutsche Freisinnige Partei* of Eugen Richter.

It was through Barth that Eyck got to know his other political teacher, Friedrich Naumann. The attraction to Naumann is not quite so obvious at first sight as that to Barth. Indeed, it may appear strange that Eyck was strongly influenced by a Protestant pastor who had earlier collaborated in the Christian Social movement with the antisemitic leader Adolf Stoecker. But he emphasised in an appreciation published in 1924 that Naumann travelled quite a distance from the Christian-Social views of his youth, by way of his intermediate programme of reconciling monarchy and democracy at the turn of the century, to the Liberal-Democratic attitude of his mature days.[92] As a young man Eyck must have been profoundly impressed by Naumann's charisma. He regarded Naumann's death just after his election to the leadership of the *Deutsche Demokratische Partei* (DDP) – the successor of the Left-Liberals of the Empire – in 1919 as a grave loss for the new regime. He believed that Naumann's ideas

[88]'Meine politischen Lehrmeister', in Erich Eyck, *Auf Deutschlands politischem Forum. Deutsche Parlamentarier und Studien zur neuesten deutschen Geschichte*, Erlenbach–Zürich 1963, pp. 65–72, which came out thanks to the initiative of his publisher, Dr. Eugen Rentsch, and appeared the year before Eyck's death in 1964.

[89]*Freisinnig* literally means free-thinking.

[90]Eyck, in *Das persönliche Regiment Wilhelms II.*, *op. cit.*, p. 71, called the Left-Liberal divisions of 1893 suicide.

[91]See Eyck's letter of 6th January 1962 to Carlheinz Gräter, who was then working on a dissertation about Theodor Barth (Erich Eyck papers). Cf. Carlheinz Gräter, *Theodor Barths politische Gedankenwelt. Ein Beitrag zur Geschichte des entschiedenen Liberalismus*, Ph.D. diss., Würzburg 1963.

[92]Erich Eyck, *Auf Deutschlands politischem Forum*, *op. cit.*, pp. 69–72.

exercised a profound effect generally on both Left and Right, which was not in any sense confined to those who had followed his banner.

To the Naumann circle Eyck owed one of his close and enduring friendships, that with Theodor Heuss (later to be the first Federal President) and with his wife Elly, the daughter of the economist Georg Friedrich Knapp. In 1903 Naumann and many of his followers joined the *Freisinnige Vereinigung* under Barth. In order to bring the two groups closer together, a fortnightly gathering was arranged at an inn. Theodor Heuss was a close collaborator of Friedrich Naumann (and later his biographer),[93] and became his aide on his journal *Die Hilfe*, to which Eyck contributed from 1906 onwards. As Heuss put it in a volume of his memoirs, Eyck turned up at the circle as a follower of Barth, "a soft, not yet firmly drawn personality".[94] Elly Heuss, who was incidentally very active in women's causes, became a mother not long before Hedwig Eyck and taught her how to swaddle a baby. Erich and Hedwig Eyck were particularly impressed by the way Elly came to the rescue, when the Nazis deprived Theodor Heuss of his livelihood. The present writer still remembers Elly Heuss when visiting the Eycks in Berlin with her husband, demonstrating the advertising techniques she pioneered to provide for them.

Through his political work Eyck also met a Left-Liberal called Vossberg, who died early, as well as Fritz Kempner, the later *Staatssekretär* of the Weimar period. Vossberg's widow, Editha, later married a senior government official, *Ministerialrat* Rau. Kempner was involved in the 20th of July 1944 plot. After its failure the Raus hid him in their home in Berlin, until he decided to surrender to the authorities. Frau Rau visited Kempner in prison before his execution. As with Theodor and Elly Heuss, the Eycks had a close relationship of great mutual warmth with Frau Rau.

Before the First World War, during some longer visits to Great Britain, Eyck was deeply impressed by what he saw there of the operation of parliamentary government. He was particularly lucky the first time, when he witnessed the Liberal landslide at the general election of January 1906[95] and formed some lasting friendships with British Liberals, particularly with the journalist Harold Spender and his wife Violet (née Schuster), and with the historian G. P. Gooch, who had just gained a seat in the House of Commons.[96] Increasingly Eyck judged the German political system by the extent to which it fell short of the standards of parliamentary responsibility set in Great Britain.

For medical reasons Eyck did not serve in the First World War. He was discharged from the army as a young man after a short period of conscription, as he had collapsed on the parade ground. Medical re-examination during the war maintained his exemption from military service. From 1915 to 1920 he was a member of the Charlottenburg *Stadtverordnetenversammlung*, until the municipality

---

[93]Theodor Heuss, *Friedrich Naumann. Der Mann, das Werk, die Zeit*, Stuttgart 1949, first published in 1937.

[94]*Idem, Vorspiele des Lebens. Jugenderinnerungen*, Tübingen 1953, pp. 281–282.

[95]He had the honour of an invitation to the National Liberal Club Dinner in February 1906 where the new Prime Minister, Sir Henry Campbell-Bannerman, delivered the address (Erich Eyck papers).

[96]See Frank Eyck, *G. P. Gooch. A Study in History and Politics*, London 1982, chap. 7 and *passim*.

was incorporated into Greater Berlin.[97] From 1928 to 1930 he served on the Berlin *Stadtverordnetenversammlung* at a critical time, earning the friendship of men like Ernst Reuter,[98] who was then responsible for the city's transport system. From its foundation Eyck belonged to the Left-Liberal DDP, one of the keenest supporters of the parliamentary system in the Weimar Republic. Eyck was also a leading member of the *Demokratischer Klub* in Berlin, which attracted excellent speakers and provided stimulating discussion. Unfortunately after a good initial showing, the DDP saw its parliamentary strength dwindle. In 1930 the party leader, Erich Koch-Weser,[99] whom Eyck knew well, believed that the only way to arrest the decline of the party was to broaden its base. He therefore proposed amalgamating with the *Jungdeutscher Orden*, which had moved from a position on the Right to greater acceptance of the democratic republican order. Many of the older members of the party, including probably Eyck himself, had grave doubts about the new partner,[100] but in the end agreed to go along and accepted fusion with the *Orden* under the name of *Deutsche Staatspartei*. Unfortunately, this rather desperate step did not bring its reward in the *Reichstag* election of September 1930. The number of seats shrank even further and the deputies drawn from the *Jungdeutscher Orden* soon seceded. August Weber,[101] a close friend of Eyck, who succeeded Koch-Weser as party leader, was faced with an almost hopeless task.

In 1915 Eyck joined the famous German-Jewish Ullstein publishing firm[102] as law correspondent (*Juristischer Mitarbeiter*) of the highly respected and oldest Berlin newspaper *Vossische Zeitung*. He founded its law section *Recht und Leben* which soon made a name for itself for its comments on legal issues, particularly on the role of law in society.[103] From the beginning of 1916 until the Nazi period Eyck contributed to the *Vossische Zeitung*, which was close to the DDP,[104] on a whole range of legal, political and historical subjects, paying particular attention

[97]Here a fellow councillor was Oscar Meyer, a prominent member of the Democratic Party in the Weimar period, who became a friend. See Röder and Strauss (eds.) *op. cit.*, vol. I, p. 498; Schwarz, *op. cit.*, p. 714.

[98]When Reuter, by then Mayor of West Berlin, came to London not long before his death in 1953, he invited Eyck to dinner, to which the author was allowed to accompany his father as the only other guest.

[99]Koch-Weser served as a *Reich* minister in the Weimar Republic. Himself a Protestant, he came under the Nazi racial laws because of Jewish descent on his mother's side. He emigrated to Brazil and helped to develop the plantation settlement at Rolandia, where he was joined by Rudolf Isay and Max Maier. For Koch-Weser see Röder and Strauss (eds.), *op. cit.*, vol. I, p. 376.

[100]When I asked my father many years later about the *Jungdeutscher Orden*, he simply replied that they were antisemites. The position of the order, which suffered severe persecution at the hands of the Nazis, is not easy to sum up.

[101]Weber, a brave opponent of the Nazis, after several *Gestapo* interrogations emigrated to Britain in 1939 and settled in London. Earlier on, he had, incidentally, been on the board of the *Hansabund* (Röder and Strauss [eds.], *op. cit.*, vol. I, p. 798).

[102]It was at Ullstein just before the Nazis came to power that Eyck met Hans Schäffer, who was appointed *Generaldirektor* in 1932, after serving as *Staatssekretär* in the *Reich* ministry of finance. Schäffer greatly assisted Eyck with material for his two-volume work on the Weimar Republic. For Schäffer see Eckhard Wandel, *Hans Schäffer. Steuermann in wirtschaftlichen und politischen Krisen. 1886–1967*, New York 1974.

[103]There is a microfilm of *Recht und Leben* for the years 1923–1931 in the Wiener Library in London.

[104]See Modris Ekstein, *The Limits of Reason. The German Democratic Press and the Collapse of Weimar Democracy*, Oxford 1975.

to Great Britain, on which he continued to look as a model for parliamentary government. In his writings he emphasised the importance of ensuring that Jews were treated fairly by the justice system.[105] Eyck played a leading role in the *Centralverein deutscher Staatsbürger jüdischen Glaubens*,[106] which saw no insuperable obstacle to combining loyalty to Germany with Jewish faith. He was a life-long opponent of Zionism, which he believed would undermine the position of Jews in the countries to which they belonged. In 1912 he was on the executive of the anti-Zionism committee, incidentally together with the Eyck family's physician *Geheimer Sanitätsrat* Dr. Peltesohn and Bernhard Weiß.[107]

Most of Eyck's energy was spent on the general defence of the rule of law and of the parliamentary and democratic system, to which he devoted a pamphlet on the crisis of German justice in 1926.[108] When, in December 1932, the National Socialists agreed to have their theory of criminal justice debated, they faced Eyck as the speaker defending the rule of law. The National Socialist lawyer and member of the *Reichstag*, Dr. Hans Frank ("Frank II"),[109] was to propound Nazi ideas. The lawyer and writer Ernst Feder noted in his diary on 12th December 1932:

> "In the evening [went] to the *Oberverwaltungsgericht* where the National Socialist theory of criminal law is to be discussed. One-sided, for Frank II bolts. Fabricius [another Nazi *Reichstag* member] spoke miserably for him in the discussion. [The speech by] Eyck is good. The crowded hall is full, [there are] many young lawyers (*Juristen*)".[110]

With the appointment of Hitler as Chancellor the following month, Eyck's influential activity as a writer and speaker on matters of concern to a democracy and a *Rechtsstaat* came to an end.

A section of anti-Jewish opinion during the Wilhelminian period "who looked to integration to remove friction between Gentiles and Jews" was often impatient with what it regarded as the "snail's pace of integration".[111] Was the latter judgement a correct assessment and was it applicable to the two generations of the Eyck family covered in this article? So far as highly-educated Jews – on whom material is available – were concerned, the very opposite is usually true. The speed of assimilation was, indeed, as with the Eyck family, often increased by the move westwards from the Eastern territories of the Prussian monarchy.

---

[105]In June 1927, Erich Eyck delivered a lecture on 'Die Stellung der Rechtspflege zu Juden und Judentum' under the auspices of the *Centralverein deutscher Staatsbürger jüdischen Glaubens*, which was published in *Deutsches Judentum und Rechtskrisis*, Berlin 1927, pp. 33–66.

[106]See Arnold Paucker, *Der jüdische Abwehrkampf gegen Antisemitismus und Nationalsozialismus in den letzten Jahren der Weimarer Republik*, Hamburg ²1969.

[107]I owe this information to Professor Klaus J. Herrmann.

[108]Erich Eyck, *Die Krisis der deutschen Rechtspflege*, Berlin 1926.

[109]Frank was Governor-General of Poland during the war and was executed as a war criminal in 1946.

[110]Arnold Paucker, 'Searchlight on the Decline of the Weimar Republic. The Diaries of Ernst Feder', in *LBI Year Book XIII* (1968), p. 233. See also Ernst Feder, *Heute sprach ich mit . . . Tagebücher eines Berliner Publizisten 1926–1932*, Herausgegeben von Cécile Lowenthal-Hensel und Arnold Paucker, Stuttgart 1971, Veröffentlichung des Leo Baeck Instituts, p. 325. For other references to Eyck in Feder's diaries see *ibid.*, pp. 29, 80, 180, 205, 224 and 323.

[111]Donald L. Niewyk, 'Solving the "Jewish Problem" – Continuity and Change in German Antisemitism 1871–1945', in *LBI Year Book XXXV* (1990), p. 346.

The events of 1933 virtually put an end to the fruitful German-Jewish interaction after some decades which – while they did not lack problems – seemed to show significant progress.* This article is an attempt to record aspects of the life of a group of well-educated Jews, who achieved high ethical and intellectual standards, marked by a true tolerance attained without compromising moral values.[112]

*For a discussion of such forms of German-Jewish relationships, the reader is referred to the essay by Werner E. Mosse, 'Integration and Identity in Imperial Germany. Towards a Typology', in this volume of the Year Book, pp. 83–99 – (Ed.).

[112]I want to thank here especially my wife, Rosemarie, who – coming from a different background – has, through her sympathy and understanding, been able to enter into my family's German-Jewish heritage. Much of the preservation of my father's books and papers, as well as making as much archival material as possible available to others, has been due to her unstinting efforts.

East and West in Orthodox German-Jewish Novels (1912–1934)

BY MICHAEL BRENNER

On the eve of the First World War a debate in one of the most prestigious German cultural journals attracted the attention of a great part of the German literary world,[*] an episode which has been treated again and again in German-Jewish historiography. A Zionist-orientated German Jew, Moritz Goldstein,[1] published an article in *Der Kunstwart* in which he criticised the "control" Jews wielded over German literature. According to Goldstein, this reflected the extremely unhealthy situation of German and Jewish culture alike. He suggested, therefore, that German Jews should retreat from their conspicuous position in German literature, and instead concentrate on Jewish culture.[2] More specifically, he called for the creation of a Jewish literature in the German language, written by Jewish authors, on Jewish topics, and for a Jewish audience. Both Zionists and liberal Jews did in fact express their different conceptions of Judaism in the form of German novels and plays. While their literary endeavour is relatively well-remembered, and some of their works have been recently reprinted, similar contributions by Orthodox Jews have gone unnoticed by historians and literary critics alike.[3]

---

[*]The author wishes to thank John Efron, New York for his assistance in preparing this article.

[1]Goldstein later published his own account of this stirring controversy in the Year Book. Cf. Moritz Goldstein, 'German Jewry's Dilemma. The Story of a Provocative Essay', in *LBI Year Book II* (1957), pp. 236–254.

[2]Moritz Goldstein, 'Deutsch-jüdischer Parnaß', *Der Kunstwart*, XXV, No. 11 (March 1912). The *Kunstwart* debate is taken up by Jehuda Reinharz, *Fatherland or Promised Land. The Dilemma of the German Jew, 1893–1914*, Ann Arbor 1975, pp. 195–199; and by Steven Aschheim, *Brothers and Strangers. The East European Jew in German and German Jewish Consciousness, 1800–1923*, Madison 1982, p. 56.

[3]Of course, the medium of the novel was used to present the various concepts of Judaism already before the appearance of Goldstein's essay. Theodor Herzl, the founder of Political Zionism was himself the author of such a novel. His *Altneuland* was an early Zionist novel, and in condensed form served as the programme of early Zionism. Among later Zionist writers in the German language, Max Brod and Arnold Zweig were the most celebrated. In *David Reubeni*, München 1925, reprinted 1979, Brod portrayed a Jewish messianic movement, as did Josef Kastein in his *Sabbatai Zewi* a few years later. The liberal Jews had their novelists, too. The most popular among them, whose characters were chosen from an assimilated Jewish milieu, was Georg Hermann, the author of *Jettchen Gebert* (1906) and *Henriette Jacobi* (1908). On the attempts of liberal Jews to create German-Jewish fiction cf. Hans Otto Horch, *Auf der Suche nach der jüdischen Erzählliteratur. Die Literaturkritik der "Allgemeinen Zeitung des Judentums" (1837–1922)*, Frankfurt a. Main – Berne – New York 1985; *idem*, 'Heimat und Fremde. Jüdische Schriftsteller und deutsche Literatur oder Probleme einer deutsch-jüdischen Literaturgeschichte', in Julius H. Schoeps (ed.), *Juden als Träger bürgerlicher Kultur in Deutschland*, Stuttgart – Bonn 1989, pp. 41–65; and Lothar Kahn, 'Neglected Nineteenth-Century German-Jewish Historical Fiction', in Mark H. Gelber (ed.), *Identity and Ethos. A Festschrift for Sol Liptzin on the Occasion of His 85th Birthday*, New York – Berne – Frankfurt a. Main 1986, pp. 156–167.

It is the intention of the present paper to redress this imbalance. Before analysing some of these Orthodox German-Jewish novels, a few background remarks on the development of German-Jewish Orthodoxy are necessary. Just as with the Zionist and liberal Jew, the expression "Orthodox Jew" was an invention of the nineteenth century. Traditional Jewish society in the early modern period did not recognise a separation between various religious and ideological streams. The term "Orthodox Jewry" was created to characterise its opposition to the religious reforms introduced in the nineteenth century. But Orthodoxy was more than just a reaction to internal Jewish developments. It was also a reaction to the external condition of German Jewry. Orthodox Jews in Germany, too, were affected by emancipation, and they, too, eventually acculturated in one form or another.

The new face of German Orthodoxy in the age of emancipation was personified by its leading figure, the Frankfurt rabbi Samson Raphael Hirsch (1808–1888), who attempted to synthesise strict observance of the Jewish law (Torah) with participation in the outside culture (*Derech Eretz*). Like liberal Jews, he basically defined Judaism as a religion, thus enabling him to emphasise his position as a member of the German nation. Hirsch's Neo-Orthodoxy seemed to suit perfectly the urban bourgeois Jews, eager to hold on to tradition, but not willing to retreat into the ghetto. While they were able to combine the readings of Schiller and the *gemarah*, they refused to pay taxes to Reform-dominated Jewish communities, who had introduced organ music into the service and whom they regarded as lax in the observance of the Sabbath and the ritual laws. Consequently, the Neo-Orthodox formed their separate congregations which were recognised by Prussian legislation in 1876.[4]

One of the major differences between traditional Judaism and Neo-Orthodoxy was the latter's adaptation of German culture. As early as the middle of the nineteenth century, Orthodox Jews were not only reading but also writing novels in German. A century earlier, this would have been entirely impossible, not only because of the *lacunae* in language skills but also because occupation with secular writings was regarded as a waste of time which could be better used for religious study.

The most famous representative of nineteenth-century German-Jewish Orthodox *belles-lettres* was Marcus Lehmann, the founder of the leading Orthodox German-Jewish journal, *Der Israelit*. Although Lehmann's novels were still

[4]A solid history of the German-Jewish Orthodoxy during the German Empire has recently been written by Mordechai Breuer, *Jüdische Orthodoxie im Deutschen Reich, 1871–1918. Die Sozialgeschichte einer religiösen Minderheit*, Frankfurt a. Main 1986. Veröffentlichung des Leo Baeck Instituts. Hermann Schwab's *The History of Orthodox Jewry in Germany*, London 1950 and Yehuda Ben Avner's *Vom orthodoxen Judentum in Deutschland zwischen zwei Weltkriegen*, Hildesheim 1987, are not based on any intensive research of the available sources and give only anecdotal accounts of Orthodox Jewish life in *inter-bellum* Germany. Two very valuable studies appeared recently by Julius Carlebach: 'Orthodox Jewry in Germany. The Final Stages', in *Die Juden im Nationalsozialistischen Deutschland/The Jews in Nazi Germany 1933–1943*, herausgegeben von Arnold Paucker mit Sylvia Gilchrist und Barbara Suchy, Tübingen 1986 (Schriftenreihe wissenschaftlicher Abhandlungen des Leo Baeck Instituts 45), pp. 75–93; and 'The Foundation of German-Jewish Orthodoxy. An Interpretation', in *LBI Year Book XXXIII* (1988), pp. 67–91. On Hirsch cf. Robert Liberles, *Religious Conflict in Social Context. The Resurgence of Orthodox Judaism in Frankfurt am Main, 1838–1878*, Westport, Conn. 1985.

reprinted as serial novels in German-Jewish Orthodox journals during the 1920s, they were found wanting, lacking both literary standard and a sense of critical contemporaneity by not addressing the burning questions of the day.[5] A more critical and indeed self-critical approach was taken only a generation later by a few Orthodox German-Jewish writers. In the following pages, I shall analyse the works of Selig Schachnowitz, Pinchas Kohn and Isaac Breuer, three Orthodox German-Jewish writers who did relate to the problems of their day and who presented, in the contemporary setting of their novels, three different perceptions of German-Jewish Orthodoxy in its last phase before destruction.

I

In 1912, the same year that Moritz Goldstein published his essay in *Der Kunstwart*, two Orthodox Jewish novels appeared in Frankfurt a. Main which were referred to as *Hirsch-Romane*, although neither of them was actually a biography of Samson Raphael Hirsch. They were different interpretations of what Neo-Orthodoxy should stand for, a generation after the death of its founder. While the journalist Selig Schachnowitz regarded an urban centre in which German culture was flourishing as the ideal environment for Neo-Orthodoxy, the Ansbach rabbi Pinchas Kohn idealised the rural Orthodox milieu of his childhood.

Selig Schachnowitz was an *Ostjude*, born in Lithuanian Georgenburg in 1874. After studying at various Lithuanian *yeshivot*, he came to Frankfurt a. Main where he attended university. He served for a few years as teacher and cantor in the rural Baden community of Endingen, before he became the editor-in-chief of *Der Israelit*. He edited *Der Israelit* from 1908 until his emigration in 1938, and died in Zürich in 1952. Schachnowitz's main works were historical novels set in different parts of the Jewish world. His topics included Jewish life in Galicia and Ethiopia, the Khazars and the life of the Chatam (Moses) Sofer, an early nineteenth-century rabbi in Pressburg.

In 1912 Schachnowitz published a novel with a contemporary setting, entitled *Luftmenschen*, in which he juxtaposed the rootless world of Eastern European Jewish intellectuals with the safe haven of German-Jewish Neo-Orthodoxy.[6] The *Luftmenschen* are the uprooted Russian *yeshivah* students Maslow, Mandes, Kaplanow and Rubin. They all leave dark Russia to find real culture in enlightened Germany. Yet only one of them, Maslow, succeeds. Mandes becomes a police officer in Kiev and is shot during revolutionary riots, Kaplanow returns to Russia as a Socialist and is sent to Siberia, and Rubin finds his fulfilment as a Zionist in Palestine. These three figures symbolise three modernist ideological options of Russian Jewry: assimilation, Socialism and Zionism.

Schachnowitz's hero, Maslow, realises that the only way to free himself from

[5]On Marcus Lehmann, see Breuer, *Jüdische Orthodoxie, op. cit.*, pp. 145–146.
[6]Selig Schachnowitz, *Luftmenschen. Roman aus der Gegenwart*, Frankfurt a. Main 1912.

his uncultivated *Luftmenschen* friends is to cut all ties with the Eastern European Jewish world. His eyes are opened by the personification of German Neo-Orthodoxy, Bergsen, who employs Maslow as a teacher for his children. The novel is basically an *Erziehungsroman* describing the metamorphosis of a rude Russian *talmud bahur* into a "civilised human being". The autobiographical traits which Schachnowitz depicts in Maslow are unmistakable. Like Maslow, the author himself fled the world of the Lithuanian *yeshivah* to find *Kultur* in Germany and, like his hero, the author first earned his living as a teacher, and found his new home in German Neo-Orthodoxy.

Maslow's employer Bergsen is an almost supernatural being. A successful merchant, he feels as at home in the world of international business and German culture as he does in Jewish tradition. This man, in whose office people from all countries and all professions meet, is a "wonderful phenomenon". While the Russian autodidact Maslow cannot hide his background and lacks concentration and clarity, Bergsen is able to "express the most complicated ideas in clear words . . . so that people of all classes come in droves to the lectures he delivers on a diversity of topics in Jewish and non-Jewish associations".[7] What was most important to Schachnowitz (alias Maslow), was the realisation that Samson Raphael Hirsch's principles are not only theory, but could be lived in practice, that "a union (*Vermählung*) of Judaism and culture [*sic!*], without any concession of the two spheres, as it is outlined in those [e.g. Hirsch's] writings is attainable in reality".[8] One may quote Gershom Scholem's ironic remark made in reference to Samson Raphael Hirsch, to describe Bergsen's place in history; "he lives where Joseph Karo, Friedrich Schiller and Judah Halevi were supposed to have met".[9]

A practical example of this union was German student life with all its traditions of student organisations. The Orthodox *Vereinigung jüdischer Akademiker* created a bizarre combination of *Kommersen* (drinking-bouts) and *shiurim* (Talmud study). Schachnowitz enthusiastically described this atmosphere, which he himself may have experienced as a student in Frankfurt a decade earlier:

> "Salvaging from a lost youth a little joy and happiness, he sang the *Gaudeamus* heartily and participated in the drinking bouts. But then he felt a particular magic, when out of the same throats, from which he first had heard joyous student songs, he now heard the learning, the old learning, out of the old books . . . Here those [Hirsch's] firm principles became reality. Knowledge and religion, Judaism and *Kultur* celebrated their union."[10]

---

[7]*Ibid.*, p. 62.
[8]*Ibid.*, p. 178.
[9]This quote appears in Gershom Scholem's review of Isaac Breuer's *Der neue Kusari*, in the *Jüdische Rundschau*, XXXIX (17th July 1934), translated into English in, Gershom Scholem, *The Messianic Idea in Judaism and Other Essays on Jewish Spirituality*, New York 1971, p. 328.
[10]This passage requires the German original: "Als galt es für ihn, einer verlorenen Jugend noch etwas Freude und Freiheit abzutrotzen, sang er kräftig den Gaudeamus mit, beteiligte er sich trinkfest und radaufroh am Salamandertreiben. Dann aber empfand er es als einen eigenartigen Zauber, aus den Kehlen, aus denen erst frohe Studentenlieder erklungen waren, das Lernen, das alte Lernen aus den alten Büchern mit etwas ungelenker Ausdrucksweise und mit der lieben Unbeholfenheit eines tastenden Kindes zu vernehmen. Hier waren jene gewagten Grundsätze Wirklichkeit geworden. Wissen und Religion, Judentum und Kultur feierten ihre Vermählung." (Schachnowitz, *Luftmenschen*, *op. cit.*, p. 179.)

Apart from these rather crude features of student life, Schachnowitz's novel had its more delicate aspects, too. Like many a good bourgeois novel this one also had its love story. Uncle Bergsen, the personification of perfection has, how could it be otherwise, a perfect niece, Fräulein Hilda, just beginning her career as a teacher. Her first student is Maslow; the subjects are Samson Raphael Hirsch's *Neunzehn Briefe über das Judentum* and his *Jeschurun* which she almost knows by heart. The *Neunzehn Briefe*, the bible of German Neo-Orthodoxy, become the ultimate means of conversion for the Russian emigrant Maslow to Samson Raphael Hirsch's creed. Fräulein Hilda, with her rootedness in German culture, her clarity of thought, her calmness and sense of humour, is the exact opposite of Maslow's former girlfriend, Sonja, who had to struggle to obtain her residence permit in Kiev where she took up her studies without any concrete goals.

The novel has a surprising conclusion. Maslow and Hilda are married and decide to go to Palestine. This, however, does not transform the book into a Zionist novel. The author's intention was to transfer German Neo-Orthodoxy to the Holy Land and was unconcerned with the ideology of Zionism. This was an approach we will see later in a more systematic manner with Isaac Breuer.[11]

II

A review of Schachnowitz's novel in the Orthodox journal *Jüdische Monatshefte* criticised the idealisation of German Neo-Orthodoxy at the expense of Eastern European Jewry:

> "It is a pity that he [Maslow] distanced himself from the Jewish spirit of his home. He thinks he has met a new form of Judaism in Germany, and feels himself to be on a higher level when he looks back on the narrow spirit of his home. This elitist consciousness is very questionable, since it affirms the position of the Reform movement which always argues that traditional Orthodoxy is dead."[12]

The appearance of a review of Schachnowitz's *Hirsch-Roman* in the *Jüdische Monatshefte* had another reason besides objective criticism. In the same year, 1912, the editor of the *Jüdische Monatshefte*, Pinchas Kohn, had presented a very different version of German-Jewish Neo-Orthodoxy in his novel *Joel Gern*, published under the pseudonym "Kopi".[13] Only a few months after the critique of Schachnowitz's *Hirsch-Roman*, the *Jüdische Monatshefte* published an enthusiastic 15-page review of Kohn's 110-page-long novel. The title of the review, 'Auch ein Hirsch-Roman', was a distinct allusion to the review of Schachnowitz's *Luftmenschen* published under the title 'Ein Hirsch-Roman'.[14]

---

[11] I am grateful to Katharina Ochse, who drew my attention to an Orthodox German-Jewish novella, *Gerson Regensburger. Ein jüdischer Bauer*, Zürich 1920, by D. Weinbaum. The hero of this novella, Gerson Regensburger, tried in vain to combine life as a farmer in a small German village with that of an Orthodox Jew. In the end, he comes to the conclusion that traditional Jewish life and return to the soil can only be united in the return to the Jewish homeland. The Zionist motive is expressed much more strongly in Weinbaum's novella than in Schachnowitz's or Breuer's novels.

[12] *Jüdische Monatshefte*, I (1914), p. 440.

[13] Pinchas Kohn, *Joel Gern. Der Werdegang eines jüdischen Mannes*, Frankfurt a. Main 1912.

[14] *Jüdische Monatshefte*, II (1915), pp. 16–31.

Just as Schachnowitz described himself in the character of Maslow, Joel Gern was an autobiographical portrait of Pinchas Kohn, who was born in the Swabian village of Klein-Nördlingen in 1867 and grew up in a rural Orthodox atmosphere. He received his Jewish education in the Orthodox house of Rabbi Auerbach in Halberstadt, and later at the Orthodox *Rabbinerseminar* in Berlin. He did not remain, however, in the big cities of Prussia, and moved back to rural Bavaria accepting a post as *Bezirksrabbiner* in Ansbach. Together with the Frankfurt rabbi Salomon Breuer, he edited the *Jüdische Monatshefte*. Kohn became quite well-known in the Eastern European Jewish world when he, together with Rabbi Emanuel Carlebach of Cologne, was sent to Poland in the First World War as an adviser on Jewish affairs to the military government established by the Germans in Warsaw. He was responsible for setting up constitutions for the Jewish communities of Poland which served many of them until their destruction in the Second World War.[15] In the inter-war period, Kohn was the director of the central office of the *Agudath Israel* World Organisation in Vienna. He returned for a short time to Ansbach serving as rabbi, before leaving Germany in 1938 for Palestine where he died three years later.

Kohn, who became an ardent advocate of Hirsch's principle of separatist Orthodox communities, was described by contemporaries as being inspired by mystical Jewish teachings, far more than his colleagues, most of whom despised kabbalistic traditions.[16] *Joel Gern* is certainly no kabbalistic novel, but it does depict the old traditions of rural Bavarian Jewry which often had their origins in kabbalistic sources. In many respects, Kohn's novel stands in opposition to Schachnowitz's idealisation of Neo-Orthodoxy. In contrast to the latter's dissociation from his original background, Kohn longed to return to the world of his childhood. Instead of the urban bourgeois atmosphere of the cosmopolitan Bergsen, Kohn's ideal was the rural Jew who upholds the traditions of his forefathers. Joel Gern does not attend a German university. Instead of drinking bouts, Kohn tells of rural Jewish customs, such as *Wachnacht*[17] and *Holekreisch*.[18] In place of German literature, Joel Gern admires his childhood readings from traditional Jewish books, such as the *Josippon* and the *Tse'ena U're'ena*.[19]

The plot of the story reflects in many ways Kohn's own life. Joel Gern grows up in the rural community of Ellerdingen, where one still uses the traditional

[15]On his mission in Poland, cf. Alexander Carlebach, 'A German Rabbi Goes East', in *LBI Year Book VI* (1961), pp. 60–121.

[16]Jakob Rosenheim, *Erinnerungen 1870–1920*, ed. by H. Eisemann and H. Kruskal, Frankfurt a. Main 1970, p. 86. On the remnants of kabbalistic teachings in rural South German Jewish communities until the end of the nineteenth century see Breuer, *Jüdische Orthodoxie, op. cit.*, p. 50, and Gershom Scholem, 'Die letzten Kabbalisten in Deutschland', *Judaica 3. Studien zur jüdischen Mystik*, Frankfurt a. Main 1973, pp. 228–246 (on Reb Hile Wechsler).

[17]The night before the circumcision of a newborn boy during which the child was guarded because evil spirits were believed to place it in special danger.

[18]Kohn uses the Franconian dialect and calls it *Holegrasch* (pp. 12–13). This ceremony of namegiving for a newborn child (especially for girls) was common in South Germany and in Alsace.

[19]The *Josippon* was an early medieval account of Jewish historical episodes and legends loosely based on the ancient historian Josephus, while the *Tse'ena U're'ena*, composed in the sixteenth century, was the most popular reading for traditional Jewish women, and in large part consisted of selected bible translations.

terms *shas* or *gemoroh* instead of the more fashionable Talmud, where the *Schulklopfer* still calls the Jews to prayer, where mystical traditions such as the *Wachnacht* are still regarded as holy. Young Joel is for the first time confronted with the outside world when his older friend, the law student Baruch Goldschmidt, comes back home for a visit and ridicules life in the Jewish village: "You in Ellerdingen, you in this awful hole, what do you understand?"[20] Baruch, who soon becomes Bernhard, "poisoned the soul of Joel Gern".[21] Joel's father, shocked by the first signs of his son's estrangement from his traditional upbringing, reacts quickly and sends him to the *yeshivah* of his old friend, Rabbi Jonas Bergenthal in Paskow, in "the East of Germany".[22]

Although Joel misses his Bavarian hills, he accustoms himself to his new environment and makes new friends, mostly East European *bahurim*, uprooted characters similar to the *Luftmenschen* in Schachnowitz's novel. His friend, Meier Pochatew, who has left the *Urtümlichkeit* of his original *hasidic* background, which Joel so much admired, is characterised by a *zerrissenes Innenleben* (torn inner life). The Paskow years are brought to an end by the outbreak of the Franco-Prussian war of 1870, in which Joel participates as a volunteer. Coming to the big city, he meets his friend Bernhard Goldschmidt who has found his way back to his Jewish roots, become the president of the local Jewish community, and wants to hire Joel as the rabbi. But Joel Gern despises the big city with its salons of assimilated Jews and decides to return to a rural Jewish community as a rabbi. This novel, too, contains a love story, which may be compared with the one in *Luftmenschen*. Unlike Maslow, who leaves his Russian friend Sonja for the modern Orthodox Hilda, Joel Gern cuts his ties with the smart and sophisticated daughter of Rabbi Bergenthal, and marries the simple and modest neighbour of his childhood days from Ellerdingen, Melitta.

The reviewer of *Joel Gern* in Kohn's journal realised that the reader might not understand why he called his review article 'Auch ein Hirsch-Roman' and asks the rhetorical question: "I hear the astonished reader ask, 'but, for heaven's sake, what has all that to do with Samson Raphael Hirsch?' " The review, which must have been published with the consent of Pinchas Kohn, tried hard to underline that Kohn stood in the Hirschian tradition, and mentioned two specific proofs for this argument; the first was a short passage in support of the Neo-Orthodox principle of separate Jewish communities: the second was the alleged implementation of Hirsch's modern methods of rabbinical education. Both arguments, however, are rather weak and unconvincing. While the support of the separatist principle is only mentioned in a few lines throughout the whole novel, it remains doubtful if Jonas Bergenthal's *yeshivah*, with its mainly Eastern European *bahurim* students, really reflected Hirsch's position on Jewish education.

It seems that the attempt at harmonising Kohn's position with Hirschian Neo-Orthodoxy was, in fact, an apologetic reaction to Hirschian critics, who rightly regarded this novel as a nostalgic longing for the old "pre-Hirschian" Jewish

---

[20]Kohn, *Joel Gern*, *op. cit.*, p. 30.
[21]*Ibid.*, p. 32.
[22]*Ibid.*, p. 34.

world.[23] It is noteworthy that the same review scoffed at a "super-Hirschianism" (*Überhirschianismus*) of a materialistic urban world as represented in Schachnowitz's *Luftmenschen*. It defended rural Jewish life with all its superstitions and backwardness against "those Hirschians who do not admit that one can also enjoy bliss in Ellerdingen".[24]

While the attempt to make Joel Gern into a Neo-Orthodox Hirschian seems extremely artificial, there is a clear connection with the Eastern European Jewish world in this novel. More than once, Kohn voiced his admiration for the *Urtümlichkeit* of this world and its ideas. While Joel Gern ridicules the modern German rabbinical seminaries which only produce *Hanswürste* (clowns) in an atmosphere lacking any sense of spirituality, he is full of praise for the Eastern European tradition of Jewish learning. In a letter to Jonas Bergenthal's daughter in the "East of Germany", he writes: "We have lost the intimacy of loyalty (*Innigkeit der Treue*) which our fathers regarded as the climax of their happiness on earth. In the East, but further East than where you live, there it is still alive."[25]

For Kohn, Eastern European Jewry represented the vanishing world of German rural Jewish life. He realised that the world of his father was slowly disappearing. When Joel Gern comes back one day to Ellerdingen he is confronted with the fact that most of the Jews have left the village; there were not even enough men for a *minyan* left behind. But the same world could still be found in the East, and especially among the *hasidim*. When Joel Gern discovers a *hasidic* book in the *yeshivah* of Paskow he reads it with great pleasure and the narrator asks: "Where did he read something like this before? Where did he admire so much unselfish devotion? Was this not the picture of his father and his mother?"[26]

The earthiness of the Bavarian village Jews was preserved in the East European *shtetl*, not in Frankfurt or Berlin. This point highlights the unbridgeable gap between Schachnowitz and Kohn. Schachnowitz came from Eastern Europe, but left the world of his youth and was absorbed by the bourgeois notion of German Neo-Orthodoxy.[27] Kohn, on the other hand, grew up in Germany, but felt much closer to the traditional Jew of Galicia, with all his superstitious rituals and his lack of *Bildung*, than to the "civilised" Jew, who went from his *talmud shiur* to the Goethe circle.

In some way, Kohn's approach, as romantic as it may appear, was more "modern" than Schachnowitz's. Since the beginning of the twentieth century, the "discovery" of *Ostjudentum* was in progress. It was fashionable to read Martin

---

[23]The reviewer stresses that "Hirsch is celebrated against his own will as the founder of a sort of bourgeois Orthodoxy"; *Jüdische Monatshefte*, II (1915), p. 29.

[24]*Ibid.*

[25]Kohn, *Joel Gern, op. cit.*, p. 85.

[26]*Ibid.*, p. 45.

[27]A later novel by Schachnowitz, *Feuerzeichen*, Frankfurt a. Main 1928, turned the Neo-Orthodox ideals back to a former period. This novel depicts the early eighteenth-century Jewish community of Frankfurt a. Main as strictly religious, but open-minded and integrated in general society. In this idealised atmosphere we see Christians attend Jewish festivals and consult the communal rabbi, just as the shady Jewish character David Grünhut chats with the philosopher Leibniz and moves freely in the house of the antisemite Eisenmenger.

Buber's *hasidic* tales, and publishing houses like the *Jüdischer Verlag* had translated many Yiddish and Hebrew novels from East European Jewish writers. As Steven Aschheim has convincingly shown, the *Ostjude* with his originality became, for a growing minority of German Jews, a counter-myth to the idealisation of the peasant by many Germans in the *völkisch* neo-romanticism of the early twentieth century.[28] Pinchas Kohn was among the first to point to the fact that one does not have to look as far as Eastern Europe to find the ideal of the "genuine" Jew, who could still be found among rural Jews in several parts of Germany.[29]

Schachnowitz, however modern he regarded his own position to be, belonged to a movement which had already passed its zenith. Hirsch's combination of full participation in society and the maintenance of strict traditions in separate Jewish communities had only a very limited effect. In only few Jewish communities did the Orthodox adhere to Hirsch's principle of strict separation from the main communities. Even most of those who belonged to the separate Neo-Orthodox congregations did not break their ties with the main Jewish communities as Hirsch had demanded.[30] Among many of the younger generation of German Orthodoxy on the eve of the First World War, Hirsch's slogans and Schachnowitz's poetic love dialogues were ridiculed.

The experience of the First World War led to a further decline in the popularity of Hirsch's essentially religious definition of Judaism. Growing antisemitism; the influx of Eastern European Jews to Germany; the encounter between German-Jewish soldiers and *Ostjuden* on the Eastern front; the diplomatic success of Zionism; and the recognition of the Jewish minority status in Eastern Europe at the Paris peace conferences had strengthened ethnic definitions of Judaism among German Jews.[31]

German-Jewish Orthodoxy, thirty years after Samson Raphael Hirsch's death, was characterised by very different fears and hopes from those of Hirsch's own lifetime. Its new leaders, such as the Frankfurt rabbi Nehemiah Anton Nobel* and Rabbi Joseph Carlebach of Altona, understood that Samson Raphael Hirsch's definition of Judaism in terms of religion, which had been attractive for many German Jews in the mid-nineteenth century, had to be adapted to the changing times. Just as liberal Jews abandoned the ideological conceptualisation of their nineteenth-century representatives, and defined Judaism as an historical or even ethnic *Gemeinschaft*, Orthodox representatives such

[28] Aschheim, *Brothers and Strangers, op. cit.*, pp. 100–138.
[29] In a more scientific way, the *Gesellschaft für Jüdische Volkskunde* established by the Hamburg rabbi Max Grunwald in 1898 tried to save Eastern European as well as rural Jewish traditions. See Christoph Daxelmüller, 'Jüdische Volkskunde in Deutschland vor 1933', in W. Brückner (ed.), *Volkskunde als akademische Disziplin. Studien zur Institutionenausbildung*, Vienna 1983, pp. 117–142.
[30] Cf. Liberles, *Religious Conflict, op. cit.*, pp. 210–219.
[31] Cf. Eva Reichmann's article, 'Der Bewußtseinswandel der deutschen Juden', in *Deutsches Judentum in Krieg und Revolution, 1916–1923*. Ein Sammelband herausgegeben von Werner E. Mosse unter Mitwirkung von Arnold Paucker, Tübingen 1971 (Schriftenreihe wissenschaftlicher Abhandlungen des Leo Baeck Instituts 25), pp. 511–612.
*On Nobel see the essay by Rachel Heuberger, 'Orthodoxy versus Reform. The Case of Nehemiah Anton Nobel of Frankfurt a. Main', in the first section of this Year Book, pp. 45–58; and also Steven E. Aschheim, 'Nietzsche and the Nietzschean Moment in Jewish Life (1890–1939)', in its preceding section, pp. 199–200 – (Ed.).

as Nobel and Carlebach adopted broader definitions for Judaism. Seeing Judaism in more than purely religious terms, they initiated reforms of Jewish education and aimed at establishing an all-embracing Jewish culture.[32]

The novels of the most important ideologue of Neo-Orthodoxy in inter-war Germany, Samson Raphael Hirsch's grandson Isaac Breuer, have to be seen against this historical background. While he claimed to be a successor to Hirsch's *Torah im Derech Eretz* concept, he actually modified his grandfather's teaching substantially.

III

As the grandson of Samson Raphael Hirsch, and the son of his successor as rabbi at the *Israelitische Religionsgesellschaft*, Salomon Breuer, Isaac Breuer (1883–1946) grew up in the innermost circle of the Frankfurt separatist Orthodox community.[33] He attended the school of the Frankfurt Orthodox community led by his uncle, the son of Samson Raphael Hirsch, Mendel Hirsch, but received his decisive education at home.[34] Instead of being sent to a German *Gymnasium*, he was educated at the *yeshivah*, which his father, whom Isaac Breuer called the "Eastern Gaon", had re-introduced in his Frankfurt home.[35] In his memoirs, Isaac Breuer describes a house full of Eastern European, mostly Hungarian, *yeshivah* students, in which talmudic learning formed the order of the day for the whole family.[36]

Breuer studied philosophy, history and German literature at the universities of

---

[32]Nobel was one of the initiators of the Frankfurt *Lehrhaus*. He exercised a great influence on such different Frankfurt Jews as Franz Rosenzweig, Ernst Simon, Leo Loewenthal and Siegfried Kracauer. See the *Gabe, Herrn Rabbiner Dr. Nobel zum 50. Geburtstag dargebracht*, Frankfurt a. Main 1922. Nobel died in the same year at the age of 51 and could not take up the appointment as lecturer at Frankfurt University. On Nobel and Carlebach cf. Carlebach, 'Orthodox Jewry in Germany', *loc. cit.*, pp. 83–93.

[33]While most works mention 1883 as the year of Breuer's birth, Salomon Ehrmann, 'Isaac Breuer', in Leo Jung (ed.), *Guardians of Our Heritage (1724–1953)*, New York 1958, pp.617–646 sets the date as 10th Elul 5642 (=1882). On Breuer see also two recent publications: Rivka Horwitz (ed.), *Yitshak Breuer: iyunim be'mishnato*, Ramat Gan 1988; and Alan L. Mittleman, *Between Kant and Kabbalah. An Introduction to Isaac Breuer's Philosophy of Judaism*, Albany 1990.

[34]Mendel Hirsch was another example of an Orthodox Jew producing literature in German. In his poems written for the annual graduation ceremony of his school, he tried to combine German literature with Jewish spirit. Mordechai Breuer writes about these poems: "In der ganzen orthodoxen Literatur gibt es wenige Schriften, die so eindringlich wie diese Gedichte versuchen, jüdischen Geist mit deutscher Kultursprache zu vermählen." (Mordechai Breuer, *Jüdische Orthodoxie*, *op. cit.*, p. 148.)

[35]This was the first *yeshivah* re-established in Germany since this form of education had disappeared in the nineteenth century. Unlike his father-in-law, Salomon Breuer did not attempt to unite Orthodox Judaism with a feeling of deep rootedness in German culture. Isaac Breuer recalls in his memoirs: "I do not think that [after the completion of his university studies] he ever took a secular book into his hands . . . Despite his phenomenal memory . . . he probably forgot most of his 'secular education', he probably wanted to forget it in order to leave his memory exclusively for traditional learning." (Isaac Breuer, *Mein Weg*, Zürich 1988, pp. 35–36.)

[36]Breuer, *Mein Weg*, *op. cit.*, pp. 36–37. See also Jacob Katz, 'Yeshivat frankfurt u'beyt breuer be'eyney talmid yoze hungaria', in Horwitz, *Yitshak Breuer*, *op. cit.*, pp. 39–49.

Giessen and Strasbourg (then part of Germany). He dedicated a whole chapter of his autobiography to his leading role in founding the *Bund Jüdischer Akademiker* (BJA), an Orthodox Jewish student organisation, such as described by Selig Schachnowitz. Although his father wanted him to become a rabbi, he did not take this into serious consideration, mainly because of his strong aversion to "preaching".[37] Since he did not want to make a "profession out of Judaism" he decided to study law and became a practising attorney.

Although Isaac Breuer was never able to realise his early student dream and become a professional writer, his publications are more numerous and manifold than those of any other representative of Orthodox German Jewry in his generation. They include newspaper articles, political pamphlets, religious polemics, novels, children's literature and an autobiography. Although they differ in form, most of his publications share one central theme: the attempt to define Judaism as a religious nation and to refute all other definitions of Judaism.

His clearest attempt at defining Judaism can be found in his book *Das Judenproblem* (1918), which is partly based on his pre-war publication, *Lehre, Gesetz und Nation*.[38] In these two works Breuer rejected any definition of Judaism in terms of race or religion. Instead, he regarded the peoplehood of the Jews, based on teaching and law, as the essential criterion for their self-definition. This approach equally refuted Reform Judaism, Zionism and a large part of German Orthodoxy. It also implied the rejection of basic principles of emancipation, as well as of the identification with the German *Volk* and European culture. Finally, Breuer's ideology led to the concept of a religious society in the Land of Israel based on a blending of messianic and anti-capitalist elements.

Most of these ideas are expressed in his first two novels, *Ein Kampf um Gott* (1920) and *Falk Nefts Heimkehr* (1923). Both deal with the central theme of alienation of young Jews growing up in the atmosphere of a purely mechanical Orthodoxy in Germany. While Heinrich Thorning, the hero of *Ein Kampf um Gott*, is alienated from traditional Judaism during his attendance at the *Gymnasium*, the decisive break from tradition for Falk Neft, the protagonist of Breuer's second novel, occurred during his war-experience. The deeper cause for their alienation, however, is the superficial Orthodoxy practised by their fathers. In the end, both, with the help of *Ostjuden*, find their way back to tradition – a tradition which is embodied in the women of the family (mother and grand-mother).[39]

In his novels, Breuer combined strong self-criticism of German Neo-Ortho-doxy and genuine praise for the Eastern European Jewish world. In particular, he singled out for attack the "pseudo-Orthodox" figures, the fathers and the rabbis, who fulfil the *mitzvot*, but are not interested in their spiritual meaning. Although they are still performing their duties, they have become shallow,

[37]Breuer, *Mein Weg, op. cit.*, p. 65.

[38]Isaac Breuer, *Lehre, Gesetz und Nation*, Frankfurt a. Main 1910; *Das Judenproblem*, Halle 1918.

[39]On the reception of Breuer's novels by German-Jewish intellectuals cf. Franz Rosenzweig's letter to Breuer, in which he states: "Die Romane haben mich sehr bewegt, weil ich aus ihnen zu spüren glaubte, daß Sie selber auch die Problematik eigenen Standpunkts empfinden und trotzdem, ohne vor den Abgründen Ihr Auge zu schließen, auf ihm stehen." Franz Rosenzweig, *Briefe*, ed. by Edith Rosenzweig, Berlin 1935, p. 496.

lacking spirituality. These pseudo-Orthodox differ only in their outward behaviour from the Reformers, but have essentially adopted their interpretation of Judaism as a religion. Thus, Falk Neft cries out:

> "How can I turn Judaism into a religion, in the ways of the nations . . . a decorative accessory for life . . . The God of Zion is no God of the synagogue, no God of the Sabbath and the Holy Days and the Fast Days. The God of Zion and Yerushalayim is a God of the (whole) order of life, a God of economic order, of political order."[40]

In his novel *Ein Kampf um Gott* Breuer has the Orthodox German rabbi define Judaism in terms of faith: "A Jew is one who believes in the only God and who feels the need to announce this God to human kind." To illustrate the insufficiency of such a "faith", Breuer lets the rich banker and community board member Baer respond: "Then I am no Jew."[41]

Breuer, who had come to Germany as a child, fulfilled all his duties as a German citizen, including three years' military service during the First World War. He wrote almost all of his books and articles in German and was educated at a German university. But it seems that his feelings of belonging to a Jewish nation were exclusive and could not be combined with any emotional commitment to another nation. The clearest remarks to underline his distance towards Germanness are to be found in his novel *Ein Kampf um Gott*. Thus, he writes about his hero Heinrich Thorning:

> "He regarded himself as deeply touched by German culture, as he knew it. But from the beginning he knew that he approached it [i.e. German culture] from outside, that it was nothing totally certain for him, that his relation to German culture was no consanguinity, but elective affinity (*nicht Blutsverwandtschaft, sondern Wahlverwandtschaft*)."[42]

In the same novel, Breuer expressed his conviction that antisemitism is related more deeply to the Germans than to any other nation.

> "But it was shown more and more that the aversion which the nations of the earth instinctively had towards the Jews was nowhere deeper engrained than in German culture. Since emancipation this aversion has often grown into real hatred."[43]

Another element of Breuer's critical posture towards German Orthodoxy was his strong aversion to bourgeois capitalist society. In his novels the alienation from true Judaism is always characterised by the social elevation of the father. In *Falk Nefts Heimkehr*, for instance, the mother complains that since the father became a wealthy merchant (*Grosskaufmann*) they never enjoyed any deep conversation and she expresses her sorrow that he did not remain "a simple man".[44] Falk Neft, the son, comes to the conclusion: "It seems to me that being Jewish does not fit with being a *Grosskaufmann*."[45] Breuer's religious Socialism

---

[40]Isaac Breuer, *Falk Nefts Heimkehr*, Frankfurt a. Main 1923, p. 182.
[41]Isaac Breuer, *Ein Kampf um Gott*, Frankfurt a. Main 1920, pp. 76–77.
[42]*Ibid.*, p. 170.
[43]*Ibid.*, p. 68. "Aber es erwies sich mehr und mehr, dass die Abneigung, die die Nationen der Erde instinktiv gegen das Volk der Juden hegten, nirgends tiefer nistete als in der deutschen Kultur, dass diese Abneigung seit der Emanzipation vielfach in wirklichen Hass sich auswuchs."
[44]Breuer, *Falk Nefts Heimkehr*, *op. cit.*, p. 62.
[45]*Ibid.*, p. 70.

and his leading role in the *Poalei Agudat Israel* must be seen in connection with this anti-bourgeois standpoint.[46]

Breuer did not only express his distance from Germanness and German culture, but also from secular culture in general. Instead of attending a *Gymnasium* he studied for six years at his father's *yeshivah* and underwent an external *Abitur* exam which was a necessary prerequisite to entering the university. He retained a life-long aversion to the *Gymnasium* education. In his novel. *Ein Kampf um Gott*, it is the *Gymnasium* which is responsible for the student Heinrich Thorning's break with traditional Judaism. Breuer called the nine years Thorning spent in the *Gymnasium* "nine years of childhood slavery" and asked: "What did all this Latin mean for his soul, for his Jewish God?"[47]

It is the encounter with Eastern European Jewry which marks the turning point in both novels. Falk Neft joins revolutionary circles and is imprisoned. While in jail he meets an Eastern European rabbi and genuine Judaism in the form of Torah study. As a *ben-tora* he returns to his hometown and takes over his father's business. In *Ein Kampf um Gott*, it is the Eastern European dairyman, Freilich, who instructs Heinrich Thorning in Talmud study and who embodies Jewish learning much more than the Orthodox German rabbi Dr. Sommerfeld, who favours the eviction of the Galician Jew Freilich from Germany.[48]

The negative description of the modern Jewish community and all of its streams sharply contrasts with his nostalgic remarks on the traditional ghetto: "In the *Judengasse*, this place of sorrow and disdain, the Jews were happy."[49] But Breuer does not want to return to the *Judengasse*, his real longings are not for the ghetto, but *Eretz Israel*. While his strong affinities with the Holy Land were already expressed in his story of 1902, *Jerusalem*, he elaborated his systematic view of the foundation of a Jewish state, whose constitution was to be framed on the basis of Jewish law, more than twenty years later in his book *Das Jüdische Nationalheim*.[50]

---

[46]On Breuer's Socialism, see Rivka Horwitz, '*Al ha'shabat ve'al shabat ha'aretz. Ha sotzialism shel Breuer*', in *idem, Yitshak Breuer, op. cit.*, pp. 77–99.

[47]Breuer, *Ein Kampf um Gott, op. cit.*, pp. 85 and 91.

[48]*Ibid.*, p. 75. Sommerfeld argues from a national-German point of view: "Freilich ist nun einmal kein Deutscher. Setzt sich unser Verein für ihn ein, so gibt er damit zu erkennen, daß er die Internationalität der Juden des Erdballes zur Grundlage hat, daß unsere Feinde im Recht sind, wenn sie behaupten, daß uns der galizische Jude näher stehe als der christliche Deutsche."

[49]*Ibid.*, p. 10.

[50]This book was translated into English under the title *The Jewish National Home*, Frankfurt a. Main 1926. One should not confound Breuer's idea of a religious Jewish state with Political Zionism whose imitation of Western Nationalism he regarded as but another form of Jewish assimilation. He distanced himself clearly from the Zionist position. See for example his statement that Zionism was "the most terrible enemy that the Jewish nation has ever had". (*Judenproblem, op. cit.*, p. 138.) His "Palestinocentrism" caused Breuer the enmity of many Orthodox Jews, especially within the *Agudath Israel* which did not favour the founding of any Jewish state in Palestine, be it secular or religious. For most Orthodox Jews the foundation of a new Jewish state was connected with the advent of the Messianic Age. Breuer was no exception in this respect. However, he did not regard the foundation of a Jewish state as an event which could take place only after the Messiah had come. On the contrary, he thought that the foundation of a Jewish state, based on *halakhah*, would hasten the coming of the Messiah.

There are many passages in Breuer's various writings which illustrate that Breuer regarded his own time to be the Messianic Age. For him the two World Wars to which he was witness were

Breuer also used the form of a novel to express his "Palestinocentric" attitude. In 1934, already under the shadow of Nazi rule in Germany, his novel *Der neue Kusari* appeared.[51] In this book the assimilated German Jew, Alfred Roden, searches for possibilities to return to Judaism. Playing on the strategies employed in Jehuda Ha-Levi's twelfth-century philosophical work *Kusari*, where a philosopher, a Muslim, a Christian and a Jew debate, Breuer's *Der neue Kusari* contains the opinions of a Reform rabbi, a non-religious Zionist, a Mizrahist and a rabbi of the Orthodox community. After rejecting all of these streams. Alfred finally finds his home in the separatist community. However, he fills the flabby separatist community with new life and creates a new movement called *Thedaismus* which stands for *Torah im Derech Eretz Israel*. In practical terms this means the importation of Breuer' Neo-Orthodoxy to Palestine. In a biting critique of this novel, Gershom Scholem accused Breuer of attempting to combine two incompatible elements by re-integrating *Kabbalah* into the ideology of German Neo-Orthodoxy of his grandfather, Samson Raphael Hirsch, Scholem argued that Breuer's "*Thedaismus* is supposed to mean the conquest of Palestine for the phantom world created by Hirsch which threatens to evaporate in a *Galut* that now shows a less favorable side than those 'mild aspects' from which it emerged".[52]

IV

We have examined here three different reactions to the crisis of German-Jewish Orthodoxy in the first third of the twentieth century. While the literary value of these novels may be questioned, they constitute an important source for the variety of options suggested by Orthodox Jewish thinkers. Selig Schachnowitz praised urban bourgeois Jewish Neo-Orthodoxy, as developed by Samson Raphael Hirsch, as the ideal union of German culture with Jewish tradition, contrasting it with the turmoil of the Eastern European Jewish world he had escaped. The other two representatives were more critical about the path German Neo-Orthodoxy had taken, and shared a sense of admiration for the Eastern European Jewish world. Pinchas Kohn expressed his longings for the vanishing world of rural Bavarian Jewish communities which he found again in the Eastern European *shtetl*. His close friend, Isaac Breuer, suggested a radical solution by establishing a religious Jewish state in Palestine. He was convinced that the German Orthodox Jew, whose Judaism had become hollow and lifeless, needed the *Ostjude* as mediator to help him regain his spirituality and ultimately adopt the "Palestinocentric" solution.

Kohn's and Breuer's idealisation of the traditional Jewish world in the

---

"messianic wars" (Breuer, *Mein Weg, op. cit.*, p. 114). His book *Messiasspuren*, Frankfurt a. Main 1918, published during the First World War, clearly characterises the previously unknown dimensions of a World War as the first sign of the Messianic Age and proposes the foundation of a Jewish state to advance the advent of the Messiah.

[51] *Der neue Kusari*, Frankfurt a. Main 1934.

[52] Cf. Gershom Scholem's review of the book, *loc. cit.* (note 9).

Bavarian *Dorf*, and the Eastern European *shtetl*, cannot disguise the fact that they, too, had long left this world. It was the German novel which had become the ideal medium for presenting their ideas, just as for liberal Jews and Zionists in Germany at the beginning of the twentieth century. While for an Eastern European *yeshivah bahur* the reading of non-traditional literature was still taboo, Orthodox German-Jewish rabbis encouraged the writing of German-Jewish novels and praised them as the culmination of Jewish literature. As the Orthodox *Jüdische Monatshefte* put it in 1912. "For Jewish pens there is no better task than the creation of such novels."[53]

[53] *Jüdische Monatshefte*, I (1914), p. 436.

War and Resistance

An Illegal Way of Life in Nazi Germany

BY AVRAHAM SELIGMANN

INTRODUCTION

Three well-known dates constitute landmarks in the process of the murder of German Jewry during the period of Nazi rule:*

1. 1st April 1933 – Boycott Day. From this day onward, the economic viability of Germany's Jews was increasingly undermined: Jews were forbidden to hold posts in the public service sector, Jewish firms began to undergo "Aryanisation", and supervision was introduced to ensure that German firms did no business with Jews.

2. 10th November 1938 – Pogrom Night. "These riots were a crucial turning point in the situation of Jews living in countries under Nazi rule. The riots were followed by a multitude of harsh decrees which aggravated the deteriorating status of the Jews and the conditions under which Jewish public life functioned. In fact, these riots were the culmination of a whole process which led from a period of relative moderation in anti-Jewish policy to a period of growing harshness, until the final stage – exile and murder."[1] On that day it was brought home with finality to Jews still living in Germany that their economic and social existence in the country was no longer possible.

3. 19th September 1941. Start of the implementation of the order of 1st September 1941, under which every Jew aged seven and up had to wear on his or her left breast a yellow Star of David, well-stitched onto the garment, on which the word *Jude* was written in black in Hebrew-like characters. "This was the most difficult day in the twelve years of hell."[2] From that day the Jews were expendable, ostracised.[3]

Shortly afterwards, German Jews began to be deported to Eastern Europe. Towards the end of 1942, increasing reports spoke about the extermination of Jews in the East. When the transports to the East began, orders were sent to the Jews – via the *kehilot* (Jewish communities) – instructing them to report two days

---

*This is the translation of an abridged version of an M.A. thesis for the Institute of Contemporary Jewry at the Hebrew University of Jerusalem. I am grateful to Dr. David Bankier of the Institute for his guidance and advice during the preparation of this study. I would also like to thank the staff of the Yad Vashem Archives in Jerusalem for their help in searching for the sources for this study.

[1]Shaul Esh, 'Historische Einführung zu [Jizchak] Schwersenz und [Edith] Wolff, "Jüdische Jugend im Untergrund"', in *Bulletin des Leo Baeck Instituts*, 12, No. 45 (1969), pp. 5–25, esp. pp. 15–16.

[2]Victor Klemperer, *LTI (Lingua Tertii Imperii). Die unbewältigte Sprache. Aus dem Notizbuch eines Philologen*, München 1947, p. 176.

[3]Ruth Andreas-Friedrich, *Schauplatz Berlin. Tagebuchaufzeichnungen 1938–1948*, Hamburg 1964, pp. 58–59 (revised and enlarged version of *Der Schattenmann. Tagebuchaufzeichnungen 1938–1945*, Berlin 1947).

later at a place of assembly, carrying only absolute necessities and a specified sum of money.

On 27th February 1943, the *Gestapo* began rounding up Jews at their forced-labour sites, on the streets and from their homes, and taking them directly to the assembly points.

In Berlin, some 5,000 Jews tried to avoid being sent to the East[4] by finding hiding places. Since about 40% of all German Jews resided in Berlin, we could make the assumption that 12,000 to 15,000 Jews throughout Germany went into hiding beginning in late 1941, but more intensively at the end of 1942 and the start of 1943.

Hence, some 8%–10% of the 153,000 Jews who were living in Germany at the end of 1941, opted for the slim chance of survival by adopting an illegal way of life. Of these, about 75% were seized by the *Gestapo*; the 3,500–4,000 who survived provided several hundred testimonies on periods of illegal life of from two to two-and-a-half years.

From the 300 written testimonies at Yad Vashem and a number of autobiographies, 65 testimonies were found from which answers could be culled to the majority of the questions relating to an illegal way of life, which were contained in a questionnaire, drawn up in a manner that overcame the problem of personal memory.

The purpose of the present work, which is based on the extant testimonies, is to examine what characterised those Jews who opted for the "illegal" course. This study, then, is concerned with biographical details and addresses the questions of how these Jews arrived at their decision to go into hiding, how their daily lives were organised, where they hid and the problems that arose as a result. At the same time, we shall examine the characteristics of the non-Jewish rescuers: who they were and what prompted them to conceal Jews. Finally, we shall consider reciprocal relations in everyday life between the Jews in hiding and their non-Jewish benefactors. By collating and summing up these features, we are able to produce an historical picture of these "illegal" Jews' lives in Nazi Germany.*

I. SURVEY OF THE STATE OF THE RESEARCH ON JEWS IN HIDING UNDER THE NAZI REGIME IN EUROPE AND THEIR RESCUERS

Systematic research on Jews who found shelter during the Nazi era and on their non-Jewish rescuers began in the late 1960s. The problem faced by historians was that the acts of rescue – that is, the concealment of Jews, whether done by individuals, families, networks of individuals or church organisations – were secret and virtually undocumented. It was only after the publication of a number

---

[4]Konrad Kwiet and Helmut Eschwege, *Selbstbehauptung und Widerstand. Deutsche Juden im Kampf um Existenz und Menschenwürde 1933–1945*, Hamburger Beiträge zur Sozial- und Zeitgeschichte, Band XIX, Hamburg 1984, p. 169.

*On Jews hiding underground see also the essay by Simone Erpel, 'Struggle and Survival – Jewish Women in the Anti-Fascist Resistance in Germany', in this section of the Year Book – (Ed.).

of books and autobiographies, after Yad Vashem's Department of Righteous Gentiles had recognised several thousand rescuers (6,948 individuals from 1962–1986), and after activity by Yad Vashem turned up rescued and rescuers who provided testimony, that research could be undertaken which was based on first-hand testimonies and interviews.[5]

Perry London is the earliest of a group of sociologists to offer explanations on the "Righteous" conduct, based on interviews of rescuers who left their native homelands and resettled in the USA, as well as on interviews with survivors who had benefited from the rescuers' help. In a 1970 study, he listed three main chracteristics which he found among these rescuers:

1) a spirit of adventure and a predilection for exciting activities.

2) an intense identification with a parent of very strong moral character – not necessarily religious, but highly opinionated on moral issues – who served as a model of moral conduct.

3) a sense of being socially marginal, such as a Seventh Day Adventist minister in the largely Calvinist or Catholic Netherlands.[6]

Eva Fogelman, in a 1985 study, found that rescuers fall into two groups: those motivated by moral values and others whose motivation was chiefly emotional and based on personal links with the victim.[7]

Nechama Tec, a sociologist, in a recent comprehensive study of the motivations of Polish rescuers, found that these fitted behaviour which she labelled as "autonomous altruism". She defined this as a sense of individuality, self-reliance and of personal commitment to the helpless and the needy; a non-heroic, matter-of-fact perception of rescue attempts; an unpremeditated and unplanned beginning of rescue activity; and a "universalistic" perception of Jews defined as helpless human beings totally dependent on the protection of others.[8]

A significant addition to the studies on this subject was provided in the papers delivered at an international conference held in Oxford in July 1988 under the title: 'Remembering for the Future'. One session was devoted to the subject of 'Helpers and Rescuers. Ethical, Psychological and Religious Factors'. Among the lecturers were Professor Nechama Tec and Dr. Mordecai Paldiel, director of the Righteous Gentiles Department at Yad Vashem.[9]

Particular importance attached to Dr. Paldiel's paper, as he disputed the conclusions reached by Perry London, Nechama Tec and Eva Fogelman. His thesis[10] is that the goodness displayed by the overwhelming majority of these Righteous Gentiles is not a mystifying phenomenon, requiring an arduous

---

[5]Eva Fogelman, *The Rescuers. A Socio-Psychological Study of Altruistic Behavior during the Nazi Era*, doctoral dissertation, City University of New York 1987, pp. 63–65.

[6]Perry London, 'The Rescuers. Motivational Hypotheses about Christians Who Saved Jews from the Nazis', in Jacqueline R. Macanlay and Leonard Berkovitz (eds.), *Altruism and Helping Behavior*, New York 1970, p. 243.

[7]Eva Fogelman and V. Lewis-Wiener, 'The Few, the Brave and the Noble', in *Psychology Today*, August 1985, pp. 61–65.

[8]Nechama Tec, *When Light Pierced the Darkness. Christian Rescue of Jews in Nazi Occupied Poland*, New York–Oxford 1986.

[9]*Remembering for the Future. Working Papers and Addenda*, Oxford 1989, vol. I, *Jews and Christians During and After the Holocaust*, pp. 475–552.

[10]Mordecai Paldiel, 'The Altruism of the Righteous Gentiles', *ibid.*, vol. I, pp. 517–522.

exercise into the intricacies of their social, psychological, ethnic, religious and economic backgrounds, in order to create models of select groups of extreme altruistic persons; but, rather, a basic human trait which needs to be aroused from its enforced slumber and cultivated – by tolerating its soothing presence in our lives, instead of repressing it. Helping others in need at great discomfort to oneself ought not to be viewed as a praiseworthy but unnatural type of human responsiveness, but as a natural and necessary predisposition, like the other legitimate intuitive drives such as competitiveness, striving for honour and wealth, and lust. Thus, what is needed is to redress the balance upset by an overzealous reliance on man's so-called depravity; not only to quote and seek support in the Genesis statement on man's innate wickedness, but in the equally forceful Psalm statement of man being but a step lower than the angels. Mordecai Paldiel does not consider the altruism of those who rescued Jews as something "marginal", but as normal human behaviour that was in a state of dormancy. That this behaviour was not implemented in practice is, in his view, due to certain rational calculations.

A summation of the studies on the subject shows that all the researchers deal with the question: why did the Righteous Gentiles risk their lives in order to rescue Jews? The researchers refer primarily to the rescuers when constructing a thesis of altruistic behaviour, and base their thesis on questionnaires relating to the rescued and the rescuers. A problem that arises in this connection is that of "collective memory" (discussed below), and from the fact that the studies were conducted twenty years or more after the events and far from their original surroundings. What is missing from these studies is a picture of the problems that cropped up in the day-to-day existence of those who decided to adopt an illegal way of life. The present study, by contrast, deals with the characteristics of life in hiding, a state of affairs that usually lasted for about two-and-a-half years: from late 1942 or early 1943 until the end of the war. This study, then, combines the historical perspective with the sociological approach towards an illegal existence under the Nazi regime.

II. RESEARCH METHOD AND SOURCES

In the past twenty years, oral documentation has become an increasingly important scholastic tool for contemporary historical research.

Oral documentation is essential in studying the period of Nazi rule in Europe and the immediate post-war years, for a number of reasons: many official documents were destroyed during the war; the *Gestapo* burned many of its records; the use of the telephone makes it difficult to trace all the steps in processes that led up to major decisions; and no written documentation exists regarding such decisions. This method is of particular importance for studying the daily life of those who went into hiding in Nazi Germany, as no historical documents whatsoever exist on this subject. At the same time, oral documentation, and the drawing of historical conclusions from that method, presents a number of problems:[11]

1. The interrogator's research level and the technique of the questions.

2. The respondent's memory and his ability to describe the facts without breaking the course and continuity of the events and his part in them.

3. (a) "Autobiographical memory". This refers to the fact that the traces of the experiences that remain in the teller's mind are influenced by the actual situation and its unfolding, and by past events in his life. (The classic example is the Japanese film *Rashomon* in which four witnesses give four completely different testimonies concerning the same event at which all of them were present.) Memory, then, is selective. But what criterion underlies that selectivity? What code causes certain events to be engraved in the memory while others are forgotten?

(b) The altered surroundings. The fact that the teller is now in surroundings that are completely different from those he is attempting to describe interferes with memory. He has no handles to grasp and, in the subject we are dealing with, few if any photographs to consult.

(c) The development of one's "personal history" affects one's value judgements about events from the past.

(d) The history of the period, as it is related in the media and in the literature of the era, also impinges on the evocation of "autobiographical memory". Thus, individual memory is "imprinted" by a "collective memory" of the surroundings and of the social context.

(e) The relating of memories is in fact a reconstruction of events from the viewpoint of one's personal state at the moment and the attendant social situation.

It is useful to spell out the problems involved in oral documentation because most of the primary sources about those who went into hiding in Nazi Germany in fact consist of oral documentation. However, this is not the appropriate place to discuss the manner in which the various historiographical schools treat oral documentation.

In order to overcome the problems noted above, and enable accurate historical conclusions to be reached, we developed a questionnaire relating to the facts that are mentioned in the testimonies, and not to assessments. The questionnaire sought to elicit personal data about those in hiding and to shed light on the process that brought about their decision to "dive", on how contact was made with the two main rescuers, their standing, their actual motivations and their attitude towards those in hiding, the total number of hiding places, and whether the person in hiding was able to get out of Germany before the end of the war. The questionnaire was drawn up so that the responses could be processed via computer, with conclusions drawn accordingly.

[11]On oral history methods see Lutz Niethammer (ed.), *Lebenserfahrung und Kollektives Gedächtnis*, Frankfurt a. Main 1985, in particular the articles by Daniel Bertaux and Isabelle Bertaux-Wiame, 'Autobiographische Erinnerungen und kollektives Gedächtnis', pp. 146–165; Ronald J. Grele, 'Ziellose Bewegung. Methodologische und Theoretische Probleme der Oral History', pp. 195–220; Lutz Niethammer, 'Postkript', pp. 471–477.

The sources for this study are testimonies in the Kaduri Collection (01) and the Wiener Collection (02), both in Yad Vashem; as well as testimonies from Yad Vashem's general collection (033) and testimonies there about Righteous Gentiles. Also used were a number of autobiographical books and essays containing relevant information.

III. THE DAILY LIFE OF THE JEWS IN GERMANY FOLLOWING THE SPECIAL REGULATIONS ON JEWS.[12] SEPTEMBER 1939– FEBRUARY 1945

On 31st October 1941 approximately 150,000 Jews remained in Germany.[13] As this number declined, life became ever more difficult for them. This emerges from a small number of diaries and other descriptions, written by non-Jews as well as Jews, that were published in the immediate post-war years, for example, *Schauplatz Berlin* by Ruth Andreas-Friedrich.

The first encumbrance on Jewish life in Germany, imposed immediately upon the war's outbreak, was a restriction on movement. Jews were forbidden to leave their apartments at night – from 8 p.m. in the winter and from 9 p.m. in the summer. They could purchase food only at certain times during the day – in Berlin, for example, between 4 and 5 p.m. – and only at certain shops. In September 1941 Jews were barred from entering markets and other uncovered commercial centres. Another decree that month forced them to obtain a special police permit in order to travel on trains throughout Germany. From the end of March 1942 Jews were forbidden to leave their town or city of residence. From September 1941 limitations were placed on Jews' use of public municipal transport: they were barred from travelling during peak hours, were restricted to the last section and made to stand. In March 1942 they were forbidden to use municipal transport unless their place of work was more than 7 km. from their home, or 5 km. in the case of schoolchildren.

Especially harsh was the reduction in food rations allotted to Jews. The whole population was subject to food rationing on the basis of coupons, but non-Jews obtained the coupons from their house supervisor, whereas Jews had to go to a municipal office for them. As already noted, they could purchase food only in particular shops during specified hours. From January 1940, Jews were denied milk, fish, fowl, rice, cocoa and other foods. Rationing for Jews became ever more stringent. In some cases individual non-Jews tried to supply their Jewish acquaintances, by roundabout means, with vegetables, fruit, milk and meat.[14]

A lengthy list of prohibitions marks the rapid deterioration in the life of

---

[12]Joseph Walk (ed.), *Das Sonderrecht für die Juden im NS-Staat. Eine Sammlung der gesetzlichen Maßnahmen und Richtlinien. Inhalt und Bedeutung*, Heidelberg–Karlsruhe 1981, 'IV. Zeitabschnitt – Vom Ausbruch des Zweiten Weltkriegs bis zur Vernichtung der deutschen Juden. 1.9.39–16.2.45', pp. 301–406.

[13]Otto Dov Kulka, *Tendencies of the Final Solution of the Jewish Problem in the Third Reich*, Jerusalem 1982 (in Hebrew), p. 16.

[14]Heinz David Leuner, *Als Mitleid ein Verbrechen war*, Wiesbaden 1967, pp. 73–76.

Germany's Jews: the halt in the distribution of clothing coupons (12th July 1939), the confiscation of radios (20th September 1939), the removal of Jews from private health-insurance funds (13th April 1940), the deduction of items arriving in food packages from outside Germany from food rations (20th April 1941), the suspension of soap rations (26th June 1941), the ban on the use of public libraries (2nd August 1941), the confiscation of typewriters, bicycles, cameras and binoculars (13th November 1941), the prohibition on selling books on the open market (14th November 1941), the ban on the use of public telephones (12th December 1941), the confiscation of woollen clothing and furs (5th January 1942), the bar on the keeping of household pets (15th February 1942), and the prohibition on supplying newspapers to Jews (17th February 1942).

Throughout Germany, Jewish-owned houses and apartments were turned into hostels in which Jews, forced to leave their previous residences, were concentrated. In some flats, eight people were crowded into a single small room, and up to twenty-eight in large rooms. The concentration of Jews into specified houses and apartments facilitated *Gestapo* supervision and the raids it carried out, mainly at night.

Jewish emigration was still being allowed as late as April–May 1940, but not to European countries. Jews were even allowed to work on farms in order to learn a new trade prior to emigrating. But those wishing to emigrate to Palestine faced formidable obstacles and stringent supervision. From August 1941, emigration of combat-fit Jews aged 18–45 was prohibited. On 23rd October 1941 Jewish emigration to countries outside Germany was banned for the duration of the war. On 1st January 1942 the Germans shut down the emigration office of the *Reichsvereinigung der Juden in Deutschland*.

Beginning in November 1940, all Jewish men and women aged 18–55, who were fit for work, were mobilised for forced labour within the framework of the *Arbeitseinsatz*, in plants that were essential for the war effort.* The forced labour, lasting ten or more hours a day, was especially difficult for the Jews, who suffered from a shortage of food. In the factories the Jews were split up into groups of twenty, separated from the other workers, and assigned the dirtiest, most menial jobs. An order was issued not to pay Jews wage "perks" such as Germans received (e.g. a special payment for national holidays, extra pay for work on holidays, bonuses for marriage and for women who gave birth, and so forth).

In the very first month of the war (25th September 1939) Jews were ordered to prepare shelters by themselves. Under a subsequent order, Jews were separated from others by a partition, or isolated in a small room inside the shelter.

Spouses in mixed marriages and their sons faced a special fate. In April 1940 all sons of mixed marriages and the husbands of Jewish women were removed from the army. The reason was that Jews were considered "enemies within". For the spouses in mixed marriages in which the husband was Jewish and the wife non-Jewish, earning a living became difficult; as Jews, they found it problematic to find work – but they were not made to do forced labour.

*On this see, in great detail, the essay by Konrad Kwiet, 'Forced Labour of German Jews in Nazi Germany', in *LBI Year Book XXXVI* (1991), pp. 389–410 – (Ed.).

On 31st July 1941, SS Commander Heydrich, was ordered to make all substantial and practical preparations for an overall solution of the Jewish problem in the German sphere of influence in Europe. At this stage the term in use was still "comprehensive solution" (*Gesamtlösung*).

On 1st September 1941 the Germans issued an order stating that as of the 19th of the month, Jews aged 7 and over must wear "the star of the Jews" in public. Moreover, Jews were forbidden to leave their area of residence without a written permit from the police, were barred from wearing medals and so forth. This order did not apply to the Jewish husband in a mixed marriage if there were any offspring who were not considered Jewish, or if they had an only son who had fallen in battle. Nor did it apply to a Jewish woman in a mixed marriage without children, as long as that marriage remained in force.

Ruth Andreas-Friedrich summed up the significance that attached to the wearing of the yellow Star of David:

> "The Jews are cast out, ostracised; they must wear on their clothing, above the left breast, a mark of shame in the form of a yellow Star of David. Inside the hexagonal star, 'Jew' is written in German, in Hebrew-like letters . . . The symbol of the Jewish star facilitates separation. It shines forth on the road to darkness . . ."[15]

Six months later the Jews were ordered to mark the door of their home with a black Star of David.

The special orders and regulations regarding Jews that were issued after 1st September 1941 had three main objectives: to make their daily life more difficult, to separate the Jewish and non-Jewish populations, and to facilitate the *Gestapo*'s transports of Jews to the East. Not all the ordinances were published in the Jews' "own" weekly, *Jüdisches Nachrichtenblatt*, the only weekly of its kind still permitted to appear after the pogroms of 10th November 1938.[16]

The mass deportation of Jews to the East got under way on 24th October 1941. Fifty thousand Jews were ordered to be sent from the *Altreich*, Austria and Bohemia-Moravia to Riga, Lodz, Kovno and Minsk. Until the autumn of 1942, the *Gestapo* sent letters to those slated for deportation via the *Gemeinde*. The letter noted the date of the transport, specified when and where to report, gave details about how much luggage and money could be taken, and concluded by informing the recipients as to when an official would visit them in order to affix a seal on their apartment and receive the keys.[17] To this the *Gemeinde* added a memorandum consisting largely of a request to implement all orders.

By the end of 1942, advance notices of deportation were no longer being sent; instead, *Gestapo* agents showed up at homes of Jews and rounded up the occupants for transports. The *Gestapo* also began detaining Jews in the street in order to send them to the East. Information about the true purpose of the transports began to filter in from the East.

> "Masses of Jews are going underground. Horrendous rumours are circulating about the fate of the evacuees. People are whispering about firing squads, about thousands who are dying of

[15]Andreas-Friedrich, *op. cit.*, pp. 58–59.
[16]Leuner, *op. cit.*, pp. 86–105.
[17]Inge Deutschkron, *Berliner Juden im Untergrund*, Berlin 1980, p. 99; *idem*, *Berlin Jews Underground*, Gedenkstätte Deutscher Widerstand, Berlin 1990.

hunger, about torture and gas chambers. Every momentary shelter becomes a God-sent gift, a way to be spared a mortal danger. Members of the 'Association' are putting up the persecuted in their homes, moving them from one person to another: one night at their place, the next at ours. Permanent guests arouse suspicion in the eyes of neighbours. The latter in any case monitor with suspicion the constant movement of those who arrive and depart."[18]

Those who were made to do forced labour were convinced that they would not be sent to Poland, but on 27th February 1943, in a surprise operation called the *Fabrik-Aktion* carried out in broad daylight, the *Gestapo* rounded up all the Jewish workers in the various factories and workshops and sent them to the East. For the first time this transport included spouses in mixed marriages. The husbands in mixed marriages were taken to a separate place of assembly while their fate was decided. In the meantime, their non-Jewish wives demonstrated outside, shouting demands for the release of their husbands. The demonstration went on for several days until the husbands were, in fact, freed.[19] This event was the final warning for all those who were already thinking about going into hiding that the time had come to act without delay.

On 19th May 1943 Berlin was declared *Judenrein*. On 19th July 1943 the police closed down the *Reichsvereinigung*. Officially, the Jewish problem had been solved.

In fact, a few thousand Jews still remained in Germany, the majority partners in mixed marriages, the minority in hiding. Some of the spouses in the mixed marriages were sent in small groups to the East, while the rest were sent to work camps that were attached to the concentration camps in Germany. Many died due to the horrific conditions in the work camps.[20] In the autumn of 1944 the authorities began considering the idea of sending all the "privileged" Jews to the East – that is, of forcibly breaking up mixed marriages.[21] Finally, on 13th January 1945 an order was issued to transfer to Theresienstadt, in a collective labour mobilisation, all Jews in mixed marriages who were fit to work, whether or not they had German nationality.

We cannot conclude this chapter without mentioning that until April 1943 there were places throughout Germany where groups of Jewish children and young adults lived in reasonable conditions. These were agricultural training centres in which some 400 young people, aged 21 to 30 worked and studied, along with 400 youngsters in the Youth *Aliyah* programme.[22] Three Zionist youth movements, to which the Youth *Aliyah* members were affiliated, still operated in Germany following the outbreak of the war: *Habonim, Makkabi Hazair*, and *Brith Chaluzim Datiim (Bachad)*. Fourteen training centres existed as late as 1940. In addition, three special schools functioned in which all the subjects on the regular curriculum were taught, but where students were also educated in values based on the spirit of the Zionist youth movements.

---

[18]Andreas-Friedrich, *op. cit.*, p. 67.
[19]Leuner, *op. cit.*, pp. 102–103. It seems that the demonstration began with a few hundred and their numbers grew, as Germans without relatives amongst the prisoners joined the demonstration.
[20]Leuner, *op. cit.*, p. 106.
[21]Andreas-Friedrich, *op. cit.*, p. 117.
[22]Jizchak Schwersenz and Edith Wolff, 'Jüdische Jugend im Untergrund'. Ein zionistische Gruppe in Deutschland während des Zweiten Weltkrieges', in *Bulletin des Leo Baeck Instituts*, 12, No. 45 (1969), pp. 61–72.

Most of these training centres and schools were closed in late 1942. By early 1943 only three centres remained, housing about 150 young people and 150 adults. In March 1943 these pioneer groups, along with the Zionist youth movement members who were in work camps, were placed on the final transport to the East and despatched to their annihilation.

If life had ostensibly proceeded "normally" in the training centres, beginning in 1941 they, too, were subjected to some of the decrees that affected all German Jews. Many at the centres were informed that their parents had been ordered to ready themselves for transport to the East within days. Most of the parents expected their children to accompany them.[23] There was no way of knowing, at this stage, whether young people and adults would be separated or whether families would be allowed to stay together. The training centres therefore decided that everyone there should remain, in order to delay transport to the East as long as possible; and thus each member became a support for the entire group. There were exceptional cases – such as a family with one parent who was ill – in which the youth was permitted to join his parent. But those who left the group on their own in order to join their parents were expelled from the movement. The majority of the parents were persuaded, in personal talks or through letters from the children and their instructors, that the best course was for their sons or daughters to remain with the group.[24]

The question then arose whether those at the training centres who wished to go into hiding should be permitted to do so. However, this option was rejected on two grounds: in order not to bring about the group's disintegration, and because the authorities would hold the centres' leaders accountable for everyone who disappeared.

At those few places that still functioned as training centres and pursued a social and cultural life even though the members were conscripted to do forced labour in the immediate area, it was known that deportation was imminent. Discussions were held about how to prepare and what to take in one's knapsack. Shortly before Passover 1943 they were informed that some would be deported in the near future; the list of names arrived on the eve of the holiday. Some volunteered to accompany those on the list, but the movement's leadership in Berlin forbade this.

> "Those in the last training centres that still existed thought, until the moment they entered the concentration camp at Auschwitz, that the deportation meant arduous work [and] a shortage of all kinds of things. They hadn't the least idea that the true meaning of the deportation was almost certain death."

As Ora Borinski wrote in the summer of 1945, a few months after she was liberated.

In the spring of 1943 the remaining training centres were liquidated and everyone in them was deported to Auschwitz. Only a few survived to tell about the events of that period in the training centres.

[23]Anneliese-Ora Borinski, *Erinnerungen 1940–1943*, Kwuzat Maagan-Zvi 1970, p. 24.
[24]*Ibid.*, p. 28.

IV. PROBLEMS OF AN ILLEGAL WAY OF LIFE IN NAZI GERMANY

By the autumn of 1941, the order that compelled Jews to wear the *Judenstern*, the concentration of Jews in the big cities in "Jewish houses", and the various restrictions on movement had rounded off the total discrimination imposed by the Nazi authorities on every Jew still living in Germany.

The *Reichsvereinigung* was instructed to send out the order to report for deportation. A sheet was appended to the order, warning that the order was to be obeyed without evasion.

The decision to escape deportation and certain death – that this was the fate the Germans planned for them was known to many Jews by early 1943 – for an uncertain destiny was not an easy one. Yet, some overcame their fear and opted for life with a new identity.[25]

The first step was to remove the Star, followed immediately by a move to new surroundings where no Jewish or non-Jewish acquaintances lived, to minimise the risk of recognition. This meant giving up work – even though it was forced labour – and the income it provided, however small.

The decision to "submerge" (*U-Boot Juden*), as the term then widespread in Germany had it, was far more difficult if one's parents were still alive, had been sent to the East, or expected to receive an order to report for deportation at any time. As for the children of couples who decided to go into hiding, the great majority of those who were of an age suitable for Youth *Aliyah* had managed to get to England or elsewhere before the war. The few small children went into hiding with their parents.

Many who went into hiding left behind "suicide notes" in order to account for their sudden disappearance. Whoever found the note would convey it to the police, who carried out a brief perfunctory search. In contrast, the *Gestapo* did not treat these suicide notes as genuine. A note that triggered even the slightest suspicion frequently caused the *Gestapo* to seize hostages from the leadership of the *Gemeinde* and shoot them. This, for example, was the pretext for the killing of eight members of the Berlin *Gemeinde* in December 1942 without a trial.[26]

The first necessity of those who decided to adopt an illegal way of life was to find a place to hide. To that end, help was required from acquaintances, or acquaintances of acquaintances, who were non-Jewish or half-Jews in mixed marriages. But even after a hiding place was located, there was no way of knowing how long it could be used. To conceal a Jew called for more than good will and courage: the very act was sufficient to endanger the lives of the rescuer's entire family. Those who were caught could expect to be thrown into a concentration camp. Thus, for example, a *Volksgerichtshof* in Königsberg sentenced five women from nearby villages to prison terms of from three-and-a-half to six years penal servitude. These women had taken in eight Jewish children from deported families and claimed they were theirs. In Freiburg, five persons

---

[25]Kwiet and Eschwege, *op. cit.*, pp. 152–153.
[26]Leuner, *op. cit.*, p. 101.

were sentenced to six, eight and ten years in prison for helping a number of Berlin Jews sneak across the border to Switzerland.[27]

A requirement of the hiding place was that it could be camouflaged if necessary. Moreover, the rescuer had to know someone who would be ready to conceal the Jew in case of a search by the *Gestapo*. The initial hiding place was often a monastery, a Catholic hospital, a hut in some remote location, and so forth. In most cases, the person in hiding was constantly on the move, occasionally sleeping in a forest or on a park bench in order to elude the Nazis.[28]

A hiding place might be an unused back room; an airless attic; a cold, dark cellar; a special shelter beneath a staircase where air was in short supply and which was too small to permit anything more than lying down; an agricultural storeroom without electricity or without a lavatory. Some of those in hiding did not emerge for lengthy periods, fearing detection by neighbours, while others were compelled to leave early every morning and to return late in the evening, spending the day wandering about the streets and parks or in cinemas. A special effort was required to maintain personal hygiene and to remove rubbish without arousing attention.[29]

When the Allies began their saturation bombing of German cities, those in concealment faced a new situation. On the one hand they were pleased that the attacks were bringing the end of the war closer, but on the other hand, if they did not have a false identity card, they could not take refuge in bomb shelters. Only when the bombing raids totally destroyed registry and documentation offices, as occurred in Hamburg for example, could those in hiding, like other refugees, receive official papers – naturally, under an assumed name and with falsified personal data. These papers included food coupons. Thus, to obtain false personal papers was the most crucial task after finding a place to live. With such papers one could walk about outside, while the rescuer could say that he had taken in a refugee from a bombed area. Some people turned to forgers, who demanded a high price for their labours – in some cases, forgers took money and then disappeared – and those who were caught by the *Gestapo* were executed.

Saying that one had come from a bombed area made it easier to obtain official papers. In a few instances papers were taken from the bodies of people who were killed in bombing raids and were then altered to conform with the necessary personal information. The bombings also saved Jewish lives. For example, on the morning of 13th February 1945 the order was issued to deport the last 70 Jews of Dresden,[30] who until then had been spared because they were spouses in mixed marriages. They were removed from the transport because Auschwitz was already in Russian hands. That evening, saturation bombing of Dresden began. Buildings collapsed, a firestorm raged, and casualties ran high, among them Jews. In the ensuing chaos, the Jews who survived escaped from the clutches of the *Gestapo*.

[27] *Ibid.*, pp. 90–91.
[28] Kwiet and Eschwege, *op. cit.*, pp. 153–159; and Philip Friedman, *Their Brothers' Keepers*, New York 1957, pp. 15–19.
[29] Paldiel, *loc. cit.*, p. 519.
[30] Klemperer, *op. cit.*, p. 272.

A third major problem – besides finding a hiding place and obtaining false papers – was food. As already mentioned, non-Jews received food coupons from the house supervisor, who was a member of the Nazi Party, but Jews had to report to special offices to get their cards. However, access to these offices was impossible for those who opted for an illegal way of life. In some cases, the rescuers shared their food with those they were hiding. In cities, food could be purchased on the black market. Food coupons could be had by presenting false papers. Some non-Jews supplied Jews in hiding with food and food coupons. There was also a network of addresses from which a certain amount of food was collected each week.

Yet another problem involved the need for cash. Some of those who hid Jews demanded payment, and people in hiding had to pay for food, essential clothing and transport. Yet, there were some who did not ask for payment in return for concealing Jews, or accepted work as a *quid pro quo*. Various people helped when fugitives ran out of money. Exactly how money was obtained is not specified in the testimonies we have.

The death of a Jew in hiding could not be reported, as this would put the rescuers in mortal danger. Usually, the deceased was buried in a field under cover of dark; the exact spot committed to memory until the liberation.[31]

Jews in hiding, even with assumed identities, who dared venture onto the streets were afraid too of being apprehended by one of the handful of Jewish "catchers" who were employed by the *Gestapo*. They also feared, rightly or wrongly, that if their rescuers did not receive the payment they demanded, they might be turned over to the *Gestapo*.

The illegal way of life demanded courage, persistence and considerable adaptability. Those in hiding had to be able to live alone and cope with the inevitable tensions that were generated between them and their benefactors.

Had it not been for those who opened their homes to Jewish fugitives, the illegal way of life would not have been possible. Some of the rescuers even obtained false documents of various kinds, such as postal certificates, work certificates and travel permits. Food coupons, for example, were valid only for a specified date, after which new cards were required. Persons of conscription age had to carry a personal document stating the reason for their exemption from military service. Some rescuers collected food and money for those in hiding, and some tried – not always successfully – to arrange for Jews to cross the German border by night across difficult terrain.

While the majority of the rescuers acted on an individual basis, there were some, particularly Protestant and Catholic clergymen such as those in the *Bekennende Kirche*, who organised in groups.[32] Many of the rescuers were betrayed, and after being tried before the notorious people's courts were hanged.[33]

After the capture of Berlin and other areas of Germany by the Allied forces,

---

[31]Martin Riesenburger, *Das Licht verlöschte nicht*, Berlin 1960, pp. 22–23.
[32]Kwiet and Eschwege, *op. cit.*, pp. 159–169.
[33]*Ibid.*, pp. 167–168.

especially those advancing from the East, the fugitives faced a new dilemma: how to prove their true identity. Jewish soldiers and officers among the Russian and American forces responded to the cry of *Shma Jisrael* or to the Yiddish language. Original papers which Jews had kept concealed on their person also saved them from prison or even death.

The experience of every person who went into hiding in Nazi Germany after September 1941 – when the order was issued to wear the *Judenstern* – is a story in itself. Yet, a perusal of the testimonies shows certain shared characteristics.

The majority of those who hid were aged between 20 and 50, and were almost equally divided between men and women. Most were offspring of Jewish parents, some of them living in mixed marriages, a smaller number the offspring of mixed marriages who were considered Jews. In most cases people went into hiding as individuals and tried to disappear in the big city. They learned about the true significance of deportation to the East in various ways in late 1942; by 1943 they knew with certainty that deportation to the East meant death. The majority decided on their own to "submerge" after their parents had been deported, or shortly before – or immediately after – receiving the order to report for transport to the East. For the most part, they found one or two hiding places where they could stay for several months or more. Others had to change their hiding places frequently, often dozens of times. The first refuge was generally with a non-Jew or with persons of mixed marriage who were previous acquaintances. Subsequent places of hiding were found by the rescuer. It was only to the first rescuer that the fugitive identified himself as a Jew. The rescuers' occupations were diverse, ranging from members of the liberal professions to a ranking Nazi who either did not know whom he had hired to work in his house or who was disgusted by the murder of Jews.

It is not true, as one testimony has it (Elsa Henk, Kaduri Collection, Yad Vashem, No. 01–58), that Germans hid Jews solely out of greed. Those who hid Jews did so for humanitarian, anti-Nazi and other reasons, including exploiting the person in hiding for work. Very few of the "submergers" succeeded in leaving Germany illegally during the war.

These shared traits will be examined in the chapters that follow.

How many of those who went into hiding in Nazi Germany survived? In Berlin, according to a number of researchers, about 1,400 of some 5,000 who "submerged" survived; in other words, 75% of them were caught by the *Gestapo* either on the street or after being informed on.[34] Since about a third of all the Jews who resided in Germany (*Altreich*) from the First World War until the end of the Second World War lived in Berlin, it is estimated that 3,500–4,000 of the Jews who decided to "disappear" survived.

---

[34] *Ibid.*, p. 169; and Kurt Großmann, *Die unbesungenen Helden. Menschen aus Deutschlands dunklen Tagen*, Berlin 1961, p. 73; and Israel Gutman (ed.), *Encyclopedia of the Holocaust*, New York–London 1990, vol. I, p. 202.

V. AN ILLEGAL WAY OF LIFE IN NAZI GERMANY

It was not only the Nazi terror or, on the other hand, appeal by Jewish institutions that deterred people from opting for the illegal way of life. There was also the fear of adopting an assumed identity in an unknown situation. Such difficulties are noted in the testimony of Ilse Rehwald:

> "By removing the yellow Star of David, we decided against the only certainty we had left – that of being deported. In 1943 for a Berlin Jew there was no other prospect than uncertainty or certain death – and the uncertainty could not be defined in any concrete terms beyond the fact that it did not hold the absolute certainty of being deported and murdered."[35]

As already noted, about 5,000 Berlin Jews mustered the courage to "submerge" and commence an illegal existence. Of the estimated 12–15,000 who went into hiding throughout Germany, some 25–28% survived; the rest were caught by the *Gestapo*.

Testimonies were taken from some of those who survived concerning their way of life, with particular reference to their non-Jewish rescuers. The majority of these statements are preserved in the Yad Vashem Archives. These testimonies, taken by trained personnel, in Israel and abroad, were also verified through comparison with parallel testimonies and through existing documents.

Testimonies given by individuals are also contained in the Kaduri Collection (16 statements), the Wiener Collection (80) and in Yad Vashem's Department for Righteous Gentiles (186 testimonies to date). Fifty of these documents were found suitable for extracting the majority of the responses to the questionnaire which I drew up for this study. In addition, there are 15 autobiographies from which information can be gleaned about the details of the illegal way of life followed by Jews in Nazi Germany. These 65 testimonies constitute the source for the description which follows of the life led by the Jews who decided to "submerge".

1. *The Fateful Decision*

October 1941 saw the start of the expulsions from Berlin and elsewhere, initially to Litzmannstadt, and, beginning the following month, to the East: Minsk, Riga, Auschwitz and elsewhere. Officially, the expulsions were called "evacuation" or "uprooting". Those being sent to the East believed that they were bound for camps where, under harsh conditions, they would labour for the good of the Third *Reich*'s war machine. As yet, they did not think their lives were in danger.

Slowly, however, via various routes, reports began filtering into Germany about the mass murder of Jews in the East. Some heard such reports on the BBC[36] or, in greater detail, from soldiers stationed in the East who came home on leave. This is indicated from a secret internal memorandum to Party members dated 9th October 1942, which stressed:[37]

---

[35]Kwiet and Eschwege, *op. cit.*, pp. 152–153.
[36]Schwersenz and Wolff, *loc. cit.*, pp. 51–53.
[37]Leuner, *op. cit.*, p. 89.

"During the work for the final solution of the Jewish problem, the population in various parts of Germany has recently begun to discuss the 'very harsh measures' taken against the Jews, particularly in the East. Investigations revealed that the opinions voiced – for the most part distortions and exaggerations – are based on stories told by soldiers on leave from units in the East, who in fact witnessed these measures. It may be that not all of our compatriots (*Volksgenosse*), especially those who have never had the opportunity to see Bolshevik brutalities first-hand, are capable of grasping that these measures are essential."

Table I, culled from the testimonies, shows the informants from whom potential "submergers" learned about the certain danger of death involved in deportation to Eastern Europe.

TABLE I
Informants about the Danger Entailed in Deportation to Eastern Europe

		In %
1. Family relation	4	7
2. Jewish friend or acquaintance	17	30
3. Non-Jewish friend or acquaintance	18	31
4. Rumour	12	21
5. First rescuer	1	2
6. Other	5	9
	n=57	100%

Thus, 60% of the potential "submergers" heard about the danger from friends or acquaintances, equally divided between Jews and non-Jews. Clearly, then, despite the authorities' rules and regulations, Jews maintained some sort of contact with non-Jews, either openly or covertly. One fifth of these persons learned about the danger from rumours that were rife throughout Germany. A few apparently decided to follow an illegal way of life even before they had definite information about the fate of the deportees.

Even though reports about the extermination began filtering in at the end of 1941, many Jews still believed that Germans were incapable of perpetrating the deeds mentioned in the rumours.[38] It was not until late 1942 and early 1943 that it became clear to the Jews still living in Germany that these rumours were in fact the terrible truth. Those who were pressed into forced labour in military industries believed they were immune from transport to the East. But on 27th February 1943 the *Fabrik-Aktion* signalled the final warning to those who were thinking about disappearing underground that now was the time to act.

The following table shows the dates, according to the testimonies, on which

[38]Borinski, *op. cit.*, p. 28; and Kwiet and Eschwege, *op. cit.*, p. 153.

potential "submergers" learned that deportation to the East entailed the prospect of death.

TABLE II
Dates on Which the Danger Involved in Deportation to the East Became Known

Year/Month	1	2	3	4	5	6	7	8	9	10	11	12	Total
1941										1		2	3
1942		1			2	2	1	1	3	5	5	8	28
1943	9	15				1	1					1	27
1944							2	1					3
													n=61

Forty-five of the 61 persons who gave these testimonies heard about the mass murder in the East between September 1942 and February 1943. A few had already heard about it in 1941, while some did not become aware of it until 1944.

The days preceding the decision to adopt an illegal way of life were filled with agonising self-questioning and consultations; rarely was a decision made from one day to the next. Preparations were required, including attempts to conceal the move from neighbours and acquaintances; indeed, it had to be kept secret from everyone. In some cases, acquaintances urged vacillators to evade deportation, thinking that the end of the Third *Reich* was imminent.[39]

The following table shows whose advice fugitives followed when they decided not to report for deportation to the East:

TABLE III
Whose Advice Was Taken When the Decision Was Made Not to Report for Deportation to the East

		In %
1. Own decision	34	52
2. Family relation	3	5
3. Jewish friend or acquaintance	4	6
4. Non-Jewish friend or acquaintance	19	29
5. The rescuer	2	3
6. Other	3	5
	n=65	100%

The figures show that more than 50% of those who gave testimony made the decision without consulting anyone. This usually occurred after their parents,

---

[39]Schwersenz and Wolff, *loc. cit.*, pp. 53–55.

siblings or other relatives had been sent East and they themselves expected to receive a similar order in the near future.

Also examined was whether a correlation exists between the person who provided the information about the danger entailed in deportation and the person advising not to report for deportation:

TABLE IV
Correlation Between Source of Information About Events in the East and Person Giving Advice to Evade Deportation

Source of information about danger of deportation	Person advising not to report for deportation						
	Own decision	Family member	Jewish acquaintance	Non-Jewish acquaintance	First rescuer	Other	Total
1. Family member	1	1		1		1	4
2. Jewish friend	12		1	3	1		17
3. Non-Jewish friend	4	1	1	12			18
4. Rumour	7	1	2	1	1		12
5. First rescuer	1						1
6. Other	4					1	5
Total	29	3	4	17	2	2	57
In %	50.9	5.3	7.0	29.8	3.5	3.5	100%

Most significant in this table is the fact that two thirds of the Jews who were the source of the information about the danger lurking in the East were also those who advised people not to report for deportation.

Those who were not at home when the *Gestapo* brought the order to report for deportation, or came to take Jews personally, heard about it from neighbours. Similarly, those who were not at work in the military plants due to sickness on the fateful day – 27th February 1943 – could no longer evade deportation. Therefore, one third of those who decided to "submerge" made the decision only after receiving the order to report for transport, as the following table shows:

TABLE V
When Was the Decision Made to "Submerge"

		In %
Before receiving an order to report for deportation	40	61.5
After receiving an order to report for deportation	24	37
Unclear	1	1.5
	n=65	100%

An analysis of the degree in which the person giving the advice to "dive" had an effect on the date of the decision turns up the following data:

TABLE VI
Who Gave the Advice, When Decision to "Submerge" Was Made

Who advised not to report for deportation	When the decision was made to "dive"				
	Before getting the order	After getting the order	Unclear	Total	In %
1. Own decision	23	10	1	34	52
2. Family member	2	1		3	5
3. Jewish friend or acquaintance	2	2		4	6
4. Non-Jewish friend or acquaintance	12	7		19	29
5. Rescuer	1	1		2	3
6. Other	1	2		3	5
Total	41	23	1	n=65	100%

Two thirds of those who decided on their own to adopt an illegal way of life, or who took the advice of a non-Jewish friend or acquaintance "disappeared" before receiving the order to report for deportation or before the *Gestapo* came to round them up for transport. About one third decided to "submerge" after getting the order to report for deportation.

2. *Personal Data on Those Who Decided to "Dive"*
"For the men, especially, it was difficult to find a place to hide. They were always suspected, if they were of army age and were not in uniform, and they were examined more thoroughly than the women."[40] In fact, there was no significant difference between the number of men and women who went into hiding. Of our 65 testimonies, 30, or 46%, are by men, and 35, or 54%, are by women. It is probable that more women than men gave testimony, and it is possible that fewer women than men were caught by the *Gestapo*.

[40]Valerie Wolffenstein, 'Shadow of a Star', in Eric H. Boehm, *We Survived*, New Haven 1949, p. 81.

Avraham Seligmann

TABLE VII
Family Status of Those in Hiding

		In %
1. Unmarried male or female	34	53
2. Married male or female	26	40
3. Widowed male or female	3	5
4. Divorced male or female	1	2
	n=64	100%

Adding up the unmarried, the widowers and the divorced, we find that 60% of those in hiding were unattached and 40% were married. Of the latter, 72% were married to a Jew and 28% to a non-Jew. In 94% of the cases, both parents were Jewish, as the following table shows:

TABLE VIII
Origin

		In %
1. Both parents Jewish	61	94
2. Only father Jewish	2	3
3. Only mother Jewish	2	3
	n=65	100%

It is surprising that among the married people who opted for an illegal way of life, 28% were in a mixed marriage, since Jews in such marriages had greater privileges and did not face the danger of deportation to the East until the end of 1944. There could have been two reasons for this decision: either the non-Jewish partner, usually the wife, became Jewish, or they educated their children as Jews.

Of those who adopted an illegal way of life, 53% did so without being accompanied by family members, as against 47% who hid out together with members of their family:

TABLE IX

Family Members Accompanying Those in Hiding

		In %
1. With wife or husband	15	50
2. With parent(s)	3	10
3. With child(ren) only	4	13
4. With wife/husband and children	8	27
	n=30	100%

An unwillingness to part with one's immediate family, particularly when families were split up during deportation, combined with boldness, led nearly 50% to find a hiding place together with family members. Brothers and sisters who decided on an illegal way of life each went their separate way,[41] although they occasionally met or otherwise kept in touch.

The ages of those in hiding ranged from 12–59, as follows:

TABLE X

Ages of Those in Hiding in 1941

		In %
1. 12–18	14	23
2. 19–30	14	23
3. 31–40	13	21
4. 41–49	17	28
5. 50–59	3	5
	n=61	100%

Forty-six per cent of those in hiding were young people up to the age of 30, about 50% were middle-aged (31–49), while only a few were in their 50s. Clearly, older people could not cope with the hardships of an illegal existence.

In 1940, 83% (53) of those in hiding lived in big cities with a population of more than 500,000. This is understandable, since during the Nazi era there was a large migration from small towns to the big cities, especially Berlin, where it was thought to be easier to get along and live as a Jew. Thirteen per cent (8) resided in middle-sized cities (100,000–500,000), and 5% (3) in towns.

---

[41] See for instance the sisters Valerie and Andreas Wolffenstein.

The occupations of those in hiding covered a very broad range, as the following table shows:

TABLE XI
Occupations

		In %
1. Schoolchildren	6	9
2. Liberal profession	14	21
3. Clerk	5	8
4. Artisan	11	17
5. Tradesman	8	12
6. Farmer	3	5
7. Other	18	28
	n=65	100%

The data on occupations should be treated cautiously, as many Jews were forced to change their occupation during the Nazi era. The figure for the liberal professions, 21%, is virtually the same as that for Jewish breadwinners in Germany in 1933.[42] As for the 17% who were artisans and the 5% who worked in agriculture, it is probable that some of them had changed occupations. The 28% of "other" relates mainly to the women, who either had no profession or whose former profession is unknown – they now worked in forced labour in different jobs.

Once the fateful decision was made, those going into hiding had to pack their most important personal belongings – no more than could fit into a knapsack or a small suitcase – while other valuables were entrusted to the safekeeping of a non-Jewish acquaintance. The Yellow Stars were then removed from all clothing, and, finally, they had to leave their neighbourhood and find a hiding place. A problem which now arose was that of name.[43] As already described, to obtain false papers was far from simple: a high price was demanded, and some forgers took the money and disappeared.[44]

The following data were discovered concerning name change:

---

[42]Esra Bennathan, 'Die demographische und wirtschaftliche Struktur der Juden', in *Entscheidungsjahr 1932. Zur Judenfrage in der Endphase der Weimarer Republik*. Ein Sammelband herausgegeben von Werner E. Mosse unter Mitwirkung von Arnold Paucker, Tübingen 1965 (Schriftenreihe wissenschaftlicher Abhandlungen des Leo Baeck Instituts 13), p. 108.

[43]Schwersenz and Wolff, *loc. cit.*, pp. 59–62.

[44]Wolffenstein, *loc. cit.*, pp. 83–84.

TABLE XII
Name of Person in Hiding

		In %
1. Original name retained	35	56
2. Changed to "Aryan" name with papers before deciding to "submerge"	5	8
3. Changed to "Aryan" name after going into hiding	23	36
	n=63	100%

More than half of those who opted for an illegal way of life continued to go by their original name, some without papers of any kind, while others obtained false papers in their name. More than a third managed to obtain false papers with an "Aryan" name – a few even before going into hiding.

3. *How the Link Was Made With the Rescuers and the Places of Hiding*
As we have said, the majority of those who went into hiding found refuge with non-Jewish acquaintances or with acquaintances of acquaintances, or with mixed couples. Some had to change the place where they slept frequently; in the morning they might not know where they would spend the night. On occasion they had to sleep outside in a forest or park.[45] The great majority found one or two main hiding places where they spent more than six months, or even the entire period of their illegal existence. Of the 65 people who gave the testimonies on which this study is based, 17, or about a quarter, found one main place of hiding, while 48 found at least two main sites. The number of places of hiding attests to the difficulty of finding a place to sleep.

TABLE XIII
Number of Additional Hiding Places of Those Who Had More Than One Main Hiding Place

Number of Hiding Places	Number of People
1	12
4	2
5	3
	17

[45]Schwersenz and Wolff, *loc. cit.*, pp. 69–73.

Seventy per cent of those in hiding spent the entire period in one location. Their benefactors provided them with a special place of concealment, brought them food and so on.

Their testimonies indicate that the hiding place was dark – it was forbidden to turn on a light – and that air was scarce. Most could emerge only at night, though some left early in the morning and returned after dark.

TABLE XIV

Number of Hiding Places of Those Who Had Two Main Hiding Places

Number of Hiding Places	Number of People	In %
2	7	
3	7	40
4	5	
5	2	
6	6	
7	1	35
8	4	
9	4	
10	6	
11	1	
12	1	
14	1	25
18	1	
21	1	
40	1	
	48	

Forty per cent of those in hiding managed during their illegal existence with up to four locations, 35% made use of from five to nine sites, and 25% had between 10 and 40 places of hiding. The testimony about 40 locations, including time spent outside, should not be thought exceptional: other testimonies, not cited in this study, mention more than 40 places of hiding.[46]

All told, the 65 persons whose testimonies are included in this study had a total of 343 hiding places. If we deduct from this nights spent outside, we arrive at a figure of about 300. In other words, some 300 non-Jews helped save the lives of 65 Jews, some of them accompanied by family members.

[46]Großmann, *op. cit.*, p. 73; Max Krakauer, *Lichter im Dunkel*, Stuttgart 1947, mentions 60 hiding places – 37 of them in 1943.

As already mentioned, it was difficult to find a place to hide. The manner in which contact was made with the first main rescuer is shown in Table XV.

TABLE XV
How Contact Was Made With the First Main Rescuer

		In %
1. Via a relative	3	5
2. Via a Jewish friend/acquaintance	9	14
3. Via a Non-Jewish friend/acquaintance	36	55
4. Via a friend at work or some economic tie	9	14
5. Personal search	4	6
6. Other	4	6
	n=65	100%

The table indicates that contact with the first main rescuer was made through a non-Jew. If we include also a non-Jewish friend at work who helped find a place of refuge, it emerges that in 69% of the cases, contact with the main rescuer was effected with the help of a non-Jew.

As for contact with the second rescuer, Table XVI shows some differences:

TABLE XVI
How Contact Was Made With the Second Rescuer

		In %
1. Via a relative	5	10
2. Via a Jewish friend/acquaintance	7	15
3. Via a Non-Jewish friend/acquaintance	14	29
4. Via a friend at work or some economic tie	1	2
5. Personal search	6	13
6. Via the first main rescuer	14	29
7. Other	1	2
	n=48	100%

In 29% of the cases the first rescuer helped find a new hiding place. As noted, in most instances the rescuers did not belong to an organisation. A few were rescued by the members of the *Bekennende Kirche* and the clergymen who organised at Württemberg to conceal Jews. According to this table, 60% of those who helped Jews find a hiding place were non-Jews. It should be noted that the number of those who opted to find a place by themselves increased from 6% to 13%.

The location of the first hiding place differed from the second:

TABLE XVII
Location of the First and Second Main Hiding Places

	First Hiding Place	In %	Second Hiding Place	In %
1. City of over 500,000	36	55	24	51
2. City of 100,000–500,000	7	11	3	6
3. Town	8	12	4	8
4. Village	12	18	16	33
5. Christian institution	1	2		
6. Solitary house outside a city or town	1	2	1	2
	n=65	100%	n=48	100%

Second hiding places were more in small towns, with a third of them in villages.
A change is also discernible in the ethnic identification of the Jew in hiding *vis-à-vis* the second rescuer.

TABLE XVIII
How the Person in Hiding Identified Himself

	To first rescuer	In %	To second rescuer	In %
1. Openly as a Jew	55	85	27	56
2. Not revealing Jewishness	2	3	5	11
3. As a Christian	7	10	15	31
4. Unclear	1	2	1	2
	n=65	100%	n=48	100%

Severe punishment was in store for anyone discovered hiding a Jew. Therefore, the majority of those in hiding – 85% – not wishing to entrap the first rescuer, revealed their Jewishness. But when the situation deteriorated and it became increasingly difficult to find a hiding place, nearly one third of those in hiding were forced to pass themselves off as anti-Nazi Christians, and only about half admitted their Jewishness.

4. *Personal Data of the Rescuers*
Although the authorities declared in late 1943 that Germany was *Judenrein*, they were well aware, as press articles at the end of 1943 and the beginning of 1944

make clear, that some Jews were still in hiding (besides those in mixed marriages).

Who were the rescuers? All the testimonies suggest that there were more women – the majority living alone – than men. As noted, apart from a few exceptional cases, no organised groups existed, not even Church groups, who operated to rescue Jews.[47] Organised rescue work would have increased the danger of discovery.

Were all those who hid Jews from the outset ready to give shelter to anyone who might happen to arrive at their home? Table XIX deals with this issue:

TABLE XIX
Who Were Rescuers Willing to Hide?

	First main rescuer	In %	Second main rescuer	In %
1. Only friends/acquaintances	37	57	16	33
2. Previous ties unimportant	28	43	32	67
	n=65	100%	n=48	100%

In the first period of hiding, more than half of the rescuers were willing to take into their home only acquaintances or persons referred to them by acquaintances; but later, as the war drew to a close, there was no prior connection between the rescuers and two thirds of those to whom they gave shelter.

Also of interest is whether the rescuers had any previous connection with Jews.

TABLE XX
Previous Connection with Jews

	First main rescuer	In %	Second main rescuer	In %
1. Family tie	6	9	4	8
2. Friendship	10	16	1	2
3. Acquaintance	23	37	18	38
4. Work or economic tie	6	10	3	6
5. Other	2	3	4	8
6. None	16	25	18	38
	n=63	100%	n=48	100%

[47]Leuner, *op. cit.*, on the *Bekennende Kirche* (*Bekenntniskirche*), pp. 162–167, on Württemberg, pp. 172–176.

Fewer than 10% of all the ties were forged by family connections resulting from mixed marriages. While 16% of those in hiding had previous friendly relations with the first rescuer, this was true in only 2% of the cases involving a second rescuer. The reason was that considerable caution was required in choosing a benefactor, and it was no longer possible to choose a friend who was willing to grant shelter to a Jew.

Mobilisation to the army and work in factories that were producing for the war effort effected a radical change in the sources of livelihood in Germany. Hence, it is pointless to compare the pre-war occupation picture with that which developed during the war. To try to arrive at common characteristics of the rescuers, we shall look also at their occupation or status.

TABLE XXI
Occupation or Status of Rescuers

	First main rescuer	In %	Second main rescuer	In %
1. Liberal profession	5	8	6	13
2. Merchant-industrialist	10	16	6	13
3. Owner of workshop	6	9	3	6
4. Clerk	4	6	3	6
5. Labourer or farmer	5	8	7	15
6. Pensioner or housewife	17	27	13	27
7. Cleric	5	8	4	8
8. Ranking Nazi	1	2	1	2
9. Other	10	16	5	10
	n=63	100%	n=48	100%

Strikingly, more than a quarter of the rescuers were pensioners or housewives. The latter generally lived alone, whether as widows or because their husbands were at the front. As the war continued, an increasing number of persons in the liberal professions showed a willingness to hide Jews. As the war progressed, the number of hiding places in smaller towns and villages increased, and there was a concomitant increase in the number of labourers and farmers who offered refuge – from 8% to 15%. For the same reason, there was a decrease in the number of merchants and industrialists among benefactors of Jews. The rescuers included some ranking Nazis who, as mentioned, either did not know that the person in question was a Jew or were disgusted by the murder of Jews.

The broad range of the rescuers' occupations was matched by the range of their motives for concealing Jews.

TABLE XXII
Motivations for Hiding Jews

	First main rescuer	In %	Second main rescuer	In %
1. Anti-Nazi	16	23	17	35
2. Religious	10	14	6	13
3. Family tie	3	4	1	2
4. Personal tie	20	28	7	14
5. Humanitarian reasons	11	16	7	14
6. For use as a workforce	4	6	7	14
7. For money	4	6	3	6
8. Other	2	3	1	2
	n=70	100%	n=49	100%

Here we have noted the leading motive; naturally, some motives overlapped.

A good many of the rescuers opposed the Nazi regime; this motive for rescuing Jews rose from 23% to 35% in the war's final years. Only 10% to 13% were prompted by a religious outlook to hide Jews. Few could hide with relatives who had mixed marriages. If at the outset those in hiding found shelter with non-Jews with whom they had previous ties, the proportion of such rescuers was halved, from 28% to 14%. Naturally, the demand for labour constantly increased during the war, reflected in the increase – from 6% to 14% – in the number of those who hid Jews, both men and women, so that they would work in their homes. Only 6% hid Jews in order to increase their income. (Some first rescuers had more than one motive for hiding Jews, hence n=70.)

An examination of motives cannot ignore the rescuers' political affiliation prior to the Nazis' rise to power. Information on this is available in only about half of the testimonies; the absolute majority of the rescuers voted for parties on the Left, or were active in them.

TABLE XXIII
Rescuers' Political Affiliation

	First main rescuer	In %	Second main rescuer	In %
1. Right-wing parties	6	19	9	36
2. Left-wing parties	19	59	13	52
3. Centre parties	7	22	3	12
	n=32	100%	n=25	100%

It is noteworthy that the number of rescuers who once supported Right-wing parties but were appalled by their actions during the war grew steadily, comprising more than a third of the second main rescuers.

In many cases the place of hiding was separate from the rescuer's residence. In order to camouflage the hiding place, windows had to be covered, cupboards had to be moved to conceal doors, and so forth. Air and light were scarce commodities under such conditions. Lavatory facilities were minimal or non-existent.[48]

Thus it was impossible to give shelter to Jews without one's family knowing about it.

TABLE XXIV
Attitude of Rescuer's Family Towards Concealment of Jews

	First main rescuer	In %	Second main rescuer	In %
1. Supportive	40	64	22	48
2. Unaware	3	5	6	13
3. Rescuer lived alone	19	31	18	39
	n=62	100%	n=46	100%

No cases were found in which a family objected to the concealment of Jews. Even husbands or sons who came from the front on leave accepted the new situation in the house. In some cases Jews were hidden in garden shacks, in a summer home, even in a boat on a lake; or in an underground shelter which the head of the family or the landlady prepared in advance for this purpose and which was unknown to the rest of the family. From many standpoints, it was convenient to go into hiding in the house of someone who lived alone. Such persons constituted more than a third of the rescuers. At all events, the majority of the families concerned supported the hiding of the Jew.

Naturally, the rescuers, aware of the danger that faced them and the punishment they could expect if caught, did everything possible to keep their neighbours in the dark about their action. The movements of the person in hiding were limited; he could venture out only at night. A neighbour who turned up unexpectedly and saw a stranger in the house was told that he was a relative – a refugee whose home had been destroyed in a bombing raid. If fear arose about an informer, or if it was learned that the police or the *Gestapo* were about to carry out an inspection, the person in hiding was moved to a different location.

---

[48]Kwiet and Eschwege, *op. cit.*, pp. 154–155.

In their daily behaviour, those in hiding showed they were conscious of their rescuers' fears, as the following table shows:

TABLE XXV
Degree of Fear of the Rescuers

	First main rescuer	In %	Second main rescuer	In %
1. Very frightened	6	9	3	6
2. Frightened but disregarded it	21	32	12	25
3. Was not afraid	35	54	31	64
4. Not known	3	5	2	5
	n=65	100%	n=48	100%

The absolute majority of the rescuers evinced no signs of fear, according to the testimonies of those in hiding. More than a quarter were frightened but did not show it openly. Only among a few of the rescuers could fear be sensed in daily contact. Since these findings are based on the personal impressions of those in hiding, they must be treated with caution.

5. *Personal Relations Between the Jew in Hiding and His Non-Jewish Rescuer*
The relations between the two sides – rescuer and person in hiding – were quite complex. One side was the giver, in some cases giving everything required for day-to-day existence, such as lodging, food and clothing, whereas it was beyond the capacity of the other side to offer a suitable *quid pro quo* or indeed to give anything at all in return. This situation was marked by constant tension: the Jew was haunted by thoughts of whether he would be able to cope with this way of life and whether he would endanger his non-Jewish rescuer. The latter was preoccupied with taking constant cautionary measures to ensure that his actions were not discovered.

Our analysis of the testimonies showed that the rescuers' attitude towards those to whom they gave shelter could be divided into three categories: 1. A "very good attitude", meaning that the rescuers saw to everything, including lodging and food, perhaps obtaining forged food coupons or false identity papers. 2. A "reasonable attitude", meaning primarily that they arranged for lodgings, at least for the nights, while the Jew had to find ways to obtain food – and money, if needed – on his own. 3. "Exploiting for work", meaning that the rescuer demanded that the Jew do hard work in or around the home in return for shelter.

TABLE XXVI
Rescuers' Attitude Towards Those They Hid

	First main rescuer	In %	Second main rescuer	In %
1. Very good attitude	47	72	22	46
2. Reasonable attitude	17	26	23	48
3. Exploited for work	1	2	3	6
	n=65	100%	n=48	100%

Three quarters of all the first rescuers had a "very good attitude" towards those to whom they gave shelter. But this was true of only about half of the second rescuers. A "reasonable attitude" was initially demonstrated by only about a quarter of those in hiding, but this increased to about half as the difficulties caused by the war grew.

An examination of the link between the rescuer's motives for hiding a Jew and his attitude towards that Jew turn up the following findings:

TABLE XXVII
Comparison of the Motives for Hiding Jews with Attitude Towards Them

	First main rescuer			Second main rescuer		
Attitude:	Very good	Reasonable	Exploit for work	Very good	Reasonable	Exploit for work
1. Anti-Nazi	13	3		15	2	
2. Religious	7	2	1	3	2	1
3. Family tie	2	1			1	
4. Personal tie	18	2		4	3	
5. Humanitarian reasons	7	4		3	4	
6. As workforce	2	2		4	3	
7. For money		4		2	1	
8. Other	2			1		

Nearly all those who hid Jews for political reasons evinced a "very good attitude" towards those they sheltered. Similarly, the majority of those who hid Jews due to personal ties showed a "very good attitude". The testimonies[49] suggest that the few who exploited Jews to do hard work belonged to the *Bekennende Kirche*. Initially they concealed only Jews who had converted to Christianity, and subsequently full-fledged Jews, too, in the hope of getting them to renounce their faith.

[49]Yad Vashem Archives Jerusalem, Collection Wiener, File 02/558 – Lilly Neumark.

Questions relating to payment for food and lodgings, and other money matters that arose from an illegal way of life, went unanswered in all the testimonies. In some cases mention is made of the large amounts that were demanded as payment for false papers. Hardly any testimonies refer to the sources of the necessary funds, although occasionally it is said that money was received from friends. The testimonies on which this study is based show that about a quarter of the rescuers received a *quid pro quo* in the form of work or money, while in three-quarters of the cases the rescuers made no monetary demands and there was no fear of being handed over or informed on due to non-payment. All these data must be treated with reservations; a separate study of this subject is merited. In fact, though, it is questionable whether sufficient data exist to form conclusions about the money needed by those living an illegal existence.

Of the 65 persons whose testimonies are included in this study, six succeeded in leaving Germany illegally before the end of the war. All six made their way to Palestine – one before the end of the war, one between 1945 and 1948, and four after the establishment of the State of Israel.

CONCLUSION

The Jews in Germany who survived the war were quick to register in the *Gemeinde* that were re-organised, particularly in the cities under the rule of the victorious powers. Their purpose was to be recognised as Jews who were local residents and had been victims of the Nazi regime. Based on this registration, Konrad Kwiet and Helmut Eschwege found that there were 1,402 Jews in post-war Berlin. Hence, it was estimated that throughout Germany some 3,500–4,000 Jews who had led an illegal way of life survived. This group constitutes 25%–28% of the Jews who opted to go into hiding.

From the 27 tables presented above, which were worked out after the questionnaires were processed via computer, we can discover the characteristics of the illegal way of life in Nazi Germany.

1. *Personal data about the "submergers" (Tables VII–XII)*
The majority of those who opted for an illegal way of life were born as Jews to two Jewish parents (94%). In age they ranged from 12 to 59, although surprisingly 23% were aged 12–18, 72% were 19–49, and 5% were in their 50s. They were equally divided between males and females. Their occupations were quite diversified: 9% were still in school, 21% practised the liberal professions, 22% were artisans and farmers, who undoubtedly changed their profession during the period of Nazi rule, and only 12% were merchants.

Eighty-three per cent resided in cities with populations of more than 500,000, 13% in cities of between 100,000 and 500,000, and 5% in small towns. More than half (53%) were unmarried, while 28% of those who were married had mixed marriages. Nearly 50% went into hiding with family members. Forty-four per cent took "Aryan" names, the majority only after finding a hiding place; 50% retained their original names, usually with false papers.

2. *Process leading up to the decision to go into hiding (Tables I–VI)*
When rumours increased about the mass murder of the Jews who were deported to Eastern Europe – rumours which were confirmed in late 1942 and early 1943 – a few thousand Jews began thinking about the choice between certain death and the chance of survival. Some arrived at the fateful decision after consulting with Jewish and non-Jewish acquaintances (29%), some on their own (52%). In some cases – when the order to report for deportation was received or was about to be received – the decision was made virtually overnight. Sixty-two per cent decided to "disappear" even before receiving the order to report for deportation.

3. *Making contact with rescuers (Tables XV–XVIII)*
Twenty-nine per cent of those who went into hiding succeeded in remaining with one main rescuer throughout most of the period, or with someone to whom they could always return. Others had two main hiding places in each of which they remained for six months or more. Sixty-nine per cent found the first rescuer through non-Jewish acquaintances, 19 per cent through Jewish relatives or acquaintances, and only 6% as a result of their own personal search. Thirty-one per cent reached the second main rescuer via non-Jewish acquaintances, 29% via the first rescuer, 13% by means of their own search, and 25% through Jewish relatives or acquaintances.

If at first 66% of the hiding places were located in cities and only 18% in villages, as the war progressed the village locations increased to 33%, with only 57% remaining in cities. This was due to the saturation bombings of German cities in the war's later stages. While 85% disclosed their Jewishness to the first rescuer, only 56% did so to the second rescuer, while 42% did not disclose their true identity at all.

4. *Personal data on the rescuers and their attitudes towards those in hiding (Tables XIX–XXVII)*
Of the first rescuers, 57% were willing to take in only acquaintances or acquaintances of acquaintances, while 28% attached no importance to this aspect. In contrast, as the war progressed, 67% of the rescuers attached no importance to a previous personal tie. It is noteworthy that more than 50% of the rescuers belonged to Left-wing parties before the war; and that 25% to 38% had no previous contact with Jews.

The rescuers' professions were quite diverse; 27% were pensioners, the majority of them housewives. There were also several ranking Nazis among them who did not know that the housekeeper was Jewish or who were disgusted by the extermination of Jews.

The motives for hiding Jews were very different: 23% to 35% are classifiable as anti-Nazi, some 30% were motivated by a religious outlook or for humanitarian reasons. At first, about 30% of the rescuers had a personal or even family tie with those they hid, but only 16% of the second rescuers had a previous personal connection. In the first stage 6% of the rescuers saw those they hid as a work force, but this subsequently rose to 14%. Only 6% hid Jews in order to increase their income. No case is known in which the rescuing family, which in some cases included a soldier – the father or a son – opposed the hiding of a Jew. It is also important that 31% to 39% of the rescuers lived alone.

Seventy-two per cent of the rescuers treated the Jews they hid very well, sharing with them everything from their home to their food, while 17% provided a place to stay, but left the person in hiding to tend to all his other needs alone.

In the case of the second rescuer, the percentage of those showing a "good attitude" towards those in hiding decreased to 46%, and the proportion of those offering only lodgings rose to 48%. Very few – and precisely those who were motivated by religious reasons to conceal Jews – took advantage of the situation to make those in hiding do hard work.

As for money – sources and payments – the testimonies do not provide sufficient information.

5. *Number of hiding places (Tables XIII–XIV)*
Two thirds of those who hid in one main location did not have to seek out another location; the others changed hiding places four or five times. Of those who hid in two main locations, 40% changed their place of hiding two to four times, 35% five to nine times, and 23% 10 to 21 times. Two per cent were compelled to change their places of hiding 40 times or more.

Only six – 9% of the total – succeeded in leaving Germany illegally before the end of the war, and all six eventually settled in Israel.

The results of our data were processed via computer. Using this method, we were able to discover the shared and differing traits among the rescuers and among those to whom they gave shelter; to illuminate the process that led certain Jews to decide to "submerge"; to examine how the connection was effected between the Jews and the rescuers; to find out the motivations of the latter for hiding Jews; to analyse the personal relations between the two groups; and finally, to learn how many places of hiding there were.

The method did not enable us to discover details about places where Jews assumed they might be able to hide but where they were in fact turned away. Nor was it possible to detail the reasons which abruptly forced those in hiding to leave one location and seek out another. Moreover, the method affords no answers to questions about how those in hiding managed to get food, clothing and other daily necessities, and how they went about obtaining money. No data exist on how they got false personal papers. Because the testimonies contain nothing in common about all these subjects, it was impossible to feed the material into a computer for processing. Yet, despite the missing details, a reliable historical description emerges about the common experiences of the Jews who opted for an illegal way of life in Nazi Germany.

A Muted Protest in War-Time Berlin

Writing on the Legal Position of German Jewry throughout the Centuries – Leo Baeck – Leopold Lucas – Hilde Ottenheimer

BY ALBERT H. FRIEDLANDER

Year Book III of the Leo Baeck Institute contains an Appendix in which some pages from a Leo Baeck manuscript (selected by Hans Liebeschütz) are brought to the attention of the scholarly community. The introduction to these selections was written by Hans Reichmann and records the conversations he and Robert Weltsch had in August 1955 with Leo Baeck relating to this material. If we return to these texts more than thirty years later, it must be made clear that this does not constitute a challenge to these eminent men; it is more of an attempt to enlarge our understanding of the mystery which still surrounds that text, and to be true to the principles of scholarship which have dominated the LBI Year Book from the first issue to this volume, which also marks the end of an era.*

The manuscript to be discussed first came to Robert Weltsch and Arnold Paucker at the Leo Baeck Institute in London. It was guarded and cared for and Arnold Paucker later arranged for the transcript of the material so that the latter could then be transmitted for permanent safe-keeping to the Archives of the Leo Baeck Institute in New York. The story of how the original text survived against all odds is told in Year Book III.[1] The task of this essay is more to examine the actual texts and to ask the necessary questions, which can only be answered in part and with some uncertainty.

---

*It is both essential and proper to pay tribute here to Arnold Paucker, whose monumental labours and profound scholarship saw these Year Book volumes through the second phase of their development. This is the last volume to be edited by him and the variety of contributions are, as ever, an enlargement in the field of Jewish historiography where the hand of the editor is also clearly visible.

[1]Hans Reichmann, 'Excerpts from Leo Baeck's Writings. Foreword: The Fate of a Manuscript', in *LBI Year Book III* (1958), pp. 361–363, Appendix of texts, pp. 363–372; see also *idem*, 'Aufzeichnung über eine Unterredung', in *Worte des Gedenkens für Leo Baeck*. Im Auftrag des Councils of Jews from Germany – London. Hrsg. von Eva G. Reichmann, Heidelberg 1959, pp. 237–241, esp. pp. 238–239.

Italic page numbers in the text refer to sections and pages of the manuscript.

I

First, one must look at the five volumes of typescript which are available to us. (The titles will be cited in German, since the assessment of the language itself must be part of the evaluation.) The first typescript is entitled *Juden und Judentum in den geistigen und religiösen Strömungen des Altertums* and contains 165 pages. The first part, 'Die Volkskunde', deals with the first encounters between Greek and Jewish thought, and one can easily distinguish Baeck's individual style in these descriptions. "Wege auf denen sie Kunde von einander gewannen" (*p. 2*); "'Philosophen' standen vor ihnen wie in ihrem Lande, so dort." (*p. 7*); "Pythagoras, diesen Mann der alten Zeit, um dessen Gestalt sich mehr als um andere sehr bald Sage und Dichtung schlangen . . ." (*p. 11*); "Ihr Besonderes sollte ein Wertvolles sein und zu den Werten die man selbst besaß in einer Beziehung stehen . . ." (*p. 44*). Even more than the style, one finds here the great themes which always occupied Baeck; the great historians and the response to the Hebrew Bible through translations. (The reason for stressing Baeck's authorship will be covered in the second section, where we concern ourselves with the nature of the co-operative enterprise which created the whole manuscript.) From *Volkskunde*, this text turns to *Weltanschauung* where one moves from 'Wandel des Denkens' to 'Wandel des Glaubens' and then to the philosophies. Again, the stress lies upon the interplay between the Jews and the civilisations they have encountered in antiquity, with the stress upon acceptance gained from outside and appreciation of the outer culture within Jewish life – even though sharp delineations had to be made in terms of self-preservation. The largest section of this text is, therefore, called 'Geistige Ausbreitung und Ablehnung', which comes to the more familiar encounter with rejection. Nevertheless, the emphasis is clearly positive, particularly when one notes that the presentation centres upon "the Jewish Mission" and explores Jewish contributions in the field of *chochma* (wisdom) and of philosophy. Baeck's own love of the pseudepigrapha comes to the fore here, as he sees Jewish authors addressing their neighbours in a style of writing not unfamiliar to Greek thought (". . . der Verfasser trat zurück, und er liess Männer mit klassischen Namen, Männer der Vorzeit sprechen, sie erzählten von der Vergangenheit, um aus ihr dann die Zukunft aufsteigen zu lassen", *p. 134*). The closing section 'Mission und Gegnerschaft' is a superb description of the interplay between two cultures, each of which attempted to absorb the other, had profound influence on the opponent, but could not succeed in their ultimate aims. Evidence for the partial success of the Jewish mission was easy to find – even in the success of the Christian mission which used the Jewish communities as outposts for their new missionary work. Yet the Jewish mission work never ended, even though, as this text closes, Judaism had to turn back into itself: "aber im wesentlichen ist in dieser Epoche die intensive Selbsterhaltung, das Fürsichsein zur Aufgabe und zur Geschichte der Juden geworden" (*p. 150*). The largest section of the material – 370 pages – is entitled *Rechtsstellung der Juden in Europa bis zur Aufklärung*. Here, we come to the purpose of the text as indicated in Leo Baeck's conversation with Robert Weltsch and Hans Reichmann, which was, in fact, at the behest of the German "conservative" resistance circles with whom Leo Baeck (as well as other members of the *Reichsvertretung/Reichsvereinigung*) was in contact. The co-operative nature of the enterprise was also indicated:

> "In this connection [for 'The Day After' the Nazi regime when guidance for portraying the Jew properly would be needed], it was suggested that a book on the development of the position of the Jews in Europe should be written for the information of the public after the liberation. I was given this assignment. I worked on it from 1938 to 1941. The writing could be done only in the very early morning hours; for this purpose I rose at 4 a.m. My assistants were Rabbi Dr. Lucas, Glogau and Dr. Hilde Ottenheimer, an able historian."[2]

One might doubt that the weighty tome resulting out of this sacrificial work would really open itself to the public in the manner envisaged. At the same time, we are not really able to place ourselves in the position of these Jewish scholars after 1938. The massive propaganda efforts of the Nazis had eliminated most positive portrayals of the Jew and of Jewish life within the universities as well as within public awareness. There was an almost prophetic insight in their vision of a world where ignorance would prevail. We can appreciate this text all the more when we realise this.

The attempt to place the Jew into the framework of European law throughout the centuries can be viewed as a cautious attempt at self-justification which might escape the attention of a government more concerned with direct challenges to its authority. At the same time, it belongs to that region of spiritual resistance which knows that to place the Jew into the structure of the law is a challenge to a lawless society. The subtitle to this part of the text (*II, p. 1*) is 'Die Entwicklung der Rechtsstellung und des Platzes der Juden in Europa, vornehmlich in Deutschland, vom Altertum bis zum Beginn der Aufklärungszeit'. The first chapter deals with the "Altertum und Vormittelalter" and describes the early settlements of Jewish life, the developing Christian *imperium*, and the changes within the legal system as the milder Theodosian system gives way to the stringent Justinian legal code.

One need not go into the various details of the text here, which is primarily a straightforward account of historical events and of legal developments. My own impression of this clear and cogent style with its careful attention to detail is that it is not dissimilar to the classic text by Leopold Lucas, *Zur Geschichte der Juden im vierten Jahrhundert*,[3] but one cannot always distinguish between competent writers working on a joint project. In any event, this text moves on to "Das frühere Mittelalter", which examines the Jews in the developing legal systems of the rest of Europe, and then enters "Das spätere Mittelalter". Here, too, one finds a careful, detailed depiction of Jewish life as seen in the various legal systems, where one deals not only with regulations concerning Jewish settlements but also with the various tax structures in which Jews are seen as a productive – and carefully controlled – part of their society. Areas of Jewish activities which had been particularly attacked by Nazi propaganda; i.e., "usury" were treated with particular care:

---

[2]Reichmann, 'Fate of a Manuscript', *loc. cit.*
[3]Leopold Lucas, *Zur Geschichte der Juden im vierten Jahrhundert. Der Kampf zwischen Christentum und Judentum*, Berlin 1910, reprinted 1985 and 1991.

"Trotz der finanziellen Eingriffe König Wenzels waren Juden aber auch noch an dem Aufschwunge des Geldhandels im 15. Jahrhundert beteiligt, da das kirchliche Zinsverbot in strenger Geltung war und die Tätigkeit der Lombarden erst allmählich ihren Raum gewann." (*II, p. 268*)

The section on 'Die jüdische Gemeinde' is particularly rich in detail and deals with the internal structure of law as well as with the outer laws contained from the earliest *Judenprivilegien* (and the *Privilegium* Friedrich II of 1236) and the situation of the Jewish community under the emperors or under the control of the cities. The wealth of detail is re-inforced through copious notes, which does indicate that the authors had access to (their own) library resources and were able to make significant scholarly contributions through this work. There was also the library of the *Hochschule für die Wissenschaft des Judentums* in Berlin. Here, as in all areas, scholarship has advanced significantly in the last sixty years (most scholarly works quoted here are pre-1930). Behind the sometimes dry and scholarly presentation of the Jewish community one can distinguish the defence of a separate Jewish life which had maintained itself through the centuries; and we would read this text today more as a dignified presentation of Jewish identity to be given to a reading public which knew only the distortions of the Third *Reich*. Whether or not Baeck ever said: "The thousand year history of the Jews in Germany has come to an end", this document places the Jews so solidly into the framework of German law and history that it reclaims their history and life for that millennium of German history – which was not the totality of Jewish history in Germany! But this right was not reclaimed for them at the expense of their individuality:

"Uebersehen werden darf nicht, dass die Juden sich in Wesentlichem auch selbst absonder-ten. Schon in der Tatsache war dies gegeben, dass sie, aufs Ganze gesehen, an ihrer Religion unbedingt festhielten und oft sich in sie zurückzogen. Sie wussten und fühlten sich darin als die Besonderen, sie hatten darin ihre eigenen Lebensformen und auch ihre eigene Mystik, die sie pflegten. Sie haben zudem nie die innere Verbundenheit mit dem Lande der Väter aufgegeben; schon im täglichen Gebet und in der Feier der drei alten Erntefeste Palästinas, die von den Händlern weiter begangen wurden, war sie bewahrt. Eine spätere Zeit hat darin Veränderungen gebracht, aber im geschichtlichen Gange waren sie vorüberziehend, die Verbundenheit blieb." (*II, p. 317*)

Once again, one might say that Baeck's style and thoughts meet in this paragraph; and, again, this is almost irrelevant.

This particular section has an especially rich scientific apparatus attached to it in terms of sources, encyclopaedias, authors and periodicals, together with an index of persons and events. Some of the references do enter the 1930s, but most of them are part of that vast body of scientific writings on Jewish themes which characterised the *Wissenschaft des Judentums* in the nineteenth century. The period covered extends through the seventeenth century; and the massive work which went into this text – set against the conditions under which it was composed – deserves the absolute appreciation of the contemporary generation.

The third bundle of manuscript pages (314 pp.) is entitled *Das Jahrhundert nach dem Westfälischen Frieden*. In assessing the spirit of the time from the beginning of the Reformation to the end of the Thirty Years' War, the author stresses what he calls

". . . eine Jenseitigkeit. Von neuem waren es die Aengste und die Wünsche der zu einer anderen Welt hingewandten Frömmigkeit, die Gefühle und Vorstellungen eines Sündenpessimismus und auf ihrem Grunde dann die Fragen und Anliegen von Kirche und Theologie, die das Dasein der Menschen erfassten und durchdrangen. Sie haben damals nicht nur das geistige Schaffen auch weithin bestimmt, sondern ebenso und vor allem die staatliche Wirksamkeit; Bekenntnisfragen lenkten oder beeinflussten zum mindesten die Innen- und Aussenpolitik. Es war die Zeit des konfessionellen Staats- und Kultursystems, des geschlossenen Bekenntnisstaates und des konstituierten Staatsbekenntnisses mit ihrem Bemühen, die 'reine Lehre' im Lande zur Herrschaft zu bringen, das Territorium zum Gebiete des rechten Gotteswortes und Sakramente zu machen." (*III, p. 2*)

This delicate understanding of the religious trends of that time dominates this section, but there is also a careful historical analysis of the Jews in the Brandenburg/Prussian state, to which is added a review of the legal situation of the Jews in Austria and in the Netherlands. In similar fashion, this document delineates the various intellectual streams which can be seen in the time of the Enlightenment and its particular revolution. The vast changes and developments in France, particularly at the time of the French Revolution and in the new legal structure of the Napoleonic legislation receives full attention here. Dohm and Mirabeau's work and their influence upon France in that vital time is assessed, and one might particularly note the quote from Clermont-Tonnerre:

". . . dass man den Juden als Menschen die Rechte gewähren, sie ihnen als Nation aber versagen müsse, denn es dürfe 'keine Nation in der Nation' geben . . . dass das Wort 'Jude' so eine Nation bezeichne, dass ihnen daher die Menschenrechte, aber nicht die Franzosenrechte zuteil werden sollten. Der Grundsatz der Aufklärung in dem, was er geben wollte, und dem, was er dafür forderte, trat hier im Wider hervor (Zitat: 'Il faut tout refuser aux juifs, comme nation, il faut tout leur accorder comme individus.' Halphen (J): a.a.O. S. 185; Dubnow: (J): a.a. O S. 92 ff." (*III, p. 132*)

The stress upon the "difference" between the Jew as an individual and the Jew as a people is, of course, of particular importance in the analysis of Jewish life within the framework of European law, and related to the purpose of this work. The use of the letter "J" following Jewish authors will be commented upon later.

The next chapter of Section III is entitled 'Der Uebergang vom Ständestaat zum Verfassungs- und Rechtsstaat', and shows the gradual dissolution of the old "Römische Reich deutscher Nation" between 1792 and 1806 within the struggles of the French Revolution and its aftermath. The chapter on Russia which follows utilises much of Dubnow's work, but also goes into much detail in regard to the difficult legislation under which Jews had to live. Then, once more, we come to a section which is much more *Geistesgeschichte* and turns to those German scholars who had a particular influence upon Leo Baeck: Friedrich Meinecke and Wilhelm Dilthey (*pp. 258ff.*). The concepts "state" and "nation" were joined together by Fichte, the new "prophet" (*p. 263*). But the text prefers to move on to Schelling and Hegel, clearly more compatible to the author who turns to another authority, Ernst Troeltsch (*p. 264*), who appears often in other writings by Leo Baeck. A typical passage:

"So traten die Kräfte gegeneinander und aus ihnen hervor die Menschen, die der alten, nun neu gewordenen Zeit gegen die der neuen, nun zur alten gewordenen. Die Weltanschauung der Romantik, welche die strengen Bindungen der Gemeinschaft, die gegebenen Abhängigkeiten und die Macht der Gefühle begreifen hiess, die die Unterordnungen, den Glauben und die vertrauende Hingabe an die Gnade verkündete, stand gegenüber der Weltanschauung der Aufklärung, die den freien, von der autonomen Vernunft geleiteten, nur sich selbst verantwortlichen Menschen lehrte. Die Staatslehre der Romantik, für die der Staat ein Organisches, die Gemeinschaft der Generationen war, voller Sinn und Heiligkeit, eine Offenbarung der göttlichen Vernunft, war gegen die Staatslehre der Aufklärung getreten, für die der Staat durch den Vertrag freier und gleicher Menschen entstanden und als ein nach rationalen Gesetzen aufgebautes, zweckvolles Gebilde hingestellt war." (*III, pp. 266–267*)

The "Jewish Crisis" is then placed into the middle of these intellectual struggles dominating the outside world, and one comes to see how much of Jewish life dissolved in a world where a closed enclave of Jewish existence disappeared to leave the Jewish community with many possible options to pursue. Jews were invited to join the new world by abandoning their Judaism; and, in a typically Baeckian phrase:

"Es war eine schwere Krisis im Gesamtwesen der Juden. Die Jahrtausende wurden durch die Jahrzehnte verdrängt, und eine solche Verdrängung bedeutet seelische Störung." (*III, p. 273*)

At the same time, the text rightly hails this moment in Jewish history as a time of re-birth in which the old tradition was re-discovered, and where new links between the people Israel and the ancient land of promise were again forged. (Part of this text is given in the appendix of this presentation.) Once again, a large and careful scientific apparatus of various indexes is part of this section.

The penultimate section of the manuscript contains 313 pages and covers the period from 1830 to 1930. The subtitle is: *Die Rechtsstellung der Juden in Europa, vornehmlich in Deutschland, von 1830–1930*. It is the third of the major sections of this manuscript which has an introduction to the ancient world and a concluding review. This third section begins with an over-view of Europe after the Congress of Vienna, and gives a careful account of the various political parties and the reshaping of the German political structure. While this is a general over-view, it does keep the central motif of Jews within the laws of the states in the foreground. Thus, describing the Prussian *Landtag* of 1847, it cites the delegate Bismarck-Schoenhausen:

"Ich glaube in meinem Recht zu sein, wenn ich einen solchen Staat einen christlichen nenne, welcher sich die Aufgabe gestellt hat, die Lehre des Christentums zu realisieren . . . dass wir aber mit Hülfe der Juden diesem Zweck näher kommen sollten als bisher, kann ich nicht glauben." (*IV, p. 12*)

The way offered to the Jews was generally conversion; and, as State Secretary von Thiele put it plainly at that Conference:

"völlige Emanzipation, aber unter der Bedingung, dass die Juden ihr separates und separierendes Gesetz aufgeben. Wenn dieses Problem gelöst werden kann und gelöst wird, dann bin ich der erste, der für völlige Emanzipation stimmt." (*IV, p. 14*)

Our text indicates that many Jews did travel down that road, and gives the example of Friedrich Julius Stahl, who not only converted but became the pillar of the Conservative party which basically opposed the Jews. August Neander (previously David Mendel), the church historian, was another example of this kind of accommodation where Conservative concepts of the "*Erweckungsbewegung*" entered evangelical theology (*IV, p. 18*). It is fascinating, though, that these and other former Jews are linked with Benjamin Disraeli who, according to our text, also united Conservative politics with the Church (*IV, pp. 18–19*). And our text honours these various figures who were genuine in their faith and made significant contributions to the thought and politics of their time. One need not read special significance into the fact that Jewish contributions to the Conservative cause are delineated here; there is a similar treatment of Liberalism and the Jewish participation in that movement. Hans Liebeschütz[4] reprints some of the text of this manuscript recording the Jewish participation in the Liberal movement, since this aspect of Jewish life within the politics of German culture is really presented with great perception. However, it might also be underscored that the far more interesting section which follows the description of Liberalism deals with radicalism and its rejection and enmity towards the Jews and Judaism. Also, of course, there is Hegel's negative judgement on Judaism as an inferior faith, contained in his *Vorlesungen über die Philosophie der Religion*; but an understanding of Jewish suffering is not absent there. As our text states:

> "[Hegel] lässt das jüdische Volk nach seiner Zerstreuung 'auf den Standpunkt des Schmerzes der menschlischen Natur zurückgeworfen' sein. 'Die jüdische Empfindung bildet das Verneinte in sich selbst, weshalb sie wesentlich in sich den unendlichen Schmerz empfindet'. (Hegel Gesam. Werke IX, 334)."

In any event, as our text indicates, the influence of Hegel upon his society and the following generations was enormous, and his view of the Jews had its effect upon Jewish life in Europe.

One need not go through all the text to recognise the sensitive approach to ideology and religion which gives importance to this document. Here, in a short survey, one might note that from ideology the text moves back to the legal systems, describing the legal position of the Jews between 1870 and 1930, not only in Germany and the individual states, but also in Austria-Hungary, Western Europe, and Eastern Europe. The chapter on antisemitism which follows is short and cautious, although the NSDAP is mentioned at the very end of the survey which began with Heinrich von Treitschke. The most cautious comment merely states:

> "aus dieser Zeit hervor ist die 'Nationalsozialistische Deutsche Arbeiterpartei' erwachsen, welche vor allem von der Rasselehre her die Ausscheidung der Juden zur nationalen Aufgabe machte". (*IV, p. 260*)

Only the fact that this statement about the Nazis is made in the past tense gives an indication that this work is indeed intended for a post-Nazi period.

The final section in this bundle 'Das Wiederaufleben im Judentum' is partially reproduced in the selection chosen by Liebeschütz,[5] and is indeed representative of the spirit and scope of the book. The indexes which follow are particularly rich in their use of non-Jewish sources.

One final section of manuscript remains to be evaluated. Entitled 'Ueberblick über die Entwicklung der Rechtsstellung der Juden in Europa, vornehmlich in

---

[4]Hans Liebeschütz, selections of chapters in Reichmann, 'Fate of a Manuscript', *loc. cit.*, pp. 363–371.
[5]*Ibid.*

Deutschland', it is more or less a review of the material covered, 85 pages long, and constitutes a succinct restatement of the body of the work. One cannot say that there are new insights added, but reformulations and emphases upon what is deemed of greatest importance in the previous 1,000-plus pages do of course give some insights into the intentions of the authors. Part of it will re-appear in our appendix. In any event, one might draw attention to the description of xenophobia – or racial antisemitism – which is observed in the neighbour:

> "Mit diesem allen verband sich eine andere, schärfer wirkende Fremdheit, die, welche sich, besonders für die Menschen der nördlichen Lande, im Typus der Juden darbot. Die mediterrane vorderasiatische Körperbeschaffenheit der Juden musste hier also die einer anderen Zone und Art erscheinen. Sie trat auch im Geistigen und Emotionalen hervor und mit ihr zusammen das, womit sich Beschäftigung und Beruf im Typus auswirkten. Auch dadurch und dadurch nicht am wenigsten standen die Juden als die Unterschiedenen da.
>
> So war es ein Gegebenes, dass Leben und Lebensformen der mittelalterlichen Welt zu einer immer schärferen Dissimilation und Ausgliederung der Juden hinführten." (*V, p. 53*)

It appears odd to see the pseudo-scientific description of the German racialist theories crop up here – "mediterrane vorderasiatische Körperbeschaffenheit" – but it was also realistic to see that in the Middle Ages the differences between Christians and Jews were viewed not only on the theological level, but also on the encounter with "the other" and the strangeness of other groups which had its impact upon the host country. Nevertheless, when reviewing the changing laws under which Jews lived, this summary stresses again that the legal structure was far more concerned with the role of the Jew in the economy rather than as an individual :

> "... sie erhielten durch die weltliche Gesetzgebung fast ein Monopol (im Geld- und Kreditwesen), und das Monopol konnte einen Zwangsauftrag bedeuten. Die Rechtsbestim-mungen für Juden befassten sich dann auch im Laufe der Zeit immer ausschliesslicher mit diesem ihrem Handel als ihrer eigentlichen Tätigkeit." (*V, p. 46*)

It took the Black Death to push the Jews out of this monopoly and turn them into small money lenders and pedlars.

How, then, shall one judge this manuscript in its totality, when we have worked our way through more than a thousand pages? It was undoubtedly a major achievement, regardless of who participated in the writing of it. Considering the difficult time in which it was written, and the limited facilities for scholarship which must have plagued the authors, one can and should view this as a text which is part of the literature of "spiritual resistance" of that period. Clearly, Leo Baeck was the major author and director of this enterprise, although the differences in style, concepts and areas of special interest strongly suggest multiple authorship. Also, once the achievement of writing this text, under oppression and with limited facilities, has been acknowledged, the question of whether or not to publish the manuscript is not that easy to answer. Half a century later, one can only indicate that scholarship has moved on, and that much of the history covered has received more than adequate treatment elsewhere. The Leo Baeck Institute Year Books themselves have responded to the challenge of Baeck and made contributions in these areas. More than that, the intention of the text was to present Jewish history and the life of the Jew within the general structure of law to a public which knew little about Jews – and what they did know was wrong and prejudged! This is no longer the case, and there is probably more study of the Jewish communities of Europe than there was in the time of Baeck. The discussion regarding the use of this manuscript has to continue; we will also return to it at the end of the essay, once we have enlarged our knowledge of that dedicated small team which wrote with such devotion in dark times. Nevertheless, I must already state my conviction that a full publication of this manuscript now would give a false picture of the scholarship of Rabbi Baeck, Rabbi Lucas, and Hilde Ottenheimer. It was a special text, for a special time, and should be viewed in that context.

II

There is a minor mystery in regard to the text which cannot be fully resolved: the use of the letter (J) to identify Jewish sources. It does not appear in the narrative, but is more a note on a note, printed behind the Jewish name listed. One cannot be totally certain that this notation (J) was not added later.[6] This however, really appears too unlikely. If we then assume that the authors added this identification in their notes, one must ask for an explanation. This work about Jews and by Jews is clearly directed to the non-Jews – most Jews would identify the Jewish names. Leo Baeck indicated, as we have said, that the book was written at the suggestion of the German Resistance, and that it was in fact a dangerous enterprise: he would rise at 4 a.m. to work on the text.[7] It could not be, as some people have supposed, that this (J) was added for a censor or that the work might even have been intended for some Nazi archive. The history of that period argues against any such suppostion.

One need only look at the *Germania Judaica* and its fate during that time. The *Gesellschaft zur Förderung der Wissenschaft des Judentums* (founded in 1902 by Leopold Lucas) had undertaken a task quite similar to that of Baeck and his associates: the writing of a history of Jews in Germany to be divided in three sections – from the beginnings to 1238; from Friedrich II's *règlement* on the Jews (1238) to the beginnings of modern history (1500); and from 1500 to 1815 and the Vienna Congress. Zvi Avneri records that by November 1938 almost 400 articles had come into the office.[8] That office was raided and closed shortly before the outbreak of war in 1939, and the material found was confiscated. One of those minor miracles of Jewish life took place when Miss Johanna Nathan, the secretary, appeared after the war with much of that material – which she had

---

[6]It has been assumed hitherto that the only copy, of the original four, to survive was the one taken to Theresienstadt by Leo Baeck and eventually deposited with the Leo Baeck Institute. Leo Baeck knew that two copies were destroyed, but the fourth manuscript, which must have fallen into the hands of the Nazi authorities, has now surfaced in Prague. Konrad Kwiet was shown the manuscript in 1990 at the Military Archives in Prague. However, recent attempts to study it there have been fruitless. (Information supplied by Professor Konrad Kwiet, Sydney.)

[7]Reichmann, 'Fate of a Manuscript', *loc. cit.*

[8]Zvi Avneri. 'Germania Judaica', in *Bulletin des Leo Baeck Instituts*, 1, Nos. 2–3 (1958), pp. 111ff.

removed to her home!⁹ In 1939, Leo Baeck was certainly aware of what had happened; the text he supervised, more of a celebration of Jewish life and an assertion of Jewish identity, would certainly have been destroyed by the Nazis if found. *It could not have been written for them.* Then why the letter (J) in the manuscript?

The simple explanation I would suggest, fully realising that it is at best an informed guess, is that the authors followed a common practice which in our time seems to have been forgotten. Baeck was involved in the *Jüdisches Lexikon* and in the *Philo-Lexikon*, which was published in 1935. In that text (the *Philo-Lexikon*) various annotations are listed at the beginning: a triangle for a non-Jew; a special mark for someone who is of Jewish descent in some way; and even an arrow designating an antisemite or a text with antisemitic content. The *Jüdisches Lexikon* basically served the needs of the Jewish community, and it was unnecessary to define Jews in such a text. This historical survey was for non-Jews; and, somehow, the need was felt to indicate where a Jewish source was used. If it was intended for the post-Nazi period, as seems evident, the (J) was not a negation but an affirmation of Jewish scholarship. And, in any event, one should not make too much of this!

Who were the authors of our text? Granted that Leo Baeck, both in terms of the personal statement made by him, and by the imprint his style and person made upon this writing, is clearly established as the main writer, one must still turn to his comment: "My assistants were Rabbi Dr. Lucas, Glogau, and Dr. Hilde Ottenheimer, an able historian." Baeck continues:

> "Dr. Lucas and Dr. Ottenheimer were most useful to me in obtaining the details, but we were at a disadvantage due to the lack of sources and literature. I wrote and practically finished the book myself, but some parts were fragmentary. . . Dr. Lucas died a natural death in Theresienstadt, but Dr. Ottenheimer was deported. . ."[10]

Far too little is known about Dr. Hilde Ottenheimer. Dr. Arnold Paucker was able to approach a number of scholars within the Leo Baeck Institute "circle", and the following information emerged:

> "Hilde Ottenheimer was an official of the *Reichsvertretung der Juden in Deutschland* in Berlin, most likely in the social service department. I believe she was a social worker by training. Last I saw of her was an article in *Jewish Social Studies* (see ref. in *YB II, LBI*, p. 56) vol. III, 1941. If I remember her byline, she was identified as a social worker and as an émigré to England or the USA. I think she was unmarried . . . with a friendly disposition and a factual mind and research orientation . . ."[11]

The reason for assuming that she had escaped from Germany was, of course, the article in *Jewish Social Studies* in 1941.[12] However, it seems quite clear that this article made its way from Germany to the USA and was translated there – but Hilde Ottenheimer did not escape. The article itself is a superb piece of scholarship, exacting and accurate, using all available sources. Judged by this,

⁹*Ibid.*, p. 115.
[10]Reichmann, 'Fate of a Manuscript', *loc. cit.*, p. 362.
[11]Letter from Professor Herbert A. Strauss, New York, to Arnold Paucker, 12th August 1991.
[12]Hilde Ottenheimer, 'The Disappearance of Jewish Communities in Germany, 1900–1938', in *Jewish Social Studies*, vol. III (1941), pp. 189–206.

Leopold Lucas
(1872–1943)

Leo Baeck
(1873–1956)

Leo Baeck was fortunate to have her as a research associate and assistant in his task.

As Arnold Paucker points out:

> "The internal evidence of her study shows that it was completed in October 1938 just before the 'Kristallnacht' and meant for publication in Germany. It does not say, for instance, that the Jewish communities gradually disappeared for reasons other than 'Binnenwanderung' and emigration. What really happened 1933–1938 in rural areas due to Nazi persecution and pressure is not stated for the obvious reasons that it could not be published in Nazi Germany. Therefore the essay could not have been written by a surviving Hilde Ottenheimer in the USA in 1941, as it would then have been more outspoken . . ."[13]

Paucker was quite right; and corroboration arrived in a letter written to him in August 1991:

> "Deine erneute Anfrage vom 14 d.M. . . . Ich habe sofort das grosse Gedenkbuch des Bundesarchivs, etwa von 1980 (1986), konsultiert und folgende Eintragung gefunden: 'Ottenheimer, Hilde, Berlin, 14.12.96, verschollen, Riga'."[14]

This, of course, fits with Leo Baeck's recollection that Dr. Ottenheimer was deported. On the basis of her text for *Jewish Social Studies*, and in line with Baeck's statement that she supplied him with details, it is not unreasonable to assume that the material dealing with Jewish communities from 1900 to 1938 (in Germany) was supplied by her and that the texts needed little editing. Her essay of 1941 is frequently cited by scholars in her field; and it is good and important to find still more reasons for restoring her place within the awareness of the scholarly community. (Incidentally, Zvi Avneri also reports Dr. Ottenheimer's death in a concentration camp and discusses her work with the *Germania Judaica* prior to her deportation.[15]) Finally, there are her three contributions to *Juden im Deutschen Kulturbereich*.[16] One would like to think that she will be remembered.

Rabbi Dr. Leopold Lucas died in Theresienstadt. He *is* remembered, both as a rabbi of compassion and dedication, and as a scholar. His book, *Zur Geschichte der Juden im vierten Jahrhundert* first appeared in Berlin in 1910, and was reprinted by the Georg Olms Verlag in 1985 and 1991. One of his disciples and admirers is Rabbi N. Peter Levinson, whose eulogy of Leopold Lucas appears in his most recent collection of funeral sermons. Dr. Levinson also wrote a preface to the republished Lucas book. In that preface, he indicates that Leopold Lucas was a pioneer in a field of historical research where a totally new approach was needed. The Lucas book showed that the brutal antisemitism of the fourth century was not solely due to political causes, but rose out of specific teachings of the Church fathers of that century: their Christology, the teachings of asceticism, their response to the Jewish propaganda, and the clear recognition that the Jew was the enemy.[17]

---

[13]Arnold Paucker in a letter to the author, 28th August 1991.
[14]Professor Ernst G. Lowenthal, Berlin, to Arnold Paucker, 16th August 1991.
[15]Avneri, *loc. cit.*, p. 15.
[16]Hilde Ottenheimer, 'Pädagogik und Sozialpädagogik'; 'Soziale Arbeit'; 'Gemeinnützige Stiftungen', in Siegmund Kaznelson (ed.), *Juden im Deutschen Kulturbereich*, Berlin 1959 (publication stopped at the presses in 1935).
[17]See N. Peter Levinson's introduction to the 1991 edn. of Lucas, *Zur Geschichte der Juden im vierten Jahrhundert, op. cit.*

The particular relevance of this book to our exploration of the work done by Leo Baeck and his associates is that Leopold Lucas did not merely record the sufferings of a Jewish people helpless against the onslaught of anti-Jewish actions. He stresses the Jewish attempt to preserve their individuality and to fight back, both in terms of propaganda and by actual rebellion and the use of arms. In the fourth century, it was not deemed a matter of course that Christianity had won permanent rule and that the function of the Jew and of Judaism was to submit quietly and to turn inwards in terms of their faith. On the contrary: Jewish missionary work continued, had its successes, and left the Christian rulers with the uneasy thought that the religion from which they had taken so much of their own strength might yet prevail. The legislation of that time fought against circumcision of slaves, against mixed marriages, and tried to make membership in the synagogue of proselytes a dangerous and unhappy situation. If we see the work of creating a post-Nazi text on Jewish life as an act of spiritual resistance, one can then begin to see the contributions of Leopold Lucas as governed by his earlier work on Jewish self-awareness. Leo Baeck's challenge to Adolf Harnack, *Das Wesen des Judentums* (*The Essence of Judaism*), was written in Oppeln in 1905, the work of a congregational rabbi concerned with preserving Jewish identity. Lucas's book appeared in 1910, the work of a rabbi in Glogau. And it is not unimportant to indicate that these men were joined together in the tasks of the rabbi as the teacher and representative of Judaism in a difficult time.

Leo Baeck and Leopold Lucas were friends and partners in the task of preserving Judaism. In a letter written to Rabbi Lucas, Leo Baeck congratulates him on the quarter century of service to Glogau, and comments on the founding of the *Gesellschaft zur Förderung der Wissenschaft des Judentums* in 1902:

> "Ihre wissenschaftliche Leistung und der weittragende Verdienst, den Sie durch die Gründung der Gesellschaft zur Förderung der Wissenschaft des Judentums erworben haben, gibt Ihnen Ihren Platz im deutschen Judentum."[18]

It is therefore not surprising, and is closely related to the production of the manuscript under discussion, that Leo Baeck called Leopold Lucas to Berlin to assist him closely with the running of the *Hochschule* (*Lehranstalt*) up to the bitter end. Not only the style, but also the situation in which the two found themselves argues strongly that much of the text – particularly the early sections which were Leopold Lucas's special area of competence – were in fact written by him. The final chapter of their friendship was written by Leo Baeck in a letter to Franz Lucas:

> ". . . Ihr Herr Vater war, wie fast alle im Lager, von Krankheiten heimgesucht, aber er hatte sie zuerst immer überwunden. Er blieb geistig rege und frisch und hat durch Vorträge, die er den Kranken in den Krankenhäusern hielt, Aufrichtung geschenkt. Ich hatte ihn immer lieb gehabt und habe ihn in den harten, schweren Tagen noch mehr liebgewonnen. Es war für mich auch ein tiefer Schmerz, dass er dann einer Lungenentzündung erlag. Sein Bild bleibt mir in treuer Erinnerung . . ."[19]

---

[18] Letter of 4th July 1924 to Leopold Lucas. See also *Philo-Lexikon. Handbuch des jüdischen Wissens*, Berlin 1935, col. 228.

[19] Leo Baeck to Leopold Lucas's son, Franz D. Lucas, 30th October 1945. The author is very grateful to Franz Lucas for his assistance in the preparation of this essay.

When one recalls the lectures given by Baeck himself in Theresienstadt, the image of Leopold Lucas as a partner in the work of "Seelensorge" as well as in their scholarly enterprise is delineated in even clearer fashion. A memorial book, produced in Marburg in 1987 (after the re-naming of the "Schwangasse" to "Leopold-Lucas-Strasse") gives full details of the Lucas *curriculum vitae* and the history of a distinguished family. One comment, by the *Oberbürgermeister*, is indicative of the respect and love evoked by this rabbinic life:

> "Es passt in das Bild von der 'grossen Güte' die ein 'hervorstehender Charakterzug' von Leopold Lucas gewesen sei, wie Überlebende des Holocausts berichten, dass Lucas von Berlin aus eine umfangreiche Hilfskampagne für seine inzwischen deportierte Glogauer Gemeinde organisierte."[20]

A final word about Leopold Lucas must come from N. Peter Levinson who honours Rabbi Dr. Lucas as his teacher in Berlin during the final days of the *Hochschule*, and writes:

> "Leben und Idee, das körperliche und das geistige Überleben des jüdischen Volkes fand Lucas in den Seiten der jüdischen Geschichte, und das gab er seinen Studenten mit auf dem Weg in einer Zeit, wo viele nur Dunkelheit zu sehen vermochten, wo sie nicht die Kraft hatten, über den jetzigen Tag und seine Not hinwegzublicken."[21]

Leopold Lucas, Hilde Ottenheimer, and most particularly Leo Baeck were joined together in a scholarly task in which resistance against evil and the evocation of the greatness of Jewish life in Germany linked their lives and thoughts in a task that was not completed but deserves to be remembered.

Again, we come back to the concept of this text as part of resistance literature. This can, of course, be over-stated. Michael Meyer's introduction to Year Book XXXVI of the Leo Baeck Institute rightly states that:

> "In short, historians of the Jews have been mainly interested in German Jews as Jews while modern German historians have been interested in them as Germans."[22]

The text we have been considering was a matter of self-definition in a time when the break between Jews and the land in which they lived seemed absolute. Both Baeck and Lucas were speaking out of a Judaism deeply aware of its German traditions (when Baeck congratulated Lucas in 1924 on his place "im deutschen Judentum" he spoke from a stance which was never totally abandoned, but which, then and now, began with a Jewish identity where "German" was an adjective of great importance, but was not the total definition). During the years of oppression when they worked on this manuscript, Baeck also wrote his *Dieses Volk. Jüdische Existenz*; and the dimension of writing out of Jewish existence is present in both texts.

Nevertheless, there are differences. *Dieses Volk* is seamless writing, realising itself within its complexities as one clear-cut statement and vision. The historical manuscript we have been examining, with all its greatness, is at times a laboured

---

[20]See Erhart Dettmering (ed.), *Rabbiner Dr. Leopold Lucas, Marburg 1872–1943 Theresienstadt. Versuch einer Würdigung*, Marburger Stadtschriften zur Geschichte und Kultur, 21, Marburg 1987, p. 11.

[21]N. Peter Levinson, *Dem Andenken der Gerechten. Nachrufe*, Munich 1988, pp. 97–100, here p. 100.

[22]Michael A. Meyer, 'Introductory Essay. Jews as Jews versus Jews as Germans: Two Historical Perspectives', in *LBI Year Book XXXVI* (1991), pp. XV–XXII, here p. XVII.

text where different styles and agendas are blended together. On occasion, one has the odd feeling of a language translated out of and into German. This is not carping or criticism; it is more an acknowledgement of the difficult task under impossible conditions which brought these Jewish scholars together, and one must be deeply grateful that this text was preserved and is available to scholars at the Leo Baeck Institute. I do come back to my conclusion that, at this time, it should not be published. The problematics of German-Jewish history as outlined by Michael Meyer bring us into a structure of historiography where one can applaud the unquenchable spirit of self-definition to which this text gives witness, but one will not see this manuscript addressing the contemporary questions of modern German-Jewish history. Perhaps, just as it was written for another time and place, it must be approached in a future time and place. In the meantime, the two short selections appended here may give a feeling of that sensitive self-examination in a time of trial, which is at times too cautious, at times too calm within its tower of objective scholarship – but which often permits us to glimpse the passion of the Jewish scholar maintaining dignity and identity as destruction moved upon Jewish life.

APPENDIX I

*Mission und Gegnerschaft**

Im Zusammentreffen und Zusammenkommen des Judentums und Griechentums war es das Geschehen, daß griechischer Geist von dem jüdischen Denken aufgenommen wurde, und daß jüdischer Geist den griechischen für sich zu gewinnen strebte. Die Zeit des Hellenismus und dann die des imperium romanum ist die einer großen Mission, welche das Judentum trieb, und ebenso auch einer Hinwendung zu ihm, die in der nichtjüdischen Welt einsetzte. Von der Sympathie, welche die griechische Philosophie ihm bewies, geht ein Weg zu dem Eintritt in das Judentum hin.

Von der Stetigkeit und dem Erfolg dieser Mission zeugen die Stimmen der Zeit. Überall sind in den jüdischen Gemeinden die Proselyten und die, die unterwegs waren, es zu werden, die "Gottesfürchtigen", wie man sie damals nannte.[1] Die Mission und Ausbreitung des Christentums in seinen ersten Jahrhunderten ist auf den Wegen und nach der Weise der jüdischen erfolgt und hat die jüdischen Gemeinden, die überall in den Provinzen entstanden waren, als Stützpunkte gehabt, die jüdischen Heiligen Schriften und die jüdische Predigt als Vorbereitung. Ohne das alles wäre sie, so wie sie weitergelangt ist, kaum möglich gewesen. Da auch die Menschen, die ihr dienten, zum Beginn fast alle aus dem jüdischen Volke kamen, war auch sie in dem Blicke und dem Urteil der Welt zunächst ein Jüdisches, von diesem nicht geschieden, und hat auch die Meinung über dieses mit bestimmt.

Nach dem ersten Drittel des zweiten Jahrhunderts, nach dem großen jüdischen Aufstande unter Hadrian (132–135), hat die jüdische Mission, die bis dahin mit dem Weitergehen der Bildung neuer Gemeindekolonien einen gleichen Schritt gehalten hatte, ein Ende genommen. Unter der tiefen Wirkung

---

*Source: *Juden und Judentum in den geistigen und religiösen Strömungen des Altertums.*
[1] J. Bernays (J): Gesammelte Abhandlungen (1885) II, S. 71–81.

der Ereignisse begann sich ein Gegensatz und ein innerer Widerspruch gegen die griechisch-römische Welt aufzutun. Der erste Krieg gegen Rom (66–70) hatte es so nicht bewirkt. Er hatte die harten, schweren Opfer auferlegt, aber ihm war ein Friedensschluß gefolgt; er hatte trotz allem keine innere Trennung gebracht, vor allem nicht von der hellenistischen Welt. Schon die Schriften des Josephus, durch die er ihr von dem Krieg erzählen und für die Vergangenheit und Wesensart seines Volkes ein Verständnis bringen wollte, legen davon Zeugnis ab. Als dann aber, sechs Jahrzehnte danach, die große leidenschaftliche Erhebung in der östlichen Diaspora und im Mutterlande die gegenseitigen Leidenschaften gegen einander geführt hatte und als danach eine gewaltsame Unterdrückung sich in den Hadrianischen Edikten auch gegen das Religiöse kehrte, trat eine innerliche Abwendung ein. Volk und Religion zogen sich auf sich selber zurück.

Das, was mit der Epoche Alexanders des Großen eingesetzt hatte, riß nun ab. Die mannigfaltige Mission hörte auf, wenigstens in ihrem planvollen Willen und ihrer Stetigkeit; man hörte auf, sich den Völkern rings umher zu verkünden. Auch die Scheidung von der christlichen Lehre und von den Christen, die bis dahin innerhalb des jüdischen Gesamtkreises einen Platz behalten hatten, geschah jetzt, nachdem sie schon nach dem ersten Kriege und unter dem Eindruck der Zerstörung des Tempels begonnen hatte. Man ging auseinander. Die Kirche, die sich gebildet hatte und ein Eigenes sein wollte, zog in die verlassenen Felder der Mission ein und nahm sie für sich in Besitz. Mission wurde jetzt im wesentlichen christliche Mission. Die jüdische hellenistische Literatur, dieser Bund mit der griechischen Sprache, diese Verbindung und Auseinandersetzung mit dem griechischen Denken, wurde nicht fortgeführt. Auch hier trat die Kirche in das Erbe ein.

Als später die Erinnerungen an die Tage des Bruches ihre Gewalt verloren hatten, war inzwischen die Kirche die Nachfolgerin Roms und Griechenlands geworden, und sie beanspruchte den Raum und die Zeit ganz für sich. Wohl gab es noch eine jüdische Mission und auch eine Annäherung an das Judentum und eine Hinwendung zu ihm; die Kirche mußte oft das "judaizare" der Ihren und der Anderen anklagen. Aber diese Mission hatte nicht mehr den beständigen und breiten Weg, sie war ein Gelegentliches nur. Hier und dort traten auch jüdische und griechische Gedanken zu einander, im Neuplatonismus fanden sie sich noch einmal. Aber der Wunsch des Judentums, sich in der griechischen Form auszudrücken, sich in ihr darzustellen, hat aufgehört. Die Welt war eine andere geworden, und man war selbst anders geworden.

Der jüdischen Mission und ihrer Literatur hatte sich das weite Gebiet, in das sie hineintraten, vielfach verschlossen. Allein auch der Widerspruch gegen Juden und Judentum ist schon lange vorher mannigfach geweckt worden und hat den mannigfachen Ausdruck gefunden. Es ist deutlich zu erkennen, wogegen er sich hinwendete.[2]

Er richtete sich zunächst und besonders gegen die Exklusivität des Judentums. In der Weigerung der Juden, sich an dem Kultus der Städte, in denen sie ihren Wohnsitz erlangt hatten, zu beteiligen, den Göttern, die die Götter der Bürgerschaft waren, die Verehrung zu gewähren, und ebenso dem allgemeinen Herrscherkult, der als ein freies Geschenk den Kaisern entgegengebracht wurde, den Tribut zu zollen, sah man einen Mangel an Religion. Der Vorwurf der Verachtung der Götter oder, wie man es auch benannte, des "Atheismus" kehrt immer wieder, und aus ihm sind bisweilen die Konflikte erwachsen. Außer der

---

[2]Die Texte sind gesammelt von Th. Reinach (J): Textes d'auteurs Grecs et romains, relatifs au Judaisme (1895).

Gottlosigkeit erblickte man in dieser Weigerung auch noch ein Fehlen der Loyalität gegen Stadt und Staat. Daneben war es ein Befremden, welches die Bildlosigkeit, die ganze Andersartigkeit der jüdischen Gottesverehrung weckte. Bald mit Staunen bald mit Spott wurde sie betrachtet, um dann auch bisweilen den Gedanken wachzurufen, daß hinter ihr merkwürdige Geheimnisse verborgen sein müßten.

Zu der Anklage der religiösen Abschließung trat die der sozialen, dieses Fürsichlebens, wie es das jüdische "Gesetz" so vielfach mit sich brachte. Hatte man in jener ersten eine Irreligiosität gesehen, so sah man in dieser nun eine Inhumanität, einen Mangel an wahrer Menschenliebe, ja ein odium generis humani. Auch dieser Vorwurf wiederholte sich in diesen Jahrhunderten. Und auch hier kam wieder das Befremdliche hinzu, als das die zahlreichen jüdischen Satzungen, die Feier der Sabbate und Feiertage, die Beschneidung, die Speisevorschriften beobachtet und empfunden wurden. Spott und Witz vor allem und auch die Satire der Dichter haben hier ihr Gebiet gefunden, und hier auch hat das Merkwürdige bisweilen ein Verborgenes vermuten lassen.

Aufs ganze gesehen ist jedoch die Linie der Sympathie oder zum mindesten des Interesses im Altertum die hervortretende und bezeichnendere. In ihr ist ein Unterschied von der Zeit gegeben, in der die Kirche das Empfinden und das Denken lenkte und bestimmte. Für sie war das Judentum der Anstoß und der Vorwurf, für sie waren die Juden die Leugnenden und Verleugnenden, die Verurteilten und Verworfenen. Die Kirche als Kirche hat das Mittelalter hindurch gegen sie beständig gekämpft, bald in der Heftigkeit bald in der Stille, wenn sie auch wieder, als Nachfolgerin römischer Kaisermajestät und Hüterin römischen Rechts und römischer Verwaltung, sie schützte oder zum mindesten duldete. Auch in der Stellung zu den Juden, der geistigen und der staatlichen, scheiden sich Altertum und Mittelalter. Und auch in der Einstellung der Juden selbst. Im islamischen mittelalterlichen Kulturgebiet sind zwar griechischer und jüdischer Geist in der jüdischen Religionsphilosophie einander wieder nahe begegnet, und eine beachtenswerte Einwirkung ist von dieser Philosophie auf die Scholastik ausgegangen. Aber im wesentlichen ist in dieser Epoche die intensive Selbsterhaltung, das Fürsichsein zur Aufgabe und zur Geschichte des Judentums geworden.

APPENDIX II

*Das Wiederaufleben im Judentum**

Der Ausgang aus der mittelalterlichen Zeit mit seinem oft plötzlichen und jähen Übergang hatte das Judentum, zunächst in Mittel- und Westeuropa und dann Jahrzehnte danach in Osteuropa, innerlich erschüttert. Die feste, bestimmte Richtung war verloren. Eine Entscheidung für ein Neues schien verlangt zu sein, und sie schien die Entscheidung gegen den alten Glauben und gegen alles Überlieferte zu bedeuten. Eine Zeit der Ratlosigkeit und Hilflosigkeit bei den einen, der Gedankenlosigkeit und Veräußerlichung bei den anderen, bei nicht wenigen auch der Flucht begann.

Das Bild, welches das Judentum anderen und sich selbst bot, war ein befremdliches. Man mochte und mußte glauben, daß es entwurzelt sei, daß es

---

*Source: *Die Entwicklung der Rechtsstellung der Juden in Europa, vornehmlich in Deutschland, vom Beginn der Neuzeit bis in das XIX. Jahrhundert.*

den Zusammenhang mit sich selber verloren habe. Seine Menschen schienen ohne den wahren Mittelpunkt ihres Lebens zu sein, ohne Ehrfurcht vor dem Geheimnis, vor dem Ewigen. Ein eigener Typus von Menschen entwickelte sich und bot sich den Blicken nur zu oft dar. Menschen waren die einen, für die das Gelingen allein und in allem Recht geben sollte, und die, wenn sie den Erfolg hatten, auch über alles ein Urteil zu besitzen glaubten und für alles die starke Meinung bereit hatten, denen als ein Letztes der Witz, auch der gewöhnlichste, jedes Erhabene und Heilige erledigen wollte. Menschen waren die anderen gewissermaßen von feuilletonistischer Sinnesart, denen alles, weil sie nie in die Tiefe dringen wollten oder konnten, zum Feuilleton wurde, alles hienieden und droben, kleine artistische Adepten jeder Modernität, die immer nur die Oberfläche erfaßten und zu den Andern nur gelangten, die darum alles banalisierten und daher im Höchsten und Ernstesten auch nur ein Banales und Plattes fanden, die alles ins Gewöhnliche zogen und den Vorwurf Schopenhauers, von der mangelnden vericundia wahrmachten. Menschen waren die einen und die anderen, welche sich dem Materialismus des Weltbildes, der Lebensauffassung und des Daseinswegen zugewandt hatten, die im Diesseitigen der Arbeit, des Erwerbes und des Genusses aufgingen, mochten sie auch bisweilen das Künstlerische als einen dünnen Schein oder das Wohltun als abgefundene Sühne darüber legen. Eine Vorhersagung hätte im zweiten Drittel des Jahrhunderts dem Judentum, zumal in Mitteleuropa, das Aufhören, den innerlichen Untergang verkündet, sie hätte ihm keine Zeit der Enkel mehr zugesprochen.

Die Wirklichkeit ist eine andere geworden. Die befreiende Wendung, erst von wenigen vollzogen und wenigen dann begriffen, kam, wie auch anderswo, durch die Erkenntnis der Geschichte. Die Vergangenheit wurde entdeckt und damit auch das Fundament der Gegenwart gewonnen. Das Judentum trat in das Bewußtsein wieder und in sein Selbstbewußtsein. Das Prinzip des Lebens wurde wieder gewonnen, das alte wurde zum neuen. Die Menschen entdeckten wieder sich selber, entdeckten ihre geschichtliche Art, ihre persönliche Besonderheit. Sie begannen die Assimilation, die nach dem Innern greifen wollte, abzulehnen, das Verlangen nach dem Eigenen erwachte.

Es hat sich überall verwirklichen wollen. Neuer Ausdruck, neue Formen des Religiösen wurden gesucht, neue Wege des Sozialen durchdacht, der Sinn der Geschichte und des Volkstums neu vor die Seele geführt. Die stärkste, lebendigste Kraft alles dessen wurde der Zionismus,[1] die Idee und die Sehnsucht, ein jüdisches Gemeinwesen im Lande der Väter, in Palästina aufzubauen, Idee und Sehnsucht einer nationalen Wiedergeburt. Seit den sechziger Jahren sind Gedanken und Forderung dessen immer wieder lebendig geworden bis ihnen Theodor Herzl (1896) die Klarheit und die politische Gestalt, Ascher Ginzberg (Achad Haam) (1899) den geistigen, kulturellen Gehalt und schließlich die Balfour Deklaration[2] das Fundement brachte. Es war eine Erhebung der Jugend, der Jugend unter den Jungen und Alten, eine innere Revolution, und eine opferwillige, oft heroische Arbeit begann mit ihrer Aufgabe zu kämpfen; Kräfte, die entschlummert schienen, waren wieder erweckt und waren erneut; ein Genie der Geduld, die sich durch nichts enttäuschen, sich niemals ermüden ließ, sollte sich bewähren.

[1]A. Böhm (J): Die Zionistische Bewegung², (1935ff.).
[2]Vergl. für den Eindruck nach außen Richtlinien der "Deutsch-Soziale Partei" vom 4.5.1924, angeführt bei F. Salomon (J): a.a.O. S.159: "Wir fordern daher in Übereinstimmung mit den Zionisten (politische Juden) die Zuweisung eines besonderen Staatsgebiets an die jüdische Nation im Wege internationaler Übereinkunft durch Ausbau der englischen Balfour-Akte, welche den Juden bereits eine "Nationale Heimstätte" in Palästina eingeräumt hat."

Alle die Gedanken, in denen die innere Wiederbelebung auch hier geschah, der religiöse Gedanke, der nationale Gedanke, der Gedanke der bleibenden Heimat, der Gedanke der Selbständigkeit und der Selbsthilfe, der Gedanke der sozialen Pflicht, der Gedanke der Geschichte und der geschichtlichen Kontinuität verbanden sich zum Zionismus. Sein Sinn ist, das Judentum, das jüdische Volk, den jüdischen Menschen wieder auf eigenen Boden zu stellen, innerlich und äußerlich. Sein Losungswort ist die Nationale Heimstätte auf dem Boden Palästinas, des Landes der Väter. Er hat damit den Juden die eigene geschichtliche Aufgabe wieder gestellt, sie auf den Weg der Weltgeschichte geführt. Er hat sie vor ein Ziel und damit in einen geschichtlichen Kampf hineingestellt, das will sagen: in den Kampf nicht des Einzelnen für sich selbst, sondern des Ganzen um sich selbst. Wohin das Geschick, welches die Geschichte ist, leiten will, ist im Ungewissen. Aber jede wahre, große Aufgabe ist gesetzt um zu bleiben, vor allem in ihrer Gewißheit zu bleiben.

Liberals of Jewish Background in the Anti-Nazi Resistance

BY HORST R. SASSIN

I. INTRODUCTION

The contribution of the Jews to the German resistance movement against the Hitler regime has been an important subject of historical research after the Second World War, especially since about 1970.[1] The newest comprehensive publication[2] about the Jewish resistance[3] provides a somewhat one-sided picture in its chapter about the political and social origin of Jews in the organised German resistance.[4] Konrad Kwiet and Helmut Eschwege only consider the working-class parties: Social Democrats, the various Socialist groups (*Sozialistische Arbeiterpartei, Internationaler Sozialistischer Kampfbund, Neu Beginnen*) and the Communists, which is followed by two sections on the Jewish exile, dealing with Jewish labour resistance and a summary about the Herbert Baum group.[5] With its Communist background this greatest and best known German-Jewish resistance organisation[6] is also in line with the political orientation of the Jews in the organised resistance as it is presented by Kwiet/Eschwege.* It is striking that these authors treat the Liberal Robinsohn-Strassmann group, not in the chapter

---

[1]Helmut Eschwege, 'Resistance of German Jews against the Nazi Regime', in *LBI Year Book XV* (1970), pp. 143–180; Lucien Steinberg, *La Révolte des Justes. Les Juifs contre Hitler 1933–1945*, Paris 1970; *Jewish Resistance during the Holocaust*. Proceedings of the conference on manifestations of Jewish resistance, Jerusalem 1971; Arnold Paucker and Lucien Steinberg, 'Some Notes on Resistance', in *LBI Year Book XVI* (1971), pp. 239–248.

[2]Konrad Kwiet and Helmut Eschwege, *Selbstbehauptung und Widerstand. Deutsche Juden im Kampf um Existenz und Menschenwürde 1933–1945* (Hamburger Beiträge zur Sozial- und Zeitgeschichte 19), Hamburg 1984, here 2nd edition 1986.

[3]Compare Eric Brothers, 'On the Anti-Fascist Resistance of German Jews', in *LBI Year Book XXXII* (1987), pp. 369–382; and Arnold Paucker, *Jüdischer Widerstand in Deutschland*, Beiträge zum Widerstand 1933–1945, Gedenkstätte Deutscher Widerstand Berlin, Heft 37, Berlin 1989, revised and expanded English version, *Jewish Resistance in Germany. The Facts and the Problems*, Berlin 1991.

[4]Kwiet and Eschwege, *op. cit.*, pp. 61–139.

[5]*Ibid.*, pp. 114–139.

[6]See also Konrad Kwiet, 'Problems of Jewish Resistance Historiography', in *LBI Year Book XXIV* (1979), pp. 37–60; Wolfgang Wippermann, *Die Berliner Gruppe Baum und der jüdische Widerstand*, Berlin 1981; Bernhard Mark, 'The Herbert Baum Group. A Jewish Resistance Group in Germany in the Years 1937–1942', in *Bletter far Geshikte*, vol. 14, Warsaw 1961, pp. 27–64 (in Yiddish). For the Communist view: Margot Pikarski, *Jugend im Berliner Widerstand. Herbert Baum und Kampfgefährten*, Berlin (GDR) 1978.

*On this Left-wing resistance see now also Simone Erpel, 'Struggle and Survival. Jewish Women in the Anti-Fascist Resistance in Germany', which follows in this section of the Year Book – (Ed.).

about Jews in the organised resistance, but in the more general chapter setting out the framework on which their analysis is based.[7] Quite obviously the Liberal majority of German Jewry has no place in the literature about Jewish resistance.

Yet, as is well known, there was a close affinity between Jewry and Liberalism in Germany's history of the nineteenth and twentieth centuries.[8] Jewish emancipation could be described as a success of Liberal policy. In the second half of the nineteenth century about 90% of German Jews adhered to the tenets of the Liberal parties,[9] opting first for the National Liberals and after 1878 defecting largely to the Progressives. The *Deutsche Demokratische Partei* (DDP), that collected the former Left-wing Liberals after 1918 as well as parts of the National Liberal Party and Independent Democrats, was always dubbed a *Judenpartei*.[10] Many members of the DDP were in fact Jews or of Jewish origin.[11] This affinity between Jewry and Liberalism was broken only when the DDP and the political branch of the antisemitic *Jungdeutscher Orden* joined to form the *Deutsche Staatspartei* in 1930 and with the collapse of the Liberal Centre the Jewish voters moved to the Social Democrats.[12] Organised political Liberalism that would have been predestined to oppose antisemitic and racial ideology had lost all its power.[13]

Consequently the Liberal part of the German resistance movement against National Socialism is an almost unknown subject in the historical research on Liberalism as well as on resistance. In the last years of the Weimar Republic the Liberal parties, above all the progressive DDP and the (National Liberal) *Deutsche Volkspartei* (DVP), turned to the Right and lost elections, members, financiers and influence. Each of the two parties gained 1% of the votes in the

---

[7]Kwiet and Eschwege, *op. cit.*, p. 47.

[8]Compare George L. Mosse, 'German Jews and Liberalism in Retrospect', in *LBI Year Book XXXII* (1987), pp. XIII–XXV.

[9]Jacob Toury, *Die politischen Orientierungen der Juden in Deutschland. Von Jena bis Weimar*. Tübingen 1966 (Schriftenreihe wissenschaftlicher Abhandlungen des Leo Baeck Instituts 15), p. 138; Heinz Holeczek, 'The Jews and the German Liberals', in *LBI Year Book XXVIII* (1983), pp. 77–91.

[10]See for example in the session of the DDP executive committee of 15th June 1928 the members of the *Reichstag*, Friedrich Wachhorst de Wente (*Judenpartei*) and Hartmann Freiherr von Richthofen (*Partei des jüdischen Kapitalismus*): *Linksliberalismus in der Weimarer Republik. Die Führungsgremien der Deutschen Demokratischen Pártei und der Deutschen Staatspartei 1918–1933*, ed. by Konstanze Wegner and Lothar Albertin, Düsseldorf 1980, pp. 464f. The characterisation as a *Judenpartei* is rejected by Werner E. Mosse, 'Der Niedergang der Weimarer Republik und die Juden', in *Entscheidungsjahr 1932. Zur Judenfrage in der Endphase der Weimarer Republik*. Ein Sammelband herausgegeben von Werner E. Mosse unter Mitwirkung von Arnold Paucker, 2nd edition, Tübingen 1966 (Schriftenreihe wissenschaftlicher Abhandlungen des Leo Baeck Instituts 13), pp. 3–49, here p. 10. The entire problem is described in: Bruce B. Frye, 'The German Democratic Party and the "Jewish Problem" in the Weimar Republic', in *LBI Year Book XXI* (1976), pp. 143–172.

[11]Prominent Jews in the DDP were Theodor Wolff (Editor-in-chief of the *Berliner Tageblatt* and co-founder of the DDP), Hugo Preuß (father of the Weimar Republic constitution of 1919), Walther Rathenau (Foreign Minister in 1922). See Rainer Erkens and Horst R. Sassin (eds.), *Dokumente zur Geschichte des Liberalismus in Deutschland 1930–1945*, Sankt Augustin 1989, pp. 267–305.

[12]Ernest Hamburger and Peter Pulzer, 'Jews as Voters in the Weimar Republic', in *LBI Year Book XXX* (1985), pp. 3–66, here p. 65.

[13]Mosse, 'Der Niedergang', *loc. cit.*, pp. 3–49, here p. 32.

last free *Reichstag* elections of 1933. Once the Nazi dictatorship was established they had to dissolve. Many leading Liberals of Jewish origin emigrated between 1933 and 1941, among them Erich Koch-Weser,[14] August Weber,[15] Oscar Meyer,[16] Ottilie Schoenewald,[17] Theodor Wolff[18] and Gustav Stolper.[19] Several Liberals joined anti-Fascist organisations abroad; for instance Georg Bernhard in the *Volksfront* (Popular Front) of 1936,[20] August Weber and Hans Albert Kluthe in the Liberal-Conservative *Deutsche Freiheitspartei*[21] and August Weber in the Left-wing *Freies Deutschland* (Free German Movement) in Great Britain.[22] Their loss was felt not only in the resistance movement within Germany, but also in the reconstruction of organised German Liberalism after 1945. On the other hand, some prominent members of both Liberal parties worked for Hitler: the former DVP member Franz Seldte became Minister of Labour 1933–1945, the former DDP member Hjalmar Schacht, Minister of Economy 1934–1937 and then Minister without Portfolio 1937–1943. None of the prominent Democrats (Theodor Heuss; Minister of Finance, Hermann Dietrich; *Reichswehrminister* Otto Gessler) became active members of the anti-Nazi resistance inside Germany, although there were some contacts. None of the prominent resistance fighters

[14]Koch-Weser's mother was of Jewish origin; he was President of the DDP, *Reich* Vice Chancellor in 1920 and *Reich* Minister 1919–1921 and 1928–1929; in 1933 he emigrated to Brazil. Gerhard Papke, *Der liberale Politiker Erich Koch-Weser in der Weimarer Republik*, Baden-Baden 1989; Ernst Portner, 'Erich Koch-Wesers Verfassungsentwurf. Ein Beitrag zur Ideengeschichte der Emigration', in *Vierteljahrshefte für Zeitgeschichte*, 14 (1966), pp. 280–298.

[15]Weber was married to a wife of Jewish origin; he was a member of the *Reichstag* fraction of the *Deutsche Staatspartei*; in 1939 he emigrated to Britain. Werner Röder and Herbert A. Strauss (eds.), *International Biographical Dictionary of Central European Emigrés 1933–1945*, vol. I, München–New York–London–Paris 1980, p. 798.

[16]Meyer was a baptised Jew; he was Prussian State Secretary 1919–1921; he emigrated to Switzerland in 1933. See Oscar Meyer, *Von Bismarck zu Hitler. Erinnerungen und Betrachtungen*, 2nd edn., Offenbach 1948.

[17]Ottilie Schoenewald was a member of the *Reich* party committee of the DDP and of the *Deutsche Staatspartei*; after 1933 she was president of the *Jüdischer Frauenbund*; in 1939 she emigrated to Britain. See Marion A. Kaplan, *Die jüdische Frauenbewegung in Deutschland. Organisation und Ziele des jüdischen Frauenbundes 1904–1938* (Hamburger Beiträge zur Geschichte der Juden, vol. 7) Hamburg 1981, pp. 145–148.

[18]Wolff was co-founder of the DDP and a member of the presidium of the DDP; in 1933 he emigrated to France. See Theodor Wolff, *Marsch durch zwei Jahrzehnte*, Amsterdam 1936; Gotthart Schwarz, *Theodor Wolff und das Berliner Tageblatt. Eine liberale Stimme in der deutschen Politik 1906–1933*, Tübingen 1968. Cf. the problematic document of Theodor Wolff, *Die Juden. Ein Dokument aus dem Exil 1942–1943*, ed. by Bernd Sösemann, Königstein 1984.

[19]Stolper was a member of the *Reichstag* (*Deutsche Staatspartei*); in 1933 he emigrated to the USA. See Toni Stolper, *Ein Leben in Brennpunkten unserer Zeit. Wien, Berlin, New York – Gustav Stolper 1888–1947*, Tübingen 1960.

[20]Bernhard was a member of the *Reichstag* (DDP); in 1933 he emigrated to France. See Ursula Langkau-Alex, *Volksfront für Deutschland?*, vol. I, *Vorgeschichte und Gründung des "Ausschusses zur Vorbereitung einer deutschen Volksfront", 1933–1936*, Frankfurt a. Main 1977.

[21]Kluthe was a member of the *Reich* party committee of the DDP and of the *Deutsche Staatspartei*; in 1936 he emigrated to Britain. See Gerlinde Runge, 'Ein liberaler Einzelgänger. Hans Albert Kluthe', in *liberal*, 26 (1984), pp. 113–118; *idem*, 'Linksliberale Emigranten in Großbritannien. Überlegungen zu Gesellschaft und Demokratie im Nachkriegsdeutschland', in *Vierteljahrshefte für Zeitgeschichte*, 37 (1989), pp. 57–84; Beatrix Bouvier, *Die Deutsche Freiheitspartei (DFP). Ein Beitrag zur Geschichte der Opposition gegen den Nationalsozialismus*, unpubl. diss., Frankfurt a. Main 1969.

[22]Werner Röder, *Die deutschen sozialistischen Exilgruppen in Großbritannien. Ein Beitrag zur Geschichte des Widerstands gegen den Nationalsozialismus*, Bonn-Bad Godesberg 1973.

(Carl Goerdeler,[23] Ludwig Beck, Wilhelm Leuschner, Julius Leber, Claus Graf Stauffenberg) was a former member of the DDP or DVP. The prevailing opinion is that Liberalism as an ideology was too weak and not self-confident enough to resist a totalitarian dictatorship.[24] Some years ago these views came under scrutiny in two publications: a short essay about a small Liberal resistance group[25] and a small exhibition about the persecution, the resistance waged and the emigration of Liberals in 1933–1945, under the auspices of a German Liberal foundation, supplemented by an exhibition catalogue.[26] Nevertheless, there is so far no detailed scientific work about Liberal resistance up to now.

II. THE ROBINSOHN-STRASSMANN-GROUP

The present author's dissertation about the resistance of the Robinsohn-Strassmann group will, it is hoped, partly close the gap.[27] This group is an example of the resistance stemming from Liberals: the leaders were former members of the DDP and of its youth organisation and the programme that was formulated in 1934 already emphasised Liberal aims such as human rights, a representative government and a free economy, with a strong social component. The foreign aims of the group were moderate – they sought to overcome national frontiers and establish a united Europe.

The first years of the group (1934–1937) were used to establish a proper organisation. From the beginning there were contacts with Socialist resistance groups in Northern Germany, and, once properly set up, co-operation with the Socialist resistance in Berlin and with the Sopade (Social Democratic Party in Exile) in Copenhagen became closer. On the other hand Strassmann collaborated with the former Mayor of Leipzig, Carl Goerdeler (*Deutschnationale Volkspartei*), with generals and officers of the *Oberkommando der Wehrmacht* such as General Ludwig Beck and with Admiral Wilhelm Canaris as well as with representatives of German industry. The position of the Robinsohn-Strassmann group as a link in anti-Fascist resistance in the years 1938–1941 can be compared with the position of the Kreisau circle in 1941–1944: necessary for a political and

---

[23]The attempt of his biographer Gerhard Ritter to classify him as a Liberal must be rejected. Gerhard Ritter, *Carl Goerdeler und die deutsche Widerstandsbewegung*, Stuttgart 1954, pp. 296f. Cf. Klaus Schwabe and Rolf Reichard (eds.), *Gerhard Ritter. Ein politischer Historiker in seinen Briefen* (Schriften des Bundesarchivs, vol. 23), Boppard 1984.

[24]Hans Mommsen, 'Der Widerstand gegen Hitler und die deutsche Gesellschaft', in Jürgen Schmädeke and Peter Steinbach (eds.), *Der Widerstand gegen den Nationalsozialismus. Die deutsche Gesellschaft und der Widerstand gegen Hitler*, München 1985, pp. 3–23, here p. 14; Agnes Blänsdorf, 'Gerhard Ritter 1942–1950. Seine Überlegungen zum kirchlichen und politischen Neubeginn in Deutschland', part 2, in *Geschichte in Wissenschaft und Unterricht*, 42 (1991), pp. 67–91, here p. 79.

[25]Wolfgang Benz, 'Eine liberale Widerstandsgruppe und ihre Ziele', in *Vierteljahrshefte für Zeitgeschichte*, 29 (1981), pp. 437–447.

[26]Horst R. Sassin, *Widerstand, Verfolgung und Emigration Liberaler 1933–1945*, ed. by the Friedrich Naumann Stiftung, Bonn 1983.

[27]This concise survey is part of the author's dissertation, submitted to Düsseldorf University in 1991, which will be published at a later date.

ideological *modus vivendi* between the Conservative Goerdeler and the Generals and the Socialist partisans of Leuschner and Leber.

Although the connections of the Robinsohn-Strassmann group were mainly within Germany there were foreign contacts, too, to anti-Nazi circles in Austria and in Danzig (before these areas were annexed), with German émigrés in Denmark, Switzerland, Sweden, the United Kingdom and the United States of America, and with the government authorities in Austria (1938) and in London.

The Robinsohn-Strassmann group was involved in the resistance activities during the crises amongst the high-ranking officers of the General Staff and that of the Austrian *Anschluss* (January to March 1938). In the abortive preparation for a *coup d'état* from the summer of 1939 up to the winter of 1939/1940 it played an important role in the civilian branch of the resistance. The central organisation of the group was thrown into disarray when Strassmann was apprehended in the summer of 1942.

It is, perhaps, worth reminding the reader that this small Liberal group was able to continue its fight against antisemitism despite the suppression of the (official) Liberal parties and that leading members of that group had Jewish backgrounds.

III. JEWISH FAMILY BACKGROUNND

The group was founded in 1934 by the Hamburg merchant Dr. Hans Robinsohn, the Berlin lawyer Dr. Ernst Strassmann and the Berlin unemployed journalist Dr. Oskar Stark. The last named left the group in the following year. Hans Robinsohn, born in 1897, was co-partner of the prominent Hamburg fashion house *Gebr. Robinsohn*.[28] He was a member of a Jewish family which had emigrated in the nineteenth century from the Poznań district to Frankfurt a. Main, where two brothers founded the fashion house. Two brothers of the following generation moved from Frankfurt to Hamburg in 1892 and founded their own fashion house which grew from a small store to become one of the foremost Hamburg fashion venues before the First World War.[29] Like his family, Hans Robinsohn became a member of the Jewish community and of its *Neuer Israelitischer Tempelverein in Hamburg*, a liberal Reform movement directed against the Orthodox *Synagogenverband*.[30] The three autonomous congregations of the Hamburg Jews – the *Tempelverband*, the *Synagogenverband* and the moderate conservative *Neue Dammtor-Synagoge* – had to find a certain balance because they were incorporated in the *Deutsch-Israelitischer Gemeindeverband in Hamburg*. The Hamburg Jews, therefore, had to execute a more moderate community policy –

[28]For Hans Robinsohn's dates see *International Biographical Dictionary of Central European Emigrés 1933–1945*, vol. I, *op. cit.*, p. 607.

[29]Hans J. Robinsohn, 'Ein Versuch, sich zu behaupten', in *Tradition. Zeitschrift für Firmengeschichte und Unternehmerbiographie*, 3 (1958), pp. 197–206, here p. 197.

[30]Ina Lorenz, *Identität und Assimilation. Hamburgs Juden in der Weimarer Republik*, Hamburg 1989, pp. XX–XXII. Cf. Stephen M. Poppel, 'The Politics of Religious Leadership. The Rabbinate in Nineteenth-Century Hamburg', in *LBI Year Book XXVIII* (1983), pp. 439–470.

an excellent basis for the growth of liberalism and tolerance. It is remarkable that the Robinsohn family was in the *Tempelverband*, an organisation of a minority of the Jewish *Kultusverbände*, as only a minority of the Hamburg Jews overall were members of the Jewish community and a minority of these members belonged to the *Kultusverbände*:[31]

Hamburg, 1927, total	19,904 Jews
members of the *Gemeindeverband*	8,000 Jews
members of the *Kultusverbände*	2,800 Jews
members of the *Tempelverband*	700 Jews

Membership of a central liberal synagogue community was a characteristic feature of the immigrating Jews from the East who longed to be integrated in the aspiring Jewish social milieu of the big cities.[32] Hans Robinsohn regarded himself in the first place as a German; his Jewish identity was of no significance.[33] He rejected all forms of religious cult, and, when he married in 1922, he only went through a civil ceremony although his wife was Jewish as well. Zionism or any form of religious Orthodoxy and fundamentalism he rejected totally.[34] In the last years of the Weimar Republic he considered leaving the *Tempelverband* but remained out of solidarity under the impact of the growing antisemitism. When Hitler's government came to power all thought of religious dissidence became irrelevant.

The other founder of the resistance group who had a Jewish family background was Ernst Strassmann – but his was an extremely complicated one. The Strassmanns were an originally Jewish family who produced some famous doctors in the cities of Berlin[35] and Breslau. Like the Robinsohns they came from Poznań. Again like Hans Robinsohn, Ernst Strassmann was born in 1897. He met Robinsohn in the new democratic youth organisation of the DDP, *Deutsche Demokratische Jugend (Jungdemokraten)*, in 1919; they soon became close friends and worked together supporting the new democratic republic. In 1929 Strassmann was appointed *Amtsgerichtsrat* in Berlin, and in 1931, he became *Landgerichtsrat*. In 1932, Robinsohn's and Strassmann's attempt to found an anti-Nazi resistance organisation failed because of disagreement with their political friends of the *Klub vom 3. Oktober*. After the Nazis had come to power Ernst Strassmann, as a civil servant, had to state his racial descent. It was at this time that he learned that *Sanitätsrat* Dr. Arnold Strassmann was not his biological father. Ernst's real father had left his mother before his birth; because both parents were Christians Ernst was baptised as a Protestant. Two years later Arnold Strassmann married Ernst's mother, adopted Ernst and accepted him as his son; hoping thereby that

---

[31]Helga Krohn, *Die Juden in Hamburg. Die politische, soziale und kulturelle Entwicklung einer jüdischen Großstadtgemeinde nach der Emanzipation 1848–1918* (Hamburger Beiträge zur Geschichte der deutschen Juden, vol. 4), Hamburg 1974, p. 124.

[32]Shulamit Volkov, *Jüdisches Leben und Antisemitismus im 19. und 20. Jahrhundert*, München 1990, p. 174.

[33]Information on the Jewish identity of Hans Robinsohn obtained from his son F. Peter Robinsohn.

[34]Cf. Francis R. Nicosia, 'Ein nützlicher Feind. Zionismus im nationalsozialistischen Deutschland 1933–1939', in *Vierteljahrshefte für Zeitgeschichte*, 37 (1989), pp. 367–400.

[35]Wolfgang Strassmann, chairman of the municipal council, was the object of antisemitic attacks in 1880, see Michael A. Meyer, 'Great Debate on Antisemitism. Jewish Reaction to New Hostility in Germany 1879–1881', in *LBI Year Book XI* (1966), pp. 137–170, here p. 167.

Ernst would never come across anything that would connect him with his "biological" real father. This case was of legal interest because Ernst Strassmann was – in the terminology of racial antisemitism – not a "half-Jew" but a full Aryan.

Ernst's father, Arnold Strassmann, described his situation of being the "non-biological" father of a beloved step-son, in a small book about his own father and people he had known in Poznań.[36] It seems that he wanted to prepare Ernst for his own destiny. In one of the stories he described the situation of a man whose wife had a son by a wealthy nobleman while her husband believed himself to be the real father. Arnold Strassmann stressed the dear love of his "cheated" father for his son and – without mentioning the Nazi "blood and soil" ideology – he asked three times where was the vaunted "voice of blood"?[37] He continued in this vein, making use of his experience as a doctor: when two newly born babies are switched in a hospital each mother will keep the changeling and say that it is the cleverest, the most beautiful, the best and the most virtuous. His conclusion was: "The everyday life that is spent together as well as the joyful devotion and parents' readiness to make sacrifices and the fact that children take such behaviour for granted; the common environment with its tiny trivialities and secrets, all these things unify, not common blood."[38] This was the environment of liberalism and tolerance in which Ernst Strassmann grew up. It was just like the situation which Lessing portrayed in his Enlightenment drama *Nathan der Weise*: a Jewish father (Nathan, Arnold Strassmann) adopts a Christian child (Recha, Ernst) whom he loves as his own, and does not try to influence the child religiously. Arnold Strassmann could have taken his words from the dialogue between Nathan's daughter Recha and Sultan Saladin in the final act of Lessing's *Nathan*:

> "Recha. 'Aber macht denn nur das Blut
> den Vater? nur das Blut?'
> (. . .)
> Saladin. 'Jawohl: das Blut, das Blut allein
> Macht lange noch den Vater nicht! macht kaum
> Den Vater eines Tieres! gibt zum höchsten
> Das erste Recht, sich diesen Namen zu
> Erwerben!' "

The first years of the Third *Reich* were, to some extent, years of a holding operation for both Robinsohn and Strassmann. The reaction of the Robinsohn family[39] shows that they believed in a future within even Nazi Germany: they extended their business premises in the summer of 1933. Under the bourgeois Ministers of Economy Kurt Schmitt (1933–1934) and Hjalmar Schacht (1934–1937) Jews were tolerated by the ministerial bureaucracy but assailed by the Nazis – for example by the organisation *Arbeitsgemeinschaft deutscharischer Fabrikanten der deutschen Bekleidungsindustrie*. Hans Robinsohn found himself in a paradoxi-

---

[36]Arnold Strassmann, *Allerlei Ostmärkisches. Geschichten und Geschichtchen aus der verlorenen Heimat*, Leipzig n.d. [1932].
[37]*Ibid.*, pp. 158f.
[38]*Ibid.*, p. 160. [Translated by H. S.]
[39]See Robinsohn, 'Ein Versuch, sich zu behaupten', *loc. cit.*, *passim*.

cal situation because of the Nazi *Gesetz zur Ordnung der nationalen Arbeit*:[40] while he was more and more oppressed in his political and personal rights, he became something of an economic dictator in his firm as the *Betriebsführer* of Gebr. *Robinsohn* – a Jew as overlord to over 700 employees, most of them "Aryans". This situation required skilful handling, especially since the works council was made up of Nazi members. Hans Robinsohn accepted the challenge and resisted Nazi influence wherever he could. He feared no case brought against him at the labour court (*Arbeitsgericht*) and won each of them; he even managed to convince the works council that a "Jewish" firm had to employ more Jews than an "Aryan" firm.

For Ernst Strassman it was easier to hold his ground. In the compulsory official declarations he did not mention his Jewish step-father in order not to alert the Nazi authorities.[41] He was successful during the first years of the Third *Reich*, but later he had to prove his "Aryan" claim legally. His brother Reinhard, the "biological" son of Arnold Strassmann, was, however, known to be a "half Jew"; as a *Patentanwalt* he tried to safeguard his profession by an extraordinary step: he put forward the proposition that the Strassmann family was of Jewish origin only by religion but not racially because they claimed descent from the Turkish Khazar tribe. By this means he hoped to play off one irrationality of racial antisemitism against another. But it did not work; he lost his licence as a patents' lawyer in September 1933.[42]

Ernst Strassmann supported his more vulnerable Jewish friend Robinsohn as much as he could. A small anecdote shows his defiance of Nazi ordinances: Robinsohn and Strassmann visiting a small German town went to a restaurant at noon to have lunch. Next to the entrance there was a sign "Jews not wanted here!" With Strassmann's reaction "one cannot meet every request", they ignored the sign and went in.[43]

It is no surprise that these two Liberals were able to find support among other Liberal Jews:[44] there were more than twenty Jews, people of Jewish origin or people married to Jews in their group which means that 7% of the group's approximately 300 members were faced with race problems. But Hans Robinsohn was the only member of a Jewish community in the leading circle of the group. One of its eminent members was the former Mayor of Berlin, Dr. Fritz Elsas.[45] He was descended from a Jewish textile entrepreneur family in Stuttgart, but was baptised as a child. His importance for the resistance group derived from his extraordinary contact with the "chancellor" of the German anti-

---

[40]Gesetz zur Ordnung der nationalen Arbeit, 20th January 1934, *Reichsgesetzblatt*, I (1934), p. 45.

[41]Bundesarchiv, Koblenz, R 22, Personalakte E. Strassmann.

[42]Private papers of Reinhard Strassmann. For the Khazars cf. Douglas M. Dunlop, *The History of the Jewish Khazars*, Princeton 1954; Arthur Koestler, *Der Dreizehnte Stamm. Das Reich der Khasaren und sein Erbe*, Bergisch-Gladbach 1989 (English: *The Thirteenth Tribe. The Khazar Empire and its Heritage*, London 1976).

[43]Told by F. Peter Robinsohn.

[44]In our broad definition of the term "Jew" we follow the definition as applied by Kwiet and Eschwege, *op. cit.*, pp. 19f. and by Paucker, *op. cit.*, p. 15.

[45]See the biographical introduction in *Auf dem Stuttgarter Rathaus 1915–1922. Erinnerungen von Fritz Elsas (1890–1945)*, ed. by Manfred Schmidt (Veröffentlichungen des Archivs der Stadt Stuttgart, vol. 47), Stuttgart 1990, pp. 9–22.

Fritz Elsas

Margarethe Lachmund

Liberal resistance in Germany

Ernst Strassmann

Hans Robinsohn

Liberal resistance in Germany

Fascist resistance, Carl Goerdeler. In Berlin the economic journalist Egon Bandmann, a so-called "half Jew", supported the inner circle with his economical and financial knowledge. Another Jew who brought important connections to the group was the professor of co-operative trading systems (*Genossenschaftswesen*), Ernst Grünfeld,[46] who lost his chair at the University of Halle-Wittenberg in 1933 because of his Jewish religion and of his membership in the DDP and *Deutsche Staatspartei*. In 1934 Grünfeld moved to Berlin where he joined the Strassmann circle. He created new contacts for the group in Halle, Naumburg and, helped by being Austrian, in Austria.[47] The famous professor of international law at Halle, Max Fleischmann,[48] joined the group as well; he was born a Jew but later baptised. Despite the solidarity of the Robinsohn-Strassmann group these two could not withstand the pressure of the growing antisemitism that steadily became more extreme and committed suicide.[49]

It would go too far to name all the Jews, baptised Jews, "half Jews" and so on who worked in the resistance group in towns like Berlin, Hamburg,[50] Kiel, Wismar and München. On the other hand it is important to know that the Jewish members of the resistance group had contacts with foreign countries, especially Britain. One German Jew living in London was Dr. Robert Kauffmann, director of the Berlin electricity supply company up to 1933, who had been a prominent member of the DDP and protector of some of the young Democrats who founded and joined the resistance group. Kauffmann was not only Jewish but joined an Orthodox Jewish community, although he himself never became Orthodox.[51] In order to aid persecuted German Jews he worked for the Jewish Refugees Committee.[52] In the last months before the Second World War broke out he established vital connections in order to bring the Robinsohn-Strassmann group into contact with British government authorities. Robinsohn emigrated to Copenhagen (Denmark) after the November Pogrom in 1938; there he remained in contact with Strassmann as well as with the British authorities, so that information about planned German aggression after the beginning of the war and about activities of the resistance movement could be transmitted.[53] The "half Jew" Dr. Rudolf Reissert in Munich, like Robinsohn

[46]*Neue Deutsche Biographie*, vol. 7 (1966), pp. 197f.

[47]Information by Frank Hoernigk.

[48]The most comprehensive biography is Hans Wehberg, 'Vorkämpfer der Völkerverständigung und Völkerrechtsgelehrte als Opfer des Nationalsozialismus: 5, Professor Max Fleischmann', in *Die Friedens-Warte*, 46 (1946), pp. 381–384. An impressive general introduction is given by Detlev F. Vagts, 'International Law in the Third Reich', in *The American Journal of International Law*, 84 (1990), pp. 661–704.

[49]Grünfeld in 1938, Fleischmann in 1943. For the problematics of suicide see Konrad Kwiet, 'The Ultimate Refuge. Suicide in the Jewish Community under the Nazis', in *LBI Year Book XXIX* (1984), pp. 135–167.

[50]The fate of a Christian-Jewish family in Hamburg which was supported by members of the Robinsohn-Strassmann group is shown in Ursula Büttner, *Die Not der Juden teilen. Christlich-jüdische Familien im Dritten Reich. Beispiel und Zeugnis des Schriftstellers Robert Brendel* (Hamburger Beiträge zur Sozial- und Zeitgeschichte, vol. 24), Hamburg 1988.

[51]Information from his daughter Carole Liston.

[52]Bundesarchiv, Koblenz, Moritz Julius Bonn papers 55, letter of the Jewish Refugees Committee, March 1935.

[53]Harold C. Deutsch, *The Conspiracy against Hitler in the Twilight War*, Minneapolis 1966, pp. 74–77.

and Kauffmann a former member of the DDP, was another member of the group who maintained contact with British officials. Several times he obtained an exit permit to Switzerland, where his family lived. In fact he channelled the group's information to the British legation in Berne.[54]

It may have been on these grounds that a member of the leading circle gave the group the "biblical" pseudonym "Rotte Korah" ("The Korah Gang"), an allusion to a Jewish opposition group mentioned in the Torah.[55]

IV. THE "JEWISH QUESTION" IN THE GROUP'S PROGRAMME

In the late spring of 1933, a year before the resistance group was formed, Hans Robinsohn wrote an essay[56] on the question: whether the triumphant National Socialism could compel him to modify his political conviction, to give up Liberal Democracy and to turn towards the new system? His conclusion was that Liberal Democracy is the superior political system because it has an inherent corrective opposition, different from the Nazi dictatorship in which faults cannot be corrected and grow out of hand. Robinsohn's essay can be considered the ideological foundation of the Robinsohn-Strassmann group. What was Robinsohn's position towards the "Jewish Question"?

Robinsohn emphasised the following four aspects. 1) The "Jewish Question" monopolised the attention of political observers and diverted it from the essential question, the anti-Liberal and anti-Democratic conviction, of which racial antisemitism was only one aspect. Its anti-Liberalism and anti-Democracy were obvious because it demanded inequality of rights but equality of duties. 2) The non-Jews, including Liberal Democrats, who regarded antisemitism as a private affair of the Jews, misunderstood its anti-Liberal and anti-Democratic dimension. 3) The Jews were to a large degree Philistine in their behaviour and reactionary pre-capitalistic in outlook. This part of German Jewry refused to support Liberalism although it was their only succour, and thus they were in part accessories to the victory of National Socialism. 4) Robinsohn defined the gap between Liberalism and Judaism according to the degree to which each feared being compromised by the other. He refused to see the Jewish Question as the key to his position towards National Socialism: "At most we can take aspects of it [antisemitism] as symptomatic of the attitude of the new regime towards Democracy and Liberalism as a whole and use this to draw conclusions."[57] With this point of view Robinsohn managed to turn the particular Jewish Question (concerning only a small segment of German society) into a general question of principle regarding Democracy or dictatorship.

The position Robinsohn outlined in his essay remained the position of the

---

[54]Private papers of Reissert.
[55]Numbers: XVI. The codename was discovered by Dr. Walter Dudek, the former Mayor of Harburg-Wilhelmsburg (near Hamburg); letter of Else Dudek, private papers of Dudek.
[56]Hans Robinsohn, 'Der Nationalsozialismus', in the Institut für Zeitgeschichte (IfZ), Munich, ED 166.
[57]*Ibid*. [Translation by H.S.]

group in the following years. In a paper of April 1936,[58] in his first report for friends abroad in October 1937,[59] and in a long memorandum written between March and August 1939,[60] Robinsohn reiterated his view of the Jewish Question as only marginal compared with that of German dictatorship. His paper of April 1936, which contains a distillation of political experience gained by a journey through Central and Southern Germany, lays stress upon the deprivation of the rights of the German Jews in order to demonstrate that the Conservative design of taming or civilising Hitler and the Nazis had failed and would fail in future. From 1937 onwards the group tried to inform friends abroad about the situation in Germany and about German opposition by using several reports and the long memorandum of 1939 – here the Jewish Question is treated characteristically in the epilogue. In these news letters for friends who had emigrated, Robinsohn characterised the Jewish Question as suitable for a) showing the consequences of giving up humanity and the concept of equality of rights and turning towards violence, b) showing how far the Nazi propaganda reached. Though a Jew himself, he considered the central and local leaders of the Nazi Party, not the German people, to be responsible for boycotts and pogroms. The Nazi leaders had often enough incited the people to expel the Jews, but the response had remained tepid. In his report of February 1939 Robinsohn cites the opinion of a taxi driver about the "*Reichskristallnacht*": "It wasn't the German people; ordinary Germans sleep between three and four o'clock in the morning."[61] In fact Robinsohn noticed a deep disgust amongst the people. In the epilogue to his memorandum of 1939 he emphasised the importance of Hitler's antisemitism for the whole world. German antisemitism, considered an internal affair of Germany, had produced one of the greatest international migration movements of history followed by social tension in many countries. His list is impressive: from 1933 onwards the foreign powers tolerated antisemitism in Germany as an internal affair; 1938 they accepted this system in Austria, in the Sudetenland and in Italy; 1939 in the rest of Czechoslovakia, and an end was nowhere in sight. Robinsohn's pessimistic vision was that the Jews could be used as scapegoats even in countries where antisemitism was hitherto unknown.[62] He did not call directly upon foreign countries to draw political conclusions, but the indirect consequence could only be the consideration of the human rights issue as a matter of international significance (like the Helsinki Conference on Security and Co-operation in Europe did later).

Although there are a number of documents from the Robinsohn-Strassmann group for the first six years of the Third *Reich* this situation changes in the Second World War. After a visit from a confidant Robinsohn wrote a new report in November 1939 in which he described the lack of discipline amongst German

---

[58]*Idem*, 'Überblick über die Lage des Nationalsozialismus in Deutschland!', IfZ, ED 166.
[59]'Bericht No. 1', private papers of Alfred Vagts, in future in the Bundesarchiv, Koblenz, Vagts papers.
[60]Published in *Vierteljahrshefte für Zeitgeschichte*, 29 (1981), pp. 447–471.
[61]Hans Robinsohn, 'Bericht No. 7', IfZ, ED 166. [Translated by H.S.]
[62]*Vierteljahrshefte für Zeitgeschichte*, 29 (1981), pp. 469f.

soldiers in Poland who were busy enriching themselves; he explained that the elevation of the cult of ownership had led to this moral decline.[63]

In a memorandum written in the autumn of 1941 Robinsohn compiled a list of all the measures that a new post-Hitler government would have to take immediately in order to make a good start.[64] There is no evidence that Strassmann received this memorandum, but we can presume so because Robinsohn kept loose contacts with the resistance group. This is the only document in which a member of the group expounded his ideas for rulings on the "Jewish Question" once the anti-Fascist opposition had taken over government, because up to then the Liberal conviction made any special reflections about the legal status of the Jews unnecessary.[65] In the sphere of constitutional law Robinsohn postulated: 1. the reconstituting of equality of rights, 2. the restoration of the unity of rights (*Rechtseinheit*), 3. the reconstitution of the independence of the judiciary, 4. compensation and restitution for the past. The first point, the only one of interest in our context, is primarily in the nature of a clarion call. Here Robinsohn referred to the Jewish Question: "After the propaganda of the past it might be advisable for the new government not to rock the boat completely on this even when taking all considerations into account."[66] This statement by a Liberal is surprising. Here Conservative resentments against Jews seem to have their echo.[67] Robinsohn's following lines may explain his opinion: "It is likely that enough people will raise their voices demanding that the government stand firm concerning its proclamation of equality of rights. Then a tactical situation might be better."[68] Here Robinsohn's political point of view becomes obvious: rights and liberties should not be granted by the new government which will draw its legitimation from a *coup d'état*, but people should fight for their rights and liberties in order to appreciate their value. This is a point of view that relates not only to the Jewish Question but to all human rights. Then Robinsohn refers to the measures that should be taken immediately:

> ". . . it is essential to repeal the special treatment of Jews as regards food supplies and the wearing of distinguishing marks in public. Proceedings based on the special legislation against Jews must be suspended (. . . until further regulation), and the public prosecutors and the police departments are to be told to discontinue accusations and other official acts which are based on this legislation for the time being".[69]

The differences from Conservative programmes are significant: while Goerdeler[70] regarded the Jews as a separate race who had to be treated as aliens in the

---

[63]Hans Robinsohn, 'Bericht aus Deutschland Anfang November 1939', IfZ, ED 166.
[64]Untitled paper in the Bundesarchiv, Robinsohn papers 31.
[65]Christof Dipper, 'Der Widerstand und die Juden', in Schmädeke and Steinbach, *op. cit.*, pp. 611f.
[66]Robinsohn's untitled paper, p. 35. [Translated by H.S.]
[67]For the Conservatives see Dipper, *loc. cit., passim.*
[68]Robinsohn's untitled paper, p. 35. [Translated by H.S.]
[69]*Ibid.*
[70]Goerdeler was in contact with representatives of the *Reichsvertretung/Reichsvereinigung der deutschen Juden*: see Leonard Baker, *Hirt der Verfolgten. Leo Baeck im Dritten Reich*, Stuttgart 1982, pp. 333–335. Otto Hirsch, the Director of the *Reichsvertretung*, was a Liberal. See Paul Sauer, *Für Recht und Menschenwürde. Lebensbild von Otto Hirsch (1885–1941)*, Gerlingen 1985; *idem*, 'Otto Hirsch (1885–1941). Director of the Reichsvertretung', in *LBI Year Book XXXII* (1987), pp. 341–368.

Germany after Hitler's fall,[71] Robinsohn emphasised that the reintroduction of the emancipation of the Jews should be obtained by strife, showing his ideal was the combative civilian of the European 1848 Revolutions. Therefore his proposals were restrained: the mere announcement of equal rights, only suspension of trials and persecution by the police. Equal treatment in law had to be a process that should be affirmed by the citizens fighting for it.

Another aspect is significant for the difference it indicates between the Conservative and Liberal anti-Fascist opposition. The diplomat Ulrich von Hassell, dismissed in 1938, a close collaborator of Goerdeler and strongly Conservative, stated as first principle that all European states should follow "the tenets of Christian ethics".[72] No document of the Liberal, secular Robinsohn-Strassmann group displays any similar religious foundation which would have excluded Jewish ethics.

The comparison with other groups influenced by Liberalism is revealing. The proposals of the Right-wing Liberal Freiburg circle concerning the "Jewish Question" accept the ecclesiastical definitions of race as well as a racial policy of the state including the de-nationalising of the Jews. It is obvious that their perspective was only apparently Liberal.[73] The Kreisau circle which included Liberal, Socialist and Christian members rejected race ideology generally and proposed to cancel all antisemitic laws and proscriptions immediately after coming to power.[74] This position is close to that of the Robinsohn-Strassmann group, but lacks the combative impulse that ought to deepen the value of human rights as an achievement of the people.

V. SUPPORT FOR JEWS

Supporting the persecuted was a matter-of-course for the members of the Robinsohn-Strassmann group. Thomas Dehler,[75] the head of the group in Northern Bavaria, demonstrated solidarity with Jews such as the president of the Jewish community in Bamberg, Willy Lessing.[76] In Berlin the group worked together with the Christian churches' relief work for Jews. Several members of

---

[71]Memorandum 'Das Ziel', from the beginning of 1941, in Bodo Scheurig (ed.), *Deutscher Widerstand 1938–1944. Fortschritt oder Reaktion?*, 2nd edn., Munich 1984, pp. 53–129, here pp. 75–77; Dipper, *loc. cit.*, pp. 606f.

[72]Confidential paper for J. Lonsdale Bryans, 23rd February 1940, printed in *Die Hassell-Tagebücher 1938–1944. Ulrich von Hassell: Aufzeichnungen vom Anderen Deutschland*, revised edition, ed. by Friedrich Freiherr Hiller von Gaertringen, Berlin 1988, p. 172.

[73]Dipper, *loc. cit.*, pp. 608f. The paper written by Constantin von Dietze is published in *In der Stunde Null. Die Denkschrift des Freiburger "Bonhoeffer-Kreises": Politische Gemeinschaft. Ein Versuch zur Selbstbesinnung des christlichen Gewissens in den politischen Nöten unserer Zeit*, ed. by Philipp von Bismarck, Tübingen 1979, p. 149.

[74]Ger van Roon, *Neuordnung im Widerstand. Der Kreisauer Kreis innerhalb der deutschen Widerstandsbewegung*, Munich 1967, p. 570.

[75]Federal Minister of Justice, 1949–1953.

[76]Friedrich Henning, 'Thomas Dehler (1897–1967)', in *Fränkische Lebensbilder*, vol. 10 (1982), pp. 239–257. About the Jewish community in Bamberg see Baruch Z. Ophir and Falk Wiesemann, *Die jüdischen Gemeinden in Bayern 1918–1945. Geschichte und Zerstörung*, Munich–Vienna 1979, pp. 109–119.

the group, such as Fritz Elsas in Berlin and Maximilian Fuchs in Munich advised Jews on emigration questions. Fuchs had the exclusive representation for Southern Germany for Jewish emigration via the Palestine & Orient Lloyd.[77] The Hamburg section of the Robinsohn-Strassmann group was in contact with the Fairplay pilot-boat firm (*Lotsenbootreederei*) of Lucy Borchard (DDP), a Jew who gave instruction to young Jews in her firm in order to prepare their emigration to Palestine.[78] The Jewish Robinsohn family in Hamburg is an example of the little-known fact that support for the persecuted was not a one-way street from "Aryans" for Jews. When in 1933 Christian Liberal opponents of National Socialism were put out of work, the Robinsohn family and other Jewish families supported them with food provisions.[79] An "Aryan" member of the group in Hamburg apprenticed his daughter to the fashion house *Gebr. Robinsohn*.[80] Hans Robinsohn financed the founding of the Hamburg cabaret *Broncekeller* by unemployed "half Jewish" members of a Hamburg resistance group.[81]

In an extraordinarily intensive way Margarethe Lachmund[82] cared for persecuted Jews in Mecklenburg and Pomerania. She was one of the Religious Society of Friends (Quakers) in Germany.[83] She helped Jews with advice, with funds, by keeping Jewish children in her home, by negotiating with Nazi authorities. Her fight for the rights of the Jews was open and risky, her sense of justice left room for no consideration of her own safety. Her selfless dedication is demonstrated by the example of the protection she gave to a Jewish doctor who lived in a small town near Schwerin. He had been a volunteer in 1914, had lost a leg by a grenade and had been decorated with the high Prussian order of the *Roter Adler*. When he lost his licence as a doctor in 1938, Margarethe Lachmund negotiated with the Vice *Gauleiter* of the Nazi Party in Mecklenburg, von Koerber, and with a ministerial official in Berlin. As she was not successful she wrote a long letter to von Koerber. In this letter of 24th August 1938 she described the situation of the persecuted doctor as well as that of the German Jews in general and emphasised that the Jews were part of the German nation:

> " 'Nation' can only be conceived as a succession of generations. As I feel quite strongly that I can never dissociate from my nation and that no outside power could dissociate me from it; as I am connected with my nation today and always, whether I be a National Socialist or not, and just as I have to bear the responsibility for everything with my nation, that nation cannot deny a period of its history; if one of its generations has endured hardship and has sacrificed

---

[77] Archiv des Deutschen Liberalismus, Gummersbach, Fuchs papers.
[78] *International Biographical Dictionary of Central European Emigrés 1933–1945*, vol. I, *op. cit.*, p. 80.
[79] Information from Dr. Wolfgang Plat; his father was the secretary of the *Deutsche Staatspartei* in Hamburg up to 1933.
[80] Private papers of Erich Wentker.
[81] Information from Alfred Johann Levy. The *Broncekeller* was a foundation of the *Gruppe Q*, which was linked with the Robinsohn-Strassmann group.
[82] Heinrich Carstens (ed.), *Margarethe Lachmund zum 80. Geburtstag. Ein Lebensbild, zusammengestellt aus ihren eigenen Buchbeiträgen, Briefen und Vorträgen zwischen 1935 und 1973* (Stimmen der Freunde, vol. 4), Bad Pyrmont 1976.
[83] Anna Sabine Halle, ' "Alle Menschen sind unsere Brüder . . ." – Nahezu unbekannter religiöser Widerstand im "Dritten Reich" ', in *Widerstand und Exil 1933–1945* (Schriftenreihe der Bundeszentrale für politische Bildung, vol. 223), Bonn 1985, pp. 127–133.

blood and life for the nation then that nation owes a debt to all the people of generations to come."[84]

In this way she showed the immorality of Nazi antisemitism. In the passage that followed she gave examples of the disavowal of antisemitism by nameless people, and she suggested that the Nazi leaders should, like Harun al Raschid, secretly find out what the real opinion of the people was. Then Margarethe Lachmund uttered her most heartfelt request:

"You will ask, Herr von Koerber, why I say all this, even though the laws already exist. I believe that within the supreme might of our land lies a monstrous demon, and I believe that because of it we are now being led astray, and I also believe that there is always a way back for real statesmen, that confessing and correcting a mistake gives, in the long run, moral superiority over all matters of tactic and all desires to seem infallible and all apparent outward loss of prestige."[85]

The man to whom this letter was addressed undoubtedly understood the frank criticism of the Nazi leaders, beginning with Hitler. The measures von Koerber took were minimal: control of her post for three months and a note in his personal card-file. This example illustrates that resistance, though dangerous, has a chance to change an adversary's mind.

After the *"Reichskristallnacht"*, Margarethe Lachmund became the official Pomeranian representative of the Protestant Bureau Grüber which supported the Jews in all official questions and furthered their emigration.[86] Her husband, Hans Lachmund, who was the Mecklenburg representative of the Robinsohn-Strassmann group, was well qualified as a lawyer to stand by her in many difficult cases. In the Second World War Margarethe Lachmund organised a group of fifty German Quakers who sent gift-parcels to the Jews in ghettos and concentration camps.[87] This humanitarian work was even continued after Strassmann's arrest in 1942 when the central co-ordination of the group collapsed.

It was no coincidence that a Liberal resistance group collaborated closely with a religious society which stresses individualism, democracy and pacifism, and that a Quaker was a member of the group. There are other hints that there were more contacts between the leading circle of the Robinsohn-Strassmann group and Berlin Quakers.

VI. CONCLUSION

The Robinsohn-Strassmann group was a specifically Liberal resistance group, recruited largely from former members of the Left-wing Liberal DDP and which

---

[84]Margarethe Lachmund to Gerd von Koerber, 24th August 1938, private Lachmund papers. [Translated by H.S.]

[85]*Ibid.*

[86]Hartmut Ludwig, *Die Opfer unter dem Rad verbinden. Vor- und Entstehungsgeschichte, Arbeit und Mitarbeiter des "Büro Pfarrer Grüber"* (theological dissertation), Berlin (GDR) 1988.

[87]Egon Larsen (ed.), *"Und doch gefällt mir das Leben" – Die Briefe der Clara Grunwald 1941–1943*, Mannheim 1985; Else Rosenfeld and Gertrud Luckner (eds.), *Lebenszeichen aus Piaski. Briefe Deportierter aus dem Distrikt Lublin 1940–1943*, München 1968, pp. 99–164.

developed its own Liberal programme for government after the collapse of the Third *Reich*. Its founders and several leading members were of Jewish origin or even Jews themselves. For the group, as such, this Jewish element was not of religious import,[88] but it created an additional driving force. Such impulses were of great importance because of the long period of the group's existence and because of the many disappointments about the success of their illegal work. Helmut Neuberger[89] has analysed Eastern German Jewry according to their innovative contribution to German progressive politics, especially to the Revolutions of 1848/1849 and 1918/1919 as well as to the foundation of new parties and organisations and we can add that men of Eastern German-Jewish origin made a dominant contribution to the Liberal anti-Fascist resistance in Germany. An important difference from that of the Conservative resistance is their aim of the complete re-integration of the Jews – a goal shared by the Kreisau circle, however. Obviously Jews played an important role in the Liberal anti-Fascist resistance in Germany.[90] The Robinsohn-Strassmann group, though part of the German resistance, operated independently as well and was conspicuous for its efforts to support the persecuted Jews.

---

[88]It is the more significant for the approach to religious organisations that Hans Robinsohn became a member of the German Society for Christian-Jewish Co-operation (*Gesellschaft für christlich-jüdische Zusammenarbeit*) after the Second World War.

[89]Helmut Neuberger, 'Der Beitrag des ostdeutschen Judentums zur deutschen Politik', in Gotthold Rhode (ed.), *Juden in Ostmitteleuropa von der Emanzipation bis zum Ersten Weltkrieg* (Historische und landeskundliche Ostmitteleuropastudien, vol. 3), Marburg 1989, pp. 115–150, here pp. 149f.

[90]Paucker, *Jüdischer Widerstand in Deutschland, op. cit.*, p. 19.

Struggle and Survival:
Jewish Women in the Anti-Fascist Resistance in Germany

BY SIMONE ERPEL

I

This essay is based upon the lives of four German-Jewish women who fought against National Socialism. All of them were involved in a Jewish resistance group as active Communists or, at least, were Communist in orientation. In order to document and describe their resistance struggle accurately, it is essential to look briefly at the extent and conditions of women's resistance as a whole.

Women from all social classes took an active part in the organised resistance and – with various motives – were to be found in all the anti-Fascist camps. Not infrequently they engaged in personal forms of resistance and performed individual acts of civil courage. However, most of the women involved in the resistance had already been politically engaged before 1933 and came from the ranks of the labour movement. It is clear that only a few women occupied leading positions, while most women resistance fighters were active in the infrastructure of the resistance. They took over the work of organisation which made resistance possible in the first place, and took continuing responsibility for it.

There was resistance from the labour movement during the entire Nazi era. However, the most active period of Communist and Socialist opposition came in the early years of the Third *Reich*. Until 1936, there were efforts in several parts of the labour movement to maintain banned organisations on an illegal basis.[1] Women were well represented in organisations close to the workers' parties, such as *Arbeiterwohlfahrt*, the *Internationale Arbeiterhilfe* and the *Rote Hilfe*, all of which were also banned and their members criminalised and persecuted.[2]

Inevitably, the persecution of known opponents of the regime tore gaps in the ranks of these organisations. These were filled by young Communist and Socialist women as well as by members of the movement still unknown to the National Socialists. After the first wave of persecutions in February 1933, important positions in the infrastructure and organisation of anti-Fascist resistance were taken over by those people who had managed to avoid arrest.

---

[1]Martin Broszat, 'Zur Sozialgeschichte des deutschen Widerstandes', in *Vierteljahrshefte für Zeitgeschichte*, 34, 3 (1986), p. 296.
[2]See Florence Hervé, 'Brot und Frieden, Frauenbewegung in der Weimarer Republik', in *idem* (ed.), *Geschichte der deutschen Frauenbewegung*, Cologne 1982, pp. 131, 142.

Among them were many women.[3] The Communist functionary Käthe Popall was finally arrested in 1935 during the leadership meeting of the illegal *Kommunistische Partei Deutschlands* (KPD) in Berlin, and was imprisoned for ten years until the liberation. On the subject of women's part in the resistance, she wrote that women were strongly represented in the entire movement, but that there were no groups specifically for women.[4]

It is a reasonable estimate that, up to the outbreak of war in 1939, a million women and men were imprisoned for political reasons, for shorter or longer periods. Hanna Elling claims that around 800,000 men and women offered resistance against National Socialism. More women from the big cities than from agricultural areas joined the resistance movement. Unfortunately, the available statistics provide little information about the proportion of women in the organised resistance. Hanna Elling believes that some 20% of those engaged in the struggle were women.[5] Among these were a significant number of German-Jewish resistance fighters. Those who were known to the Nazis as active opponents of the regime were in the gravest danger of all.

Ruthless force was used by the new rulers against female political representatives of the Weimar Republic and against *Reichstag* deputies. The Social Democrat deputy Leni Rosenthal, Thälmann's colleague Franziska Kessel, the Communist deputy Helene Fleischer – all were either murdered by the *Gestapo* or died as a result of the appalling ill-treatment they had suffered. Minna Cammens, who had formerly been a *Reichstag* deputy of the *Sozialdemokratische Partei Deutschlands* (SPD), was also killed by the *Gestapo* whilst in "protective custody".[6]

Other women political opponents of the regime were forced to emigrate. The Communist Elsa Vierling-Fugger had taken part, with her husband Carl Fugger, in illegal activity for the banned *Rote Hilfe Deutschlands* since 1933. When her husband was arrested in Spring 1934, the *Gestapo* also began to hunt for Elsa. She was forced to leave for France through the Saarland.[7] Other well-known opponents of the regime, such as the German-Jewish Communist Olga Benario, emigrated to the Soviet Union.[8]

Representatives of the bourgeois women's movement were also forced to choose the path of emigration. They included Alice Salomon, the founder of professional social work, and the scientist Alice Rühle-Gerstel, who had written about the condition of the German women's movement before 1933. These women fled from Germany into exile in America and Mexico.[9]

[3]See Hanna Elling, *Frauen im deutschen Widerstand 1933–1945*, Frankfurt a. Main 1978, pp. 44–45.
[4]See *ibid.*, pp. 150–151.
[5]*Ibid.*, pp. 50,71f.
[6]Sybil Milton, 'Deutsche und deutsch-jüdische Frauen als Verfolgte des NS-Staates', in *Dachauer Hefte, Frauen – Verfolgung und Widerstand*, 3 (1987), p. 3.
[7]See Sigrid Jacobeit, 'Elsa Fugger. Das Leben einer Widerstandskämpferin', in *Dachauer Hefte*, 3 (1987), *op. cit.*, pp. 208–209.
[8]Fernando Morais, *Olga – Das Leben einer mutigen Frau*, Cologne 1989.
[9]See Joachim Wieler, *Er-Innerung eines zerstörten Lebensabend. Alice Salomon während der NS-Zeit (1933–1937) und im Exil (1937–1948)*, Darmstadt 1987; Alice Rühle-Gerstel, *Das Frauenproblem der Gegenwart*, Berlin 1932.

The impetus and first initiatives for a broad-based women's movement against National Socialism emerged from the International Women's Congress held in Paris during 1934. Over 1,000 delegates from 24 countries agreed on joint action in the struggle against Fascism; they included 15 women from Germany who had travelled illegally to the Congress, which was close to the Socialist and trade union movement.[10] However, the Congress was the last of its kind during this period.

An especially precarious position was faced by those German-Jewish women in the resistance who either could not or would not emigrate. As members of the Jewish population, they were subjected to sporadic violence after 1933, and were also the victims of official abuse and antisemitic propaganda.[11] "They were subjected to a 'creeping persecution', by which they were eliminated from the professions by legislative means and excluded from the social, cultural, intellectual and economic life of Germany."[12]

Young Jews such as Marianne Prager-Joachim from the Baum Group, who was only 13 years old in 1933, felt the impact of the antisemitic legislation with particular force. In their schooling, as in their vocational training, they were deprived of any real choice. By means of legislation, decrees and state-promoted antisemitism, the professional prospects and entire futures of young German Jews were destroyed step by step.[13] Repression of this kind led to the recognition that life in Germany was becoming impossible, but it also radicalised the resistance to National Socialism within some sections of the German-Jewish population.

Helga Beyer was 13 years old when she joined the resistance to the Nazi regime. She was a member of the German-Jewish youth group *Kameraden* which resisted the Nazi terror under the sign of the *Weisse Möwe* (White Gull). Helga worked in Breslau as a courier in a resistance group until her arrest in 1938.[14]

Jewish anti-Fascist women fought in mixed resistance groups, such as Helga Beyer in the Breslau *Kommunistische Parteiopposition*(KPO) and in exclusively Jewish groups. For example, a number of active women resistance fighters belonged to the Jewish resistance organisation set up by the young Communist Herbert Baum.[15] Additionally, there were other women who initially concentrated on personal acts of resistance. One of these was the Zionist Edith Wolff, whose individual campaign involved leaving her own anti-Nazi leaflets in public places, such as telephone booths. Finally, when the first Berlin Jews were deported in autumn 1941, Edith decided to take part in organised forms of resistance. She found ways to help young Jews and her friends to go underground or to leave the country. After the "factory action" of February 1943, when all remaining Jewish forced labourers in munitions factories were deported, the

---

[10]Elling, *op. cit.*, pp. 56–57.

[11]Milton, *loc. cit.*, p. 5.

[12]*Ibid.*, p. 6; Joseph Walk (ed.), *Das Sonderrecht für die Juden im NS-Staat. Eine Sammlung der gesetzlichen Maßnahmen und Richtlinien – Inhalt und Bedeutung*, Karlsruhe 1981.

[13]See Werner T. Angress, *Generation zwischen Furcht und Hoffnung. Jüdische Jugend im 3. Reich 1933–1945*, Hamburg 1985, p. 9.

[14]Antje Dertinger, *Weisse Möwe, gelber Stern. Das kurze Leben der Helga Beyer*, Berlin–Bonn 1987.

[15]See Margot Pikarski, *Jugend im Berliner Widerstand. Herbert Baum und Kampfgefährten*, East Berlin 1978.

Chug Chaluzi was set up in her home to co-ordinate help for Jews attempting to escape.[16]

Those Jewish women who offered resistance in German concentration camps also deserve to be remembered. One group of Jewish women forced labourers managed to smuggle gunpowder out of the "Union" munitions factory in Auschwitz under the most difficult conditions, and passed it on to the resistance group which organised the camp uprising in Auschwitz-Birkenau on 7th October 1944.[17]

Of course, most Jewish men and women in Germany did not – and could not possibly – fight actively against the Nazi regime. In addition, the assimilated middle-class Jewish community conformed to bourgeois behavioural norms. Many reacted with incomprehension to their expulsion from the Gentile majority society, which began at every level in 1933. Against this background, previously unregarded aspects of Jewish self-assertion and the struggle for human dignity gain in significance. One example was the *Jüdischer Frauenbund*, led by Bertha Pappenheim, which belonged to the moderate wing of the women's movement until the *Bürgerliche Frauenbewegung* disbanded itself in 1933. Because of the increasingly German Nationalist tone in the umbrella organisation of the *Bürgerliche Frauenbewegung*, the *Bund Deutscher Frauenvereine*, the largely middle-class *Jüdischer Frauenbund* declared its departure from the organisation. Leading members of the *Jüdischer Frauenbund*, among them Cora Berliner and Hannah Karminski, instead sought closer ties with Jewish organisations, which continued to exist until 1938. Though Jewish women were denied the opportunity to take active part in shaping community life, they took the initiative in questions of welfare and supported emigration after 1936. These women led a struggle for self-assertion and fought against the destruction of their human dignity.[18]

Whilst we are fully aware that there were Jewish women of different political persuasions who resisted the Nazi regime,* this contribution is restricted to the Left of the political spectrum: to those Jewish women, active anti-Fascists, who felt an affinity to the German working-class movement. In this respect they were typical of the majority of those Jews who were engaged actively in the political struggle against National Socialism. The profiles that follow are of four young Jewish women in the anti-Nazi resistance.

II

Alongside Herbert Baum and Marianne Cohn, Sala Rosenbaum-Kochmann was a leading figure in one of the biggest anti-Fascist resistance groups of young

---

[16]Edith Wolff, 'Lasst euch nicht deportieren', in Ferdinand Kroh, *David kämpft. Vom jüdischen Widerstand gegen Hitler*, Reinbek bei Hamburg 1988, pp. 103–117.

[17]Hana Weisblum, 'Widerstand in Auschwitz', in *Dachauer Hefte*, 3 (1987), *op. cit.*, p. 250.

[18]Marion Kaplan, *Die jüdische Frauenbewegung in Deutschland. Organisation und Ziele des Jüdischen Frauenbundes 1904–1938*, Hamburg 1981.

*See in this context the preceding essay by Horst Sassin, 'Liberals of Jewish Background in the Anti-Nazi Resistance', in this Year Book – (Ed.).

Jews in Germany, the pro-Communist Herbert Baum Group in Berlin.[19] "Yes, Herbert and Sala, they were models for me", remembered their former colleague Walter Sack.[20] Sala Rosenbaum-Kochmann encouraged young Jews to stick together in conditions of increasing isolation and exclusion under the Nazi regime. She was one of eleven group members who participated in the arson attack against the Nazi propaganda exhibition *Das Sowjetparadies* in Berlin's Lustgarten on 18th May 1942.[21] With 27 others, Sala was captured in the wave of arrests which began only three days after the action. She was condemned at a summary trial and executed on the morning of 18th August 1942.[22] Her husband Martin Kochmann, tipped off by an acquaintance, managed to evade his Nazi persecutors until October 1942, when he was arrested by the *Gestapo* and murdered in Plötzensee.[23]

Marianne Prager-Joachim used false papers to go underground near Berlin after the arson attack. Her husband Heinz Joachim had already fallen victim to the first wave of arrests on 22nd and 23rd May. On 9th July, the *Gestapo* also tracked Marianne down and captured her. Her friend Hanni Lindenberger-Meyer and the sisters Alice and Hella Hirsch suffered the same fate, along with eight other members of the group. The first interrogations were unproductive; the accused, according to a secret letter from the *Gestapo* to the *Oberreichsanwalts-chef*, were thereupon subjected to "intensified interrogation in the form of blows with sticks".[24] In a summary trial lasting only one day, the second Senate of the People's Court sentenced Marianne to death. She was kept in her cell for eight months before her execution, unaware that her husband had been put to death on 18th August 1942.[25] On 4th March 1943, the 21-year-old woman was executed in Berlin-Plötzensee.

[19]Important literature on the Baum Group: Bernhard Mark, 'Die Gruppe Baum. Aus der Geschichte des anti-faschistischen Kampfes der jüdischen Jugend in Deutschland in den Jahren 1937–1942', in *Bulletin des jüdischen historischen Instituts Warschau* (in Polish), No. 33 (January/March 1960), pp. 3–45; Margot Pikarski, *Sie bleiben unvergessen. Widerstandsgruppe Herbert Baum*, East Berlin 1968; Pikarski, *Jugend im Berliner Widerstand, op. cit.*; Helmut Eschwege, 'Resistance of German Jews against the Nazi Regime', in *LBI Year Book XV* (1970), pp. 143–180; Arnold Paucker and Lucien Steinberg, 'Some Notes on Resistance', in *LBI Year Book XVI* (1971), pp. 239–248; Lucien Steinberg, 'The Herbert Baum Campaign', in *Not as a Lamb. The Jews Against Hitler*, London 1974, pp. 26–53; Kurt Schilde, *Jugendorganisationen und Jugendopposition in Berlin-Kreuzberg 1933–1945*, Berlin 1983; Konrad Kwiet and Helmut Eschwege, *Selbstbehauptung und Widerstand 1933–1945. Deutsche Juden im Kampf um Existenz und Menschenwürde*, Hamburg 1984; Wolfgang Scheffler, 'Der Brandanschlag im Berliner Lustgarten im Mai 1942 und seine Folge. Eine quellenkritische Betrachtung', in *Berlin in Geschichte und Gegenwart. Jahrbuch des Landesarchivs Berlin*, Berlin 1984, pp. 91–118; Eric Brothers, 'On the Anti-Fascist Resistance of German Jews', in *LBI Year Book XXXII* (1987), pp. 369–382; *idem*, 'Profile of a German-Jewish Resistance Fighter: Marianne Prager-Joachim', in *The Jewish Quarterly*, vol. 34, No. 1 (1987), pp. 31–36. See also, Paucker, *Jüdischer Widerstand* (note 31), pp. 7–8 and *passim*.
[20]I held this conversation with Walter Sack at the beginning of December 1989 in Berlin-Adlershof.
[21]In his essay 'On the Anti-Fascist Resistance', Eric Brothers points out that most of the literature on the Baum Group deals mainly with the arson attack of 1942 and much less with the many anti-Fascist activities of the group between 1933 and 1938. Exceptions are Margot Pikarski, Konrad Kwiet and Helmut Eschwege.
[22]See Pikarski, *Sie bleiben unvergessen*, p. 55; and 'Führerinformation', No. 81 (1942), quoted in Scheffler, *loc. cit.*, p. 99.
[23]See Kwiet and Eschwege, *Selbstbehauptung und Widerstand*, p. 136.
[24]Secret letter of 5th May 1942, quoted in Schilde, *Jugendorganisationen und Jugendopposition*, p. 127.
[25]Secret message of Marianne Prager-Joachim, cited in Pikarski, *Sie bleiben unvergessen*, p. 92.

Rita Resnik-Meyer had helped Martin Kochmann in his temporary escape from the Nazi authorities before herself being discovered, arrested and transported to Auschwitz. She was among the few survivors of the extermination camp.

Help and support was also needed by the numerous Jews who escaped the threat of deportation by going into hiding. A contemporary witness stressed the mortal danger facing the German Jews at this time: "We found the escalating deportations particularly demoralising . . . for we knew that our time was up . . . We all prepared ourselves for an illegal life."[26] Ellen Compart and Ursula Ehrlich, two members of the Baum Group, likewise acquired false papers and went into hiding. With them, Rosel Dzsida-Bibo, an acquaintance of Marianne and Herbert Baum, was also one of the few to survive in hiding.[27] Together with her husband, she had chosen to resist deportation.

Rosel Dzsida-Bibo (in hiding), Rita Resnik-Meyer (helping escapees), Marianne Prager-Joachim (the organiser) and Sala Rosenbaum-Kochmann (the functionary) – all these women belonged to the Baum Group or were close to it. They can be regarded as representative of many active Jewish women in the group.[28] Until now, that women made up nearly half the Baum Group has been virtually ignored, despite the fact that this proportion far exceeded the overall share of both Jewish and non-Jewish women in the anti-Fascist resistance, which was between 15% and 20%.[29]

Is this fact insignificant? Are the resistance struggles of Jewish Communist women unworthy of detailed examination? Clearly, this is not the case. Instead, the neglect of their role reflects the dominating concerns of historical research. It has virtually ignored the women resistance workers in a threefold sense: as Communists, as Jews and as women.[30]

Despite the increase in detailed studies of the Jewish resistance since the 1970s,[31] West German research into the resistance took little account of its results. On one hand, German-Jewish historiography failed to make the resistance of Jewish women into a special object of its investigations and for many years marginalised the role of the Communist resistance; and on the other, feminist research into women's history in the Federal Republic since the 1970s, though recognising that women in general played a part in the resistance,

[26]Emmi Löwenthal, 'Verurteile nicht deinen Nächsten, bis du dich in seiner Lage gesehen hast', in Henryk M. Broder and Michel R. Lang (eds.), *Fremd im eigenen Land. Juden in der Bundesrepublik*, Frankfurt a. Main 1979, p. 280.

[27]See Kwiet and Eschwege, *Selbstbehauptung und Widerstand*, p. 151.

[28]See short biographies of women resistance fighters by Margot Pikarski.

[29]See Elling, *op. cit.*, pp. 50, 71–72; Milton, *loc. cit.*, p. 5.

[30]Ingrid Strobl, *Sag nie du gehst den letzten Weg. Frauen im bewaffneten Widerstand gegen Faschismus und deutsche Besatzung*, Frankfurt a. Main 1989, pp. 19–34.

[31]Arnold Paucker, *Jüdischer Widerstand in Deutschland. Tatsachen und Problematik*, Beiträge zum Widerstand 1933–1945, Gedenkstätte Deutscher Widerstand Berlin, Heft 37, Berlin 1989, pp. 4–5. Revised and expanded English version, *Jewish Resistance in Germany. The Facts and the Problems*, Berlin, pp. 4–5.

devoted little attention to the resistance of Jewish women.[32] The impulse for such research, as well as studies on the subject, came from Jewish feminists mainly from the USA and France.[33]

What new aspects can be revealed by bringing a feminist perspective to bear on the well-documented activities of the Baum Group? First and foremost, the task of "making visible" the role of women in the resistance – in this case, the resistance of Jewish Communists – is essential for its own sake. For too long these women have been deemed of little relevance by researchers. Placing Jewish women resistance fighters at the centre of research requires an investigation of the specific conditions, forms, locations and motives of their resistance and their awareness of themselves as Communists, Jews and women. Often these women defined themselves by their Socialist outlook, were not religious, regarded their ethnic identity as relatively insignificant until the outbreak of war and their gender as a matter of chance.[34]

In the Left-wing Zionist organisations, women were granted the same degree of equality as in other Socialist movements. As Viola Roggenkamp has indicated, this was never full equality.[35] In this respect, their experience in the Baum Group resembled the situation elsewhere.

Each of the following biographical portraits reveals one facet of the history of the Baum Group and its struggle. The life stories of Sala Rosenbaum-Kochmann, Marianne Prager-Joachim, Rita Resnik-Meyer and Rosel Dzsida-Bibo are significant both for the individual experiences they describe and as representative of a generation of German-Jewish women who embraced active resistance. Many voices, not one, are to be heard in each biography. The sources used are the published documents of the Nazi prosecuting authorities and the (auto)biographical reports of the resistance fighters and witnesses of both sexes.[36]

The individual biographies deal with the different forms of resistance: struggle, organisation, support and survival. Struggle meant an attempt to disrupt the smooth running of the Nazi terror regime by resorting to direct action; organisation and support were modes of conduct in the infrastructure of the resistance, of vital importance to establish and maintain communications and personal ties: survival should be understood as an element of Jewish resistance to the policy and practice of the Nazi regime, which aimed at the annihilation of all Jewish life.[37]

Such drawing of distinctions between various forms of resistance is intended to

---

[32]Few exceptions: *Dachauer Hefte*, 3 (1987) *op. cit.*; Jessica Jacoby and Gotlinde Magiriba Lwanga, 'Was "sie" schon immer über Antisemitismus wissen wollte, aber nie zu denken wagte', in *Beiträge zur feministischen Theorie und Praxis*, 27 (1990): *Geteilter Feminismus*, pp. 95–105.

[33]Vera Laska, *Women in the Resistance and the Holocaust. The Voices of Eyewitnesses*, Connecticut 1983; Debra Seideman, *Die Stimmen überlebender Frauen. Der Holocaust, Frauen und Widerstand*, Division III Thesis, Hampshire College 1982; Rita Thalmann, *Frausein im Dritten Reich*, Frankfurt a. Main 1987.

[34]See Paucker, *Jüdischer Widerstand*, p. 8; *idem*, *Jewish Resistance*, p. 7.

[35]Viola Roggenkamp, 'Jüdinnen', in *Emma*, 10 (1988), p. 41.

[36]Brothers, 'On the Anti-Fascist Resistance', investigates the significance and value of witness accounts as historical sources.

[37]See Kwiet and Eschwege, *Selbstbehauptung und Widerstand*, p. 150.

prevent a hierarchical definition of resistance and to cut across the previous dichotomy between active (fighting) and passive (supporting) resistance. Instead, the aim is to facilitate a view of resistance activities across a wide spectrum.

The order of the life stories reflects the chronological shifts in women's resistance and implicitly reveals its different phases.[38] The sequence begins in 1933 with the resistance struggle of Sala Rosenbaum-Kochmann and ends with Rosel Dzsida-Bibo, who went into hiding in December 1942.

III

Sala Rosenbaum-Kochmann

"Sala was a remarkable woman. I will never forget her voice or her smile. Her voice had a special tone, soft, clear, expressive. We all admired her. And if people had troubles, they went to her."[39] These are the warm memories of her former colleague Walter Sack, who worked with Sala Rosenbaum-Kochmann until his emigration in 1939, and made a vain attempt to organise a chance for Sala to emigrate to Sweden.[40]

Born in Rzeszow near Poznań in 1912, Sala Rosenbaum joined the *Deutsch-jüdische Jugendgemeinschaft* when she was 13 years old. Here in 1928 she met Herbert Baum, Marianne Cohn and Martin Kochmann, who later became her husband. Sala trained as a kindergarten teacher and worked at the Jewish kindergarten in Jerusalemer Straße until her arrest on 22nd May 1942. She is remembered as an excellent teacher in her profession, in the *Kommunistischer Jugendverband* (KJVD) which she joined in 1932, and in the group which coalesced round Baum in 1935–1936. In this group she was chiefly responsible for youth work.[41]

For young Communists, the resolutions of the Brussels Conference of 1935 were highly significant. This was concerned mainly with the KPD's united front policy and with the attempt to create legal openings for political work. After the ban on the KJVD, the young Jews associated with Baum sought to gain a foothold in the existing Jewish organisations such as the *Ring – Bund deutsch-jüdischer Jugend* and the Left-wing Zionist *Hashomer Hazair*, which remained legal until 1937 and 1938 respectively. Walter Sack recalled: "This was above all an attempt to recreate legal possibilities. Our best prospect was to go into a Jewish organisation again and build up legal possibilities where we could meet."[42]

Also very important was the KPD directive at the end of 1936 and the beginning of 1937, which ruled that Jewish comrades were excluded from the

---

[38]I obtained suggestions for the application of these categories from the team of researchers working on women in the Austrian resistance. Elisabeth Holzinger *et al.*, *Der Himmel ist blau. Kann sein. Frauen im Widerstand, Österreich 1938–1945*, Vienna 1985.

[39]Walter Sack, unpublished and undated manuscript, p. 29.

[40]*Ibid.*

[41]See Sack, interview.

[42]Sack, manuscript, p. 29.

Edith Fränkel
Murdered in Auschwitz

Rosel Dzsida-Bibo
Survived

Marianne Prager-Joachim
Executed 4th March 1943

Jewish women of the anti-Fascist resistance

Sala Rosenbaum-Kochmann
Executed 18th August 1942

Helga Beyer
Murdered in Ravensbrück in 1942

Rita Resnik-Meyer
Survived

Jewish women of the anti-Fascist resistance

remaining illegal cadres and forced to decide either to emigrate or to form separate Jewish groups.[43] This decision, ostensibly taken to reduce the dangers facing non-Jewish comrades involved in illegal activity,[44] has received little attention from historians; it has not been analysed adequately against the background of the Nuremberg Laws of 1935.

Sala had already done educational and political work in the illegal KJVD and had run training evenings. From 1935/1936 she was also involved in legal work in the *Ring – Bund deutsch-jüdischer Jugend*. Her aim was to provide a "Heimstatt"[45] for increasingly isolated young Jews. "We were often at Sala's house. Nor will I forget that we used to read Heine with her, *Wintermärchen* and *Harzreise* and found pleasure in this . . . We also wanted to enjoy the beauty of life, fully enjoy it."[46]

Sala also took charge of the organisation's *Heimabende*, which took place every week until 1938 in the Jewish community house in Oranienburger Strasse. Various Zionist organisations also met here.[47] At the *Heimabende* for Jewish schoolchildren between the ages of 12 and 16, political themes were debated, literature was discussed, books were read aloud and songs were sung.[48] As well as suggesting reading material, Sala also gave political instruction to the young Jews. Walter Sack recalled that they read Marx's *Das Kapital* from pages torn out of books: "It was really crazy, but in the home in Oranienburger Strasse everything happened . . . We had provided some cover, though, securing the entrance to the room as well as having another book lying within reach on the table. We had torn the relevant pages out of the study material so it would be very quick to make them disappear."[49]

In discussions at the *Heimabende*, the causes of antisemitism and the persecution of the Jews became a subject of constant debate. Sala was convinced that equal rights could be achieved only after the dismantling of the Fascist dictatorship, in a Socialism for all people irrespective of the religious and ethnic affiliations. Thus Socialism itself offered a "solution of the Jewish Question".[50] This view was held by the convinced Communists among the group, but was not shared by all its members.

Political debate was not restricted to theoretical questions of antisemitism. It was also related directly to the realities of daily life for young Jews, increasingly confronted by exclusion and rejection. At meetings, "the events of the day and the situation and concerns of the Jews were discussed".[51] Alongside the *Heimabende*, there were regular excursions to the outlying areas of Berlin at weekends, which became an increasingly important "counter-reality" for the young members. "The trips were to Buchow, Mierdorf, Wildenbruch, Fried-

---

[43]Kwiet and Eschwege, *Selbstbehauptung und Widerstand*, pp. 113–114, 116.
[44]See Pikarski, *Sie bleiben unvergessen*, p. 30.
[45]Sack, interview.
[46]*Ibid.*
[47]Sack, manuscript, p. 5.
[48]*Ibid.*, p. 15.
[49]*Ibid.*, p. 26.
[50]See Pikarski, *Sie bleiben unvergessen*, p. 18.
[51]From the sentence on Heinz Rotholz *et al.*, quoted in Karl-Heinz Jahnke and Michael Buddrus, *Deutsche Jugend 1933–1945*, Hamburg 1989, p. 447.

richsthal . . . We went bathing at the Stössensee mostly . . . Almost every weekend and on feast days we would be on our way. These joint expeditions were also linked with discussions and group learning."[52] Even after the ban on Jewish youth organisations, Sala kept her links with these young people. During the period of illegality, hikes, training evenings and educational courses remained important elements of the communication between them. At this time of isolation, this was the only chance the young Jews had to maintain contact.[53] It signified their fighting for an aspect of the quality of life which was being denied them.

Marianne Prager-Joachim

"And despite everything I pull myself together again",[54] wrote Marianne Prager-Joachim to her friend Hanni Lindenberger-Meyer, who had also been arrested.

Marianne Prager, born in 1921, grew up in Berlin-Prenzlauer Berg, an area with a large Jewish population. She had a sister, four years younger than herself. In 1936, with her closest schoolfriend Inge Gerson, she joined the *Ring – Bund deutsch-jüdischer Jugend* in which Sala Rosenbaum-Kochmann was already involved. In the *Ring* Marianne came into contact with Socialist literature, and she and Inge participated in secret political meetings and literary evenings until the imposition of the ban. Works of literature as well as political themes were presented and analysed at these *Heimabende*.[55] Marianne was already interested in Zionism and developed an increasing sympathy for Communism during the period. Her sister Ilse Prager-Kessler recalls that, shortly after the "*Kristallnacht*", Marianne decided she could no longer endure the personal restrictions and humiliations of life in silence. Resolutely, she told her family: "If they ever come for my books or my piano, they will have to take me first!"[56]

When Jewish youth organisations were disbanded by the Nazis in 1938, members continued to meet in secret. Marianne was now convinced that only Communism could defeat the Nazi regime. Her friend Inge, however, was less sympathetic to the Communist and atheist tendency of the group and ceased to attend its meetings. Despite political differences, their friendship survived.[57] "What kept us close was the bond created by growing up together, doing the same things and liking each other so very much."[58] Even after they had finished school the two friends did not drift apart. They met often after work and, when forbidden to telephone they wrote to each other.[59]

In the summer of 1940 Marianne met Heinz Joachim, a jazz saxophonist,

[52]Günter Prager, unpublished and undated manuscript, p. 3; see also Sack, manuscript, pp. 19–20.
[53]Scheffler, 'Der Brandanschlag', p. 98.
[54]Secret message from Marianne Prager–Joachim to her friend Hanni Lindenberger-Meyer, *loc. cit.*
[55]See Brothers, 'Profile', p. 33.
[56]*Ibid.* This was a conversation which her sister Ilse Prager-Kessler remembered in 1985 in an interview with Eric Brothers.
[57]See letter from Inge Gerson-Berner, quoted in Arno Klönne, *Jugend im Dritten Reich. Die Hitlerjugend und ihre Gegner*, Cologne–Düsseldorf 1984, pp. 276–278.
[58]From the letters of Inge Gerson-Berner in May, July and August 1985, in Brothers, 'Profile', p. 34.
[59]*Ibid.*, p. 33.

during forced labour in agriculture and forestry. When both had to do forced labour at *Siemens Electromotorenwerk Spandau* at the beginning of 1941,* a group of 8–10 young forced labourers of both sexes gathered round them.[60] The resistance circle established by Herbert Baum also included Lotte Jastrow-Rotholz and her husband Siegbert Rotholz, Hildegard Loewy, Ursula Ehrlich and the sisters Hella and Alice Hirsch.[61] From summer 1941, Marianne and Heinz tried to buy identity papers from French and Belgian forced labourers. The price for a set of forged papers was RM150.[62] Marianne obtained papers in the name of André Alla and used them to rent legal quarters near Berlin.[63]

In August 1941, Marianne Prager married Heinz Joachim in the synagogue in Oranienburger Strasse, which had been damaged during the *"Kristallnacht"*. Significantly, the ensuing celebrations at their home had a strong traditional and religious element;[64] Jewish men and women often turned to traditional forms of their faith as a reaction to the destruction of Jewish identity by the Nazi regime.[65] But what persuaded German-Jewish women to marry in 1941? Hanni Lindenberger-Meyer and Lotte Jastrow-Rotholz, two more women from the resistance circle, also chose to marry that year. Inge Deutschkron, who survived, judges that such marriages were a reflection of the determination to survive with a committed partner in a profoundly hostile and destructive environment. Looking back, Inge Deutschkron wrote: "The narrower our freedom of action became, the more I clung to him. Apart from my mother I had no-one, and it was good to be able to trust someone. If many Jewish marriages were made in those days, that was often an important reason."[66]

Shortly after the wedding, the *Gestapo* arrested Marianne's friend Inge. During her three months of detention she was allowed no visitors, only letters. Inge recalled that Marianne was the only one "who wrote on an open postcard and with her full address telling me to be brave and not to despair. She signed off with the initials M.P. But that didn't mean Marianne Prager, but was an old sign between us referring to Marquis Posa and his call for freedom of thought."[67]

When Marianne was herself under arrest in 1942, she wrote to encourage another friend enclosing a secret message which she hoped to smuggle to Hanni Lindenberger-Meyer, who was also under arrest. It is not known whether it reached the addressee. What is certain is that the information fell into the hands

---

*On Jewish forced labour in general see now Konrad Kwiet, 'Forced Labour of German Jews in Nazi Germany', in *LBI Year Book XXXVI* (1991), pp. 389–410 – (Ed.).

[60]See Pikarski, *Sie bleiben unvergessen*, p. 32.

[61]Kwiet and Eschwege, *Selbstbehauptung und Widerstand*, pp. 117–118.

[62]*Ibid.*; and extracts from the report by Ilse Haak-Stillmann, quoted in Pikarski, 'Die Rolle der Parteiorganisation', appendix pp. 42–43.

[63]See Pikarski, *Jugend im Berliner Widerstand*, pp. 116–117; Allgemeiner Studentenausschuss der Technischen Universität Berlin (ed.), *Die Berliner Widerstandsgruppe um Herbert Baum*, Berlin 1984, p. 43.

[64]*Ibid.*, p. 35.

[65]Walter Sack, whose family was not religious, himself turned more towards Jewish traditions. See Sack, manuscript, p. 8.

[66]Inge Deutschkron, *Ich trug den gelben Stern*, Munich 1985, p. 79.

[67]Letter of Inge Gerson-Berner, in Klönne, *op. cit.*, p. 278. On Inge Gerson-Berner see also Paucker, *Jüdischer Widerstand*, p. 14; and *Jewish Resistance*, pp. 13 and 19.

of the *Gestapo*. The secret message was included in the judgement against Marianne as evidence of her stubborn adherence to her convictions. "Even during her detention Marianne Joachim . . . used the secret message to encourage the accused Hanni Meyer to adhere to her treasonable position."[68] Thus the language of the Nazi prosecuting authorities! The actual content of the secret message concerned the limited possibilities for these arrested to meet each other and their families. Despite the dreadful news of the execution of her colleagues in the resistance – perhaps including her husband – and despite the knowledge that her own death was imminent, Marianne still found the strength to encourage her fellow prisoners. She was just 21 years old.

Her farewell letter to her parents, which has survived, expresses the same spirit. It is dated 4th March 1943, the day of her execution. She expressed her concern for the welfare of her parents and urged them to be brave, for the sake of her sister Ilse. "If you receive this letter, I will no longer be alive. You can believe that I was courageous to the last second. How I would like to be certain that you too will have the strength to face what cannot be changed . . . For the last time I kiss you in my thoughts."[69]

Rita Resnik-Meyer

Until shortly before her death in 1983, Rita Resnik-Meyer continued to pass on to others all that she knew about the Baum Group. She was particularly concerned that young people should become aware of it. "That is my only task, to tell of what I have experienced and seen."[70]

Rita Resnik was born in Kishinev, Russia, in 1915. At the age of 12 she joined the *Deutsch-jüdische Jugendgemeinschaft*. There she met Herbert Baum and Sala Rosenbaum-Kochmann, with whom she maintained contact when she joined the illegal KJVD. When Jewish Communists looked for opportunities to organise legally in 1936, Rita joined a drama group.[71]

After the arson attack of May 1942 and the subsequent wave of arrests, Rita and her husband set up a base for those group members who were still at liberty.[72] However, in October the *Gestapo* discovered the small band of helpers and Rita was arrested with her husband Herbert, Charlotte Abraham-Holzer and Martin Kochmann.[73] By the time Rita and eight other defendants from the escape-helpers group went on trial before the *Strafsenat* on 25th June 1943, her husband had already been murdered while in detention.[74] The Nazis sent Rita to the extermination camp of Auschwitz. Her five-year-old daughter was murdered; Rita was never able to discover exactly when and where.

---

[68]Judgement against Heinz Rotholz *et al.*, in Jahnke and Buddrus, *op. cit.*, p. 448.
[69]Farewell letter from Marianne Prager-Joachim to her parents, quoted in Paucker and Steinberg, 'Some Notes on Resistance', p. 248.
[70]Miriam Lilina, 'Rita Zocher', in *Sowjetisch Heimatland*, 12, Moscow 1978, p. 40.
[71]*Ibid.*, p. 37.
[72]See undated and unpublished report by Charlotte Abraham-Holzer, p. 2.
[73]See Scheffler, 'Der Brandanschlag', p. 95.
[74]*Ibid.*, p. 104; Kwiet and Eschwege, *Selbstbehauptung und Widerstand*, p. 137.

Any discussion of the merciless persecution of those who assisted the resistance fighters must also include mention of the *Gestapo* reprisals against the Jewish population of Berlin after the arson attack on *Das Sowjetparadies*. Many Jews completely unconnected with any resistance activities or helping fugitives fell victim to the Nazi thirst for revenge. On 27th May 1942, shortly after the Baum Group launched its attack, the *Gestapo* arrested 154 Jewish men in Berlin. They were shot in Sachsenhausen concentration camp along with at least 96 other Jewish camp inmates. Relatives of the murdered hostages were sent to Theresienstadt. In a further measure, 250 Berlin Jews of both sexes were sent to Sachsenhausen, where most were tortured to death. The survivors were dispatched to certain death in Auschwitz in October 1942.[75] The Berlin representatives of the Jewish community were instructed by the *Reichssicherheitshauptamt* to inform the Jewish population "that further measures of this kind can be expected if one more act of sabotage in which Jews are involved should take place".[76] It was in this climate of fear and persecution that Rita and her husband had declared themselves willing to help fugitives and to assist those attempting to go underground.[77] When Martin Kochmann fell gravely ill, he was cared for by Charlotte Abraham-Holzer in Rita's house.

Rita also provided contact to the families of these who had gone into hiding, passed on ration cards, and organised quarters for Charlotte Abraham-Holzer and Martin Kochmann. Furthermore, she attempted to obtain false papers on the black market.[78] To finance the ration cards and false identity papers, Rita sold "requisitioned" valuables at the beginning of May 1942; Herbert Baum, disguised as a *Gestapo* official, had gained entry into the home of a Jewish family named Freundlich and had "confiscated" carpets and silver.[79] The obtaining of ration cards was already fraught with difficulties, as is shown by this comment by Ruth Andreas-Friedrich, a member of the "*Onkel Emil*" group: "Hundreds, thousands, tens of thousands, risking their necks every hour and every day for a couple of miserable bread coupons, a temporary emergency shelter. A little, a little more, a little more again . . . wrested pertinaciously in defiance of all bans, laws and propaganda orders. No-one who did not go through it themselves can imagine how difficult it can be to provide even the simplest assistance under such circumstances."[80]

Rita asked her schoolfriend Ursula Reinke and a non-Jewish couple named Milkert to hide Martin Kochmann. Only a few days later they were arrested by

---

[75]The reprisals were carried out partly as revenge for the assassination of Heydrich only a few days after the attack. They rapidly became the stuff of legend. Wolfgang Scheffler has provided a detailed reconstruction of events. See Scheffler, 'Der Brandanschlag', pp. 106, 110. Also Heinz Boberach (ed.), *Meldungen aus dem Reich. Die geheimen Lagerberichte des Sicherheitsdienstes der SS*, vol. 10, Berlin 1984, pp. 3754–3755.

[76]Memorandum of the Vienna representative Dr. Josef Löwenherz of 1st June 1942, quoted in Scheffler, 'Der Brandanschlag', p. 111.

[77]Report of Abraham-Holzer, p. 2.

[78]See Kwiet and Eschwege, *Selbstbehauptung und Widerstand*, p. 136; report of Abraham-Holzer, p. 2.

[79]See *Charlottenburger Zeitung*, 13th May 1942: 'Bandenstreich falscher Kriminalbeamter'. This incident was also mentioned in the judgement against Heinz Rotholz *et al.*, in Jahnke and Buddrus, *op. cit.* See also Kwiet and Eschwege, *Selbstbehauptung und Widerstand*, pp. 124–125.

[80]Ruth Andreas-Friedrich, *Der Schattenmann*, Frankfurt a. Main 1986, pp. 128–129.

the *Gestapo*. From October to December, the resistance fighters and their helpers still at liberty fell into the clutches of the *Gestapo*. On 22nd December, *Amt IV* of the *Reichssicherheitshauptamt* reported the arrest of 18 people "who belonged to the Communist organisation founded by the Jew Herbert Israel Baum".[81] The list contained the names of Rita, her husband Herbert, Martin Kochmann and Charlotte Abraham-Holzer.

Dreadful sessions of interrogation followed. After sentence in June 1943, Rita was transported to Auschwitz. She recalled with great clarity the condition in which she arrived there. "When I opened my eyes a Soviet woman doctor named Klawa was standing next to me. She bent over me and said that I was still alive. If it had not been for Klawa and the other friends, German, Soviet, Polish Communists, I would not have survived. I never doubted who would win the struggle, but whether I would stay alive . . . I thought, that was not so important. But as you see, I did survive."[82]

Rosel Dzsida-Bibo

Looking back, Rosel Dzida-Bibo says of her decision to go into hiding: "With all our strength we tore ourselves out of our lethargy and resolved to act. We wanted to stop just impotently letting everything happen to us."[83]

Rosel Dzsida was born in Basle in 1913, but grew up in Berlin. There she trained as a tailor, joined her union, became involved in the *Internationale Arbeiterhilfe* (IAH) and was active in sport through the workers' sport association *Fichte*. Rosel was friendly with Herbert and Marianne Baum, who suggested that Rosel and her husband Siegfried should join them. The idea came to nothing, because the resistance work of the Baum couple would have drawn Rosel and her husband into great danger.[84] In December 1942, with the deportation trains leaving Berlin for the East, Rosel and Siegfried decided to go into hiding.

By the end of 1941 the social and physical segregation of the Jewish population was complete. They were robbed of their rights, denied employment, driven from their homes and subject to supervision and persecution by the Nazis. From autumn 1940, German-Jewish women and men were compelled to do forced labour. Rosel was one of approximately 900 women forced labourers in the electro-motor works of *Siemens-Schuckert-Werke AG*.

Rosel remembers: "We had to assemble at the factory gate, were fetched to work all together and brought out again together. First of all I was in the *Entgraterei*. You had to meet your target or else you were in danger of being picked up. So you always got the older people's work from the box and trimmed it, since they could not do the set amount. Later I was at the tin bath, I had to tin with both hands. Aryan women only with one hand, and they got an extra litre of

---

[81]Report of 22nd December 1942, cited in Margot Pikarski, *Gestapo-Berichte. Über den antifaschistischen Widerstand der KPD 1939–1943*, vol. 2, East Berlin 1989, pp. 323–324.
[82]Rita Resnik-Meyer, quoted in Lilina, 'Rita Zocher', p. 40.
[83]Rosel Bibo, 'Angst – Verfolgung – Illegalität', in Gerda Szepansky, *Frauen leisten Widerstand 1933–1945*, Frankfurt a. Main 1988, p. 241.
[84]*Ibid.*, p. 229.

full milk each day. My food ration consisted of six or seven potatoes with some salt. Sometimes I only worked automatically, was really ill with exhaustion, but we were not allowed to sit down."[85] In addition there was the constant fear of being taken from work and deported. "If we were led through dark alleys before we reached our places of work, I always thought: something will happen to us here some day. So I always had a feeling of fear. One no longer felt like a human being, in this constant awareness of fear."[86]

Ellen Compart, a Jewish forced labourer with *I. G. Farben* who joined the resistance group round Herbert Baum,[87] witnessed the arrest of Hella and Alice Hirsch after the arson attack of May 1942. The Hirsch sisters both came from the *Ring – Bund deutsch-jüdischer Jugend* and were subsequently active in the resistance.[88] "Meanwhile I had been 'conscripted' to I. G. Farben acetate works at Rummelsburg. Hella Hirsch had been sent there too, we saw each other every day, were very close to each other . . . One week later she was arrested at work. This gentle little person was taken away in handcuffs by two gigantic bulls of *Gestapo* men. That same day Hella's younger sister Alice was taken as well. I stood alongside, scarcely grasping that the same thing was not happening to me."[89] Ellen Compart was one of the few members of the Baum Group to go into hiding and survive.[90]

At the beginning of the deportations, 72,972 Jews were still living in Berlin. By September 1943 there were only 6,790 left. Konrad Kwiet and Helmut Eschwege estimate that some 7% of Berlin Jews went underground. A quarter of all those in hiding survived.[91] From the beginning of 1943 until July of that year, the percentage of those in hiding rose from 13% to 42%. Consequently, of the Berlin Jews registered in 1941, only 2% survived underground. Among the few survivors was Rosel Dzsida-Bibo.

After the onset of the deportations and the ban on emigration in October 1941, escape usually meant going into hiding or ended in suicide. Rosel was told by a neighbour, a soldier home on leave, that Jewish men and women were being gassed in lorries[92] and that he himself had been involved as a co-driver. She knew that the deportations led to certain death. "No one has come back to tell us anything."[93] Even in early March 1940, Else Behrend-Rosenfeld had written in her diary of her terrible suspicions about the real fate of the deportees. "And what are these people to do in Poland? Is the idea to give them specific work? So why have they taken the very old with them? But what use is it to ask questions upon questions!"[94] Rumours about the whereabouts of the deportees leaked out, as

---

[85]*Ibid.*, p. 226; on working conditions see Pikarski, *Sie bleiben unvergessen*, pp. 31–32.
[86]Bibo, 'Angst', p. 233.
[87]Pikarski, *Jugend im Berliner Widerstand*, p. 94.
[88]See judgement against Heinz Rotholz *et al.*, in Jahnke and Buddrus, *op. cit.*, p. 450.
[89]Letter from Ellen Compart-Salinger to Charlotte Abraham-Holzer, 28th February 1968.
[90]Apart from her, Ursula Ehrlich also survived in hiding; see Kwiet and Eschwege, *Selbstbehauptung und Widerstand*, p. 137.
[91]See *ibid.*, p. 151.
[92]Bibo, 'Angst', pp. 234–235.
[93]*Ibid.*, p. 229.
[94]Else Rahel Behrend-Rosenfeld, *Ich stand nicht allein. Erlebnisse einer Jüdin in Deutschland 1933–1944*, Munich 1988, p. 80.

Ruth Andreas-Friedrich – a Christian who helped Jews to go into hiding – noted in her diary on 19th September 1941. "Some days ago the third and last Jewish departures began. Fetched from their homes. Compulsory evacuations with unknown destinations. 'To Polish camps', some say, 'To certain death', others prophesy."[95] These rumours proliferated and, by the end of 1942, had become dreadful certainty. From July 1942 onwards, Else Behrend-Rosenfeld had no doubt that the people deported to Poland were being murdered.[96] Inge Deutschkron heard about the gassings and mass-shootings on the BBC in November 1942.[97]

Irrespective of how much each individual knew, deportation itself was certain; Else Behrend-Rosenfeld referred to it as the "abyss". The move into hiding was thus a decision to oppose the only certainty which still existed – the certainty of deportation.[98] Rosel Dzsida-Bibo calculated that "all who stayed at home would be taken eventually".[99] She therefore resolved not to wait for the deportation order, but to act. "Yes, we dropped everything, just packed a rucksack, took off the [yellow] star and, very early on the morning of 12th December 1942, went by tram to the home of friends in Kreuzberg. On the way I cried so much that Siegfried said: 'The way you are behaving, we'll never get there.' . . . And I looked at all the people on the way, because I always thought they were already on our track."[100] They spent the night with their friends and took the train to Alt-Hüttendorf next day, to Rosel's friend Hanne, who ran a tailor's workshop with her partner Jupp. Hanne insisted that only Rosel could work for her and that Siegfried would have to hide somewhere else. When Rosel refused point blank – "either both, or neither of us" – Hanne agreed to give refuge to Siegfried as well.[101]

Shortly after Rosel went underground, the Nazis deported all Jewish forced labourers from the *Elmo-Werke*. Thanks to the support of her friend Hanne, who surmounted the many difficulties involved in giving shelter to "illegals", Rosel and her husband survived to see the collapse of the Nazi dictatorship.[102]

IV

All the women described here were fundamentally opposed to the National Socialist regime. Their active resistance was based on their Communist

---

[95] Andreas-Friedrich, *Der Schattenmann*, p. 83.

[96] Behrend–Rosenfeld, *Ich stand nicht allein*, p. 166.

[97] See Deutschkron, *Ich trug den gelben Stern*, p. 100.

[98] See Ilse Rewald, in Kwiet and Eschwege, *Selbstbehauptung und Widerstand*, p. 152.

[99] Bibo, 'Angst', p. 235.

[100] *Ibid.*, p. 236.

[101] *Ibid.*, p. 231.

[102] The experiences and strategies of those who went underground form a unique subject which has been little researched as yet and is only touched on in this essay.* See Kwiet and Eschwege, *Selbstbehauptung und Widerstand*, pp. 152–159.*

* However, see the essay by Avraham Seligmann, 'An Illegal Way of Life in Nazi Germany', which is the first essay in this section of the Year Book – (Ed.).

convictions, or at the very least their pro-Communist sentiments. However, the exclusion of the entire Jewish population from the majority Gentile society also had an impact on their self-image. As Walter Sack explains, many of them made the sudden "discovery" that they were Jews.[103]

In the case of these German-Jewish resistance fighters, the struggle against National Socialism overlapped with the dangers they faced because of their ethnic identity. The following two testimonies are taken from the resistance circle round Herbert Baum, and clearly demonstrate how the two motives became interlinked. Hildegard Loewy, a member of the Left-wing Zionist *Hashomer Hazair* until 1938 and subsequently involved in the Baum Group, was "questioned" by the *Gestapo* about the reasons for her illegal work: "We saw . . . our only salvation lay in Germany sometime acquiring another state constitution."[104] Similar motives for resistance can be detected in the record of the interrogation of Lotte Jastrow-Rotholz, who was barely 19 years old: "So far as I know it was clear to all of us that one could have no positive relationship to the current regime because of the persecution of the Jews by the government of Germany, and that every opportunity to fight against the regime had to be taken. I am not personally politically educated . . . but one thing was clear to me, that as a Jewess I cannot stand back . . . We were and are linked with Baum."[105]

The progressive exclusion of the Jewish population limited its freedom of action to an ever greater degree and particularly the choices for Jewish resistance fighters. While non-Jewish women could always withdraw from the struggle in the hope of escaping further political persecution, this route was never open to Jewish women in the resistance.[106] Because of their ethnic identity they were the target of racist persecution whatever they did.

Jewish defendants faced drastically lower chances of survival and much harsher punishment following their arrest. Lotte Jastrow-Rotholz, who was only involved on the periphery of resistance activity, was first sentenced to eight years' imprisonment, then very likely sent to Theresienstadt and subsequently murdered. Edith Fränkel, sentenced to five years' imprisonment by the People's Court, probably suffered the same fate.[107] From July 1943 the German courts were no longer responsible for the sentencing of Jews, which passed instead to the SS.[108]

The avoidance of deportation orders was a specifically Jewish form of self-defence undertaken in defiance of the persecutors' intention to extinguish all Jewish life.[109] Yet the step towards an "illegal" existence was far from easy and was not lightly regarded as an acceptable alternative.[110] Often it was women

[103]See Sack, manuscript, p. 8.
[104]Quoted in Pikarski, *Sie bleiben unvergessen*, p. 58.
[105]Quoted in Mark, 'Die Gruppe Baum', p. 40.
[106]See Gerda Zorn, 'Mein alltäglicher Faschismus', in Charles Schüddekopf (ed.), *Der alltägliche Faschismus. Frauen im Dritten Reich*, Berlin 1982, pp. 33–67.
[107]See Kwiet and Eschwege, *Selbstbehauptung und Widerstand*, p. 132; judgement against Heinz Rothholz *et al.*, in Jahnke and Buddrus, *op. cit.*, p. 448.
[108]Kwiet and Eschwege, *Selbstbehauptung und Widerstand*, p. 137.
[109]*Ibid.*, p. 150.
[110]See Ilse Rewald, *ibid.*, p. 153.

who decided against going underground out of concern for other members of their families. Walter Sack remembers Regina Gänzel, leader of a children's group in the *Ring – Bund deutsch-jüdischer Jugend*, who refused to go into hiding because it would mean leaving her mother. "She could still have left Germany in 1939 with her mother. Floh (cover name) made contact with her in 1943 and advised her to go underground. She told him she could not go into hiding because she had to look after her mother. Both were then deported to Auschwitz."[111]

Rather less attention has been paid to the social implications of resistance faced by women as mothers. Charlotte Abraham-Holzer, Rita Resnik-Meyer and Lotte Jastrow-Rotholz all had small children to care for. Charlotte Abraham-Holzer told of the difficulties of housing and feeding her daughter Eva, especially during the period of persecution. For a time she even lived in hiding with her child.[112] Overall, the special problems facing such women deserve closer investigation. It should be directed both at the women who went into hiding and were forced to leave members of their families without anyone to care for them, and at others who actually refused to go underground for that reason.

In the last analysis it is almost impossible to define the exact motivation of the Jewish women who joined the resistance against National Socialism. Certainly the racist persecution which threatened all Jewish life was a decisive factor. However, rather than creating a hierarchy of motives, I believe it is valid to refer to an interaction between Communist conviction, ethnic identity and gender to explain the courageous struggle waged by Sala, Marianne, Rita and Rosel.

[111]Sack, manuscript, p. 13. Ingrid Strobl noted similar experiences among the women who resolved to join the armed resistance.
[112]See Irene Runge, 'Das Wort Held mag ich nicht', in *DDR-Revue*, 25, Jg. 2 (1980), p. 19; report of Abraham-Holzer, pp. 1–2.

German and Austrian Jews in Britain's Armed Forces and British and German Citizenship Policies 1939–1945

BY JOHN P. FOX

The United Kingdom's declaration of war on Germany on 3rd September 1939 was to have a profound effect upon the situation of the thousands of Jewish refugees who had sought refuge there from the Third *Reich*. The new situation of war exacerbated all the elements involved in the strict application of United Kingdom alien law, although some public pressure was directed at government for it to be applied more humanely. Most often this conflict of interests concerned, in the words of Frank Newsam, a senior Home Office official, "the widest possible liberty consistent with law and order", the balance of which it was incumbent upon the Home Office to uphold.[1] During the war this conflict was epitomised in the subject of internment,[2] together with that of the naturalisation, and its corollary, the repatriation of aliens, including those who had served in the British armed forces. The conflict of laws and the position of the individual was particularly intense insofar as "enemy aliens" of Jewish origin from Germany and Austria were concerned. Yet for the United Kingdom, the management during the Second World War of the Jewish-alien question was not unique, since from the massive wave of Russian-Jewish immigrants during the 1880s and beyond, there had always been a Jewish alien "question" in one form or the other.[3]

Having known Arnold Paucker well for almost twenty years, and often been encouraged in pursuing my particular lines of argument by him, my only regret about my present contribution is that it should be the first and the last to appear in a volume of the Year Book edited by him. The chapter is therefore particularly dedicated to Arnold Paucker for two reasons: to express my thanks for his friendship and support to a Gentile friend and colleague in the study of modern Jewish history; and to acknowledge the debt the chapter owes to his suggestions.

[1]Peter and Leni Gillman, *'Collar the Lot!' How Britain Interned and Expelled Its Wartime Refugees*, London 1980, p. 92.

[2]Cf. Gillman, *op. cit.*, *passim*; Miriam Kochan, *Britain's Internees in the Second World War*, London 1983; François Lafitte, *The Internment of Aliens*, London 1988, new edn.

[3]Cf. Shmuel Almog, 'Antisemitism as a Dynamic Phenomenon: The "Jewish Question" in England at the End of the First World War', in *Patterns of Prejudice*, vol. 21, No. 4 (Winter 1987), pp. 3–18; C. C. Aronsfeld, 'Jewish Enemy Aliens in England During the First World War', in *Jewish Social Studies*, vol. XVIII, No. 4 (1956), pp. 275–283; Marion Berghahn, *German-Jewish Refugees in England. The Ambiguities of Assimilation*, London 1984; Eugene C. Black, *The Social Politics of Anglo-Jewry 1880–1920*, Oxford 1988, in particular chap. 9: 'The Alien Question', pp. 243–270; Joseph Buckman, *Immigrants and the Class Struggle. The Jewish Immigrant in Leeds 1880–1914*, Manchester 1983; David Cesarani, 'Anti-Alienism in England After the First World War', in *Immigrants and Minorities*, vol. 6, No. 1 (March 1987), pp. 5–29; Bernard Gainer, *The Alien Invasion. The Origins of the Aliens Act of 1905*,

Yet whatever detail of British policy concerning aliens was involved, British official discussions were necessarily conducted from the perspective of "government" and how "British interests" were interpreted by politicians and the bureaucracy, rather than by any abstract notions of "humanity". In this respect, the United Kingdom was no different from any other twentieth-century State, the chief characteristic of which is the unlimited power it abrogates to itself to determine virtually every aspect of its citizens' lives, something especially acute in a time of war,[4] even to the extent of involving its citizens and others, as did the Third *Reich*, in a policy of Europe-wide mass murder. In the United Kingdom, the power of government to regulate the lives of its citizens was confirmed by the Emergency Powers (Defence) Act, which became law on 25th August 1939, and the subsequent Defence Regulations designed to restrict civil liberties.[5] The State and its servants thus also have extensive powers to determine the nature and numbers of its citizen body, as well as of others "permitted" to reside within its borders under certain conditions.[6]

It is necessary also to acknowledge the fact that in national or international political life there is no sense of "imperative responsibility" on the part of groups and governments for the fate of specific minority groups in other societies, or even in their own societies if those groups are "outsiders" to begin with. Statements such as "the plight of Jews was perceived as a problem of immigration rather than a duty of rescue" underline the sense of naivety with

---

London 1972; John A. Garrard, *The English and Immigration 1880–1910. A Comparative Study of the Jewish Influx*, Oxford 1971; Lloyd P. Gartner, *The Jewish Immigrant in England 1870–1914*, London 1960, especially the section, 'Native Jewry and Immigration', pp. 49–56; Colin Holmes, *Anti-Semitism in British Society 1876–1939*, London 1979; idem, *John Bull's Island. Immigration and British Society 1871–1971*, London 1988; Sharman Kadish, 'Boche, Bolshie and the Jewish Bogey: The Russian Revolution and Press Antisemitism in Britain 1917–21', in *Patterns of Prejudice*, vol. 22, No. 4 (Winter 1988), pp. 24–39; Tony Kushner, *The Persistence of Prejudice. Antisemitism in British Society During the Second World War*, Manchester 1989; Louise London, 'British Government Policy and Jewish Refugees 1933–45', in *Patterns of Prejudice*, vol. 23, No. 4 (Winter 1989–90), pp. 26–43; idem, 'Jewish Refugees, Anglo-Jewry and British Government Policy, 1930–1940', pp. 163–190 in David Cesarani (ed.), *The Making of Modern Anglo-Jewry*, Oxford 1990; idem, 'British Immigration Control Procedures and Jewish Refugees 1933–1939', in Werner E. Mosse (co-ordinating ed.), Julius Carlebach, Gerhard Hirschfeld, Aubrey Newman, Arnold Paucker and Peter Pulzer (eds.), *Second Chance. Two Centuries of German-speaking Jews in the United Kingdom*, Tübingen 1991 (Schriftenreihe wissenschaftlicher Abhandlungen des Leo Baeck Instituts 48), pp. 485–517; Aubrey Newman (ed.), *The Jewish East End 1840–1939. Proceedings of the Conference held on 22 October 1980 jointly by the Jewish Historical Society of England and the Jewish East End Project of the Association for Jewish Youth*, London 1981; Panikos Panayi, 'Anti-German Riots in London During the First World War', in *German History*, vol. 7, No. 2 (August 1989), pp. 184–203; Jill Pellew, 'The Home Office and the Aliens Act, 1905', in *The Historical Journal*, vol. XXXII, No. 2 (1989), pp. 369–385; A. J. Sherman, *Island Refuge. Britain and Refugees from the Third Reich 1933–1939*, London 1973; Bill Williams, *The Making of Manchester Jewry 1740–1875*, Manchester 1976.

[4]On the question of the power of the modern State, cf. Robert Justin Goldstein, *Political Repression in 19th Century Europe*, London 1983; Neil Stammers, *Civil Liberties in Britain During the Second World War. A Political Study*, London 1983.

[5]*Ibid.*, pp. 11–22.

[6]Although it is open to criticism, this subject is dealt with quite well in Michael R. Marrus, *The Unwanted. European Refugees in the Twentieth Century*, London–New York 1985. See also the collection of essays in Anna C. Bramwell (ed.), *Refugees in the Age of Total War*, London 1988.

which many observers approach these subjects.[7] This is not to say that humanitarian feelings do not exist, but their influence upon policy comes to depend entirely upon what one might term "pragmatic responsibility", i.e. what is politically and practically possible at any one time to help those in need, within the strict limitation that such responsibility can never be universal or total.[8]

A case in point of the inherent conflict between "imperative" and "pragmatic" responsibilities of governments and individuals in the modern world, and indeed of the conflict of interests referred to by Newsam, is that of the German and Austrian Jews who served in the British Armed Forces during the Second World War and the attempts by some to gain British citizenship at its conclusion. Yet their efforts in this direction came to be submerged in a vast complex of difficult political and legal issues with international dimensions. Moreover, it was a German law of 25th November 1941 which acted as a further catalyst for the hardening of British official attitudes towards them when their position in the United Kingdom was seen to be in potential conflict with "British interests".

One immediate consequence of the United Kingdom's declaration of war on Germany was the classification of the 70,000 Germans and Austrians resident in the country as enemy aliens. At least 55,000 of those were refugees from Hitler's *Großdeutschland*, a large proportion of whom were Jews. On 4th September 1939 the Secretary of State for the Home Office, Sir John Anderson, informed the House of Commons that the Aliens Order of 1920 had been strengthened to provide closer controls over both enemy and neutral aliens, resulting in the detention of several hundreds. On the other hand, there was to be an immediate review of all Germans and Austrians in the United Kingdom, through special Aliens Tribunals established in London and the provinces, to establish who could be left at large, who interned, and who subjected to other restrictions.

In stating that discussions were proceeding with the Ministry of Labour "as to the manner in which use can be made of the services of aliens who are not at present at liberty to take employment", Sir John Anderson was in part answering, and at the same time deflecting, the unsuccessful attempt on 3rd September in the House of Commons by Josiah Wedgwood MP, to persuade the government to allow German and Austrian refugees to volunteer for military service.[9]

Of particular interest was Anderson's refusal to answer immediately Wedgwood's question about which category stateless Jews were to be placed in, Czech or German. Anderson's comment that he desired notice of the question, or at least time to investigate the matter,[10] indicated the political importance of the precise nationality of alien Jewish refugees. Two days later the Home Secretary supplied a written answer, a preliminary statement of the government's position

---

[7]London, 'Jewish Refugees, Anglo-Jewry, and British Government Policy, 1930–1940', *loc. cit.*, p. 163.
[8]John P. Fox, 'German and European Jewish Refugees 1933–1945: Reflections on the Jewish Condition under Hitler and the Western World's Response to their Expulsion and Flight', in Bramwell, *op. cit.*, pp. 69–85, esp. p. 80.
[9]*Parliamentary Debates*, 5th Series, House of Commons (= HC), vol. 351, col. 303, 3rd September 1939.
[10]HC, vol. 351, cols. 366–370, 4th September 1939; *ibid.*, vol. 351, col. 970, 20th September 1939.

on what, in subsequent years, was to become one of the most fractious questions it had to deal with. The government's position was that refugees retained their original nationality and hence were the legal responsibility of their countries of origin, not of the United Kingdom, wherein they resided on a temporary basis only: "refugees from Germany and Austria who were nationals of those countries are registered as either Germans or Austrians and must therefore be so classified for the purpose of the review of all German and Austrian cases, notwithstanding that they may have been deprived of German nationality by some German law".[11]

Nevertheless, an inkling of the other directions in which such issues could develop was indicated a month later during exchanges in the House of Commons when the question of the naturalisation of aliens was discussed. On 3rd October, Osbert Peake, the Home Office Minister, denied there was any connection between the grant of work permits to aliens and eligibility for naturalisation. Yet when Peake stated that if "an alien renders good service to this country during the war, account must obviously be taken of this, together with all other relevant considerations, should he subsequently apply for naturalisation", and Sir John Anderson replied in a similar vein on 5th October to a question about military service by aliens affecting their chances of naturalisation,[12] the British government seemed to be offering positive hope for the future to alien refugees in the United Kingdom. Nevertheless, for those prescient enough, a word of warning was contained in Anderson's statement that "none of the persons naturalised in 1938 were persons who came here under the recent arrangements for the temporary admission of refugees with a view to re-emigration".[13] This was followed on 23rd November by his statement that applications for naturalisation received before the outbreak of war would be processed, but those received after the outbreak of war would not.[14] Thus, the key planks of British policy on the naturalisation of alien refugees, Jewish or otherwise, were set out and remained so for the duration of the war.

Yet Wedgwood's efforts on 3rd September seemed to have struck a chord in the Home Office. On 4th September, Sir Alexander Maxwell, Permanent Under-Secretary of State at the Home Office, proposed to Sir James Grigg, Permanent Under-Secretary of State for War, an inter-department meeting to discuss the question of utilising the services of refugees in a military sense.[15] That meeting took place on 12th September at the Home Office, with representatives from the War Office, and the Ministries of Health and Labour. Sir James Grigg

[11]HC, vol. 351, col. 548, 6th September 1939.
[12]HC, vol. 351, cols. 1823–1824, 3rd October 1939, col. 2127, 5th October 1939.
[13]HC, vol. 351, col. 2073, 5th October 1939.
[14]HC, vol. 353, cols. 1434–1435, 23rd November 1939.
[15]Public Record Office, Kew. Home Office Documents, principally Alien Department Papers (= HO). HO 213/262. GEN. 29/15/127, Sir Alexander Maxwell to Sir James Grigg, 4th September 1939. An echo of the nature of some jingoistic anti-alien feeling in the United Kingdom was sounded in the House of Commons on 4th September when Mr. William Sampson Cluse, MP, asked Sir John Anderson, "will the right hon. Gentleman see to it that where aliens are proved to be enemy aliens and have to be interned, they will be put to productive work instead of acting as parasites on the nation?" Anderson replied, "that will be considered": HC, vol. 351, col. 370, 4th September 1939.

said the War Office was prepared to accept aliens in the Army, provided that if they were Germans, Austrians, or Czechs they had been vetted and passed by one of the new aliens tribunals. Yet aliens were to be kept out of the Royal Navy and Air Force, where it was easier to perform acts of sabotage than in the Army. Doctors, however, could form an exception to this rule and be allowed into any of the services. The meeting agreed that all aliens – Germans, Austrians and Czechs only after having been passed by a tribunal – could enrol in the Civil Defence Services, other than in the Police War Reserve or as Air Raid Wardens. It was considered to be "obvious that aliens, however trustworthy, would not inspire confidence in either of these occupations".[16] Following customary practice, an announcement of this decision was made the following day in the House of Commons in reply to an apparently random question by Geoffrey le Mesurier Mander, MP.[17]

This decision eventually paved the way for the recruitment of aliens into the Auxiliary Military Pioneer Corps following the announcement by the Secretary of State for War, Leslie Hore-Belisha, in the House of Commons on 11th October 1939.[18] In the meantime, the conditions laid down on 12th September were met by the work begun on 28th September 1939 by the aliens tribunals. Some 120 tribunals were established in order to divide enemy aliens into three categories: "A", to be interned; "B", exempt from internment but subject to the restrictions decreed by a Special Order relating to the notification of the residence, travel, and ownership of cameras etc. of enemy aliens; and "C", exempt from both internment and restrictions. The tribunals also had to make a supplementary decision whether the individual in question should be classified as "a refugee from Nazi oppression" or placed in a class of "non-refugees". Their findings were stamped on the alien's registration card.[19]

During the final months of 1939, however, the tentative steps taken in the direction of a more sensible and less "war hysteria" approach to the problem of alien "investigation", itself symptomatic of a growing realisation that the final months of 1939 would not see a repetition of those of 1914, was accompanied by increasing demands that the British government utilise the service of refugees from Nazism in the British war effort, however that might be defined in the opening stages of what ultimately became "a total war" for all societies involved.[20] Whilst in December 1939 those demands concerned the civilian employment of enemy aliens (or "refugees" – and hereafter referred to as alien

---

[16]HO 213/262. GEN. 29/15/127, Unsigned Record of Meeting in Home Office, 12th September 1939.
[17]HC, vol. 351, cols. 648–649, 13th September 1939. On 2nd November, Sir John Anderson repeated this point in the House of Commons: HC, vol. 352, cols. 295–296, 2nd November 1939.
[18]HC, vol. 352, cols. 347–348, 11th October 1939.
[19]These paragraphs are based on Kochan, *op. cit.*, chap. 1: 'The Sheep and the Goats' and chap. 2: 'The Greatest Possible Expedition'. For the Home Office guidelines to the chairmen of the Aliens Tribunals concerning the main types of enemy aliens, see Gillman, *op. cit.*, pp. 43–44. For more on the vetting process, see *ibid.*, pp. 44–45; Kochan, *op. cit.*, pp. 16–17.
[20]Cf. Arthur Marwick, *Britain in the Century of Total War. War, Peace and Social Change 1900–1967*, London 1968; *idem, War and Social Change in the Twentieth Century. A Comparative Study of Britain, France, Germany, Russia and the United States*, London 1974.

refugees), it is the process begun in November which is of particular concern here.

In November 1939, alien refugees were finally permitted to enlist in certain branches of the armed forces[21] and this granted them exemption from registration under article 22 of the Aliens Order, although it did nothing to change their nationality particulars. This followed a government statement that aliens approved by the Military Intelligence Branch of the War Office would be allowed to join a new army formation of the Auxiliary Military Pioneer Corps (AMPC), known from 1940 simply as the Pioneer Corps.[22] The AMPC, formed on 17th October 1939 under Army Order 200 of 1939, was essentially a military labour unit whose members, often known as "Sappers", were "of course, the jacks-of-all-trades".[23] As such, it was regarded as "the dumping ground of the British army; all human dross, it was once unkindly said, was there. It was the natural home of illiterates and former criminals."[24] But not always. Arthur Koestler, the influential writer, was once a Pioneer, while other writers, musicians, actors and intellectuals helped to mark out the Corps as something different in the annals of the British army.[25]

Nevertheless, many alien refugees were quick to take up such an opportunity. First, many desperately wanted to leave the institutionalised environment of transit camps, especially when the chances of civilian unemployment remained so uncertain. Second, by joining such a unit, despite its shortcomings, there was at least generated a feeling of "getting back" at the Nazi regime of Germany. And third, there was the positive encouragement (at least in the way they read it) concerning future naturalisation procedures contained in statements in the House of Commons in October.

The new AMPC was the only branch of Britain's armed forces open to such alien refugees. An alien could not hold a rank higher than that of Warrant Officer. Although the restrictions of the Army Act were suspended by the Defence Regulations, which gave authority for the unrestricted enlistment and commission of aliens, in practice and for three years at least, the military authorities were unwilling, for security reasons, to admit them to any combatant, intelligence, and technical unit – except the Commandos and Parachutists – nor did they ever favour the idea which had long been adopted in France of a fighting foreign legion.[26]

---

[21] Kochan, *op. cit.*, p. 17.

[22] Norman Bentwich, *I Understand the Risks. The Story of the Refugees from Nazi Oppression who fought in the British Forces in the World War*, London 1950, p. 31. The change of title was announced in the House of Commons on 26th November 1940 by Anthony Eden, Secretary of State for War: HC, vol. 367, col. 131.

[23] Major E. H. Rhodes-Wood, *A War History of the Royal Pioneer Corps 1939–1945*, Aldershot 1960, pp. 9, 86.

[24] Gillman, *op. cit.*, p. 257; Rhodes-Wood, *op. cit.*, pp. 17–19, 83–84.

[25] Bentwich, *Risks, op. cit.*, pp. 52–62, esp. p. 56 for Koestler. See also, J. M. Ritchie, 'Germans and Austrians in Exile in Great Britain. Inaugural Lecture delivered on 31 October 1988', in *Aberdeen University Review*, 181 (Spring 1989), pp. 18–29, esp. p. 23. I am extremely grateful to Professor J. M. Ritchie, Director of the Research Centre for Germans and Austrians in Exile in Great Britain, of the University of Aberdeen, for having sent me a copy of his inaugural lecture.

[26] Bentwich, *Risks, op. cit.*, pp. 63–64; Rhodes-Wood, *op. cit.*, p. 22.

Upon its formation, the AMPC established five Training and Reception Centres (TRCs), each designed to produce four trained companies a month, in addition to providing reinforcements for companies already in France.[27] One TRC for special "Alien Companies" (ACs) was actually established at a well-known transit camp for (in the main) Jewish refugees from Germany and Austria, at Richborough on the Kent coast adjoining Sandwich, although it actually consisted of two camps, the Kitchener and Haig Camps.[28] On 25th October 1939, when the Marquis of Reading assumed command of Number 3 TRC at Richborough, and 16th November, when the first alien was enlisted, it could be said that German- and Austrian-Jewish refugees from the Third *Reich* resident in the United Kingdom were at last "taking up arms" against the enemy, albeit in unarmed units popularly known as the "King's Own Enemy Aliens".[29] That, however, served to increase the frustration many professional alien refugees felt at being forced to serve in a unit which, for many, wasted their intelligence and abilities.[30] Use of the English language was made compulsory, although of course the moment any member of an Alien Company spoke, the rest of the British Army could hardly ignore the new phenomenon of German and Austrians in British uniform.[31] By 6th January 1940, some 905 aliens had been accepted for service in the British army.[32]

While about half of Richborough's 3,000 inmates eventually signed up, many felt misgivings about wearing uniform, fearful for their relatives still in Germany and Austria. Others held back from such a commitment because they hoped to emigrate to the United States of America and elsewhere, while yet others were fortunate to be taken into civilian employment.[33] At Richborough, those who did not volunteer for the Pioneers took some part in the war effort by providing services (cooking, tailoring, cobbling) for those who were enlisted. About 150 men were employed on special work for the Army, recording day and night broadcasts from all the German stations.[34]

Until May 1940, Richborough camp was a hive of activity, particularly for the training of recruits for the Alien Companies of the AMPC who, when trained, were intensively prepared for overseas service. In the event, the Alien Companies fully retained their individual identities only up to 1942, after which it was policy to dissolve them gradually.[35] Of the first six Companies formed in the early months of 1940, all but one went overseas, after a few weeks training, as part of the British Expeditionary Force in France, and later in other arenas of war. Whilst their main function was indeed that of unarmed "labourers" employed on

[27] *Ibid.*, p. 21.
[28] Bentwich, *Risks, op. cit.*, pp. 26–27. On the Richborough Camp, see also *idem, They Found Refuge. An Account of British Jewry's Work for Victims of Nazi Oppression*, London 1956, pp. 102–110.
[29] *Ibid.*, p. 108.
[30] Rhodes-Wood, *op. cit.*, pp. 21–22, 66.
[31] *Ibid.*, pp. 22–23.
[32] HC, vol. 356, cols. 8–9, 16th January 1940, statement by Mr. Oliver Stanley, Secretary of State for War.
[33] Bentwich, *Risks, op. cit.*, p. 31.
[34] *Ibid.*, p. 32.
[35] *Ibid.*, p. 35.

camp and railway construction, in the heat of battle in May 1940 members of the fourth and fifth Companies, Numbers 87 and 88, were given rifles and fifty rounds per man by their Commander, Colonel Arthur Evans, MP, in order to play an active role in the defence of Le Havre. Within a short time, however, they were also manning machine-guns and anti-tank rifles. But just as the Duke of Wellington expressed himself more nervous about the common soldier under his command than of the opposing French, so some Naval officers at Le Havre were more fearful of these newly-armed aliens in the British army. One alien sentry with his newly-acquired rifle was asked by the Commanding Officer what he would do if a German appeared. He said he would call "Halt" and, if the man still came on, would further say: "advance, and produce your AB [Army Book] 64, Part 2".[36]

In the withdrawal from France and Belgium the Pioneers brought out from France every weapon they could carry, but were forced to hand them over to the authorities upon landing at Southampton or later in the TRCs. The pervasive doubts about the political reliability of men of the Alien Companies was compounded by irrational fears of their handling arms,[37] a galling point for alien members of the ACs, compounded on 30th July 1940 when Anthony Eden, the Secretary of State for War, announced that it had been decided to arm only the British members of the Corps.[38] For a short while the Companies were sent to the Westward Ho TRC, and thereafter employed in various home defence measures, mainly assisting the Engineers, as well as the Ordnance and Army Service Corps. During the summer of 1940, when invasion was daily expected, some were engaged in more direct military service constructing pill-boxes, tank-traps, and digging trenches. When the Blitz began later in the year, many worked in London and other major cities on clearance and rescue tasks.

From 1940 to 1943, the fifteen Alien Companies eventually established were sent all over the United Kingdom, except for the East coast where it was thought the imminent threat of invasion would involve them in too great a peril, and were engaged in a variety of construction and labour tasks. The dominant Jewish character of many of these Companies was signified by the strong adherence to all aspects of Jewish religious life, and by the fact that when they were eventually transferred overseas, the men were strongly advised to change their foreign names for their own security in case of capture. To this end, the Army authorities furnished them with new paybooks which concealed their German and Austrian origins.[39]

This slightly positive side to the aliens question in the United Kingdom changed in May and June 1940. With the German conquest of the Netherlands, Belgium, and France, not only was Richborough closed down because it was on the classic invasion coast of England and the TRC moved to other sites, but the

[36]*Ibid.*, pp. 35–37; Rhodes-Wood, *op. cit.*, pp. 45–46. On the role of the AMPC in France and Belgium, cf. also J. R. M. Butler (ed.), *History of the Second World War. United Kingdom Military Series*: Major L. F. Ellis, *The War In France and Flanders 1939–1940*, London 1953, pp. 21, 79, 153, 263.
[37]Rhodes-Wood, *op. cit.*, p. 65.
[38]Lafitte, *op. cit.*, p. 243.
[39]Bentwich, *Risks*, *op. cit.*, pp. 37–51; Rhodes-Wood, *op. cit.*, pp. 69–70, 76–82.

recruitment of alien refugees to the British armed forces ceased. That occurred in conjunction with the popular cry against enemy aliens, "intern the lot", which had steadily gained ground in the early months of 1940, as a result of the "Fifth Column" scare whipped up by the popular press because of the widespread fear that the United Kingdom was next on Hitler's list of conquests.[40]

Nor could such campaigns be entirely divorced from the undercurrent of anti-Jewish feeling which permeated certain classes of British society.[41] On 21st February 1940, for example, Colonel Charles Ponsonby, MP, later Parliamentary Private Secretary to Anthony Eden,[42] wrote to Prime Minister Neville Chamberlain to express the concern of himself and others about the increase in the United Kingdom's Jewish population, the increase in antisemitism, and indeed the power of the Jewish lobby in contemporary British political life: "most of us feel that we would rather hand down to Posterity a slowly diminishing number of people of British stock than provide now [sic] material for increasing the stock of Jewish or Jew-British population".[43] Ponsonby and the people he spoke for requested an assurance from the government that, "except in exceptional cases of distinguished scientists, teachers, inventors and the like, and, possible [sic], as a reward for active service in combatant units, no Naturalisation certificates will be granted to Jewish refugees".

Ponsonby's letter clearly misread government intentions and policy concerning the use of alien refugees in combatant units. Nevertheless, coinciding with a general anti-alien campaign, he had obviously focused on one special worry for some: the possibility that alien Jewish refugees enlisting in the British armed forces would be issued with naturalisation certificates. According to the terms of the British Nationality Act, 1914, such certificates were normally granted on the basis of five years' residence in His Majesty's Dominions or five years in the service of the Crown.

The Prime Minister's Office at Number 10, Downing Street, following correct procedures, requested a draft reply from the Home Office. Sent on 8th March by Norman Brook, this reiterated the government's general policy on favouring the further emigration of refugees to other countries, even during the war. So far as naturalisation policy was concerned, the draft went on: "it has never been the policy of His Majesty's Government to consider racial origin or religious faith as a relevant factor in deciding whether or not an applicant for naturalisation is so imbued with British sentiments and with loyalty to British institutions as to be worthy of the privilege of being granted a Certificate of Naturalisation. Naturalisation is never granted to an alien unless it has already been decided

[40]Gillman, *op. cit.*, pp. 73–80.
[41]Cf. Kushner, *op. cit., passim.*
[42]The Rt. Hon. the Earl of Avon, *The Eden Memoirs. The Reckoning*, London 1965, p. 188.
[43]This statement needs to stand alongside that of William Greene, MP, in the House of Commons on 11th February 1925: "I feel that it is our duty . . . to keep our race pure. We have established a race of which I am proud . . . and I want to keep that race as it is as pure as possible. I feel that it is absolutely essential to preserve the purity of our race and to prevent contamination with the riff-raff of Eastern Europe, the stiffs of the Mediterranean, and the dead-beats of the world": cf. John P. Fox, 'British Attitudes to Jewish Refugees from Central and Eastern Europe in the Nineteenth and Twentieth Centuries', in *Second Chance, op. cit.*, pp. 465–484, esp. p. 465.

that he can properly be allowed to reside permanently in this country, and permission to reside permanently is never granted unless the authorities are satisfied that the alien is an acquisition to our population. I need hardly assure you that naturalisation is not lightly granted and is limited to those cases where the Home Secretary is satisfied that an alien has so identified himself with British life, sentiments and habits as to be already a British subject in all but name."[44] Although Ponsonby would have been correct to see this letter as a typical civil service "holding operation", nevertheless, it probably satisfied him in some respects, since it confirmed the government's intention to be the final arbiter of such matters, a point reiterated by Sir John Anderson in the House of Commons on 25th April 1940 concerning the government's complete authority over that other contentious matter, internment.[45]

The public campaign for internment was accompanied by a far more powerful one within government, and the Home Office soon found itself isolated against the War Office, the Foreign Office, the Chiefs of Staff, the Joint Intelligence Committee, and MI5 (the Intelligence Service).[46] Beginning on 12th May 1940 with the arrest of every male alien aged between sixteen and sixty found in the coastal strip "likely, if invasion took place, to be affected", internment policy proceeded apace. In the latter half of May 1940, this was extended to cover all Category B aliens, and by 11th June Category C aliens were added, thus completing a policy of mass internment. At its peak, the policy affected 27,000 enemy aliens, with over 7,000 sent overseas.[47]

Nevertheless, just as internment policy reached a peak in the summer of 1940 – when the strength of the Pioneer Corps was some 56,000, of whom 1,091 were Germans and 628 Austrians[48] – and escalated by the intense House of Commons debate on 10th July on an Adjournment motion concerning refugees,[49] public opinion began to force its reversal on the government. That was partly due to the fears of immediate invasion fading, and by revulsion at the sinking of the *Arandora Star*, a ship transporting Italian and German internees to Canada, which went down with the loss of over 650 aliens.[50] Yet it proved easier to have created the apparatus of internment than to dismantle it, the policy of release being described as "erratic".[51] Its abandonment began with the White Paper issued by the Home Office on 31st July, Cmd. 6217, *German and Austrian Civilian Internees. Categories of Persons Eligible for Release from Internment and Procedure to be Followed in Applying for Release*, revised and reissued as Cmd 6233 on 17th October 1940. This specified eighteen categories of internee who could be considered for release, with the proviso that release could be refused on security grounds. In August a

[44]HO 213/44, GEN. 7/49/43, Colonel Charles Ponsonby to Neville Chamberlain, 21st February 1940; Norman Brook, Home Office to A. N. Rucker, 10 Downing Street, 8th March 1940.
[45]HC, vol. 360, col. 366, 25th April 1940.
[46]Gillman, *op. cit.*, p. 93.
[47]Cf. *ibid.*, pp. 91ff; Kochan, *op. cit.*, pp. 22ff.; Kushner, *op. cit.*, pp. 145ff.; Stammers, *op. cit.*, chap. 2: 'The Internment of Enemy Aliens'.
[48]Rhodes-Wood, *op. cit.*, p. 65.
[49]HC, vol. 362, cols. 1207–1306, 10th July 1940.
[50]Kushner, *op. cit.*, p. 147. On the sinking of the *Arandora Star*, see Gillman, *op. cit.*, pp. 185–201.
[51]Kushner, *op. cit.*, p. 148.

nineteenth category was added; that of political refugees. Thereafter, the policy of release proceeded steadily, although the new Home Secretary from 8th October 1940, Herbert Morrison, agreed with the conclusions of the Joint Intelligence Committee, that "the ruling factor must always be the security and military needs of the country".[52]

The process of alien refugee recruitment into the British armed forces, begun in November 1939 and interrupted in 1940, was permitted to resume under categories 11 and 12 of the White Paper of 31st July 1940. These allowed for the release of persons "who, having served in His Majesty's Forces (including the Auxiliary Military Pioneer Corps), had been discharged on grounds not reflecting on their loyalty to the country or their personal character"; and of "internees who were accepted for enlistment in the Pioneer Corps".[53]

Posters explaining and encouraging enlistment in the Corps were soon displayed in all the male internment camps, although since its poor reputation obviously carried all before it, the notices at first met with a mixed response. There were other reasons for this hesitancy. Recruitment in the ACs would mean Jews serving side-by-side with Gentile Germans who, although anti-Nazi, could not always be assumed to be philosemitic. Moreover, both the Jewish alien refugees who wished to fight against National Socialism and the British government were exercised by one key question, which became more acute the closer victory became: what was it they were fighting for, what kind of Germany would replace the Third *Reich*?[54]

On 19th August 1940 the first notices that Category C internees could join up were posted in Onchan Internment Camp on the Isle of Man. But since this did not produce the expected (or required) quota of applicants and, as has been noted, "there was an unsavoury hint of blackmail in the next notice to appear, on 17th October": "a small number of internees are delaying their applications for the AMPC in the hope of being released under some category of the White Paper. In this they may be disappointed as firms engaged in work of national importance have shown no particular desire to re-employ aliens now in internment and medically fit for service in the Auxiliary Military Pioneer Corps. In their own interest internees should be informed that delay in making up their minds whether or not they wish to join the AMPC may result in their internment for the duration of the war. It is proposed to close recruiting after the 30th November."[55]

Since even this pressure failed to achieve its purpose, the government issued a sharp warning. In the House of Commons on 26th November, the Home Secretary, Herbert Morrison warned that the government regarded enlistment in the Pioneer Corps as the appropriate method of obtaining release for men between the ages of eighteen and fifty. It was, he declared, "an opportunity clearly to demonstrate their friendliness to the Allied cause by offering their services to this Corps". However, "they should not, therefore, defer offering their

[52]Gillman, *op. cit.*, pp. 257, 260; Kochan, *op. cit.*, pp. 123–124; Kushner, *op. cit.*, pp. 148–149.
[53]Cf. also Kochan, *op. cit.*, pp. 123–124.
[54]*Ibid.*, p. 165; Lafitte, *op. cit.*, p. 244.
[55]Gillman, *op. cit.*, pp. 257–258.

services to the Corps in the expectation that there may be enlargements, affecting them, of the existing categories set out in the White Paper".[56]

While eventually the number of aliens enlisting in the Pioneer Corps slowly grew, there were several difficulties accompanying the process and their experience within it. First, the government was adamant that control over the wives and children of aliens recruited into the British armed forces should continue, albeit "in such a way as to avoid unnecessary hardship or interference with law-abiding persons".[57] Second, in principle and until their cases were considered individually by the police, until the end of 1940 and the beginning of 1941, alien refugees discharged from the Pioneer Corps on medical grounds were still subject to the same restrictions applicable to aliens in general[58] – although alien members of the AMPC were not subject to the ordinary restrictions of aliens during their periods of leave.[59] Third, it appeared that a number of difficulties confronted would-be applicants to the AMPC since, as Wedgwood claimed in the House of Commons on 3rd December 1940, "it is very difficult now to get into the Pioneers. It is both difficult to pass the medical test and having passed it, to get accepted. It is even more difficult to get into the Pioneers than into the R[oyal] A[ir] F[orce]."[60] Fourth, great dissatisfaction was expressed at the fact that aliens with high technical qualifications were being forced to enter the AMPC, whereas they were better qualified to serve in other Corps of the British army.[61]

At the end of 1940 as well, there was raised the one question which, as the government probably realised, amounted to the chickens of 3rd and 5th October 1939 coming home to roost and was likely to become more rather than less awkward to deal with as time went on. Given the more positive attitude towards alien refugees in society, as a consequence of the slow abandonment of internment and especially the praise heaped upon the AMPC for its role in the withdrawal from France and Belgium in the summer and the blitz later,[62] possibly the only surprise about the question raised by Wedgwood in the House of Commons on 12th December 1940 was that it had been so long delayed. He asked the Home Secretary, "whether any aliens now serving in His Majesty's Forces and who were resident in this country for more than five years, can apply for naturalisation; whether, in the case of German or Austrian anti-Nazis, such a naturalisation will be granted during the war; and, if not, will their requests be noted for preferential treatment after the cessation of hostilities?" Morrison, however, deftly side-stepped the question by pointing out that naturalisation had

[56]HC, vol. 367, cols. 79–81, 26th November 1940; Kochan, *op. cit.*, p. 165.

[57]HC, vol. 367, cols. 330–331, 28th November 1940, statement by Mr. Herbert Morrison. This matter was raised again a fortnight later: HC, vol. 367, col. 1025, 12th December 1940.

[58]HC, vol. 368, col. 200, 22nd January 1941.

[59]HC, vol. 368, col. 665, 30th January 1941.

[60]HC, vol. 367, col. 468, 3rd December 1940.

[61]HC, vol. 367, cols. 478–479, 3rd December 1940.

[62]HC, vol. 369, col. 1059, 6th March 1941, statement by Captain H. D. R. Margesson, Secretary of State for War.

been suspended during the war, and that it was impossible "to make any statement as to what the future policy may be".[63]

Yet there were some small positive developments. Civilian communities responded well to ACs when they were employed locally. During 1941, the War Office agreed to the granting of commissions to alien refugees in the Pioneer Corps, although this has been described as "a niggardly concession". The Alien Pioneers could be officers only in that Corps, and not more than one alien officer could be posted to a Company, nor could he occupy a higher rank than subaltern. Gradually, other restrictions were lifted: transfer to other Army technical units, except Signal formations, was finally permitted as from 2nd March 1943,[64] as was alien employment in skilled tradesmen's posts. From March 1943 as well, the War Office declared itself willing to permit alien recruits with special qualifications to bypass the Pioneer Corps and be posted direct to units needing their special skills.[65] Moreover, the self-esteem of many German and Austrian Jews in the ACs grew enormously when, from 1941, they were consulted by Intelligence personnel in preparation for the Royal Air Force's early raids on Germany's industrial centres.[66] By 2nd May 1941, the number of aliens in the Pioneer Corps with medical qualifications was 65, 39 doctors and 26 dental surgeons.[67]

Nor was recruitment of German- and Austrian-Jewish refugees into the British armed forces limited to the United Kingdom. On 20th November 1940, Herbert Morrison announced that it might be possible to extend the facilities for enlistment in the AMPC to German and Austrian internees in Category C sent to Canada and Australia;[68] something which he confirmed for the Australian case on 6th February 1941.[69] Later, a telegram from Sir Archibald Clark Kerr, British Ambassador to China, on 9th October 1941 to the Foreign Office prompted lengthy discussions on whether and how to utilise the German- and Austrian-Jewish refugees in Shanghai,[70] "large numbers of whom are keen anti-Nazis and eager to serve our cause".[71]

As always, though, the positive was accompanied by the negative, at least from a non-governmental perspective. During 1941 and beyond, the British

[63]HC, vol. 367, col. 1060, 12th December 1940.
[64]HC, vol. 369, col. 789, 4th March 1941; HC, vol. 370, cols. 9–10, 18th March 1941; HC, vol. 372, col. 1183, 1st July 1941; HC, vol. 374, col. 855, 7th October 1941; HC, vol. 382, col. 1206, 6th August 1942; HC, vol. 387, cols. 477–478, 2nd March 1943.
[65]HC, vol. 387, cols. 1046–1047, 16th March 1943.
[66]Bentwich, *Risks, op. cit.*, p. 69; Rhodes-Wood, *op. cit.*, pp. 138–139.
[67]HC, vol. 371, col. 716, 6th May 1941.
[68]HC, vol. 365, cols. 1990–1991, 20th November 1940.
[69]HC, vol. 368, cols. 1096–1097, 6th February 1941.
[70]Cf. the detailed study by David Kranzler, *Japanese, Nazis and Jews. The Jewish Refugee Community of Shanghai, 1938–1945*, New York 1976. For a more populist examination of Japan and Jewish refugees from Nazi Germany, see Marvin Tokayer and Mary Swartz, *The Fugu Plan*, London 1979.
[71]Public Record Office, Kew. Foreign Office Correspondence (= FO). FO 371, vol. 29235. W12102/12102/48, Sir Archibald Clark Kerr to Foreign Office, Hong Kong, 9th October 1941; Comments by A. Walker, 13th October 1941; A. Walker, Foreign Office to War Office, 18th October 1941; *ibid.*, W14678/12102/48, War Office to Foreign Office, 18th October 1941; *ibid.*, W12102/12102/48, Foreign Office to Sir Archibald Clark Kerr, London, 26th November 1941.

government repeatedly emphasised, as did Herbert Morrison in the House of Commons on 31st July 1941 and on other occasions, "service in the Pioneer Corps could not of itself be regarded as a special ground for naturalisation".[72] On 14th August this prompted John Parker, MP, to forward to Morrison an article sent to him by an Austrian serving in the Pioneer Corps and entitled, 'Enemy Aliens for Oversea? [*sic*] Von einem Pioneer'. This argued against such statements by demanding that naturalisation certificates should be granted to all Austrians serving in the Pioneer Corps. There was, however, more to the statement than any hint of pique. The unknown author of the article focused on a key issue which was to pre-occupy the British authorities and especially Jewish alien refugee members of the Pioneer Corps for several years to come. As and when refugees might be actively engaged in fighting Germans, this could lead to severe treatment in the case of capture and reprisals against their relatives in Germany or German-occupied countries. It was suggested that if, in the meantime, they had been granted naturalisation as British subjects, they would be granted the normal status of Prisoners of War. This would also avoid the risk of reprisals against relatives.

The Home Office's immediate response on 14th August, in Morrison's absence, was to repeat its arguments to Ponsonby in March 1940, that certificates of naturalisation were only granted to males when it was considered to be "in the public interest". More illuminating was the draft for Morrison's reply by D. R. S. Davies. Beyond correcting some inaccuracies of the original article, the draft tackled the central issue by stating that "this argument that the cases of aliens sent to fight overseas should receive special treatment merits very sympathetic consideration. It raises, of course, a question extending far beyond the confines of the Pioneer Corps and affects not merely all those aliens serving in all branches of the forces but also those serving in the mercantile marine."

Yet one key point of the draft and of Morrison's reply of 22nd September 1941, that the grant of British nationality in such cases was hardly likely to afford alien refugees any real protection against the brutality of the Nazis in the case of capture, was intended to divert attention away from far more serious matters for the government. This diversionary tactic was confirmed by the deletion – authorised by Charles Gustavus Markbreiter on 17th September – from Davies's draft of a passage referring to "the very complicated issues which are bound to arise should we begin to change our naturalisation policy at this juncture" by the issue of naturalisation certificates or other means in order to protect those aliens in question.[73] The Home Office realised that to grant naturalisation certificates to aliens in the British armed forces on the grounds presented to it would be tantamount to abandoning any official control over naturalisation policy. If it were to accede to such demands then, it would be unable to control the floodgates. It desired, therefore, as little public airing of that matter as possible.

---

[72] HC, vol. 373, col. 1525, 31st July 1941; HC, vol. 373, cols. 2113–2114, 7th August 1941.
[73] HO 213/48. GEN. 7/49/84, John Parker to Herbert Morrison, 14th August 1941, with enclosure; Home Office to John Parker, 14th August 1941; Draft by D. R. S. Davies; Herbert Morrison to John Parker, 22nd September 1941.

Neither did it feel able to ignore the sense of some British opinion, which Ponsonby's letter early in 1940 had confirmed.

The Home Office's position by the end of 1941 on the naturalisation of alien refugees, Jewish or otherwise, even for those serving in the Pioneer Corps, was that the British government had a completely free choice in the matter because the people concerned were of foreign nationality. They could be "accepted", which meant they would remain in the United Kingdom or elsewhere in the Empire. Or, they could be "rejected", in which case it would be expected they would eventually return to their original homelands. Yet at the end of 1941 a shadow was cast over some basic assumptions of British policy which, slowly merging with a number of negatives inherent in the British situation, produced by 1943 and 1944 an atmosphere of such great suspicion as to cause many German- and Austrian-Jewish refugees in the British armed forces to doubt whether there had been any real point to their contribution to the British war effort.[74] But that shadow was of German, not British, making and took the form of the Eleventh Ordinance in Pursuance of the *Reichsbürgergesetz* (*Reich* Citizenship Law) of 25th November 1941.

The real significance of the German Ordinance of 25th November 1941 was that for the first time it made *de jure* what until then had generally been taken as *de facto* in the wake of the Nuremberg Laws of 15th September 1935, at least by most German (and Austrian) Jews who left Germany: that German Jews living beyond the boundaries of the *Reich* were that special pariah of the twentieth century, stateless persons.

Until November 1941 that was not actually the case in German law, whatever the realities of social life may have been and the interpretation of later observers. Indeed, and including the Nuremberg Laws, so much of National Socialist lawmaking was framed in such ambiguous and indeterminate language as to make even German jurists hang their heads in despair.[75] Despite enacting an *Ausbürgerungsgesetz* as early as 14th July 1933 – one target of which was obviously the immigrant *Ostjuden* and others granted German citizenship between 9th November 1918 and 30th January 1933 – by 31st July 1939 the National Socialist regime had only de-naturalised 10,882 German citizens.[76] There are two special points to be noted about that figure. First, the majority of those de-naturalised

---

[74] For one memorial volume dedicated to those Jews who fought and died in the British war effort, see Henry Morris, *We will remember them. A Record of the Jews Who Died in the Armed Forces of the Crown 1939–1945*, ed. by Gerald Smith, London 1989.

[75] Cf. Marianne Sigg, *Das Rassestrafrecht in Deutschland in den Jahren 1933–1945 unter besonderer Berücksichtigung des Blutschutzgesetzes*, Aarau 1951; Joseph Walk, *Das Sonderrecht für die Juden im NS-Staat. Eine Sammlung der gesetzliche Maßnahmen und Richtlinien. Inhalt und Bedeutung*, Heidelberg–Karlsruhe 1981. In 1939, Julius Streicher, the infamous Jew-baiter and editor of the pornographic anti-Jewish tabloid, *Der Stürmer*, published his version of the Third *Reich*'s anti-Jewish legislation from 1933: Julius Streicher, *Die Judengesetze Großdeutschlands*, Nürnberg 1939.

[76] John P. Fox, 'Nazi Germany and German Emigration to Great Britain', in Gerhard Hirschfeld (ed.), *Exile in Great Britain. Refugees from Hitler's Germany*, Leamington Spa–Atlantic Highlands, N.J. 1984, pp. 29–62, esp. p. 44; Diemut Majer, *"Fremdvölkische" im Dritten Reich. Ein Beitrag zur nationalsozialistischen Rechtssetzung und Rechtspraxis in Verwaltung und Justiz unter besonderer Berücksichtigung der eingegliederten Ostgebiete und des Generalgouvernements*, Boppard am Rhein 1981, pp. 195–199.

were not Jews but German political émigrés who had left Germany, voluntarily or under duress, to fight elsewhere for "das andere Deutschland".[77] Second, that figure has to be related to the total of nearly 400,000 German citizens who left the *Reich* from 1933 to 1939–1941, although figures for emigration from Germany after January 1933 are not totally accurate.[78]

While the *Reich* Citizenship Law of 15th September 1935 and paragraph four of its First Supplementary Decree dated 14th November 1935 effectively disenfranchised German Jews – in pursuance of the Party Programme of 1920 – by disbarring them from being German "citizens" (*Reichsbürger*) and effectively made them second-class persons of "subject" or "nationals" (*Staatsangehöriger*) status,[79] the National Socialist regime struggled indecisively for many years over how to proceed further and more precisely with the anti-Jewish thrust of its citizenship (= nationality) laws; a process which came to determine the fate of millions controlled by Germany.[80] In other words, how to define in law, and to achieve in practical politics, the removal of even "German subject" status from Jews. Beyond difficulties caused by the vagueness of National Socialist rhetoric, there were problems about how to proceed with an authoritative separation of the distinction between "citizen" and "subject", although in reality all Jews and Gypsies knew what the rules were. The law and decree of 15th September and 14th November 1935, for example, forecast the issue of citizenship papers, but these were never distributed. Another problem concerned the precise definition of who was a Jew, exacerbated by the exclusion from the body politic of Jews, but the inclusion (in varying degrees) of the "*Mischlinge*" as *Reich* citizens – something which also bothered the regime throughout the European phase of the *Endlösung* programme.[81]

The process to redefine the acquisition and removal of German citizenship in the wake of the Nuremberg Laws began on 14th February 1938 with a *Reich* Ministry of the Interior draft for a new citizenship law. On 3rd February 1938, however, the *Reich* promulgated a law which, although directed at German émigrés and hardly applicable to Jews, nevertheless gave notice to those German-Jewish subjects residing abroad that in the long run the spectre of *de jure*

---

[77]Cf. Lothar Kettenacker, *Das "Andere Deutschland" im Zweiten Weltkrieg. Emigration und Widerstand in internationaler Perspektive* (Veröffentlichungen des Deutschen Historischen Instituts London, Band 2), Stuttgart 1977. See also Bundeszentrale für politische Bildung, Bonn (Hrsg.), *Widerstand und Exil 1933–1945*, Bonn 1985; Herbert E. Tutas, *Nationalsozialismus und Exil. Die Politik des Dritten Reiches gegenüber der deutschen-politischen Emigration 1933–1939*, München 1975.

[78]For the difficulties in attempting to arrive at a precise figure for all those who left Germany from 1933 for a variety of racial, political, or religious reasons, see Werner Röder, *Die deutschen sozialistischen Exilgruppen in Großbritannien 1940–1945. Ein Beitrag zur Geschichte des Widerstandes gegen den Nationalsozialismus*, Bonn–Bad Godesberg 1973, pp. 15–19. See also Kurt G. Grossmann, *Emigration. Die Geschichte der Hitler-Flüchtlinge 1933–1945*, Frankfurt a. Main 1969.

[79]Cf. Majer, *op. cit.*, pp. 199–207; Jeremy Noakes and Geoffrey Pridham, *Nazism 1919–1945. Volume 2: State, Economy and Society 1933–39. A Documentary Reader* (Exeter Studies in History, Number 8), Exeter 1984, pp. 536–539; Kurt Pätzold, *Verfolgung, Vertreibung, Vernichtung. Dokumente des faschistischen Antisemitismus 1933 bis 1942*, Frankfurt a. Main 1984, pp. 114, 117–118.

[80]Cf. Majer, *op. cit.*, *passim*.

[81]Majer, *op. cit.*, pp. 201ff. For a useful discussion of the *Mischlinge* question, see H. G. Adler, *Der verwaltete Mensch. Studien zur Deportation der Juden aus Deutschland*, Tübingen 1974, pp. 278–322.

statelessness would also hang over them like the sword of Damocles. But that spectre was as much a worry for foreign governments with German Jews residing in their territory. That law required all German nationals abroad to report to local German authorities. Paragraph 5 stated: "anyone persistently failing to carry out his obligation to report such as to amount to an infringement of his duty of loyalty to People and *Reich* in accordance with the existing provisions of the law, may be declared to have lost his German nationality".

This sent tremors as well through Whitehall, because of the many German citizens, Gentile and Jewish, resident in the United Kingdom, almost all of whom could be expected to decline any return to a National Socialist Germany and who would therefore ignore such regulations. Such a prospect was accurately pinpointed by C. B. McAlpine of the Home Office in February 1938: "this law opens up a very serious prospect. It is to be anticipated that most of the refugees from Germany will refuse to report and will be only too glad to be deprived of their German nationality. The practical effect, so far as we are concerned, will be that the refugees who are here will become stateless and we shall be unable to send them back to Germany even if they are convicted of serious criminal offences." He continued by suggesting that the new law came at a time when, "for other reasons", it might be "desirable to consider the question of German refugees as a whole". This would involve stopping, or drastically reducing the inflow of refugees, particularly since its Jewish component raised the "real danger of the spread of anti-Jewish feeling". Since the Nazi regime was increasing its persecution of German Jews, more of whom could be expected to flee Germany, McAlpine acknowledged that the refugee question was essentially a Jewish one, so that undoubtedly "the restriction of Jewish immigration is deemed to be a national necessity". He therefore proposed a tightening of landing procedures at points of entry, so that *all* Germans were only granted "a short time condition" of time in the United Kingdom; "this would be only a very partial solution of the difficulty, as the real point is to prevent potential refugees from getting here at all".[82] In the event, the real significance of McAlpine's reference to a "serious prospect" only began to be realised in the wake of the German Ordinance of 25th November 1941.

The chief purpose of the *Reich* Ministry Interior draft of 14th February 1938 was to ensure that henceforth, no Jew or person of "alien blood" could be described as a German subject. Amazingly, inter-Ministerial negotiations dragged on for at least three years without agreement. From 1940, disunity over fine points of interpretation was accentuated by new problems concerning the legal status of the conquered peoples of the East within the new German empire. In the event, so controversial and extensive were the problems that no definitive law could be passed. All that was possible was a series of half-measures, at least to April 1943, to which belongs the Ordinance of 25th November 1941.[83]

[82]HO 213/157. GEN. 20/36/22. Details of German Law of 3rd February 1938, and Minute by C. B. McAlpine.
[83]Uwe Dietrich Adam, *Judenpolitik im Dritten Reich*, Düsseldorf 1972, pp. 292ff.; Majer, *op. cit.*, pp. 207–209.

On 11th December 1940, in an effort to break the long-standing deadlock, the *Reich* Ministry of the Interior proposed a supplementary decree to the *Reich* Citizenship Law. This would declare that all German Jews resident in the *Reich* would lose the status of "subject" and be demoted to "protectee" of the *Reich*. Thus, German Jews would not be perceived in a more favourable position *vis-à-vis* those "kindred foreigners" gathered together in the new German European empire. Two days later Dr Wilhelm Kritzinger, State Secretary in the *Reichskanzlei* (and later to be that Office's representative at the Wannsee Conference of 20th January 1942[84]), following discussions with his Chancellery colleague, Hans Heinrich Lammers, found it unreasonable to grant Jews protectee status in view of their forthcoming disappearance from the *Reich*. Instead, he proposed that Jews who had forsaken or lost their domicile in the *Reich* should be declared stateless. On 20th December, Hitler supported Kritzinger's opposition to protectee status for Jews, and on 27th December the *Reichskanzlei* issued instructions to the *Reich* Ministry of the Interior to draw up regulations concerning the withdrawal of German citizenship from Jews no longer domiciled in Germany. Behind such a move lay another intention, the "legal" appropriation of the property of those Jews.[85]

Further drafts from that Ministry and inter-Ministerial meetings on 15th January and 15th March 1941 followed in quick succession. By 8th April, the Ministry of the Interior had prepared yet another draft which it forwarded to the *Reichskanzlei* for a *Führer* decision. Yet that document served only to underline once again a basic difference between the Ministry and the *Reichskanzlei*. Whereas the latter, and hence Hitler himself, proposed the withdrawal of citizenship from Jews who had already departed the *Reich*, the Ministry of the Interior wished the full force of such a measure to be applied simultaneously to Jews still *in situ*. Paragraph 1 of the Ministry's draft proposed, therefore, the denaturalisation of German subject Jews (*staatsangehörige Juden*) in the *Reich* and abroad. Both groups would thus be declared stateless persons, a condition to be applied also to the "privileged *Mischlinge*". This move would ease the deportation of Jews, besides paving the way for the appropriation of their property and cessation of pension rights.[86]

Much to the frustration of the Ministry of the Interior, this was hardly the end of the matter. As a direct result of *Reichskanzlei* action, other individuals and Ministries now became directly involved in discussions: *Reichsmarschall* Hermann Göring in his capacity as Commissioner Plenipotentiary for the Four Year Plan, Reinhard Heydrich of the *Reichssicherheitshauptamt*, the Ministry of Justice, and even the military authorities. Throughout, Interior Ministry arguments stumbled against the opposing views of Hitler. Matters came to such a pass that by 11th May 1941, even Kritzinger began to wonder whether the best solution might not be a *tabula rasa*, especially since further discussions with the *Führer*

---

[84]Cf. *Akten zur deutschen auswärtigen Politik 1918–1945*, Series E. vol. I, Document 150, Undated Protocol of the Wannsee Conference [20th January 1942].
[85]Adam, *op. cit.*, pp. 294–295.
[86]*Ibid.*, pp. 295–298; Majer, *op. cit.*, pp. 210–211.

would clarify whether a law along the extensive and complicated lines suggested by the Interior and Justice Ministries was indeed necessary.

By 29th May this negative view was indeed the *Führer*'s standpoint, while on 7th June both the Interior Ministry (and later, historians) learnt more about the leader's standpoint from two directions. First, Lammers informed the Ministry of the Interior of Hitler's unchanged opinion that Jews who resided abroad should be de-naturalised and their property appropriated. Second, and more confidentially, Lammers informed Martin Bormann of the real reason why Hitler had rejected the Ministry of the Interior's proposed legislation: "he is of the opinion that after the war there would not be any Jews left in Germany anyhow and that, therefore, it is not necessary to issue now a regulation which would be difficult to enforce, which would tie up personnel and which would not bring about a solution in principle".[87]

The Interior Ministry had no choice but to comply with the *Führer*'s wishes. It revised its draft and submitted it to further inter-Ministerial meetings on 14th July and 22nd October 1941, until in the *Reichsgesetzblatt*, Part I, page 722 of 26th November 1941, and dated 25th November, there was published the Eleventh Ordinance in Pursuance of the *Reichsbürgergesetz* concerning the de-naturalisation of Germany's Jewish subjects residing abroad. It stated: "By virtue of article 3 of the *Reich* Citizenship law of the 15th September 1935 (*Reichsgesetzblatt*, Part I, page 1146),[88] it is ordered as follows: Article 1: A Jew who has his ordinary abode abroad may not be a German national. Ordinary abiding abroad exists when a Jew stays abroad in circumstances which make it clear that he is not staying there merely temporarily. 2. A Jew loses German nationality: a) on the entry into force of the present ordinance, if he has his ordinary abode abroad at the date when the ordinance enters into force; b) on the transfer of his ordinary abode abroad, if he subsequently takes up such abode abroad."[89]

Interestingly, the Ministry of the Interior and other authorities still managed to target those Jews remaining in Europe since a week later, on 3rd December 1941, there was issued a confidential ordinance, not for publication, which extended Article 13 of the Eleventh Decree of 25th November. Paragraph 1 of the subsequent ordinance stated: "the loss of citizenship and the forfeiture of property refers also to such Jews coming under this decree who have their permanent place of residence, or who will reside later on, in territories occupied by German troops or such territories which are under German administration, especially also in the Government General or in the *Reich* Commissariats Ostland and Ukraine".[90] What this meant, of course, was that when the killing process

[87]Adam, *op. cit.*, pp. 298–300; *Trials of War Criminals Before The Nuremberg Military Tribunals Under Control Council Law No. 10*, Washington 1952, vol. XIII: "The Ministries Case" (= TWC), pp. 167–169, Dr. Hans Lammers to Martin Bormann, Berlin, 7th June 1941.

[88]Adam, *op. cit.*, pp. 114ff.

[89]HO 213/160. GEN. 20/36/47, D. Seaborne Davies to H. Ward, Nationality Division, Home Office, 12th December 1941; HO 213/945. GEN. 461/2/4, German Citizenship Laws. See also TWC, pp. 189–190, Extracts from the 11th Decree on the *Reich* Citizenship Law, 25 November 1941.

[90]TWC, pp. 191–92, Confidential Ordinance, 3 December 1941, concerning execution of the 11th Decree to the *Reich* Citizenship Law.

began in the fixed extermination sites beyond the borders of Germany, in territories defined as *Ausland*, the German authorities could be assured juridically they were not destroying German "subjects" as such, but merely stateless persons of the Jewish faith. In this sense, the date of 25th November 1941 deserves to be considered alongside other significant dates along the slippery path to *Endlösung*.[91]

In the United Kingdom, the reactions of individual Jews to the German law of November 1941 were obviously mixed. For those who had left their homeland in the hope of returning one day to a free and democratic Germany, the new law was yet another discriminatory measure added to those which had contributed to their leaving their country of origin, and which would need to disappear with the eventual demise of the regime. For others who had no intention of returning, the new measure meant nothing so far as emotional ties to Germany were concerned. It served merely to intensify their efforts to find new roots – and a new nationality – elsewhere. Yet both kinds of reaction were to change irrevocably by the news which emerged with certainty during 1942, of the Nazi *Endlösung der Judenfrage in Europa*. For most, that closed the door for ever on notions of returning home.

Certainly, the British government could not ignore this new development. In January 1942 the Home Office instructed Chief Constables throughout the United Kingdom on the powers to intern stateless persons under the Royal Prerogative with particular reference to the German Ordinance of 25th November 1941. Despite its circumlocutory nature, the instructions said, in effect, that while the British government was bound to take note of the legal measures of other governments, there was no requirement upon it to apply those measures within the United Kingdom: "an alien who does not possess enemy nationality is not liable to internment under the Royal Prerogative notwithstanding the fact that he may be registered for the purposes of the Aliens Order as of that nationality".

While this appeared to be a judicious mix of law and politics, the rest of the document dealt with other important matters of nationality and internment policy in such a manner, as is the wont of such documents, as to clarify some points and to confuse others. First, that British law reserved to itself the right to determine, under Article 21 (1) of the Aliens Order of 1920, the "apparent nationality" of an alien. This was to reaffirm the implied Home Office stance that the United Kingdom could choose to recognise or ignore foreign legal measures insofar as consequent actions within the United Kingdom were concerned. Second, that aliens could only be interned under the Royal Prerogative if they possessed the nationality of a state at war with the United Kingdom, although this observation appeared to be at odds with the ultimate part of the first paragraph of the circular. If such "enemy nationality" was not

---

[91]Majer, *op. cit.*, pp. 213, 215.

possessed, aliens could only be interned under Article 12 (5A) of the Aliens Order or Defence Regulation 18B. Third, and most essentially, there was to be no automatic or general issue of the status of statelessness to all and sundry: "a) that any person who claims to be stateless may, if previously registered wth Home Office authority as stateless, be so registered again on application to the police; b) any other application to be registered as stateless should be referred to the Aliens Department, Home Office, for decision". And fourth, that it remained within the power of the British government to decide its own criteria for "the imposition of special restrictions", i.e. internment.[92]

It was this fourth point which the Foreign Office chose to stress in its reactions to the German move and the Home Office's standpoint. On 7th February, William Eric Beckett, Legal Adviser to the Foreign Office, emphasised to Sir Oscar Dowson at the Home Office that although English law had to recognise the nationality laws of other countries, it remained the right of the British legal system to state that certain persons should not cease to be classed as enemy aliens within the United Kingdom, notwithstanding their *de jure* loss of German nationality under the 25th November 1941 decree; and that the continued legality of the internment under the Royal Prerogative of German Jews deprived of their German nationality by that ordinance was not affected.[93]

There were, however, other important considerations behind these initial reactions which, when victory over the Third *Reich* became certain by 1944, were to dominate government thinking. If foreign governments acknowledged the nationals of other States as stateless, this opened up four possibilities for the individual refugee and the government of the State in which refuge had been sought. First, the individual applied for, and was granted, naturalisation and the right of residence by the State of refuge. Second, the individual applied for, and was granted, naturalisation by another State, in which case he moved to that other State. Third, the State of refuge and other States refused naturalisation, in which case real problems arose for the State of refuge and the individual. And fourth, in the special case of the Third *Reich*, with its defeat and the abolition of all discriminatory laws, so-called "stateless Jews" would "recover" German nationality, in which case they would be expected to return to Germany.

So seriously were the implications of the November 1941 Ordinance regarded that on 4th May 1942 an opinion was requested of the Law Officers of the Crown concerning the continued legality of the internment of enemy aliens and the right of aliens to challenge their detention. The Law Officers concluded that, notwithstanding the fact that these people might have lost German nationality under German law, it was lawful for the Crown to continue to intern them as enemy aliens because it was contrary to public policy that an enemy State should be able, by its legislation during the war, to remove disabilities from persons in

[92]FO 371, vol. 32616. W664/6/48, Home Office to Foreign Office, 8th January 1942, Copy of Circular Letter to Chief Constables.
[93]HO 213/945. GEN. 461/2/4. W. E. Beckett, Foreign Office to Sir Oscar Dowson, Home Office, 7th February 1942.

England who were on the outbreak of war that State's subjects, or to deprive the Crown of powers over them.[94]

Yet while the Law Officers' Opinion of 4th May 1942 implicitly acknowledged that German and Austrian Jews residing in the United Kingdom were indeed stateless, they side-stepped the issue of whether, especially with regard to the acquisition of other nationalities, there was anything the British government need initiate to resolve all the uncertainties in the situation. This was an implicit recommendation for a policy of delay, if not of passivity. However, government offices could hardly have been surprised, beginning in the summer of 1942, when the nationality-statelessness thrust to the consequences of 25th November 1941 came to land on their desks with increasing frequency, particularly so far as it concerned Jewish alien refugees serving in the British armed forces. On 3rd July 1942, for example, D. MacLeod of Section AG3B of the War Office directly confronted A. J. Tudor of the Aliens Department in the Home Office with precisely this problem. The Commanding Officer of a Pioneer Company had wanted to know whether the papers of German and Austrian personnel serving with His Majesty's Forces as German and Austrian subjects should be altered to classify them as stateless. But this was precisely the kind of general and indiscriminate step which, in a tentative manner, the Home Office circular of January was meant to block, because it opened the way for applications by such people for naturalisation as British citizens.

The reply to MacLeod vouchsafed by Ernest N. Cooper of the Aliens Department on 25th July 1942 indicated how far the Home Office realised the full implications of Berlin's actions the previous November. Cooper acknowledged the doubts surrounding the whole issue which could only finally be resolved by the High Court of Justice. Nevertheless, he then appeared to contradict directly that part of the January circular in which the Home Office had allowed individual applications to the Aliens Department of the Home Office for registration as stateless when he stated: "we do not feel ourselves bound to recognise German wartime legislation purporting to deprive German nationals in this country of their nationality, and it has been decided that we should not grant a request by a civilian registered under the Aliens Order as a German, who claimed that he had become stateless by virtue of the decree in question, to have his registration particulars amended. In these circumstances we certainly do not wish the military documents of Germans and Austrians serving in the Forces to be amended." Not only was there to be no change to the abandonment of processing naturalisation applications during the war, but Cooper also concluded: "so far it had not been possible to make arrangements for dealing exceptionally with applications by men serving in His Majesty's Forces".

If Cooper thought his reply and Herbert Morrison's statement in the House of Commons on 30th July, that Britain was unable to recognise any act of deprivation of German nationality by a general decree, would simply brush the

---

[94]FO 371, vol. 36545. W5068/134/49, W. E. Beckett, Foreign Office to Sir J. Moylan, Home Office, 23rd March 1943; HO 213/945. GEN. 461/2/4. T.5131/1223/378/1942, Home Office, 4th May 1942, Case for the Opinion of the Law Officers of the Crown.

matter under the carpet, he was soon disabused of any such notion. Morrison made it quite clear that it was an axiom of British "public policy" not "to recognise the power of an enemy State by its legislation in time of war to relieve persons who were its nationals at the outbreak of war from any disabilities, liabilities or restrictions imposed by our law on aliens of enemy nationality".[95]

MacLeod, trying to press what he thought was one advantage, wrote again on 8th August quoting the case of one Private Hirsch, told on 25th April 1942 that he and his family were to be registered as stateless. Yet as Cooper informed MacLeod on 14th August, the Hirsch case came under the German *Ausbürgerungsgesetz* of 14th July 1933 by which individual deprivations under the law were published in Germany's Official Gazette in a period prior to the outbreak of war. The German Ordinance of November 1941, was, however, "on a different footing and if we were to give it full recognition His Majesty's Government would be in the position of permitting a foreign government with which it is at war to deprive the King of using the Royal Prerogative". To underline his point, Cooper referred to Morrison's statement of 30th July.

This and subsequent correspondence between MacLeod and Cooper further established a number of important points about British policy and the national status of alien refugees serving in the British armed forces. First, that the British government recognised only specific German acts of "named" denaturalisation carried out under the law of 14th July 1933 but not under the generalised decree of 25th November 1941. Second, applications by serving Germans and Austrians to be recognised as stateless, if made only on the basis of the 14th July 1933 law and when accepted by the Home Office, would result in changes to their army records showing them as stateless persons rather than people of German or Austrian nationality. Third, all other German and Austrian alien refugees serving in the British armed forces – and for the majority that still meant service in the Pioneer Corps – were still to be classified as German and Austrian nationals for the foreseeable future.[96]

That policy was confirmed privately and declared publicly in the winter of 1942–1943 during Parliament's consideration of the British Nationality and Status of Aliens Bill which received its Second Reading in the House of Commons on 17th March 1943. What prompted further reiteration of the Home Office's restrictive standpoint was the proposal in Clause 4 of that Bill for authority to grant certificates of naturalisation to French nationals serving in Britain's armed forces, but to deny the same facility to any other serving foreigner, a point confirmed at the Second Reading.[97]

On 18th December 1942, the day after the House of Commons stood for a minute's silence out of respect for the Jewish victims of the Nazi policy of

[95]HC, vol. 382, cols. 707–708, 30th July 1942.
[96]HO 213/946. GEN. 461/2/9. D. MacLeod, War Office to A. J. Tudor, Home Office, 3rd July 1942 with enclosure; E. N. Cooper to D. MacLeod, 25th July 1942; D. MacLeod to E. N. Cooper, 8th August 1942; E. N. Cooper to D. MacLeod, 14th August 1942; E. N. Cooper to D. MacLeod, 7th September 1942; War Office to Officer in charge of Pioneer Records, 10th September 1942; D. MacLeod to E. N. Cooper with enclosure of 10th September letter, 30th October 1942.
[97]HC, vol. 387, cols. 1258–1287, 17th March 1943.

extermination and when it heard the government declare its intention to bring the perpetrators of that crime to book,[98] the Lord Chancellor, Viscount Simon, wrote to Herbert Morrison and Anthony Eden, Foreign Secretary, to express his concern at the proposed limitations of Clause 4. He even felt the matter serious enough to merit discussion in Cabinet. In his memorandum, the Lord Chancellor felt that in the wake of the statement of 17th December the government had at least a moral duty to extend the same facility of Clause 4 to stateless Jews serving in Britain's armed forces and who wished to become British.

While the Lord Chancellor's motives were undoubtedly honourable, he considerably weakened his negotiating position by arguing from assumptions which the Home Office had for long regarded as invalid. In that Office's view, there were few stateless foreign Jews serving in Britain's armed forces but many of German and Austrian nationality. The Home Office's reply to the Lord Chancellor, sent by Morrison on 30th December, disingenuously opposed the extension of Clause 4 to all serving foreigners except the French, whatever their nationality, because it would require extra police and work in the Home Office to establish the applicants' *bona fides* according to the British Nationality Act, 1914. Moreover, the Home Office argued it would be "unjustifiable" to grant "exceptional facilities for naturalisation to foreigners in general who are serving in His Majesty's Forces without granting similar facilities to those who are helping the Allied cause in civilian occupations" as part of the broader war effort. As to the latter, no secret was made of the fact that "the policy of His Majesty's Government has been to utilise the services of all foreigners who are prepared to help us in those directions in which their services are likely to be most valuable".

However, this apparent even-handedness was accompanied by evidence of the firmness with which the government was determined to maintain its total control over the composition of the population of the United Kingdom: "most of the persons possessing German and Austrian nationality who are serving with His Majesty's Forces were admitted to this country as refugees on the understanding that their residence here would be temporary, until such time as they could find a place of settlement overseas. The policy of admitting refugees in 1938 and 1939 was accepted by Parliament on this understanding, and the government would not be justified at the present date in departing from this understanding and including in the present Bill a provision which implies that refugees who are assisting in the war effort have established a claim to British nationality and permanent settlement in this country."

Nor was the Home Office convinced by the Lord Chancellor's arguments "that there are special arguments for granting facilities to stateless Jews" since it suggested it was "quite impracticable" to draw a distinction between stateless aliens and other aliens. It then repeated its opposition to any blanket, as opposed to particularist, approaches to the problem: "all Germans, Austrians and Czechs who are Jews under the provisions of the German law [of 25th November 1941]

---

[98]Cf. John P. Fox, 'The Jewish Factor in British War Crimes Policy in 1942', in *The English Historical Review*, vol. XCII, No. 362 (January 1977), pp. 82–106; Bernard Wasserstein, *Britain and the Jews of Europe 1939–1945*, Oxford 1979.

and are residing outside the Reich have been declared en bloc to have forfeited German nationality, but it is by no means easy to ascertain which particular individuals are Jews under German law, and even if this were practicable it would be most invidious to discriminate in their favour against other refugees who, though they may not have been deprived of their original nationality, have made no smaller sacrifices and have given no less help to the Allied cause".[99]

Public expression of the government's unwillingness to entertain the notion of naturalisation for aliens serving in the Pioneer Corps was given in Herbert Morrison's reply in the House of Commons on 18th February 1943 to a question on this very point by Mr. Price.[100] From the beginning of 1943, however, this negative approach was accompanied by developments which, while entirely positive in themselves, served to underline the twin-track policy of the British government towards serving German- and Austrian-Jewish alien refugees.

On 22nd February 1943, Lieutenant-Colonel V. C. Bawden of the War Office informed Mr. M. G. Kirk of the Home Office that the War Office now proposed to allow aliens and dual nationals of enemy origin to serve in any arm or branch of the service, except the Royal Corps of Signals and Chemical Warfare Battalions of Royal Engineers, on exactly the same terms as British soldiers. This would not mean the wholesale abandonment of the Pioneer Corps, since requests for transfer from that unit by aliens would only be considered if it was felt the individual could give better service in another branch, and whether he could be spared from the Pioneer Corps.

There were three points to the memorandum written in the Home Office on 24th February by Cooper for Sir John Moylan's consideration of this communication: there appeared to be no objection to these War Office proposals; the principle should be established that only those aliens who volunteered should be accepted for duty in combatant units, especially since Jews would have special reasons for not wanting to be captured by the Germans; while the Home Office should be aware that "if German and Austrian refugees are transferred at their request to combatant units, they are in a measure building up for themselves a claim to be allowed to establish themselves in this country at the end of the war, and if they desire to do so to apply for naturalisation as British subjects in due course". Yet to avoid an over-exposure of sensitive issues, this third point was omitted when Sir John Moylan replied to Colonel Bawden on 25th February.

Yet when Cooper further discussed the unit disposition of aliens in the British armed forces with one Captain Davidson, who had been responsible for the recruitment of nearly all Germans and Austrians serving in the Pioneer Corps – whose total by March 1943 was between 4,000 and 5,000 – he did so with undoubted knowledge of Herbert Morrison's letters of 5th March to Lord Nathan of Churt and Sir Percy Hurd, MP, which reiterated the government's constant opposition to the naturalisation of refugees of enemy nationality serving

[99]HO 213/191. GEN. 20/105/11. Viscount Samuel to Herbert Morrison, 18th December 1942; Herbert Morrison to Viscount Samuel, 30th December 1942.
[100]HC, vol. 386, cols. 1959–1960, 18th February 1943.

in the Pioneer Corps.[101] It was Davidson's other proposals about identity documents, however, which undoubtedly caused Cooper some disquiet. Since it could be expected that the Germans would treat captured German and Austrian Jews as traitors and not as prisoners of war, despite having deprived them of their German nationality, Davidson proposed the issue to every foreigner serving in the Pioneer Corps of an identity document which would be indistinguishable from that held by British soldiers – a notion put to the Secretary of State for War, Sir James Grigg, in the House of Commons on 23rd February.[102] Davidson believed it would not be sufficient protection simply to strike out the word "British" from the identity documents of aliens since this would make it obvious that the person concerned was not a British subject. Moreover, the War Office intended to allow alien soldiers who served overseas to change their names under a new Army Order.[103]

That such matters were common knowledge was confirmed the day before the important House of Commons debate on 17th March on the British Nationality and Status of Aliens Bill when, on 16th March, Lord Wedgwood asked in the House of Lords whether German-Jewish members of the Pioneer Corps would be sent abroad unnaturalised, and what their position would be in the event of capture. The answer given by Lord Cranborne, Secretary of State for Dominion Affairs and Leader of the House of Lords, was hardly calculated to improve the temper of those in the Home Office who felt confident they had established, without question, the substance of British policy on the nationality and statelessness issues for Jews of German and Austrian nationality.

Lord Cranborne argued that the treatment of members of the British armed forces taken prisoner was determined by the Prisoners of War Convention, under which it was not necessary that members of armed forces should be nationals of the Power in whose forces they served in order to benefit by its provisions. But he then went on to state that "the vast majority of German Jews in this country are therefore Stateless" according to the provisions of the German Law of 25th November 1941. According to him, this meant that "any Jews of the Pioneer Corps who still possess German nationality might legally be prosecuted by the Germans for treason if they were captured as the Prisoners of War Convention does not prevent this. However, as British nationality would not have caused them to lose their German nationality under the Decree I have already mentioned their position would not be improved, in the event of their being taken prisoners, by British naturalisation."

Nothing in Lord Cranborne's somewhat convoluted reply satisfied Lord Wedgwood, who then advised adoption of the American system whereby, after

---

[101]HO 213/1015. GEN. 480/2/12. Herbert Morrison to Lord Nathan of Churt, 5th March 1943; Herbert Morrison to Sir Percy Hurd, MP, 5th March 1943.

[102]HC, vol. 387, col. 14, 23rd February 1943.

[103]HO 213/1011. GEN. 480/1/9. Lieutenant-Colonel V. C. Bawden, War Office to M. G. Kirk, Home Office, 22nd February 1943; E. N. Cooper to Sir John Moylan, 24th February 1943; Sir John Moylan, Home Office to Lieutenant-Colonel V. C. Bawden, War Office, 25th February 1943; Lieutenant-Colonel V. C. Bawden to Sir John Moylan, 4th March 1943; Note by E. N. Cooper, 6th March 1943; Sir John Moylan to Lieutenant-Colonel V. C. Bawden, 9th March 1943.

ninety days' service in the armed forces, aliens were permitted to apply for American citizenship, prompting even further confusions from Cranborne.* It was, however, left to Lord Wedgwood to articulate popular sentiments as opposed to the niceties of the law when he declared, 'if they are Stateless, there is no one to speak for them. If they are British subjects they have the whole power of the British Empire behind them.'[104]

Despite its apparent incoherence, Cranborne's reply confirmed the British government's implacable opposition to the granting of British naturalisation to German and Jewish alien refugee members of the Pioneer Corps. This was confirmed the following day in the House of Commons debate on 17th March on the British Nationality and Status of Aliens Bill, when the Attorney General, Sir Donald Somervell, made it clear that the government would not amend Clause 4, which allowed for applications for naturalisation to be received only from members of the French forces who threw their lot in with the British in 1940 by joining Britain's armed forces – and thus to exclude all other aliens.[105]

In the event, neither the government's supporters nor detractors were at all pleased with Lord Cranborne's performance. Both Otto M. Schiff, Secretary of the Jewish Refugees Committee,[106] and Sir John Moylan of the Home Office,[107] pointed out to the Home and Foreign Offices respectively on 22nd and 23rd March that it was declared British policy not to acknowledge as stateless those German and Austrian Jews in the United Kingdom who were clearly affected by the German Ordinance of 25th November 1941. Of particular interest was Schiff's support of this policy for one important reason: "in my opinion this decision is a correct one and in the interests of the refugees as the same decree contains a paragraph which deprives all such persons of their property in Germany which becomes the property of the State". Clearly, retention of German citizenship, which meant ignoring the Nazi edict of November 1941, was the best means of substantiating later claims for the restitution of such property. This view fitted logically with Schiff's other important point, which was undoubtedly central to official British thinking, although some historians wilfully deny its existence: "moreover, it is certain that a number of political refugees will want to return to Germany when the Nazi regime is overthrown, and if the British government accepted the German decision, the British government could hardly insist on repatriation of refugees who according to the German decree, recognised by the British government, are [sic] no longer German nationals".

Nevertheless, Schiff came out strongly in support of the proposal that those alien (German-Jewish) members of the Pioneer Corps sent overseas should be

---

*On military service in the USA by refugees from Germany, see the following essay by Guy Stern, 'In the Service of American Intelligence. German-Jewish Exiles in the War against Hitler', in this section of the Year Book – (Ed.).

[104]*Parliamentary Debates*, 5th Series, House of Lords, vol. 126, cols. 698–699, 16th March 1943.

[105]HC, vol. 387, cols. 1258–1287, 17th March 1943.

[106]HO 213/1015. GEN. 480/2/12. Otto M. Schiff to E. N. Cooper, Home Office, 22nd March 1943.

[107]FO 371, vol. 36545. W5068/134/49, Sir John Moylan, Home Office to Sir W. Malkin, Foreign Office, 23rd March 1943.

granted British nationality since, according to him, German law would recognise them as British and they would be treated in accordance with international law as British prisoners-of-war. But there was also a moral issue involved. While these people had enlisted voluntarily to fight against Nazism, and in doing so swore allegiance to the British King in whose service some might be killed, still the British government regarded them as aliens of enemy nationality. What would happen to their families in the event of their deaths on active service? What, also, was to be their fate at the end of the war: "if they remain aliens they are not likely to earn a livelihood after the war, when there is bound to be unemployment and they may even be asked to leave the country".

The Foreign Office's reaction to Moylan's letter of 23rd March on the question of nationality was to confirm, in the words of W. E. Beckett, that there could be no doubt that the "vast majority of German Jews in this country are stateless, and that, not under Nuremberg decrees, but under the Reich Citizenship Law of 25th November 1941". Yet the clear implication of Beckett's reference to Lord Cranborne's answer in the House of Lords on 16th March and in relation to the Opinion of the Law Officers of the Crown on 4th May 1942, was that while the British government had, perforce, to acknowledge the statelessness of the German and Austrian Jews in question, this was altogether different from needing to undertake any initiatives within the United Kingdom which might lead to these people acquiring British nationality.[108]

Yet if the Foreign Office felt no need for government initiatives in this matter, the Home Office was even more firmly set against any official action. That emerged time and again in the quite lengthy correspondence which, at Mr Schiff's persistence, was conducted with the Home Office during March and April 1943, and which generally covered old ground and familiar arguments: government rejection of the demand that German and Austrian Jews serving in the Pioneer Corps or elsewhere in the British armed forces be granted certificates of British naturalisation to "protect" them in case of capture by the Germans, and because they were fighting for the United Kingdom. Part of Schiff's frustration was due to the fact, as Sir Alexander Maxwell freely admitted to him on 6th April, that "there is nothing in our law to prevent us in time of war naturalising persons who are of enemy nationality or are stateless, and in a limited number of cases we have during the war granted certificates of British nationality where the Home Secretary was satisfied that there was some special and important reason in the interests of the war effort for conferring such nationality". In Schiff's view, nothing could be a more "special and important reason" for granting British nationality than service in the British armed forces during a period of total war against an enemy which was wiping out the physical existence of European Jewry. That the British government steadily refused to do or promise any such thing was, naturally enough, a cause of great "despondency" among serving alien refugees.[109]

---

[108]FO 371, vol. 36545. W5068/134/49, W. E. Beckett, Foreign Office to Sir John Moylan, Home Office, 23rd March 1943.
[109]Bentwich, *Risks, op. cit.*, p. 70.

For their part, government authorities were suspicious that the demand to grant British nationality to Jewish alien refugees in the British armed forces was probably a backdoor attempt to achieve naturalisation for all German- and Austrian-Jewish refugees in the United Kingdom. This suspicion undoubtedly accounts for the note of irritation, and indeed warning, which crept into some of the correspondence from the Home Office. On 6th April, for example, Sir Alexander Maxwell stated that "had it been anticipated when the government allowed a number of aliens to come here for temporary refuge that, as a consequence, a large proportion would establish a claim to naturalisation and permanent settlement here, this would have been a serious obstacle to the policy adopted in 1938 and 1939 of admitting refugees. The liberal policy which was adopted in this matter before the war rests on the principle that the admission of these refugees should not necessarily give them a claim to permanent settlement in the United Kingdom."

Maxwell's suspicions were probably increased by Schiff's firm rejection of this interpretation, but above all by his apparent note of understanding for the current position of the British government which, nevertheless, viewed from the Home Office perspective, undoubtedly carried a nasty sting in the tail: "I fully realise that wholesale naturalisation would be impossible during wartime, owing to the staff which would have to be employed, apart from other considerations, and in the first instance, naturally, all our efforts must be concentrated on winning the war". As worrying for the Home Office was his observation that, "I do hope and feel sure that the liberal policy adopted by Sir Samuel Hoare will be carried on after the war and that Sir Herbert Emerson's [High Commissioner for Refugees, Director of Inter-Governmental Committee on Refugees] personal feelings that no refugee will be forced by the British government to go back to his country of origin, particularly not Jews to Germany and Austria, will become a fact".

Two days later, Maxwell actually warned Schiff not to "rock the boat" any more: "my own view is that whatever may be your hopes for a liberal policy after the war, any agitation at the present time for the naturalisation of aliens with a view to ensuring for them the right to permanent settlement in this country may do more harm than good".[110]

As if to press this message home in an unmistakable manner, on 19th April Lord Cranborne informed Schiff of the totality of British government powers over aliens residing in the United Kingdom: "His Majesty's Government can continue to treat persons who have lost their German nationality under [the] Decree of November 1941, as if they had not lost their German nationality, in the sense that HMG can continue to impose upon these persons those disabilities and restrictions to which enemy aliens are subject in this country. Thus, if any of

[110]HO 213/1015. GEN. 480/2/12. E. N. Cooper to Otto Schiff, 26th March 1943; Otto Schiff to E. N. Cooper, 29th March 1943, and comments on by D. R. S. Davies, 1st April 1943; Sir Alexander Maxwell to Otto Schiff, 6th April 1943; Otto Schiff to Sir Alexander Maxwell, 8th April 1943; Sir Alexander Maxwell to Otto Schiff, 8th April 1943; Otto Schiff to Sir Alexander Maxwell, 9th April 1943; Sir Alexander Maxwell to Otto Schiff, 10th April 1943; Lord Cranborne to Otto Schiff, 19th April 1943.

these people are interned as enemy aliens, HMG can continue to intern them as persons in this category."[111]

While the somewhat tetchy correspondence between Maxwell and Schiff hardly shifted either side from its entrenched position, other developments in British policy concerning Jewish alien refugees in the United Kingdom actually served to strengthen, in a moral sense, some of the positions adopted by Schiff and others and to complicate some of those propounded by the Home Office. Of course, whether morality would ever manifest itself in practical politics was another question altogether. In the House of Commons on 22nd April 1943, Sir James Grigg announced that, from 1st May, aliens of enemy origin would be considered for direct enlistment into any corps of the armed services other than the Royal Corps of Signals.[112] As of 2nd June 1943, it was established that there were approximately 4,760 aliens of enemy origin in the Pioneer Corps, of whom 112 had already been transferred to more actively combatant units while applications for transfer from a further 218 were then under consideration.[113]

Initially, this announcement acted like a sprinkler system on the discussion of British nationality for Jewish alien refugees serving in the British armed forces, underlined by Herbert Morrison's refusal once more on 23rd September 1943 to reopen the naturalisation process.[114] Nor was he any more forthcoming on 14th October when Miss Eleanor Rathbone, that indefatigable crusader on behalf of Jewish refugees, asked him to give assurances about the grant of naturalisation to aliens serving in the British armed forces. As she pointed out, these people were uncertain "as to whether, after the war is over, they will not be bundled out of this country".[115] That, of course, was something Morrison was hardly likely to declare as a major plank of British policy at a time when the United Kingdom needed all the moral and manpower support it could get to achieve final victory over the Third *Reich* in an Allied coalition. Thereafter, however, Morrison continued to be bombarded with questions along the lines of that raised by Rathbone, and about the government's attitude towards alien refugees at the end of the war. Morrison continually responded by refusing to reopen the naturalisation process for anybody, including aliens serving in Britain's armed forces, or to move away from previously stated positions on the whole complex.[116]

In the event, other political developments during 1943 and 1944 tended to strengthen official British attitudes about the aliens and nationality issue in such a way, apparently, as to counter the threats posed by the moral implications which its opponents might have argued were contained in the change of policy implemented from 1st May 1943. These new developments concerned the

[111]HO 213/1015. GEN. 480/2/12. Lord Cranborne to Otto Schiff, 19th April 1943.
[112]HC, vol. 388, col. 1837, 22nd April 1943.
[113]Public Record Office, Kew. War Office Papers (= WO). WO 32/10676. 27/GEN/2884. Note of 2nd June 1943: Direct Enlistment of Aliens into Arms other than the Pioneer Corps. Cf. also Bentwich, *Risks, op. cit.*, pp. 74ff.
[114]HC, vol. 392, cols. 448–449, 23rd September 1943.
[115]HC, vol. 392, col. 1042, 14th October 1943.
[116]Cf. HC, vol. 395, cols. 555–556, 2nd December 1943; HC, vol. 396, cols. 387–388, 20th January 1944; HC, vol. 400, cols. 1494–1495, 8th June 1944; HC, vol. 403, cols. 1143–1144, 5th October 1944.

manner in which aliens were registered in the United Kingdom under the Aliens Order of 1920. Although, by virtue of Article 22 of the Aliens Order, aliens serving in the British and Allied armed forces were exempt from having to register with the authorities, such exemption did nothing to alter their national status which, as had been confirmed time and again, remained German or Austrian and not one of statelessness. When, beginning in August 1943, there was some tentative discussion about whether the total exemption from registration of this first group might be abandoned or modified,[117] it indicated how firmly the British authorities, cognisant of the impetus towards victory of the Allied forces and the nature of some peace-time problems they would be confronted with, wished to reaffirm government "control" over aliens as an integral part of the complex of nationality and refugee questions. Implicit in this was concern how the British government might divest itself of the refugees at the war's end.

It was an international proceeding which accelerated the domestic resolution of the registration issue. In Moscow from 18th–31st October 1943 there took place the Foreign Ministers' Conference, one of whose decisions was to denounce as null and void the German annexation of Austria on 15th March 1938.[118] This allowed the British government to decide by the end of the year that "any alien now registered as German who can furnish satisfactory evidence that at the above date [of 15th March 1938] he possessed Austrian citizenship may on application be regarded as Austrian".[119]

The thrust of this decision was perfectly clear then and later: to substantiate as many cases as possible of non-British nationality within the refugee community as a means of diverting attention and applications away from the position of statelessness, seen always as the backdoor to British naturalisation. In February and March 1944, for example, the Foreign, Home, and War Offices reached agreement in principle on the point summarised by Geoffrey Wedgwood Harrison of the Foreign Office's Central Department to Lieutenant Colonel J. C. Denton Carlisle of the War Office on 17th February: "we can see no objection to the proposal that Austrian soldiers now serving in His Majesty's Forces who can furnish satisfactory evidence that on 15 March 1938 they possessed Austrian citizenship should similarly have this fact entered in their military records".[120]

Since aliens serving in the armed forces were exempt from the duty of registration under Article 22 of the Aliens Order, agreement that their army records could be amended showed that the authorities (or at least the Home Office) were seeking ways and means of ensuring that upon discharge from military service, when such aliens would once more become subject to the Aliens Order, those aliens would have their specific national status – not that of

[117]HO 213/1013. GEN. 480/1/15. Minute by J. Tudor, 19th August 1943.

[118]Cf. Earl of Avon, *op. cit.*, pp. 410–418; Sir Llewellyn Woodward, *British Foreign Policy in The Second World War*, London 1962, p. 244.

[119]FO 371, vol. 36627. W17334/7/48. Home Office Circular, 14th December 1943.

[120]HO 213/1014. GEN. 480/1/16. G. W. Harrison, Foreign Office to Lieutenant Colonel J. D. Carlisle, War Office, 17th February 1944; Minute by L. Barnes, Home Office, 24th February 1944; H. A. Smith, War Office to H. H. C. Prestige, Home Office, 7th March 1944.

statelessness – confirmed in an official document, their discharge papers.[121] By confirming the special case of Austrian citizenship where they could, the authorities clearly hoped to substantiate their previous arguments that, from the point of view of British law at least, the German Ordinance of 25th November 1941 had no standing.[122] Nevertheless, a bureaucratic note of caution about procedure was sounded when Herbert A. Smith of the War Office wrote to H. H. C. Prestige in the Home Office on 26th May 1944: "what we had in mind was not to invite aliens who are entitled to Austrian nationality to apply for the fact to be entered on their Army records, but to deal with such applications as arise".[123]

Not long afterwards, and in the wake of D-Day on 6th June 1944 when the tide of war slowly turned against Germany, the other long-term concern of the British authorities was reaffirmed in instructions issued to army recruiting staffs in August. It was to be made clear to aliens enlisting into the British Army that acceptance for service carried no right to British nationality. While this information had previously been communicated to Polish Military Representatives in London on 3rd March, on 8th August the War Office informed the Foreign Office that it then preferred a more public statement of the policy to be issued in the press.[124]

This was followed shortly afterwards by renewed discussions about the policy to be adopted towards the requests for British nationality from aliens residing in the United Kingdom, especially from those serving in the British armed forces. That a special meeting on this subject was convened in the Home Office on 5th September 1944 indicated the extent of government concern about the likely proportions this question might assume in the run-up to final victory over the Third *Reich*. By the autumn of 1944, it was estimated that the alien population of the United Kingdom was some 275,000 persons, of whom around 150,000 were not subject to residence conditions and could, therefore, be regarded as permanent residents. Of these, there were some 57,000 Germans or Austrians registered with the police in the United Kingdom, "of whom the vast majority are recognised as refugees from Nazi oppression".[125] Of the approximately 10,000 alien members of the British armed forces, it was accepted that "it is certain that there is a very considerable number of persons who are anxious to be naturalised and whose claims will be vigorously stressed from certain quarters".[126]

---

[121] In a circumlocutory fashion, this was the essence of a Home Office minute on 11th April 1944: cf. HO 213/1014. GEN. 480/1/16. Minute by Leven (?), 11th April 1944. The point was then confirmed by H. H. C. Prestige of the Home Office to H. A. Smith of the War Office in a letter of 9th May 1944, HO 213/1015. GEN. 480/2/12: "I agree that the Army documents of Austrians serving in the Army should show their nationality as Austrian if they, as civilians, would be registered with the Police as Austrians under current practice . . ."

[122] HO 213/1015. GEN. 480/2/12. H. H. C. Prestige, Home Office to H. A. Smith, War Office, 9th May 1944.

[123] HO 213/1015. GEN. 480/2/12.

[124] FO 371, vol. 39487A. C10504/918/55. Major A. Dru, War Office to D. Allen, Foreign Office, 8th August 1944.

[125] FO 371, vol. 39188. C13128/12432/18, Mr. H. Prestige, Home Office to Mr. Mason, Foreign Office, 26th September 1944.

[126] HO 213/52. GEN 7/49/133. Memorandum by D. Seaborne Davies, 11th September 1944.

The general sense of the Home Office meeting on 5th September was that the practice followed at the end of the Great War, when aliens who had served in the British armed forces were naturalised, could not be followed at the conclusion of the present conflict and demands for this were to be resisted. The point was made that naturalisation was not to be regarded as a reward for service in the Forces, "or for that matter for other service of national importance".[127] Besides which, it was agreed that "a very considerable proportion of the aliens serving in His Majesty's Forces have been thereby serving their own 'cause' as much as 'Britain's cause' in the narrow sense", in that many joined the Pioneer Corps simply to escape the burden of internment. Moreover, naturalisation could hardly be extended to aliens in the armed forces, only for it to be denied to those "who have given valuable aid to the war effort in other directions".

Another matter the meeting dealt with concerned how, or indeed whether, to arrange for the disposal of the country's refugee population at the war's end, given the assumption they possessed their original nationality. Yet it was acknowledged that two moral issues were involved: "would it be defensible to require refugees who had performed important war service to leave the country?" was how one aspect of the matter was presented, especially since there appeared to be no doubt "that the majority of refugees from Germany had no wish to return to that country". Yet the corollary of such thoughts, from a purely *Realpolitik* point of view for the Allies, was summed up thus: "could we allow Germany to be populated exclusively by Germans who had experience of the war only from inside Germany?".

Other nuances to these questions involved the strong possibility that enemy aliens who had served in the British armed forces might be subject to persecution if ordered back to their own country, especially Germany and Austria. Although unspoken, many present undoubtedly projected another consideration onto that likelihood: was the United Kingdom really to be responsible for their fate, once they had left British shores? Yet as the meeting also acknowledged, political factors would always outweigh whatever moral considerations were weighed in the balance. Unbeknown to the participants, however, the manner in which this primacy of politics was presented in the discussion was to lead in 1945 to specific "repatriation" policies of special anguish sited in Austria, the historical and private legal consequences of which reverberate to the present day: "if it was laid down in principle, that asylum should be afforded to refugees who have taken arms against their own country, we should be in a weak position in securing the disposal of the many Russian prisoners-of-war who have been captured on the Western Front while serving in the German Army or paramilitary organisations and whom the Soviet Government wish to be sent back to Russia".[128]

The meeting also defined broadly how the naturalisation issue was to be approached in the immediate future: naturalisation policy should not arouse

[127]HO 213, Files 55 and 71 deal in more detail with Home Office opposition to concede any preferential treatment for naturalisation to aliens (Germans, Austrians, Czechs) who had fought in the British armed forces, even in exemplary cases.

[128]Cf. Nicholas Bethell, *The Last Secret. Forcible Repatriation to Russia 1944–1947*, London 1974; Nikolai Tolstoy, *Victims of Yalta*, London 1977.

apprehensions or create hostility and inflame prejudices during the difficult period of the demobilisation of the armed forces and industrial resettlement; it should not proceed in advance of policy on the settlement of aliens in the United Kingdom; nor should the administration of naturalisation policy lead to the "clogging of the machinery of the Home Office and the Police".[129]

That the Home Office was perpetually discussing other aspects of the matter from the premise that German- and Austrian-Jewish refugees had never lost their German nationality which would be reaffirmed once Nazi discriminatory laws had been repealed, and indeed was anxious to formulate a fixed policy for the United Kingdom, emerged from a letter of 26th September from H. Prestige of the Home Office to the Foreign Office. This was an invitation to a conference scheduled for 9th October to discuss the issue of "what classes of German (including Austrian) civilians it might be expedient after cessation of hostilities in Europe to repatriate or retain in the United Kingdom".[130] The clear intent was to declare the United Kingdom an "alien and refugee-free zone" at the end of the war because nationals of other nations belonged in their own countries, not in the United Kingdom, particularly when the original cause of their flight – Nazi persecution – no longer existed.

Coincidentally, these matters also became a matter of public knowledge. British authorities could hardly have been surprised when, in the midst of their own discussions, they were apprised of the letter sent on 5th October 1944 to Sir Herbert Emerson, High Commissioner for Refugees under the Protection of the League of Nations, by Adolf Schoyer, Chairman of the Association of Jewish Refugees in Great Britain. Referring to reports that the Allied military authorities in occupied Germany had decreed that the racial and anti-Jewish laws of the Nazi regime were no longer valid, Schoyer expressed the hope that the authorities would find a formula for new German laws which avoided imposing, without any individual choice, German nationality upon Jewish refugees from Nazi Germany who had been expatriated by the Nazis. Certainly, Schoyer spoke for many when he declared: "the great number of us who do not trust that there will be a quick change of mind of the German people and do not want to return wish most earnestly not to be forced back into the status of German nationals by well-meant but rash legislation".[131]

While Sir Herbert Emerson told Paul Mason of the Foreign Office that he could not conceive that their original nationality would be reimposed upon alien refugees without consultation with those concerned,[132] the conference scheduled for 9th October discussed at length the "disposal after the war of enemy aliens in

[129]HO 213/52. GEN 7/49/133. Note of Meeting in Sir Alexander Maxwell's room in the Home Office on "the Disposal of Aliens after the Cease Fire", 5th September 1944; Memorandum by D. Seaborne Davies, 11th September 1944.
[130]FO 371, vol. 39188. C13128/12432/18, Mr H. Prestige, Home Office to Mr Mason, Foreign Office, 26th September 1944.
[131]HO 213/199. GEN. 20/114/4. A. Schoyer, Chairman, Association of Jewish Refugees in Great Britain to Sir Herbert Emerson, High Commissioner for Refugees under the Protection of the League of Nations, 5th October 1944.
[132]FO 371, vol. 42837, WR1364/9/48 and HO 213/199. GEN. 20/114/4: Sir Herbert Emerson to Paul Mason, Foreign Office, 11th October 1944.

the United Kingdom". Two key points of British policy concerning alien refugees were confirmed by this meeting. First, that although there were strong reservations about a general policy of repatriation at the cessation of hostilities, nevertheless it was a desired objective that the majority of German refugees permitted in the United Kingdom on a temporary basis – i.e. as refugees from Nazism – should "be required to leave the country in due course when circumstances permit unless in individual cases (a) being unable to secure admission to a country other than Germany they may still be exposed to the risk of persecution in Germany or (b) they can establish a case for being allowed to prolong their stay or to settle here". Among its recommendations concerning "other grounds" on which consideration might be given to allowing individuals, subject to satisfactory records, to prolong their stay or even to settle in the United Kingdom, was: "(6) that the alien has willingly and zealously cooperated in the war effort, whether as a member of the armed forces or as a civilian, according to his qualifications and physical capacity".[133]

During October and November 1944 these questions went back and forth between the Home and Foreign Offices, the wide-ranging discussions also confirming the continuing validity of the previous British position on the German Ordinance of 25th November 1941, as represented in the Law Officer's opinion of 4th May 1942 and reaffirmed by Foreign Office interpretations of the judgement of the King's Bench Divisional Court of 26th July 1944 in the case of an application for writ of *habeas corpus* by "LH and OH". That case, the King v. the Home Secretary, *ex parte* LH and OH (*in camera*), was taken by both the Home and Foreign Offices to have substantiated British policy on the alien-refugee issue *vis-à-vis* the German Ordinance since, as W. E. Beckett of the Foreign Office concluded on 18th October, it confirmed that Austrians became Germans in 1938, that an interned enemy alien could not apply for a writ of *Habeas Corpus*, and that a person who was an enemy alien at the outbreak of war did not cease to be one because an enemy decree made during the war deprived him of his enemy nationality.[134]

Whilst there appeared to be general agreement between the Foreign and Home Offices at the meeting of 9th October and subsequently, nevertheless there was a tendency for each of their special responsibilities to dominate the general interpretation given to specifics of policy when they arose. On 10th November, for example, Ian Henderson of the Foreign Office wrote to the Under Secretary of State at the Home Office, that "the present intention of His Majesty's Government as expressed in their proposals to the EAC [European Advisory Commission] is that the legislation repealing the present German discriminatory laws should be worded in such a way as automatically to restore German nationality to those Jews who have been deprived of it inter alia under

---

[133]FO 371, vol. 39188. C14797/12432/18, Mr. Prestige, Home Office to Mr. Mason, Foreign Office, 24th October 1944, with enclosure of record of meeting of 9th October.
[134]FO 371, vol. 38830. C10210/30/3, Minute by Beckett, 18th October 1944; HO 213/941. GEN 60/7/2, Foreign Office to Home Office, 2nd November 1944.

the decree of 1941 which divests of German nationality German Jews resident abroad".

This seemed to imply that since such German Jews would again be considered German citizens after the necessary rescinding laws, their chances of remaining in the United Kingdom or of obtaining British naturalisation were slim indeed. Yet observations by the Foreign Secretary, Anthony Eden, acknowledged the effect upon government of what might be described as the "humanitarian" campaign, by Gentiles as well as Jews, to consider the feelings and position of the Jewish alien refugees in the wake of the Nazi campaign to exterminate European Jewry. Eden's view was that "it will be for governments which have given asylum to German-Jewish refugees to decide whether to let them remain resident in their territories and also the conditions on which such refugees may become naturalised in the countries where they are now living. Insofar as governments allow their refugees to remain on to become naturalised, the automatic restoration of German nationality will not prejudice them."[135]

Although the Home Office concurred, nevertheless it continued, as it did on 18th December, to repeat time and again the official standpoint that the German Ordinance of 25th November 1941 had never been recognised by the British government. This meant that "the alien has therefore remained liable to repatriation to his country of origin", because there had never been any change in his nationality, according to British law, and that "the annulment of the 1941 decree would bring the position in German law into alignment with the policy which was adopted by the Government". The opportunity was also taken to stress another guiding light for British policy, that "by far the greater number are refugees here on a temporary basis pending emigration or other arrangements being approved".[136]

If anything, these frequent exchanges between the Home and Foreign Offices at the turn of 1944–1945 indicated how necessary it was to attain a "final formulation" of British policy. Yet if officials were worried about "getting the thing right", their concerns were as nothing compared to the uncertainties experienced by the Jewish alien refugees themselves. A majority had more than mixed feelings about returning to a Germany from which the *Endlösung der Judenfrage in Europa* had originated to culminate in the activities of the *Einsatzgruppen* in Russia[137] and the gas camps established in what was formerly Poland.[138] Most feared that the compulsory reinstatement of German and Austrian nationality by the Allies would also mean their compulsory repatriation to their former homelands without any choice in the matter.[139]

[135]FO 371, vol. 42837, WR1364/9/48 and HO 213/199. GEN 20/114/4: Ian L. Henderson, Foreign Office to Under Secretary of State, Home Office, 10th November 1944.

[136]HO 213/950. GEN. 461/2/19. Minute by (?) Lyon, 18th December 1944.

[137]Helmut Krausnick and Hans-Heinrich Wilhelm, *Die Truppe des Weltanschauungskrieges. Die Einsatzgruppen der Sicherheitspolizei und des SD 1938–1942*, Stuttgart 1981.

[138]Cf. Yitzhak Arad, *Belzec, Sobibor, Treblinka. The Operation Reinhard Death Camps*, Bloomington, Ind. 1987.

[139]See FO 371, vol. 51157, in particular the following papers: WR1593/WR 1616/WR1789/139/48. See also *ibid.*, WR 1406/4/48. Mr N. Barou, World Jewish Congress, London to Mr Paul Mason, Foreign Office, 7th May 1945.

In January 1945, for example, the Board of Deputies of British Jews opposed continuation of forms of statelessness, but urged that Jews "should be as a whole naturalised in their present country of domicile",[140] a wholly unacceptable proposition for the British. Through Sir Herbert Emerson, Schoyer maintained his opposition to German and Austrian Jews being treated as nationals of those nations in any future peace agreement, a thought he described as "the leading idea" of his associates.

In official circles this prompted the immediate riposte, "how should such people be classified?". On 20th January, Ian Henderson of the Foreign Office agreed that while the British authorities had no wish to recognise statelessness imposed upon these Jews, neither was it the intention of the British government "to treat them as belonging to a category of persons specially privileged among their compatriots". This indicated agreed bureaucratic policy that post-Nazi German and Austrian nationality would automatically accrue to all Germans and Austrians, irrespective of race or religion. Yet Henderson's further remarks betrayed something of the inherent antipathy towards Jews in British society which, nevertheless, could not be said to be the mainspring of British policy on the nationality issue: "It is by no means clear that all German and Austrian Jews have actively favoured the cause of the United Nations, still less that no Jews have favoured the cause of the enemy, and there might therefore be moral arguments against our concurring in the 'leading idea' mentioned above."

Paul Mason, however, on 9th February not only argued the case for German and Austrian Jews never having lost their nationality, but accepted that these refugees should be given a choice in the matter of their future nationality. While not proposing any easing of procedures for obtaining British nationality, he was concerned that if the Allied governments were inflexible about the automatic resumption of German and Austrian nationality for these people, with its implications of population transfer, they might be placed in the invidious position of forcing the repatriation of Jews against their will, leading to an unwelcome "public feeling which will undoubtedly be aroused". The following day another colleague, Mr Vyvyan, pointed out that if these refugees were not returned to their original nationality, which in effect would be to acknowledge them as stateless, this would not resolve the ambiguous position of Jews remaining in Germany. Again the message was clear: all Jews, wherever they were, should be classed as Germans or Austrians.[141]

International developments by the turn of the year 1944–1945 inclined the Foreign Office more to the international repercussions of whatever form British policy took, whereas the Home Office remained concerned about how such matters would relate to the whole complex of domestic British politics in the transition from war to peace. Not surprisingly, the Home Office reply of 27th February 1945 to the Foreign Office letter of 10th November 1944, as set out by Frank A. Newsam, was an attempt at retrenchment on the fundamental issue

---

[140]FO 371, vol. 51157, WR 139/139/48, Board of Deputies of British Jews to Foreign Office, 11th January 1945.
[141]For this correspondence and comments, see FO 371, vol. 51157. WR 140/139/48.

that the post-war restoration of German nationality to Jewish alien refugees should be without individual choice in the matter. This implied that one consequence would be their early departure from the United Kingdom. While it was acknowledged that such restoration of nationality would not necessarily involve compulsory repatriation, the Home Office was adamant that refugees should understand that the country of refuge was not "under some obligation to allow the refugee to continue his residence in that country with a view to his eventual naturalisation therein", especially since in the case of the United Kingdom most of the refugees had been admitted on a temporary basis. And, to ensure a clean sweep of Nazi legislation leading to a *tabula rasa* of the whole refugee-nationality-statelessness question, the Home Office wanted confirmation that not only the decree of 1941 but also the law of 1933 would be repealed.[142]

Newsam's letter, phrased as coming from the Home Secretary, and showing some divergence from Foreign Office thinking, prompted the realisation in the Foreign Office that it was high time for British policy makers "to get their act together". Sir George Rendel, Superintending Under-Secretary of State for Prisoners-of-War and Refugees questions, proposed on 1st March a meeting to discuss the full ramifications, on the eve of victory over the Third *Reich*, of all the issues raised by Jewish refugees in the United Kingdom and their future nationality in a post-Nazi Germany. He emphasised that matters should not be considered from the purely Jewish point of view since not all refugees were Jews, although future conditions in Germany and Austria would have to be such as to secure the safety of those returning. But he rejected out of hand as a reason for accepting the presence of refugees in the post-war period their desire simply to live in the United Kingdom: "that is hardly a sufficient reason to justify us in continuing indefinitely to give our hospitality to a large number of foreigners who are no longer threatened by the dangers which originally led us to admit them".

Yet there were two points in Rendel's *obiter dicta* which underlined how far aspects of British *Realpolitik* also determined the management of the refugee-nationality issue. While he felt it was probably too early to decide whether conditions in Germany were sufficiently tolerable "to justify us in bringing pressure to bear on German refugees to return to that country", it might be "very useful to us to have a certain proportion of the population of Germany in future consisting of people who may be presumed to be well disposed towards this country, and to be violently hostile to a Nazi regime". Nevertheless, doubts about forcing Jews back to a Germany responsible for the murder of European Jewry had to be balanced by the consideration that "the majority of the Jewish organisations concerned would be very glad to see these people stateless, since this would strengthen their hand in trying to play up the principle of a separate Jewish nationality based on Palestine. This seems to me to make it all the more

---

[142]HO 213/950. GEN 461/2/19. F. A. Newsam, Home Office to Under Secretary of State, Foreign Office, 27th February 1945.

important to get all these various issues carefully sorted out and considered, one at a time."[143]

The upshot of the Rendel meeting on 8th March 1945 was that the Refugee Department was to draft, for Foreign Office circulation, with a view to eventual consideration by the Committee on Armistice Terms and Civil Administration,[144] a memorandum on the problems involved "so far as ex-enemy refugees were concerned in the repeal of Nazi legislation abrogating their nationality". Its purpose was to indicate what practical steps were required to prevent such refugees being inequitably treated following the repeal of Nazi laws, and it would include a draft direction to the appropriate Allied authorities.[145]

While the Foreign Office prepared its submission, other developments added to the pressures exerted upon the British government. On 21st March 1945, for example, the *Daily Express* carried an article with the eye-catching title, 'Germans To Stay Here', which claimed a plan for the 40,000 German and Austrian refugees on temporary permits in the United Kingdom was being officially discussed: one-third would remain to become British citizens, one-third would return to the Continent, and one-third would emigrate to the British Empire.[146] Such leaks hardly ensured a calm or balanced public discussion. More to the point, at least from an official perspective, was the memorandum submitted to the European Advisory Commission on 9th April by Sir Herbert Emerson and clearly at odds with entrenched Home Office views, suggesting that if a decision were taken for the rescission of discriminatory legislation and consequent restoration of nationality, there should either be an option to the individual to renounce within a specified period or, conversely, the restoration should become operative only if the individual exercised an election within a specified period.[147] This kind of moral pressure on the British authorities was accompanied by equally urgent Jewish representations. At the beginning of May, Dr. Gerhard Riegner of the World Jewish Congress in Switzerland pressed his London representative, Noa Barou, to oppose any automatic reintegration of German and Austrian Jews "into former undesirable nationality but [that they] should be granted right of repudiation or option".[148]

By 11th May, the Foreign Office memorandum, entitled 'Status of Ex-Enemy Refugees In View of Impending Repeal of Nazi Discriminatory Legislation', was ready and circulating as document ACAO/P(45)48 to the appropriate authorities. It pulled together the main arguments of the moment – repeal of Nazi legislation, restoration of German and Austrian citizenship, the temporary basis ("asylum because they were in danger") on which most Jews had been admitted to the United Kingdom before the war, and the issue of repatriation to Germany.

---

[143]FO 371, vol. 51157. WR 140/139/48.

[144]Cf. Woodward, *op. cit.*, pp. lii-liii, 445; *ibid.* generally for other committees established to oversee future administration of a defeated Germany.

[145]For the record of the meeting of 8th March 1945, see FO 371, vol. 51157. WR1489/139/48.

[146]See FO 371, vol. 51157, WR 140/139/48.

[147]HO 213/951. GEN 461/2/20.

[148]FO 371, vol. 51117. WR 1406/4/48. Mr. N. Barou, Secretary of the World Jewish Congress in London to Mr. Paul Mason, Foreign Office, 7th May 1945.

Paragraph 7 contained the key recommendations for the final form of British policy. While there should be no forcible repatriation, nevertheless the United Kingdom was not to be considered an automatic repository for Europe's refugees: "the mere fact that the ex-German refugees in this country may now have to resume their German nationality does not imply that they will be forcibly repatriated to Germany, irrespective of the conditions existing in that country. It will not, in fact, materially alter their status as refugees any more than that status was, in fact altered before. . . On the other hand, if some special arrangements were made to allow these people to remain technically 'stateless', it might well become more difficult to insist upon their leaving this country once conditions for their re-admission to Germany are satisfactory, and they would, no doubt, claim a sort of right to remain here and to acquire British nationality, irrespective of whether they were still in any personal danger elsewhere, which might be exceedingly embarrassing to His Majesty's Government. . . It is clearly impossible for us to give them any right or claim to permanent settlement in this country once the acute danger from which they were escaping when they first sought asylum here is past . . . the decision on this point must clearly rest with the Governments concerned and not with the refugees themselves. These Governments [of asylum] will not be automatically debarred from a decision to retain or naturalise refugees simply because the refugees re-acquire German nationality. On the other hand, if the refugees remain 'stateless', the universal desire to abolish as far as possible the condition of 'statelessness' may well affect their situation and hamper the Governments of the countries of asylum in what should be their unfettered right to decide whether or not they are prepared to retain and to naturalise any or all of these refugees."

So as not to create any "privileged" groups, the memorandum recommended (paragraph 8) that all Nazi legislation, even that "affecting the nationality of these particular victims of German persecution", be rescinded. Moreover, the assumption should be, not that the refugees lost their nationality and then passed through a period of "statelessness" before regaining their original nationality, but that they never lost their nationality at all. Finally, the document strongly suggested "the issue of a directive discouraging the premature repatriation from Allied countries and re-admission of such persons into Germany before the Allied Commanders-in-Chief are satisfied that the conditions existing there are such as to guarantee their safety".[149]

Official discussion of these questions was accompanied by a broad range of public discussion which was divided between pro- and anti-alien sentiment. Following up another Member of Parliament's question in the House of Commons on 21st March 1945 about naturalisation for Polish citizens serving in the British armed forces, Eleanor Rathbone, as did Colonel Wedgwood once before, expressed a great deal of public opinion when, in widening out the scope of the subject, asked whether the United Kingdom could "afford to reject gallant

---

[149]FO 371, vol. 51157. WR 1487/139/48. Paper WR 1488/139/48 contains working papers and drafts during April and May for WR 1487.

men who have been thought good enough to fight for us, but apparently are not thought good enough to bear the responsibility of becoming citizens?".[150]

Typical of the other approach was the Commons question put down in May 1945 by Austin Hopkinson for a reply from the Prime Minister: "whether, in view of the destruction of National Socialism, arrangements can be made for the immediate repatriation of all Jewish refugees who had been the victims of persecution in their country of origin?". That the Home Office (and the Foreign Office) were still not prepared, at that stage, to commit themselves publicly on the fine points of policy, was confirmed by the fact that immediately on 14th May, R.J.P. Hewison of the Home Office informed Miss Edith M. Watson of the Prime Minister's Department that "any answer given at this date should be non-committal – except so far as it may refer to the practical difficulties of arranging for immediate repatriation apart from any other considerations".[151]

On 15th May Hopkinson's question was answered by Churchill in the House along the lines suggested by Hewison, i.e. "there would be very considerable practical difficulties in carrying out" the suggestions. Hopkinson, clearly dissatisfied, returned to the fray by asking whether "the frequent assurances given by Home Secretaries in previous days that these men were to be repatriated at the earliest possible moment still remains the policy of the government?". While Churchill acknowledged that was still the government's intention, it was a matter which depended entirely on the restoration of order in Europe and certain practicalities. Churchill then agreed with Sydney Silverman, who suggested, "it would be difficult to conceive of a more cruel procedure than to take people who have lost everything they have – their homes, their relatives, their children, all the things that made life decent and possible – and compel them against their will, to go back to the scene of those crimes".[152]

The following day, Commander Oliver Locker-Lampson asked the Foreign Secretary about government policy "in regard to repatriating Jewish refugees from Germany and in regard to Jews in Germany". In reply, Mr George H. Hall explained that "it is still too early for me to be able to make any statement", while as regards the second part "it is the policy of His Majesty's Government that all discrimination hitherto applied in Germany, on grounds of race, religion, or political belief, should be abolished".[153] Yet a month later, on 6th June when the Attorney-General confirmed the general line indicated by Churchill on 15th May, it was obvious that clear signals were being sent out as to the form which future British policy would assume on these issues. Replying to a question by Captain Shaw as to whether the government could give assurances that "every effort [will be made] to expedite the departure of the large number of war refugees in this country?", Sir Donald Somervell stated that "civilians who found refuge here when the countries of North and North-West Europe were overrun

[150]HC, vol. 409, cols. 803–804, 21st March 1945.
[151]FO 371, vol. 51117. WR 1464/4/48, R. J. P. Hewison, Home Office to Miss E. M. Watson, Prime Minister's Department, 14th May 1945.
[152]HC, vol. 410, col. 2266, 15th May 1945.
[153]HC, vol. 410, col. 2441, 16th May 1945.

by the Nazis will be expected to return to those countries as soon as local conditions permit". Nevertheless, he also warned that "many others now lack houses to which they can return and that in any case the rate of return must be limited by difficulties of transport".[154]

For some time, thereafter, neither the Home nor Foreign Offices felt they could progress much further, either with the question of the departure of refugees because of the total chaos in occupied Germany, or with any purely British approach to the question of their former and new nationality since those questions necessarily dove-tailed with complex questions of international law and Allied policy. These concerned the abrogation of one sovereign nation's law, that of Nazi Germany, and its replacement by occupation decrees designed to de-Nazify Germany, how to cope with immediate post-war problems, and how to ensure the establishment of a free and democratic Germany.[155]

The Foreign Office position, that repeal of Nazi discriminatory legislation should be wholesale and result in the "legal" restoration of German nationality to refugees who had lost it through Nazi legislation, while there should be no general policy of forcible repatriation unless conditions guaranteed the safety of the refugee and a reasonable opportunity of earning his livelihood, seemed to carry the day in further discussions with the Home Office and Control Commision for Germany.[156] Its position was further stated on 20th June when John Monro Troutbeck wrote to Ivone Kirkpatrick of the Control Commission for Germany: "the attitude of the United Nations to this German discriminatory legislation is that it is legislation which should never have been passed, and the validity of which they have never admitted. The Nuremberg laws were contrary to elemental principles and by arranging for their repeal we are restoring the situation to what it was, and removing something which never should have been done. There is in fact no question of new legislation imposing, or re-imposing a nationality on someone who had validly lost it. It is rather a case of rescinding illegal, unjust, and fundamentally invalid legislation and thus restoring all the rights (and obligations) which that legislation had attempted to remove. This alone is sufficient to take the case out of any general rules limiting a State's power with regard to nationality legislation."[157]

Troutbeck's shift of angle towards emphasising the illegality of Nazi law was, of course, clearly intended to focus the future debate on the fate of Jewish refugees in the United Kingdom on the Government's long-standing view that the Jewish refugees only resided in the country on a temporary basis. If the original cause of their flight, the National Socialist regime, its persecution of Jews and discriminatory legislation, were not only removed but were considered not to have existed at all, then the stage was set for a restoration of the pre-1933

---

[154]HC, vol. 411, col. 912, 6th June 1945.
[155]Cf. FO 371, vol. 51157. WR1493/139/48. Mr. Kirkpatrick, Control Commission for Germany to Troutbeck, Foreign Office, 17th May 1945.
[156]See the October 1945 memorandum on the restoration of German and Austrian nationality in HO 213/951. GEN 461/2/20.
[157]FO 371, vol. 51157. WR 1493/139/48. J. M. Troutbeck to Ivone Kirkpatrick, 20th June 1945.

domiciliary and legal status of such people – in their original homelands and not in the United Kingdom.

Although by the end of June 1945 there still seemed to be some uncertainty as to the exact method of repealing Nazi Laws,[158] a month later the Allied occupying powers had issued ordinances "to revoke forthwith all discriminatory legislation". That, however, was not to be the final word on the nationality question.[159] As to the linked question, at least in the view of some Members of Parliament and British public opinion, of the immediate "repatriation" of the refugees, pressure continued to be exerted on the government through questions in the House of Commons. But again, as on 10th October when the new Labour Prime Minister, Clement Attlee, dealt with the matter, the new dual emphasis to British policy was once more stated: "it is the policy of His Majesty's Government to create conditions in Europe which will enable and encourage foreigners who are here on a temporary basis to return to their own countries. Many thousands have already gone under arrangements made by the various Allied Governments, but in the present state of international transport there is no prospect of the possibility of a mass emigration from the United Kingdom at an early date." And, as Churchill had previously agreed with Sydney Silverman, so on that occasion Attlee likewise confirmed to Silverman that "in no circumstances will any refugee from political oppression abroad be compelled to return to the scene of that oppression".[160]

Such statements, if the fine print had been read as such, amounted to a tacit admission by the British government that practical, and perhaps even moral, conditions by the end of the war – exacerbated by the daily revelations of Nazi crimes against humanity – was forcing upon it a realisation that the black-and-white stance it had adopted since 1939 on the linked question of "temporary refuge" being no grounds for a more liberal naturalisation policy, had now to be replaced by a policy position where nuances had to be the order of the day. That such was the case was clearly signalled in the House of Commons on 18th October when Eleanor Rathbone and others asked for a statement regarding "the future policy regarding naturalisation of aliens", especially for those who had no real hope of safe repatriation for themselves, but above all for those "who have served creditably in the British or allied forces" or in other ways in the British war effort, to which Mr Chuter Ede, Secretary of State at the Home Office, replied: "I hope to make a statement on future policy at an early date".[161]

From the British point of view, the long-running linked questions of "refuge" and "naturalisation", forged in a special relationship because of the peculiar conditions of a total war since 1939, reached a conclusion of sorts in the somewhat surprising statement of government policy on naturalisation, with particular reference to aliens serving in the British armed forces, presented in the House of Commons on 15th November 1945 by Mr Chuter Ede. Given the

[158]FO 371, vol. 51117. WR 1406/4/48. Ian L. Henderson to Mr. N. Barou, 27th June 1945.
[159]Cf. the October 1945 memorandum in HO 213/951. GEN. 461/2/20.
[160]HC, vol. 414, cols. 225–226, 10th October 1945.
[161]HC, vol. 414, cols. 1343–1347, 18th October 1945.

nature of official consideration of this question over several years which, on more than one occasion, had betrayed degrees of jingoism, Ede's statement was surprisingly generous. Yet it was also an acknowledgement of the horrendous tasks of reconstruction in Europe that confronted the Allied governments which also prevented any fanciful schemes of wholesale repatriation for most refugees from being implemented, let alone proposed – although not of course for other national groups in detention in Austria. As it was, many former members of the Pioneer Corps found new employment in the various units of Military Government and the Control Commissions in Germany and Austria, and even in the preparation of the post-war trials of Nazi war criminals through the work of the British War Crimes Executive and as translators of the many tons of German records which were recovered.[162] That being so, it would have appeared invidious for them to have been rewarded by immediate repatriation to Germany and Austria, or even being refused re-entry into the United Kingdom after their work for the Allied governments in this respect.

Of those aliens resident in the United Kingdom and desirous of becoming British subjects, Ede acknowledged the "many" who had become assimilated in the British way of life and had "special claims to be admitted to British citizenship". These had served in the British armed forces "and have earned their share of the gratitude which we all feel to the fighting services", while others had contributed in various ways to the civilian war effort. Given that it was government policy to resume as quickly as possible the naturalisation policy which had been suspended in 1940, it was intended that those groups which Ede had singled out would be given priority treatment because they stood out "as deserving special attention". Nevertheless, Ede's warning that applications for naturalisation needed to be based on solid grounds, that the bureaucratic machinery would "be settled as quickly as possible" (i.e. as "quickly" as such matters were normally managed in the bureaucratic machinery of government), that first attention would be given to the 6,500 cases for naturalisation already on hold at the time of suspension in 1940, and that "consequently the work will have to be spread over a comparatively lengthy period", was an indication of at least two hidden thrusts to the government's strategy: choice in the matter remained firmly in government, not in refugee, hands, and that as the process was perhaps drawn out, so many of those waiting in the wings would be discouraged and try their luck for new nationalities elsewhere than in the United Kingdom.[163]

In the final analysis, however, it could be said that outside conditions and temporary expediencies and not real degrees of altruism from within the confines of British bureaucracy had contributed to this final form of British policy on the "refuge" and "nationality" issues for alien Jewish refugees which had been approached with such firmness and rigidity since the outbreak of war on 3rd September 1939. If so, such a position was consistent with the manner in which the State excludes considerations of "humanity" in the determination of its

---

[162]Bentwich, *Risks, op. cit.*, pp. 160–168.
[163]HC, vol. 415, cols. 2305–2310, 15th November 1945.

domestic and foreign policies. From this perspective, and regarded objectively, the principal *leit-motifs* of British policy on the Jewish issue during the Second World War had a logical basis. This also forces a consideration of something else. The United Kingdom, despite its liberal traditions and democratic freedoms, clearly exercised the full powers of the State – in the interests of the State – to pursue an official policy of severity and stringency towards these refugees from Nazi persecution. Whatever criticisms may be levelled about this, it is necessary to bear in mind that those traditions and freedoms, even during a period of total war, ensured that the exercise of State power in the United Kingdom was an entirely different matter from that most extreme case of the State's power to determine absolutely the life of its citizens and other residents, Nazi Germany. The manner in which the Third *Reich* exercised State power did not result in parliamentary debates, but in control over its citizens to the extent that, in the name of the German State, its servants committed mass murder on a pan-European scale.

In the Service of American Intelligence
German-Jewish Exiles in the War against Hitler

BY GUY STERN

The recent appearance of Arno Lustiger's detailed study of the participation of Jews in the Spanish Civil War[1] highlights once again the need for a global history of Jews serving in the Second World War. Predictably this would extend over many volumes and, in all probability, would require the energies of a large team of researchers.* But even the far more modest task outlined in the title of this article, will ultimately require a sizable monograph that no doubt could not exhaust its subject: Jews from Nazi Germany and Austria served in all branches and at every level of US Intelligence, with the possible exception of Signal Intelligence,[2] in the gathering and dissemination of information, in cryptography and psychological warfare, in military government and the planning for the short-term and long-term future of the defeated enemy.

A further complication in such an undertaking is the often highly individualistic nature of the exploits of the exiles which are not reflected even in the half-a-dozen voluminous holdings of the records of the Second World War assembled in the National Archives in Washington. An interesting example is provided by an obscure, twenty-two-year-old infantryman and interpreter with the American

---

This essay is in appreciation of Arnold Paucker's more than twenty years of inspired editing.

[1] Arno Lustiger, *Schalom Libertad! Juden im spanischen Bürgerkrieg*, Frankfurt a. Main 1989; Köln 1991; Frankfurt a. Main 1991 (Büchergilde Gutenberg); *Shalom Libertad! Les Juifs dans la guerre civile d'Espagne*, Paris 1991. See also *idem*, 'German and Austrian Jews in the International Brigade', in *LBI Year Book XXXV* (1990), pp. 297–320. On German Jews in the war against Nazi Germany and in the resistance see a.o. Arnold Paucker, *Jüdischer Widerstand in Deutschland. Tatsachen und Problematik*, Beiträge zum Widerstand 1933–1945, Gedenkstätte Deutscher Widerstand Berlin, Heft 37, Berlin 1989. Revised and expanded English version, *Jewish Resistance in Germany. The Facts and the Problems*, Berlin 1991. A magisterial work which also deals with German Jews in the war against Hitler is: Konrad Kwiet and Helmut Eschwege, *Selbstbehauptung und Widerstand. Deutsche Juden im Kampf um Existenz und Menschenwürde 1933–1945*, Hamburg 1984.

*Some spadework towards such a comprehensive history is being done by the Leo Baeck Institute. See John P. Fox, 'German and Austrian Jews in Britain's Armed Forces and British and German Citizenship Policies 1939–1945', which precedes this essay in the current volume of the Year Book; and previously Yoav Gelber, 'Central European Jews from Palestine in the British Forces', in *LBI Year Book XXXV* (1990), pp.321–332 – (Ed.).

[2] A telephone interview with Professor Paul K. Whitaker, one of the principal sources for Thomas Parish, *The Ultra Americans. The U.S. Role In Breaking the Nazi Code*, New York 1986, indicated that in all likelihood no German-Jewish refugee was involved in the joint British-American success of breaking the German code.

84th Infantry Division who was catapulted suddenly to the post of reorganiser, then of chief adviser to the municipal government of Krefeld and then of the Bergstrasse District. He was charged also with ferreting out local Nazis and, finally, was entrusted with the teaching of high-ranking American officers on "how to find Nazis who were hiding in the community and taking refuge underground".[3] But this lowly GI's meteoric and spectacular rise, all outside official military government channels, would never have been chronicled, if the erstwhile private had not re-emerged later as US Secretary of State Henry Kissinger.

Unfortunately, the adventures of numerous exiles who have been too busy with the routine tasks of post-war life or too reticent to wax autobiographical are likely to be lost. Such individual achievements to be recorded are not merely anecdotes; they are chips making up a complex mosaic. The means by which Sgt. Thomas Werner Angress of US Military Intelligence, later a noted historian and a Fellow of the Leo Baeck Institute, hid his German-Jewish provenance from his German captors in Normandy may shed light on the workings of the minds of his interrogators. Then again there is the gallant story of Sgt. Karl Frucht who, under the aegis of Varian Fry, organised an escape route through France and Germany for trapped German, French and Czech Jews, mostly artists and intellectuals, and brought this experience to bear on his subsequent interrogations of German prisoners-of-war during his service in American Military Intelligence. Mentioned briefly for his exploits in a book by Eric Sevareid, he himself delayed the writing of his autobiography until his retirement from the World Health Organisation and the Animal Protection League.[4]

Other Jewish exiles have been "discovered" and honoured, but only decades after the end of the Second World War. William Perl's rescue mission of thousands of Austrian Jews following the _Anschluss_ and his service in Military Intelligence – he rose from private to lieutenant-colonel – finally gained recognition in 1990 from the US House of Representatives. The full story of his heroism was carried ultimately and belatedly by the _New York Times_ in a full-page feature story.[5]

Even the most exclusive of all US intelligence services, Naval Intelligence, which prior to the Second World War was closed to non-native Americans, numbered among its war-time members the colourful journalist, theatre critic and cultural historian Curt Riess. He brought some life into the staid and somnolent Washington establishment of Naval Intelligence. On his own initiative he started to interrogate the first German prisoners-of-war to come into American hands: the survivors of sunk submarines and surface vessels. He did not concentrate on the then standard military intelligence information, but

[3]See Charles R. Ashman, _Kissinger, the Adventures of Super Kraut_, Secaucus, N.J. 1972, pp. 56–57.
[4]Angress's activities were told to me in personal conversations during and after the Second World War. For Karl Frucht see Eric Sevareid, _Not So Wild a Dream_, New York 1946, pp. 97, 112, 134, 154, 183 and 200. Frucht's book was scheduled for publication by the Kremayer Verlag of Vienna late in 1991. For Varian Fry's rescue mission see his autobiography, _Surrender On Demand_, New York 1945.
[5]See Ralph Blumenthal, 'Decades After Helping Jews Escape, A Psychologist Gains Honor As a Hero', _New York Times_, National Ed., 18th November 1990, p. 32L; see also William R. Perl, _Operation Action. Rescue from the Holocaust_, New York 1983.

elicited gossip about Germany's naval officers which ranged from sexual misbehaviour to financial defalcations. Then he broadcast these choice bits along with some serious news to German ships at sea. He heard subsequently from prisoners that these broadcasts created jealousies, suspicion and several fist fights among German naval personnel.[6]

Riess's enterprise earned him a laudatory mention in the memoirs of Admiral Ellis M. Zacharias, Chief of Naval Intelligence,[7] and a subsequent posting to Allan Dulles's Office of Strategic Services (OSS) headquarters in Basel. Based in Switzerland, he undertook several cloak-and-dagger return trips to Germany in 1943, trying to assess the willingness of the average German to continue the war. Infiltrated by train, he was retrieved each time by a small craft traversing the Rhine. But on his last trip he missed his rendezvous; on sighting a German border patrol, he swam back to safety, contracting pneumonia as a result.[8]

However, the most sizable group of German-Jewish exiles were the backbone of that sector of Army Military Intelligence which was charged with the interrogation of German prisoners-of-war. Typically, a soldier endowed with certain essential skills (fluency in German, Italian or Japanese, competence in the analysis of aerial photographs, intimate knowledge of German geography, politics and history) would be culled out of one or another branch of service and sent, after the requisite clearance by the Federal Bureau of Investigation (FBI) or other agencies, to the Military Intelligence Training Camp at Camp Ritchie, Maryland, located in the picturesque Blue Ridge Mountains and within commuting distance of Baltimore and Washington.

According to Hans Habe, "about 80 percent of the Intelligence recruits were not yet American citizens, about half of them were refugees from Hitler and less than 5 percent had been born in America".[9] The training programme, a rigorous preparation for the vetting of German prisoners, has been described in various autobiographies by the exile-trainees. A particularly graphic description appears in Hanuš Burger's *Der Frühling war es wert*.

"In dieses Camp, das gewiß über dreitausend Mann faßte, wurde man aufgenommen, wenn man irgendwelche Sprachen Europas halbwegs passabel meisterte. Es wimmelte hier also nicht nur von Ex-Deutschen, Ex-Österreichern, Ex-Franzosen und -Italienern, sondern die Lochkartenmaschinen des Pentagon hatten darüber hinaus alle ausgespuckt, die diese Sprachen aus den verschiedensten Gründen irgendwann gelernt hatten. Außer Emigranten konnten also ebensogut Ur-Amerikaner hierher verschlagen werden, Universitätsdozenten zum Beispiel, die Germanistik lehrten und Spezialisten für Walther von der Vogelweide waren, oder Hotelportiers, die fünfundzwanzig gängige Sätze in vier verschiedenen Sprachen beherrschten, die mit ihrem Beruf zusammenhingen. Lochkarten sind da unparteiisch . . .

In einer Sonderbaracke lagerten zentnerweise erbeutete Dokumente, Briefe, Landkarten und Ausrüstungsstücke. Hier wurde unterrichtet, wie man solches Fallobst des Schlachtfeldes ausdeutet, auswertet und archiviert. Als ich Anfang 1943 nach Ritchie kam, lag bereits die erste Frucht dieser Auswertungen vor: eine dicke Broschüre, in der man nachschlagen konnte, wie der deutsche Abschnittskommandeur von St. Sauveur in der Normandie hieß, wie lange er im Dienst war, ob ihn seine Mannen schätzten und warum, ob er verheiratet, ein

---

[6]See Curt Riess, *Das waren Zeiten. Eine nostalgische Autobiografie mit vielen Mitwirkenden*, Vienna–Munich–Zurich–Innsbruck 1977, chaps. 20–23.
[7]Ellis M. Zacharias, *Secret Missions. The Story of an Intelligence Officer*, New York 1946, p. 305.
[8]See Riess, *op. cit.*, chap. 3, especially pp. 32–38.
[9]See Hans Habe, *All my Sins. An Autobiography*, transl. by E. Osers, London–Toronto 1957, p. 324.

lauer oder scharfer Nazi war. Das ganze Ding hieß 'German Order of Battle', und es gab Kameraden, die es auswendig kannten. Aber was konnte sich alles geändert haben, bis wir selbst in Frankreich landen würden!"[10]

Burger might have added that a trainee also had to master, for later instantaneous recognition, Italian army organisation and foreign maps. He had to prove his map-reading skill by locating a designated position in the middle of the night. He had the chance to take a refresher course in German stenography under Staff Sergeant Tengood[11] who, like many of the other instructors, was in exile from Nazi Germany.

While some of the "Ritchie Boys", as they were called by the natives of the Blue Ridge Mountain area, were established professionals already, many others would achieve prominence after the war. Before entering the service, Curtis Bieber had started to climb the ladder towards a distinguished career in the music department of CBS, Stefan Heym had written one best-seller, and Hanuš Burger was an established theatre director. After the war Kurt Jasen became an avid art collector, his hobby supported by successful business enterprises, Fred Howard (Fritz Ehrlich) established, through Howard Displays, the largest display company in the US;[12] and Benno Frank became a US theatre officer in West Berlin. Countless Ritchie graduates, including the German-Jewish exiles, began successful careers in American colleges and universities. One of these post-war luminaries, the writer Walter Hasenclever, described in his autobiography the arcane activities at Camp Ritchie.

> "Das Lager war ein wahres Babel. Wir wurden aufgefordert und ermutigt, uns in der jeweiligen Fremdsprache zu unterhalten, die für unsere Abwehrtätigkeit wichtig werden sollte. Englisch sprach man nur mit den Wachen und den Offizieren, oder mit den Angehörigen anderer Sprachgebiete, um überhaupt eine Verständigung zu ermöglichen. Sonst hörte man an jeder Straßenecke und an jedem Barackenwinkel eine andere Fremdsprache – wobei Fremdsprache gleich Nichtenglisch ist – die fließend und mit Leidenschaft gesprochen wurde."[13]

Once in the European Theatre of Operations and after the invasions of Italy and Normandy, the Ritchie graduates found themselves attached to intelligence units (S-2 and G-2) ranging from regimental to army level. And, depending upon their assignment, they were handed the task of ferreting out important tactical and strategic information. At the regimental level, a Prisoners-of-War Interrogator (PWI) might be charged with eliciting the exact location of an enemy artillery position; at the army level he was to assess German morale inside the *Reich*, locate industrial targets for the air force, pinpoint supply and troop replacement routes, report on the effect of air raids and of psychological warfare and, towards the end of the war, unmask perpetrators of atrocities and war crimes.

---

[10]Hanuš Burger, *Der Frühling war es wert. Erinnerungen*, München 1977, pp. 32 and 34.
[11]These observations are confirmed by my own experiences as a graduate of the eighth class at Camp Ritchie and as a participant in Sgt. Tengood's course.
[12]Several of the above-named are mentioned in Karl Frucht, 'We Were a PWI Team', *Commentary*, I (January 1946), pp. 69–76.
[13]Walter Hasenclever, *Ihr werdet Deutschland nicht wieder erkennen. Erinnerungen*, Munich 1978, p. 42.

I may speak from my own experience for a moment. I was part of a six-man PWI-team (Team 41), attached with four other teams to the First Army of General Courtney Hodges and his G-2 and Assistant G-2, Colonel Benjamin A. ("Monk") Dickson and Lieutenant-Colonel Specht. The vast majority of the officers and enlisted men in our teams were German-Jewish refugees, all of whom felt that the war against Hitler Germany was a personal crusade. We used various tactics to extract information from prisoners, ranging from preferential treatment such as providing extra food, to the psychological ploy of threatening to hand them over to the Russians with the consequent shipment to Siberia, a threat never carried out, of course. A daily forty-page report, at first reproduced on gelatin mats, was the average product of a day's interrogation.

The commander of our unit, Lieutenant, later Captain, Edgar Kann, also a German-Jewish refugee, designated me as chief of our survey section. We would receive a variety of complicated questionnaires from the different higher headquarters, e.g. from the Air Force, Engineers, Medical Corps and Psychological Warfare units, inquiring about such matters as the methods employed by the Germans to replace damaged railway tracks and bombed-out rolling stock, or the make-up of newly formed German divisions. (I was decorated for the accuracy and value of these reports.) One of our reports, recently rediscovered in the National Archives, is attached to this article as an example of our methods (see Appendix).[14] And one of our "reports", which we wrote as comic relief in the form of an overly broad satire (it detailed our purported discovery of Hitler's "latrine orderly" at the *Führer Hauptquartier*), was taken at face value, as a factual document, in a serious history of the US Counter Intelligence Corps![15]

But more demanding concerns occupied us. Fred Howard and I were among the first to identify and interrogate one of the Third *Reich*'s mass murderers, a German Army physician named Gustav Wilhelm Schuebbe, whose lethal injections of morphine preparations doomed more than 25,000 concentration camp inmates.[16] The uncovering of murderers, small-scale and large-scale, caused recurrent shock waves among us, Jewish soldiers formerly from Germany and Austria.

[14]See National Archives, M1623, Roll 2 (=War Diary, M[orale] O[perations] Branch, OSS London Psychological Warfare Division, Vol. V, Book 1. For a helpful guide to pertinent sections of the National Archives, see Steven W. Siegel, 'U.S. War Department', in Herbert A. Strauss (ed.), *Jewish Immigrants of the Nazi Period in the USA*, New York–Munich–London–Paris 1978, vol. I, p. 97.
[15]Ian Sayer and Douglas Botting, *America's Secret Army. The Untold Story of the Counter Intelligence Corps*, New York–Toronto 1989, pp. 193–194, mistook our satire as "one of the strangest cases ever to have involved the CIC in World War Two". Another history, quoting our satire, did point out that it was spurious. See Charles B. MacDonald, *A Time for Trumpets. The Untold Story of the Battle of the Bulge*, New York 1985, p. 56: "The strain [between First Army Headquarters and OSS] increased when somebody at the First Army headquarters wrote a parody of a prisoner-of-war report, allegedly representing an interrogation of Hitler's latrine orderly. Finding it amusing, Captain Wainwright sent it to his OSS superiors at the 12th Army Group, where everybody missed the point and took the parody seriously. An order was soon on the way to the First Army to fly the prisoner back to SHAEF for further questioning, much to the subsequent embarrassment of the OSS."
[16]Our discovery of Schuebbe was reported by a major news-magazine. See 'Out of the Pit', *Time* (7th May 1945), p. 35.

Unfortunately, our reports did not receive the attention they deserved. Had they been more closely heeded, they could have forewarned our troops of the German counter-attack that came at the end of 1944.[17]

Our work at army level constituted a war of the minds with the Germans which was dangerous only during the Normandy Invasion and the German counter-offensive, the "Battle of the Bulge". Our comrades in the lower echelons, however, incurred casualties and some performed deeds of valour. Perhaps the most remarkable feat was performed by Captain Walter Midener who, Maurice R. Davie noted, single-handedly induced 340 German soldiers to surrender to him.

> "M/Sgt. Walter Mitener [sic], a sculptor in civilian life, who learned after his arrival here that his parents had committed suicide to avoid deportation to Poland, said that he knew what he was fighting for. He received the Silver Star and a commission as lieutenant for capturing 400 Germans. 'I just talked them into surrender.' "[18]

Midener returned to the United States to become a prestigious American sculptor, represented in major museums and public institutions. In a recent interview, I elicited the details of his exploit. At the battle of Falaise-Argentan, then-Sgt. Midener learned through the interrogation of a German Catholic priest of the whereabouts of several wounded enemy soldiers. But when he arrived at the outskirts of Argentan, he found that not only disabled German soldiers but also uninjured troops were in the vicinity. Through the force of his personality and with shouted German commands, he brought about their surrender. At first completely alone, and then with the help of a platoon of the 90th Division, he convinced this batch of POWs to induce more and more German soldiers to surrender. For this daring exploit, Major William Falvey, S–2 of the 358th Regiment, and General James van Fleet recommended him for the Silver Star and a battlefield commission.

Another German-Jewish exile, Staff Sergeant Walter ("Putty") Eichelbaum, achieved a spectacular surrender of a very special German unit. In bringing it about he employed a most canny strategem. During the Battle of the Bulge he spotted a platoon-sized German unit, dressed in American uniforms, which had penetrated the American lines as far as Thionville, France. Although he lacked training in psychological warfare – he had been transferred to Military Intelligence from a combat unit without the benefit of Camp Ritchie – he hit on an ingenious plan. He commandeered a few military policemen, a searchlight and a loudspeaker. Then, he assumed the role of part of a German division in disguise asking American troops to surrender. Since the unit of Germans in American combat dress had nothing to fear from their own countrymen, they

---

[17]See MacDonald, *op. cit.*, p. 70, who shows that the warning by Colonel Benjamin A. ("Monk") Dickson, G-2, First Army, was predicated in part on our interrogation "of an extremely intelligent PW" and on our observations "that morale among recently captured prisoners of war had 'achieved a new high' ". MacDonald's favourable account of the contributions of the German-Jewish exiles is marred by an insensitive observation (p. 55): "[American Intelligence Officers] might employ as interrogators refugee German-Jews whose appearance belied their race".

[18]Maurice R. Davie, *Refugees in America*, New York–London 1947, p. 189.

came out, singly and unarmed – and received the shock of their lives when their captors turned out to be Americans. Because of his feat in disarming a potentially exceedingly troublesome cadre of saboteurs and disruptors, Sgt. Eichelbaum was decorated by General George Patton and mentioned in despatches.[19] His heroism also proved that ingenuity plus language skills could substitute for formal intelligence training.

Not all of us were as fortunate. Two interrogators, captured by an SS-unit during the German counter-attack, were identified in the prison camp as Jews from Berlin, were taken out, and shot.[20]

Another US intelligence agency, which also sent personnel to Camp Ritchie as part of a trainee's "curriculum", was the American Counter Intelligence Corps (CIC).[21] In brief, the agency's mission was counter espionage or, as one of the directives put it: "The primary purpose of these agents is undercover operation for the detection and investigation of espionage, sabotage, disaffection, disloyalty and general subversion."[22] In practice, it meant that they investigated suspect civilians overtaken by the Allied advance, or, in more dramatic situations, they were instrumental in unmasking German soldiers disguised as Americans during the German counterattack. These infiltrators behind the US lines had been charged to disrupt the Allied effort and some with the assassination of high-ranking US officers, including General Eisenhower.[23]

Several of the German-Jewish exiles served with the CIC throughout the war. Near war's end, one of them, Special Agent Arnold Weiss, teamed up with Major Hugh Trevor-Roper in an attempt, ultimately successful, to determine the events surrounding Hitler's last days. Weiss and Trevor-Roper interrogated *SS-Standartenführer* Wilhelm Zander and learned the whereabouts of Hitler's personal last will and political testament. For this extraordinary coup, Weiss received numerous medals and citations.[24] Finally, Captain Walter Rothschild capped his OSS war-time service as one of the supervisors for the training of future CIC agents at the counter-intelligence school at Fort Holabird, Maryland.[25] It was there that I met him.

Several more German-Jewish refugees were recruited for service in occupied Germany shortly after the cessation of hostilities: "A few of the newer CIC men did manage to bring linguistic ability and a familiarity of the German background to their jobs. Mostly these were German refugees, generally of Jewish origin, who had sought sanctuary in the USA during Hitler's rise to power before the war."[26]

---

[19]See Bernt Engelmann, *Die unfreiwilligen Reisen des Putti Eichelbaum*, Munich 1986, pp. 300–307.
[20]My unit received news of this war crime from the reports of lower echelons.
[21]As detailed by Sayer and Botting, *op. cit.*, p. 36.
[22]*Ibid.*, pp. 24 and 134.
[23]*Ibid.*, p. 178.
[24]*Ibid.*, p. 308.
[25]See 'Rothschild, Walter', in Werner Röder and Herbert Strauss (eds.), *Biographisches Handbuch der deutschsprachigen Emigration nach 1933*, Munich–New York–London–Paris 1980–1983, vol I, p. 622.
[26]Sayer and Botting, *op. cit.*, p. 276.

The contributions of the CIC to the war effort have been chronicled in only one monograph, published as late as 1989, while the exploits of the OSS have been recalled, even celebrated, in numerous voluminous studies.[27] And there is some justice in an often repeated complaint by CIC personnel: "To the OSS fell the glamour; to the CIC fell the grind."[28]

The OSS was created with the vague mandate "to plan and operate such special services as may be directed by the Joint Chiefs of Staff". Its ultimate charge – to perform "research, secret intelligence and subversive activities" – was only slightly more precise.[29] Working under these ambiguous directives and with a visionary at its helm, the legendary "Wild" Bill Donovan, the OSS engaged in all types of intelligence operations, from spy missions to sabotage, from library research to front-line telephone monitoring, from fighting with underground units in France and Yugoslavia to attempting high-level and/or surreptitious diplomacy, in short from the gathering of information to acting upon it. In all of its operations, but especially in its research and analysis branch, the OSS drew on the exiles from Nazi Germany. Toni Sender, the exiled German-Jewish labour leader, supplied Arthur Goldberg, Head of the OSS-Labour Desk and future Supreme Court Justice, with invaluable lists of anti-Nazi union officials within Germany and Austria;[30] Robert Kempner, as early as 1944, assembled a similar list "of anti-Nazis who might be selected for administrative posts by the American Military Government".[31]

When Allan Dulles was sent by OSS to Berne to build up "an intelligence network that stretched from Algiers to Prague", his priority, set by Washington, was to contact resistance groups. He used Gerald Meyer to establish contact with Fritz Kolbe, a German foreign office official who would become Dulles's eyes and ears in the *Auswärtiges Amt*. Meyer, the first liaison person, "was an OWI [Office of War Information] propagandist of German-Jewish extraction who had been co-opted by Dulles for his OSS-staff".[32] Another Dulles recruit, at least equally valuable as a contact with resisters and resistance groups in Germany, was Gero von Schulze-Gaevernitz. Described in one of the histories of the OSS as Dulles's "principal link to the anti-Nazi opposition in Germany", he was the son of a liberal Weimar legislator who, because of his Jewish wife, had left Germany after Hitler's accession to power. His son, despite his "non-Aryan" background, "was well-connected in German elite circles . . . When Dulles arrived, Gaevernitz was already prepared to introduce him to anti-Nazi émigrés in Berne."[33]

---

[27]Bradley F. Smith, *The Shadow Warriors. OSS and the Origins of the C.I.A.*, New York 1983, p. xiv.
[28]Sayer and Botting, *op. cit.*, p. 31.
[29]See R. Harris Smith, *OSS. The Secret History of America's First Central Intelligence Agency*, Berkeley–Los Angeles–London 1972; and Bradley Smith, *op. cit.*, p. 161.
[30]See Guy Stern, ' "Hitler besiegen – das genügt nicht". Zusammenarbeit zwischen amerikanischen und exilierten Gewerkschaftlern', in Thomas Koebner, Gert Sautermeister and Sigrid Schneider (eds.), *Deutschland nach Hitler*, Opladen 1988, p. 153, where Sender's work for the OSS is detailed.
[31]See R. Harris Smith, *op. cit.*, p. 222. For a fuller account of Kempner's remarkable achievements, see Röder and Strauss, *op. cit.*, vol. I, pp. 360f.
[32]See R. Harris Smith, *op. cit.*, p. 219.
[33]*Ibid.*, pp. 230 and 211.

Finally a few exiles, such as the aforementioned Curt Riess, took part in the missions carried out in enemy territory. The need for strategic intelligence about and from within Germany surfaced in October 1944; no plans for such missions had been made by Supreme Headquarters. "The OSS fell back in desperation upon the small German operation section formed by the Labor Section . . . By the spring of 1945 OSS had sent more than 150 men into Germany." For these missions Arthur Goldberg "enlisted a host of German-speaking agents [including] a few German exiles. Missions of those kinds raised the image and prestige of OSS in the eyes of Eisenhower and other Allied commanders."[34]

But, as I previously indicated, the German-Jewish exiles made their most palpable impact on the OSS within the confines of its Research and Analysis (R. and A.) Division under the command of William Langer, the noted Harvard historian. Their recruitment and performance have been summarised in the most recent history of the OSS:

> "By 1943, there was a large and influential German refugee contingent in R. and A. featuring, among others, Hajo Holborn, Franz Neumann, and Otto Kirchheimer. Many of these people were distinctly leftist in their political predilections, and nearly all had been classified as non-Aryan by the Nazis, although few were practising Jews . . . But in R. and A., they were respected, and such men as Neumann and Holborn (the latter having already been taken aboard at Yale), enjoyed a status of special esteem and honor. This phenomenon constituted a real breakthrough in extending the social base of American academia (in the social sciences and the humanities) and would contribute to the further broadening of the social groups represented in American high educational faculties during the postwar university boom."[35]

Beyond this relatively terse account, the contributions of the Jews from Germany to Research and Analysis have been commemorated in a chapter-length account within a specialised study of that division. Entitled 'The Frankfurt School Goes to War', the chapter details how the Marxist scholars with "their distinctive theory of the inner mechanism of Fascism" and with "their deep reservoir of political, regional and linguistic expertise"[36] came up with, at least in the first phase of the war, infinitely detailed and profound studies of the Third *Reich* and its capabilities for warfare.

> "Throughout 1943 the Senior Analysts were concerned with the functioning of the New Order in Germany and Nazi-occupied Europe. Their studies, based on reports in the European press, radio broadcasts from the Reich monitored by the Federal Comunications Commission, cables from the OSS Mission to London and outposts in neutral Lisbon, Algiers, Stockholm, and Bern, prisoner-of-war interrogations, and – most prosaic of all – published materials excavated from the Library of Congress, dealt with the potential significance of everything from the effects of bomb damage on civilian morale to changes in ladies' fashions. While struggling to define their task and to be heard within the organization, they assembled a minutely detailed picture of the social, economic, political, and cultural structure of totalitarianism, and of points of vulnerability and resistance within it."[37]

---

[34]*Ibid.*, p. 225.
[35]Bradley Smith, *op. cit.*, p. 379.
[36]Barry M. Katz, *Foreign Intelligence Research and Analysis in the Office of Strategic Services, 1942–1945*, Cambridge, Mass.–London 1989, p. 31.
[37]Katz, *op. cit.*, p. 34. One of the most astute analysts was Franz Neumann. About his leadership, see Robin W. Winks, *Cloak and Gown, 1939–61. Scholars In the Secret War*, New York 1987, p. 85.

But it can also be argued that the brilliant thinkers of German-Jewish origin who found themselves in the R. and A. division, from the Frankfurt School and beyond – Franz Neumann, Felix Gilbert, Otto Kirchheimer, Friedrich Pollock, Richard Krautheimer, and Henry Kellerman – had an impact on American thinking much beyond the war years. The German scholar Alfons Söllner, analysing the papers by representative members of the Frankfurt School, concedes that their influence, if measured by the parameters of mega-politics, might be negligible. But he adds that a smaller, more subtle influence might still have prevailed: "Es ist vielleicht nur verdeckte Wirklichkeit oder gar eine Wirklichkeit, die sich selbst verdecken mußte."[38] Much the same can be argued for the non-Marxist scholars and thinkers of OSS.

While these contributions of the exiles to the war-time OSS have not gone unnoticed, their numbers do not stop there. Several exiles, as can be extrapolated from a recently acquired collection at the New York Leo Baeck Institute,[39] were drawn into the orbit of the OSS as special consultants. Specifically Emil J. Gumbel, an avowed Socialist and, before Hitler's rise to power, a mathematician at the University of Heidelberg and an analyst of National Socialism virtually from its beginnings, was asked repeatedly to supply historical information needed by the Research and Analysis branch. In letters of 11th September 1944 and 7th February 1945, signed by William B. Kip of the OSS, Gumbel is asked to contribute to a "List of a Thousand" and to write a "day-by-day history of Munich from November 1918 to November 1919". We may infer from this example that other German-Jewish exiles were similarly approached.

As to the refugees' contributions and essential value during the war-years there was never any doubt in the mind of the founder and commander of the OSS, General Donovan. One of the early historians of the OSS, Ladislav Farago, recalls a conversation with Donovan during a train ride in December, 1942. "We talked about the big mistake France had made when it interned without discrimination the bulk of German refugees instead of utilizing the cream of the crop in the war against the Nazis. He mentioned a book he had read recently on the subject and that stirred him to considerable thinking. It was Arthur Koestler's *Scum of the Earth*. 'I will never make that mistake', he said."[40] The German-Jewish exiles of the OSS more than repaid his farsightedness.

The OSS, while never abandoning propaganda exploits entirely, had relinquished most of its psychological warfare missions to the Office of War

---

[38]Alfons Söllner, 'Archäologie der deutschen Demokratie. Eine Forschungshypothese zur theoretischen Praxis der kritischen Theorie im amerikanischen Geheimdienst', in his anthology *Zur Archäologie der Demokratie in Deutschland. Analysen politischer Emigranten im amerikanischen Geheimdienst. Band I: 1933–1945*, Frankfurt a. Main 1982, p. 35; see also *idem*, for the United Kingdom, 'On Transit to America. Political Scientists from Germany in Great Britain after 1933', in Werner E. Mosse (co-ordinating ed.), Julius Carlebach, Gerhard Hirschfeld, Aubrey Newman, Arnold Paucker, Peter Pulzer (eds.), *Second Chance. Two Centuries of German-speaking Jews in the United Kingdom*, Tübingen 1991 (Schriftenreihe wissenschaftlicher Abhandlungen des Leo Baeck Instituts 48), pp. 121–135.

[39]The papers are filed as the Emil J. Gumbel Collection of the New York LBI Archives.

[40]Ladislav Farago, *Burn After Reading. The Espionage History of World War II*, New York 1962, p. 219.

Information (OWI) by 1944. Some of the most talented writers and speakers of German-Jewish origin were recruited for this task by the incredibly adroit "manager" Hans Habe, who was able to commandeer an abandoned army post, Camp Sharpe, in Pennsylvania, for training purposes and to utilise to the utmost his troupe of Jewish intellectuals for the three major phases of psychological warfare: direct loudspeaker addresses to front-line enemy units, the composing of propaganda leaflets, and the manning of propaganda radio stations.[41]

The work of these Jewish intelligence officers and enlisted men was prodigious, sometimes death-defying, and often under-appreciated. Oskar Seidlin, in later years a friend and colleague, told me that he found leaflet-writing as demanding a task as the composition of the most scholarly Germanist articles and books.[42] While he has left no written account of these activities, two of his Jewish comrades-in-arms, Hanuš Burger and Stefan Heym, the latter a highly acclaimed novelist before and after the war, have given us graphic descriptions of all three phases of psychological warfare. Here is Burger's narrative of a loudspeaker mission:

"Der Anflug [amerikanischer Flugzeuge] dauerte fünf ohrenbetäubende, dröhnende Minuten. Im gleichen Augenblick, da der Lärm erstarb, begann ich: 'Achtung, Achtung . . . !' Komisch, wie meine Stimme klingt. Der Lautsprecher steht etwa 40 Meter weiter. Ich sage denen da drüben, wie sie rüberkommen sollen. Ich erzähle ihnen keine Lügen. Alles, was ich sage, muß stimmen. Sie können es ja nachprüfen . . .

Ja, und dann geschieht tatsächlich das Unglaubliche. Aus den Büschen kommen mit aufgehobenen Händen vier Deutsche in verdreckten Tarnuniformen. Sie sind völlig betäubt . . .

[Es sind] Jungs von einer Einheit, die erst heute eingesetzt wurde, und schon haben unsere Intelligence-Leute ein Muster zur Verfügung.

Ich reiße das Mikrophon wieder hoch.

'Achtung. Achtung! Die erste Gruppe eurer Kameraden ist schon bei uns. Sie sind der Hölle entgangen. Sie sind in Sicherheit.'

Die zweite Gruppe kommt aus den Büschen. Noch dreizehn Fallschirmjäger und ein Panzergrenadier."[43]

Stefan Heym recalls the composition of propaganda leaflets; literally hundreds were devised by psychological warfare:

"Folglich sind die ersten Flugblätter, die er [Stefan Heym] und der Sergeant [Hanuš] Burger und ein oder zwei andere in Colombières zu schreiben beginnen, höchst einfach: dem Gegner wird seine Situation dargelegt, er ist eingekreist, oder abgeschnitten, oder steht einer Streitmacht gegenüber, die ihm an Material und Feuerkraft weit überlegen ist; ein Hinweis auf die russischen Siege im Osten mag von Nutzen sein, denn daraus läßt sich schlußfolgern, daß größere Reserven hier an der Westfront kaum zu erwarten sind, und daß Görings Luftwaffe nur noch begrenzt eingreifen kann, sieht der Landser selber, da genügt eine kurze Bemerkung, ein Nebensatz oft . . . [Die] Mädchen im Bayeux des Jahres 1944 rollen die Bündel der Flugblätter nun und stopfen sie in die Hülsen von Rauchgranaten, Kaliber 105 mm, die dann, aus den entsprechenden Haubitzen gefeuert, ihren papierenen Segen über den deutschen Linien herabflattern lassen."[44]

---

[41]See Habe, *op. cit.*, pp. 340–350.
[42]Virtually all US propaganda leaflets of the Second World War directed at enemy forces have been reprinted in a remarkable folio-size volume. See Klaus Kirchner, *Flugblattpropaganda im zweiten Weltkrieg Europas, Band 6: Flugblätter aus den USA 1943–44*, Erlangen 1980.
[43]Burger, *op. cit.*, pp. 179–180.
[44]Stefan Heym, *Nachruf*, Munich 1988, p. 292.

Radio Luxemburg, captured intact by the rapid Allied advance, devoted itself to the dissemination of news, openly attributed to its American source, for the consumption of soldiers and the German homeland. It maintained credibility by being scrupulously truthful. But the general news was merely background for the most potent psychological tool, the detailed, individual slice-of-life accounts, retold during the broadcasts by Americans, occasionally by German POWs:

> "Die Einzelschicksale . . . [sind] der eigentliche Stoff der Sendungen . . . die Schicksale von Einheiten, die zerrieben, von Menschen, die geopfert werden in einem Kampf, der längst verloren ist. Solche Schicksale erfährt man *zu Tausenden in den Lagern der Kriegsgefangenen*, aus Verhören und Berichten über Verhöre, oder man liest sie ab aus den Papieren, die die deutschen Stäbe zurückgelassen haben beim Rückzug, aus den vergeblichen Rufen nach Verstärkung, Munition, Lebensmitteln, den dürren Angaben der Ärzte in den Sanitätsstellen und Feldhospitälern. Und dann die Briefe: Briefe, die die an der Front nach Hause schicken an Frau und Mutter und Kind, und Briefe, die von zu Haus gesandt wurden an die Männer vorn, Briefe, die sämtlich ihre Adressaten nicht mehr erreichten – jeder Brief ein Schicksal."[45]

The sensitivity and the intimate knowledge of the German psyche of a Heym, a Burger, a Peter Weidenfeld and, yes, a Hans Habe were required to turn this mostly prosaic detritus of the crumbling Third *Reich* into an effective tool of psychological warfare.[46]

The intelligence work of the German-Jewish exiles did not end with the close of the Second World War. An appreciable number applied their rare talents, honed during the war, to the war-crime trials and to such tasks as the supervision of the reviving German media, to military government, or to temporary new assignments. A spot check of a standard reference work reveals time and again the initials "OMGUS" (Office of Military Government [for Germany] US) or the item "Nuremberg Trials" in its biographical entries.[47] Still other exiles made the US Army their career. But that is another story and of another time.[48] Most of these exile warriors, like Cincinnatus of early Roman times, would return to their peace-time occupations with the satisfaction of having done their part in a war about which they felt intensely personal.

---

[45] *Ibid.*, pp. 310–311.

[46] See Röder and Strauss, *op. cit.*, *passim*.

[47] A part of this early post-war history has already been documented and analysed by Ulrich Borsdorf and Lutz Niethammer, *Zwischen Befreiung und Besatzung. Analysen des US-Geheimdienstes über Positionen und Strukturen deutscher Politik 1945*, Wuppertal 1976. See for example p. 12: "Auch die Abwehrabteilungen der nach Deutschland einmarschierenden Armeen (CIC) beschäftigten vielfach Emigranten oder Amerikaner deutscher bzw. jüdischer Abstammung als Führer, Dolmetscher, Untersuchungsbeamte, etc." The quote's dichotomy between "German" and "Jewish" deserves criticism. It only recently came to my attention that Professor Gustave Mathieu (Fullerton, California) assumed important responsibilities as a member of the Information Control Branch of Military Government and of the radio station, RIAS, in Berlin.

APPENDIX

FIRST ARMY
SPECIAL REPORT

5/6 Nov 44

EFFECTS OF ALLIED PROPAGANDA – A SURVEY

Introduction

Since there was a lull in the fighting prior to the attack of 28th Inf Div of 2 Nov 44, US forces had ample time to subject the enemy in that sector to diverse methods of propaganda. It was the purpose of this survey to determine

1. what effect our propaganda had
2. reaction of the Germans
3. strength and weaknesses of this particular propaganda campaign
4. suggestions for future psychological warfare; see paragraph entitled "Ideas for new propaganda" (p. 27)

315 PWs were questioned for this survey, including 2 officers. All PWs belonged to the 275 Div and its auxiliaries, e.g. KG WEGLEIN and TRIER. The 275 Div held sector SCHMIDT-VOSSENACK-HUERTGEN which is the sector on which our attack as well as our propaganda concentrated. Depth of propaganda penetration could not be determined as no PW captured belonged to echelons higher than Bn Hq.

Effects

Deserters. Out of 315 PWs interrogated, 17 claim to have come over to our lines voluntarily, 9 claim that leaflets had some bearing on their decision to desert. The promise of good treatment, coupled with their already punctured morale, effected their desertion. Said a Cpl from 1 Co 983 Regt "I had been toying with the idea to desert for some time, but I formed a fixed plan after I had read your leaflet 'Wir bitten um Auskunft'". A NCO claims that the night following our leaflet barrages 4 Volksdeutsche disappeared. All in all interrogators won the impression that leaflets rarely are the sole or even primary cause for desertion, but that they are often the "weight that tips the balance". PWs state the reason many Germans do not desert is the sharp supervision by officers and NCOs.

Range of Leaflets

Distribution seems to have been best in the vicinity of UNTER-MAUBACH-F 095375, worst in sector of 3 Co 983 Regt vicinity VOSSENACK where out of 41 PWs questioned only 3 had seen our leaflets. The leaflet that circulated most and was retained by many PWs was the "Safe Conduct leaflet", with "Was nicht geht, das geht nicht" running a not too close second. Our "Frontpost" – pamphlet in newspaper form – and "Wen schuetzt der Westwall?" follow in this order. It should also be mentioned that none of the pamphlets addressed to the 1412 Bn – now 1 Bn 983 – "Das war ein Traum" ever reached this unit. Altogether 257 PWs saw our leaflets in one form or another.

Source: National Archives, M1623, Roll 2 (= War Diary, M[orale] O[perations] Branch, OSS London Psychological Warfare Division, Vol. 5, Book I).

Distribution

PWs claim distribution could have been enhanced by more precise release from planes. In many instances leaflets were either blown back to our lines or 10–12 km behind the German lines.

Range of Frontline Broadcasts

The broadcast which was released before the attack was more or less ineffective. Only 31 of PWs questioned heard the transmission, all but 2 EM – on an advanced post – failed to understand the words. Reason for this failure seems to have been threefold:

1. unfavorable wind conditions
2. the distance between loudspeaker and German lines
3. the fact that a forest was located in the path of the sound

Criticism of Existing Leaflets

What they liked:

1. The veracity of the leaflets is generally believed by PWs. 257 PWs saw the leaflets, and their reaction upon receipt was as follows:

Credence without reservations	185
Credence of most points	32
Doubtful – between belief and disbelief	19
Disbelief	21

2. The Safe Conduct leaflet was by far the most popular. Without exception did the PWs refer to it as a "document". It frequently happened during the survey that when asked whether they had seen any propaganda leaflets PWs answered "No, but we saw some of those documents signed by General Eisenhower". The official-looking make-up, the seals, the military language, plus aforementioned signature – underneath explicit instructions to Allied troops on how to treat PWs – appealed to the German psychology. They are sure that our troops will follow a signed order and they have faith in the integrity of our CG. PWs suggest more leaflets on the same order.

3. PWs on the front are always receptive to news and appreciate news items even if disseminated by the enemy. The fact that the German "Wehrmachtsbericht" is constantly being "scooped" by our "Frontpost" is believed to be good propaganda. Including news-items in the small-form leaflets is suggested by several PWs.

4. The mentioning of the names of COs and telling about their foibles gives the Germans the satisfaction to see their favorite gripes rehashed. This plays havoc with their morale. – Leaflet "General Model spricht zum Landser" in which the cowardice of Lt PRYM is mentioned.

They didn't like:

1. Mistakes in spelling often jar the unconscious belief that the writer is a German "Comrade" and gives rise to ridicule. For example, many of the PWs had noticed the faulty abbreviation of artillery in the leaflet mentioned above. Sentence-structure, although usually painstakingly correct, is not loose enough. Wording at times, without talking down to the soldiers, could be less formal. A NCO states that f.i. the leaflet "So fiel Aachen" is written over the head of the average soldier.

2. Of dubious propaganda value, according to PWs, is our "advertising" – on a leaflet entitled "Frage den Frontsoldaten" that PWs no longer are sent to the

States. Many of the PWs, especially the younger ones, consider the alternative of being taken prisoner a "good bet" because it would offer an opportunity to go to the States. The fact that remaining in Europe would mean being close to home at the end of the war did not compensate for the advantages which they believe accompany internment in the States.

3. PWs state that sometimes our leaflets promise too much. The implications in the leaflet entitled "Fuenf Minuten English" are just "too good to be true".

4. Gen Eisenhower's name should be printed underneath his signature. Many PWs couldn't make out his name on the Safe Conduct leaflets.

Ideas for New Propaganda

PWs brought up diverse suggestions on what they would like to hear through the leaflets as well as proposals on how to influence their comrades still fighting:

1. Treatment in PW Camps. German counter propaganda has constantly harped that PWs will be sent to Siberia, turned over to the French, or guarded by the Armée Blanche. This, PWs claim, keeps many men from deserting. Assurance that treatment is humane and food adequate – and constant repetition of this assurance – would dispel the Nazi claims of castration, famine and hard labor in Allied PW camps.

2. An appeal to the specialists in the German Army. Thousands of German airplane technicians, signal men, interpreters, medical technicians, flying personnel, etc., have been deprived of their jobs and have been committed as infantry. Their resentment, a PW formerly with the Navy claims, can be increased by our propaganda. That would be on the order of the leaflet entitled "Das war ein Traum".

3. Apparently German soldiers are more concerned about setbacks on the E. front than on the W. front. Constant accentuation of Russian progress, a soldier from the 1 Co 275 Fues Bn, believes, would lessen the fighting spirit of troops committed on the W. front.

4. The soldiers having seen our treatment of German civilians were greatly impressed. They believe that it would be good propaganda to inform the "Landser" about this point. Perhaps illustrate this leaflet with some good photos.

5. PWs were divided in their opinion on introducing music on the loudspeaker programs. Perhaps, one PW comments, at the end of this program we should make an appeal like this "Do you like music? If you do, come over to us because where you are you'll soon hear a different tune – played by our Arty".

6. The German soldier, for some reason or other, is afraid of our colored troops. Perhaps the fact that the average German has never seen a negro accounts for it. PWs claim that our colored line troops would take more prisoners if we assured the Jerries that treatment of PWs by our colored soldiers is equal to that accorded them by the white troops.

7. One NCO from 275 Medics states that it would be wise to stress in our propaganda that wounded and sick PWs receive good medical treatment. Also that they are frequently treated by their own doctors and medics who have the best US medical supplies at their disposal.

8. PWs passing through our lines are always impressed by the vastness of our supply system. In order to let the troops in the line know, we could perhaps send leaflets over giving detailed information about the rations Allied soldiers receive and stating the fact that PWs are being issued the same. Furthermore good pictures and descriptions of American war plants, ship yards and other military supply installation – without, of course, revealing exact locations – would convince Germans more than anything about the futility of their continued resistance.

9. "Tell the Germans", an Austrian deserter suggests, "that after the war they'll be sent home to a post-war Germany. You'll increase your number of deserters that way."

10. Many Germans are afraid to desert because that would mean walking into our Arty fire. Several PWs suggest that we drop leaflets telling Heinies that upon a pre-arranged signal or noise – which may come at any time – our firing will cease for a few minutes and that deserters can come without being endangered.

11. PW Michel JOVY suggests an appeal to the young German soldier. As he appears to be highly intelligent he was allowed to develop this theme himself and it is reproduced in ANNEX A.

12. All in all it appears that leaflets addressed to specific units, mentioning particular names, and calling attention to special events have more propaganda value than those on a general level. Although no specific poll was taken on this point, it appears that 70% of the PWs preferred leaflets like "Offener Brief", to more general ones like "Wer kann bis 3 zaehlen?"

Enemy Counterpropaganda and How to Combat It.

1. One of the ways in which the German High Command tries to curb circulation of leaflets is by ordering the immediate collection of leaflets. They have to be turned in to Os and NCOs. This fact, one PW points out, Allied propaganda could utilize by asking "Why are they anxious not to let you see our leaflets? Is it because they are afraid of the truth?"

2. Effective German counter propaganda followed our leaflet "Fragt den Frontsoldaten". We called attention to the fact that we are no longer sending PWs to the States. This was pounced upon by the Politischer Orientierungs-Offizier – propaganda officer – who told troops "Damn right, you're not going to the States, you're headed for Siberia as PWs". This bears out the inadvisability to continue this particular propaganda slogan.

3. Germany threatens its deserters with the prospect of famine for their families by withdrawal of ration cards. PWs suggest to throw great quantities of allied fabricated ration cards down over Germany to confuse the ration offices and thus render this threat ineffective.

4. Threats of death or imprisonment for families of deserters could be deprived of their sting by telling prospective German deserters that there are so many soldiers coming to our lines as to make the execution of these threats well-nigh impossible.

5. Orders have been issued in many sub-units of the 275th that advance-guards are to shoot at anyone trying to advance further than their posts. Deserters state that they circumvented this danger by either participating in patrols and then deserting, or by running over when they knew that the guard was a friend of theirs. Perhaps this advice should be passed on to German troops.

6. One officer of the 275 Fues Bn told his men in the way of counter-propaganda 'They must be pretty desperate if they have to resort to such methods as leaflets to try to win the war". Recommended propaganda to counteract statements like these was suggested by EM from the same unit: "Tell our troops that you're only 'resorting' to leaflets because you want to save lives".

7. "As PWs you'll be employed to blow up mines" is a rumor now circulated in 275 Div. PWs suggest we might tell this unit that this is not the case.

Allied Propaganda Methods

PWs claim that our distribution of leaflets by Arty shells was by far more precise than dropping them by nickel bombs which frequently open too early. It is significant that no one bothered to counteract our broadcast before our attack. PWs suggest that our broadcasts would be more effective if mobile radio units would follow closely behind Allied front-line troops, promising protection to surrendering pillbox crews. Other means to increase effectiveness would be to use a battery of loudspeakers instead of the single instruments used up to now. Leaflets are generally preferred to radio because as many PWs claim "leaflets are more personal and you can frequently refer to them".

Other Means of Propaganda

PWs state that letters received from PWs already in our base camps have always been "a plug" in our favor and one PW claims that he deserted because his cousin now in a Texas PW camp described his life there as very comfortable. One PW wisecracks "The best propaganda I have ever seen up to date was observing your airplanes overhead". Exchanged medics have frequently spread stories about the fair treatment in Allied PW camps.

Summary

Two officer PWs, one was 1st Lt E. STORK of the 275 Arty Regt – state that Allied leaflets have improved considerably since those first propaganda campaigns in Normandy. There can be no doubt that our leaflets give the Germans something to ponder about, and that generally they have to admit, even if they are Nazis like an NCO from the 1 Co 275 Fues Bn, "that there is something to the statements and claims made by the Allies". We also seem to have been able to convince the Germans that it is undoubtedly safer to desert than to try to hide somewhere in the homeland. Leaflets do succeed in many cases to further undermine an already shaky morale and to lessen "Kampfwillen" – willingness to fight – of a great many of our opponents.

Annex A
POLL conducted by: S/Sgt Guy STERN
                      Cpl V. SETTELEN   E. W. KANN
                                                          1st Lt FA

[Comment added by higher headquarters]

The front picked for this survey was not one which had been subjected to more than usual treatment by the First Army PW Combat Team. Therefore it gives a picture of the results of psychological warfare on an average German unit facing our troops along the border.

Out of the 315 prisoners interrogated, 257 had seen our leaflets. Of these, 186 believe in the veracity of the leaflets without reservation, 32 believed most points, 19 were doubtful and 21 expressed disbelief. Out of 17 prisoners who claimed they came over to our lines voluntarily, 9 said that leaflets had influenced them.

RADIO

Tactical Radio

Radio had never been used successfully for combat psychological warfare purposes until 12th Army Group PW put it to work in this campaign, first at Lorient and then at Luxembourg. It has turned out to be one of the most powerful.

Attitudes to Prejudice

The United States and the Jewish Question in Austria

BY BRUCE F. PAULEY

The recent Waldheim affair produced numerous articles in the United States about a revival of Austrian antisemitism.[1] Senator Daniel Patrick Moynihan of New York went so far as to equate Kurt Waldheim's election to the Austrian presidency with a "symbolic amnesty for the Holocaust".[2] Edgar Bronfman, the President of the World Jewish Congress, called Waldheim an "amoral and unrepentant man" and charged that some Austrians had "deliberate[ly] exploit[ed] the Waldheim affair . . . to promote anti-Jewish sentiments".[3] Actually, the Waldheim affair and its reverberations in the US are only the latest incidents in a long history of American concern with Austrian antisemitism; and some Austrians have not hesitated to make counter-charges with regard to American antisemitism and to use American racism as a legitimisation for their own proposed discriminatory legislation between the 1880s and the 1930s.*

CONFLICTS BEFORE THE FIRST WORLD WAR

Jewish issues disturbed Austro-American relations only rarely prior to the collapse of the Austro-Hungarian Monarchy in 1918. In part this may have been due to the still relatively modest Jewish population in the United States, at least before the end of the nineteenth century, and in part it no doubt reflected American isolationism and lack of knowledge about domestic affairs in European countries. American journalists reporting from Austria were also far more inclined to describe the marriages and hunting expeditions of the imperial and royal family than they were to recounting antisemitic incidents. Nevertheless, *The New York Times*, at least, did from time to time carry stories about anti-Jewish riots in Croatia or ritual murder trials in Hungary or Bohemia. The first story emanating from the German-speaking part of the Austrian Empire concerned anti-Jewish riots in Vienna in June 1885 accompanying a municipal election

---

[1] See, for example, the perceptive article in the *Washington Post*, 29th November 1987, p. A–10.
[2] *The New York Times* (hereafter *NYT*), 10th June 1986, p. 27.
[3] *Ibid.*
*This article is an expansion of a paper read at the German Studies Association meeting in Buffalo, New York in October 1990. For Austrian antisemitism, see also Bruce F. Pauley, *From Prejudice to Persecution. A History of Austrian Anti-Semitism*, Chapel Hill, N.J. 1992.

campaign. A "howling mob" at the Karmeliterplatz was said to have raided and ruined a number of Jewish shops.[4]

The year 1885 also marked the first of two diplomatic incidents which, for a brief time, seriously disturbed relations between the United States and Austria-Hungary. In May, Anthony M. Kelley, a lawyer from Virginia, was named the American envoy of the United States to Vienna by President Grover Cleveland. The appointment was rejected by the Austro-Hungarian Foreign Minister, Count Gustav Kalnoky, on the grounds that "the position of a foreign envoy wedded to a Jewess by civil marriage would be untenable and even impossible in Vienna".[5] Secretary of State Thomas F. Bayard was not mollified by Kalnoky's later explanation that the appointment was also refused out of deference to the Italian government, because of criticisms of the Italian takeover of the Papal States which Kelley had made in a public speech in 1871. In a note to the Austro-Hungarian envoy in Washington, Baron Schaeffer, Secretary Bayard angrily noted that:

> "The case we are now considering is that of an envoy of the United States, unquestionably fitted, morally and intellectually, and who has been duly accredited to a friendly Government, towards which he is thoroughly well affected; who in accordance with the laws of this country, has long since contracted and has maintained an honourable marriage, and whose presence near the foreign Government in question is objected to by its agents on the sole ground that his wedded wife is alleged to entertain a religious faith which is held by very many of the most honored and valued citizens of the United States.
>
> It is not believed by the President that a doctrine and practice so destructive of religious liberty and freedom of conscience so devoid of catholicity, and so opposed to the spirit of the age in which we live can for a moment be accepted by the great family of civilized nations or be allowed to control their diplomatic intercourse."[6]

The incident ultimately led to the United States not replacing its envoy to Vienna for more than a year and then only after the Austrians had made the first advances.[7]

A similar incident occurred in 1893 when Max Judd, a Jewish businessman from Missouri, was named American envoy during the second administration of President Cleveland. Coming as it did during a high point in antisemitic agitation in Vienna, the nomination caused a petition to be sent to Emperor Franz Joseph and the Austro-Hungarian Foreign Office asking that the appointment be refused. The Foreign Office, however, rejected Judd's appointment on the again unusual grounds that he was a former Austro-Hungarian subject and was engaged in the apparently disreputable emigration business. The controversy ended when the American Minister to Austria, Grant, said that his government would withdraw the nomination, but would appoint another Jew, conceding only that this time the nominee would not be a former Austro-Hungarian.[8]

[4]*NYT*, 3rd June 1885, p. 5.
[5]Telegram from Count Kalnoky (Vienna) to Baron Schaeffer (Washington), 8th May 1885, *Foreign Relations of the United States. Diplomatic Papers* (hereafter *FRUS*) (1885), p. 48.
[6]Letter from Thomas F. Bayard (Department of State) to Baron Schaeffer, 18th May 1885, *FRUS* (1885), p. 50.
[7]*NYT*, 3rd April 1893, p. 8.
[8]*NYT*, 2nd April 1893, p. 8; *NYT*, 3rd April 1893, p. 8; *NYT*, 22nd April 1893, p. 8.

The above episodes notwithstanding, American diplomatic representatives in Vienna usually ignored the existence of antisemitism in their reports back to Washington in the 1880s and 1890s. However, the electoral victories of the Catholic and conservative Christian Social Party and its leader, Karl Lueger, during the middle 1890s, did not escape the attention of *The New York Times*. A rare editorial about Austrian domestic politics in 1895 criticised Lueger for saying that the possessions of Jewish financiers were "not sacred" and that "the least Jew in Austria had more influence than the most powerful Christian". For the *Times* it was "quite clear that a country in which sentiments such as these were allowed to prevail would be a country in which no attention was paid to the rights of property, a country which was given over to anarchy . . ." Fortunately, however, there was "no longer thought to be any danger that Dr. Lueger [would] again be elected Burgomaster of Vienna".[9] In 1898, only a year after this prophecy proved unfounded, the *Times*'s reporter in Vienna, Johannes Horowitz, called Vienna's antisemitic movement "retrograde" and held the clergy and aristocracy responsible for making Vienna's once liberal population reactionary and clerical. Horowitz went on to note, however, that the antisemitic leaders had not kept their promises.[10] After this report nothing further was heard about Austrian antisemitism in *The New York Times*, prior to outbreak of the First World War, and even the death of Mayor Lueger in 1910 was almost ignored.[11]

Pre-war American influences on the Jewish question in Austria were not always as positive as these few incidents and editorial comments would imply. As early as 1885, Georg von Schönerer, the founder of Austrian pan-Germanism and one of Hitler's own acknowledged forerunners, proposed a bill in the *Reichsrat*, the lower house of the Austrian Parliament, which would have sharply restricted Jewish immigration to Austria. The bill was, in fact, a verbatim copy of the Chinese exclusion law which had recently been approved by the American Congress. The one difference was that the word "Jew" was substituted for the word "Chinese". Jewish immigrants, however, were evidently viewed with less alarm in Austria than Chinese newcomers were in the United States because Schönerer's bill was supported by only 19 deputies out of 572.[12]

THE AMERICAN RESPONSE TO POST-FIRST WORLD WAR AUSTRIAN ANTISEMITISM

The previously infrequent American interest in Austrian antisemitism changed radically immediately after the First World War. At that time, desperate food,

[9]*NYT*, 19th December 1895, p. 4.
[10]*NYT*, 13th January 1898, p. 19.
[11]*NYT*, 11th March 1910, p. 9.
[12]John W. Boyer, *Political Radicalism in Late Imperial Vienna. Origins of the Christian Social Movement, 1848–1897*, Chicago 1981, p. 98; Jonny Moser, *Von der Emanzipation zur antisemitischen Bewegung. Die Stellung Georg Ritter von Schönerers und Heinrich Friedjungs in der Entwicklungsgeschichte des Antisemitismus in Österreich (1848–1896)*, Ph.D. diss., University of Vienna 1962, pp. 63–64; George E. Berkley, *Vienna and its Jews. The Tragedy of Success, 1880s–1980s*, Cambridge, Mass. 1988, p. 94.

fuel, and housing shortages caused by the war induced many Austrian politicians to call for the deportation of Galician Jews who had fled to Vienna during the war to evade the army of notoriously antisemitic tsarist Russia. In February 1919, Dr. Anton Jerzabek, along with nineteen of his colleagues in the Christian Social Party, proposed a bill in the Austrian Parliament which would have expelled Jewish refugees if they had infectious diseases, were guilty of financial misdemeanours, or had carried out political subversion. The sponsors of the bill warned that if it were not enacted the outraged masses would resort to "self-help". The Jews were not singled out in the language of the bill, but the motivation was clear and the alleged habits and customs of the Jewish refugees were openly discussed by the parliamentary deputies. In March an antisemitic group of German Nationalist clubs called the *Deutscher Volksrat* for Vienna and the federal state of Lower Austria, demanded that all refugees have their ration cards and freedom to conduct business withdrawn. Then on 10th September the Social Democratic Governor of Lower Austria, Albert Sever, ordered the expulsion by the 20th of the same month of all foreigners who had not been residents at the start of the World War, on the grounds that there was not enough housing and work available for them. Already on the 23rd, however, he claimed that the shortage of trains and the coal to fuel them made this order impractical.[13]

It is possible that Governor Sever was never serious about expelling the foreigners and had only made a gesture to appease the antisemites. It is also likely, however that he was reacting to a warning the American Consul General in Vienna, Albert Halstead, gave to Chancellor Karl Renner on 25th September, that American opinion would be prejudiced against Austria if the expulsion should actually occur. The warning came at a time when Austria was desperately dependent on the United States for famine relief. A few weeks later (in November) Halstead repeated his implied threat, this time to the Austrian Foreign Ministry, saying that reports coming out of Vienna about anti-Jewish agitation had created a very unfavourable impression in the United States, which could make it difficult in the future for Austria to obtain American credit.[14]

THE WORLD ZIONIST CONGRESS OF 1925

With the return of at least a modicum of prosperity in 1924 Austrian antisemitism tended to decline until the next economic crisis, the Great Depression, struck the country with its full fury in 1930. This six-year lull was

---

[13]Hermann Holzmann, *Antisemitismus in der österreichischen Innenpolitik 1918–1933. Der Umgang der drei politischen Lager mit diesem Phänomen*, Diplomarbeit, University of Vienna 1986, pp. 104–106; Anton Staudinger, 'Christlichsoziale Judenpolitik in der Grundungsphase der österreichischen Republik', in Karl Stuhlpfarrer (ed.), *Jahrbuch für Zeitgeschichte 1978*, Vienna 1979, p. 28.

[14]*NYT*, 28th September 1919, 2:1; Elisabeth Streibel, *Judenfrage und Antisemitismus im Spiegel der "Reichspost" in den Jahren 1918–1923*, Hausarbeit am Institut für Geschichte, University of Vienna 1981, p. 73.

seriously interrupted only once, in the late winter and summer of 1925. In March of that year, the murder of Hugo Bettauer, the popular Jewish-born author of *Die Stadt ohne Juden. Ein Roman von Übermorgen,* combined with the trial of his assassin, were the first two of three major incidents which reawakened antisemitic feelings. For the United States, however, it was the XIVth Zionist Congress, which met in Vienna in August, which was by far the most significant event.

The Congress was accompanied by antisemitic parades and violent demonstrations. Some 6,000 policemen were needed to protect the 8,000 delegates. Hundreds of demonstrators were arrested and $4 million worth of property damage was caused in the rioting, not counting the lost revenue from thousands of would-be delegates who were too frightened to come to the Austrian capital. In the United States the Congress was front-page news in *The New York Times,* which reported that in one parade ten thousand men, women and children marched down Vienna's Ringstrasse shouting "Clear out the Jews" and "Kill the Jews".[15] The paper printed a telegram from an American member of the Executive Committee of the Congress, Louis N. Jaffe, to President Calvin Coolidge, complaining about the riots and asking the American government to issue a formal protest. An even more prominent American Zionist, Stephen S. Wise, who was one of the Vice Presidents of the Congress as well as the President of the American Jewish Congress, was quoted by the *Times* as saying that " 'the Zionist Congress must never again be held in a land which grants police protection rather than extends hospitality' ". Wise went on to denounce the riots saying: " 'May Austria be spared the shame and curse of the reaction which would follow in the wake of anti-Semitism triumphant.' "[16] The Austrian Consul in New York, however, responded to these reports by saying that they were "grossly exaggerated" in the US press.[17]

AMERICAN STUDENTS AND ANTISEMITIC VIOLENCE AT THE UNIVERSITY OF VIENNA

Anti-Jewish feelings were by far the most pronounced in inter-war Austria at the University of Vienna. Although academic antisemitism was already commonplace in pre-war Vienna, especially during the last two decades of the nineteenth century, it was the post-war economic crisis, especially the virtual absence of openings in the liberal professions, along with terribly overcrowded classrooms, which made student hostility towards Jews particularly virulent. Consequently, numerous student organisations, above all the (*völkisch*) *Deutsche Studentenschaft*, called for the implementation of a *numerus clausus* or cap on representation for Jewish students at the University of Vienna and other Austrian institutions of higher learning. The Austrians were hardly alone in such demands, however. Almost certainly they were inspired by already existing policies in Hungary,

[15]*NYT*, 13th October 1925, p. 8.
[16]*NYT*, 20th August 1925, p. 7.
[17]*NYT*, 23rd August 1925, p. 24.

Poland, and the Baltic States during the 1920s and 1930s. Austrians were also well aware that private American universities on the East Coast, including Harvard, Yale and Princeton, informally restricted Jewish enrolment, starting between 1919 and 1923 and lasting into the mid-1940s. For example, Harvard's freshman class, which was 27.6 per cent Jewish in 1925, was only 15 per cent or less Jewish a few years later.[18]

Consequently, the American government was in no position to complain about demands for the restriction of Jewish enrolment. Antisemitic violence, however, was another matter, especially when it involved American students. From the beginning of 1919 until the eve of the *Anschluss* in March 1938 *The New York Times* printed over sixty articles concerning Austrian antisemitism, the majority of which concerned violence at Austria's universities, above all at the University of Vienna. Antisemitic violence was especially common in the first four years following the end of the First World War. It appears to have eased somewhat between the beginning of 1924 and the autumn of 1928, without ever disappearing altogether, before resuming in November of the latter year. It then reached epidemic proportions between 1930 and early 1933 with the coming of the Great Depression, the increase in strength of the Austrian Nazi Party, and Hitler's takeover of power in Germany in January 1933.

The climax of academic violence came in June 1931 when the constitutional court of Austria declared that a ruling dividing the student body of the University of Vienna into "nations", including one for Jews, was unconstitutional. The decision touched off three days of the worst academic violence in the history of the First Austrian Republic, during which hundreds of well-armed Nazi students attacked Jewish and Socialist students with rubber truncheons and steel clubs, seriously injuring fifteen of them.[19]

The violent demonstrations induced the Board of Directors of the *Israelitische Kultusgemeinde* in Vienna to send a sharp protest to the Federal Chancellor and caused Jewish students to hold a massive demonstration of their own on 27th June.[20] Such Jewish protests in the past had rarely led to effective measures being taken to prevent further disturbances. This time, however, the Viennese Jews received backing from a surprising quarter. The Executive Committee of the American League for the Protection of Foreign Students in Vienna, which consisted of prominent members of the American Medical Association, issued a strongly-worded protest note. Copies were sent to the Austrian government, to the Rector and College of Professors of the University of Vienna, to the American Minister in Austria (the American diplomatic representative did not have ambassadorial status in the inter-war period), to President Herbert Hoover, and

---

[18]Helge Zoitl, *Kampf um Gleichberechtigung. Die Sozialdemokratische Studentenbewegung in Wien 1914–1925*, Ph.D. diss., University of Salzburg 1976, p. 378; *Wiener Morgenzeitung*, 27th September 1920, p. 1; Marcia Graham Synott, 'Anti-Semitism and American Universities. Did Quotas follow the Jews?', in David A. Gerber (ed.), *Anti-Semitism in American History*, Urbana, Ill. 1986, pp. 233–235, 239.

[19]*Arbeiter-Zeitung* (Vienna), 24th June 1931, p. 5; *Arbeiter-Zeitung*, 25th June 1931, p. 4; *NYT*, 24th June 1931, p. 48.

[20]*Bericht der Israelitischen Kultusgemeinde Wien über die Tätigkeit in der Periode 1929–1932*, Vienna 1932, pp. 11–12; *Die Stimme* (Vienna), 3rd July 1931, p. 7.

to all important newspapers in the United States. The note denounced the "cowardly, inhuman and unsportsmanlike" conduct of the Nazi students. It also objected to the absence of protection provided for the victims by the Rector of the University. The American Minister, Gilchrist Baker Stockton, also made an informal complaint to Foreign Minister Johannes Schober which was apparently instrumental in preventing serious disturbances for the next year.[21]

American interest in Austrian antisemitism during the First Republic was high because of the relatively large numbers of Americans who were studying in Vienna at the time, the great majority of whom were Jewish medical students. Vienna had long been a Mecca for such scholars. Between 1870 and 1914 two thirds of all Americans who came to Central Europe to study medicine – between 200 and 300 a year in the decade before the outbreak of the First World War – came to Vienna, a number which held at approximately 250 during the inter-war period. No doubt some of the students were simply following in the footsteps of their fathers. Others, however, were there because of increasingly restrictive quotas against Jews at American medical colleges, where Jewish enrolment fell from 16.4 per cent in 1918 to 12.7 per cent in 1946.[22]

By the time the next major round of antisemitic violence at the University of Vienna occurred in October 1932, the American Legation in Vienna was prepared to take an even firmer stance to protect American students. A Nazi attack with steel rods, whips, brass knuckles and knives on Jewish students at the Anatomy Institute of Professor Julius Tandler – a prominent Socialist welfare reformer of Jewish origins – resulted in fifteen being injured, three of them Americans. Following the attack, twenty American students called on Stockton to demand the protection of the American government.[23]

Consequently, the American Minister had a series of three meetings with the Austrian Chancellor, Dr. Engelbert Dollfuss, to protest about Nazi violence. During the first meeting the Chancellor was visibly irritated by the "gross stupidity of the National Socialist students" and promised to do everything he could to prevent a recurrence. Nevertheless, the disturbances continued, causing Stockton to seek a second interview in which he "expressed the opinion that if the University authorities were unable to extend protection the state should intervene". Stockton asked for a third meeting with the Chancellor after four more American students were injured in yet another incident. This time Dollfuss was defensive, blaming the unruly spirit of the students on their lack of discipline, which in turn, he claimed, was the result of Austria not having compulsory military service. Stockton was not impressed with this argument, however, and replied that university officials in the United States managed to maintain law and order despite a similar absence of compulsory military service. The meeting ended with Stockton again saying that it was the duty of the

[21]*Ibid.*; *NYT*, 1st July 1931, p. 52; 'The Minister in Austria to the Secretary of State', 2nd March 1932, *FRUS* (1932), vol. II, p. 122.

[22]*NYT*, 21st May 1933, p. 25; E. Wilder Spaulding, *The Quiet Invaders. The Story of the Austrian Impact upon America*, Vienna 1968, p. 271; Synott, *loc. cit.*, p. 251.

[23]*NYT*, 18th October 1932, p. 7; *NYT*, 27th October 1932, p. 8.

Austrian State to intervene if the authorities at the University of Vienna could not extend adequate protection to students.[24]

The formal *démarche* of the American Minister along with similar protests from the envoys of Poland, Bulgaria, Yugoslavia and Romania to the Federal Chancellery was widely publicised, both in Austria and abroad. The recently elected *völkisch* Rector of the University of Vienna, Professor Othenio Abel, was forced to make a formal and public apology to the American envoy. Abel also issued a proclamation at the University of Vienna urging students not to precipitate further disorders, threatening to expel students who disturbed the academic peace and even having them prosecuted criminally.[25]

The pro-Nazi *Deutschösterreichische Tages-Zeitung* called Abel's apology a "humiliation" and warned ominously that "the time in which such things are impossible is just around the corner". It went on to allege that, based on their surnames, at least 74 per cent of the American students were Jewish and therefore not really Americans. "The Jew belongs to a nation with special characteristics like no other people. It is therefore irrelevant where he happens to live, he still remains a Jew."[26]

The protests of the American Minister to Austria appear to have quietened antisemitism at the University of Vienna for a few months. However, Hitler's appointment as Chancellor in January 1933 convinced Austrian Nazis that they, too, would soon be able to take over political and educational institutions. Consequently, Nazi violence increased rapidly in the spring of 1933, not only at the University of Vienna, but also throughout the whole country. Following two waves of attacks by Nazi students on Professor Tandler's Anatomy Institute in March and May and a new protest from Minister Stockton over the injuring of American students, Dollfuss revoked the Institute's academic autonomy, thus allowing police to enter the premises in order to protect students. Nazi students were also forbidden to wear their insignia, although they did so anyway.[27]

In November 1933, the new American Minister to Austria, George H. Earle, stated publicly that Austria could count on the sympathy of and better trade relations with the United States if it rejected antisemitism. (The minister received eighty-two threatening letters in response to this admonition.) A more direct, semi-official warning was published in the Austrian press in January, stating that the American government could not co-operate with a country which persecuted people because of their birth. The warning may have been partially responsible for Dollfuss making a radio broadcast to the American people the next month.[28]

[24]'The Minister in Austria to the Secretary of State', 22nd October 1932, 27th October 1932, 29th October 1932, *FRUS* (1932), vol. II, pp. 124–129, 132–133. The quotations are from pp. 125 and 128.

[25]*Die Wahrheit* (Vienna), 4th November 1932, p. 1; *NYT*, 27th October 1932, p. 8; 'The Minister in Austria to the Secretary of State', 29th October 1932, *FRUS* (1932), vol. II, pp. 124–129, 130–133.

[26]*Deutschösterreichische Tages-Zeitung*, 20th October 1932, p. 3.

[27]Karl Sablik, *Julius Tandler. Mediziner und Sozialreformer*, Vienna 1983, p. 300; *NYT*, 11th May 1933, p. 10; *NYT*, 21st May 1933, p. 25.

[28]*NYT*, 15th November 1933, p. 4; *NYT*, 18th November 1933, p. 34; *Die Wahrheit*, 23rd February 1934, p. 1.

Although the documentary evidence reveals no hostility towards Jews by either Engelbert Dollfuss, or his successor, Kurt von Schuschnigg, the Chancellors' attitude towards the Jewish community cannot be attributed to personal feelings alone. Both men were subjected to numerous domestic and foreign influences on questions regarding Jews, which made it politically opportune to avoid at least obvious signs of antisemitism. As practising Catholics and convinced Austrian patriots, the Chancellors ardently sought to preserve the independence of both Austria and the Roman Catholic Church. But to do so they desperately needed political, economic and military assistance from both domestic and foreign sources. After Dollfuss abolished parliamentary democracy in March 1933, the renunciation of antisemitism was one important way in which Dollfuss and Schuschnigg could put ideological distance between themselves and Hitler. Aid was unlikely from either the United States or Great Britain if Austria were perceived as an antisemitic country at a time when antisemitism and Nazism were increasingly being equated in the popular mind.

AUSTRIAN RESPONSES TO AMERICAN ANTISEMITISM AND RACISM

Not everyone in Austria appreciated the stern warnings of the American Ministers in Vienna. Not surprisingly, to some Austrians such lectures sounded hypocritical. The Catholic weekly, *Schönere Zukunft*, observed that Minister Earle's comments were strange coming from a country which practised strict racial segregation in the Southern states against people having only a trace of Negro blood. Only dirty railroad cars were available for such people; and they were forced to drink from separate fountains. Even in some of the Northern states, marriage between whites and Negroes was forbidden. Another article in the same journal pointed out that the 1.6 million Jews of New York were so thoroughly rejected socially that not even the richest among them could get into the most prestigious private clubs.[29] A similar article in the thinly-disguised Nazi newspaper, *Deutsches Volksblatt*, reported a speech by Rabbi J. X. Cohen to the American Jewish Congress in which the rabbi noted the high number of large businesses, utility companies and banks in New York which discriminated against Jews in their hiring practices.[30]

Schönere Zukunft and the *Deutsches Volksblatt* were not alone in taking note of American racism. Austrian antisemites, including Adolf Hitler, were especially impressed with the antisemitic publications of the American automobile magnate, Henry Ford, especially his book, *The International Jew*.[31] The *Deutschösterreichische Tages-Zeitung* was particularly enthusiastic about Ford's chapter which dealt with American Jews taking over the film industry.[32] The viciously

---

[29]*Schönere Zukunft*, 14th January 1934, p. 396; *Schönere Zukunft*, 28th February 1937, p. 575.
[30]*Deutsches Volksblatt*, 23rd August 1937, p. 3.
[31]Norman Cohn, *Warrant for Genocide. The Myth of Jewish World Conspiracy and the Protocols of the Elders of Zion*, Providence 1969, 1981, p. 162.
[32]*Deutschösterreichische Tages-Zeitung*, 12th April 1930. Reprinted in Alexander Schilling[-Schletter], *Dr. Walter Riehl und die Geschichte des Nationalsozialismus*, Leipzig 1933, p. 134.

antisemitic *Eiserner Besen* was equally approving of Ford's claim that there was a Jewish "shadow government" in Washington which prevented the federal government from publishing any statistics about Jewish immigration.[33] *Der Stürmer*, another poorly disguised Nazi newspaper published in Vienna (not to be confused with Julius Streicher's newspaper of the same name in Bavaria) included quotations from Ford's *The International Jew* along with anti-Jewish statements by other famous historical figures.[34]

An umbrella organisation in Austria known as the *Antisemitenbund*, which flourished in the early 1920s and again shortly before the *Anschluss*, was convinced that its proposals for discriminatory legislation against Jews were moderate in comparison to the rights accorded to Negroes, Indians, and Chinese in the United States who were not even allowed to sit next to whites on streetcars or in restaurants; the *Bund* also stated that American whites thought that racial segregation was essential for their self-protection.[35] The *Deutsche Arbeiter-Presse*, an official organ of the Austrian Nazi Party, was pleased to report on the existence of the Ku Klux Klan with its five million members who were opposed to Jews of every description.[36] Unfortunately, these descriptions of American racism were probably more accurate than one published by the great opponent of Austrian antisemitism, Irene Harand, who, after a trip to New York, reported in her newspaper, *Gerechtigkeit*, that Americans considered it "ridiculous" to restrict someone's career because of their origins or because they did not belong to the majority.[37]

THE UNITED STATES AND THE DEPORTATION OF AUSTRIAN JEWS

Following the annexation of Austria by Nazi Germany in March 1938, the persecution of Jews progressed so rapidly that within a few months, and in some cases within just a few days, most Jews had been deprived of their livelihoods and were forced to try to emigrate. Obtaining an immigration visa from a potential host country, including the United States, was no easier for Austrian Jews than it had been earlier for Jews in Germany. The German Ambassador to the United States, Hans Dieckhoff, when reporting to Berlin on the American reaction to the *Anschluss*, noted with apparent glee that: "The realization that large numbers of Austrian refugees, especially of the Jewish race, would constitute no blessing for America, might also have contributed to this sobering up [of hostile public opinion]; and it was interesting to note the letters to the papers, especially from

[33] *Eiserner Besen*, 16th October 1924, p. 2.
[34] *Der Stürmer*, 16th September 1933, p. 3.
[35] Karl Peter, *Der Antisemitismus*, Vienna 1936, p. 11.
[36] *Deutsche Arbeiter-Presse*, 21st February 1925, p. 5.
[37] *Gerechtigkeit*, 17th December 1936, p. 1.

the middle strata of the population, criticizing the American Government's readiness to admit such refugees and thus further depress the labor market."[38]

Once an immigrant's visa had been obtained, there were still other obstacles to overcome before a Jew could leave Austria. The Nazis hoped to export antisemitism and enrich the Third *Reich* by allowing only penniless Jews to leave. Therefore Jews were allowed to take only thirty Marks (later reduced to ten) in German and foreign currency when they left Austria. This problem could be surmounted only with the aid of Jewish organisations abroad. The American Jewish Joint Distribution Committee, the Jewish Agency for Palestine, as well as the Central British Fund for Refugees all set up soup kitchens for Jews while they remained in Vienna and paid all the costs of Jewish emigration. Unfortunately, such aid ended with the outbreak of the war.[39]

Of the 128,500 Austrian Jews who managed to escaped the Holocaust through emigration (or slightly more than twice the number murdered) only 28,615 moved to the United States before America virtually closed its doors to further immigration in July 1940. This figure was actually less than the 30,850 who emigrated to Great Britain. Nevertheless, these immigrants, together with another 65,000 Jewish refugees from Germany, probably represented the largest single influx of talent in American history even before another 12,000 Austrian-Jewish immigrants entered the US between the end of the Second World War and 1958.[40]

THE UNITED STATES, AUSTRIA AND JEWISH ISSUES SINCE 1945

Jewish issues have been generally less disruptive of overall Austro-American relations in the forty-five years since the end of the Second World War than during the two decades of the inter-war period. Austria's Jewish population of around 8,000 is less than four per cent of the 220,000 who lived in the First Republic. And although Austrian antisemitism has been far from dead in the Second Republic it has been much less vocal and almost entirely non-violent. Finally, there is no longer a large contingent of Jewish-American students studying in Austria to get caught in the crossfire of radical student politics as was the case in the 1920s and 1930s. Nevertheless, there have been several issues of interest to Jews which have at times seriously disturbed Austro-American relations.

By far the most enduring and aggravating of these divisive issues has been the question of restitution for the Jewish victims of Nazi persecution following the

[38]'The German Ambassador in the United States (Dieckhoff) to the German Foreign Ministry', Washington, 18th April 1938, in *Documents on German Foreign Policy, 1918–1945*, Series D, vol. I, *From Neurath to Ribbentrop*, Washington 1949, p. 619.

[39]Gerhard Botz, *Wien vom "Anschluss" zum Krieg*, Vienna–Munich 1978, p. 254; idem, *Wohnungspolitik und Judendeportation in Wien 1938 bis 1945*, Vienna 1975, p. 101.

[40]Herbert Rosenkranz, 'The Anschluss and the Tragedy of Austrian Jewry', in Josef Fraenkel (ed.), *The Jews of Austria. Essays on their Life, History and Destruction*, London 1967, pp. 510, 514; *NYT*, 23rd May 1958, p. 22.

Anschluss. The persistence of at least private prejudicial feelings toward Jews, as revealed in numerous public opinion polls conducted in Austria since 1945, has made the Austrian government reluctant to compensate those former Austrian Jews who lost their homes, jobs and property after the *Anschluss.** Only in 1953, after some diplomatic pressure had been put on the Austrian government by the State Department of the United States and the British Foreign Office, did the Austrian government even agree to negotiate the demands of the Jewish Claims Committee which had its headquarters in New York. After nine years of negotiations Vienna settled on a sum of $6 million plus 10 per cent to cover administrative costs. Jews who lost land in 1938 (a relatively small number since Jews were not large land owners) received only two thirds of its actual value; those who had lost property were awarded only one fourth of its real value.[41]

Victims of Nazism, especially those who were forced to leave their homes and jobs and emigrate, were incensed by the Austrian government restoring the property of former Austrian Nazis before the Jewish victims themselves had been compensated. Still worse was the granting of an amnesty to 90 per cent of the 500,000 former members of the Party in 1948 and nearly all the others, including the *Gestapo* and the SS by 1957.[42]

Jewish-American critics of the Austrian de-Nazification record, such as George Berkley,[43] have neglected to point out, however, that the post-war American government considered it counter-productive to dwell on Austria's Nazi and antisemitic past at a time when Soviet Communism was rapidly engulfing East and Central Europe. From 1946 on the American policy towards Austria was based on the half-truth, originally formulated in the Allies' own "Moscow Declaration" of November 1943, that Austria was the "first victim" of Nazi aggression. Even the very real differences between the American and Austrian governments over the issue of compensation for Jewish victims were, therefore, kept out of the public's view because of the Cold War. This factor alone, of course, limited the amount of pressure the United States could put on Austria to compensate Nazi victims. Consequently, foreign pressure to make restitution to the Jews steadily declined after early 1947, whereas domestic pressures against such compensation correspondingly increased. The United States, joined by Britain and France, did not press the issue of reparations because it wanted a stable Austria; the Soviet Union likewise was not insistent because it wanted a neutral Austria.[44]

---

*On this reluctance see the essay by Robert Knight, 'Restitution and Legitimacy in Post-War Austria 1945–1953', in *LBI Year Book XXXVI* (1991), pp. 413–442 – (Ed.).

[41]Berkley, *op. cit.*, p. 351; Dietmar Walch, *Die jüdischen Bemühungen um die materielle Wiedergutmachung durch die Republik Österreich*, Vienna 1971, pp. 5, 229–230; *NYT*, 22nd December 1953, p. 16; Robert Knight, *Ich bin dafür, die Sache in die Länge zu ziehen. Wortprotokolle der österreichischen Bundesregierung von 1945–52 über die Entschädigung der Juden*, Frankfurt a. Main 1988, p. 52.

[42]*NYT*, 19th December 1953, p. 2; Walch, *op. cit.*, p. 148; Dieter Stiefel, 'Nazifizierung plus Entnazifizierung in Österreich', in Sebastian Meissl, Klaus-Dieter Mulley and Oliver Rathkolb (eds.), *Verdrängte Schuld – verfehlte Sühne. Entnazifizierung in Österreich 1945–1955*, Munich 1986, p. 34.

[43]Berkley, *op. cit.*, pp. 347–350.

[44]Knight, *op. cit.*, pp. 34, 50, 55; *idem*, 'Kalter Krieg, Entnazifizierung und Österreich', in Meissl *et al.* (eds.), *op. cit.*, p. 46.

The two decades after the mid-1960s saw a steady diminution in Austrian antisemitism and the virtual disappearance of the Jewish question in Austro-American relations. This happy state of affairs was disrupted, however, by the official welcome accorded, by the Austrian Minister of Defence, to the return to Austria of the convicted SS war criminal, Walter Reder and more seriously by the international uproar over the election of the former *Wehrmacht* officer and Secretary General of the United Nations, Kurt Waldheim, to the Presidency of Austria.

Walter Reder, a former major in the SS had been convicted in 1951 for his role in the deaths of at least 600 and perhaps as many as 1,830 civilians in and around the village of Marzabotto in Northern Italy in September 1944. Senator Gianfranco Maris, the President of the Italian Association of the Former Political Deportees in Nazi Camps, said at the time of Reder's release that " 'in forty years of detention, [Reder] had never expressed a precise refusal of Nazism or a clear repentance for his guilt' ". Reder was released five months before the scheduled end of his term on humanitarian grounds, because of his suffering from hardening of the arteries in his brain. Reder's release from prison and return to Austria might have gone relatively unnoticed were it not for the fact that the country's Minister of Defence, Friedhelm Frischenschlager, a member of the Right-wing Freedom Party, went to Graz to greet Reder officially and then compounded the ensuing controversy by saying that he had done so as a "humanitarian gesture". At a news conference he went on to say that " 'by far the largest part of the population will be happy when someone belonging to this nation returns after years in prison' ".[45]

The timing of this episode could not have been worse as far as Austro-American-Jewish relations were concerned. At that very moment 2,000 members of the World Jewish Congress were meeting for the first time ever in Vienna. The President of the WJC, Edgar M. Bronfman, denounced Frischenschlager's actions and called for his dismissal. The affair came to a relatively amicable ending, however, when the Austrian Chancellor, Fred Sinowatz, censured his Minister of Defence and apologised to all the leaders of world Jewish organisations. A few days later Frischenchlager himself apologised and Bronfman declared the matter closed.[46]

If the matter was closed, it was certainly not forgotten when revelations about the war-time career of presidential candidate Kurt Waldheim became public little more than a year later, in the spring of 1986. The Waldheim affair and its impact on Austrian antisemitism and relations between Austria and the world Jewish community have been thoroughly discussed elsewhere.[47] Although the issue was exposed by an article in the popular Austrian magazine, *Profil*, it was American-Jewish organisations, especially the World Jewish Congress, which pursued the matter most vigorously thus leaving many Austrians with the false

[45]*NYT*, 25th January 1985, p. 2.
[46]*NYT*, 28th January 1985, p. 4; *NYT*, 30th January 1985, p. 3.
[47]See especially Robert E. Herzstein, *Waldheim. The Missing Years*, New York 1988; Richard Bassett, *Waldheim and Austria*, New York 1989.

impression that the whole affair was part of an international or at least American-Jewish conspiracy. Consequently the Waldheim campaign reacted by printing posters saying that no one was going to tell the Austrian people how to vote. Edgar Bronfman outraged many Austrians by threatening to block Austria's admission into the European Community, a move which was even criticised by Paul Grosz, President of the *Israelitische Kultusgemeinde* in Vienna.[48] Simon Wiesenthal, the world-famous investigator of Nazi war criminals, also accused the World Jewish Congress of stirring up antisemitism in Austria and denied that Waldheim was a war criminal.[49] Waldheim, for his part, inflamed Jewish opinion in the United States by attempting to brush off the accusations against him as having been made by "some interest groups in New York".[50]

The question about whether President Waldheim was a war criminal in the Nuremberg sense of the term appears to have been answered in the negative by Robert Herzstein in his book, *Waldheim. The Missing Years*, as well as by the findings of a special historical commission. There is also no clear evidence that Waldheim exploited antisemitism during his presidential campaign. On the other hand, he was criticised for not denouncing the phenomenon, at least not until after the first ballot in May, and not vigorously until after the second ballot the next month when he promised to oppose discrimination against Jews. Moreover, *The New York Times* described his apparent nonchalance about his military assignments in the Balkans as "staggering".[51] Even more caustic was the *Times*'s commentary on Waldheim's reaction to the report of the historical commission in February 1988. The commission concluded that Waldheim had committed no crimes himself, but had repeatedly gone along with crimes perpetrated by others. When the Austrian President interpreted this finding as a clear statement that he was not guilty, the *Times* declared him "unfit for leadership" and unfavourably compared him with President Richard von Weizsäcker of West Germany, who in a recent speech had warned his countrymen about the dangers of forgetting and distorting their Nazi past.[52]

IN RETROSPECT

In looking back over the last hundred years or so of Austro-American relations it is obvious that Jewish issues often played an important role in that relationship long before anyone had heard the name Kurt Waldheim. Although incidents involving Jews only rarely disturbed relations between Austria-Hungary and the United States prior to the First World War the American government already established a clear policy of defending the rights of its Jewish citizens in Austria. It was only after the fall of the Habsburg Monarchy, however, that the United

[48]*A-Z* (new name for *Arbeiter-Zeitung*, reprinted in the *Österreich-Bericht*, No. 58 (10th March 1988), p.1.
[49]*NYT*, 17th May 1986, p. 4.
[50]Herzstein, *op. cit.*, p. 252; *NYT*, 12th June 1986, p. 3.
[51]*NYT*, 29th March 1986, p. 20.
[52]*NYT*, 12th February 1988, p. 34.

States, now playing a much greater role in world affairs than before the war, began to take an active interest in the welfare of Austrian Jews and not just Americans who happened to be in Austria. The presence of a relatively large number of Jewish students at the University of Vienna, as well as the concern American Jews had for the large Jewish community in the Austrian capital, provided much of the motivation for American involvement. Austria's pitiful economic circumstances in the early post-First World War years and its need for diplomatic support in the face of the growing Nazi threat in the early 1930s gave the United States substantial leverage in persuading the Austrian government to restrain antisemitism. Unfortunately, however, the moral authority of the United States was tarnished in the eyes of many Austrians by its own record of antisemitism and racism.

The American government again played a positive role after the Second World War in supporting the claims for restitution by Austrian-Jewish refugees now living in the United States. Once more, however, its effectiveness was somewhat limited, this time by its desire to place Cold War interests above those of Jewish refugees. Perhaps the biggest change in American involvement in Austrian antisemitism in the Second Republic has been the greater role played by Jewish organisations, especially the World Jewish Congress, as seen during both the Reder affair and the Waldheim affair.

The Austrian government in recent years has not been insensitive to its international image with regard to Jewish issues. During the fiftieth anniversary of the *Anschluss* in 1988 it sponsored a number of international scholarly symposia – in which Austria was no longer depicted as being purely the victim of Nazi aggression as had been done so frequently in the past. The fiftieth anniversary of the "*Kristallnacht*" in November 1988 was commemorated in Vienna by a special exhibition at the Museum of the History of Vienna which graphically portrayed the horrors of that event. A Jewish museum in Vienna's Seitenstettengasse in the First District, which was founded in 1895 and completely destroyed by the Nazis in 1938, was reopened in March 1990 through the financial support of the municipal and federal governments; plans call for it undergoing a major expansion by 1995.[53] The federal government has also assisted in the restoration of a synagogue in St. Pölten. Unfortunately, none of these events has received much publicity in the United States.

Whether these recent attempts by the Austrian government to improve its image *vis-à-vis* the "Jewish Question" will be successful remains to be seen. The decision by President Waldheim not to seek a second six-year term in 1992 should improve Austria's relations with the United States and its Jewish population. The same should be true of Chancellor Franz Vranitzky's unequivocal condemnation of pro-Nazi statements made in June 1991 by the Governor of Carinthia, Jörg Haider.[54] Thus, it would be fair to say that the "Jewish

---

[53] *A-Z*, reprinted in the *Österreich-Bericht*, No. 186 (12th August 1991), p. 2.
[54] *Die Presse* (Vienna), 9th July 1991, p. 1.

Question" in Austria is, at least temporarily, on the "back burner" so far as American Jews are concerned. Given the considerable, albeit largely personal, antisemitism still existing in Austria today, however, the possibilities for friction in the future cannot be ruled out.

The Churches and the Jews in the German Democratic Republic

BY HELMUT ESCHWEGE

For church leaders in Germany as for the Christian congregations and the population as a whole, the end of the war brought an awareness of the appalling crime of Auschwitz. Even more, it involved the need to recognise that their own past attitudes had helped to bring the crime about. This element of guilt has been an important topic of debate for many years, both privately and in public. From small beginnings, meetings were organised between Christians and Jews, and church leaders increasingly strove to come to terms with the past. The publication of numerous books and articles bears eloquent witness to this development.[1] Christian groups with an interest in the religion, history and culture of the Jews were founded in many areas – from 1948 in the Federal Republic and after 1965 in the German Democratic Republic. All these groups were led either by individual theologians or by priests from the lower ranks of the church hierarchy.[2]

When the detainees returned home from the prisons and concentration camps in 1945, non-Jews were accepted and supported by their families. They also received assistance from the state, which in the Eastern Zone (later the GDR) was usually in the hands of Communists. However, the Jews had no families they could return to, and were entirely dependent on outside help. In localities where

This essay is dedicated to Dr. Arnold Paucker, my close friend and colleague for many decades. I am also grateful to him for stimulating my own work on the resistance of German Jews.

[1] On the attitude of the churches from 1933 to 1945 see a.o.: Wolfgang Gerlach, *Als die Zeugen schwiegen. Bekennende Kirchen und die Juden*, Berlin 1987; Jochen-Christoph Kaiser and Martin Greschat (eds.), *Der Holocaust und die Protestanten. Analysen einer Verstrickung*, Frankfurt a. Main 1988; *Die evangelische Kirche und die Judenfrage*, Genf 1943; Kurt Meier, *Kirche und Judentum. Die Haltung der evangelischen Kirche zur Judenpolitik des Dritten Reiches*, Halle 1968; Eberhard Röhm and Jörg Thierfelder, *Evangelische Kirche zwischen Kreuz und Hakenkreuz*, Stuttgart 1982; Landeskirchliches Archiv in Nürnberg (Hrsg.), *Wo ist dein Bruder Abel? Fünfzig Jahre Novemberpogrom. Christen und Juden in Bayern in unserem Jahrhundert*. (Exhibition catalogue compiled by Helmut Baier *et al.*), Nürnberg 1988; Rolf Hochhuth, *Der Stellvertreter*, Hamburg 1963; Guenter Lewy, *Die katholische Kirche und das Dritte Reich*, München 1965; Fritz J. Raddatz (ed.), *Summa iniuria oder durfte der Papst schweigen?*, Hamburg 1963; Günther Bernd Ginzel (ed.), *Auschwitz als Herausforderung für Juden und Christen*, Heidelberg 1980; Hans Müller (ed.), *Katholische Kirche und Nationalsozialismus*, München 1965.

[2] Siegfried Theodor Arndt, 'Das christlich-jüdische Gespräch in der DDR', in *idem et al.*, *Juden in der DDR. Geschichte – Probleme – Perspektiven*, Duisburg 1988, pp. 11ff.; Helmut Eschwege, 'Zusammenarbeit von Christen und Juden', in *Kirche in Sachsen. Wirkungen des Evangeliums zwischen Elster und Neiße*, Berlin 1990, pp. 126ff.

assistance was refused, such as Leipzig and Halle, returning Jews began the first post-war Jewish emigrations from the Eastern Zone.[3]

According to a census of 1946 which requested details of religious affiliation, approximately 3,000 Jews were then living in the territory of what became the GDR (656 in Saxony, 428 in Thuringia, 153 in Mecklenburg, 900 in East Berlin, 435 in Saxony-Anhalt and 424 in the rest of Prussia and Brandenburg. These Jews were not a homogeneous group. They came from many different lands of origin and varied widely in their attitudes towards Jewry and their knowledge of it.

After the war, the East German government adhered strictly to the Potsdam agreement on the de-Nazification, demilitarisation and democratisation of Germany, and the elimination of militarism, chauvinism and racial abuses by means of the liquidation of the armaments industry and the destruction of monopolies. But the attack on great wealth and property meant that many firms, houses and businesses which had once belonged to Jews were nationalised or left in the hands of their Nazi "trustees". A leading politician of the *Sozialistische Einheitspartei Deutschlands* (SED), Paul Merker, did advocate the return to Jewish owners of property looted by the Nazis. However, he was imprisoned in 1952 for his pains.[4]

Nevertheless, in justice to the East German leadership, it must be admitted that able Jews quickly achieved senior positions in politics, the economy, academic and cultural life, the police and the armed forces. In the first decade after the war, almost all directors and producers of the Berlin theatre were Jews. Others, or men of Jewish ancestry, reached senior positions as civil servants and even government ministers.

During this period, an unsavoury role was played by the *Vereinigung der Verfolgten des Naziregimes*, which excluded large groups of persecuted Jews and denied them the support which had been conceded to persecuted Communists.[5]

As Jewish communities were being established or re-created in the Federal Republic, others were emerging in the Eastern Zone and later the GDR. At the outset these were composed of Jews who had managed to survive (usually "*Mischlinge*"), surviving non-Jewish spouses, returning deportees and the first re-emigrants from abroad. All the Jews from the surrounding area joined these communities. Consequently, many of the communities chose to refer to them-

---

[3]Helmut Eschwege, 'Die jüdische Bevölkerung der Jahre nach der Kapitulation Hitlerdeutschlands auf dem Gebiet der DDR bis zum Jahre 1953', in Arndt *et al., op. cit.*, pp. 63ff.

[4]'Lehren aus dem Prozeß gegen das Verschwörerzentrum Slánský', in *Beschluß des Zentralkomitees der SED vom 20. Dezember 1952*, Berlin 1953. Merker was convicted for his campaign for compensation for Jewish citizens whose property had been confiscated by the Nazis; for supporting the foundation of a Jewish national state; his view of Jews as a national minority in Germany; his support for unrestricted emigration of Jews to Israel; for speaking out in favour of Jews in the GDR joining Jewish communities and other abstruse charges.

[5]Helmut Eschwege, 'Juden nach 1945 weiter ausgegrenzt. Der VVN spielte dabei eine unrühmliche Rolle', in *Sächsische Zeitung*, 3rd August 1990; *idem*, 'Ein zweites Mal verfolgt, dann aus den Geschichtsbüchern verbannt', *ibid.*, 8th June 1990; *idem*, 'Mit bewußtem Schweigen deckte die SED ihre Verbrechen zu. Vielen Juden wurden in der DDR die Anerkennung als "Opfer des Faschismus" vorenthalten', in *Allgemeine jüdische Wochenzeitung*, 28th June 1990.

selves as *Landesgemeinde*, as did the Mecklenburg community based in Schwerin, and the Thuringia community in Erfurt. With the start of the infamous Slánský trial in Prague at the end of 1952, and the accusations that Jewish doctors had killed leading Soviet functionaries in Moscow, an onslaught against Jews also began in the GDR. In its aftermath Jews were imprisoned in East Germany, some for years. All the declarations of solidarity with the Jewish victims of Nazism, made by leading SED politicians, were suddenly forgotten. The Jews were closely watched; I, personally, went through five years of interrogation and persecution. After the Slánský trial, therefore, a new flight of Jews from the GDR began. It involved Jews from the communities and those who belonged to none, and included leading functionaries of Party and State.[6]

The boards of the communities took with them the library of the Jewish community in Oranienburger Strasse. Shortly afterwards, the remaining *Gesamtarchiv der deutschen Juden* was moved by the *Zentrales Staatsarchiv* to Potsdam, where it remained inaccessible until early 1990.

After the exodus of 1953, the eight Jewish communities of the GDR contained only some 1,000 members compared with 3,000 in 1946. Some five years previously, the leading East German statesmen and politicians had sent congratulations to the communities on the foundation of the Jewish state,[7] while the Israeli national flag had hung from Jewish community rooms and synagogues. The abrupt change of policy in the GDR was clear to see.

By 1957 the Jewish communities were again being left in peace. However, at the same time the SED leadership and the government were intensifying their support for the Palestine Liberation Organisation; anti-Zionism had begun to reveal certain traces of antisemitism. Israel was declared to be an imperialist and criminal state and the Zionists were accused of complicity with the Nazis.

During this period, the Evangelical Church in Germany issued its first reflections on its silence during the Nazi crimes and, in the words of its synod at Berlin-Weissensee on 27th April 1950, on "the obligation to Israel". The declaration was also prefaced by a call for a "rejection of antisemitism". It ended with these words:

"We ask all Christians to renounce any antisemitism and to oppose it wherever it stirs afresh, and to greet Jews and Jewish Christians in a spirit of brotherhood.

We ask the Christian communities to take into their protection the Jewish cemeteries in their parishes if these are untended.

We ask the God of mercy to bring the day of fulfilment in which we will praise the victory of Jesus Christ with a redeemed Israel."

This last sentence made it crystal clear that the Evangelical Church still regarded the mission to the Jews as the main objective. Significantly, no Christian community responded to the request to take care of Jewish cemeteries.

---

[6]*Idem*, 'Die erneute Vertreibung der Juden. Voller Angst verließ 1952/53 ein Drittel der jüdischen Gemeindemitglieder die DDR', in *Leipziger Volkszeitung*, 21st/22nd July 1990.

[7]*SED-Information* (mid-1948), 'Erdöl-Krieg in Palästina', with greetings from Wilhelm Pieck and Paul Merker a.o. Also contains report by the *SED-Pressedienst*, 12th June 1948, which called for immediate recognition of the Jewish State of Israel, suspension of the supply of weapons to and support for Arab states etc.

Yet it must be borne in mind that the declaration had a number of forerunners. The first was the *Stuttgarter Schuldbekenntnis* which appeared at the end of 1945, but failed to mention the persecution of the Jews. At that stage the church leaders were still too deeply entangled with the past. Then in 1948 came the Darmstadt declaration of the *Bruderrat*, which still contained the following type of argument: "By crucifying the Messiah, Israel lost its position as the Elect and its destiny"; "the fact that God's justice has followed Israel in persecution until today is a sign of his forbearance".[8] In this declaration, the Jews themselves were virtually blamed for the destruction of their people, almost as atonement for the death of Christ, for which they were still being blamed even in 1948. Seen in this light, the synod declaration of 1950 was a great step forward.

Only a year after the war, the evangelical group *Mission unter Israel* became active again in Saxony, Berlin and Mecklenburg. The groups of the *Christlich-jüdische Begegnung*, which emerged in about 1965, were assigned to this organisation. Not until September 1968 were the anachronistic *Mission unter Israel* offices in Saxony and elsewhere disbanded and renamed the *Arbeitsgemeinschaft Kirche und Judentum*. At an earlier stage the cathedral preacher in Schwerin, Karl Kleinschmidt, had achieved this reorganisation in Mecklenburg.

The attitude of the East German government and its organisations towards the Jews was marked by ambivalence. On the one hand, the state had given generous help to the Jewish communities since the end of the war, building or renovating their synagogues and providing money to help them rebuild their communities and care for their cemeteries. On the other hand, however, all the state media were urged to castigate Israel and Zionism in a policy which lasted almost until the fall of the Socialist regime.

Literature on the persecution of the Jews began to appear in both East and West Germany shortly after the end of the war. Though in the Federal Republic the literature was extensive, in East Germany it was restricted to two meagre booklets which were quickly withdrawn from the market. One of the authors was the economist Siegbert Kahn.[9] He was strongly criticised for arguing, like Paul Merker before him, that the property stolen by the Nazis should be returned to the Jews. The second author was Stefan Heymann,[10] who was Deputy Foreign Minister of the GDR for a time. Almost twenty years passed before a first full-scale academic work on the theme appeared. It was written by the present author, and it is thanks to pressure from Arnold Zweig, Jürgen Kuczynski, Stefan Heymann and some twenty other leading East German Jews that a publishing house was forced to print it. The book was *Kennzeichen J*, on the persecution of the German Jews.

Jewish religious services were held regularly on the Sabbath in Berlin, and on feast days in Dresden, Leipzig and Erfurt. In Leipzig and Dresden a choir consisting of Christian women has joined the service and added to its appeal.

---

[8]Ginzel, *op. cit.*, pp. 541ff.
[9]Siegbert Kahn, *Antisemitismus und Rassenhetze. Eine Übersicht über ihre Entwicklung in Deutschland*, Berlin 1948.
[10]Stefan Heymann, *Marxismus und Rassenfrage*, Berlin 1948.

IN SCHAM UND TRAUER
GEDENKEN CHRISTEN
DER JÜDISCHEN BÜRGER DIESER STADT·
1933 LEBTEN IN DRESDEN 4675 JUDEN·
1945 WAREN ES 70·
WIR SCHWIEGEN,
ALS IHRE GOTTESHÄUSER
VERBRANNT, ALS JUDEN
ENTRECHTET, VERTRIEBEN
UND ERMORDET WURDEN·
WIR ERKANNTEN IN IHNEN
UNSERE BRÜDER
UND SCHWESTERN NICHT·

WIR BITTEN
UM VERGEBUNG UND SCHALOM

NOVEMBER 1988

A memorial tablet at the Dresden Kreuzkirche
for the Jewish victims of Nazism

The children of members of the community usually remained within it and were joined by young people whose parents had broken away from the communities in the past. There were various reasons for this expression of solidarity, but the anti-Israel propaganda of the mass media certainly played a significant part. When the attacks became too harsh and unrelenting, protests were made by individual members of the community and by others who did not belong to it. Only rarely, however, did these protests meet with a response from the authorities.

One extreme case may be cited to indicate the approach to Jewish questions from individual community leaders. This concerned the attitude towards the chairwoman of the Jewish community in Halle. Her father had been a policeman between 1933 and 1945, mostly in Halle, and there was outrage when the daughter later buried her parents in a place of honour in the town's Jewish cemetery. Only the late president of our community supported this woman until 1987. To crown it all, the Chairman of the *Verband der Jüdischen Gemeinden in der DDR*, Helmut Aris, sent her son to train as a *Chasan* at the rabbinical school in Budapest. Not until 1987 did I manage to obtain the dismissal of the chairwoman in Halle.[11]

An investigation into the condition of some 220 Jewish cemeteries in the GDR revealed that 74 had been completely destroyed and 34 badly damaged after the defeat of the Nazi regime. In the mid 1970s, groups from the *Begegnung mit dem Judentum* began to hold talks on Jewish religion, history, culture and science for interested Christians in the big towns. They were usually run by priests and theologians with Jewish academics, often rabbis from abroad, as speakers. At this time, priests and their communities in many places began to tend the Jewish cemeteries in their parishes, re-erecting fallen and scattered gravestones. In Jessnitz and in Guben, Christian communities renovated the cemetery buildings for use as their chapels. They also took responsibility for tending the attached Jewish cemeteries. In Guben a belfry was set up and one of the bells engraved with the phrase, in Hebrew and German, "Peace with Israel".

It must have been 1967 or 1968 when the pastor Fritz Schulz, leader of the Dresden group of *Begegnung mit dem Judentum*, asked me to attend a meeting of Evangelical pastors in Krummenhennersdorf, a meeting place of the Evangelical *Landeskirche* in Saxony. In response to his request for a talk on the history of the German Jews and their religion, I gave the first of several lectures on Jewish themes here. Quite soon I was being asked to do the same elsewhere, even abroad, Fritz Schulz was then appointed representative of the *Landeskirche* of Saxony to the Jewish community. He was a self-educated man of wide knowledge, able to speak on varied aspects of Jewish affairs.

Over the years it became customary for Christian institutes to devote one of their meetings each year to Jewish themes. The practice was also adopted by student communities, theological colleges, priests' conferences and other bodies. In the last decade, the leaders of the *Begegnung mit dem Judentum* were the pastors

[11]The publication of an article in *Aufbau* (New York) about the usurper Karin Mylius and the production of birth and baptism certificates persuaded the leader of the Jewish community in the GDR, Helmut Aris, and East German State Security to dismiss her.

Hildebrand in Berlin, Theodor Arndt in Leipzig, and Siegfried Reimann in Dresden, with the catechist Christiane Neumann in Rostock. All of them maintained close links with the Jewish communities of their cities. The chairmen of our Jewish communities in Erfurt and Magdeburg also kept in close contact with the Christian communities of the surrounding area and gave talks to them. The committees of all the *Begegnung mit dem Judentum* groups included Evangelical and Catholic friends, frequently priests, working together in true brotherhood. If a Jew lived in the town concerned, he would be invited to join the committee.[12]

During this period a number of resolutions were adopted by Catholic meetings and bishops' conferences, for instance on the Eichmann trial in 1961 and on the need for reparation. These also included a prayer for the murdered Jews and their persecutors, to be read out in every church.

A strong impetus for co-operation within the Catholic community was provided by the declaration *Nostra aetate* issued by the Second Vatican Council of 28th October 1965 and relating to relations with the non-Christian religions. Article 4 dealt extensively with the Old and New Testaments and with Christians and Jews. An extensive literature on the Council declaration rapidly appeared in both German states, influencing Catholics in the GDR to take an active part in meetings of the *Begegnung mit dem Judentum*. Catholic dignitaries also appeared in our synagogues on special occasions.

In the 1970s and 1980s, meetings of the *Begegnung mit dem Judentum* were held, at which the collections were dedicated to the Jewish libraries, the rebuilding of our cemetery walls, or other Jewish needs. Many officials duplicated my lectures and made them available to the communities of the area. Some of the subjects, such as Zionism, contradicted the line taken by official propaganda.

For Jews in the communities outside Berlin, the talks given by *Begegnung mit dem Judentum* groups offered the only opportunity to become acquainted with their history, culture and religion. Our Jewish communities were amalgamated in one national association. Its first president was Hermann Baden in Halle; his successor from 1962–1987 was Helmut Aris of Dresden. The latter was a loyal citizen of his Socialist state who led the communities in a high-handed manner.

Nine years after the Vatican Council declaration *Nostra aetate*, in December 1974, guidelines were issued for its implementation. These pointed to the spiritual bonds and historic ties linking the Church with Jewry. Such bonds ruled out all forms of antisemitism and discrimination as contrary to the spirit of Christianity, just as they were also to be condemned on the basis of human dignity and worth. Moreover, these ties created the obligation to forge "better mutual understanding and a new mutual respect". Elsewhere it was noted that "Jews and Christians should work together in the spirit of the prophets to promote justice and peace in the local, national and international sphere".[13] Further exposition of the declaration appeared in the following year. Thereafter, the Christian-Jewish dialogue was no longer confined to the *Begegnung mit dem Judentum* and to academic gatherings, but spread increasingly into everyday life.

[12]Arndt *et al.*, *op. cit.*; Eschwege, 'Zusammenarbeit von Christen und Juden', *loc. cit.*, pp. 126ff.
[13]Ginzel, *op. cit.*, pp. 296ff.

In 1975 the tide of propaganda against Israel reached new heights in the German Democratic Republic, and the condemnation of the Jewish state became intolerable. For example, the press reported that Israeli scientists were working with West German scientists on plans to sterilise the Arabs there (*Neues Deutschland*, 4th October 1968). Shortly afterwards it was claimed that 4,000 West German armaments experts were working in Israel, including 52 nuclear scientists (*Allgemeiner Deutscher Nachrichtendienst*, 30th December 1968). These slanders were continued in the following years. Thus the East German government was a co-sponsor of the United Nations resolution of 10th November 1975, attacking Zionism as a form of racial discrimination and racialism.

Greatly to the honour of the Evangelical bishops and the Free Churches of the GDR, on 27th December 1975 they published a declaration expressing deep dismay over the UN resolution. The bishops declared that they could not accept "the equation of racism and Zionism". They explained that "as Germans, in the past we denied the right to existence of the Jewish people to a terrifying degree; as a church in the GDR we have expressly supported the programme of the Ecumenical Council to combat racism."[14]

The gatherings of the *Begegnung mit dem Judentum* subsequently became more political and topical. Several attempts by Christian communities to hold discussions with Jewish citizens ended in failure simply because there were no Jewish citizens in the town or the surrounding area. In 1970 there were fewer than ten Jews in Mecklenburg, in Brandenburg outside Berlin, and in Saxony-Anhalt. Many big cities did not contain a single Jewish inhabitant. If we were to look at a similar Christian community of 50 members, how many of them would be capable of giving a talk on their religion, history or culture? Consequently, many of our bigger meetings depended on the help of outsiders. These had to be genuine enthusiasts; with our East German Marks we could not pay them a fee or even travelling expenses in their currency. At best we were able to present them with books to show our appreciation.

Only rarely did the average East German have the opportunity to meet with Jews. The pastor Theodor Arndt commented: "Knowledge of Jewry is almost nil in the younger generation. Where knowledge is available, Jewry is understood largely as an historical factor, Israel as the modern state of today; the Jewish people is an alien concept. In this respect much uncertainty and ignorance prevails . . . Judaism is not seen as a living religion, but as a 'rudiment' which has survived for an incomprehensibly long time."[15] In 1977, a series of annual meetings of the Saxony *Begegnung mit dem Judentum* groups began, which was devoted exclusively to Jewish problems.

The 40th anniversary of the so-called "*Kristallnacht*" led for the first time to reflections on this crime in all the churches. Special preparations were made in various places. On 24th September 1978, the conference of the Evangelical Church leaders in the GDR issued a statement to all its members: "In view of the failure and the guilt of Christianity this [i.e. '*Kristallnacht*'] revealed, every effort

[14]Complete text in Arndt *et al.*, *op. cit.*, pp. 52, 53.
[15]Arndt, 'Das christlich-jüdische Gespräch', *loc. cit.*, p. 28.

must be made to spread knowledge about historical and contemporary Jewry; to gain a new insight into the relationship between Jews and Christians from the Holy Scriptures; to expose concealed hostility to the Jews in Christian preaching; and to strive for a genuine mastery of the calamitous past."[16]

This was followed by the suggestion for the following addition to the Common Prayer service: "Today we remember the 40th anniversary of the '*Kristallnacht*' on 9th November 1938, when so many terrible and appalling things were done to our Jewish fellow citizens. We confess that Christians too burdened themselves with much guilt in those times. We ask you, Lord, to forgive all of us who were guilty and help us all so that we may not again do wrong to our Jewish brothers and sisters. Let us be on our guard when today among us are the victims of our prejudices, where the individuality of human beings, the apparent strangeness of their modes of conduct, becomes the cause of attacks on their dignity."

The prayer was a rebuff to the official attitude of the state, which had rejected the idea that its citizens bore any responsibility for the crimes of the Nazis by arguing that theirs was an anti-Fascist people and that all the guilty men – every last man jack of them – were living in the Federal Republic.

In Dresden, the Ecumenical Commission of the Catholic Berlin Conference of Bishops had its headquarters. Its secretary, Michael Ulrich, suggested that the injustice done to Jewish citizens should be remembered in church services before the 40th anniversary of the "*Kristallnacht*". Dr Ulrich had also collected material dealing with the crimes of 1938, including the call to repentence by the German bishops in 1962, which had already been forgotten by many Chrisitians. The collection also contained documents about the courageous Berlin provost, Bernhard Lichtenberg, who died in Dachau as a result of his public protest against the November Pogrom. Ulrich ended by suggesting the inclusion of three prayers of intercession for the Jews, one of which had been written by Pope John XXIII.[17]

In Magdeburg, headquarters of the *Landeskirche* of Saxony-Anhalt, High Consistory member Christfried Berger made great efforts to prepare for the anniversary. He established a working group comprising representatives of all the local churches and members of the Jewish community. Berger's group contributed two volumes of material on the events of 1938 and the attitude of the population towards them. There were also declarations from the churches on the relationship of Christians with their Jewish neighbours. The book was also published in the Federal Republic.

Along with representatives of the government, bishops from all the churches took part in the commemorations of the *Verband der jüdischen Gemeinden der DDR*. After the anniversary, the working group in Saxony-Anhalt began work on an exhibition on the history of the Jews in the two *Länder*. This was first displayed in the *Marktkirche* in the centre of Halle in 1982. Since then it has been sent to

---

[16] *Evangelischer Pressedienst* (Frankfurt a. Main), No. 44 (16th October 1978), p. 135.
[17] *Ökumenische Kommission der Berliner Bischofskonferenz*, Secretariat, mimeograph, Dresden 3rd October 1978.

various churches in Saxony-Anhalt to explain Jewry and Jewish tradition to the congregations and visitors.

After the opening of the exhibition, the same working group began a detailed investigation into the history of the Jews in the area. Several short monographs about the Jews in individual towns have since been published by this commission, of which I am privileged to be a member.

More than any other declaration, work of literature, or play, the television series "Holocaust" (1978) served to awaken dormant public interest in the greatest crime in Germany's history. Many books and articles were published, both on the film and on the Nazi crimes against the Jewish people. These have led a number of young Germans to involve themselves in the study of Jewish history, religion and culture.

On 24th April 1979, the discussion group *Christen und Juden* of the *Zentralkomitee der deutschen Katholiken* issued its "Theological foci of the Jewish-Christian dialogue", containing the conditions for a dialogue between Christians and Jews. At the same time, Christian friends began to support those few members of the Jewish community who had protested against the anti-Zionist, anti-Israeli propaganda of the media.[18]

The work of the *Aktion Sühnezeichen* had already begun in the GDR some years before. Its members frequently took responsibility for Jewish cemeteries, cleared them of weeds and mended broken gravestones. This Christian youth organisation worked to increase its awareness of Jewish issues. Its members worked with Jewish communities outside the GDR and in erstwhile concentration camps. They demonstrated on the streets of Germany along which the "death marches" of concentration camp prisoners had been driven across the country before the end of the war; the majority of these prisoners had either died of malnutrition or had been murdered by their SS guards when they fell behind.

Since the 40th anniversary of the "*Kristallnacht*", noticeably more Christian communities have come forward to tend our cemeteries. In many places, the local councils have felt obliged to follow their lead and to rebuild cemetery walls. The Jewish communities themselves are so small in number, and so depleted by age and emigration, that they have been unable to play an active role in looking after the cemeteries. A few statistics will serve to demonstrate the position: the Jewish community in Magdeburg has 12 members to look after 42 cemeteries in the former provinces of Prussian Saxony and Anhalt; the city of Erfurt also has 12 members to care for 35 cemeteries, in the former province of Thuringia; in Mecklenburg there are more than 30 cemeteries, but only 4 Jews in the entire region. The cemeteries of Frankfurt a. der Oder, Potsdam and Cottbus are maintained from Dresden.

The Evangelical *Sophiengemeinde*, under the leadership of its pastor Johannes Hildebrand, also helped to deal with the problems of the local Jewish community. For example, it was Hildebrand who intervened to prevent the SED from building a major road through the Jewish cemetery of Berlin-Weissensee.

---

[18]Klemens Richter (ed.), *Die Katholische Kirche und das Judentum. Dokumente 1945–1980*, Frankfurt a. Main 1980, pp. 53ff.

For some thirty years, the *Verband der jüdischen Gemeinden der DDR* has held an annual children's holiday camp on the Baltic coast. Since 1989 the holiday has included telling the children of the community about Jewry and teaching them Jewish and Hebrew songs and the Hebrew language. This strong educational element first became possible in 1989, when the *Zentralrat der Juden in Deutschland* sent an Israeli woman teacher to the camp. The experiment was repeated in 1990. This year the care of the children was undertaken by my daughter, who had herself attended the Jewish holiday camp during her childhood.

The community in Berlin maintained a butcher who sold kosher meat and came to us regularly from Budapest. Among his customers were the members of all the city's Arab embassies and institutions. However, it was the state which financed the 40-strong Christian synagogue choir in Leipzig. To a journalist who asked about the meaning of the choir, its leader and conductor, Helmut Klotz, replied: "We want to retain what Fascist hatred sought to exterminate – it is a form of restitution to those who remain." Many members of the choir are either soloists or chorus members at the Leipzig theatres.

Christian communities and our joint working groups spent much time discussing the resolution of the synod of the Evangelical Church in the Rhineland "On the renewal of relations between Christians and Jews", adopted on 11th January 1980. This referred directly to the responsibility and guilt of Christians in Germany for the Holocaust. The theologians in the GDR generally reached the same conclusion as the church in the Rhineland. The Christian-Jewish dialogue, begun by individual pastors, now has the official blessing of church leaders everywhere and is given both material and ideological support.

The Rhineland resolution was followed, on 28th April 1980, by a declaration by the German Catholic bishops "On the relationship of the Church with Jewry". It covered the following themes:[19]
I. Jesus Christ – our access to Jewry
II. The spiritual legacy of Israel for the Church
III. The fundamental message of the scriptures and the Church on the relationship between Church and Jewry
IV. Differences of faith
V. Changes in thinking concerning Jewry
VI. Common tasks

In 1983, during the Christian community's Luther Year, Luther's teaching and its effects on Christianity were at the centre of discussion. This was also true of our meetings of the *Begegnung mit dem Judentum*, where seminars and symposia were devoted to Luther's changing attitudes towards Jewry. Distinguished Jewish and Christian theologians and other academics attended our meetings as speakers, helping to analyse Luther from both a Christian and a Jewish point of view. I myself spoke at ten evening meetings on this theme. Previous sessions had been devoted to the theme of Jesus and the Jews, sometimes under the heading "bringing Jesus home for us Jews".

---

[19]Deutsche Bischofskonferenz (ed.), *Über das Verhältnis der Kirche zum Judentum. Erklärung der deutschen katholischen Bischöfe, 28th April 1980*, Bonn 1980.

In 1984, two colleagues in the *Begegnung mit dem Judentum* were awarded the Buber-Rosenzweig medal by the Society for Christian-Jewish Cooperation in recognition of long years of work. In the following year, several of our groups and the *Aktion Sühnezeichen* made a journey to Theresienstadt and to visit the Jewish museums in Prague. Shortly afterwards, in October 1985, we visited Auschwitz. Everyone who made that journey had prepared long and carefully. The exhibition staged there by the GDR was thoroughly depressing with only passing reference to the Jews murdered there. It consisted mainly of a hymn of praise to the Communists; only a few of the people mentioned or pictured had ever been incarcerated in Auschwitz. Nevertheless, all our members came away determined to continue the work of explaining history so that the experience of Auschwitz can never be repeated.

It was at Auschwitz that the Dresden group decided to follow the example set by their friends in Saxony-Anhalt, and to mount an exhibition on the history of the Jews in Saxony. This was completed in time to be displayed in the Dresden Kreuzkirche on the 50th anniversary of the "*Kristallnacht*" and was subsequently shown in the cathedrals and Catholic churches of Dresden before being sent to the larger churches of the *Land*. The exhibition showed its audiences the enormous intellectual and economic loss Saxony had sustained as a result of the senseless destruction and expulsion of the Jews during the Nazi regime.

Other areas had also prepared carefully for the 50th anniversary of the "*Kristallnacht*", for example by improving the condition of Jewish cemeteries, renovating our synagogues, setting up memorials or memorial tablets on the site of shattered synagogues and cemeteries. The great wall round the cemetery in Berlin Weissensee was rebuilt and the Jewish cemetery in Rostock superbly repaired, to name only two of many examples.

In the centre of Dresden, the *Landeskirche* placed a memorial tablet at the front of the Kreuzkirche. It was unveiled on 9th November 1989. The inscription, which we had worked on for several weeks, was as follows: "In shame and sorrow Christians remember the Jewish citizens of this city. In 1933 4,675 Jews lived in Dresden. In 1945 there were 70. We were silent as their houses of God were burned down, as Jews were deprived of their rights, driven out and murdered. We failed to recognise them as our brothers and sisters. We ask for forgiveness and Shalom, November 1988."[20]

Between October 1987 and May 1988, our third rabbi was Isaac Neumann from the United States. Though he was welcomed by state dignitaries, by East German Jews, and by Christians of the GDR who were glad at the arrival of a Jewish theologian, his stay was not a complete success. Rabbi Neumann was not satisfied with the conduct of the state, while further problems were caused by his attempt to introduce a reformed religious service without the agreement of the local community. The visit was cut short and the rabbi returned home with his new wife, the daughter of the Deputy Minister of the Interior.

All the *Landeskirchen* of the GDR, and the ecumenical office of the Catholic

---

[20]For the memorial plaque which was unveiled in the main entrance to the *Kreuzkirche* in Dresden on 9th November 1988, see illustration opp. p. 500.

Church, provided detailed reports for the 50th anniversary of the "*Kristallnacht*". In these they encouraged Christians to reflect on their relations with the Jews and to debate the attitude the Church had taken during the Nazi era. This material also suggested ways in which Christians might conduct themselves today in their relations with Jews.

An identical declaration was published by the Evangelical Church leadership in both parts of Germany. All church newspapers contained long articles on the anniversary. The media, including television and radio, were filled with the views of politicians, historians and local historians on the crime which had been committed 50 years before.

The three bishops' conferences of Berlin, the Federal Republic and Austria jointly published a document "Accepting the burden of history". As well as examining the conduct of the Church in the past, this called the Jews "our favoured brothers" and emphasised the need to strive for reconciliation.[21] In a pastoral letter on the 50th anniversary, all the Catholic bishops of the GDR urged their flocks to remember the Jews in a prayer of intercession, and to devote the collections taken on 13th November to the rebuilding of the *Neue Synagoge* in Berlin.[22] In the same spirit, the *Konferenz landeskirchlicher Arbeitskreise*, the *Arbeitsgemeinschaften Kirche und Judentum* and the *Aktion Sühnezeichen* also published a declaration on the 50th anniversary of the "*Reichskristallnacht*". This urged Christians not to relax their efforts to achieve understanding with the Jews.[23]

Our Jewish communities in the GDR now numbered only about 400 members. Many of the old people among them received a generous pension. There was no discrimination against them because they were Jews; if anything, the opposite was the case for a number of years. Jews were treated with respect and efforts were made to help them with any problems they encountered, in a reversal of the experience of earlier years. For some years, Jews in the GDR had been permitted to visit their relatives in Israel. Older Jews, regarded as victims of Fascism, were granted certain advantages in changing their homes and receiving medical treatment, and were entitled to free travel tickets in the GDR for themselves and those accompanying them. It is doubtful whether these privileges will be maintained after unification with the Federal Republic. Towards the end, Jews also gained a much greater influence in academic, cultural and artistic circles in East Germany than might have been expected given their small share of the total population.

At the end of 1987, the leading East German politicians became convinced that the necessary economic relations with the United States could best be achieved by reaching an understanding with Jewish Congressmen. These could be influenced by an improvement in relations with Israel. In consequence, the reluctant Honecker regime prepared to bite the bullet. In June 1988, the

---

[21]*Hirtenwort der Berliner Bischofskonferenz zum 50. Jahrestag der Reichspogromnacht, November 1988*, mimeograph, Berlin 1988.

[22]*Hirtenwort*, mimeograph, Graal-Müritz (6th September 1988).

[23]*Friede den Fernen und Frieden den Nahen. Friedensdekade der Evangelischen Kirchen in der DDR, 6.–16. November 1988*, mimeograph, pp. 39, 40.

Chairman of the *Zentralrat* in the Federal Republic, Heinz Galinski, and the President of the World Council of Jews, Edgar M. Bronfman, were invited to visit the GDR. The aim was to present a changed situation to them as part of a wider campaign to convince the Jewish Congressmen. The media began to curb their strictures against Israel, while the communities were granted additional money to renovate dilapidated synagogues.

Mario Offenberg, the son or grandson of a former member of the *Austrittsgemeinde Adas-Jisroel* in Berlin, made use of the new atmosphere to re-establish the organisation. Though he had little success in West Berlin, he proved highly successful in the East of the city. The services of a talented lawyer, Lothar de Maizière, were retained. Through him, the former property of the *Adas Jisroel* in East Berlin was returned to Mario Offenberg as its representative. His community had between four and six members in both parts of the city and others in the surrounding area, including former Jewish Stalinists and people who had previously tried unsuccessfully to be accepted into the city's Jewish community. When de Maizière was elected *Ministerpräsident* by the first free election in the GDR in March 1990, Offenberg received a large subvention from the state for this group. However, it appears that the representatives of the former *Adas* community abroad moved quickly to dissociate themselves from Offenberg. Ultimately he asked to be accepted into the existing Jewish community under Dr Peter Kirchner.

Over recent years, surviving synagogues have been restored to their former condition with great care by Free Church communities and then used as their own churches. The early example of Jessnitz and Guben has thus been followed by Zwickau and Schönebeck. (Even before the war, local Catholics had turned the modern synagogue in Plau, Mecklenburg, into their church without changing it.) All these Christian communities also committed themselves officially to tending the Jewish cemeteries. In the same spirit, a Jewish museum was created in the former synagogue at Gröbzig. A memorial was set up to the Jews of Anhalt in the synagogue at Wörlitz, a circular building designed by one of the most famous architects of the period.

The Jewish community of East Berlin had long endeavoured to offer cultural performances as well as religious care for its members, in an attempt to acquaint them with knowledge of Jewish life. Separate performances were offered to young people and children. A library with a large selection of books was opened, mainly for the benefit of non-Jews with an interest in Jewish life. It was certain that unification with the Jewish community of West Berlin would enrich the cultural life of Jews in the East, and the need for two Jewish libraries here in future must be regarded as doubtful.[24] Almost since its inception, the *Verband der jüdischen Gemeinden der DDR* maintained a newsletter which improved its standards each year. Its Jewish calendar was dropped in 1990.

On the 50th anniversary of the "*Kristallnacht*", the government invited numerous representatives of Jewish organisations to visit the GDR. They had the

---

[24]The amalgamation of the Jewish communities of both East and West Germany was announced in the *Allgemeine jüdische Wochenzeitung*, 22nd November 1990.

opportunity to see an informative exhibition on the history of the Jews, especially in Berlin, based in the superb palace once built for the Court Jew Ephraim. The building was completely destroyed in the war and had recently been rebuilt and restored to its former glory. The foundation stone was also laid for the rebuilding of the *Neue Synagoge* in Oranienburger Strasse, which is so important to the Jews both historically and artistically. An appeal was made to Jews abroad to help meet the cost. Foreign visitors were also made aware of the only Jewish community of any size in the GDR, that of East Berlin.

Erich Honecker and Horst Sindermann, who were the official representatives of the State at the *"Kristallnacht"* ceremony, were eloquent in praise of the contribution made by Jewish citizens to the development of the German economy, technology, science and culture. They also spoke of the persecution of the workers' movement and the churches by the Nazis, and described the powerlessness of the workers' movement to stand by the Jews in their distress.[25] (This argument, of course, requires some qualification. At a Party conference in 1939, Wilhelm Pieck conceded that the Communists too had been passive bystanders during the violence on 9th November 1938.)[26]

During this ceremony it was left to Heinz Galinski to point out what the speakers had omitted, and which lay at the heart of Jewish concern. He argued that it was essential to combat upsurges of antisemitism in both German states, just as both states bore a common responsibility for the past. Galinski continued: ". . . from our point of view, an element of this common responsibility is also the obligation to advocate the unconditional right to exist of the State of Israel".[27]

Additional money for the construction of the *Neue Synagoge* was provided by the Honecker government, and still more by the government of de Maizière. Appeals for support were also made to firms and organisations.

As in the Weimar Republic, our Jewish communities are composed of both religious and non-religious Jews. The latter choose to attend synagogue sometimes, either out of a sense of solidarity with the parental home or because they feel the ties of a common history. For them, Israel is often a substitute religion. They confess to being Jews, are frequently proud of it, but reject the religion of their fathers. This is nothing new in Jewish history. We need only remember the large Jewish Socialist *Bund* movement in Eastern Europe and America, for whose members Jewish culture replaced the Jewish religion as the guiding principle. As in many other countries, numerous mixed marriages pose a

---

[25] *Neues Deutschland* (Berlin), 9th November 1988.
[26] That is not to deny, of course, that the German Communist Party abroad and the Communist underground press in Germany demonstrated their solidarity with and sympathy for the Jewish community in the aftermath of the November Pogrom. Cf. Helmut Eschwege (ed.), *Kennzeichen J. Bilder, Dokumente, Berichte zur Geschichte der Verbrechen des Hitlerfaschismus an den deutschen Juden 1933–1945*, 2nd revised edn., Berlin 1981, p. 331; Arno Lustiger, 'German and Austrian Jews in the International Brigade', in *LBI Year Book XXXV* (1990), pp. 300–301; Arnold Paucker, *Jüdischer Widerstand in Deutschland. Tatsachen und Problematik*, Beiträge zum Widerstand 1933–1945, Gedenkstätte Deutscher Widerstand Berlin, Heft 37, Berlin 1989, p. 9, revised and expanded English version, *Jewish Resistance in Germany. The Facts and the Problems*, Berlin 1991, p. 8.
[27] Heinz Galinski in *Neues Deutschland*, 10th November 1988.

problem which is exacerbated by the small size of our communities. These communities will inevitably change in future. It is difficult to predict whether the Jews who have fled here from the Soviet Union in recent months – there are now about 800 of them[28] – will increase the size of our communities and bring us gain. After two decades of atheist education, these emigrants have been alienated from the Jewish religion and from Jewish culture.

Nevertheless, our communities regard it as their Jewish and humanitarian duty to help these people as best they can. The *Zentralrat* supports us and has provided two workers from the Central Welfare Office to help take care of the Russian Jews. But finding work for them is difficult, since the reorganisation of our economy means that thousands of manual workers, white-collar workers, academics and artists are losing their jobs every month.

The political upheaval has changed the lives of East German Jews in other unforeseen ways. At its first sitting of 12th April 1990, the various factions of the first democratically elected *Volkskammer* united to address the Jews of all nations, especially in Israel. The delegates confessed the responsibility of the citizens of the GDR for German crimes against the Jews and other peoples. The deputies asked for pardon in the name of the people, and asked the people of Israel to forgive them for the hostility of East German politicians and for the persecution and indignity suffered by Jewish citizens in the GDR. The declaration continued: "We know that we are under a special obligation to promote and protect the Jewish religion, culture and tradition in Germany, and to tend and maintain Jewish cemeteries, synagogues and memorials in the future.

We see a special task as lying in educating the youth of our country to respect the Jewish people and giving them knowledge of Jewish religion, tradition and culture.

We therefore support the granting of asylum in the GDR to persecuted Jews. We declare our desire to strive for the establishment of diplomatic relations and for many-sided contacts with the State of Israel."[29]

Three weeks after this declaration, the *Zentralrat* and the *Verband der Jüdischen Gemeinden in der DDR* jointly instituted in commemoration the "Day of the Holocaust" in the East Berlin synagogue in Rykestrasse. The ceremony was attended by representatives of the government and by a delegate from the *Amcha-Stiftung*, which is concerned with the psychological damage suffered by the victims of Nazi persecution. The Health Minister of the GDR handed over to it 6.2 million Marks, taken from the estate of the SED, in the name of the government.[30]

On 1st April 1990, a *Gesellschaft DDR–Israel für Verständigung und Zusammenarbeit*

---

[28]By the beginning of 1991 there were already 10,000 Soviet Jews. In April the German government gave in to the demands and pressures of the Israeli government and imposed a ban on the immigration of Jews from the Soviet Union. Up to this time Heinz Galinski, President of the *Zentralrat der Juden in Deutschland*, had welcomed their immigration into Germany, seeing it as strengthening the many small communities in the country. But even his enthusiasm waned as many Jewish communities became anxious about the financial implications.

[29]*Allgemeine jüdische Wochenzeitung*, 19th April 1990.

[30]*Ibid.*, 3rd May 1990.

was founded in East Berlin. Its aim was to provide a true picture of Israel for the GDR in order to fight antisemitism, racism and neo-Nazism and to cultivate cultural exchanges with Israel. On the 4th July, a meeting was held in Dresden for people with an interest in Jewish history and culture. The circle, which is limited to Dresden and the surrounding area, contains 31 members including four from the Jewish community. Similar groups are currently meeting in several places.

This paper on the Jews in the GDR was concluded shortly before the unification of the two Germanies. It is inevitable that the process will change their position in a fundamental way. The first change will be structural. In the GDR there were eight Jewish communities. However, in united Germany, the East Berlin community will join with the much larger community of West Berlin, and the remaining seven will amalgamate into two communities. The Jewish community in Erfurt will join with that of Hesse.

Over forty years of rule by Ulbricht and Honecker have left the GDR with an illegal but continuing legacy of antisemitism and neo-Nazism, which was never combatted officially nor even acknowledged. In East German schoolbooks, there was little mention either of the history of the Jews or of antisemitism; the persecution of the Jews by the Nazis was dealt with very briefly, without any attempt to provide a historical context either before 1933 or after 1945. The dogma that the population of the GDR was always anti-Fascist, and was even among the victors over the Nazi regime, was doggedly maintained. Indeed, it virtually produced the grotesque notion that the GDR was actually the first state to be invaded by the Nazis. Concepts such as defeat and capitulation were held to apply only to the Nazis, who were all deemed to reside in the territory of the Federal German Republic.

Antisemitism and neo-Fascism thus blossomed along with the fall of Honecker. East German Jews were profoundly shocked by the appearance of antisemitic graffiti, the desecration of cemeteries and the abuse of Jews. Though all these had occurred in the past, they had been denied because they were not supposed to exist. But it should be emphasised that both Christian denominations are striving to come to terms with their past. A recent synod declaration of the Evangelical Church in Brandenburg on 24th April 1990 was devoted to the renewal of relations between Jews and Christians. It devoted much attention to the special kinship between followers of the two religions, and included a critical appraisal of Christian tradition and references to the lasting significance of the Old Testament for the Christian faith. Pastors and theologians were asked to reflect on the Jewishness of Christ more than in the past, and to respect Jewry. The same synod also resolved to observe each 9th November as a "day of repentance and remembrance".

The foregoing survey should be viewed as an initial attempt to evaluate the situation of the diminutive Jewish community in the now defunct German Democratic Republic and to chart the development of church attitudes to the

"Jewish Question", the German-Jewish past and Jewry today. To a lesser degree it examines the position adopted *vis à vis* the Jews by the ruling elites of the GDR during more than four decades of post-war rule. No one is more aware than this author that much remains to be done in this respect[31] and that his own analysis inevitably retains a strong personal note. The reason for this is obvious: the Jewish group in post-war "Eastern" Germany was such a small one that a Jewish "activist" necessarily played a disproportionately large role.*

The course of German history underwent a crucial change in 1990. The end of an era in the Eastern half of the country surely heralds the hour for a critical assessment of the way in which its inhabitants came – or rather failed to come – to terms with what befell German Jewry in the twelve years after the victory of Nazism in 1933.

---

[31]We cannot append here a full bibliography of work already undertaken, but special mention should be made of an essay published in this Year Book: Monika Richarz, 'Jews in Today's Germanies', in *LBI Year Book XXX* (1985), pp. 265–274; and see also *idem*, 'Juden in der Bundesrepublik Deutschland und in der Deutschen Demokratischen Republik Deutschland seit 1945', in Micha Brumlik *et al.* (eds.), *Jüdisches Leben in Deutschland seit 1945*, Frankfurt a. Main 1986; Lothar Mertens, 'Juden in der DDR. Eine schwindende Minderheit', in *Deutschland Archiv*, Jg. 19, Köln (November 1986), pp. 1192–1203; Robin Ostow, *Jüdisches Leben in der DDR* (transl. by Wolfgang Lotz), Frankfurt a. Main 1988; *idem*, *Jews in Contemporary East Germany. The Children of Moses in the Land of Marx*, Basingstoke 1989. See now also Willi Jasper, 'Schrumpfende Gemeinde unter Zionismus-Verdacht. Jüdisches Leben in der ehemaligen DDR', in *Das Parlament*, No. 33 (9th August 1991), p. 4.

*The author's memoirs were published after the completion of this manuscript, when the Year Book was at the printers. See Helmut Eschwege, *Fremd unter meinesgleichen. Erinnerungen eines Dresdner Juden*, Berlin 1991 – (Ed.).

Refugees and the Film Industry

Jews and Exiles in British Cinema

BY KEVIN GOUGH-YATES

"By the end of the war, a positive reading of 'mainstream' British cinema for the first time became convincingly available, both in Britain and abroad. It was a cinema unproblematically British in personnel (after a decade of foreign infiltration that was resented by many) . . ."
Charles Barr, 'Introduction. Amnesia and Schizophrenia', in *All Our Yesterdays. 90 Years of British Cinema*, London 1986.

In his historiographic survey of British cinema Charles Barr repeats many of the myths which are associated with its development. The Second World War, so the argument goes, created a cinema which subordinated "individual desire and ambition to the team and the job" to produce "the classic films of the period (*In Which We Serve, Millions Like Us, Fires Were Started, The Way to the Stars, San Demetrio London*) . . . [films which] could be grouped together as achievements of a national cinema to be proud of".[1] Drawing an analogy with politics, Barr argues that the contradictions and conflicts which had existed in film production, between rival factions within the documentary and commercial feature film, were resolved by integrating documentary personnel into the industry.

Barr is only one recent exponent of a line which has been consistently lengthening since 1945 and has become sanctified as embodying truths about nationhood. The distinguished film journalist Dilys Powell was writing similarly immediately after the war when she identified a change in audience appreciation, towards "the semi-documentary film [which] has gained a hold over British imaginations"[2] and histories of British cinema, those by George Perry and Rachel Low, for example,[3] have so fuelled the myths that they have found their way into works of social history. The British at war had the Spitfire and the Hurricane, the British cinema fought the battle for the nation with the documentary and its descendant, British realism.

They contribute to a partial and misleading representation of the period and, when we look more closely, a more complex picture emerges, in which the dominant creative forces in the cinema are émigrés, frequently refugees, and often, in so far as it is valuable to identify them, Jews. For a more complete picture we need to consider a whole range of factors, which includes other components of Britain's history, in particular, the debate over Empire Free

---

[1]Charles Barr, 'Introduction. Amnesia and Schizophrenia', in *idem* (ed.), *All Our Yesterdays. 90 Years of British Cinema*, London 1986, pp. 10–11.
[2]Dilys Powell, 'Films since 1939', in *Since 1939. Ballet, Films, Music, Painting*, London 1948, pp. 94ff.
[3]George Perry, *The Great British Picture Show*, London 1974; Rachel Low, *The History of British Film 1929–1939. Film Making in 1930s Britain*, London 1985.

Trade, which dominated so much economic thinking in the nineteen thirties and played its part in shaping Britain's weak role in Europe.

The reasons for the large number of Jews, émigrés and refugees being associated with the development of British cinema in the 1930s is only in part due to the rise of Hitler and Nazism.[4] Many had arrived in Britain after the introduction of sound in 1929 which, along with the Wall Street Crash, had had a devastating effect on German film production. Others, Alexander Korda for example, had tried Hollywood and failed. Some, the film producers Ludwig Blattner and Julius Hagen, had been in Britain since the beginning of the century. Others: Michael Balcon, Victor Saville, Oscar Deutsch and Isidore Ostrer, had been here all along.

One of the exiles, Filippo Del Giudice, the managing director of Two Cities, is reputed to have learnt the little English he knew by teaching it to the children of Italian waiters in Soho, one step ahead of them in the manual. Yet he was at once "the architect of British film renaissance"[5] in the 1940s and "a big spender with large domestic staffs, motor cars, and a huge entertainment account" whose films had to make a small fortune before they could show a profit.[6] He not only purchased the rights to Winston Churchill's *Life of Marlborough* from Korda but paid Churchill a further £50,000 for them. An Italian lawyer, he had been a member of the Christian Democratic Party and came to Britain in 1933, apparently for political reasons. Antisemitic legislation would have prevented him from practising later and, indeed, Two Cities was banned from making a film in Italy as it had "a Jewish Board of management".[7] After advising Ludovico Toeplitz, Alexander Korda's old partner, on details of Italian law in the Bette Davis contract suit with Warner Bros., he and Toeplitz set up Two Cities Films Ltd., with £5,000 of borrowed money. As had Gabriel Pascal, the producer-director who is closely associated with the film adaptations of the plays of George Bernard Shaw, Del Giudice moved from rags to riches. He was similarly profligate and his personal expenditure was in the region of £50,000 a year. When he gave a dinner-party, there were seldom less than thirty round the table and among the frequent guests were Ernest Bevin and Stafford Cripps. Sir Robert Bruce Lockhart, who was introduced to Del Giudice at an archetypically improvident dinner party, thought him a cynical exploiter of politicians, at his best in the election of 1945. Expecting Churchill to win he had filled his house with "the tough boys of the Tory party. Two weeks later they had been replaced by the Labour victors."[8] More of an impresario than a producer, he was cavalier about money, and J. Arthur Rank, his financier after 1942, tired of his personal

[4]On the role of Jews in the German cinema see Hans Feld, 'Jews in the Development of the German Film Industry – Notes from the Recollections of a Berlin Film Critic', in *LBI Year Book XXVII* (1982), pp. 337–365.

[5]Alan Wood, *Mr Rank. A Study of J. Arthur Rank and British Films*, London 1952, p. 128. Filippo Del Giudice (1892–1962).

[6]Sir Robert Bruce Lockhart, *Friends, Foes and Foreigners*, London 1957, p. 178.

[7]*Manchester Guardian*, 8th September 1938.

[8]Bruce Lockhart, *op. cit.*, pp. 176–177; Hugh Gaitskell, *The Diary of Hugh Gaitskell 1945–56*, ed. by Philip M. Williams, London 1979, pp. 176–177, considered him to have "no morals whatsoever" and to be "quite unsound from every point of view".

excesses and the rising cost of his productions and stopped financing him.[9] Del Giudice had been responsible for some of the best British films of the decade, *In Which We Serve, This Happy Breed, Henry V, The Way to the Stars* and *Odd Man Out* amongst them but, as with all the inspirational schemes of British film production, there was no firm industrial base and his courting of influential people provided his company with no long-term stability.

In general, film executives have sought large profits in America, a market with strong barriers against foreign film products. Their few successes have encouraged others, all of whom have had their fingers burnt. In the nineteen thirties Alexander Korda, the most visionary of all film producers in Britain, came close to achieving the complete integration of British film production into the American market. But it failed to work out, partly a consequence of poor management, partly that of the British financial markets, and partly a feature of the more complex economic failure of the country. Others, Max Schach for example, "The Pocket Battleship of British films", pinned their hopes on success in the United States, but assumed it would happen by osmosis and had no assured distribution outlets. He, as others have, felt he had an absolute sense of the man in the street. "If I make a picture to please myself, I make money. If I try to make a picture to please the public, I lose."[10] His press officer, Monja Danischewsky, describes the much-publicised charity première for the Czinner-Bergner film, *Dreaming Lips*, in February 1937, which was attended by "the late Queen Mary, then Queen Mother", at her first public appearance since the death of King George V in 1936. Schach wanted to abandon the National Anthem for the occasion and get the Kneller Hall Trumpeters' Band to play 'Pack Up Your Troubles in Your Old Kit Bag'. "I have lived in zis country for two years – and look vere I am, and look vere you are", he chided the apprehensive Danischewsky.[11] The slump which hit the film industry in 1937 and helped cause his downfall marked the end of many film careers, his own included.

A year later, after his film companies had collapsed, he was exploring other avenues and came close to establishing a commercial radio station in Ostende. After the war he tried, unsuccessfully, to set up a bi-lingual film with George Höllering, the co-producer of *Kuhle Wampe* (1932), producer/director of *Murder in the Cathedral* (1951), and owner of Academy Cinemas in Oxford Street. Schach died in 1957, in virtual obscurity, whilst his life-time associate Karl Grune, whom he had invited to write and direct his first film for Friedrich Zelnik at Stern Film after the First World War,[12] managed to co-produce only one more, *The Silver Darlings* (Holyrood 1947, dir. Clarence Elder and Clifford Evans), a film set in the Hebrides of the eighteenth century, but which exhibited some of the stage-like costuming and designs for films which he had directed in the 1930s.

[9]The cost of *Henry V* for example, rose to £475,000.
[10]Campbell Dixon, *Daily Telegraph*, [?] March 1935, undated clipping, British Film Institute.
[11]Monja Danischewsky, *White Russian – Red Face*, London 1966, pp. 108–109.
[12]Schach's wife, Beate (née Schoch), had written film scripts and collaborated on Grune's first film, *Der Mädchenhirt* [The Shepherdess] (1919). She became Grune's companion. After Schach's death they married. When Grune died in 1962 she took her own life and his estate went to the JNF Charitable Trust "for the purpose of settling poor immigrant people in the State of Israel".

Grune's long-running biblical project, *From Beginning to Beginning*, came to nothing.

Schach, who has been described by David Stewart Hull as one of "Germany's three top pre-Nazi producers", along with Erich Pommer and Seymour Nebenzahl,[13] had aspired to be another Korda, the Hungarian film director, who had had a career in Budapest, Berlin and Hollywood, before settling in London in 1931, initially to make "Quota" films for Paramount. In 1933 Korda had directed *The Private Life of Henry VIII* for his own company, London Film Productions (LFP), for a figure which was said to be £60,000, but was, in fact, more than half as much again, and helped launch a boom in British film production of which Schach was one of the beneficiaries. Schach, with no studio facilities of his own, is sometimes painted as the villain, the film industry's Horatio Bottomley, but the bubble was created less by film makers than by banks and finance houses eager for easy money. Believing that an international success was available for £60,000, they rushed to finance films which, whatever their other shortcomings, were under-financed and, consequently, ran over budget.

After 1933, refugees from Hitler's Germany arrived in Britain often, but not always, with a contract from Korda in their hands. For every Elisabeth Bergner and Conrad Veidt, who found it easy to establish themselves, there were half a dozen actors and actresses who did not;[14] for every Korda there were two or three producers and directors who found it less than easy and some, Leo Lasko for example, with a long writing and directing career behind him,[15] never worked in the film industry again.[16] In 1938, he was reported to have opened a factory for the manufacture of hair colouring. Loo Hardy, a prominent actress in Weimar Germany, took to running a boarding house for refugees in Cleveland Square.

[13]David Stewart Hull, *Film in the Third Reich*, Berkley–London 1969, p. 128.

[14]The list of actors and actresses includes: Josef Almas, Gitta Alpar, Charlotte Ander, Sybille Binder, Jacques Brunius, Paul Demel, Tamara Desni, Ernst Deutsch, Josef Durham, Erich Freund, Marta Eggerth, Carl Esmond (Willy Eichberger), Amy Frank, Charles Goldner, Paul Grätz, Guy Guy-Maas, Dolly Haas, Loo Hardy, Gerard Heinz, Paul Henreid, Oscar Homolka, Carl Jaffé, Lilly Kann, Jan Kiepura, Fritz Kortner, Hella Kurty, Marta Labarr, Albert Lieven, Tatiana Lieven, Jan Van Loewen, Herbert Lom, Peter Lorre, Arthur Mainzer-Reinholds, Lucie Mannheim, Andrew Marton, Meinhart Maur, Ferdi Mayne, Martin Miller, Lilli Palmer, Irène Prador, Friedrich Richter, Walter Rilla, Gerik Schelderup, Josef Schmidt, Karel Stepanek, Richard Tauber, Frederick Valk, Hans Wengraf and Adolf Wohlbrück (Anton Walbrook).

[15]Among Lasko's early films were *Der Dolch der Malaien* (1919) and *Der Sträfling von Cayenne* (Zelnik 1921), but he continued to be associated with feature films in Germany until 1935 (pseudonymously, after 1933, as Frank Wysbar).

[16]The list of directors and producers includes: Kurt Alexander, Rudolph Becker, Paul Czinner, Rudolph Bernauer, Kurt Bernhardt, Hans Brahm (John Brahm), Fritz Brunn (asst. dir), Hans Casparius, Alberto Cavalcanti, Henry Cornelius, Filippo Del Giudice, Richard Eichberg, Alexander Esway, Friedrich Feher, Hermann Fellner, Alexander Galperson, Isadore Goldschmidt, Karl Grune, Julius Haimann, Marcel Hellmann, George Höllering, Leopold Jessner, Victor Katona, Rudolf Katscher (Rudolph Cartier), Count von Keller, Alexander Korda, Zoltan Korda, Otto Kreisler, Carl Lamac, Leo Lasko, Arthur Lassally, Ivan Lassgallner, Kurt Lewenhak, Max Mack, Carl Mayer, Lothar Mendes, Olaf Olsen, Richard Oswald, Gabriel Pascal, Erich Pommer, Arnold Pressburger, Max Schach, Victor Skutezky, Henry Sokal, Josef Somlo, Paul Soskin, Sam Spiegel, Günther Stapenhorst, Paul Stein, Stefan and Franciszka Themerson, Wilhelm Thiele, André de Toth, Eugene Tuscherer, Berthold Viertel, Jiri Weiss, Fritz Wendhausen, Robert Wiene, Alfred Zeisler and Friedrich Zelnik.

Figures who had been important to the development of German cinema, Max Mack and Carl Mayer, for example, did little creative work in England. Mack directed only one film, *Be Careful Mr. Smith* (Union 1935); Mayer, the screenwriter of *Das Cabinett des Dr Caligari* and *Der letzte Mann* had had his talents wasted on the Bergner-Czinner films and died in 1944. Del Giudice, probably through the good offices of Emeric Pressburger, employed him at Two Cities as a scenario editor but, in England, he had only one screen credit, as consultant to Paul Rotha's *The Fourth Estate* (Realist 1940), a film which, because it satirised its sponsor, Times Newspapers, was never publicly shown. For other writers,[17] composers,[18] designers and technicians,[19] and commentators,[20] it was little different. When they could, many made their way to Hollywood, where the prospects seemed better: Gitta Alpar, Elisabeth Bergner, Martha Eggerth, Willy Eichberger, Paul Grätz, Dolly Haas, Oscar Homolka, Peter Lorre, Paul Henreid, Fritz Kortner and Conrad Veidt, among the actors; Paul Czinner, Kurt Bernhardt, Hans Brahm, Richard Eichberg, Friedrich Feher, Leopold Jessner and Richard Oswald, among the directors; Hanns Eisler and Karol Rathaus among the composers; and Laszlo Benedek, Curt Courant, Rudi Fehr, Franz Planer and Eugen Schüfftan among the technicians. It was, however, a mixed blessing and whilst some prospered, others fell by the wayside. Paul Grätz and Conrad Veidt died soon after arriving in Hollywood; Elisabeth Bergner's career foundered, in substantial part, because she had fled to the USA in the middle of making the Michael Powell-Emeric Pressburger film *49th Parallel*;[21] and Leopold Jessner, a major figure in German theatre, found it impossible to find any kind of footing.[22]

[17]The list of writers includes: Lajós Biró, Ernest Borneman, Fritz Gottfurcht (Frederick Gotfurt), Herbert Juttke (Herbert Victor), Paul Merzbach, Carl Mayer, Maurice Moiseiwitsh, Emeric Pressburger, Erwin Reiner, Walter Reisch, Paul Tabori, Akos Tolnay, Hans Wilhelm, Wolfgang Wilhelm and Carl Zuckmayer.

[18]The list of composers includes: Ludwig Brav, Nikolaus Brodszky, Francis Chagrin, Hanns Eisler, Walter Goehr, Allan Gray, Hans May, Ernst Hermann Meyer, Karol Rathaus, Miklós Rózsa, Kurt Schroeder, Matyas Seiber, Mischa Spoliansky, Vilhelm Tausky and Ernst Toch.

[19]The list of designers and technicians includes: Josef Ambor, Andrei Andrejew, Kyril Arapov, Josef Bato, Laszlo Benedek, Francis Bieber, Max Brenner, Ulrich Cassirer, Curt Courant, Helga Cranston, Dragutin Domac, Henry Elwis, Tony Etienne, Rudi Fehr, Alice Fenyues, Ignaz Fleminger, Kurt Goldberger, Ulf Greeber, Mutz Greenbaum (Max Greene), Philippo Guidobaldi, Oswald Hafenrichter, John Halas, Albert Haymsen, Hein Heckroth, Heinrich Heitfield, Otto Heller, Walter Jentzsch, Albert Jullion, Alfred Junge, Otto Kanturek, Karl Kayser, Vincent Korda, Günter Krampf, Nicholas Krass, Andrew L. Mazzei, Lazare Meerson, Laszlo Meitner, Ernö Metzner, László Moholy-Nagy, Kurt von Molo, F. I. Neuenberg, Georges Périnal, Franz Planer, Peter Sachs, Hans Schneeberger, Eugen Schüfftan, Jan Stallich, Walter Stokvis, Alex Strasser, Joe Strasser, Peter Straussfield, Wolfgang Suschitzky, Franz Weihmayer, Fritz Weiss and Oscar Werndorff.

[20]Hans Feld, Heinrich Fraenkel, Egon Larsen, Pem (Paul Marcus) and Hans H. Wollenberg.

[21]She smuggled jewellery out of England sewn into the hems of her clothes and, although she was already British, gives one of her reasons as "I didn't want to report to police any more". Others on *49th Parallel* revealed a different spirit. Walbrook gave his salary to the British Red Cross and Pressburger, who was now classified as an enemy alien, only agreed to go to Canada in the first place on the understanding that he would be given a re-entry permit to Britain, see *Kinematograph Weekly*, 5th December 1940.

[22]Jessner directed one film in Britain, *Children of the Fog* (Jesba Films 1937), photographed by Eugene Schüfftan with music by Allan Gray.

Other producers who arrived in England in the early 1930s include Isadore Goldsmith and Fred Zelnik who had been associates in Germany. Their companies had Rudolph Bernauer and Fritz Kortner as their main writers, and Paul Czinner and Karl Grune as their star directors. Grune claimed that it was watching the faces and gestures of foreign soldiers during the First World War, that had attracted him to the pictorial language of the cinema. With Schach as producer, he directed *Die Straße* (1923), a film from a Carl Mayer scenario, which established his reputation. Schach and Grune continued together with a long series of films, including *Schlagendes Wetter* (*Trapped in the Mine*, 1923), which was later to kindle an interest in the A. J. Cronin novel, *The Stars Look Down*.[23] Together they went via UFA (Universum Film AG) to Munich, where in the late twenties, Grune was in charge of production for Emelka and Schach was its executive producer. In England Schach formed the Capitol Film Corporation. Its "programme for 1936 includes . . . *I Pagliacci* [sic] and *The Stars Look Down*, both to be made by that master director Karl Grune . . ."[24] He had reputedly paid £18,000 for the film rights to the former, which was to be the first in a series of filmed operas.

Ludwig Blattner (like Schach, a diminutive film producer) had arrived from Germany in 1897 aged thirteen and was in the film business from 1907. He rose from an assistant cinema manager until he controlled several small circuits which included the Gaiety Theatre, Manchester. In December 1927, he sold them to British International Pictures, established the Ludwig Blattner Picture Corporation and entered film production. It was in financial difficulties from the beginning, but the young Michael Powell, who was working for him at the time, identified Blattner as "a promoter of genius with far-seeing ideas about technical developments in Sound and Colour".[25] He controlled the non-American rights to the Keller-Dorian lenticular colour process as well as the North American and British rights to the Stille Recording System to which he had been introduced by the great German cine-photographer Karl Freund.[26] The former was a relatively inexpensive, if complicated, method of producing colour and, as early as 1926, the financier E. Beddington-Behrens, who was attempting to open a film studio in Brighton, had written enthusiastically about it to the writer/producer Ivor Montagu.[27] The Stille patents Blattner incorporated into the Blattnerphone, an early method of recording sound on steel tape, a number of which were leased by the BBC,[28] but both systems had severe limitations and Blattner soon lost

---

[23]Originally a Schach-Grune project, when Capitol collapsed, it was taken up by their associate Isadore Goldsmith (Goldschmidt) at Grafton Films.

[24]*Kinematograph Weekly*, 9th January 1936.

[25]Michael Powell, *A Life in Movies. An Autobiography*, London 1986, p. 199.

[26]Karl Freund (1890–1969) was co-director of Walter Ruttmann's *Berlin – Die Symphonie einer Großstadt* (1927), and photographer on Murnau's *Der letzte Mann/The Last Laugh* (1924), E. A. Dupont's *Variété* and Fritz Lang's *Metropolis* (1926).

[27]Letter, 15th March 1926. The lenticular colour system continued to have advocates, but was really unsuitable for feature films. A good description of the system is to be found in Brian Coe, *The History of Movie Photography*, London 1981, which notes its success in amateur film making.

[28]For more information on the development and history of the Blattnerphone see William Lafferty, 'The Blattnerphone. An Early Attempt to Introduce Magnetic Recording Into the Film Industry', in *Cinema Journal*, Summer 1983, pp. 18–37.

control of them. Unable to meet his purchasing commitments from Keller-Dorian, he sold his rights to Technicolor in February 1930, and, unable to develop the Blattnerphone which offered only a low quality of recording, he sold the machines to the BBC who cannibalised them for spare parts. The most important film in Blattner's programme was an adaptation of Lion Feuch-twanger's novel, *Jew Süss*, but, in the end, he was forced to sell it to Gaumont-British for £6,000, the price he had originally paid and a good one considering that sound and dialogue rights were not included.

Lothar Mendes, its director, had seen *Jew Süss* on the stage in New York, but could raise no interest in it as a film subject in Hollywood and had brought the idea to Michael Balcon, who found himself negotiating with the playwright, Ashley Dukes,[29] the publisher Martin Secker for the dialogue rights according to the book and with Feuchtwanger himself. In the end, the cost of acquiring them helped force the production well over its estimated £85,000 and the film eventually cost around £120,000. It was for Gaumont-British a massive and expensive production, with four of the Shepherd's Bush and Islington stages simultaneously in use and 214 technical and production personnel in continuous employment for five months. By the time it was about to be made, Hitler was securely in power in Germany and Goebbels attempted to prevent Conrad Veidt, who had been completing *Wilhelm Tell* (1934 dir. Heinz Paul), returning to England to appear in it.[30]

It is often thought that British cinema did little to alert audiences to the political crisis of the nineteen thirties, but, hemmed in by censorship and press manipulation on the one hand and commercial considerations on the other, it is remarkable that any films were able to echo the European situation at all.[31] Balcon and Mendes, the director of *Jew Süss*, although they denied it at the time, considered the theme of major importance.[32] It was the first Gaumont-British picture "on a epic scale", wrote Balcon in his memoirs. "I had to fight much resistance on the ground that it was a 'dangerous' subject." The Ostrers (Isidore, Mark and Maurice) saw financial viability as the prime consideration, and as the "sales overseas were relatively insignificant" for the films of Gaumont-British, they looked to him for assurance that it would make its money back in Britain alone. In the end, a variety of compromises led to it being an artistic and financial failure. Balcon had originally intended to cast Elisabeth Bergner and Emil Jannings, but the idea had to be dropped and the film failed commercially, Conrad Veidt feeling that the natural audience for the film kept away because of the racial issues it raised. "The Jews are too deeply concerned with the

[29] In whose play the sound rights were partly vested.

[30] Heinrich Fraenkel, *Unsterblicher Film*, Munich 1957, pp. 100–102. Veidt was kept in Germany and Balcon was sent a doctor's certificate from Germany claiming he was too ill to travel and had to send a distinguished doctor to declare him well.

[31] For more on censorship and control see Nicholas Pronay, 'The Political Censorship of Films in Britain between the Wars', in Nicholas Pronay and D. W. Spring (eds.), *Propaganda, Politics, and Film, 1918–45*, London 1982; James C. Robertson, *The British Board of Film Censors*, London 1985; *idem*, *The Hidden Cinema. British film censorship in action, 1913–1972*, London 1989; Richard Cockett, *Twilight of Truth. Chamberlain, Appeasement and the Manipulation of the Press*, London 1989.

[32] Michael Balcon, *Michael Balcon Presents . . . A Lifetime of Films*, London 1969, pp. 83–84.

persecution question . . . to patronise pictures . . . that deal with the problem."[33] If Jews turned their backs on it so did everyone else, and James Agate, who was uncomfortable with "films extolling" Jews "at unbearable length", thought it should not have been made in the first place. He was, he wrote, an "anti-anti-semite", who believed in not raising the subject and treated the film cruelly, arguing that there had been quite enough "of these Wandering Jews, Roth-schilds, and Süsses".[34]

Jew Süss was to have been the first of a number of films on Jewish subjects, but the programme came to nothing. Victor Saville wanted to make a version of Louis Golding's novel *Magnolia Street*, but it was finally abandoned. In the spring of 1933, when Gaumont-British was in the throes of producing *Jew Süss*, it was also considering three other Jewish themes, one of them from Lion Feucht-wanger, which dealt with the fate of a German-Jewish family after the rise of Hitler to power, to be produced by the impresario and producer, Hermann Fellner, but the problems of *Süss* and the attitude of the British Board of Film Censors led to all three being dropped. Fellner visited Feuchtwanger in Bandol, France, and invited him to produce a suitable screen subject, as "Ramsay MacDonald wanted an anti-Nazi film". He sent down Gaumont-British's "best man" Sidney Gilliat to write it as a "narrative-treatment", but Gilliat recalled that it was an impossible subject for the time and "I never heard another word about it". One of the others, *City Without Jews*, was taken from the novel by the murdered Austrian writer Hugo Bettauer and set in contemporary Vienna. When the Jews are expelled from Austria by the Christian Socialist and German Nationalists, it loses all its foremost brains in the sciences, the arts and finance and the country moulder until a new election leads to the repeal of the legislation. A crude, propagandist idea, *City Without Jews* was dropped from the Gaumont-British programme along with the third film, *A German Tragedy*, the story of a Jewish doctor in Germany, who loses everything, including his family, as a result of persecution.[35]

Jew Süss was the stimulus for the making of two other films. Even whilst it was in preparation Basil Dean revived John Galsworthy's play *Loyalties* (ATP 1933 dir. Dean) for the screen. It was already more than ten years old and the screen version, the only example of its kind, had more than a touch of British middle-class antisemitism. The haughty Ferdinand de Levis (Basil Rathbone), made "effeminate" in the view of *Variety*,[36] is tolerated in society because of his wealth,

[33] *World Film News*, October 1936. Earlier, with regard to *The Wandering Jew* (Twickenham 1933, dir. Maurice Elvey) in which he had also played, he denied its topicality, *Picturegoer*, 19th August 1933. "Our job was not concerned with propaganda or the production of a political or ethnological problem-film, we were working on a document which reveals the soul of a human being and his vicissitudes."

[34] James Agate, *Around Cinemas*, 2nd Series, London 1948, pp. 104–107.

[35] Geoff Brown, *Launder and Gilliat*, London 1987, p. 50; interview with author 8th January 1990. The story was published as *Die Geschwister Oppenheim* in 1933 and translated as *The Oppermanns* in Britain. A Soviet film version was made in 1939, before the Non-Aggression Pact with Germany, directed by Grigori Roshal; Jeffrey Richards, 'The British Board of Film Censors and Content Control in the 1930s: Foreign Affairs', in *Historical Journal of Film, Radio and Television*, vol. 2, No. 1, 1982. Richards describes other films which were not made.

[36] *Variety*, 21st October 1936.

but intensely disliked as a Jew and *Loyalties* is unusual in exploiting a mass of antisemitic clichés. Jews "stick together"; apart from working harder, "they're everywhere"; Jews are both easily recognised on a jury and considered to be biased in favour of the Jewish defendant; de Levis is seen as a *parvenu* who is sharp with money; his membership application to an exclusive club is blocked because "you have to draw the line somewhere". He is aware of the surrounding animosities and contemptuously defiant, but when £1,000 is taken from his room and he is expected to act like a "gentleman" and not allow a scandal to occur, he is immediately confronted with a forked antisemitic challenge. If he fails to pursue the matter he, as a Jew, will suffer further humiliations; if he braves it he will open a Pandora's box full of prejudice which portrays Jews as exaggeratedly money-conscious. When he publicly accuses Captain Ronald Ramsey (Miles Mander) of the theft and is called a "damned Jew", he is provoked beyond endurance; he refuses to withdraw his accusation and forces an action for slander. De Levis, as some already knew, was right all along and, when the truth finally emerges, Ramsey protests to his wife that he was doing no wrong as he "was only looting a looter". The contrast between de Levis, as an edgy unsociable snob, and the comfortable, clubbable and even lazy personalities who surround him makes him seem less unaccepted than out of place, but the list of antisemitic slurs which he arouses are intended as irony only in part and, finally, after Ramsey has comitted suicide, the audience is left in no doubt that de Levis, who is shown in a huge close-up walking past the camera, remains the cause of the Captain's ruin.

Whereas Ramsey is both a womaniser and a scoundrel, he is shown to have a personal life with a young and devoted wife as well as a number of loyal friends who continue to support him. On the other hand, de Levis is unpleasantly and sneeringly arrogant and has little other than money to recommend him. Except for the acid aside that his father made his money by selling carpets, nothing of his family or personal life is seen or discussed and we are left with the assumption that his only bond is an attachment to a mysterious Jewish brotherhood. The rapacious antisemitism which *Loyalties* describes is shown critically but sympathetically, without the balance or contrast of the play, and the audience is left in little doubt that the turmoil which has been created is a direct conseqence of de Levis being proudly Jewish, that he provoked it all. James C. Robertson, in writing of Süss's "unsavoury character during his quest for power", illustrates the gap that may exist between the intended and received theme of a film, for he observes, that "at some points the message appears rather to be [that] the Jews can bring persecution upon themselves by their own dubious conduct".[37] These considerations probably struck a chord with Dean who finds no redeeming qualities in de Levis, but many in Ramsey and his friends.

The other film for which *Jew Süss* was indirectly responsible, *The Wandering Jew*, was similarly ambiguous. Two of its actors, Felix Aylmer and Abraham Sofaer had appeared in *Loyalties* on the stage, the former as General Canynge in

[37]Robertson, *The Hidden Cinema, op. cit.*, pp. 60–62.

the 1922 New York production, the latter as de Levis on tour in Britain in 1929, and one of its actresses, Peggy Ashcroft, had starred as Naemi in the original 1929 London production of *Jew Süss*. Taken from the play by E. Temple Thurston, *The Wandering Jew*, which starred Conrad Veidt as Matathias, was made in the hurry so characteristic of films at Twickenham, and was completed almost a year before *Süss* was first seen. Julius Hagen, its producer, was, according to the American-born director Bernard Vorhaus, semi-literate and never read a script; Maurice Elvey, its director was never noted for his subtlety. The latter had directed a silent version for Stoll Picture Productions in 1923 with Matheson Lang in the Veidt part[38] and Hagen, characteristically, saw it as an opportunity to produce a film version without too great an outlay. It is pretty dull stuff and apart from Veidt, who according to Elvey could speak no English at the time and learnt the verse phonetically, there is little in the film to admire.[39]

Julius Hagen,[40] lived on until 1940. He had been brought to England as a child and, after a period in distribution, went into production, eventually forming Twickenham Film Productions. His tiny studio backed onto a railway line and the shooting was frequently interrupted by passing trains, but in the early and mid-1930s he produced a long series of inexpensive "Quota" films, often adaptations of West-End successes, on a single sound stage which was in use twenty-four hours a day. One film was shot during the day, another at night. The films made in such conditions were noticeably poor and, in spite of their cheapness, frequently lost money. On the other hand, Hagen took a salary and percentages on each production and was said to be one of the most highly paid men in the country, his gross income rivalling that of Korda, who was running London Film Productions (LFP), the most exalted film company in Britain, and producing a range of prestigious feature films for the American and British market. Whilst Korda produced films such as *The Rise of Catherine the Great* (1934 dir. Paul Czinner), *Sanders of the River* (1935 dir. Zoltan Korda) and *Things to come* (1936 dir. William Cameron Menzies), Twickenham's titles are mostly unremembered.

Hagen, however, made one other film which clearly refers to racial persecution, a remake of D.W.Griffith's *Broken Blossoms*, directed in 1936 by Hans Brahm,[41] at that time known only as a stage director in Germany, and starring Dolly Haas as Lucy Burrows. According to Brahm, he happened to be around at the point when Griffith, who was originally to direct it, dropped from the scene and was given his opportunity, supervised by Bernard Vorhaus, who thought little of the completed film and considered Emlyn Williams an anachronism in the part of the Chinese missionary. The photography, by Curt Courant who had

[38] Lang was later to play Süss on the British stage.
[39] Maurice Elvey in Conversation with John Sharp', in Linda Wood (ed.), *The Commercial Imperative in the British Film Industry. Maurice Elvey, a Case Study*, London 1987, p. 57.
[40] Né Kleinenhagen (1884–1940).
[41] John Brahm (1893–1982) in America.

worked for Jean Renoir and Marcel Carné in France,[42] and the score by Karol Rathaus,[43] however, distinguish it from most of the Twickenham product. Although it lacks the visual elegance of the Griffith version, its design resonates with the influences of Pabst's *Die Dreigroschenoper* and some of the crowd scenes are clearly modelled on Fritz Lang. In many respects it is more closely associated with the persecution of Jews in Germany than any other British film of the period, its interest lying less in its qualities as a film, more in its connections to the events in Europe, from which Haas and Brahm had recently escaped,[44] and in the ambivalent reception which Britain offered to refugees.[45] As with many films which had been rushed out at Twickenham, it failed and when, in 1937, a severe slump hit British film production, Twickenham was one of the first companies to collapse.

Early in Schach's British career, *The Times* identified the correspondence between the story of Karl Grune's *Abdul the Damned* (Capitol-BIP 1935, dir. Karl Grune),[46] the rise of Hitler and the killing of Röhm. It had been adapted from a story by Robert Neumann and Ashley Dukes, the playwright, had collaborated on the screenplay. *The Jewish Chronicle* considered "the whole of the political side is excellent".[47] Campbell Dixon, in the *Daily Telegraph*, thanked Max Schach, Karl Grune, BIP and Adolf Hitler, "but for whom it would probably never have been made".[48] Although clearly a film about exile, the fussy allusion to Hitler is childish and Hanns Eisler, the film's composer, hated working on it. He had composed the scores for half a dozen important sound films in the early 1930s[49] and it "was meant to ridicule the 'Führer' ", with Abdul Hamid being Adolf Hitler, but he found it a ghastly experience. In the summer of 1934, he wrote to Bertolt Brecht that the film was

"politically 'respectable', but unfortunately still rubbish. . . After fighting for a whole day I had (for decency's sake!) to give in. I have never so much regretted not having money. I would dearly like to throw the whole rubbishy thing in the swine's faces. After a day in the film world

---

[42]Curt Courant (1899–1968), also the photographer of numerous German films, went to America.

[43]Karol Rathaus (1895–1954) went to America.

[44]For more on Haas, Brahm and *Broken Blossoms*, see Ann Jesperson, 'Exil. Six Actors from Germany in Retrospect', in *Kino (German Film)*, No. 11 (Summer 1983); 'Interview. Dolly Haas im Gespräch mit Gero Gandert', in *Dolly Haas. Mit Beiträgen von Gero Gandert, Karsten Witte, Angelika Kaps*, Berlin 1983.

[45]This topic is dealt with in great detail in the recent publication of the Leo Baeck Institute, Werner E. Mosse (co-ordinating ed.), Julius Carlebach, Gerhard Hirschfeld, Aubrey Newman, Arnold Paucker and Peter Pulzer (eds.), *Second Chance. Two Centuries of German-speaking Jews in the United Kingdom*, Tübingen 1991 (Schriftenreihe wissenschaftlicher Abhandlungen des Leo Baeck Instituts 48).

[46]*The Times*, 3rd March 1935.

[47]*Jewish Chronicle*, 8th March 1935.

[48]Unidentified newspaper clipping, British Film Institute.

[49]These were Alexander Granowsky's *Das Lied vom Leben* (1931); Victor Trivas's *Niemandsland* (1931); and Slaton Dudow's *Kuhle Wampe* (1931); two films by Joris Ivens, *Die Jugend hat das Wort*, and *Nouvelle Terre*; a second film for Victor Trivas, *Dans les Rues*; and Jacques Feyder's *Le Grand Jeu*. His first film score had been for Walter Ruttmann's *Opus III* in 1927.

the much-abused Skovbostrand seems like a marvellous paradise to which I look back regretfully. It is more loathsome than laughable, that's the tricky thing."[50]

It failed on other accounts: it was, like all the films with which Schach was closely associated, callow, loosely conceived and, in the end, frivolous. The costumes, by the fashion designer Joe Strassner, who had designed for Ludwig Berger and Kurt Bernhardt, are stylish but distracting. Wedded to an idea that authoritarianism could be equated with Hitlerism and the Nazis, Schach acquired the rights to Maurice Collis's *Siamese White*, a novel set in the seventeenth century about a "fantastically cruel monarch" which, had it been made, would again, most likely, have looked like something derived from operetta.[51] The Richard Tauber film *Land Without Music* was no different. Graham Greene's now infamous review of another film of Schach's, *The Marriage of Corbal* in 1936, asked whether it should be considered an English film at all, directed as it was by "Karl Grune and F[ritz] Brunn, photographed by Otto Kanturek, and edited by E. Stokvis [*sic*], with a cast which includes Nils Asther, Ernst Deutsch, and the American Noah Beery".[52] Greene, who was courting the GPO Film Unit at the time, thought there were "English technicians capable of producing films of high enough standard to take their place", technicians who had made *Song of Ceylon*, *The Voice of Britain*, *The Turn of the Tide*, *Nightmail* and *Midshipman Easy*. This was the standard, if inaccurate, gripe of the Association of Cinematographic Technicians (ACT) and, although it is certainly a feeble film, Greene is wrong about both Kanturek's photography and Stokvis's continuity editing which are far ahead of almost anything that British technicians were capable of at the time. *The Marriage of Corbal* is, in the Schach-Grune tradition, set in a stage version of France in which the costumes, the textures, and exteriors all take on the ersatz appearance of provincial theatre; the actors wear their make-up like masks, Grune's direction shows no grasp of sound technique and the actors stand, as on the stage in twos or threes, expressively looking towards the proscenium arch and the audience.[53] Although the film is set during the Terror of the French Revolution and the dictatorial style of Citizen Varenne (Nils Asther), another character, is intended to embody the qualities of Nazi tyranny, he is actually closer to a musical-comedy representation of Robespierre, a victim of decorative symbolism. Marching citizens are heard singing 'La Marseillaise', conducted like a musical chorus and the film rapidly deteriorates

[50]Letter, from around August 1934, quoted in Albrecht Betz, *Hanns Eisler*, London 1982, p. 141. In spite of his unhappy experiences on *Abdul* he agreed to arrange the music for another of Karl Grune's films, *Pagliacci*, which was seen as the first of a possible cycle based on the world's "greatest operas", see *Kinematograph Weekly*, 13th August 1936. Once more it was not a good experience. Eisler helped Brecht find work assisting on the adaptation of *I Pagliacci*. He was offered £500, but argued and was paid off. Furious, he tried to take Kortner and Eisler with him. Brecht had been looking for work in films, but a scenario with Leo Lania (who had, with Béla Balácz and Ladislaus Vajda, adapted the film version of *Die Dreigroschenoper*), about Semmelweiss the Viennese doctor who had specialised in puerperal fever, was turned down by Korda.
[51]*Kinematograph Weekly*, 12th March 1936.
[52]Included in Graham Greene, *The Pleasure Dome. The Collected Film Criticism 1935–40*, ed. by John Russell Taylor, London 1972, pp. 78–79. E. Stokvis should be Walter Stokvis.
[53]The same faults are apparent in *Pagliacci*, which had virtually no movement. Kanturek tried to compensate by moving the camera.

into the kind of silly love story of the period in which the hero finds himself falling in love with a young boy, only to find, to his great relief, that he is a girl in trousers.

One of Schach's writers, Rudolph Bernauer, also associates all authoritarian personalities with Hitler. Films based on his scenarios have a unified idea, but lack a genuine sense of character and the story-writing skills of a committed film maker. He had been a well-known figure in German theatre but exile in England left him in a no-man's-land in which his film scenarios and screenplays muddle together continental and British themes. *Southern Roses* and *The Lilac Domino*[54] show clearly how deep the cultural isolation in Britain could be, but even those films which are seemingly set in a recognisable world lack characterisation, wit and irony and are a self-pityingly defeatist partner to the policies of appeasement. Bernauer's version of *The Lilac Domino* (Grafton Films 1937, dir. Fred Zelnik) and his *Mademoiselle Docteur* (Grafton Films 1937, dir. Edmund T. Gréville), for example, attempt to revive an already archaic tradition of operetta and simultaneously introduce immature and obvious references to Hitler's Germany. *The Lilac Domino* had been written for the stage at the end of the First World War, but a sequence was added to the "Ballroom scene" in which "shadows of men dressed in Ku Klux Klan costume [are thrown] on wall". Any contemporaneous association which Schach, Goldsmith or Bernauer were hoping to introduce, however, is swallowed inside the ludicrously silly plot of a playboy baron who, although close to finanical ruin through adventuring and gambling, is trying to discover the identity of the masked girl with whom he has fallen in love. Bernauer's was the original scenario for *The Stars Look Down* (Grafton 1940, dir. Carol Reed) but the collapse of Schach's companies meant that he had no influence on the final screenplay and it is uncertain whether it was used at all. Almost certainly, the character of Barras, the mine owner, would have been more tyrannical had Grune directed it.

Bernauer also adapted a second Cronin novel, *Hatter's Castle*. "I was given 'a treatment' ", writes Rodney Ackland, with typical disdain for the film industry, "already written by two eminent German refugees (whose names were to be used inconspicuously in the credits), and told I must work from that."[55] This heavy irony is a reminder that both the names of Paul Merzbach and Bernauer figure above his own and he, anyway, considered that: "The German treatment was . . . a travesty of Cronin's story." Ackland, who had been described as the English Chekhov, would have been expected to produce lively dialogue and was shocked that some of the strongest dramatic situations, specifically those arising from the incest theme in which the son and the father have an affair with the same woman, were diluted or dropped entirely. Bernauer's and Merzbach's adaptation had not been intended as a screen transcription of Cronin's novel, but as a moral tale showing how tyrants eventually destroy themselves.

James Brodie (Robert Newton), a sadistic and cruel hatter who erroneously

[54]Both directed by Fred Zelnik.

[55]Rodney Ackland and Elspeth Grant, *The Celluloid Mistress: or the Custard Pie of Dr. Caligari*, London 1954, p. 121. I am grateful to Kevin MacDonald, Emeric Pressburger's grandson, for details relating to this. Bernauer was engaged in Black Propaganda at Woburn Abbey during the war.

believes he is related to the aristocracy, builds a hideous Gothic mansion in Levenford, a market town near Glasgow, as a self-aggrandising monument. Whilst ruining himself with debt and drink, he treats his wife and family with brutal contempt and builds up a string of enemies within the town community. He is conducting a liaison with a barmaid (classily, but inappropriately, played by Enid Stamp-Taylor), whom he introduces into the household, which finally causes the death of his already terminally ill wife. In the process of losing everything, he throws his pregnant daughter (Deborah Kerr) out of the house and refuses an offer to buy out his failing business. There are compressions and changes from the novel which, in spite of Ackland's complaints, do not damage the story, although the casting of Emlyn Williams as the sly Dennis, an ex-lover of the father's mistress and the callous seducer of Brodie's daughter, Mary, makes one wonder if Goldsmith or his team could distinguish between a Scottish and a Welsh accent. As the father of Mary's child, he is a completely transformed figure for the film, but, as in the novel, is killed when a railway bridge collapses as he is about to abandon her. *Hatter's Castle*, however, takes place in the never-never land of German studio-Scotland and much of the film, with vignettes quivering on the screen, suggests early expressionist cinema. The design, although transparently inexpensive, combines with the lighting to create a dark and threatening world, like the London which its designer, James Carter, had created for *Broken Blossoms*.[56] Above all, the emphasis in the script on the irrational and dissolute tyrant, the "mad hatter" who builds himself a grotesque memorial, catches the preoccupation of Schach and his colleagues with what was happening in Germany and Austria, and often to their own families.

When the bank manager calls to advise Brodie that his debt is about to be called in and that he would have been better to have built a house than a "sham castle", there is an immediate change of tone as we see the face of Brodie, shot from below and now clearly fanatical, whilst the underscoring rises to accentuate his developing madness. "Sham castle? Aye, that's what it is to you, just bricks and mortar and heaps of stone, but to me it is the realisation of a dream." Paintings hang at a crazy angle, the shadows get longer and, when his son shoots himself, Brodie is finally compelled to recognise that his "dream" has been the cause of his ruin and he destroys everything in a fit of blazing and drunken insanity. At the funeral service the minister describes him as "a man who was made of the stuff of which the great tyrants of history are made". It was another film about Hitler, but, as with the films from the Capitol camp, it was ultimately hollow. Whilst it reflects the desperation of the refugee, it provides no help to understanding and Brodie simply destroys himself. *Hatter's Castle* turns out to be a cautionary tale about a boy who plays with fire whilst offering nostalgia for a world that is lost, but it makes no attempt to come to terms with the present.

In this respect there is a great difference between the writings of Bernauer and Emeric Pressburger. The latter adopted England as his home, took to many of its rituals, and was at once clubbable and an enthusiastic football fan. His films of the war, all "written, produced and directed" with Michael Powell; *The Life and*

[56]Carter had been art director at Twickenham. He also designed *The Stars Look Down*. Later he became an executive producer.

Death of Colonel Blimp, *A Canterbury Tale* and *I Know Where I'm Going* engage with the present whilst not abandoning his past. *A Canterbury Tale*, for example, is often seen as revealing Michael Powell's tendency towards romanticism, yet it is one of Pressburger's most personal films and was written out of his memories and experience as a child living on a farm in Hungary.[57]

There are no figures of the numbers or the proportion of Jews within the film industry and those who were sensitive to antisemitism may have exaggerated its significance. Nevertheless, those who were less so have certainly underestimated it. When the *Jewish Chronicle* criticised H. G. Wells for contriving "a new world" in *Things to Come*, "from which the Jews, as a body, were eliminated" and in which he referred to this "antiquated obdurate culture",[58] he repudiated any suggestion that he was antisemitic. He had, he pointed out, "a considerable number of Jewish friends – I may count Freud and Einstein among them – and I doubt if anyone will find me ignorant of the splendid record of men and women of Jewish origin . . . I am always telling people that Defoe was a Jew – look at his portrait. I am inclined to give a large element of Dickens to Judaism." He found the "isolationist Jewish tradition", which had irritated diverse peoples through the ages, to be "mentally mischievous". He had been, he claimed, dishonestly misquoted and asked, "are we Gentiles never to be allowed to utter any impression of this ancient, narrow and racially egotistical Jewish culture, except in terms of cringing admiration and subservience?"[59] Needless to say, the *Jewish Chronicle* had the last word and considered the self-examination of the Jewish tradition which Wells advocated Jews to undertake to be simply "a pretext or cover for xenophobia. The truth is, Mr. Wells is really distressingly obsessed by this 'tradition' . . ."[60]

Dolly Haas, who had initially been invited to Britain by BIP to play a "trouser role" in *Girls Will be Boys* (BIP 1934, dir. Marcel Varnel), and not herself Jewish, describes its producer, Walter Mycroft, as a "small German sympathiser, enthusiastic about the Nazis". She found "noticeable antisemitism in the studio", provided, she felt, to "test" her and to which she "reacted very sharply".[61] Berthold Viertel, "another Jewish Wanderer" as the *Jewish Chronicle* described him,[62] had noticed it too. "Here in England", he wrote to his wife in California, some "papers are openly anti-semitic. Only the Quakers perform miracles of

---

[57]For more on Pressburger's approach to the representation of exile, see Kevin Gough-Yates, 'The British Feature Film as a European Concern. Britain and the Emigré Film-Maker, 1933–45', in Günter Berghaus (ed.), *Theatre and Film in Exile. German Artists in Britain, 1933–1945*, Oxford 1989.

[58]Watchman, *Jewish Chronicle*, 29th May 1936.

[59]*Jewish Chronicle*, 12th June 1936.

[60]Watchman, *Jewish Chronicle*, 19th June 1936.

[61]Dolly Haas, 'Interview with Gero Gandert', *loc. cit.*, pp. 16–17. After *Girls Will be Boys*, Haas returned to Berlin where the *Gestapo* interrogated her over her connection with the Jewish Hans Brahm, whom she was later to marry. She had attended a Jewish school as a child and they were also interested in her own "possible Jewish origins". Mycroft (1891–1959), producer and screenwriter, was much disliked and came close to being interned in 1940.

[62]Interview, *Jewish Chronicle*, 4th October 1935.

helpfulness."[63] Carl Zuckmayer, also, found "lax, indifferent, cynical" people in London and Paris. In London, working for Korda after the *Anschluß*, an MP had patted him on the back and described Hitler as "quite a good chap . . . a bulwark against Communism".[64]

There was antisemitism, certainly, but it was hardly present in the film industry and the Association of Cinematographic Technicians (ACT), the film technicians' union, although formed with the specific purpose of combatting the employment of foreign workers in British films, showed no hint of it. As usual in these situations, there are contradictions to be found and whilst the two active trade unionists, the editor Sidney Cole and the director Thorold Dickinson, nominated the famous Czech cine-photographer Otto Heller for union membership, they were simultaneously part of a delegation to the Ministry of Labour which protested at his employment. On the other hand, the documentary film-maker Paul Rotha, who had researched his pioneering *The Film Till Now* in Berlin, was a friend of Berthold Viertel, Ernö Metzner and Fritz Kortner among others. When internment threatened the already terminally ill Carl Mayer, Rotha put him on the pay-roll.

In January 1940, the film trade-journal *Kinematograph Weekly* reported Sir Kenneth Clark, the newly appointed Director of the Films Division at the Ministry of Information, as saying: "If we lose the war . . . let the essential non-British and Jewish element in the Industry realise what would happen to them." He was soon made to eat humble pie and there were immediate rejoinders and a front-page apology. He had intended his comment as an incentive, but had lapsed into a typical example of societal inelegance. George Archibald, a Scotsman and a joint Managing Director of United Artists (England), reminded Clark that it would be unbearable for others as well and "that in the Film Industry we do not think of a man as 'non British' because he is Jewish".[65] George Elvin, Secretary of ACT and a leading activist in the campaign to restrict the employment of foreigners and refugees in the British film industry, considered that Clark had spoilt

> "a promising debut . . . by the use of a phrase similar to those which fall so glibly from the mouths of the leaders of the forces against whom the war is being waged . . . ACT would never support an allegation that those [foreigners] who work here and have adopted British nationality are less good citizens . . . Similar allegations [*sic*] concerning the many Jews in the Industry is an insult."[66]

Indeed ACT, despite its campaign, displayed no trace of antisemitism, even whilst its target group "the foreigners", was being steadily eroded as earlier exiles and refugees from Nazism: the producer-director Alexander Korda, his brothers Zoltan and Vincent, Paul Czinner, Elisabeth Bergner, Conrad Veidt and others,

---

[63]Quoted in Salka Viertel, *The Kindness of Strangers*, New York 1969, pp. 224–225. His involvement with the *Freier Deutscher Kulturbund* and his contributions to the émigré newspapers *Die neue Weltbühne* and *Das neue Tage-Buch* were factors in the Home Office failing to renew his residency permit in May 1939. He returned to America but was unable to find film work.
[64]Zuckmayer, *A Part of Myself*, London 1970, p. 89.
[65]*Kinematograph Weekly*, 25th January 1940.
[66]*Ibid*.

'The Wandering Jew' (Twickenham 1933)
Conrad Veidt as Matathias and Peggy Ashcroft as Olalla Quintana

On the set of 'The Lilac Domino' (Grafton 1937)
The writer, Rudolph Bernauer, with the actress June Knight (centre)
and his daughter, Agnes Bernelle

By courtesy of Agnes Bernelle

Emeric Pressburger, c. 1935, newly arrived in London,
but already studying the football results

By courtesy of Margarita Stapenhorst

The entertainment journalist Pem (Paul Marcus)
and Hildegard Marcus with Fritz Lang (left) in London, 1965

By courtesy of Sylvia Ury

A greetings card from 'The Two Antons'
Anton Walbrook to the Bernauers

'A Kid for Two Farthings' (LFP/Big Ben 1955)
Sidney Tafler and David Kossoff

most of whom had left Germany before Hitler's coming to power, became naturalised.

Antisemitism did not hold much attraction for the British electorate either; there "was virtually no penetration of the trade union movement" by Oswald Mosley's British Union of Fascists.[67] The authorities, whilst generally sympathetic to Jewish refugees, were, however, anxious not to inflame antisemitic feelings or to run into conflict with certain professional groups and continually revised their criteria for entry.[68] Britain was understood to be a place of temporary abode and most refugees were expected to move on to the United States or South America.[69] The parents of the cine-photographer Walter Lassally, for example, came to Britain, supposedly in transit to Canada, his mother with a forged Peruvian visa.[70] The papers to Canada had not come by the time war was declared. "Special care" had to be taken in dealing with visa applications when it appeared that the "real object is . . . to remain indefinitely . . ."[71] and Rudolph Katscher was issued with a one-month visa;[72] "England" said Emeric Pressburger "is a very, very difficult country for foreigners to come to". He wrote a sequence into one of his most individual films, *The Life and Death of Colonel Blimp*, in which a voluntary exile from Hitler's Germany (Anton Walbrook) is given a hard time by the immigration authorities. "Of course, when I came my intention was to stay in England but you have to lie straight away . . . you're not only dying to stay in England, you can't go anywhere else . . . And you know to the question, 'How long do you intend to stay here?' you mustn't say, 'I intend to stay for ever' . . . so you answer 'Six months', and then you extend the six months."[73] It was a similar story for many others. The then young animator Peter Sachs, who had worked with Georges Pal and Oskar Fischinger, came later, in July 1939, when the refugee crisis was at its height. He and his wife were allowed into

[67]John Stevenson and Chris Cook, *The Slump*, London 1977, pp. 213–217.

[68]For figures see Bernard Wasserstein, *Britain and the Jews of Europe 1939–1945*, Oxford 1979, p. 7.

[69]On this see Louise London, 'British Immigration Control Procedures and Jewish Refugees 1933–1939', in *Second Chance, op. cit.*, pp. 483–517.*

  * See now also the essay by John Fox, 'German and Austrian Jews in Britain's Armed Forces and British and German Citizenship Policies 1939–1945', in this volume of the Year Book – (Ed.).

[70]Lassally's father, an engineer, had made industrial films in Germany, but was only able to get back into film making after the war.

[71]Public Record Office, Kew, HO 213/94 150872 [1938]. Abstracting from official records may make the relevant departments seem callous, but this is not the case and they tempered logic with realism. Leading persons in scientific or medical research, established artists, well-established industrialists, non-refugee students and refugee students with places in higher education establishments, would "not be refused entry". Whilst C. B. McAlpine, a Home Office official, observed on 1st March 1938, "that from a financial point of view refugees are becoming steadily less desirable . . .", this seemingly hard-nosed approach was tempered in the same memorandum: "Sooner or later we come up . . . against the ultimate difficulty, are we prepared to send back to Germany a refugee who tells us, probably with truth, that he will be sent to a concentration camp . . . ?" *Ibid.*

[72]On 30th September 1935, Rudolph Cartier (Ruldoph Katscher), interview with author, 31st October 1988.

[73]Emeric Pressburger, interview 12th November 1970, in Kevin Gough-Yates, *Michael Powell in Collaboration with Emeric Pressburger*, London 1971.

the country to work as servants for two elderly ladies in Worthing,[74] an episode he considered to be "a joke", especially as the hospitality which Britain offered was followed by a period of internment.[75]

Of the many refugee organisations before and during the war, the film industry associated itself with the Lord Baldwin Fund for refugees.[76] Elisabeth Bergner made a personal appearance at a screening of "the Paramount-Orion presentation" of *Stolen Life* on 18th January 1939.[77] Eddie Cantor, priding "himself justifiably on his success as a 'schnorrer'", collected £100,000 in England for the fund for Austrian-Jewish refugee children.[78] And over 3,000 "kinemas took part in the effort for the Earl Baldwin's Refugee Fund on Saturday last. The result of the 10% contribution from takings and the collections of kinemas will not be known until the end of the week . . ."[79]

There were many film personalities, Oscar Deutsch,[80] the creator of the Odeon cinema circuit, among them, who played a part in the rescue of people from the clutch of the Nazis. His Hungarian-born parents had prospered in scrap-metal in Birmingham and, after a spell in distribution, he turned to buying Midland cinemas in the 1920s. In 1933 he set up the Odeon Theatres Ltd., and devised an original approach to cinema architecture and exhibition, not only by introducing new standards of comfort to British cinemas, but also in the manner in which local finance was raised to help pay for their construction. The Odeons, mostly designed by the Birmingham architect Harry W. Weedon and Andrew Mather, were influenced in their interior design by his wife, Lily Deutsch. Each cinema was unique, adapted to local conditions, but externally, distinguished by its single tower and the use of cream, square-glazed tiles. Rachel Low, the film historian, sourly describes them as "antiseptic", but, in aspiring to provide "homes" for the latest and most progressive entertainment in the modern world, Deutsch created some of the most enduring symbols of 1930s and 1940s British architecture.[81] In 1938, he was a link in the chain which included Lord Rothschild, Lionel Rothschild, Neville Laski and Otto Schiff, which sent Sir Michael Bruce, the colourful Scottish adventurer and film stunt man, to Europe. Bruce, whilst working as Deutsch's public relations officer, went to Berlin to meet Wilfrid Israel, who was trying to set up avenues of rescue for Jews in

[74]On the experience of refugees who came as servants see Tony Kushner, 'An Alien Occupation – Jewish Refugees and Domestic Service in Britain, 1933–1948', in *Second Chance, op. cit.*, pp. 553–578.

[75]Peter Sachs, interview with author, 11th May 1989. Sachs arrived in England without a word of English, took advantage of internment to smarten up his drawing skills, and volunteered, but was rejected on health grounds, for the Pioneer Corps, and eventually found himself back in animation, working on films for the Ministry of Information and the Ministry of Defence.

[76]It was a non-denominational fund, administered through the Christian Council for Refugees and the Council for German Jewry.

[77]This raised £3,600 for the Baldwin Fund and other organisations. Among the eminent who attended were Sir Robert and Lady Vansittart, Mrs Beddington-Behrens, Oscar Deutsch, the Brothers Ostrer and Michael Redgrave. Bergner had earlier led an appeal "at the home of Mrs. Anthony de Rothschild", which raised £8,000. *Kinematograph Weekly*, 12th January 1939; *The Times*, 19th January 1939.

[78]*Kinematograph Weekly*, 28th July 1938.

[79]*Kinematograph Weekly*, 19th January 1939.

[80]Oscar Deutsch (1893–1940).

[81]Oscar Deutsch, 'Supplement' to *Design and Construction*, March 1937.

Europe. When the old army camp at Richborough was refurbished to provide temporary accommodation for refugees from Germany, Deutsch gave it its cinema.[82]

"We don't have to tell you", noted the entertainment journalist Pem (Paul Marcus), "how helpful [Korda] always was to everybody who knocked at his door – he even bought a script by the late Alfred Kerr before the war."[83] This, it transpires, was about Napoleon's mother,[84] the first of at least two unsuccessful attempts by Kerr to write for the screen. Pem, who used to meet Kerr for coffee at the Mount Royal prior to their slipping across the road to eat at Lyons, gave the title of another as *Cagliostro*, the story of the eighteenth-century Italian charlatan whose "spagyric food" offered eternal youth to those foolish enough to eat it. There is no evidence that Korda had any intention of making it, but he bought it nevertheless.

Much has been written about Korda and his involvement with British Intelligence both before and during the war. There has been a great deal of exaggeration and a number of false claims, but unquestionably he allowed London Films to be used as a cover organisation in the gathering of intelligence in the 1930s. In the early part of the war, he personally took a number of uncomfortable flights across the Atlantic as a courier for Churchill and immediately after it surrounded himself with old colleagues, people he felt he could trust, from the period. Just as important, he helped provide a channel for members of the film industry and friends to leave continental Europe in the 1930s. Kerr and his family were able to make their way to England on the strength of the £1,000 he received from Korda. Carl Zuckmayer, in Vienna in the spring of 1934, had earned his "bread doing movie work for . . . Korda" and, having made it to Zürich, was brought to London by Korda, who sent him "a handsome sum in sterling – although he owed me no money . . ." It was a genuine advance and was not deducted from the next contract, but from the one after that.[85]

The end of the 1930s brought many changes in cinema, associated in part with world-wide political changes and, also, with the industry's own technological developments. When in 1943 the French film director Jean-Pierre Melville arrived in London, he saw twenty-seven films within the space of a week's leave and realised that the war had turned everything upside down; not only had a "certain form of civilisation suddenly disappeared . . . [but also] a certain form of cinema . . . The tempo, the pace, of the pre-war comedies had disappeared."

---

[82]More complete accounts are to be found in Naomi Shepherd, *Wilfrid Israel. German Jewry's Secret Ambassador*, London 1984, pp. 150–154; Norman Bentwich, *I Understand the Risks. The Story of the Refugees from Nazi Oppression Who Fought in the British Forces in the World War*, London 1950; Sir Michael Bruce, *Tramp Royal*, London 1954.

[83]*Pem's Personal Bulletins*, 7th September 1953; 21st April 1972.

[84]Described by Judith Kerr, *When Hitler Stole Pink Rabbit*, London 1971, pp. 174–192.

[85]Zuckmayer, *op. cit.*, pp. 38–75. Bergner, although he didn't take it, also offered him money. Karol Kulik, *Alexander Korda. The Man Who Could Work Miracles*, London 1975, remains the best source for information on Korda and the scripts were, Kulik tells us, narrative treatments of eight-to-ten pages, written in German which Korda reworked.

Welles, Kazan, Wilder, Wise, Preminger, Mankiewicz, "people who really came out of American cinema", could be "felt in the air".[86]

The changes were not simply aesthetic, a different sense of rhythm or visual awareness, they were also technological: sound, film stock, the developments at Technicolor, improvements in cine-cameras, special effects and general photographic technique, for example, were developments which the British film industry could not ignore. Even the manner of exhibition, which the large cinema chains had developed in response to changes in film-going habits, expressed their own internal ideological rationale. Once more, developments had a direct effect on careers.

Just as some directors and actors, Karl Grune and Leo Lasko for example, had been left behind when sound was introduced, others now saw their careers thinning out. Allan Gray and Mischa Spoliansky, both composers of incidental music in the cinema, were gradually replaced by the composers of quasi-symphonic scores, which demanded larger orchestras and improved recording equipment. Korda, already an infrequent director before 1940, directed only one film after it, *An Ideal Husband* (LFP 1947), a hapless attempt to capture, through Oscar Wilde's play, some of the Lubitsch touch which had always eluded him. Universally more realistic than previously, the cinema reflected many of the contradictions within British society: of affluence and poverty, of crime and law enforcement, of industry and unemployment.

The seeds had been present before the war; in 1936, Wolfgang Wilhelm had seen the possibilities within a true incident when a troopship with hundreds of British servicemen put into Southampton, only to be sent off again immediately with everyone on board;[87] Korda reacted to the charge that he was turning his back on "indictment and indignation" which was to be found in the distressed areas of the country and had Erich Pommer produce *Farewell Again*. John Grierson, no admirer of foreign film makers in Britain, admired it, ironically, as: "The only first-rate British script that has been seen recently . . ."[88] As the ship sails away to its new destination and families and lovers are left to cheer and wave from the quay, the band playing 'Pack Up Your Troubles' moves into 'Old Lang Syne'. The creation of a patriotic response to social misery was allotted a particular space in British cinema during the 1930s and was bound up with a vision of Empire. Whilst film makers aspired to make the ideal genre film which operated within a set of other co-existing values and beliefs, there was also a conflict; for the cinema of exiles and Jews in Britain introduced contradictory areas of concern which derived from the political problems in Europe.

Such was the impact of the exile and refugee on British cinema of the 1930s

---

[86] *Melville on Melville*, ed. by Rui Nogueira, London 1971, p. 16.
[87] Wilhelm had worked for Decla Bioscope, Berlin, and UFA and arrived in England in 1933, where, without his knowing a word of English, he was given the job of polishing the dialogue of knockabout British comedies. A brilliant initiator of ideas, in 1944 he unsuccessfully approached Launder and Gilliat with a project, *The Red Prophet*, in which Karl Marx was to be portrayed as a henpecked husband.
[88] *Kinematograph Weekly*, 13th January 1938.

and 1940s that it is difficult to find examples from the "better" films with which they were not closely associated. The films which were written and directed by Launder and Gilliat, *Millions Like Us*, *The Rake's Progress* and *I See a Dark Stranger* are amongst the few, but they nevertheless lack the finish which a Mutz Greenbaum or an Otto Heller would have provided. Even Olivier's *Henry V*, which the film writer Dilys Powell considered the only British film of the first rank to be made in Britain during the war, is made radiant by the designs of Paul Sherriff,[89] the Russian-born protegé of two others from the same country, Lazare Meerson and Andrei Andrejew; the former the designer for René Clair's great pre-war French successes, *Sous les Toits de Paris* and *A Nous la Liberté*; the latter the designer on Robert Wiene's *Raskolnikow* and G. W. Pabst's *Die Dreigroschenoper*. The large number of Jews already active in the industry should not disguise the impact of those who had come to Britain in the 1930s and most of whom had started their careers in Germany. The most important British director in Britain before the war, Alfred Hitchcock, and the most important one to emerge during the early 1940s, Michael Powell, both identified the inspiration of German cinema in their own film making and worked closely with designers and photographers from Europe. When, after the war, Powell and Pressburger decided to part from their designer Alfred Junge, they turned to the stage designer Hein Heckroth, whose career had been closely associated with the Ballets Jooss. His experience in film had been minimal: the costumes for Gabriel Pascal's *Caesar and Cleopatra* (Independent Productions–Pascal 1946) and for their own *A Matter of Life and Death* (1946) and *Black Narcissus* (1947). Whereas Junge had been at UFA and "a marvellous" film technician, Heckroth knew nothing. He was "marvellous with colour . . . but in those days knew hardly anything about film or film technique or what you could do with film". The way in which the camera worked, opticals, matte shots, hanging miniatures, which had become second nature to Junge, were unknown areas to Heckroth. Powell and Pressburger wanted an artist more than a technician.[90]

Through Heckroth, Powell saw the opportunity to revert to an idea which had first been achieved with animation by Walt Disney and attempted with live actors by Ludwig Berger. Both had successfully combined music, design and picture into an integrated whole using pre-recorded soundtracks. Pem identified "Hein Heckroth's Disney-like decors" for *The Red Shoes*, but Berger, the theatre and film director who had made *Walzerkrieg* for UFA in 1933, with Renate Müller, Adolf Wohlbrück and Willy Frisch, was an even more important and, although unrecognised, efficacious teacher of Powell, who had been his second-unit director on *The Thief of Bagdad*. Coincidentally, Berger had been the intended director for a Korda project, which Powell was later to take over, *The*

---

[89]Né Shouvalov.
[90]For more on Heckroth's film career, see interview in Kevin Gough-Yates, *Michael Powell*, Brussels 1973; Powell, *op. cit.*; Hilmar Hoffmann and Walter Schobert (eds.), *Hein Heckroth. Film-Designer*, Frankfurt a. Main 1991.

Red Shoes.[91] The war and Korda's financial fortunes put an end to many projects and he was already planning to move production to America in late May 1939 when Powell was taken on to *The Thief of Bagdad*. It had been in production for over three months and Berger, who had another two and a half months on it, left Denham on 16th August 1939, along with Natalie Kalmus, the Technicolor expert on the film.[92] All the interiors had been completed. We can now see that the "striking *consistency* of imagery and theme" that has been attributed to Powell, in spite of six directors having worked on it,[93] is a consequence of Berger's desire for organic unity. The popular story about *The Thief of Bagdad* is that Berger was forced from the film as Korda became dissatisfied with his approach, but it is now clear that Korda, for financial reasons, was closing down on all projects and that a wholesale move to Hollywood was his only option.[94] He behaved badly to Berger, did not pay him fully, and did not take him to America. He was often appalling to directors, but it is more than possible that he was driven by anxieties about money and was clumsily trying to hurry him along.

The post-war scene in British cinema brought figures such as Henry Cornelius[95] into direction. He had studied with Max Reinhardt and entered the film industry in France. When he arrived in England he was still in his early twenties and became assistant editor on *The Ghost Goes West* (1935), the film which René Clair directed for Korda. He rose to direct two Clair-influenced comedies, *Passport to Pimlico* (1949) and *Genevieve* (1951), among the most perennially popular of all British films, as well as a less successful adaptation, *I am a Camera* (1955), of the play version of Christopher Isherwood's stories. *En route*, Cornelius had produced *It Always Rains on Sunday* (1947) for Ealing, directed by Robert Hamer. Taken from the novel by Arthur La Bern, it is set amongst the working-class communities of London's East End which, a few years later, had already taken on a mythological status, and provided the background for Wolf Mankowitz's Jewish folk stories, *Make Me an Offer* (1954 dir. Cyril Frankel) and *A Kid for Two Farthings* (London Films 1955 dir. Carol Reed), in both of which a host of Jewish actors, including David Kossoff and the refugee actress Lily Kann are given their heads.[96]

At one level *It Always Rains on Sunday* is a straight-forward working-class crime story in which an escaped convict, played by John McCallum, drifts back to his old haunts and his old girlfriend (Googie Withers) in East London, before being

[91]Described as "the Ballet Film", it was originally planned as a Günther Stapenhorst production, to star Vivien Leigh, later changed to a vehicle for Merle Oberon. Pressburger worked on it, reworking the scenario by the popular novelist G. B. Stern, but it was abandoned by Korda in August 1939 and Powell and Pressburger bought the rights to it soon after the war. Korda was committed by an earlier contract to give Powell full director credit and thus he shares full credit with Berger and Tim Whelan on *The Thief of Bagdad*.

[92]*Kinematograph Weekly*, 17th August 1939.

[93]See, for example, Ian Christie, *Arrows of Desire. The Films of Michael Powell and Emeric Pressburger*, London 1985, p. 50.

[94]For more details, see Kulik, *op. cit.*, pp. 238–242.

[95]Heinz Cornelius (1913–1958), was born in Berlin and educated in South Africa where, during the Second World War, he worked on propaganda films.

[96]The cast of these films includes Sidney James, Lou Jacobi, Harold Berens, Danny Green, Irene Handl, Alfie Bass, Sidney Tafler, Meier Tzelniker, Vic Wise and Meier Leibovitch.

finally run to earth. At another, however, it stands up as one of the most authentic and persuasive creations of immediate post-war British cinema, in which the working-class life of Bethnal Green is centred around street markets with a high proportion of Jewish traders and their families, played, amongst others, by John Slater, Sydney Tafler, Alfie Bass and Meier Tzelniker, making his first film appearance.[97] Tzelniker, as an old immigrant newspaper seller, despairs at the shady activities of his son (Slater), the owner of an entertainment arcade, who fixes boxing matches and gives his winnings to the local Christian-run youth club. Assimilation and intermarriage threaten the end of a cohesive integrated community as the more prosperous and successful Jews abandon the East End for the suburbs of North London. His other son (Tafler), a dance band leader and record shop owner finds his marriage on the rocks, another consequence of the Jewish community being dispersed by assimilation. He has taken up with a young non-Jewish girl, who is desperate to grasp at the opportunity to escape from poverty, and believes in his offer of a singing career. It is not just the Jewish community which is threatened, it is also working-class life. Her sister, a secretary at the Gas Board opts not to leave her family and friends for an uncertain future. The hunt for the prisoner, escaped from Dartmoor, provides the direct dramatic component, but the centre-piece of the film is the character of London's East End, something of a ghetto, with its Jewish community, small-time criminals, and church missions packed tight within a railway line, with its cul-de-sacs in the north and the Isle of Dogs and the river Thames in the south.

The most notable Jewish film director to appear in England since the war is John Schlesinger, whose career has swung from success to disaster and has, apart from *Midnight Cowboy*, been unsuccessful with his American films. Indeed two of his films, *The Day of the Locust* and *Honky Tonk Freeway* are financial disasters on an epic scale and two others, *The Falcon and the Snowman* and *Madame Sousatzka* are films which fell quickly from sight. His humble films of the nineteen sixties, such as *A Kind of Loving*, express strongly felt personal themes which have failed to transfer to the commercial cinema of Hollywood and some feel that his most effective work has been for television, where his career as a film maker began. Once an actor, he began making short films for the BBC art programme *Monitor* and sprang to notice with *Terminus*, a well-observed documentary made for British Transport Films, set in Waterloo Station. One of his main qualities as a director, namely a patience and sympathy with actors and a sense of detail, is immediately apparent. The railway station suggests another theme in his work; his characters compulsively move on, to the big city or to another country, in the hope of a better future but, also, simply to escape from stultifying restrictive environments. His most personal film *Sunday Bloody Sunday* (1971), and his last film in Britain for eight years, is the story of a homosexual Jewish doctor played by Peter Finch, who is involved in a triangular relationship with a bisexual male commercial sculptor (Murray Head) and a female employment executive (Glenda Jackson). It has all of his virtues and reveals only some of his tendency

---

[97] Tzelniker first appeared on the British stage in 1928 and was a leading actor in Yiddish Theatre at the Grand Palais, Whitechapel.

towards a cynicism about the values within human relationships. The doctor remains an outsider in all communities; non-religious, his sense of being Jewish extends no further than a partiality for chopped liver; homosexual, he is excluded from a conventional domestic life. Schlesinger, often criticised for a tendency to exploit easy dramatic devices and to attack merely modish targets, is certainly prone to shots through prisms. This visual condemnation of a contemporary drug-obsessed Britain in which the drug dependents hang around all-night chemists, fashionable Hampsteaders provide marijuana for their precocious children and doctors casually prescribe drugs for their patients is, perhaps, facile, but Schlesinger sees this world as an insider and his films, therefore, have their compensations. The idealism which fires personal relationships is inevitably dashed as underlying social values assert themselves; links between people are devoid of communication, and here the telephone rings but remains unanswered. The opening words of *Sunday Bloody Sunday*, heard over the titles: "Tell me if you feel anything, anything at all", echo through a film which depicts an anomic community, its central characters haunted by anxiety about death and isolation. His central figures despair for a society which is invariably repressive and in which people have become consumers of trashy fashions in art, drugs and attitudes. Schlesinger's emphasis is always on the characters at the centre of his story and not on abstract analysis and, for the young and hopeful, there is always a possible future somewhere else.

Why is it that British cinema, which has continued to have a large number of Jews working within it, should have produced so few films with Jewish themes? The answer lies in the complex interplay of ideologies which exist in England in which Jews are not identified as a single cohesive social group and in which, at some levels, at least partial or complete assimilation occurs. Only in Britain could a film on the life of Benjamin Disraeli, *The Prime Minister* (Warner Bros. 1940, dir. Thorold Dickinson), a film indirectly critical of the Nazi-Soviet pact, be made without a mention, and barely a hint, of his Jewish background. He is only "a self-made man" who, at worst, has "oriental sympathies". Questions in the House of Commons in the 1930s, as to the number of Jews entering the country, invariably received the reply that such statistics were not kept. Throughout the 1930s and 1940s, the subject of antisemitism, even of Jewish life, does not occur in British cinema within a contemporary context. There was more than one reason for this; one external to British society and one internal. The policy of the Foreign Office throughout most of the period was such as to encourage the dampening down of subjects and references in films which might be received as critical of Nazi Germany. At home, official policy, at the BBC and the Ministry of Information during the war, for example, was not to have the subject of antisemitism raised at all on the grounds that it might prove inflammatory. There were individual examples of it, but Arthur Koestler, for example, who had experienced a great deal in France, whilst chiding the British and their institutions for their narrowness, experienced none at all.[98] When, in

[98]Arthur Koestler in Kay Gladstone interviews, *British Service Cameramen, 1939–1945*, Accession no. 005393, Imperial War Museum. He was "requisitioned" by the Ministry of Information, for whom he wrote *Lift Your Head Comrade* (1943, prod. Basil Wright, dir. Michael Hankinson).

1945, Sidney Gilliat completed one of the most interesting films of the war, *The Rake's Progress* (Individual),[99] its charmingly near-psychopathic, playboy hero (Rex Harrison), finds himself broke in Vienna at the time of the *Anschluß*, and agrees to marry a young Jewish girl (Lilli Palmer) who is desperate to get out of the country, although his primary consideration is to swindle her out of her money. A brief conversation at his hotel in Vienna provides the film's only reference to her being Jewish and when he brings her to England his upper-class family take to her with only a passing reference to her being a foreigner and none at all to her being Jewish. "I thought you would have married an English girl", says the father, already suspicious of his son's motive, "You didn't have to marry her, I suppose?" British cinema, consistent with other institutional systems in Britain has been officially blind to cultural, racial and religious differences. Being Jewish has mattered little to British institutions; being British has mattered a great deal.

[99]Written by Gilliat and Frank Launder early in the war, from a story by Val Valentine, it was based on a real personality, a musician, who tricked and swindled everyone in sight.

Post-War Publications on German Jewry

A Selected Bibliography of Books and Articles 1991

Compiled by

BARBARA SUCHY and ANNETTE PRINGLE

Leo Baeck Institute
4 Devonshire Street
London W1N 2BH

CONTENTS

<table>
<tr><td></td><td>Page</td></tr>
</table>

I. HISTORY

    A. General 545

    Linguistics/Western Yiddish 551

    B. Communal and Regional History 552

      1. Germany 552

      1a. Alsace 562

      2. Austria 562

      3. Czechoslovakia 564

      4. Hungary 565

      5. Switzerland 565

    C. German Jews in Various Countries 566

II. RESEARCH and BIBLIOGRAPHY

    A. Libraries and Institutes 567

    B. Bibliographies and Catalogues 569

III. THE NAZI PERIOD

    A. General 569

    B. Jewish Resistance 588

IV. POST WAR

    A. General 588

    B. Restitution 591

    C. Antisemitism, Judaism, Nazism in Education and   592
      Teaching ....

V. JUDAISM

    A. Jewish Learning and Scholars 592

    B. The Jewish Problem 595

    C. Jewish Life and Organisations 596

    D. Jewish Art and Music 598

VI. ZIONISM and ISRAEL 598

VII. PARTICIPATION in CULTURAL and PUBLIC LIFE

    A. General 601

    B. Individual 605

VIII. AUTOBIOGRAPHY, MEMOIRS, LETTERS, GENEALOGY 614

IX. GERMAN-JEWISH RELATIONS

    A. General 617

    B. German-Israeli Relations 619

    C. Church and Synagogue 619

    D. Antisemitism 620

    E. Noted Germans and Jews 625

X. FICTION and POETRY 626

    INDEX 629

BIBLIOGRAPHY 1991

I. HISTORY

A. General

27914. AGETHEN, MANFRED: *Bekehrungsversuche an Juden und Judentaufen in der frühen Neuzeit.* [In]: Aschkenas, Bd. 1, Wien, 1991, Pp. 65–94, footnotes.

27915. ARNSBERG, GAD: *Gabriel Riesser als deutsch-jüdischer Intellektueller und liberaler Ideologe.* [In]: Menora, Bd. 2, München, 1991. Pp. 81–104, notes.

27916. *Aufklärung und Haskala in jüdischer und nichtjüdischer Sicht.* Hrsg. von Karlfried Gründer und Nathan Rotenstreich. Heidelberg: Lambert Schneider, 1990. 193 pp., notes, illus. [Incl.: Das Verhältnis der jüdischen Aufklärung zur mittelalterlichen jüdischen Philosophie (Amos Funkenstein, 13–22). Isachar Falkensohn Behr, 1746–1817 (Gerhard Alexander, 57–66; I. F. Behr, Polish doctor, poet, great admirer of Moses Mendelssohn, converted to Russian-Orthodoxy in St Petersburg in 1781.) Judentum als Religion – Judentum als Wissenschaft. Kontinuität oder Bruch (Michael Graetz, 123–130). Das Bild der Aufklärung bei der deutsch-jüdischen Orthodoxie (Mordechai Breuer, 131–142). Aufklärung, Emanzipation, Selbstemanzipation (Moshe Zimmermann, 143–152). Aufklärung als Emanzipation? (Rudolf Vierhaus, 161–172).]

27917. BAECK, LEO. ARONSFIELD, C. C.: *Schon 1933 oder erst 1946? Historiographische Anmerkungen zu einem vielzitierten Ausspruch Leo Baecks.* [In]: Tribüne, Jg. 30, H. 120, Frankfurt am Main, 1991. Pp. 217–221. [On Leo Baeck's much-quoted dictum 'Die 1000jährige Geschichte der deutschen Juden ist zu Ende'; previously published in Die Zeit, No. 46, Hamburg, Nov. 8, 1991, p. 67.]

27918. BĂLEANÚ, AVRAM ANDREI: *Die Geburt des Ahasver.* [In]: Menora, Bd. 2, München, 1991. Pp. 15–43, notes, bibl. [Cont. transcription of Kurtze Beschreibung und Erzehlung von einem Juden mit Namen Ahasverus (1602).]

27919. BARKAI, AVRAHAM: *Zur Wirtschaftsgeschichte der Juden in Deutschland. Historiographische Quellen und Tendenzen vor und nach 1945.* [In]: Tel Aviver Jahrbuch für deutsche Geschichte, Bd. 20, Gerlingen, 1991. Pp. 195–214, notes. [Extended and annot. version of a paper given at the conference of the Leo Baeck Institute and the Max-Planck-Stiftung für Geschichte at Schloß Ringberg (Tegernsee), November 25–28, 1987.]

27920. BERDING, HELMUT: *Aufklären durch Geschichte. Ausgewählte Aufsätze.* Mit einem Vorwort von Hans-Peter Ullmann und Heinz Schilling. Göttingen: Vandenhoeck & Ruprecht, 1990. 352 pp. [Incl.: Judenemanzipation im Rheinbund (247–264); orig. publ. in 1984 [in]: Reformen im rheinbündischen Deutschland. Hrsg. von E. Weis. München: 1984. Pp. 269–284.]

—— BERING, DIETZ: *Kampf um Namen. Bernhard Weiß gegen Joseph Goebbels.* [See No. 28902.]

27921. BODIAN, MIRIAM: *The Gomperz family in the 17th and 18th centuries: toward emancipation?* [In Hebrew]. [In]: Proceedings of the 10th World Congress of Jewish Studies, 1989, Division B, Vol. 1: *The history of the Jewish people.* Jerusalem, 1990. Pp. 177–182.

27922. BOSKIN, JUDITH R.: *Some parallels in the education of medieval Jewish and Christian women.* [In]: Jewish History, Vol. 5, No. 1, Leiden, Haifa Univ., Spring 1991. Pp. 41–51, notes. [Incl. German Jews.]

27923. BRUER, ALBERT A.: *Geschichte der Juden in Preußen (1750–1820).* Frankfurt am Main; New York: Campus. 531 pp., notes, tabs. (377–466), bibl. (468–525), index of persons (526–531).

27924. *Der Davidstern; Zeichen der Schmach – Symbol der Hoffnung; ein Beitrag zur Geschichte der Juden.* Hrsg.: Wolf Stegemann/S. Johanna Eichmann. Red. Elisabeth Cosanne-Schulte-Huxel [et al.]. Wiss. Berater: Michael Brocke. 4270 Dorsten: Dokumentationszentrum für jüd. Geschichte u. Religion (Postfach 622), 1991. 206 pp., illus., docs., facsims., maps, notes, index of persons, places. [Cont. texts, documents and articles dealing with the origin and history of the Magen David from antiquity to present times in the context of Jewish history and antisemitism. Incl. (titles abr.): Letztlich ein jüdisches Symbol (Gerbern S. Oegema,

28–29). Die Synagoge als Magd der Ecclesia (S. Johanna Eichmann OSU, 30–37). Magen David und Brauerzeichen (Peter Freimark, 100–107). Further contributions are listed according to subject.]

27925. DORON, JOACHIM/ SHMUEL, GAN: *'Der Geist ist es, der sich den Körper schafft!' Soziale Probleme in der jüdischen Turnbewegung (1896–1914).* [In]: Tel Aviver Jahrbuch für deutsche Geschichte, Bd. 20, Gerlingen, 1991. Pp. 237–258, notes.

27926. DOTHAN, ESTHER: *Glückel of Hameln after 300 years.* In the aftermath of a study day at the 92nd Street Y. [In Hebrew, title transl.]. [In]: Hadoar, Vol. 70, No. 10, New York, Jan. 11, 1991. Pp. 16–18.

27927. ENGEL, EVA J.: *Das Geburtsjahr Moses Mendelssohns.* [In]: Aschkenas, Bd. 1, Wien, 1991. Pp. 151–157, footnotes, illus.

27928. ENGEL HOLLAND, EVA: *The world of Moses Mendelssohn.* [In]: LBI Year Book XXXVI, London, 1991. Pp. 27–43, footnotes.

27929. GRAB, WALTER: *Obrigkeitliche und revolutionäre Formen der Judenemanzipation.* [In]: Tel Aviver Jahrbuch für deutsche Geschichte, Bd. 20, Gerlingen, 1991. Pp. 127–134, notes.

27930. GRAB, WALTER: *Warum die Judenemanzipation in Deutschland scheiterte.* [In]: Evangelische Kommentare, Jg. 23, Nr. 11, Stuttgart, 1990. Pp. 674–676.

27931. GRAB, WALTER: *Juden und Demokratie; zwei Jahrhunderte sozialen und politischen Engagements in Deutschland* [In]: Jüdische Lebenswelten [see No. 27946]. Frankfurt am Main: Jüdischer Verlag, Suhrkamp, 1991. pp. 336–352, illus.

27932. GRAB, WALTER: *Der deutsche Weg der Judenemanzipation 1789–1938.* Orig.-Ausg. München: Piper, 1991. 204 pp. (Serie Piper 1008.)

——— GROSSMAN, AVRAHAM: *On the ban of Rabbenu Gershom.* [See No. 28521.]

27933. GUGGENHEIM, YAKOV: *Social stratification of Central European Jewry (Ashkenaz) at the end of the Middle Ages: the poor.* [In Hebrew]. [In]: Proceedings of the 10th World Congress of Jewish Studies, 1989, Division B. Vol. 1: *The history of the Jewish people.* Jerusalem, 1990. Pp. 130–136.

27934. HERZBERG, WOLFGANG: *Überleben heißt Erinnern; Lebensgeschichten deutscher Juden.* Berlin: Aufbau, 1991. 438 pp., illus., facsims. [Incl.: Nachbemerkung (425–435; also on the author's own biography).] [Recollections of three women and three men about surviving in Nazi Germany and thereafter living in the GDR, compiled and written by Wolfgang Herzberg, himself the son of German-Jewish refugees who fled to England from Nazi persecution, where he was born in 1944; returned to Eastern Germany after the war.] [Cf.: Chronik nicht stattgefundener Tode (Sulamith Sparre). [In]: Tribüne, Jg. 30, H. 118, Frankfurt am Main, 1991. Pp. 213–214. Deutsche Juden erzählen. Überlebende, die ihre Hoffnung auf Ostberlin setzten (Karin Hartewig) [in]: Süddeutsche Zeitung, Nr. 34, München, 11. Feb. 1992, p. 11.]

27935. HERZIG, ARNO: *Die Anfänge der deutsch-jüdischen Geschichtsschreibung in der Spätaufklärung.* [In]: Tel Aviver Jahrbuch für deutsche Geschichte, Bd. 20, Gerlingen, 1991. Pp. 59–75.

27936. HERZIG, ARNO: *Die erste Emanzipationsphase im Zeitalter Napoleons.* [In]: Juden in Deutschland [see No. 27940]. Hamburg: Christians, 1991. Pp. 130–163, notes.

27937. HILGER, MARIE-ELISABETH: *Probleme jüdischer Industriearbeiter in Deutschland.* [In]: Juden in Deutschland [see No. 27940]. Hamburg: Christians, 1991. Pp. 304–325, notes.

27938. JERSCH-WENZEL, STEFI: *Juden in Preußen – Preußische Juden?* [In]: Tel Aviver Jahrbuch für deutsche Geschichte, Bd. 20, Gerlingen, 1991. Pp. 437–448, notes.

27939. *The Jewish legacy and the German conscience: essays in memory of Rabbi Joseph Asher.* Ed. by Moses Rischen and Raphael Asher. Berkeley, Ca.: Judah L. Magnes Museum, 1991. X, 357 pp., illus., ports., bibl. ref. [J.A., 1921–1990, Berlin, came to U.S. via Australia, reform rabbi.]

27940. *Juden in Deutschland. Emanzipation, Integration, Verfolgung und Vernichtung.* 25 Jahre Institut für die Geschichte der Juden, Hamburg. Hrsg. von Peter Freimark, Alice Jankowski, Ina S. Lorenz. Hamburg: Hans Christians Verlag, 1991. 486 pp., notes, index (persons). (Hamburger Beiträge zur Geschichte der deutschen Juden, XVII). [Incl.: Geleitwort (Henning Voscherau), Grusswort (Baruch Z. Ophir), Vorwort (by the editors). Cont. the sections: *Juden in Hamburg und Altona* (15–129). *Emanzipation – Antisemitismus – Zionismus* (130–251). *Zur Sozial-, Wirtschafts- und Mentalitätsgeschichte* (252–374). *Nationalsozialismus und Versuche einer 'Bewältigung'* (375–465). Anhang (466–477), see No. 28200. Contributions are listed according to subject.] [Cf.: Besprechung (Ernst Gottfried Lowenthal) [in]: Israelitisches Wochenblatt, Nr. 32, Zürich, 9. Aug. 1991. P. 19.]

27941. *Judentum im deutschen Sprachraum.* Hrsg. von Karl E. Grözinger. Frankfurt am Main:

Suhrkamp. 435 pp., notes, illus. (edition suhrkamp, 1613). [Papers delivered at a symposium held at the opening of the Frankfurt Jewish Museum in Dec. 1988, organised by the universities of Frankfurt am Main, Jerusalem and Tel Aviv, by the Jüdisches Museum Frankfurt and by the Jüdische Gemeinde Frankfurt.] [Cont.: Einleitung (Karl E. Grözinger, 7–14); the 20 essays are arranged under the headings: *Recht, Politik und Gesellschaft im Mittelalter*: titles partly condensed: Die Stellung der Juden in Recht und Verfassung der mittelalterlichen Stadt (Gerhard Dilcher, 17–35). Das Bild des Juden in der deutschen Literatur des Mittelalters (Winfried Frey, 36–59). Die politischen Entwicklungen im mittelalterlichen deutschen Judentum (Ivan G. Marcus, 60–88). Jüdisch-deutsche Symbiose? Kokem-Loschem und Rotwelsch (R. J. Zwi Werblowsky, 89–99). *Religion, Brauchtum und Kultur vor der Aufklärung*: Aschkenasische Frömmigkeit in Synagoge und Lehrhaus (Mordechai Breuer, 103–116). Normative und volkstümliche Frömmigkeit im Sefer Chasidim (Ithamar Gruenwald, 117–126). Jüdische Mystik im mittelalterlichen Deutschland (Joseph Dan, 127–172). Magie und Kabbala im ausgehenden Mittelalter (Israel Jacob Yuval, 173–189). Jüdische Wundermänner (Karl E. Grözinger, 190–221). Rabbi Ja'akov Emdens Autobiographie (Maurice R. Hayoun, 222–236). Synagogale Kunstmusik in Europa (Israel Adler, 237–255, music scores). *Emanzipation und Moderne*: Judentum und Moderne (Michael Graetz, 259–279). Jüdische Rechtsgelehrte (Hans-Peter Benöhr, 280–308). Die Halacha unter dem Druck der modernen Verhältnisse (Jakob Katz, 309–324). Der Religionsreformer A. Bernstein und die Anfänge der jüdischen Reformbewegung (Julius H. Schoeps, 325–346). Jüdisches Lernen und die Wissenschaft des Judentums (Zeev W. Falk, 347–356). Theodor Herzl; Zionismus und Journalismus (Johannes Wachten, 357–370). Zur Zweideutigkeit deutsch-jüdischen Geistes: Hermann Cohen (Micha Brumlik, 371–382). Die Synagoge in Augsburg – Architektur und Symbolik (Hannelore Künzl, 382–405. *Neubeginn nach der Zerstörung*: Die 4. jüdische Gemeinde in Frankfurt am Main – Zukunft oder Zwischenspiel (Salomon Korn, 409–433).]

27942. *Die Juden in ihrer mittelalterlichen Umwelt.* Hrsg.: Alfred Ebenbauer/Klaus Zatloukal. Wien; Köln: Böhlau, 1991. 322 pp., notes. [Incl.: Die Juden in ihrer mittelalterlichen Umwelt (Frantisek Graus, 53–66). Juden und Christen als Geldgeber im hohen und späten Mittelalter (Markus J. Wenninger, 281–300). Further articles pertinent to German-Jewish history are listed according to subject.]

27943. *Jüdische Lebenswelten. Jüdisches Denken und Glauben, Leben und Arbeiten in den Kulturen der Welt.* Katalog. Hrsg. von Andreas Nachama und Gereon Sievernich im Auftrage der Berliner Festspiele. Red.: Michaela Diener [et al.]. Berlin: Berliner Festspiele GmbH & Jüdischer Verlag/Suhrkamp Verlag, 1991. XIV, 7 pp., illus., index. [Catalogue for an exhibition held in Berlin Jan. 12 – April 26, 1992. Incl. the sections: Aschkenas – Mittelalter in rheinischen Städten (108–134). Von Osteuropa nach Berlin [and] Berlin (167–232). Moses Mendelssohn und die Aufklärung (474–492). Tradition und Wandel im Judentum (493–530). Heinrich Heine, Ludwig Börne, Rahel Varnhagen und Henriette Herz (531–543). Politik und jüdisches Leben (544–577). Aufbruch in die Moderne: Berlin, Prag, Wien, Warschau (611–680). Shoa (681–683). Enzyklopädie der Judenfeindschaften (Willi Jasper, 712–724). Jüdische Friedhöfe in Berlin (Hermann Simon, 725–729).]

27944. *Jüdische Lebenswelten. Jüdisches Denken und Glauben, Leben und Arbeiten in den Kulturen der Welt.* Programme [&] Journal. Hrsg. im Auftrag der Berliner Festspiele von Runze & Caspar. Red.: Bernd Krüger [et al.]. Berlin: Berliner Festspiele, 1992. 62 pp., illus.

27045. *Jüdische Lebenswelten. Jüdisches Denken und Glauben, Leben und Arbeiten in den Kulturen der Welt.* Wegweiser durch die Ausstellung der Berliner Festspiele im Martin-Gropius-Bau 12. Januar bis 26. April 1992. Hrsg.: Andreas Nachama und Gereon Sievernich. Zusammenstellung: Rudolf Stegers. Berlin: Argon, 1992. 96 pp., illus. [Published also in English under the title: Patterns of Jewish life; Jewish thought and beliefs, life and work within the cultures of the world.]

27946. *Jüdische Lebenswelten. Essays.* Hrsg. aus Anlaß der Ausstellung "Jüdische Lebenswelten" im Martin-Gropius-Bau Berlin, 12. Jan. – 26. April 1992 von Andreas Nachama, Julius H. Schoeps, Edward van Voolen im Auftrag der Berliner Festspiele GmbH. Frankfurt am Main: Jüdischer Verlag, Suhrkamp, 1991. 406 pp., illus., index. [Incl. Juden und Demokratie; zwei Jahrhunderte sozialen und politischen Engagements in Deutschland Walter Grab, 336–351). Other essays relevant to German Jewry are listed according to subject.]

27947. KAHLER, ERICH VON: *Judentum und Judenhass; drei Essays.* Wien: Österreichischer Bundesverlag (ÖBV), 1991. 141 pp., port., notes (137–141). [Cont. the essays: *Ursprung und Wandlung des Judenhasses*, first published in 1939. *Die Juden in Europa*, first published in 1945. *Was sind die Juden?*, first published in 1950.] [E.v.K., Oct. 14, 1885 Prague – June 28, 1970 Princeton, literary critic, philosopher of history, emigrated in 1933 via Vienna and Zurich to the USA.]

27948. KANARFOGEL, EPHRAIM: *Jewish education and society in the High Middle Ages.* Detroit: Wayne State Univ. Press, 1991. 160 pp. [Incl. German Jews.]

27949. KAPLAN, MARION A.: *The making of the Jewish middle class. Women, family, and identity in Imperial Germany.* New York; Oxford: Oxford University Press, 1991. XVI, 351 pp., illus., tabs., notes (235–303), bibl. (304–319), index of subjects, names, places (321–351).

27950. KATZ, JAKOB: *Zur jüdischen Sozialgeschichte: epochale und überepochale Geschichtsschreibung.* [In]: Tel Aviver Jahrbuch für deutsche Geschichte, Bd. 20, Gerlingen, 1991. Pp. 429–436, notes.

27951. KAYSERLING, MEYER: *Die jüdischen Frauen in der Geschichte, Literatur und Kunst.* Unveränd. Nachdr. der Ausg. Leipzig 1879. Hildesheim; Zürich: Olms, 1991. 383 pp. (Nachdruck in der Bibliothek des deutschen Judentums, hrsg. im Auftrag des Salomon Ludwig Steinheim-Instituts für deutsch-jüdische Geschichte von Julius H. Schoeps.)

27952. KRAUS, ELISABETH: *"Mietbürger" ohne Kündigungsschutz; neuere Literatur zur Geschichte der Juden in Deutschland.* [In]: Archiv für Sozialgeschichte, Nr. 31, Bonn, 1991. Pp. 645–647, footnotes. [Review article.]

27953. LANGE, HERMANN: *Die christlich-jüdische Ehe. Ein deutscher Streit im 19. Jahrhundert.* [In]: Menora, Bd. 2, München, 1991. Pp. 47–80, notes.

27954. LIVNÉ-FREUDENTHAL, RACHEL: *Der 'Verein für Cultur und Wissenschaft der Juden' (1819–1824) zwischen Staatskonformismus und Staatskritik.* [In]: Tel Aviver Jahrbuch für deutsche Geschichte, Bd. 20, Gerlingen, 1991. Pp. 103–125, notes.

27955. LÖWENBRÜCK, ANNA-RUTH: *Zalkind Hourwitz. Vom polnischen Ghetto zur französischen Revolution.* [In]: Tel Aviver Jahrbuch für deutsche Geschichte, Bd. 20, Gerlingen, 1991. Pp. 77–101, notes. [Z.H., 1740 Lublin – 1812 Paris, writer, advocate of emancipation of the Alsatian Jews, went to Paris via Berlin and Metz.]

27956. LOTTER, FRIEDRICH: *Geltungsbereich und Wirksamkeit des Rechts der kaiserlichen Judenprivilegien im Hochmittelalter.* [In]: Aschkenas, Bd. 1, Wien, 1991. Pp. 23–64, footnotes.

27957. LOTTER, FRIEDRICH: *Die Juden im Kirchenrecht des Mittelalters; Bericht über neuere Literatur.* [In]: Aschkenas, Bd. 1, Wien, 1991. Pp. 161–172, footnotes.

27958. MAGNUS, SHULAMIT S.: *German Jewish history.* [In]: Modern Judaism, Vol. 11, No. 1, Baltimore, Feb. 1991. Pp. 125–146, notes. [An overview of recent literature dealing with different aspects of German-Jewish history.]

27959. MALINO, FRANCIS/SORKIN, DAVID, eds.: *From east and west: Jews in a changing world 1750–1870.* Oxford: Blackwell, 1991, 336 pp., map [Incl. Joseph Wolf and the ideology of emancipation (David Sorkin, 107–125; J.W., b. 1762, Sandersleben in Anhalt, Dessau, d. 1826). Mordechai Aaron Günzburg: a Lithuanian Maskil faces modernity (Israel Bartal, 126–150; M.A.G., b. 1795, Salait, Lithuania, d. 1846). Jewish upper crust and Berlin Jewish enlightenment: the family of Daniel Itzig (Steven M. Lowenstein, 182–201, footnotes; D.I., 1723–1799, financier to Frederick the Great). Work, love and Jewishness in the life of Fanny Lewald (Deborah Hertz, 202–220, footnotes). Towards a biography of the Hatam Sofer (Jacob Katz, 223–266, footnotes; H.S., rabbi, 1763–1839). Zevi Hirsch Kalischer and the origins of religious Zionism (Jody Elizabeth Myers, 264–294, footnotes; Z.H.K., b. 1795, Lissa, Posen, d. 1874, Judaist). The Anglicization of orthodoxy: the Adlers, father and son (Eugene C. Black, 295–325, footnotes; Nathan Marcus Adler, Chief Rabbi of Hanover and Oldenburg, 1803–1890, Hermann Adler, his son, 1839–1911, moved to Britain in 1845. Father and son became the first two Chief Rabbis of Great Britain.).]

27960. MATTENKLOTT, GERT: *Jettchen Gebert und das Schtetl. Jüdische Lebenswelten in der deutschen Literatur.* [In]: Jüdische Lebenswelten. Essays [see no. 27943]. Frankfurt am Main: Jüdischer Verlag, Suhrkamp, 1991. Pp. 221–238, illus., notes. [On Jewish life as depicted in the works of numerous German-speaking Jewish authors.]

27961. MAURER, TRUDE: *'Sehr wichtig sind Bücher von der Jüdischen Geschichte'. Zu den Lebensverhältnissen und Lektüreinteressen jüdischer Kriegsgefangener aus dem Russischen Reich (1917/18).* [In]: Tel Aviver Jahrbuch für deutsche Geschichte, Bd. 20, Gerlingen, 1991. Pp. 259–286, notes. [Covers also the founding and activity of the 'Ausschuß zur Beschaffung jidischer (sic) und hebräischer Literatur für russische kriegsgefangene Juden unter dem Protektorat der Kgl. Spanischen Botschaft'.]

27962. MAURER, TRUDE: *Partnersuche und Lebensplanung. Heiratsannoncen als Quelle für die Sozial- und

Mentalitätsgeschichte der Juden in Deutschland. [In]: Juden in Deutschland [see No. 27940]. Hamburg: Christians, 1991. Pp. 344–374, notes. [Advertisements for a marriage partner in 'Israelitisches Familienblatt' and 'Der Israelit' as a source for Jewish social history.]

27963. MOKOTOFF, GARY/SACK, SALLYANN AMDUR: *Where once we walked: a guide to the Jewish communities destroyed in the Holocaust*. Teaneck, N. J.: Avotaynu, 1991. XXVIII, 514 pp., illus., maps. [Gazetteer of towns with statistics on the Jewish population, incl. many German and Austrian communities.]

27964. MONZ, HEINZ: *Samuel Hirsch (1815–1889). Ein jüdischer Reformator aus dem Hunsrück*. [In]: Jahrbuch für westdeutsche Landesgeschichte, 17, 1991, pp. 159–180.

27965. MOSSE, GEORGE L.: *Ebrei in Germania fra assimilazioni e antisemitismo*. Traduzione di Paola e Cristina Candela. Firenze: La Giuntina, 1991. 273 pp., index of names. (Collana 'Schulim Vogelmann'; 26.) [A collection of nine essays translated into Italian, for the most part taken from English publications of the Leo Baeck Institute.]

27966. OCH, GUNNAR: *Jüdische Leser und jüdisches Lesepublikum im 18. Jahrhundert. Ein Beitrag zur Akkulturationsgeschichte des deutschen Judentums*. [In]: Menora, Bd. 2, München, 1991. Pp. 298–336, notes.

27967. PRESTEL, CLAUDIA: *Jüdische Unterschichten im Zeitalter der Emanzipation; dargestellt anhand der Gemeinde Fürth 1826–1870*. [In]: Aschkenas, Bd. 1, Wien, 1991. Pp. 95–134, footnotes. [And]: *Zwischen Tradition und Moderne. Die Armenpolitik der Gemeinde zu Fürth (1826–1870)*. [In]: Tel Aviver Jahrbuch für deutsche Geschichte, Bd. 20, Gerlingen, 1991. Pp. 135–162.

27968. RAHE, THOMAS: *Religionsreform und jüdisches Selbstbewußtsein im deutschen Judentum des 19. Jahrhunderts*. [In]: Menora; Bd. 1, München: Piper, 1990. Pp. 89–121, notes. [This entry has been inadvertently ommitted in the bibliography of LBI Year Book XXXVI; see No. 27166/YBXXXVI.]

27969. REINER, ELCHANAN: *Jewish fate: the adventures of an itinerant preacher in the Thirty Years' War and the hellish tortures of an apostate* [In Hebrew, title transl.] [In]: Eit-mol, No. 100, Tel-Aviv, Dec. 1991. Pp. 15–17. [On Abraham ha-Darshan (the Preacher) from Brisk and Lublin, who lived in Vienna in the mid-17th century and wrote about Hayyim of Engelberg.] [Hayyim of Engelberg, orig. Ferdinand Engelberger, apostate, converted to Christianity in 1636 to evade penalty for theft, executed for further theft in Vienna in 1642.]

27970. REINHARZ, JEHUDA/SCHATZBERG, WALTER, eds.: *The Jewish response to German culture: from the Enlightenment to the Second World War*. Nahover, N. H.; London: Univ. Press of New England (publ. for Clark University), 1991. XII, 362 pp., footnotes. [Paperback edn. of collection of essays orig. publ. in 1985, see No. 21832/YBXXXI.]

27971. RICHARZ, MONIKA: *Jüdische Lehrer auf dem Lande im Kaiserreich*. [In]: Tel Aviver Jahrbuch für deutsche Geschichte, Bd. 20, Gerlingen, 1991. Pp. 181–194, notes.

27972. RICHARZ, MONIKA, ed.: *Jewish life in Germany. Memoirs from three centuries*. Translated by Stella P. Rosenfeld and Sidney Rosenfeld. Sponsored by the Leo Baeck Institute. Bloomington, Ind.: Indiana University Press, 1991. 484 pp., notes, glossary, illus., index of names. (The Modern Jewish Experience, Paula Hyman and Deborah Dash Moore, eds.) [Cont.: Introductory essay (Monika Richarz, 1–40) and 51 autobiographical texts from the archives of the LBI New York, reflecting five generations of Jewish life in Germany from the ghetto to the destruction during the Nazi period, arranged under the headings: *The age of emancipation, 1780–1871* (41–164). *Imperial Germany, 1871–1918* (165–300). *Weimar Republic and National Socialism, 1918–1945* (301–474). This volume is a translation of 'Bürger auf Widerruf: Lebenszeugnisse deutscher Juden 1780–1945'. München: Beck, 1989, see No. 25958/YBXXXV, which was an abridged version of an earlier three-volume edition 'Jüdisches Leben in Deutschland'. Bd. 1–3, Stuttgart: Deutsche Verlagsanstalt, 1976–1982, see No. 18824/YBXXVIII.]

27973. ROSENTHAL, MALKA: *Süßkind von Trimberg – ein Jude? Mutmaßungen über den berühmten Minnesänger des 13. Jahrhunderts*. [In]: Tribüne, Jg. 30, H. 118, Frankfurt am Main, 1991. Pp. 176–185, illus.

27974. SCHRECKENBERG, WILHELM: *Literaturbericht: Das Judentum in Geschichte und Gegenwart*. Teil 4. [In]: Geschichte in Wissenschaft und Unterricht, 42. Jg., H. 1, Stuttgart, 1991. Pp. 39–64.

27975. *Second Chance. Two Centuries of German-speaking Jews in the United Kingdom*. Eds.: Werner E. Mosse (Co-ordinating ed.), Julius Carlebach, Gerhard Hirschfeld, Aubrey Newman, Arnold Paucker, Peter Pulzer. Preface by Claus Moser. Tübingen: Mohr, 1991. XII, 654 pp., footnotes, index of names (623–650). (Schriftenreihe wissenschaftlicher Abhandlungen des Leo Baeck Instituts 48.) [Papers presented at the International Historical Conference held by the Leo Baeck Institute in association with the German Historical Institute London and the Jewish Historical Society of England at Clare College in Cambridge, Sept. 14–19, 1988 (see No. 24908/YBXXXIV). Cont.: Emigration and reception. Foreigners: the immigrant in Britain (Peter Pulzer, 3–9). Immigrants and refugees in Britain (Colin Holmes, 11–30). German Jews in Britain: a prologue (Aubrey Newman, 31–36). German-Jewish settlement in Victorian England (Todd M. Endelman, 37–56). Areas of departure from Nazi Germany and the Social Structure of the Emigrants (Doron Niederland, 57–68). Areas of reception in the United Kingdom: 1933–1945. (Bob Moore, 69–80). Jewish Emmigration in the Nazi period: some aspects of acculturation (Herbert A. Strauss, 81–95). Social and cultural impact. Central European Emigré Psychologists and Psychoanalysts in the United Kingdom (Mitchell G. Ash, 101–120). On transit to America: political scientists from Germany in Great Britain after 1933 (Alfons Söllner, 121–135). The contribution of German-speaking Jewish refugees to German studies in Britain (Rodney Livingstone, 137–152). The contribution of German-speaking Jewish Immigrants to British Historiography (Christhard Hoffmann, 153–175). Jews of German background in British politics (Rudolf Muhs, 177–194). German, Czech and Austrian Jews in English publishing (Uwe Westphal, 195–208). German-speaking Jews as patrons of the arts and sciences in Edwardian England (Peter Alter, 209–219). The history of the contribution to law by German-speaking Jewish refugees in the United Kingdom (Kurt Lipstein, 221–227). Some contributions to physics by German-Jewish émigrés in Britain and elsewhere (Paul K. Hoch, 229–241). The contribution of Central European Jews to medical science and practice in Britain, the 1930s–1950s (Paul Weindling, 243–254). The impact of German-speaking refugees in Britain on the fine arts (Peter Lasko, 255–274, illus.). The German-Jewish contribution to musical life in Britain (Erik Levi, 275–295, illus.). The émigrés from Nazi Germany and their contribution to the British theatrical scene (Günter Berghaus, 297–314, illus.). The image of the German Jew in English fiction (Pauline Paucker, 315–333, illus.). Merchants and bankers (Stanley D. Chapman, 335–346). Engineers from Germany in exile in Britain, 1933–1945 (Wolfgang Mock, 347–359). German Jews in British industry (Harold Pollins, 261–377). Refugees from the Third Reich and industry in the depressed areas of Britain (Herbert Loebl, 379–403). The impact of German Jews on Anglo-Jewry – Orthodoxy, 1850–1950 (Julius Carlebach, 405–423). The German influence on progressive Judaism in Great Britain (Albert H. Friedlander, 425–435). The contribution of German-Jewish scholars to Jewish studies in the United Kingdom (Raphael Loewe, 437–462). Paths to acceptance. British attitudes to Jewish refugees from Central and Eastern Europe in the nineteenth and twentieth centuries (John P. Fox, 465–484). British immigration control procedures and Jewish refugees 1933–1939 (Louise London, 485–517). Anglo-Jewish attitudes to the refugees from Central Europe 1933–1939 (Vivian D. Lipman, 519–531). German-Jewish Women in England (Jillian Davidson, 533–551). An alien occupation – Jewish refugees and domestic service in Britain, 1933–1948 (Tony Kushner, 553–578). Jewish refugee organisations (Ronald Stent, 579–598, illus.). British non-Jewish organisations in support of refugees (Gerhard Hirschfeld, 599–610). To give and to take: a balance sheet (Werner E. Mosse, 611–622)] [Selected reviews: Sie hatten gewiß das "richtige" Land gewählt; die Geschichte der deutschen Juden in England ist größtenteils eine Erfolgsstory (Robert Jütte) [in]: Allgemeine Jüdische Wochenzeitung, Nr. 46/24, Bonn, 13. Juni 1991, p. 5. One-way Channel crossing (David Maier) [in]: AJR Information, Vol. 46, No. 6, London, June 1991, p. 4. Dislocations and new beginnings: the experience of German-speaking Jews (Peter Wende) [in]: German Historical Institute London, Bulletin, Vol XIV, No. 2, May 1992, pp. 3–7. Safe Haven? (James Joll) [in]: Government and Opposition, Vol. 26, No. 4, London, Autumn 1991, pp. 549–554. 'Fearsome virus' view of German refugees (David Cesarani) [in]: Jewish Chronicle, London, 19 July, p. 13. Review (Sharman Kadish) [in]: Hamaor. Journal of the Federation of Synagogues, Vol. 27, No. 1, London, Pesach 1992, pp. 33–34. Deutschstämmige Juden in Großbritannien (Jobst Knigge) [in]: Leipziger Volkszeitung, 15. Juni 1991. German Jews and Anglo-Jewry (DLM) [in]: Our Congregation (Belsize Square Synagogue), No. 430, London, June 1991, p. 2. Deutschprachige Juden in England (Christoph Stamm) [in]: Das Parlament, Nr. 46, Bonn, 1991, p. 17. Juden in England (SH) [in]: Stuttgarter Zeitung, 23 März 1991. A benign bargain (Bernard Wasserstein) [in]: Times Literary Supplement, London, 20 March 1992, pp. 3–4.

27976.   SIMON, HERMANN: *Vernachlässigte Quellen zur Sozial-und Wirtschaftsgeschichte der deutschen Juden.* [In]: Juden in Deutschland [see No. 27940]. Hamburg: Christians, 1991. Pp. 273–285, notes. [About A. F. Thiele's book, 'Die jüdischen Gauner in Deutschland, Berlin 1841–1843', as a source for Jewish social history.]

27977. TOURY, JACOB: *Die bangen Jahre (1887/1891). Juden in Deutschland zwischen Integrationshoffnung und Isolationsfurcht.* [In]: Juden in Deutschland [see No. 27940]. Hamburg: Christians, 1991. Pp. 164–185, notes.

27978. VOLKOV, SHULAMIT: *Die Erfindung einer Tradition. Zur Entstehung des modernen Judentums in Deutschland.* [In]: Historische Zeitschrift, Bd. 253, München, 1991. Pp. 603–628.

—— WALK, JOSEPH: *Jüdische Schule und Erziehung im Dritten Reich.* [See No. 28440.]

27979. YUVAL, ISRAEL JACOB: *Hospices and their guests in Jewish medieval Germany.* [In Hebrew]. [In]: Proceedings of the 10th World Congress of Jewish Studies, 1989. Division B. Vol. 1: *The history of the Jewish people.* Jerusalem, 1990. Pp. 125–129.

27980. *Zerbrochene Geschichte; Leben und Selbstverständnis der Juden in Deutschland.* Hrsg. von Dirk Blasius und Dan Diner. Frankfurt am Main: Fischer, 1991, 238 [2]pp., notes. [Incl. (titles partly condensed): Einleitung (Dirk Blasius/ Dan Diner, 7–10). Lebensbedingungen der Juden im spätmittelalterlichen Deutschland (Alfred Haverkamp, 11–31). Lage und Selbstverständnis der deutschen Juden (Rainer Walz, 32–52). Die Juden im Zeitalter der Aufklärung (Stefi Jersch-Wenzel, 53–63). Die Dynamik der Dissimilation (Shulamit Volkov, 64–78). Jüdische Geschichte in Deutschland (Reinhard Rürup, 79–101). Die Juden in der Weimarer Republik (Trude Maurer, 102–120). All other contributions are listed according to subject.]

27981. ZIMMERMANN, MOSHE: *Biography as a historical monograph.* [In]: Tel Aviver Jahrbuch für deutsche Geschichte, Bd. 20, Gerlingen, 1991. Pp. 449–457, notes.

Linguistics/Western Yiddish

27982. ALLERHAND, JAKOB: *Die jüdisch-deutsche Mundart als Sprache der Aschkenasim – ihre Opposition im aschkenasischen Raum am Ausgang des Mittelalters.* [In]: Die Juden in ihrer mittelalterlichen Umwelt [see No. 27942]. Wien; Köln: Böhlau, 1991. Pp. 11–16.

27983. ALT, ARTHUR TILO: *Yiddish and Berlin's Scheunenviertel* [In]: Shofar, Vol. 9, No. 2, West Lafayette, In., Purdue Univ., Winter 1991. Pp. 29–43, footnotes.

27984. BECHTEL, DELPHINE: *Les revues modernistes Yiddish à Berlin et à Varsovie de 1922 à 1924: la quête d'une nouvelle Jérusalem.* [In]: Etudes Germaniques, Vol. 46, No. 2, Paris 1991. Pp. 161–177.

27985. GILMAN, SANDER L.: *Chicken soup, or the penalties for sounding too Jewish.* [In]: Shofar, Vol. 9. No. 2, West Lafayette, In., Purdue Univ., Winter 1991. Pp. 55–69, footnotes. [Deals with the prejudices and hostilities between German and Austrian Jews and Eastern European Jews, specifically relating to the differences in the use of languages, specially Yiddish. This essay served as keynote address at conference on the relationship between German Jews and East European Jews held in the spring of 1990 by the German Department at Columbia University.]

27986. HOBERMANN, JIM: *Jenseits von Galizien, diesseits von Hollywood; der jiddische Film aus Wien.* [In]: Babylon, H. 8, Frankfurt am Main, Febr. 1991. Pp. 116–132, notes.

27987. *Jiddistik-Mitteilungen: Jiddistik in deutschsprachigen Ländern.* Nr. 5 & 6. Hrsg. von der Jiddistik im Fachbereich Sprach- und Literaturwissenschaften der Universität Trier (Postfach 3825, D–5500 Trier). Red.: Gabriele Brünnel. Trier. Apr. & Nov. 1991. 2 issues, notes, bibl. (H. 6 incl.: "Killeberger" als Quelle für Sprache und Brauchtum deutscher Juden im 19. Jahrhundert (Walter Röll, 7–22, footnotes.]

27988. MATRAS, YARON: *Zur Rekonstruktion des jüdischdeutschen Wortschatzes in den Mundarten ehemaliger "Judendörfer" in Südwestdeutschland.* [In]: Zeitschrift für Dialektologie, Jg. 58, H. 3, Stuttgart, 1991. Pp. 267–293.

27989. SIMON, BETTINA: *Judendeutsch und Jiddisch* [In]: Die Juden in ihrer mittelalterlichen Umwelt [see in No. 27942]. Wien: Böhlau, 1991. Pp. 251–260.

27990. STENBERG, PETER: *Journey to oblivion: the end of the East European Yiddish and German worlds in the mirror of literature.* Toronto: Toronto Univ. Press, 1991. IX, 213 pp., bibl. [Author uses literature to trace the destinies of Eastern European speakers of German and Yiddish.]

27991. TIMM, ERIKA: *Die Bibelübersetzungssprache als Faktor der Auseinanderentwicklung des Jiddischen und des deutschen Wortschatzes.* [In]: Deutsche Bibelübersetzungen des Mittelalters. Beiträge eines Kolloquiums im deutschen Bibel-Archiv unter Mitarbeit von Nikolaus Henkel hrsg. von Heimo Reinitzer. Bern: Lang, 1991. Pp. 59–75, notes, tabs.

27992. TIMM, ERIKA: *Wie Elia Levita sein Bovobuch für den Druck überarbeitete: ein Kapitel aus der italo-*

jiddischen Literatur der Renaissancezeit. [In]: Germanisch-Romanische Monatsschrift, N. F., Bd. 41, H. 1, Heidelberg, 1991. Pp. 61–81, notes.

—— WERBLOWSKY, ZWI R. J.: *Jüdisch-deutsche Symbiose? Bemerkungen zum Kokem-Loschem und Rotwelsch.* [See in No. 27941.]

27993. WULFF, MICHAL: *Das Sprichwort im Kontext der Erziehungstradition. Dargestellt am Beispiel deutsch-jüdischer Sprichwörter.* Frankfurt am Main: Lang, 1991. 317 pp., Sprichwörterbeispiele (264–293), bibl. (297–317). (Europäische Hochschulschriften, Reihe XI, Pädagogik, Bd. 44;). [On German-Jewish proverbs, their origin and their role in the Jewish educational tradition.]

B. Communal and Regional History

1. Germany

—— AACHEN. [See also No. 28220.]

27994. —— LUCAS, ERIC: *Jüdisches Leben auf dem Lande. Eine Familienchronik.* Aus dem Engl. übertragen von Hildegard & Ernst Cassel. Mit einem Vorwort von Rudolf Dieregsweiler. Frankfurt am Main: Fischer Taschenbuch Verl., 1991. 155 pp. (Lebensbilder. Jüdische Erinnerungen und Zeugnisse. Hrsg. von Wolfgang Benz). [Memoirs, orig. written in 1945, of a cattle dealer's son, born in 1915 in Aachen, grew up in Forst near Aachen, emigrated after the November Pogrom via Belgium and England to Palestine.]

—— ALDINGEN [see No. 28058.]

27995. ALTENA. PETRASCH, FRIEDRICH: *Siegmund Heinemann (1878–1951) – ein jüdischer Kaufmann in Altena.* [In]: Der Märker, Jg. 40, H. 5, Altena Sept./Okt. 1991. Pp. 202–208, illus., footnotes.

27996. ALTENKUNSTADT. ANGERSTORFER, ANDREAS: *'Herbstmarder gelten nicht viel': ein Brief [von 1845] des Fellhändlers Michel Lindner, gefunden in der Geniza von Altenkunstadt.* [In]: Vom Main zum Jura (Postfach 41, D-8628 Weismain), H. 6, Lichtenfels, 1991. Pp. 135–147, illus., notes. [Incl. chap.: Zur Geschichte der Juden in Thüringen (145–146).]

27997. ALTENSTADT. JOHANN, ELISABETH: *Unsere jüdischen Nachbarn; ein fast vergessener Teil der Ortsgeschichte von Altenstadt (Hessen), Hoechst a. d. Nidder und Lindheim, 14. bis 20. Jahrhundert.* Altenstadt: Vorstand der Gemeinde Altenstadt, 1991. 442 pp., illus., facsims., plans, ports., bibl. [Incl. persecution of Jews during Nazi period.]

27998. ALTONA. GILLIS-CARLEBACH, MIRIAM: *Aus der Vorgeschichte der hochdeutschen-israelitischen Gemeindeschule zu Altona – ca. 1583–1843. Thesen – Dokumente – Zusammenhänge.* [In]: Juden in Deutschland [see No. 27940]. Hamburg: Hans Christians Verlag, 1991. Pp. 15–35, notes.

27999. —— ZÜRN, GABY: *Die fotografische Dokumentation von Grabinschriften auf dem jüdischen Friedhof Königstrasse/Altona (1942–1944) und ihr historischer Kontext.* [In]: Juden in Deutschland [see No. 27940]. Hamburg: Christians, 1991. Pp. 116–129, notes.

28000. ANDERNACH. *Andernacher Juden im Mittelalter.* Begleitheft zur Ausstellung Andernacher Juden im Mittelalter im Stadtmuseum Andernach vom 6. Okt. – 16. Dez. 1990. Hrsg.: Klaus Schäfer. Andernach: Stadtmuseum, 1990. 71 pp., illus.

28001. ARNSBERG. *Juden in Arnsberg.* Eine Dokumentation. Herausgegeben im Auftrag der Stadt Arnsberg und des Arbeitskreises 'Geschichtswerkstatt' von Michael Gosmann, Arnsberg: Der Stadtdirektor, 1991. 334 pp., notes, illus., maps, tabs., bibl., index (names, places, subjects, 309–333). (Städtekundliche Schriftenreihe über die Stadt Arnsberg 18) [Incl.: (titles abbr.) Frühgeschichte (bis 1803) (Michael Gosmann, 11–20). Unter Hessen (bis 1816) und Preußen (bis 1933) (Fritz Timmermann, 21–30). Das Dritte Reich (Ernst Heinrich Rehermann, 31–46). Erste Kontakte mit der Heimat nach dem Holocaust (Karl Föster, 47–48). Der Besuch ehemaliger jüdischer Bürger in Arnsberg 1988 (Willi Kleine-Büning, 49–52). Die Arnsberger Synagogengemeinde (Horst Hoven, 55–67). Die Synagoge in der Schloßstraße (Michael Gosmann, 69–76). Die jüdische Schule und ihre Lehrer (Michael Gosmann, 77–85). Der jüdische Friedhof (Karl Föster (87–92). Jüdische Bürger als Mitglieder der Arnsberger Bürgerschützengesellschaft (Bert Collas, 93–94). Jugenderinnerungen einer Arnsbergerin (Ottilie Ebert, 95–96). Der Novemberpogrom (Michael Gosmann, 97–104). Ein Zwölfjähriger erlebt den Novemberpogrom (Alexander Primavesi, 105–106). Die 'Reichskristallnacht' in Zeitzeugenberichten (107–111). Antisemitische Zeitungsartikel in der lokalen Presse 1938–1944 (Michael Gosmann, 112–129). Erinnerungen eines Arnsberger Juden bis 1933 (Ewald Steinmann, 130–132 [28]). Jüdische Familien in Arnsberg (136–229). Juden in Arnsberg – ein Thema für den Unterricht (Eckhard Kotthaus/Jürgen Müller, 233–248); list of Nazi victims (285–286), Namensverzeichnis der Grabsteine auf dem Friedhof Seltersberg (299–304).] [Cf.: Besprechung (Ursula Homann) [in]: Allgemeine Jüdische Wochenzeitung, Nr. 47/10, Bonn, 5 März 1992, p. 10.]

—— AUGSBURG. KÜNZL, HANNELORE: *Die Synagoge in Augsburg – Architektur und Symbolik.* [See in No. 27941.]

—— BADEN. KAUFMANN, URI: *The impact of the French Revolution on rural Jewry in Alsace, Baden and Switzerland.* [See No. 28124.]

28002. BECHHOFEN. PROSCH, BERNHARD: *Ein Pilotprojekt gerät ins Stocken. Der jüdische Friedhof in Bechhofen wird renoviert und inventarisiert.* [In]: Tribüne, Jg. 30, H. 117, Frankfurt am Main 1991. Pp. 54–58.

28003. BERLIN. ALEXANDER, GABRIEL: *Die Entwicklung der jüdischen Bevölkerung in Berlin zwischen 1871 und 1945.* [In]: Tel Aviver Jahrbuch für deutsche Geschichte, Bd. 20, Gerlingen, 1991. Pp. 287–314, tabs., notes, [Based on the author's Diss. (in Hebrew), History of the Jewish Community of Berlin in the Weimar Republic.]

28004. — BERTZ, INKA: *'Keine Feier ohne Meyer'. Die Geschichte der Firma Hermann Meyer & Co. 1890– 1990.* Mit einem Vorwort von Rolf Bothe. Berlin: Berlin Museum, 1990. 120 pp., illus. (Schriftenreihe des Berlin Museums zur Geschichte von Handel und Gewerbe in Berlin, Bd. 2) [On the food and beverages chainstore company, founded in Berlin in 1890 by Hermann Meyer, together with Louis Licht and Max Warschauer, all three originally from Poznań.]

28005. — HERTZ, DEBORAH: *Die jüdischen Salons im alten Berlin.* Aus dem Amerikanischen von Gabriele Neumann-Kloth. Frankfurt am Main: Hain, 1991. 349 pp., ports., tabs., bibl. notes (339–344). [Footnotes of the original edn. omitted] [For American edn., Jewish high society in old régime Berlin, 1988, see No. 24980/YBXXXIV.] [Cf.: Als die Standesgrenzen fielen (Ulrike Wahlich) [in]: Aufbau, Vol. 57, No. 11, New York, May 24, 1991, p. 7. Besprechung (Ludger Heid) [in]: Das Historisch-Politische Buch, 40. Jg., H. 1&2, Göttingen, 1992. P. 87.]

28006. — KOCH, URSULA E.: *Der Teufel in Berlin. Von der Märzrevolution bis zu Bismarcks Entlassung; illustrierte politische Witzblätter einer Metropole 1848–1890.* Köln: informationspress – c.w. leske verlag, 1991. 880 pp., illus., notes (671–786), bibl. (787–828), index of persons and periodicals. [Incl. passim numerous references to Jewish personalities in the Berlin newspaper world; also the sections: Jüdischer Wortwitz in Berliner Stadtzeitungen (32–41). 'Vom jüdischen Kriegsschauplatz' (242–256). Die alte Leier: der Jude als Sündenbock (538– 542).]

28007. — LAUSCH, HANS: *A. S. Gumpertz und die Académie Royale des Sciences et Belles-Lettres in Berlin. Zum Auftakt der Euler-Dollondschen Achromasie-Kontroverse.* [In]: Bulletin des LBI, 88, Frankfurt am Main, 1991. Pp. 11–26, notes. [A.S.G., Dec. 10, 1723 Berlin – 1766 (or 1770) Hamburg, physician, man of letters.]

28008. — LOWENSTEIN, STEVEN M.: *Two silent minorities: orthodox Jews and poor Jews in Berlin 1770– 1823.* [In]: LBI Year Book XXXVI, London, 1991. Pp. 3–25, footnotes.

28009. — MICHAEL, REUVEN: *The enlightenment in the period of the French Revolution – the demise of the 'Berlin Enlightenment'?* [In Hebrew, with English summary]. [In]: Zion, Vol. 56, No. 3, Jerusalem, 1991. Pp. 275–298. [On the radicalisation of the Berlin maskilim, influenced by the French Revolution.]

28010. — SIMON, HERMANN: *Die Neue Synagoge Berlin. Geschichte, Gegenwart, Zukunft.* Berlin: Edn. Hentrich, 1991. 49 pp., illus., plans, ports.

28011. — SIMON, HEINRICH: *Hebrew studies at the University of Berlin.* [In Hebrew]. [In]: Brit Ivrit Olamit: the 7th Hebrew Scientific European Congress, October 1986. Ed.: Efrat Naor. [In Hebrew]. Jerusalem: Brit Ivrit Olamit, 1990. Pp. 154–158. [A short overview of the 19th– 20th centuries.]

28012. — *Juden in Kreuzberg; Fundstücke . . . Fragmente . . . Erinnerungen.* Hrsg.: Berliner Geschichts- werkstatt (Konzept und Projektleitung: Christine Zahn, Katalogredaktion: Andreas Ludwig, Bildredaktion: Carola Jüllig). Berlin: Edn. Hentrich, 1991. 436 pp., illus., facs., docs. [Cont.: Liste der aus Kreuzberg deportierten Juden (13–50), and 52 contributions dealing with the religious, social, economic and business life of Jews in Kreuzberg, incl. personal memoirs and articles on individual personalities, on the synagogues, organisations, Jüdischer Kulturbund, forced labour.]

—— — GUTMANN, JOSEPH: *The Kirschstein Museum of Berlin.* [See No. 28586.]

28013. BRAUNSCHWEIG. MEYER, WALTER: *Der Braunschweiger Landesrabbiner Samuel Levi Eger (1769–1842):* Auszüge aus Walter Meyers Familiengeschichte Eger, bearb. von Ralf Busch. Stadtarchiv Braunschweig. Braunschweig: Stadtarchiv; Stadtbibliothek, 1991. 38 pp., illus. (Kleine Schriften/Stadtarchiv und Stadtbibliothek Braunschweig; 20.)

28014. BRESLAU. *Mitteilungen des Verbandes ehemaliger Breslauer in Israel.* Hrsg.: Mosche Goldstein [et al.]. No. 55. Tel-Aviv (P.O.B. 3591), 1991. 16 pp. [Incl.: Die Synagoge 'Zum Weissen Storch' verfällt in Breslau (Jerzy Kos, 6 & 10, illus.).]

28015. COESFELD (Kreis). *Juden im Kreis Coesfeld.* Hrsg.: Kreis Coesfeld. Der Oberkreisdirektor. Red.: Diethard Aschoff. Mit Beiträgen von Gertrud Althoff [et al.]. Coesfeld: Kreis Coesfeld, Der Oberkreisdirektor, 1990. 351 pp., illus., tabs. (Beiträge zur Landes- und Volkskunde des Kreises Coesfeld; Bd. 24.)

28016. COLOGNE. LAUF, PETER: *Jüdische Studierende an der Universität zu Köln: 1919–1934.* Köln: Böhlau, 1991. X, 275 pp., tabs. (Studien zur Geschichte der Universität zu Köln; Bd. 11). Zugl.: Köln, Univ., Diss., 1990.

28017. — MAGNUS, SHULAMIT S.: *"Who shall say who belongs?": Jews between city and state in Prussian Cologne, 1815–1828.* [In]: AJS Review, Vol. 16, Nos. 1–2, Cambridge, Ma., Spring-Fall 1991. Pp. 57–105, footnotes, tabs. [Deals with the legal battle between the city of Cologne and the Prussian provincial government about control over the status of the Cologne Jews as expressed in the law of 1809, which required Jews to obtain 'Jew licences' in order to set up a business.]

28018. — REUTER, URSULA: *Studien zu Profil und Funktion Kölner jüdischer Zeitungen in den Jahren 1921–1938.* Magisterarbeit (Universität zu Köln), 1990. 175 pp. [Mimeog., obtainable at Germania Judaica, Kölner Bibliothek zur Gesch. d. dt. Judentums.] [Also by the same author: Jüdische Zeitungen in Köln, 1919–1938. [In]: Geschichte in Köln, H. 29, Köln, Juli 1991. Pp. 83–118.]

28019. CUXHAVEN. DETTMER, FRAUKE: *Juden im Amt Ritzebüttel und der Stadt Cuxhaven.* [Frauke Dettmer]. [Cuxhaven]: [Verl.-Ges. Cuxhaven], [1991?]. 179 pp., illus. [Incl. Nazi period.]

28020. DARMSTADT. GOWER, DAVID/STEINBECK, UDO: *Jüdische Spuren in Darmstadt.* Darmstadt: D. Gower (Brüder-Knauss-Str. 60), 1990. 35 pp.

—— DÜSSELDORF. *Tatjana Barbakoff, 1899 Libau – 1944 Auschwitz.* [See No. 26683.]

28021. EDENKOBEN. SCHMIDT, FRANZ: *Juden in Edenkoben; Spuren ihrer Geschichte 1660 – 1942.* Hrsg.: Sparkasse Südliche Weinstraße in Landau. 6737 Sparkasse Edenkoben 1991. 191 pp., illus., notes, docs., facsims. [Incl. the chaps.: Judenordnung und Judenrecht; Die wirtschaftlichen und sozialen Verhältnisse der Edenkobener Juden im 18. und 19. Jahrhundert; Kehilla Kedosha. Das innere System der jüdischen Gemeinde Edenkoben; Zwischen Judengasse und Assimilation; Verfolgung und Vernichtung 1933–1942; Ein berühmter Edenkobener: Franz Weidenreich.] [F.W., June 7, 1873 Edenkoben – July 11, 1948 New York, professor of anthropology in Frankfurt am Main, emigrated in 1934 to the USA, from 1935 until 1941 Visiting Professor of Anatomy in Peking.]

—— EIFEL [See No. 28220.]

28022. ELBERFELD. KASTNER, DIETER: *Die Elberfelder Zeitung und die Judenfrage im Jahre 1843. Ein Beitrag zur Ablehnung der Emanzipation aus evangelischer Sicht.* [In]: Monatshefte für Evangelische Kirchengeschichte des Rheinlandes, Jg. 39, Düsseldorf, 1990. Pp. 247–276.

28023. EPPINGEN. *Der jüdische Friedhof in Eppingen. Eine Dokumentation.* Hrsg. von Ralf Bischoff und Reinhard Hauke. Mit Beiträgen von Wolfram Angerbauer [et al.]. 7519 Eppingen: Heimatfreunde Eppingen (Geranienstr. 19), 1989. 351 pp., illus., index of persons, list of names, inserted map. (Rund um den Ottilienberg; 5) [Incl.: Zur Geschichte der Jüdischen Gemeinde in Eppingen (Wolfram Angerbauer, 10–16). Die Entstehungsgeschichte des Friedhofs (Reinhard Hauke, 17–23). Zur Grabstein-Symbolik des jüdischen Friedhofs (Joachim Hahn, 24–30). Die Belegungsgeschichte des Friedhofs und die Veränderungen bis heute (Ralf Bischoff, 31–42). Dokumentation der Grabinschriften (43–327; incl. Einleitung und Übersetzung von Andreas Gotzmann, with Hebrew inscriptions and their German translation; Grabsteinaufnahme und Photographien von Ralf Bischoff).]

28024. ESSEN. BRAUN, UTE: *Das Damenkapitel läßt eine neue Synagoge bauen (1685).* [In]: Das Münster am Hellweg. Mitteilungsblatt des Vereins für die Erhaltung des Essener Münsters, Jg. 44, Essen, Jan.–Dec. 1991. Pp. 33–40, notes, illus.

28025. — BROCKE, EDNA: *Die 'Alte Synagoge' in Essen; Reflexionen zum Selbstverständnis.* [In]: Zerbrochene Geschichte. [See No. 27980.] Pp. 187–200, illus. [On the history of the Essen synagogue and its present function as a memorial and museum.]

28026. — ZIMMERMANN, MICHAEL: *Zur Geschichte der Essener jüdischen Gemeinde vor 1933.* [In]: Zerbrochene Geschichte. [See No. 27980.] Pp. 172–186.

—— EUSKIRCHEN. [See No. 28220.]

—— FRANCONIA. FRANGER, GABY: *Aufnahme und Vertreibung: zur Geschichte der jüdischen Gemeinden* [in Erlangen, Fürth, Nürnberg, Schwabach]. [See No. 28283.]

28027. — HOFFMAN, JOSEPH: *A mohel book from Lower Franconia from the years 1814–1868.* [In Hebrew]. [In]: Mechkerei Yerushalayim be-Folklor Yehudi (Jerusalem Studies in Jewish Folklore), No. 11–12, Jerusalem, June 1990. Pp. 152–157.

28028. — SIEGISMUND, WALTER: *Die jüdische Bevölkerungsgruppe im Seebachgrund.* [In]: Der Weisendorfer Bote aus dem Seebachgrund. Weisendorf, 1987. Pp. 52–72.

28029. — VÖLKL, BÄRBL: *Jüdisch-fränkische Familiensaga; von Scheßnitz in alle Welt.* [In]: Nordbayerischer Kurier, Nr. 166, Bayreuth, 20./21. Juli 1991. [Personal recollections of Kurt Land (formerly Landauer) about his family.]

28030. FRANKFURT am Main [See also No. 28286]. Frankfurt am Main. *Die Geschichte der Stadt in neun Beiträgen.* Hrsg.: Frankfurter Historische Kommission. Sigmaringen: Thorbecke, 1991. 631 pp., illus., notes, tabs., bibl. (585–589), index (persons, places, subjects; 591–630). [Refers passim and in special sections resp. chapters to Jews (131–136; 229–247; 269–277; 507–511). Incl. Nazi persecution.]

28031. — FRIEDRICHS, CHRISTOPHER R.: *The anti-Jewish movements in Frankfurt and Worms, 1612–1617: local crisis and Imperial response.* [In]: Proceedings of the 10th World Congress of Jewish Studies, 1989, Divisions B, Vol. 2: The history of the Jewish people. Jerusalem, 1990. Pp. 199–206.

28032. — HEIL, JOHANNES: *Vorgeschichte und Hintergründe des Frankfurter Pogroms von 1349.* [In]: Hessisches Jahrbuch für Landesgeschichte, Bd. 41, Marburg, 1991. Pp. 105–151, footnotes.

—— — KLEEBLATT, NORMAN L.: *Illustrating Jewish lifestyles on opposite banks of the Rhine: Alphonse Lévy's Alsatian peasants and Moritz Daniel Oppenheim's Frankfurt burghers.* [See No. 28588.]

28033. — WACHTEN, JOHANNES: *The historical background of the Frankfurt Haggadah, 1731.* [In Hebrew]. [In]: Proceedings of the 10th World Congress of Jewish Studies, 1989, Division B, Vol. 1: The history of the Jewish people. Jerusalem, 1990. Pp. 183–186.

28034. FÜRTH. [See also No. 27967.] GIERSCH, ROBERT: *Zwischenbericht zur Hausforschung Königstrasse 89: ein Fürther Anwesen und seine Bewohner.* [In]: Fürther Heimatblätter, N.F., Jg. 41, Nr. 3, Fürth, 1991. Pp. 81–91, geneal. tab., notes. [Refers to the family Fromm, founders of the first Hebrew printing-office.]

28035. — ROSSMEISSL, RALF: *Spuren des 'Fränkischen Jerusalem': zur jüdischen Geschichte Fürths.* [In]: Gerd Walther/Ralf Rossmeissl: Fürth – die Kleeblattstadt; Rundgänge durch Geschichte und Gegenwart. Fürth: Städtebilder Verlag, 1991. Pp. 25–37, illus.

28036. — *Nachrichten für den jüdischen Bürger Fürths,* Isr. Kultusgemeinde Fürth (Blumenstr. 31). Hrsg.: Ruben J. Rosenfeld (Blumenstr. 31). Sept. 1991. 47 pp., illus. [Incl.: Das Fürther jüdische Museumsgebäude (Siegfried Ziegler, 11–12). Zwischen Assimilation und traditionellem jüdischen Leben – zur Familie-Ortenau-Sammlung im jüdischen Regionalmuseum Fürth (Monika Bertholt, 16–18). Zur Genealogie des Rabbi David Dispeck (Mosche N. Rosenfeld, 28–31). Zebi Hirsch ben Chaim aus Fürth, Autor und Buchdrucker: ein Beitrag zum 300jährigen Fürther jüdischen Buchdruck (Mosche N. Rosenfeld, 34–40, facsims., geneal. tab.). Die Rolle der Fürther Juden im Ersten Weltkrieg (Werner Heymann, 42–46). Eine Liedflugschrift um 1800 mit hebräischen Lettern (Hermann Süss, 46–47, facsims.).]

28037. GELDERN (Kreis). ALBERT SPITZNER-JAHN: *Die Hoerstgener Juden – die 'älteste israelitische Gemeinde im Kreise Geldern'.* [In]: Der Niederrhein, 57. Jg., H. 2, Krefeld, April 1990. Pp. 103–106.

28038. GEVELSBERG. KAPPEL, ROLF: *unbekannt wohin verzogen: Jüdinnen und Juden in Gevelsberg.* Hrsg.: Gesellschaft für christlich-jüdische Zusammenarbeit Hagen und Umgebung e.V. Hagen: Reiner Padligur Verl., 1991. 135 pp., illus., docs., facsims. [Incl. Nazi period.]

28039. GIESSEN. BREITBACH, MICHAEL [et al.]: *Der Ausschluß der Juden aus den Gießener Märkten. Eine Untersuchung über das Verwaltungshandeln im Nationalsozialismus, zugleich ein Beitrag zur Geschichte des jüdischen Kleinhandels in der nationalsozialistischen Zeit.* [In]: Archiv für hessische Geschichte und Altertumskunde. Neue Folge, Bd. 48, Gießen 1990. Pp. 191–244, notes (239–244).

28040. GLOGAU. LUCAS, FRANZ D./HEITMANN, MARGRET: *Stadt des Glaubens. Geschichte und Kultur der Juden in Glogau.* Hildesheim: Olms, 1991. 582 pp., footnotes, illus., ports., maps, facsims., docs., lists of names, bibl., index of persons (567–581). (Wissenschaftliche Abhandlungen des Salomon Ludwig Steinheim-Instituts für deutsch-jüdische Geschichte, Bd.3: Beiträge zur Geschichte der Juden in Schlesien I.) [Cont. the history from the 13th century until 1942; also short biographies of 27 personalities (384–484).] [Cf.: Glogau – Stadt der Weisen und der Schriftgelehrten. Franz D. Lucas über Juden in seiner schlesischen Vaterstadt (Nathan Peter Levinson) [in]: Allgemeine', 47. Jg., Nr. 47, Bonn, 16. April 1992, p. 9.]

28041.   GODESBERG, BAD. BONDY, DAN: *Die jüdischen Grabsteine am Fuße des Godesberges – Dokumentation der Inschriften.* [In]: Godesberger Heimatblätter, Heft 29, Bad Godesberg, 1991. Pp. 5–39, illus.

28042.   GROSS-GERAU (Kreis). SCHLEINDL, ANGELIKA: *Verschwundene Nachbarn: jüdische Gemeinden und Synagogen im Kreis Gross-Gerau.* [Hrsg. vom Kreisausschuss des Kreises Gross-Gerau; Kreisvolkshochschule Gross-Gerau]. Gross-Gerau: Kreisvolkshochschule, 1990. 398 pp., illus., tabs. [Incl. Nazi period.]

———   HAMBURG. [See also No. 28200.]

28043.   — DOMKE, ELIEZER: *Yehude Hamburg 1928–1933: Kehilah be-'itot mashber.* Dissertation. Jerusalem: Hebrew University, 1990. 416 pp. [In Hebrew, with abstract in English: "Hamburg's Jewry 1928–1933: a community at a time of crisis".]

28044.   — *Ehemals in Hamburg zu Hause: Jüdisches Leben am Grindel.* Ursula Wamser/Wilfried Weinke (Hrsg.). Mit Beiträgen von Ulrich Bauch [et al.]. Hamburg, VSA-Verlag, 1991. 248 pp., illus., facsims., docs., index of names. [Covers also Nazi period.] [Cf.: Der Erinnerung ein Zuhause geben (Matthias Heyl) [in]: 'Allgemeine', Nr. 47/17, Bonn, 23. April 1992, p. 8.]

28045.   — FREIMARK, PETER: *Porträts von Rabbinern der Dreigemeinde Altona-Hamburg-Wandsbek aus dem 18. Jahrhundert.* [In]: Juden in Deutschland [see No. 27940]. Hamburg: Christians, 1991. Pp. 36–57, notes, ports.

28046.   — LOOSE, HANS DIETER: *Wünsche Hamburger Juden auf Änderung ihrer Vornamen und der staatliche Umgang damit. Ein Beitrag zur Geschichte des Antisemitismus im Hamburger Alltag 1866–1938* [In]: Juden in Deutschland [see No. 27940]. Hamburg: Christians, 1991. Pp. 58–80, notes.

28047.   — LOUVEN, ASTRID: *Vierhundert Jahre Juden in Hamburg;* Programm der Gedenkveranstaltungen zum 25. Okt. 1991 im Museum für Hamburgische Geschichte. Hamburg: Museum für Hamburgische Geschichte, 1991. 49 pp., illus., ports.

28048.   — STEIN, IRMGARD: *Lazarus Gumpel und seine Stiftungen für Freiwohnungen in Hamburg.* Hamburg: Christians, 1991. 236 pp., illus., notes, index of persons. (Hamburger Beiträge zur Geschichte der deutschen Juden, Bd. 18.)

28049.   — VIETH, HARALD: *Von der Hallerstraße 6/8 zum Isebek und Dammtor; jüdische Schicksale und Alltägliches aus Harvestehude-Rotherbaum in Hamburg seit der Jahrhundertwende.* Verbesserte Neuauflage. Hamburg: Selbstverlag Harald Vieth [Hallerstr. 8, 2000 Hamburg 13], 1991. 110 pp., illus., facsims., docs. [First edn. see No. 27036/YBXXXVI.]

28050.   — *Die Juden in Hamburg.* Wissenschaftliche Beiträge der Universität Hamburg zur Ausstellung 'Vierhundert Jahre Juden in Hamburg'. Hrsg. von Arno Herzig in Zusammenarbeit mit Saskia Rohde. Hamburg: Dölling und Galitz, 1991. 735 pp., notes, illus., tabs., facsims. (Die Geschichte der Juden in Hamburg 1590–1990; Bd. 2.) [Incl. English summaries of all articles. Cont. (titles condensed): Die Sephardim in Hamburg (Günter Böhm, 21–40). Die aschkenasischen Juden bis 1780 (Günter Marwedel, 41–60). Die Juden in Hamburg 1780–1860 (Arno Herzig, 61–76). Die jüdische Gemeinde 1860–1943 (Ina S. Lorenz, 77–100). Die jüdische Gemeinde seit den 50er Jahren (Raoul Wenzel Michalski, 101–112). Jüdisches Schulwesen in Hamburg 1780–1942 (Ursula Randt, 113–130). Jüdische Vereine in Hamburg (Erika Hirsch, 131–142). Synagogen im Hamburger Raum 1680–1943 (Saskia Rohde, 143–176). Das Oberrabbinat Altona-Hamburg-Wandsbek (Peter Freimark, 177–186). Schutzjuden und Betteljuden in Hamburg im 17. und 18. Jahrhundert (Peter Kromminga, 187–194). Die Gründung des Hamburger Tempels und seine Bedeutung für das Reformjudentum (Michael A. Meyer, 195–208). Die jüdische Gemeinde und ihr Armenwesen (Sybille Baumbach, 209–220). Glückel (von) Hameln (Andrea Misler, 221–226;. Fromet Gugenheim (Eva J. Engel, 227–236). Johanna Goldschmidt (Maya Fassmann, 237–248). Martha Freud (Astrid Louven, 249–262). Margarete Susman (Charlotte Ueckert, 263–274). Aus den Erinnerungen (Emma Isler, 275–276). Ein von Moses Mendelssohn gespendeter Toravorhang in der Altonaer Synagoge (Hermann Simon, 277–282). Sprachverhalten und Assimilation der portugiesischen Juden (Michael Studemund-Halévy, 283–298). Juden im Musikleben Hamburgs (Peter Petersen, 299–310). Jüdische Künstler an der Hamburger Oper (Stefan Wulf, 311–322). Jüdische Kulturgeschichte des Hauses Hartungstraße 9–11 (Barbara Müller-Wesemann, 323–332). Jüdische

Autoren im Exil (Rolf Eigenwald, 333–344). Jüdische Künstler im Nationalsozialismus (Maike Bruhns, 345–360). Die 'Gesellschaft für jüdische Volkskunde' in Hamburg (Christoph Daxelmüller, 361–382). Erwin Panofsky und das Kunsthistorische Seminar (Karen Michels, 383–392). Ernst Cassirer und Aby Warburg (Claudia Naber, 393–406). William Stern und das Psychologische Institut (Helmut E. Lück, 407–418). Hamburger jüdische Oberschicht im 19. Jahrhundert (Daniela Tiggemann, 419–430). Drei Juden in der Wirtschaft Hamburgs: Heine-Ballin-Warburg (Werner E. Mosse, 431–446). Jüdische Wohnstifte (Angela Schwarz, 447–458). Hamburg und die jüdische Auswanderung; Teil I: Um die Mitte des 19. Jahrhunderts (Cornelia Östreich, 459–466); Teil II: Von 1881–1914 (Karin Schulz, 467–474). Die antisemitische Bewegung in Hamburg 1873–1918 (Daniela Kasischke, 475–486). Forcierte Auswanderung und Enteignung 1933–1941 (Gaby Zürn, 487–498). Hamburgs öffentliche Fürsorge und die Juden 1933–1939 (Uwe Lohalm, 499–514). Die antisemitische Kampagne gegen die Firma Beiersdorf (Frank Bajohr/Joachim Szodrzynski, 515–526). Schülerschicksale während der NS-Zeit: Rolf Arno Baruch (Christiane Pritzlaff, 527–536). Der einsame Protest des Walter Gutmann (Beatrix Herlemann, 537–544). Jüdische Gefangene in Hamburger Konzentrationslagern (Detlef Garbe/Sabine Homann, 545–560). Juden in Wandsbek (Astrid Louven, 561–576). Die Verfolgung der Juden in Altona nach 1933 (Susanne Goldberg/Ulla Hinnenberg/ Erika Hirsch, 577–588). Der Untergang der jüdischen Gemeinde in Altona (Günter Hönicke, 589–600). Ausgrenzung, Vertreibung und Ermordung der Eimsbütteler Juden (Beate Meyer, 601–612). Juden in Hamburg in den ersten Nachkriegsjahren (Ursula Büttner, 613–632). Zur Entstehung der neuen Jüdischen Gemeinde 1945–1948 (Ina S. Lorenz/Jörg Berkemann, 633–656). Das Budge-Palais. Entziehung jüdischer Vermögen und Rückerstattung (Günter Könke, 657–668). Synagoge und Gemeindezentrum der neuen Jüdischen Gemeinde (Saskia Rohde, 669–678).]

28051.   — *Spuren der Vergangenheit sichtbar machen:* Beiträge zur Geschichte der Juden in Hamburg. Landeszentrale für Politische Bildung in Hamburg in Verbindung mit dem Institut für die Geschichte der deutschen Juden, Hamburg. Hrsg.: Peter Freimark/Franklin Kopitzsch. Hamburg: Landeszentrale für Politische Bildung, 1991. 123 pp., illus.

28052.   HAMM. BRAND, MECHTHILD: *Geachtet – geächtet: aus dem Leben Hammer Juden in diesem Jahrhundert.* Hamm: Stadt Hamm, 1991. 330 pp., illus., tabs.

————   HANOVER. [See also No. 28834.]

28053.   — SCHULZE, PETER: *Turnbruder und Chawer; zur Geschichte der jüdischen Sportbewegung in Hannover.* [In]: Sport in Hannover von der Stadtgründung bis heute. Hrsg.: Niedersächsisches Institut für Sportgeschichte Hoya e.V. Hoya: Niedersächsisches Institut für Sportgeschichte, 1991. pp. 153–158, illus.

28054.   HERFORD. *Juden in Herford:* 700 Jahre jüdische Geschichte und Kultur in Herford. Hrsg.: Christian Brade. Bielefeld: AJZ, 1990. 133 pp., illus., tabs. (Herforder Forschungen; Bd. 4.). [See also No. 28493.]

28055.   HESSE. BERDING, HELMUT/SCHIMPF, DOROTHEE: *Assimilation und Identität; Probleme des jüdischen Schul- und Erziehungswesens in Hessen-Kassel im Zeitalter der Emanzipation.* [In]: Nationale und kulturelle Identität. Studien zur Entwicklung des kollektiven Bewußtseins in der Neuzeit. Hrsg. von Bernhard Giesen. Frankfurt am Main: Suhrkamp, 1991. Pp. 350–387, footnotes.

28056.   — HEINEMANN, HARTMUT: *Wissenschaftliche Bearbeitung jüdischer Friedhöfe in Hessen.* [In]: Aschkenas, Bd. 1, Wien, 1991. Pp. 211–215, footnotes.

28057.   — *Juden – Hessen – Deutsche.* Beiträge zur Kultur- und Sozialgeschichte der Juden in Nordhessen. Hrsg. von Helmut Burmeister und Michael Dorhs. 3520 Hofgeismar: Verein für hessische Geschichte und Landeskunde e.V. 1834, Zweigverein Hofgeismar, 1991. 207 pp., notes, illus., index (198–204). (Die Geschichte unserer Heimat; Bd. 8) [A collection of articles partly original, partly reprinted from regional periodicals as a continuation of Fremde im eigenen Land [see No. 21900/YBXXXI], publ. by the same editors in 1985. On the religious, social and economic life of Jews in the villages and small towns. Incl. Jüdische Opfer der Nazizeit aus den Gemeinden der Altkreise Hofgeismar, Kassel und Wolfhagen; der Forschungsstand 1991 (Michael Dorhs, 163–176); also memoirs by émigrés.]

28058.   HOCHBERG. BICKHOFF-BÖTTCHER/BOLAY, GERTRUD/THEINER, EDUARD: *200 Jahre jüdisches Leben in Hochberg und Aldingen 1730–1930.* 7148 Remseck: Gemeinde Remseck am Neckar, 1990. 78 pp., illus., facsim., docs., tabs. (Heimatkundliche Schriftenreihe der Gemeinde Remseck am Neckar; Landschaft, Natur, Geschichte; 10.)

558 Bibliography

558 *Bibliography*

28059. HOHENFELD. SIEGISMUND, WALTER: *Der Ärger des Weisendorfer Seckendorff mit der Judenfamilie in Hohenfeld.* [In]: Der Weisendorfer Bote aus dem Seebachgrund, Weisendorf, 1987, Pp. 73–89.

28060. ICHENHAUSEN. *Juden auf dem Lande. Beispiel Ichenhausen.* Katalog zur Ausstellung. Herausgegeben vom Haus der Bayerischen Geschichte. München: Haus der Bayerischen Geschichte, 1991. 173 pp., illus. (Veröffentlichungen zur bayerischen Geschichte und Kultur, 22/91.) [Catalogue of an exhibition held in the former Synagogue in Ichenhausen, July 9 – Sept. 29, 1991. Obtainable at Stiftung Ehemalige Synagoge Ichenhausen, Landratsamt Günzburg, Postfach 249, 8870 Günzburg.] [Also refers to Nazi period.] [Cf.: Die Juden von Ichenhausen und die Mär von guter Nachbarschaft (Hanna Rheinz) [in]: Allgemeine Jüdische Wochenzeitung, Nr. 46/31, Bonn, 1. Aug. 1991, p. 3.]

28061. — WEGLEIN, ROLF: *Erinnerungen an Ichenhausen* [In]: Aufbau, Vol. 57, No. 16, pp. 5 & 16. [Also on Nazi persecution.]

28062. ISERLOHN. BETTGE, GÖTZ/KIRSTE, REINHARD: *Quellen zur Geschichte der Juden im Raum Iserlohn.* Hrsg.: Evang. Schulreferat; Stadtarchiv Iserlohn. Iserlohn: Evang. Schulreferat; Stadtarchiv, 1989, 42 pp., illus. (Beiträge und Mitteilungen/Stadtarchiv Iserlohn; H. 5.)

28063. ISSUM. BENGER, RUTH: *Die ehemalige Synagoge in Issum.* [In]: Geldrischer Heimatkalender 1990, Geldern, 1989. Pp. 35–39, illus.

28064. — VOGT, HANS: *Die einzige erhalten gebliebene Synagoge am Niederrhein – jetzt eine Gedenkstätte in Issum.* [In]: Der Niederrhein, 57. Jg., H. 4, Krefeld, Okt. 1990. Pp. 247–248, illus.

28065. JÜLICH. BERS, GÜNTER: *Jüdisches Vereinswesen in der Stadt Jülich 1892–1907.* [In]: Neue Beiträge zur Jülicher Geschichte, Hrsg.: Günter Bers [et al.], Bd. II, Jülich, 1991. Pp. 64–81, footnotes.

28066. KAIRLINDACH. GOLLWITZER, RAINER: *Ein Verzeichnis Kairlindacher Juden vom 1. Mai 1834.* [In]: Der Weisendorfer Bote aus dem Seebachgrund, Weisendorf, 1989. Pp. 217–220, facsims.

28067. — SIEGISMUND, WALTER: *Die geheimnisvolle Kairlindacher Judenurkunde.* [In]: Der Weisendorfer Bote aus dem Seebachgrund, Weisendorf, 1989. Pp. 209–216, illus. [On a document issued during the Thirty Years' War by the municipal council of Nuremberg as a pass for non-Jewish citizens, erroneously considered to be a Jewish document because of the citizens' biblical first names.]

28068. KAMEN. ASCHOFF, DIETHARD: '. . . *der ungehorsamen Juden wegen'. Zur Geschichte der Kamener Juden im Mittelalter.* [In]: Der Märker. Jg. 40, H. 1, Altena Jan./Feb. 1991. Pp. 3–11, footnotes.

28069. KASSEL. WATANABE-O'KELLY, HELEN: *"Mit dem höflichen Hut in der furchtsamen Hand". Die Beteiligung der Juden am fürstlichen Hochzeitsfest in Kassel (1740).* [In]: Bulletin des LBI, 88, Frankfurt am Main, 1991. Pp. 3–10, notes.

28070. KELSTERBACH. FREILING, HARALD: *Juden in Kelsterbach; jüdische Familien und jüdische Gemeinde in Kelsterbach zwischen 1774 und 1945.* 6092 Kelsterbach (Mörfelfelder Str. 52): H. Freiling, 1990. 44 pp.

28071. KISSINGEN (BAD). BECK, HANS-JÜRGEN/WALTER, RUDOLF: *Jüdisches Leben in Bad Kissingen.* Hrsg.: Stadt Bad Kissingen. 8740 Bad Neustadt: Rötter Druck & Verlag, 1990, 220 pp., illus., facsims., maps, notes (199–211), bibl., index. [Incl. errata sheet.] [Cont. the sections: I. Die jüdische Gemeinde in Bad Kissingen. Ein geschichtlicher Überblick (13–54). II. Antisemitismus in der Weimarer Republik (55–64). III. Ausgrenzung und Entrechtung unter dem NS-Regime (65–162). IV. Einzelschicksale (163–192). V. Jüdisches Leben in Bad Kissingen nach dem Krieg (193–194). VI. Zeittafel (195–198).

28072. KLEVE. PUYN, ALOIS: *Rabbiner überwachte 'Tomor'-Produktion.* [In]: Kalender für das Klever Land auf das Jahr 1991. 41. Jg. Kleve: Boss, 1990. Pp. 54–56. [On the margarine factory in Kleve, owned by the Jewish family van den Bergh, where a.o. products the only kosher margarine in Germany was produced.]

28073. KREUZNACH (BAD). MOLITOR, MATTHIAS/REISEK, JÖRG JULIUS: *Neue Erkenntnisse über den ältesten jüdischen Friedhof in Bad Kreuznach.* [In]: Beiträge zu jüdischen Geschichte in Rheinland-Pfalz, Jg. 1, Heft 1, Bad Kreuznach, 1991. Pp. 36–41, illus.

28074. KUNREUTH. WOLF, GERHARD PHILIPP: *Aus der Geschichte der ehemaligen Judengemeinde Kunreuth.* (Ofr.) bis zu ihrer Auflösung. [In]: Jahrbuch für fränkische Landesforschung, Bd. 51, Neustadt (Aisch), 1991. Pp. 71–102, notes.

28075. LADENBURG (Nordbaden). ARBEITSKREIS JÜDISCHE GESCHICHTE: *Die jüdischen Ladenburger. Ein Beitrag zur Stadtgeschichte.* Mannheim: Peter Wagener, 1991. 324 pp., illus., bibl., list of names (279–306), map. (Jüdische Bibliothek; Bd. 2.) [Compiled and written by a team, who started in 1983. The documentation was completed and written by Ulrike Haß-Zumkehr, Ulrich Schäfer, Ingrid Wagner, Sybille Wagner and Jürgen Zieher.]

28076. LANGENLONSHEIM. Höffler, Karl-Wilhelm: *Die Geschichte der jüdischen Gemeinde zu Langenlonsheim.* [In]: Beiträge zur jüdischen Geschichte in Rheinland-Pfalz, Jg. 1, Heft 1, 1991. Pp. 4–35, notes, illus. [Incl. Nazi period.]

28077. LEIPZIG. Grubel, Frederick: *Die Leipziger jüdische Gemeinde von Hitlers Machtübernahme (1933) bis zum Pogromwinter (1938/39).* Leipzig: Thomas, 1991. 18 pp. (Kirchliche Hochschule Leipzig; Forschungsstelle Judentum. Mitteilungen und Beiträge; 2.)

28078. — Klotz, Helmut/Weiss, Anne: *Leipziger Synagogalchor.* Red.: Helmut Klotz [et al.]. Leipzig: Juette, 1991 [?]. 25 pp., illus., music, ports. [Obtainable at the LBI New York.]

28079. LIMBURG. *Juden im Kreis Limburg-Weilburg.* Red.: Eugen Caspary. Limburg an der Lahn: Kreisausschuss des Landkreises Limburg-Weilburg, 1991. 135 pp., illus. (Schriftenreihe zur Geschichte und Kultur des Kreises Limburg-Weilburg.)

28080. LINNICH. Paulissen, Hermann Josef: *Die Israelitische Volksschule in Linnich 1926–1938.* [In]: Neue Beiträge zur Jülicher Geschichte, Hrsg.: Günter Bers [et al.]. Bd. I, Jülich, 1990. Pp. 27–59, illus.

28081. LIPPE. '. . . *dennoch Menschen von Gott erschaffen'. Die jüdische Minderheit in Lippe von den Anfängen bis zur Vernichtung.* Katalog und Arbeitsbuch zur Wanderausstellung. Hrsg. von der Stadt Detmold [et al.]. Bearbeitet von Dina van Faassen und Jürgen Hartmann. Bielefeld: Verlag für Regionalgeschichte, 1991. 133 pp., illus., facsims. [Incl.: Gedenkverzeichnis. Die Opfer der nationalsozialistischen Judenverfolgung in Lippe (127–133).]

28082. — *Vom Schutzjuden zum Staatsbürger jüdischen Glaubens*: Quellensammlung zur Geschichte der Juden in einem deutschen Kleinstaat (1650–1900). Bearb. von Klaus Pohlmann. Hrsg.: Herbert Stöwer [et al.]. [Detmold]: Lippischer Heimatbund, 1990. XXVII, 453 [11]pp., illus., bibl.

28083. LIPPSTADT. *Leben und Leiden der jüdischen Minderheit in Lippstadt.* Dokumentation zur Ausstellung der Stadt Lippstadt. Hrsg.: 4780 Stadt Lippstadt. Der Stadtdirektor: Stadtarchiv Lippstadt (Postfach 2540). 195 (?) pp., illus. (Lippstädter Spuren. Schriftenreihe des Heimatbundes Lippstadt; Sonderband/1991.)

28084. MARBURG. Schlich, Thomas: *Marburger jüdische Medizin- und Chirurgiestudenten*, 1800–1832; Herkunft, Berufsweg, Stellung in der Gesellschaft. Marburg: Elwert, 1990. 278 pp., ports., bibl. (237–264). (Academia Marburgensis; Bd. 6.)

28085. MECKLENBURG. Rohlén-Wohlgemut, Hilde: *Rapport om en rapport: Tychsens origineller Bericht über die Mecklenburgischen Juden von 1769.* [In]: Nordisk Judaistik, Jg. 11, H. 1–2, Abo, 1990. Pp. 81–84.

28086. MEDEBACH. Schäfer, Klaus: *Medebach und seine Ortschaften. Die Geschichte der jüdischen Gemeinde Medebach. Vom Anfang bis nach dem bitteren Ende.* Medebach: N. Schäfer, 1990. 192 pp., docs., facsim., notes, index of persons. (Schriften des Heimat- und Geschichtsvereins Medebach; H. 10). [Mimeog., obtainable at the Germania Judaica, Cologne.] [Covers also Nazi period.]

28087. METTMANN. Rauchenbichler, Ulrich/Schöttler, Gisela: *Juden im Kreis Mettmann: Bibliographie, Zeitzeugen zur Geschichte.* Hrsg.: Kreis Mettmann, Der Oberstadtdirektor, Kreisarchiv. Mettmann: Kreisarchiv, [1990]. 36 pp., illus.

—— MOERS. [See No. 28367.]

—— MONSCHAU. [See No. 28220.]

28088. MONTABAUR. Wild, Markus: *Montabaur. Die Geschichte der jüdischen Gemeinde.* Eine Dokumentation. Hrsg.: Stadt Montabaur. Montabaur, 1991. 184 [& 26] pp., illus., docs. [Covers also Nazi period.] [Revised and augmented version of No. 23045/YBXXXII.]

28089. MÜNSTER. Lindner, Erik: *Ein Schüler der Marks-Haindorfstiftung. Zu den Memoiren des Westfälischen Juden Jakob Ostwald (1838–1930).* [In]: Westfälische Zeitschrift, 141. Bd., Paderborn, 1991. Pp. 255–262.] [Memoirs from the archival collections of the Leo Baeck Institute in New York reflecting the social and economic life of Jews in Westphalia.]

28090. NIENBURG. Sabelleck, Rainer: *Jüdisches Leben in einer nordwestdeutschen Stadt:* Nienburg. Göttingen: Vandenhoeck & Ruprecht, 1991. 406 pp., tabs., footnotes, tabs., bibl., index of persons, index of places. (Veröffentlichungen des Max-Planck-Instituts für Geschichte, 99; D 7: Göttinger Philosophische Dissertation.) [Refers also to Nazi period.]

—— ODENBACH. Künzl, Hannelore: *Die Synagoge in Odenbach.* [See No. 28589.]

28091. OFFENBACH. Werner, Klaus: *Offenbach – eine jüdische Gemeinde der Einwanderer. Notizen von*

der Gründung bis zum Vorsitzenden Max Willner. [In]: Max Willner. Würdigung eines
verdienten Mannes [see No. 28582]. Frankfurt am Main: Landesverband der Jüdischen
Gemeinden in Hessen, 1991. Pp. 124–132.

28092. PAPENBURG. Eissing, Uwe: *Rückkehr in die Heimat. Ehemalige jüdische Bürger im Emsland oder
Gedanken zum Thema Heimat nach 'Auschwitz'*. [In]: Jahrbuch des Emsländischen Heimatbundes, Bd. 37, 4475 Sögel, 1991. Pp. 298–303.

28093. POSEN. Trzeciakowski, Lech: *Social and political changes among Jews of Poznan in the early 19th
century*. [In]: Proceedings of the 10th World Congress of Jewish Studies, 1989, Division B,
Vol. 2: The history of the Jewish people. Jerusalem, 1990. Pp. 289–296.

28094. RECKLINGHAUSEN. Peter, Jan Henning: *Jüdische Schüler am Gymnasium Petrinum in
Recklinghausen*. [In]: Vestische Zeitschrift. Zeitschrift der Vereine für Orts- und Heimatkunde im Vest Recklinghausen, Bd. 88/89, Recklinghausen, 1990. pp. 197–214. [Incl. list of
names.]

28095. REGENSBURG. Keil, Martha: *Ein Regensburger Judensiegel des 13. Jahrhunderts; zur
Interpretation des Siegels des Peter bar Mosche haLewi*. [In]: Aschkenas, Bd. 1, Wien, 1991. Pp.
135–150, footnotes.

28096. REMAGEN. Kleinpass, Hans: *Die Einweihung der Synagoge in Remagen anno 1869. Bereits 1863
Hauskollekte für den Neubau genehmigt*. [In]: Heimatjahrbuch 1991. Kreis Ahrweiler, Jg. 48,
Monschau, 1991. Pp. 111–115, notes.

28097. RHAUNEN. Weirich, Hilde/Stoll, Erich: *Beiträge zur Geschichte der Juden in Rhaunen*. [In]:
Mitteilungen des Vereins für Heimatkunde im Landkreis Birkenfeld und der Heimatfreunde Oberstein, Jg. 65, Birkenfeld, 1991. Pp. 95–184, illus., tabs., bibl. [Incl. cemetery.]

28098. RHINELAND. Heid, Ludger [et al.]: *Juden im Rheinland. I. Das antisemitische Vorurteil bis
1933*. Hrsg. von Lutz E. Reutter. Bearb. von Manfred Kremers. Düsseldorf: Landschafts-
verband Rheinland; Landesbildstelle, 1991. 80 pp., illus. [Accompanying publication to
slides series.]

28099. — Kirsch-Schäfer, H.: *Russische Juden im Rheinland*. [In]: Evangelische Kommentare, Jg.
23, Nr. 9, Stuttgart, 1990. Pp. 528–531.

28100. SAXONY. Muhs, Rudolf: *Verfassungsgebung und Judenfrage*. [In]: Dresdner Hefte. 8 Jg., H.
26, 2/91, Beiträge zur Kulturgeschichte 26. Pp. 31–35, illus.

——— SCHLEIDEN. [See No. 28220.]

28101. SCHLESWIG-HOLSTEIN. *Zwischen gestern und heute;* Erinnerungen jüdischen Lebens
ehemaliger Schleswig-Holsteiner zusammengestellt und eingeleitet von Gerhard Stolz.
Herausgegeben von der Jüdischen Gemeinde Hamburg. Heide: Boyens, 1991. 154 pp.,
illus. [Cont. 20 personal recollections (three written in English) of former citizens of Altona,
Flensburg, Friedrichstadt, Kiel, Lübeck.] [Cf.: Besprechung [in]: Allgemeine Jüdische
Wochenzeitung, Nr. 46/14, Bonn, 4. April 1991, p. 9.]

28102. SCHMIEHEIM. Pommerening, Günther: *Die Juden in Schmieheim*; Untersuchung zur
Geschichte und Kultur der Judenheit in einer badischen Landgemeinde. Hamburg, Univ.,
Diss., 1990. 228 [31] pp., illus., notes. [Incl.: Liste der jüdischen Bürger (167–182).]

28103. SCHÖNEBECK. Kuntze, Günter: *Juden in Schönebeck*. Hrsg.: Kreismuseum Schönebeck,
1991. Schönebeck: Kreismuseum, [1991]. 84 pp., illus.

28104. SCHWÄBISCH-GMÜND. Seidel, Ortrud: *Mut zur Erinnerung: Geschichte der Gmünder
Juden*; eine persönliche Spurensuche. Schwäbisch-Gmünd: Einhorn, 1991. 207 pp., illus.

28105. SIEGEN. *Die jüdischen Friedhöfe im Kreis Siegen-Wittgenstein*. Hrsg.: Gesellschaft für Christ-
lich-Jüdische Zusammenarbeit Siegerland e.V. in Zusammenarbeit mit Klaus Dietermann,
Johanna Morgenstern-Wulff und Ruth Röcher. Siegen: Gesellschaft für Christlich-Jüdische
Zusammenarbeit, 1991. 56 pp., illus., map.

28106. SIEGERLAND. Dietermann, Klaus: *Jüdische Begräbnisplätze im Siegerland. Vom Zerfall
bedroht – Denkmalschutz gefordert*. [In]: Siegerland, Blätter des Siegerländer Heimat- und
Geschichtsvereins, Bd. 68, H. 3–4, 5900 Siegen, 1991. Pp. 59–69, illus.

——— SINGEN (Hohentwiel). [See No. 28421.]

28107. SOBERNHEIM. Berkemann, Hans-Eberhard: *Sobernheims jüdischer Friedhof auf dem
Domberg*. [In]: Landeskundliche Vierteljahrsblätter, Jg. 36, Trier, 1990. Pp. 5–22, notes,
illus., facsims.

28108. STEINFURT (Kreis). Feld, Willi: *Die Geschichte der Juden im Kreis Steinfurt [Westphalia] von
den Anfängen bis zur Vernichtung*. Unter zeitweiliger Mitarbeit von Thomas Starosta. Hrsg.:
Kreis Steinfurt, Der Oberkreisdirektor. Steinfurt: Kreis Steinfurt, Oberkreisdirektor, 1991.
155 pp., illus. (Steinfurter Hefte; 13.)

28109. STOLP. SALINGER, GERHARD: *Zwischen Zeit und Ewigkeit: ein Rückblick und Beitrag zum Leben und Schicksal der Juden in Stolp in Pommern*. With English Summary. D-2000 Wedel: Prismaoffice, 1991. IV, 152 pp., illus. [Cf.: Besprechung (Adolf Diamant) [in]: 'Allgemeine', Nr. 47/18, Bonn, 30. April 1992, p. 11.]

28110. STUTTGART. KLÖPPING, KARL: *Historische Friedhöfe Alt-Stuttgarts. Sankt Jakobus bis Hoppenlau*. Ein Beitrag zur Stadtgeschichte mit Wegweiser zu den Grabstätten des Hoppenlaufriedhofs. Hrsg.: Landeshauptstadt Stuttgart, Friedhofsamt. Stuttgart: Klett-Cotta, 1991. 391 pp., illus., maps, names lists, notes, index. [Refers also to the Jewish cemetery, opened in 1834 in the vicinity of the Hoppenlau-Friedhof. See also No. 25132/YBXXXIV.]

28111. SULZBURG. GROSSPIETSCH, JOST, ed.: *Spuren: Ehemalige Synagoge Sulzburg*. Sulzburg: Freundeskreis Synagoge Sulzburg, 1991. [20] pp., illus., facsims., maps, table.

28112. TRIER. HAVERKAMP, ALFRED: *Die Juden im Erzstift Trier während des Mittelalters*. [In]: Die Juden in ihrer mittelalterlichen Umwelt [see No. 27942]. Wien: Böhlau, 1991. Pp. 67–90.

28113. ULM. *Zeugnisse zur Geschichte der Juden in Ulm. Erinnerungen und Dokumente*. Hrsg. vom Stadtarchiv Ulm. Ulm, 1991. 271 pp., illus., facsims., ports., index (269–270). [Incl. memoirs; covers also Nazi period.]

28114. VIERSEN. *Geschichte der Juden im Kreis Viersen*. Hrsg. Oberkreisdirektor. Red.: Gerhard Rehm. 455 pp., illus., tabs. Viersen: Kreis Viersen, 1991. (Schriftenreihe des Kreises Viersen (vormals Kempen-Krefeld); Bd. 38.) [Cont.: Judenpolitik in den niederrheinischen Territorien in der frühen Neuzeit (Andreas Schneider, 11–24, footnotes). Die erste kurkölnische Judenordnung von 1592; zur Situation der Juden in Kurköln am Ende des 16. Jahrhunderts (Horst Dinstühler, 25–38, footnotes). Die französische Judenpolitik und Judengesetzgebung im Rheinland (Jörg Engelbrecht, 39–49, footnotes). Das rheinische Judentum unter preußischer Herrschaft im 19. und 20. Jahrhundert (Arie Nabrings, 51–80, footnotes, bibl.). Zum Schicksal der rheinischen Juden 1933–1945 (Hans Kaiser, 81–106, footnotes). Zur Verwaltungsgeschichte der Synagogengemeinde im heutigen Kreis Viersen 1808–1939 (Paul Günter Schulte, 107–126, footnotes). Gemeindeleben, Volksfrömmigkeit und religiöses Brauchtum (Uwe Cordt, 127–143, footnotes). Juden in Schwalmtal (Johann Jakob Manten, 145–157, footnotes, illus., facs.). Zur Geschichte der Juden in Brüggen, Born und Bracht (Gerhard Rehm, 159–174, footnotes, illus.) Aus der Geschichte der Juden im Gebiet der heutigen Stadt Nettetal (Leo Peters, 175–207, footnotes, illus., facsims., lists of names). Geschichte der Oedter Juden (Johannes Lipp, 209–254, footnotes, illus., geneal. tabs., lists of names). Juden in Grefrath (Johannes Lipp/Gerhard Rehm, 255–271, footnotes, illus., facsim., geneal. tabs.). Geschichte der jüdischen Gemeinde Kempen (Friedhelm Weinforth, 273–306, footnotes, illus., list of names). Juden in Viersen (Jochem Ulrich 307–338, footnotes, illus., tabs., list of names). Die Geschichte der Juden in Süchteln (Arie Nabrings, 339–354, footnotes, illus., docs., lists of names). Die Geschichte der Juden in Dülken (Arie Nabrings, 355–388, footnotes, illus., lists of names). Die Vorster Juden und ihr Schicksal im 3. Reich (Willi Schmidt, 389–399, footnotes, illus.). Aus der Geschichte der jüdischen Bürger von St Tönis (Paul Wietzorek, 401–428, footnotes, illus., tabs., lists of names). Jüdische Gemeinden in Anrath, Neersen, Schiefbahn und Willich (Ludwig Hügen, 429–455, footnotes, illus.).]

28115. WALLDORF. HERRMANN, DIETER: *Geschichte und Schicksal der Walldorfer Juden*. Hrsg.: Vereinigung Walldorfer Heimatfreunde; Stadtverwaltung Walldorf. 1985. 48 pp., illus. [Incl. Nazi period.]

28116. WESTPHALIA. ASCHOFF, DIETHARD: *Niemand soll sein Haar in nichjüdischer Weise schneiden. Christlich-jüdische Beziehungen bis zum 13. Jahrhundert in Westfalen*. [In]: Der Davidstern; Zeichen der Schmach – Symbol der Hoffnung [see No. 27924]. Dorsten, 1991. Pp. 40–43.

28117. — NAARMANN, MARGIT: *Daß Jude und Christ ihr Brot gemeinsam in Eintracht brechen . . .'. Die antijüdischen Ausschreitungen in Geseke und Störmede im Jahr 1844 als historischer Hintergrund für Else Lasker-Schülers Drama Arthur Aronymus und seine Väter*. [In]: Menora, Bd. 2, München, 1991. Pp. 339–370, notes.

28118. — *Auch Selbstdarstellung. Mit breiter Krempe und hornartiger Verlängerung; Judenhut und Judenring in Westfalen* [no author]. [In]: Der Davidstern; Zeichen der Schmach – Symbol der Hoffnung [see No. 27924]. Dorsten, 1991. Pp. 50–54.

28119. WEYERBUSCH. MOOG, HORST: *Gesuch zur Errichtung einer Synagoge in Weyerbusch*. [In]: Heimat-Jahrbuch des Kreises Altenkirchen (Westerwald), Jg. 34, Altenkirchen, 1991. Pp. 163–164.

28120. WIESBADEN. *Osteuropäisches Judentum in Wiesbaden.* Hrsg. vom Förderkreis Aktives Museum Deutsch-Jüdischer Geschichte in Wiesbaden. Red.: Dorothee Lottmann-Kaeseler. Wiesbaden: Seyfried, 1991. 224 pp., illus., tabs.

—— WITTEN. [See No. 28442.]

28121. WORMS. EIDELBERG, SHLOMO: *R. Juspa, shammash of Worms: Jewish life in 17th-century Worms.* [In Hebrew]. Jerusalem: Magnes Press, Hebrew University, 1991. 242, 111 (English) pp. [An edition of three works by Yiftah Joseph Juspa Halevy (1604–1678), known as Juspa Shammash ("Schammes", see No. 26675/YBXXXV), here given in Hebrew and English, and facsimile of the original Hebrew manuscript (pp. 107–242 of the Hebrew section). Contents of the English section: Introduction (9–14). "Minhagim" of the Holy Community Warmaisa (15–45). Sefer Ma'ase Nissim – The Book of Wonder Stories (47–93). Pinkas Hakehila – The Ledger of Commercial Contracts, Community of Worms (excerpts) (95–108).]

—— — FRIEDRICHS, CHRISTOPHER R.: *The anti-Jewish movements in Frankfurt and Worms, 1612–1617.* [See No. 28031.]

28122. — FRIEDRICHS, CHRISTOPHER R.: *Anti-Jewish politics in early modern Germany: the uprising in Worms, 1613–17.* [In]: Central European History, Vol. 23, Nos. 2/3, Atlanta, Ga., June/Sept. 1990. Pp. 91–152, footnotes.

1a. Alsace

28123. HYMAN, PAULA E.: *The emancipation of the Jews of Alsace: acculturation and tradition in the nineteenth century.* New Haven, Ct.: Yale Univ. Press, 1991. VIII, 214 pp., map, tabs., notes, bibl. (191–208).

28124. KAUFMANN, URI: *The impact of the French Revolution on rural Jewry in Alsace, Baden and Switzerland: a comparison.* [In]: Proceedings of the 10th World Congress of Jewish Studies, 1989, Division B, Vol. 2: The history of the Jewish people. Jerusalem, 1990. Pp. 239–242.

—— KLEEBLATT, NORMAN L.: *Illustrating Jewish lifestyles on opposite banks of the Rhine: Alphonse Lévy's Alsation peasants and Moritz Daniel Oppenheim's Frankfurt burghers.* [See No. 28588.]

2. Austria

28125. ALTENSTADT (FELDKIRCH). BURMEISTER, KARL HEINZ: *Die Juden in Altenstadt (Feldkirch) 1663–1667.* [In]: Montfort, 43. Jg., H. 4, Dornbirn, 1991. Pp. 250–260.

28126. GALICIA. HÖDL, KLAUS: *Vom Shtetl an die Lower East Side. Galizische Juden in New York.* Wien: Böhlau, 1991, 305 pp., illus., bibl. (Böhlaus zeitgeschichtliche Bibliothek; 19.)

28127. HOHENEMS. BURMEISTER, KARL HEINZ: *Der Musikverein der Israeliten in Hohenems von 1831.* [In]: Montfort, 43, Jg., H. 3, Dornbirn, 1991. Pp. 185–188, notes, facsim.

28128. — BURMEISTER, KARL HEINZ: *Hohenems zur Jugendzeit Salomon Sulzers.* [In]: Salomon Sulzer – Kantor, Komponist, Reformer. [And]: PURIN, BERNHARD: *Die Levi-Sulzer. Geschichte einer jüdischen Familie in Vorarlberg* [see in No. 28591]. Bregenz, 1991. Pp. 16–25 [&] 38–51.

28129. — GRABHERR, EVA: *'was wir fir bicher habn wie folgt!': eine bürgerliche Bibliothek [der Familie Levi-Löwenberg, Hohenems, um 1830].* [In]: Montfort, Jg. 42, Dornbirn, 1990. Pp. 288–292, notes.

28130. — JÜDISCHES MUSEUM HOHENEMS: *Texte im Museum. – Texts in the museum.* Transl. by Michael Hastik. A-6845 Hohenems: Jüdisches Museum Hohenems, 1991. 23 leaves, illus.

28131. — STUMPF, JOSEF: *Das neue Jüdische Museum in Hohenems: Haus der Toleranz gegenüber Minderheiten.* [In]: Allgemeine Jüdische Wochenzeitung, Nr. 46/31, Bonn, 1. Aug. 1991. P. 5, illus.

28132. *(Das) Jüdische Echo.* Zeitschrift für Kultur und Politik. Hrsg.: Vereinigung Jüdischer Hochschüler und Jüdischer Akademiker Österreichs. Wien (Gonzagagasse 22). Okt. 1991. 270 pp., illus., notes. [Cont. the sections: Zum Geleit (pp. 5–23; incl. the essays): Schatten: das jüdische Erbe Mitteleuropas – das mitteleuropäische Erbe der Juden (Steven Beller, 5–7). Jüdisches Mitteleuropa bis 1938 (Erhard Busek, 10–13). Tradition als Zukunftsaufgabe: das jüdische Erbe Wiens (Helmut Zilk, 13–14). Mitteleuropa und die Juden (pp. 26–165; incl.): Die Leopoldstadt (Ernst Molden, 26–28). 'Österreicher – sans phrase . . .': jüdische Positionen in der Nationalitätenfrage (Klaus Hödl, 28–36), Auf Mitteleuropas Wegen und

Irrwegen: Notizen zu jüdischen Denkmälern in Mitteleuropa (Alfons Dalma, 37–41). 'Für Juden, Sesselträger und Fiaker': der Kampf um die Einheit der Wiener jüdischen Gemeinde (Jonny Moser, 48–51). Selbstaufgabe und Selbstbehauptung: europäische Identität und jüdischer Geist (Norbert Leser, 69–72). Wider die falsche Idylle: Österreich, Wien um 1900 (Anton Pelinka, 77–79). Fröhliche Apokalypse: jüdische Intellektuelle, Modernität und Massenpolitik im Wien des Fin de siècle (Robert S. Wistrich, 79–84). Lemberg, Krakau, Kolomea . . .: Galizien zum Gedenken (Lola Blonder, 129–131). Gilgul und Galizien: über den Schriftsteller Hermann Blumenthal (Gabriele Kohlbauer-Fritz, 140–144). Jüdische Ruinen: eine Reise nach Galizien und in die Bukowina (Rüdiger Wischenbart, 144–149). Literatur, Kunst, Wissenschaft (pp. 168–236). Israel heute (238–270). Further essays are listed according to subject.]

28133. LICHTBLAU, ALBERT: '*Man kann einen Menschen aus der Heimat vertreiben, aber nicht die Heimat aus dem Menschen.*' Die Österreicher und die Zweite Republik im Blickfeld der Lebensgeschichte von Autoren österreichisch-jüdischer Herkunft. [In]: Zeitgeschichte, Jg. 18, H. 7/8, Wien, 1990/1991. Pp. 209–223, notes [incl. bibliographical references] (217–222).

28134. LOHRMANN, KLAUS: *Judenpolitik in Österreich bis 1420.* [In]: Die Juden in ihrer mittelalterlichen Umwelt [see No. 27942]. Wien: Böhlau, 1991. Pp. 113–130.

28135 LOHRMANN, KLAUS: *Eine schwierige Emanzipation. Die Lage der Juden in Österreich 1848–1867* [in]: Salomon Sulzer – Kantor, Komponist, Reformer [see in No. 28591]. Bregenz, 1991. Pp. 38–51.

28136. *Österreichisch-jüdisches Geistes- und Kulturleben.* Bd. 3. Hrsg.: Liga der Freunde des Judentums (A-1090 Wien, Postfach 150). Wien: Literas-Universitätsverlag, 1990. 117 pp. [Cont.: Großhändler, Bankiers und Industrielle – Juden in der ersten Hälfte des 19. Jahrhunderts (Gertrude Wagner, 1–16). . . . auch nicht von der Frau Hinterhuber (Alexander A. Bankier, 17–38). Jüdische Sozialwissenschaftler (Norbert Leser, 86–117).]

28137. PALME, RUDOLF: *Zur spätmittelalterlichen und frühneuzeitlichen Sozial- und Rechtsgeschichte der Juden in Tirol.* [In]: Die Juden in ihrer mittelalterlichen Umwelt [see No. 27942]. Wien: Böhlau, 1991. Pp. 183–204.

28138. SALMON, YOSEF: *The emergence of a Jewish nationalist consciousness in Eastern Europe during the 1860s and 1870s.* [In]: AJS Review, Vol. 16, Nos. 1–2, Cambridge, Ma., Spring–Fall 1991. Pp. 107–132, footnotes. [Incl. Galicia; also deals with Yiddish and Hebrew press in parts of Germany; the Hebrew journalist David Gordon.]

28139. SCHASER, ANGELIKA: *Die Juden Siebenbürgens vom 16. bis zum 18. Jahrhundert.* Mathias Bernath zum 70. Geburtstag. [In]: Südost-Forschungen, Bd. IL, München 1990, Pp. 57–94, footnotes, docs., facsims, bibl.

28140. SPITZER, SHLOMO: *The study of the Torah in the yeshivot in Austria during the 14th–15th centuries.* [In Hebrew]. [In]: Proceedings of the 10th World Congress of Jewish Studies, 1989, Division B., Vol. 1: The history of the Jewish people. Jerusalem, 1990. Pp. 137–144.

28141. STERNFELD, ALBERT: *Betrifft: Österreich. Von Österreich betroffen.* Wien: Löcker, 1990. 253 pp., facsims., docs., [On post-war Austrian attitudes to the Jews, denazification, return of expellees, restitution, antisemitism.]

28142. SULZ. PURIN, BERNHARD: *Die Juden von Sulz. Eine jüdische Gemeinde in Vorarlberg 1676–1744.* [In]: Studien zur Geschichte und Gesellschaft Vorarlbergs; 9. Bregenz: Vorarlberger Autoren Gesellschaft, 1991.

28143. VIENNA. FREIDENREICH, HARRIET PASS: *Jewish politics in Vienna, 1918–1938.* Bloomington: Indiana Univ. Press, 1991, VII, 272 pp., illus., maps, tabs., appendix, bibl. (259–263), notes.

28144. — FREIDENREICH, HARRIET PASS: *Jewish nationalist politics in Vienna: the failure of Landespolitik.* [In]: Shofar, Vol. 9, No. 2, West Lafayette, In., Purdue Univ., Winter 1991. Pp. 44–54, footnotes.

28145. — GILBOA, MENUHA: *The Hebrew press in Vienna in the second half of the 19th century.* [In Hebrew, with English summary]. [In]: Qesher, No. 10, Tel-Aviv, Nov. 1991. Pp. 49–54.

28146. — VARON, BENNO WEISER: *The Jews in fin-de-siècle Vienna.* [In]: Midstream, Vol. 37, No. 5, New York, Aug./Sept. 1991. Pp. 24–27.

28147. — *Vienna 1900: from Altenberg to Wittgenstein.* Ed. by Edward Timms and Ritchie Robertson. Edinburgh: Edinburgh Univ. Press, 1990. XIV, 216 pp., illus. [First annual vol. about the cultural traditions of the Habsburg Empire and Austrian Republic, emphasises Viennese literary studies at the turn of the century; articles range from Altenberg's fabricated photographs to Herzl's and Freud's Jewish identity; incl. (titles condensed): Five unpublished Sketches by Peter Altenberg (Leo A. Lensing, 47–72). The tendentious reception of (Schnitzler's) Professor Bernhardi (W. E. Yates, 108–125). Cont. also review articles.]

28148. WISTRICH, ROBERT S.: *The Jews and nationality conflicts in the Habsburg lands.* An inaugural lecture for the Jewish Chronicle Chair of Jewish Studies delivered at University College London, 13 November 1991. London: University College London, 1991. 29 pp.

28149. WISTRICH, ROBERT S.: *Habsburg, Jews and the Holy Land.* [In]: The Jewish Quarterly, Vol. 37, No. 4, London, Winter 1990–1991. Pp. 43–44. [Speech on the occasion of Otto von Habsburg's visit to the Hebrew University where he was awarded an honorary fellowship.]

B. Czechoslovakia

28150. BOHEMIA. WLASCHEK, RUDOLF M.: *Jüdisches Leben in Trautenau/Nordostböhmen; ein historischer Rückblick.* Dortmund: Forschungsstelle Ostmitteleuropa (4600 Dortmund 50, Universität, Postfach 50 05 00), 1991. 74 pp., illus., facsims., tabs., bibl. (Veröffentlichungen der Forschungsstelle Ostmitteleuropa an der Universität Dortmund, Reihe B, Bd. 44.) [Covers also Nazi period.]

28151. HAHN, FRED: *Masaryk und die Juden.* [In]: Das Jüdische Echo, Vol. 40, Nr. 1, Wien, Okt. 1991. Pp. 101–106, notes. [Also in this issue]: Verspätet, aber dennoch zeitgemäss: die Geschichte der slowakischen Juden (Juraj Spitzer, 108–113, illus.). Der unvergessene Prager Kreis (Alfred Joachim Fischer, 113–119).

28152. HOFFER, GERDA: *The Utitz legacy: a personalized history of Central European Jewry.* Jerusalem: Posner and Sons, 1988. 187 pp. [On the Utitz family of Bohemia and Prague. For German version and author's data see No. 27778/YBXXXVI.]

28153. IVANOVA, TATIANA: *Eine altmodische Geschichte: Sigmund Steiner, Bratislava, Buch- und Musikalienhandlung, wissenschaftliches Kunstantiquariat, gegründet 1847.* [In]: Börsenblatt für den Deutschen Buchhandel, Jg. 158, H. 67, Frankfurt am Main & Leipzig, 23. Aug. 1991. Pp. 2714–2717. [On the history of the once famous new and antiquarian book shop, reopened in 1991.]

28154. *Judaica Bohemiae.* Vol. 27, Nos. 1–2. Publié par le Musée juif d'Etat, Prague. Secrétaire de la rédaction: Jirina Sedinová. Praha: Státni zidovské muzeum v Praze, 1991, 111 pp., illus., footnotes. [1 issue.] [Incl.: Comenius and MaHaRal; the historical background of the parallels in their teachings (Otto D. Kulka, 17–30). Jewish Hebrew studies in the Czech lands in the pre-enlightenment and enlightenment periods; part III: beginnings of modern teaching of Hebrew at the main Jewish school in Prague (Bedrich Nosek, 31–44). The Jewish cemetery in Trebic (Vlastimila Hamacková/Jirina Sedinová, 82–91). Further contributions are listed according to subject.]

28155. KIEVAL, HILLEL JOSEF: *Die Geschichte der Juden in Böhmen, Mähren und der Slowakei bis 1918.* [In]: Das Jüdische Museum in Prag [see No. 28166]. Berlin: Dietz Nachf., 1991. Pp. 38–60.

28156. MANN, VIVIAN: *Symbole des Vermächtnisses; aus jüdischem Gemeindeleben in Böhmen und Mähren.* [In]: Das Jüdische Museum in Prag [see No. 28166] Berlin: Dietz Nachf., 1991. Pp. 152–220.

28157. NAZI PERIOD. FATRAN, GILA: *Dr. Franz Kahn.* [In Hebrew, with English summary]. [In]: Yalkut Moreshet, No. 51, Tel-Aviv, Nov. 1991. Pp. 69–79. [F.K., Zionist leader in Czechoslovakia, deported to Theresienstadt, perished in Auschwitz.]

28158. PRAGUE. IGGERS, WILMA A.: *Die Prager Juden zwischen Assimilation und Zionismus.* [In]: Berlin und der Prager Kreis [see No. 28666]. Pp. 19–30.

28159. — KAFKA, FRANTISEK: *Zur Geschichte der jüdischen Gemeinde in Prag.* [In]: Berlin und der Prager Kreis [see No. 28666]. Pp. 9–18.

28160. — OEGEMA, GERBERN S.: *Von Prag aus in die ganze Welt. Kaiser Karl schenkte der Judenschaft eine Fahne mit goldenem Stern.* [In]: Der Davidstern; Zeichen der Schmach – Symbol der Hoffnung [see No. 27924]. Dorsten, 1991. Pp. 70–73.

28161. — OLMEROVA, HELENA: *Ritualbad bei der Pinkas-Synagoge in der Prager Altstadt.* [In]: Judaica Bohemiae, Vol. 27, No. 1–2, Prague, 1991, pp. 69–78.

28162. — SADEK, VLADIMIR: *Silber als Symbol der Thora.* [In]: Judaica Bohemiae, Vol. 27, No. 1–2, Prague, 1991, pp. 49–53. [On the exclusive use of silver for religious objets d'art in Prague during the early modern and pre-Enlightenment period.]

28163. — SEDINOVA, JIRINA: *Volksdruck der Megilla Esther.* [In]: Judaica Bohemiae, Vol. 27, No. 1–2,

Prague, 1991, pp. 45–48. [On woodcuts from the collection housed in the Klausen Synagogue in Prague since 1984.]

28164. — SMEJKALOVA, JANA: *The message of the banner of Marcus Mordecai Mayzl.* [In]: Judaica Bohemiae, Vol 27, No. 1–2, Prague, 1991, pp. 54–64. [M. M. Mayzl, financier, tradesman, mayor of the Jewish town in the second half of the sixteenth century.]

28165. — VILIMKOVA, MILADA: *Le ghetto de Prague.* Prague: Artia, 1990. 231 pp.

28166. — *Das Jüdische Museum in Prag. Von schönen Gegenständen und ihren Besitzern.* Hrsg. von der Alten Synagoge Essen; Edna Brocke/Michael Zimmermann. Berlin: Dietz Nachf., 1991, 239 pp., illus. [Accompanying catalogue book to an exhibition held at the Alte Synagoge in Essen from Sept. 22 with the same title, 1991 until Jan. 2, 1992. Incl.: Von schönen Gegenständen und ihren Besitzern. Eine Ausstellung in der Alten Synagoge in Essen (Edna Brocke/ Michael Zimmermann, 10–37). Das jüdische Museum 1906–1942 (Arno Parik, 113–126). Das Schicksal des Jüdischen Museums während der deutschen Besatzung (Hana Volavková, 129–151). Das Staatliche Jüdische Museum der Nachkriegszeit (Ludmila Kybalová, 221–223). Further contributions are listed according to subject.]

28167. — *Judaica Prag. Aus dem Staatlichen Jüdischen Museum Prag.* Hrsg.: Berthold Roland [&] Bundeskanzleramt. Mainz: Zabern, 1991. 96 pp., illus. [Catalogue of an exhibition held at Bonn, Bundeskanzleramt May 8–June 14, 1991 and Nürnberg, Germ. Nationalmuseum June 20–July 31, 1991.] [Incl.: Zum Geleit (Helmut Kohl, 7). Vorwort (Gerhard Bott, 8). Judaica aus den Sammlungen des Staatlichen Jüdischen Museums in Prag (Vladimir Sadek, 9–14). Zur Ausstellung und zum Katalog (Klaus Pechstein, 14–15).]

28168. — *Die Prager Judenstadt.* Text von Milada Vilímkova. Zum Andenken an Dr Otto Muneles. 2. Aufl. Ins Deutsche übertragen von Helena Tomanová-Weisová. Hanau: Dausien, 1991. 234 pp., illus., notes, bibl., index of names, of subjects (228–234). [Incl. the chaps.: I. Geschichte; II. Das Prager Ghetto; III. Hervorragende Persönlichkeiten der Judenstadt; IV. Die Prager Synagogen; V. Der Alte Jüdische Friedhof; VI. Die Kunst im Prager Ghetto.] [1st edn. Aventinum 1990.]

28169. ROTHKIRCHEN, LIVIA: *Die tschechoslowakische Judenheit: Aufstieg und Niedergang 1919–1989.* [In]: Das Jüdische Museum in Prag [see No. 28166]. Berlin: Dietz Nachf., 1991. Pp. 90–112.

28170. TEUFEL, HELMUT: *Neuere Literatur zur Geschichte der Juden in Böhmen und Mähren* (Berichtszeitraum 1945–1990). [In]: Aschkenas, Bd. 1, Wien, 1991. Pp. 173–193.

4. Hungary

——— BUDAPEST. PRESSBURGER, GIORGIO & NICOLA: *Die Gesetzestafeln der Selma Grün. Geschichten aus dem achten Bezirk.* [See No. 28828.]

28171. CONGDON, LEE: *Exile and social thought: Hungarian intellectuals in Germany and Austria, 1891–1933.* Princeton, N.J.: Princeton Univ. Press, 1991. 329 pp., illus. [Incl., a.o.: Georg Lukács, Alexander Korda, Karl Mannheim, G. W. Pabst.]

28172. KONRAD, GYÖRGY: *Unsere Galuth-Insel: Juden in Ungarn.* [In]: Das Jüdische Echo, Vol. 40, Nr. 1, Wien, Okt. 1991. Pp. 89–92. [Also in this issue]: Spion der Seele: auf den Spuren György Konráds (Hans-Henning Paetzke, 94–99) Ungarische Biographie (Gábor Székély, 99–100).

28173. KÜHNER, CLAUDIA: *Das Rabbinerseminar von Budapest: Geschichte einer Hochburg jüdischer Wissenschaft.* Bilder [von] Verena Eggmann. [In]: Neue Zürcher Zeitung, Nr. 142, 22./23. Juni 1991. Pp. 85–87, illus. [Deals also with recent events.]

28174. SANDERS, IVAN: *Jewish revival in Central Europe: a survey of recent Hungarian Judaica.* [In]: Jewish Book Annual, Vol. 49 (1991–1992), New York, 1991. Pp. 34–47, footnotes.

5. Switzerland

28175. KAUFMANN, URI: *Geschichte der Juden im Bereich der heutigen Schweiz in Mittelalter und früher Neuzeit*; ein Bericht über die 1945–1990 erschienene Literatur. [In]: Aschkenas, Bd. 1, Wien, 1991. Pp. 195–202.

——— KAUFMANN, URI: *The impact of the French Revolution on rural Jewry in Alsace, Baden and Switzerland.* [See No. 28124.]

28176. KOHN, MICHAEL: *Die Schweiz und die Juden; Affinitäten und Kontraste.* [In]: Isr. Wochenblatt, 92. Jg., Nr. 22, Zürich, 31. Mai 1991. Pp. 25–28.

28177. WEINGARTEN, RALPH: *Acht Jahrhunderte schwweizerisch-jüdische Geschichte*. [In]: Isr. Wochenblatt, Jg. 91, Nr. 46, Zürich, 15. Nov. 1991. Pp. 25–39, illus.

C. German Jews in Various Countries

28178. ALLFREY, PAUL: *Edward VII and his Jewish court*. London: Weidenfeld & Nicolson, 1991. XIV, 321 pp., illus., ports. geneal. tabs., bibl. (307–309). [Incl. relations with Jews of German descent, such as the Rothschild, Bischoffsheim, Goldschmidt families, and also Baron Moritz von Hirsch, Sir Ernest Cassell a.o. Deals also with the hostility towards them during World War I.]

28179. ARGENTINE. SCHWARCZ, ALFREDO JOSÉ: *Y a pesar de todo . . .; los judíos de habla alemana en la Argentina*. Buenos Aires: Grupo editor Latinoamericano, 1991, 328 pp., notes, bibl. [About immigration of German-speaking Jew to the Argentine, including Nazi period.]

28180. *Authors of their own lives: intellectual autobiographies by twenty American sociologists*. Ed. and with an introd. by Bennett M. Berger. Berkeley, Univ. of California Press, 1990. CCVIII, 503 pp., bibl. ref. [Incl. many of German-Jewish origin: Reinhard Bendix, Guenther Roth, a.o.]

28181. AVISAR, ILAN: *Die Mischpoche von Hollywood; Juden vor und hinter der Kamera*. [In]: Jüdische Lebenswelten. Essays [see No. 27946]. Frankfurt am Main: Jüdischer Verlag, Suhrkamp, 1991. Pp. 203–220, illus. [Also on German-Jewish film producers, directors and actors.]

—— BENZ, WOLFGANG, ed.: *Das Exil der kleinen Leute. Alltagserfahrungen deutscher Juden in der Emigration*. [See No. 28265.]

28182. BÖHM, GÜNTER: *Judíos alemanes en la República Argentina durante el siglo XIX*. [In]: Proceedings of the 10th World Congress of Jewish Studies, 1989, Division B, Vol 2: The history of the Jewish people. Jerusalem, 1990, Pp. 473–479.

28183. BURMEISTER, KARLHEINZ: *Die jüdische Gemeinde am Eschnerberg* [Liechtenstein] *1637–1651*. [In]: Jahrbuch des Historischen Vereins für das Fürstentum Liechtenstein. Bd. 89. Vaduz: Selbstverl. des Hist. Vereins, 1991. Pp. 153–176, footnotes.

28184. EXILE. *An interrupted past. German-speaking refugee historians in the United States*. Ed. by Hartmut Lehmann and James J. Sheehan. Washington D.C.; Cambridge: German Historical Institute & Cambridge University Press, 1991. 234 pp., footnotes, names index. [Cont.: Introduction (James J. Sheehan, 1–3). Part I.: German and American historiography in the nineteenth and twentieth centuries (Ernst Schulin, 8–31). German historiography during the Weimar Republic and the émigré historians (Wolfgang J. Mommsen, 32–66). The historical seminar of the university of Berlin in the twenties (Felix Gilbert, 67–70). Part II: Refugee historians in America: preemigration Germany to 1939 (Michael H. Kater, 73–93). "Uphill work": the German refugee historians and American institutions of higher learning (Karen J. Greenberg, 94–101). Everyday life and emigration; the role of women (Sybille Quack, 102–108). The special case of Austrian refugee historians (Fritz Fellner, 109–115). Schicksalsgeschichte: refugee historians in the United States (Catherine Epstein, 116–135). German historians in the Office of Strategic Services (Barry M. Katz, 136–139). The refugee scholar as intellectual educator: a student's recollections (Carl E. Schorske, 140–146). Part III: German émigré historians in America: the fifties, sixties, and seventies (Kenneth D. Barkin, 149–169). The americanization of Hajo Holborn (Otto P. Pflanze, (Hanna Schissler, 180–187). Ernst Kantorowicz and Theodor E. Mommsen (Robert E. Lerner, 188–205). Refugee historians and the German historical profession between 1950 and 1970 (Winfried Schulze, 206–225). Conclusion (James J. Sheehan, 226–228).]

28185. —— *Dunera News*. A quarterly publication for refugees from Nazi and Fascist persecution (mistakenly shipped to and interned in Australia at Hay and Tatura, many serving later in the 8th AERC, AMF), their relations and friends. Ed. by Eric Eckstein [et al.]. Dandenong: Hay-Tatura Association, c/o Eric Eckstein, 87 Clow Street, Dandenong, Vic. 3175. 4 issues [mimeog.] [Incl. [a.o.] personal recollections of German-Jewish refugees shipped to Australia from Great Britain as "enemy aliens" on the Dunera in 1940.]

—— *Exilforschung. Ein Internationales Jahrbuch. Bd.: Exil und Remigration*. München, Ed. Text und Kritik, 1991. [See No. 28643.]

28186. —— HARTENSTEIN, ELFI: *Heimat wider Willen*. Emigranten in New York; Begegnungen. Fotografiert von Thomas K. Müller. D-8137 Berg am See: Verlagsgemeinschaft Berg, 1991. 350 pp., illus. [Cont. 27 interviews of German-Jewish and Austrian-Jewish émigrés.]

28187. —— *Hitlerflüchtlinge im Norden: Asyl und politisches Exil 1933–1945*. Hrsg. von Hans Uwe Petersen.

Kiel: Neuer Malik Verlag, 1991. 373 pp., notes, bibl. (Veröff. d. Beirats f. Geschichte der Artbeiterbewegung u. Demokratie in Schleswig-Holstein; Bd. 7.) [Incl.: Norwegen und die jüdischen Flüchtlinge. 1933–1940 (Harald Skjönsberg, 25–32). Hitlerdeutschland, Schweden, Skandinavien und die Juden (Wolfgang Wilhelmus, 33–40). Finnland ein Flüchtlingsland ? (Hannes Saarine, 41–54). Dänemark und die antinazistischen Flüchtlinge 1940/41 (Hans Uwe Petersen, 55–78). Die Flüchtlingspolitik in der dänischen Aussenpolitik. 1933–1940 (Brian Klitgaard/Jens Melson, 79–92). Exil in Schweden (Helmut Müssener, 93–122). Der institutionelle und organisierte Widerstand gegen die Flüchtlinge in Schweden. 1933–1945 (Heléne Lööw, 123–144). Frauen im Exil in Dänemark nach 1933 (Birgit S Nielsen, 145–168). Das Mateotti-Komitee und die Hitlerflüchtlinge (Minna Steffen Pedersen, 169–180). Max Hodann im Exil. Die Max-Hodann-Materialien in der Universitätsbibliothek Oslo (Ivar Sagmo, 181–196); also pertinent to the history of the Jewish refugees from Germany and elsewhere: section III. Quellen und Archive zur Erforschung der Hitlerflüchtlinge im Norden, pp. 279–348.]

28188. — KINROSS, ROBIN: *Emigré graphic designers in Britain: around the Second World War and afterwards.* [In]: Journal of Design History, Vol. 3, No. 1, 1990, pp. 35–57, illus. [Incl. a.o. John Heartfield, Hans Schleger, Berthold Wolpe, Hans Schmoller.]

28189. — KNIGHT, MAX: *Emigration und Identität.* [In]: Aufbau, 57, New York, Oct. 25, 1991, pp. 8, 14. [Autobiographical essay; Max Knight (orig. Max Kühnel), author, born June 8, 1909 Pilsen, translator.]

28190. — KREISSLER, FRANÇOISE: *Das 'Pariser Tagblatt': ein Spiegel jüdischen Lebens 1933–1939.* [In]: Das Jüdische Echo, Vol. 40, Nr. 1, Wien, Okt. 1991. Pp. 151–154.

28191. — KROCH, ERNESTO: *Exil in der Heimat, Heim ins Exil. Erinnerungen aus Europa und Lateinamerika.* Frankfurt am Main: Dipa, 1990. 205 pp., plates, ports. (Edition Zeta; Zeugnisse.) [Memoirs of German-Jewish refugees in Uruguay.]

28192. — MOLTMANN, GÜNTER: *Auf dem Auswandererschiff. Zur jüdischen Komponente der deutschen Amerikaauswanderung im 19. Jahrhundert.* [In]: Juden in Deutschland [see No. 27490]. Hamburg: Christians, 1991. Pp. 286–303, notes.

28193. — STIEFEL, ERNST C./MECKLENBURG, FRANK: *Deutsche Juristen im amerikanischen Exil (1933–1950).* Tübingen: Mohr, 1991. VIII, 236 pp., notes, bibl. (214–228), index of persons (229–236).

28194. PANAYI, PANIKOS: *The enemy in our midst: Germans in Britain during the First World War.* Oxford: Berg, 1991. XII, 312 pp., bibl. (292–302). [Incl. prominent German-Jewish figures in society; Sir Ernest Cassell, a.o.]

—— REINHARZ, JEHUDA: *Die Ansiedlung deutscher Juden im Palästina der 1930er Jahre.* [See No. 28620.]
—— *Second Chance. Two centuries of German-speaking Jews in the United Kingdom.* [See No. 27975.]
—— TOURY, GIDEON/TOURY, JACOB: *Namensänderungen deutschsprachiger Einwanderer in Palästina.* [See No. 28627.]

28195. TROPP, ASHER: *Jews in the professions in Great Britain 1891–1991.* London: The Maccabaeans, 1991. VI, 104 pp. [Incl. Jewish refugee professionals from Germany, Austria etc.]

II. RESEARCH AND BIBLIOGRAPHY

A. Libraries and Institutes

28196. BUNDESARCHIV, ABTEILUNG POTSDAM. GRAHN, GERLINDE: *Der Teilbestand des Reichssippenamtes im Bundesarchiv, Abteilungen Potsdam.* [In]: Archivmitteilungen, H.6, Potsdam 1991. Pp. 269–274. [Refers also to registers of Jews and the enforcement of Nuremberg Laws.]

28197. FLEMING, GERALD: *The Auschwitz archives in Moscow.* [In]: The Jewish Quarterly, Vol. 38, No. 3, London, Autumn 1991. Pp. 9–12. [On the administrative archives of Auschwitz, which were transported to Moscow after the war.]

28198. FREIMARK, PETER: *Jüdische Bibliotheken und Hebraica-Bestände in Hamburg.* [In]: Tel Aviver Jahrbuch für deutsche Geschichte, Bd. 20, Gerlingen, 1991, Pp. 459–467, notes.

28199. HOCHSCHULE FÜR JÜDISCHE STUDIEN, Heidelberg. *Trumah.* 2. Hrsg. von Julius Carlebach. Wiesbaden: Reichert, 1990. VIII, 15 pp., illus. [Contributions relevant to German-Jewish history are listed according to subject.]

28200. INSTITUT FÜR DIE GESCHICHTE DER DEUTSCHEN JUDEN, Hamburg. FREIMARK, PETER: *Vom Hamburger Umgang mit der Geschichte einer Minderheit. Vorgeschichte und Gründung des Instituts für die Geschichte der deutschen Juden* [in]: Juden in Deutschland [see No. 27940. Orig. publ. in 1989, see No. 26197/YBXXXV.]. [Cf.: Rückschauende Zwischenbilanz (Ernst G. Lowenthal) [in]: 'Allgemeine', Nr. 46/33, Bonn, 15. August 1991, p. 8.]

28201. INSTITUT FÜR DEUTSCHE GESCHICHTE, Universität Tel-Aviv. *Tel Aviver Jahrbuch für deutsche Geschichte*. Bd. 20. *Sozialgeschichte der Juden in Deutschland* [Festschrift zum 75. Geburtstag von Jacob Toury]. Hrsg. im Auftrag des Instituts für deutsche Geschichte von Shulamit Volkov; Frank Stern. Gerlingen: Bleicher, 1991. 494 pp. [Cont.: Jacob Toury – zum 75. Geburtstag (Shulamit Volkov, 13–21). Bibliographie der Schriften von Jacob Toury (Gideon Toury, 469–485). Individual contributions are listed according to subject.]

28202. KLEIN, HANS-GÜNTER: *25 Jahre Mendelssohn-Archiv*. [In]: Jahrbuch Preußischer Kulturbesitz 1990, Bd. 27, Berlin: Gebr. Mann, 1991. Pp. 333–346. [Mendelssohn Archiv, Staatsbibliothek Preußischer Kulturbesitz, founded March 26, 1965; cont. Mendelssohniana (musical and non-musical collections related to Felix Mendelssohn) and the Moses-Bibliothek (collection of books, manuscripts and pictures related to the Mendelssohn family).]

—— LEO BAECK INSTITUTE. HOFFMANN, CHRISTHARD: *Deutsch-jüdische Geschichtswissenschaft in der Emigration: das Leo-Baeck-Institut*. [In]: Die Emigration der Wissenschaften nach 1933 [See in No. 28267.].

28203. — *Bulletin des Leo Baeck Instituts*. Nr. 88 [1991] & 85 [1990].: Hrsg. von Joseph Walk, Jacov Guggenheim und Itta Shedletzky. Frankfurt am Main: Hain, 1990 [&] 1991. 80 [&] 91 pp., notes. [2 issues.] [Individual contributions are listed according to subject.] [No. 85, does not, as announced in No. 27159/YBXXXVI, contain the index of Nos. 50 (1974) – 84 (1989), which will be published later.]

28204. — *Leo Baeck Institute Year Book XXXVI*. A community assailed. Ed.: Arnold Paucker. London: Secker & Warburg, 1991. XIII, 615 pp., illus., footnotes, bibl. (501–592), general index (597–615). [Cont.: Preface (Arnold Paucker, VII–XIII; incl. obituaries for Lux Furtmüller, p. XI–XII; Nahum N. Glatzer, p. XII; Lothar Kahn, p. XII; Fred W. Lessing, p. XII; Hans Seidenberg, p. XIII). Jews as Jews versus Jews as Germans. Two historical perspectives: introduction to Year Book XXXVI (Michael A. Meyer, XV–XXII, notes). Individual contributions are listed according to subject. [Cf.: Besprechung (Claudia Prestel) [in]: MB, Jg. 60, Nr. 79, Tel Aviv, Mai 1992, pp. 4–5. Review article (Glenn Sharfman) [in]: Shofar, Vol. 9, No. 4, West Lafayette, In., Purdue Univ., Summer 1991. Pp. 145–147.]

— *LBI Information*. Nachrichten aus den Leo Baeck Instituten in Jerusalem, London, New York und der Wissenschaftlichen Arbeitsgemeinschaft in der Bundesrepublik. Hrsg. von den Freunden und Förderern des LBI e.V. in Frankfurt/M. Redaktion: Arno Lustiger. Nr. 1, Frühjahr 1991 – Frankfurt am Main (Liebigstr. 24): Freunde und Förderer des LBI e.V., 1991. 20 pp. illus. [Cont. reports on events and activities of the LBI in general and in Germany in particular. Incl.: Zum Geleit – 35 Jahre Leo Baeck Institut (Arno Lustiger, 1). Neue Aspekte der deutsch-jüdischen Geschichtsschreibung (Reinhard Rürup, 3–5). Ein Ost-West-Treffen (Monika Richarz, 6–9).]

— LBI New York. *Library & Archives News*. Ed.: Gabrielle Bamberger. No. 30. New York: Leo Baeck Institute, Winter 1991. [8] pp.

– *LBI News*. Ed.: Gabrielle Bamberger. No. 59. New York: Leo Baeck Institute, Fall 1991. 16 pp., front illus., ports., facsims. [Incl.: Researching family roots at the LBI (pp. 2–4). Ismar Schorsch new president of the LBI (p. 5). Jewish soldiers under the double eagle (pp. 6–7). Reports on the LBI New York events and on its collections in library and archives. Obituaries: Lucy S. Dawidowicz; Gerson D. Cohen; Alfred S. Oppenheimer; Felix Gilbert (p. 10).]

28205. SALOMON LUDWIG STEINHEIM-INSTITUT FÜR DEUTSCH-JÜDISCHE GESCHICHTE, Universität Duisburg *Menora*. Jahrbuch für deutsch-jüdische Geschichte 1991. Bd. 2 Im Auftrag des 'Salomon-Ludwig-Steinheim-Institutes für deutsch-jüdische Geschichte' hrsg. von Julius H. Schoeps in Verbindung mit Arno Herzig und Hans Otto Horch. Red.: Ludger Heid. München: Piper, 1991. 419 pp., notes, index (names). (Serie Piper Bd. 1345.) [Cont.: Einführung (eds., 7–14). Individual contributions are listed according to subject.] [Cf.: Besprechung (Thomas Brechenmacher) [in]: Das Historisch-Politische Buch, 40. Jg. H. 1 & 2, Göttingen, 1992. P. 16.]

28206. — *Dialog*. Mitteilungen für die Freunde und Förderer des Salomon Ludwig Steinheim-Instituts für deutsch-jüdische Geschichte e.V. Erlangen: Union-Aktuell Verlags- und Werbeges. Red.: Elisabeth Heid. Jg. 4, Nr. 1–4 (Feb.–Nov. 1991). 4 issues (8 pp. each), illus.

28207. WIENER LIBRARY, London: *The Wiener Library Newsletter.* Published by the Institute of Contemporary History and Wiener Library. No. 17 (Winter), London, 1991. 4 pp. [Reports on Wiener Library events.]

28208. ZENTRALARCHIV ZUR ERFORSCHUNG DER GESCHICHTE DER JUDEN IN DEUTSCHLAND, Heidelberg. *Jüdische Friedhöfe in der DDR.* Sammlung Ruthenberg/Schulenburg (1987–1991) B, 3/ 20. Bearb. und hrsg. von Monika Preuss. Heidelberg, 1991. 92 pp. [Typescript.]

—— ZENTRUM FÜR ANTISEMITISMUSFORSCHUNG der Technischen Universität Berlin. [See No. 28944.]

B. Bibliographies and Catalogues

—— BERGMANN, JOACHIM: *Die Schaubühne/Die Weltbühne 1905–1933*: Bibliographie und Register mit Annotationen. Teil 1. [See No. 28634.]

28209. CHARNY, ISRAEL W., ed.: *Genocide: a critical bibliographic review*, volume 2. New York: Facts on File, 1991, XXVIII, 432 pp. [Chaps. incl. 'Righteous people in the Holocaust'; 'The psychology of denial of known genocides'; 'Denial of the Holocaust'.]

28210. DINNER, CHAVA/GOELL, YOHAI: *The history of Zionism and the State of Israel*: a selected and annotated bibliography for 1990. [In]: Studies in Zionism, Vol. 12, No. 2, Tel-Aviv, 1991. Pp. 203–293. [Incl. indexes of authors, journals, yearbooks and anthologies. Lists many titles on German Jewry and German Zionists.]

28211. EDELHEIT, ABRAHAM J./EDELHEIT, HERSHEL, eds.: *Bibliography on Holocaust literature*: supplement. Boulder, Co.: Westview Press, 1990. 684 pp., authors & periodicals indexes. [Supplement to bibliography publ. in 1986, see No. 23193/YBXXXII.]

28212. *Hebräische Handschriften der Stadt- und Universitätsbibliothek Frankfurt am Main.* Teil b. (sic) Beschrieben von Ernst Roth und Leo Prijs. Stuttgart: Steiner, 1990. XXII, 206 pp., bibl. (Verzeichnis der orientalischen Handschriften in Deutschland, Bd. 6, 1b) [For Part a see No. 18978/YBXXVII.]

28213. HOLOCAUST MEMORIAL RESOURCE AND EDUCATION CENTER OF CENTRAL FLORIDA: *Bibliography of the Holocaust. Memorial Resource and Education Center of Central Florida.* Maitland, Fla., 1990. 399 pp.

28214. *Index of articles on Jewish studies (and the study of Eretz Israel).* Vol. 30: 1988. Comp. and ed. in 'Kiryat Sefer', the Jewish National and University Library. Ed. board: Bitya Ben-Shammai, Susie Cohen [et al.]. Jerusalem: The Jewish National and Univ. Library Press, 1990. XLVII, 454 pp., author and subject indexes (365–454). [A selective bibliography incl. articles on German-speaking Jewry.]

28215. *Oral history of contemporary Jewry: an annotated catalogue.* New York: Garland, 1990. XV, 245 pp., indexes. [Catalogue contains descriptions of more than 900 taped interviews conducted between 1960 and 1986, and housed at the Oral History Division of the Institute of Contemporary Jewry of the Hebrew Univ., Jerusalem. The listings are arranged under five major headings: Jewish communities: World War II – the Holocaust, resistance and rescue; the Yishuv and the State of Israel, youth movements; culture and education. Incl. German Jews.]

28216. *Post-war publications on German Jewry; a selected bibliography of books and articles 1990.* Compiled by Barbara Suchy and Annette Pringle. [In]: LBI Year Book XXXVI, London, 1991. Pp. 501–592, index (572–592).

28217. SALAMANDER, RACHEL, ed.: *Literatur zum Judentum: Nachtrag 1991.* München: Literaturhandlung (Fürstenstr. 17), 1991. 74 pp.

III. THE NAZI PERIOD

A. General

—— GENERAL. Communal & regional Histories referring to the Nazi period and fully listed in other sections: Altenstadt (No. 27997). Arnsberg (No. 28001). Berlin-Kreuzberg (No. 28012). Coesfeld (No. 28015). Cuxhaven (No. 28019). Frankfurt am Main (No. 28030). Gevelsberg (No. 28038). Glogau (No. 28040). Gross-Gerau (No. 28042). Hamburg (Nos. 28044, 28049, 28050). Hamm (No. 28052). Hesse (No. 28057). Kelsterbach (No. 28070).

Kissingen (Bad) (No. 28071). Kunreuth (No. 28074). Ladenburg (No. 28075). Langenlonsheim (No. 28076). Lippe (No. 28081). Lippstadt (No. 28083). Medebach (No. 28086).
Mettmann (No. 28087). Montabaur (No. 28088). Nienburg (No. 28090). Steinfurt (No.
28108). Stolp (No. 28109). Ulm (No. 28113). Viersen (No. 28114). Walldorf (No. 28115).

——   *Aber das Leben marschiert weiter und nimmt uns mit; Briefwechsel zwischen Roth und dem Verlag De*
Gemeenschap 1936–1939. [See No. 28800.]

——   *Adult education in crisis situations.* Eds.: Franz Pöggeler/Kalman Yaron. [See No. 28561.]

28218.   ALTENA. SCHÜTTE, LEOPOLD: *Politisch unzuverlässig? Eine Notarsernennung in Altena im Jahre*
1935. [In]: Der Märker. 39. Jg., H. 3, Altena, Mai/Juni 1990. Pp. 87–95, footnotes. [On the
Jewish lawyers Heinrich and Albert Simons.]

28219.   ANGERMUND, RALPH: *Deutsche Richterschaft 1919–1945. Krisenerfahrung, Illusion, politische*
Rechtsprechung. Frankfurt am Main: Fischer Taschenbuch Verl., 1990. 280 pp., notes.
[Refers to the expulsion of Jewish judges. Incl. Juden vor Gericht (chap. V: 104–132).]

28220.   ARNTZ, HANS-DIETER: *Judenverfolgung und Fluchthilfe im deutsch-belgischen Grenzgebiet: Kreisge-*
biet Schleiden, Euskirchen, Monschau, Aachen und Eupen/Malmedy. 5350 Euskirchen: Kümpel,
1990. 784 pp., illus., facsims., docs., tabs., notes (744–769), index of persons (771–779),
index of places (781–784). [Incl. the chaps.: 1. Juden im Eifel-Ardennen-Gebiet (1–11). 2.
'Israeliten' mit dem erwünschten Bürgerrecht (12–37). 3 Kein Antisemitismus im Regie-
rungsbezirk Aachen (38–53). 4. Getreidehändler Levano aus Kommern gerät in die
deutsche Innenpolitik (54–63). 5. Die 'Machtergreifung' der Nationalsozialisten in der Eifel
(64–86). 6. Judendiskriminierung und erste Verfolgungen (87–110). 7. Antijüdisches im
Eifeler Platt (111–122). 8. Gegen die jüdischen Metzger! (123–149). 9. Ausschaltung des
jüdischen Viehhandels (150–179). 10. Rassentrennung (180–204). 11. Jüdische und arische
Jugend im Strudel der NS-Hetze (205–223). 12. Der Nationalsozialismus im deutsch-
belgischen Grenzgebiet (224–241). 13. Das Eupener 'Grenz-Echo' im Kampf gegen den
Nationalsozialismus (242–256). 14. Illegaler Grenzübertritt vor 1937 (257–270). 15.
Aufbruchsstimmung in der jüdischen Betgemeinde Mechernich (271–302). 16. Der Untergang der jüdischen Familien in Schleiden (303–323). 17. Gemünd vor dem 'großen Sturm'
(324–356). 18. Die 'Kristallnacht' in Gemünd (357–383). 19. Der 'Prangermarsch' von
Hellenthal (384–418). 20. Der Novemberpogrom in Mechernich (419–445). 21. Verbrechen
nach der 'Judenaktion' von 1938 (446–472). 22. Judenverfolgung in Kall und Aachen (472–
498). 23. Die 'grüne Grenze' (1937/38) nach Belgien (499–527). 24. Flucht nach Belgien:
Fluchtvarianten, Flüchtlingskomitees, Lagerleben, Rettungsaktionen (528–568). 25. Die
Ausplünderung der Daheimgebliebenen (569–595). 26. Isidors Briefe – eine dokumentar-
ische Erzählung (596–621). 27. Deportation und Holocaust (622–651). 28. Die allerletzte
Chance: Organisierte Fluchthilfe nach 'Altbelgien' (1942). (652–678). 29. 'Privilegierte
Mischehen' (679–691). 30. Rettung und Widerstand (692–716). 31. Epilog – Der Versuch
der 'Wiedergutmachung' (717–743).] [Cf.: Schmuggler und 'Judenschlepper im Grenzgebiet' (Reinhold Weitz) [in] Allgemeine Jüdische Wochenzeitung, Nr. 46/16, Bonn, 18. April
1991, p. 9.]

28221.   AUSCHWITZ. CZECH, DANUTA: *The Auschwitz chronicle, 1939–1945.* Foreword by Walter
Laqueur. London: Tauris; New York: Holt, 1990. XXI, 855 pp., illus., maps, glossary, bibl.
(831–838), list of names. [A detailed, day-to-day documentation of the construction,
operation and destruction of Auschwitz, based on documents from the archives of the
Auschwitz Memorial and the German Federal Archives. Incl. biographical sketches of some
of the camp leaders. Preliminary work on the chronicle was previously published in Polish
and German.]

28222.   — LAGNADO, LUCETTE MATALON/DEKEL, SHEILA COHN: *Children of the flames: Dr Josef*
Mengele and the untold story of the twins of Auschwitz. London: Sidgwick & Jackson; New York:
William Morrow, 1991. 320 pp., illus., bibl. [On Mengele's experiments with twins. Incl.
personal histories of survivors.]

28223.   AUSTRIA. STREIBEL, ROBERT: *Plötzlich waren sie alle weg. Die Juden der 'Gauhauptstadt Krems'*
und ihre Mitbürger. Mit einem Vorwort von Erika Weinzierl und einem Beitrag von Gabriele
Anderl. Wien: Picus, 1991. 291 pp., illus., footnotes, lists of names [incl. Nazi victims,
refugees and interviewees]. (Schriftenreihe des Waldviertler Heimatbundes; 33.) [Incl. the
sections: Vom Alltag zur Vertreibung (15–76). Familienschicksale (77–164; incl. letters of
émigrés). Lebendige Geschichte (165–208; incl. the cemetery of Krems; also on 'Vergangenheitsbewältigung' in Austria). Tagebuch einer Flucht (Abraham & Josef Nemschitz, 209–
251; about illegal immigration to Palestine).]

28224. — *Innsbruck im Spannungsfeld der Politik 1918–1938.* Berichte – Bilder – Dokumente. Von Franz-Heinz Hye unter Mitwirkung von Josefine Justic. Innsbruck: Stadtmagistrat, 1991. 893 pp., notes, illus., facsims., docs., index (persons, places, subjects, 871–893). [Incl. passim references to Jews resp. antisemitism in Innsbruck.]

— BAECK, LEO. ARONSFELD, C.C.: *Schon 1933 oder erst 1946? Historiographische Anmerkungen zu einem vielzitierten Ausspruch Leo Baecks.* [see No. 27917.]

28225. BALDWIN, PETER, ed.: *Reworking the past: Hitler, the Holocaust, and the historians' debate.* Boston: Beacon Press, 1990. VII, 308 pp. Cont.: The Historikerstreit in context (Peter Baldwin, 3–37). Immoral equivalence: revising the past for the Kohl era (Charles S. Maier, 38–44). The Jewish Question in the German Question (Anson Rabinbach, 45–73). A plea for the historization of National Socialism (Martin Broszat, 77–87). Some reflections on the historization of National Socialism (Saul Friedländer, 88–101). A controversy about the historization of National Socialism (Martin Broszat/Saul Friedländer, 102–132). Between aporia and apology: on the limits of historizing National Socialism (Dan Diner, 133–145). Singularity and its relativization: changing views in German historiography on National Socialism and the 'Final Solution' (Otto Dov Kulka, 146–170). Reappraisal and repression: the Third Reich in West German historical consciousness (Hans Mommsen, 173–184). Explaining the German catastrophe: the use and abuse of historical explanations (Hagen Schulze, 185–195). Warding off the past: a problem only for historians and moralists? (Wolfgang Benz, 196–213). Unburdening the German past? A preliminary assessment (Hans-Ulrich Wehler, 214–223). The Historikerstreit and social history (Mary Nolan, 224–248). Negative symbiosis: Germans and Jews after Auschwitz (Dan Diner, 251–261). Coping with the past: the West German Labor Movement and the Left (Andrei S. Markovits, 262–275). German identity and historical comparison: after the Historikerstreit (Jürgen Kocka, 279–293). Bibliography on the Historians' Debate and related topics (295–304).

28226. BANKIER, DAVID: *Jewish society through Nazi eyes 1933–1936.* [In]: Holocaust and Genocide Studies, Vol. 6, No. 2, Oxford, 1991. Pp. 111–127, notes. [On the image of the German-Jewish society as reflected in the Gestapo reports on public opinion.]

28227. BANKIER, DAVID: *Fluchtweg in die innere Emigration abgeschnitten? Reaktionen auf die Einführung des gelben Sterns im Deutschen Reich.* [In]: Der Davidstern; Zeichen der Schmach – Symbol der Hoffnung [see No. 27924]. Dorsten 1991. Pp. 122–131.

28228. BANKIER, DAVID: *German public responses to the Holocaust: the reactions to the Yellow Badge.* [In]: Proceedings of the 10th World Congress of Jewish Studies, 1989, Division B, Vol. 2: The history of the Jewish people. Jerusalem, 1990. Pp. 395–402.

28229. BARKAI, AVRAHAM: *Max Warburg im Jahre 1933. Missglückte Versuche zur Milderung der Judenverfolgung.* [In]: Juden in Deutschland [see No. 27940]. Hamburg: Christians, 1991. Pp. 390–405, notes.

28230. BARKAI, AVRAHAM: *Max Warburg in 1933: a Jewish magnate in Germany versus the Nazis' anti-Jewish policy.* [In Hebrew, with English summary, title transl.]. [In]: Yalkut Moreshet, No. 51, Tel-Aviv, Nov. 1991. Pp. 51–64.

28231. BAUER, YEHUDA: *Antisemitismus und Krieg.* [In]: Der nationalsozialistische Krieg. Hrsg. von Norbert Frei/Hermann Kling. Frankfurt am Main: Campus, 1990. Pp. 146–172, notes.

28232. BAUER, YEHUDA: *Who was responsible and when? Some well-known documents revisited.* [In]: Holocaust and Genocide Studies. Vol. 6, No. 2, Oxford, 1991. Pp. 129–149. [On Nazi policy to annihilate the Jews.]

28233. BEJARANO, ESTHER: *"Man nannte mich Krümmel"; eine jüdische Jugend in den Zeiten der Verfolgung.* Hrsg. vom Auschwitz-Komitee in der Bundesrepublik e.V. Hamburg: Curio-Verl., 2, Aufl., 1991. 36 pp., illus. [E.B., born Dec. 15, 1924 in Saarlouis, singer, music educator, from 1941 in forced labour, deported to Auschwitz in April 1943, member of the 'Mädchenorchester', Oct. 1943 deported to Ravensbrück, emigrated to Palestine in 1945. Living in Hamburg from 1960.]

28234. BERGEN-BELSEN. *Bergen-Belsen.* Ausstellungsbegleitheft. Hrsg.: Niedersächsische Landeszentrale für politische Bildung, Hannover, 1990. Recherchen, Bildauswahl und Textentwürfe von Monika Gödecke, Rolf Keller, Thomas Rahe, Wilfried Wiedemann. 96 pp., illus. [Published also in English, French, Danish, Dutch, Hebrew, Polish and Russian.]

28235. — LAQUEUR, RENATA: *Bergen-Belsen; Tagebuch 1944/1945.* 2. erg. Aufl., Hannover: Fackelträger, 1989. 144 pp. [R.L., data see No. 28353.]

28236. — *The relief of Belsen, April 1945; eyewitness accounts.* Published by the Imperial War Museum (comp.: Paul Kemp), Lambeth Road, London SE1 6HZ. London, 1991. 32 pp., illus. [Accompanying a permanent exhibition on the same theme in the Imperial War Museum, opened in April 1991. See also PAUL KEMP: The liberation of Bergen-Belsen concentration camp in April 1945: the testimony of those involved. [In]: Imperial War Museum Review, No. 5. London: Imperial War Museum, 1990. Pp. 28–41.]

28237. BERLIN. DEUTSCHKRON, INGE: *Berlin Jews underground.* Transl. by Hanna Silver. Berlin: Gedenkstätte deutscher Widerstand/German Resistance Memorial, 1990. [8] pp., ports. (German Resistance 1933–1945.)

28238. — KNOBLOCH, HEINZ: *Der beherzte Reviervorsteher. Ungewöhnliche Zivilcourage am Hackeschen Markt.* Berlin: Morgenbuch Verl., 1990. 177 pp., illus. [On a Berlin policeman who prevented the destruction of the synagogue, Oranienburger Straße, during the November Pogrom. Also on the origin of the famous photograph of the burning synagogue which the author proves to be a forgery.]

28239. — KÖNIG, JOEL: *'Du trägst ja gar keinen Judenstern!' Erinnerungen an Berlin.* [In]: Der Davidstern; Zeichen der Schmach – Symbol der Hoffnung [see No. 27924]. Dorsten, 1991. Pp. 134–135.

28240. — SCHILDE, KURT/TUCHEL, JOHANNES: *Columbia-Haus: Berliner Konzentrationslager 1933–1936.* Mit einem Geleitwort von Klaus Wowereit. Hrsg. vom Bezirksamt Tempelhof von Berlin anläßlich der geplanten Errichtung eines Mahnmals zur Erinnerung an die Geschichte des Gefängnisses und Konzentrationslagers Columbia-Haus. Berlin: Edn. Hentrich, 1990. (Reihe deutsche Vergangenheit. Stätten der Geschichte Berlins; 43.) 228 pp., illus. [Incl. persecution of Jews and Jewish politicians.]

28241. BLASIUS, DIRK: *Zwischen Rechtsvertrauen und Rechtzerstörung; Deutsche Juden 1933–1935.* [In]: Zerbrochene Geschichte [See No. 27980.], pp. 121–137.

28242. BREMEN. *Deportation Bremer Juden nach Minsk.* Hrsg. vom Initiativkreis Gedenkfahrt nach Minsk. Bremen: Edn. Temmen, 1991. [25] pp. [Incl.: Deportation und Ermordung Bremer Juden (Klaus Wedemeier, 13-25).]

28243. BRONOWSKI, ALEXANDER: *Es waren so wenige; Retter im Holocaust.* Aus dem Hebr. übersetzt von Zeev Eshkolot. Stuttgart: Quell Verl., 1991. 256 pp. [Orig. publ. 1989 in Israel by Beit Lochamei Hagethaot under the title They were few (in Hebrew). Incl.: Zur deutschen Ausgabe (Richard von Weizsäcker, 5–6). Vorwort (Yoav Gelber, 7–11). Als Verfolgte von Christen gerettet (12–75). Die Gerechten dieser Welt. Der Plan zur Vernichtung der Juden und seine Umsetzung (76–85). Die Gedenkstätte Yad Vashem und das Komitee für die Ehrung der 'Gerechten dieser Welt' (86–93). Österreich (94–122; a.o. Hermann Langbein). Deutschland (123–172; a.o. Prälat Hermann Maas, Berthold Beitz). Dänemark (173–180). Holland (181–189). Ungarn (190–210); a.o. Raoul Wallenberg). Litauen (211–215). Polen (216–254). Die 'Gerechten dieser Welt'; Aufteilung nach Ländern der Herkunft und ethnischem Ursprung. Stand 1988 (255–256).] [The author, a lawyer, co-founder and director of Yad Vashem gives an account of his and his family's own story of surviving Nazi persecution in Lublin and elsewhere with the help of non-Jewish Poles; see chap. 1: Als Verfolgte von Christen gerettet (12–75).] [Cf.: Zeugnisse der Nächstenliebe (Maria Stiefl-Cermak) [in]: Allgemeine Jüdische Wochenzeitung, Nr. 46/19, Bonn, 26. Dez. 1991, p. 14.]

28244. BROWDER, GEORGE C.: *Foundations of the Nazi police state: the formation of Sipo and SD.* Lexington, Ky.: Univ. Press of Kentucky, 1990. 378 pp., notes (252–309), bibl. (310–331). [Incl. actions against Jews, November Pogrom, Nuremberg Laws.]

28245. BUCHENWALD. EICHMANN, BERND: *KZ-Gedenkstätten in der ehemaligen DDR (2): Das Konzentrationslager Buchenwald bei Weimar* [title condensed]. [In]: Das Parlament, Nr. 9, Bonn, 21. Feb. 1991. P. 17.

28246. BÜTTELBORN. *'Juden sind keine mehr vorhanden': fünfzig Jahre nach der Reichspogromnacht;* eine Dokumentation. Friedensgruppe Büttelborn [Hrsg.]. Red.: Erika Bopp [et al.]. Büttelborn: Friedensgruppe Büttelborn, 1990. 103 pp., illus.

28247. BURLEIGH, MICHAEL/WIPPERMANN, WOLFGANG: *The racial state: Germany 1933–1945.* Cambridge: Cambridge Univ. Press, 1991. 368 pp., illus., maps, notes (308–357), bibl. essay (358–379). [Incl. chaps.: 'Barbarous utopias' racial ideologies in Germany (23–43); barbarism institutionalised; racism as state policy (44–73); the persecution of the Jews (75–112), bibliographical and historiographical surveys of research on the history of the national socialist regime [incl. history of racism in Germany: Nazi racial policy; the persecution of the Jews] (358–379). [Cf.: History Today, Vol. 41, London, Nov. 1991, pp. 35–36.]

28248. CHURCH. May, Georg: *Kirchenkampf oder Katholikenverfolgung? Ein Beitrag zu dem gegenseitigen Verhältnis von Nationalsozialismus und christlichen Bekenntnissen.* Stein am Rhein: Christiana-Verl., 1991. 799 pp. [Cf. critical review, especially of the author's apologetical presentation of the attitude of Christians towards the Jews during the Nazi period: Ein Zerrbild des Kirchenkampfs im Dritten Reich (Ferdinand Seibt) [in]: Neue Zürcher Zeitung, Nr. 90, 16. Apr. 1992, p. 71.]

28249. COLOGNE. Pracht, Elfi: *Jüdische Kulturarbeit in Köln 1933–1941.* [In]: Geschichte in Köln, H. 29, Köln, Juli 1991. Pp. 119–156.

28250. CZECHOSLOVAKIA. Makarova, Elena: *"There is no sun here": the life and art of Friedl Dicker-Brandeis.* [In]: Ariel; a review of arts and letters in Israel, No. 85–86, Jerusalen, 1991. Pp. 54–67.

28251. DACHAU. [See also in No. 28455.] Sack, Joel: *Dawn after Dachau.* New York: Shengold, 1990. 141 pp. [Author, survivor of Dachau, describes his experiences in Germany following his liberation by American troops.]

28252. Dale Jones, Priscilla: *British policy towards German crimes against German Jews, 1939–1945.* [In]: LBI Year Book XXXVI, London, 1991. Pp. 339–366, footnotes.

28253. DANZIG. Bogacz, Daniel: *Emigration der Juden aus der Freien Stadt Danzig im Lichte der Politik der Nationalsozialisten (1938–1939).* [In]: Studia nad faczyzmen i zbrodniami Hitlerowskimi, XIV, Wroclaw: Uniwersytet Wroclawski – Wydawnictwo, 1991. Pp. 219–252.

28254. — Stauffer, Paul: *Carl J. Burckhardt und das Danziger NS-Regime, Aufschub für die Juden dank dem Völkerbundkommissar?* [In]: Neue Zürcher Zeitung, Nr. 179, 6. Aug. 1991, p. 15 [Excerpts from a forthcoming book by Paul Stauffer about Burckhardt's attitude towards Nazi policies and the Jews and his role as the League of Nations High Commissioner, which is seen in a different light from Burckhardt's own Meine Danziger Mission (1960).]

—— DEPORTATIONS. [See also No. 28220.]

28255. — Büchler, Yehoshua: *The deportation of Slovakian Jews to the Lublin district of Poland in 1942.* [In]: Holocaust and Genocide Studies, Vol. 6, No. 2, Oxford, 1991. Pp. 151–166, maps, tabs., notes, appendix.

28256. — Kruglow, Aleksander: *Von den Hitlernazis unternommene Deportationen von Juden aus Deutschland, Österreich, und Böhmen nach dem Osten vom November 1941 bis November 1942.* [In Polish, with German and French summaries.] [In]: Studia nad faczyzmen i zbrodniami Hitlerowskimi, XIV, Wroclaw: Uniwersytet Wroclawski – Wydawnictwo, 1991. Pp. 373–396, footnotes.

28257. — Scheffler, Wolfgang: *Die Deportation war Auftakt für den Massenmord;* Im Herbst 1941 begann die 'Aussiedlung' der deutschen Juden nach Polen. [In]: Allgemeine Jüdische Wochenzeitung, Nr. 46/42, Bonn, 17. Okt. 1991. P. 11.

28258. — *Soviel der Einzelne tragen kann.* Zum Gedenken an die Deportation der badischen und pfälzischen Juden im Jahr 1940. Mit Beiträgen von Hanna Meyer-Moses, Albrecht Lohrbächer, Kurt Witzenbacher, Peter Noah, Paul Sauer, Hans Maass, Johannes Obst und Albert Friedlander. Hrsg.: Evangelische Akademie Baden (7500 Karlsruhe, Postfach 2269). Karlsruhe, 1991. 111 pp. (Herrenalber Protokolle; 82.)

28259. Diner, Dan: *Die Katastrophe vor der Katastrophe;* Auswanderung ohne Einwanderung. [In]: Zerbrochene Geschichte. [See No. 27980.] Pp. 138–160. [On emigration after the November Pogrom up to 1941.]

28260. DRESDEN. Klemperer, Victor: *Nirgends eine Kränkung, aber das qualvollste, bitterste Gefühl.* Tagebuchnotizen. [In]: Der Davidstern; Zeichen der Schmach – Symbol der Hoffnung [see No. 27924]. Dorsten 1991. Pp. 136–141. [On the imposition of the Jews' badge in Dresden in Sept. 1941. Reprint of No. 27782/YBXXXVI.]

28261. Dreyfuss, Louis: *Emigration nur ein Wort? Ein jüdisches Überlebensschicksal in Frankreich 1933–1945.* Hrsg. von Erhard Roy Wiehn. Konstanz: Hartung-Gorre, 1991. 150 pp.

28262. Dwork, Deborah: *Children with a star; Jewish youth in Nazi Europe.* New Haven; London: Yale Univ. Press, 1991. XLVI, 354 pp., illus., notes, map, bibl. (313–334), index. [Based on interviews conducted with persons, among them many German Jews, who had survived Nazi oppression during World War II in hiding or with false identity, and as inmates of ghettos, extermination and forced labour camps; author also used as source material diaries, letters, family albums and archival records. [Cf.: The echoes from our lost generation (Richard Overy) [in]: The Observer, London, June 2, 1991.]

28263. Edelheit, Hershel/Edelheit, Abraham J.: *A world in turmoil:* an integrated chronology of the Holocaust and World War II. Westport, Ct.: Greenwood Press, 1991. 450 pp., glossary, index of places and subjects, bibl. (406–422). (Bibliographies and indexes in world history, No. 22.) [Chronology starts in 1933 and ends in 1948, incl. an introductory essay on the historical background of the Holocaust and the war.]

28264. EICHMANN, ADOLF. MALKIN, PETER Z.: *Ich jagte Eichmann.* Der Bericht des israelischen Agenten, der den Organisator der 'Endlösung' gefangennahm. Unter Mitarbeit von Harry Stein. Aus dem Engl. von Dietlind Kaiser. München: Piper, 1991. 313 pp., illus. [Translation of MALKIN, PETER Z./STEIN, HARRY: Eichmann in my hands. New York: Warner Books, 1990. See No. 27241/YBXXXVI.] [Cf.: Wer jagte Eichmann? (Schalom Ben-Chorin) [in]: Tribüne, Jg. 30, H. 120, Frankfurt am Main, 1991. Pp. 244–248. Nochmals: ein Geheimagentenbericht über Eichmann (lfd) [in]: 'MB', Nr. 77/78, Tel Aviv, März/April 1992, p. 10.]

28265. EMIGRATION. BENZ, WOLFGANG, ed.: *Das Exil der kleinen Leute; Alltagserfahrungen deutscher Juden in der Emigration.* Hrsg. von Wolfgang Benz. München: Beck, 1991. 341 pp. [Cont. (titles condensed): Das Exil der kleinen Leute (Wolfgang Benz, 7–38). Die Hühnerzüchter von New Jersey (Gert Niers, 39–46). Siedler in Bolivien (Patrik von zur Mühlen, 47–54). 'Viva México' (Irene Lorisika, 55–60). Von Memmingen nach Rio de Janeiro (Gernot Römer, 61–68). Emigrantenalltag in Stockholm (Hilde Rohlén-Wohlgemut, 69–79). Amtsarzt in Jamaika (Rudolf Aub, 80–98). In Südafrika (Angelika Tramitz, 99–108). Wartezimmer Shanghai (Frank Stern, 109–120). Die Grünfelds in Israel (Angelika Schardt/Juliane Wetzel, 121–125). Ein Lehrer und Kaufmann in Istanbul (Dietrich Gronau, 126–133). Eine Leipzigerin in Haifa (Christiane Schütz, 134–142). Ein Journalist in Paris (Anna-Patricia Kahn, 143–150). Else Kapp in Kfar Shmaryahu (Elisabeth Keil, 151–159). Ein Danziger Kaufmann in Italien (Klaus Voigt, 160–170). Elisabeth Young in Sidney (Frauke Meyer-Gosau, 171–181). Eine Wienerin in Australien (Sabine Berloge, 182–187). Eine Kunstlehrerin in England (Bernd Ulrich/Angelika Tramitz, 188–197). Chicago (Catherine Stodolsky, 198–202). Mit dem Kindertransport nach England (Jenny Kreyssig, 203–232). Auf der Suche nach meiner Identität (Herbert Liffman, 233–244). Lebensjahre in Belgien, Frankreich, Australien (Sophie Caplan, 245–260). In Argentinien (Kurt Fischbein, 261–278). Eine neuseeländische Identität (Antony Barta, 279–286). Ein Amerikaner aus Berlin in Australien (Klaus Loewald, 287–300). Eine jüdische Familie in der Schweiz (Barbara Distel, 301–308). In der DDR (Salomea Genin, 309–325). Lucy Geigers Auswanderung und Rückkehr (Ute Benz, 326–331). Rückkehr auf Zeit: Erfahrungen deutsch-jüdischer Emigranten mit Einladungen in ihre ehemaligen Heimatstädte (Wolfgang Benz, 332–340). [Cf.: Die schwere Last des Exils (Julius H. Schoeps) [in]: Die Zeit, Nr. 42, Hamburg, 11. Okt. 1991, p. 34.]

——— — JÜTTE, ROBERT: *Die Emigration der deutschsprachigen 'Wissenschaft des Judentums'. Die Auswanderung jüdischer Historiker nach Palästina 1933–1945.* [See No. 28530.]

28266. — MANN, KLAUS & ERIKA: *Escape to Life. Deutsche Kultur im Exil.* Hrsg. von Herbert Hoven. München: Edn. Spangenberg, 1991. 421 pp., illus. [Escape to life was published for the first time in April 1939 in Boston; dealing with ca. 400 émigrés in the USA, most of them German-Jewish; first edn. of the original German version.] [Cf.: 'Escape to Life' auf Deutsch (Henry G. Proskauer) [in]: Aufbau, Vol. 58, No. 1, New York, Jan. 3, 1992, p. 7. Zeugnis der Selbstbehauptung (Uwe Wolff) [in]: Neue Zürcher Zeitung, Nr. 294, 18. Dez. 1991, p. 17.]

28267. — *Die Emigration der Wissenschaften nach 1933*; disziplingeschichtliche Studien. Hrsg. von Herbert A. Strauss [et al.]. München; London [et al.]: Saur. 282 pp., notes. [Incl.: Einleitung: Wissenschaftsemigration als Forschungsproblem (Herbert A. Strauss, 7–23). The following essays refer passim to many German-speaking Jewish émigré scientists (titles condensed): Die Emigration deutschsprachiger Physiker nach 1933 (Klaus Fischer, 25–72, notes). Die Emigration deutschsprachiger Naturwissenschaftler 1933–1945 in die Türkei (Regine Erichsen, 73–104, notes, tabs.). Vom Staatsrecht zur 'political science' – die Emigration deutscher Wissenschaftler nach 1933 (Alfons Söllner, 137–164, notes). Zur Typisierung von Emigrationsverläufen; Emigration deutschsprachiger Sozialwissenschaftler (Ilja Sjrubar, 165–182, notes). Die Emigration deutschsprachiger Ökonomen (Claus-Dieter Krohn, 183–192, notes). Der Einfluß der deutschen Kunstgeschichte in England (Peter Lasko, 219–233, notes; deals with Sir Ernst Gombrich, Sir Nikolaus Pevsner. Zur Remigration des Germanisten Richard Alewyn (Regina Weber, 235–256). Deutsch-jüdische Geschichtswissenschaft in der Emigration: das Leo-Baeck-Institut (Christhard Hoffmann, 257–279, notes).

28268. *Engpass zur Freiheit. Aufzeichnungen der Frau Hilde Huppert über ihre Erlebnisse im Nazi-Todesland und ihre wundersame Errettung aus Bergen-Belsen.* Manuskriptbearbeitung von Arnold Zweig. Mit einem Essay von Detlev Claussen. Hrsg. von Heidrun Loeper. Berlin: Kontextverl., 1990. 160 pp., illus., notes. (Texte zum 9. November in Zusammenarbeit mit der Jüdischen Gemeinde Berlin.) [Incl.: Zum Geleit (Heidrun Loeper, 5–6). Vorwort & Vorrede nach 16 Monaten & Nachwort (Arnold Zweig, 9–16 & 108–145). Wir wurden vernichtet (Hilde Huppert, 17–107). Aufklärung in der Wüste (Detlev Claussen, 146–157).] [The memoirs (orig. written in German) of a Czech woman about life in several ghettos and concentration camps, the last of which was Bergen-Belsen, from where she was evacuated and then liberated by the Americans near Magdeburg. Orig. edn. in Czech in 1949, revised and with a preface by Arnold Zweig. First published in Germany, with a revised preface and a new epilogue by Arnold Zweig, under the title Fahrt zum Acheron in 1951. The two prefaces and the essay by Detlev Claussen were first publ. by Detlev Claussen under the title 'Blick zurück nach vorn' in 'Freibeuter', Nr. 39, Berlin 1988, pp. 96–103.]

28269. ERMLAND. Sommerfeld, Aloys: *Juden in Ermland: ihr Schicksal nach 1933.* Hrsg.: Historischer Verein für Ermland. Osnabrück: fromm, 1991. 142 pp., illus. (Zeitschrift für die Geschichte und Altertumskunde Ermlands; Beiheft 10.)

28270. EXILE. Hermann, Georg: *Unvorhanden und stumm, doch zu Menschen noch reden.* Briefe aus dem Exil 1933–1941 an seine Tochter Hilde. Weltabschied, ein Essay. Hrsg. von Laureen Nussbaum. Mannheim: Persona, 1991. 269 pp., ports. [Cf.: Angst vor dem Vergessenwerden; Georg Hermanns Briefe aus dem Exil (Heribert Seifert) [in]: Neue Zürcher Zeitung, Nr. 265, 14. Nov. 1991, p. 30.]

——— — Herzfelde, Wieland: *Prag – Moskau.* Briefe von und an Wieland Herzfelde 1933–1939. Hrsg. von Giuseppe De Siati und Thies Ziemke. [See No. 28817.]

——— — Kreissler, Françoise: *Das 'Pariser Tagblatt': ein Spiegel jüdischen Lebens 1933–1939.* [See No. 28190.]

28271. FINAL SOLUTION. Bartoszewski, Wladyslaw: *Polen und Juden in der Zeit der 'Endlösung'.* 1070 Wien, Burggasse 35: Informationszentrum im Dienste der Christl.-Jüd. Verständigung, 1991. 31 pp. (IDCIV-Vorträge, 41.)

28272. — Breiman, Richard: *The architect of Genocide: Himmler and the Final Solution.* New York: Knopf, 1991. XII, 335 pp., glossary.

28273. — Longerich, Peter: *Vom Massenmord zur 'Endlösung'. Die Erschiessung von jüdischen Zivilisten in den ersten Monaten des Ostfeldzuges im Kontext des nationalsozialistischen Judenmords.* [In]: Zwei Wege nach Moskau. Vom Hitler-Stalin-Pakt zum 'Unternehmen Barbarossa'. Im Auftrag des Militärgeschichtlichen Forschungsamt hrsg. von Bernd Wegner. Orig.-Ausg. Piper: München, 1991. Pp. 251–274, notes.

28274. — Mommsen, Hans: *Die Realisierung des Utopischen: Die 'Endlösung der Judenfrage' im 'Dritten Reich'.* [In]: Mommsen, Hans: Der Nationalsozialismus und die deutsche Gesellschaft; ausgewählte Aufsätze. Zum 60. Geburtstag hrsg. von Lutz Niethammer und Bernd Weisbrod. Orig.-Ausg. Reinbeck b. Hamburg: Rowohlt Taschenbuch Verlag, 1991. (Sachbuch; 8857.) Pp. 184–232, notes. [Reprint of No. 20034/YBXXIX.]

28275. — Padfield, Peter: *Himmler.* London, New York: Macmillan, 1991. XII, 656 pp., illus., ref. notes (613–634), glossary, bibl. (635–638). [Cf.: The Reichsfuehrer SS (Anthony Storr) [in]: Dimensions, Vol. 6, No. 2, New York, 1991, pp. 29–31, illus.]

28276. — Pätzold, Kurt/Schwarz, Erika: *Die Organisation der 'Endlösung'. Vor 50 Jahren: Die Wannsee-Konferenz der Judenmörder.* [In]: Tribüne, Jg. 30, H. 120, Frankfurt am Main, 1991. Pp. 193–198.

——— — Segal, Lilli: *Die Hohenpriester der Vernichtung. Anthropologen, Mediziner und Psychiater als Wegbereiter von Selektion und Mord im Dritten Reich.* [See No. 28929.]

28277. — Streit, Christian: *Ostkrieg, Antibolschewismus und 'Endlösung'.* [In]: Geschichte und Gesellschaft, 17. Jg., Göttingen, 1991. Pp. 242–255, footnotes.

28278. — *'Vernichtungspolitik': Eine Debatte über den Zusammenhang von Sozialpolitik und Genozid im nationalsozialistischen Deutschland.* Wolfgang Schneider (Hrsg.). Hamburg: Junius, 1991. 198 pp., notes. (Schriftenreihe des Hamburger Instituts für Sozialforschung.) [Essays presented at a symposium under the title Wissenschaft und Massenvernichtung – zur Rationalität nationalsozialistischer Vernichtungspolitik, held by the Hamburger Institut für Sozialforschung in June 1989. Cont. contributions about mass extermination in the context of Nazi economic and demographic policies by the following authors: Susanne Heim, Götz Aly, Ulrich Herbert, Christopher Browning, Walter Grode, Dan Diner, Reinhard Kreissl, Ernst Köhler, Ludger Weiß, Götz Rohwer, Werner Röhr, Jan Philipp Reemtsma, Karl Heinz

Roth.] [Cf.: Nicht nur rational: über den Zusammenhang von Sozialpolitik und Genozid im 'Dritten Reich' (Hans Mommsen) [In]: Die Zeit, Nr. 43, Hamburg, 18. Okt. 1991, p. 83.]

28279. FORCED LABOUR. Perz, Bertrand: *Projekt Quarz. Steyr-Daimler-Puch und das Konzentrationslager Melk*. Industrie, Zwangsarbeit und Konzentrationslager in Österreich. Band 3. Wien: Verlag für Gesellschaftskritik, 1991. 500 pp. [On one of the largest concentration camps in Austria, 70 km east of Mauthausen, built as its Außenlager in 1944.] [Cf.: Jüdische Todesrate: 43 Prozent (Anton Maegerle) [in]: Tribüne, Jg. 30, H. 120, Frankfurt am Main, 1991. Pp. 230–232.]

28280. — *Deutsche Wirtschaft. Zwangsarbeit von KZ-Häftlingen für Industrie und Behörden*; Symposion 'Wirtschaft und Konzentrationslager'. Hrsg.: Hamburger Stiftung zur Förderung von Wissenschaft und Kultur. Hamburg: VSA-Verlag, 1991. 227 pp., illus. [A collection of papers delivered at a conference held in Hamburg in June 1989 on forced labour of concentration camp prisoners. Incl. (titles partly condensed): Der Arbeitseinsatz von KZ-Häftlingen und die Perspektive der Industrie (Rainer Fröbe, 33–78). Auschwitz – Normalität oder Anomalie eines kapitalistischen Entwicklungssprungs ? (Karl Heinz Roth, 79–96). Das Beispiel Auschwitz (Franciszek Piper, 97–140, docs.). Häftlingsarbeit: Profit, Produktion und Rassenideologie (Falk Pingel, 141–152). Das Beispiel Neuengamme (Hermann Kaienburg, 187–201). Häftlinge des KZ Neuengamme bei den Reichswerken 'Hermann Göring' (Gerd Wysocki, 203–211). Daz KZ-Aussenlager Drägerwerk (Stefan Romey, 213–219). Zwangsarbeit und Konzentrationslager bei den Volkswagen-Werken (Hans Mommsen, 221–225).]

28281. FRANCE. Caron, Vicki: *Loyalties in conflict: French Jewry and the refugee crisis, 1933–1935*. [In]: LBI Year Book XXXVI, London, 1991. Pp. 305–338, footnotes.

28282. — Klarsfeld, Serge & Beate: *Die Kinder von Izieu; eine jüdische Tragödie*. Aus dem Französichen übersetzt von Anna Mudry; mit Beiträgen von Johanna Attah und Manfred Richter. Berlin: Edn. Hentrich, 1991. 189 pp., illus. [On Klaus Barbie and the fate of the 44 children (16 from Austria and Germany) who were at the children's hostel near Izieu until they were deported and murdered.]

28283. FRANCONIA. *Flucht – Vertreibung – Exil – Asyl: Frauenschicksale im Raum Erlangen, Fürth, Nürnberg, Schwabach*. (Begleitband zur Ausstellung. Hrsg.: Feministisches Informations-, Bildungs- und Dokumentationszentrum, Nürnberg. Red.: Brigitte Fischer-Brühl [et al.].) Nürnberg: Fibidoz, 1990. 429 pp., illus., notes. bibl. [Incl. section on persecution and exile of Jewish women and their families during the Nazi period: Exil, Vertreibung, Vernichtung im Nationalsozialismus (pp. 53–212). Also essay on pre-Nazi persecution: Aufnahme und Vertreibung: zur Geschichte der jüdischen Gemeinden (Gaby Franger, 45–52).]

28284. FRANK, ANNE. Lindwer, Willy: *The last seven months of Anne Frank*. Transl. from the Dutch by Alison Meersschaert. New York: Pantheon Books, 1991. XIII, 204 pp., illus. [Covers the period from the time when Anne was arrested to her death in Bergen-Belsen; based on eyewitness accounts of six Jewish women who were imprisoned with her and who survived.]

28285. — Rosenfeld, Alvin H.: *The Anne Frank we remember*. [In]: Dimensions, Vol. 5, No. 2, New York, 1990. Pp. 3–6, illus, notes.

28286. FRANKFURT am Main. Drechsler, Siegmund/Kalinski, Siegmund/Mausbach, Hans: *Ärztliches Schicksal unter der Verfolgung 1933–1945 in Frankfurt am Main und Offenbach*. Eine Denkschrift erstellt im Auftrag der Landesärztekammer. Frankfurt am Main: Verlag für akad. Schriften, 1990. 179 pp., illus., facsims. [Cf.: 'Ich kann Frankfurt nicht verlassen . . .' (Adolf Diamant) [in]: 'Allgemeine', Nr. 46/13, Bonn, 28. März 1991, p. 9.]

28287. — Freise, Judith/Martini, Joachim: *Jüdische Musikerinnen und Musiker in Frankfurt 1933–1942: Musik als Form geistigen Widerstandes*. Ausstellungsbegleitheft. Frankfurt am Main: Verl. Dr Otto Lembeck, 1990. 359; 73; 84 pp. [Cont. annotated programmes of musical events extracted from advertisements and reviews in the Frankfurter Israelitisches Gemeindeblatt (from Oct. 1937: Jüdisches Gemeindeblatt für die Israelitische Gemeinde zu Frankfurt am Main) and list of names of Jewish musicians in Frankfurt am Main, incl. biographical data.]

28288. FREEDEN, Herbert: *The Jewish press in Nazi Germany*. Oxford: Berg, 1991. 208 pp., bibl. [Translation of Die jüdische Presse im Dritten Reich; see No. 24236/YBXXXIII.]

28289. FÜRTH. Zuckermann, Hanny: *Erinnerungen an die Nazizeit*. [In]: Nachrichten für den jüdischen Bürger Fürths, Isr. Kultusgemeinde Fürth (Blumenstr. 31), 31. Sept. 1991. Pp. 19–24.

28290. FULDA. Renner, Gerhard [et al.], eds.: *". . . werden in Kürze anderweit untergebracht . . .".*

Das Schicksal der Fuldaer Juden im Nationalsozialismus; eine Dokumentation. Fulda: Ulenspiegel, 1990. 160 pp. (Regionalgeschichtliche Schriften der Geschichtswerkstatt Fulda.)

28291. GALLAGHER, HUGH G.: *Patients, physicians, and the license to kill in the Third Reich*. New York: Holt, 1990. IX. 342 pp., illus., bibl. [Author sees Nazi euthanasia programme as a testing ground for the mass murder of the Jews.]

28292. GELLATELY, ROBERT: *Rethinking the Nazi terror system: a historiographical analysis*. [In]: German Studies Review, Vol. 14, No. 1, Tempe, Az., Feb. 1991. Pp. 23–38. [Incl. 'historians' debate'.]

28293. GEMÜNDEN. REIS, STEFAN: *Wie Hass entsteht und wohin er führen kann: vom Leben und Sterben der Juden im Raum Gemünden*. Hrsg.: Historischer Verein Gemünden und Umgebung. Anh.: Auszüge aus der Facharbeit von Martin Kaiser. Gemünden am Main: Historischer Verein Gemünden am Main und Umgebung, 1990. 55 pp., illus. (Schriftenreihe des Historischen Vereins Gemünden am Main und Umgebung; H. 3.)

28294. GIESSEN. *Antisemitismus und Nationalsozialismus in der Giessener Region*. [Katalog zur Ausstellung der Arbeitsgruppe 'Soziale und Politische Geschichte Giessens'.] Red.: Bruno W. Reimann [et al.]. Giessen: Arbeitsgruppe 'Soziale und Politische Geschichte Giessens', Inst. für Soziologie, 1990. 434 pp., illus., tabs. (Materialien zur sozialen und politischen Geschichte; Bd. 2.)

28295. GILBERT, MARTIN: *Auschwitz and the allies*. New York: Holt, 1990. 368 pp., illus., plates, map. [For orig. 1981 edn. see No. 18114/YBXXVII.]

—— GOEBBELS, JOSEPH. BERING, DIETZ: *Kampf um Namen. Bernhard Weiss gegen Joseph Goebbels*. [See No. 28902.]

28296. GÖRLITZ. OTTO, ROLAND: *Die Verfolgung der Juden in Görlitz unter der faschistischen Diktatur: 1933–1945*. Hrsg.: Stadtverwaltung Görlitz. Görlitz: Stadtverwaltung, 1990. 119 pp., illus. (Schriftenreihe des Ratsarchivs der Stadt Görlitz; 14.)

28297. GOLDSTEIN, JACOB/LUKOFF, IRVING F. /STRAUSS, HERBERT A.: *Individuelles und kollektives Verhalten in Nazi-Konzentrationslagern*. Soziologische und psychologische Studien zu Berichten ungarisch-jüdischer Überlebender. Frankfurt am Main: Campus, 1991. 198 pp. [Based on 728 interviews with Hungarian-Jewish surviving inmates of Nazi concentration camps conducted in 1945. Cont. three additional case studies on the long-term consequences of persecution.]

28298. GOTTSCHALK, GERDA: *Der letzte Weg*. Konstanz: Südverlag, 1991. 168 pp. [Recollections of an actress of partly Jewish descent in Leipzig, who survived Nazi forced labour camps with the help of non-Jewish friends. Incl. excerpts from the diary of a friend, Dora Hansen, who was deported to Riga in 1941 and murdered in 1944.]

28299. GRÜBER, HEINRICH. *Bevollmächtigt zum Brückenbau. Heinrich Grüber; Judenfreund und Trümmerprobst. Erinnerungen, Predigten, Berichte, Briefe*. Hrsg. von Jorg Hildebrandt. Leipzig Evangelische Verlagsanstalt, 1991. 427 pp., illus., ports., facsims., index of names. Incl.: "So gehe hin und tue desgleichen". Zur Geschichte des "Büros Pfarrer Grüber" 1938–1940 (Hartmut Ludwig, 11–40). An der Stechbahn. Erlebnisse und Berichte aus dem Büro Grüber in den Jahren der Verfolgung (41–75). Erinnerungen aus einem halben Jahrzehnt (1940–1945) (Heinrich Grüber, 76–171). Ein Partner der Vernunft (Günter Wirth, 180–275; incl. the section: Eichmann-Prozess in Jerusalem, pp. 251–257). Das unischerste und schwerste Amt; Predigten, Briefe, Reden, Aufsätze (1938–1970) (Heinrich Grüber, 276–370; incl. contributions on anti-Judaism, antisemitism and Martin Buber). [See also No. 28399.]

28300. GUGGENHEIM, JULIUS & LINI: *Auch das geht vorüber*. Bearbeitet von Lilo Guggenheim Levine. Frankfurt am Main: Haag & Herchen, 1991. 113 pp., illus. [Cont. letters written by Julius and Lini Guggenheim from Stuttgart to their children who escaped from Nazi Germany with the Kindertransport to England.]

28301. GURS. PHILIPP, MICHAEL, ed.: *Gurs – ein Internierungslager in Südfrankreich 1939–1943*. Literarische Zeugnisse, Briefe, Berichte. Hamburg: Hamburger Institut für Sozialforschung, 1991. 87 pp., illus., fascims. [Incl. the sections: Internierung der 'feindlichen Ausländerinnen' (19–31). Deportation der badischen und pfälzischen Juden nach Gurs (33–43). Lagerleben 1940–1942 (45–71) Deportationen nach Auschwitz (73–81). Chronologie (83–85).]

28302. — *Ein Internierungslager in Südfrankreich 1939–1943*. Ausstellungskatalog mit Zeichnungen, Aquarellen und Fotografien. Sammlung Elsbeth Kasser. Viborg: Skovgaard Museets Forlag, 1989. 63 pp., illus.

28303. HAAS, PETER J.: *The healing-killing paradox.* [In]: Dimensions, Vol. 5, No. 2, New York, 1990. Pp. 8–10. [On Nazi doctors and medical experiments.]

28304. HADAMAR. SCHWEITZER, PETER PAUL [et al.]: *Das Schicksal der Hadamarer Juden: Schule und Öffentlichkeit erneuern gemeinsam das Gedächtnis an jüdische Mitbürger von 1933–1945.* Fuldatal: Hess. Inst. für Lehrerfortbildung, Hauptstelle Reinhardswaldschule, 1991. 146 pp., illus., music scores. (Ergebnisse regionaler Lehrerfortbildung; Aussenstelle Limburg.)

28305. HAMBURG. LORENZ, INA S.: *Die Gründung des 'Jüdischen Religionsverbandes Hamburg' (1937) und das Ende der jüdischen Gemeinden zu Altona, Wandsbek und Harburg-Wilhelmsburg.* [In]: Juden in Duetschland [see No. 27940]. Hamburg: Christians, 1991. Pp. 81–115.

28306. HEIBER, HELMUT: *Universität unterm Hakenkreuz. Teil 1. Der Professor im Dritten Reich; Bilder aus der akademischen Provinz.* München: Saur, 1991. 652 pp., notes, bibl., index of persons, of places. [Incl. detailed account of attitudes of German professors towards their Jewish colleagues and students.] [Cf.: Besprechung (Manfred Funke) [in]: Das Parlament, Nr. 43, Bonn, 18. Okt. 1991, p. 15.]

28307. HERSHAN, STELLA K.: *Rethinking the American Jewish experience: a memoir of Nazi Austria and the Jewish refugee experience in America.* [In]: American Jewish Archives, Vol. 43, No. 2, Cincinnati, Fall/Winter 1991. Pp. 181–206, footnotes, illus.

28308. HERZBERG, ARNO: *The Jewish press under the Nazi regime. Its mission, suppression and defiance. A memoir.* [In]: LBI Year Book XXXVI, London, 1991. Pp. 367–388, footnotes. [Personal recollections of the author, a manager and editor of the Jewish Telegraphic Agency in Berlin from 1934–1937.]

28309. HISTORIOGRAPHY & 'HISTORIANS' DEBATE'. *Amoklauf: gegen die Wirklichkeit. NS-Verbrechen und 'revisionistische' Geschichtsschreibung.* Hrsg.Dokumentationsarchiv des österreich-ischen Widerstandes: Bundesministerium für Unterricht und Kunst. Wien: Dokumen-tationsarchiv des österreichischen Widerstandes, 1991. 135 pp., footnotes, docs., facsims. [Incl. various articles on the denial of the Holocaust and 'revisionist' historiography by Brigitte Bailer-Galanda, Josef Bailer, Florian Freund, Thilo Geisler, Wilhelm Lasek, Wolfgang Neugebauer, Gustav Spann, Werner Wegner.]

28310. — BERGHAHN, VOLKER: *The unmastered and unmasterable past.* [In]: The Journal of Modern history. Vol. 63, No. 3, Chicago, Sept. 1991. Pp. 546–554. [Review essay on various recent books about the historians' debate.]

28311. — BOCK, GISELA: *Krankenmord, Judenmord und nationalsozialistische Rassenpolitik: Überlegungen zu einigen neueren Forschungshypothesen.* [In]: Zivilisation und Barbarei. Die widersprüchlichen Potentiale der Moderne. Detlev Peukert zum Gedenken. Hrsg. von Frank Bajohr [et al.]. Hamburg: Christians 1991. (Hamburger Beiträge zur Zeitgeschichte; Bd. 27.) Pp. 306, notes.

28312. — *Der historische Ort des Nationalsozialismus. Annäherungen.* Mit Beiträgen von Dirk Blasius, Dan Diner, Saul Friedländer, Raul Hilberg, Hans Mommsen, Lutz Niethammer, Wolfgang Schieder und Heinrich August Winkler. Hrsg. von Walter H. Pehle. Frankfurt am Main: Fischer Taschenbuch Verlag, 1990. 182 pp., notes. [Incl. historiography about the Nazi persecution and mass extermination of the Jews and the 'historians' debate'.]

28313. — DINER, DAN: *Historisches Verstehen und Gegenrationalität. Der Judenrat als erkenntnistheoretische Warte.* [In]: Zivilisation und Barbarei. Die widersprüchlichen Potentiale der Moderne. Detlev Peukert zum Gedenken. Hrsg. von Frank Bajohr [et al.]. Hamburg: Christians, 1991. Pp. 307–321. [Augm. and revised version of a lecture given at a conference on historiography of the Holocaust, held at the Univ. of California in 1990.]

28314. — DONAT, HELMUT/WIELAND, LOTHAR, eds.: *'Auschwitz erst möglich gemacht?' Überlegungen zur jüngsten konservativen Geschichtsbewältigung.* Bremen: Donat, 1991. 214 pp. [13 essays, incl.: Holocaust und 'Historikerstreit' (Leonidas E. Hill, 23–37, notes). Brüderlichkeit nach Auschwitz? Zum Verhältnis von Juden und Christen in Deutschland (Klaus Wedemeier, 83–93). Der Holocaust – ein transzendentaler Vernichtungsprozess? Kritische Anmerkun-gen zu Ernst Noltes Interpretation des Mordes an den Juden im Zweiten Weltkrieg (Hans-Walter Schmuhl, 119–133, notes). Treitschke redivivus? Ernst Nolte und die Juden (Julius H. Schoeps, 134–139). Bibliographie zum 'Historikerstreit' (Helmut Donat/Diether Koch/Martin Rohrkrämer, 150–214). [Cf.: Blick zurück nach vorn; Bestandsaufnahme zwischen zwei Historikerdebatten (Klaus Neumann) [in]: Die Zeit, Jg. 47, Nr. 12, Hamburg, 13. März 1992, p. 55.]

28315. — EBBINGHAUS, ANGELIKA/ROTH, KARL HEINZ: *Deutsche Historiker und der Holocaust.* [In]:

1999. Zeitschrift für Sozialgeschichte des 20. und 21. Jahrhunderts. H. 3, Köln, 1991. Pp. 7–10.

28316. — GEISS, IMMANUEL: *'Wende' und Ende im 'Historikerstreit'*. [In]: Historische Mitteilungen, 4, Jg., H. 1, Stuttgart 1991. Pp. 101–142.

28317. — LIPSTADT, DEBORAH E.: *Deniers, Relativists and pseudo-scholarship*. [In]: Dimensions, Vol. 6, No. 1, New York 1991, Pp. 4–9, illus., notes. [Examines how Holocaust denial has become more aggressive in the last decade and has assumed a pseudo-academic format.]

28318. — *Nationalsozialismus und Modernisierung*. Hrsg. von Michael Prinz und Rainer Zitelmann. Darmstadt: Wiss. Buchges., 1991. 337 pp., notes, bibl. [A collection of essays dealing with the impact of National Socialism on modern German society. Refers also passim to the 'Historians' Debate'.] [Cf.: Modernisierung des Nationalsozialismus (Christoph Dipper) [in]: Neue politische Literatur, Jg. 36, Frankfurt am Main, 1991. pp. 450–456; a critical discussion of Rainer Zitelmann's concept of National Socialism in the context of modernisation.]

28319. — OVERY, RICHARD: *The 'Historikerstreit'*. [In]: The Jewish Quarterly, Vol. 37, No. 3, London, Autumn 1990. Pp. 13–15, illus.

28320. — SENFFT, HEINRICH: *Kein Abschied von Hitler; ein Blick hinter die Fassaden des 'Historikerstreits'*. Hrsg. von der Hamburger Stiftung für Sozialgeschichte des 20. Jahrhunderts. Köln: Volksblatt Verlag, 1990. 145 pp., bibl., index of persons. (Kleine historische Bibliothek, Bd. 2.)

28321. — SHAPIRO, SHELLEY, ed.: *Truth prevails: demolishing Holocaust denial: the end of 'The Leuchter report'*. Latham, N.Y. 12110, 800 New Loudon Road, suite 400): Beate Klarsfeld Foundation and Holocaust Survivors and Friends in Pursuit of Justice, 1990. XI, 135 pp., illus., facsims., bibl. [Leuchter report denied that Germans used gas chambers during Holocaust. F. A. Leuchter, Massachusetts businessman, claims to be an expert in gas-chamber technology.]

28322. — THOMAS, LAURENCE: *Characterizing and responding to Nazi Genocide: a review essay*. [In]: Modern Judaism, Vol. 11, No. 3, Baltimore, Oct. 1991. Pp. 371–379, notes. [Reviews various recent publications on the Holocaust.]

28323. — *(The) unresolved past: a debate in German history*. A conference sponsored by the Wheatland Foundation. Chaired and introduced by Ralf Dahrendorf. Ed. by Gina Thomas. London: Weidenfeld and Nicholson, 1990. 138 pp. [Conference on the 'historians' debate' held in Sept. 1987 at Leeds Castle. Cf.: A collection of tribes with little but language in common (Daniel Johnson) [in]: The Spectator, London, Feb. 9, 1991.]

28324. — WICKHAM, CHRISTOPHER J.: *Representation and mediation in Edgar Reitz's 'Heimat'*. [In]: The German Quarterly, Vol. 64, No. 1, Cherry Hill, N.J., Winter 1991. Pp. 35–45.

28325. HOFFMANN, CHRISTHARD/SCHWARTZ, DANIEL R.: *Early but opposed – supported but late*. Two Berlin seminaries which attempted to move abroad. [In]: LBI Year Book XXXVI, London, 1991. Pp. 267–304, footnotes, port., illus. [On the Rabbinerseminar für das Orthodoxe Judentum, the 'Hildesheimer Seminary', and the Hochschule (Lehranstalt) für die Wissenschaft des Judentums.]

28326. HOLOCAUST. ALY, GÖTZ/HEIM, SUSANNE: *Vordenker der Vernichtung. Auschwitz und die deutschen Pläne für eine neue europäische Ordnung*. Hamburg: Hoffmann & Campe, 1991. 544 pp., notes, chronol. table, index of persons. [On the interrelation between Nazi economic and demographic policies and the plans for mass annihilation; authors discuss also whether systematic mass murder of Jews and other groups of the population would be repeatable.] [Cf.: Ist der Holocaust wirklich nicht wiederholbar? (Torsten Borchers [in]: Allgemeine Jüdische Wochenzeitung, Nr. 47, Bonn, 9. Jan. 1992, p. 5. Rationalität und Vernichtung (Siegbert Wolf) [in]: Tribüne, Jg. 30, H. 118, Frankfurt am Main, 1991. Pp. 226–228.]

28327. — ARAD, YIZHAK, ed.: The pictorial history of the Holocaust. London, New York: Macmillan, 1990. 396 pp. illus. [A compilation of photographs, maps and text, incl. section on persecution of German Jews 1933–1939.]

28328. — BENZ, WOLFGANG, Hrsg.: *Dimension des Völkermords. Die Zahl der jüdischen Opfer des Nationalsozialismus*. München: Oldenburg, 1991. 584 pp., index of persons (565–571), of places (572–584). [Cont.: Die Dimension des Völkermords. Einleitung (Wolfgang Benz, 1–22). Deutsches Reich (Ino Arndt/Heinz Boberach, 23–66). Österreich (Jonny Moser, 67–94). Luxemburg (Ino Arndt, 95–104). Frankreich und Belgien (Juliane Wetzel, 105–136). Niederlande (137–166). Dänemark (Hermann Weiß, 167–186). Norwegen (187–198). Italien (Liliana Picciotto Fargion, 199–228). Albanien (Gerhard Grimm, 229–240). Griechenland (Hagen Fleischer, 241–274). Bulgarien (Hans-Joachim Hoppe, 275–310). Jugoslawien (Holm Sundhaussen, 311–330). Ungarn (László Varga, 331–352). Tschechoslowakei (Eva Schmidt-Hartmann, 353–380). Rumänien (Krista Zach, 381–410). Polen (Frank Golczewski, 411–498). Sowjetunion (Gert Robel, 499–560).] [Cf.: Zahlen des Grauens; ein Standardwerk zum Holocaust (Eberhard Jäckel) [in]: Die Zeit, Nr. 27, Hamburg, 28. Juni 1991, p. 47. Dimension des Völkermords. Zu einer Neuerscheinung des Instituts für Zeitgeschichte (Klaus Hildebrand) [in]: Geschichte in Wissenschaft und Unterricht, 42. Jg., H. 11, Seelze, 1991. Pp. 710–713. See also: Zahlenbeispiele mit den Auschwitz-Opfern? Mit Wahrheit ist der Erinnerung am besten gedient (Michael Wolffsohn) [in]: Frankfurter Allgemeine Zeitung, Nr. 7, 9. Jan. 1991, p. 10.]

28329. — COHN-SHERBOK, DAN: *Jewish faith and the Holocaust.* [In]: Religious Studies, Jg. 26, H. 2, Cambridge, 1990. Pp. 277.

28330. — FRIEDLÄNDER, SAUL: *Die Dimension des Völkermords an den europäischen Juden.* [In]: Merkur, 45. Jg., H. 508, Stuttgart 1991. Pp. 557–634. [Review article of RAUL HILBERG: Die Vernichtung der europäischen Juden [See No. 27274/YBXXXVI] and WOLFGANG BENZ: Dimension des Völkermords. Die Zahl der jüdischen Opfer des Nationalsozialismus [see No. 28328.]

28331. — *Generations of the Holocaust.* Ed. by Martin S. Bergmann and Milton E. Jucovy. Irvinton, N.Y.: Columbia Univ. Press, 1991. 360 pp. [Psychoanalytic study of the effect of the Holocaust on the second generation. Also incl. a section on the children of Nazis who frequently identify with the Jewish victims.]

28332. — GOTTLIEB, ROGER S., ed.: *Thinking the unthinkable; meanings of the Holocaust.* New York: Paulist Press, 1990, XI, 446 pp.

28333. — HENNINGSEN, MANFRED: *Die Pest, der Holocaust und die europäische Hemmungslosigkeit des Tötens.* [In]: Merkur, Jg. 45, H. 3, Stuttgart, 1991. Pp. 239–245. [Review essay.]

28334. — KLEE, ERNST [et al.], eds.: *'Those were the days': the Holocaust through the eyes of the perpetrators and bystanders.* Foreword by Lord Dacre of Glanton. London: Hamish Hamilton, 1991, 288 pp. [American edn. under the title: 'The good old days': the Holocaust as seen by its perpetrators and bystanders. Foreword by Hugh Trevor-Roper. New York: Free Press, 1991. 288 pp.] [For orig. German edn. see No. 25346/YBXXXIV.]

28335. — KUSHNER, TONY: *Rules of the game: Britain, America and the Holocaust in 1944.* [In]: Holocaust and Genocide Studies, Vol. 5, No. 4, Jerusalem, 1990. Pp. 381–402. [In the same issue also: Technical analysis of methods to bomb the gas chambers at Auschwitz (Richard Foregger, 403–422). David Wyman and the historiography of America's response to the Holocaust: counter-considerations (Frank W. Brecher, 423–446).]

28336. — LANGER, LAWRENCE: *Holocaust testimonies: the ruins of memory.* New Haven, Ct.: Yale Univ. Press, 1991. 240 pp., illus. [Drawing on the Fortunoff Video Archives for Holocaust Testimonies at Yale University, author shows how oral Holocaust testimonies complement historical studies.]

28337. — LEVKOVITZ, ELLIOT, ed.: *Dimensions of the Holocaust.* Evanston, Ill.: Northwestern Univ. Press, 1990. 90 pp. [First publ. in 1977, contains essays by Elie Wiesel, Lucy Dawidowicz, a.o. Deals with society's inability to comprehend the Holocaust and its unwillingness to remember.]

28338. — ULLRICH, VOLKER: *'Wir haben nichts gewußt'; ein deutsches Trauma.* [In]: 1999. Zeitschrift für Sozialgeschichte des 20. und 21. Jahrhunderts. H. 3, Köln, 1991. Pp. 11–46.

28339. — WOLLASTON, I.: 'Starting all over again'? The criteria for a Christian response to the Holocaust. [In]: Theology, 93, No. 756, London, 1990. Pp. 456–461.

28340. — YOUNG, JAMES E.: *Erinnern und Gedenken. Die Schoa und die jüdische Identität.* [In]: Jüdische Lebenswelten. Essays [see No. 27946]. Frankfurt am Main: Jüdischer Verlag, Suhrkamp, 1991. Pp. 149–164, illus., bibl. [On the Holocaust as a base for Jewish identity and on Holocaust memorials in Israel, Poland, Germany and elsewhere.]

28341. ITALY. CAVAGLION, ALBERTO: *Nella notte straniera: gli ebrei di St.-Martin-Vésubie 8 Settembre – 21 Novembre 1943.* Cuneo: Edizioni l'Arciere Cuneo. 159 pp. [Incl. deportations of German and Austrian Jews.]

28342. — PICCIOTTO FARGION, LILIANA: *Il libro della memoria; gli ebrei deportati dall'Italia (1943–1945).* Milano: Mursia, 1991. 950 pp., illus., notes, bibl., index of names. (Ricerca del Centro di Documentazione Ebraica Contemporanea.) [The lists of deportees include the names of all the German- and Austrian-Jewish refugees who were sent from Italy to the death camps in the East.]

28343. — VOLPE, FRANCESCO: *Ferramonti: un lager nel sud.* Atti del Convegno internazionali di studi 15/16 maggio 1987. Cosenza: Edizionii Orizzonti meridionali, 1990. 207 pp. [Contains much material on Jewish refugees from Germany and elsewhere in internment camps in Calabria.]

28344. KAPLAN, MARION: *Alltagsleben jüdischer Frauen in Deutschland 1933–1938.* [In]: Frauen und Faschismus in Europa. Der faschistische Körper. Hrsg. von Leonore Siegele-Wenschke-witz/Gerda Stuchlik. Pfaffenweiler: Centaurus 1990, pp. 137–149, footnotes. (Frauen in Geschichte und Gesellschaft, Bd. 6.]

28345. KAPLAN, MARION: *Jewish women in Nazi Germany: daily life, daily struggles, 1935–1939.* [In]: Juden in Deutschland [see No. 27940]. Hamburg: Christians, 1991. Pp. 406–434, notes. [Article is also published in Feminist Studies, 1990. College Park, Md., Fall 1990. Pp. 579–606.]

28346. KARLSRUHE. WERNER, JOSEF: *Hakenkreuz und Judenstern: das Schicksal der Karlsruher Juden im Dritten Reich.* Hrsg.: Stadt Karlsruhe, Stadtarchiv. 2., überarb, und erw. Aufl. Karlsruhe: Badenia, 1990. 558 pp., illus. [For first edn. see No. 25343/YBXXXIV.]

28347. KATTOWITZ. KONIECZNY, ALFRED: *Struktur und Tätigkeit der Gestapo-Stelle Kattowitz zur Zeit des Zweiten Weltkrieges.* [In Polish, with German and French summaries.] [In]: Studia nad faczyzmen i zbrodniami Hitlerowskimi, XIV, Wroclaw: Uniwersytet Wroclawski – Wydawnictwo, 1991. Pp. 309–348.

28348. KLEVE. SCHÜÜRMANN, HERBERT: *Als Schilder erschienen: 'Juden nicht erwünscht'.* [In]: Kalender für das Klever Land auf das Jahr 1991. 41. Jg. Kleve: Boss, 1990. Pp. 50–53.

28349. KOCH, GERTRUD: *The angel of forgetfulness and the black box of facticity: trauma and memory in Claude Lanzmann's film Shoah.* [In]: History and Memory, Vol. e, No. 1, Tel Aviv, Spring 1991. Pp. 119–134, notes.

28350. KWIET, KONRAD: *Forced labour of German Jews in Nazi Germany.* [In]: LBI Year Book XXXVI, London, 1991. Pp. 389–410, footnotes, illus., document. [Incl., published here for the first time, a historical key-document of March 1939, revealing the long-term Nazi planning of the disposal of the Jewish population of Germany.]

28351. KWIET, KONRAD: *'Ich verpflichte mich, das Kennzeichen sorgfältig zu behandeln . . .'. Verordnungen bestimmten die Details.* [In]: Der Davidstern; Zeichen der Schmach – Symbol der Hoffnung [see No. 27924]. Dorsten, 1991. Pp. 112–121. [On the imposition of the Jews' badge in Sept. 1941.]

28352. LANGBEIN, HERMANN: *Diskussion über die Zahl der Opfer. Trotz allem: Auschwitz bleibt Inbegriff der Vernichtung.* [In]: Tribüne, Jg. 30, H. 117, Frankfurt am Main, 1991. Pp. 38–46. [Confirms the estimate of a minimum of 1.35 million Jews murdered in Auschwitz.]

28353. LAQUEUR, RENATA: *Schreiben im KZ; Tagebücher 1940–1945.* Bearb. von Martina Dreisbach und mit einem Geleitwort von Rolf Wernstedt. Hrsg.: Niedersächsische Landeszentrale für politische Bildung. Bremen: Donat, 1991. 168 pp., illus., bib. (153–166), map. [About 13 concentration camp inmates, their biographies and diaries, collected and analysed by Renata Laqueur, who, herself, had written a diary during her internment in Bergen-Belsen, see No. 28235.] [R.L., born Nov. 3, 1919 in Brieg, Silesia, daughter of the pharmacologist Ernst Laqueur, grew up in the Netherlands, from where she was deported to Bergen-Belsen in March 1944. Liberated by the Red Army near Tröbitz. Lives in New York.]

28354. LASKIER, MICHAEL M.: *Between Vichy antisemitism and German harassment: the Jews of North Africa during the early 1940s.* [In]: Modern Judaism, Vol. 11, No. 3, Baltimore, Oct. 1991. Pp. 343–369, tabs., notes. [Jewish population included many German-Jewish refugees.]

28355. LEE, BARBARA SCHWARZ: *Heroic and shameful behavior in the Nazi concentration camps.* [In]: Journal of Psychology and Judaism, Vol. 14, No. 2, New York, Summer 1990. Pp. 109–124, notes.

28356. LEMBERG. KAHANE, DAVID: *Lvov Ghetto diary.* Transl. from the Hebrew by Jerzy Michalowicz. Amherst: Univ. of Massachusetts Press, 1990. 176 pp. [The memoirs cover the period from July 1, 1941 to July 27, 1944. The author escaped and survived in hiding.]

28357. LEPSIUS, JULIANE: *Es taucht in Träumen wieder auf.* Schicksale seit 1933. Düsseldorf: Droste, 1991. 259 pp., illus. [Narrative interviews incl. Jews resp. persons of Jewish descent who were persecuted by the Nazis: Es gab ja keine Fragen (Sonja Teller, 47–93; S.T., born in Prague, deported to Theresienstadt and Auschwitz). Denken und überwinden (Lajos Skékely, 95–144; psychoanalyst, born in Budapest, emigrated to the Soviet Union). Doppelte Glaubenskraft (Siegfried Borris, 145–177; of partly Jewish descent, born in Berlin, composer, musicologist, son of the statistician Salomon Zuckermann). Es taucht in

Träumen wieder auf (Gertrude Milch-Meyer, 179–259; orig. Kantorowicz, emigrated from Berlin to Brazil in 1936).]

28358. LEVIN, NORA: *The Holocaust years: the Nazi destruction of European Jewry 1933–1945.* Malabar, Fla.: Krieger, 1990. X, 373 pp., illus., maps, tabs. [Incl. persecution of German Jewry, November Pogrom, Jewish resistance. Part 1 consists of a concise history of the period, part 2 consists of 100 official Nazi and Allied documents illustrating these events.]

——— LEYENS, ERICH/ANDOR, LOTTE: *Die fremden Jahre. Erinnerungen an Deutschland.* [See No. 28823.]

28359. LITHUANIA. HAASE, NORBERT: *". . . eine Sportveranstaltung, wenn auch etwas besonderer Art . . .".* Der Mord an den Libauer Juden im Sommer 1941. Aus dem Tagebuch eines Augenzeugen. [In]: Tribüne, Jg. 30, H. 120, Frankfurt am Main, 1991. Pp. 200–208.

28360. LODZ (Ghetto). ZONABEND, NACHMAN: *The truth about the saving of the Lodz ghetto archive.* Published by the author. Stockholm, 1991. 20 pp., illus. [On how the author saved the documents of the Lodz ghetto.]

28361. LÜDENSCHEID. SCHMIDT, HANS-GÜNTER: *'Es war die uns von Gott gegebene Obrigkeit'.* Studien und Materialien zur Zeit des Nationalsozialismus in Lüdenscheid. Pfaffenweiler: Centaurus, 1991. 199 [35] pp., notes (163–186), tabs., stats., bibl. (187–196). (Bibliothek der historischen Forschung; 3.) [Incl. the chap.: Antisemitismus und Judenverfolgung in Lüdenscheid (139–145).]

28362. MAIN-SPESSART (Landkreis) *Gedenkbuch für die Opfer der Verfolgung der Juden unter der nationalsozialistischen Gewaltherrschaft im Gebiet des Landkreises Main-Spessart 1933–1945.* Hrsg.: Förderkreis Synagoge Urspringen. Zusammenstellung: Martin Harth. Urspringen: Förderkreis Synagoge, 1991. 30 pp., illus.

28363. — *'. . . auf höhere Weisung abgewandert'. Leben und Leiden der Juden im Landkreis Main-Spessart.* [Hrsg.: Landkreis Main-Spessart]. Karlstadt: Landkreis Main-Spessart, 1990. 62 pp., illus.

28364. *M.d.R. Die Reichstagsabgeordneten der Weimarer Republik in der Zeit des Nationalsozialismus. Politische Verfolgung, Emigration und Ausbürgerung 1933–1945.* Eine biographische Dokumentation, bearbeitet von Katharina Lübbe (et al.). Hrsg.: Martin Schuhmacher. Droste: Düsseldorf, 1991. 686 pp., illus., tabs., stat., indexes. [Incl. politicians of Jewish and partly Jewish descent.] [Cf.: Besprechung (Ralph Uhlig) [in]: Das Historisch-Politische Buch, 40. Jg., H. 1 & 2, Göttingen, 1992. Pp. 48–49.]

28365. MEHL, STEFAN: *Das Reichsfinanzministerium und die Verfolgung der deutschen Juden 1933–1945.* Berlin: Zentralinstitut für Sozialwiss. Forschung, 1990. VII, 117 pp., bibl. (Berliner Arbeitshefte und Berichte zur sozialwissenschaftlichen Forschung; 38.)

28366. MELCHIOR, IB/BRANDENBURG, FRANK: *Quest: searching for Germany's Nazi past, a man's story.* Novato, Ca.: Presidio Press, 1990. XII, 330 pp., illus., ports. [Personal account by Brandenburg, a young German non-Jew, on his discovery of the Nazi past, his visit to Auschwitz, and his subsequent interviews with Nazi war criminals.]

28367. MOERS. WIRSBITZKI, BRIGITTE: *Geschichte der Moerser Juden nach 1933.* Mit einem Beitrag von Michael Brocke zum jüdischen Friedhof. Herausgegeben von der Gesellschaft für Christlich-Jüdische Zusammenarbeit. Moers: Brendow, 1991. 264 pp., illus., map, ports.

28368. MOLL, MICHAEL/WEILER, BARBARA, eds.: *Lyrik gegen das Vergessen. Gedichte aus Konzentrationslagern.* Mit Illustrationen von Tina Stolt. Marburg: Schüren, 1991. 174 pp., notes, bibl. [Collection of poems by Jewish and non-Jewish inmates of Nazi ghettos and concentration camps, partly unknown. Incl. also biographies of authors as far as their names and fate could be established.]

28369. MOMMSEN, HANS: *Was mit der Ausgrenzung begann, endete im Verbrechen gegen die Menschen. Das Ende der deutsch-jüdischen Symbiose.* [In]: Der Davidstern; Zeichen der Schmach – Symbol der Hoffnung [see No. 27924]. Dorsten, 1991. Pp. 162–169.

28370. MOMMSEN, HANS: *From Weimar to Auschwitz: essays in German history.* Transl. by Philip O'Connor. Princeton, N.J.; Princeton Univ. Press, 1991. 367 pp., notes (279–353), glossary. [Essays incl.: National Socialism: continuity and change (141–162; also antisemitism). The realization of the unthinkable: the 'Final Solution of the Jewish Question' in the Third Reich (224–253). Hannah Arendt and the Eichmann trial (254–278).]

28371. MÜLLER, INGO: *Hitler's justice: the courts in the Third Reich.* Transl. by Deborah Lucas Schneider. Introd. by Detlev Vagts. Cambridge, Ma.: Harvard Univ. Press, 1991. 368 pp., illus., tab.

28372. *Musik in Konzentrationslagern.* Konzeption und Durchführung [Hrsg.]: Projektgruppe Musik in Konzentrationslagern, Andrea Baaske [et al.]. Freiburg i. Br. 1991, 84 pp., illus.

[Accompanying brochure to a series of concerts, films, lectures and an exhibition held in Freiburg i. Br. Oct. 21 – Dec. 18, 1991.]

28373. NELKI, ERNA & WOLFGANG: *Geschichten aus dem Umbruch der deutschen Geschichte zwischen Assimilation und Asyl*. Hannover: Revonnah, 1991. 58 pp. [About the Nelki family from Berlin, incl. the story of a friend, Edith Ehrlich, who survived in hiding.]

28374. NETHERLANDS. MOORE, BOB: *Jewish refugee entrepreneurs and the Dutch economy in the 1930s*. [In]: Immigrants and Minorities. Vol. 9, No. 1, London, March 1990. Pp. 46–63, tabs., notes. [Deals mainly with German-Jewish refugees and some Dutch misgivings about their role in the economy.]

28375. — STOOP, PAUL: *Das tödliche Dilemma des Judenrats. Kooperation und Verantwortung während der deutschen Besatzung der Niederlande*. [In]: Tribüne, Jg. 30, H. 118, Frankfurt am Main, 1991. Pp. 154–162, illus., footnotes.

28376. NEUENGAMME. KAIENBURG, HERMANN: *'Vernichtung durch Arbeit': der Fall Neuengamme*; die Wirtschaftsbestrebungen der SS und ihre Auswirkungen auf die Existenzbedingungen der KZ-Gefangenen. Bonn: Dietz, 1990. 503 pp., illus., notes. Zugl.: Hamburg, Univ., Diss. 1989.

28377. — *Arbeit und Vernichtung: das Konzentrationslager Neuengamme 1938–1945*. Katalog zur ständigen Ausstellung der KZ-Gedenkstätte Neuengamme, Aussenstelle des Museums für Hamburgische Geschichte. 2., überarb. Aufl., hrsg. von Ulrich Bauche. Hamburg: VSA-Verlag, 1991. 260 pp., illus., bibl.

28378. NORWAY. SOKOLL, GABRIELE: *Julius Elias, Halvdan Koht und das jüdische Exil in Norwegen*. [In]: Skandinavistik, 21, Glückstadt, 1991. Pp. 116–130. [On the jurist and literary historian Dr. Julius Elias, Berlin, Sept. 19, 1891 – Dec. 1942 (?) Auschwitz, who emigrated with his mother Julie Elias in 1938 to Norway with the assistance of the Norwegian foreign minister, Halvdan Koht, and was deported by the Germans to Auschwitz in Oct. 1942. In the same issue: ERIK M. CHRISTENSEN: Brandes, Berlin und Bismarck; pp. 131–135. [See also on Georg Brandes No. 27856/YBXXXVI.]

——— NOVEMBER POGROM. [See also Nos. 28220 and 28501.]

28379. — BENZ, WOLFGANG: *Trauern oder Feiern. Der schwierige 9. November*. [In]: Journal Geschichte, Jg., H. 5, Weinheim, 1990. Pp. 38–45, illus.

28380. — DICK, LUTZ: Der Attentäter: Herschel Grynszpan und die Vorgänge um die 'Kristallnacht'. Orig.-Ausg. Reinbek b. Hamburg: Rowohlt, 1991. 216 pp., bibl. (rororo-Rotfuchs; 527.) [On the pre-history of the November Pogrom.]

28381. — HAMMERSTEIN, FRANZ VON: *Das Pogrom vom 9./10. November 1938 als Problem und Aufgabe in Deutschland heute*. [In]: Judaica, Jg. 47, H. 1/2, Basel, Juni 1991, pp. 103–106.

28382. — JONCA, KAROL: *Die 'Kristallnacht': Studium über die moderne Pogromtechnik vom 9. – 10. November 1938 im Dritten Reich* [in Polish, title transl.]. [In]: Acta Universitatis Wratislaviensis, No. 1169, Wroclaw, 1991. Pp. 195–218, notes. (Studia nad Faszyzmem i Zbrodniami Hitlerowskimi 14.) [Incl. German and French abstract of article.]

28383. — JONCA, KAROL: *Die "Kristallnacht" und der Fall des Herschel Grynszpan* [in Polish, title transl.]. (Acta Universitatis Wratislaviensis No. 1312). Wroclaw: Uniwersytet Wroclawski – Wydawnictwo, 1992. 398 pp., illus., notes, bibl. (371–380), index. [Incl. German summary.]

28384. — JONCA, KAROL: *Die Radikalisierung des Antisemitismus; der Fall Herschel Grynszpan und die 'Reichskristallnacht'*. [In]: Karl Dietrich Bracher [et al.], ed.: Deutschland zwischen Krieg und Frieden. Beiträge zur Politik und Kultur im 20. Jahrhundert. Festschrift für Hans-Adolf Jacobsen. Düsseldorf: Droste, 1991. Pp. 43–55.

28385. — MOMMSEN, HANS: *Die Funktion des Antisemitismus im 'Dritten Reich'; Das Beispiel des Novemberpogroms*. [In]: Zerbrochene Geschichte [See No. 27980]. Pp. 161–171.

28386. — SHAMIR, HAIM: *The 'Crystal Night' pogrom in relation to Nazi domestic and foreign policy at the end of 1938*. [In Hebrew, with English summary]. [In]: Yalkut Moreshet, No. 50, Tel-Aviv, Apr. 1991. Pp. 111–118.

28387. — TOMASZEWSKI, JERZY: *The deportation of Jews of Polish citizenship from Germany October 28 – October 29, 1938*. [In Polish, with German and French summaries]. [In]: Studia nad faczyzmen i zbrodniami Hitlerowskimi, XIV, Wroclaw: Uniwersytet Wroclawski – Wydawnictwo, 1991. Pp. 167–193, footnotes.

28388. OEGEMA, GERBERN S.: *Die Geschichte des Davidsterns. Zum 50. Jahrestag der Einführung des Judensterns am 1. September 1941*. [In]: Tribüne, Jg. 30, H. 120 Frankfurt am Main, 1991. Pp. 209–214.

584   Bibliography

28389.   OLDENBURG. *Mahnmal für alle Opfer des Nationalsozialismus in Oldenburg, 9. November 1990;*
         eine Dokumentation. Hrsg. von der Stadt Oldenburg, Kulturdezernat. Oldenburg: Holzberg,
         1990. 60 pp., illus.
28390.   PAWELZIK, FRITZ/SCHILD, GÜNTHER: *Frankreich ohne Rückfahrkarte.* Wuppertal; Zürich:
         Brockhaus, 1990. 208 pp. [Memoirs of Günther Schild, who played an active role as a Berlin
         lawyer in defending anti-Nazis before 1933; emigrated to France, where he survived in
         hiding.]
28391.   PEHLE, WALTER H., ed.: *November 1938: from 'Kristallnacht' to Genocide.* Transl. from the
         German by William Templer. Oxford, New York: Berg, 1991. X, 259 pp.
28392.   PINGEL, FALK: *The destruction of human identity in concentration camps: the contribution of the social*
         sciences to an analysis of behaviour under extreme conditions. [In]: Holocaust and Genocide Studies,
         Vol. 6, No. 2, Oxford, 1991. Pp. 167–184. notes.
28393.   POMERANIA. FRANKIEWICZ, BOGDAN: *Zur Lage der Juden in Pommern nach Hitlers Machtüber-*
         nahme. [In]: Studia nad faczyzmen i zbrodniami Hitlerowskimi, XIV, Wroclaw: Uniwersy-
         tet Wroclawski – Wydawnictwo, 1991. Pp. 267–279, footnotes.
28394.   PORAT, DINA: *Jews from the Third Reich in the Ninth Fort near Kowno, 1941–1942.* [In]: Tel Aviver
         Jahrbuch für deutsche Geschichte, Bd. 20, Gerlingen, 1991. Pp. 363–392, notes.
28395.   PROCTOR, ROBERT N.: *Racial hygiene: the collaboration of medicine and Nazism.* [In]: Dimensions,
         Vol. 5, No. 2, New York, 1990. Pp. 3–6, illus., notes.
28396.   RAVENSBRÜCK. BRUHA, ANTONIA: *Chronik des Konzentrationslagers Ravensbrück anhand der*
         im DÖW befindlichen Aktensammlung. [In]: Dokumentationsarchiv des österreichischen
         Widerstandes. Jahrbuch 1991. Wien: [Österreichischer Bundesverl. ?], 1991. Pp. 101–107,
         footnotes.
28397.   REFUGEE POLICY. BAUMEL, JUDITH TYDOR: *The Jewish refugee children from Europe in the*
         eyes of the American press and public opinion 1934–1945. [In]: Holocaust and Genocide Studies,
         Vol. 5, No. 3, Jerusalem, 1990. Pp. 293–312.
28398.   — FREEDEN, HERBERT: *Tausende danken ihr das Leben. Eleanore Rathbone und die Tragödie der*
         europäischen Juden. [In]: Tribüne, Jg. 30, H. 119, Frankfurt am Main, 1991. Pp. 80–82. [E.R.
         British MP, actively involved in organising immigration for Jewish refugees from Nazi
         oppression to Great Britain and Palestine.]
28399.   — JOLLES, CHARLOTTE: *Probst Grüber und die Flüchtlingshilfe in England; Erinnerungen aus den*
         Jahren 1939 bis 1945. [In]: Standpunkt; Evangelische Monatsschrift, 17. Jg., H. 2, Berlin
         [East], Feb. 1989. Pp. 44–46. [On the 'Büro Grüber' and the 'Church of England Committee
         for "Non-Aryan" Christians', which organised the rescue of Christian children of Jewish
         descent from Nazi Germany and elsewhere.] [An English version of this article (typescript)
         is available in the LBI London; on the 'Büro Grüber' see also No. 28300.]
————   — KAMBAS, CHRYSSOULA: *Bulletin de Vernuches: neue Quellen zur Internierung Walter Benjamins.*
         [See No. 28685.]
28400.   — KOHLER, ERIC D.: *Relicencing Central European refugee physicians in the United States, 1933–*
         1945. [In]: Simon Wiesenthal Center Annual, Vol. 6, White Plains, N.Y., 1989. Pp. 3–32.
         [Chiefly on German Jews.]
28401.   — LASSERRE, ANDRÉ: *Les réfugiés de Bergen-Belsen et Theresienstadt ou les déboires d'une politique*
         d'asil en 1944–1945. [In]: Schweizerische Zeitschrift für Geschichte/Revue Suisse d'Histoire/
         Rivista Storica Svizzera, Vol. 40, Basel, 1990. Pp. 307–317.
28402.   REFUGEES. HOLMES, COLIN: *A tolerant country? Immigrants, refugees and minorities in Britain.*
         London: Faber, 1991. 127 pp., notes, bibl. (118–122). [Covers German-Jewish refugees as
         well.]
28403.   — LEHNSEN, HEINRICH: *Flucht über die niederländische Grenze bei Elmpt*; aus den Erinnerungen
         des Heinrich Lehnsen 1939 bis 1945; herausgegeben von Manfred Backhausen. [In]:
         Heimatbuch des Kreises Viersen 1991, 42. Folge, Viersen, 1990. Pp. 144–150, illus. [Also on
         Jewish refugees fleeing illegally across the German-Dutch border.]
28404.   — THALMANN, RITA: *La mise au pas; idéologie et stratégie sécuritaire dans la France occupée.* Paris:
         Fayard, 1991. 395 pp., docs., facsims., notes, bibl. [Covers also fate of German-Jewish
         refugees in France.]
28405.   — ZARIZ, RUTH: *Berthold Storfer and his role in rescuing Jews from Germany.* [In Hebrew, title
         transl.] [In]: Shapira, Anita, ed.: Ha'apalah. [Illegal immigration: an anthology on the
         history of the rescue, the escape, the illegal immigration and the Holocaust survivors.] Tel
         Aviv: Tel Aviv University; Am Oved, 1990. Pp. 124–142. [B. Storfer, data see No. 27394/
         YBXXXVI.]

28406. — *AJR Information*: Special fiftieth anniversary issue. London: July 1991. AJR Information, Vol. 46, No. 7, London, July 1991. [The history of the Association of Jewish Refugees on the occasion of its 50th anniversary. Incl.: From foundation to maturity (David Maier, 6–7). Thanking Britain (Hans Feld, 11). Gems from the archives (M.N., 12–13). Endurance and optimism; the spadework of the founder members (Werner Rosenstock, 18–19).]

—— — *Dunera News* [see No. 28185.].

28407. — *Escape to the rising sun*. A 95-minute film written and directed by Diane Perelsztejn. Belgium 1990. [This documentary was shown on Oct. 22, 1991, in London, as part of the 7th Jewish Film Festival. The film, on the 20,000 Jews from Europe who escaped from Nazi persecution to Shangai, incl. German- and Austrian-Jewish refugees.]

—— — *Hitlerflüchtlinge im Norden. Asyl und politisches Exil 1933–1945*. Hrsg. von Hans Uwe Petersen. [See No. 28187.]

28408. REMSCHEID. BREIDENBACH, ARMIN: *Judenverfolgung in Remscheid: 1933–1945*. Hrsg.: Die Grünen, Kreisverband Remscheid. Remscheid; Berlin: Die Grünen, Kreisverband Remscheid, 1990. 51 pp.

—— RESISTANCE BY NON-JEWS. DEUTSCHKRON, INGE: *Berlin Jews underground*. [See No. 28237.]

28409. — REWALD, ILSE: *Berliners who helped us to survive the Hitler dictatorship*. Berlin: Gedenkstätte deutscher Widerstand/German Resistance Memorial Center, 1990. [12] pp. (German Resistance 1933–1945.)

28410. — STOPNIAK, FRANCISZEK: *Bemerkungen zu Hilfsaktionen geistlicher Personen für Juden im Zweiten Weltkrieg*. [In Polish, with German and French summaries.] [In]: Studia nad faczyzmen i zbrodniami Hitlerowskimi, XIV, Wroclaw: Uniwersytet Wroclawski – Wydawnictwo, 1991. Pp. 253–265, footnotes.

28411. — SCHMALHAUSEN, BERND: *Berthold Beitz im Dritten Reich. Mensch in unmenschlicher Zeit*. Essen: Pomp, 1991. 111 pp., illus. [About the mass executions of Jews in Drohobycz and Boryslaw in Eastern Galicia, and the attempts of Berthold Beitz, at that time director of an oil company in Boryslaw, to save Jews. Also on the mass exterminations of Belzec. Also on Beitz: THOMAS SANDKÜHLER: Wer mit dem Teufel handelt . . . Menschlichkeit im Holocaust: Die bitteren Erfahrungen des Berthold Beitz in Ostgalizien 1941–44. [In]: Die Zeit, Nr. 8, Hamburg, 14. Feb. 1992. P. 49.]

28412. REWALD, RUTH. KRÜGER, DIRK: *Wider das Vergessen. Erinnerungen an die deutsch-jüdische Kinder- und Jugendbuchautorin Ruth Rewald*. [In]: Menora, Bd. 2, München, 1991. Pp. 270–297, notes. [Abstract of the author's dissertation about Ruth Rewald, published in 1990, see No. 27244/YBXXXVI.]

28413. ROMANIA. STEPHANI, CLAUS: *'War einer Hersch, Fuhrmann'. Leben und Leiden der Juden in Oberwischau*; Erinnerungsgespräche. Frankfurt am Main: Hain, 1991. 191 pp., glossary, chronol. table, maps, bibl. [Narrative interviews of Germans about life before and during Nazi period in Oberwischau, a small market town in Transylvania (today: Viseu des Sus) with a mixed population of four ethnic groups (Germans, Jews, Romanians and Ruthenians) and about the deportations of the Jews between 1942 and 1944.]

28414. ROSE, PAUL LAWRENCE: *Joel Brand's interim agreement and the course of Nazi-Jewish negotiations 1944–1945*. [In]: The Historical Journal, Vol. 34, No. 7, Cambridge, 1991. Pp. 909–929, footnotes, glossary of Hebrew, Yiddish and code words, appendixes. [On J.B.'s agreement with Eichmann to save Hungarian Jews for money: incl. letters by Brand.]

28415. ROSENHEIM. *Rosenheim im Dritten Reich*; Beiträge zur Stadtgeschichte. Red.: Walter Leicht; Peter Miesbeck. Hrsg. vom Kulturamt der Stadt Rosenheim. Mit Beiträgen von Robert Berberich [et al.]. 8200 Rosenheim: Kulturamt der Stadt Rosenheim, 1989. 112 pp., illus. [Incl.: Antisemitismus und Judenverfolgung in Rosenheim 1920–1942 [and] Die Kaufmannsfamilie Fichtmann (Wolfgang Stäbler, 37–40, notes [&] 41–42, notes). Elisabeth Block aus Niedernburg (Manfred Treml, 43). Schicksale Rosenheimer Juden. Eine Dokumentation (Peter Miesbeck, 44–47, notes).]

28416. SCHLOSS, EVA/KENT, EVELYN JULIA: *Evas Geschichte; Anne Franks Stiefschwester erzählt*. Der Bericht einer Frau, die Verfolgung, Deportation und Lager überlebte. Aus dem Englischen von Angela Gaumér. München: Heyne, 1991. 216 pp., illus., map. [E.Sch., orig. Eva Geiringer, born May 11, 1929 in Vienna, fled with her family to Amsterdam in 1938, deported with her mother to Auschwitz in 1944. After the liberation her mother married Otto Frank, Anne Frank's father. For English orig. see No. 26522/YBXXXV.]

28417. SCHWAB, GERALD: *The day Holocaust began: the odyssey of Herschel Grynszpan.* New York: Praeger, 1990. XIII, 226 pp., bibl.

28418. SCHWEINFURT. *Dokumente jüdischen Lebens in Schweinfurt.* Ausstellung des Stadtarchivs Schweinfurt aus Anlass des Gedenkens an den 50. Jahrestag des Judenpogroms vom November 1938. Schweinfurt: Stadtarchiv, 1990. 132 pp., illus. (Veröffentlichungen des Stadtarchivs Schweinfurt; Nr. 4.)

28419. SILESIA. JONCA, KAROL: *The destruction of German Jews in Upper Silesia (1933–1945)* [in Polish, title transl., with German summary]. [In]: Sobótka, 2, Wroclaw, 1991. Pp. 219–249, footnotes. [Incl. lists of deportees, abstract in German.]

28420. *Simon Wiesenthal Center Annual. Vol. 6.* Eds.: Henry Friedlander and Sybil Milton. White Plains, N.Y.: Kraus Internat. Publ., 1989. 1 vol. [Incl.: Inside Auschwitz: four memoirs (Dagmar C.G. Lorenz, 113–142). Jews, Nazis, and the law: the case of Julius Streicher (Dennis E. Showalter, 143–163). *Review essays*: The German Jews under Hitler (Donald L. Niewyk, 235–247; review of 'Die Juden im Nationalsozialistischen Deutschland', Hrsg. Arnold Paucker, S. Gilchrist, B. Suchy, 1986). On the historiography of the SS (Charles W. Sydnor, 249–262). Cooperation, compliance, resistance: German diplomats in the Third Reich (George O. Kent, 263–276). Jewish life as stigma (Jack Zipes, 277–285). Interpretations of the Holocaust (Michael Berenbaum, 287–294). The bitter legacy of the Holocaust (Carl Steiner, 295–307). Further articles are listed according to subject.]

28421. SINGEN (Hohentwiel). KAPPES, REINHILD: *. . . und in Singen gab es keine Juden?* Eine Dokumentation. Hrsg. vom Kulturamt der Stadt Singen (Hohentwiel). Sigmaringen: Thorbecke, 1991. 112 pp., illus., facsims., plan, ports., tabs., bibl. (Hegau Bibliothek; Bd. 84.)

28422. SONNENBLUCK, HENRI: *J'avais 16 ans à Auschwitz.* Bruxelles: Librairie Alain Ferraton, [1991?]. 94 pp. [Cf.: Besprechung (Ulrich Brochhagen) [in]: Das Historisch-Politische Buch, Jg. 39, H. 12, Göttingen, 1991. P. 389.] [Recollections of how a young Belgian Jew in Antwerp was caught in hiding, deported to Auschwitz and later to Mauthausen, where he was liberated in 1945 by the Allied troops.]

28423. STEGEMANN, WOLF: *'Dagegen ist ihnen das Zeigen der jüdischen Farben gestattet'. Verordnungen bestimmten die Details.* [In]: Der Davidstern; Zeichen der Schmach – Symbol der Hoffnung [see No. 27924]. Dorsten, 1991. Pp. 108–111.

28424. STEGEMANN, WOLF: *Auch Kinder im Kinderwagen mußten den gelben Stern tragen. Die Verbreitung der Judenkennzeichen in den besetzten Ländern.* [In]: Der Davidstern; Zeichen der Schmach – Symbol der Hoffnung [see No. 27924]. Dorsten, 1991. Pp. 144–149.

———— STUTTGART. GUGGENHEIM, JULIUS & LINI: *Auch das geht vorüber* [See No. 28300.]

28425. — *Damit kein Gras drüber wächst . . . Eine Stadtrundfahrt durch Stuttgart auf den Spuren von Faschismus und Widerstand.* [Comp. by] Stafan Best [et al.]. Hrsg. vom Kreisverband Stuttgart der Gewerkschaft Erziehung und Wissenschaft. Ludwigsburg: Süddeutscher Päd. Verl., 1991. 74 pp., illus., maps. [Incl. persecution of Jews.]

28426. SUNNUS, MICHAEL: *Der NS-Rechtswahrerbund (1928–1945); zur Geschichte der nationalsozialistischen Juristenorganisation.* Frankfurt am Main: Lang, 1990. 180 pp. (Rechtshistorische Reihe; 78.) [Refers also to the expulsion of Jewish judges and lawyers.] [Cf.: Besprechung (Heinz Boberach) [in]: Das Historisch-Politische Buch, 40. Jg., H. 1 & 2, Göttingen, 1992. P. 69.]

28427. SWITZERLAND. BORNSTEIN, HEINI: *Aid and rescue activities from Switzerland.* [In Hebrew, with English summary; title transl.] [In]: Yalkut Moreshet, No. 51, Tel-Aviv, Nov. 1991. Pp. 81–90.

———— — GUGGENHEIM, KURT: *Wir waren unser vier.* [See No. 28975.]

28428. THERESIENSTADT. GOLDSCHEIDER, FRANZ: *'Die Juden und die Radfahrer sind an allem Schuld.'* Erinnerungen an das Theater im Ghetto in Theresienstadt. [In]: Berlin und der Prager Kreis [see No. 28666]. Würzburg: Königshausen & Neumann, 1991. Pp. 291–301.

28429. — KARNY, MIROSLAV: *Geschichte des Theresienstädter Transports in die Schweiz, Februar 1945.* [In]: Judaica Bohemiae, Vol. 27, No. 1–2, Prague, 1991, pp. 4–16, footnotes.

28430. — MAKAROVA, LENA: *Friedl Dicker-Brandeis remembered.* [In]: Jewish Art, Vol. 16/17, Jersualem, 1991. Pp. 122–129. [F.D.-B (also Brandejsová), July 30, 1898 Vienna – Oct. 1944 Auschwitz, artist (decorative art), emigrated in 1934 to Czechoslovakia, deported to Theresienstadt in 1942, art instructor for children, collected some 4,000 drawings of her pupils, now at the State Jewish Museum in Prague.]

28431. — MAKAROVA, ELENA: *'There is no sun here': the life and art of Friedl Dicker-Brandeis.* [In]: Ariel, No. 85–86, Jersualem, 1991. Pp. 54–67.

28432. — *Seeing through 'paradise': artists and the Terezin concentration camp.* [Exhibition at the] Massachusetts College of Art, Boston, March 6 – May 4, 1991. Boston: Massachusetts College of Art, 1991. 88 pp., illus.

28433. — SHLEIN, MARGALIT: *German efforts at deception in Theresienstadt as reflected in a document dated October 1942.* [In Hebrew]. [In]: Massuah: a yearbook on the Holocaust and heroism, Vol. 19, Tel-Aviv, Apr. 1991. Pp. 105–113. [The document is dated 28 Oct. 1942 and headed: Alterstransporte nach dem Osten.]

28434. — TROLLER, NORBERT: *Theresienstadt: Hitler's gift to the Jews.* Transl. by Susan E. Cernyak-Spatz. Ed. by Joel Shatzky. Chapel Hill: The Univ. of North Carolina, 1991. XXXVI, 182 pp., illus., notes, glossary. [Author, a Czech-Jewish architect (1896–1981), describes his two years in Theresienstadt from 1942–1944, after which he was deported to Auschwitz when Nazis discovered he and other artists were smuggling out drawings. Some of these drawings are published here for the first time. After liberation T. lived in the U.S. The original German manuscript and drawings are deposited at the Leo Baeck Institute in New York.]

28435. — WEBER, ILSE: *In deinen Mauern wohnt das Leid: Gedichte aus dem KZ Theresienstadt.* Gerlingen: Bleicher, 1991. pp., illus. docs. [Ilse Weber-Herlinger, Jan. 11, 1903 Witkowitz, Moravia – 1944 Auschwitz, date of death not known, worked as a nurse in the ghetto of Theresienstadt, from where she was deported with her son Tommy to Auschwitz in 1944.]

28436. — *Terezín, místa utrpení a vzdoru.* [In Czech, with English summary under the title: *Terezín; the places of suffering and resistance.*] [Eds.]: Miroslava Benesová [et al.]. Prague: Památník Terezín, 1991. 80 pp., illus., docs., facsims.

28437. — *Vom Bauhaus nach Theresienstadt; Friedl Dicker-Brandeis und die Kinderzeichnungen aus dem Ghetto-Lager Theresienstadt.* Hrsg. vom Jüdischen Museum im Auftrag des Magistrats der Stadt Frankfurt am Main. Hrsg.: Georg Heuberger. Frankfurt am Main: Jüdisches Museum, 1991. 120 pp., illus., bibl. [Catalogue to an exhibition held at the Jüdisches Museum in Frankfurt am Main April 25 – July 28, 1991. Incl.: Friedl Dicker-Brandeis: Ein großartiger Mensch (Elena Makarova, 11–12). Im Ghetto-Lager Theresienstadt (Georg Heuberger, 47–60). Friedl Dicker-Brandeis: Vom Bauhaus nach Terezín (Ljuba Beran-kova/Ursula Thürich, 61–115).]

28438. TUCHEL, JOHANNES: *Konzentrationslager. Organisationsgeschichte und Funktion der 'Inspektion der Konzentrationslager' 1934–1938.* Boppard a. Rhein: Boldt, 1991. 438 pp. [Cf.: Kalkulierter Terror (Peter Longerich) [in]: Frankfurter Allg. Zeitung, No. 88, April 13, 1992, p. 13.]

28439. *Verfolgung und Vernichtung der europäischen Juden unter der nationalsozialistischen Gewaltherrschaft.* Tondokumente aus den Jahren 1930–1946. Berlin/Frankfurt am Main: Funkhaus Berlin/ Deutsches Rundfunkarchiv (Bertramstr. 8, D-6000 Frankfurt am Main 1), 1991. 41 pp., index of names. [Annotated list of 225 original recordings (incl. records from radio, film and other media) by Hitler, Goebbels, Himmler and other Nazi officials; incl. also some BBC and radio recordings of the Nuremberg Trial 1946.]

28440. WALK, JOSEPH: *Jüdische Schule und Erziehung im Dritten Reich.* Frankfurt am Main: Hain, 1991. 371 pp., illus., tabs., notes [incl. bibl. references] (271–361), index. [Incl. reprint of 'Richtlinien zur Aufstellung von Lehrplänen für jüdische Volksschulen' (1937) and 'Erläuterungen zu den "Richtlinien" ' (Adolf Leschnitzer).] [Cf.: Besprechung (Konrad Fuchs) [in]: Tribüne, Jg. 30, H. 120, Frankfurt am Main, 1991. Pp. 242–244.]

28441. WEISS, YFAAT: *Schicksalsgemeinschaft im Wandel: jüdische Erziehung im nationalsozialistischen Deutschland 1933–1938.* Hamburg: Christians, 1991. 225 pp., docs., notes, bibl., index of persons. (Hamburger Beiträge zur Sozial- und Zeitgeschichte Bd. 25.) [Cont. the chaps: 1. Rahmenbedingungen jüdischer Erziehung (12–22). 2. Die öffentliche Diskussion über die jüdische Schule (23–36). 3. Erziehung als Politkum (37–51). 4. Die Reichsvertretung und die jüdischen Interessengruppen (52–69. 5. Die Aufgaben der Reichsvertretung (70–85). 6. Die Lehrinhalte an der jüdischen Schule (86–104). 7. Schule als Identitätsstifter (105–111).]

28442. WITTEN. KLINER-LINTZEN, MARTINA/PAPE, SIEGFRIED: '. . . *vergessen kann man das nicht'. Wittener Jüdinnen und Juden unter dem Nationalsozialismus.* Herausgegeben von der Stadt Witten. Bochum: Winkler, 1991. 413 pp., illus., ports., facsims., maps, tabs., notes. [Incl. historical and demographical introduction (XI–XXXIX), alphabetically listed biographies (1–294), memoirs and interviews (297–379).]

28443. ZIEGLER, MONIKA/PICHLER, HERMANN: *Eine Kindheit, die sie nie hatten.* [In]: Aufbau, Vol. 57, No. 11, New York, May 24, 1991. Pp. 1, 2, 17. [Recollections of childhood in hiding in Germany and other Nazi-occupied countries.]

28444. ZIRNDORF. MAHR, HELMUT: *Es geschah in der Kleinstadt Zirndorf im Jahr 1938.* [In]:

Nachrichten für den jüdischen Bürger Fürths, Isr. Kultusgemeinde Fürth (Blumenstr. 31), 31. Sept. 1991. Pp. 25–26.

B. Jewish Resistance

28445.　BROTHERS, ERIC: *Our secular heritage: remembering resistance scholar Yuri Suhl (1908–1986).* [In]: Jewish Currents, Vol. 44, No. 10 (487), New York, Nov. 1990. Pp. 24–25; 28. [About the author of They fought back; the story of the Jewish resistance in Nazi Europe, published in 1968 in London.]

28446.　FITTKO, LISA: *Escape through the Pyrenees.* Transl. by David Koblich. Evanston, Il.: Northwestern Univ. Press, 1991. IX, 221 pp., illus. [Author is an Austrian Jewess, who lived in Berlin, Prague; emigrated to France, escaped to Cuba during the war, then USA; book describes her escape and her involvement in left-wing resistance to the Nazis.]

28447.　HERMAN-FRIEDE, EUGEN: *Für Freudensprünge keine Zeit. Erinnerungen an Illegalität und Aufbegehren 1942–1948.* Mit einem Nachwort von Barbara Schieb-Samizadeh. Berlin: Metropol, 1991. 222 pp. (Zentrum für Antisemitsmusforschung Berlin: Reihe Dokumente, Texte, Materialien; Bd. 2.) [Incl.: Die Gemeinschaft für Frieden und Aufbau (Barbara Schieb-Samizadeh, 189–222).] [Personal recollections of survival in hiding in Berlin from 1943 and joining the resistance group Gemeinschaft für Frieden unD Aufbau, otherwise known as Arbeitsgemeinschaft für Frieden und Freiheit.] [Cf.: Besprechung (Kurt Schilde) [in]: Die Mahnung, 38. Jg., Nr. 12, Berlin, 1. Dez. 1991, p. 5. Die deutsche Misere; einer hat es aufgeschrieben: Leben und Leid unter zwei Diktaturen (Günter Kunert) [In] Die Zeit, Nr. 41, Hamburg, 3. Okt. 1991, p. 87.]

28448.　*(Der) Kampf um die Ätherwellen: Feindpropaganda im Zweiten Weltkrieg.* Hrsg.: Hans Sakowicz und Michael Crone unter Mitarbeit des Deutschen Rundfunkarchivs. Frankfurt am Main: Eichborn, 1991. 6 Kassetten (420 Minuten) mit Begleitbuch (96 S.). [Incl. the contribution of Jewish and anti-Fascist refugees from Germany and Austria to the propaganda war against Nazi Germany.] [Cf.: Krieg auf Ätherwellen (Uwe Naumann) [in]: Die Zeit, Nr. 33, Hamburg, 9. Aug. 1991, p. 27.]

28449.　KREISSLER, FELIX: *Österreicher im französischen Widerstand 1940–1945.* [In]: De Gaulles europäische Größe: Analysen aus Österreich. Jahrbuch für Zeitgeschichte 1990/91. Wien: Geyer, 1991. Pp. 17–21, footnotes. [Incl. Jewish refugees.]

28450.　NETHERLANDS. BRABER, BEN: *Zelfs als wij zullen verliezen: Joden in verzet en illegaliteit in Nederland, 1940–1945.* Amsterdam: Uitgeverij Balans, 1990. 192 pp. [Cf.: Review (Rena G. Fuks-Mansfeld) [in]: Studia Rosenthaliana, Vol. 25, No. 1, Assen, The Netherlands, Spring 1991, pp. 120–121.] [Also on German-Jewish refugees who went into hiding or lived during the Nazi occupation.]

28451.　PAUCKER, ARNOLD: *Jewish resistance in Germany; the facts and the problems.* Berlin (Stauffenbergstrasse 13/14): Gedenkstätte deutscher Widerstand/German Resistance Memorial Center, 1991. 20 pp., notes. Revised, extended and transl. version of Jüdischer Widerstand in Deutschland: Tatsachen und Problematik. Gedenkstätte deutscher Widerstand, 1989. (Beiträge zum Widerstand 1933–1945, 37.) [For German version see No. 26554/YBXXXV.]

28452.　SCHAFRANEK, HANS: *Zwischen NKWD und Gestapo. Die Auslieferung deutscher und österreichischer Antifaschisten aus der Sowjetunion an Nazideutschland 1937–1941.* Frankfurt am Main: ISP-Verl., 1990. 220 pp., index of persons, bibl. [Documentation on the fate of German- and Austrian-Jewish and non-Jewish Socialists and Communists, who had found refuge from Nazi persecution in the Soviet Union, and were handed over to Nazi Germany.]

28453.　VILNA (Ghetto).: *'ss firt kein weg zurik . . . Geschichte und Widerstand des Ghettos von Wilna 1941–1943.* Mit einem Vorwort von Simon Wiesenthal. Hrsg.: Florian Freund; Hans Safrian. Wien: Picus, 1991. 167 pp., illus., music. [Documentation on the ghetto of Vilna, incl. texts and music of resistance songs.]

IV. POST WAR

A. General

28454.　BAUMEL, JUDITH TYDOR: *The politics of spiritual rehabilitation in the DP camps [in Germany].* [In]: Simon Wiesenthal Center Annual, Vol. 6, White Plains, N.Y., 1989. Pp. 57–79.

28455. BENZ, WOLFGANG: *Zwischen Hitler und Adenauer. Studien zur deutschen Nachkriegsgesellschaft.* Frankfurt am Main: Fischer Taschenbuch Verl., 1991. Orig.-Ausg. 248 pp., notes. [Incl.: Zwischen Befreiung und Heimkehr. Das KZ Dachau im Mai und Juni 1945 (41–62, notes pp. 219–222; orig. publ. in the Dachauer Hefte 1, 1985). Jüdisches Leben in Deutschland nach Auschwitz (63–78, notes pp. 222–224). Der Wollheim-Prozess. Entschädigung für Zwangsarbeit in Auschwitz (128–154, notes pp. 230–232; orig. publ. in 1989 in HERBST, LUDOLF/GOSCHLER, CONSTANTIN: Wiedergutmachung in der Bundesrepublik Deutschland, 1989. See No. 26585/YBXXXV).]

28456. BLOCH, BENJAMIN: *Glaube an eine neue jüdische Existenz. Max Willner und die Zentralwohlfahrtsstelle der Juden.* [In]: Max Willner. Würdigung eines verdienten Mannes [see No. 28582]. Frankfurt am Main: Landesverband der Jüdischen Gemeinden in Hessen, 1991. Pp. 106–115, illus.

28457. BODEMANN, MICHAEL Y.: *Gedächtnistheater; Zu den Grußadressen für Rosch Haschana.* [And]: *Grüße zu Rosch Haschana in der Allgemeinen Jüdischen Wochenzeitung, 1950–1988.* Eine Chronologie. [In]: Babylon, H. 8, Frankfurt am Main, Febr. 1991. Pp. 100–104 [and] 105–115.

28458. BODEMANN, MICHAEL Y.: *Die Endzeit der Märtyrer-Gründer; an einer Epochenwende jüdischer Existenz in Deutschland.* [In]: Babylon, H. 8, Frankfurt am Main, Februar 1991. Pp. 7–14. [Deals with Jewish leadership and their function in post-war Germany between 1945 and 1951.]

28459. *Deutsche Juden – Juden in Deutschland.* [In]: Das Parlament, 41, Jg., Nr. 33, Bonn, 9. Aug. 1991. 19 pp., illus. (Konzeption und Zusammenstellung: Michael Wuliger. Redaktion: Peter Juling.) [The special topic of this issue is Jewish life in post-war Germany. Incl. (titles condensed): Auf dem Weg in die Normalität (Michael Wolffsohn, 1). Generationenkonflikte prägen den jüdischen Alltag (Hanna Rheinz, 1). Die Münchner Gemeinde (Ellen Presser, 2). Die Düsseldorfer Gemeinde (Doris Bulau, 3). Jüdische Organisationen in Deutschland (Judith Hart, 3). Schrumpfende Gemeinde unter Zionismus-Verdacht, jüdisches Leben in der ehemaligen DDR (Willi Jasper, 4). Berlin, Synagoge Oranienburger Straße (Heiderose Leopold, 4). Die neue Potsdamer Gemeinde (Doris Bulau, 5). Sowjetische Juden in Berlin (Burgel Langer, 5). Zur Geschichte des deutsch-jüdischen Verhältnisses (Julius H. Schoeps, 6). NS-Verbrechen und deutsche Justiz (Heiner Lichtenstein, 7). Zum Dialog zwischen Christen und Juden (Günther Bernd Ginzel, 8). Israel-Vergessenheit oder Verdrängung (Martin Stöhr, 8). Deutschland und Israel, das schwierige Verhältnis (Fritz Schatten, 9). Jüdisches Museum in Frankfurt (Annette Hornung, 13). Bibliothek Germania Judaica in Köln (Monika Richarz, 14). Salomon Ludwig Steinheim-Institut für deutsch-jüdische Geschichte (14). Antisemitische Vorurteile: nicht alles, was so aussieht, ist antisemitisch (Ursula Homann, 15). Theorien des Antisemitismus (Werner Bergmann/Rainer Erb, 15–16). Deutsche Juden in Israel (Fritz Schatten, 16).]

—— *Exilforschung.* Ein Internationales Jahrbuch. *Bd. 9: Exil und Remigration.* München, Ed. Text und Kritik, 1991. [See No. 28643.]

—— FRANKFURT am Main. KORN, SALOMON: *Die 4. jüdische Gemeinde in Frankfurt am Main; Zukunft oder Zwischenspiel?* [See in No. 27941.]

28460. GREENBERG, GERSHON: *From 'Hurban' to redemption: orthodox Jewish thought in the Munich area, 1945–1948.* [In]: Simon Wiesenthal Center Annual, Vol. 6, White Plains, N.Y., 1989. Pp. 81–112.

28461. HECHT, INGEBORG: *Von der Heilsamkeit des Erinnerns; Opfer der Nürnberger Gesetze begegnen sich.* Mit einem Vorwort von Heinz Knobloch. Hamburg: Hoffmann & Campe, 1991. 199 pp. [About the response the author met to her autobiographical book, Als unsichtbare Mauern wuchsen, publ. in 1984 (see No. 21100/YBXXX), in which she described how her youth in Nazi Germany had been affected by her partly Jewish descent.]

28462. HERMAN, DAVID: *'Ruinboys' or rainbows? Survivors of the Holocaust and their children.* [In]: The Jewish Quarterly, Vol. 38, No. 2, London, Summer 1991. Pp. 21–26, illus.

28463. HOLOCAUST TRAUMA. KAMINER, ISIDOR J.: *Spätfolgen bei jüdischen KZ-Überlebenden.* [And]: LEMPP, REINHART: *Die Wandlungen der Spätfolgen nach Verfolgungsträumen im Kindesalter.* Die Bedeutung der Sequenz für Traumatisierung und Stabilisierung. [And]: JUELICH, DIERK: *Wer ist eigentlich betroffen?* Aspekte zur psychoanalytischen Kulturkritik nach Auschwitz. [In]: Geschichte als Trauma [See in No. 28743]. Hrsg.: Dierk Juelich. Frankfurt am Main: Nexus, 1991. Pp. 19–34 [&] 35–48 [&] 75–94.

28464. KOCHAVI, ARIEH J.: *British policy on non-repatriable Displaced Persons in Germany and Austria,*

1945–7. [In]: European History Quarterly, Vol. 21, No. 3, London, July 1991. Pp. 365–382, notes.

28465.   KROPAT, WOLF-ARNO: *Jüdische Gemeinden, Wiedergutmachung, Rechtsradikalismus und Antisemitismus nach 1945.* Beobachtungen und Feststellungen aus historischer Sicht. [In]: Max Willner. Würdigung eines verdienten Mannes [see No. 28582.]. Frankfurt am Main: Landesverband der Jüdischen Gemeinden in Hessen, 1991. Pp. 143–170. [Incl. a section on the post-war Jewish communities in Hesse.] [Abbr. version, authorised by the author of an article published under the same title in No. 19832/YBXXIX.]

28466.   KUGELMANN, CILLY: *Stapelläufe, Orden und Kriegsverbrecher; der Wiederbeginn jüdischen Lebens in Deutschland.* Eine Chronik interessanter Ereignisse von 1945–1958. [In]: Babylon, H. 8, Frankfurt am Main, Febr. 1991. Pp. 85–99. [Based on the events covered by the Allgemeine Jüdische Wohenzeitung.]

28467.   LEVINSON, PETER: *Western Europe fifty years on.* [In]: European Judaism, Vol. 24, No. 1, London, Spring 1991. Pp. 34–37. [Speech made by the Chief Rabbi of Hamburg at the 25th International Conference of the World Union for Progressive Judaism held in London in the Spring of 1990; discusses present-day German-Jewish communities.]

28468.   LICHTENSTEIN, HEINER: *Nicht auf gepackten Koffern sitzend. Die Minderheit der 30 000 Juden in der neuen Bundesrepublik Deutschland.* [In]: Tribüne, Jg. 30, H. 117, Frankfurt am Main, 1991. Pp.116–125.

28469.   MALZAHN, MANFRED: *Germany 1945–1949: a sourcebook.* London; New York: Routledge, 1991. 239 pp., illus., tabs., notes. [Incl. the de-Nazification process, also post-war German attitudes towards returning Jews.]

28470.   MASER, PETER: *Juden und jüdische Gemeinden in der DDR bis in das Jahr 1988.* [In]: Tel Aviver Jahrbuch für deutsche Geschichte, Bd. 20, Gerlingen, 1991. Pp. 393–426, notes. [Based on lecture at Münster University, May 14, 1990.]

28471.   MILTON, SYBIL: *In fitting memory: the art and politics of Holocaust memorials.* Photographs by Ira Nowinski. Detroit: Wayne State Univ. Press, 1991. 368 pp., 136 black-and-white photographs. [Incl. also memorials to German Jews.]

28472.   MÜNSTER. *Begegnung ehemaliger jüdischer Mitbürger in und mit Münster. 5. bis 12. Juni 1991.* Dokumentation. Hrsg.: Der Oberstadtdirektor der Stadt Münster. Münster: Der Oberstadtdirektor, 1991. 64 pp., illus., facsims. [Also available in English under the title, Meeting of the former Jewish citizens in and with the city of Münster from June 5th to 12th, 1991.]

28473.   PROSECUTION OF NAZI CRIMES. BAUER, YEHUDA: *Who was responsible and when? Some well-known documents revisited.* [In]: Holocaust and Genocide Studies, Vol. 6, No. 2, Oxford, 1991. Pp. 129–149, notes. [Deals with documents used during the Nuremberg Trials.]

28474.   — BUSCHER, FRANK M.: *Kurt Schumacher, German Social Democracy and the punishment of Nazi crimes.* [In]: Holocaust and Genocide Studies, Vol. 5, No. 3, Jerusalem, 1990. Pp. 261–273.

28475.   — GIEFER, RENA/GIEFER, THOMAS: *Rattenlinie; Fluchtwege der Nazis, eine Dokumentation.* Frankfurt am Main: Hain, 1991. 280 pp.

38476.   — KLEE, ERNST: *Persilscheine und falsche Pässe. Wie die Kirchen den Nazis halfen.* Frankfurt am Main: Fischer Taschenbuchverlag, 1991. 192 pp. [Also on this topic: KLEE, ERNST: Vergebung ohne Reue. Heimliche Hilfe der Kirchen für Massenmörder und Schreibtischtäter [in]: Die Zeit, Nr. 9, Hamburg, 21. Feb. 1992. P. 49.]

28477.   — LICHTENSTEIN, HEINER: *Vor dem Ende der NS-Prozesse. "Wir haben die Mörder wenigstens erschreckt".* [In]: Tribüne, Jg. 30, H. 120, Frankfurt am Main, 1991. Pp. 184–192.

28478.   — RENZ, ULRICH: *Schlampereien in einem NS-Prozess.* Hauptverhandlung gegen ehemaligen SS-Schergen nach 10 Jahren abgebrochen. [In]: Tribüne, Jg. 30, H. 118, Frankfurt am Main, 1991. Pp. 54–60. [On the Hanover trial of Heinrich Niemeier.]

28479.   — SCHWARBERG, GÜNTHER: *Der Juwelier von Majdanek.* Göttingen: Steidl, 1991. 254 pp. [On the Majdanek trial and the Slovakian jeweller Samuel Antmann, who survived Majdanek because his expertise and skill were indispensable to the SS personnel.]

28480.   — WEMBER, HEINER: *Umerziehung im Lager; Internierung und Bestrafung von Nationalsozialisten in der britischen Besatzungszone Deutschlands.* Essen: Klartext, 1991. 430 pp. [Cf.: Die Täter als Opfer; wie hochbelastete Nazis nach 1945 davonkamen und wer ihnen half (Volker Ullrich) [in]: Die Zeit, Nr. 51, Hamburg, 13. Dez. 1991, p. 41.]

28481.   — ZAYAS, ALFRED-MAURICE DE: *Der Nürnberger Prozeß vor dem internationalen Militär Tribunal*

(1945–1946). [In]: Macht und Recht. Große Prozesse in der Geschichte. Hrsg. von Alexander Demandt. München: Beck, 1990. Pp. 249–270.

——— RICHARZ, MONIKA: *Luftaufnahme – oder die Schwierigkeiten der Heimatforscher mit der jüdischen Geschichte.* [See No. 28867.]

28482. SALLEN, HERBERT/SILBERMANN, ALPHONS: *Bekenntnis zur jüdischen Identität.* Selbstbild und Fremdbild der Juden in Westdeutschland 1990. [In]: Tribüne, Jg. 30, H. 118, Frankfurt am Main, 1991. Pp. 122–130.

28483. SCHOEPS, JULIUS H.: *Jüdisches Leben in Nachkriegsdeutschland; von den Jahren des Aufbaus bis zum Ende der Teilung.* [In]: Jüdische Lebenswelten. Essays [see No. 27946]. Frankfurt am Main: Jüdischer Verlag, Suhrkamp, 1991. pp. 352–383, illus., bibl.

28484. SELIGMANN, RAFAEL: *Mit beschränkter Hoffnung; Juden, Deutsche, Israelis.* Hamburg: Hoffmann und Campe, 1991. 316 pp. [Essays on Jews in post-war Germany, their attitudes and the political and psychological climate of opinion surrounding them; also on antisemitism, philosemitism, German-Israeli relations and the immigration of Jews from the (former) Soviet Union.) [Cf.: 'Wie können Sie hier leben?' (Gabriele von Arnim [in] Die Zeit, Nr. 46, Hamburg, 8. Nov. 1991, p. 22. Wider das deutsch-jüdische Ritual (Michael Wolffsohn) [in]: Frankfurter Allgemeine Zeitung, Nr. 274, 26. Nov. 1991, p. 37. Versuch einer Standortbestimmung (Michael Zeller) [in]: Aufbau, Vol. 57, Dec. 20, 1991, p. 7.]

28485. SHAFIR, SHLOMO: *Henry Morgenthau and his involvement in rescue in Germany and in Eretz, Israel.* [In Hebrew, with English summary, title transl.]. [In]: Yalkut Moreshet, No. 51, Tel-Aviv, Nov. 1991. Pp. 35–49. [On Henry Morgenthau Jr.'s activities in the 1940s–50s on behalf of German Jewry, the DPs, and the State of Israel.]

——— STERN, FRANK: *Im Anfang war Auschwitz. Antisemitismus und Philosemitismus im deutschen Nachkrieg.* [See No. 28932.]

28486. SURVIVAL SYNDROME. EICKHOFF, FRIEDRICH-W.: *Über das 'unbewußte entlehnte Schuldgefühl'.* Einige fallbezogene Nachgedanken zum 34. Kongress der IPV in Hamburg. [In]: Geschichte als Trauma [see No. 28743]. Hrsg.: Dierk Juelich. Frankfurt am Main: Nexus, 1991. Pp. 49–58.

28487. *'Vergangenheitsbewältigung'* [Editorial] [In]: The Jewish Quarterly, vol. 38, No. 3, London, Autumn 1991. Pp. 3–4. [On German re-unification and German-Jewish relations.]

28488. WROBEL, HANS: *Verurteilt zur Demokratie; Justiz und Justizpolitik in Deutschland 1945–1949.* Heidelberg: Juristischer Verlag, 1989. 400 pp. [Deals also with prosecution of Nazi crimes.] [Cf.: Opfer oder Täter; die Rolle der Juristen im 'Dritten Reich' (Ralph Angermund) [in]: Das Parlament, Nr. 27, Bonn, 28. Juni 1991, pp. 22–23.] [See also No. 26386/YBXXXV.]

28489. *Zwischen Antisemitismus und Philosemitismus; Juden in der Bundesrepublik.* Hrsg. von Wolfgang Benz. Berlin: Metropol, 1991. 118 pp. (Reihe Dokumente, Texte, Materialien; Zentrum für Antisemitismusforschung, Bd.1.) [Incl. (titles condensed): Der schwierige Status der jüdischen Minderheit in Deutschland nach 1945 (Wolfgang Benz, 9–21, footnotes). Zur Lage der jüdischen Minderheit in der Bundesrepublik (Charlotte Knobloch, 23–27). Die jüdische Minorität in der ehemaligen DDR (Peter Kirchner, 29–38). Jüdische Geistigkeit und Kultur in der Bundesrepublik (Julius Carlebach, 39–45, notes). Philosemitismus statt Antisemitismus (Frank Stern, 47–61, footnotes). Die Anfänge der Gesellschaften für Christlich-Jüdische Zusammenarbeit (Josef Foschepoth, 63–70). Three autobiographical essays: In der Haut der Eltern (Richard Chaim Schneider, 71–86). Rückkehr aus der Emigration: Leben in Deutschland (Werner T. Angress, 87–97). Aus der Sowjetunion nach Deutschland (Ljudmila Duwidowitsch, 99–118).]

B. Restitution

——— BENZ, WOLFGANG: *Der Wollheim-Prozess.* [See in No. 28455.]

28490. BROTHERS, ERIC: *Why the German Democratic Republic never paid reparations to Holocaust survivors.* [In]: Jewish Spectator, Vol. 56, No. 1, Calabasas, Ca., Spring 1991. Pp. 19–20.

28491. FROHN, AXEL, ed.: *Holocaust and Shilumim: the policy of Wiedergutmachung in early 1950s.* Ed. by Axel Frohn, with the assistance of Anne Hope. Washington, D.C.: German Historical Institute, 1991. VII, 66 pp., bibl. ([63]–66). (Occasional paper, No. 7.)

28492. KNIGHT, ROBERT: *Restitution and legitimacy in post-war Austria 1945–1953.* [In]: LBI Year Book XXXVI, London, 1991. Pp. 413–441, footnotes.

28493. SAHRHAGE, NORBERT: '. . . *weil wir hofften, daß nach all dem Erlebten uns nunmehr Gerechtigkeit widerfahren würde.*' Reintegration und Entschädigung der jüdischen Bevölkerung des Kreises Herford nach 1945. [In]: Menora, Bd. 2, München, 1991. Pp. 371–404, notes.

28494. STEIN, ERWIN: *Befreiung und Betreuung. Beginn der Wiedergutmachung in Hessen und der 'Fall Dr. Epstein'*. [In]: Max Willner. Würdigung eines verdienten Mannes [see No. 28582]. Frankfurt am Main: Landesverband der Jüdischen Gemeiden in Hessen, 1991. Pp. 133–142.

28495. SYWOTTEK, ARNOLD: *Über die Anfänge der deutsch-israelischen Wirtschaftsbeziehungen.* Eine erste Annäherung. [In]: Juden in Deutschland [see No. 27940]. Hamburg: Christians, 1991. Pp. 450–464, notes, tabs.

28496. VOGT-HEYDER, BARBARA: *Einige Gedanken zur deutschen Wiedergutmachung.* [In]: Geschichte als Trauma [see No. 28743]. Hrsg.: Dierk Juelich. Frankfurt am Main: Nexus, 1991. Pp. 59–68.

C. Antisemitism, Judaism, Nazism in Education and Teaching

28497. BEIMEL, MATTHIAS: *Die Karikatur als Ersatzhandlung. Antisemitismus in der NS-Propaganda und ihre Vorbilder.* [In]: Geschichte lernen, 3. Jg., H. 18, Velber, 1991. Pp. 28–33, illus.

28498. *Besucherforschung und Vermittlungsstrategien in historischen Ausstellungen*; Kolloquiumsbericht zu den Ergebnissen der Ausstellung 'Geschichte und Kultur der Juden in Bayern'. Hrsg. vom Haus der Bayerischen Geschichte. Redaktion: Manfred Treml. München: Haus der Bayerischen Geschichte, 1991. 52 pp. [Incl.: Stereotype Vorstellungen über Juden in der Bundesrepublik Deutschland heute (Rainer Erb, 20–24). Juden und Antisemitismus in der öffentlichen Debatte. Einige empirische Ergebnisse zum Einstellungswandel in der Bundesrepublik Deutschland (Werner Bergmann, 25–32).]

28499. DONESON, JUDITH E.: *Teaching the Holocaust with film.* [In]: The Jewish Quarterly, Vol. 38, No. 1, London, Spring 1991. Pp. 58–63, notes. [Incl. 'Shoah', 'Jud Süss' a.o.]

28500. GRUBER, HELMUT: *Antisemitismus im Medienkurs: die Affäre 'Waldheim' in der Tagespresse.* Wiesbaden: Dt. Univ.-Verl., 1991. 268 pp., bibl. (256–268).

—— HEID, LUDGER [et al.]: *Juden im Rheinland.* I. *Das antisemitische Vorurteil bis 1933.* [See No. 28098.]

28501. HOMEIER, JOBST-H.: *9. November 1938. Wie eine Schule in ein Projekt 'hineinrutscht'.* [In]: Geschichte lernen, Jg. 4, H. 23, Velber, 1991. Pp. 46–50.

28502. MATTHÄUS, WOLFGANG: *'Zu der Zeit war es für uns unmöglich, weiter zu lernen'; jüdische Schülerinnen im Nationalsozialismus.* [In]: Geschichte lernen, Jg. 4, H. 24, Velber, Nov. 1991. Pp. 16–19, illus.

28503. STEINBACH, PETER: *Selbstbehauptung als Widerstand. Widerstand von Juden als Thema deutsch-jüdischer Beziehungsgeschichte im 20. Jahrhundert.* [In]: Geschichte, Politik und ihre Didaktik, 18. Jg., H. 1/2, Paderborn, 1990. Pp. 158–166.

28504. WOLF, SIEGBERT: *Mühsames Erinnern. Hearing zum geplanten Lern- und Dokumentationszentrum des Holocaust.* [In]: Tribüne, Jg. 30, H. 120, Frankfurt am Main, 1991. Pp. 59–64. [On an international hearing held in Frankfurt am Main Oct. 23–25, 1991 about a future German national Holocaust memorial.]

V. JUDAISM

A. Jewish Learning and Scholars

28505. BEN-CHORIN, SCHALOM: *Porträts bekannter und verkannter Zeitgenossen.* Hrsg. von Verena Lenzen. Gerlingen: Bleicher, 1991. 179 pp. [A selection of previously published articles; incl. about: Theodor Herzl, Vladimir Jabotinsky, Martin Buber, Franz Rosenzweig, Richard Beer-Hofmann, Arnold Zweig, Josef Kastein, Lion Feuchtwanger, Klaus Mann, Else Lasker-Schüler, Franz Werfel, Joseph Roth, Oskar Goldberg, Alfred Mombert, David Frankfurter, Max Brod, Felix Weltsch, Sammy Gronemann, Gabriel Stern, Hans Lamm.]

28506. BLEICH, JUDITH: *Menahem Mendel Steinhardt's 'Divrei Iggeret' [Rödelheim, 1812]: harbinger of reform.* [In]: Proceedings of the 10th World Congress of Jewish Studies, 1989, Division B, Vol. 2: The history of the Jewish people. Jerusalem, 1990. Pp. 207–214.

——— BREUER, MORDECHAI: *Ausdrucksweisen aschkenasischer Frömmigkeit in Synagoge und Lehrhaus.* [See in No. 27941.]

28507. BUBER, MARTIN. BRESLAUER, S. DANIEL: *Silence and language in Hasidism: Martin Buber's view.* [In]: Shofar, Vol. 9, No. 2, West Lafayette, In., Purdue Univ. Winter 1991. Pp. 16–28, footnotes. [Also focuses on Heschel and Scholem.]

——— — FRIEDENTHAL-HAASE, MARTHA: *Martin Buber's and Ernst Simon's concept of adult education in crisis situations.* [See in No. 28561.]

28508. — FRIEDMANN, MAURICE: *Encounter on the narrow ridge.* New York: Paragon House, 1991. 512 pp., illus., ports. [Biography focussing on Buber's encounters with other personalities of his time.]

28509. — GRIES, ZEEV: *The Jewish background to Buber's rewriting of hasidic tales.* [In Hebrew, with English summary]. [In]: Mechkerei Yerushalayim be-Folklor Yehudi (Jerusalem Studies in Jewish Folklore), No. 11–12, Jerusalem, June 1990. Pp. 45–56. [On Buber's youth in his grandfather's house in Lemberg, and the impact of the Eastern European maskilim on him.]

28510. — KATZ, STEVEN T.: *Laurence Perlman's 'Buber's anti-Kantianism': a reply.* [In]: AJS Review, Vol. 15, No. 1, Cambridge, Ma., Spring 1990. Pp. 109–117.

28511. — LEVENSON, JON D.: *The hermeneutical defense of Buber's Hasidism:* a critique and counter statement. [in]: Modern Judaism. Vol. 22, No. 3, Baltimore, Oct. 1991. Pp. 297–320, notes.

28512. PERLMAN, LAURENCE: *Buber's anti-Kantianism.* [In]: AJS Review, Vol. 15, No. 1, Cambridge, Ma., Spring 1990. Pp. 95–108, footnotes.

28513. — SHAPIRA, AVRAHAM: *Time and eternity in Buber's concept of redemption.* [In Hebrew, with English summary]. [In]: Doar, No. 27, Ramat-Gan, Summer 1991. Pp. 61–71.

28514. — SHAPIRA, AVRAHAM: *Political messianism in Buber's conception of redemption.* [In]: Journal of Jewish Studies, Vol. 42, No. 1, Oxford, Spring 1991. Pp. 92–107, footnotes.

28515. COHEN, HERMANN. KURZWEIL, ZVI/BEN-CHORIN, ZVIA: *The educational innovations of Ezekiel Hermann Cohen.* [In Hebrew, with English summary]. [In]: Iyyunim be-Chinukh (Studies in Education), No. 55–56, Haifa, June 1991. Pp. 169–176. [On Cohen's educational work.]

28516. EISENSTADT, MEIR. SPITZER, SHLOMO Y.: *On the activities of the 'Panim Meirot' in the 'seven communities'.* [In Hebrew, title transl.]. [In]: Tzfunot: Tora quarterly, Vol. 3, No. e, Benei-Beraq, Teveth 5751 [= Dec. 1990–Jan. 1991]. Pp. 83–87. [M.E., ca. 1670 Poland – 1744 Eisenstadt, rabbinical authority, rabbi of Eisenstadt and its 'seven communities' from 1714.]

28517. ELEAZAR BEN JUDAH of Worms. HERSCHLER, MOSHE: *'Sodot ha-Tefillah' by Rabbi Eleazar of Worms – author of the 'Rokeach'.* [In Hebrew, title transl.] [In]: Moriah, Vol. 18, No. 1–2, Jerusalem, Tishrei 5752 [= Sept. – Oct. 1991]. Pp. 5–11. [Cont. excerpts from the 'Sodot ha-Tefillah', collected from five manuscripts, from the author's Nachlass.] [E.b.J., data see No. 26622/YBXXXV.]

28518. ELIEZER BEN NATHAN of Mainz. SHAPIRO, ALEXANDER M.: *An anti-Christian polemic of the 12th century.* [In Hebrew, with English summary]. [In]: Zion, Vol. 56, No. 1, Jerusalem 1991. Pp. 79–85. [On a polemic by Eliezer ben Nathan, found in a manuscript of his halakhic work 'Even ha-ezer' in the library of Wolfenbüttel.]

28519. *Essential papers on Hasidism.* Ed. by Gershon Hundert. New York: New York Univ. Press, 1991. XI, 546 pp. [Incl. papers by Buber, Dubnow, Shmuel Ettinger, Maimon, Scholem.]

——— FALK, ZEEV W.: *Jüdisches Lernen und die Wissenschaft des Judentums.* [See in No. 27941.]

28520. FORMSTECHER, SALOMON. KRATZ-RITTER, BETTINA: *Salomon Formstecher. Ein deutscher Reformrabbiner.* Hildesheim: Olms, 1991. 223 pp, notes, ports., bibl., index of names. (Wissenschaftliche Abhandlungen des Salomon Ludwig Steinheim-Instituts für deutsch-jüdische Geschichte, Bd. 1.) [S.F., Offenbach 1808–1889, philosopher, rabbi of Offenbach from 1842 until his death.]

——— FRIEDLANDER, ALBERT H.: *Von Berlin in die Welt. Personen und Stationen der jüdischen Reformbewegung.* [In]: Jüdische Lebenswelten. Essays [See No. 27946.].

28521. GERSHOM BEN JUDAH ME'OR HA-GOLAH. GROSSMAN, AVRAHAM: *On the ban of Rabbenu Gershom.* [In Hebrew, title transl.] [In]: Eit-mol, No. 98, Tel-Aviv, Aug. 1991. Pp. 3–5. [On Gershom ben Judah's ban on polygamy.] [Gershom ben Judah Me'or Ha-Golah, ca. 960 Metz [?] – 1028 Mainz, one of the first great German talmudic scholars and a spiritual moulder of German Jewry.]

28522. GÖTZINGER, CATARINA: *Fromme und Gerechte: der osteuropäische Chassidismus und seine mystische Bedeutung.* [In]: Das Jüdische Echo, Vol. 40, Nr. 1, Wien, Okt. 1991. Pp. 220–224, notes.

28523. GOLDBERG, ARNOLD: *Ist Gott allmächtig? Was die Rabbinen Hans Jonas antworten können.* [In]: Judaica, Jg. 47, H. 1/2, Basel, Juni 1991, pp. 51–58, notes. [Dedicated to Kurt Hruby on the occasion of his 70th birthday.]

28524. HANAU, SOLOMON ZALMAN. YITSHAKI, DAVID: *Prayer-book redactors in Ashkenaz; the grammarian Rabbi Zalman Hanau and his falsifications.* [In Hebrew, title transl.]. [In]: Tzfunot; Tora quarterly, Vol. 3, No. 3, Benei-Beraq, Nissan 5751 [= March–April 1991]. Pp. 72–81. [Solomon Zalman Hanau, 1687 Hanau – 1746 Hanover, Hebrew grammarian.)

28525. HANDELMAN, SUSAN A.: *Fragments of redemption: Jewish thought and literary theory in Benjamin, Scholem, and Levinas.* Bloomington: Indiana Univ. Press, 1991. 416 pp., notes.

—— HAYOUN, MAURICE R.: *Rabbi Ja'akov Emdens Autobiographie oder der Kämpfer wider die sabbatianische Häresie.* [See in No. 27941.]

28526. HELIN, RAPHAEL. LEHMANN, MENASHE (MANFRED) RAPHAEL: *Remembrance in a book: on an exegesis manuscript on the Mishnah by rabbi Raphael Helin of Glogau.* [In Hebrew, title transl.]. [In]: Moriah, Vol. 17, No. 9–10, Jerusalem, Teveth 5751 [Dec. 1990–Jan. 1991]. Pp. 109–111. [A description of the manuscript.] [R.H., data see No. 27491/YBXXXVI.]

28527. HESCHEL, ABRAHAM JOSHUA. SCHORSCH, REBECCA: *The hermeneutics of Heschel in Torah min Hashamayin.* [In]: Judaism, Vol. 40, No. 3, New York, Summer 1991. Pp. 301–308.

28528. HEZEKIAH BEN JACOB (of Magdeburg). HAVAZELET, AVRAHAM: *The halachic decisions of Rabbi Hezekiah of Magdeburg.* [In Hebrew, title transl.]. [In]: Moriah, Vol. 17, No. 11–12, Jerusalem, Iyar 5751 [= April 1991]. Pp. 9–14. [H.b.J., 13th-century, tosafist, was appointed as reader of the Magdeburg community.]

28529. HILDESHEIMER, ESRIEL. ELLENSON, DAVID: *Rabbi Esriel Hildesheimer and the creation of modern Jewish orthodoxy.* Tuscaloosa: Univ. of Alabama Press, 1990. XV, 212 pp. (Judaic studies series.)

—— HOFFMANN, CHRISTHARD/SCHWARTZ, DANIEL R.: *Early but opposed – supported but late. Two Berlin seminaries which attempted to move abroad.* [See No. 28325.]

28530. JÜTTE, ROBERT: *Die Emigration der deutschsprachigen 'Wissenschaft des Judentums'. Die Auswanderung jüdischer Historiker nach Palästina 1933–1945.* Stuttgart. Steiner, 1991. 247 pp., tabs., lists of names, bibl., index of persons.

28531. KATZ, JACOB. SINGER, DAVID: *Homage to Jacob Katz.* [In]: Commentary, Vol. 92, No. 4. New York, Oct. 1991. Pp. 50–51. [Discusses Katz's numerous writings on Jewish topics.]

28532. MORAD, MIRJAM: *The contribution of Friedrich S. Krauss to general and Jewish folkloristics.* [In]: Proceedings of the 10th World Congress of Jewish Studies (Jerusalem, 1989), Division D, Vol. 2: Art, folkore and music. Jerusalem, 1990. Pp. 141–148. [F.S.K., Oct. 7, 1859 Pozega, Austria–May 30, 1938 Vienna [?], ethnographer and folklorist, lived in Vienna.]

28533. LUBARSKY, SANDRA B.: *Tolerance and transformation: Jewish approaches to religious pluralism.* Cincinnati: Hebrew Union College Press (distrib. Behrman House), 1990. X, 149 pp. [Among those discussed are Baeck, Buber, Rosenzweig.]

28534. MEIR BEN BARUCH of Rothenburg. HAVATZELET, AVRAHAM YOSEF: *'Piskei Maharam' or 'Drashot Maharach': an unknown work by Maharam of Rothenburg.* [In]: Moriah, Vol. 17, No. 9–10, Jerusalem, Teveth 5751 [= Dec. 1990–Jan. 1991]. Pp. 105–108. [Discusses the authorship of a manuscript by Meir of Rothenburg or Chaim Or Zaru'a]

—— MENDELSSOHN, MOSES. ENGEL HOLLAND, EVA: *The World of Moses Mendelssohn.* [See No. 27928.]

—— — KLEIN, HANS-GÜNTHER: *25 Jahre Mendelssohn-Archiv.* [See No. 28202.]

28535. — PELLI, MOSHE: *The biographical genre of Hebrew literature in Germany in the 18th century*: Moses Mendelssohn in the image of the New Jew in Isaac Euchel's biographical model. [In Hebrew]. [In]: Bitzaron, No. 45–48, New York, April 1990–April 1991. Pp. 118–127. [On Euchel's biography of Mendelssohn, 'Toledoth ha-Rambaman', publ. in Berlin 1788.]

28536. — *Rezensionsartikel in 'Allgemeine deutsche Bibliothek' (1765–1784). Literarische Nachträge.* Bearb. von Eva J. Engel. Stuttgart: Frommann-Holzboog, 1991. LXIX, 327 pp. (Moses Mendelssohn: Gesammelte Schriften: Jubiläumsausgabe. Bd. 5,2.)

28537. MUNK, MOSES. BREUER, MORDECHAI: *Rabbi Moses Munk: on the 20th anniversary of his death.* In Hebrew, title transl.] [In]: Ha-Ma'yan, Vol. 32, No. 1, Jerusalem, Tishrei 5752 [= Sept.–Oct. 1991]. Pp. 43–48. [Lecture delivered at a memorial service.] [M.M., educated in Cologne and Frankfurt, emigrated to Palestine.]

28538. NORDHEIMER, ISAAC. GOLDMAN, SHALOM: *Isaac Nordheimer (1809–1842): 'an Israelite truly in whom there was no guile'.* [In]: American Jewish History, Vol. 80, No. 1, Waltham, Ma., Winter 1990–91. Pp. 213–229, footnotes. [I.N., talmudic and Hebrew scholar, b. Memelsdorf, Bavaria. Studied in Würzburg and Munich, emigrated to New York, where he taught at New York University and Union Theological Seminary.]

28539. PREUSS, JULIUS: Biblisch-talmudische Medizin. Beiträge zur Geschichte der Heilkunde und der Kultur überhaupt. Germering/München: S. Karger, 1989. VII, 736 pp. [Reprint of the 1911 edition.]

—— *Rabbinische Responsen zum Synagogenbau*. [See No. 28574.]

28540. ROSENZWEIG, FRANZ. AMIR, YEHOYADA: *The foundations of Franz Rosenzweig's theory of knowledge*. [In Hebrew, with English summary]. [In]: Iyyun, Vol. 39, Jerusalem, Oct. 1990. Pp. 381–422.

28541. — HALLO, WILLIAM W.: *Two centenaries*. [In]: LBI Year Book XXXVI, London, 1991. Pp. 491–500, footnotes. [On the centenaries of the birth of Franz Rosenzweig (1986) and the philosopher Eugen Rosenstock-Huessy (1988) and some aspects of their respective philosophies of language.]

28542. — MEINEKE, STEFAN: *A life of contradiction. The philosopher Franz Rosenzweig and his relationship to history and politics*. [In]: LBI Year Book XXXVI, London, 1991. Pp. 461–489, footnotes.

28543. — MORGAN, MICHAEL L.: *Franz Rosenzweig: objective truth and the personal standpoint*. [In]: Judaism, Vol. 40, No. 4, New York, Fall 1991. Pp. 521–530, footnotes.

28544. RÜLF, ISAAC. MARON, AVRAHAM: *'Arukhat bat ami'*. [In Hebrew]. [In]: Eit-mol. No. 99, Tel-Aviv, Oct. 1991. Pp. 17–18. [On the life and activities of Isaac Rülf, rabbi, Zionist, data see No. 18319/YBXXVII.]

28545. SCHÄFER, PETER: *Judaistik – jüdische Wissenschaft in Deutschland heute. Historische Identität und Nationalität*. [In]: Saeculum. Jahrbuch für Universalgeschichte, Freiburg: Karl Alber, 1991. Pp. 199–216, footnotes.

28546. SCHLÜTER, MARGARETE: *Jüdische Geschichtskonzeptionen der Neuzeit. Die Entwürfe von Nachman Krochmal und Heinrich Graetz*. [In]: Frankfurter Judaistische Beiträge, H. 18, Frankfurt am Main, Okt. 1990, pp. 175–205.

28547. SCHOLEM, GERSHOM. IDEL, MOSHE: *Rabbinism versus Kabbalism: on G. Scholem's phenomenology of Judaism*. [In]: Modern Judaism, Vol. 11, No. 3, Baltimore, Oct. 1991. Pp. 281–296, notes.

28548. SCHWARZSCHILD, STEVEN S. NETO, JOSE R. MAIA: *The string that leads the kite: Steven S. Schwarzschild's (1924–1989) view of Jewish philosophy*. [In]: Judaism, Vol. 40, No. 2, New York, Spring 1991. Pp. 226–238, footnotes.

28549. SEESKIN, KENNETH: *Jewish philosophy in the 1980s*. [in]: Modern Judaism, Vol. 11, No. 1, Baltimore, Feb. 1991. Pp. 151–172, notes. [Incl. Emil Fackenheim, Steven S. Schwarzschild.]

—— SIMON, ERNST AKIBA. FRIEDENTHAL-HAASE, MARTHA: *Martin Buber's and Ernst Simon's concept of adult education in crises situations*. [See in No. 28561.]

28550. SORKIN, DAVID: *From context to comparison. The German Haskalah and Reform Catholicism*. [In]: Tel Aviver Jahrbuch für deutsche Geschichte, Bd. 20, Gerlingen, 1991. Pp. 23–58, notes.

28551. VÖLKER, HEINZ-HERMANN: *Die Gründung und Entwicklung der Hochschule für die Wissenschaft des Judentums 1869–1900*. [In]: Trumah, 2, Wiesbaden, 1990. Pp. 24–46, notes. [Based on M.A. thesis, TU Berlin 1987; continuation (1900–1942) in H. Walravens, ed.: Bibliographie und Berichte, see No. 27522/YBXXXVI.]

28552. WELTSCH, ROBERT. *MB*, Jg. 59, Nr. 70 [with the issue title]: *Sondernummer Robert Weltsch 1891–1991*. Tel Aviv, Juni 1991. [Incl.: Robert Weltsch in seiner Zeit. Bemerkungen zu seinem hundertsten Geburtstag (Heinz Gerling, 1–2, port.) Äußerungen von [und über] Robert Weltsch (3–4).]

B. The Jewish Problem

28553. ARKUSH, ALLAN: *Judaism as egoism: from Spinoza to Feuerbach to Marx*. [In]: Modern Judaism, Vol. 11, No. 2, Baltimore, May 1991. Pp. 211–223. notes.

28554. BOROWITZ, EUGENE B.: *Rethinking our Holocaust consciousness*. [In]: Judaism, Vol. 40, No. 4, New York, Fall 1991. Pp. 511–520. [Deals with the theological implications of the Holocaust and earlier persecutions of Jews; incl. the views of Buber, Fackenheim, Heschel, Rosenzweig.]

28555. CASSIRER, ERNST. SIEG, ULRICH: *Deutsche Kulturgeschichte und jüdischer Geist. Ernst*

Cassirers Ausseinandersetzung mit der völkischen Philosophie Bruno Bauchs. Ein unbekanntes Manuskript. [In]: Bulletin des LBI, 88, Frankfurt am Main, 1991. Pp. 59–91, notes.

28556. DÖBLIN, ALFRED: *Journey to Poland.* Transl. by Joachim Neugroschel. New York: Paragon House, 1991. XXVIII, 274 pp., map. [D.'s 1924 search for his Polish-Jewish roots. Orig. publ. in Berlin in 1925.]

28557. FACKENHEIM, EMIL L.: *The Jewish bible after the Holocaust: a re-reading.* Manchester: Manchester Univ. Press, 1990; Bloomington: Indiana Univ. Press, 1991. CII, 122 pp.

28558. GARBER, ZEV: *The problem of Edith Stein: Jewess and Christian martyr.* [In]: Jewish Spectator, Vol. 56, No. 2, Calabasas, Ca., Fall 1991. Pp. 13–14.

28559. MARMUR, DOW: *The star of return: Judaism after the Holocaust.* Westwood, Ct.: Greenwood Press, 1991. XIII, 156 pp., illus., bibl. [Author asserts that Judaism is in the midst of a paradigm shift due to the establishment of Israel. The views of Baeck, Buber, Heschel, Rosenzweig are discussed in this context.]

28560. ZIPES, JACK: *Die kulturellen Operationen von Deutschen und Juden im Spiegel der neueren deutschen Literatur.* [In]: Babylon, H. 8, Frankfurt am Main, Febr. 1991, Pp. 34–44.

C. Jewish Life and Organisations

28561. *Adult education in crisis situations.* Proceedings of the third international conference on the history of adult education. Eds.: Franz Pöggeler & Kalman Yaron. Jerusalem: Magnes Press, Hebrew University, 1991. 238 pp. [Incl.: Martin Buber's and Ernst Simon's concept of adult education in crisis situations (Martha Friedenthal-Haase, 34–53). Adult education in Palestine among German Jewish immigrants (Michael Volkmann, 201–211; covers the years 1933–1944).]

28562. BERLINER, CORA. LOWENTHAL, ERNST G.: *In Berlin bis zum bitteren Ende geblieben. Professor Cora Berliner wäre jetzt 100 geworden.* [In]: Mitteilungen des Vereins für die Geschichte Berlins, 86. Jg., H. 2, Berlin, April 1990. Pp. 278–280, port. [C.B., social scientist, social worker, member of the Reichsvertretung der Juden in Deutschland, data see No. 27532/YBXXXVI.]

28563. BORUT, JACOB: *The rise of Jewish defence agitation in Germany, 1890–1895: a pre-history of the C.V.?* [In]: LBI Year Book XXXVI, London, 1991. Pp. 59–96, footnotes, tabs. [On the Centralverein and its antecedents.]

28564. BORUT, JACOB: *Vereine für Jüdische Geschichte und Literatur: the popularisation of Judaism and the science of Judaism.* [In Hebrew]. [In]: Proceedings of the 10th World Congress for Jewish Studies, 1989, Division B, Vol. 1: The history of the Jewish people. Jerusalem, 1990. Pp. 251–258.

28565. COHEN, EVELYN M./SCHRIJVER, EMILE G. L.: *The Esslingen Mahzor. A description of the 'New Amsterdam' and 'Old Amsterdam' volumes.* [In]: Studia Rosenthaliana, Vol. 25, No. 1, Assen, The Netherlands, Spring 1991, pp. 55–82, notes. [On the earliest recorded dated and localised Hebrew manuscript written in Germany, one volume currently housed in the Bibliotheca Rosenthaliana in the Amsterdam University Library, the other volume in the Jewish Theological Seminary in New York.]

—— DORON, JOACHIM/SHMUEL, GAN: *Soziale Probleme in der jüdischen Turnbewegung (1896–1914).* [See No. 27925.]

28566. FRIEDHABER, ZVI: *Dance in Ashkenazic Jewry as reflected in the ethical literature and the community sumptuary laws of the 17th–18th centuries.* [In Hebrew]. [In]: Proceedings of the 10th World Congress of Jewish Studies, 1989, Division D, Vol. 2: Art, folklore and music. Jerusalem, 1990. Pp. 21–28.

28567. FRIESEL, EVYATAR: *The Centralverein and the American Jewish Committee: a comparative study.* [In]: LBI Year Book XXXVI, London, 1991. Pp. 97–125, footnotes, illus.

28568. HETKAMP, JUTTA: *Die jüdische Jugendbewegung in Deutschland von 1913–1933.* Essen, Univ., Diss., 1991. 281 pp.

—— KARTELL-CONVENT (K.C.) SCHINDLER, THOMAS: *Der Kampf des K.C. gegen den Antisemitismus.* [See No. 28928]

28569. KROHN, HELGA: *'Du sollst dich niemals beugen': Henriette Fürth, Frau, Jüdin, Sozialistin.* [In]: Juden in Deutschland [see No. 27940]. Hamburg: Christians, 1991. Pp. 327–342, notes.

28570. LEVITT, CYRIL: *The prosecution of antisemites by the courts in the Weimar Republic: was justice served?*

[In]: LBI Year Book XXXVI, London, 1991. Pp. 151–167, footnotes. [On the efficacy of legal means and the organised Jewish defence to curb antisemitic agitation.]

28571. MARX, BETTINA: *Juden Marokkos und Europas: das marokkanische Judentum im 19. Jahrhundert und seine Darstellung in der zeitgenössischen jüdischen Presse in Deutschland, Frankreich und Grossbritannien.* Frankfurt am Main; New York [et al.]: Lang, 1991. VI, 342 pp. (Judentum und Umwelt; Bd. 32.) Zugl.: Köln, Univ., Diss., 1990.

—— MATTENKLOTT, GERD: *Jettchen Gebert und das Schtetl. Jüdische Lebenswelten in der deutschen Literatur.* [See No. 27960.]

28572. MORGENTHALER, SIBYLLE: *Countering the pre-1933 Nazi boycott against the Jews.* [In]: LBI Year Book XXXVI, London, 1991. Pp. 127–149, footnotes. [On the efforts to combat anti-Jewish boycott agitation by legal means in the Weimar Republic.]

28573. ORT. *ORT 1921–1991. 70 Jahre ORT in Deutschland.* [In]: ORT, Nr. 5, Winter 1991/92, Frankfurt am Main: 1991. Pp. 31–60. [Documents on the liquidation of ORT during Nazi period and personal memoirs; incl.: Ein Rückblick auf die Geschichte (Nele Löw Beer, 31–37). Aus der Frühgeschichte von ORT in Deutschland. Erinnerungen von Prof. Dr Ernst G. Lowenthal (43–45).]

28574. *Rabbinische Responsen zum Synagogenbau. Teil I. Die Responsentexte.* Übers. und eingeleitet von Brigitte Kern-Ulmer. Olms: Hildesheim; New York, 1990. 233 pp. (Studien zur Kunstgeschichte; Bd. 56.)

28575. SALMEN, WALTER: *Jüdische Musikanten und Tänzer vom 13. bis 20. Jahrhundert.* [At head of title: '. . . denn die Fiedel macht das Fest'.] Innsbruck: Edn. Helbling, 1991. 224 pp., illus., facsims., music scores, plans.

—— SCHLICH, THOMAS: Marburger jüdische Medizin- und Chirurgiestudenten, 1800–1832; Herkunft, Berufsweg, Stellung in der Gesellschaft. [See No. 28084.]

—— SEEWANN, HARALD: *'Mit Wort und Wehr für Judas Ehr'!': jüdisch-nationale Studentenverbindungen* [in Österreich] *als Wegbereiter des Zionismus.* [See No. 28624.]

28576. SELIGSOHN, JULIUS L. LOWENTHAL, ERNST G.: *Ein vergessener Berliner. Julius L. Seligsohn, Anwalt und Sozialarbeiter.* [In]: Mitteilungen des Vereins für die Geschichte Berlins, 86. Jg., H.3, Berlin, Juli 1990. Pp. 311–312. [J.L.S., lawyer, member of the board of the Reichsvereinigung der Juden in Deutschland, May 7, 1890 Berlin – Feb. 28, 1942 Sachsenhausen.]

28577. STRAUSS, HERBERT A.: *Robert Weltsch und die Jüdische Rundschau.* [In]: Berlin und der Prager Kreis [see No. 28666]. Pp. 31–44.

28578. TEMKIN, SEFTON D.: *How Reform Judaism developed.* [In]: Judaism, Vol. 40, No. 3, New York, Summer 1991. Pp. 369–377, footnotes. [Incl. review of Michael Meyer: Response to modernity: a history of the reform movement in Judaism, see No. 24922/YBXXXIV.]

28579. TOURY, JACOB: *Anti-Anti 1889/1892.* [In]: LBI Year Book XXXVI, London, 1991. Pp. 47–58. [On the first individual and organised attempts at fighting antisemitism by Jews and non-Jews.]

28580. TSCHOETSCHEL, MICHAEL: *Die Diskussion über die Häufigkeit von Krankheiten bei den Juden bis 1920.* Mainz, Univ., Diss., 1990. XI, 454 pp.

—— WEISS, YFAAT: *Schicksalsgemeinschaft im Wandel: die jüdische Erziehung im nationalsozialistischen Deutschland 1933–1938.* [See No. 28441.]

28581. WIESEMANN, FALK: *'Masal tow' für Braut und Bräutigam. Der Davidstern auf Hochzeitssteinen.* [In]: Der Davidstern. Zeichen der Schmach – Symbol der Hoffnung [see No. 27924]. Dorsten, 1991. Pp. 86–91, notes [p. 194], illus. [About chuppa stones as found in some parts of the Palatinate, Hesse, Franconia, Schwaben, Württemberg and Baden.]

28582. WILLNER, MAX. *Max Willner. Würdigung eines verdienten Mannes.* Hrsg. von Moritz Neumann im Auftrag des Landesverbandes der Jüdischen Gemeinden in Hessen. Frankfurt am Main (Hebelstr. 17): Landesverband der Jüdischen Gemeinden in Hessen, 1991. 216 pp., illus. [Incl.: Beschreibung und Würdigung eines verdienten Mannes [13 contributions dealing with the life and work of M.W.] (19–76). Ausgewählte Reden und Schriften (Max Willner, 173–200). Zum 85. Geburtstag: Reden auf Max Willner [5 contributions] (201–216). Further contributions are listed according to subject.] [M.W., born 24. July, Gelsenkirchen, from 1939 until 1945 forced labourer in Auschwitz, Sachsenhausen, Flossenbürg and Dachau, from 1945 co-founder and president of the Jüdische Gemeinde Offenbach am Main, from 1954 until 1985 Geschäftsführer des Landesverbandes der Jüdischen Gemeinden in Hessen, from 1979 Stellvertreter Vorsitzender des Zentralrats der Juden in Deutschland.]

D. Jewish Art and Music

28583. AMISHAI-MAISELS, ZIVA: *Innenseiter, Außenseiter; moderne jüdische Künstler im Portrait.* [In]: Jüdische Lebenswelten. Essays [see No. 27946]. Frankfurt am Main: Jüdischer Verlag, Suhrkamp, 1991. Pp. 165–184, illus., bibl. [Also [a.o.] on Moritz Oppenheim, Max Liebermann, Ludwig Meidner.]

28584. GOTTLIEB, MAURICY.: *Mauricy Gottlieb 1856–1879; Meisterwerke.* Herausgegeben vom Jüdischen Museum Frankfurt im Auftrag des Magistrats der Stadt Frankfurt am Main. Hrsg.: Georg Heuberger. Frankfurt am Main: Jüdisches Museum, 1991, 95 pp., illus., notes, bibl. [Catalogue book to an exhibition held at the Jüdisches Museum Frankfurt Nov. 28, 1991 – Feb. 23, 1992.] [M.G., Feb. 21, 1856 Drohobycz, Galicia – July 17, 1879 Cracow, painter, lived in Galicia and Vienna.]

28585. GRADENWITZ, PETER: *'So singet uns von Zijons Sang!' Jüdische Musik und Musiker in ihrer Umwelt.* [In]: Jüdische Lebenswelten [see No. 27946]. Frankfurt am Main: Jüdischer Verlag, Suhrkamp, 1991, Pp. 185–202, illus. [Also on the music tradition of the Aschkenasim and on German-Jewish composers.]

28586. GUTMANN, JOSEPH: *The Kirschstein Museum of Berlin.* [In]: Jewish Art, Vol. 16/17, Jerusalem, 1991. Pp. 172–176. [Salli Kirschstein, July 26, 1869 Kolmar, Poznań – Jan. 11, 1935 Berlin, merchant, art collector, expert on Jewish art, most of his important collection of Jewish art and cult objects was bequeathed to the Hebrew Union College, Cincinnati.]

—— HOBERMANN, JIM: *Jenseits von Galizien, diesseits von Hollywood: der jiddische Film aus Wien.* [See No. 27986.]

28587. ISZAK, ANDOR: *Das europäische Zentrum für Jüdische Musik in Augsburg.* [In]: Aschkenas, Bd. 1, Wien, 1991. Pp. 217–219. [On the initiative of two Hungarian cantors and organists, Marcel Lorand and Andor Izsak, who founded the Europäisches Zentrum für Jüdische Musik in Augsburg in 1988.]

—— *Judaica Prag.* Aus dem Staatlichen Jüdischen Museum Prag. [See No. 28167.]

28588. KLEEBLATT, NORMAN L.: *Illustrating Jewish lifestyles on opposite banks of the Rhine: Alphonse Lévy's Alsatian peasants and Moritz Daniel Oppenheim's Frankfurt burghers.* [In]: Jewish Art, Vol. 16/17, Jerusalem, 1991. Pp. 53–63.

—— KLOTZ, HELMUT/WEISS; ANNE: *Leipziger Synagogalchor.* [See No. 28078.]

28589. KÜNZL, HANNELORE: *Die Synagoge in Odenbach.* [In]: Trumah, 2, Wiesbaden, 1990. Pp. 1–23, illus., notes.

28590. METZGER, THÉRÈSE: *L'iconographie de la bible hébraïque médiévale.* [In]: Die Juden in ihrer mittelalterlichen Umwelt [see No. 27942]. Wien: Böhlau, 1991. Pp. 151–172.

—— *(Die) Prager Judenstadt.* Text von Milada Vilímková. [See No. 28168.]

—— *Rabbinische Responsen zum Synagogenbau. Teil I. Die Responsentexte.* Übers. und eingeleitet von Brigitte Kern-Ulmer. [See No. 28574.]

—— SALMEN, WALTER: *Jüdische Musikanten und Tänzer vom 13. bis. 20. Jahrhundert.* [See No. 28575.]

28591. SULZER, SALOMON. *Salomon Sulzer – Kantor, Komponist, Reformer.* Katalog zur Ausstellung des Landes Vorarlberg. Red.: Bernhard Purin. Bregenz: Land Vorarlberg, 1991. 142 pp., index. [Incl.: Die Levi-Sulzer. Der Liedkomponist und Liedinterpret Salomon Sulzer (Walter Pass, 52–73). Der 'Sulzerkantor' – ein Phänomen seiner Epoche (Thomas Dombrowski, 74–83); further articles are listed according to subject.]

—— WIESEMANN, FALK: *'Masal tow' für Braut und Bräutigam; der Davidstern auf Hochzeitssteinen.* [See in No. 27924].

VI. ZIONISM AND ISRAEL

28592. AGNON. SAMUEL JOSEF. HOFFMANN, ANNE GOLOMB: *Between exile and return: S.Y. Agnon and the drama of writing.* Albany: State Univ. of New York Press, 1991. 256 pp., bibl. (Modern Jewish literature and culture.)

28593. —— WINEMAN, ARYEH: *Agnon and Rabbi Nahman.* [In]: Jewish Book Annual, Vol. 49 (1991–1992), New York, 1991. Pp. 97–106, footnotes. [Agnon's treatment of the 'Tales of Rabbi Nahman'.]

28594. BERNSTEIN, EDUARD. Hildesheimer, Esriel: *The socialist Eduard Bernstein and Zionism.* [In Hebrew, title transl.] [In]: Machbarot 1-Machshava Sotsialistit, No. 14, Tel-Aviv, Summer 1990. Pp. 82–91. [Reprinted from 'Me'assef', 9, Givat Haviva, Aug. 1977.]

28595. BODENHEIMER, MAX ISIDOR. Bodenheimer, Henriette Hannah: *Max Isidor Bodenheimer (1865–1940).* [In]: Rheinische Lebensbilder. Bd. 12. Im Auftrag der Gesellschaft für Rheinische Geschichtskunde hrsg. von Franz-Josef Heyen. Köln: Rheinland Verl., 1991. Pp. 233–256, bibl. [Henriette Hannah Bodenheimer, 1898 Cologne – March 25, 1992 Jerusalem, daughter of M.I.B. *Obituary:* (Schalom Ben-Chorin) [in]: MB, Jg. 60, Tel Aviv, May 1992, p. 9.]

28596. — Valder-knechtges, Claudia: *Max Isidor Bodenheimer; Wegbereiter für den jüdischen Staat.* Hrsg. von Klaus Kunkel. Köln: Kölner Universitätsverlag, 1990. 35 pp.

28597. Carmel, Alex: *Gustav Bauernfeind – an unknown painter of Eretz Israel.* [In Hebrew]. [In]: Cathedra, No. 57, Jerusalem, Sept. 1990. Pp. 52–75. [See also No. 28617.]

——— Dinner, Chava/Goell, Yohai: *The history of Zionism and the State of Israel*: a selected and annotated bibliography for 1990. [See No. 28210.]

28598. Eliav, Mordechai, ed.: *Siege and distress: Eretz Israel during the First World War.* [In Hebrew]. Jerusalem: Yad Izhak Ben-Zvi, 1991. 290 pp. [Incl.: The activities of German and Austrian diplomatic representatives on behalf of the Jews of Eretz Israel (Mordechai Eliav, 157–167). German and American intervention on behalf of the Yishuv (Isaiah Friedman, 168–188).]

28599. Eloni, Yehuda: *Der unsterbliche Schlemiel.* [In]: MB. Jg. 59, Nr. 68, Tel Aviv, April 1991, pp. 4–5. [On the Zionist satirical periodical, founded in 1903 in Berlin by Max Grundmann [et al.] and its vicissitudes.]

28600. Friedman, Isaiah: *The involvement of Germany in the expulsion of Jews from Jaffa in 1914 and 1917.* [In Hebrew]. [In]: Proceedings of the 10th World Congress of Jewish Studies, 1989, Division B, Vol. 1: The history of the Jewish people. Jerusalem, 1990. Pp. 339–344.

28601. Gordon, Louis A.: *Arthur Koestler and his ties to Zionism and Jabotinsky.* [In]: Studies in Zionism, Vol. 12, No. 2, Tel-Aviv, 1991. Pp. 149–168, footnotes.

28602. GOTTGETREU, ERICH. Guney, Erol: *Erich Gottgetreu a different kind of foreign correspondent.* [In Hebrew and English.[[In]: Qesher, No. 10, Tel-Aviv, Nov. 1991. Pp. 30–34 (English) & 75–79 (Hebrew). [E.G., July 31, 1903 Chemnitz – Nov. 13, 1981 Jerusalem, studied journalism in Berlin, emigrated to Palestine in 1933, AP representative and head in Jerusalem.]

28603. HERZL, THEODOR. Beller, Steven: *Herzl.* London: Peter Halban, 1991. XIV, 161 pp., bibl., index. (Jewish Thinkers.)

28604. — Schäfer, Barbara: *Theodor Herzl und die 'Araberfrage'.* [In]: Menora, Bd. 2, München, 1991. Pp. 141–162, notes. [Incl. letters of Jacob de Haas, Herzl and Yusuf al-Khalidi, deputy and former mayor of Jerusalem.]

——— — Wachten, Johannes: *Theodor Herzl: Zionismus und Journalismus.* [See in No. 27941.]

28605. — *Briefe und Tagebücher.* Hrsg. von Alex Bein (s.A.), Hermann Greive (†), Moshe Scharf, Julius H. Schoeps, Johannes Wachten. Bd. 5: *Briefe; Anfang Dezember 1898 – Mitte August 1900.* Bearb. von Barbara Schäfer in Zusammenarbeit mit Sofia Gelman [et al.]. Frankfurt am Main: Propyläen, 1991. 774 pp., index of persons, of subjects (757–774).

28606. Ilsar, Yehiel: *Hermann Badt – Von der Vertretung Preußens im Reichsrat zum Siedlungsprojekt am Genezareth-See.* [In]: Tel Aviver Jahrbuch für deutsche Geschichte, Bd. 20, Gerlingen, 1991. Pp. 339–362, notes. [H.B., July 13, 1887 Breslau – Sept. 1946 Jerusalem, lawyer, Prussian Ministerialdirektor, Zionist, emigrated to Palestine in 1933.]

28607. IRGUN OLEI MERKAS EUROPA. *Fünfzig Jahre Solidaritätswerk.* [In]: MB: Mitteilungsblatt des Irgun Olei Merkas Europa, Jg. 59, Nr. 72, Tel-Aviv, Okt. 1991. Pp. 1–3. [Solidaritätswerk, founded on March 21, 1941 by the Irgun Olei Merkas Europa to help German- and Austrian-Jewish refugees from Nazi Europe to settle in Palestine.]

——— Jütte, Robert: *Die Emigration der deutschsprachigen 'Wissenschaft des Judentums'. Die Auswanderung jüdischer Historiker nach Palästina 1933–1945.* [See No. 28530.]

28608. Kling, Simcha: *Zionist leaders in Germany before the First World War.* [In Hebrew, title transl.] [In]: Hadoar, Vol. 70, No. 4, New York, 23 Nov. 1990. Pp. 22–23.

28609. Lavsky, Hagit: *The distinctive path of German Zionism.* [In]: Art and its uses: the visual image and modern Jewish society. Studies in Contemporary Jewry. An annual; VI, 1990. Ed.: Ezra Mendelssohn; guest symposium ed.: Richard I. Cohen. New York; Oxford: Oxford University Press, 1990. Pp. 254–271, notes.

28610. Lavsky, Hagit: *Before catastrophe: the distinctive path of German Zionism.* Jerusalem: Magnes and Hassifriyah Hazionit, 1990. 292 pp. (in Hebrew). [Cf.: Review article (Jehuda Reinharz) [in]: Studies in Zionism, Vol. 12, No. 1, Tel-Aviv, Spring 1991. Pp. 93–95.]

28611. MENDES-FLOHR, PAUL: *Zion und die Diaspora; vom babylonischen Exil bis zur Gründung des Staates Israel.* [In]: Jüdische Lebenswelten. Essays [see No. 27946]. Frankfurt am Main: Jüdischer Verlag, Suhrkamp, 1991. Pp. 257–284, bibl. [Also on the development of messianism and Zionism in Germany and Austria.]

28612. NAOR, MORDECAI: *The comptroller's report.* [In Hebrew, title transl.] [In]: Eit-mol, No. 97, Tele-Aviv, June 1991. Pp. 3–6. [On Franz Oppenheimer's criticism of collective settlements in Palestine.] [F.O., economic theorist, data see No. 22676/YBXXXI.]

28613. NICOSIA, FRANCIS R.: *The end of emancipation and the illusion of preferential treatment: German Zionism, 1933–1938.* [In]: LBI Year Book XXXVI, London, 1991. Pp. 243–265, footnotes.

28614. NORDAU, MAX. SÖDER, HANS-PETER: *Disease and health as contexts of modernity: Max Nordau as a critic of fin-de-siècle modernism.* [In]: German Studies Review, Vol. 14, No. 3, Tempe, Az., Oct. 1991. Pp. 473–487, notes.

28615. OEGEMA, GERBERN S.: *'Juden, nehmt ihn auf, den Davidschild, und tragt ihn in Ehren'. Als Zionsstern weltweit zum Symbol der Heimkehr geworden.* [In]: Der Davidstern; Zeichen der Schmach – Symbol der Hoffnung [see No. 27924]. Dorsten, 1991. Pp. 94–99.

28616. OFER, DALIA: *Escaping the Holocaust: illegal immigration to the land of Israel, 1939–1944.* Oxford, New York: Oxford Univ. Press, 1991. XIII, 408 pp., illus., appendixes, notes (329–380), bibl. (381–391). [Rescue efforts by the Palestinian Jewish community in the context of general Zionist policy.]

28617. *(Der) Orientmaler Bauernfeind 1848–1904. Leben und Werk = The life and work of Gustav Bauernfeind. Orientalist painter 1848–1904.* Hrsg. in Zusammenarbeit mit d. Gottlieb-Schuhmacher-Inst. zur Erforschung d. christl. Beitrags zum Wiederaufbau Palästinas im 19. Jahrhundert an d. Univ. Haifa, Israel. Stuttgart: Dr. Ernst Hauswedell & Co, 1990. 368 pp., illus., facsims., plates. [Incl.: Der Orientmaler Gustav Bauernfeind. Eine historische Einführung (Alex Carmel, XI-XII, 1–17; English version transl. by Ted Gorelick, 78–157).] [The non-Jewish architect and painter G.B., Sept. 4, 1848 Sulz am Neckar – Dec. 24, 1904, Jerusalem, lived in Munich, made several trips to Palestine between 1881–1889, emigrated to Palestine in 1896; he also did in 1891 an oil painting commissioned by the Nuremberg Jewish community: Das Innere der Synagoge in Nürnberg darstellend; see also No. 28597.]

28618. PENSLAR, DEREK JONATHAN: *Zionism, colonialism and technocracy: Otto Warburg and the Commission for the Exploration of Palestine, 1903–7.* [In]: Journal of Contemporary History, Vol. 25, No. 1, Jan. 1990.

28619. RADKE, RUDOLF: *Teddy Kollek. Ein Leben für die Menschlichkeit.* München: List, 1991. 244 pp., bibl. [T.K., orig. Theodor, born May 27, 1911 in Nagyvaszony, Hungary, emigrated from Vienna to Palestine in 1935, since 1965 mayor of Jerusalem.]

28620. REINHARZ, JEHUDA: *Die Ansiedlung deutscher Juden im Palästina der 1930er Jahre.* [In]: Menora, Bd. 2, München, 1991. Pp. 163–184.

28621. REINHARZ, JEHUDA: Zionismus und die österreichische Linke vor dem Ersten Weltkrieg. [In]: Juden in Deutschland [see No. 27940]. Hamburg: Christians, 1991. Pp. 229–251, notes. [Übers. von Barbara Gerber.]

28622. RIEMER, JEHUDA: *Fritz Perez Naphtali, Sozialdemokrat und Zionist.* Aus dem Hebr. von Magali Philippsborn. Gerlingen: Bleicher, 1991. 400 pp. (Schriftenreihe des Instituts für deutsche Geschichte, Universität Tel Aviv.) [P. (orig. Fritz) N., March 29, 1888 Berlin – April 30, 1961 Tel Aviv, economist, Socialist politician, Israeli welfare minister.] [Cf.: Besprechung (Chaim Seeligmann) [in]: MB, Nr. 74, Tel Aviv, Dez. 1991, pp. 7–8.]

28623. SCHINDLER, THOMAS: *Ein 'zionistischer' Verbandsbruder.* [In]: CC-Blätter, Jg. 106, Nr. 3, Bonn, 1991. Pp. 70–71. [On the German author Alfons Paquet, 1881–1944.]

28624. SEEWANN, HARALD: *'Mit Wort und Wehr für Judas Ehr'!': jüdisch-nationale Studentenverbindungen [in Österreich] als Wegbereiter des Zionismus* [In]: Das Jüdische Echo, Vol. 40, Nr. 1, Wien, Okt. 1991. Pp. 42–47, ports.

——— SHAFIR, SHLOMO: *Henry Morgenthau and his involvement in rescue in Germany and in Eretz Israel.* [See No. 28485.]

28625. SIMMER, EBERHARD: *Eine Oase für Kinder: 'Neve Hanna'.* Der Staat Israel würdigt das Lebenswerk von Hanni Ullmann. [In]: Tribüne, Jg. 30, H. 119, Frankfurt am Main, 1991. Pp. 118–124, illus. [On the kindergarten teacher Hanni Ullmann, who emigrated from Berlin in 1929 to Palestine and founded the family home, Neve Hanna.]

28626. STRAUSS, HERBERT A.: *Zum zeitgeschichtlichen Hintergrund zionistischer Kulturkritik: Scholem,*

Weltsch und die Jüdische Rundschau. [In]: Juden in Deutschland [see No. 27940]. Hamburg: Christians, 1991. Pp. 375–389, notes.

28627. TOURY, GIDEON/TOURY, JACOB: *Namensänderungen deutschsprachiger Einwanderer in Palästina bis 1942.* [In]: Menora, Bd. 2, München, 1991. Pp. 185–212, notes.

—— VOLKMANN, MICHAEL: *Adult education in Palestine among German Jewish immigrants [1933–1944].* [See in No. 28561.]

28628. WALLAS, ARMIN A./LAURITSCH, ANDRES M., eds.: *Israel II.* A-9500 Villach (Rennsteiner Str. 118): Armin A. Wallas, Mai 1991. 64 pp. (Mnemosyne, H. 11.) [Cont. prose texts and poems by German- and Austrian-Jewish writers now living in Israel, incl. short biographies.]

28629. WEINER, HANNA: *The first kibbutzim established by pioneers from Germany.* [In Hebrew]. [In]: Shoraskim (Roots), Vol. 6, Tel-Aviv, 1991. Pp. 163–175. [On the kibbutzim Heftzibah and Beit Zera.]

28630. WOLF, ARIE: *Arnold Zweigs Zionismus; einiges über Zweigs zionistische Gesinnung und sein aktives zionistisches Engagement.* [In]: heinrich mann jahrbuch 8, 1990. Hrsg. von Helmut Koopmann [et al.]. Senat der Hansestadt Lübeck: Amt für Kultur, 1990. Pp. 171–187, notes.

28631. ZADEK, WALTER: *Verpaßte Chancen. Palästina konnte eine deutsch-jüdische 'Weltbühne' nicht brauchen.* [In]: Tribüne, Jg. 30, H. 119, Frankfurt am Main, 1991. Pp. 182–187. [On the short-lived German-language periodical 'Orient', first published in Haifa in 1942.]

—— ZARIZ, RUTH: *Berthold Storfer and his role in rescuing Jews from Germany.* [See No. 28405.]

VII. PARTICIPATION IN CULTURAL AND PUBLIC LIFE

Due to the wealth of studies in the history of German-speaking Jews and antisemitism published in 1991 and listed comprehensively in the preceding sections and below, this section has to be curtailed. [Ed.]

A. General

28632. AUSTRIA. BLAU, PAUL: *Die Sozialdemokratie als Heimat: jüdische Politiker* [in Österreich] *von der Frühzeit bis zum Ende der Ersten Republik.* [In]: Das Jüdische Echo, Vol. 40, Nr. 1, Wien, Okt. 1991. Pp. 53–60, notes. [Also in this issue: Europäische Dimensionen: die Ideen Otto Bauers (Herbert Steiner, 52–53).]

28633. — WALTER, FRITZ: *'Im Kino erlebe ich die Welt': jüdische Filmkünstler aus Österreich.* [In]: Das Jüdische Echo, Vol. 40, Nr. 1, Wien, Okt. 1991. Pp. 177–183, ports. [Also in this issue: Die lebenden Toten: Juden auf der Wiener Bühne (Peter Loos, 171–176).]

—— BENÖHR, HANS-PETER: *Jüdische Rechtsgelehrte in der deutschen Rechtswissenschaft.* [See in No. 27941.]

28634. BERGMANN, JOACHIM: *Die Schaubühne/Die Weltbühne 1905–1933:* Bibliographie und Register mit Annotationen. *Teil 1: Bibliographie mit biographischen Annotationen. Alphabetisches Titelregister.* Mit einem Essay von Axel Eggebrecht. München; London [et al.]: Saur, 1991. XXIII, 382 pp. [Ed.: Siegfried Jacobsohn (until 1926); Kurt Tucholsky; Carl von Ossietzky. Cf.: Besprechung (Alfred Estermann) [in]: Buchhandelsgeschichte. 1992/1. [Beilage zum] Börsenblatt für den Deutschen Buchhandel, Nr. 24, Frankfurt & Leipzig, 24. März 1992, pp. B 30 – B 33.] [See also No. 26745/YBXXXV.]

28635. BERGMAN, SCHMUEL HUGO: *Dialogical philosophy from Kierkegaard to Buber.* Transl. by Arnold A. Gerstein. Foreword by Nathan Rotenstreich. Albany: State Univ. of New York, 1991. XVI, 257 pp. (SUNY series in Jewish philosophy.). [Incl. also Rosenzweig.]

28636. BLOOM, HAROLD: *Kafka, Freud, Scholem.* Aus dem amerikanischen Englisch von Angelika Schweikhart. Basel/Frankfurt am Main: Stromfeld/Roter Stern. 80 pp. [Orig. American edn. appeared in 1987 under the title, The strong light of the canonical. Kafka, Freud, Scholem as revisionists of Jewish culture and thought.]

28637. BOTSTEIN, LEON: *Judentum und Modernität; Essays zur Rolle der Juden in der deutschen und österreichischen Kultur 1848–1938.* Köln: Böhlau, 1990. 240 pp. [On Felix Mendelssohn, Richard Wagner, Fritz Mauthner, Arnold Schönberg, Karl Kraus, Ludwig Wittgenstein, Sigmund Freud, Gustav Mahler, Max Nordau, Theodor Herzl, Egon Friedell, Martin Buber.] [Cf.: Mehr als eine Kultusgemeinde (Elisabeth Endres) [in]: Süddeutsche Zeitung, München, 20. Sept. 1991, p. 11.]

28638. CASSIRER. family. BRÜHL, GEORG: *Die Cassirers: Streiter für den Impressionismus.* Leipzig: Verlag Edn. Leipzig, 1991. 500 pp., 378 illus., geneal. tab.

28639. CHRIST, KARL: *Geschichte und Existenz.* Berlin: Wagenbach, 1991. 89 pp. [Incl. the essay: Die Verdrängten – zur Existenz des Historikers (pp. 51–89; a.o. on Elias Bickermann, Eugen Täubler, Richard Laqueur, Victor Ehrenberg).] [Cf.: Wahrheitsethos [in]: Neue Zürcher Zeitung, Nr. 255, 2./3. Nov. 1991, p. 27.]

28640. COCKS, GEOFFREY: *Partners and pariahs: Jews and medicine in modern German society.* [In]: LBI Year Book XXXVI, London, 1991. Pp. 191–205, footnotes.

28641. ERNST, HEIKO, ed.: *Der innere Kosmos. Gespräche mit Psychologen.* Weinheim: Beltz, 1991. 279 pp. (Beltz Psychologie heute.) [Interviews with 18 psychologists, orig. publ. between 1974 and 1991 in 'Psychologie Heute', a.o.: Rudolf Arnheim (12–27). Bruno Bettelheim (44–52). Marie Jahoda (132–141). Manès Sperber (237–250).

28642. ESCHWEGE, HELMUT: *Die Dresdner Bank und der Anteil der Juden an ihrer Geschichte.* [In]: Sächsische Heimatblätter, Sonderheft 1, Dresden, 1991. Pp. 29–31. [Incl. list of names of important Jewish bankers of the Dresdner Bank 1872–1933.]

28643. EXIL. *Exilforschung.* Ein internationales Jahrbuch. Bd. 9: *Exil und Remigration.* Hrsg. im Auftrag der Gesellschaft für Exilforschung/Society for Exile Studies von Claus-Dieter Krohn [et al.] München: Edn. Text und Kritik, 1991. 263 pp., notes. [Incl. (titles condensed): Exil und Remigration als öffentliches Ärgernis. Zur Soziologie eines Tabus (Sven Papcke, 9–24). Reise zurück aus der Zukunft: intellektuelle USA-Remigranten in den fünfziger Jahren (Axel Schildt, 25–45). Die Weiderkehr der Traumata im Versuch sie zu bearbeiten: die Remigration von Horkheimer und Adorno. (Wolfgang Kraushaar, 46–67). Adorno und Eisler (Claudia Albert, 68–80). Wiedereinbürgerung, Rehabilitation und Wiedergutmachung nach 1945 (Hans Georg Lehmann, 90–103). Rückkehr auf Zeit. Erfahrungen deutsch-jüdischer Emigranten mit Einladungen in ihre ehemaligen Heimatstädte (Wolfgang Benz, 196–207). Zum Paradigmenwechsel in der Exilliteraturforschung (Ernst Loewy, 208–217). Erzählung als Erfahrungsrettung: Anna Seghers Exilroman 'Transit' (Jürgen Barkhoff, 218–235).]

28644. EXILE LITERATURE. *Exil. Forschung, Erkenntnisse, Ergebnisse.* Jg. 10, Nr. 2 & Jg. 11, Nr. 1. Hrsg. von Edita Koch. 6457 Maintal (Goethestr. 122): E. Koch, 1990 & 1991. 2 issues, notes. [Jg. 10, Nr. 2 (1990) incl., titles condensed: Der Moskauer Schriftstellerkongress 1934 und seine deutschen Gäste (Michael Rohrwasser, 45–58). Buchbesprechungen in 'Das Wort' (Michael Grunewald, 59–75). Jg. 11, Nr. 1 (1991): Paul Ludwig Landsberg – ein Name in Vergessenheit (Verena Lenzen, 5–22; P.L., Dec. 3, 1901 Bonn – Apr. 2, 1944 Oranienburg concentration camp, philosopher, emigrated to France in 1933). Zu Celans Gedichte "Die Fleissigen" [Yoshihiko Hirano, 41–45). Diskussionen um den Freiheitsbegriff im englischen Exil 1944/45 [Dieter Schiller, 93–99). Index für Jg. 10, 1990 (110–112). Further essays are listed according to subject.] Sonderband: *Exiltheater und Exildramatik 1933–1945*; Tagung der Hamburger Arbeitsstelle für deutsche Exilliteratur 1990. Hrsg. von Edita Koch und Frithjof Trapp. Unter Mitarbeit von Anne-Margarete Brenker. 326 pp., notes, index of persons. (*Exil; Forschung, Erkenntnisse, Ergebnisse*, Sonderband 2.) [Incl. (titles partly condensed): Exilland Österreich? (Hilde Haiger-Pregler, 13–40, notes). 'Bleiben doch die ewgen Juden . . .'. Max Reinhardts Exil (Leonhard M. Fiedler, 41–62, notes). Deutschsprachige Exilierte und das englische Theatersystem (J. M. Ritchie, 63–79, notes). Die exilierten Theaterleute und das Broadwaysystem (Henry Marx, 80–103, notes). Das Neue Deutsche Theater Prag in den dreißiger Jahren (Hansjörg Schneider, 104–117). Zwischen Unterhaltungsfunktion und der Erwartung politischer Stellungnahme: die 'Freie Deutsche Bühne' Buenos Aires (Frithjof Trapp, 118–137, notes). Der Internationale Revolutionäre Theaterbund (Peter Diezel, 155–171, notes). Hermann Greid und das deutschsprachige Theater im schwedischen Exil (Helmut Müssener, 182–202, notes; Hermann Greid, orig. Grabscheid, 1892 Vienna – 1975 Stockholm). Ernst Tollers Beziehungen zu englischen und amerikanischen Theaterleuten nach 1933 (Richard Dove, 203–218, notes). Die Kurt-Weill-Stiftung und ihre Wirkung auf die amerikanische Theaterwelt (Guy Stern, 294–306, notes).]

28645. — EISENBERG-BACH, SUSI: *Holland als Verlagsland deutscher Literatur des Exils.* [In]: Aus dem Antiquariat, 5, [Beilage zum] Börsenblatt für den deutschen Buchhandel, Nr. 43, Frankfurt am Main, 31. Mai 1991, pp. A 184-A 186, notes.

28646. — HAARMANN, HERMANN: '*. . . nur meines Kummers Gewalt sänftigen können sie nicht./Seit ich die Heimat verließ . . .*'. Exil, Exilliteratur und Exilpublizistik. Für Leo Löwenthal zum 90.

Geburtstag. [In]: Internat. Archiv für Sozialgeschichte der deutschen Literatur, 16. Bd., 1.H., Tübingen, 1991. Pp. 79–93, footnotes. [Incl. German-Jewish exiles.]

28647. — HERZFELDE, WIELAND: *Prag-Moskau; Briefe von und an Wieland Herzfelde 1933–1938*. Hrsg. von Guiseppe de Siati und Thies Ziemke. Kiel: Neuer Malik Verlag, 1991. 220 pp. [Cf.: Grämliche Genossen (Fritz J. Raddatz) [in]: Die Zeit, Nr. 2, Hamburg, 3. Jan. 1992, p. 41.]

28648. — *'Ich war für all das zu müde'*. Briefe aus dem Exil. Orig.-Ausg. Gesammelt von Peter Härtling. Hamburg: Luchterhand. 1991. 197 pp. (Sammlung Luchterhand; 998) [Cont.: 68 letters of Jewish and non-Jewish exiled authors, poets and artists. Nachwort (Peter Härtling, 167–175). Die Absender, Adressaten und Quellen (176–197).]

28649. — *Im Fluchtgepäck die Sprache: deutschsprachige Schriftstellerinnen im Exil*. Hrsg. von Claudia Schoppmann. Berlin: Orlanda Frauenverl., 1991. 245 pp., illus., bibl. (238–243). (Der andere Blick.) [Cont.: Einleitung (Claudia Schoppmann, 11–22, notes); short stories, letters, excerpts from diaries, memoirs and other texts [a.o.] by Jenni Aloni, Ruth Landshoff-Yorck, Ilse Losa, Erika Mann, Hilde Rubinstein, Lessie Sachs, Hedda Zinner; with biographical introductions by the editor.]

28650. — MAAS, LIESELOTTE: *Handbuch der deutschen Exilpresse 1933–1945. Bd. 4: Die Zeitungen des deutschen Exils in Europa von 1933–1939 in Einzeldarstellungen*. München: Hanser, 1990. 527 pp., illus. [Incl.: many newspapers and periodicals edited by German-Jewish and Austrian-Jewish exiles, also Jewish papers such as Golus (Prague), Freiland (Paris), Birobidjan im Bau (Brünn; Prague), Jüdische Revue (Mukacevo), Ordo (Paris).] [Cf.: Besprechung (Maria Kühn-Ludewig) [in]: Buchhandelsgeschichte, 1991/1, [Beilage zum] Börsenblatt für den dt. Buchhandel, Nr. 24, Frankfurt am Main, 24. März 1991. Pp. B45–B48, notes.]

28651. — SOCIETY FOR EXILE STUDIES = GESELLSCHAFT FÜR EXILFORSCHUNG, ed.: *Nachrichtenbrief = Newsletter*. 12/Dez. 1990.: Nr. 12/Dez. 1990. Bearb. von Barbara Seib [et al.]. Frankfurt am Main (Postfach 550207): Ernst Loewy, 1990. 246 pp., index (229–246). [Issue incl. reports on symposia, review articles and bibliography of current books and articles pertaining to exile literature and historiography.]

—— WALDINGER, ERNST: *Noch vor dem Jüngsten Tag; ausgewählte Gedichte und Essays*. [See No. 28986.]

28652. — WOLFFHEIM, ELSBETH: *'Heinrich Mann war leider nicht auf diesem Kongress'*. Deutsche Exilautoren als Gäste auf dem 'Ersten Allunionskongress der Sowjetschriftsteller' in Moskau im Jahre 1934. [In]: heinrich mann jahrbuch 8, 1990. Hrsg. von Helmut Koopmann [et al.] Senat der Hansestadt Lübeck: Amt für Kultur, 1990. Pp. 59–80, notes. [Incl. many German-Jewish exiled authors.]

28653. — *(Der) Zweite Weltkrieg und die Exilanten*. Eine literarische Antwort. World War II and the Exiles. A literary response. Hrsg. [Ed.by] Helmut F. Pfanner. Bonn: Bouvier, 1991. 324 pp., notes. [A collection of essays based on an international symposium of the same title, at the University of Nebraska-Lincoln, April 6–9, 1989. Incl. (titles partly condensed): Exile: the modern epidemic (Frederick Morton, 7–12). From premonition to portrayal: Franz Werfel and World War II (James C. Davidheiser, 13–22, notes). Zum lyrischen Werk von Günter Anders (Johann Holzner, 37–42, notes). Yvan Goll im amerikanischen Exil (Silvia Schlenstadt, 43–51, notes). Das Frankreichbild des Exils (Wulf Koepke, 53–61, notes). Frankreich-Kritik in den literarischen Werken von Bertolt Brecht und Lion Feuchtwanger (Reinhold Jaretzky, 73–83, notes). Die Dialektik der Moral: Anna Seghers Roman Das siebte Kreuz (Heike A. Doane, 85–95). Manès Sperbers Jugoslawienbild (Mirjana Stancic, 133–148, notes). Gefangen im Geistesreich der Idee: Arnold Zweigs Das Beil von Wandsbek (1938–44) (Helga Schreckenberger, 149–158, notes). Musik von Kurt Weill im Dienste der amerikanischen Kriegführung 1942–1945 (Jürgen Schebera, 169–176, notes). Hans Habe und Stefan Heym in der Psychological Warfare (Reinhard K. Zachau, 177–186, notes). Der unverwüstliche Gefreite Hirnschal und die treudeutschen Hörer/innen der BBC. (Gerhard Bauer, 187–195, notes; about Robert Lucas and his war-time satirical BBC-series). Hans Habes und Alfred Döblins Erlebnisberichte über den Krieg in Frankreich (Helmut Peitsch, 273–293, notes, bibl.). The exiles and the war of the minds (Guy Stern, 311–322, notes).

28654. *Freie Volksbühne Berlin 1890–1990*. Beiträge zur Geschichte der Volksbühnenbewegung in Berlin. Hrsg. von Dietger Pforte. Berlin: Argon, 1990. 276 pp., notes, index of names. [A collection of essays on the history of the Volksbühne. Refers passim to numerous actors, musicians and theatre directors of Jewish descent, a.o. Otto Brahm, Leopold Jessner, Max Reinhardt.]

28655. *(The) global anthology of Jewish women writers*. Robert and Roberta Kalechofsky, eds.:

Marblehead, Ma.: Micah Publications, 1990. V, 426 pp. [Incl. Hannah Arendt, Else Lasker-Schüler, Nelly Sachs, Rahel Varnhagen, a.o.]

28656. GROSSKURTH, PHYLLIS: *The secret ring: Freud's inner circle and the politics of psychoanalysis.* London: Cape, 1991. 245 pp., illus., notes, chronology. [On Freud's relationship with his closest disciples, such as Alfred Adler, Sandor Ferenczi, Ernest Jones, Melanie Klein, and the secret committee that they founded.] [Incl. comprehensive review of Peter Gay: Freud: a life for our time. See No. 25752/YBXXXIV.] [Cf.: Historicizing psychoanalysis: Freud in his time and for our time (John E. Toews) [in]: The Journal of Modern History, Vol. 63, No. 3, Chicago, Sept. 1991, pp. 504–545, footnotes.]

28657. HEINE, JENS ULRICH: *Verstand und Schicksal: die Männer der I.G Farbenindustrie A.G. in 161 Kurzbiographien.* Weinheim: VCH Verlagsgesellschaft, 1990. 341 pp. [Incl. short biographies of the Jewish members of the board and the board of directors; deals also with the Nuremberg Trial.] [Cf.: Besprechung (Wilhelm Treue) [in]: Das Historisch-Politische Buch, Jg. 39, H. 10, Göttingen, 1991. Pp. 330–331.]

28658. HIRSCH, HELMUT: *Rosa Luxemburg in Kunst und Literatur unter besonderer Berücksichtigung des jüdischen Aspekts.* [In]: Beiträge zur Geschichte der Arbeiterbewegung, 33. Jg., Hamburg: Demokratie und Recht, Zeitschriftenverlag, 1991, H. 4. Pp. 479–482. [Issue incl. 14 essays under the heading Luxemburg – Bild im Meinungsstreit; Materialien des Rosa-Luxemburg-Symposiums in Berlin am 5./6. März 1991.]

28659. JÄGER, LORENZ: *Zwischen Soziologie und Mythos: Hofmannsthals Begegnung mit Werner Sombart, Georg Simmel und Walter Benjamin.* [In]: Hugo von Hofmannsthal: Freundschaften und Begenungen mit deutschen Zeitgenossen. Hrsg.: Ursula Renner [u.] G. Bärbel Schmid. Würzburg: Königshausen & Neumann, 1991. Pp. 95–107, footnotes. [In the same book also: 'Elektra' und 'Ödipus': Hofmannsthals 'Erneuerung der Antike' für das Theater Max Reinhardts (Wolfgang Nehring, 123–142, footnotes).]

28660. JARAUSCH, KONRAD H.: *Jewish lawyers in Germany, 1848–1938. The disintegration of a profession.* [In]: LBI Year Book XXXVI, London, 1991. Pp. 171–190, footnotes.

28661. KRACH, TILLMANN: *Jüdische Rechtsanwälte in Preussen. Über die Bedeutung der freien Advokatur und ihre Zerstörung durch den Nationalsozialismus.* München: Beck, 1991. XXXIV, 441 pp., notes, tabs., index of persons. [Incl. biographical data (429–438).]

28662. LEIMKUGEL, FRANK: *Wege jüdischer Apotheker. Die Geschichte deutscher und österreichisch-ungarischer Pharmazeuten.* 6236 Eschborn: Govi, 1991. 212 pp. [Incl. persecution during Nazi period.]

28663. LORENZ, DAGMAR, C.G.: *Autobiographie und Fiktion bei Aichinger und Fried.* [In]: Modern Austrian Literature, Vol. 24, Nos. 3/4, Riverside, Ca., 1991. Pp. 43–53. [Author examines Ilse Aichinger's and Erich Fried's fiction as it reflects their experiences during the Nazi period.]

——— MANN, KLAUS & ERIKA: *Escape to life – Deutsche Kultur im Exil.* [See No. 28266.]

28664. MENGS, ANTON RAPHAEL. GRAFINGER, CHRISTINE MARIA: *Anton Raphael Mengs – ein Künstler jüdischer Abstammung und das Papyruskabinett der Bibliotheca Apostolica Vaticana.* [In]: Jewish Art, Vol. 16/17, Jerusalem, 1991. Pp. 30–45. [A.R.M., March 22, 1728 Aussig, Bohemia – June 29, 1779 Rome, painter.]

28665. PAPCKE, SVEN: *Gesellschaftsdiagnosen; klassische Texte der deutschen Soziologie im 20. Jahrhundert.* Orig.-Ausg. Frankfurt am Main; New York: 1991. 238 pp., footnotes, index of persons. [11 essays on selected 'classical' texts of German sociologists reflecting the biographical and political context; incl. Eduard Heimann, Siegfried Kracauer, Karl Mannheim, Erich von Kahler, Emil Lederer.]

28666. PAZI, MARGARITA/ZIMMERMANN, DIETER: *Berlin und der Prager Kreis.* Würzburg: Königshausen & Neumann, 1991. [Incl. (titles partly condensed): Der verzweifelte Parodist: Fritz Mauthner (Hans Dieter Zimmermann, 45–56). Franz Werfel und der Expressionismus (Rio Preisner, 111–126). Paul Kornfeld und Berlin (Margarita Pazi, 127–144). Max Brod und Berlin (Donald G. Daviau, 145–158). Berlin – Die Illusion der Freiheit für Franz Kafka (Ernst Pawel, 159–171). Berlin in Werk und Leben von Ernst Weiß (Peter Engel, 171–188.) Das verdrängte Judentum im Werk von Ernst Weiß (Franz Haas, 189–198; E.W., Aug. 28, 1882 Brünn/Brno, doctor, author.) Bruno Adler (Joachim W. Storck, 211–224; B.A., (pseud.: Urban Roedl) author, Karlsbad Oct. 14, 1888 – Dec. 28, 1968, emigr. 1933 from Berlin via Prague to England in 1936). Egon Erwin Kisch und das Theater in Berlin (Josef Polácek, 243–265). Über Willy Haas (Norbert Abels, 265–280). Emil Faktor und die Theaterkritik (Klaus Siebenhaar, 281–290). Further essays pertinent to German-speaking Jewry are listed according to subject.]

28667. *Prager deutschsprachige Literatur zur Zeit Kafkas.* Kafka-Symposiom 1989, Klosterneuburg. Hrsg.: Österreichische Franz Kafka-Gesellschaft Wien-Klosterneuburg. Wien, Braumüller, 1991. 112 pp., notes. (Schriftenreihe der Franz Kafka-Gesellschaft 4.). 13 essays referring passim to many Jewish authors, a.o. Brod, Kafka, Mauthner. Essays incl.: Nachrichten vom Krankenbett; Neue Kafka-Briefe aus den Jahren 1922–1924 (Josef Cermák, 27–36).

28668. RINGER, FRITZ K.: *Academics in Germany: German and Jew.* Some preliminary remarks. [In]: LBI Year Book XXXVI, London, 1991. Pp. 207–212, footnotes.

28669. ROBERTS, DAVID/THOMSON, PHILIP, eds.: *The modern German historical novel: paradigms, problems and perspectives.* Oxford; New York: Berg, 1991. 240 pp. [Incl. Hermann Broch, Alfred Döblin, Stefan Heym, Georg Lukács, Anna Seghers.]

28670. SAYERS, JANET: *Mothering psychoanalysis: Helene Deutsch, Karen Horney, Anna Freud, Melanie Klein.* London: Hamish Hamilton, 1991. XII, 319 pp., illus. [American edn. under the title: Mothers of psychoanalysis. New York: Norton, 1991.] [Cf.: Mind over mater (Julia Neuberger) [in]: The Sunday Times, London, Feb. 10, 1991.]

28671. SCHÜTZ, HANS J.: *Jüdische Schriftsteller und deutsche Literatur.* Folge 1–11. [In]: Börsenblatt für den Deutschen Buchhandel, Jg. 158, H. 3; 5; 6; 9; 10; 11; 13; 14; 15; 17; 20; 21; 23; 27; 39; 43; 46; 47; 49; 51; 59; 63. Frankfurt am Main & Leipzig, 11. Jan. – 9. Aug. 1991. 22 pts. (various pagings), ports., notes. [On the Jewish contribution to German literature from the Middle Ages to the exile during the Nazi period in the German-speaking European countries, with special chaps. for Vienna and Prague. This series is scheduled to be published as a volume of the 'Serie Piper'. Munich 1992.]

28672. SCHULZE, FRIEDRICH: *Der deutsche Buchhandel und die geistigen Strömungen der letzten hundert Jahre.* Hildesheim: Olms, 1990. VI, 296 pp., tabs., illus. [Reprint of the Leipzig edn. of 1925. Refers also to German-Jewish publishers and booksellers.]

28673. SILLO-SEIDL, GEORG: *Pioniere der modernen Medizin – Jüdische Ärzte deutscher Sprache.* Koblenz: Fölbach, 1991. 184 pp., illus. [Cf.: Besprechung (Janos Paál) [in]: Tribüne, Jg. 30, H. 120, Frankfurt am Main, 1991. Pp. 227–230.]

28674. STRUBE, ROLF, ed.: *Sie sassen und tranken am Teetisch. Anfänge und Blütezeit der Berliner Salons 1789–1871.* Orig.-Ausg. Piper: München, 1991. 326 pp., illus. (Serie Piper; 1204.) [Incl. texts from memoirs, letters and novels reflecting social and cultural life in the Berlin salons incl., a.o. those of the Mendelssohn families. Henriette Herz and Rahel Varnhagen.]

28675. TRAVERS, MARTIN: *The parameters of commitment: the German literary intelligentsia on the eve of the Third Reich.* [In]: Journal of European Studies, Vol. 21, No. 8, Chalfont St. Giles, March 1991. Pp. 19–41. [Incl. German-Jewish intellectuals such as Kurt Hiller, Erich Mühsam, Max Tau, Ernst Toller.]

28676. ULLSTEIN family. WALTER, HANS-ALBERT: *Ein Bruderzwist im Hause Ullstein. Anatomie eines Presseskandals Ende der Weimarer Republik.* [Funkmanuskript zur Sendung 'Kultur und Wissenschaft' am 21. Feb. 1991.] Red.: Lothar Fend. Köln (Appellhofplatz 1): Westdeutscher Rundfunk, 1991. 29 pp. [Mimeog.]

28677. WIGODER, GEOFFREY, ed.: *Dictionary of Jewish biography.* New York: Simon & Schuster, 1991. 568 pp., illus. [Biographical dictionary contains almost 1,000 entries on Jews from biblical times to the 20th century, excluding the living. Entries cover figures from politics, religion, science, the arts, i.a. many German Jews.]

28678. WIMMER, REINER: *Vier jüdische Philosophinnen: Rosa Luxemburg, Simone Weill, Edith Stein, Hannah Arendt.* 2. Aufl., Tübingen: Attempto, 1991. 308 pp.

B. Individual

28679. ADORNO, THEODOR W.: *Alban Berg: master of the smallest link.* Transl. by Juliane Brand and Christopher Hall. Cambridge: Cambridge Univ. Press, 1991. XVIII, 156 pp., illus., musical scores.

28680. AMÉRY, JEAN. HESS, A.: *Jean Améry und der Nationalsozialismus.* [In]: Zeitschrift für Religions- und Geistesgeschichte, Jg. 43, H. 1, Leiden, 1991. Pp. 49–68.

28681. ARENDT, HANNAH. *Israel. Palästina und der Antisemitismus.* Aufsätze. Hrsg. von Eike Geisel und Klaus Bittermann. Berlin: Wagenbach, 1991. 125 pp. [Collection of essays originally publ. between 1943 and 1964. For first German edn. see No. 26747/YBXXXV.] [Cf.: Eine Moralistin; über persönliche Verantwortung in der Diktatur: wie wappnet man sich gegen das Mitmachen? (Judith Klein) [in]: Die Zeit, 47. Jg., Nr. 15, Hamburg, 3. April 1992, p. 50.]

28682. ARNSTEIN, FANNY. SPIEL, HILDE: *Fanny von Arnstein: a daughter of Enlightenment, 1758– 1818.* Transl. from the German by Christine Shuttleworth. Oxford; New York: Berg, 1991. X, 368 pp., bibl. (343–351). [For first German edn. see No. 3226/YB VIII and No. 15424/ YB XXIV.]

28683. BARBAKOFF, TATJANA. *Tatjana Barbakoff – 1899 Libau – 1944 Auschwitz.* Ausstellung des Stadtmuseums, Düsseldorf, 17. Oktober – 24. November 1991. (Vorwort: Annette Baumeister, Text: Günter Goebbels.) Hrsg.: Landeshaupstadt Düsseldorf, Stadtmuseum, Düsseldorf 1991. 32 pp., illus. [T.B., orig. Cilly Edelberg, Libau (Lettland) 1899 – 1944 Auschwitz, dancer, emigrated from Düsseldorf to Paris in 1933 (together with the painter Gert Wollheim), interned in 1940 and murdered in Auschwitz in 1944.]

——— BENJAMIN, WALTER [See also No. 28953.]

28684. ——— BOLZ, NORBERT/REIJEN, WILLEM VAN: *Walter Benjamin.* Frankfurt am Main. Campus, 1991. 148 pp. (Reihe Campus Einführungen.) [On life and work of W.B.]

28685. ——— KAMBAS, CHRYSSOULA: *Bulletin de Vernuches: neue Quellen zur Internierung Walter Benjamins.* [In]: Exil, Jg. 10, Nr. 2, Maintal, 1990. Pp. 5–30, notes. [Incl. the French text of the draft for the camp-journal 'Bulletin de Vernuches'.]

28686. ——— PUTTNIES, HANS/SMITH, GARY (eds.): *Benjaminiana. Eine biographische Recherche.* Im Zusammenhang mit der Ausstellung 'Bucklicht Männlein und Engel der Geschichte; Walter Benjamin, Theoretiker der Moderne' im Werkbundarchiv, Berlin 28.12.1990– 28.4.1991. Giessen: Anabas, 1991. 56 pp.

28687. ——— SMITH, GARY: *'Das Jüdische versteht sich von selbst': Walter Benjamins frühe Auseinandersetzung mit dem Judentum.* [In]: Deutsche Vierteljahrsschrift für Literatur und Geistesgeschichte, Jg. 65, Stuttgart 1991. Pp. 318–334, Engl. summary (318).

28688. ——— TIMMS, EDWARD: *Shop till you drop: Walter Benjamin's philosophy of history* [In]: The Jewish Quarterly, Vol. 38, No. 3, London, Autumn 1991. Pp. 37–41, illus., notes.

28689. ——— WITTE, BERND: *Walter Benjamin: an intellectual biography.* Transl. by James Roleston. Detroit: Wayne State Univ. Press, 1991. 256 pp., illus.

28690. ——— *Erinnern an Walter Benjamin.* [In]: Kulturberichte, 1/1991. Hrsg. vom Arbeitskreis selbständiger Kulturinstitute e.V. (AsKI). 5300 Bonn: AsKI, Prinz Albert Str. 34, 1991. Pp. 2–5, illus. [On the memorial by the Israeli artist Dani Karavan for Walter Benjamin in Port Bou, the Spanish border village, where Benjamin committed suicide on Sept. 26, 1940.]

28691. BETTELHEIM, BRUNO. MEHLHAUSEN, JOACHIM: *Leben lernen; Gedenken an Bruno Bettelheim.* Tübingen: J. C. B. Mohr, 1991. 68 pp.

28692. BLOCH, ERNST: *Heritage of our times.* Transl. by Neville and Stephen Plaice. Oxford; Cambridge, Ma.: Polity Press, 1991. XIV, 377 pp. [First publ. as 'Erbschaft dieser Zeit', book reads as a contemporary observation of the rise of Nazism.]

28693. BÖRNE, LUDWIG: *Leben ist Differenz*: Nachgelesenes bei Ludwig Börne. Von Peter Hossfeld und Michael Strich. Berlin: Verl.-Anst. Union, 1991. 151 pp., illus.

28694. BORCHARDT, RUDOLF. ROHDE, FRIEDRICH: *Rudolf Borchardt (1877–1945). Abiturient am Weseler Gymnasium im Jahr 1895.* [In]: Heimatkalender des Kreises Wesel 1990. 11. Jg., Kleve: Boss, 1989. Pp. 79–84, illus.

28695. ——— SCHUHMACHER, KLAUS: *Der messianische Liebhaber Rudolf Borchardt.* Für Gabriella Harley-Peterich. [In]: Jahrbuch der deutschen Schillergesellschaft. 35. Jg., 1991. Stuttgart: Kröner, 1991. Pp. 234–256. [Discusses also his attitude towards his Jewish origin and his conversion.]

——— BROD, MAX [See No. 28964.]

28696. CASSIRER, ERNST: *Versuch über den Menschen.* Aus dem Englischen von Reinhard Kaiser. Frankfurt am Main: S. Fischer, 1990. 381 pp. [Cf.: Was ist er, der Mensch (Ernst Wolfgang Orth) [in]: Die Zeit, Nr. 42, Hamburg, 11. Okt. 1991, p. 46.]

28697. CELAN, PAUL. ANDERSON, MARK M.: *The 'impossibility of poetry': Celan and Heidegger in France.* [In]: new german critique, No. 53, Ithaca, N.Y., Spring/Summer 1991. Pp. 3–18, footnotes. [On the recent debate in France on the relationship between politics and culture in Nazi Germany, illustrated by the examples of Celan and Heidegger; also on the influence of the Holocaust on Celan's work.]

——— COHEN, HERMANN. BRUMLIK, MICHA: *Zur Zweideutigkeit deutsch-jüdischen Geistes: Hermann Cohen.* [See in No. 27941.]

28698. DEUTSCH, HELENE. ROAZEN, PAUL: *Helene Deutsch: a psychoanalyst's life.* New Brunswick,

N.J.: Transactions Publisher, 1991. 371 pp., notes (paperback). [H.D. 1885–1982, went to U.S. in 1935. First publ. in 1985, incl. relationship with Freud.]

28699.　DÖBLIN, ALFRED. Prangel, Matthias: *Alfred Döblins Konzept von der geistigen Gesamterneuerung des Judentums.* [In]: Interbellum und Exil. Hrsg. von Sjaak Onderdelinden. Amsterdam 1991. (Amsterdamer Publikation zur Sprache u. Literatur, 90.) Pp. 162–180.

28700.　EINSTEIN, CARL. *Carl Einstein. Prophet der Avantgarde.* Hrsg. von Klaus Siebenhaar [et al.]. Berlin: Fannei & Walz, 1991. 91 pp., port., illus., facsims. [A collection of autobiographical texts, letters, essays and poems.] [C.E., April 26, 1885 Neuwied – July 5, 1940 France (suicide), writer, literary critic, art historian, emigrated to France in 1934, took part in the Spanish Civil war, 1940 interned in Bordeaux.] [Cf.: Prophet der Avantgarde (Reto Sorg) [in]: Neue Zürcher Zeitung, Nr. 303, 31. Dez. 1991, p. 18.]

28701.　ELIAS. NORBERT: *The society of individuals.* Transl. by Edmund Jephcott. Ed. by Michael Schröter. Oxford; Cambridge, Ma.: Blackwell, 1991. X, 247 pp. [Part I: 'The society of individuals', written in 1939; part II: 'Problems of self-consciousness and the image of man', written in the 1940s and 1950s; part III: 'Changes in the we-I balance', written in 1987. First publ. in German in 1987.]

28702.　FELDMANN, ELSE. Exenberger, Herbert: *Auf den Spuren von Else Feldmann: Eine Wiener Schriftstellerin – Opfer des Holocaust.* [In]: Dokumentationsarchiv des österreichischen Widerstandes. Jahrbuch 1991. Wien: Österreichischer Bundesverl., 1990. Pp. 56–75, footnotes, illus., facsims.; incl. bibl. of E.F.'s works. [E.F., Feb. 25, 1884 Vienna – 1942 deported to Izbica, date of death not known, Socialist, writer.]

28703.　FEUCHTWANGER, LION. Kröhnke, Karl: *Lion Feuchtwanger: Der Ästhet in der Sowjetunion; ein Buch nicht nur für seine Freunde.* Stuttgart: Metzler, 1991. 321 pp., footnotes, bibl. (301–321). [A critical survey of Feuchtwanger's life and oeuvre, incl. his visit to Moscow in 1937 and his attitudes to Communism and Stalin.]

28704.　FLECHTHEIM, OSSIP K./Joos, Egbert: *Ausschau halten nach einer besseren Welt: Biographie, Interview, Artikel.* Berlin: Dietz, 1991. 189 pp., bibl. [O.K.F., born May 5, 1909 in Nikolayew (Russia), professor of political sciences, emigrated to Switzerland and the USA in 1935, lives in Berlin.]

28705.　Flechtheim, Ossip K.: *Vergangenheit im Zeugenstand der Zukunft.* Hrsg. und mit einem Nachwort versehen von Egbert Joos. Berlin: Joos, 1991. 551 pp. (Soziales Denken des 19. und 20. Jahrhunderts.)

28706.　FREUD, SIGMUND. Bakan, David: *Sigmund Freud and the Jewish mystical tradition.* New York: Free Association Books (distr. Columbia Univ. Press), 1991. XXXI, 326 pp. [Reissue (in paperback with new preface) of book first publ. in 1958.]

28707.　— Gresser, Moshe: *Sigmund Freud's Jewish identity: evidence from his correspondence.* [In]: Modern Judaism, Vol. 11, No. 2, Baltimore, May 1991. Pp. 225–240, notes.

28708.　— Grubrich-Simitis, Ilse: *Freuds Moses-Studie als Tagtraum.* München: Verlag Internationale Psychoanalyse, 1991. 96 pp.

28709.　— Haselstein, Ulla: *Poets and prophets: the Hebrew and the Hellene in Freud's cultural theory.* [In]: German Life and Letters, Vol. 45, No. 1, Oxford, Jan. 1991. Pp. 50–65, footnotes. [Based on Freud's 'Der Mann Moses und die monotheistische Religion'.]

28710.　— Luprecht, Mark: *'What people call pessimism': Sigmund Freud, Arthur Schnitzler and nineteenth-century controversy at the University of Vienna Medical School.* Riverside, Ca.: Ariadne Press, 1991. 172 pp., bibl. (149–165). (Studies in Austrian literature, culture and thought.)

28711.　— Reines, Alvin J.: *Freud's concepts of reality and God: a text study.* [In]: Hebrew Union College Annual, Vol. 61, Cincinnati, 1990. Pp. 219–270, footnotes.

28712.　— Rice, Emanuel: *Freud and Moses: the long journey home.* Albany: State Univ. of New York Press, 1990. 256 pp. [Examines Freud's Jewish origins, the more orthodox aspects in his family background, and his own education in religious matters.]

28713.　— Yerushalmi, Yosef Hayim: *Freud's Moses: Judaism terminable and interminable.* New Haven, Ct.: Yale Univ. Press, 1991. XIX, 159 pp., illus., facsims., bibl. [Author presents Freud's 'Moses and monotheism' as a psychoanalytic history of the Jews, Judaism and the Jewish psyche.] [Cf.: Freuds Auseinandersetzung mit dem Judentum (Sigmund Bendkower) [in]: Neue Zürcher Zeitung, Nr. 5, 8. Jan. 1992, p. 21.]

28714.　FRIED, ERICH. *Einer singt aus der Zeit gegen die Zeit; Erich Fried 1921–1988;* Materialien und Texte zu Leben und Werk. Zusammengestellt und bearbeitet von Volker Kaukoreit und Heidemarie Vahl. Darmstadt: Häusser, 1991. 124 pp., illus., facsims. (Eine Publikation des Heinrich-Heine-Instituts, Düsseldorf. Hrsg. von Joseph A. Kruse, anläßlich der Gedenkausstellung für Erich Fried im Sommer 1991.) [Cont. selected texts and poems by Fried, contributions about him by Catherine Fried-Boswell, Alexander von Bormann, Peter Rühmkorf, Dick van Stekelenburg; Zeittafel und Werkverzeichnis (Volker Kaukoreit, 105–122). Nachwort (Volker Kaukoreit/Heidemarie Vahl, 123–124).]

28715. FRIEDELL, EGON. INNERHOFER, ROLAND: *Kulturgeschichte zwischen den beiden Weltkriegen. Egon Friedell.* Mit einem Beitrag von Johann Hinterhofer. Wien Böhlau: 1990. 177 pp., bibl. (162–173), Werkverzeichnis (156–162). (Literatur in der Geschichte, Geschichte in der Literatur; 20.)

28716. FRIEDEN, KEN: *Y.L. Teller's 'lider fun der Tsayt(ung)'.* [In]: AJS Review, Vol. 15, No. 2, Cambridge, Ma., Fall 1990. Pp. 269–289, footnotes. [American Yiddish poet and journalist of the 1930s, who published many articles and poems relating to the Jews in Germany, the Nazi period; also contains a cycle of six poems dealing with his friendship with Freud.]

28717. FROMM, ERICH. *Erich Fromm und die Kritische Theorie.* Hrsg.: Internationale Erich-Fromm-Gesellschaft. Münster: Lit-Verl., 1991, 351 pp., illus., ports., notes, bibl. (Wissenschaft vom Menschen = Science of man; Jahrbuch der Internationalen Erich-Fromm-Gesellschaft, Bd. 2.) [Cont. 12 essays, incl.: Messianic thinking in the Jewish intelligentsia of the twenties (Micha Brumlik, 20–32).]

28718. GANS, EDUARD. WASZEK, NORBERT: *Eduard Gans (1797–1839): Hegelianer – Jude – Europäer.* Texte und Dokumente. Frankfurt am Main: Lang, 1991. 199 pp., notes, bibl., index of persons. (Hegeliana; Studien und Quellen zu Hegel und zum Hegelianismus, hrsg. von Helmut Schneider, Bd. 1.) [Incl. Gans's three lectures in the 'Kulturverein' and a letter and obituary of Heinrich Heine.]

28719. — WASZEK, NORBERT: *Zwischen Hegel und Marx; Eine Würdigung Eduard Gans' anläßlich der 150. Wiederkehr seines Todestages (5. Mai 1839).* [In]: Dialektik, Nr. 17, Köln, 1989. Pp. 162–176.

28720. GEIGER, LUDWIG. HOLZHAUSEN, HANS-DIETER: *Ludwig Geiger (1849–1919).* Ein Beitrag über sein Leben und sein Werk unter dem Aspekt seiner Bibliothek und weiterer Archivalien. [In]: Menora, Bd. 2, München, 1991. Pp. 245–269, notes, bibl.

28721. GILBERT, FELIX. GUGGISBERG, HANS R.: *Für Offenheit und Pluralismus: zum Tod von Felix Gilbert.* [In]: Neue Zürcher Zeitung, Nr. 49, 28. Feb. 1991. P. 30. [F.G. May 21, 1905 Baden-Baden – Feb. 14, 1991 Princeton, historian, emigrated in 1933 via England to the USA, professor at the Institute of Advanced Study in Princeton, board member of the New York Leo Baeck Institute. For memoirs, 1905–1945, see No. 26804/YBXXXV.]

28722. GUMBEL, EMIL JULIUS. JANSEN, CHRISTIAN: *Emil Julius Gumbel; Portrait eines Zivilisten.* Heidelberg: Das Wunderhorn, 1991. 420 pp., illus., docs., notes, bibl. [Cf.: 'Apostel der Justiz'; Eine Dokumentation über E. J. Gumbel (Will Schaber) [in]: Aufbau, Vol. 58, No. 10, New York, May 8, 1992, p. 8. Der Zivilist als Aussenseiter. Emil Julius Gumbel verkörperte wie kaum ein zweiter die in Deutschland so seltene Tugend der Zivilcourage (Volker Ullrich) [in]: Die Zeit, Nr. 30, Hamburg, 19. Juli 1991, p. 36.] [E.J.G., July 18, 1891 Munich – Sept. 10, 1966 New York, mathematician, statistician, pacifist, dismissed from Univ. Heidelberg in 1932, emigrated to the USA via France.]

28723. HASENCLEVER, WALTER. HELMETAG, CHARLES H.: *Walter Hasenclever: a playwright's evolution as a film writer.* [In]: The German Quarterly, Vol. 64, No. 4, Cherry Hill. N.J. Fall 1991. Pp. 452–463, notes.

28724. HEIMLER, BRIGITTE: *Eugene Heimler: in memoriam.* [In]: European Judaism, Vol. 24, No. 2, London, Summer 1991. Pp. 52–58. [An address given at a memorial evening at the Leo Baeck College in London on June 5, 1991; E.H., b. 1922, Hungary; d. 1991, London. Imprisoned in Buchenwald in 1944, came to England in 1947, psychiatric social worker, developed the Heimler method used in assessing the mentally ill.]

28725. HEINE, HEINRICH. HASUBEK, PETER: *Dreiecksverhältnis: Campe – Immermann – Heine.* Mit 28 unveröffentlichten Briefen Julius Campes an Immermann. [In]: Heine Jahrbuch 1991, Jg. 30, Hamburg 1991. Pp. 11–68, notes (64–68).

28726. — HERMAND, JOST: *Mehr als ein Liberaler: über Heinrich Heine.* Frankfurt am Main: Lang, 1991. 211 pp. (Forschungen zur Literatur- und Kulturgeschichte; Bd. 31.)

28727. — PFEIFER, CHRISTIANE BARBARA: *Heine und der islamische Orient.* Wiesbaden: Harrassowitz, 1991. 124 pp. (Mîzân; Studien und Texte zur Literatur des Orients, 1.)

28728. — REGENSTEINER, HENRY: *Heine on Shylock.* [In]: Midstream, Vol. 37, No. 3, New York, April/May 1991. Pp. 37–39. [Based on Heine's 'Shakespeares Mädchen und Frauen' from his collected works.]

28729. — ROSE, PAUL LAWRENCE: *Heine and Wagner revisited: art, myth and revolution.* [In]: Heine

Jahrbuch 1991. Jg. 30, Hamburg, 1991. Pp. 93–122, notes (118–122). [On Heine's relationship with Richard Wagner.]

28730. — Söhn, Gerhart: *Von gereizter Höflichkeit zu gehässiger Gegnerschaft. Zum Verhältnis Wolfgang Menzel – Heinrich Heine.* [In]: Heine Jahrbuch 1991, Jg. 30, Hamburg, 1991. Pp. 69–92, notes (89–92).

28731. — *The Lazarus poems.* Transl. by Alistair Elliot. Manchester: Carcanet, 1990. 79 pp. (paperback). [First publ. in 1979. Cf.: Vigorous equivalents (S. S. Prawer) [in]: TLS, London, Oct. 28, 1990.]

28732. HENSEL, FANNY [MENDELSSOHN]. Rebmann, Jutta: *Fanny Mendelssohn.* Biographischer Roman. 7130 Mühlacker: Stieglitz, 1991. 275 pp., illus.

28733. — *Fanny Mendelssohn: ein Porträt in Briefen.* Hrsg. und mit einem Nachwort versehen von Eva Weissweiler. Orig.-Aus. Frankfurt am Main: Ullstein, 1991. 250 pp., illus. (Ullstein-Buch 30241; Die Frau in der Literatur.)

—— HERMANN, GEORG: *Unvorhanden und doch stumm, doch zu Menschen noch reden.* Briefe aus dem Exil 1933–1941 an seine Tochter Hilde. [See No. 28270.]

28734. HERMLIN, STEPHAN. Villain, Jean: *Gespräch mit Stephan Hermlin.* [In]: Neue deutsche Literatur; Monatsschrift für deutschsprachige Literatur und Kritik, 38. Jg., H. 454, Berlin, Okt. 1990. Pp. 37–49.

28735. HILDESHEIMER, WOLFGANG: *Gesammelte Werke in sieben Bänden.* Hrsg. von Christiaan Lucus Hart Nibbrig und Volker Jehle. Frankfurt am Main: Suhrkamp, 1991. *Bd. 1: Erzählende Prosa.* 550 pp. *Bd. 2: Monologische Prosa.* 415 pp. *Bd. 3: Essayistische Prosa.* 508 pp. *Bd. 4: Biographische Prosa.* 302 pp. *Bd. 5: Hörspiele.* 561 pp. *Bd. 6: Theaterstücke.* 883 pp. *Bd. 7: Vermischte Schriften.* 853 pp. [Vol. 7 incl. Mein Judentum (159–169.] [Cf.: Gegen Befehl und Schrei (Beatrice von Matt) [in]: Neue Zürcher Zeitung, Nr. 273, 23./24. Nov. 1991, p. 65.] [W.H., Dec. 9, 1916 Hamburg – 21. Aug. 1991 Poschiavo (Switzerland), writer, translator, artist, emigrated to England in 1933, later to Palestine, returned to England in 1946. *Obituaries:* Endlich allein; die Literatur deutscher Sprache ist um einen zu wenig bekannten Autor ärmer (Rolf Michaelis) [in]: Die Zeit, Nr. 36, Hamburg, 30. Aug. 1991, p. 59. Verstummen angesichts des Selbstvernichtung (Sigurd Baecker) [in]: Allgemeine Jüdische Wochenzeitung, Nr. 46/35, Bonn, 27. Aug. 1991, p. 7.]

28736. — Jehle, Volker, ed.: *Wolfgang Hildesheimer.* Herausgegeben von Volker Jehle. Frankfurt am Main: Suhrkamp, 1989. 384 pp., chronol. tab., bibl. [A collection of essays by W.H. and about him and his books.]

28737. HUSSERL, EDMUND. Bell, David: *Husserl.* London: Routledge, 1990. XV, 266 pp., illus. [Cf.: The mind in Husserl: intentionality in the fog (Hubert L. Dreyfus) [in]: TLS, London, June 12, 1991.]

28738. KAFKA, FRANZ. Bar-David, Yoram: *Kafka's Hebrew studies: on Hebrew language and hidden Judaism.* [In Hebrew, with English summary]. [In]: Am Vasefer, Vol. 6, Jerusalem, Winter 1990–1991. Pp. 59–84. [Incl. discussion of Kafka's attitude to Judaism.]

28739. — Bodoff, Lippman: *Letters to Felice – Kafka's quest for Jewish identity.* [In]: Judaism, Vol. 40, No. 3, New York, Summer 1991. Pp. 263–280, footnotes.

28740. — Northey, Anthony: *Kafka's relatives: their lives and his writing.* Transl. from the German. New Haven, Ct.: Yale Univ. Press, 1991. 115 pp., illus.

28741. — Stölzl, Christoph: *Kafkas böses Böhmen. Ein Prager Jude, Antisemit, Zionist.* [In]: Das Jüdische Museum in Prag. Von schönen Gegenständen und ihren Besitzern [see in No. 28166]. Berlin: Dietz, 1991. Pp. 61–89. [Discusses Kafka's 'Jewish antisemitism' and his attitude to Judaism and Zionism.]

28742. KANTOROWICZ, ERNST H. Boureau, Alain: *Kantorowicz: Geschichten eines Historikers.* Aus dem Franz. übers. von Annette Holoch. Mit einem Nachwort von Roberto delle Donne. Stuttgart: Klett-Cotta, 1991. 173 pp. [Biography of the historian Ernst H. Kantorowicz.] [E.H.K., historian, May 3, 1895 Posen – Sept. 9, 1963 Princeton, emigrated in 1938 from Frankfurt am Main to the USA, professor at the Institute for Advanced Study.]

28743. KEILSON, HANS. *Geschichte als Trauma.* Festschrift für Hans Keilson zu seinem 80. Geburtstag. Hrsg.: Dierk Juelich. Frankfurt am Main: Nexus. 191 pp. [Incl.: Vorwort: Jüdische Deutsche und nichtjüdische Deutsche – Ein Brief (Dierk Juelich, 7–18). An Hans Keilson – Ein Brief. [Und]: Sprache als Objekt. Vernichtung, Unterdrückung und Wiederfinden der eigenen Sprache – Ein Entwurf (Norbert Freedman, 69–74). Die Genese des Hasses. Zu Hans Keilsons Roman 'Der Tod des Widersachers' (Frithjof Trapp, 151–164). Humanität: ein gescheiterter Versuch? Hans Keilsons Erzählung 'Dissonanzen-

Quartett' (Franz Hebel, 165–174). Further contributions are listed according to subject.]
[H.K., born in Freienwalde an der Oder Dec. 12, 1909, musician, psychiatrist, psychoanalyst, writer, poet, studied medicine and physical education in Berlin, emigrated in 1936 to the Netherlands, survived in hiding, working for the Dutch resistance. Lives near Amsterdam.]

28744. KERR, ALFRED: *Werke.* Werke in Einzelbänden. Berlin: Argon, 1989–1991. *Bd. I, 1: Erlebtes 1; Deutsche Landschaften, Städte und Menschen.* Hrsg. von Günther Rühle. 559 pp. [1989]. *Bd. I,2: Erlebtes 2; Reisen in die Welt.* Hrsg. von Hermann Haarmann. 597 pp. [1989]. *Bd. II: Liebes Deutschland; Gedichte.* Hrsg. von Thomas Koebner. 406 pp. [1991]. *Bd. III: Essays; Theater, Film.* Hrsg. von Hermann Haarmann und Klaus Siebenhaar. 479 pp. [1991]. [Cf.: Alfred Kerrs Leben als Werk, neu ediert (Gerhard Stadelmaier) [in]: Frankfurter Allgemeine Zeitung, Nr. 280, 3. Dez. 1991, p. L 9. Besprechung (Paul F. Proskauer) [in]: Aufbau, Vol. 57, New York, Dez. 20, 1991, p. 8.] [A.K. (orig. Kempner), Dec. 25, 1867 Breslau – Oct. 12, 1948 Hamburg, writer, theatre critic, emigrated in 1933 to France via Switzerland, 1936 to U.K.; chairman German PEN Club, London 1939–1947.]

——   KIRSCHSTEIN, SALLI. GUTMANN, JOSEPH: *The Kirschstein Museum of Berlin.* [See No. 28586].

28745. KORDA, ALEXANDER. KULIK, KAROL: *Alexander Korda: The man who could work miracles.* London: Virgin, 1991. 428 pp., illus. [A.K., Hungarian-Jewish film director/producer, 1893–1956, came to England in 1932.]

28746. LANG, FRITZ. GEHLE, FRED/KASTEN, ULLRICH: *Fritz Lang; die Stimme von Metropolis.* Berlin: Henschel, 1991. 295 pp., illus. [Personal memoirs, documents and essays about life and work of Fritz Lang on the occasion of his 100th birthday.] [F.L., Dec. 5, 1890 Vienna – Aug. 2, 1976 Los Angeles, film director and producer, of partly Jewish origin, emigrated 1933 via France to the USA.]

——   LASKER-SCHÜLER, ELSE. [See also No. 28117.]

28747. — SCHWERTFEGER, RUTH: *Else Lasker-Schüler: inside this deathly solitude.* Oxford; New York: Berg, 1991. IX, 116 pp., notes, bibl. (110–113).

28748. — YUDKIN, LEON, I.: *Else Lasker-Schüler: a study in German-Jewish literature.* Chicago: Science Review Limited (distrib. by Henchek & Associates, 68 East Wacker Place, Suite 800, Chicago, Il. 60601), 1991. 97 pp., bibl.

28749. LASSALLE, FERDINAND. COMO, FRANK: *Die Diktatur der Einsicht; Ferdinand Lassalle und die Rhetorik des deutschen Sozialismus.* Frankfurt am Main: Lang, 1991. 186 pp. (Europäische Hochschulschriften: Reihe 3, Geschichte und ihre Hilfswissenschaften, Bd. 455.) [Cf.: Besprechung (Ludger Heid) [in]: Das Historisch-Politische Buch, Jg. 39, H. 10, Göttingen, 1991. Pp. 315–316.]

28750. LÖWENSTEIN, KURT. EPPE, HEINRICH: *Kurt Löwenstein: ein Wegbereiter der modernen Erlebnispädagogik?* Lüneburg: Neubauer, 1991. 22 pp., illus. (Schriftenreihe 'Wegbereiter der modernen Erlebnispädagogik'; H. 23.) [K.L., Bleckede May 18, 1885 – May 8, 1939 Paris, educationalist, pacifist, Socialist, USPD member of the Reichstag, emigrated to Paris in 1933.]

28751. LUKÁCS, GEORG. KADARKY, ARPAD: *Georg Lukács: life, thought and politics.* Oxford: Blackwell, 1991. XV, 538 pp., illus., ports. [Cf.: After the age of sinfulness: Lukács and the mystical roots of revolution (Daniel Bell) [in]: TLS, No. 4608, London, 26 July 1991, pp. 5–8.]

28752. LUXEMBURG, ROSA. SALUS, CAROL: *R. B. Kitaj's 'The murder of Rosa Luxemburg'; a personal metaphor.* [In] Jewish Art, Vol. 16/17, Jerusalem, 1991. Pp. 130–138. [On the painting by R. B. Kitaj, also discusses R. L.'s career, her Jewish identity and antisemitism in Germany.]

28753. MARX, KARL. FISCHMAN, DENNIS: *Political discourse in exile: Karl Marx and the Jewish question.* Amherst: The Univ. of Massachusetts Press, 1991. VIII, 145 pp.

28754. MASANI, P. R.: *Norbert Wiener: 1894–1964.* Basel: Birkhäuser, 1990. 416 pp., illus. [N.W., mathematician, inventor of the science of cybernetics.]

28755. MAYER, GUSTAV. NIEDHART, GOTTFRIED: *Identitätskonflikte eines deutschen Juden an der Wende vom 19. zum 20. Jahrhundert: Gustav Mayer zwischen jüdischer Herkunft und ungewisser deutscher Zukunft.* [In]: Tel Aviver Jahrbuch für deutsche Geschichte, Bd. 20, Gerlingen, 1991. Pp. 315–326, notes. [G.M., Oct. 4, 1871 Prenzlau – Feb. 21, 1948 London, historian.]

28756. MAYER, HANS/FAURE, ULRICH: *Kein Ende der Utopie.* [Interview.] [In]: Börsenblatt für den Deutschen Buchhandel, Jg. 158, H. 65, Frankfurt am Main & Leipzig, 16. Aug. 1991. Pp. 2662–2666. [On literary life in the former GDR and now after unification.]

28757. MENDELSSOHN, FELIX. TODD, LARRY R., ed.: *Mendelssohn and his world*. Princeton: Princeton Univ. Press, 1991. XIII, 401 pp. [Series of essays exploring different aspects of F.M.'s life, incl. the nature of a Jewish identity in his music. Also contains memoirs and reviews by his contemporaries, and selections from his letters.]

28758. MENDELSSOHN, MOSES: *Rezensionsartikel in 'Briefe, die neueste Litteratur betreffend'* (1759–1965). Bearb. von Eva J. Engel. Stuttgart: Frommann-Holzboog, 1991. XXXIII, 700 pp. (Moses Mendelssohn: Gesammelte Schriften: Jubiläumsausgabe. Begonnen von Ismar Elbogen [et al.]. Fortgesetzt von Alexander Altmann in Gemeinschaft mit Fritz Bamberger [et al.]. Bd. 5,1.)

28759. MEYER, EDUARD. CALDER III, WILLIAM/DEMANDT, ALEXANDER: *Eduard Meyer: life and achievement of a universal historian*. Leiden: Brill, 1990. 537 pp.

28760. MEYERBEER, GIACOMO. FISCHER, JENS MALTE: *Wirkung ohne Ursache? Giacomo Meyerbeer und die Grosse Oper*. [And]: GIER, ALBERT: *Einzig dastehende Popularität: Meyerbeers Welterfolg, Paris und die deutschen Bühnen*. [In]: Neue Zürcher Zeitung, Nr. 201, 31. Aug./1. Sept. 1991. Pp. 69 [&] 70.

28761. — ZIMMERMANN, RAINER: *Giacomo Meyerbeer; eine Biographie nach Dokumenten*. Berlin: Henschel, 1991. 480 pp., illus., music scores.

28762. — *Giacomo Meyerbeer – Weltbürger der Musik*. Eine Ausstellung der Musikabteilung der Staatsbibliothek Preußischer Kulturbesitz Berlin zum 200. Geburtstag des Komponisten vom 31. Okt. 1991 bis zum 5. Jan. 1992. Wiesbaden: Reichert, 1991. 219 pp., illus., facsims., bibl., notes, index of persons, genealog. tree. [Incl. contributions by Heinz Becker, Gudrun Becker, Reinhold Becker and Sieghart Döhring on the life, work and reception of Meyerbeer.]

28763. MOSES, JULIUS. NEMITZ, KURT: *Weimarer Profile: Julius Moses*. [In]: Die Neue Gesellschaft. Frankfurter Hefte, H. 5, Frankfurt am Main, Mai 1991. Pp. 451–456, port., illus.

28764. PICARD, JACOB: *Werke*. In zwei Bänden hrsg. von Manfred Bosch. CH-8598 Bottighofen: Faude, 1991. 2 Vols., 616 pp., illus., ports. [Cont.: *Vol. 1: Erzählungen aus dem süddeutschen Landjudentum. Literarische Essays über Berthold Auerbach, Albert Ehrenstein, Julius Bab, Alfred Mombert, Ernst Blass, Gertrud Kolmar. Vol. 2: Gedichte, autobiographische Erzählungen; Nachwort* (Manfred Bosch; on life and work of Picard); Register der jiddischen Wortwendungen.]

28765. RATHENAU, WALTHER. BUDDENSIEG, TILMANN/HUGHES, THOMAS/KOCKA, JÜRGEN [et al.]: *Ein Mann vieler Eigenschaften. Walther Rathenau und die Kultur der Moderne*. Berlin: Wagenbach, 1990. 143 pp., port., notes. (Kleine Kulturwissenschaftliche Bibliothek; Bd. 21) [The 10 essays incl.: Krieg und Modernisierung. Rathenau als philosophierender Industrieorganisator im Ersten Weltkrieg (Ernst Schulin, 55–69). Der unschlüssige Staatsmann. Rathenaus letzter Tag und die Krise der Weimarer Republik (Gerald D. Feldman, 84–98). Überlegungen zur Ermordung Rathenaus als symbolischem Akt (Shulamit Volkov, 99–105). Der Vater, der Sohn und der künstlerische Beirat (Tilmann Buddensieg, 123–139).] [Cf.: Unbegrenzt flexibel: Kontroverse über Rathenau (Karlheinz Dederke) [in]: Die Zeit, Nr. 41, Hamburg, 3. Okt. 1991, p. 54; this review mistakenly names Wolf Lepenies as editor.]

—— RIESSER, GABRIEL. [See No. 27915.]

28766. ROTH, JOSEPH. GORDIMER, NADINE: *The empire of Joseph Roth*. [In]: The New York Review of Books, Vol. 38, No. 20, Dec. 5, 1991. Pp. 16–20.

28767. — PFABIGAN, ALFRED: *Geistesgegenwart. Essays zu Joseph Roth, Karl Kraus, Adolf Loos, Jura Soyfer*. Wien: Österr. Bundesverl., 1991. 153 pp. (Edn. Falter im ÖBV.)

28768. — REICH-RANICKI, MARCEL: *Der Romancier Joseph Roth*. [In]: Das Jüdische Echo, Vol. 40, Nr. 1, Wien, Okt. 1991. Pp. 200–204.

28769. — ROTH, JOSEPH: *Werke*. Hrsg. von Klaus Westermann und Fritz Hackert. Köln: Kiepenheuer & Witsch, 1991. Bd. 3: *Das journalistische Werk 1929–1939*. 107 pp. Bd. 6: *Romane und Erzählungen 1936–1940*. 814 pp. [Cf.: Neue Joseph-Roth-Ausgabe komplett (Paul F. Proskauer) [in]: Aufbau, Vol. 57, New York, Oct. 11, 1991, p. 9. Ich zeichne das Gesicht der Zeit (Hanns-Josef Ortheil) [in]: Die Zeit, Nr. 8, Hamburg, 14. Feb. 1992, p. 67.]

28770. — ROTH, JOSEPH: *Right and left*. Transl. by Michael Hofmann. London: Chatto & Windus, 1991. 235 pp. [Orig. publ. in German in 1929. Cf.: Self-concealment in Berlin (Philip Brady) [in]: TLS, London, Jan. 18, 1991. Before the brown shirts (Christopher Wordsworth) [in]: Guardian Weekly, London, Jan. 27, 1991.]

28771. SACHS, NELLY. HAMM, PETER: *Unser Gestirn ist vergraben im Staub*; zum 100. Geburtstag der Dichterin Nelly Sachs am 10. Dezember. [In]: Die Zeit, Nr. 50, Hamburg, 6. Dez. 1991, p.

76. [And] KÖNIG, FRANK: *Leben unter Bedrohung*; zum 100. Geburtstag von Nelly Sachs am 10. Dezember [in]: Neue Zürcher Zeitung, Nr. 287, 10. Dez. 1991, pp. 23–24.]

28772.   — SPARRE, SULAMITH: *Geflohen vor den Meistern des Todes*. Die Dichterin Nelly Sachs wäre am 10. Dezember 1991 hundert Jahre alt geworden. [In]: Tribüne, Jg. 30, H. 120, Frankfurt am Main, 1991. Pp. 76–79.

28773.   SCHINDLER, THOMAS: *Ein vergessener Held des Ersten Weltkrieges: Grab von Fliegerleutnant Max Pappenheimer auf dem jüdischen Friedhof Unterbalbach*. [In]: Amtsblatt der Stadt Lauda-Königshofen [Baden], 9. Aug. 1991.

————   SCHNITZLER, ARTHUR. [See also No. 28710.]

28774.   — THOMPSON, BRUCE: *Schnitzler's Vienna: image of a society*. London: Routledge. Chapman & Hall, 1990. VII, 213 pp., illus., map, notes, bibl. (206–209). [Incl. chaps.: 'The Freudian connection' (32–54); 'Politics and the Jewish question' (160–176).]

28775.   SCHÖNBERG, ARNOLD. GREENBAUM, KYLA: *Reflections on Schoenberg*. [In]: The Jewish Quarterly, Vol. 38, No. 1, London, Spring 1991. Pp. 22–25.

————   SCHOEPS, HANS-JOACHIM. LEASE, GARY: *Der Briefwechsel zwischen Karl Barth und Hans-Joachim Schoeps (1929–1946)*. [See No. 28830.]

28776.   SEGHERS, ANNA. KUCZYNSKI, JÜRGEN: *Für Anna Seghers*. [And]: JANKA, WALTER: *Über Anna Seghers und andere*. [And]: SCHWARZ, FREIMUT: *Über Seghers 'Der gerechte Richter'*. [In]: europäische ideen, H. 76, Berlin, 1991. Pp. 54–59 [&] 60–61 [&] 62–63.

28777.   SIMMEL, GEORG. GROSSHEIM, MICHAEL: *Von Georg Simmel zu Martin Heidegger*. Philosophie zwischen Leben und Existenz. Bonn: Bouvier, 1991. VII, 136 pp. (Abhandlungen zur Philosophie, Psychologie und Pädagogik; 230.)

28778.   SOYFER, JURA. *Zwischenwelt. Die Welt des Jura Soyfer*. Hrsg. von der Jura Soyfer Gesellschaft in Zusammenarbeit mit der Theodor Kramer Gesellschaft (1210 Wien, Obere Jungenberggasse 27). Wien: Verl. für Gesellschaftskritik, 1991. 259 pp., illus., bibl. [Cont. texts by, and contributions on, Jura Soyfer.] [J.S., 1912 Charkow – Feb. 1939 Buchenwald, author, satirist, playwright, lived in Vienna, imprisoned on charges of Communist activity from Nov. 1937 until Feb. 1938. Arrested attempting to flee illegally to Switzerland in 1939.]

28779.   SOYFER, JURA: *Sturmzeit. Briefe 1931–1939*. Herausgegeben von Horst Jarka. Hrsg.: Verein zur Förderung und Erforschung der antifaschistischen Literatur. Wien: Verl. für Gesellschaftskritik, 1991. 255 pp., index of persons.

28780.   SPIEL, HILDE. REICH-RANICKI, MARCEL: *Reden auf Hilde Spiel*. München: List, 1991. 117 pp., illus., bibl. (103–106).

28781.   STERN, WILLIAM. DEUTSCH, WERNER, Hrsg.: *Über die verborgene Aktualität von William Stern*. Frankfurt am Main: Lang, 1991. 141 pp. (Beiträge zur Geschichte der Psychologie; Bd. 3.) [A collection of 10 essays about the life and work of William Stern. Incl.: William Stern – Günther Anders: zwei Generationen – zwei Welten (Wilfred H.O. Schmidt, 117–130). Erinnerungen an meine Eltern (Eva Michaelis-Stern, 131–141).] [W.S., Apr. 29, 1871 Berlin – March 27, 1938 Durham, N.C., psychologist, founder of personalistic psychology, engaged in child psychology, together with his wife Clara (1877–1945), emigrated in 1933 via the Netherlands to the USA.] [Cf.: Pionierarbeit zur Begabungsforschung (Yizhak Ahren) [in]: Allgemeine Jüdische Wochenzeitung, Nr. 46/24, Bonn, 13. Juni, 1991, p. 6.]

28782.   STRAUSS, LUDWIG: *Land Israel*. Gedichte. Herausgegeben und mit einem Nachwort versehen von Hans Otto Horch. Aachen: Rimbaud, 1991. 96 pp. [Orig. publ. under the same title by Schocken, Berlin 1935 (Bücherei des Schocken Verlags 41).]

28783.   STROUSBERG, BETHEL HENRY. BORCHART, JOACHIM: *Der europäische Eisenbahnkönig Bethel Henry Strousberg*. München: Beck, 1991. 354 pp., illus., maps, notes (259–326), bibl. (327–343), index of names. [B.H.St., orig. Baruch Hirsch Straussberg, Nov. 20, 1823 Neidenburg – May 31, 1884 London, industrialist.] [Cf.: So übel nicht: der Fall des legendären Eisenbahnkönigs Bethel Henry Strousberg (Hans-Joachim Neubauer) [in]: Die Zeit, Nr. 11, Hamburg, 6. März 1992, p. 53.]

————   TOURY, JACOB. [See also No. 28201.]

28784.   — TOURY, GIDEON (comp.): *Bibliographie der Schriften von Jacob Toury*. [In]: Tel Aviver Jahrbuch für deutsche Geschichte, Bd. 20, Gerlingen, 1991. Pp. 469–485.

28785.   VALENTIN, VEIT. *Geschichte der Deutschen*. Mit einem Appendix: Erhard Klöss: Deutsche Geschichte 1945–1990. Köln: Kiepenheuer & Witsch, 1991. 830 pp. [Orig. publ. in 1946 in New York; first German edn. in 1947 in Berlin.] [Cf.: Ein liberaler Patriot; Veit Valentins 'Geschichte der Deutschen' in einer leider unkommentierten Neuauflage (Volker Ullrich)

[in]: Die Zeit, Jg. 47, Nr. 13, Hamburg, 20. März 1992, p. 53.] [V. V., historian, March 25, 1885 Frankfurt – Jan. 12, 1947 Washington D.C.]

28786. VARNHAGEN, RAHEL. WEISSBERG, LILIANE: *Stepping out: the writing of difference in Rahel Varnhagen's letters*. [in]: new german critique, No. 53, Ithaca, N.Y., Spring/Summer 1991. Pp. 149–162, footnotes. [Discusses R.V.'s attitude towards her Jewishness as expressed in some of her letters.]

28787. — PATSCH, HERMANN: *'Als ob Spinoza sich wollte taufen lassen'. Biographisches und Rechtsgeschichtliches zu Taufe und Trauung Rahel Levins*. [In]: Jahrbuch des Freien Deutschen Hochstifts 1991. Tübingen: Niemeyer, 1991. Pp. 149–178, notes.

28788. WARBURG, ABY M. DIERS, MICHAEL: *Warburg aus Briefen; Kommentar zu den Kopierbüchern der Jahre 1905–1918*. Weinheim: VCH, Acta Humaniora, 1991. VIII, 249 pp., illus. (Schriften des Warburg-Archivs im Kunstgeschichtlichen Seminar der Universität Hamburg; Bd. 2.) Zugl.: Hamburg, Univ., Diss., 1990.

——— WEIDENREICH, FRANZ. [See in No. 28021.]

28789. WEILL, KURT. TAYLOR, RONALD: *Kurt Weill; composer in a divided world*. London. Simon & Schuster, 1991. 342 pp., illus., music scores, bibl., index.

28790. WEISS, PETER *Peter Weiss; Leben und Werk*. Hrsg.: Gunilla Palmstierna-Weiss [et al.] Frankfurt am Main: Suhrkamp, 1991. 346 pp., illus. [Catalogue book to an exhibition of the Akademie der Künste, Berlin and the Moderna Museet, Stockholm, held in Berlin Feb. 24, – April 28 and Stockholm Aug. 31 – Oct. 13, 1991. Cont. excerpts of an unpubl. manuscript and essays on the life and work of Peter Weiss.] [P.W., Nov. 18, 1916 Nowawes near Berlin – May 10, 1982 Stockholm, author and painter of partly Jewish descent, emigrated in 1934 to England, Prague and Sweden.]

28791. WERFEL, FRANZ. *Franz Werfel. 1890–1945*. Ausstellung der Österreichischen Nationalbibliothek. Gestaltung der Ausstellung und Katalog: Marianne Jobst-Rieder. Wien: Österr. Nationalbibliothek, 1990. 117 pp., illus.

28792. WICCLAIR, WALTER. ASPER, HELMUT G.: *Walter Weinlaub und die Gerhart Hauptmann-Bühne in Kreuzburg 1932/33*. Eine Dokumentation zum 90. Geburtstag von Walter Wicclair am 24. Januar 1991 von Helmut G. Asper. Dortmund: Helmut G. Asper, 1991. 42 pp., illus., port., facsims. [Obtainable through Dr. Helmut G. Asper, Univ. Bielefeld, Postfach 8640, 4800 Bielefeld.) [Walter Wicclair, orig. Walter Weinlaub, born in Gleiwitz [?] Jan. 24, 1901, actor, emigrated in 1939 via various countries to the USA. Lives in Los Angeles.]

28793. WOLFF, KURT. *Kurt Wolff: a portrait in essays and letters*. Ed. by Michael Ermarth. Transl. by Deborah Lucas Schneider. Chicago: Univ. of Chicago Press, 1991. XXVIII, 233 pp., notes, bibl. of K.W.'s works (199–200). [Incl. list of selected titles from the publishing houses of K.W.] [Cf.: The prince of publishers (D. J. R. Bruckner) [in]: New York Times Book Review, Jan. 5, 1992, pp. 12 and 14.] [K.W., 1887–1963, German-Jewish publisher, founder of the Kurt Wolff Verlag and later in New York of Pantheon Books, also published many Jewish authors like Brod, Kafka, Kraus. For publication of essays and letters see No. 5246/ YBXI and No. 5858/YBXII.]

28794. WOLFSKEHL, KARL. VOIT, FRIEDRICH: *Tomi heisst auf Englisch Auckland: zum Leben und Werk von Karl Wolfskehl im neuseeländischen Exil*. [In]: Exil, Jg. 11, Nr. 1, Maintal, 1991. Pp. 23–29, notes.

——— ZWEIG, ARNOLD. [See also No. 28268.]

28795. — HILDEBRANDT, KLAUS: *Arnold Zweig*. [In]: Schlesische Lebensbilder. Hrsg. von der Historischen Kommission für Schlesien. Bd. 6. Schlesier des 15. bis 20. Jahrhunderts. Im Auftrag der Historischen Kommission für Schlesien hrsg. von Josef Joachim Menzel und Ludwig Petry. Sigmaringen: Thorbecke, 1990. Pp. 254–264, bibl.

28796. — ZADEK, WALTER: *Der 'verstaatlichte' Dichter. Hatte der Schriftsteller Arnold Zweig Angst in der DDR?* [In]: Tribüne, Jg. 30, H. 117, Frankfurt am Main, 1991. Pp. 144–150.

28797. ZWEIG, MAX. WALLAS, ARMIN A.: *Sie starben im Nirgendwo'. Ein Drama des jüdischen Widerstands: 'Ghetto Warschau' von Max Zweig*. [In]: Sprachkunst, Jg. 21/1990, 2. Halbband, Wien, 1991. Pp. 251–283, footnotes. [M.Z., born June 22, 1892 Prossnitz, Moravia, writer, cousin of Stefan Zweig, emigrated in 1934 from Berlin via Czechoslovakia to Palestine, lives in Jerusalem. His drama 'Ghetto Warschau' was written in 1947.]

28798. ZWEIG, STEFAN. LIPTZIN, SOL: *Remembering Stefan Zweig: on the semicentennial of his death*. [In]: Jewish Book Annual, Vol. 49/1991–1992, New York, 1991. Pp. 145–151.

28799. — ZOHN, HARRY: *Stefan Zweigs Mittlerrolle: zum fünfzigsten Todestag des Dichters im Februar 1992*. [In]: Das Jüdische Echo, Vol. 40, Nr. 1, Wien, Okt. 1991. Pp. 206–212.

VIII. AUTOBIOGRAPHY, MEMOIRS, LETTERS, GENEALOGY

28800. *Aber das Leben marschiert weiter und nimmt uns mit*; Briefwechsel zwischen Joseph Roth und dem Verlag De Gemeenschap 1936–1939. Hrsg. und eingeleitet von Theo Bijvoet und Madelaine Rietra. Köln: Kiepenheuer & Witsch, 1991. 329 pp. [Cf.: Joseph Roths Zäsur (Will Schaber) [in] Aufbau, Vol. 57, No. 12, New York, June 7, 1991, pp. 6–7.]

28801. AMBURGER, ERIK: *Protestantische und katholische Familien jüdischer Herkunft in Rußland.* [In]: Genealogisches Jahrbuch, Bd. 30, Neustadt a.d. Aisch 1990. Pp. 27–67. [Incl. Jewish families from Germany and Russian-Jewish immigrants to Germany.]

28802. BRAND, HERMANN: *Die Tournee geht weiter: ein jüdisches Schauspielerschicksal in Deutschland und in der Schweiz 1898–1966.* Hrsg. Schmuel Brand und Erhard Roy Wiehn. Konstanz: Hartung-Gorre, 1990. 270 pp., facsims., illus., ports. [Hermann Samuel Brand-Rademacher, actor, 1898 Galicia – Sept. 14, 1966 Zurich, after 1900 in Karlsruhe, emigrated 1933 to Switzerland, 1955–1961 in Düsseldorf, 1961–1966 in Zurich.]

28803. EGER FAMILY. *The Eger family association 1913–1990.* [In Hebrew]. Kibbutz Netzer Sereni, 1990. [40] pp. [Consists of family trees of Rabbi Akiva Eger's descendants.]

28804. ESCHWEGE, HELMUT: *Fremd unter meinesgleichen. Erinnerungen eines Dresdner Juden.* Berlin: Ch. Links, 1991. 288 pp., index of persons. [Cf.: Nicht ohne Ecken und Kanten: Wider den Strom (Werner Klöpper) [in]: Allgemeine Jüdische Wochenzeitung, Nr. 47/17, Bonn, 23. April 1992, p. 9.] [H.E., born in Hanover, July 10, 1913, Socialist, publicist, historian, emigrated in 1934 to Palestine via Denmark and Estonia, returned to (Eastern) Germany in 1946, lives in Dresden.]

28805. FAERBER, MEIR MARCELL: *Statt einer Autobiographie.* [In]: Mnemosyne (Hrsg. und Red.: Armin A. Wallas, A-9500 Villach, Rennsteiner Str. 118), H. 9, Villach, Okt. 1990. Pp. 26–31. [See also No. 28973.] [M.M. Faerber (pseud.: Meir Reubeni), born Apr. 29, 1908 Mährisch-Ostrau, writer, journalist, emigrated to Palestine in 1934, founder and chairman of the 'Verband deutschsprachiger Schriftsteller in Israel', lives in Tel Aviv.]

28806. FEUCHTWANGER, LION. FEUCHTWANGER, MARTA: *Leben mit Lion.* Gespräch mit Reinhart Hoffmeister in der Reihe 'Zeugen des Jahrhunderts'. Hrsg. von Ingo Hermann. Red.: Jürgen Voigt. Göttingen: Lamuv, 1991. 117 pp., notes., bibl. [Based on the ZDF television series Zeugen des Jahrhunderts.]

28807. — *Briefwechsel mit Freunden, 1933–1958.* Hrsg. von Harold von Hofe und Sigrid Washburn. Berlin: Aufbau, 1991. 2 Vols., 988 pp. [Cf.: Autorenschicksale im Exil (Willi Jasper) [in] Neue Zürcher Zeitung, Nr. 233, 8. Okt. 1991, p. 28.]

28808. FISCHER, ALFRED JOACHIM: *In der Nähe der Ereignisse.* Berlin: Transit, 1991. 260 pp. [Cf.: Immer auf der Hut (Dorothea Hilgenberg) [in]: Die Zeit, 47. Jg., Nr. 13, Hamburg, 20. März 1992, p. 54.] [A.J.F., born Nov. 27, 1909 in Altkloster, Posen, 1933 flight, via numerous European countries, to U.K. in 1939; after the war in Switzerland; lives in Berlin.]

28809. FISCHER, RUTH: *Stalin und der deutsche Kommunismus. Bd. 1: Von der Entstehung des deutschen Kommunismus bis 1924. Bd. 2: Die Bolschewisierung des deutschen Kommunismus ab 1925.* Mit einer Vorbemerkung von Klaus Konner. Berlin: Dietz, 1991. 2 Vols., 457; 355 pp. [Reprint, first publ. in 1948 by Verlag Frankfurter Hefte.] [Autobiographical account of the inner development of the KPD.] [R.F., orig. Elfriede Eisler, Communist politician and publicist, data see No. 27770/YBXXXVI.]

28810. FISHER, JOSEY G., ed.: *The persistence of youth: oral testimonies of the Holocaust.* From the Holocaust Oral History Archive of Gratz College [Melrose Park, Pa.]. Introd. by Nora Levin. Westport, Ct.: Greenwood Press, 1991. XXI, 171 pp., illus. [Vol. is a collection of fifteen first-person accounts of growing up during the Nazi era. Incl. testimonies from the daughter of an anti-Nazi German family, a son of a mixed German-Jewish family, a Czech-Jewish teenager. Also discusses anti-Jewish measures in general in both Germany and Czechoslovakia.]

28811. FRANK, ANNE: *Anne Frank Tagebuch*; autorisierte und ergänzte Fassung von Otto H. Frank und Mirjam Pressler. Frankfurt am Main: S. Fischer, 1991. 315 pp., illus. [Authorised edn. of Anne Frank's diary as publ. by her father Otto Frank, enlarged by hitherto unpubl. parts of diary 'a' and diary 'b'.] [Cf.: Die Text- und Editionsgeschichte bleibt problematisch. Das Wort bewahren. (Willi Jasper) [in] Die Zeit, Nr. 40, 26. Sept. 1991, p. 49.]

28812. FREEDEN, HERBERT: *Leben zur falschen Zeit.* Berlin: Transit, 1991. 277 pp. [Cf.: Besprechung

(Reuven Assor) [in]: MB, Nr. 74, Tel Aviv, Dez. 1991, p. 8. Die unsichtbare Kette (Henryk M. Broder) [in]: Die Zeit, Nr. 9, Hamburg, 21. Feb. 1992, p. 53.] [H.F. (orig. Friedenthal), born Jan. 22, 1909 in Posen, journalist, writer, emigrated 1939 to U.K. Since 1951 lives in Jersualem.]

28813. FRIEDLÄNDER, SAUL: *Wenn die Erinnerung kommt.* Aus dem Franz. von Helgard Oestreich. Ungekürzte Ausgabe. Frankfurt am Main: Fischer Taschenbuch-Verl., 1991. 191 pp. [For English and German translation first publ. 1978, see No. 16765/YB XXV.] [S.F., orig. Pavel Friedländer, born Oct. 11, 1932 in Prague, professor of history, emigrated to France in 1939, where he spent 4 years as a Catholic in a boarding school; after 1946 became a Zionist and emigrated to Palestine 1948. Lives in Jersualem.]

28814. GINSBERG, ERNST: *Abschied: Erinnerungen, Theateraufsätze, Gedichte.* Hrsg. von Elisabeth Brock-Sulzer. Zürich: Arche, 1991. 259 pp. [E.G., Feb. 1902 Berlin – Dec. 3, 1964 Zurich. Actor, stage director, author, converted to Catholicism 1935, emigrated 1933 via Austria to Switzerland.]

28815. GOLDSCHMIDT, GEORGES-ARTHUR: *Die Absonderung.* Erzählung. Mit einem Vorwort von Peter Handke. Zürich: Ammann, 1991. 178 pp. [Narrative account of the author's childhood years during the time of Nazi persecution in Hamburg and in a children's hostel in Savoy, where he lived with his brother. Continuation of his early childhood memoirs: *Ein Garten in Deutschland.* Eine Erzählung. Aus dem Französischen von Eugen Helmlé. Zürich: Ammann, 1988. 192 pp.; paperback edn.: Frankfurt: Suhrkamp, 1991. 186 pp.] [G.-A.G., born 1928 in Hamburg, author, translator, high school teacher of German literature, lives in Paris.]

—— GOMPERZ FAMILY. [See No. 27921.]

28816. HAMBURGER, MICHAEL: *String of beginnings: intermittent memoirs, 1924–1974.* London: Skoob Books, 1991. 338 pp. [M.H., born 1924 in Berlin. Volume was first publ. in 1973.]

—— HENSEL, FANNY [MENDELSSOHN]: *Fanny Mendelssohn: ein Porträt in Briefen.* Hrsg. und mit einem Nachwort versehen von Eva Weissweiler. [See No. 28732.]

—— HERZFELDE, WIELAND. [See also No. 28647.]

28817. —— *Prag – Moskau: Briefe von und an Wieland Herzfelde 1933–38.* Hrsg. von Guiseppe de Siati und Thies Ziemke. Kiel: Neuer Malik Verl., 1991. 200 pp., illus. [Orig. Wieland Herzfeld, born Weggis, Switzerland April 11, 1896, writer, publisher, brother of John Heartfield, emigrated 1933 to Czechoslovakia, France, England, USA. Returned to Germany (East) in 1949.]

28818. —— *Tribüne und Aurora: Briefwechsel Wieland Herzfelde und Bertold Viertel.* [Hrsg. von der Akad. der Wiss. und der Literatur, Mainz. Klasse der Literatur.] Hrsg. von Friedrich Pfäfflin unter Mitarbeit von Heidemarie Gruppe. Mainz: v.Hase & Kohler, 1990. 286 pp. (Die Mainzer Reihe; Bd. 71.)

28819. HEYMANN, FRITZ. SCHOEPS, JULIUS H.: *'Wer mich auf die rechte Wange schlägt, dem haue ich zwei auf die linke'.* Unveröffentlichte Briefe des Schriftstellers Fritz Heymann aus den niederländischen Exil. [In]: Geschichte als Trauma [see No. 28743]. Hrsg.: Dierk Juelich. Frankfurt am Main: Nexus, 1991. Pp. 175–184. [Letters addressed to Hans-Joachim Schoeps.] [F.H., Aug. 28, 1897 Bocholt – 1942/43 Auschwitz, journalist, historian. See also No. 21828/YBXXXI.]

—— *'Ich war für all das zu müde'. Briefe aus dem Exil.* Gesammelt von Peter Härtling. [See No. 28648.]

28820. IWENS, SIDNEY: *How dark the heavens: 1400 days in the grip of Nazi terror.* New York: Shengold, 1990. 291 pp. [Author's experiences in a ghetto in Lithuania, Dachau, then liberation. Written in diary form.]

28821. JOSEPH, ALBRECHT: *Ein Tisch bei Romanoff's: vom expressionistischen Theater zur Westernserie. Erinnerungen.* Mit einem Nachwort von Stefan Weidle. Mönchengladbach: Juni Verl., 1991. 246 pp. [And]: *Wie ich Cutter wurde.* [In]: Juni, das Magazin für großangelegte Kultur, 5. Jg., Nr. 2, Mönchengladbach, 1991. [Cf.: Odyssee eines Lebens (Will Schaber) [in]: Aufbau, Vol. 58, No. 5, New York, Feb. 28, 1992, p. 8.]

—— KOLLEK, TEDDY. RADKE, RUDOLF: *Teddy Kollek.* [See No. 28619.]

28822. LANDSHOFF, FRITZ H.: *Amsterdam, Keizersgracht 333, Querido Verlag; Erinnerungen eines Verlegers.* Berlin: Aufbau, 1991. 559 pp., illus. [Memoirs of the co-owner and director of the German department of the Querido Publ. House, founded in 1933 in Amsterdam, which was one of the main publishers of German exile literature.] [Cf.: Amsterdam, Keizersgracht 333; ein Stück Kulturgeschichte – die Memoiren des Verlegers Fritz H. Landshoff (Fritz J. Raddatz)

[in]: Die Zeit, Nr. 34, Hamburg, 16. Aug. 1991, p. 45. Die Rettungsstation. Büchermachen aus dem Nichts: der große Exilverleger Fritz H. Landshoff (Walter Hinck) [in] Frankfurter Allgemeine, Nr. 208, 7. Sept. 1991. Fritz H. Landshoff: Erinnerungen eines großen Verlegers (Ulrich Faure) [in]: Börsenblatt für den Deutschen Buchhandel, Jg. 158, H. 77, Frankfurt am Main & Leipzig, 27. Sept. 1991. Pp. 3284–3286, illus.] [F.H.L., July 29, 1901 Berlin – March 28 (or 30?), 1988 Haarlem.]

28823. LEYENS, ERICH/ANDOR, LOTTE: *Die fremden Jahre. Erinnerungen an Deutschland.* Eingeleitet von Wolfgang Benz. Frankfurt am Main: Fischer Taschenbuch Verl., 1991. 120 pp. Orig.-Ausg. (Lebensbilder; Jüdische Erinnerungen und Zeugnisse. Hrsg. von Wolfgang Benz. Fischer Taschenbuch: Geschichte.) [Cont.: Vorbemerkung (Wolfgang Benz, 11–14 & 57–58). Unter dem NS-Regime 1933–1938. Erlebnisse und Beobachtungen (Erich Leyens, 15–53). Memoiren einer unbekannten Schauspielerin oder Ich war nie ein Bernhardiner (Lotte Andor, 59–120).] [E.L., born 1898 in Wesel, owner of a department store in Wesel, emigrated 1935 via Italy, Switzerland, Cuba to the USA. Living since 1942 in New York.] [L.A., Bochum 1903 – July 8, 1991 New York, actress, emigrated in 1934 via Paris, Amsterdam, Barcelona, Prague and London to the USA. Lived from 1937 in New York.]

28824. LIND, JAKOV: *Crossing.* London: Methuen, 1991. 224 pp. [J.L., born 1927 Vienna, left Austria 1938, came to London via Holland and Israel; book is autobiographical account.]

—— LUCAS, ERIC: *Jüdisches Leben auf dem Lande.* Eine Familienchronik. [See No. 27994.]

28825. LUCÁCS, GEORG: *Tagebuch 1910/11.* Berlin: Brinkmann & Bose, 1991. XVIII, 364 pp.

28826. MAHLER, GUSTAV. MAHLER, ALMA: *Gustav Mahler; Erinnerungen.* Frankfurt am Main: Fischer Taschenbuch Verl., 1991. 238 pp., ports. [Orig. publ. 1940 by Allert de Lange in Amsterdam. Reprinted 1949 by Berman Fischer/Querido-Verlag in Amsterdam. These first edns. were enlarged by love letters of Mahler to Alma, not included now.]

28827. MAYER, HANS: *Der Turm von Babel; Erinnerung an eine Deutsche Demokratische Republik.* Frankfurt am Main: Suhrkamp, 1991. 272 pp., index of names.

—— PAWELZIK, FRED/SCHILD, GÜNTHER: *Frankreich ohne Rückfahrkarte.* [See No. 28390.]

28828. PRESSBURGER, GIORGIO & NICOLA: *Die Gesetzestafeln der Selma Grün. Geschichten aus dem achten Bezirk.* Aus dem Ital. von Michaela Wunderle. Frankfurt am Main: Verl. Neue Kritik, 1989. 133 pp. [Memoirs of Jewish life in Budapest during the fifties and sixties.]

28829. SCHNEIDER, GERTRUDE, ed.: *The unfinished road: Jewish survivors of Latvia look back.* New York: Praeger, 1991. 232 pp., illus., maps, bibl. [Many Jews from Germany, Austria, Czechoslovakia and Hungary were transported to Latvia. The book collects the remembrances of thirteen survivors.]

28830. SCHOEPS, HANS-JOACHIM: LEASE, GARY: *Der Briefwechsel zwischen Karl Barth und Hans-Joachim Schoeps (1929–1946).* [In]: Menora, Bd. 2, München, 1991. Pp. 105–137, notes. [Cont. 16 letters from the Karl-Barth-Archiv, Basle.]

28831. SCHWARZ-GARDOS, ALICE: *Von Wien nach Tel Aviv. Lebensweg einer Journalistin.* Gerlingen: Bleicher, 1991. 240 pp. [A.Sch.-G., born ca. 1915 in Vienna, journalist, emigrated illegally from Preßburg to Palestine in 1939. From 1974 chief editor of the German daily newspaper 'Israel Nachrichten'.] [Cf.: Besprechung (Eberhard Otto) [in]: Tribüne, Jg. 30, H. 119, Frankfurt am Main, 1991. Pp. 209–210.]

—— SOYFER, JURA: *Sturmzeit. Briefe.* [See No. 28779.]

28832. SPERBER, MANÈS: *The unheeded warning, 1918–1933.* Transl. by Harry Zohn. New York: Holmes & Meier, 1991. 216 pp. (All our yesterdays, vol. 2.) [This vol. of memoirs describes the author's life in inter-war Vienna and Berlin.]

28833. SPIRA, STEFFIE: *Trab der Schaukelpferde. Autobiographie.* Unveränd. Nachdr. d. Ausg. Berlin [East] 1984. Freiburg: Kore, 1991. 249 pp., illus. [For orig. edn. and data see No. 21726/ YBXXX.]

28834. STEINBERG, GEORG: *Kriegs- und Friedenserlebnisse eines Hannoverschen Jägers. 1866.* Georg Steinbergs 'Beim 3. Jägerbataillon'. 2. unveränd. Aufl. Hrsg. und mit einem Nachwort versehen von Rainer Sabelleck. Mannheim: Peter Wagener, 1991. 212 pp., illus., Nachwort (Rainer Sabelleck, 182–210, notes), bibl. (Jüdische Bibliothek; Bd. 1.) [Memoirs by the shop-owner and writer Georg Steinberg (1840–1919), who served in the Hanoverian army and fought in the war between Hanover [a.o.] and Prussia in 1866. Orig. publ. in 1898.]

28835. TOLLER, ERNST: *I was a German: the autobiography of a revolutionary.* Transl. from the German by Edward Crankshaw. New York: Paragon House, 1991. XVII, 302 pp. [Orig. edn. 1933.]

28836. VIERTEL, BERTHOLD: *Kindheit eines Cherub.* Autobiographische Fragmente. Hrsg. von Siglinde Bolbecher und Konstantin Kaiser. Wien: Verl. f. Gesellschaftskritik, 1991. 376 pp., notes. (Berthold Viertel-Studienausgabe in vier Bänden, Bd. 2; Antifaschistische Literatur und Exilliteratur, Studien und Texte; Bd. 4.) [Cf.: Bilanzfälscher von Beruf (Ulrich Weinzierl) [in]: Frankfurter Allgemeine Zeitung, Nr. 268, 18. November, 1991, p. 34. Wider den Schein der Geschlossenheit (Wendelin Schmidt-Dengler) [in]: Mit der Ziehharmonika. Zeitschrift der Theodor Kramer Gesellschaft, 9. Jg., Nr. 1, Wien, März 1992, p. 20. Scham, Erinnerung (Erich Hackl) [in]: Die Zeit, Nr. 46, Hamburg, 8. Nov. 1991, p. 12.] [B.V., Vienna June 28, 1885 – Sept. 24, 1953, poet, theatre director, essayist, emigrated in 1939 to the USA, returned in 1947.] [Vol. 1 was published in 1989: Studienausgabe Bd. 1: Die Überwindung des Übermenschen: Exilschriften. Hrsg. von Konstantin Kaiser und Peter Roessler in Zusammenarbeit mit Siglinde Bolbecher. Wien: Verl. f. Gesellschaftskritik, 1989. 420 pp., notes, index of persons. (Antifaschistische Literatur und Exilliteratur; Bd. 2).]

——— VIERTEL, BERTHOLD *Tribüne und Aurora: Briefwechsel 1940–1949.* Wieland Herzfelde und Berthold Viertel. [See No. 28818.]

——— WALDINGER, ERNST: *Noch vor dem Jüngsten Tag:* ausgewählte Gedichte und Essays. [See No. 28986.]

28837. WALLERSTEIN, SUSANNE: *Alle meine Jahre.* Erinnerungen 1910–1988. Rosengarten: Dagmar Dreves Verl., 1989. 200 pp.

28838. WEISS, PETER: *Aus unveröffentlichten Tagebüchern.* Aus den Aufzeichnungen des Jahres 1970. [In]: ndl. neue deutsche literatur, Jg. 39, H. 464, Berlin, August 1991, pp. 5–15.

28839. WEISSKOPF, VICTOR: *Mein Leben. Ein Physiker, Zeitzeuge und Humanist erinnert sich an unser Jahrhundert.* Aus dem Amerikan. von Liselotte Julius. München: Scherz, 1991. 383 pp., index of names. [V.W., born Sept. 19, 1908 in Vienna, physicist, emigrated via various countries to the USA in 1937, worked during World War II on the atomic bomb project in Los Alamos, from 1961 until 1965 president of CERN, Geneva, thereafter head of physics department of MIT, Boston.]

28840. WHITE, IRENE: *I came as a stranger.* Preface by James Herriot. London: Hazelwood (London NW4, 122 Sunningfields Road), 1991. 112 pp. [Autobiography of a German-Jewish refugee.]

28841. WITTGENSTEIN, LUDWIG: *Geheime Tagebücher 1914–1916.* Hrsg. und dokumentiert von Wilhelm Braun. Vorwort von Hans Albert. Wien: Turia & Kant, 1991. 176 pp., illus.

28842. WOLF, MARKUS. RUNGE, IRENE/STELBRINK, UWE: *Markus Wolf: 'Ich bin kein Spion';* Gespräche mit Markus Wolf. Berlin: Dietz, 1990. 126 pp.

28843. WOLF, MARKUS: *In eigenem Auftrag; Bekenntnisse und Einsichten.* München: Schneekluth, 1991. 358 pp., index of persons. [M.W., born Jan. 19, 1923 Hechingen, former head of the intelligence service in the former GDR, son of the physician and writer Friedrich W., emigrated in 1933 with parents via Switzerland and France to Soviet Russia, from 1945 in the Russian occupied zone resp. GDR.]

IX. GERMAN-JEWISH RELATIONS

A. General

28844. APPLEGATE, CELIA: *A nation of provincials: the German idea of Heimat.* Berkeley: Univ. of California Press, 1990. XI, 273 pp., illus., bibl. (247–268). [Incl. German antisemitism; National Socialism and 'Heimat'; 'Vergangenheitsbewältigung'.]

28845. *Babylon.* Beiträge zur jüdischen Gegenwart. Hrsg.: Micha Brumlik [et al.]. Frankfurt am Main: Verlag Neue Kritik, H. 8 & 9, Feb. & Nov. 1991. 2 issues. [Essays are listed according to subject.] [Cf.: Babylon, Israel, Zion; jüdische Intellektuelle in Deutschland (Richard Chaim Schneider) [in]: Die Zeit, Nr. 48, Hamburg, 22. Nov., 1991, p. 69.]

28846. BANKIER, DAVID: *The Germans and the Holocaust.* [In]: The Jewish Quarterly, Vol. 37, No. 3, London, Autumn 1990. Pp. 7–11, illus.

28847. BAUMAN, ZYGMUNT: *Modernity and ambivalence.* Ithaca, N.Y.: Cornell Univ. Press, 1991, 285 pp. [Author uses the Jewish experience as a paradigm of modern experience itself and in this context provides re-readings of Freud, Kafka and Simmel. He examines anti-Jewish thought and policy in the last century and addresses the sociology of assimilation using the example of German Jews.]

28848. BENZ, WOLFGANG: *Die Verfolgung und Vernichtung der Juden im Bewußtsein der Deutschen.* [In]: Juden in Deutschland [see No. 27940]. Hamburg: Christians, 1991. Pp. 435–449, notes.

28849. BENZ, WOLFGANG: *Die Legende von der deutsch-jüdischen Symbiose.* [In]: Merkur, Jg. 45, Stuttgart, 1991. Pp. 168–174. [For an English version, publ. under the title The legend of German-Jewish symbiosis, see in LBI Year Book XXXVII, London, 1992, pp. 95–102, footnotes.]

28850. BODEMANN, Y. MICHAL/OSTOW, ROBIN: *Federal Republic of Germany & German Democratic Republic.* [Report]. [In]: American Jewish Yearbook 1991. Vol. 91, New York 1991. Pp. 302–315; 316–323.

28851. BRIN, HERB: *Where are the children? Conversations in Germany.* Middle Village, N.Y., Jonathan David, 1991. 172 pp. [Author, publisher of Jewish newspapers in California, records his impressions and conversations with Germans from all walks of life and ages. Conversations centred mainly around events during the Nazi period.]

28852. COULMAS, CORINNA/FRIEDLÄNDER, SAUL: *German leftists come to grips with the past: a case study.* [In]: Holocaust and Genocide Studies, Vol. 6, No. 1, Oxford, 1991. Pp. 33–44, footnotes. [Authors analyse recent articles in German leftist journals and examine antisemitism by the Left, as well as changing leftist attitudes to the Nazi past.]

—— *Deutsche Juden – Juden in Deutschland.* [See No. 28459.]

28853. EVANS, RICHARD, J.: *German unification and the new revisionism.* [In]: Dimensions, Vol. 6, No. 1, New York, 1991. Pp. 6–14, illus., notes. [Incl. historians' debate, Republikaner, etc.]

28854. FOX, THOMAS C.: *A 'Jewish Question' in GDR literature?* [In]: German Life & Letters, Vol. XLIV/1990–1991, Oxford, 1991. Pp. 58–70.

28855. *Germans and Jews: an interview with Elie Wiesel and Sidney Zion.* [In]: Dimensions, Vol. 5, No. 2, New York, 1990. Pp. 20–22. [Interview with E.W. and the New York Times journalist S.Z. on how American Jews feel about German re-unification.]

28856. GILMAN, SANDER L.: *German reunification and the Jews.* [In]: new german critique, No. 52, New York, 1991. Pp. 173–191.

28857. GOLDMANN, ROBERT B.: *German reunification: its meaning for Jews.* [In]: ADL Bulletin, Vol. 48, No. 1, New York, Jan. 1991. Pp. 6–7, illus.

28858. GOSCHLER, CONSTANTIN: *The attitude towards Jews in Bavaria after the Second World War.* [In]: LBI Year Book XXXVI, London, 1991. Pp. 443–458, footnotes.

28859. HURWITZ, EMANUEL: *Christen und Juden; Tagebuch eines Mißverständnisses.* Zürich: Nagel und Kimche, 1991. 170 pp. [On the author's experiences with anti-Zionism and antisemitism of the Swiss Left especially during and after the Gulf War.] [Cf.: Nachwirkungen eines bösen Erbes; über die neue Judenfeindschaft (Elisabeth Endres) [in]: Süddeutsche Zeitung, Nr. 242, München, 18. Okt. 1991, p. 45.]

28860. KASTNER, DIETER: *Die Elberfelder Zeitung und die Judenfrage im Jahre 1843.* Ein Beitrag zur Ablehnung der Emanzipation der Juden aus evangelischer Sicht. [In]: Monatshefte für evangelische Kirchengeschichte des Rheinlandes, Jg. 39, Düsseldorf, 1990. Pp. 247–276.

28861. LEA, CHARLENE A: *Tolerance unlimited: 'the noble Jew' on the German and Austrian stage (1750–1805).* [In]: The German Quarterly, Vol. 64, No. 2, Cherry Hill, N.J., Spring 1991. Pp. 166–177, notes. [Incl. Lessing's 'Nathan der Weise'.]

28862. LEVINAS, EMMANUEL: *Difficult freedom: essays on Judaism.* Transl. by Sean Hand. Baltimore, Md.: Johns Hopkins Univ. Press, 1990. XIV, 306 pp. [Topics incl. Jewish-Christian relations, the works of Hegel, Heidegger; the works of Rosenzweig.]

28863. MOSSE, GEORGE L.: *The nationalization of the masses: political symbolism and mass movements in Germany from the Napoleonic wars through the Third Reich.* Ithaca, N.Y.: Cornell Univ. Press, 1991. XIV, 252 pp., illus., ports., notes (219–246). (Paperback.) [First publ. in 1975 by Fertig, New York. Incl. German antisemitism and treatment of Jews.]

28864. NA'AMAN, SHLOMO: *Die Bedeutung der Judenfrage in der frühen Arbeiterbewegung.* Eine Erweiterung der Studie von Jacob Toury 'The Jewish Question, a semantic approach'. [In]: Tel Aviver Jahrbuch für deutsche Geschichte, Bd. 20. Gerlingen, 1991. Pp. 163–180, notes.

28865. PATSCH, SYLVIA M.: *Artfremd und undeutsch: jüdische Dichtung in österreichischen Lesebüchern.* [In]: Das Jüdische Echo, Vol. 40, Nr. 1, Wien, Okt. 1991. Pp. 215–220, ports.

28866. PLAUT, W. GUNTHER: *Germans and Jews – the symbiosis that failed.* [In]: Judaism, Vol. 40, No. 4, New York, Fall 1991. Pp. 531–542, footnotes.

28867. RICHARZ, MONIKA: *Luftaufnahme – oder die Schwierigkeiten der Heimatforscher mit der jüdischen Geschichte.* [In]: Babylon, H. 8, Frankfurt am Main, Februar 1991. Pp. 27–33. [An abridged version publ. [in]: MB, Jg. 60, Tel Aviv, März/April 1992, p. 5, 12.]

28868. SERENY, GITTA: *Into that darkness: from mercy killing to mass murder.* London: André Deutsch, 1991. 379 pp., ports., illus., maps. bibl. (369–372). [Incl. the Catholic Church's and the Vatican's silence about Nazi atrocities. For orig. publ. in 1974 see No. 12038/YB XX.]

28869. STERN, FRANK: *The 'Jewish question' in the 'German question', 1945–1990.* [In]: new german critique, No. 52, New York, 1991. Pp. 155–172.

28870. *Survey of Jewish Affairs 1990.* Ed. by William Frankel. London: Institute of Jewish Affairs; Oxford: Blackwell, 1990. XII, 303 pp., bibl. [Subjects incl. the impact of German re-unification and the controversy over the Carmelite convent at Auschwitz.]

28871. *Tribüne.* Zeitschrift zum Verständnis des Judentums. Jg. 30, H. 117–120. Hrsg. von Elisabeth Reisch. Frankfurt am Main: Tribüne Verl., 1991. 4 issues. [*H. 117* incl.: Die Deutschen und der Golfkrieg (Elvira Grözinger, 6–8). *H. 118*: Mehr Kontinuitäten als Brüche. Realität und Utopie im Verhältnis zwischen Juden und Nichjuden (Birgit Seemann, 30–36). Anne Frank als Humanitätssymbol; von speziellen Schwierigkeiten im Umgang mit der Vergangenheit (Wolfgang Boeckh, 60–66, illus.). *H. 119*: 'Opfer' und 'Täter'; ein Gesprächsversuch zwischen Juden und Deutschen (Birgit Seemann, 54–57). Offener Dialog bleibt unverzichtbar (Brigitte Meer, 57–60). Gefühle der Schuld und der Abwehr; Begegnungen zwischen Nachkriegsdeutschen und Juden der Nach-Shoah (Björn Krondorfer, 130–139, notes). Further contributions are listed according to subject.]

28872. VOGT, ROLF: *Eine typische Fehlleistung.* [In]: Geschichte als Trauma [see No. 28743]. Hrsg.: Dierk Juelich. Frankfurt am Main: Nexus. Pp. 107–110. [On the author's personal experience of Vergangenheitsbewältigung.]

28873. WOLFFSOHN, MICHAEL: *Spanien, Deutschland und die 'Jüdische Weltmacht'.* Über Moral, Realpolitik und Vergangenheitsbewältigung. Gütersloh: Bertelsmann, 1991. 190 pp. [Essays dealing also with German-Jewish relations, and post-war antisemitism.]

B. German-Israeli Relations

28874. DEUTSCHKRON, INGE: *Israel und die Deutschen; das schwierige Verhältnis.* Köln: Verl. Wissen-schaft u. Politik, 516 pp. (Aktualisierte Neuauflage.) [Orig. publ. in 1970.]

28875. FEINBERG, ANAT: *Rays of light and the shadows of history.* [In]: Modern Hebrew Literature, No. 7, Tel-Aviv, Fall-Winter 1991. Pp. 8–10. [This issue of the journal is devoted to the reception of Hebrew literature abroad. The contribution of A.F. deals with the reception in Germany.]

28876. HANSEN, NIELS: *Image im Widerspiegel; Partnerschaft bedarf gegenseitigen Vertrauens.* [In]: Tribüne, Jg. 30, H. 120, Frankfurt am Main, 1991. Pp. 108–116, notes.

28877. MEROZ, YOHANAN: *Israel und Deutschland. Ein Jahr nach der Vereinigung.* [In]: Tribüne, Jg. 30, H. 120, Frankfurt am Main, 1991. Pp. 96–106.

—— SELIGMANN, RAFAEL: *Mit beschränkter Hoffnung: Juden, Deutsche, Israelis.* [See No. 28484.]

C. Church and Synagogue

28878. BARTOSZEWSKI, WLADYSLAW T.: *The convent at Auschwitz.* New York: George Braziller, 1991. IX, 169 pp. [An account of the controversy which arose in 1984 when a group of Carmelite nuns tried to establish a convent adjacent to Auschwitz.]

28879. EHRLICH, ERNST LUDWIG: *Christen und Juden in neuen Gesprächen im Geiste von Hermann Maas.* [In]: Judaica, Jg. 47, H. 1/2, Basel, Juni 1991, pp. 107–115. [Dedicated to Kurt Hruby.]

28880. EICHMANN, JOHANNA S.: *Enterbt und entrechtet – ihr Stab ist zerbrochen. Die Synagoge als Magd der Ecclesia.* [In]: Der Davidstern; Zeichen der Schmach-Symbol der Hoffnung [See No. 27924]. Dorsten 1991. Pp. 30–37.

28881. *Essential papers on Judaism and Christianity in conflict.* Ed. by Jeremy Cohen. New York: New York Univ. Press, 1991. 578 pp, notes. [Incl. papers by Hans Liebeschütz, Jacob Katz, among 18 essays. Covers the Holy Roman Empire and Luther's anti-Judaism.]

28882. *Israel und Kirche heute.* Beiträge zum christlich-jüdischen Gespräch. Festschrift zum 70. Geburtstag von Ernst Ludwig Ehrlich. Hrsg. von Marcel Marcus [et al.]. Freiburg i.Br.: Herder, 1991. 439 pp.

28883. IV. *Laterankonzil; das Merkmal der Demütigung tragen.* Juden als Schuldige in der Erniedrigung halten [no author]. [In]: Der Davidstern; Zeichen der Schmach – Symbol der Hoffnung [see No. 27924]. Dorsten 1991. Pp. 44–49.

28884. LEVINSON, PNINA NAVÈ: *Kirche und Synagoge. Der schwierige Dialog zwischen Juden und Christen.* [In]: Jüdische Lebenswelten. Essays [see No. 27946]. Frankfurt am Main: Jüdischer Verlag, Suhrkamp, 1991. Pp. 134–148, illus., bibl. [On the dialogue between Jews and Christians in post-war Germany.]

28885. RITTNER, CAROL/ROTH, JOHN K., eds.: *Memory offended: the Auschwitz convent controversy.* New York: Praeger, 1991. XIV, 289 pp.

28886. SANDERS, W.: *Das Passionsspiel von Oberammergau 1990 im Kontext des christlich-jüdischen Dialogs.* [In]: Una Sancta, Jg. 45, H. 4, Meitingen, 1990. Pp. 291–296.

28887. SCHANDL, FELIX: *Jüdische Bezüge im Leben und Werk Edith Steins 1891–1942.* Wien: Felix Schandl, 1070 Wien, Burggasse 35: Informationszentrum im Dienste d. Christl.-Jüd. Verständigung, 1991. 30 pp. (IDCIV-Vorträge, 43.)

28888. SCHUBERT, KURT: *Das christlich-jüdische Religionsgespräch im 12. und 13. Jahrhundert.* [In]: Die Juden in ihrer mittelalterlichen Umwelt [see No. 27942]. Wien: Böhlau, 1991. Pp. 223–250.

—— WEDEMEIER, KLAUS: *Brüderlichkeit nach Auschwitz?* Zum Verhältnis von Juden und Christen in Deutschland. [See No. 28314.]

28889. WITTSTADT, KLAUS: *Zwischen Vergangenheitsbewältigung und interdisziplinären Neuansätzen – neuere Forschungen zur kirchlichen Zeitgeschichte.* [In]: Neue politische Literatur, Jg. 36, Frankfurt am Main, 1991. Pp. 185–215. [Review article; incl. the role of the Christian churches during the Nazi period and their attitude to Jews and Judaism.]

D. Antisemitism

28890. AHREN, YIZHAK/HORNSHOJ-MOLLER, STIG: *'Der ewige Jude': wie Goebbels hetzte*; Untersuchungen zum nationalsozialistischen Propagandafilm. Aachen: Alano, 1990. 112 pp., bibl.

28891. ALMOG, SHMUEL: *'Judentum als Krankheit'. Antisemitisches Stereotyp und Selbstdarstellung.* [In]: Tel Aviver Jahrbuch für deutsche Geschichte, Bd. 20, Gerlingen, 1991. Pp. 215–235, notes. [Extended version of a paper given at the 10th Judaistik-Kongress, Jerusalem, August 1980.]

28892. AUSTRIA. ANDICS, HELLMUT: *Der Ungeist der Neuerung* [in Österreich]; *ein Jahrhundert 'Rerum Novarum': die Erben der Bergpredigt und ihr Judenhass.* [In]: Das Jüdische Echo, Vol. 40, Nr. 1, Wien, Okt. 1991. Pp. 61–66, illus.

28893. — LOHRMANN, KLAUS: *Stufen des Antisemitismus in Österreich von 1890–1938.* Wien: Burggasse 35: Informationszentrum im Dienste d. Christlich-Jüdischen Verständigung, 1990. 24 pp. (IDCIV-Vorträge; 32.)

28894. — SCHWARZ, JOSEF JAKOB: *Eine/keine (?) Geheime Reichssache! Eine Zeitungscollage [mit Anmerkungen].* A-2700 Wiener Neustadt: Josef Schwarz, Friedr. Holzer-Gasse 3, 1989, 90 pp. [A documentation on Austrian antisemitism from 1933 until 1938 consisting of annotated newspaper clippings (facsims.); also on post-war antisemitism and Vergangenheitsbewältigung in Austria, incl. the 'Waldheim-Affäre'.]

28895. — 'Wir sind alle unschuldige Täter'. Diskurshistorische Studien zum Nachkriegsantisemitismus. Von Ruth Wodak, Peter Bowak, Johanna Pelikan, Helmut Gruber, Rudolf de Cillia und Richard Mitten. Orig.-Ausg. Frankfurt am Main: Suhrkamp, 1990. 401 pp., footnotes, bibl. (374–394). (Suhrkamp-Taschenbuch Wissenschaft; 881.) [An analysis of post-war Austrian antisemitism, referring also [a.o.] to Bruno Kreisky, Friedrich Peter and Simon Wiesenthal, and the presidential election campaign from 1985 and thereafter (the 'Waldheim affair').]

28896. BARTELS, KARL: *Dämme oder: Der projektiv verschobene Haß.* Frankfurt am Main: Verl. f. Akad. Schriften (VAS), 1991, 271 pp., docs. (237–258), notes, bibl. (259–271). [On the origin, history and recent manifestations of xenophobia in Germany, incl. many references to antisemitism.]

—— BAUER, YEHUDA: *Antisemitismus und Krieg.* [See No. 28231.]

28897. BEN-AVNER, YEHUDAH: *Antisemitism in the Weimar Republic in Germany according to the Jewish press.* [In Hebrew, title transl.]. [In]: Sinai, Vol. 107, Jerusalem, Shvat-Adar 5751 [=Feb.-March 1991]. Pp. 265–283. [Based on accounts in 'Der Israelit' and the 'Jüdische Rundschau'.]

28898. BENDA, FRANZ: *Der Deutsche Turnerbund 1889. Seine Entwicklung und Weltanschauung.* Wien:

VWGÖ, 1991 (Dissertationen der Universität Wien; 216.) (Zugl.: Wien, Univ., Diss., 1990). 336 [13] pp., bibl. (310–335). [Incl. chap. on antisemitism.]

28899. BERGMANN, WERNER/ERB, RAINER: *Antisemitismus in der Bundesrepublik Deutschland*. Ergebnisse der empirischen Forschung von 1946–1989. Opladen: Leske & Budrich, 1991. 328 pp., graphs, tabs. [Based on extensive public opinion research initiated by the Anti-Defamation League (ADL), New York in co-operation with the Zentrum für Antisemitismusforschung, Berlin and the Institut für Demoskopie, Allensbach.]

28900. BERGMANN, WERNER/ERB, RAINER: *Extreme Antisemiten in der Bundesrepublik Deutschland*. [In]: Jahrbuch Extremismus & Demokratie (E & D). 3, Jg. 1991, Bonn: Bouvier, 1991. Pp. 70–93, footnotes.

28901. BERGMANN, WERNER/ERB, RAINER: *'Mir ist das Thema Juden irgendwie unangenehm'*; Kommunikationslatenz und die Wahrnehmung des Meinungsklimas im Fall des Antisemitismus. [In]: Kölner Zeitschrift für Soziologie und Sozialpsychologie, H. 3, Opladen, 1991. Pp. 503–519, footnotes, bibl.

28902. BERING, DIETZ: *Kampf um Namen. Bernhard Weiß gegen Joseph Goebbels*. Stuttgart: Klett-Cotta, 1991. 527 pp. [& insert], illus., notes (405–481), bibl. (485–506), index of first names, of surnames (509–517), index of subjects and persons (518–527). [Cont.: I. Einleitung (17–28). II. Biographische Exposition (29–144; incl. Bernhard Weiß – Aspekte eines Lebensweges; Joseph Goebbels – Perspektiven einer Biographie). III. Namensysteme (145–228). IV. Der Namenkampf (229–352; incl. Der Kampfplatz Berlin; Namenkampf gegen Bernhard Weiß oder: 'Isidor' – die Symbolfigur des 'Systems'; Kampf vor Gericht). V. Biographischer Schluß (353–394; incl. Endkampf in Berlin; Der staatenlose Emigrant). VI. Blick aufs Ganze (395–402). [About the battle between Goebbels and Bernhard Weiß, police vice-president of Berlin during the Weimar Republic, based on onomastic, socio-psychological and historical analysis, the essence of which the author laid down in Der Name als Stigma [see No. 24811/YBXXXIII]. [B. Weiss data see No. 18075/YBXXVII.]

28903. BIBÓ, ISTVÁN: *Die deutsche Hysterie: Ursachen und Geschichte*. Aus dem Ungarischen von Hans-Henning Paetzke; mit einem Nachwort von György Dalos. Frankfurt am Main: Insel, 1991. 197 pp. [Covers also antisemitism and the 'Jewish Question'.] [Cf.: Von der Moderne überrannt (Thomas Schmid) [in]: Die Zeit, Nr. 33, Hamburg, 9. Aug. 1991, p. 34. See also No. 27861/YBXXXVI.]

28904. BLUMENKRANZ, BERNHARD: *Die Juden im Mittelalter: Geschichte und Geschichtsschreiber. Judenhaß und Antisemitismus*. [In]: Die Juden in ihrer mittelalterlichen Umwelt [see No. 27942.]. Wien: Böhlau, 1991. Pp. 17–26.

28905. BODEK, JANUSZ: *Die Fassbinder-Kontroverse: Entstehung und Wirkung eines literarischen Textes; zu Kontinuität und Wandel einiger Erscheinungsformen des Alltagsantisemitismus in Deutschland nach 1945, seinen künstlerischen Weihen und seiner öffentlichen Inszenierung*. Frankfurt am Main; New York [et al.]: Lang, 1991. 438 pp. Zugl.: Bielefeld, Univ., Diss., 1991. [On the controversy about the staging of Rainer W. Fassbinder's theatre play Der Müll, die Stadt und der Tod in Frankfurt am Main between 1976 and 1986.]

28906. BRAUN, CHRISTINA VON/HEID, LUDGER, eds.: *Der ewige Judenhass. Christlicher Antijudaismus, deutschnationale Judenfeindlichkeit, rassistischer Antisemitismus*. Mit Beiträgen von Wolfgang Gerlach, Ludger Heid, Christina von Braun. Stuttgart: Burg, 1990. 244 pp., illus., bibl. (214–236), index of names. [Cont.: Vorwort (Christina von Braun/Ludger Heid, 7–10). Essays (titles condensed): Siebzehnhundert Jahre christlicher Antijudaismus (Wolfgang Gerlach, 11–69, notes). Jüdische Emanzipation und Judenfeindlichkeit 1750–1880 (Ludger Heid, 70–109, notes). Der moderne Antisemitismus in Kaiserreich und Weimarer Republik (Ludger Heid, 110–130, notes). Die 'Ostjudenfrage' als neue Variante des Antisemitismus (Ludger Heid, 131–148, notes). Der rassistische Antisemitismus (Christina von Braun, 149–213, notes.) [Based on a TV-series produced by the Westdeutscher Rundfunk (WDR) and the Norddeutscher Rundfund (NDR) in co-operation with the Landeszentrale für politische Bildung Nordrhein-Westfalen.]

28907. ERB, RAINER/LICHTBLAU, ALBERT: *'Es hat nie einen jüdischen Ritualmord gegeben'*. Konflikte um die Abschaffung der Verehrung des Andreas von Rinn. [In]: Zeitgeschichte, Jg. 7, H. 1–12, Salzburg, Okt. 1989 – Sept. 1990. Pp. 127–162.

28908. EYBL, FRANZ M: *Das Anderle von Rinn in barocken Predigten*. [In]: Die Juden in ihrer mittelalterlichen Umwelt [see No. 27942.]. Wien: Böhlau, 1991. Pp. 27–34.

28909. *Fremdenfeindlichkeit, Rassismus, Antisemitismus*. Mit Beiträgen von Jacques Picard, Berthold Rothschild, Walter Schmid, Michael Kohn. Geleitwort von Alfred A. Häsler. Einleitung von Gaby Rosenstein. Hrsg.: Israelitische Cultusgemeinde Zürich/Gesellschaft Minderheiten in der Schweiz. Konstanz: Hartung-Gorre, 1991. 73 pp. [Based on the 'Zürcher Symposium', held on Dec. 2, 1990. Incl.: Vom modernen zum neuen Antisemitismus; Tendenzen und Formenwandel rassistischer und antidemokratischer Bewegungen im Europa des 20. Jahrhunderts.]

28910. FREY, WINFRIED: *Gottesmörder und Menschenfeinde. Zum Judenbild in der deutschen Literatur des Mittelalters.* [In]: Die Juden in ihrer mittelalterlichen Umwelt [see No. 27942.]. Wien: Böhlau, 1991. Pp. 223–250. Pp. 35–52.

——— FRIEDRICHS, CHRISTOPHER R.: *The anti-Jewish movements in Frankfurt and Worms, 1612–1617.* [See No. 28031.]

28911. GILMAN, SANDER L./KATZ, STEVEN T., eds.: *Anti-Semitism in times of crisis.* New York: New York Univ. Press, 1991. VII, 406 pp., illus. [Incl.: The origins of anti-semitism: ancient evidence and modern interpretations (Nicolas de Lange), 21–37, notes. The dehumanization of the Jews in medieval propaganda imagery (Moshe Lazar), 38–80, notes. The theological and historical foundations of Luther's anti-Judaism (Jeremy Cohen), 81–102, notes. Responses to anti-semitism in Midrashic literature (Pinchas Hacohen Peli, 103–114, notes. Jews as magicians in Reformation Germany (R. Po-chia Hsia), 115–139, notes. The writing of difference in Rahel Varnhagen's letters (Liliane Weissberg), 140–153, notes. Dualistic thinking and the rise of ontological antisemitism in nineteenth-century Germany: from Schiller's Franz Moor to Wilhelm Raabe's Moses Freudenstein (Walter H. Sokel, 154–172, notes). The theme of anti-semitism in the work of Austrian Jews (Ruth Kluger, 173–187, notes). The role of racial antisemitism in the Nazi analysis of the Weimar Republic (Steven T. Katz, 227–256, notes). Jewish writers in contemporary Germany (Sander L. Gilman, 311–342, notes). German reunification and the Jews (Sander L. Gilman, 372–390, notes). Index (395–406).]

28912. GINZEL, GÜNTHER B., Hrsg.: *Antisemitismus. Erscheinungsformen der Judenfeindschaft gestern und heute.* Köln: Verl. Wiss. & Politik, 1991. 527 pp., illus., notes, index (subjects, persons, places, 503–519). [Cont. the sections (titles condensed): Einleitung: Über Antisemiten und Antisemitismus in Deutschland (Günther B. Ginzel, 15–32). I. 'Ihr habt den Teufel zum Vater': Das judenfeindliche Dogma und seine Entstehungsgeschichte (Reinhold Mayer, 34–52). Judenfeindschaft von der frühen Kirche bis zu den Kreuzzügen (Wolfgang Wirth, 53–70). Antisemitismus im Mittelalter (Willehad Paul Eckert, 71–99; incl. editor's note on usury, 85–86). Die Theologie der Reformationszeit und die Juden (Paul Gerhard Aring, 100–122, bibl.). II. Vom Gottesmörder zum Weltfeind: Vom religiösen zum rassischen Judenhaß (Günther B. Ginzel, 124–169). Zur Entstehung der deutschen Antisemitenparteien in Deutschland und Österreich (Kurt Düwell, 170–180). Die deutsche Gesellschaft der Weimarer Republik und der Antisemitismus (Heinrich August Winkler, 181–191). Die Judenpolitik des Dritten Reiches 1933–1942 (Uwe Adam, 193–218). III. Von der Aktualität eines Vorurteils: Antisemitismus in Polen (József Niewiadomski, 220–233; incl. Polnisches Bischofswort zum Verhältnis von Christen und Juden, 231–233). Antijüdisches im christlichen Alltag (Wilhelm Salberg, 234–248). Antisemitismus – auch von Links? (Hans G. Glasner, 249–268). Antisemitismus von Rechts (Günther B. Ginzel, 269–284). Zur Akzeptanz pogromistischer Judenwitze. Eine repräsentative Umfrage (Michael Selbmann, 285–287). Judenstaat und Judenhaß (Schalom Ben-Chorin, 288–302). IV. Spezialthemen: Der Talmud; Zielscheibe und Ausgangspunkt antisemitischer Polemik (Hermann Greive, 304–310). Soziologische Erkenntnisse zur Rassenfrage (Alphons Silbermann, 311–319). Antisemitismus und 'Ostjudenfrage' (Ludger Heid, 320–326). Kleine Mediengeschichte des Joseph Süß Oppenheimer 1737/38 bis 1984 (Friedrich Knilli/Siegfried Zielinski, 327–335). Antisemitismus – eine Männerkrankheit? Psychoanalytische Betrachtungen (Margarete Mitscherlich-Nielsen, 336–342). Jüdischer Selbsthaß; Spezialfall des Antisemitismus (Hans Lamm, 343–355). V. Antisemitische Bildersterotypen: Antijudaismus in der christlichen Kunst (Willehad Paul Eckert, 358–388). Der nationalsozialistische Antisemitismus im Spiegel des politischen Plakates (Jürgen Benatzky, 389–417). Stereotype Darstellungen von Juden, Judentum und Israel in der neuzeitlichen Karikatur (Henry Wassermann, 418–437). VI. Anhang: Kommentierte Bibliographie zur Antisemitismusforschung (Günther B. Ginzel et al., 440–448). Antisemitismus-Umfrage I & II, Herbst 1949 & Herbst 1987 (449–461). Tabellen (reprinted from public opinion poll projects, 462–502).]

28913. GROLLE, JOIST: *'Deutsches Geschlechterbuch' – Ahnenkult und Rassenwahn.* [In]: Juden in Deutschland [see No. 27940]. Hamburg: Christians, 1991. Pp. 207–228, notes, illus.

—— GRUBER, HELMUT: *Antisemitismus im Medienkurs: die Affäre 'Waldheim' in der Tagespresse*. [See No. 28500.]

28914. HEILBRONNER, ODED: *Where did Nazi anti-Semitism disappear to? Anti-Semitic propaganda and ideology of the Nazi party, 1929–1933*; a historiographic study. [In]: Yad Vashem Studies, Vol. 21, Jerusalem, 1991. Pp. 263–286. [For an extended version see: *The role of Nazi antisemitism in the Nazi party's activity and propaganda; a regional historiographical study* [in]: LBI Year Book XXXV, London, 1990. Pp. 397–439, footnotes.] [This article was inadvertently not listed in the Bibliography of LBI Year Book XXXVI, London, 1991; see No. 27160/YB XXXVI.]

28915. HOFMEISTER, WERNFRIED: *Das 'Jüdel' im Kontext mittelhochdeutscher literarischer Kindesdarstellungen*. [In]: Die Juden in ihrer mittelalterlichen Umwelt [see No. 27942.]. Wien: Böhlau, 1991. Pp. 91-104.

—— KAHLER, ERICH VON: *Ursprung und Wandlung des Judenhasses* [See No. 27947.]

28916. KATZ, JACOB: *Accounting for antisemitism*. [In]: Commentary, Vol. 91, No. 6, New York, June 1991. Pp. 52–54. [Incl. German antisemitism.]

28917. KRONDORFER, BJÖRN: *Ist die deutsche Kultur antisemitisch? Gedanken zur (Fremd-) Bestimmung des Judentums*. [In]: Tribüne, Jg. 30, H. 117, Frankfurt am Main, 1991. Pp. 131–143. [On antisemitism in post-war Germany with special emphasis on the situation after re-unification.]

—— LEVITT, CYRIL: *The prosecution of antisemites by the courts in the Weimar Republic: was justice served?* [See No. 28570.]

28918. LITTELL, FRANKLIN H.: *The future of anti-semitism*. [In]: Judaism, Vol. 40, No. 4, New York, Fall 1991. Pp. 511–520. [Incl. German antisemitism, both historical and present-day.]

—— LOOSE, HANS DIETER: *Wünsche Hamburger Juden auf Änderung ihrer Vornamen und der staatliche Umgang damit*. [See No. 28046.]

28919. LUTHER, MARTIN. WENZEL, EDITH: *Martin Luther und der mittelalterliche Antisemitismus*. [In]: Die Juden in ihrer mittelalterlichen Umwelt [see No. 27942]. Pp. 301–319.

28920. *(The) meaning of antisemitism*. [In]: The Jewish Quarterly, Vol. 38, No. 1, London, Spring 1991. Pp. 33–43. [A series of short articles on the recent increase in antisemitic incidents in Europe, incl. Germany.]

28921. MIKLAUTSCH, LYDIA: *Der Antijudaismus in den mittelalterlichen Legenden am Beispiel der Silvesterlegende in der Fassung des Konrad von Würzburg*. [In]: Die Juden in ihrer mittelalterlichen Umwelt [see No. 27942]. Pp. 173–182.

28922. NA'AMAN, SHLOMO: *Social Democracy on the ambiguous ground between antipathy and antisemitism: the example of Wilhelm Hasenclever*. [In]: LBI Year Book XXXVI, London, 1991. Pp. 229–240, footnotes, illus.

28923. NEUBAUR, CAROLINE: *Wahnsystem Antisemitismus*. [In]: Merkur, H. 508, Stuttgart, 1991. Pp. 634–642.

28924. PAULEY, BRUCE F.: *From prejudice to persecution. A history of Austrian anti-semitism*. Chapel Hill; London: The University of North Carolina Press, 1991. 426 pp., illus., notes, bibl., index. [From the Middle Ages to present times.]

28925. REIF, ADALBERT/STRAUSS, HERBERT A: *Der antisemitische Wahn*. Adalbert Reif im Gespräch mit dem Antisemitismus-Experten Herbert A. Strauss. [In]: Universitas, Jg. 46, H. 11, Stuttgart, Nov. 1991, pp. 1099–2006.

28926. REUTH, RALF GEORG: *Goebbels*. München: Piper, 1991. 760 pp. [Cf.: Joseph Goebbels – gerissener Demagoge und hetzerischer Antisemit (Diethard Henning) [in]: Süddeutsche Zeitung, Nr. 110, München, 14. Mai 1991, p. 11.]

28927. ROHRBACHER, STEFAN/SCHMIDT, MICHAEL: *Judenbilder; Kulturgeschichte antijüdischer Mythen und antisemitischer Vorurteile*. Orig.-Ausg. Reinbek b. Hamburg: Rowohlt Taschenbuch Verl., 1991. 441 pp., illus., notes, index of subjects, of persons, 428–439). (kulturen und ideen; rowohlts enzyklopädie 498.)

28928. SCHINDLER, THOMAS: *Der Kampf des Kartell-Convents* [der Verbindung deutscher Studenten jüdischen Glaubens] *(K.C.) gegen den Antisemitismus*. Dargestellt am Beispiel von Hellmuth Schreiber Spreviae, Nassoviae. [In]: Einst und Jetzt, Bd. 36, Nürnberg, 1991. Pp. 189–203, illus, notes.

28929. SEGAL, LILLI: *Die Hohen Priester der Vernichtung. Anthropologen, Mediziner und Psychiater als Wegbereiter von Selektion und Mord im Dritten Reich*. Berlin: Dietz, 1991. 241 pp., illus., facsims., notes, index of persons. (Schriftenreihe Geschichte.) [Also on antisemitism and the mass extermination of Jews.] [L.S., born 1913, biologist, survivor of Auschwitz, where she herself had to undergo 'selection' by Dr. Josef Mengele.]

624   Bibliography

28930. SIEGLER, BERND: *Auferstanden aus Ruinen. Rechtsextremismus in der DDR.* Berlin: Edn. Tiamat, Verl. Bittermann, 1991. 191 pp., bibl. (Critica Diabolis; 32.) [Incl. the chap.: Der 'getarnte' Antisemitismus (120–137).]

28931. SPEIER, SAMMY: *Manifestationen der totgeschwiegenen Vergangenheit 1933–1945 im heutigen Alltagsbewußtsein: Die BRD – ein politisch-menschlicher Krisenherd?! Kehrt vor der eigenen Tür!* [In]: Geschichte als Trauma [see No. 28743]. Frankfurt am Main, 1991. Pp. 95–196. [Discusses Vergangenheitsbewältigung and antisemitism of the Left.]

28932. STERN, FRANK: *Im Anfang war Auschwitz. Antisemitismus und Philosemitismus im deutschen Nachkrieg.* Gerlingen: Bleicher, 1991. 388 pp., footnotes, bibl. (359–380), index (persons, subjects, 382–388). (Schriftenreihe des Instituts für deutsche Geschichte, Universität Tel Aviv, 14.)

28933. STERN, FRANK: *Philosemitismus; Stereotype über den Feind, den man zu lieben hat.* [in]: Babylon, H. 8, Frankfurt am Main, Februar 1991. Pp. 15–26.

28934. STERN, GUY: *Nazi book burning and the American response.* Distinguished lecture to the Friends of the Wayne State Universities Libraries, November 1, 1989. Detroit: Wayne State University, 1989. 17 pp., illus.

28935. STRÖLE-BÜHLER, HEIKE: *Studentischer Antisemitismus in der Weimarer Republik*; eine Analyse der Burschenschaftlichen Blätter 1918–1933. Frankfurt am Main: Lang, 1991. 197 pp., notes, bibl. (177–197). [Europäische Hochschulschriften; Reihe 3, Geschichte und ihre Hilfswissenschaften; Bd. 486.)

28936. SUALL, IRWIN: *Skinhead update: whether they follow the neo-Nazi line or not, German gangs share many of its beliefs.* [In]: ADL Bulletin, Vol. 48, Nos. 4/5, New York, April/May 1991. Pp. 5–6, illus.

——   TOURY, JACOB: *Anti-Anti 1889/1892.* [See No. 28579.]

28937. *(The) value of the human being: medicine in Germany 1918–1945.* An exhibition in the Ärztekammer Berlin in connection with the Bundesärztekammer. Concept and text: Christian Pross and Goetz Aly. Berlin: Ärztekammer; Edn. Hentrich, 1991. 52 pp., illus., facsims. [Incl. references to racial and antisemitic ideology.]

28938. WASSERMANN, HENRY: *An essay on Haman, Risches, Judenhass and antisemitism.* [In]: Juden in Deutschland [see No. 27940]. Hamburg: Christians, 1991. Pp. 186–195, notes.

28939. WINNECKEN, ANDREAS: *Ein Fall von Antisemitismus; zur Geschichte und Pathogenese der deutschen Jugendbewegung vor dem Ersten Weltkrieg.* Köln: Verlag Wissenschaft und Politik, 1991. 160 pp., illus., index of subjects, of persons. [Deals with nationalistic and antisemitic leanings of the German youth movement and also with the emergence of the Jewish Wanderbund Blau-Weiß.]

28940. WISTRICH, ROBERT S.: *Vom 'Christusmord' zur 'Weltverschwörung'. Motive des europäischen und arabischen Antisemitismus.* [In]: Jüdische Lebenswelten. Essays [see No. 27946]. Berlin: Jüdischer Verlag, Suhrkamp 1991. Pp. 123–133, notes. [Also on antisemitism in Germany.]

28941. WISTRICH, ROBERT S.: *Antisemitism: the longest hatred.* London: Thames Methuen, 1991. XXVI, 341 pp., illus., notes. [Cf.: Anti-Judaism and antisemitism (Geoffrey Alderman) [in]: Jewish Journal of Sociology, Vol. 33, No. 2, London, Dec. 1991, pp. 117–121, notes.]

28942. WITTENBERG, REINHARD/PROSCH, BERNHARD/ABRAHAM, MARTIN: *Antisemitismus in der ehemaligen DDR. Überraschende Ergebnisse der ersten Repräsentative Umfrage und einer Befragung von Jugendlichen in Jena.* [In]: Tribüne, Jg. 30, H. 118, Frankfurt am Main, 1991. Pp. 102–120, tabs.

——   WOLFFSOHN, MICHAEL: *Spanien, Deutschland und die 'jüdische Weltmacht'. Über Moral, Realpolitik und Vergangenheitsbewältigung.* [See No. 28873.]

28943. ZELINSKY, HARTMUT: *Kaiser Wilhelm II., die Werk-Idee Richard Wagners und der 'Weltkampf'.* [In]: Der Ort Kaiser Wilhelms in der deutschen Geschichte. Hrsg. von John C. G. Röhl unter Mitarbeit von Elisabeth-Müller Luckner. München: Oldenbourg, 1991. (Schriften des Historischen Kollegs; Kolloquien 17.) Pp. 297–356, footnotes. [On the antisemitism of Wagner and the Wagner circle, incl. Hitler, Wilhelm II, Eulenburg, Chamberlain, Langbehn, Bernhard Förster (Nietzsche's brother-in-law).] [An earlier version was published under the title Sieg oder Untergang: Sieg und Untergang: Kaiser Wilhelm II., die Werk-Idee Richard Wagners und der 'Weltkampf'. München: Keyser, 1990. 112 pp. illus. (Querschüsse.)]

28944. ZENTRUM FÜR ANTISEMITISMUSFORSCHUNG. *News Letter, No. 1 & 2,* Berlin, May & Oct. 1991. Red.: Juliane Wetzel. 2 issues [8 & 6 pp.] [Incl. reports on special events, research activities and recent publications of the Zentrum für Antisemitismusforschung.]

28945. ZIMMERMANN, MOSHE: *Antisemitismus im Kaiserreich zwischen Modernität und Antimodernismus im*

Urteil der Renegaten. [In]: Juden in Deutschland [see No. 27940]. Hamburg: Christians, 1991. Pp. 196–206.

E. Noted Germans and Jews

28946. ANDREAS-SALOMÉ, LOU. MARTIN, BIDDY: *Woman and modernity: the (life) styles of Lou Andreas-Salomé.* Ithaca; London: Cornell Univ. Press. 1991. XIV, 250 pp., illus. [L.A.-S., writer, thinker, lay analyst; book incl. her many friendships with Jewish personalities, Sigmund and Anna Freud, Peter Altenberg, Richard Beer-Hofmann, Arthur Schnitzler. These associations brought her into conflict with the Nazis who were about to confiscate her property when she died in 1937.]

28947. ARNIM, BETTINE VON. NEUHAUS-KOCH, ARIANE: *Bettine von Arnim im Dialog mit Rahel Varnhagen, Amalie von Helvig, Fanny Tarnow und Fanny Lewald.* [In]: 'Stets wird die Wahrheit hadern mit dem Schönen'; Festschrift für Manfred Windfuhr zum 60. Geburtstag. Hrsg.: Gertrude Cepl-Kaufmann [et al.]. Köln: Böhlau, 1990. 506 pp.

28948. BEETHOVEN, LUDWIG VAN. BLOOM, CECIL: *Beethoven's Jewish connection.* [In]: The Jewish Quarterly, Vol. 38, No. 1, London, Spring 1991. Pp. 22–25. [Deals with B.'s correspondence with his Jewish publisher and his friendship with Rahel Varnhagen; also on antisemitic comments in his letters.]

28949. — GRADENWITZ, PETER: *Ludwig van Beethoven und die hebräische Liturgie.* [In]: Menora, Bd. 2, München, 1991. Pp. 215–244, notes.

28950. CALHOON, KENNETH S.: *The education of the human race: Lessing, Freud and the savage mind.* [In]: The German Quarterly, Vol. 64, No. 2, Cherry Hill, N.J., Spring 1991. Pp. 178–189, notes.

28951. DOHM, CHRISTIAN WILHELM VON. EISSING, UWE J.: *Christian Wilhelm von Dohm, die bürgerliche Verbesserung der Juden und die Vision einer 'judenfreien' Welt.* [In]: Bulletin des LBI, 88, Frankfurt am Main, 1991. Pp. 27–58, notes.

28952. HAUBEN (NEVO), JOSEPH: *Lessing, Herder, Goethe, Schiller and Nietzsche (also Heine and Dostojewski) on the Jews.* [In Hebrew]. Jerusalem: Academon – the Hebrew Univ. Students' Printing and Publ. House, 1990. 226 pp. [Cont. excerpts from these writers on the Jews. The Hebrew title incl. also the names of Moses Mendelssohn and Rabbi Moses Sofer which were omitted on the English title-page.]

28953. HEBEL, JOHANN PETER. HORCH, HANS OTTO: *'Haggadisches Erzählen'. Johann Peter Hebels 'jüdische' Kalendergeschichten und ihre Deutung durch Walter Benjamin.* [In]: Juden in Deutschland [see No. 27940]. Hamburg: Christians, 1991. Pp. 252–272, notes.

28954. HEGEL, GEORG FRIEDRICH. SMITH, STEVEN B.: *Hegel and the Jewish Question: between tradition and modernity.* [In]: History of Political Thought, Vol. XII, Issue 1, London, Spring 1991. Pp. 87–106.

28955. HEIDEGGER, MARTIN. LYOTARD, JEAN-FRANÇOIS: *Heidegger and 'the Jews'.* Transl. from the French by Andreas Michel and Mark S. Roberts. Minneapolis: Univ. of Minnesota Press, 1990. XXIX, 106 pp., bibl. [Examines H.'s relationship to Nazism]

28956. — WOLIN, RICHARD: *Introduction to: 'Herbert Marcuse and Martin Heidegger: an exchange of letters'.* [Followed by the letters which were transl. by R. Wolin.] [In]: new german critique, No. 53, Ithaca, N.Y., Spring/Summer 1991. Pp. 19–27; 28–32. [Exchange of letters dating from 1947–1948 and dealing mainly with Marcuse's disappointment at his mentor's involvement with the Nazis and Heidegger's lack of remorse.]

28957. — WOLIN, RICHARD, ed.: *The Heidegger controversy: a critical reader.* Irvington, N.Y.: Columbia Univ. Press, 1991. 304 pp. [Heidegger's alliance with the Nazi regime.]

28958. HEYM, GEORG. BRIDGEWATER, PATRICK: *Poet of expressionist Berlin; the life and work of Georg Heym.* London: Libris, 1991. 305 pp. [Heym's circle included many Jewish artists and writers, such as Hiller, Loewenson, Wolfsohn, Guttmann, Meidner.]

28959. HIPPEL, THEODOR GOTTLIEB VON. KOHNEN, JOSEPH: *Hippel und die Juden.* [In]: Recherches Germaniques, Vol. 21, Strasbourg, 1991. Pp. 79–95, footnotes. [On the mayor of Königsberg, Theodor Gottlieb von Hippel, who, in spite of being known as a supporter of the Enlightenment and humanitarian ideas, exposed in a mémoir, written in 1791, a fervent antisemitism which is close to some ideas of National Socialism.]

28960. HUMBOLDT, ALEXANDER VON. BECKER, HEINZ: *Vertrauliche Indiskretionen; Alexander von Humboldt und Giacomo Meyerbeer.* [In]: Jahrbuch Preußischer Kulturbesitz 1990, Bd. 27, Berlin: Gebr. Mann, 1991. Pp. 477–513.

28961. JUNG, C. G. Neumann, Micha: *On the problem of Jung's antisemitism: Carl Gustav Jung's attitude toward Jews, based on his writings and his correspondence with Erich Neumann.* [In Hebrew, with English summary, title transl.]. [In]: Sichot – Dialogue, Israel journal of psychotherapy, Vol. 5, No. 3, Ramat Hasharon, June 1991. Pp. 201–208. [Erich Neumann, psychologist, data see No. 17612/YB XXVI, corresponded with Jung from his emigration to Palestine in 1934 until 1959.]

28962. LESSING, GOTTHOLD EPHRAIM. Strohschneider-Kohrs, Ingrid: *Vernunft als Weisheit; Studien zum späten Lessing.* Tübingen: Niemeyer, 1991. 304 pp., notes. (Hermaea. Germanistische Forschungen. N.F.; Bd. 65.) [Incl. the sections: 1. Lessings Nathan-Dichtung mit ihren Hinweisen auf eine authentische, personale religio-Erfahrung und deren Konnotation in der Hiob-Thematik. 2. Lessings kritisch-denkerische Verständigung mit Mendelssohn über die fides historica und die Wahrheit 'unter mehr als einer Gestalt'.]

―――― LUTHER, MARTIN. Wenzel, Edith: *Martin Luther und der mittelalterliche Antisemitismus.* [See No. 28919.]

28963. MANN, THOMAS. Darmaun, Jacques: *Crise révolutionnaire et problème juif à travers le JOURNAL (1918–1921) de Th. Mann.* [In]: Cahiers d'Études Germaniques, Vol. 19, Institut d'Études Germaniques de l'Université Lumière – Lyon II [et al]., 1990. Pp. 147–158, footnotes.

28964. ―― Gelber, Mark: *Indifferentism, anti-semitism, the Holocaust, and Zionism; Thomas Mann and Max Brod.* [In]: Tel Aviver Jahrbuch für deutsche Geschichte, Bd. 20, Gerlingen, 1991. Pp. 327–337, notes.

28965. ―― Hoelzel, Alfred: *Thomas Mann's attitudes toward Jews and Judaism: an investigation of biography and oeuvre.* [In]: Art and its uses. The visual image and modern Jewish society. Studies in Contemporary Jewry. An annual; VI, 1990. Ed. by Ezra Mendelsohn. Guest Symposium ed.: Richard I. Cohen. New York; Oxford: Oxford University Press, 1990. Pp. 229–253, notes.

28966. ―― Lubich, Frederick Alfred: *'Fascinating Fascism': Thomas Manns 'Das Gesetz' und seine Selbst(de)montage als Moses-Hitler.* [In]: Zeitschrift für Literaturwissenschaft und Linguistik, Jg. 20, Heft 79, Göttingen 1990. Pp. 129–133, footnotes.

28967. NIEBUHR, REINHOLD. Littell, Franklin: Essay: *Reinhold Niebuhr and the Jewish people.* [In]: Holocaust and Genocide Studies, Vol. 6, No. 1, Oxford, 1991. Pp. 45–62

28968. NIETZSCHE, FRIEDRICH. Ansell-Pearson, Keith: *Nietzsche the rebel: 'non legar, non legar'.* [In]: The Jewish Quarterly, vol. 37, No. 3, London, Autumn 1990. Pp. 27–31, notes. [Incl. N.'s views on Jews.]

28969. ―― *De Sils-Maria à Jérusalem; Nietzsche et le Judaisme.* Les intellectuels juifs et Nietzsche. Sous la direction de Dominique Bourel et Jacques le Rider. Paris: Les éditions du cerf, 1991. 275 pp., index of names. [Incl. the essays (titles condensed): Philohellénisme et antisémitisme en Allemagne: le cas Nietzsche (Hubert Cancik/Hildegar Cancik-Lindemaier, 21–46). Nietzsche dans les revues culturelles juives de langue allemande, de 1900 à 1938 (Gert Mattenklott, 93–110). De Lemberg à Jérusalem: Nietzsche et Buber (Dominique Bourel, 121–130). Fritz Mauthner et Nietzsche (J. Edgar Bauer, 131–146). Nietzsche vu par Gustav Landauer (Christine Holste, 147–180). Les intellectuels juifs viennois et Nietzsche; autour de Sigmund Freud (Jacques le Rider, 181–200). Les débuts de la réception de Nietzsche parmi les intellectuels hongrois (Endre Kiss, 201–226). Lectures de Nietzsche à Prague; autour de Brod et Kafka (Mark Anderson, 211–226).]

28970. SOMMER, FRED: *Nostalgia, francophilia and the agony of Hitlerism*: the autobiographies of Heinrich Mann and Stefan Zweig. [In]: New German Studies, No. 2, Hull, 1990–1991. Pp. 109–123, notes. [Deals with parallels in their literary careers and personal lives.]

28971. WAGNER, RICHARD. Rose, Paul Lawrence: *One of Wagner's Jewish friends.* Berthold Auerbach and his unpublished reply to Richard Wagner's antisemitism (1881). [In]: LBI Year Book XXXVI, London, 1991. Pp. 219–228, footnotes. [Incl. Auberbach's Richard Wagner und die Selbstachtung der Juden, 1881 (in German).]

X. FICTION AND POETRY

28972. Canetti, Veza: *Yellow street.* Transl. by Ian Mitchell. With a foreword by Elias Canetti. London: Halban, 1990; New York: Norton, 1991. 144 pp. [For German edn. see No. 27903/YBXXXVI.]

28973. FAERBER, MEIR MARCELL: *Aus unbekannten Motiven.* Drama. A-9020 Klagenfurt (Mozartstr. 61/6/19): Mnemosyne, 1991. 50 pp. (Mnemosyne-Schriften, Bd. 1.) [Based on the author's autobiography. A young Slovak Jew joins an illegal transport to Palestine, organised by Zionists; his non-Jewish girl friend is accompanying him; both are drowned near the Palestinian shore. See also No. 28805 and Was ich sagen wollte (Meir Marcell Faerber) [in]: Mit der Ziehharmonika. Zeitschrift der Theodor Kramer Gesellschaft, 9. Jg., Nr. 1, Wien, März 1992, p. 7, port.]

28974. FINK, IDA: *Die Reise.* Roman. Aus dem Polnischen von Klaus Staemmler. München: 1991. 236 pp. [Autobiographical novel, orig. publ. in Polish in London 1990, about two Jewish sisters who escape from a ghetto in Poland during World War II, and survive with false identity as Poles in forced labour camps in Germany. [I.F., writer, born 1921 in Zbaraz, Poland, emigrated from Poland to Israel in 1957.]

——— GOLDSCHMIDT, GEORGES-ARTHUR: *Die Absonderung.* [See No. 28815.]

28975. GUGGENHEIM, KURT: *Wir waren unser vier.* Roman. Frankfurt am Main: Suhrkamp, 1990. 256 pp., illus. [Incl.: Charles Linsmayer: Nachwort (217–255). First published in 1949. Autobiographical novel about four friends, one of them a Swiss Jew, and their life in Switzerland between 1939 and 1945.]

28976. KANIUK, YORAM: *Der letzte Jude.* Roman. Aus dem Hebräischen von Ruth Achlama. Frankfurt am Main: Dvorah Verl., 1990. 420 pp. [On the failure of two authors, a German and an Israeli, to write jointly a book about a Holocaust survivor. See also: Dreieinhalb Stunden und fünfzig Jahre mit Günter Grass in Berlin (Yoram Kaniuk) [in]: Die Zeit, Nr. 26, Hamburg, 21. Juni 1991, p. 53.]

28977. LANG, RUDOLF: *Nur der Tod ist so deutsch wie der Traum.* Roman. München: Ehrenwirth, 1991. 175 pp. [About the young German soldier, Alfons Beyer, who becomes deeply traumatised by his participation in mass executions of Jews during World War II and who later joins the resistance against the Nazi regime.]

28978. LEVIN, MEYER/LOEW, IDA: *Die Geschichte der Eva Korngold.* Nach Aufzeichnungen von Ida Loew. Mit einem Nachwort von Andrzey Szczypiorski. München: Kunstmann, 1990. 316 pp. [First publ. 1959 in New York under the title: Eva; a novel of the Holocaust.]

28979. LIVELY, ADAM: *The snail.* London: Hutchinson, 1991. 117 pp. [Novel about Austrian-Jewish refugees in Britain.]

28980. LOSA, ILSE: *Unter fremden Himmeln.* Roman. Von der Autorin aus dem Portugiesischen übersetzt und überarbeitet. Freiburg: Beck & Glückler, 1991. [Autobiographical novel. Cf.: Unter fremden Himmeln. Probleme der exilierten Autorinnen (Will Schaber) [in]: Aufbau, Jg. 5, New York, April 24, 1992, p. 12.] [I.L., orig. Ilse Lieblich, born 1913 in Westphalia, emigrated to Portugal in 1934, author of numerous books and articles in Portuguese.] [See also No. 28649.]

28981. LOWY, LIESEL: *Mein Leben – eine vergangene Gegenwart.* Roman. Berlin: Edition q, 1991. 190 pp. [Autobiographical novel; L.L., born in 1918 in Berlin, writer, emigrated in the thirties to Australia; lives in Sydney.]

28982. MASSIE, ALLAN: *The sins of the father.* London: Hutchinson, 1991. 299 pp. [Novel about a present-day relationship between the daughter of a former German-Jewish economist in Germany's post-war government and the son of a former SS officer implicated in war crimes.]

28983. MENASSE, ROBERT: *Selige Zeiten, brüchige Welt;* Roman. Salzburg: Residenz, 1991. 325 pp. [Story about a young man whose parents had emigrated to Brazil and returned with him to Vienna in the Sixties.] [Cf.: Weltgeist zu Besuch (Erich Hackl) [in]: Die Zeit, Nr. 42, Hamburg, 11. Okt. 1991, p. 6 L.]

28984. PLAUT, GUNTHER: *The man who would be messiah.* Cincinnatti: Mosaic Press, 1991. 257 pp., glossary. [Novel explores the life of Jacob Frank, 18th-century founder of the Frankist sect.]

28985. POLLAK, FELIX. GRIMM, REINHOLD: *Ein Aphoristiker im Gehäus: neues aus dem Nachlaß von Felix Pollak.* [In]: Modern Austrian Literature, Vol. 24, Nos. 3/4, Riverside, Ca., 1991. Pp. 17–41, notes. [F.P. 1909 Vienna – 1987 Madison, Wi., writer and poet. Publ. poetry in English and a collection of aphorisms in German.]

28986. WALDINGER, ERNST: *Noch vor dem Jüngsten Tag;* ausgewählte Gedichte und Essays. Hrsg. und mit einem Nachwort von Karl-Markus Gauß. Salzburg: Otto Müller, 1990. 232 pp., port., facsims. [Incl.: Mein Bruder Ernst Waldinger; Skizze seines Lebens (Theodor Waldinger, 5–40). Gedichte; eine Auswahl aus acht Bänden (43–114). Aus dem Nachlaß (115–152). Essays (153–214). Ernst Waldinger; Versöhnung und Zerrissenheit (Karl-Markus Gauß,

218–229).] [E.W., Oct. 16, 1896 Vienna – Feb. 1, 1970 New York, poet, essayist, emigrated in 1938 to the USA, from 1947 until 1964 professor of German Literature in Saratoga Springs.]

28987. WANDER, FRED: *Hôtel Baalbek*. Roman. Berlin: Aufbau, 1991. 223 pp. [Autobiographical novel about a hotel in Marseille during the Nazi period.] [F.W., author, born Jan. 1, 1917 Wien, emigrated to France in 1938, deported to Auschwitz and Buchenwald in 1942, returned to Vienna after the war, from 1955 until 1982 in the German Democratic Republic. Lives in Vienna.] [Cf.: Sie waren nicht ohne Namen. Fred Wanders Emigrations-Roman (Klemens Renoldner) [in]: Mit der Ziehharmonika. Zeitschrift der Theodor Kramer Gesellschaft, 9. Jg., Nr. 1, Wien, März 1992. pp. 4–6.]

Index to Bibliography

Aachen, 27994, 28220
Abels, Norbert, 28666
Abraham Ha Darshan, 27969
Abraham, Martin, 28942
Acculturation, Assimilation, 27916, 27966, 28055, 28123, 28158, 28966
Adam, Uwe, 28912
'ADL Bulletin', 28857, 28936
Adler, Alfred, 28656
Adler, Bruno, 28666
Adler, Israel, 27941
Adler, Nathan Marcus & Hermann, 27959
Adorno, Theodor W., 28643, 28679
Agethen, Manfred, 27914
Agnon, Samuel Josef, 28592, 28593
Ahasverus, 27918
Ahren, Yizhak, 28781, 28890
Aichinger, Ilse, 28663
'AJR Information', 27975, 28406
'AJS Review', 28017, 28138, 28510, 28512, 28716
Albany, 28328
Albert, Claudia, 28643
Albert, Hans, 28841
Alderman, Geoffrey, 28941
Aldingen, 28058
Alexander, Gabriel, 28003
Alexander, Gerhard, 27916
Allerhand, Jakob, 27982
Allfrey, Anthony, 28178
'Allgemeine' Jüd. Wochenzeitung, 27975, 28001, 28040, 28044, 28060, 28109, 28131, 28200, 28220, 28243, 28257, 28286, 28326, 28457, 28466, 28735, 28781
Almog, Shmuel, 28891
Alsace, 27955, 28123, 28124, 28588
Alt, Arthur Tilo, 27983
Altena, 27995
Altenberg, Peter, 28147, 28946
Altenkunstadt, 27996
Altenstadt (Feldkirch), 28125
Altenstadt (Hesse), 27997
Alter, Peter, 27975
Althoff, Gertrud, 28015
Altona, 27998, 27999, 28045, 28050, 28101, 28305
Aly, Goetz, 28326, 28278, 28937
'Am Vasefer', 28738
Amburger, Erik, 28801
'American Jewish Archives', 28307
American Jewish Committee, 28567

'American Jewish History', 28538
'American Jewish Year Book', 28850
Amir, Yehoyada, 28540
Amishai-Maisels, Ziva, 28583
Amsterdam, 28822
'Amtsblatt der Stadt Lauda-Königshofen (Baden)', 28773
Améry, Jean, 28680
Anderl, Gabriele, 28223
Andernach, 28000
Anders, Günther, 28653, 28781
Anderson, Mark M., 28697
Andics, Hellmut, 28892
Andor, Lotte, 28823
Andreas von Rinn, 28907, 28908
Andreas-Salomé, Lou, 28946
Angerbauer, Wolfram, 28023
Angermund, Ralph, 28219, 28488
Angerstorfer, Andreas, 27996
Angress, Werner T., 28489
Anrath, 28114
Ansell-Pearson, Keith, 28968
Anti-Defamation League, New York (ADL), 28899
Anti-Judaism, 28118, 28299, 28847, 28880, 28881, 28883, 28906, 28911, 28912, 28927, 28941
Antisemitism (see also Austria; Switzerland), 27943, 27947, 27977, 28001, 28006, 28031, 28046, 28098, 28117, 28122, 28294, 28415, 28459, 28554, 28681, 28752, 28844, 28891, 28894, 28903, 28904, 28906, 28908, 28913, 28916, 28918, 28922, 28923, 28924, 28926, 28934, 28938, 28940, 28941, 28944, 28945, 28955, 28959, 28961, 28964
— Defence, 28230, 28563, 28567, 28570, 28572, 28579, 28902, 28928, 28971
— Imperial Germany, 28050, 28863, 28898, 28906, 28912, 28939, 28943
— Jewish, 28741
— Middle Ages (see also Anti-Judaism; Blood Libel), 28032, 28116, 28880, 28910, 28912, 28919, 28927
— Nazi, 28231, 28247, 28384, 28439, 28497, 28863, 28890, 28896, 28902, 28912
— Post War, 28141, 28459, 28465, 28482, 28484, 28489, 28498, 28500, 28852, 28853, 28858, 28859, 28873, 28896, 28899, 28900, 28901, 28905, 28909, 28911, 28912, 28917, 28918, 28920, 28925, 28930, 28931, 28932, 28936, 28942

— Weimar Republic, 28863, 28897, 28902, 28906, 28912, 28914, 28935
Antisemitismus, 28912
Antizionism, 28859
Applegate, Celia, 28844
Arad, Yizhak, 28327
'Archiv f. Hessische Geschichte u. Altertums-kunde', 28039
'Archiv f. Sozialgeschichte', 27952
'Archivmitteilungen',
Arendt, Hannah, 28370, 28655, 28678, 28681
Argentine, 28179, 28182
— Refugees, 28265
'Ariel', 28250, 28431
Aring, Paul Gerhard, 28912
Arkush, Allan, 28553
Armed Forces, Jews in, 28773, 28834
Arndt, Ino, 28328
Arnheim, Rudolf, 28641
Arnsberg, 28001
Arnstein, Fanny von, 28682
Arntz, H.-Dieter, 28220
Aronsfeld, C.C., 27916, 17917, 28920
Art and its uses, 28965
Art Historians, 28050, 28267, 28700, 28788
Art, Jewish, 28162, 28584, 28586
Arts, Jews in, 28188, 28430, 28432, 28434, 28583, 28588, 28638
Aryanisation, 28050
'Aschkenas', 27914, 27927, 27956, 27957, 27967, 28095, 28170, 28175, 28587
Aschoff, Diethard, 28015, 28068, 28116
Ash, Mitchell G., 27975
Asher, Joseph, 27939
Asher, Raphael, 27939
Asper, Helmut G., 28792
Association of Jewish Refugees (AJR), 28406
Assor, Reuven, 28812
Attah, Johann Ofori, 28282
Auerbach, Berthold, 28971
'Aufbau', New York, 27934, 28005, 28061, 28189, 28266, 28443, 28722, 28744, 28821
Aufklärung und Haskala, 27916
Augsburg, Europ. Zentrum f. Jüdische Musik, 28587
Auschwitz, 28221–28222, 28233, 28280, 28295, 28352, 28416, 28420, 28422, 28870, 28878, 28885
Ausgburg, 27941
Australia, Refugees, 28185, 28265, 28981
Austria (see also Bohemia; Bukowina; Galicia; Moravia; Vienna), 27963, 28126, 28131, 28132–28135, 28140, 28147–28148, 28171, 28621, 28624, 28632, 28637
— Antisemitism, 28224, 28500, 28892–28895, 28912, 28924, 28941
— Nazi Period, 28223–28224, 28243, 28279, 28307, 28328
— Post War, 28141, 28464, 28492, 28983

Autobiographies, Memoirs, Diaries, Letters, 27972, 27994, 28189, 28191, 28215, 28235, 28265, 28268, 28270, 28334, 28353, 28356–28357, 28366, 28390, 28416, 28434, 28446, 28556, 28605, 28647–28648, 28677, 28700, 28742, 28764, 28800, 28802, 28804–28843, 28851, 28981, 28986, 28987
Avisar, Ilan, 28181

'Babylon', 28845; 27986, 28458, 28466, 28560, 28933
Backhausen, Manfred, 28403
Baden, 28102, 28111, 28124, 28258, 28764
Badt, Hermann, 28606
Baeck, Leo, 27916–27917, 28533, 28559
Baecker, Sigurd, 28735
Bailer, Josef, 28309
Bailer-Galanda, Brigitte, 28309
Bajohr, Frank, 28050, 28311
Bakan, David, 28706
Baldwin, Peter, 28225
Baleanu, Avram Andrei, 27918
Ballin, Albert, 28050
Bamberger, Gabrielle, 28204*
Bankier, Alexander A., 28136
Bankier, David, 28226–28228, 28846
Banking, Jews in, 27975, 28050, 28136, 28230, 28642
Bar-David, Yoram, 28738
Barbakoff, Tatjana, 28683
Barbie, Klaus, 28282
Barkai, Avraham, 27919, 28229–28230
Barkhoff, Jürgen, 28643
Barkin, Kenneth D., 28184
Bartal, Israel, 27959
Bartels, Karl, 28896
Barth, Karl, 28830
Bartoszewski, Wladyslaw, 28271, 28878
Baruch, Rolf Arno, 28050
Bauche, Ulrich, 28044
Bauer, Edgar J., 28969
Bauer, Gerhard, 28653
Bauer, Otto, 28632
Bauer, Yehuda, 28231, 28232, 28473
Bauernfeind, Gustav, 28597, 28617
Bauman, Zygmunt, 28847
Baumbach, Sybille, 28050
Baumeister, Annette, 28683
Baumel, Judith Tydor, 28397, 28454
Bavaria, 28060, 28858
Bechhofen, 28002
Bechtel, Delphine, 27984
Beck, Hans-Jürgen, 28071
Becker, Gudrun, 28762
Becker, Heinz, 28762, 28960
Becker, Reinhold, 28762
Beer-Hofmann, Richard, 28505, 28946
Beethoven, Ludwig Van, 28948–28949

Beiersdorf (Co.), 28050
Beimel, Matthias, 28497
'Beiträge zur Gesch. d. Arbeiterbewegung', 28658
'Beiträge zur Jüd. Geschichte in Rheinland-Pfalz', 28073, 28076
Beitz, Berthold, 28243, 28411
Bejarano, Esther, 28233
Belgium, Nazi Period, 28328, 28422
— Refugees, 28220, 28265
Bell, Daniel, 28752
Bell, David, 28737
Beller, Steven, 28132, 28603
Belzec, 28411
Ben-Avner, Yehudah, 28897
Ben-Chorin, Schalom, 28264, 28505, 28595, 28912
Ben-Chorin, Zvia, 28515
Ben-Shammai, Bitya, 28214
Benda, Franz, 28898
Bendix, Reinhard, 28180
Bendkower, Sigmund, 28713
Benesová, Miroslava, 28436
Benger, Ruth, 28063
Benjamin, Walter, 28525, 28659, 28684–28690, 28953
Benoehr, Hans-Peter, 27941
Benz, Wolfgang, 28225, 28265, 28328, 28330, 28379, 28455, 28489, 28643, 28823, 28848–28849
Berankova, Ljuba, 28437
Berding, Helmut, 27920, 28055
Berenbaum, Michael, 28420
Berg, Alban, 28679
Bergen-Belsen, 28234–28236, 28268, 28284, 28401
Berger, Bennett M., 28180
Berghahn, Volker, 28310
Berghaus, Günter, 27975
Bergman, Schmuel Hugo, 28635
Bergmann, Joachim, 28634
Bergmann, Martin S., 28331
Bergmann, Werner, 28459, 28498, 28899–28901
Bering, Dietz, 28902
Berkemann, Hans-Eberhard, 28107
Berkemann, Joerg, 28050
Berlin, 27943, 27959, 27983–27984, 28003–28011, 28237–28240, 28409, 28447, 28459, 28586, 28654, 28666, 28674, 28676, 28720, 28832, 28902
— Berlin Museum, 28004
— Cemeteries, 27943
— Kreuzberg, 28012
Berlin und der Prager Kreis, 28666; 28158–28159, 28428, 28577
Berliner, Cora, 28562
Bernatzky, Jürgen, 28912
Bernstein, Aron, 27941
Bernstein, Eduard, 28594

Bers, Günter, 28065, 28080
Berthold, Monika, 28036
Bertz, Inka, 28004
Best, Stefan, 28425
Bettelheim, Bruno, 28641, 28691
Bettge, Goetz, 28062
Bible, 28590
Bibliographies, Catalogues, Inventories, 28201, 28209–28217, 28314, 28634, 28784
Bibliographies, Personal, 28201, 28714
Bibó, István, 28903
Bickermann, Elias, 28639
Bickhoff-Böttcher, Nicole, 28058
Bischoff, Ralf, 28023
Bischoffsheim Family, 28178
Bittermann, Klaus, 28681
'Bitzaron', 28535
Black, Eugene C., 27959
Blasius, Dirk, 27980, 28241, 28312
Blau, Paul, 28632
Blau-Weiss (org.), 28939
Bleich, Judith, 28506
Bloch, Benjamin, 28456
Bloch, Ernst, 28692
Block, Elisabeth, 28415
Blonder, Lola, 28132
Blood Libel, 28907–28908, 28927
Bloom, Cecil, 28948
Bloom, Harold, 28636
Blumenkranz, Bernhard, 28904
Blumenthal, Hermann, 28132
Boberach, Heinz, 28328, 28426
Bock, Gisela, 28311
Bodek, Janusz, 28905
Bodemann, Michal Y., 28457–28458, 28850
Bodenheimer, Henriette Hannah, 28595
Bodenheimer, Max Isidor, 28595–28596
Bodian, Miriam, 27921
Bodoff, Lippman, 28739
Boeckh, Wolfgang, 28871
Boehm, Günter, 28050, 28182
Börne, Ludwig, 27943, 28693
'Börsenblatt f. d. Deutschen Buchhandel', 28153, 28634, 28645, 28650, 28671, 28756, 28822
Bogacz, Daniel, 28253
Bohemia (see also Austria; Czechoslovakia), 28150, 28152, 28154–28156, 28170
Bolay, Gertrud, 28058
Bolbecher, Sieglinde, 28836
Bolivia, Refugees, 28265
Bolz, Norbert, 28684
Bondy, Dan, 28041
Bopp, Erika, 28246
Borchardt, Rudolf, 28694, 28695
Borchart, Joachim, 28783
Bormann, Alexander von, 28714
Born (Krs. Viersen), 28114
Bornstein, Heini, 28427

Borowitz, Eugene B., 28554
Borris, Siegfried, 28357
Borut, Jacob, 28563, 28564
Bosch, Manfred, 28764
Boskin, Judith R., 27922
Bothe, Rolf, 28004
Botstein, Leon, 28637
Bott, Gerhard, 28167
Boureau, Alain, 28742
Bourel, Dominique, 28969
Braber, Ben, 28450
Bracher, Karl-Dietrich, 28384
Bracht (Krs. Viersen), 28114
Brade, Christian, 28054
Brady, Philip, 28770
Brahm, Otto, 28654
Brand, Hermann, 28802
Brand, Joel, 28414
Brand, Mechthild, 28052
Brand, Schmuel, 28802
Brandenburg, Frank, 28366
Brandes, Georg, 28378
Bratislava (Pressburg), 28153
Braun, Christina von, 28906
Braun, Ute, 28024
Braun, Wilhelm, 28841
Braunschweig, 28013
Brazil, Refugees, 28265, 28983
Brechenmacher, Thomas, 28205
Brecher, Frank W., 28335
Breidenbach, Armin, 28408
Breitbach, Michael, 28039
Breitman, Richard, 28272
Bremen, 28242
Brenker, Anne-Margarete, 28644
Breslau, 28014
Breslauer, S. Daniel, 28507
Breuer, Mordechai, 27916, 27941
Brind, Herb, 28851
Brit Ivrit Olamit, 28011
Broch, Hermann, 28669
Brock-Sulzer, Elisabeth, 28814
Brocke, Edna, 28025, 28166
Brocke, Michael, 28367
Brod, Max, 28505, 28666–28667, 28964, 28969
Bronowski, Alexander, 28243
Broszat, Martin, 28225
Brothers, Eric, 28445, 28490
Browder, George C., 28244
Browning, Christopher, 28278
Bruckner, D.J.R., 28793
Brüggen, 28114
Brühl, Georg, 28638
Brünnel, Gabriele, 27987
Bruer, Albert A., 27923
Bruha, Antonia, 28396
Bruhns, Maike, 28050
Brumlik, Micha, 27941, 28717, 28845
Buber, Martin, 28299, 28505, 28507–28514,

28519, 28533, 28554, 28559, 28561, 28635, 28637, 28969
Buchenwald, 28245
Budapest, 28828
— Rabbinical Seminar, 28173
Buddensieg, Tilmann, 28765
Büchler, Yehoshua, 28255
Büttelborn, 28246
Büttner, Ursula, 28050
Bukowina, 28132
Bulau, Doris, 28459
Bulgaria, 28328
'Bulletin de Vernuches', 28685
Burckhardt, Carl J., 28254
Burleigh, Michael, 28247
Burmeister, Helmut, 28057
Burmeister, Karl Heinz, 28183, 28125, 28127–28128
'Burschenschaftliche Blätter', 28935
Buscher, Frank M., 28474
Busek, Erhard, 28132

Cabbala, 27941
Cahiers d'Études Germaniques', 28963
Calder III, William, 28759
Calhoon, Kenneth S., 28950
Campe, Julius, 28725
Cancik, Hubert, 28969
Cancik-Lindemaier, Hildegard, 28969
Canetti, Veza, 28972
Caricatures, Jews depicted in, 28006, 28497, 28927
Carlebach, Julius, 27975, 28199, 28489
Carmel, Alex, 28597, 28617
Caron, Vicki, 28281
Caspary, Eugen, 28079
Cassel Family, 28178, 28194
Cassell, Sir Ernest, 28178
Cassirer Family, 28638
Cassirer, Ernst, 28050, 28555, 28696
Catalogues, of Exhibitions, 27943, 28000, 28081, 28166–28167, 28294, 28377, 28418, 28432, 28584, 28591, 28683, 28762
'Cathedra', 28597
Cattle Trade, 28039, 28220
Cavaglion, Alberto, 28341
'CC-Blätter', 28623
Celan, Paul, 28644, 28697
Cemeteries, 27943, 27999, 28002, 28023, 28041, 28056, 28097, 28105–28107, 28110, 28154, 28168, 28208, 28367, 28773
'Central European History', 28122
Centralverein dt. Staatsbürger Jüd. Glaubens (C.V.), 28563, 28567, 28570, 28572, 28579
Cermak, Josef, 28667
Cesarani, David, 27975
Chapman, Stanley D., 27975
Charny, Israel W., 28209
Chassidism see Hasidism

Christ, Karl, 28639
Christensen, Erik M., 28378
Church and Synagogue, 27957, 28880, 28883, 28941
Church, Christians and Jews, 28116, 28882, 28888, 28908
— Nazi Period, 28248, 28299, 28399, 28830, 28868, 28889
— Post War, 28314, 28459, 28476, 28878–28879, 28884–28886, 28932, 28941
Cillia, Rudolf de, 28895
Claussen, Detlev, 28268
Cocks, Geoffrey, 28640
Coesfeld, 28015
Cohen, Evelyn M., 28565
Cohen, Gerson D., 28204
Cohen, Hermann, 27941, 28515
Cohen, Jeremy, 28881, 28911
Cohen, Susie, 28214
Cohn-Sherbok, Dan, 28329
Cologne, 28016–28017, 28249
Comenius, Jan Amos, 28154
'Commentary', 28531, 28916
Communists, 28452, 28658, 28809, 28842–28843
Como, Frank, 28749
Concentration Camps, Ghettos, 28050, 28221–28222, 28234–28235, 28240, 28251, 28262, 28279–28280, 28284, 28297–28298, 28302, 28313, 28343, 28353, 28355–28356, 28360, 28368, 28372, 28376–28377, 28392, 28394, 28396, 28411, 28416, 28432, 28434, 28438, 28453, 28455, 28479, 28974
Congdon, Lee, 28171
Conversion from Judaism, Baptism, 27914, 27916, 27969, 28399, 28695, 28787
Cordt, Uwe, 28114
Coulmas, Corinna, 28852
Cracow, 28132
Crone, Michael, 28448
Cuxhaven, 28019
Czech, Danuta, 28221
Czechoslovakia (see also Bohemia; Prague; Slovakia), 28157, 28169, 28328, 28810

Dachau, 28251, 28455, 28820
Dacre, Lord of Glanton, 28334
Dahrendorf, Ralf, 28323
Dale Jones, Priscilla, 28252
Dalma, Alfons, 28132
Dan, Joseph, 27941
Danzig, 28253–28254
Darmaun, Jacques, 28963
Darmstadt, 28020
Daviau, Donald G., 28666
Davidheiser, James C., 28653
Davidson, Jillian, 27975
(Der) Davidstern, 27924; 28116, 28118, 28160, 28227, 28239, 28260, 28351, 28369, 28423–28424, 28581, 28615, 28880, 28883

Dawidodowicz, Lucy, 28204, 28337
Daxelmüller, Christoph, 28050
Dederke, Karlheinz, 28765
Dekel, Sheila Cohn, 28222
Demandt, Alexander, 28481, 28759
Demetz, Peter, 28666
Demography, Statistics, 27963, 28003
Denmark, Nazi Period (see also Scandinavia), 28243, 28328
— Refugees, 28187
Department Stores, 28823
Deportations, 28050, 28220, 28242, 28255–28258, 28290, 28301, 28341–28342, 28419
Dettmer, Frauke, 28019
Deutsch, Helene, 28670, 28698
Deutsch, Werner, 28781
'Deutsche Vierteljahrsschrift f. Literatur u. Geistesgesch.', 28687
Deutschkron, Inge, 28237, 28874
'Dialog', 28206
Diamant, Adolf, 28109, 28286
Dick, Lutz, 28380
Dicker-Brandeis, Friedl, 28250, 28430–28431, 28437
'Die Zeit', Hamburg, 28647, 28696, 28976, 28983
Diers, Michael, 28788
Dietermann, Klaus, 28105–28106
Diezel, Peter, 28644
Dilcher, Gerhard, 27941
Dimension des Völkermords, 28328
'Dimensions', 28275, 28285, 28303, 28317, 28395, 28853
Diner, Dan, 27980, 28225, 28259, 28278, 28312–28313
Dinner, Chava, 28210
Dinnerstein, Leonard, 28911
Dinstühler, Horst, 28114
Dipper, Christoph, 28318
Directories, Lists of Names, 28001
Dispeck, David, 28036
Displaced Persons, 28454, 28460, 28464, 28485
Doane, Heike A., 28653
'Doat', 28513
Döblin, Alfred, 28556, 28653, 28669, 28699
Döhring, Sieghart, 28762
Dohm, Christian Wilhelm von, 28951
Dokumentationsarchiv d. Österr. Widerstandes, 28309, 28396
Dombrowski, Thomas, 28591
Domke, Eliezer, 28043
Donat, Helmut, 28314
Doneson, Judith E., 28499
Dorhs, Michael, 28057
Doron, Joachim, 27925
Dorsten, Dokumentationszentrum f. jüd. Geschichte, 27924
Dostoevsky, Feodor M., 28952
Dothan, Esther, 27926

Dove, Richard, 28644
Dreisbach, Martina, 28353
Dresden, 28260
'Dresdner Hefte', 28100
Drexler, Siegmund, 28286
Dreyfus, Hubert L., 28737
Dreyfuss, Louis, 28261
Dubnow, Simon, 28519
Dülken, 28114
Düsseldorf, 28459, 28683
Düwell, Kurt, 28912
'Dunera News', 28185
Duwidowitsch, Ljudmilla, 28489
Dwork, Debórah, 28262

Early Modern Period (Pre-Enlightenment), 27969, 27980, 28031, 28121–28122, 28160, 28516, 28566, 28881, 28911
Eastern Jewry, 27980, 27985, 28120, 28906
Ebbinghaus, Angelika, 28315
Eckert, Willehad Paul, 28912
Eckstein, Eric, 28185
Edelheit, Abraham J., 28211, 28263
Edelheit, Hershel, 28211, 28263
Edenkoben, 28021
Education, 27948, 27971, 27993, 27998, 28001, 28050, 28055, 28080, 28094, 28140, 28440–28441, 28564
Eger Family, 28013, 28803
Eggebrecht, Axel, 28634
Ehrenberg, Victor, 28639
Ehrlich, Edith, 28373
Ehrlich, Ernst Ludwig, 28879
Ehrlich, Ernst Ludwig (Festschrift), 28882
Eichmann, Adolf, 28264, 28299, 28370
Eichmann, Bernd, 28245
Eichmann, Johanna S., 27924, 28880
Eickhoff, Friedrich-W., 28486
Eidelbert, Shlomo, 28121
Eifel, 28220
Eigenwald, Rolf, 28050
'Einst und Jetzt', 28928
Einstein, Carl, 28700
Eisenberg-Bach, Susi, 28645
Eisenstadt, Meir, 28516
Eisler, Hanns, 28643
Eissing, Uwe J., 28092, 28951
'Eit-Mol', 27969, 28521, 28544, 28612
Elberfeld, 28022, 28860
Eleazar ben Judah of Worms, 28517
Elias, Julius, 28378
Elias, Norbert, 28701
Eliav, Mordechai, 28598
Eliezer ben Nathan of Mainz, 28518
Ellenson, David, 28529
Eloni, Yehuda, 28599
Emancipation, 27915–27916, 27920–27921, 27923, 27929–27930, 27932, 27936, 27941, 27953, 27959, 27966–27968, 27972, 27980,

28005, 28022, 28055, 28123, 28135, 28459, 28860, 28906, 28966
Emden, Jacob, 27941
Emigration, 28050, 28179, 28192, 28259, 28265, 28267, 28446
(Die) Emigration der Wissenschaften nach 1933, 28267
Emsland, 28092
Endelman, Todd M., 27975
Endres, Elisabeth, 28637
Engel (Holland), Eva (J.), 27927–27928, 28050, 28536–28537, 28758
Engelbrecht, Jörg, 28114
Enlightenment, 27923, 27927–27928, 27935, 27943, 27955, 27980, 28007, 28009, 28535, 28951, 28959
Eppe, Heinrich, 28750
Eppingen, 28023
Epstein, Catherine, 28184
Erb, Rainer, 28459, 28498, 28899–28901, 28907
Ermarth, Michael, 28793
Ermland, 28269
Ernst, Heiko, 28641
Eschnerberg (Liechtenstein), 28183
Eschwege, Helmut, 28642, 28804
Essen, 28024–28026
Esslingen Mahzor, 28565
Estermann, Alfred, 28634
Es waren so wenige; Retter im Holocaust, 28243
Ettinger, Shmuel, 28519
'Etudes Germaniques', 27984
Euchel, Isaac, 28535
Eulenburg-Hertefeld, Philipp Fürst zu, 28943
Eupen/Malmedy, 28220
'Europäische Ideen', 28776
'European History Quarterly', 28464
'European Judaism', 28467, 28724
Euskirchen, 28220
Euthanasia, 28291
'Evangelische Kommentare', 27930, 28099
Evans, Richard, 28853
Exenberger, Herbert, 28702
(Das) Exil der Kleinen Leute, 28265
Exil. Forschung, Erkenntnisse, Ergebnisse, 28644
'Exil', 28644, 28685, 28794
Exile (see also Emigration, Refugees), 28190, 28266, 28651
— Literature and Arts, 27975, 28050, 28270, 28412, 28592, 28628, 28643–28653, 28671, 28743, 28793, 28800, 28807, 28822, 28986
— Theatre, Film, 27975, 28644, 28746, 28802
'Exilforschung, Int. Jahrbuch', 28643
Exiltheater und Exildramatik 1933–1945, 28644
Eybl, Franz M., 28908

Faassen, Dina van, 28081
Fackenheim, Emil L., 28549, 28554, 28557
Faerber, Meir Marcell, 28805, 28973
Faktor, Emil, 28666

Falk, Zeev W., 27941
Falkensohn-Behr, Isachar, 27916
Fassbinder, Rainer W., 28905
Fassmann, Maya, 28050
Fatran, Gila, 28157
Faure, Ulrich, 28822
Feinberg, Anat, 28875
Feld, Hans, 28406
Feld, Willi, 28108
Feldman, Gerald D., 28765
Feldmann, Else, 28702
Fellner, Fritz, 28184
'Feminist Studies', 28345
Ferenczi, Sandor, 28656
Ferramonti, 28343
Festschrift, 28384, 28582, 28743, 28882, 28947
Feuchtwanger, Lion, 28505, 28653, 28703, 28806, 28807
Feuchtwanger, Marta, 28806
Feuerbach, Anselm, 28553
Fichtmann Family, 28415
Fiedler, Leonhard M., 28644
Final Solution (see also Holocaust), 28232, 28233, 28243, 28271–28277, 28311, 28330, 28350, 28358, 28369–28370, 28868, 28929
Fink, Ida, 28974
Finland, Refugees, 28187
Fischer, Alfred Joachim, 28151, 28808
Fischer, Jens Malte, 28760
Fischer, Klaus, 28267
Fischer, Ruth, 28809
Fischer-Brühl, Brigitte, 28283
Fischman, Dennis, 28753
Fisher, Josey G., 28810
Fittko, Lisa, 28446
Flechtheim, Ossip K., 28704, 28705
Fleming, Gerald, 28197
Flensburg, 28101
Förster, Bernhard, 28943
Forced Labour, 28012, 28262, 28279, 28280, 28298, 28350, 28376, 28974
Foregger, Richard, 28335
Formstecher, Salomon, 28520
Foschepoth, Josef, 28488
Fox, John P., 27975
Fox, Thomas C., 28854
France, Nazi Period, 28302, 28328, 28404
— Refugees, 28190, 28261, 28265, 28281–28282, 28301–28302, 28341, 28354, 28390, 28404, 28449, 28685, 28700, 28813, 28815, 28987
Franconia, 28002, 28027–28029, 28059, 28283
Franger, Gaby, 28283
Frank, Anne, 28284–28285, 28416, 28811
Frank, Jacob, 28984
Frankel, William, 28870
Frankfurt am Main, 27941, 28030–28033, 28286–28288, 28588, 28905
— Jüdisches Museum, 28437, 28459, 28584
Frankfurt School, 28717

'Frankfurter Allg. Zeitung', 28328, 28438, 28744
'Frankfurter Hefte', 28763
'Frankfurter Judaistische Beiträge', 28546
Frankfurter, David, 28505
Frankiewicz, Bogdan, 28393
Freeden, Herbert, 28288, 28398, 28812
Freedman, Norbert, 28743
Frei, Norbert, 28231
Freidenreich, Harriet Pass, 28143–28144
Freiling, Harald, 28070
Freimark, Peter, 27924, 27940, 28045, 28050–28051, 28198, 28200
Freise, Judith, 28287
Freud, Anna, 28670, 28946
Freud, Martha, 28050
Freud, Sigmund, 28147, 28636, 28656, 28698, 28706–28712, 28847, 28946, 28950, 28969, 28713
Freund, Florian, 28309, 28453
Frey, Winfried, 27941, 28910
Fried, Erich, 28663, 28714
Fried-Boswell, Catherine, 28714
Friedell, Egon, 28637, 28715
Frieden, Ken, 28716
Friedenthal-Haase, Martha, 28561
Friedhaber, Zvi, 28566
Friedländer, Saul, 28225, 28312, 28330, 28813, 28852
Friedlander, Albert H., 27975, 28258
Friedlander, Henry, 28420
Friedman, Isaiah, 28600
Friedmann, Maurice, 28508
Friedrichs, Christopher R., 28031, 28122
Friedrichstadt, 28101
Friesel, Evyatar, 28567
Fröbe, Rainer, 28280
Frohn, Axel, 28491
Fromm Family, 28034
Fromm, Erich, 28717
Fuchs, Konrad, 28440
Fürth, 28034–28036, 28289, 27967
Fürth, Henriette, 28569
Fürth, Jüdisches Regionalmuseum, 28036
'Fürther Heimatblätter', 28034
Fuks-Mansfeld, Rena G., 28450
Fulda, 28290
Funke, Manfred, 28306
Funkenstein, Amos, 27916
Furtmüller, Lux, 28204

Galicia, 28126, 28132, 28138
Gallagher, Hugh G., 28291
Gans, Eduard, 28718–28719
Garbe, Detlef, 28050
Garber, Zev, 28558
Gauss, Karl-Markus, 28986
Gehler, Fred, 28746
Geiger, Ludwig, 28720
Geisel, Eike, 28681

Geisler, Thilo, 28309
Geiss, Imanuel, 28316
Gelber, Yoav, 28243
Geldern, 28037
'Geldrischer Heimatkalender', 28063
Gellately, Robert, 28292
Gelman, Sofia, 28605
Gemünd, 28220
Gemünden, 28293
'Genealogisches Jahrbuch', 28801
Genealogy, 27921, 28027, 28036, 28801, 28803
Genocide, 28209
Gerlach, Wolfgang, 28906
Gerling, Heinz, 28552
German Democratic Republic, 28245, 28265, 28459, 28470, 28489, 28490, 28756, 28796, 28804, 28827, 28850, 28854, 28930, 28942
German Historical Institute London, 'Bulletin', 27975
'German Life & Letters', 28709, 28854
'(The) German Quarterly', 28324, 28723, 28861, 28950
German Re-Unification, 28487, 28850, 28853, 28855, 28856–28857, 28870, 28911, 28917
'German Studies Review', 28292
German-Israeli Relations, 28459, 28871, 28874, 28876, 28877, 28976
German-Jewish Relations (see also Antisemitism; Acculturation; Church), 27958, 27970, 28370, 28459, 28467, 28487, 28489, 28845, 28847, 28849, 28851, 28854–28855, 28857, 28866, 28871, 28873, 28955, 28982
Germania Judaica, Köln, 28459
'Germanisch-Romanische Monatsschrift', 27992
Germany (see also Early Modern Period; Enlightenment; German Democratic Republic; German Re-Unification; Imperial Germany; Middle Ages; Weimar Republic),
— Immigration, 28459, 28489
— Post War, 27941, 28050, 28092, 28314, 28366, 28454–28489, 28493–28495, 28845, 28848, 28852–28854, 28858, 28867, 28869–28870, 28873, 28899, 28932, 28936, 28982
— Remigration, 28469, 28484, 28489
Gershom b. Judah Me'or Ha-Golah (of Mainz), 28521
Geschichte als Trauma (Festschrift Hans Keilson), 28743; 28463, 28486, 28496, 28819, 28872, 28931
'Geschichte in Köln', 28249
'Geschichte in Wissenschaft und Unterricht', 27974, 28328
'Geschichte Lernen', 28497, 28501–28502
'Geschichte und Gesellschaft', 28277
'Geschichte, Politik und ihre Didaktik', 28503
Geseke, 28117
Gesellschaft Minderheiten Schweiz, 28909
Gestapo, 28226, 28452
Gevelsberg, 28038

Giefer, Rena & Thomas, 28475
Gier, Albert, 28760
Giersch, Robert, 28034
Giesen, Bernhard, 28055
Giessen, 28039, 28294
Gilbert, Felix, 28184, 28204, 28721
Gilbert, Martin, 28295
Gilboa, Menuha, 28145
Gillis-Carlebach, Miriam, 27998
Gilman, Sander L., 27985, 28856, 28911
Ginsberg, Ernst, 28814
Ginzel, Günther Bernd, 28459, 28912
Glasner, Hans, 28912
Glatzer, Nahum N., 28204
Glogau, 28040
Glückel von Hameln, 27926, 28050
Godesberg (Bad), 28041
'Godesberger Heimatblätter', 28041
Goebbels, Günter, 28683
Goebbels, Joseph, 28890, 28902, 28926
Gödecke, Monika O., 28234
Goell, Yohai, 28210
Görlitz, 28296
Goethe, Johann Wolfgang, 28952
Götzinger, Catarina, 28522
Golczewski, Frank, 28328
Goldberg, Arnold, 28523
Goldberg, Oskar, 28505
Goldberg, Susanne, 28050
Goldman, Shalom, 28538
Goldmann, Robert B., 28857
Goldscheider, Franz, 28428
Goldschmidt, Georges-Arthur, 28815
Goldschmidt, Johanna, 28050
Goldstein, Jacob, 28297
Goll, Yvan, 28653
Gollwitzer, Rainer, 28066
Gomperz Family, 27921
Gordimer, Nadine, 28766
Gordon, David, 28138
Gordon, Louis A., 28601
Goschler, Constantin, 28858
Gosmann, Michael, 28001
Gottgetreu, Erich, 28602
Gottlieb, Maurycy, 28584
Gottlieb, Roger S., 28332
Gottschalk, Gerda, 28298
Gotzmann, Andreas, 28023
'Government and Opposition', 27975
Gower, David, 28020
Grab, Walter, 27929–27932, 27946
Grabherr, Eva, 28129
Gradenwitz, Peter, 28949, 28585
Graetz, Heinrich, 28546
Graetz, Michael, 27941, 27916
Grafinger, Christine Maria, 28664
Grahn, Gerlinde, 28196
Grass, Günter, 28976
Graus, Frantisek, 27942

Great Britain, 27959, 27975, 28178, 28194–28195, 28745, 28979
— Refugees, 27975, 28188, 28196, 28252, 28265, 28398–28399, 28402, 28406, 28644
Greece, 28328
Greenbaum, Kyla, 28775
Greenberg, Gershon, 28460
Greenberg, Karen J., 28184
Grefrath, 28114
Greid, Hermann, 28644
Greive, Hermann, 28912
Gresser, Moshe, 28707
Gries, Zeev, 28509
Grimm, Gerhard, 28328
Grimm, Reinhold, 28985
Grode, Walter, 28278
Grözinger, Elvira, 28871
Grözinger, Karl E., 27941
Grolle, Joist, 28913
Gronemann, Sammy, 28505
Gross-Gerau, 28042
Grossheim, Michael, 28777
Grosskurth, Phyllis, 28656
Grossman, Avraham, 28521
Grosspietsch, Jost, 28111
Grubel, Frederick, 28077
Gruber, Helmut, 28500, 28895
Grubrich-Simitis, Ilse, 28708
Grüber, Heinrich, 28299, 28399
Gründer, Karlfried, 27916
Gruenwald, Ithamar, 27941
Grundmann, Max, 28599
Grunewald, Michael, 28644
Gruppe, Heidemarie, 28818
Grynszpan, Herschel, 28380, 28384, 28417
'Guardian, Weekly', 28770
Günzburg, Mordechai Aaron, 27959
Gugenheim, Fromet, 28050
Guggenheim Levine, Lilo, 28300
Guggenheim, Julius & Lini, 28300
Guggenheim, Kurt, 28975
Guggenheim, Yacov (Jakov), 28203, 27933
Guggisberg, Hans R., 28721
Gumbel, Emil Julius, 28722
Gumpel, Lazarus, 28048
Gumpertz, Aron Salomon Emmerich, 28007
Guney, Erol, 28602
Gurs, 28301, 28302
Gutmann, Joseph, 28586
Gutmann, Walter, 28050
Guttmann, Simon, 28958
György, Konrád, 28172

Ha'Apalah, 28405
'Ha-Ma'yan', 28537
Haarmann, Hermann, 28646, 28744
Haas, Franz, 28666
Haas, Peter J., 28303

Haas, Willy, 28666
Haase, Norbert, 28359
Habe, Hans, 28653
Habsburg, 28149, 28147
Hackert, Fritz, 28769
Hackl, Erich, 28983
Hacohen Peli, Pinchas, 28911
Hadamar, 28304
'Hadoar', 27926, 28608
Härtling, Peter, 28648
Häsler, Alfred A., 28909
Haggadah, 28033
Hahn, Fred, 28151
Hahn, Joachim, 28023
Haider-Pregler, Hilde, 28644
Halakha, 27941, 28528
Hallo, William W., 28541
Hamacková, Vlastimila, 28154
'Hamaor', 27975
Hamburg, 27999, 28043–28051, 28198, 28200, 28305
Hamburger, Michael, 28816
Hamm, 28052
Hamm, Peter, 28771
Hammerstein, Franz von, 28381
Hanau, Solomon Zalman, 28524
Handbuch der Deutschen Exilpresse, 28650
Handelman, Susan A., 28525
Handke, Peter, 28815
Hanover, 28053, 28834
Hansen, Niels, 28876
Harburg, 28305
Hart, Judith, 28459
Hartenstein, Elfi, 28186
Hartewig, Karin, 27934
Harth, Martin, 28362
Hartmann, Jürgen, 28081
Haselstein, Ulla, 28709
Hasenclever, Walter, 28723
Hasenclever, Wilhelm, 28922
Hasidism, 27941, 28507, 28511, 28519, 28522
Haskalah, 27916, 28009, 28550
Hasubek, Peter, 28725
Hauben (Nevo), Joseph, 28952
Hauke, Reinhard, 28023
Havatzelet, Avraham (Yosef), 28528, 28534
Haverkamp, Alfred, 27980, 28112
Hay-Tatura Association, 28185
Hayoun, Maurice R., 27941
Hayyim of Engelberg, 27969
Hebel, Franz, 28743
Hebel, Johann Peter, 28953
Hebräische Handschriften, 28212
Hebrew Literature, 28212, 28574
'Hebrew Union College Annual', 28711
Hecht, Ingeborg, 28461
Hegel, Friedrich Wilhelm, 28862, 28954
Heiber, Helmut, 28306
Heid, Elisabeth, 28206

Heid, Ludger, 28005, 28098, 28205, 28749, 28906, 28912
Heidegger, Martin, 28697, 28777, 28862, 28955, 28956–28957
Heil, Johannes, 28032
Heilbronner, Oded, 28914
Heim, Susanne, 28278, 28326
Heimann, Eduard, 28665
'Heimat-Jahrbuch d. Kreises Altenkirchen', 28119
'Heimatbuch d. Kreises Viersen', 28403
'Heimatjahrbuch', 28096
'Heimatkalender d. Kreises Wesel', 28694
Heimler, Brigitte, 28724
Heimler, Eugene, 28724
'Heine Jahrbuch', 28725, 28729–28730
Heine, Heinrich, 27943, 28725–28731, 28952
Heine, Jens Ulrich, 28657
Heine, Salomon, 28050
Heinemann, Hartmut, 28056
Heinemann, Siegmund, 27995
Heitmann, Margret, 28040
Helin, Raphael, 28526
Hellenthal, 28220
Helmetag, Charles H., 28723
Henning, Diethard, 28926
Henningsen, Manfred, 28333
Hensel, Fanny, 28732, 28733
Herbert, Ulrich, 28278
Herder, Johann Gottfried, 28952
Herford, 28493, 28054
Herlemann, Beatrix, 28050
Herman, David, 28462
Herman-Friede, Eugen, 28447
Hermand, Jost, 28726
Hermann, Georg, 28270
Hermann, Ingo, 28806
Hermlin, Stephan, 28734
Herrmann, Dieter, 28115
Herschler, Moshe, 28517
Hershan, Stella K., 28307
Hertz, Deborah, 27959, 28005
Herz, Henriette, 27943, 28674
Herzberg, Arno, 28308
Herzberg, Wolfgang, 27934
Herzfelde, Wieland, 28647, 28817–28818
Herzig, Arno, 27935, 27936, 28050, 28205
Herzl, Theodor, 27941, 28147, 28505, 28603–28605, 28637
Heschel, Abraham Joshua, 28507, 28527, 28554, 28559
Hess, A., 28680
Hesse, 28055–28057, 28465
'Hessisches Jahrbuch f. Landesgeschichte', 28032
Hetkamp, Jutta, 28568
Heuberger, Georg, 28437
Heyl, Matthias, 28044
Heym, Georg, 28958

Heym, Stefan, 28669
Heymann, Fritz, 28819
Heymann, Werner, 28036
Hezekiah ben Jacob (of Magdeburg), 28528
Hilberg, Raul, 28312, 28330
Hildebrand, Klaus, 28328
Hildebrandt, Jörg, 28299
Hildebrandt, Klaus, 28795
Hildesheimer Seminary, 28325
Hildesheimer, Esriel, 28529, 28594
Hildesheimer, Wolfgang, 28735, 28736
Hilgenberg, Dorothea, 28808
Hilger, Marie-Elisabeth, 27937
Hill, Leonidas E., 28314
Hiller, Kurt, 28675, 28958
Himmler, Heinrich, 28272, 28275
Hinnenberg, Ulla, 28050
Hippel, Theodor Gottlieb von, 28959
Hirano, Yoshihiko, 28644
Hirsch Family, 28178
Hirsch, Baron Moritz von, 28178
Hirsch, Erika, 28050
Hirsch, Helmut, 28658
Hirsch, Samuel, 27964
Hirschfeld, Gerhard, 27975, 28328
Historians, 27975, 28184, 28201, 28267, 28530–28531, 28639, 28715, 28721, 28742, 28755, 28759, 28785
Historians' Debate, 28225, 28292, 28309–28324, 28853
'(The) Historical Journal', 28414
Historiography, 27919, 27935, 27950, 27952, 27957, 27958, 27974, 27981, 28170, 28175, 28184, 28204, 28292, 28313, 28320, 28546, 28867, 28904
— 'Revisionism', 28209, 28309, 28317, 28321
'(Das) Historisch-Politische Buch', 28005, 28205, 28364, 28422, 28426, 28657, 28749
'Historische Mitteilungen', 28316
'Historische Zeitschrift', 27978
'History and Memory', 28349
'History of Political Thought', 28954
'History Today', 28247
Hitlerflüchtlinge im Norden, 28037, 28187
Hobermann, Jim, 27986
Hoch, Paul K., 27975
Hochberg, 28058
Hochschule f. d. Wissenschaft d. Judentums, Berlin, 28551, 28325
Hochschule f. Jüdische Studien, Heidelberg, 28199
Hodann, Max, 28187
Hoechst a. d. Nidder, 27997
Hoedl, Klaus, 28126, 28132
Hoeffler, Karl-Wilhelm, 28076
Hoelzl, Alfred, 28965
Hönicke, Günter, 28050
Hoerstgen, 28037
Hofe, Harald von, 28807

Hoffer, Gerda, 28152
Hoffman, Joseph, 28027
Hoffmann, Anne Golomb, 28592
Hoffmann, Christhard, 27975, 28267, 28325
Hoffmeister, Reinhart, 28806
Hofgeismar, 28057
Hofmannsthal, Hugo von, 28659
Hofmeister, Wernfried, 28915
Hohenems, 28129, 28127, 28128, 28131
— Jüd. Museum, 28130
Hohenfeld, 28059
Holborn, Hajo, 28184
Hollywood, 28746
Holmes, Colin, 27975, 28402
Holocaust, 28213, 28215, 28243, 28263, 28291, 28326–28328, 28337, 28340, 28355, 28392
— Art, 28471
— Denial of, 28209, 28309, 28317, 28321
— Historiography, 28204, 28209, 28211, 28225, 28314–28315, 28322, 28333, 28336, 28338, 28420
— Knowledge, 28295, 28338
— Reaction, 28335, 28846, 28852
— Teaching, 28499, 28504
— Theological and Philosophical Impact, 28329, 28332, 28339, 28523, 28554, 28557, 28559, 28697
— Trauma, 28331, 28349, 28462, 28463, 28977
'Holocaust and Genocide Studies', 28226, 28232, 28233, 28255, 28335, 28392, 28397, 28474, 28852, 28967
Holste, Christine, 28969
Holzhausen, Hans-Dieter, 28720
Holzner, Johannes, 28653
Homann, Sabine, 28050
Homann, Ursula, 28001, 28459
Homeier, Jobst-H., 28501
Hope, Anne, 28491
Hoppe, Hans-Joachim, 28328
Horch, Hans Otto, 28205, 28782, 28953
Horkheimer, Max, 28643
Horney, Karen, 28670
Hornung, Annette, 28459
Hossfeld, Peter, 28693
Hoven, Herbert, 28266
Hsia, R. Po-Chia, 28911
Hügen, Ludwig, 28114
Hughes, Thomas, 28765
Humboldt, Alexander von, 28960
Hundert, Gershon, 28519
Hungary, 28171–28174
— Nazi Period, 28243, 28297, 28328, 28414
Huppert, Hilde, 28268
Hurwitz, Emanuel, 28859
Husserl, Edmund, 28737
Hye, Franz-Heinz, 28224
Hyman, Paula E., 28123

Ichenhausen, 28060–28061
Idel, Moshe, 28547
Identity, Jewish, 27941, 27947, 27949, 28132, 28147, 28189, 28204, 28265, 28340, 28484, 28556, 28560, 28601, 28687, 28707, 28712, 28713, 28739, 28741, 28752, 28755, 28757, 28786
Iggers, Wilma A., 28158
Ilsar, Yehiel, 28606
Immermann, Carl, 28725
'Immigrants and Minorities', 28374
Immigration, see Argentine, Australia, Great Britain, USA, Refugees
Imperial Germany, 27925, 27949, 27971, 27972, 27977, 28563, 28579, 28755, 28939, 28945
Imperial War Museum, 28236
Index of Articles on Jewish Studies, 28214
Industrialists, 27975, 28136, 28657, 28783
Industry, Jewish Workers, 27937
Innerhofer, Roland, 28715
Innsbruck, 28224
Institut f. d. Gesch. d. Juden in Deutschland, 27940, 28200
Institut f. Demoskopie, 28899
'Int. Archiv. f. Sozialgeschichte d. Deutschen Literatur', 28646
Interbellum und Exil, 28699
Internment Camps, 28185, 28685
(An) Interrupted Past, 28184
Irgun Olei Merkas Europa, 28607
Iserlohn, 28062
Isler, Emma, 28050
'Israel Nachrichten', 28831
Israel und Kirche Heute, 28882
Israel, State of (see also Zionism), 28210, 28265, 28484, 28495, 28602, 28615, 28619, 28628–28629, 28681, 28831, 28805
'(Der) Israelit', 27962, 28897
Israelitische Cultusgemeinde Zürich, 28909
'Israelitisches Familienblatt', 27962
'Israelitisches Wochenblatt', 28176, 28177
Issum, 28063–28064
Italy, Nazi Period, 28328
— Refugees, 28265, 28341–28343
Ivanová, Tatiana, 28153
Iwens, Sidney, 28820
'Iyyun', 28540
'Iyyunim be-Chinukh' ('Studies in Education'), 28515
Izieu, 28282
Izsak, Andor, 28587

Jabotinsky, Vladimir S., 28505, 28601
Jacobsen, Hans-Adolf (Festschrift), 28384
Jacobsohn, Siegfried, 28634
Jäckel, Eberhard, 28328
Jaeger, Lorenz, 28659
Jahoda, Marie, 28641
'Jahrb. d. Emsländischen Heimatbundes', 28092

'Jahrbuch d. Deutschen Schillergesellschaft', 28695
'Jahrbuch d. Freien Deutschen Hochstifts', 28787
'Jahrbuch d. Hist. Vereins f. d. Fürstentum Liechtenstein', 28183
'Jahrbuch Extremismus & Demokratie', 28900
'Jahrbuch f. Zeitgeschichte', 28449
'Jahrbuch f. Fränkische Landesforschung', 28074
'Jahrbuch Preussischer Kulturbesitz', 28202, 28960
Jamaica, Refugees, 28265
Janka, Walter, 28776
Jankowski, Alice, 27940
Jansen, Christian, 28722
Jarausch, Konrad H., 28660
Jaretzky, Reinhold, 28653
Jarka, Horst, 28779
Jasper, Willi, 27943, 28459, 28807
Jehle, Volker, 28736
Jersch-Wenzel, Stefi, 27938, 27980
'Jerusalem Studies in Jewish Folklore', 28027, 28509
Jessner, Leopold, 28654
'Jewish Art', 28430, 28586, 28588, 28664, 28752
'Jewish Book Annual', 28174, 28593, 28798
'Jewish Chronicle', 27975
Jewish Councils, 28313
'Jewish Currents', 28445
Jewish Historical Society of England, 27975
'Jewish History', 27922
Jewish Identity, see Identity, Jewish
'Jewish Journal of Sociology', 28941
Jewish Life in Germany, 27972
Jewish Problem, 27947, 28610, 28713, 28864, 28869, 28891
'(The) Jewish Quarterly', 28197, 28319, 28462, 28487, 28499, 28688, 28775, 28846, 28948, 28969
Jewish Question (see also Antisemitism), 28774, 28753, 28922
'Jewish Spectator', 28490, 28558
'Jiddistik-Mitteilungen', 27987
Jobst-Rieder, Marianne, 28791
Johann, Elisabeth, 27997
Johnson, Daniel, 28323
Joll, James, 27975
Jolles, Charlotte, 28399
Jonas, Hans, 28523
Jonca, Karol, 28382–28384, 28419
Jones, Ernest, 28656
Joos, Egbert, 28704–28705
Joseph, Albrecht, 28821
'Journal Geschichte', 28379
'Journal of Contemporary History', 28618
'Journal of European Studies', 28675
'Journal of Jewish Studies', 28514
'(The) Journal of Modern History', 28310, 28656

'Journal of Psychology and Judaism', 28355
Journalists, 28602 28808
Jucovy, Milton E., 28331
'Judaica Bohemiae', 28154; 28161–28164, 28429
'Judaica', 28381, 28523, 28879
Judaism, 27941, 27943, 28011, 28173, 28524, 28526–28529, 28547, 28553, 28559, 28862
'Judaism', 28527, 28543, 28548, 28554, 28578, 28739, 28866, 28918
Judaism, Jewish History, in Teaching, 28051 28098, 28545
Juden – Hessen – Deutsche, 28057
Juden im Deutschen Sprachraum, 27941
Juden in Deutschland, 27940; 27936, 27937, 27962, 27976, 27977, 27998, 28045, 28046, 28192, 28200, 28229, 28305, 28345, 28495 28569, 28621, 28626, 28848, 28913, 28938, 28945, 28953
Juden in Hamburg 1590–1990, 28050
(Die) Juden in ihrer mittelalterlichen Umwelt, 27942; 27982, 27989, 28112, 28134, 28137, 28590, 28888, 28904, 28908, 28910, 28915, 28919, 28921
Juden in Kreuzberg, 28012
Judenräte see Jewish Councils
'(Das) Jüdische Echo', 28132, 28151, 28172, 28190, 28522, 28624, 28632–28633, 28768, 28799, 28865, 28892
Jüdische Lebenswelten, 27943–27945
Jüdische Lebenswelten: Essays, 27946; 27931, 27960, 28181, 28340, 28483, 28583, 28585, 28611, 28884, 28940
(Das) Jüdische Museum in Prag, 28166; 28155, 28156, 28169, 28741
'Jüdische Rundschau', 28552, 28577, 28626, 28897
Jülich, 28065
Juelich, Dierk, 28463, 28743
Jüllig, Carola, 28012
Jütte, Robert, 27975, 28530
Juling, Peter, 28459
Jung, C.G., 28961
Juspa Halevy, Yiftah Joseph, 28121

Kabbalah, 28547
Kadarkay, Arpad, 28751
Kadish, Sharman, 27975
Kafka, Frantisek, 28159
Kafka, Franz, 28636, 28666–28667, 28738–28741, 28847, 28969
Kahane, David, 28356
Kahler, Erich von, 27947, 28665
Kahn, Franz, 28157
Kahn, Lothar, 28204
Kaienburg, Hermann, 28280, 28376
Kairlindach, 28066, 28067
Kaiser, Hans, 28114
Kaiser, Konstantin, 28836
Kaiser, Martin, 28293

Kalechofsky, Robert, 28655
Kalechofsky, Roberta, 28655
'Kalender f. d. Klever Land', 28072, 28348
Kalinski, Siegmund, 28286
Kalischer, Zevi Hirsch, 27959
Kall, 28220
Kambas, Chryssoula, 28685
Kamen, 28068
Kaminer, Isidor J., 28463
Kanarfogel, Ephraim, 27948
Kaniuk, Yoram, 28976
Kantorowicz, Ernst H., 28184, 28742
Kaplan, Marion A., 27949, 28344–28345
Kappel, Rolf, 28038
Kappes, Reinhild, 28421
Karavan, Dani, 28690
Karlsruhe, 28346
Karny, Miroslav, 28429
Kartell-Convent d. Verb. dt. Stud. jüd. Glaubens (K.C.), 28928
Kasischke, Daniela, 28050
Kassel, 28057, 28069
Kasser, Elsbeth, 28302
Kastein, Josef, 28505
Kasten, Ullrich, 28746
Kastner, Dieter, 28022, 28860
Kater, Michael H., 28184
Kattowitz, 28347
Katz, Barry M., 28184
Katz, Jakob (Jacob), 27941, 27950, 27959, 28531, 28881, 28916
Katz, Steven T., 28510, 28911
Kaufmann, Uri, 28124, 28175
Kaukoreit, Volker, 28714
Kayserling, Meyer, 27951
Keil, Martha, 28095
Keilson, Hans (Festschrift), 28743; 28463, 28486, 28496, 28819, 28872, 28931
Keller, Rolf O., 28234
Kelsterbach, 28070
Kemp, Paul, 28236
Kempen (Krs. Viersen), 28114
Kent, Evelyn Julia, 28416
Kent, George O., 28420
Kern-Ulmer, Brigitte, 28574
Kerr, Alfred, 28744
Kiel, 28101
Kierkegaard, Soren, 28635
Kieval, Hillel Josef, 28155
Kindertransport, 28265, 28300, 28399
Kinner, Klaus, 28809
Kinross, Robin, 28188
Kirchner, Peter, 28489
Kirsch-Schäfer, H., 28099
Kirschstein, Salli, 28586
Kirste, Reinhard, 28062
Kisch, Egon Erwin, 28666
Kissingen (Bad), 28071
Kitaj, R.B., 28752

Klarsfeld, Beate & Serge, 28282
Klee, Ernst, 28334, 28476
Kleeblatt, Norman L., 28588
Klein, Hans-Günter, 28202
Klein, Melanie, 28656, 28670
Kleinpass, Hans, 28096
Klemperer, Victor, 28260
Kleve, 28072, 28348
Kliner-Lintzen, Martina, 28442
Kling, Hermann, 28231
Kling, Simcha, 28608
Klitgaard, Brian, 28187
Klöpping, Karl, 28110
Klotz, Helmut, 28078
Kluger, Ruth, 28911
Knigge, Jobst, 27975
Knight, Max, 28189
Knight, Robert, 28492
Knilli, Friedrich, 28912
Knobloch, Charlotte, 28489
Knobloch, Heinz, 28238
Koch, Dieter, 28314
Koch, Edita, 28644
Koch, Gertrud, 28349
Koch, Ursula E., 28006
Kochavi, Arieh J., 28464
Kocka, Jürgen, 28225, 28765
Koebner, Thomas, 28744
Köhler, Ernst, 28278
'Kölner Zeitschrift f. Soziologie u. Sozialpsychologie', 28901
König, Frank, 28771
König, Joel, 28239
Könke, Günter, 28050
Koepke, Wulf, 28653
Koestler, Arthur, 28601
Kohl, Helmut, 28167
Kohlbauer-Fritz, Gabriele, 28132
Kohler, Eric D., 28400
Kohn, Michael, 28176, 28909
Kohnen, Joseph, 28959
Koht, Halvdan, 28378
Kollek, Teddy, 28619
Kolomea, 28132
Kommern, 28220
Konieczny, Alfred, 28347
Koopmann, Helmut, 28630
Kopitzsch, Franklin, 28051
Korda, Alexander, 28171, 28745
Korn, Salomon, 27941
Kornfeld, Paul, 28666
Kos, Jerzy, 28014
Kowno, 28394
Kracauer, Siegfried, 28665
Krach, Tillmann, 28661
Kratz-Ritter, Bettina, 28520
Kraus, Elisabeth, 27952
Kraus, Karl, 28637, 28767
Krauss, Friedrich Salomo, 28532

Kreisky, Bruno, 28895
Kreissl, Reinhard, 28278
Kreissler, Felix, 28449
Kreissler, Françoise, 28190
Krems, 28223
Kreuznach (Bad), 28073
Kroch, Ernesto, 28191
Krochmal, Nachman, 28546
Kröhnke, Karl, 28703
Krohn, Claus-Dieter, 28643
Krohn, Helga, 28569
Kromminga, Peter, 28050
Krondorfer, Björn, 28871, 28917
Kropat, Wolf-Arno, 28465
Krüger, Bernd, 27944
Krüger, Dirk, 28412
Kruglow, Aleksander, 28256
Kuczynski, Jürgen, 28776
Kühner, Claudia, 28173
Künzl, Hannelore, 27941, 28589
Kugelmann, Cilly, 28466
Kulik, Karol, 28745
Kulka, Otto Dov, 28154, 28225
'Kulturberichte', 28690
Kulturbund, Jüdischer, 28012, 28249, 28812
Kulturverein, 28718
Kunkel, Klaus, 28596
Kunreuth, 28074
Kuntze, Günter, 28103
Kurköln, 28114
Kurzweil, Zvi, 28515
Kushner, Tony, 27975, 28335
Kwiet, Konrad, 28350–28351

Ladenburg (Nordbaden), 28075
Lagnado, Lucette Matalon, 28222
Lamm, Hans, 28505, 28912
Landauer Family, 28029
Landauer, Gustav, 28969
'Landeskundliche Vierteljahrsblätter', 28107
Landesverband der Jüdischen Gemeinden in Hessen, 28582
Landsberg, Paul Ludwig, 28644
Landshoff, Fritz H., 28822
Lang, Fritz, 28746
Lang, Rudolf, 28977
Langbein, Hermann, 28243, 28352
Lange, Hermann, 27953
Lange, Nicholas de, 28911
Langenlonsheim, 28076
Langer, Burgel, 28459
Langer, Lawrence, 28336
Lanzmann, Claude, 28349
Laqueur, Renata, 28235, 28353
Laqueur, Richard, 28639
Laqueur, Walter, 28221
Lasek, Wilhelm, 28309
Lasker-Schüler, Else, 28505, 28655, 28747–28748

Laskier, Michael M., 28354
Lasko, Peter, 27975
Lassalle, Ferdinand, 28749
Lasserre, André, 28401
Latvia, 28911
Lauf, Peter, 28016
Lauritsch, Andres M., 28628
Lausch, Hans, 28007
Lavsky, Hagit, 28609–28610
Lazar, Moshe, 28911
Le Rider, Jacques, 28969
Lea, Charlene A., 28861
Lease, Gary, 28830
Lederer, Emil, 28665
Lee, Barbara Schwarz, 28355
Lefkovitz, Elliot, 28337
Legal History, 27920, 27941, 27953, 27956–27957, 28017, 28095, 28100, 28114, 28134–28135, 28137, 28420, 28883
Legal Professions, Jews in, 27941, 27975, 28193, 28218–28219, 28426, 28660–28661
Lehmann, Hans Georg, 28643
Lehmann, Hartmut, 28184
Lehmann, Menashe (Manfred) Raphael, 28526
Lehnsen, Heinrich, 28403
Leicht, Walter, 28415
Leimkugel, Frank, 28662
Leipzig, 28077, 28078, 28298
'Leipziger Volkszeitung', 27975
Lemberg (Lvov), 28132, 28356
Lempp, Reinhart, 28463
Lenzen, Verena, 28505, 28644
Leo Baeck Institute, 27972, 28267
— 'Bulletin', 28203; 28007, 28069, 28555, 28951
— 'Year Book', 28204; 27928, 28008, 28216, 28252, 28281, 28308, 28325, 28350, 28492, 28541–28542, 28563, 28567, 28570, 28572, 28579, 28613, 28640, 28660, 28668, 28858, 28914, 28922, 28971
— LBI Information. Nachrichten aus den Leo Baeck Institutionen
— London, 27975
— New York, 'Library and Archives News', 28204
— — 'LBI News', 28204
— Schriftenreihe, 27975
Leopold, Heiderose, 28459
Lepsius, Juliane, 28357
Lerner, Robert E., 28184
Leser, Norbert, 28132, 28136
Lessing, Fred W., 28204
Lessing, Gotthold Ephraim, 28861, 28950, 28952, 28962
Leuchter Report, 28321
Levenson, Jon D., 28511
Levi, Erik, 27975
Levi-Löwenberg Family, 28129
Levi-Sulzer Family, 28128
Levin, Meyer, 28978

Levin, Nora, 28358
Levinas, Emmanuel, 28525, 28862
Levinson, Nathan Peter, 28040, 28467
Levinson, Pnina Navé, 28884
Levitt, Cyril, 28570
Levy, Alphonse, 28588
Lewald, Fanny, 27959, 28947
Lewis, Bernard, 28911
Leyens, Erich, 28823
Libau, 28359
Libraries and Archives, 28187, 28197–28198,
    28200, 28202, 28204, 28336, 28720, 28944
Lichtblau, Albert, 28133, 28907
Lichtenstein, Heiner, 28459, 28468, 28477
Liebermann, Max, 28583
Liebeschütz, Hans, 28881
Liechtenstein, 28183
Limburg, 28079
Lind, Jakov, 28824
Lindheim, 27997
Lindner, Erik, 28089
Lindwer, Willy, 28284
Linnich, 28080
Lipman, Vivian D., 27975
Lipp, Johannes, 28114
Lippe, 28081, 28082
Lippstadt, 28083
Lipstadt, Deborah E., 28317
Lipstein, Kurt, 27975
Liptzin, Sol, 28798
Literary Studies, Jews in, 28378, 28637, 28663,
    28720, 28744, 28986
Literature, Hebrew, 27941, 28121, 28535, 28911
Literature, Jews Depicted in, 27918, 27941,
    27960, 27975, 28560, 28854, 28861, 28905,
    28910, 28911, 28915, 28921, 28927, 28952–
    28953, 28966
Literature, Jews in, 27959–27960, 27990, 28132,
    28133, 28151, 28601, 28644, 28655, 28667,
    28669, 28671, 28675, 28702, 28714, 28731,
    28735, 28740, 28743, 28747, 28791, 28797,
    28836, 28854, 28911, 28985, 28986, 28987
Lithuania, 27959, 28243, 28359
Littell, Franklin H., 28918, 28967
Litzmannstadt see Lodz
Lively, Adam, 28979
Livingstone, Rodney, 27975
Livné-Freudenthal, Rachel, 27954
Lodz, 28360
Loebl, Herbert, 27975
Lööw, Heléne, 28187
Loeper, Heidrun, 28268
Löw Beer, Nele, 28573
Loew, Ida, 28978
Loewe, Raphael, 27975
Löwenbrück, Anna-Ruth, 27955
Loewenson, Erwin, 28958
Löwenstein, Kurt, 28750
Löwenthal, Leo, 28646

Loewy, Ernst, 28643, 28651
Lohalm, Uwe, 28050
Lohrbächer, Albrecht, 28258
Lohrmann, Klaus, 28134, 28135, 28893
London, Louise, 27975
Longerich, Peter, 28273, 28438
Loos, Peter, 28633
Loose, Hans Dieter, 28046
Lorenz, Dagmar C.G., 28420, 28663
Lorenz, Ina S., 27940, 28050, 28305
Losa, Ilse, 28980
Lotter, Friedrich, 27956–27957
Lottmann-Kaeseler, Dorothee, 28120
Louven, Astrid, 28047, 28050
Lowenstein, Steven M., 27959, 28008
Lowenthal, Ernst G., 28200, 28562, 28573,
    28576
Lowy, Liesel, 28981
Lubarsky, Sandra B., 28533
Lubich, Frederick Alfred, 28966
Lucas, Eric, 27994
Lucas, Franz D., 28040
Lucas, Robert, 28653
Ludwig, Andreas, 28012
Ludwig, Hartmut, 28299
Lübbe, Katharina, 28364
Lübeck, 28101
Lück, Helmut E., 28050
Lüdenscheid, 28361
Lukács, Georg, 28171, 28669, 28751, 28825
Lukoff, Irving F., 28297
Luprecht, Mark, 28710
Lustiger, Arno, 28204
Luther, Martin, 28881, 28911, 28919
Luxembourg, 28328
Luxemburg, Rosa, 28658, 28678, 28752
Lyotard, Jean-François, 28955

Maas, Hermann, 28243
Maas, Lieselotte, 28650
Maass, Hans, 28258
'Machbarot le-Machshava Sotsialistit', 28594
Maegerle, Anton, 28279
'(Der) Märker', 27995, 28068, 28218
Magen David, 27924, 28615
Magnus, Shulamit S., 27958, 28017
Maharal, Rabbi Judah Loeb, 28154
Mahler, Gustav, 28637, 28826
Mahler-Werfel, Alma, 28826
'(Die) Mahnung', 28447
Mahr, Helmut, 28444
Maier, Charles S., 28225
Maier, David, 27975, 28406
Maimon, Salomon, 28519
Main-Spessart, 28362–28363
Mainz, 28521
Majdanek, 28479
Makarova, Lena (Elena), 28250, 28430–28431,
    28437

Malino, Francis, 27959
Malkin, Peter Z., 28264
Malzahn, Manfred, 28469
Mann, Erika, 28266
Mann, Heinrich, 28652, 28970
Mann, Klaus, 28266, 28505
Mann, Thomas, 28963–28966
Mann, Vivian, 28156
Mannheim, Karl, 28171, 28665
Manten, Johann Jakob, 28114
Marburg, 28084
Marcus, Ivan G., 27941
Marcus, Marcel, 28882
Marcuse, Herbert, 28717, 28956
Markovits, Andrei S., 28225
Marmur, Dow, 28559
Maron, Avraham, 28544
Marseille, 28987
Martin, Biddy, 28946
Martini, Joachim, 28287
Marwedel, Günter, 28050
Marx, Bettina, 28571
Marx, Henry, 28644
Marx, Karl, 28753
Masani, P.R., 28754
Masaryk, Thomas Garrigue, 28151
Maser, Peter, 28470
Massie, Allan, 28982
'Massuah', 28433
Matras, Yaron, 27988
Mattenklott, Gert, 27960, 28969
Matthaeus, Wolfgang, 28502
Maurer, Trude, 27961–27962, 27980
Mausbach, Hans, 28286
Mauthausen, 28422
Mauthner, Fritz, 28637, 28667, 28969
May, Georg, 28248
Mayer, Gustav, 28755
Mayer, Hans, 28756, 28827
Mayer, Reinhold, 28912
Mayzl, Marcus Mordecai, 28164
'MB', Mitteilungsblatt des Irgun Olei Merkas Europa, 28204, 28264, 28552, 28595, 28607, 28812, 28867
Mechernich, 28220
Mecklenburg, 28085
Mecklenburg, Frank, 28193
Medebach, 28086
Medicine, Jews in, 28084, 28286, 28400, 28539, 28580, 28640, 28673
Mehl, Stefan, 28365
Mehlhausen, Joachim, 28691
Meidner, Ludwig, 28583, 28958
Meineke, Stefan, 28542
Meir b. Baruch of Rothenburg, 28534
Melchior, Ib, 28366
Melson, Jens, 28187
Memorials, 28025, 28245, 28340, 28389, 28471, 28504, 28690

Menashri, David, 28911
Menasse, Robert, 28983
Mendelsohn, Oskar, 28328
Mendelssohn Family, 28674
Mendelssohn, Felix, 28637, 28757
Mendelssohn, Moses, 27916, 27927–27928, 27943, 28050, 28202, 28535–28537, 28758, 28952, 28962
Mendelssohn-Archiv, Berlin, 28202
Mendes-Flohr, Paul, 28611
Mengs, Anton Raphael, 28664
'Menora', 28205; 27915, 27918, 27953, 27968, 28117, 28412, 28493, 28604, 28620, 28627, 28720, 28830, 28949
Menzel, Wolfgang, 28730
Merchants, 27975
'Merkur', 28330, 28333, 28849, 28923
Meroz, Yohanan, 28877
Messianism, 27941, 28204, 28514, 28611, 28984
Mettmann, 28087
Metzger, Therese, 28590
Meyer, Beate, 28050
Meyer, Eduard, 28759
Meyer, Hermann, 28004
Meyer, Michael A., 28050, 28204, 28578
Meyer, Walter, 28013
Meyer-Moses, Hanna, 28258
Meyerbeer, Giacomo, 28760–28762, 28960
Michael, Reuven, 28009
Michaelis, Rolf, 28735
Michaelis-Stern, Eva, 28781
Michalski, Raoul Wenzel, 28050
Michels, Karen, 28050
Middle Ages, 27918, 27922, 27933, 27941–27943, 27948, 27956–27957, 27973, 27979–27980, 27982, 27989, 27991, 28000, 28032, 28068, 28095, 28112, 28114, 28134, 28137, 28140, 28517–28518, 28521, 28524, 28528, 28534, 28565, 28574, 28590, 28880–28881, 28883, 28888, 28911–28912, 28915, 28921
'Midstream', 28146, 28728
Miesbeck, Peter, 28415
Miklautsch, Lydia, 28921
Milch-Meyer, Gertrud, 28357
Milton, Sybil, 28420, 28471
Minsk, 28242
Mishnah, 28526
Misler, Andres, 28050
'Mit der Ziehharmonika. Zeitschr. d. Th.K. Gesellschaft', 28836, 28973, 28987
Mitscherlich-Nielsen, Margarete, 28912
'Mitt. d. Vereins f. Heimatkunde im Landkreis Birkenfeld', 28097
'Mitteilungen des Verbandes ehem. Breslauer in Israel', 28014
'Mitteilungen d. Vereins f. d. Geschichte Berlins, 28562, 28576
Mitten, Richard, 28895
Mixed Marriages, 27953, 28220

— Children of, 28298, 28461
'Mnemosyne', 28628, 28805
Mock, Wolfgang, 27975
'Modern Austrian Literature', 28663, 28985
'Modern Hebrew Literature', 28875
'Modern Judaism', 27958, 28322, 28354, 28511, 28547, 28549, 28553, 28707
Moers, 28367
Mohel Book, 28027
Molden, Ernst, 28132
Molitor, Matthias, 28073
Moll, Michael, 28368
Moltmann, Günter, 28192
Mombert, Alfred, 28505
Mommsen, Hans, 28225, 28274, 28278, 28280, 28312, 28369–28370, 28385
Mommsen, Theodor E., 28184
Mommsen, Wolfgang J., 28184
'Monatshefte f. Evangel. Kirchengesch. d. Rheinlandes', 28022, 28860
Money Lending, 27942
Monschau, 28220
Montabaur, Hilde, 28088
'Montfort', 28125, 28127, 28129
Monz, Heinz, 27964
Moog, Horst, 28119
Moore, Bob, 27975, 28374
Morad, Mirjam, 28532
Moravia, 28155–28156, 28170
Morgan, Michael L., 28543
Morgenstern-Wulff, Johanna, 28105
Morgenthaler, Sibylle, 28572
Morgenthau, Henry, 28485
'Moriah', 28517, 28526, 28528, 28534
Morocco, 28571
Morton, Frederic, 28653
Moser, Jonny, 28132, 28328
Moser, [Sir] Claus, 27975
Moses, Julius, 28763
Mosse, George L., 27965, 28863
Mosse, Werner E., 27975, 28050
Motokoff, Gary, 27963
Mühsam, Erich, 28675
Müller, Ingo, 28371
Müller-Luckner, Elisabeth, 28943
Müller-Wesemann, Barbara, 28050
Münster, 28472
'(Das) Münster am Hellweg', 28024
Müssener, Helmut, 28187, 28644
Muhs, Rudolf, 27975, 28100
Muneles, Otto, 28168
Munich, 28459
Munk, Moses, 28537
Museum, Jewish, Hohenems, 28131
Museums, 28010, 28025, 28036, 28130, 28586
Music, 27941, 28127, 28372, 28575
Music, Jewish, 28078, 28287, 28566, 28585, 28587, 28591, 28949
Musicians, Composers, 27975, 28050, 28287,

28585, 28591, 28637, 28679, 28732–28733, 28757, 28760–28762, 28789, 28826, 28960
Myers, Jody Elizabeth, 27959
Mysticism, 27941

Na'Aman, Shlomo, 28864, 28922
Naarmann, Margit, 28117
Naber, Claudia, 28050
Nabrings, Arie, 28114
Nachama, Andreas, 27943, 27945–27946
'Nachrichten f. d. jüd. Bürger Fürths', 28036, 28289, 28444
Name, Change of, 28046, 28627
Names, 28067, 28902
Naor, Efrat, 28011
Naor, Mordecai, 28612
Naphtali, Fritz Perez, 28622
Nationalism, 28148, 28863, 28941
Nationalsozialismus und Modernisierung, 28318
Nazi Crimes, Prosecution of, 28252, 28264, 28366, 28459, 28473–28481, 28488
Nazi Medicine, 28222, 28291, 28303, 28395, 28868, 28929, 28937
Nazi Period (see also Exile, Refugees), 28050, 28114, 28157, 28165–28166, 28218–28444, 28661, 28912
— In Film, Radio, Theatre, 28349, 28407, 28499
— Jewish Life in Germany, 27934, 27970, 27972, 28039, 28050, 28215, 28220, 28226, 28239, 28241, 28243, 28260, 28286–28287, 28298, 28300, 28305, 28308, 28344–28345, 28351, 28423, 28440, 28451, 28810, 28835, 28847
— Jewish Youth, 28440–28441, 28502, 28810
— Jurisprudence, 28371
— Latvia, 28829
— Lithuania, 28359
— Survival in Hiding, 28237, 28243, 28262, 28356, 28373, 28409, 28443, 28447
— Teaching, 28001, 28025, 28497, 28501–28504
— Universities, 28306
Nazi Politics and Propaganda, 28039, 28165, 28219, 28228–28229, 28232–28233, 28244, 28247, 28253, 28272, 28275, 28326, 28350–28351, 28365, 28370, 28375, 28380, 28386, 28424, 28426, 28433, 28439, 28570, 28572, 28810, 28890, 28912, 28914, 28929, 28934
'NDL, Neue Deutsche Literatur', 28734, 28838
Neersen, 28114
Nehring, Wolfgang, 28659
Neisser, Ulrich, 28641
Nelki, Erna & Wolfgang, 28373
Nemitz, Kurt, 28763
Nemschitz, Abraham & Joseph, 28223
Netherlands, Nazi Period, 28243, 28270, 28328, 28374–28375, 28450, 28645
— Refugees, 28403, 28416, 28811, 28819, 28822
Neto, Jose R. Maia, 28548

Nettetal, 28114
Neubaur, Caroline, 28923
Neuberger, Julia, 28670
'Neue Beiträge z. Jülicher Geschichte', 28065, 28080
'Neue Politische Literatur', 28889
Neuengamme, 28280, 28376–28377
Neugebauer, Wolfgang, 28309
Neuhaus-Koch, Ariane, 28947
Neumann, Erich, 28961
Neumann, Klaus, 28314
Neumann, Micha, 28961
Neumann, Moritz, 28582
'1991. Zeitschrift f. Sozialgesch. d. 20. u. 21. Jahrhunderts', 28315, 28338
'New German Critique', 28697, 28786, 28856, 28869, 28956
'New German Studies', 28970
New York, 28186
'(The) New York Review of Books', 28776
'New York Times Book Review', 28793
New Zealand, Refugees, 28265, 28794
Newman, Aubrey, 27975
Nicosia, Francis R., 28613
Nieburg, Reinhold, 28967
Niederland, Doron, 27975
Niedernburg, 28415
'(Der) Niederrhein', 28037, 28064
Niedhart, Gottfried, 28755
Nielsen, Birgit S., 28187
Nienburg, 28090
Niethammer, Lutz, 28312
Nietzsche, Friedrich, 28952, 28968, 28969
Niewiadomski, Józef, 28912
Niewyk, Donald L., 28420
Noah, Peter, 28258
Nolan, Mary, 28225
Nolte, Ernst, 28314
'Non-Aryan' Christians, 28299, 28399
Nordau, Max, 28614, 28637
'Nordbayerischer Kurier', 28029
Nordheimer, Isaac, 28538
'Nordisk Judaistik', 28085
North Africa (see also France, Refugees), 28354
Northey, Anthony, 28740
Norway, Nazi Period, 28328
Norway, Refugees, 28187, 28378
November Pogrom, 28001, 28220, 28238, 28244, 28259, 28358, 28379–28387, 28391, 28501
Nowinski, Ira, 28471
Nuremberg Laws, 28244
Nuremberg Trial, 28439, 28473, 28481, 28657
Nussbaum, Laureen, 28270
'NZZ' (Neue Zürcher Zeitung), 28173, 28248, 28254, 28266, 28270, 28639, 28713, 28721, 28760, 28771, 28807

Oberammergau, 28886
Oberwischau, 28413

'(The) Observer', 28262
Obituaries, 28204, 28724, 28735, 28595
Obst, Johannes, 28258
Och, Gunnar, 27966
Odenbach, 28589
Oedt (Krs. Viersen), 28114
Oegema, Gerbern S., 27924, 28160, 28388, 28615
Österreichisch-Jüdisches Geistes- und Kulturleben, 28136
Oestreich, Cornelia, 28050
Ofer, Dalia, 28616
Offenbach, 28091, 28286, 28520
Oldenburg, 28389
Olmerova, Helena, 28161
Onderdelinden, Sjaak, 28699
Ophir, Baruch Zwi, 27940
Oppenheim, Moritz Daniel, 28583, 28588
Oppenheimer, Alfred S., 28204
Oppenheimer, Franz, 28612
Orbach, Alexander, 28911
Organisations, 28050, 28065, 28305, 28440, 28456, 28459, 28563–28564, 28567–28570, 28573, 28579, 28624, 28928, 28939
— Refugees, 27975, 28406, 28607
Ort, 28573
Orth, Ernst Wolfgang, 28696
Orthodoxy, 27916, 27975, 28008, 28460, 28529
Ossietzky, Karl von, 28634
Ostow, Robin, 28850
Ostwald, Jakob, 28089
Otto, Eberhard, 28831
Otto, Roland, 28296
'Our Congregation (Belsize Square Synagogue)', 27975
Overy, Richard, 28262, 28319

Paál, Janos, 28673
Pabst, G.W., 28171
Padfield, Peter, 28275
Pätzke, Hans-Henning, 28172
Pätzold, Kurt, 28276
Palatinate, 28258
Palestine, 28149, 28265, 28405, 28597–28598, 28600, 28612, 28616–28618, 28620, 28625, 28627, 28631, 28831
— Refugees, 28223, 28530, 28607
Palme, Rudolf, 28137
Palmstierna-Weiss, Gunilla, 28790
Panayi, Panikos, 28194
Panofsky, Erwin, 28050
Papcke, Sven, 28643, 28665
Pape, Siegfried, 28442
Papenburg, 28092
Pappenheimer, Max, 28773
Paquet, Alfons, 28623
Parik, Arno, 28166
'Pariser Tagblatt', 28190

'(Das) Parlament', 27975, 28245, 28306, 28459, 28488
Pass, Walter, 28591
Patsch, Hermann, 28787
Patsch, Sylvia M., 28865
Paucker, Arnold, 27975, 28204, 28420, 28451
Paucker, Pauline, 27975
Pauley, Bruce F., 28924
Paulissen, Hermann Josef, 28080
Pawel, Ernst, 28666
Pawelzik, Fritz, 28390
Pazi, Margarita, 28666
Pechstein, Klaus, 28167
Pehle, Walter H., 28312, 28391
Pelikan, Johanna, 28895
Pelinka, Anton, 28132
Pelli, Moshe, 28535
Penslar, Derek Jonathan, 28618
Perelsztejn, Diane, 28407
Perlman, Laurence, 28510, 28512
Perz, Bertrand, 28279
Peter, Friedrich, 28895
Peter, Jan Henning, 28094
Peters, Leo, 28114
Petersen, Hans Uwe, 28037, 28187
Petersen, Peter, 28050
Petrasch, Friedrich, 27995
Peukert, Detlev, 28311
Pfabigan, Alfred, 28767
Pfäfflin, Friedrich, 28818
Pfanner, Helmut F., 28653
Pfeifer, Christiane Barbara, 28727
Pflanze, Otto E., 28184
Pforte, Dietger, 28654
Pharmacists, 28662
Philipp, Michael, 28301
Philosemitism, 28484, 28489, 28932–28933
Philosophy and Learning, Jews in, 28508, 28541, 28542, 28548–28549, 28553, 28555, 28635, 28637, 28644, 28678, 28688, 28696, 28709, 28737, 28753
Philosophy, Jewish, 27916, 28511, 28514, 28519, 28525, 28547–28549, 28635, 28706
Picard, Jacob, 28764
Picard, Jacques, 28909
Picciotto Fargion, Liliana, 28328, 28342
Pichler, Hermann, 28443
Pingel, Falk, 28280, 28392
Piper, Franciszek, 28280
Plaut, W. Gunther, 28866, 28984
Pöggeler, Franz, 28561
Poetry, 28744, 28782
Pohlmann, Klaus, 28082
Polacek, Josef, 28666
Poland, Nazi Period, 28243, 28255, 28271, 28328, 28387, 28410
Politics, Jews in, 27931, 27975, 28143–28144, 28364, 28632, 28765
Pollak, Felix, 28985

Pollins, Harold, 27975
Pomerania, 28393
Pommerening, Günther, 28102
Porat, Dina, 28394
Posen, 28093
Potsdam, 28459
Pracht, Elfi, 28249
Prague, 27943, 28151, 28158–28168, 28671, 28740, 28969
— Jewish Museum, 28166–28167
Prangel, Matthias, 28699
Prawer, S.S., 28731
Preisner, Rio, 28666
Press, 28006, 28831
Press, Jewish, 27962, 28138, 28145, 28288, 28308, 28457, 28466, 28571, 28577, 28599, 28626, 28631, 28845, 28897, 28969
Pressburger, Giorgio & Nicola, 28828
Presser, Ellen, 28459
Pressler, Mirjam, 28811
Prestel, Claudia, 27967, 28204
Preuss, Julius, 28539
Preuss, Monika, 28208
Prijs, Leo, 28212
Pringle, Annette, 28216
Printers, Hebrew, 28034, 28036
Prinz, Michael, 28318
Pritzlaff, Christiane, 28050
'Proceedings of the 10th World Congress of Jew. Studies', 27921, 27933, 27979, 28031, 28033, 28093, 28124, 28140, 28182, 28228, 28506, 28532, 28564, 28566, 28600
Proctor, Robert N., 28395
Prosch, Bernhard, 28002, 28942
Proskauer, Henry G., 28266
Proskauer, Paul F., 28744
Pross, Christian, 28937
Prussia, 27923, 27938, 28661, 28959
Psychoanalysts, Psychologists, 27975, 28050, 28641, 28656, 28670, 28691, 28698, 28708, 28711–28713, 28724, 28781
Publishers, Printers, 27975, 28145, 28647, 28672, 28676, 28793, 28822
Pulzer, Peter, 27975
Purin, Bernhard, 28128, 28142
Puttnies, Hans, 28686
Puyn, Alois, 28072

'Qesher', 28145, 28602
Quack, Sybille, 28184

Rabbinical Seminaries, 28325
Rabbis, 27939, 27959, 28045, 28050, 28520, 28544
Rabinbach, Anson, 28225
Racism, 28247, 28311, 28395, 28896, 28906, 28909, 28913, 28929
Raddatz, Fritz J., 28647, 28822

Radke, Rudolf, 28619
Rahe, Thomas, 27968, 28234
Randt, Ursula, 28050
Rathbone, Eleanore, 28398
Rathenau, Emil, 28765
Rathenau, Walther, 28765
Rauchenbichler, Ulrich, 28087
Ravensbrück, 28233, 28396
Rebmann, Jutta, 28732
'Recherches Germaniques', 28959
Recklinghausen, 28094
Reemtsma, Jan Philipp, 28278
Reform Judaism, 27939, 27941, 27968, 27975,
    28050, 28506, 28520, 28533, 28578
Refugee Policy, 27975, 28187, 28354, 28401,
    28405, 28485
Refugees, 28179, 28265–28266, 28307, 28374,
    28403, 28407, 28450, 28616, 28620, 28645,
    28840 28979
Regensburg, 28095
Regensteiner, Henry, 28728
Rehm, Gerhard, 28114
Rehwald, Ruth, 28412
Reich-Ranicki, Marcel, 28768, 28780
Reichsvereinigung d. Juden in Deutschland,
    28576
Reichsvertretung d. Juden in Deutschland,
    28440, 28562
Reif, Adalbert, 28925
Reijen, Willem van, 28684
Reimann, Bruno W., 28294
Reiner, Elchanan, 27969
Reines, Alvin J., 28711
Reinhardt, Max, 28644, 28654, 28659
Reinharz, Jehuda, 27970, 28610, 28620–28621
Reis, Stefan, 28293
Reisch, Elisabeth, 28871
Reisek, Jörg Julius, 28073
'Religious Studies', 28329
Remagen, 28096
Remigration, 28643, 28983
Remscheid, 28408
Renner, Gerhard, 28290
Renner, Ursula, 28659
Renoldner, Klemens, 28987
Renz, Ulrich, 28478
Resistance, Jewish, 28237, 28243, 28358, 28436,
    28445–28453, 28503, 28797
Resistance, Non-Jewish, 28209, 28220, 28238,
    28243, 28409–28411
Restitution, 28050, 28455, 28465, 28490–28496,
    28643
Re-unification see German Re-unification
Reuter, Ursula, 28018
Revolution and Jews, 27955
Rewald, Ilse, 28409
Rheinz, Hanna, 28060, 28459
Rhineland, 27943, 28098–28099, 28114
Rice, Emanuel, 28712

Richarz, Monika, 27971–27972, 28204, 28459,
    28867
Richter, Manfred, 28282
Riemer, Jehuda, 28622
Riesser, Gabriel, 27915
Riga, 28298
Ringer, Fritz K., 28668
Rischin, Moses, 27939
Ritchie, J.M., 28644
Rites and Ceremonies, 28114, 28162, 28532,
    28566, 28581
Rittner, Carol, 28885
Ritual Bath, 28161
Ritzebüttel, 28019
Roazen, Paul, 28698
Robel, Gert, 28328
Roberts, David, 28669
Robertson, Ritchie, 28147
Röcher, Ruth, 28105
Röhl, C.G., 28943
Röhr, Werner, 28278
Röll, Walter, 27987
Rössler, Peter, 28836
Rohde, Friedrich, 28694
Rohde, Saskia, 28050
Rohkrämer, Martin, 28314
Rohlen-Wohlgemuth, H., 28085
Rohrbacher, Stefan, 28927
Rohrwasser, Michael, 28644
Rohwer, Götz, 28278
Romania, 28328, 28413
Romey, Stefan, 28280
Rose, Paul Lawrence, 28414, 28729
Rosenberg, Hans, 28184
Rosenfeld, Alvin H., 28285
Rosenfeld, Ruben J., 28036
Rosenfeld, Sidney, 27972
Rosenfeld, Stella P., 27972
Rosenheim, 28415
Rosenstein, Gaby, 28909
Rosenstock, Werner, 28406
Rosenstock-Huessy, Eugen, 28541
Rosenthal, Malka, 27973
Rosenzweig, Franz, 28505, 28533, 28540–28543,
    28554, 28559, 28635, 28862
Rossmeissl, Ralf, 28035
Rotenstreich, Nathan, 27916
Roth, Ernst, 28212
Roth, Günther, 28180
Roth, John K., 28885
Roth, Joseph, 28505, 28766–28770, 28800
Roth, Karl Heinz, 28278, 28280
Rothkirchen, Livia, 28169
Rothschild Family, 28178
Rothschild, Berthold, 28909
Rotwelsch (thieves' cant), 27941
Rühle, Günther, 28744
Rühmkorf, Peter, 28714
Rülf, Isaac, 28544

Rürup, Reinhard, 27980, 28204
Runge, Irene, 28842
Rural Jewry, 27971, 27994, 28060, 28102, 28124, 28220, 28764
Russia, 28801

Sabelleck, Rainer, 28090, 28834
Sachs, Nelly, 28655, 28771–28772
Sack, Joel, 28251
Sack, Sallyann Amdur, 27963
Sadek, Vladimir, 28162, 28167
'Saeculum', 28545
Safrian, Hans, 28453
Sagmo, Ivar, 28187
Sahrhage, Norbert, 28493
Salamander, Rachel, 28217
Salberg, Wilhelm, 28912
Salinger, Gerhard, 28109
Sallen, Herbert, 28482
Salmen, Walter, 28575
Salmon, Yosef, 28138
Salomon Sulzer – Kantor, Komponist, Reformer, 28591; 28128, 28135
Salons, 28005, 28674
Salus, Carol, 28752
Sanders, Ivan, 28174
Sanders, W., 28886
Sarkowicz, Hans, 28448
Sauer, Paul, 28258
Saxony, 28100
Sayers, Janet, 28670
Scandinavia, Refugees, 28037, 28187
Schaber, Will, 28722, 28821
Schäfer, Barbara, 28604–28605
Schäfer, Klaus, 28000
Schäfer, Nikolaus, 28086
Schäfer, Peter, 28545
Schafranek, Hans, 28452
Schandl, Felix, 28887
Schaser, Angelika, 28139
Schatten, Fritz, 28459
Schatzberg, Walter, 27970
(Die) Schaubühne/Die Weltbühne, 28634
Scheffler, Wolfgang, 28257
Schieder, Wolfgang, 28312
Schiefbahn, 28114
Schild, Günther, 28390
Schilde, Kurt, 28240, 28447
Schildt, Axel, 28643
Schiller, Dieter, 28644
Schiller, Friedrich, 28952
Schimpf, Dorothee, 28055
Schindler, Thomas, 28623, 28773, 28928
Schissler, Hanna, 28184
Schleiden, 28220
Schleindl, Angelika, 28042
Schlenstedt, Silvia, 28653
Schleswig-Holstein, 28101
Schlich, Thomas, 28084

Schloss, Eva, 28416
Schlüter, Margarete, 28546
Schmalhausen, Bernd, 28411
Schmid, G. Bärbel, 28659
Schmid, Thomas, 28903
Schmid, Walter, 28909
Schmidt, Franz, 28021
Schmidt, Hans-Günter, 28361
Schmidt, Michael, 28927
Schmidt, Willi, 28114
Schmidt-Dengler, Wendelin, 28836
Schmidt-Hartmann, Eva, 28328
Schmieheim, 28102
Schmuhl, Hans-Walter, 28314
Schneider, Andreas, 28114
Schneider, Gertrude, 28829
Schneider, Hansjörg, 28644
Schneider, Richard Chaim, 28489, 28845
Schneider, Wolfgang, 28278
Schnitzler, Arthur, 28710, 28774, 28946
Schönberg, Arnold, 28637, 28775
Schönebeck, 28103
Schoeps, Hans-Joachim, 28819, 28830
Schoeps, Julius H., 27941, 27946, 27951, 28205, 28265, 28314, 28459, 28483, 28819
Schöttler, Gisela, 28087
Scholem, Gershom, 28507, 28519, 28525, 28547, 28626, 28636
Schoppmann, Claudia, 28649
Schorsch, Ismar, 28204
Schorsch, Rebecca, 28527
Schorske, Carl E., 28184
Schreckenberg, Wilhelm, 27974
Schreiber, Hellmuth, 28928
Schrijver, Emile G.L., 28565
Schubert, Kurt, 28888
Schütte, Leopold, 28218
Schütz, Hans, 28671
Schüürmann, Herbert, 28348
Schuhmacher, Klaus, 28695
Schuhmacher, Martin, 28364
Schulin, Ernst, 28184, 28765
Schulte, Paul Günter, 28114
Schulz, Karin, 28050
Schulze, Friedrich, 28672
Schulze, Hagen, 28225
Schulze, Peter, 28053
Schulze, Winfried, 28184
Schumacher, Kurt, 28474
Schutzjuden, 28050
Schwab, Gerald, 28417
Schwäbisch-Gmünd, 28104
Schwalmtal, 28114
Schwarberg, Günther, 28479
Schwarcz, Alfredo José, 28179
Schwartz, Daniel R., 28325
Schwarz, Angela, 28050
Schwarz, Erika, 28276
Schwarz, Freimut, 28776

Schwarz, Josef Jakob, 28894
Schwarz-Gardos, Alice, 28831
Schwarzschild, Steven S., 28548–28549
Schweinfurt, 28418
Schweitzer, Peter Paul, 28304
'Schweizerische Zeitschrift f. Geschichte', 28401
Schwertfeger, Ruth, 28747
Sciences and Mathematics, Jews in, 27975, 28132, 28267, 28722, 28754, 28839
Second Chance. Two Centuries of German-Speaking Jews in the United Kingdom, 27975
Sedinová, Jirina, 28154, 28163
Seebachgrund, 28028
Seemann, Brigitte, 28871
Seeskin, Kenneth, 28549
Seewann, Harald, 28624
Sefer Hasidim, 27941
Segal, Lilli, 28929
Seghers, Anna, 28643, 28653, 28669, 28776
Seib, Barbara, 28651
Seibt, Ferdinand, 28248
Seidel, Ortrud, 28104
Seidenberg, Hans, 28204
Seifert, Heribert, 28270
Selbmann, Michael, 28912
Seligmann, Rafael, 28484
Seligsohn, Julius L., 28576
Senfft, Heinrich, 28320
Sephardim, 28050, 28571
Sereny, Gitta, 28868
Shafir, Shlomo, 28485
Shamir, Haim, 28386
Shanghai, Refugees, 28265, 28407
Shapira, Anita, 28405
Shapira, Avraham, 28513–28514
Shapiro, Alexander M., 28518
Shapiro, Shelley, 28321
Sharfman, Glenn, 28204
Shatzky, Joel, 28434
Shedletzky, Itta, 28203
Sheehan, James J., 28184
Shlein, Margalit, 28433
Shmuel, Gan, 27925
'Shofar', 27983, 28144, 28204, 28507
'Shoraskim (Roots)', 28629
Showalter, Dennis E., 28420
Siati, de, Guiseppe, 28817
'Sichot – Dialogue', 28961
Siebenbürgen see Transylvania
Siebenhaar, Klaus, 28666, 28700, 28744
Sieg, Ulrich, 28555
Siegele-Wenschkewitz, Leonore, 28344
Siegen, 28105
Siegerland, 28106
'Siegerland', 28106
Siegismund, Walter, 28028, 28059, 28067
Siegler, Bernd, 28930
Sievernich, Gereon, 27943, 27945
Silbermann, Alphons, 28482, 28912

Silesia, 28040, 28419
Sillö-Seidl, Georg, 28673
Simmel, Georg, 28659, 28777, 28847
Simmer, Eberhard, 28625
'Simon Wiesenthal Center Annual', 28400, 28420, 28454, 28460
Simon, Bettina, 27989
Simon, Ernst, 28561
Simon, Heinrich, 28011
Simon, Hermann, 27943, 27976, 28010, 28050
Simons, Heinrich & Albert, 28218
Singen (Hohentwiel), 28421
Singer, David, 28531
'Skandinavistik', 28378
Skekely, Lajos, 28357
Skjoensberg, Harald, 28187
Slovakia, 28151, 28155, 28255
Smejkalova, Jana, 28164
Smith, Gary, 28686, 28687
Smith, Steven B., 28954
Sobernheim, 28107
'Sobótka', 28419
Social and Economic Development, 27933, 27937, 27962, 27966–27967, 27976, 28004, 28966
Social Reform, 28763
Social Sciences, 28021, 28136, 28180, 28267, 28562, 28665, 28701, 28704, 28753, 28777
Social Welfare, 27967, 28048, 28050, 28456, 28625, 28750
Socialists, Social Democrats, 27931, 28452, 28594, 28632, 28647, 28749, 28804, 28864
Society for Exile Studies, 28651
Söder, Hans-Peter, 28614
Söhn, Gerhart, 28730
Söllner, Alfons, 27975, 28267
Sofer, Hatam, 27959
Sofer, Moses, 28952
Sokel, Walter H., 28911
Sokoll, Gabriele, 28378
Sombart, Werner, 28659
Sommer, Fred, 28970
Sommerfeld, Aloys, 28269
Sonnenbluck, Henri, 28422
Sorkin, David, 27959, 28550
South Africa, Refugees, 28265
Soviet Union, 28328, 28452
Soyfer, Jura, 28778–28779
Spann, Gustav, 28309
Sparre, Sulamith, 28772
'(The) Spectator', 28323
Speier, Sammy, 28931
Sperber, Manès, 28641, 28653, 28832
Spiel, Hilde, 28682, 28780
Spinoza, Baruch, 28553
Spira, Steffie, 28833
Spitzer, Juraj, 28151
Spitzer, Shlomo, 28140, 28516
Spitzner-Jahn, Albert, 28037

Sports, Jews in, 27925, 28053
'Sprachkunst', 28797
St.Tönis, 28114
Stäbler, Wolfgang, 28415
Stamm, Christoph, 27975
'Standpunkt', Evangel. Monatsschrift, 28399
Starosta, Thomas, 28108
Stauffer, Paul, 28254
Steffen Pedersen, Minna, 28187
Stegemann, Wolf, 27924, 28423–28424
Stein, Edith, 28558, 28678, 28887
Stein, Erwin, 28494
Stein, Irmgard, 28048
Steinbach, Peter, 28503
Steinbeck, Udo, 28020
Steinberg, Georg, 28834
Steiner, Carl, 28420
Steiner, Herbert, 28632
Steiner, Sigmund, 28153
Steinfurt, 28108
Steinhardt, Menahem Mendel, 28506
Steinheim-Institut, 28205, 28206, 28459
— Wissenschaftliche Abhandlungen, 28040, 28520
Stekelenburg, Dick van, 28714
Stelbrink, Uwe, 28842
Stenberg, Peter, 27990
Stent, Ronald, 27975
Stephani, Claus, 28413
Stern, Frank, 28201, 28489, 28869, 28932–28933
Stern, Gabriel, 28505
Stern, Guy, 28644, 28653, 28911, 28934
Stern, William, 28050, 28781
Sternfeld, Albert, 28141
Stiefel, Ernst C., 28193
Stiefl-Cermak, Maria, 28243
Stöhr, Martin, 28459
Stölzl, Christoph, 28741
Störmede, 28117
Stöwer, Herbert, 28082
Stoll, Erich, 28097
Stolp, 28109
Stolz, Gerd, 28101
Stoop, Paul, 28375
Stopniak, Franciszek, 28410
Storfer, Berthold, 28405
Storr, Anthony, 28275
Strauss, Herbert A., 27975, 28267, 28297, 28577, 28626, 28925
Strauss, Ludwig, 28782
Streibel, Robert, 28223
Streicher, Julius, 28420
Streit, Christian, 28277
Strich, Michael, 28693
Ströle-Bühler, Heike, 28935
Strohschneider-Kohrs, Ingrid, 28962
Strousberg, Bethel Henry, 28783
Strube, Rolf, 28674
Stuchlik, Gerda, 28344

Studemund-Halévy, Michael, 28050
'Studia nad Fasczymen i zbrodniami Hitlerowskim', 28253, 28256, 28347, 28383, 28387, 28393, 28410
'Studia Rosenthaliana', 28450, 28565
'Studien z. Geschichte u. Gesellschaft Vorarlbergs', 28142
'Studies in Contemporary Jewry', 28609, 28965
'Studies in Zionism', 28210, 28601, 28610
Stumpf, Josef, 28131
Stuttgart, 28110, 28300, 28425
'Stuttgarter Zeitung', 27975
Suall, Irwin, 28936
Suchy, Barbara, 28216
Süchteln, 28114
'Süddeutsche Zeitung', 28637, 28926
'Südost-Forschungen', 28139
'Süss, Hermann, 28036
Süsskind von Trimberg, 27973
Suhl, Yuri, 28445
Sulz, 28142
Sulzburg, 28111
Sulzer, Salomon, 28135, 28591
'(The) Sunday Times', 28670
Sundhausen, Holm, 28328
Sunnus, Michael, 28426
Survival in Hiding, see Nazi Period, Survival in Hiding
Survival Syndrome (see also Holocaust, Trauma), 28486
Susman, Margarete, 28050
Sweden, Refugees, 28187, 28265
Switzerland, 28124, 28175–28177, 28859
— Antisemitism, 28909
— Nazi Period, 28427, 28975
— Refugees, 28265
Sydnor, Charles W., 28420
Synagogues, 27941, 28010, 28012, 28014, 28024, 28050, 28060, 28063, 28096, 28111, 28119, 28163, 28168, 28238, 28459, 28574, 28589
Sywottek, Arnold, 28495
Szczypiorski, Andrzey, 28978
Székely, Gábor, 28172
Szodrzynski, Joachim, 28050

Täubler, Eugen, 28639
Tarnow, Fanny, 28947
Tau, Max, 28675
Taylor, Ronald, 28789
'Tel Aviver Jahrbuch f. Deutsche Geschichte', 27919, 27925, 27929, 27935, 27938, 27950, 27954, 27955, 27961, 27967, 27971, 27981, 28003, 28198, 28201, 28470, 28550, 28606, 28755, 28784, 28864, 28891, 28964
Teller, Sonja, 28357
Teller, Y.L., 28716
Temkin, Sefton D., 28578
Teufel, Helmut, 28170
Thalmann, Rita, 28404

Theatre, Cabaret, Cinema, Jews in, 27986, 28181, 28633, 28654, 28683, 28745, 28792, 28802, 28821, 28823
Theiner, Eduard, 28058
'Theology', 28339
Theresienstadt, 28250, 28401, 28428–28437
Thiele, A.F., 27976
Thomas, Gina, 28323
Thomas, Laurence, 28322
Thompson, Bruce, 28774
Thomson, Philip, 28669
Thürich, Ursula, 28437
Thuringia, 27996
Tiggemann, Daniela, 28050
Timm, Erika, 27991, 27992
Timms, Edward, 28147, 28688
'TLS' (Times Literary Supplement), 27975, 28731, 28737, 28752, 28770
Todd, Larry R., 28757
Toews, John E., 28656
Toller, Ernst, 28644, 28835, 28675
Tomaszewski, Jerzy, 28387
Toury, Gideon, 28201, 28627, 28784
Toury, Jacob, 27977, 28201, 28579, 28627, 28784
Trade, Jews in, 27996, 28004, 28050, 28136
Transylvania, 28139, 28413
Trapp, Frithjof, 28644, 28743
Trautenau, 28150
Travers, Martin, 28675
Trebic (Trebitsch), 28154
Treml, Manfred, 28415, 28498
Treue, Wilhelm, 28657
Trevor-Roper, Hugh see Dacre, Lord
'Tribüne', 28871; 27916–27917, 27973, 28002, 28264, 28276, 28279, 28326, 28352, 28359, 28375, 28388, 28440, 28468, 28477–28478, 28482, 28504, 28625, 28631, 28673, 28772, 28796, 28831, 28876, 28877, 28917, 28942
Trier, 28112
Troller, Norbert, 28434
Tropp, Asher, 28195
'Trumah', 28199, 28551, 28589
Trzeciakowski, Lech, 28093
Tschoetschel, Michael, 28580
Tuchel, Johannes, 28240, 28438
Tucholsky, Kurt, 28634
Turkey, Refugees, 28265, 28267
Tyrol, 28137
'Tzfunot: Tora Quarterly', 28516, 28524

Ueckert, Charlotte, 28050
Uhlig, Ralph, 28364
Ullmann, Hanni, 28625
Ullrich, Volker, 28338, 28480, 28785
Ullstein Family, 28676
Ulm, 28113
Ulrich, Jochem, 28114
'Una Sancta', 28886

'Universitas', 28925
Universities and Jews, 28016, 28084, 28306, 28623– 28624, 28668, 28722, 28928, 28935
Unterbalbach, 28773
Urspringen, 28362
Uruguay, 28191
USA, Immigration, 28126, 28181, 28192
— Refugees, 28184, 28186, 28189, 28193, 28265, 28397, 28400
Utitz Family, 28152

Vahl, Heidemarie, 28714
Valder-Knechtges, Claudia, 28596
Valentin, Veit, 28785
Varga, László, 28328
Varnhagen, Rahel, 27943, 28655, 28674, 28786, 28787, 28911, 28947, 28948
Varon, Benno Weiser, 28146
Verein f. Cultur u. Wissenschaft d. Juden, 27954
Vergangenheitsbewältigung, 28324, 28338, 28487, 28492, 28844, 28848, 28867, 28873, 28894, 28933
'Vestische Zeitschrift', 28094
Vienna, 27943, 27986, 28132, 28143–28147, 28671, 28710, 28774, 28832, 28949, 28969, 28972, 28983
Vierhaus, Rudolf, 27916
Viersen, 28114
Viertel, Berthold, 28818, 28836
Vieth, Harald, 28049
Vilimkova, Milada, 28165, 28168
Villain, Jean, 28734
Vilna, 28453
Völker, Heinz-Hermann, 28551
Völkl, Bärbl, 28029
Vogt, Hans, 28064
Vogt, Rolf, 28872
Vogt-Heyder, Barbara, 28496
Voit, Friedrich, 28794
Volavková, Hana, 28166
Volkmann, Michael, 28561
Volkov, Shulamit, 27978, 27980, 28201, 28765
Volpe, Francesco, 28343
'Vom Main zur Jura', 27996
Voolen, Edward van, 27946
Vorarlberg, 28128, 28591
Vorst, 28114
Voscherau, Henning, 27940

Wachten, Johannes, 27941, 28033
Wagner, Gertrude, 28136
Wagner, Richard, 28637, 28729, 28943, 28971
Wahlich, Ulrike, 28005
Waldheim, Bruno, 28895
Waldinger, Ernst, 28986
Waldinger, Theodor, 28986
Walk, Joseph, 28203, 28440
Wallas, Armin A., 28628, 28797
Walldorf, 28115

Wallenberg, Raoul, 28243
Wallerstein, Susanne, 28837
Walter, Fritz, 28633
Walter, Hans-Albert, 28676
Walter, Rudolf, 28071
Walther, Gerd, 28035
Wamser, Ursula, 28044
Wander, Fred, 28987
Wandsbek, 28045, 28050, 28305
Wannsee-Conference, 28276
Warburg, Aby M., 28050, 28788
Warburg, Max, 28229, 28050, 28230
Warburg, Otto, 28618
Warsaw, 27943, 27984
Warsaw, Ghetto, 28797
Washburn, Sigrid, 28807
Wassermann, Henry, 28912, 28938
Wasserstein, Bernard, 27975
Waszek, Norbert, 28718–28719
Watanabe-O'Kelly, Helen, 28069
Weber, Ilse, 28435
Wedemeier, Klaus, 28242, 28314
Weglein, Rolf, 28061
Wegner, Werner, 28309
Wehler, Hans-Ulrich, 28225
Weidenreich, Franz, 28021
Weil, Simone, 28678
Weilburg, 28079
Weiler, Barbara, 28368
Weill, Kurt, 28644, 28789
Weimar Republic, 27972, 28016, 28043, 28171,
    28570, 28572, 28675–28676, 28832, 28911,
    28935, 28937
Weindling, Paul, 27975
Weiner, Hanna, 28629
Weinforth, Friedhelm, 28114
Weingarten, Ralph, 28177
Weinke, Wilfried, 28044
Weinlaub, Walter see Wicclair, Walter
Weinzierl, Erika, 28223
Weinzierl, Ulrich, 28836
Weirich, Hilde, 28097
'(Der) Weisendorfer Bote aus dem Seebach-
    grund', 28028, 28059, 28066–28067
Weiss, Anne, 28078
Weiss, Bernhard, 28902
Weiss, Ernst, 28666
Weiss, Hermann, 28328
Weiss, Ludger, 28278
Weiss, Peter, 28790, 28838
Weiss, Yfaat, 28441
Weissberg, Liliane, 28786, 28911
Weisskopf, Victor, 28839
Weissweiler, Eva, 28733
Weitz, Reinhold, 28220
Weizsäcker, Richard von, 28243
Weltsch, Felix, 28505
Weltsch, Robert, 28626, 28552
Wember, Heiner, 28480

Wende, Peter, 27975
Wenninger, Markus J., 27942
Wenzel, Edith, 28919
Werblowsky, R.J.Zwi, 27941
Werfel, Franz, 28505, 28653, 28666, 28791
Werner, Josef, 28346
Werner, Klaus, 28091
Wesel, 28694
Westermann, Klaus, 28769
'Westfälische Zeitschrift', 28089
Westphal, Uwe, 27975
Westphalia, 28089, 28116–28118, 28269
Wetzel, Juliane, 28328, 28944
Weyerbusch, 28119
White, Irene, 28840
Wicclair, Walter, 28792
Wickham, Christopher J., 28324
Wiedemann, Wilfried O., 28234
Wiehn, Erhard Roy, 28261, 28802
Wieland, Lothar, 28314
'(The) Wiener Library Newsletter', 28207
Wiener, Norbert, 28754
Wiesbaden, 28120
Wiesel, Elie, 28337, 28855
Wiesemann, Falk, 28581
Wiesenthal, Simon, 28453, 28895
Wietzorek, Paul, 28114
Wigoder, Geoffrey, 28677
Wild, Markus, 28088
Wilhelmus, Wolfgang, 28187
William II. (Emperor), 28943
Willner, Max (Festschrift), 28582; 28091, 28456,
    28465, 28494
Wimmer, Reiner, 28678
Windfuhr, Manfred (Festschrift), 28947
Wineman, Aryeh, 28593
Winkler, Heinrich August, 28312, 28912
Winnecken, Andreas, 28939
Wippermann, Wolfgang, 28247
Wirsbitzki, Brigitte, 28367
Wirth, Günter, 28299
Wirth, Wolfgang, 28912
Wischenbart, Rüdiger, 28132
Wissenschaft des Judentums, 27941, 28530,
    28551, 28718
Wistrich, Robert S., 28132, 28148–28149,
    28940–28941
Witte, Bernd, 28689
Witten, 28442
Wittenberg, Reinhard, 28942
Wittgenstein, Ludwig, 28147, 28637, 28841
Wittstadt, Klaus, 28889
Witzenbacher, Kurt, 28258
Wlaschek, Rudolf M., 28150
Wodak, Peter, 28895
Wodak, Ruth, 28895
Wolf, Arie, 28630
Wolf, Gerhard Philipp, 28074
Wolf, Joseph, 27959

Wolf, Markus, 28842, 28843
Wolf, Siegbert, 28326, 28504
Wolff, Kurt, 28793
Wolff, Uwe, 28266
Wolffheim, Elsbeth, 28652
Wolffsohn, Michael, 28328, 28459, 28873
Wolfhagen, 28057
Wolfskehl, Karl, 28794
Wolin, Richard, 28956–28957
Wollaston, I., 28339
Women, 27922, 27949, 27951, 27975, 28005, 28050, 28184, 28187, 28283, 28344–28345, 28396, 28569, 28649, 28655, 28670, 28682, 28732–28733, 28747, 28786–28787, 28946–28947
Wordsworth, Christopher, 28770
World War II and the Exiles, 28653
Worms, 28031, 28121, 28122
Wrobel, Hans, 28488
Wulf, Stefan, 28050
Wulff, Michal, 27993
Wuliger, Michael, 28459
Wyman, David, 28335
Wysocki, Gerd, 28280

Yad Vashem, 28243
'Yad Vashem Studies', 28914
'Yalkut Moreshet', 28157, 28230, 28386, 28427, 28485
Yaron, Kalman, 28561
Yerushalmi, Yosef Hayim, 28713
Yiddish, 27941, 27982–27992
Yitshaki, David, 28524
Young, James E., 28340
Youth Movement, 28568, 28939
Yudkin, Leon I., 28748
Yugoslavia, 28328
Yuval, Israel Jacob, 27941, 27979

Zach, Krista, 28328
Zadek, Walter, 28631, 28796
Zahn, Christine, 28012
Zariz, Ruth, 28405
Zayas, Alfred-Maurice de, 28481
Zebi Hirsch ben Chaim, 28036
'(Die) Zeit', 28265, 28278, 28314, 28480, 28735,

28765, 28771, 28785, 28808, 28822, 28845, 28903
'Zeitgeschichte', 28133, 28907
'Zeitschrift f. Dialektologie', 27988
'Zeitschrift f. Literaturwissenschaft u. Linguistik', 28966
'Zeitschrift f. Religions- u. Geistesgeschichte', 28680
Zelinsky, Hartmut, 28943
Zentralarchiv z. Erforschung d. Gesch. d. Juden in Deutschland, 28208
Zentrum f. Antisemitismusforschung, Berlin, 28447, 28899, 28925, 28944
Zerbrochene Geschichte, 27980; 28025–28026, 28241, 28259, 28385
Ziegler, Monika, 28443
Ziegler, Siegfried, 28036
Zielinski, Siegfried, 28912
Zilk, Helmut, 28132
Zimmermann, Hans Dieter, 28666
Zimmermann, Michael, 28026, 28166
Zimmermann, Moshe, 27916, 27981, 28945
Zimmermann, Reiner, 28761
'Zion', 28518, 28009
Zion, Sidney, 28855
Zionism, 27941, 27959, 28149, 28157–28158, 28210, 28485, 28544, 28552, 28577, 28594, 28595–28596, 28599, 28601, 28604–28612, 28615–28616, 28618, 28620–28621, 28623–28624, 28626–28627, 28629–28630, 28637, 28681, 28964
— and Nazis, 28613
Zipes, Jack, 28420, 28560
Zirndorf, 28444
Zitelmann, Rainer, 28318
Zivilisation und Barbarei, 28311, 28313
Zohn, Harry, 28799
Zonabend, Nachman, 28360
Zuckermann, Hanny, 28289
Zuckermann, Salomon, 28357
Zürn, Gaby, 27999, 28050
Zweig, Arnold, 28268, 28505, 28630, 28653, 28795–28796
Zweig, Max, 28797
Zweig, Stefan, 28798–28799, 28854, 28970
(Der) Zweite Weltkrieg und die Exilanten, 28653
Zwischen Antisemitismus und Philosemitismus, 28489

List of Contributors

ASCHHEIM, Steven E., Ph.D., b. 1942 in Johannesburg. Senior Lecturer in German Cultural and Intellectual History, Hebrew University, Jerusalem. Author of i.a. *Brothers and Strangers. The East European Jew in German and German-Jewish Consciousness, 1800–1932* (1982); *Nietzsche in Germany, 1890–1990* (1992); and of numerous articles on German, Jewish and cultural history. (Contributor to Year Book XXVIII.)

BENZ, Wolfgang, Dr. phil., b. 1941 in Ellwangen. Director of the Zentrum für Antisemitismusforschung and Professor at the Technische Universität Berlin. Author of numerous volumes, including *Zwischen Hitler und Adenauer* (1991). Editor of i.a. *Dimension des Völkermords* (1991); *Das Exil der kleinen Leute* (1991); *Zwischen Juden und Antisemitismus* (1991).

BRENNER, Michael, M.A., b. 1964 in Weiden. Doctoral candidate in Jewish History at Columbia University, N.Y. Author of *Am Beispiel Weiden. Jüdischer Alltag im Nationalsozialismus* (1983); 'Zurück ins Ghetto?', in *Trumah* (1991); 'Wider den Mythos der "Stunde Null"', in *Menora* (1992); 'From Smyrna to Weimar', in Delphine Bechtel (ed.), *Between East and West. Cultural Contacts between German and Eastern European Jews* (1992). (Contributor to Year Book XXXV.)

EFRON, John M., Ph.D., b. 1957 in Melbourne. Assistant Professor of Modern Jewish History, Indiana University. Author of *Defining the Jewish Race. The Self-Perception and Responses of Jewish Scientists to Scientific Racism in Europe, 1882–1933* (diss., University of Columbia 1991, publ. forthcoming).

ERPEL, Simone, M.A., b. 1963 in Gütersloh. Research fellow at the Interdisziplinäre Frauengruppe Frauenforschung, Bielefeld. Author of i.a. '. . . Marianne Prager/Joachim, deutsch-jüdische Widerstandskämpferin', in *Tarantel, Bielefelder Frauenzeitung* (1990); 'Historikerinnengruppe Bielefeld, Grenzüberschreitungen', in *Frauen und Öffentlichkeit* (1991). Currently researching "Women in the Jewish Partisan Movement in Eastern Europe".

ESCHWEGE, Helmut, b. 1913 in Hannover. Historian. Author of *"Kennzeichen J", Bilder, Dokumente, Berichte zur Geschichte der Verbrechen des Hitlerfaschismus an den deutschen Juden 1933–1945* (²1979); *Die Synagogen in der deutschen Geschichte* (1980); *Fremd unter meinesgleichen, Erinnerungen eines Dresdner Juden* (1991). Co-author (with Konrad Kwiet) of *Selbstbehauptung und Widerstand. Deutsche Juden im Kampf um Existenz und Menschenwürde 1933–1945* (1984). (Contributor to Year Book XV.)

EYCK, Frank, M.A., F.R.Hist.S., b. 1921 in Berlin. Professor emeritus, University of Calgary. Author of i.a. *The Frankfurt Parliament, 1848–49* (1968); *G.P. Gooch. A Study in History and Politics* (1982). Editor of *The Revolutions of 1848–49* (1972); and Frederick Hertz, *The German Public Mind in the Nineteenth Century* (1975). Author of numerous articles on historical subjects and current affairs.

Fox, John P., Ph.D., F.R.Hist.S., b. 1937 in London. 1990–1991 Maxwell Fellow in the Teaching and Study of the Holocaust at the Oxford Centre for Postgraduate Hebrew Studies. Author of i.a. *Germany and the Far Eastern Crisis 1931–1938* (^{2}1985); 'British Attitudes to Jewish Refugees from Central and Eastern Europe in the Nineteenth and Twentieth Centuries', in *Second Chance. Two Centuries of German-speaking Jews in the United Kingdom* (1991). British editor of *Akten zur Deutschen auswärtigen Politik 1918–1945*.

FRIEDLANDER, Albert H., Ph.D., D.D., b. 1927 in Berlin. Rabbi, senior lecturer and Dean of Leo Baeck College, London. Author of i.a. *Leo Baeck. Teacher of Theresienstadt* (^{2}1973); *A Thread of Gold* (1990); *Leo Baeck. Leben und Lehre* (1990); 'The German Influence on Progressive Judaism in Great Britain', in *Second Chance* (1991); 'Berlin in die Welt', in Andreas Nachama *et al.* (eds.), *Jüdische Lebenswelten. Essays* (1991). Member of the Board of the London LBI. (Contributor to Year Book XI.)

GOUGH-YATES, Kevin, Ph.D., b. 1936 in London. Writer and lecturer on cinema. Author of i.a. *Michael Powell in Association with Emeric Pressburger* (1971); *Michael Powell* (1973); 'Moving Pictures', in *Art Monthly* (1979–1990); 'The British Feature Film as European Concern', in Günter Berghaus (ed.), *Theatre and Film in Exile. German Artists in Britain 1933–1945* (1989).

GRAETZ, Michael, Ph.D., b. 1933 in Breslau. Professor for Modern Jewish History and Head of the Dinur Institute for Research in Jewish History, Hebrew University, Jerusalem. Author of *From Periphery to Center. Chapters in 19th Century History of French Jewry* (1982); *The French Revolution and the Jews* (1989).

HERZIG, Arno, Dr. phil., b. 1937 in Albendorf, Silesia. Professor at the Historisches Seminar of the University of Hamburg since 1979. Author of i.a. *Unterschichtenprotest in Deutschland 1790–1870* (1988). Editor of *Die Juden in Hamburg 1590 bis 1990* (1991). Co-editor (with Julius H. Schoeps and Hans Otto Horch) of *Menora. Jahrbuch für deutsch-jüdische Geschichte* (1990ff.). Author of numerous essays and articles on the German workers' movement, the history of the Jews in Germany and German-Jewish historiography. (Contributor to Year Book XXVI.)

HEUBERGER, Rachel, M.A., b. 1951 in Tel-Aviv. Librarian of the Judaica and Hebraica division of the Stadt- und Universitätsbibliothek, Frankfurt a. Main. Author of i.a. 'Aron Freimann', in *Jüdische Stiftungen in Frankfurt am Main* (1988); co-author (with Helga Krohn) of *Hinaus aus dem Ghetto . . . Juden in Frankfurt am*

Main (1988). Currently working on a dissertation at the Hebrew University of Jerusalem on the Jewish Community in Frankfurt in the Weimar Republic.

KAISER, Wolf, Ph.D., b. 1948 Gelsenkirchen. Pädagogisch-wissenschaftlicher Mitarbeiter at the Gedenkstätte Haus der Wannsee-Konferenz. Author of i.a. *Palästina – Erez Israel. Deutschsprachige Reisebeschreibungen jüdischer Autoren von der Jahrhundertwende bis zum Zweiten Weltkrieg* (1992); and articles on eighteenth-century German literature, German writers in exile and pedagogical issues.

LINDNER, Erik, M.A., b. 1964 in Feuchtwangen. Doctoral candidate and author of i.a. 'Jüdische Presse und Obrigkeit am Anfang des 19. Jahrhunderts', in *Trumah* (1992); and five essays in Julius H. Schoeps *et al.* (eds.), *Wegweiser durch das jüdische Rheinland* (1992). Currently on a dissertation about patriotism and German Jews, 1813–1871.

MOSSE, Werner E., Ph.D., F.R.Hist.S., b. 1918 in Berlin. Professor emeritus, University of East Anglia, Norwich. Author of i.a. *Jews in the German Economy. The German-Jewish Economic Elite 1820–1935* (1986); *The German-Jewish Economic Elite 1820–1935. A Socio-Cultural Profile* (1989). Editor and co-editor of five symposium volumes of the Leo Baeck Institute. Chairman of the Board of the London LBI. (Contributor to Year Books IV, XV, XXIV, XXVIII, XXXIII, XXXIV and XXXV.)

PAUCKER, Arnold, Dr. phil., b. 1921 in Berlin. Director, Leo Baeck Institute, London, and Editor of the Year Book of the Leo Baeck Institute 1970–1992. Author of i.a. *Der jüdische Abwehrkampf gegen Antisemitismus und Nationalsozialismus in den letzten Jahren der Weimarer Republic* (²1969); and of many essays on historical and philological subjects. Co-editor and editor of eight symposium volumes and of other publications of the Leo Baeck Institute. (Contributor to Year Books V, VIII, XI, XIII and XVI.)

PAULEY, Bruce F., Ph.D., b. 1937 in Lincoln, Nebraska. Professor of History, University of Central Florida. Author of *Hahnenschwanz und Hakenschwanz. Steirischer Heimatschutz und österreichischer Nationalsozialismus* (1972); *The Habsburg Legacy, 1867–1939* (1972); *Hitler and the Forgotten Nazis. A History of Austrian National Socialism* (1981); *From Prejudice to Persecution. A History of Austrian Anti-Semitism* (1992).

REINHARZ, Jehuda, Ph.D., b. 1944 in Haifa. Richard Koret Professor of Modern Jewish History and Director, The Tauber Institute for the Study of European Jewry, Brandeis University. Author of i.a. *Chaim Weizmann. The Making of a Zionist Leader* (1985); *Hashomer Hazair in Germany, 1931–1939* (1989); *Chaim Weizmann. The Making of a Statesman* (1992). Editor of i.a. *Dokumente zur Geschichte des deutschen Zionismus, 1882–1933* (1981); co-editor of and contributor to many other volumes on European Jewish history. Recipient of the President of Israel

Prize for 1990. (Contributor to Year Books XXII, XXIV, XXX, XXXI, XXXII, XXXIII and XXXV.)

SASSIN, Horst R., Dr. phil., b. 1953 in Regensburg. Teacher of history and German. Author of i.a. *Widerstand, Verfolgung und Emigration Liberaler 1933–1945* (exhibition cat. 1983). Co-editor of *Dokumente zur Geschichte des Liberalismus in Deutschland 1830–1945* (1989); *Liberaler Widerstand gegen den Nationalsozialismus* (forthcoming); and articles on Liberalism, resistance and military policy. Recipient of Wolf Erich Kellner Preis (1991) and Carl von Ossietzky Preis (1992).

SCHORSCH, Ismar, Ph.D., b. 1935 in Hannover. Chancellor and Professor of Jewish History, The Theological Seminary of America, New York. Author of i.a. *Jewish Reactions to German Antisemitism 1870–1914* (1972); 'Emancipation and the Crisis of Religious Activity', in *Revolution and Evolution. 1848 in German-Jewish History* (1981); 'German Judaism: From Confession to Culture', in *Die Juden in Nationalsozialistischen Deutschland/The Jews in Nazi Germany 1933–1945* (1986). Fellow of the American Academy for Jewish Research. President of the New York LBI. (Contributor to Year Books XI, XIX, XXII, XXV, XXVIII, XXXI, XXXIII, XXXIV and XXXV.)

SELIGMANN, Abraham, M.A., b. 1915 in Hamburg. Formerly agricultural planner, now historian. Author of various articles on agricultural themes; contributor to *Pinkas Hakehillot – Germany – Hessen* (Yad Vashem, forthcoming).

SORKIN, David, Ph.D., b. 1953 in Chicago. Clore Fellow at the Oxford Centre for Postgraduate Hebrew Studies and Research Fellow of St. Antony's College, Oxford. Author of i.a. *The Transformation of German Jewry* (1987). Co-editor of *From East and West. Jews in a Changing Europe, 1750–1870* (1990). General Editor of *Jewish Society and Culture*. Currently working on an intellectual biography of Moses Mendelssohn for the series *Jewish Thinkers*. Member of the Executive Committee of the London LBI. (Contributor to Year Books XXXII and XXXV.)

STERN, Guy, Ph.D., b. 1921 in Hildesheim. Professor of Germanic Languages and Literatures, Wayne State University. Author of numerous publications, including *War, Weimar and Literature, the Story of the Neue Merkur* (1971); *Alfred Neumann* (1979); *Literatur im Exil* (1989); *Nazi Book Burning and the American Response* (1991). Recipient of the Goethe Medal in 1989. (Contributor to Year Book VI.)

STRAUSS, Herbert A., Dr. phil., b. 1918 in Würzburg. Professor emeritus, City College and City University of New York, former Director of the Zentrum für Antisemitismusforschung and Ehrenmitglied of the TU, Berlin, Fellow, Wissenschaftskolleg, Berlin and Director of Research, Research Foundation for Jewish Immigration, New York. Author of numerous publications on German-Jewish history, migration 1933–1945, antisemitism and acculturation. Fellow and Member of the Board of the New York LBI and Member of the Board of the

London LBI. (Contributor to Year Books VI, XI, XVI, XXV, XXVI and XXXV.)

Toury, Jacob, Ph.D., b. 1915 in Beuthen. Professor emeritus of Jewish History, Tel-Aviv University. Author of numerous publications including *Die politischen Orientierungen der Juden in Deutschland* (1966); two contributions to: *Das Judentum in der Deutschen Umwelt 1800–1850* (1977); *Soziale und politische Geschichte der Juden in Deutschland* (1977); *Die Jüdische Presse im Österreichischen Kaiserreich 1802–1918* (1982); *Jüdische Textilunternehmer in Baden-Württemberg 1683–1938* (1984). (Contributor to Year Books XI, XIII, XVI, XXII, XXVI, XXX, XXXIII and XXXVI.]

Wiesemann, Falk, Dr. phil., b. 1944 in Fürstenfeldbruck. Akademischer Oberrat at the Heinrich-Heine-Universität, Düsseldorf. Author of *Bibliographie zur Geschichte der Juden in Bayern* (1989). Editor of *Zur Geschichte und Kultur der Juden im Rheinland* (1985). Co-editor of *Bayern in der NS Zeit* (1977); and *Die jüdischen Gemeinden in Bayern 1918–1945* (1979). Author of various articles on the history of the rural Jews in Germany.

Wistrich, Robert S., Ph.D., b. 1945 in Lenger, USSR. Jewish Chronicle Professor of Jewish Studies, University College London. Author of i.a. *Who's Who in Nazi Germany* (1982); *Hitler's Apocalypse* (1985); *The Jews of Vienna in the Age of Franz Joseph* (1989); *Between Redemption and Perdition* (1990); *Antisemitism. The Longest Hatred* (1991). Winner of the 1989 Viznitzer Prize for research in Jewish history. Member of the Boards of the Jerusalem and London LBI. (Contributor to Year Books XXI, XXII, XXVI and XXXIII.)

Corrections

MAX PLAUT

In Year Book XXXVI, on p. 187, there is a reference to Dr. Max Plaut. According to Rabbi W. Gunther Plaut of Toronto, Max Plaut, his cousin, survived incarceration in Theresienstadt and returned after the war to Bremen, where he was a leading figure in the reconstituted community.

JULIUS HIRSCHBERG

On p. 193 of the Year Book XXXVI the reference to Julius Hirschfeld should read Julius Hirschberg.

HIRSCH FAMILY

In Year Book XXXV there is reference to the acquisition of the *Kupferhammer* in Ilsenburg by members of the Hirsch family. This took place in 1817, not in 1803 or 1829 as suggested on p. 135. The Halberstadt office of *A. Hirsch & Sohn* was transferred to Berlin in 1927 not in 1930 as stated on p. 147. The author is grateful to Dr. E. Hildesheimer of Jerusalem for indicating these two points.

Abstracts of articles in this Year Book are included in *Historical Abstracts* and *America: History and Life*.

General Index to Year Book XXXVII
of the Leo Baeck Institute

Abel, Othenio (Vienna University Rector), 487, 488

Abraham, Karl (psychoanalyst), 172

Abraham-Holzer, Charlotte (of Baum Group), 408, 409, 410, 411n, 414

'Abwehrblätter', 96, 231n. *See also* 'Mitteilungen aus dem Verein zur Abwehr des Antisemitismus'.

Abwehrverein, *see* Verein zur Abwehr des Antisemitismus

Academics, Jewish, 79, 95, 97, 296–297; dismissal, XXVII, 297, 389; in Palestine, 263, 269

Acculturation, *see* Assimilation

Ackland, Rodney (writer), 529, 530

Action Française, 115, 130, 134

Adersbach, Gerson (physician), 40

Adler, Alfred (psychologist), 186

Adler, Victor (Austrian Socialist politician), 142, 143, 144

Adler-Rudel, Shalom (social worker, Director of LBI, Jerusalem), XXVIII

Adorno, Theodor Wiesengrund (philosopher), 191

Agate, James (critic), 524

Agrarians, *see* Bund der Landwirte

Agriculture, Jews and, 62, 333, 348; in Palestine, 263–282 *passim*. *See also* Vocational training.

Agudas Jisroel, 285n

Agudath Israel, 46n, 314

Ahad Ha'Am (Asher Ginzberg) (Zionist leader, Hebrew writer), 163, 379; and Nietzsche, 209n

Ahlwardt, Hermann (antisemitic agitator), 226

Aid to the persecuted, XIII, 304, 328–361 *passim*, 393–395, 402, 409, 462, 534; by Christians, 339, 351, 352, 353, 354, 358, 393, 394–395, 412; by Jews, 389, 394, 399–400, 409; by Nazis, 340, 354, 360

Aktion Sühnezeichen, 505, 507, 508

'Alarm', 251–252

Albu brothers (South African financiers), 136

Alexander, Eleanor, 287n

'Alldeutsche Blätter', 227

Alldeutscher Verband, 142, 221n, 225, 227, 229, 230, 232, 233, 236, 483

'Allgemeine Zeitung des Judent[h]ums', 63, 196

'Allgemeiner Anzeiger', 78

Allgemeiner Deutscher Arbeiter-Verein (ADAV), 124–125

'Allgemeiner Deutscher Nachrichtendienst', 503

Allgemeiner Deutscher Rabbinerverband, 46, 50

Alliance Israélite Universelle, 150, 162

Alpar, Gitta (actress), 520n, 521

Alzey Jewish community, 28

Amcha-Stiftung, 511

American Jewish Congress, 485, 489

American Jewish Joint Distribution Committee, 491

American League for the Protection of Foreign Students in Vienna, 486

Amsterdam Jewish community, 76

Anarchism, 115, 121, 127, 143, 189, 191

Anderson, John (British politician), 417, 418, 419n, 424

Andreas-Friedrich, Ruth (Christian rescuer, Resistance worker), 332, 334, 409, 412

Andrejew, Andrei (designer), 521n, 537

Angress, Werner Thomas, XXVIII, 462

Anhalt Jewry, 509; Anhalt-Dessau Jewry, 5

Ansbach Jewry, 22, 314

Antisemitenbund (Austria), 490

Antisemitic legislation, 332–333, 334, 336, 337, 393, 399; and citizenship, 100, 429–452 *passim*; rescindment, 448–457 *passim*. *See also* Nuremberg Laws.

Antisemitism, 65–69, 81, 85, 86, 87, 88, 96, 99, 111–145, 147, 150, 157, 247, 249–250, 252n, 294, 317, 369, 386, 389, 390–391, 399, 504, 510; ADAV, 124–125; Alldeutscher Verband, 233; and Anglophobia, 129–130; anthropology and, 169, 170, 172; anti-Christian, 8, 118, 126–127, 130, 131, 194, 218; anti-Israel, 500, 501, 503, 505, 511; anti-Zionism, 100, 113, 499, 500; Arnim, 67, 68; in Austria, XV–XVI, 117, 142–145, 391, 481–496; Barrès, 133; B. Bauer, 118–119; in Bavaria, 244–245; Blanqui, 131; in Bremen, 240; in Britain, 112, 134–138, 423, 524–525, 531–533, 540–541; J. Burns, 138; H.S. Chamberlain, 213–236; A. Chirac, 132; "Jewish conspiracy", 120–121, 138–139; in Czechoslovakia, 113, 391, 499; Daumer, 118; Deckert, 231; defence, Jewish, XI, XXI, XVIII, 111, 128, 194–197, 213–236, 237–257, 266, 385. *See also* Centralverein . . ., Resistance; Drumont, 116, 129, 130, 132, 133, 137; Dühring, 126, 127–128, 139; economic, 66–67, 68, 111–145 *passim*; Eichendorff, 67;'Eiserner Besen', 490; Eisenmenger, 20n, 231; Feuerbach, 118; Fichte, 68, 231n; Finn, 125; Ford, 489; Fourier, 128–129; in France, 9, 115–116, 117, 118, 128–134; Freemasonry, 78, 134, 162; Freikorps, 245; Fritsch, 217, 223, 224, 227, 228n, 231; in German Democratic Republic, 499–511 *passim*; Ghillany, 118; Glagau, 126; Goethe and, 230–231; Guérin, 133; Guesde, 133: K. Hardie, 138; Hasenclever, 125; Hasselmann, 125–126, 139; Herder and, 231n; Hobson, 138; Hodge, 135; Holbach, 118, 131; in Hungary, 117, 481, 485; Hyndman, 136–137; Iokhelson, 122; in Italy, 391, 518; Jungdeutscher Orden, 382; Junkers, 111, 128; 'Justice', 136–137; Leroux, 129; literary, 67–68, 113, 117; Lueger, 137; Luther and, 231n; Marr, 118, 126–127; Marx, 68, 114–126 *passim*, 129; in Memmingen, 245n; T. Mommsen and, 231n; Morès, 133; in Munich, 246; Nietzsche and, XI, 190–200 *passim*; physicians and, 175n; Podolinsky, 122; in Poland, 113, 144, 486; Populists, 122–124; post-WWII, 100–101; press, German, and, 113, 124; Proudhon, 120–121, 130–131; Quelch, 137; Regnard, 132; Reichsbanner and, 249–250; religious, 118, 373; 'Revue socialiste', 132;'Reynolds News', 137; Rochefort, 133; Rohling, 231; A. Roth, 228; rural, 67, 111; in Russia, 122–124, 140–142, 144, 294, 484; in schools, 295; v. Schweitzer, 124; Selbstschutz organisation, 245; Sessa, 67, 68; Socialists and, X–XI, 92, 111–145; Sorel, 134; Stalin, 141–142; Stoecker, 85, 127, 128, 137, 294; Streicher, 429n; student, 78, 123, 156, 295, 485–488; Tölcke, 125; Toussenel, 129–130; trade unions, 135, 138, 228; Tridon, 131; in US, 481, 486, 487, 489, 490; US reaction to, 481–496; in USSR, 112–113, 499; "usury", *see* Moneylenders; Vatican II and, 502; in Vienna, 144, 481–482, 485–488, 490; Voltaire, 118, 131; Voss, 67; Wagner, 118; Wahrmund, 231; H.G. Wells and, 531; workers and, 92, 112, 113, 115–116, 132; in Würzburg, 247. *See also* Economic persecution, Nazism, Numerus clausus, Pogroms, Ritual murder accusation, Yellow Star.

Antisemitism, defence against, 96, 156–157, 394–395. *See also* Verein zur Abwehr des Antisemitismus *and under* Antisemitism, defence, Jewish.

Apt, Rudolf (metal merchant), 240, 244

Arabs and Jews, XII, XXI, 263, 266, 271–286; Arab labour, 270–276 *passim*; Bedouins, 271, 279; land purchase, 275–280, 285; riots, 274, 280, 285n, 286

'Arandora Star' (ship), 424

Arbeiterwohlfahrt, 397

'Arbeiterzeitung', 144

Arbeitsgemeinschaft deutscharischer Fabrikanten der deutschen Bekleidungsindustrie, 387

Arbeitsgemeinschaft Kirche und Judentum, 500, 508

Archibald, George (film company director), 532

Arendt, Hannah (social historian), 5, 95, 102

Aris, Helmut, 501, 502

Arndt, Ernst Moritz (writer), 230n

Arndt, Theodor, 502, 503

Arnheim family, 301

Arnim, Ludwig Achim von (poet), 67, 68

Arnim, Otto, *see* A. Roth

Aronsfeld, Caesar C., XXIIIn

Artisans, Jewish, 62, 348

Aryanisation, *see* Economic persecution

Aschaffenburg Jewry, 22

Ascher, Saul (writer), 11

Aschheim, Steven, 317

Ashcroft, Peggy (actress), 526

Assimilation, IX, 5, 11, 30, 31, 57, 61, 63, 67, 73, 75, 83–93, 95–102 *passim*, 107, 118, 124, 140, 142, 159n, 170, 174, 186, 197, 198, 291, 293, 310, 311, 321n, 400, 540;'assimilationism', X, XI, XII, XXI, 84, 86, 154–163 *passim*, 186, 187, 188, 198; and disease, 180, 183–188; and Zionism, 147–167 *passim. See also* Symbiosis.

Association of Cinematographic Technicians (ACT), 528, 532

Association of Former Political Deportees in Nazi Germany (Italy), 493

Association of Jewish Refugees in Great Britain, 448

Attlee, Clement (British Prime Minister), 457

Auerbach family, 90

Auerbach, Benjamin Hirsch (rabbi), 314

Auerbach, Philipp (of Reichsbanner), 244

Auschwitz extermination camp, 100, 336, 338, 341, 400, 402, 408, 409, 497, 507; women in, 400, 408, 410, 414

Austerlitz, Friedrich (Socialist editor), 144

Austria; Nazis in, 486–488, 489–491, 492, 495

Austrittsgesetz, -gemeinde, 45–46, 53, 56; Adas Jisroel, 509

Auxiliary Military Pioneer Corps (AMPC), *see* Pioneer Corps

Avenarius, Ferdinand (editor), 225–226

Avneri, Zwi, 371, 373

AW (organisation for defence groups), 238

Axelrod, Paul (Russian Social Democrat), 123

Baal-Shem-Tov (Israel ben Eliezer) (founder of Hasidism), 211

Baden Jewry, 7, 23

Baden, Hermann (Halle community leader), 502

Baeck, Leo (rabbi, scholar, President of Reichsvertretung), XIII–XIV, XXIII, 56, 299, 363–379

Bäumler, Alfred (Nietzschean Nazi), 195n

Bakunin, Michael Alexandrovich (Russian revolutionary), 115, 120, 121, 122, 125, 132
Balácz, Bela (Hungarian poet, scriptwriter), 528n
Balcon, Michael (film producer), 518, 523
[Lord] Baldwin Fund for Refugees, 534
Balfour, Arthur James (British statesman), 137; Balfour Declaration, 154, 281, 285, 379
Bamberg Jewish community, 19, 393
Bamberger, Julius (department store owner, active in Bremen C.V.), 239–240, 241, 244
Bamberger, Ludwig (Liberal politician), 192n
Bamberger, Nathan (Würzburg rabbi), 29–30
Bambus, Willy (Zionist writer), 261
Bandmann, Egon (economic journalist), 389
Bankers, Jewish, 61, 75, 79, 84–88, 102, 129
Bankier, David, 327n
Baptism, *see* Conversion
Bar Kochba; in Hamburg, 244; Verein Jüdischer Hochschüler in Prag, 163
Barkai, Avraham, XXVIII
Barmat family, 253, 256
Barnato, Barnett Isaacs "Barney" (South African financier), 136
Barou, Noa (economic consultant), 453, 457n
Barr, Charles, 517
Barrès, Maurice (French nationalist), 116, 133
Barth, Theodor (Liberal politician), 302–303, 304
Basedow, Johann Bernhard (educationalist), 76
Bass, Alfie (actor), 538n, 539
Bauer, Bruno (Protestant theologian, historian), 118–119, 126, 127, 131
Bauer, Otto (Austrian Socialist leader and theoretician), 142, 144
Baum, Herbert (Resistance leader), 399, 400–401, 402, 404, 407, 408, 409, 410, 411, 413; Baum Group, 381, 399–413 *passim*; and Sowjetparadies exhibition, 401, 408, 409, 410
Baum, Marianne (née Cohn, of Baum Group), 400, 402, 404, 410
Bavarian Jewry, XVIII, 23–26, 62, 64, 71, 73, 185, 244–245, 248–249, 314, 322–323. *See also* Franconian.
Bawden, V.C. (British officer), 439, 440n
Bayard, Thomas F. (US Secretary of State), 482
Bayerdörfer, Hans-Peter, 67
Bayerische Volkspartei (BVP), 246, 247n, 249
Bayle, Pierre (French liberal writer), 39
Beadles, Cecil (British psychiatrist), 174
Bebel, August (Socialist politician), 111, 119–120, 127, 139–140
Beck, Ludwig (general, in Resistance), 384
Becker, Rafael (Zionist psychiatrist), 176–177, 184–188
Becker, Werner, XXVIII
Beckett, William Eric (British official), 435, 442, 449
Beddington-Behrens, E. (financier), 522, 534n

Beethoven, Ludwig van (composer), 98
Begegnung mit dem Judentum, 501–502, 503, 506–507
Beggars, Jewish, 7, 61
Behrend-Rosenfeld, Else Rahel (memoirist), 411, 412
Behrendt-Beuthen, Ernst (union secretary, active in Reichsbanner and C.V.), 251n
Beit, Alfred (South African financier), 136
Belke, Ingrid, XXVIII
Ben-Baruch, Benjamin, 154n
Ben-gavriêl, Moshe Ya-akov (Eugen Hoeflich) (writer), 231, 283, 285
Benario, Olga (Communist), 398
Bendavid, Lazarus (writer, mathematician, headmaster), 11, 40
Bendix, Hirsch Nathan (Berlin Jewish leader), 74
Benedek, Laszlo (cinema technician), 521
Benedikt, Moritz (psychiatrist), 174–177, 179, 187
Benjacob, Isaac, 41
Bennathan, Esra, XXVIII
Bentwich, Norman (historian), XVn
Benz, Wolfgang, X, 104, 107–108
Berdiczevski (bin Gorion), Micha Yoseph (folklorist, Hebrew writer), 197, 209–211
Berens, Harold (actor), 538n
Berger, Christfried, 504
Berger, Ludwig (film director), 528, 537–538
Bergman[n], Hugo Samuel [Shmuel Hugo] (Zionist philosopher), 163n, 285
Bergner, Elisabeth (actress), 519, 520, 521, 523, 532, 534, 535n
Bergner, Samuel (of Reichsbanner), 254
Bergson, Henri (French philosopher), 197
Berkley, George E., 492
Berl, Heinrich (writer), 201
Berlin Jewish community, 5, 6, 7, 55, 72, 73, 75, 78, 87, 88, 107, 108, 241, 250–251, 287–307 *passim*, 328, 335, 336, 337, 338, 386, 409, 411; deportation, 399, 409, 410; Freischule, 9, 11, 40, 80; Rabbiner-Seminar, 47, 314; R.j.F. in, 238, 239; Resistance, 384, 389, 393–394. *See also* Baum Group; scholars, 363–379; synagogues, 80, 289–290, 508, 510; underground life in, 328, 340–341, 347, 359, 401, 411; post-WWII, 498–512 *passim*.
'Berliner Tageblatt', 233, 382n
Berliner, Cora (educationalist, communal worker), 400
Bernauer, Rudolph (film director), 520n, 522, 529, 530
Berner, Inge, *see* I. Gerson
Bernhard, Georg (editor), 251, 383
Bernhardi, Friedrich (militarist writer), 221
Bernhardt, Kurt (film director), 520n, 521, 528
Bernstein, Eduard (Socialist politician), 91, 120
Berth, Edouard (French syndicalist), 134

Bertram, Ernst (literary historian), 192
Bettauer, Hugo (writer), 485, 524
Beuthen Jewish community, 252n
Bevilacqua, Giuseppe, XXVIII
Bevin, Ernest (British politician), 518
Beyer, Helga (of Resistance), 399
Biale, David, 205n, 210
Bible, 8, 9, 10, 11, 364, 502, 504; Christian study of, 39, 48, 199; Nietzsche and, 195, 199n
Bibo, Siegfried (of Resistance), 402, 410, 412
Bieber, Curtis, 464
Bielefeld Jewish community, 68
Bier (of Cologne, R.j.F. leader), 238
Biluim (Russian-Jewish pioneer group), 270
Birnbaum, Nathan (Mathias Acher) (politician, writer), 164
Birnbaum, Salomon A. (Yiddishist), XXIX
Bismarck, Otto von (German Chancellor), 117, 128, 231n, 232, 295, 303
Bismarck-Schoenhausen, Otto Eduard Leopold Graf von (Prussian statesman), 368
Blach, Friedrich (writer), 198
Blanqui, Louis Auguste (French Socialist), 115, 126, 131; Blanquists, 131–132, 133
Blattner, Ludwig (film producer), 518, 522–523
Blau-Weiss, 283
Blech, Leo (composer), 102
Bleichröder, Gerson von (banker), 120
Bleuler, Eugen (psychiatrist), 172, 184
Bloch, Ernst (philosopher), 191
Blüher, Hans (youth leader, antisemite), 205
Blumenbach, Johann Friedrich (anthropologist), 169
Blumenfeld, Kurt (German Zionist leader), 153, 253
Board of Deputies of British Jews, 451
Bodenheimer, Max Isidor (German Zionist leader), 151, 153
Börne, Ludwig (Löb Baruch) (writer), 40, 78
Bohemian Jewry, XII, 163–164, 166, 334, 481
Borchard, Lucy (owned pilot boat firm), 394
Borinski, Annaliese-Ora (memoirist), 336
Bormann, Martin (Nazi leader), 433
Borochov, Ber (founder "Poale Zion"), 144
Boulanger, Georges (French general), 132, 133
Boycotts; by Arabs, 274; by Jews, 272, 275; by Nazis, 99, 101, 327, 391
Brahm, Hans (John) (film director), 520n, 521, 526–527, 531n
Brandenburg Jewry, 5, 72, 367, 498, 503
Brandes, Georg (Danish-Jewish scholar), 190, 197
Braun, Heinrich (Austrian Socialist, editor), 143
Brecher, Daniel, XXVIII
Brecht, Bertolt (poet, playwright), 527, 528n
Bremen Jewish community, XII, 238, 239–241, 242, 244, 245, 252, 255
Brenner, Michael, XII
Brenner, Yoseph Chaim (workers' leader), 209n

Brentano, Clemens von (poet), 67, 68
Breslau Jewish community, 22, 30, 80, 107, 238, 386
Breuer, Isaac (rabbi, writer), 313, 318–322
Breuer, Mordechai, 45n, 310n
Breuer, Raphael (rabbi, Orthodox leader), 4
Breuer, Salomon (rabbi in Frankfurt), 314, 318
Brief, [Dr.] (writer), 220–221
Brinker, Menachem, 210n, 211n
Brith Chaluzim Datiim (Bachad), 335
Brith Shalom, 285
British Broadcasting Corporation, 412, 522–523
British Evangelical Alliance Committee, 221
British International Pictures, 522, 527, 531
Brod, Max (philosopher, writer), 309n
Brod, Peter, XXVIII
Broncekeller (Hamburg cabaret), 394
Bronfman, Edgar 481, 493, 494, 509
Brook, Norman (British official), 423, 424n
Brothers, Eric, 401n, 406n
Bruce, Michael (stunt man), 534
Brunn, Fritz (film director), 520n, 528
Brunswick Jewish community, 6
Buber, Martin (philosopher), 51n, 102, 152, 153, 164, 281, 316–317; Buber-Rosenzweig Medal, 507; and Nietzsche, 205–207, 210n, 211
'Bühne und Welt', 226, 230
Büren Jewish community, 64
Bürgerliche Frauenbewegung, 400
Büttner, Ursula, XXVIII, 255n, 257n
Bund (Jewish Socialist movement), 140, 141, 166, 510
Bund der Landwirte, 226, 298
Bund Deutscher Frauenvereine, 400
Bund jüdischer Akademiker (BJA), 319
[Vaterländischer] Bund jüdischer Frontsoldaten, 237, 238, 239, 242, 243
Bund Schwarz-Rot-Gold, 247
Burger, Hanuš, 463–464, 471, 472
Burgpreppach Jewish community, 30
Burials, Jewish, IX, 17–31, 74, 79; cremation, 29–30; decorum, IX, 25; regulations, 20–21, 22–26
Burns, John (British Labour leader), 138
Businessmen/traders, Jewish, 61, 62, 73, 75, 79, 88–92, 101, 102

Cahan, Abraham (American-Jewish Socialist), 144
Cahen, Richard Maximilian (jurist), 197, 198
Cahnmann, Werner (sociologist, C.V. functionary), 246, 270, 275, 285–286
Calé family, 293, 302
Calé, Walter (poet), 293, 302
Calendar, Jewish, 43n, 509
Calvary, Moses (Zionist educationalist), 265, 278
Calwer, Richard (Socialist writer), 139
Cammens, Minna (Socialist deputy), 398

Canaris, Wilhelm (admiral, of Resistance), 384
Cantor, Eddie (actor), 534
Capitalism and Jews, 62, 88, 111–145 *passim*, 225, 246, 255, 319, 320
Carlebach, Emanuel (Cologne rabbi), 314
Carlebach, Joseph Zvi (Hamburg rabbi), 317–318
Carlebach, Julius, XVII, XXVIII, 116–117
Caro, Joseph (rabbi, mystic), 41
Cartier, Rudolph (Katscher) (film director), 520n, 533
Cassel Jewish community, 6, 237, 238
Catholics and Jews, 12–14, 15, 16, 339, 502–508 *passim*
Celle Jewish community, 75
Cemeteries, Jewish, 17–31, 37, 499, 500, 501, 502, 505, 507, 509, 512
Central British Fund for Refugees, 491
Centralverein deutscher Staatsbürger jüdischen Glaubens (C.V), XI, XVIII, XXIV, 96, 97, 150, 153, 154–155, 156, 200, 213, 216, 235, 239, 262, 270, 271, 306; historiography, XXI–XXII; and Nietzsche, 195n; and republican defence organisations, 241–256 *passim*
Cesarani, David, XXVIII, 3n
Chamberlain, Houston Stewart (racist writer), XII, 213–236; and 'Frankfurter Zeitung', 231–233; and Goethe, 226, 231, 233; and Reichstag, 223–224, 228, 235; Wilhelm II and, 227, 229, 234, 235
Chamberlain, Joseph (British politician), 137
Chamberlain, Neville (British Prime Minister), 423, 424n
Chevra Kaddisha (burial society), 19, 22, 30
Children, Jewish, 335, 337, 405, 414, 534
Chirac, Auguste (Socialist, antisemite), 132
Christians and Jews, 3–16, 17–19, 77, 118–119; Bekennende Kirche, 339, 351, 358; "Christian state", 65, 68, 118, 368; in GDR, XV–XVI, 497–513; "Jewish Christians", XIX. *See also* Aid to the persecuted, Catholics, Protestants, Resistance.
Christlich-jüdische Begegnung, 500
Christlichsoziale Partei/Bewegung, 127, 303
Christlich-soziale Partei (Austria), 143, 483, 484, 524
Chug Chaluzi (escape organisation), 400
Churchill, Winston Spencer (British statesman), 277, 455, 457, 518, 535
Civil servants; German, 26, 99, 386; Jewish, 95, 100
Clair, René (film director), 537, 538
Clark, Kenneth Mackenzie (art historian), 532
Claß, Heinrich (Daniel Frymann) (Pan-German leader, antisemite), 232, 233, 234n
Clermont-Tonnerre, Stanislaus, comte de (French statesman), 95, 367
Cluse, William Sampson (British MP), 418n
Cobbett, William (radical writer), 136

Cohen, Gerson D. (Judaist), XXVII
Cohen, Hermann (philosopher), 33, 35, 47–49, 155
Cohen, J.X. (US rabbi), 489
Cohen, Raphael (Altona rabbi), 76
Cohen, Robert A., 202n
Cohen, Susie, XXVIII
Cohn, Abraham (preacher, author), 41
Cohn, Bertha (bibliographer), XXVII
Cohn, Oscar (lawyer, Socialist politician), 253
Cole, Sidney (film editor), 532
Cologne Jewish community, 30, 47, 52, 55, 238
Columbus, Christopher (explorer), 34, 40
Communists, XVI, XXIII, 249, 252, 255, 274, 497, 498, 507, 510; emigration, 405, 510; in Resistance, XIII, XIV, XV, 381, 397–414, 510n; women, 397–414; youth, 404, 405, 408. *See also* Kommunistische Partei Deutschlands.
Community structure, Jewish in Germany, X, 7, 46n, 51, 73, 74, 90, 104, 106–107, 147, 157n, 161, 321, 327, 366; post-WWII, 498, 500; Zionists and, 147, 157n, 161, 165, 166–167. *See also* individual communities.
Compart, Ellen (of Baum Group), 402, 411
Concentration camps, XXIII, 98, 100, 335, 336, 337, 373, 395, 400, 409, 505, 533n. *See also* individual camps.
Congress of Vienna, 61, 63, 77, 368, 371
Conservatives, Conservatism, XIII, 88, 223n, 224n, 368–369, 391, 392–393; in Resistance, XIII–XIV, 364, 385, 393, 396
Control Commission for Germany/Austria, 456, 458
Conversion, converts, XIX, 40, 48, 65, 85, 88, 92, 95, 97, 101, 118, 179n, 191n, 302, 358, 368, 383n, 386, 388, 389
Cooper, Ernest N. (British official), 436–437, 439–440, 441n, 443n
Cornelius, Henry (Heinz) (film director), 538
Cottbus Jewish community, 505
Courant, Curt (photographer), 521, 526–527n
Court Jews, 6, 61, 73, 75
Cranborne, [Viscount] (British politician), 440–441, 442, 443–444n
Crémieux, Adolphe (French justice minister, president Alliance Israélite Universelle), 121
Criminals, Jewish, 7, 61, 182
Croatian Jewry, 481
Crohn, Paul (Magdeburg merchant), 250
Cronin, A.J. (novelist), 522, 529
Culture, German; in Jewish life, 288, 293, 319; Jewish part in, XIX, 101, 102, 193, 199, 226. *See also* Jewry (German – symbiosis).
'C.V.-Zeitung', 96, 155, 235, 252
Czech-Jewish National Union, 163
Czinner, Paul (film director), 519, 520n, 521, 522, 526, 532

Dachau concentration camp, 504

'Daily Express', 453
'Daily Mail', 222
'Daily Telegraph', 226, 527
Danischewsky, Monja (press officer), 519
Darwin, Charles (British scientist), 234n; Social Darwinism, 215
Daumer, Georg Friedrich (religious philosopher), 118, 126, 131
Davidson (British officer), 439–440
Davie, Maurice R. (writer), 466
Davies, D.R. Seaborne (British official), 428, 433n, 443n, 446n, 448n
Deckert, Joseph (priest, antisemite), 231
Defoe, Daniel (novelist), 531
Dehler, Thomas (of Resistance), 393
Dehmel, Richard (poet, playwright), 217
Del Giudice, Filippo (film company director), 518–519, 520n, 521
Delbrück, Hans (historian), 301
Demokratischer Klub Berlin, 305
Demps, Laurenz, 92n
Department stores, 88, 239, 241, 255
Deportation, XIII, XXV, 327–350 *passim*, 372, 373, 399, 402, 410–412, 493; Fabrik-Aktion, 335, 342, 399; post-WWI, 484
Derrida, Jacques, 191
Dessau, Jewish community, 6
Deutsch, Ernst (actor), 520n, 528–529
Deutsch, Lily (wife of Oscar D.), 534
Deutsch, Oscar (film director), 518, 534
'Deutsch-Israelitische Zeitung', 247n. *See also* 'Die Laubhütte'.
Deutsch-jüdische Jugendgemeinschaft, 404, 408
'Deutsche Arbeiter-Presse', 490
Deutsche Bank, 84
Deutsche Demokratische Jugend (Jungdemokraten), 386
Deutsche Demokratische Partei (DDP), XIX, 237, 248, 251, 305, 382, 383, 384, 386, 389, 390, 394, 395
Deutsche Demokratische Republik, *see* German Democratic Republic
Deutsche Fortschrittspartei, 297, 303
Deutsche Freiheitspartei, 383
Deutsche Freisinnige Partei, 303
'Deutsche Heimat', 230n
Deutsche Staatspartei (DStP), 305, 382, 383n, 389, 394n
Deutsche Studentenschaft, 485
'Deutsche Tageszeitung', 224n
Deutsche Volkspartei (DVP), 256n, 300, 382, 383, 384
'Deutsche Zeitung', 231
Deutscher Automobil Club, 257n
Deutscher Republikanischer Reichsbund, 241, 248n
Deutscher Volksrat (Nationalist club), 484
'Deutsches Volksblatt', 489
Deutschkron, Inge, 407, 412

'Deutschlands Erneuerung', 230
Deutschnationale Volkspartei (DNVP), 240, 384
Deutschnationaler Handlungsgehilfenverband, 228
'Deutschösterreichische Tages-Zeitung', 488, 489
'Deutschvölkische Blätter', 222, 228
Dickens, Charles (novelist), 531
Dickinson, Thorold (film director), 532, 540
Dickson, Benjamin A. "Monk" (US officer), 465, 466n
Diderot, Denis (encyclopedist), 8
Dieckhoff, Hans (German Ambassador), 490–491n
Dienemann, Max (writer), 276n
Dietrich, Theodor (Weimar finance minister), 383
Dilthey, Wilhelm (philosopher), 367
Dinshaw, Avi, XXVIII
Disconto-Gesellschaft, 86–87
Diseases of Jews, *see* Pathology
Displaced persons, 497, 498
Disraeli, Benjamin (British statesman), 369, 540
Dixon, Campbell (film critic), 527
Dohm, Christian Wilhelm von (civil servant, archivist), 8–9, 11, 62, 367
Dollfuss, Engelbert (Austrian Chancellor), 487, 488–489
Donovan, "Wild" Bill (US general, founder of OSS), 468, 470
Dowson, Oscar (British official), 435
Dresden Jewish community, 6, 502, 507
Dreyfus Affair, 115, 128, 131–132, 133–134, 135
Drumont, Edouard Adolphe (French antisemite), 116, 129, 130, 131, 132–133, 137
Dubnow, Simon (historian), 367
Dühring, Eugen (racist philosopher), 120, 126, 127–128, 139
Dürer, Albrecht (artist), 225
Düsseldorf Jewish community, 28, 68
Dukes, Ashley (playwright), 523, 527
Dulles, Allan Welsh (head of OSS), 463, 468
Dunker, Ulrich, 237–238, 252n
Dupont, E.A. (film director), 522n
Durkheim, Émile (French sociologist), 81
Dzsida-Bibo, Rosel (of Resistance), 402, 403, 404, 410–412, 414

Earle, George H. (US diplomat), 488, 489
Eberhard, Helga, XXVIII
Ebert, Friedrich (President, Weimar Republic), 249n
Economic persecution, 100, 102, 327, 432
Ede, Chuter (British Home Secretary), 457–458
Eden, Anthony (Earl of Avon) (British politician), 420n, 423, 438, 450
Education, Jewish; in Germany, 11, 45, 76, 77, 80, 294–296, 298, 300, 311, 318, 320–321; in

Palestine, 268; religious, 11, 45, 76, 77, 80, 176, 178, 316, 318, 321

Efron, John, XI, 309n

Eger, Akiba (Halberstadt/Poznań rabbi), 107

Eggerth, Marta (actress), 520n, 521

Ehrenberg, Samuel Meyer (headmaster), 42

Ehrlich, Fritz, *see* Fred Howard

Ehrlich, Ursula (of Baum Group), 402, 407, 411n

Eichberg, Richard (film director), 520n, 521

Eichberger, Willy, *see* C. Esmond

Eichelbaum, Walter "Putty" (of US Intelligence), 466–467

Eichendorff, Josef Frhr. von (poet), 67

Eichmann, Adolf; Eichmann Trial, 502

Eigenbrodt, August (Nationalist writer), 232n

Einstein, Albert (physicist), 101, 102, 531

Einwohnerwehren (Republican defence groups), 242–243, 245

Eisenhower, Dwight David (US general), 467, 469, 475

Eisenmenger, Johann Andreas (orientalist, antisemite), 20n, 231, 316n

'Eiserner Besen', 490

Eisler, Hanns (composer), 521, 527–528

Eisner, Kurt (Socialist politician, Bavarian prime minister), 192, 245

Eitingon, Max (psychoanalyst), 172

Elbogen, Ismar (historian), XXVII

Ellend[t] (Nazi woman propagandist), 247

Elling, Hanna, 398

Elsas, Fritz (Mayor of Berlin), 388, 394

Elvey, Maurice (film director), 524n, 526

Elvin, George (trade union secretary), 532

Emancipation, 5–16 *passim*, 20, 22, 26, 33, 39, 61–69, 71–82, 83–93, 95–102, 103–108, 147, 161, 165, 180, 310, 319; Autoemancipation, 149, 150, 151, 160, 166, 174; effects on health, 183–184; historiography of, 103–108; and French Revolution, 65, 95, 128, 150; post-WWII, XIII–XIV, 393

Emancipation, laws on, 64, 104, 105; in Austria (Toleranzpatent), 11, 13, 76; in Baden (1808–09), 64; in Bavaria (1813), 64, 71; Germany (1870–71), 69; Hanseatic cities, 63, 64; Kölner Toleranzpatent, 13; in Prussia: (1812), 63, 71, (1836), 65, (1847, projected), 65, 71, 107, 368; in Westphalia (1836), 65; after World War II, XIV

Emden, Jacob Israel (Altona rabbi, talmudist), 15, 20, 42

Emerson, Herbert (High Commissioner for Refugees), 443, 448, 451, 453

Emigrants; in Allied forces, XV, XXIV, XXV; British camps for, 420–421, 535; in British cinema, XVI, 517–541; in British forces, XV, 415–459; in British Intelligence, XV, 529n, 535; internment, 415, 417, 419, 423, 424–425, 434–435, 444, 447, 449, 531n, 532, 534; intern-

ment in France, 470; physicians, 419, 427; Polish, 446; repatriation/restoration of nationality, 415, 448–457 *passim*; statelessness, 429, 431, 435–436, 438, 440–442, 445, 451–452; in US Intelligence, XV, 461–477. *See also* Jewry (British), Jewry (United States), Naturalisation, Pioneer Corps, United States Intelligence.

Emigration; from Austria, 490–491, 492; banned, 338, 411; to Brazil, 305n, 383n; to Britain, XII, XV, XVI, XX, 287, 293, 337, 383, 385, 415–459, 491; to Denmark, 385, 389; from East Germany, 498; to France, 383n, 398, 470; illegal, 359; to Mexico, 398; money regulations, 287, 491; from Nazi Germany, XIII, 102, 197, 248n, 263, 269, 333, 383, 394, 395, 398, 430, 431; to Palestine/Israel, XXI, 148–149, 151, 153, 157, 177, 187, 205, 253, 261–286 *passim*, 313, 314, 333, 394, 498n; re-emigration, 418, 421, 423, 521n, 533; to Shanghai, 427; to Sweden, 385; to Switzerland, 311, 383n, 385; to USA, XV, 91, 338, 383n, 385, 398, 490–491, 495; to USSR, 398

Endingen Jewish community, 311

Engel, Eduard (writer), 226

Engelhard, Karl (völkisch writer), 226

Engels, Friedrich (Socialist theoretician), 111, 116, 119, 120, 127, 128, 140, 143, 300

Engländer, Martin (Zionist physician), 179–181

Enlightenment (Aufklärung), IX, XI, 3–16, 18–19, 31, 61, 62, 67, 68, 73–74, 75, 79, 188, 367; French, 118; Nietzsche and, 193; opponents, X

Ephraim, [Nathan] Veitel Heine (court banker, communal elder), 74, 510

Erfurt Jewish community, 499, 500, 502, 505, 512

Erhardt, Hermann (naval officer), 253n

Erpel, Simone, XIII, XIV

Erzberger, Matthias (Zentrum politician), 243

Eschwege, Helmut, XV, 359, 381, 401n, 411, 461n, 500

Esmond, Carl (Willy Eichberger) (actor), 520n, 521

Estreicher, Ze'ev, XXVIII

Euchel, Isaac Abraham (editor 'Hame'asef'), 42, 75, 79

Evans, Arthur (British MP), 422

Extermination, IX, X, XVI, XXV, 98, 100, 327, 341, 342–343, 360, 430, 434, 442, 450, 459, 465; death marches, 505; extermination camps, 434, 450; Wannsee Conference, 432

Eyck family, XII, 287–307

Eyck, Anna (née Veitel, wife of James E.), 293n

Eyck, Erich (historian), XII, 287, 288, 292, 293, 295–296, 297, 299, 300–306

Eyck, Ernst (businessman, son of Joseph E.), 288, 292, 294–295

Eyck, F. Gunther, 287n

Eyck, Hans (patent lawyer, son of Joseph E.), 288, 292, 296, 298
Eyck, Hedwig (née Kosterlitz, wife of Erich E.), 287, 301–302, 304
Eyck, Helene (wife of Joseph E., née Veitel), 287–290, 292, 293–295, 296, 297–298, 299–300
Eyck, Jakob (father of Joseph E.), 290n, 292
Eyck, James (fl. 1890), 293n
Eyck, Joseph (grain broker, brewery manager), 287–294, 296, 297, 298–300, 302
Eyck, Rosemarie, 307n
Eyck, U.F.J. (Frank), XII

Fabricius (Nazi deputy), 306
Falk, Alfred ("Cohn") (youth leader), 248n
Fanon, Frantz (Afro-American writer), 108
Farago, Ladislas, 470
Feder, Ernst (publicist, editor), 306
Feher, Friedrich (film director), 520n, 521
Feit (Veitel), Fedor (architect), 288, 299
Feit, Erna (wife of Fedor F.), 288, 292, 299–300
Feld, Hans, XVI, XXVIII, 521n
Fellner, Hermann (film director), 520n, 524
Fetscher, Iring (writer), 234n
Feuchtwanger, Lion (novelist), 102, 523, 524
Feuerbach, Ludwig (philosopher), 118, 126
Fichte (workers' sport association), 410
Fichte, Johann Gottlieb (philosopher), 68, 193n, 229n, 230n, 231n, 367
Field, Geoffrey G., XIIn, 214, 215, 234, 235
Films, XVI, XVIII, 517–541; anti-Nazi, 524, 527–529; on Jewish subjects, 523–527, 538–541. *And see* lists in text: of film actors, actresses, directors, 520n; of writers, composers, technicians, 521n.
Finch, Peter (actor), 539
Finn, Carl (ADAV agitator, antisemite), 125
Fischer, Grete (travel writer), 263, 284
Fischer, Samuel (publisher), 101
Fischinger, Oskar (film director), 533
Fishberg, Maurice (writer on race), 170n
Fleischer, Helga (Communist deputy), 398
Fleischmann, Max (professor of law), 389
Floß Jewish community, 18
Foerg, Irmgard, XXVII–XXVIII
Fogelman, Eva, 329
Forced labour, 328, 333, 335, 337, 342, 348, 399, 400, 407, 410, 411, 412; Elmo-Werke, 412; I.G. Farben, 411; Siemens factories, 407, 410; Union munitions factory, 400
Ford, Henry (motor manufacturer), 489–490
Fortschritt/Freisinn, XIX, 297, 298, 303. *See also* Progressives.
Fould, Achille (French Minister), 120, 121, 130
Fourier, Charles (economist), Fourierists, 114, 115, 128–129, 131, 139
Fox, John, XV
Fränkel, Edith (of Resistance), 413

Fraenkel, Heinrich (writer, film critic), 521n
Franckel, Leo (associate of Herzl), 204n
Franconian Jewry, 248; Lower Franconia, 18, 23, 25, 26, 30; Middle Franconia, 27
Frank, Benno (of US Intelligence), 464
Frank, Hans (lawyer, Nazi leader), 306
Frankel, Cyril (film director), 538
Frankfurt a. Main Jewish community, 4, 5, 46, 48, 49, 53, 55–56, 73, 75, 76, 78, 316n, 318, 385; Einheitsgemeinde, 53, 56; Israelitische Gemeinde, 49, 50n, 55–56; Israelitische Religionsgesellschaft, 46n, 52, 318
Frankfurt a.d. Oder Jewish community, 505
Frankfurt School (Institut für Sozialforschung), 191, 468–469
Frankfurt National Assembly, 4, 298n
'Frankfurter Zeitung', 231–233, 300, 301
Frankl, Ludwig August (Jewish functionary, poet), 261
Franklin, Benjamin (natural philosopher, politician), 40
Franklin, Dan, XXVIII
Freemasons, 77, 78, 133, 134, 162
Freiburg; rescuers in, 337–338; Resistance, 393
'(Die) Freie Hanse', 241, 244
Freier Deutscher Kulturbund, 532n
Freies Deutschland (Free German Movement in Great Britain), 383
Freiheitspartei (Austria), 493
Freikorps, 245
Freisinnige Vereinigung, 303, 304
Freud, Sigmund (founder of psychoanalysis), 171n, 172, 184, 185, 186, 205, 531
Freund, Karl (photographer), 522
Freundlich family, 409
Freystadt Jewish community, 288, 290–291
Friedemann, Adolf (jurist, Zionist politician), 153, 271
Friedländer, Albert H., XIII, XIV, XXVIII
Friedländer, David (Berlin manufacturer, Jewish reformer), 9, 73, 74, 265
Friedländer, Joseph Abraham (Brilon rabbi), 27n
Friedrich II (Hohenstaufen Emperor), 366, 371
Friedrich II (Frederick the Great), 39, 72
Friedrich III (Emperor of Germany), 297
Friedrich Wilhelm (Great Elector), 6, 72
Friedrich Wilhelm I (King of Prussia), 72
Friedrich Wilhelm III (King of Prussia), 19, 30, 71
Friedrich Wilhelm IV (King of Prussia), 35, 65, 71, 105
Fries, Jakob (historian), 68
Friesel, Evyatar, XXVIII–XXIX
Frisch, Willy (actor), 537
Frischenschlager, Friedhelm, 493
Frischman, David (Hebrew writer), 209n
Fritsch, Theodor (antisemitic agitator), 217, 223, 224, 227, 228n, 231

Fromm, Erich (psychoanalyst), 49
Frucht, Karl, 462
Frühwald, Wolfgang, 67
Fry, Varian (rescued European Jews), 462
Fuchs, Eugen (jurist, C.V. Chairman), 155
Fuchs, Maximilian (of Resistance), 394
Fugger, Carl (of Resistance), 398
Fugger, Elsa Vierling- (Communist, in Resistance), 398
Furtmüller, Lux (translator), XXVIII

Gänzel, Regina (leader of childrens' group), 414
Galician Jewry, 144, 159, 311, 316, 484
Galinski, Heinz, 509, 510, 511n
Gans, David ben Salomo (astronomer, mathematician, historian), 41
Gans, Eduard (jurist, philosopher), 40, 75
Gans, Isaac Jacob (grandfather of Eduard G.), 75
Gardiner, Kate, XXIX
Gavron, Robert, XXIX
Gedud Haavodah, 269
Gellert, Christian Fürchtegott (poet), 8
George, Stefan (poet), 191, 192
'Gerechtigkeit', 490
German Democratic Republic, XV, 497–513
German language, 30, 72, 309, 310
'Germania Judaica', 371, 373
Geroda Jewish community, 30
Gerolzhofen Jewish community, 248
Gerson[-Berner], Inge, 406, 407
Gesellschaft DDR-Israel für Verständigung und Zusammenarbeit, 511–512
Gesellschaft der Freunde [of Enlightenment], 79
Gesellschaft für christlich-jüdische Zusammenarbeit, 396n, 507
Gesellschaft für jüdische Volkskunde, 317n
Gesellschaft zur Förderung der Wissenschaft des Judentums, 371, 374
Gessler, Otto (Reichswehrminister), 383
Gestapo, 305n, 328, 330, 333–341 passim, 344, 345, 356, 398, 401, 407–413 passim, 492, 531n
Geula (Redemption) (land purchase society), 276v
Ghettos, 97, 98, 334, 341, 395. See also individual ghettos.
Ghillany, Friedrich Wilhelm (writer), 118, 131
Gibson, Mary, XXVIII
Gidal, Nachum Tim, XXIX
Giese, Therese (actress), 102
Giessen Jewish community, 28
Gilbert, Felix (historian), 470
Gilchrist, Sylvia, XXVII
Gilliat, Sidney (scriptwriter), 524, 536n, 537, 541
Gilman, Sander L., 169n, 177n
Ginat, Jochanan (educationalist, Director of LBI, Jerusalem), XXVIII
Ginzel, Günter, XXIX

Glagau, Otto (antisemitic writer), 126
Glatzer, Nahum N. (Judaist, historian), 49
Gmeiner, Franz Xavier (professor), 14, 16
Gobineau, Joseph-Arthur, comte de (orientalist, racist), 131, 132, 217, 233–234n
Goebbels, Joseph (Nazi leader), 102, 523
Goedeke, Karl (Germanist), 225
Goerdeler, Carl (Nationalist politician, in Resistance), 384, 385, 389, 393, 394
Göring, Hermann (Nazi leader), 432
Görlitz Jewish community, 238
Goethe, Johann Wolfgang von (poet), 30, 50–51, 192, 193n, 226, 230, 231, 233, 288, 316
Goetz, Helmut, 302n
Goeze, Johann Melchior (Hamburg pastor), 12–13
Goldberg, Arthur (jurist, of OSS), 468, 469
Golding, Louis (novelist), 524
Goldmann, Nahum (Zionist statesman), 193n, 267, 272, 279
Goldschmidt, Trude (née Arnheim), 301
Goldschmitt (wrote on cremation), 29n
Goldsmith, Isadore (Isidor Goldschmidt) (film director), 520n, 522, 529, 530
Goldstein, Moritz (writer), 309, 311
Golomb, Jacob, 192n
Gooch, George Peabody (historian), 304
Gordon, Judah Leib (Loeb) (Hebrew poet), 33n
Goslar, Hans (Pruss. civil servant, Zionist), 254
Gottfurcht, Fritz (Frederic Gotfurt) (scriptwriter), 521n
Gough-Yates, Kevin, XVI
Gräter, Carlheinz, 301n, 303n
Graetz, Michael, X, 103, 104, 106–107
Grätz, Paul (actor), 520n, 521
Graham ('The Times' correspondent), 223
Grant (US diplomat), 482
Gray, Allan (composer), 521n, 536
Green, Danny (actor), 538n
Greenbaum, Mutz (Max Greene) (cinema technician), 521n, 537
Greene, Graham (novelist), 528
Greene, William (British MP), 423n
Greive, Gisela, XXIX
Grenville, John A.S., XVII, XXVIII
Gréville, Edmund T. (film director), 529
Grierson, John (film director), 536
Griffith, David Wark (film director), 526, 527
Grigg, James (British politician), 418, 440, 444
Grimm, Jacob Ludwig Karl and Wilhelm Karl (philologists), 225
Gröbzig Jewish community, 509
Grosz, Paul, 494
Grubel, Fred, XXVIII, 299n
Grüber, Heinrich; Büro Grüber, 395
Grünewald, Hirsch Lazarus (butcher), 23
Gruenewald, Max (rabbi, International President of the Leo Baeck Institute), XXVIII
Grünfeld, Ernst (sociologist, professor), 389

Grune, Karl (film director), 519–520, 522, 527, 528, 536
Grunwald, Max (Hamburg rabbi), 317n
Gruppe Q (Resistance group), 394n
Guben Jewish community, 501, 509
Guérin, Jules (French antisemitic leader), 133
Guesde, Jules [Bazile] (French politician), 133
Gumbel, Emil Julius (mathematician), 97, 470
Gumpertz, Ruben Samuel (banker), 74
Gundolf, Friedrich (literary historian), 191

Haas, Dolly (actress), 520n, 521, 526, 527, 531
Haas, Ludwig (Liberal politician), 249n, 251
Habe, Hans (Békessy) (writer), 463, 471, 472
Haber, Fritz (chemist), 102
Habonim, 335
Hafenrichter, Oswald (cinema technician), 521n
Hagen, Julius (Kleinenhagen) (film producer), 518, 526
Haider, Jörg, 495
Haig Camp (for refugees), 421
Halberstadt Jewish community, 47, 90–91, 314
Halevi, Yehuda (Jehudah Ha-Levi) (poet, religious philosopher) , 200, 312
Hall, George H. (British MP), 455
Halle Jewish community, 6, 501, 502
Halle, Aron Wolfsohn (satirist), 75
Hallo, Rudolf (art historian), 51n
Halstead, Albert (US diplomat), 484
Hamburg Jewish community, 48, 76, 385–386; Alsterpavillon pogroms, 66; Reichsbanner in, XII, 238–239, 240, 242–244, 245; Resistance, 389, 394; synagogues, 80, 385; veterans' groups, 238, 239, 242–243, 252
Hamburger, Oskar (involved in trial), 249n
'Hame'asef', 9, 42, 79
Hamer, Robert (film director), 538
Hamilton, Gordon, 299n
Hamm Jewish community, 68
'(Der) Hammer, Blätter für deutschen Sinn', 223, 224
Handl, Irene (actress), 538n
Hansabund für Gewerbe, Handel und Industrie, 298, 305n
Hapoel Hazair, 281
Harand, Irene, 490
Harburger, Perez (memoirist), 98
Harden, Maximilian (journalist, editor), 236n
Hardenberg, Karl August Fürst von (Prussian statesman), 64, 67
Hardie, Keir (British Labour leader), 138
Hardy, Loo (actress), 520
Harnack, Adolf (Protestant theologian), 374
Harrison, Geoffrey Wedgwood (British official), 445
Hasenclever, Walter, jr, 464
Hasenclever, Wilhelm (Socialist politician), 125
Hashomer Hazair, XII, 205, 274, 404, 413

Hasidism, 152, 207, 211, 283, 315, 316, 317
Haskalah (Jewish Enlightenment), 3, 5, 9–12, 14–15, 16, 21, 52, 75, 173–174, 188
Hassel, Ulrich von (Resistance leader), 393
Hasselmann, Wilhelm (Socialist politician, editor), 125–126, 127, 139
Haverkamp, Alfred, 103n
Herberstein (Bishop of Laibach, fl. 1782), 13
Hebrew language, 9–11, 19, 29, 30, 42, 160, 165–166, 177, 263, 292; in cemeteries, 19, 29, 30
Hebrew literature, 41, 208, 209, 317
Hechawer (Swiss Zionist fraternity), 184
Heckroth, Hein (designer), 521n, 537
Hegel, Georg Wilhelm Friedrich (philosopher), 193n, 202, 367; and Judaism, 369; Hegelians, 118, 126, 131
Heid, Ludger, XXIX
Heidegger, Martin (philosopher), 192
Heifetz, Lillian, 214n
Heimann, Felix (lawyer), 250
Heimschutz Groß-Hamburg, 243
Heine, Heinrich (poet), XI, 40, 121, 125, 195, 405
Heine, Wolfgang (Socialist politician), 139
Heinemann (publishers), XXVIII
Heinemann, Isaac (religious philosopher), 200–201
Held, Heinrich (Bavarian politician), 247, 255
Heller, Otto (photographer), 521n, 532, 537
Heller, Yomtov Lipman (rabbinic scholar), 41
Helphand, Alexander Israel, see Parvus-Helphand
Henderson, Ian (British official), 449–450n, 451, 457n
Henk, Elsa (memoirist), 340
Henreid, Paul (actor), 520n, 521
Hentrich, Gerhard, XXIX
Herder, Johann Gottfried (philosopher), 231n
Hermann, Georg (novelist), XIII, 309n
Herrman, Hugo (Zionist journalist), 266, 272–274, 280–281
Herrmann, Klaus J., 306n
Hertz, Friedrich (writer), 216–217, 233
Herz, Marcus (physician), 21, 27, 41, 73–74
Herzig, Arno, IX, 103, 104–105
Herzl, Theodor (founder of Zionist movement), 50, 134, 150–151, 161, 162, 163, 166, 204, 263, 264, 309n, 379; "Altneuland", 309n
Herzstein, Robert, 494
Hess, Moses (Socialist philosopher), 120, 131
Hessian Jewry, 5, 64, 512
Heuberger, Rachel, IX
Heuss, Elly (née Knapp, wife of Theodor H.), 304
Heuss, Theodor (Liberal politician, German Fed. President), 304, 383
Hewison, R.J.P. (British official), 455
Heydrich, Reinhard (Nazi leader), 34, 409n, 432
Heym, Stefan (Hellmuth Flieg), 464, 471, 472

Heymann, Stefan (GDR minister), 500
Hibbat Zion, 148, 151, 261n
Hildebrand, Johannes (pastor), 502, 505
Hildesheimer family, 90
Hildesheimer, E., 659
Hildesheimer, Esriel (rabbi, leader of Orthodoxy), 47, 53
'(Die) Hilfe', 304
Hindenburg, Paul von Benneckendorf und von (German field-marshal, President of Weimar Republic), 97, 235, 291
Hirsch (Halberstadt) family, 84, 90–91, 659
Hirsch, Alice and Hella (of Baum Group), 401, 407, 411
Hirsch, Benjamin (metal merchant), 90–91, 93
Hirsch, Julie-Julchen (née Auerbach), 90, 91
Hirsch, Mendel (headmaster), 318
Hirsch, Samson Raphael (rabbi, leader of Orthodoxy), 4, 45, 48n, 310, 311, 312, 313, 314, 315–316, 317, 318, 322; Hirsch-Romane, 311–317. *See also* Orthodox (Neo-Orthodoxy).
Hirschberg, Alfred (editor'C.V.-Zeitung'), 254
Hirschberg, Julius (ophthalmologist), 659
Hirschberg, Max (lawyer), 245
Hirschfeld, Gerhard, XXIX
Hirschfeld, Max (sexologist), 183
Historiography, XII, 33–43, 101, 111–112, 116, 513n; Bochum meeting, IX; of emancipation, 103–108; German-Jewish, X, XVII–XXVI, XXIX, 309, 402; Holocaust studies, XXII, 500; Left-wing, 112; under Nazism, 363–379; Nietzsche and, 210; Resistance, XIV, 381; underground life, 328–332, 361; Zionist, XXI
Hitchcock, Alfred (film director), 537
Hitler, Adolf, XIV, XXV, 97, 247n, 306, 386, 395, 417, 423, 432–433, 467, 483, 488, 489, 523, 527, 529, 530, 532; Conservatives and, 391; Hitler-Stalin Pact, XV, 538
Hoare, Samuel (British politician), 443
Hobson, John A. (journalist, economist), 138
Hochschule (Lehranstalt) für die Wissenschaft des Judentums, Berlin, 366, 374, 375
Hochschule für Jüdische Studien Heidelberg, XVII
Hodge, John (trade union leader), 135
Hodges, Courtney (US General), 465
Hoeflich, Eugen, *see* M.Y. Ben-Gavriêl
Hölderlin, Friedrich (poet), 204
Höllering, George (film director), 519, 520n
Hoernigk, Frank, 389n
Hörsing, Otto (Reichsbanner Chairman), 239, 249–250, 256
Hoetzsch, Otto (journalist), 232n
Höxter Jewish community, 64
Hoffmann, Christhard, XVIIn, XXIX
Hofmannsthal, Hugo von (poet, dramatist), 227
Holbach, Paul Heinrich Dietrich Baron von (philosopher, encyclopedist), 8, 118, 131
Holborn, Hajo (writer), 469

Holitscher, Arthur (writer), 268–269, 271, 273, 280
Holländer, Ludwig (C.V. director, lawyer, publisher), 246
"Holocaust" (TV film), 101
Holzer, Charlotte, *see* Abraham-H., C.
Holzer, Eva, 414
Homolka, Oscar (actor), 520n, 521
Honecker, Erich, 508, 510, 512
Hoover, Herbert (US President), 486
Hopkinson, Austin (British MP), 455
Hoppe, Hugo (Jewish physician), 182–183
Hore-Belisha, Lesley (British politician), 419
Horkheimer, Max (social philosopher), 191
Horovitz, Marcus (rabbi), 46n, 48, 56, 76, 231
Horowitz, Johannes (journalist), 483
Horwitz, Nathan (physician), 34
Hovevei-Zion, 148–149, 156
Howard, Fred (Fritz Ehrlich), 464, 465
Hull, David Stewart, 520
Humboldt, Alexander Frhr. von (scientist), 40
Humboldt, Wilhelm Frhr. von (Prussian statesman), 65, 192
Hurd, Percy (British MP), 439–440n
Hyndman, Henry (editor), 136–137

"I.St." (nom-de-plume), 217, 230–231
ibn Ezra, Abraham (medieval philosopher), 41
ibn Khaldun, Abd ar-Rahman (medieval historian), XXVII
'Im deutschen Reich', 155, 235
Intermarriage, 11, 81, 86, 92, 98, 100, 137, 374, 383n, 482, 498, 510; in Third Reich, 333–335, 338, 340, 346, 349, 353, 354, 355, 359
International Brigades, XXIV
International Women's Congress (1934), 399
Internationale Arbeiterhilfe (IAH), 397, 410
'Internationale Monatsschrift', 224n
Internationaler Sozialistischer Kampfbund, 381
Iokhelson, Vladimir (Russian Socialist), 122
Isay, Rudolf (lawyer, convert), 302, 305n
Isherwood, Christopher (writer), 538
Israel, State of, XII, XX, XXII, 167, 500, 501, 503 505, 510, 511
Israel, Wilfrid (merchant, philanthropist), 534
'(Der) Israelit', 310, 311
Itzig, Daniel (banker), 74–75

Jacob ben Meir Tam (French scholar), 41
Jacobi, Lou (actor), 538n
Jacobs, Robert A., XXVIII
Jacobsen, Alfred (Right-wing lawyer), 232
Jacoby family, 84–85
Jaffe, Louis N. (Zionist), 485
Jaffé, Philipp (medieval historian), 40
James, Sidney (actor), 538n
Jannings, Emil (actor), 523
Janvion, Emile (French syndicalist), 134
Jasen, Kurt (art collector), 464

Jaspers, Karl (philosopher), 192
Jastrow-Rotholz, Lotte (of Baum Group), 407, 413, 414
Jaurès, Jean (French Socialist politician), 115, 133, 134
Jersch-Wenzel, Stefi, XXIX
Jerzabek, Anton (of Christlich-Soziale Partei), 484
Jessner, Leopold (film director), 520n, 521
Jessnitz Jewish community, 501, 509
Jewish Agency for Palestine, 167, 491
Jewish Brigade, XXVn
'Jewish Chronicle', 527, 531
Jewish Claims Committee, 492
Jewish disabilities, 6–7, 9; special laws, 63–64, 72; special taxes, 7, 72, 100, 287. See also Antisemitism, Nuremberg Laws.
Jewish Legion, 282
Jewish mysticism, 41, 314, 322; Zohar, 41, 42
Jewish National Council in Palestine, 281
Jewish National Fund (Keren Kayemeth le'Israel), 271, 275, 277, 278, 519n
Jewish Refugees Committee, 389, 441
'Jewish Social Studies', 372, 373
Jewish Territorial Organisation (ITO), 166
Jewry, Austrian, XII, XIX, XXVn, 142–144, 159n, 367, 462, 524; in Britain, XV, 415–459 passim, 534; deportation, 334; restitution, 491–492, 495; in US Intelligence, 461, 463, 465
Jewry, Austro-Hungarian, 149, 158–161, 162–164, 166, 367, 369; education, 11; Jewish immigration, 483. See also Joseph II.
Jewry, British, XX, 3, 69, 90, 134–138, 176, 389, 518, 526; H.S. Chamberlain and, 219–220; East European immigrants, 135, 137, 177; in press, 136, 137; Trade Unions and, 135, 138. See also Emigrants, Emigration.
Jewry, Czech, 163–165, 462; in Britain, 417, 419, 438, 447n. See also Bohemian, Moravian.
Jewry, Danish, 384. See also Emigration.
Jewry, East European, 57, 96, 107, 142, 149, 154, 161, 162, 166, 197–198, 255, 311–323 passim, 369, 386, 429; intellectuals, 208–209; Nietzsche and, 190, 198, 208–209; pathology of, XI, 171–179, 183–188 passim; and Zionism, 149, 151, 152, 155, 157, 167, 208
Jewry, Ethiopian, 311
Jewry, French, 3, 9, 69, 220, 367, 462, 463
Jewry, German; Communists, 397–414; demography, 7, 31, 498, 503, 505; Gesamtarchiv der deutschen Juden, 499; insanity, 169–188; Landjudenschaften, 63; legal position, 363–380; patriotism, IX, XII, XVIII, XXIII, XXV, 48–49, 68, 87, 97–98, 99, 101, 154–155, 159. 199, 220, 234, 306; political allegiances, XI, XIII–XV, XIX–XX, XXIII, 88, 91–92, 162, 192, 237–257 passim, 297, 298, 300, 302–305, 320, 368–369, 381–382, 390, 396. See also

Liberals; post-WWII, 359; rural, 7, 24, 26, 30, 31, 62, 107, 311, 313n, 314–316, 322–323, 373. See also Emigrants, Symbiosis. See also Anhalt, Ansbach, Aschaffenburg, Baden, Bavarian, Brandenburg, Franconian, Hessian, Kurhessen, Mecklenburg, Pomeranian, Poznań, Prussian, Rhineland, Saxonian, Schleswig-Holstein, Silesian, Thuringian, Westphalian and under individual communities.
Jewry, Hungarian, 159, 318, 481
Jewry, Italian, 40, 220, 463
Jewry, Lithuanian, 311, 312
Jewry, Netherlands, 69, 367
Jewry, Polish, 119, 135, 140, 283, 314; physicians and, 171, 174, 187–188
Jewry, Portuguese, 39
Jewry, Romanian, 148, 149, 151, 158, 230
Jewry, Russian/Soviet, X, 119, 121, 135, 140–142, 151, 156, 158, 162, 179, 311, 511; in Britain, 415; Hovevei-Zion, 148–149, 156; in Palestine, 270, 271; pathology, 176, 178–179
Jewry, South African, 136–137, 138
Jewry, Spanish, 34, 39
Jewry, Ukrainian, 140
Jewry, United States, XX; students, 485–488, 491, 495. See also United States Intelligence.
Jewry, Western European, 198, 369; pathology of, XI, 171–188 passim
Jewry, Yemeni, 283
Joachim, Heinz (of Baum Group), 401, 406–407
Jochmann, Werner, XXIX
John XXIII (Pope), 504
John, Johannes (writer), 226–227
Joll, James, XXIX
Joseph II (Emperor of Austria), 40; Toleranzpatent, 11, 13, 76
Josephus Flavius (historian), 314
'Journal für Psychologie und Neurologie', 178
Judaism, 302, 500–501; abandonment, 291–293, 299, 386, 501; Cherem, 74, 76; circumcision, 27, 35, 36, 374; conservative, 46n, 385; dietary laws, 27, 291, 292, 506; liberal, 26–27, 28, 53, 89, 309, 310; liturgy, 45; Memorbuch, IX, 34–43; music, 310; ritual, 200, 204, 290, 310; sermons, 3, 53, 55n; Zunz and, 35–37, 41. See also Burial, Cemeteries, Orthodox Judaism, Reform.
Judd, Max (US Jewish diplomat), 482
'Jüdische Monatshefte', 313, 314, 315, 323
'Jüdische Presse', 49
'Jüdische Rundschau', 96
Jüdische Volkspartei, 254
Jüdischer Frauenbund, 383n, 400
Jüdischer Kulturbund, see Kulturbund deutscher Juden
Jüdischer Verlag, 317
'Jüdisches Echo', 253n
'Jüdisches Literaturblatt', 29n
'Jüdisches Nachrichtenblatt', 334

'Jüdisches Wochenblatt', 250
Jung, Carl Gustav (psychologist), 192
Jungdeutscher Orden, 305, 382
Junge, Alfred (designer), 521n, 537
Jurists, Jewish, 73, 100, 191, 297, 300–302
'Justice', 136–137

Kabbalah, *see* Jewish mysticism
Kälnoky von Köröspatak, Gustav Graf (Austro-Hungarian politician), 482
Kafka, Franz (writer), 98
Kahn, Siegbert (economist), 500
Kahr, Gustav von (Bavarian statesman), 246
Kaiser, Erich (of Reichsbanner), 254n
Kaiser, Wolf, XII
Kalmus, Natalie (cinema technician), 538
Kameraden (youth movement), 238, 251n, 399
Kameradschaften (republican groups), 242–244, 254; Kameradschaft jüdischer Frontsoldaten (Hamburg), 243
Kann, Edgar W. (of US Intelligence), 465, 477
Kann, Lily (actress), 520n, 538
Kanowitz, Siegfried (Shimon) (Zionist leader), 153
Kant, Immanuel (philosopher), 4, 41, 48n, 192, 193n, 202; Kantians, 74; Neo-Kantianism, 47
Kanturek, Otto (cameraman), 521n, 528
Kaplan, Marion A., XXIX
Kapp, Wolfgang; Kapp Putsch, 242, 243, 252n, 253
Karaites, 41
Kareski, Georg (Zionist politician), 254n
Karminski, Hannah (social worker), 400
Karo, Joseph (Spanish-Jewish theologian), 312
Kastein, Josef (writer), 309n
Katscher, Rudolph, *see* R. Cartier
Kauffmann, Robert (company director), 389, 390
Kaufmann, Walter, 194n
Kautsky, Karl (Socialist theoretician), 140, 143
Kazan, Elia (Kazanjoglou) (film director), 536
Kellerman, Henry, 470
Kelley, Anthony M. (US diplomat), 482
Kempner, Fritz (state secretary, in July Plot), 304
Kempner, Robert (jurist), 468
Keren Hayesod, 266, 271, 274, 280
Keren Kayemeth le'Israel (KKL), *see* Jewish National Fund
Kerr, Alfred (Kempner) (writer, critic), 191, 535
Kerr, Archibald Clark (British diplomat), 427
Kershaw, Ian, XXIX
Kessel, Franziska (associate E. Thälmann), 398
Keyserling, Hermann Graf (philosopher), 218n
Khazars, 311, 388
Kibbutz movement, 58, 266, 268–269, 270, 271, 273, 274
Kiel Jewish community, 389
Kip, William B. (of OSS), 470

Kirchheimer, Otto (sociologist), 469, 470
Kirchner, Peter, 509
Kirdorf, Emil (Managing Director of GBAG), 87
Kirkpatrick, Ivone (British official), 456
Kissinger, Henry, 462
Kitchener camp (for refugees), 421
Klages, Ludwig (poet), 192
Klee, Alfred (Berlin Jewish leader), 252–254
Kleinbardorf Jewish community, 18
Kleinschmidt, Karl (Christian preacher), 500
Klemperer, Otto (conductor), 102
Klotz, Helmut, 506
Klub vom 3. Oktober, 386
Kluthe, Hans Albert (anti-Fascist), 383
Knapp, Georg Friedrich (economist), 304
Knoblauch, Eduard (architect), 289
Koch-Weser, Erich (Liberal politician), 305, 383
Kochmann, Martin (of Resistance), 401, 402, 404, 408, 409, 410
'Kölnische Volkszeitung', 215–216, 220
König, Eduard (Bonn Geheimrat), 217
Königsberg Jewish community, 52, 55, 68, 238; Adass Isroel, 47, 52; rescuers, 337
Königswarter family, 120
Koerber, Gerd von (Nazi vice-Gauleiter), 394–395
Koestler, Arthur (writer), 420, 470, 540
'Kohelet Musar' (The Preacher of Morals), 10
Kohn (rabbi, wrote on cremation), 29n
Kohn, Hans (historian), 204–205
Kohn, Pinchas (Ansbach rabbi, kabbalist), 311, 313–317, 322–323
Kolbe, Fritz (German official, OSS contact), 468
Kommunistische Partei Deutschlands (KPD), 240, 404; under Nazism, 398, 405, 510n
Kommunistische Parteiopposition (KPO), 399
Kommunistischer Jugendverband Deutschlands (KJVD), 404, 405, 408
Konferenz landeskirchlicher Arbeitskreise, 508
Korda, Alexander (film director), 518, 519, 520, 526, 528n, 532, 535, 536, 537–538
Korda, Vincent (designer), 521n, 532
Korda, Zoltan (film director), 520n, 526, 532
Kortner, Fritz (actor), 102, 520n, 521, 522, 528n, 532
Kossoff, David (actor), 538
Kosterlitz, Adolf (demolition firm owner), 302
Kovno ghetto, 334
Kracauer, Siegfried (writer, film expert), 49
Kraepelin, Emil (psychiatrist), 170–171, 172, 180, 181
Krafft-Ebing, Richard von (psychiatrist), 170, 171, 172, 180, 181
Krakauer, Moritz (wrote on cremation), 29n
Krautheimer, Richard, 470
Kreisau-Kreis, 384, 393, 396
Kreuzschar (Upper Silesian Centre Party), 250n
'Kreuzzeitung', 223n, 232n

Kritzinger, Wilhelm (state secretary), 432
Krochmal, Nachman (historian, philosopher), 34, 41, 42
Ku Klux Klan, 490, 529
Kuczynski, Jürgen (economic historian), 500
Kulturbund deutscher Juden, 4
'Kunstwart', 225, 226, 309, 311
Kupferberg, Alfred (editor), 269
Kurhessen Jewry, 5
Kuttner, Erich (journalist), 251, 254n
Kwiet, Konrad, XXIX, 359, 371n, 381, 401n, 411, 461n

'Labour Leader', 223
Lachmund, Hans (lawyer), 395
Lachmund, Margarete (Quaker), 394–395
Lammers, Hans Heinrich (head of Reich Chancellery), 432, 433
Landauer, Carl (Socialist journalist), 245–246, 247
Landauer, Gustav (anti-Marxist Socialist), 191, 205
Landsberg, Otto (Socialist politician), 254
'(Das) Landvolk', 257
Lang, Fritz (film director), 522n, 527
Langer, William (historian), 469
Langmaid, Janet Barbara, XXVIII, 214n
Lania, Leo (cinema writer), 528n
Larsen, Egon (writer, film critic), 521n
Laski, Neville (judge), 534
Lasko, Leo (Frank Wysbar) (film director), 520, 536
Lassalle, Ferdinand (Socialist politician), 120, 124–125, 127, 140, 300
Lassally, Walter (photographer), 533
Laube, Heinrich (writer), 40
'(Die) Laubhütte', 247. See also 'Deutsch-Israelitische Zeitung'.
Launder, Frank (cinema writer), 536n, 537, 541n
Lavrov, Pyotr Lavrovich (sociologist), 121
Lazarus, Moritz (Moses) (philosopher), 155
Leber, Julius (Socialist politician), 384, 385
Lehmann, Marcus Meir (rabbi, editor), 310
Leibniz, Gottfried Wilhelm (philosopher), 193n, 230, 316n
Leibovitch, Meir (actor), 538n
Leigh, Vivien (actress), 538n
Leipzig Jewish community, 6, 48
Lenin, Vladimir Ilyich (Soviet statesman), 141
Lent, Alfred (in Disconto-Gesellschaft), 87
Lentschutz, Efraim, 41
Leo Baeck Institute, XVII, XIX, XX, XXII, XXIV, XXVI–XXVII, XXIX, 103, 372, 376; archives, 363, 371n, 470; bibliographies, XXVII; conferences, Xn, 145n; publications, XVI, 527n; Year Books, XVI–XXII, XXIV–XXVI, XXVII, XXIX, 103n, 363, 370, 372

Leroux, Pierre (French Socialist), 115, 129
Lessing, Gotthold Ephraim (poet, dramatist), 4, 8, 12, 80, 192;'Nathan der Weise', 4, 67, 387
Lessing, Theodor (philosopher), 97, 207–208, 293n
Lessing, Willy (Bamberg community leader), 393
Lettow-Vorbeck, Paul von (Prussian general), 242
Leuschen-Seppel, Rosemarie, 113
Leuschner, Wilhelm (Socialist politician), 384, 385
Leuß, Hans (Reichstag deputy, antisemite), 236
Levin, Shmaryahu (Zionist writer, politician), 149
Levinger, Wilhelm (Munich C.V. leader), 245
Levinson, N. Peter, 373, 375
Levy, Alfred Johann, 394n
Lévy, Bernard-Henri, 116
Lewkowitz, Albert (theologian, teacher), 196n
Liberalism, X, XIX, 113, 154, 155, 156–157, 162–163, 166, 233, 369, 383–396 *passim*; in Austria, 143, 164; British, 304; after 1945, 383; Left Liberals, *see* Progressives
Liberals, Jewish, XIII, XIX, XX, XXIII, 147, 150, 151, 155–165 *passim*, 192, 194, 213; Resistance, XIV, 381–396
Liberation of Labour (Russian Social Democratic organisation), 123
Liberman[n], Aron (Hebrew Socialist), 122
Lichtenberg, Bernhard (Berlin provost), 504
Lichtheim, George (writer), 114–115
Lichtheim, Richard (Zionist politician), 153
Liebermann, Max (painter), 102
Liebeschütz, Hans (historian), 363, 369
Liebknecht, Wilhelm (Socialist politician), 145
Lindenberger-Meyer, Hanni (of Baum Group), 401, 406, 407–408
Lindner, Petra, 214n
Lipiner, Siegfried (writer), 190
Lissauer, Ernst (poet), 222
List, Guido von (racist theoretician), 214
Liston, Carole, 389n
Literature, 309; depiction of Jews, 8, 113; Orthodox, XII–XIII, 262, 265, 275, 309–323; on Palestine, 261–286
Litthauer, Ernest K., XXIX
Locke, John (English philosopher), 15, 76
Locker-Lampson, Oliver (British MP), 455
Lockhart, Robert Bruce (diplomat), 518
Łódź ghetto, 334, 341
Loeb, Walter (banker), 249n, 255
Löwenfeld, Philipp (lawyer), 245
Löwenherz, Josef (of Vienna), 409n
Löwenthal, Leo (of Frankfurt School), 49
Loewy, Hildegard (of Baum Group), 407, 413
London, Perry, 329
Lonsbach (pseud.), *see* R.M. Cahen
Lorenz, Ina, 242

Lorre, Peter (actor), 520n, 521
Louis Philippe (King of the French), 129
Louzon, Robert (French syndicalist), 134
Low, Rachel, 517, 534
Lowenthal, Ernst Gottfried, XXIIIn, XXIX, 373n
Lowenthal-Hensel, Cécile, XXIX
Loyola, Ignatius (founder of Jesuits), 219, 229
Lubitsch, Ernst (film director), 536
Lucas family, 375
Lucas, Franz D., 374
Lucas, Leopold (rabbi, historian), XIV, 363, 365, 371, 372, 373, 374–375
Lübeck Jewish community, 63
Lueger, Karl (Mayor of Vienna), 137, 143, 144, 483
Lukács, Georg (philosopher), 192
Luppe, Hermann (Mayor of Nuremberg), 247, 249
Luria, Isaac (Ha'ari) (Kabbalist), 41
Luschan, Felix von (eugenicist), 219
Lustiger, Arno, XXIX, 461
Luther, Martin (religious reformer), 40, 231n, 506; Lutheran Church, XVI
Luxemburg, Rosa (Socialist leader), 139

McAlpine, C.B. (British official), 431, 533n
Maccabaea (Czech-Jewish student association, later Verein der jüdischen Hochschüler), 163
MacDonald, James Ramsay (British Prime Minister), 524
MacDonald, Kevin, 529n
Mack, Max (film director), 520n, 521
MacLeod, D. (British official), 436–437
Magdeburg Jewish community, 243, 250, 502, 504, 505
Maier, Max (lawyer), 302, 305n
Maimonides, Moses (Rambam) (medieval philosopher), 10, 42, 174n, 200
Maizière, Lothar de, 509, 510
Makkabi Hazair, 335
Malbim, Meir Leibusch (Meir Loeb ben Jechiel Michael) (rabbi, talmudist), 52
Malon, Benoît (editor), 132
Mander, Geoffrey le Mesurier (British MP), 419
Mankiewicz, Joseph L. (film director), 536
Mankowitz, Wolf (writer), 538
Mann, Thomas (writer), 96–97, 191–192
Mapu, Abraham (novelist), 40
Marburg Jewish community, 47
Marcus, Paul, *see* "Pem"
Marcuse, Herbert (philosopher), 191
Marcuse, Moshe (Königsberg physician), 174
Maris, Gianfranco, 493
Markbreiter, Charles Gustavus (British official), 428
Marr, Wilhelm (antisemitic agitator), 118, 126–127
Marriage, 171, 181–182, 188, 293, 407

Martov, L. (Iulii Ossopovich Zederbaum) (Russian politician), 141
Marx, C.T., XXIX
Marx, Karl Heinrich (founder of scientific Socialism), 68, 114, 116–117, 118–121, 124, 125, 126, 128, 129, 139–140, 142, 300, 405, 536n; "Zur Judenfrage", 114, 116–117, 118, 126, 129, 139, 144
Marx, Wilhelm (Zentrum politician, German Chancellor), 250n
Marxism, XII, 113–128 *passim*, 133–134, 140–143, 192, 469; Austro-Marxists, 140; and Nietzsche, 205
Masaryk, Thomas Garrigue (Czechoslovak statesman), 164
Maskilim, 12, 15, 75–76, 149, 174, 180
Maslow, Abraham, 153–154
Mason, Paul (British official), 446n, 448–449n, 450n, 451
Massing, Paul W. (writer), 111–112, 113
Mather, Andrew (architect), 534
Mathieu, Gustave, 472n
'(Le) Matin', 222, 226
Matthias, Adolf (educationalist), 227
Maurer, Trude, 253n
Maxwell, Alexander (British official), 418, 442, 443, 444, 448n
Mayer, Carl (film director, writer), 520n, 521, 522, 532
Mayer, Eugen (writer), 57n
Mayer, Paul "Yogi", XXIX
Mayer, Shlomo, XXVIII
Me'asfim, 52
Mecklenburg Jewry, 394, 498, 499, 503, 505, 509; Mecklenburg-Schwerin, 19, 20, 74
Medieval Jewry, 5, 18, 38, 39, 65, 67, 72, 77, 185–186, 365–366, 370
Meerson, Lazare (designer), 521n, 537
Mehring, Franz (Socialist politician), 139, 140
Meinecke, Friedrich (historian), 193n, 367
Meitner, Lise (physicist), 102
Melchior, Carl J. (Hamburg lawyer, banker), 255
Melville, Jean-Pierre (film director), 535
Memmingen Jewish community, 245n
Mendelssohn (banking house), 120
Mendelssohn, Joseph (banker), 79
Mendelssohn, Moses (philosopher), 3, 4, 10, 15, 16, 41, 42, 62, 73, 75, 76, 79, 80, 169–170; Bible translation, 9, 11; and burial regulations, 20–21, 27, 74
Mendes, Lothar (film director), 520n, 523
Mendes-Flohr, Paul R., 202n, 206n
Merker, Paul (Communist politician), 498, 499n, 500
Merzbach, Paul (cinema writer), 521n, 529
Messer, (Professor, of Giessen), 215–216, 224
Metzner, Ernö (designer), 521n, 532
Meyer, Gerald (of OSS), 468

Meyer, Herbert (of Resistance), 408, 409, 410
Meyer, Michael A., XXVI, XXVIII, 45n, 169n, 375, 376
Meyer, Oscar (Liberal politician), 305n, 383
Meyer, Seligmann (rabbi, editor), 246
Meyers, Julie (Nuremberg C.V. secretary), 246n, 247, 248, 249, 254n
Michael, Jakob (Weimar businessman), 256
Midener, Walter (sculptor, of US Intelligence), 466
Military service, 47, 85–86, 95, 98, 99, 107, 250, 296; dismissal, 100; in Turkey, 265. *See also* Emigrants, World War . . .
Milkert family, 409
Minden Jewish community, 66
Minsk ghetto, 334, 341
Mirabeau, Honoré Gabriel Riquetti, comte de (French statesman), 367
Misrachi, 50, 58, 322
Misrahi, Robert (French philosopher), 116
Mission unter Israel, 500
'Mitteilungen aus dem Verein zur Abwehr des Antisemitismus' (later 'Abwehrblätter'), 213–236 *passim*
Model, Walther (German field-marshal), 474
Moest, Gerhard, XXIX
Moholy-Nagy, László (artist), 521n
Mommsen, Theodor (historian, jurist), 231n
Moneylenders, Jewish, 61, 62, 67, 124, 129, 160, 365–366
Montagu, Ivor (writer, film critic), 522
Montefiore, Judith (wife of Moses M.), 41
Montefiore, [Sir] Moses (philanthropist), 41
Montesquieu, Charles de (philosopher), 8
Moravian Jewry, 334
Morès, Marquis de (French writer), 133
Morgan, Emma, XXVIII
Morrison, Herbert (British politician), 425, 426–427, 428, 436–437, 438, 439, 440n, 444
Mosbacher, Elias (wine merchant), 24
Moses, Siegfried (President, Leo Baeck Institute, Zionist politician, Israeli minister), XXII
Mosheim, Johann Lorenz von (historian, theologian), 12, 16
Mosley, Oswald (British Fascist politician), 533
Mosse, George L., XIX, XXIX, 45n, 115, 193
Mosse, Rudolf (publisher), 257n
Mosse, Werner E., X, XII, XXVIII, 103, 104, 107
Motzkin, Leo (Zionist politician), 149
Moylan, John (British official), 439, 441, 442
Moynihan, Daniel Patrick, 481
Mühlen, Patrick von zur, 236n
Müller, Renate (actress), 537
'Münchener Post', 245
Münsterberg, Hugo (philosopher), 216, 233
Muhr, Abraham (reformer, businessman), 41, 107

Munich Jewish community, 55, 98, 238, 245–246, 247; Resistance, 389, 394
Munk, Leo (Orthodox rabbi, Marburg), 55n
Mycroft, Walter (pro-Nazi film producer), 531
Mylius, Karin, 501

Nagy-Atad Jewish community, 47
Names, Jewish, 38; change of, 348–349, 359
Namier, Lewis Bernstein (historian), 107
Napoleonic era, 3, 61, 63–64, 68, 130, 367
Narodnaya Volya (The People's Will) (Tsarist Russian terrorist movement), 122–123
Nathan, Harry Louis (1st Baron), 439
Nathan, Johanna (secretary), 371–372
Nathan, Paul (politician, publisher), 246
'(Die) Nation', 302
Nationalism, German, 48–49, 51, 68, 97, 142, 143, 189, 193, 245, 253, 291, 484
Nationalism, Jewish, *see* Zionism
Nationalliberale Partei, XIX, 298, 382
Naturalisation, XV, 6, 74–75; of refugees in Britain, XV, 415, 418, 423–424, 426, 428–429, 436, 438–448, 450–451, 454–455, 457–458
Naumann, Friedrich (Liberal politician), 303, 304
Nazism, 96, 97, 189, 369, 510; before 1933, 244, 247–248; Ausbürgerungsgesetz (1933), 429, 437; Machtergreifung, XX, 158, 192; propaganda, 121, 247, 365, 366, 391, 401; racial policy, 99, 101, 391, 403, 430–434
Nazism, Jews under X, XIII, XXII–XXV, 262, 269, 322, 327–361, 363–380, 381–396, 397–414, 510 businessmen, 387–388; Jewish historiography, 363–380; specific prohibitions, 332–333, 334, 336, 337. *See also* Underground life, Yellow Star.
Neander, August (David Mendel) (church historian), 368
Neu Beginnen, 381
Neuberger, Helmut, 396
'Neue Freie Presse', 143, 162, 264
'(Das) neue Tage-Buch', 532n
'(Die) neue Weltbühne', 532n
'Neuer Social-Demokrat', 125
'Neues Deutschland', 503
Neumann, Christiane (catechist), 502
Neumann, Franz (lawyer, trade unionist), 469, 470
Neumann, Isaac, 507
Neumann, Oskar (Slovak Zionist), 277
Neumann, Robert (writer), 527
New York Jewish community, 489
'(The) New York Times', 462, 481, 483, 485, 486, 494
Newsam, Frank (British official), 415, 451, 452
Newton, Isaac (scientist), 11
Nicosia, Francis R., XXIX
Nietzsche, Friedrich Wilhelm (philosopher), and Jewry, XI–XII, 189–212, 221; and anti-

semitism, XI, 190, 191, 193–197, 198, 200; and Zionism, 196n, 203–212
Niewyk, Donald L., 252
Nobel family, 47
Nobel, Nehemiah Anton (Orthodox leader), IX, 45–58, 199–200, 317–318; and Zionism, 48, 50
'Nord und Süd', 176
Nordau, Max (physician, Zionist leader), 192, 204
Northcliffe, Alfred Charles Harmsworth, Viscount (newspaper proprietor), 230, 231n
Nothnagel, Hermann (physician), 171n
Numerus clausus, 485–486, 487
Nuremberg Jewish community, 245, 246n, 247, 248
Nuremberg Laws, 99, 100, 101, 388, 405, 429, 430, 456. *See also* Antisemitic legislation.
Nussbaum, Arthur (jurist), 288, 296–297
Nussbaum, Trude (née Eyck), 288, 296, 298

Oberland (reactionary group), 245
Ochse, Katharina, 313n
Offenberg, Mario, 509
Onchan Internment Camp (Isle of Man), 425
"Onkel Emil" (rescue group), 409
Oppenheim, Gertrud (cousin of Rosenzweig), 202n
Oppenheim, Hermann (neurologist), 174, 178–179
Oppenheim, Moritz (painter), 80
Oppenheimer, Franz (sociologist), 151
Oppenheimer, Josef Süss (Jud Süss) (court Jew), 524, 525; 'Jew Süss' (film), 523–524, 526
Oppenheimer, Max (painter), 102
(Die) orientalische Buchdruckerei (publishing house of Berliner Freischule), 11
Orthodox Judaism, IX, XII–XIII, 4, 28, 29–30, 41, 45–58, 63, 76, 90, 106, 107, 151, 165, 175, 178n, 188, 199, 385, 389; and Jewish defence, 238n; under Nazi regime, XXIII; Neo-Orthodoxy, 310–318, 319–320, 322; novels, 309–323; in Palestine, 262, 265, 266, 275, 285n; and Zionists, 148
'Ost und West', 197–198
Ostrer brothers, 523, 534n
Ostrer, Isidore (film director), 518, 523
Oswald, Richard (film director), 520n, 521
Ottenheimer, Hilde (historian), XIV, 363, 365, 371, 372–373, 375

Pabst, G. W. (film director), 527, 537
Pacifism, 90
Paderborn Jewish community, 64, 68
Pál, George (puppet-film maker), 533
Paldiel, Mordecai, 329–330
Palestine Jewish Colonisation Association (PICA), 270–271
Palestine Liberation Organisation, 499
Palestine/Israel, 157, 162, 167, 261–286, 322;

British Mandatory Government, 167, 263, 277, 282; German-Jewish immigration, 262–286 *passim*; German-Jewish visitors, XII, 261–286; Jewish nationality, 452; Orthodox immigrants, 262, 285n; Jewish peasants, 266–268, 276. *See also* Arabs, Emigration.
Palmer, Lilli (actress), 520n, 541
Pan-Germanism, *see* Alldeutscher Verband
Pappenheim, Bertha (social worker), 400
Parker, John (British MP), 428
Parti Ouvrier Français, 134
Partial Jews, XIX, 340, 394, 430, 432, 468, 498; Strassmann case, 386–387, 388, 389
Pascal, Gabriel (film director, producer), 518, 520n, 537
Pataud, Emile (French syndicalist), 134
Pathology, Jewish, XI, 169–188, 266; alcoholism, 171, 182–183, 185, 187; inbreeding, 171, 181–182, 185, 188; mental illness, 169–188; religious practice and, 171, 173, 174, 175, 176, 178n, 185–186, 188; sexual life and, 171, 175, 181–183, 185; statistics, 185, 187
Patton, George (US general), 467
Paucker, Arnold, XVIIn, 3n, 103n, 111n, 147n, 189n, 237n, 246n, 287n, 363, 372, 373, 415n, 461n, 497n
Paucker, Pauline, XXVIII
Paul, Heinz (film director), 523
Paul, Hermann (philologist), 225
Pauley, Bruce F., XV
Paulsen, Friedrich (educationalist), 301
Paulus-Bund, Vereinigung nichtarischer Christen, XIX
Peake, Oswald (British politician), 418
Peled, Rina, 205n
Peltesohn (physician), 293–294, 306
"Pem" (pseudonym of Paul Marcus, journalist), 521n, 537
Péreire, Isaac (financier), 130
Perl, William (rescued Austrian Jews), 462
Pernerstorfer, Engelbert (Austrian Socialist politician), 143
Perry, George, 517
Pestalozzi, Johann Heinrich (educationalist), 76
Philippson, Ludwig (editor), 28, 29, 63
Phillips, Lionel (South African financier), 136
Philo Judaeus (Jewish philosopher), 200, 231n
Physicians, German, 170–171; psychiatrists, 170–171, 172
Physicians, Jewish, 73, 79, 100, 386, 487; Maskilic, 174, 188; psychiatrists, XI, 169–188; Zionism and, 172, 176–177, 179–180, 183–184, 186–187, 188; Zionism as symptom, 177, 186
Picard, Edmond (Belgian Socialist), 127
Picciotto Fargion, Liliana, XXIX
Pieck, Wilhelm (Communist leader), 499n, 510
Pikarski, Margot, 401n
Pineas, Hermann (physician), 288, 299, 300

Pineas, Lilli (née Eyck), 288, 292, 297, 299, 300
Pinner, Felix (journalist), 266n, 268, 271
Pinsker, Leon (physician, Zionist politician), 149
Pioneer Corps (Auxiliary Military Pioneer Corps), 419–421, 424, 425–429, 437, 439, 440, 441, 442, 444, 447, 458, 534; statistics, 424, 444
Planer, Franz (cinema technician), 521
Plat, Wolfgang, 394n
Plaut, W. Gunther, 659
Plaut, Max (jurist), 659
Plekhanov, Georgii Valentinovich (Social Democratic theoretician), 141
Poale Zion, 144
Poalei Agudas Israel, 321
Pococke, Edward (English Orientalist), 42
Podolinsky, Serge (Ukrainian Socialist), 122
Pogroms in Eastern Europe, 148, 176; Croatia, 481; Galicia, 144; Russia, 123, 135, 140, 145, 178: (1881), 121, 122, 294, (1905), 89, 140
Pogroms in Germany/Austria, 66, 69, 105, 135, 391; medieval, 38–39; "Hep-Hep" (1819), 66, 105; Hamburg (1830), 66; Minden, Prague (1844), 66; (1848), 66, 69, 105; Vienna (1885), 481–482; Kapp Putsch (1920) and, 252, 253; Beuthen (1923), 252n
Pogrom (November 1938), 99, 100, 290n, 327, 334, 373, 389, 391, 395, 406, 407, 495, 504, 510n; commemoration, 503–504, 507–508, 509–510
Poliakov, Léon (writer), 234
Police, German; and republican defence organisations, 238–249 *passim*
'Politisch Anthropologische Monatshefte', 230
Pollock, Friedrich (sociologist, economist), 470
Pomeranian Jewry, 394
Pommer, Erich (film director), 520, 536
Ponsonby, Charles (British MP), 423, 424, 428, 429
Popall, Käthe (Communist functionary), 398
Popular Front, XXIV, 383
Populist Movement (Russia), 121, 122
Potsdam Jewish community, 505
Powell, Dilys (film critic), 517, 537
Powell, Michael (film director), 521, 522, 530–531, 537, 538
Poznań Jewry, 86, 88, 107, 291, 385, 386
Prager, Günter, 406n
Prager-Joachim, Marianne (of Baum Group), 399, 401, 402, 403, 406–408, 414
Prager-Kessler, Ilse (sister of M. P.-Joachim), 406, 408
Prague Jewish community, 66, 163–164, 507
Preminger, Otto (film director), 536
Press Agencies, 222
Press, Austrian, Jews in, 143, 144
Press, British, 215, 226; Jews in, 215, 222–223. *See also* individual titles.

Press, French, 222, 226
Press, German, 113, 124; Conservative, 223n, 224n; Jews in, 124, 125, 220; underground, 510n. *See also* individual titles.
Press, Jewish, 216. *See also* individual titles.
Pressburger, Emeric (Emmerich) (film director, writer), 521, 529n, 530–531, 533, 537, 538n
Prestige, H.H.C. (British official), 445n, 446, 448, 449n
Preuß, Hugo (political scientist), 382n
Price (British MP), 439
Pringle, Annette, XXVIII
Prisoners of war, 452; German, 462–477 *passim*; refugees, 428, 440, 442, 467; Russian, 447
'Profil', 493
Progressives, XX, 88, 89, 90, 297, 300, 302–305, 382, 396. *See also* Deutsche Demokratische Partei, Fortschritt/Freisinn.
Protestants, XVI, 8, 12–13, 15, 16, 54, 105, 293, 339, 395, 499–509 *passim*
Proudhon, Pierre-Joseph (French Socialist philosopher), 115, 120–121, 125, 128, 130–131, 132, 134
Prussian Jewry, 6, 7, 62, 63–64, 65, 69, 72, 107, 185, 290–291, 367, 498
Psychiatrists, XI, 169–188
Public opinion, German, X, 342, 391, 395
Pulzer, Peter J.G., XIX, XXVIII, 112

Quakers, *see* Society of Friends
Quelch, Harry (radical writer), 137

Rabbinate, German, 45–58, 72, 74–75, 77, 209, 210
Rabinowitz, Shaul Pinchas (writer), 43n
Rade, Martin (*not* Michael) (Protestant theologian), 57n
Radio Luxembourg, 472, 477
Rank, J. Arthur (industrialist), 518
Raphael family, 120
Rapoport, Solomon Judah Leib (Shlomo Yehudah Löb) (rabbi, scholar), 41, 42
Rashi (Solomon Yitzhaki) (medieval scholar), 41
Rathaus, Karol (composer), 521, 527
Rathbone, Eleanor (British MP), 444, 454, 457
Rathenau family, 99
Rathenau, Fritz (civil servant), 253
Rathenau, Walther (German statesman, philosopher), 101, 237, 243, 245, 250, 295, 382n
Rationalists, 62, 74, 76, 118, 151
Rations, 332–333; and forced labour, 411; and underground life, 339, 409
Rau, Editha (aided Resistance), 304
Reder, Walter (war criminal), 493, 495
Reform Judaism, IX, 4, 28–29, 31, 33, 36, 45–58, 63, 73, 80, 91, 151, 165, 310, 319, 320, 322, 385
Reformfreunde, Reformverein, *see* Verein für Reformfreunde Frankfurt a. Main
Regnard, Albert (racist French writer), 132

Rehwald, Ilse, 341
Reibmayer, (physician), 182
Reichmann, Eva G., XIX, XXIX
Reichmann, Hans (lawyer, C.V. Syndikus), XXIIIn, 363, 364
Reichsadler (youth group), 241
'(Das) Reichsbanner', 243, 251
Reichsbanner Schwarz-Rot-Gold, XII, 237–257
'Reichsbote', 223n
Reichsbund jüdischer Frontsoldaten (RjF), 99, 237–252 *passim*, 256
Reichsfluchtsteuer, 287
Reichshammerbund, 217, 228n
Reichsorganisation der deutsch-demokratischen Jugend, 250
Reichsvertretung der deutschen Juden (Reichsvereinigung der Juden in Deutschland), XIII, 333, 335, 337, 365, 372
Reif, Hans (of Hansabund), 299n
Reimann, Siegfried (pastor), 502
Reinhardt, Max (impresario), 538
Reinharz, Jehuda, XI, XXIn, XXIX
Reinke, Ursula, 409
Reissert, Rudolf (Resistance worker), 389–390
Renan, Ernest (French historian), 131, 132
Rendel, George (British official), 452–453
Renner, Karl (Austrian Chancellor), 484
Rentsch, Eugen (publisher), 303n
Republikanische Beschwerdestelle e.V., 248
Republikanischer Jugendbund Schwarz-Rot-Gold, 248n
Republikanischer Reichsbund, 248
Republikanisches Regiment Reichstag, 253
Resistance to Nazism, general, XIII–XV, XXV; Austrian, 385; Christian, 394, 504; Communists, XIV, 397–414, 510; Conservative, XIII–XIV, 364–365, 371; against deportation, 335; in exile, 420, 421, 430, 465, 466, 468, 532n; foreign contacts, 384–385, 389–390, 391, 468; Liberal, XIV, 381–396 *passim*; military, 384, 385; post-war planning, XIII–XIV, 391–393, 396, 405; Socialist, 384, 385; 20th July Plot, 304. *See also* Aid to the persecuted.
Resistance to Nazism/Fascism, Jewish, XIII, XIV–XV, XXIV–XXV, 363–414; Aufbau im Untergang, XXII; in concentration camps, 400; historiography, XXV; Liberal, 381–396; scholarship as, 363–380; Communist women, XIV–XV, 397–414; youth, XIV. *See also* Underground life, World War II.
Resnik-Meyer, Rita (of Resistance), 402, 403, 408–410, 414
Restitution, 491–492, 495, 498, 500, 502, 511
Reuter, Ernst (Mayor of West Berlin), 305
Reuter, Irene, 287n
Reuters, *see* Press Agencies
Reventlow, Graf Ernst zu (nationalist politician), 226

Revolution, French, 3, 22, 65, 68, 95, 114, 128, 150, 224, 367, 528
Revolution, German (1918–1919), 244–245, 396; Spartacists, 253
Revolutions (1848), 61, 71, 104–105, 393, 396
'Revue Socialiste', 132
'Reynolds News', 137
Rhineland Jewry, 64, 68–69
Ricardo family, 225
Richard Clay (printers), XXVIII
Richarz, Monika, XXIX, 45n
Richborough (refugee camp), 421, 422, 535
Richter, Eugen (Liberal politician), 303
Riegner, Agnes (née Arnheim, wife of Heinrich R.), 301, 302
Riegner, Gerhard (General Secretary of World Jewish Congress), 301n, 453
Riegner, Heinrich (lawyer), 301n, 302
Riess, Curt, 462–463, 469
Riess, Moses Aron (manufacturer), 74
Riesser, Gabriel (judge, Liberal politician), 4, 63, 155, 298n
Riesser, Jakob (jurist, banker), 298–299
Riff, Michael A., XXIX, 163n, 299n
Riga ghetto, 334, 341
Ring – Bund deutsch-jüdischer Jugend, 404, 405, 406, 411, 414
Rishon-le-Zion, 271, 272, 273
Ritter, Gerhard (writer), 384n
Ritual murder accusation, 67, 105, 131, 481
Robb, James, 112
Robert, Ludwig (writer, brother of Rahel Varnhagen), 68
Robertson, James C., 525
Robinsohn family, 385–386, 387, 385, 388, 394
Robinsohn, F. Peter, 386n
Robinsohn, Hans (merchant), 385–386, 387–388, 389, 390–393; Robinsohn-Strassmann Resistance group, 381, 384–385, 389, 391, 393–394, 395–396
Rochefort(-Luçay), Henri (de) (journalist), 133
Röhm, Ernst (SA Chief of Staff), 527
Roggenkamp, Viola, 403
Rohe, Karl, 237, 238, 239, 256
Rohleder, Hermann (sexologist), 188n
Rohling, August (antisemitic writer), 231
Romanticism, XXI, 68, 317, 367–368
Roseman, Mark, 17n
Rosenbaum-Kochmann, Sala (of Baum Group), 400–401, 402, 403, 404–406, 408, 414
Rosenberg, Curt (lawyer), 296n
Rosenberg, Else (née Stein, wife Curt R.), 296n
Rosenberg, Gerhard, 287n
Rosenheim, Jakob (Orthodox leader), 46n
Rosenstock, Werner, XXIX
Rosenthal, Alfred ("Aros") (journalist), 199n
Rosenthal, Erwin (orientalist, Judaist), XXVII
Rosenthal, Leni (Socialist deputy), 398
Rosenthal, Tom, XXIX

Rosenzweig, Franz (philosopher), 33, 49, 51n, 319n; and Nietzsche, 201–202
Rostock Jewish community, 502, 507
Rote Hilfe Deutschlands, 397, 398
Roter Frontkämpferbund, 255n
Roth, Alfred (Otto Arnim) (antisemite), 228
Rotha, Paul (film director), 521, 532
Rotholz, Siegbert (of Resistance), 407
Rothschild family, 75, 120, 121, 129, 130, 132, 133, 143, 225, 524, 534
Rothschild, [Baron] Edmond de (banker, philanthropist), 148–149, 151, 270, 271, 276
Rothschild, Amschel [Anselm] Meyer Baron von (banker, son of Mayer A.R.), 35
Rothschild, Lionel Nathan de (banker), 534
Rothschild, Mayer [Meyer] Amschel (founded banking house), 75
Rothschild, Nathaniel M.V. (3rd baron), 534
Rothschild, Walter (of OSS), 467
Rothstein, Ludwig (war veterans' leader), 243
Rothstein, Theodor (British Communist), 137
Rousseau, Jean-Jacques (philosopher), 213
Rubo, Julius (jurist), 107
Rudolphi, Karl Asmund (anthropologist), 169
Rühle-Gerstel, Alice (scientist), 398
Rühs, Christian Friedrich (antisemitic writer), 68
Rürup, Reinhard, XXVI, XXIX, 103, 113
Ruppin, Arthur (sociologist, Zionist leader), 285
Russian Democratic Party, 142
Ruttmann, Walter (film director), 522n, 527n

Sabbatai Zvi (17th-cent. pseudo-Messiah), 42
Sachs, Peter (film animator), 521n, 533–534
Sachsenhausen concentration camp, 409
Sack, Walter, 401, 404, 405, 407n, 413, 414
Saint-Simon, Claude Henri, comte de (philosopher), 129
Salomon, Alice (social worker), 398
Salomonsohn family, 84, 86–88
Salomonsohn, Adolf (banker), 86–88
Salomonsohn, Arthur (banker), 88
Salomonsohn, Sara (née Rinkel), 87, 88
Salten (Salzmann), Felix (novelist), 264, 279
Samuel, Herbert Louis (1st viscount), 439n
St. Pölten Jewish community, 495
Sartre, Jean-Paul (writer), 112
Sassin, Horst, XIII, XIV
Saville, Victor (film director), 518
Saxonian Jewry, 498, 597; Sachsen-Anhalt, 498, 503, 504–505, 507
Schach, Beate (née Schoch), 519n
Schach, Max (film producer), 519–520, 522, 527–529, 530
Schachnowitz, Selig (writer, editor), 285n, 311–314, 315, 316–317, 319, 322
Schacht, Hjalmar Horace Greeley (Reichsbank president, Reich minister), 383, 387
Schaeffer, [Baron] (Austrian diplomat), 482

Schäffer, Hans (Reich state secretary), 305n
Schatzker, Chaim, XXIn
Scheck, Marianne, 287n
Scheidemann, Philipp (Socialist politician), 249n, 253
Schelling, Friedrich Wilhelm Joseph (philosopher), 367
Scherbel, Simon (wrote on cremation), 29n
Schiff, Otto Moritz (founder of Jewish Refugees Committee), 441, 442–444, 534
Schiller, Friedrich von (poet), 4, 192, 310, 312
Schlesinger, John, 539–540
Schleswig-Holstein Jewry, 240
Schmitt, Kurt (Reich minister), 387
Schmoller, Gustav (economist), 301
Schneider, Eulogius, 14n
Schnitzler, Arthur (playwright, novelist), 159n
Schober, Johannes (Austrian politician), 487
Schocken (publishing house), 102
Schönebeck Jewish community, 509
'Schönere Zukunft', 489
Schönerer, Georg von (Austrian antisemitic politician), 143, 483
Schoenewald, Ottilie (Liberal, memoirist), 383
Scholem Gershom [Gerhard] (philosopher, authority on Jewish mysticism), X, 83–84n, 92, 95, 107–108, 202, 203n, 312, 322
Schopenhauer, Arthur (philosopher), 47, 193n, 200
Schorsch, Ismar, IX, XXVI, XXVIII, 213
Schoyer, Adolf (AJR Chairman), 448, 451
Schuebbe, Gustav Wilhelm (physician, war criminal), 465
Schüfftan, Eugen (photographer), 521
Schulin, Ernst, XXIX
Schulz, Fritz (pastor), 501
Schulze-Gaevernitz, Gero von (OSS contact with German Resistance), 468
Schuschnigg, Kurt von (Austrian Chancellor), 489
Schutzjuden, 6, 64, 72, 74
Schutzverband deutscher Schriftsteller, 254
Schweinfurt Jewish community, 28
Schweitzer, Johann Baptist von (ADAV leader), 124
Schwerin Jewish community, 499
Schweriner, Art[h]ur (jurist, C.V. functionary), 251–252, 254n
Secker & Warburg (publishers), XXVIII
Secker, Martin (publisher), 523
Secularism, 148, 151, 209
Segall, Dora, XXVIII
Segnitz Jewish community, 23
Seidlin, Oskar (of US Intelligence, writer), 471
Sejmist Party (in Poland), 166
'Selbstschutz' (reactionary group), 245
'Selbstwehr' (Prague Jewish journal), 164
Seldte, Franz (Stahlhelm leader), 383
Self-regard, Jewish, 35, 46, 82, 374, 400; Jewish

identity, IX, XIX, 31, 62, 147–167, 366, 386; self-hatred, 120, 122, 142, 186–187, 208
Seligmann, Avraham, XIII
Seligmann, Caesar (leader of Reform Judaism), 53, 55, 199
Semank, Alfred (Reichsbanner leader), 248
Sender, Toni (workers' leader), 468
Sessa, Borromäus Karl (antisemite, writer), 67, 68
Settelen, V. (of US Intelligence), 477
Sevareid, Eric (writer), 462
Sever, Albert (Austrian politician), 484
Seville Jewish community, 39
Shaw (British MP), 455
Shaw, George Bernard (playwright), 518
Sherman, Joshua A., XXIX
Sherriff, Paul (Shouvalov) (film designer), 537
Shindel, Ilse, XXVIII
Sichel, Max (Jewish psychiatrist), 181–182, 183
Sielemann, Jürgen, 242n
Silbergleit, Artur (Reichsbanner associate), 254n
Silberner, Edmund, 113–115
Silesian Jewry, 107, 238, 291
Silverman, Sydney S. (British MP), 455, 457
Simeon bar Yohai (2nd-century teacher), 41, 42
Simmel, Georg (philosopher), 82, 107, 190–191
Simon, Ernst Akiba (educationalist), 49
Simon, Heinrich Veit (lawyer), 302
Simon, Hermann, XXIX
Simon, John Allsebrook (British politician), 438
Simon, K. (member of Reichsbanner), 251
Simon, Leon (editor), 209n
Simpson, John Hope (British civil servant), 277
Sindermann, Horst (GDR politician), 510
Singer, Paul (Socialist politician), 84, 91–92, 93, 145
Sinowatz, Fred, 493
Sklarek brothers (textile merchants), 253, 256
Sklarz, Georg (Left-wing defendant), 253
Slánský Trial, 499
Slater, John (actor), 539
Smirnov (Russian Populist), 121
Smith, Herbert A. (British official), 445n, 446
Social Democracy, XIX, XX, 111–112, 113, 114, 123, 161, 223, 237, 241, 245, 246, 247, 254, 303, 381, 382, 384–385; in Austria, 142–145, 484; in Russia, 114, 123, 140–142
Social Democratic Federation (SDF), 136, 137
Social status, Jewish , XIX, 62, 63, 71–82 *passim*, 83–93, 95–102, 106–107, 147, 153, 161, 169, 180, 184; Bildungsbürgertum, 73, 106; urbanisation, 26, 31, 63, 107
Socialism, Socialists, X–XI, 92, 111–145, 189, 192, 273, 311, 320, 381, 470; and Nietzsche, 203n; and Palestinian Jewry, 268–269, 270, 271; Resistance to Nazism, XIII, 397. *See also* Antisemitism, Communism, Social Democracy.

Society of Friends (Quakers), 394, 395, 531
Söllner, Alfons, 470
Sofaer, Abraham (actor), 525–526
Sofer, Leo (Jewish psychiatrist), 181, 182
Sofer (Schreiber), Moses (Hatam Sofer) (Austro-Hungarian leader of Orthodox Jewry), 311
Solmssen, Georg (Salomonsohn) (banker), 87, 88
Sombart, Werner (economist), 224
Somervell, Donald (British politician), 441, 455–456
Sonnemann, Leopold (editor), 124, 300, 301
Sonnenfels, Joseph Reichsfrhr. von (Austrian jurist, Liberal), 40
Sophiengemeinde, 505
Sorel, Georges (French Socialist), 115, 134
Sorkin, David, IX, XXVIII
Sozialdemokratische Arbeiterpartei (SDAP), 124–125, 126; Sozialdemokratische Arbeiterpartei Österreichs (SDAP), 142
Sozialdemokratische Partei Deutschlands (SPD), X, 84, 90, 91–92, 113, 117, 124, 127–128, 139, 140, 145, 244, 246, 248, 249, 251, 252, 253, 255, 301, 398; Mehrheits-Sozialisten, 242, 245, 250, 253. *See also* Social Democracy, Socialism.
Sozialdemokratische Partei im Exil (Sopade), 384
Sozialistische Arbeiterpartei, 381
Sozialistische Einheitspartei Deutschlands (SED), 498, 499, 505, 511; SED-Pressedienst, 499n
Specht (in US Intelligence), 465
Spender, Harold (British journalist), 304
Spender, Violet (née Schuster), 304
Spengler, Oswald (philosopher), 199n
Spinoza, Baruch (philosopher), 40, 76
Spitzemberg, Baroness (diarist), 295
Spoliansky, Mischa (composer), 521n, 536
S.S, (Schutz-Staffel), 413, 492, 493, 505
Stahl, Friedrich Julius (Conservative politician), 368
Stalin, Joseph, 141–142; Hitler pact, XV, 538
Stampfer, Friedrich (editor 'Vorwärts'), 251n, 254n
'(The) Standard', 226
Stanislawski, Michael, 33n
Stanley, Oliver (British politician), 421n
Stapenhorst, Günther (film director), 520n, 538n
Stark, Oskar (journalist, co-founder of Resistance group), 385
Statistics; Hamburg community, 386; Pioneer Corps, 424, 444; on underground life, 328, 340, 341, 342–358, 359
Stauff, Philipp (antisemitic writer), 225n
Stauffenberg, Claus Philip Schenk Graf von (20th July Plot leader), 384

Steckelmacher, Moritz (wrote on cremation), 29n
Stein, Louise (née Veitel), 298n
Stein, Ludwig (delicatessen owner), 298
Steinberg, Auguste (writer), 196n
Steinheim Institut Duisburg, Xn, 145n
Steinheim, Salomo[n] Ludwig (philosopher), 41
Stepan, Nancy, 169n
Stern family, 120
Stern, Guy, XV, 477
Stern, Hayum (Segnitz businessman), 24
Stern-Taeubler, Selma (historian), 106
Sternfeld, Albert, XXIX
Sternhell, Zeev, 115
Stettin Jewish community, 255
Stockton, Gilchrist Baker (US diplomat), 487–488
Stoecker, Adolf (antisemite, preacher), 85, 127, 128, 137, 231n, 294, 303
Stokvis, Walter (film editor), 521n, 528
Stolper, Gustav (economist, Liberal), 383
Strassmann, Arnold (Sanitätsrat), 386–387, 388
Strassmann, Ernst (lawyer, Resistance group co-founder), 384, 385, 386–387, 388, 392
Strassmann, Reinhard (lawyer), 388
Strassmann, Wolfgang (local politician), 386n
Strassner, Joe (fashion designer), 521n, 528
Straus, Elias (of Memmingen), 245n
Strauss, Herbert A., X, XXIX, 372n
Streicher, Julius (Nazi leader, editor of 'Der Stürmer'), 20n, 247, 248, 429n, 490
Strelitz Jewish community, 22
Stresemann, Gustav (German statesman), 256n, 300n
Strobl, Ingrid, 414n
Student fraternities, 77–78, 156, 157, 162, 312; Orthodox, 319; in Vienna, 485
Students, Jewish, 47, 73, 77–78, 79, 85, 95, 98, 123, 156, 163, 238, 298, 312–313, 320; in Austria, 485–488, 491, 495; organisations, 319
Students, Russian, 123
'(Der) Stürmer', 20n, 429n
'(Der) Stürmer' (Vienna), 490
Stuttgart Jewish community, 388
Suchan, Erika (friend of Eyck family), 302n
Suchy, Barbara, XIX, XXVIII, 213
Suchy, Bernhard, XXIX
Süss [Jüd], *see* Oppenheimer, Josef
Suicide, 198, 337, 389, 411, 466
Symbiosis, 49, 80, 92, 95–102, 104, 108
Szántó, Simon (rabbi, editor 'Die Neuzeit'), 29

'Tägliche Rundschau', 222, 223, 224
Tafler, Sidney (actor), 538n, 539
'(Der) Tag', 257n
Talmud, 10, 11, 35–36, 53, 76, 231, 312, 313, 321; Talmud schools, 76, 77
Tandler, Julius (anatomist), 487, 488
Tauber, Richard (singer, actor), 520n, 528

Tec, Nechama, 329
'(Le) Temps', 226
Tengood (refugee, of US Intelligence), 464
Thälmann, Ernst (leader of German Communist Party), 398
Theresienstadt ghetto, 335, 371n, 373, 375, 409, 413, 507, 659
Thiele, von (Prussian state secretary), 368
Thomasius, Christian (jurist, leader of Enlightenment), 5
Thuringian Jewry, 498, 499, 505
Tietz family, 84, 88–90, 255
Tietz, Betty (wife of Oscar T.), 90n
Tietz, Georg (son of Oscar T.), 88, 89, 90
Tietz, Hermann (co-founder Tietz department store), 89
Tietz, Jakob (carter), 88, 89
Tietz, Oscar (co-founder Tietz department store), 88–90
'(The) Times', 222, 223, 226, 231n, 235n, 521, 527
Tocqueville, Charles Alexis Henri Clérel de (French political scientist), 81
Tölcke, C.W. (Socialist agitator), 125
Tönnies, Ferdinand (philosopher, sociologist), 81
Toeplitz, Ludovic (film producer), 518
Toury, Jacob, XII, XIX, XXIX, 62, 63
Toussenel, Alphonse (French Socialist), 115, 129–130, 132
Trade Unions, 124, 134, 228, 532–533
Traders, Jewish, *see* Businessmen
Treitschke, Heinrich von (historian), 221, 222n, 369
Trevor-Roper, Hugh (Lord Dacre), 467
Tridon, Gustave (follower of Blanqui), 131
Troeltsch, Ernst (Protestant theologian), 107, 367
Trotsky, Leo[n] (Lev Bronstein) (Russian revolutionary leader), 141
Troutbeck, John Monro (British official), 456
Tschernikovsky, Shaul (Hebrew poet), 209n
'Tse'ena Ure'ena' (Zena Ur'ena), 314
Tucholsky, Kurt (writer), 102
Turkish Empire, Jews in, 265, 273
Typography; Fraktur type, 225–226
Tzelniker, Meier (actor), 538n, 539

Ulbricht, Walter (Communist leader), 512
Ullstein (publishing house), 102, 305
Ulrich, Michael (Catholic official), 504
Unabhängige Sozialdemokratische Partei Deutschlands (USPD), 382
Underground life, XIII, XXIV–XXV, 327–361, 399, 401, 402, 409–412, 413–414
Union of American Hebrew Congregations, 91
United States Intelligence, Jews in, XV, 461–477; Counter Intelligence Corps (CIC), 465, 467, 468; Military Intelligence, 462–463, 466;

occupied Germany, 462, 467, 472; Office of Strategic Services (OSS), 463–470 *passim*; Office of War Information (OWI), 468, 470–471; psychological warfare, 471–477; Signal Intelligence, 461; training establishments, 463–464, 466, 467, 471

United States of America; emigration to, XV, 148, 177, 421; reaction to Austrian antisemitism, XV–XVI, 481–496

Universum Film AG (UFA), 522, 536n, 537

Untermerzbach Jewish community, 25

Urias, Siegfried (RjF leader), 242, 243

"Usury", *see* Moneylenders, Jewish

Vaad Leumi, 167

Vaillant, Edouard (French Socialist), 133

Vajda, Ladislaus (cinema writer), 528n

Vansittart, Robert Gilbert (diplomat), 534n

Varnel, Marcel (film director), 531

Varnhagen von Ense, Rahel (née Levin), 68

Vaterländischer Bund jüdischer Frontsoldaten, *see* Bund jüdischer Frontsoldaten

Veidt, Conrad (actor), 520, 521, 523, 526, 532

Veitel family, 287, 293

Veitel, Adolph (businessman), 287, 289, 298n

Veitel, Theresa (née Gottschalk), 287

Verband der Jüdischen Gemeinden der DDR, 501, 504, 506, 509, 511

Verband der orthodoxen Rabbiner Deutschlands, 53

Verband deutscher Waren- und Kaufhäuser, 88

Verband zur Erforschung der Geschichte der deutschen Juden, 103n

Verein für Cultur und Wissenschaft der Juden, 40, 63, 80

Verein für Reformfreunde Frankfurt a. Main, 36

Verein jüdischer Frontsoldaten Bremen, 238, 239–240

Verein Republik, 241, 242

Verein zur Abwehr des Antisemitismus (Abwehrverein), XII, 96, 213–236

Vereinigung der liberalen Rabbiner Deutschlands, 53

Vereinigung der traditionell-gesetzestreuen Rabbiner Deutschlands, 53

Vereinigung der Verfolgten des Naziregimes, 498

Vereinigung jüdischer Akademiker, 238n, 312

Vereinigung Republik, 237, 242

Vereinstag Deutscher Arbeitervereine, 300

Versammlung Deutscher Historiker, 1990, 103n

Vienna Jewish community, 6, 66, 158; Israelitische Kultusgemeinde, 158, 486, 494; museum, 495; physicians, 174–175, 182; students, 485–488, 495; violence against, 481–482, 485–488

Vierhaus, Rudolf, XXIX

Viertel, Berthold (writer, film director), 520n, 531, 532

Vocational training, Jewish, 263–264, 265, 333, 335–336, 394

Völkisch ideas, XXI, 96, 97, 118, 126, 157, 131, 132, 189, 208, 213–236 *passim*, 317, 485, 488

'Völkischer Beobachter', 244

Vogelstein, Heinemann (Reform rabbi), 91

Vogelstein, Ludwig (industrialist), 91

'Volkserzieher', 224n

'Volksstaat', 125

Voltaire (François-Marie Arouet) (philosopher, writer), 8, 39, 118, 126, 131

Vorhaus, Bernard (film director), 526

'Vorwärts', 223, 238

Voss, Johann Heinrich (poet, translator), 67

Vossberg (Progressive, associate of E. Eyck), 304

'Vossische Zeitung', 215, 227, 305

Vranitsky, Franz, 495

Wach- und Schließgesellschaft Bremen, 239

Wagner, Adolf (political economist), 301

Wagner, Cosima (wife of Richard W.), 213, 234

Wagner, Richard (composer), 98, 118, 217, 225, 226, 233; Wagner-Kreis, 216n

Wahrmund, Adolf (Catholic antisemite), 231

Walbrook, Anton, *see* A. Wohlbrück

Waldheim, Kurt, 481, 493–494, 495

Walk, Joseph, XXVIII

Wallich family, 84–86

Wallich, Anna (née Jacoby), 84, 85

Wallich, Henry C., 86

Wallich, Hermann (banker), 84–85, 86, 88

Wallich, Paul (banker, son Hermann W.), 85–86

Walter, Bruno (conductor), 101

Walz, Hans, XXIX

Wandervogel, 157

Wannsee Conference, 432

War Crimes Trials, 458, 472, 493

Warburg Jewish community, 64

Warburg (banking house), 255

Warburg, Fritz M. (banker), 255n

Warburg, Max Moritz (banker), 51n, 58n

Wassermann, Jakob (novelist), 98

Wassermann, Ludwig (C.V. chairman, Munich), 246

Watson, Edith M. (British official), 455

Webb, Beatrice (British Socialist), 135

Weber, August (Liberal, DDP leader), 305, 383

Weber, Max (sociologist), 95

Wedgwood, Josiah (British MP, later 1st baron), 417, 418, 426, 440–441, 454

Weedon, Harry W. (architect), 534

Weidenfeld, Peter, 472

Weill, Alexandre (writer), 121

Weimar Republic, Jews in, X–XI, XII, XVIII, XXIV, 9, 99, 157, 237–257; Republican defence, 237–257

Weinbaum, D. (novelist), 313n

Weisl, Wolfgang von (Right-wing Zionist journalist), 277, 281–283

Weiss, Arnold (of CIC), 467
Weiß, Bernhard ("Isidor") (vice-president, Berlin police), 293, 306
Weiß, Emma (mother of Bernhard W.), 293
Weisse Möwe (resistance group), 399
Weissfisch, Arye, 200n
Weizmann, Chaim (chemist, first President of Israel), 149; and Nietzsche, 203
Weizmann, Vera (née Khatzman), 203
Weizsäcker, Richard, 494
Welles, Orson (film director), 536
Wells, Herbert George (writer), 531
Wells, Tony, XXIX
'(Die) Welt', 163, 204
Weltsch, Felix (philosopher, librarian), 261, 268
Weltsch, Robert (editor'Jüdische Rundschau', Zionist, founder-editor LBI Year Book), XVI, XVII, XXIIIn, XXVIII, XXIX, 204, 363, 364
Wentker, Erich, 394n
Werfel, Franz (poet, dramatist), 98
Wessely, Hartwig (Naphtali Herz Weisel) (Hebrew writer), 9, 11, 15, 41; and education, 76
Westphalian Jewry, 64, 65, 68.
Wette, Wilhelm Martin Lebrecht de (orientalist), 39–40
Whitaker, Paul K., 461n
Wichmann, Christa, XXIX, 254n
Wiene, Robert (film director), 520n, 537
Wiener (rabbi, wrote on cremation), 29n
Wiener, Alfred (Syndikus of Centralverein, founder of Wiener Library), 263, 271, 275, 278, 281, 285
Wiener Library, XXVIII, 332, 341
Wiener, P.B., XXIX
Wiesemann, Falk, IX
Wiesenthal, Simon, 494
Wiessler, Alexandra, XXIX
Wilder, Billy (film director), 536
Wilhelm II (Emperor of Germany), 87, 97, 227, 229, 234, 235, 295, 297
Wilhelm, Wolfgang (cinema writer), 521n, 536
Willmot, Louise, XXVIII
Wilmaset (photosetters), XXVIII
Windthorst-Bund, 250
Wirth, Joseph (Zentrum politician), 250
Wise, Robert, 536
Wise, Stephen S. (US rabbi, Zionist), 485
Wise, Vic (actor), 538n
Wismar Jewish community, 389
Wissenschaft des Judentums, 81, 104, 366. See also Gesellschaft zur Förderung der . . ., Hochschule für die Wissenschaft des Judentums.
Wistrich, Robert Solomon, X, XXIX
Witkowsky, Gustav (politician, Orthodox Zionist), 49
Wittola, Marc (Jansenist), 14
Wöllner decrees, 6

Wörlitz Jewish community, 509
Wohlbrück, Adolf (Anton Walbrook) (actor), 520n, 521n, 533, 537
Wolf, Elkan Isaac (physician), 173–175, 176, 178n
Wolfenbüttel Jewish community, 37, 42
Wolff (of Aurich, wrote on cremation), 29n
Wolff, Christian Frhr. von (philosopher, mathematician), 5, 10, 11, 193
Wolff, Edith (Zionist, Resistance worker), 399–400
Wolff, Ilse, XXVII
Wolff, Theodor (editor), 251, 254n, 382n, 383
Wolffenstein, Valeria and Andreas, 347n
Wolffsohn, David (Zionist leader), 50n
Wolfsberg, Jeschayahu (writer), 48n
Wolfskehl, Karl (poet), 191
Wolfssohn, A[a]ron Halle (writer, editor), 42, 79
Women, Jewish, 41, 49, 175, 319; Resistance and, XIV–XV, 397–414
World Jewish Congress, 453, 481, 493–494, 495, 509
World War I, Jews in, XII, 48–49, 98, 99, 151–152, 243–244, 250, 265, 299, 304, 314, 317, 320; Jewish defence during, 213–236; veterans, 237–257 *passim*. See also Reichsbund jüdischer Frontsoldaten.
World War II, Jews in, XIII–XV, 415–459, 461–477; post-war planning, 425, 445–457 *passim*
World Zionist Organisation, 150, 157, 161, 166
Wormann, Curt (Germanist, librarian), XXVII
Wronkow, Ludwig (Reichsbanner associate), 254n
Württemberg, rescuers in, 351
Würzburg Jewish community, 66, 105, 245, 247, 248, 249, 252
Wyneken, Gustav (youth leader), 205

Yad Vashem; Archives, 328, 329, 332, 341
Yantsin (Ukrainian revolutionary), 121–122
Yellow Star, 100, 327, 334, 337, 338, 341, 348, 412
Yerushalmi, Yosef Hayim, 169n
Yiddish language, XI, 19, 67, 135, 141, 160, 166, 174, 177, 184, 187, 317, 340; theatre, 539n
Young, Edward (writer, theologian), 11
Youth Aliyah, 335, 337
Youth, Jewish, XIV, XV, 155, 157, 244, 399, 405, 408, 414; Resistance, XIV, 399. See also Baum Group; youth movements, XXI, XXIII, 155, 238. See also Zionism.
Youth movements, 155, 157, 190; German, 264; Liberal/Republican, 241, 248, 250, 251n, 383

Zacharias, Ellis M. (Chief of US Naval Intelligence), 463
Zander, Wilhelm (SS-Standartenführer), 467
Zangwill, Israel (Zionist writer), 166

'(Die) Zeit', 256
'Zeitfragen', 226
Zeitlin, Hillel (Hebrew writer), 209n
Zelnik, Friedrich (film producer, director), 519, 520n, 522, 529
Zentralkomitee der deutschen Katholiken, 505
Zentralrat der Juden in Deutschland, 506, 509, 511
Zentrumspartei, 215, 249, 250n, 251
Zhitlovsky, Chaim (Socialist, Yiddishist), 123–124
Ziegler, August (writer in 'Abwehrblätter'), 231n
Zimmermann, Moshe, XXIX, 45n
Zion (Austrian fraternal lodge), 163, 179
Zionism, Revisionist, 262, 277–278, 281–283
Zionism, Zionists, X, XI, XII, XXI, XXIII, 4, 30–31, 48, 50, 51, 96–97, 108, 140, 142, 143, 147–167, 211, 261–286, 310, 317, 321n, 322, 405, 413, 484–485, 502; Abwehrverein and, 235; Allgemeine Zionisten, 262; anti-Zionism, 100, 137, 177, 186, 267, 268–269, 271, 278,

280, 307, 319, 484–485, 499, 500, 503, 505; Arbeiterzionismus, 262; defence, 252–253; and Edelnazis, XXIII; historiography, XXI; Kulturzionisten, 30: literature, 261–286 *passim*; Nietzsche and, 196n, 203–212; in novels, 311, 313n; physicians and, XI, 172–188 *passim*; and Reichsbanner, 248, 253; in Resistance, 399: religious, 262, 320; Uganda plan, 50, 166; women, 399, 403; youth organisations, XXI, 244, 283, 335–336, 404. *See also* Misrachi, Palestine.
Zionistische Vereinigung für Deutschland (ZVfD), XXI, 50, 153, 155, 156, 157–158, 253
Zola, Emile (French novelist), 133
Zuckmayer, Carl (playwright), 521n, 532, 535
'(Die) Zukunft', 236n
Zunz, Leopold (Berlin scholar, headmaster), IX, 3, 33–43, 107
Zweig, Arnold (novelist), XI, 309n, 500
Zweig, Stefan (writer), 98
Zwickau Jewish community, 509

FORTHCOMING

A SYMPOSIUM VOLUME ON
JEWS AND THE GERMAN LABOUR MOVEMENT

PUBLISHED JOINTLY BY
THE STEINHEIM INSTITUTE, DUISBURG,
AND THE LEO BAECK INSTITUTE, LONDON

Ludger Heid & Arnold Paucker

Editors

**Juden und deutsche Arbeiterbewegung bis 1933
Soziale Utopien und religiös-kulturelle Traditionen**

(Schriftenreihe wissenschaftlicher Abhandlungen des
Leo Baeck Instituts 49)

With contributions by Micha Brumlik,
Hanna Delf, Laurenz Demps, Walter Grab,
Donna Harsch, Ludger Heid, Arno Herzig,
Mario Kessler, Kurt Koszyk, Susanne Miller,
Shlomo Na'aman, Gottfried Niedhart, Jacob Toury,
Klaus Dieter Vinschen, Christl Wickert,
Robert S. Wistrich

J.C.B. MOHR (PAUL SIEBECK), TÜBINGEN